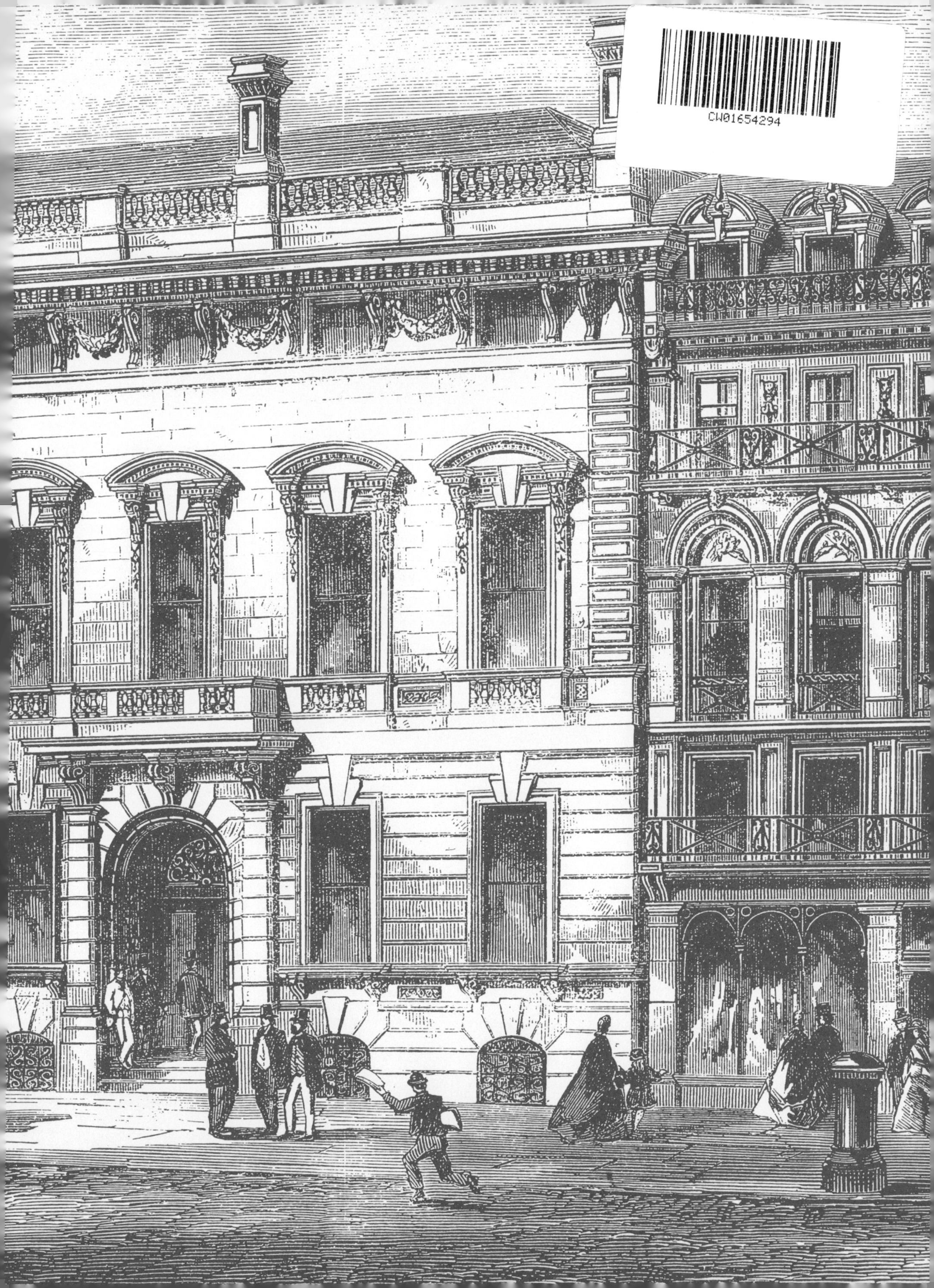

PICTURES IN THE

GARRICK CLUB

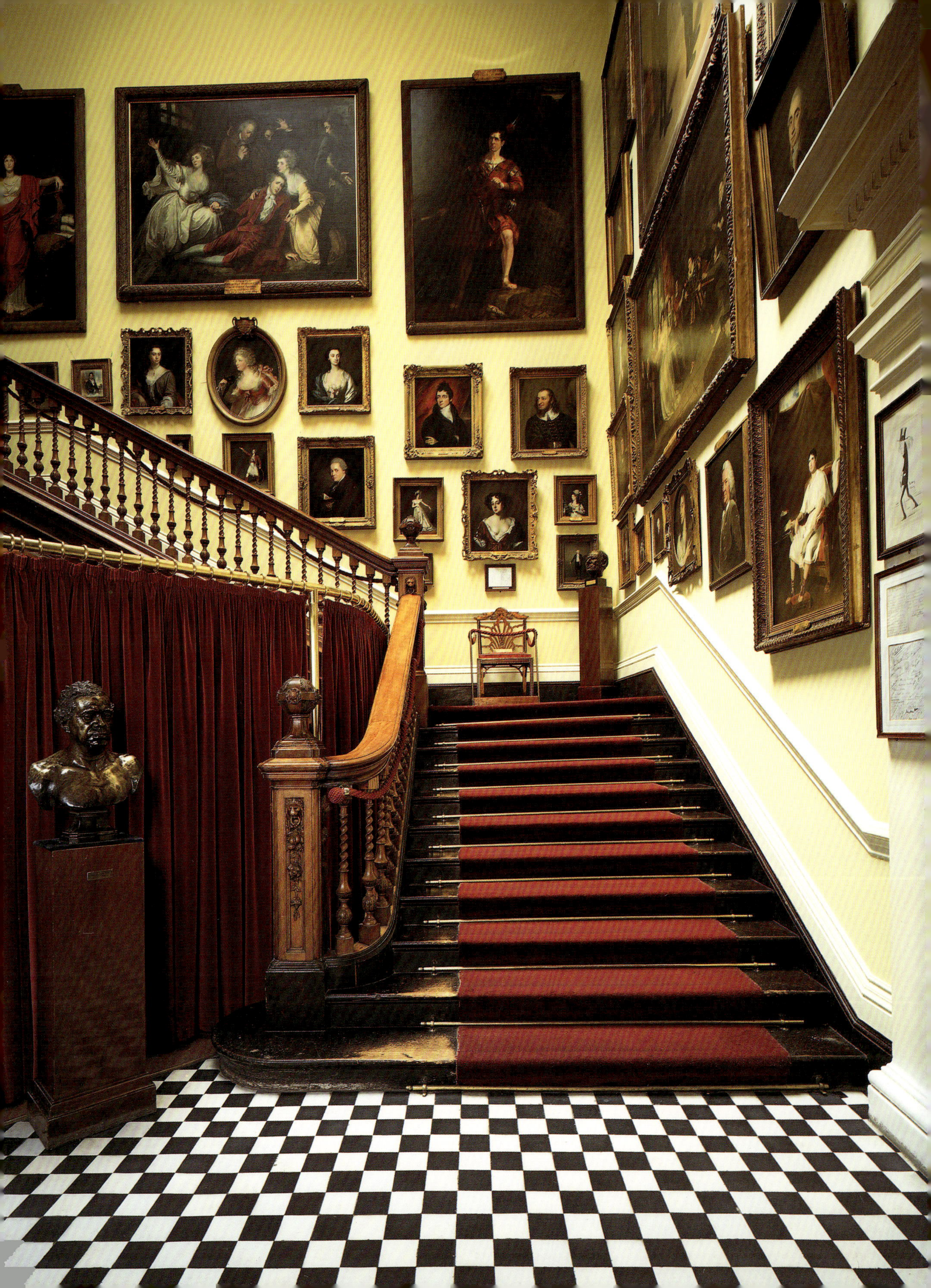

PICTURES IN THE
GARRICK CLUB

A CATALOGUE

of the paintings, drawings, watercolours and sculpture

compiled and written by

GEOFFREY ASHTON

edited by

KALMAN A. BURNIM & ANDREW WILTON

GARRICK CLUB

First published 1997 by Garrick Club, Garrick Street, London WC2E 9AY
in association with Unicorn Press, 21 Afghan Road, London SW11 2QD

ISBN 0 906290 14 7

A catalogue record of this book is available from the British Library

PICTURE CREDITS

ENDPAPERS

New building of the Garrick Club, 1864 (engraving: *The Illustrated London News*)

FRONTISPIECE

The main staircase, Garrick Club (photograph: David Parmiter)

PAGE X

The Coffee Room, Garrick Club (photograph: Derry Moore)

PAGE XXII

The Morning Room, Garrick Club (photograph: Derry Moore)

Produced by Hugh Tempest-Radford *Book Producers*
21 Afghan Road, London SW11 2QD

Designed by Gillian Greenwood

Typeset in Baskerville type by Helen Robertson
Illustrations originated by John Rawlinson

Printed and bound in Great Britain by Bath Press Colourbooks

CONTENTS

Dedicated by permission
to our Patron

HIS ROYAL HIGHNESS
THE DUKE OF EDINBURGH K.G., K.T.

by the members of
THE GARRICK CLUB

PREFACE

It is exactly 60 years since the 1936 catalogue of the Garrick Club's collection, compiled by C.K. Adams and now long since out of print, was published. The present catalogue was commissioned on behalf of the Club in 1982 by the late Sir Anthony Lousada, former Chairman of the Works of Art Sub-Committee, from the eminent theatre and art historian, the late Dr Geoffrey Ashton. Sadly, Ashton died at the early age of 39 in August 1991. During his short career he applied himself to the study of British theatrical painting and illustration, an area which had formerly been virtually ignored by art historians. He helped to mount several exhibitions dealing with different aspects of the theatre and, from 1979 to 1984, was Librarian to the Club. He was still engaged on his *magnum opus*, the present catalogue, when he was struck down by illness. Realising that he would be unable to complete the work in publishable form before his death, he asked Mr Andrew Wilton, Keeper of the British Collection at the Tate Gallery, to help see it to press. Mr Wilton and Professor Kalman A. Burnim, Fletcher Professor of Drama, Emeritus, of Tufts University, who had been introduced through the good offices of Mr Iain Mackintosh, were then invited by the Works of Art Sub-Committee to undertake a thorough editing of the author's manuscript. They performed this formidable task voluntarily over a period of four years as a memorial to their friendship with Geoffrey Ashton, and the Club wishes to express its marked gratitude to both of them. Professor Burnim also made a number of visits to England in order to check every item with Mr Wilton. Without the tireless labours of these two scholars, the catalogue could never have been published.

The Club also wishes to thank a Member, Lord Sainsbury of Preston Candover, for his generous help towards funding the publication. The catalogue was produced by another Member, Mr Hugh Tempest-Radford. Miss Betty Beesley made her intimate knowledge of the collection readily available. The care and conservation of the paintings is in the hands of Miss Anthea Pelham-Burn.

Sir Anthony Lousada was succeeded as Chairman of the Works of Art Sub-Committee by Mr John Baskett and it has been under his distinguished direction that the catalogue has been brought to completion. The Club expresses its gratitude to both of them.

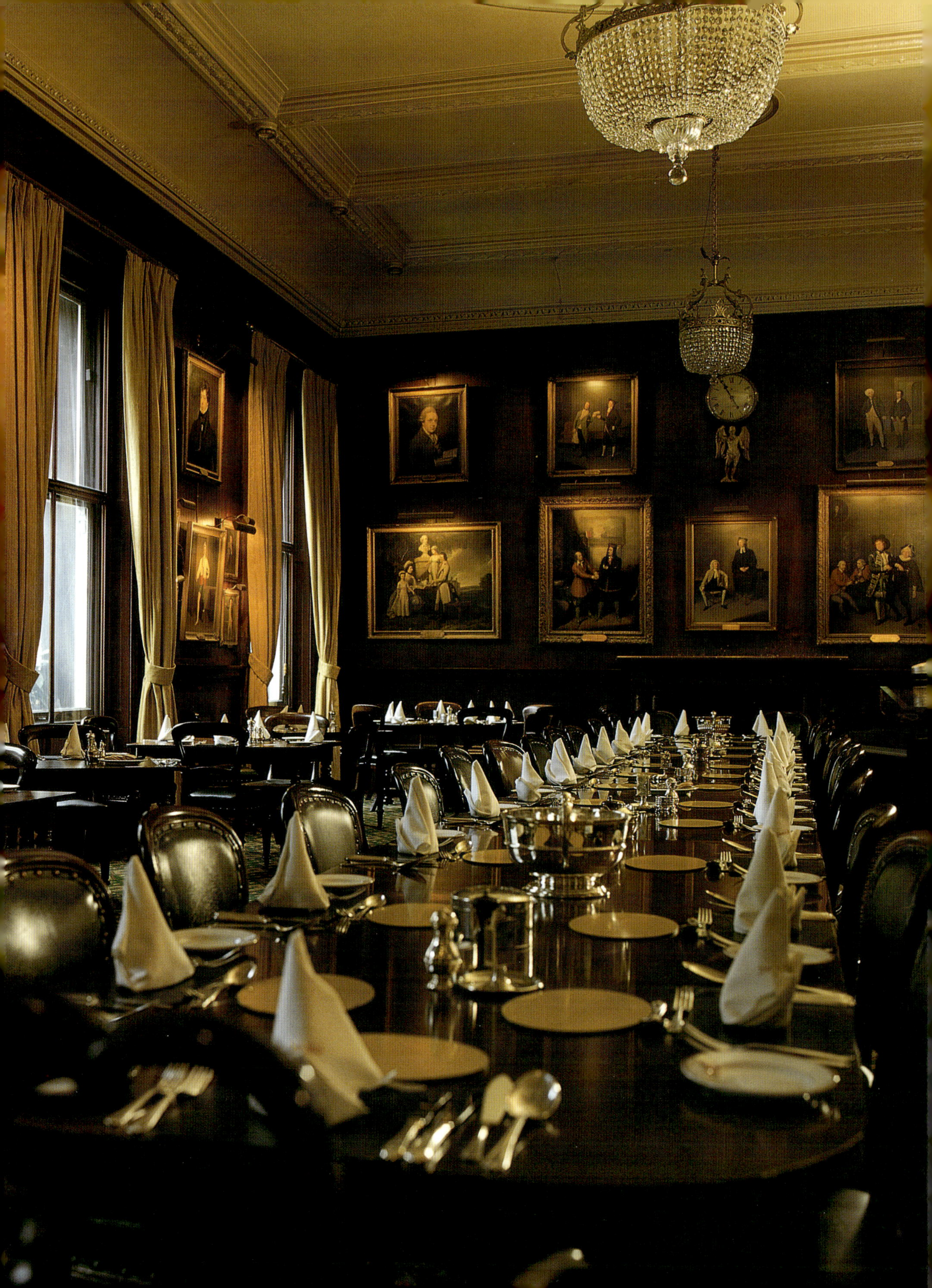

LIST OF SUBSCRIBERS

Anthony Abrahams
Michael D. Abrahams C.B.E.
Sir Timothy Ackroyd, Bt.
Jonathan Acton Davis Q.C.
Geoffrey V. Adams
R.A. Albert
Ian B. Albery
Professor W.J. Albery F.R.S.
Sir Michael Alexander G.C.M.G.
Lord Alexander of Weedon Q.C.
Thomas Allen C.B.E.
P.H.B. Allsop C.B.E.
Eric Ambler O.B.E.
Stanley Amis
Dr Peter E. Andry
Anthony Anderson Q.C.
Timothy Angel
Ben Aris
Alex Armitage
Sir Eric Ash C.B.E.
Julian F.K. Ashby
Professor Norman Ashton C.B.E., F.R.S.
Philip Attenborough C.B.E.
Lawrence P. Bachmann
Peter H. Bagnall
Robin Bailey
M. Baird-Smith D.F.C.
Richard Baker O.B.E., R.D.
Sir John Balcombe
John Bankes
David Barr
A.G.S. Barstow
Peter R. Bartlett
John Baskett
Anthony Bate
Richard Bebb
Rodney Bennett-England
Sir Christopher Benson
Francis J. Bergin
Anthony Besch
Rodney Bewes
John Bickford Smith C.B.
Claud Bicknell O.B.E.
Geoffrey Bide O.B.E.
Dr John Birch
Ellis Birk
Christopher Bishop
His Honour A.J. Blackett-Ord C.V.O.
Viscount Bledisloe Q.C.
His Excellency Leif Blomqvist
Peter Blythe
His Honour Judge Graham Boal Q.C.
Stephen W. Bonarjee
Derek Bond M.C.
Professor Gustav Born F.R.S.
Lord Borrie of Abbots Morton Q.C.
Jamie Borwick
Gerald F. Bowden
Peter Bowles
Sir Jeffery Bowman
Peter Boydell Q.C.
Mark Brackenbury
Sir Kenneth Bradshaw K.C.B.
Melvyn Bragg
Sebastian Breaks
Adrian Bridgewater
Richard Briers O.B.E.
Alan Britten
Tony Britton
Simon Broadbent
John Bromley O.B.E.
W. Michael Brown
Michael J. Brown
Rt. Hon. Sir Stephen Brown
R.N. Brueton F.R.C.S.
Barnabas Brunner
Sir Gordon Brunton
James Buckley
George Bull O.B.E.
Robin Burgess
Andrew Burns C.M.G.
Dr Nat Burstein
Anthony Butcher Q.C.
William Camp
Hugh Campbell
Simon Campbell-Smith
John B. Cannell
Sherban Cantacuzino C.B.E.
Hugh Carlisle Q.C.
Timothy Carlton
Francis Carnwath
Peter F. Carter-Ruck
Timothy Cassel Q.C.
John Casson O.B.E.
Hon. Sir Edward Cazalet
Rt. Hon. Lord Chadlington
Rt. Hon. Lord Chalfont O.B.E., M.C.
Roderick Chamberlain
Nicholas M. Chambers Q.C.
Ian S. Chapman
Kit Chapman M.B.E.
John Charlton
Michael Charlton
Kris Chatamra F.R.C.S.
Sir Christopher Chataway
David Chipp
Graham Clark

His Honour Judge Paul Clark
Rt. Hon. Kenneth Clarke Q.C., M.P.
Philip Clough
Stephen Cockburn
Nicholas Colchester
John Coldstream
Giles H.C. Cole
Tom Conti
David Conville O.B.E.
M.N. Conville
Charles A.G. Cook M.C., G.M., D.S.C., F.R.C.S.
Bryan Cooper
Christopher T.S. Cooper
Guy Cooper
Joseph E.N. Cooper O.B.E.
Leo Cooper
William Corlett
Laurence Cotterell
Ronald Coubrough
Adrian Cowell
Professor Richard Creese T.D.
Rodney J. Croft F.R.C.S.
Arthur Crook
Rt. Hon. Sir David Croom-Johnson D.S.C., V.R.D.
Laurence Cuckney
Hugh Cudlipp O.B.E.
Ian Curteis
Anthony Curtis
J.S. Curtis
Neville Cusworth
David Damant
John Darby
Ronald Davidson-Houston
Sir Michael Davies
Rowland Davies
Noel Davis
William Davis
William Gronow Davis
David Day
Eric de Bellaigue
John L.F. Dean
Martin Dean
Michael Deeley
Giles de la Mare
Lord Denham K.B.E.
Maurice Denham O.B.E.
John Denison C.B.E.
His Honour Judge Neil Denison Q.C.
José Juan de Olloqui
André Deutsch C.B.E.
Bernard P. Dewe Mathews C.B.E., T.D.
Robert de Wynter
Professor C.J. Dickinson
Professor Peter Dickinson
Peter Dimmock C.V.O., O.B.E.
Peter Dorrington-Ward
Robert Dougall M.B.E.
John Doyle M.B.E.
John Dreyfus
Nicholas Dromgoole
Maurice Druon C.B.E.
Richard Dunn C.B.E.
Hugh Dykes M.P.
H.H.G. Eastcott F.R.C.S.
Michael Edwards C.B.E., Q.C.
John Ehrman
Peter Elstob
J.H. Emlyn Jones C.B.E.
Robin Esser
Professor Martin Esslin O.B.E.
James Evans C.B.E.
Kenneth H.R. Ewing
J.O. Fairfax
Peter W. Fane
Edward Faulks Q.C.
Stephen Fay
David Fearnley
Stephen Fein
J.J. Fenwick
Christopher Fildes O.B.E.
Paul H.D. Findlay
His Honour Judge Peter Fingret
Christopher Floyd Q.C.
Dr Bruce Fogle
Michael Fone
His Honour Judge Jeremy Fordham
Sir Denis Forman O.B.E.
William Fox T.D.
Mark Fox-Andrews
N. Fox Bassett
Clive Francis
Maestro Massimo Freccia
Hon. Sir Christopher French
Martin Fuller
Roy Fullick
David Gadsby
John Gale O.B.E.
David Galloway
James Galloway
Paul Gane
Sir Edward Gardner Q.C.
Gordon Gardiner
Norman Garrod C.B.E.
Charles Neilson Gattey
Lord Gibson
Sir John Gielgud C.H.
Michael Gilbert C.B.E., T.D.
David Gilmore
Kenneth S. Giniger
David Gladwell
Kenneth D. Glancy
Ben Glazebrook
Rt. Hon. Sir Iain Glidewell
J.F. Goble
Dr J.R. Godwin-Austen
David Gordon
Giles Gordon
John Gordon
Sam Gordon Clark
Marius Goring C.B.E.
Sir John Gorst M.P.
Gerald Gouriet
Sir James Gowans C.B.E., F.R.S.
Sir Alexander Graham G.B.E.
Keith Grant
Anthony J. Gray
A.J.R. Gray
Henry Green Q.C.
Hubert Gregg
Arthur Grimwade
C.P. Grimwade
Gerald Grusin
Ivor Guest
Robin Guilleret

Gareth Gwenlan
Arnold Hagenbach
Professor Jack W.C. Hagstrom
Willis Hall
Robin G. Halwas
Adrian D. Hamilton
Eben Hamilton Q.C.
M.I.G. Hamilton D.S.C.
Ralph Hammond Innes C.B.E.
The Rev. R.F. Hannay
R.D. Harman Q.C.
Desmond Harney O.B.E.
Joseph C. Harper Q.C.
Kenneth C. Harper
W. Paul Harriman
Bruce Harris
Raymond Harris
C. Anthony Hart
William Hart
John Hartley
Richard Hartley Q.C.
St. John Hartnell
David W. Harvey
Ross Harvey
Hon. Philip Havers Q.C.
His Honour Judge Richard O. Havery Q.C.
Dr David Hay
Dr John Hayes C.B.E.
Rt. Hon. Lord Hayhoe
Richard Hayward
Brigadier Sir Gilbert Heathcote, Bt., C.B.E.
Peter Hemmings
Francis A. Henley F.R.C.S.
Raymond Henley
Hon. David Herbert
Ian Herbert
Patrick Heren
Christopher Hibbert M.C.
Graham Hill
John E.B. Hill
Rupert Hill
Professor Hillgarth
Nicholas Hilliard
His Honour Derek Hill-Smith V.R.D.
John Hilton Q.C.
Edward A. Hoare
Sir Anthony Hollis
Will Hopper
Sir Derek Hornby
J. Horsfall Turner C.B.E.
Peter Horsfield Q.C.
Anthony Howard
Luke Hughes
Kenneth Hyman
Robin Hyman
Ian A.N. Irvine
David Jacobs C.B.E.
Hon. Sir Robin Jacob Q.C.
Martin W. Jacomb
P.P. Janson-Smith
Peter Jarrold
Keith H. Jeffery
Peter Jeffrey
Julian Jeffs Q.C.
Hugh R. Jenkins C.B.E.
Toby Jessel M.P.
R.R. Jessell
Milton Johns
Hugh Johnson
Iain Johnstone
Allen Jones
Gareth Jones
John W. Keffer
E.D. Kempner
Rt. Hon. Sir Michael Kerr
Gerald le Blount Kidd O.B.E.
Paul H. Kiernan
Sir John Killick G.C.M.G.
David R. Kilpatrick
David King-Farlow
Dr Paul Knapman
Dr Roman S. Kocen T.D., F.R.C.P.
Peter Land
Paul Langridge
Dr Peter T. Lascelles
Sir Frank Layfield Q.C.
Rt. Hon. Lord Lawson
Peter Leaver Q.C.
Richard Leech
Andrew Leigh
Anthony Leonard
Hon. Sir John Leonard
Bernard H. Leser
John N.C. Lewis
J.W. Lewis
Clive Lindley
Nigel Lindsay-Fynn
Christopher Lloyd
Oliver A.W. Lodge T.D.
Oliver R.W.W. Lodge
Anthony Loehnis
David Long
His Honour Richard Lowry Q.C.
Terence Lucas
William Lund
P.M. Luttman-Johnson
David Machin
Sir Charles Mackerras
Iain Mackintosh
Murdo Maclean
Bryan Magee
David Male C.B.E.
Dr Christopher Mallinson F.R.C.P.
Martin Mann Q.C.
Robin Marlar
Professor Alfred Marnau
Grahame Martin-Turner
Roger Marwood
Brian Masters
John Mathew Q.C.
P.C. Maxlow-Tomlinson
Lieutenant-Colonel Simon Mayall
Professor David Mayer
Hon. David McAlpine
Hon. Sir William McAlpine, Bt.
Professor Ian McDonald
Henry McGee
Lord McGregor of Durris
Dr Keith McKee
Professor James G. McMurtry
David Meddings
Cornelius Medvei
Dr V.C. Medvei C.B.E., F.R.C.P.
Andrew Merton
Peter Meyer
Leonard Miall O.B.E..

Peter Miall
R.G. Middleton D.S.C.
James P. Miller
David Milne Q.C.
Peter Mimpriss
Sir Derek Mitchell K.C.B., C.V.O.
Geoffrey Mitchell
Julian Mitchell
Stephen Mitchell T.D.
Frank R. Moat
Michael Mockridge
Alec Monteath
Viscount Montgomery of Alamein C.B.E.
Christopher Morahan
Roger Morgan C.B.E.
Sheridan Morley
Rt. Hon. Sir Andrew Morritt C.V.O.
David Mullock
Martin Muncaster
Nigel Murray
M.B. Musgrave
J.A. Nasmyth
Rt. Hon. Sir Brian Neill
Michael Nelson
Derek Nimmo
Kit Nisbet
James Noble
Robert Noel
Paddy Nolan
Dr Remington Norman
Ian Norrie
Robert Norton
Richard Odgers
Dr Michael O'Donnell
John L. Oliver
Hon. Tarquin Olivier
Dr Michael Ormerod
Richard Ormond
Dr Gordon Ostlere F.R.C.A.
Peter O'Toole
Hon. Sir John Owen
Tudor Owen
Nicholas Padfield Q.C.
Hon. Michael Pakenham C.M.G.
E. Harold Palmer C.B.E.
Geoffrey Palmer
Howard Panter
Christopher Parish
Charles G.A. Parker
Hon. Sir Jonathan Parker
Geoffrey Parkhouse
Sir Peter Parker K.B.E.
John Parry
Richard Pasco C.B.E.
David Peppercorn
Sir Edward Pickering
Mark Pitman
Jonathan Playford Q.C.
Greville Poke
Philip Pollock
Jeremy Potter
Professor Roy Pounder
D.W. Pountney C.B.E.
Dr Christopher Powell-Brett
Colin Prestige
Dr John V. Price
Robin Price
Stanley L. Prothero
André Ptaszynski
Jonathan Pym
Raymond Raikes
Simon Raison
Christopher Rawson
The Rev. Gerald Reddington
Michael Redington
His Honour Judge Paynter Reece
Gareth Rees F.R.C.S., F.R.C.P.
Max Reinhardt
Simon Relph G.M.
Peter Rice
His Honour Judge Michael Rich Q.C.
Denis Richards O.B.E.
Professor Peter Richards
Sir John Riddell, Bt.
P.J.R. Riddell
P.R. Riddle F.R.C.S.
Michael Ridley C.V.O.
A.O.B. Riviere
Stanley Rivlin
Lord Rix C.B.E.
Tim Rix
Toby Robertson O.B.E.
Robert Robinson
Vivian Robinson Q.C.
His Honour Judge John W. Rogers Q.C.
I.L.R. Romer
James Roose-Evans
Barry Rose M.B.E.
Rt. Hon. Sir Christopher Rose
Albi Rosenthal
Tom Rosenthal
Donald Ross F.R.C.S.
Anthony Rota
H. Rothenberg O.B.E.
David Rowe-Beddoe
Joshua Rozenberg
Michael Rubinstein
Sir Jack Rumbold Q.C.
Alan C. Rusbridger
Sir Charles Russell, Bt.
Vice-Admiral Malcolm Rutherford C.B.E.
Richard Sachs
Lord Sainsbury of Preston Candover K.G.
Peter Sallis
Nick Salmon
Geoffrey Samson
Ian Samuel C.M.G., C.V.O.
Jeremy Saunders
Michael Sayers Q.C.
John Schlesinger C.B.E.
Alexander Schouvaloff
Peter Scott C.B.E.
Robin H. Scutt C.B.E.
Patrick Seale
Harold Sebag-Montefiore
William Servaes
Thomas Seymour
James Sharkey
Michael Shaw
Dr Michael Shea C.V.O.
Eric Shorter
Bernard Shrimsley
Milton Shulman

David Sigall
Robin Simon
Andrew Sinclair
Donald Sinden C.B.E.
Peter J. Singer
Anthony Slingsby
Rt. Hon. Lord Slynn of Hadley
Hon. Sir Brian Smedley Q.C.
Godfrey Smith
A. Kenneth Snowman
Dr Bethel Solomons
J.M. Southern
Arthur Spencer
Sir Michael Spicer M.P.
Timothy Stanley-Clarke
Dr Richard Staughton F.R.C.P.
Professor Denis Stevens C.B.E.
Marshall Stewart
B.L.D. Stone
Evan Stone Q.C.
John Strachan F.R.C.S.
Edward Streator
J.G. Studholme
David Summers
Anthony Sumption D.S.C.
J.H.G. Sunnucks
John Sweetman C.B., T.D.
David H. Tatham O.B.E.
Selwyn Taylor F.R.C.S.
Gerald Tedder
Hugh Tempest-Radford
Norman Thackeray M.B.E.
Rt. Hon. Sir Swinton Thomas
Edward Thompson
Nicolas Thompson
Nicholas Thompson
Garry C.C. Thorne
Frank Thornton
Richard C. Thornton
Dr H. Thurston
Julian Tobin O.B.E.
Keith Topley
Dr Desmond Torrens M.B.E.
Harry Towb
Dr T.O. Treadwell
Donald Trelford
Frederick Treves B.E.M.
Ion Trewin
William S.P. Trower
Francis Tufton
His Honour Sir Stephen Tumin
Dr Barry Turner
Michael R. Turner
John Tydeman
John Underwood
Sir William Van Straubenzee M.B.E.
Sir John Vane
David Vermont
John Vernon M.B.E.
Anthony C. Vickers
Hon. Sir John Vinelott
Laurence Viney
Hugh Wace
Dr Thomas H.H. Wade
Rt. Hon. Lord Wakeham
Dr O.C. Waldron
Sir Stephen Waley-Cohen
Richard Walford
Ian Wallace O.B.E.
Rt. Hon. Sir Mark Waller
Richard Walton
Geoffrey Wansell
Michael Ward-Thomas
R.G. Ware
Sir Kenneth Warren
Keith Waterhouse C.B.E.
Hon. Sir Ronald Waterhouse
Alan Watkins
His Honour The Rev. D.B. Watling Q.C.
Jack Watling
Moray Watson
Duncan Wauchope
Ewan Wauchope
Colin Webb
David West C.B.E.
Timothy West C.B.E.
His Honour Sir David West-Russell
Anthony Whitaker
D.H. Whitaker O.B.E.
Harvey White
Romilly Whitehead
Hugh Whitemore
John Whitney
Andreas Whittam Smith
Professor Glynne Wickham
Jeffry Wickham
Jonathan Wicks
David Widdicombe Q.C.
Frank Wilding
J.H. Willcox C.B.
Nunc Willcox
Gerard M. Wilkinson
Graham Willett
J.P.Williams
Tim Wilton-Steer
Donald A.G. Wintersgill
David Wolfers M.C.
Sir Philip Woodfield K.C.B., C.B.E.
Edward Woodward O.B.E.
Sir Paul Wright K.C.M.G., O.B.E.
Robin Yapp
Peter Yates
Charles Yorke
J.S. Yorke
R.G.A. Youard
Dr Michael Zatouroff F.R.C.P.
Dr Ronald Zeegen O.B.E., F.R.C.P.

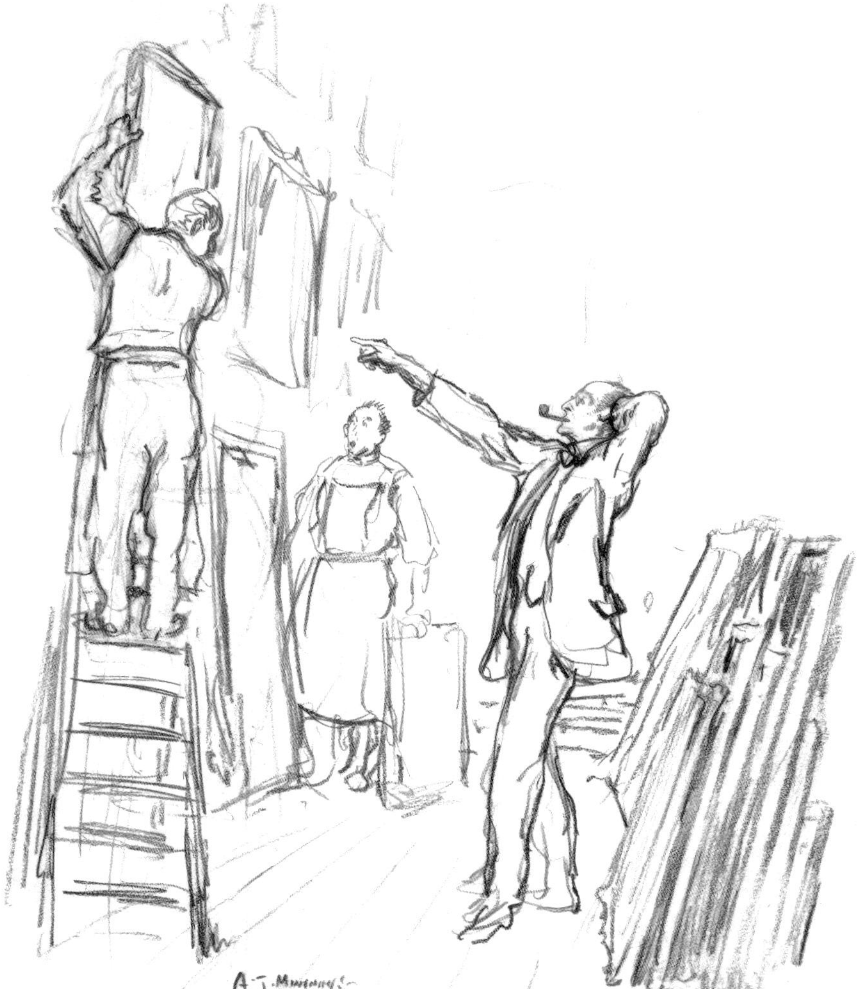
DEC. 23.

EDITORS' FOREWORD

Geoffrey Ashton's catalogue of the Garrick Club's collection is essentially an account of the Club's pictures, drawings and sculpture as documents of the history of the British stage, and of the Club itself. It does not attempt detailed descriptions or interpretations of the works primarily as objects of art history independent of those associations.

When the editors began their work early in 1993, it immediately became clear that Dr Ashton had created a landmark in theatre history studies, but because of the illness that he endured in the last years of his life, the huge manuscript was in need of a considerable amount of editing with respect to format, consistency and detail.

The text of the introduction and catalogue listings that follow is Dr Ashton's final draft, so far as the editors have been able to determine. The editors' task has been to prepare the manuscript for publication. In doing so, they have sometimes re-written text for the sake of clarification, made it consistent in format, and corrected the few errors they found. Unfortunately, Dr Ashton did not have the opportunity to revise what was a very large manuscript. The editors have therefore made some deletions of passages that did not contribute directly to an entry or to the subject in hand. They have done this in the belief that he would have approved the deletions and would have made them himself in the final text. They have attempted to verify data and references and, at the end of the main catalogue, have added the acquisitions made by the Garrick Club since 1988. They have checked each entry against the respective pictures, drawings and sculpture in the collection. As a result of this direct study of the objects themselves and because of the addition of recent acquisitions, changes were made in some instances to the catalogue entries, and several indexes had to be revised.

For their part, the editors would like to thank, in addition to those already mentioned in the Preface, the many people who made their task easier. Miss Eileen Tweedy photographed the entire collection and maintained the photographic records. Mr Hugh Kelly photographed a selection of paintings and sculpture for reproduction in colour. Mr Peter Siddons' expert knowledge of Siddons and Kemble portraiture and his generous assistance to the editors in their review of the portraits and ordering of the photographs has been invaluable. The co-operation and patience of Miss Enid Foster, the Club's Librarian, has been most appreciated. The editors gratefully acknowledge the assistance of Miss Nafisa Taylor at the Computer Centre of University College,

London in the process of retrieving and converting the files from Dr Ashton's original word-processor disks. Miss Jaki Leverson, director of the Tufts University Program in London at University College, kindly accommodated Professor Burnim with regular use of a printer and computer. Dr Brian Allen, Director of the Paul Mellon Centre for Studies in British Art, gave good advice. The skill of Miss Gillian Greenwood, designer, and the sharp eye of Helen Robertson, copy editor and typesetter, contributed substantially to the realisation of the project. Miss Marie Leahy's expert advice on copy-editing matters is also gratefully acknowledged.

The editors' greatest thanks are due to Miss Betty Beesley, secretary to the Works of Art Sub-Committee, who looked after them during the time they worked in the Club and, drawing on her unrivalled knowledge of the collection, responded to their numerous queries with patience and expertise.

K.A.B. & A.W.
June 1996

I · THE GARRICK CLUB COLLECTION

The Garrick Club houses by far the largest and most significant collection of British theatrical works of art: 972 paintings and drawings and 56 pieces of sculpture. The particular strength of the collection is the mid-to-late Georgian period, from 1760 to 1830, the golden age of theatrical portraiture. Regular gifts over the past 165 years, however, have augmented the collection so that it also includes many later 19th-century and contemporary works.

The most important event in the growth of the Garrick Club collection was the acquisition in 1835 of the paintings and drawings owned by Charles Mathews. Gathered over the previous 30 years, they formed a visual history of the Georgian theatre, and the Club – only recently having been founded and named after England's greatest actor – was seen as the ideal setting for them. In 1833 Mathews had exhibited his pictures at the Queen's Bazaar, Oxford Street, hoping to find a buyer for the collection as a single lot. It seems that some items were sold individually, as 28 of the pictures have never been part of the Garrick Club collection. As a commercial venture, however, the exhibition was a failure, and after an unsuccessful attempt to sell the pictures to the National Gallery, Charles Mathews's widow was left with a large collection of pictures and nowhere to put them. (See section 4 below for details of his collection and its acquisition.)

The pictures were hung in the original club house at what had been Probatt's Family Hotel, 35 King Street, just round the corner from the present club house. They joined a small collection of busts and paintings that included Mather Brown's scene from *The Gamester* (682), Van Bleeck's scene from *The Alchymist* (271), and Roubiliac's gilt bronze bust of David Garrick (S15).

Mathews's 1833 exhibition was provided with a catalogue of the 388 paintings and drawings compiled by his son Charles James Mathews with Mathews's assistance.[1] It became the unofficial catalogue of the Garrick Club collection until Robert Walters produced a new catalogue, published in 1909.[2] The Club had been left three or four pictures annually over the intervening 75 years, and Walters's catalogue contains 592 entries. His catalogue includes a number of engravings and photographs. The growth of the collection is a clear indication that the Club was seen as the logical resting place for theatrical pictures. It was fortunate that in 1864 the Club was able to move to much larger premises in New King Street, which was renamed Garrick Street at the request of the members of the Club.

Although most of the pictures that were given to the Club in the 19th century are still in the collection, there are very few survivors of the 30 or so busts that had been donated to the Club during that period. In the 19th century the Club attracted a number of artist members who were generous enough to donate examples of their work, usually not theatrical. In 1847 David Roberts gave his large and impressive view of Baalbec (932) and in 1857 Clarkson Stanfield gave two of his own pictures, a seascape (935) and a view of Ancona.[3] When the Club moved to the new club house in 1864, Louis Hague presented two large views for the Smoking Room, and in 1887 Sir John Gilbert gave his large picture of *The Standard Bearer.*[4]

In his 1909 catalogue Robert Walters followed the format of the Mathews catalogue by including chatty comments on many of the sitters. There is no obvious order to the numbering of the Mathews catalogue – perhaps the order in which they were hung in the Queen's Bazaar – and Walters numbered the pictures by their location in the Club, room by room.[5] C.K.Adams followed this order in his catalogue of 1936, despite frequent rearrangements of the pictures. Adams's catalogue was the first attempt to view them as works of art rather than theatrical snapshots.[6] It consisted of 632 entries for paintings and drawings with 27 more added in his 1948 supplement. He removed the engravings and photographs included in Walters's catalogue.

The present catalogue [completed in 1991 by Geoffrey Ashton and updated and revised by the editors, 1993–96] has added about 300 entries to the paintings and drawings section. This increase is caused by the number of acquisitions since 1948, and also by the fact that the De Wilde watercolours and some other drawings which had been catalogued in groups are now separately listed.[7] Also the sculpture had not previously been catalogued.

The Garrick Club collection continues to grow, although without the almost manic acquisitiveness of the 19th century. Distinguished theatrical donors at that time included Sir Henry Irving, who gave several pictures, including Clint's great scene with Edmund Kean in *A New Way to Pay Old Debts* (355) and John Collier's portrait of J.L. Toole (810), and Sir Squire Bancroft, who presented 13 works of art to the Garrick including the Boydell Macbeth picture (748) and the busts of himself and his wife by Count Gleichen (S1 and S2).

A number of pictures have been presented by a subscription of members. The first to be acquired in this manner was the portrait of Walter Lacy, bought in 1886 and no longer in the collection. More distinguished pictures acquired by subscription were Forbes-Robertson's portrait of Samuel Phelps as Wolsey (655) and John Collier's *Merry Wives of Windsor* group with Herbert Beerbohm Tree, Ellen Terry and Madge Kendal (810), both bought as memorials to the great actor-managers.

Theatrical portraiture as an independent genre really ended with the advent of theatrical photography in the 1850s, but a tenuous tradition continued, and some of the more interesting later 19th-century theatrical portraits are to be found in the Garrick. These include Henry Phillips's portrait of Charles Kean as Louis XI (344), Jenny Lee as Jo by Henry Macbeth-Raeburn (414), and Pettie's portrait of Charles Wyndham as David Garrick (860). A number of portraits of non-theatrical members of the Garrick were bequeathed to the Club in the 19th century, and in recent years a number of similar portraits have been presented by their painter, Jack Gilroy, who in the 1960s and 1970s became a sort of unofficial artist to the Club.[8] Gilroy's pictures are complemented by the work of other contemporary artists such as Feliks Topolski (202) and Mervyn Peake (643). These pictures, and the recent purchase of Anthony Devas's portrait of Sir John Gielgud as Valentine in *Love for Love* (261), indicate that the Garrick Club collection continues to play a vital role in the narrative of the English-speaking stage and its history. The Garrick Club is the Pantheon of the British Theatre.

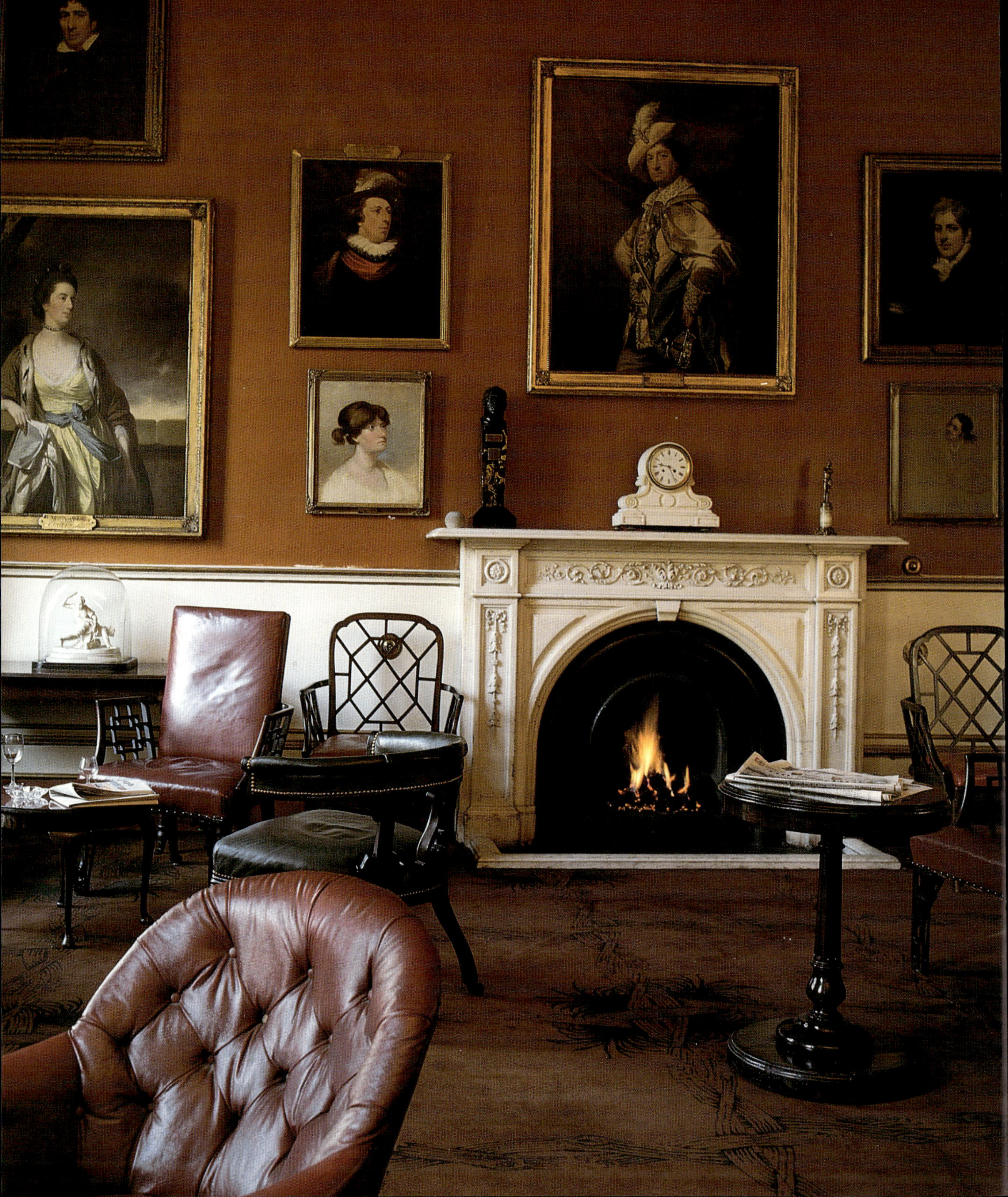

2 · THE GOLDEN AGE OF BRITISH THEATRICAL PORTRAITURE

From 1760 to 1830 there was in England a golden age of theatre painting. This golden age is best studied at the Garrick Club, where the collection of theatrical portraits is unique in terms of quality, quantity and historical importance. Artists well represented in the Garrick, such as Johan Zoffany, James Roberts, Gainsborough Dupont and Samuel De Wilde, made theatrical subjects a major feature of their work, but almost all British figurative painters living during the reigns of George III and George IV had some contact with the theatre, whether they specialised in portraits or subject pictures. And landscape artists frequently painted theatrical scenery.

Amongst the family portraits, topographical views, and sporting pictures in country house collections that survive from the 18th and early 19th centuries, it is quite usual to find the occasional theatrical portrait.[1] Similarly, libraries that have survived from the same period invariably contain volumes of theatrical plates. The less wealthy made do with individual prints. At first even these, in the form of theatrical mezzotints sold at a guinea or half a guinea, tended to be expensive, but in the late 18th century the popular stipple engraving brought theatrical portraits within the range of any theatre-lover's pocket. Penny-plain prints later extended the genre as theatrical entertainment became a popular diversion. The number of theatrical portraits in all media produced before the introduction of theatre photography in the mid-1850s was phenomenal – probably something in the region of 10,000.[2]

What did the patron who commissioned a picture or purchased a print expect from his theatrical portrait? Undoubtedly he hoped for a likeness, but a likeness rather different from that provided by an ordinary portrait. That difference derives from the two-fold nature of the portrait's subject, who is both actor and character. Painted in costume at a particular, well-known dramatic moment, the subject of a theatrical portrait inspires a sort of dual recognition on the part of the viewer. The best theatrical portraits deliver at once the spectacle of a dramatic performance and the intimacy of a recognisable likeness. In these pictures actual persons and their fictional personae coalesce to form single images. Famous actors and actresses, interesting in themselves, are set in a context which holds a separate, special fascination for the viewer – the play in performance.

The style of acting in the 18th and early 19th centuries helped the artist to match his sitter with just the right scene or moment in the play. It was a period in the history of the British theatre when the actor's position was paramount. Most people visited the theatre to see a particular performance and not to hear the play, admire the production, or discuss the direction. Performances, especially of tragedies, were planned around a number of set pieces which, if well performed, would provoke enthusiastic applause. Long speeches and significant moments were punctuated with grand dramatic poses which would be held whilst the applause lasted. Those moments and those pauses were what an audience would remember most clearly from a performance, and they were therefore reproduced in theatrical portraits.

A more difficult task was the attempt to encapsulate the spirit of the whole play in the portrait. It was perhaps only the more experienced theatrical artists such as Zoffany and De Wilde who managed to achieve this aim regularly and successfully in their group paintings. In other pictures, notably in portraits or scenes from comedies where the dramatic principle of point-making was not usually an important feature of the performance, actors were often shown in a pose that was typical rather than particular. For example, there are a number of portraits of various actors in the part of Steady in *The Quaker* in which the poses are typical of the character rather than of 'a particular moment'.[3] In many theatrical portraits, especially those sent for exhibition, a detailed background was painted in, ostensibly to give an accurate impression of the stage scene. However, some backgrounds were evidently fanciful and not theatrical, and the fact that most theatrical portraits had a plain background shows that the first consideration was the pose of the actor rather than his setting.

On the other hand, theatrical scenes, which are perhaps the most familiar form of theatrical portraiture, almost always have a pictorial background. Zoffany's first theatrical scene, which shows Garrick in his short curtain-raiser *The Farmer's Return* of 1762, depicts in careful detail all the utensils and artefacts of the stage kitchen in which the scene takes place.[4] His next theatrical scene, showing Garrick and Mrs Cibber in *Venice Preserv'd*, includes a view of the Salute and gives prominence to a street lamp.[5] Both the moon, which lights the church and the water in front of it, and the street lamp, which lights the players, are essential components of the picture. The slightly later scene from *The Provok'd Wife* also includes the suggestion of moonlight, although the main source of illumination comes from the lanterns carried by the watchmen.[6]

It is evident that Zoffany did a great deal to heighten the reality of his theatrical scenes. Although the kitchen implements in *The Farmer's Return* might have been painted on a piece of sliding scenery, they would not have appeared on stage as props in the way that Zoffany shows them. The speed of 18th-century productions, especially in a simple curtain-raiser, would not have allowed for the setting of such a complex array of objects. Zoffany's lighting of the scenes from *Venice Preserv'd* and *The Provok'd Wife* is too sophisticated for the resources of the candle-lit Drury Lane of the 1760s.[7] He gives an impression of reality to the scenery. The same heightening of reality is found in the work of other artists. For instance, portraits of actors playing Richard III in the last scene of Cibber's adaptation of Shakespeare's play – those of Garrick by Hayman and Nathaniel Dance are perhaps the most familiar – invariably show a tentatively realistic battlefield with battle in progress in the background, scenes far removed from anything that would have been possible on the 18th-century stage.[8]

Not only did Zoffany and other artists add spice to the limited visual reality of the 18th-century stage, they also reorganised the figures in the scenes they had witnessed on stage and wished to paint. Zoffany's scene from *The Clandestine Marriage* of about 1770 shows Fanny and Lord Ogleby in the foreground, standing in a garden, with Canton approaching from behind the well-stocked flower-bed in the background. On stage the flower-bed would have been a painted flat with a straight edge from which the character would have emerged, and the two foreground figures would have been standing on the forestage in front of the proscenium arch, entirely isolated from the scenery.

The 18th-century actor performed almost the entirety of his part on the forestage while some distance behind him, on the stage proper behind the proscenium arch, sliding flats would indicate the setting and context of the scene. Zoffany and his successors compress these two quite separate areas of the stage in their theatrical scenes and in their pictures of individual performers when the background is shown. Only in the early 19th century, when the forestage was removed in the major London theatres, could painted theatrical scenes bear any resemblance to what painter and audience saw on stage.[9] George Clint's theatrical scenes such as *The Clandestine Marriage* of 1819 or *Love, Law and Physic* of 1830 were undoubtedly much more precise reproductions of stage practice than anything that had been produced in the days of the forestage.[10] But even Clint's apparently accurate theatre pictures must not be viewed as depictions of actual performances. Several of his oil sketches survive to show that his theatrical scenes were carefully constructed in the studio.[11]

Likewise, Zoffany's scenes must not be viewed as pictorial stills of actual performances. A somewhat dubious oil sketch in Oxford is the only evidence that Zoffany prepared for his theatrical scenes by taking sketches of individual actors in performance.[12] Also some small full-lengths of actors were probably painted *after* rather than before they appeared in the larger theatrical scenes.[13]

Zoffany's theatrical pictures betray the artist's careful preparation in their somewhat contrived compositions. The scene from *The Provok'd Wife* shows Garrick and his attackers arranged in a neat semi-circle, an ideal conceit for Zoffany's pictorial effect but nonsensical in relation to the scene as played on the stage. Having composed the picture in this way, however, Zoffany experienced some difficulty with the central figure of Garrick as Sir John Brute. Garrick, who had commissioned the picture, was perhaps sensitive about being immortalised in a frock and anxious to present a manly countenance to the world. The first version of the picture, now in the collection of the Marquess of

Normanby, did not meet with his approval and Zoffany rubbed out the head and replaced it. This revision also seems not to have pleased the actor, so Zoffany experimented with the single figure now in the Royal National Theatre. Again Garrick demanded a repainting of the head; this third and final version of the head was reproduced in the picture that Garrick finally bought from the artist, which is now at Wolverhampton.

Some artists were less successful than Zoffany in their attempts to rearrange theatrical impressions into a satisfying composition. Francis Wheatley's scene from *Twelfth Night* of 1772, now in Manchester, displays some attempt to depict the scene on stage.[14] Individually, the characters are portrayed with considerable wit and accuracy; however, they create the impression of having been lined up with little attempt to suggest, through composition, the dramatic relationships of the play. Samuel De Wilde occasionally throws his characters together in a similar manner. For instance, his scene from *The Lord of the Manor* of 1814 consists of individual portraits joined together by a pastoral backdrop. There is only one moment in the play when the three characters depicted appear together, so the dramatic context is clear; but De Wilde clearly had difficulty in relating the figures to each other.[15]

On the other hand, the occasional theatrical scene can be by far the most literal form of theatrical portrait. For example, Benjamin Wilson's painting of the tomb scene in Garrick's version of *Romeo and Juliet*, with George Anne Bellamy and Garrick in the roles of the lovers, is probably the most accurate representation of a theatrical scene in 18th century art.[16]

Despite such exceptions, a theatrical scene generally falls into one of two categories: either it is an artificial reconstruction of a specific dramatic performance, or it is a collection of individual theatrical portraits, combined, according to the skills of the artist, to create a stronger, more artistically impressive whole.

Although the term 'theatrical portrait' may be understood to include portraits of actors and actresses out of costume, more accurately it applies to portraits of actors in character, in which the artist is trying to convey the essence of the performance by reproducing a significant moment in the play. The theatrical scene is often the most effective type of theatrical portrait because it concentrates the essence of the performance of several players into one moment.

Theatrical scenes are also invariably the most spectacular form of theatrical portrait and were more frequently chosen for exhibitions than their comparative rarity would suggest. Only 30 of the paintings and drawings in the Garrick Club depict theatrical scenes. The second largest collection of theatrical paintings from this period, the Somerset Maugham Collection at the Royal National Theatre, includes 10 theatrical scenes out of a total of 80 pictures. By their very multi-figured nature theatrical scenes are easily compared with conversation pieces and history paintings, and both these genres were investigated by artists whose main interests lay with the theatre and theatrical portraiture.

Sometimes the theatrical scene was used to serve a wider purpose. For instance, the large painting by Zoffany of the trial scene from *The Merchant of Venice* (*c.* 1768) in the Tate Gallery, depicting Charles Macklin as Shylock, includes portraits of Lord Mansfield and other Justices who were involved in the lawsuit that had recently been brought against Macklin.[17] Forty years earlier, Hogarth had added portraits of well-known contemporaries to the audience depicted in his later versions of the scene from *The Beggar's Opera*, not because the characters were seen at the play but because their presence in his paintings would increase the social relevance and therefore the value of his work.[18]

There are, in fact, close parallels between the popularity of theatrical portraits in Britain and the popularity of social and political caricatures. Both genres were at their most popular between 1750 and 1850, especially in the decades around 1800. Many political caricatures derive their impact from a theatrical allusion that the public would recognise immediately. Allusions from Shakespeare without an actual visual quotation from a theatrical scene were even more abundant.[19] Early on, satirical prints were a popular art form while theatrical prints were largely confined to the more expensive mezzotint and large line engravings. As theatrical entertainments and the resultant prints became more readily available at the end of the 18th century, however, the visual parallels between satirical and theatrical prints became closer. Dighton's slightly caricatured portraits, the precursors of the penny-plain, tuppence coloured prints, had exact equivalents in the political satires of Heath, Gillray and others.[20] The same artists adapted the group portraits of Charles Mathews – which appeared after George Henry Harlow's 1814 portrait of the actor – for their political caricatures of the 1820s.[21] By the late 1820s there was a falling-off in both quality and quantity in both genres, and the next 20 years saw the gradual emergence of commercial wood-engraving and photography – developments that effectively put an end to the satirical print and theatrical portrait as independent art forms.

One further aspect of theatrical portraiture was viewed with great interest and enthusiasm by both artist and actor as well as by the theatre-struck public. Theatrical costume is almost an end in itself in some theatrical portraits, and in many portraits in character the costume is an essential clue to identifying the part and the play. The idea of accurately dressing historical plays slowly gained ground towards the end of the 18th century, although Charles Kemble's staging of *King John* at Covent Garden in 1823 was the first occasion on which a strictly archaeological approach was applied to the whole production.[22] Of course, some 'historical' characters, such as Falstaff and Richard III, wore distinctive costumes throughout the 18th century and others could be identified by extravagant theatrical shapes such as that worn by James Quin in the well-known engraving of him as Coriolanus.[23] Although most costumes were versions of everyday dress, it would be a mistake to assume that the actors and actresses shown in contemporary costume are merely dressed in their ordinary apparel.

Contemporary fashion in both male and female dress was reproduced on stage, but often using unusually bright colours and large quantities of braid, sequins and other variegated glitter – all the better to create an effect in the subdued and somewhat unsatisfactory lighting of the theatre.[24] Theatrical portraits, therefore, often have a slight feeling of caricature about the costume as well as the sitter's person. The heightened pose or gesture is paralleled by the heightened costume.

Despite the enormous popularity of the genre at the turn of the 19th century, the taste for theatrical portraiture had been a relatively recent development. Actors and managers, as well as painters, engravers and publishers, who had a professional interest in a thriving market for theatrical portraits, had all contributed to the growth of interest. Although there had been the occasional earlier work, such as John Greenhill's pastel portraits of Restoration actors,[25] the theatrical portrait did not really assume an important place in English art until the interests of John Rich and William Hogarth combined in 1728 to produce the six pictorial versions of the Prison Scene from John Gay's *The Beggar's Opera*.[26]

The Beggar's Opera was the most successful theatrical production of the early 18th century, and Rich, the manager of Lincoln's Inn Theatre where the play was staged, was able to build a new theatre in Covent Garden in 1732 with his profits. Rich was happy to use Hogarth to propagate as well as record his success, and Hogarth was equally happy to take advantage of a situation in which he could satisfy a demand in exchange for much-needed cash and probable artistic recognition. Hogarth's pictures supplied the top end of the market for souvenirs of *The Beggar's Opera*, a market that included fans, screens and playing cards.[27] In the latest and largest versions of his picture Hogarth seems to have been persuaded by Rich to depict an image of the new theatre at Covent Garden: large and elegant and still to be built. The format developed by Hogarth in his successive versions of the scene from *The Beggar's Opera* was basically that used and adapted by Zoffany in his theatrical scenes painted for Garrick and his contemporaries 30 years later.

David Garrick was the great catalyst in the development of the theatrical portrait in the 18th century. Early in his career he was used by Hogarth as part of the painter's efforts to found a British school of history painting. Hogarth's huge portrait of Garrick as Richard III was completed in 1745, four years after Garrick's famous début in the part at Goodman's Fields Theatre. Nathaniel Dance's most ambitious portrait was later to depict Garrick in the same role, and in 1784 William Hamilton carried the tradition into the next generation with his large and impressive portrait of John Philip Kemble as Richard III.[28]

It was J.P. Kemble who inspired the most impressive of these portraits of actors as larger-than-life historical figures, the series of four massive pictures by Sir Thomas Lawrence. Lawrence described his portrait of Kemble as Coriolanus of 1798 as 'a sort of half history picture'. His portrait of Kemble as Rolla in *Pizarro* of 1800 became one of the most popular images of the war-torn, and hero-seeking, early 19th century. The Duke of Wellington later wanted to take the picture to Paris to decorate the British Embassy. The portrait of Kemble as Hamlet was bought in 1812 by William Alexander Madocks (1774–1828), a Welsh MP, to form the high altar of the church in his newly-built village of Tre Madoc; Lawrence was not alone in regarding his large 'half history' pictures as modern equivalents of the baroque altarpiece. The last portrait in the series, Kemble as Cato in Addison's *Cato*, was exhibited in 1812.[29]

These grand portraits, from Hogarth's *Richard III* to Lawrence's *Cato*, relied, for at least part of their impact, on the viewer confusing the actor playing his part with the vision of an actual historical or pseudo-historical figure. This grandiose style of theatrical portraiture ran side by side with the more intimate conversation-piece theatrical scenes and small full-length portraits. It represented, perhaps, the aspect of the genre where the artist was most completely in control of the final form of the portrait. Hogarth's use of Garrick for his own ends in the 1745 portrait of the great actor as Richard III put some strain on their usually warm and friendly relationship.

The actor, however, and not the artist, was very much in control by 1762 when Garrick began to commission the series of theatrical conversation pieces from Johan Zoffany.[30] Occasional portraits of Garrick, as well as other actors and actresses, had appeared during the late 1740s and 1750s. These included the Shakespeare scenes by Zoffany's English mentor, Benjamin Wilson.[31] Nevertheless, it was the partnership of Garrick and Johan Zoffany that established the popularity of theatrical painting as an independent genre in England. The Society of Artists, of which Garrick was a founding member, held an annual exhibition from 1761 in which Zoffany was able to show his theatrical conversation pieces to a wide public. (Its predecessor, the Society of Arts, had held an exhibition in 1760, when Francis Hayman exhibited his portrait of Garrick as Richard III.) Mezzotints after the pictures were sometimes shown at the exhibitions as well. These theatrical pictures established Zoffany's reputation, but they also brought the image of Garrick before that section of the educated public which did not attend the theatre but might be persuaded to adopt the habit. They also consolidated Garrick's reputation, not only as an actor but also as an art patron.

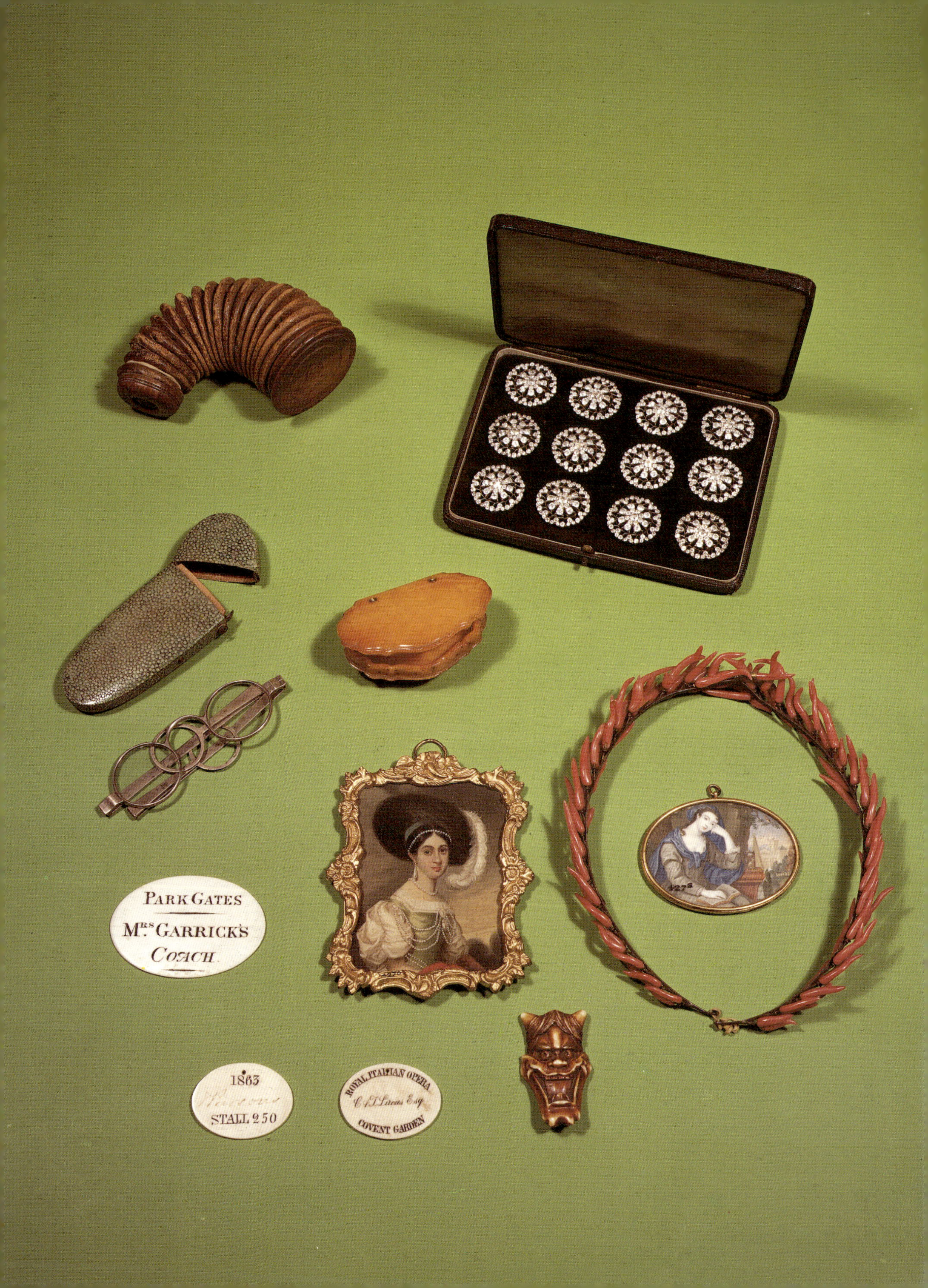
PARK GATES
MRS GARRICK'S
COACH
1863
STALL 250
ROYAL ITALIAN OPERA
COVENT GARDEN

3 · THEATRICAL PRINTS

Garrick was fully aware of the publicity value of the pictures, both in London and further afield. Whilst in Bath, for instance, in 1766, he wrote to Benjamin Wilson, mentioning the imminent arrival of a whole 'cargo' of prints of himself – probably a recent engraving of Wilson's scene from *Romeo and Juliet* with Garrick as Romeo.[1] Surprisingly few actors, however, seem to have appreciated the virtually free publicity that the exhibited portraits and the resultant engravings gave to their performances in particular and their careers in general. Samuel Foote took advantage of Garrick's absence on the Grand Tour in 1764 to commission Zoffany to paint a theatrical subject. The picture, which included a portrait of Foote himself, shows a scene from Foote's own play *The Mayor of Garratt*.[2] Foote, however, was almost as exceptional as Garrick, and later actors and actresses, even the much-portrayed Sarah Siddons, had a seemingly passive attitude to theatrical portraiture. Occasionally a remarkable theatrical début, such as Edmund Kean's in 1814, would produce a flurry of pertinent theatrical portraiture but, such inspiration apart and with the important exception of Charles Mathews, the instigators of most theatrical portraits were artists and publishers rather than actors.[3] Artists exhibited increasing numbers of theatrical portraits, and a number of publishers commissioned theatrical paintings and drawings for engravings to be sold to an ever-widening market.

The most important publisher of theatrical portraits in the late 18th century was John Bell. Although he did publish individual plates of large format, he specialised in collections of plays, each one illustrated with a theatrical portrait frontispiece. His main ventures were the three editions or collections of Shakespeare's plays of 1773–74, 1775–78 and 1785–88,[4] and the three large collections of plays, *The British Theatre* of 1776–77 (reissued with several changes in 1780), 1791–93 and (1791–)97.[5] Bell's 1797 edition of *The British Theatre*, which ran to over 100 titles before the publisher went bankrupt, established Samuel De Wilde as the leading theatrical portraitist of the day in the same way that Zoffany's reputation had been established by the theatrical conversation pieces painted for Garrick. [Kalman A. Burnim & Philip H. Highfill, Jr are preparing a catalogue of over 350 portraits published by Bell in his collections or issued separately by him. This catalogue, to be published by the Southern Illinois University Press in 1997, will also provide a comprehensive account of Bell's life, and of the various editions he published.]

In all the Bell collections, except Shakespeare 1773–74, each play was prefaced by a small full-length of an actor or actress in costume. In a number of cases either the plays were never performed or the actor shown never played the part.[6] These are exceptions, but they illustrate the dubious veracity of some theatrical portraits. The full-length theatrical portrait was used in collections similar to Bell's *British Theatre*, from Cawthorn's *British Theatre*, the immediate successor to Bell, to George Cumberland's *British Theatre*, the last collection with full-length theatrical portrait frontispieces. Later collections, such as those of Lacy and French, were initially illustrated with a frontispiece, often from the spidery hand of George Cruickshank, showing a scene from the play.[7] Eventually even these unsatisfactory illustrations were abandoned. The problem was not only the change of fashion but also the need for cheaper editions and huge print runs that were beyond the technical capacity of subtly engraved portrait plates.

The portrait frontispieces to the 1785–88 ('literary') edition of Bell's *Shakespeare* and the 1791–97 edition of Bell's *British Theatre* were each supplemented with a plate illustrating a scene from the play. Although some attempts have been made by the artist to connect various of them with stage productions, it is more realistic to treat the scenes as literary subject pictures rather than theatrical portraits.[8] *Parsons's Minor Theatre*, a collection of 27 plays published about the same time as the third edition of Bell's *British Theatre*, also included title-page scenes with decorative borders. The corresponding theatrical portrait for each play, however, was an oval bust portrait of an actor or actress in everyday dress.[9] This perhaps somewhat surprising alternative to full-length portraits in costume was adopted in a number of theatrical publications at the turn of the century, such as *The Thespian Dictionary* of 1802 and 1805.[10]

The simple bust or half-length theatrical portrait was preferred in later publications, such as William Oxberry's weekly periodical *Oxberry's Dramatic Biography*, of 1824–27, and his *Dramatic Mirror* of 1827 and 1828.[11] Oxberry's publications were extremely popular. Some of the portraits were reduced from full-length and all the actors and actresses were shown in character. The most sophisticated series of half-length illustrations were those to another of Oxberry's publications, *Oxberry's New English Drama* of 1818–21.[12] Most of the engravings were taken from pencil drawings by Thomas Charles Wageman, whose work in this period forms a theatrical portrait gallery second only to that of Samuel De Wilde for sensitive characterisation and theatrical immediacy.

Apart from the frontispieces to collections of plays, the main outlets for engraved theatrical portraits were illustrated theatrical periodicals and collections of theatrical biographies. There was also a handful of illustrated theatrical biographical dictionaries, including the already-mentioned *Thespian Dictionary*. Although there were many theatrical periodicals in the late 18th and early 19th centuries, in fact relatively few of them were illustrated; only about 20 titles in the period 1770 to 1840, from *The Macaroni; and Theatrical Magazine* (1772-74)[13] to *Actors by Daylight* (1838)[14], contained illustrations. About half the titles were published in the 1820s, including *Oxberry's Dramatic Biography*, which was one of the three most heavily illustrated periodicals. The other two were *The Monthly Mirror* (1795–1811),[15] which had half-length portrait frontispieces in the style of Parsons's *Minor Theatre* and *The Thespian Dictionary*, and *The Theatrical Inquisitor* (1812–1820),[16] which had full-length portrait frontispieces in the style of Bell's *British Theatre*.

The biographical collections also came into their own in the 1820s with *Oxberry's Dramatic Biography*, easily the most profusely illustrated.[17] Previous collections such as *Roach's Authentic Memoirs* (1796), and *Authentic Memoirs of the Green Room* (1806) were less copiously illustrated.[18] At the other end of the spectrum were the collections of large-scale engraved theatrical portraits. Daniel Terry's *British Theatrical Gallery* (1825), a collection of 20 full-length quarto plates of actors and actresses in character, was the first such collection to be published since John Smith's *Dramatic Characters, or Different Portraits from the English Stage in the Days of Garrick etc.* in 1772 and 1773, with engravings after De Fesch.[19] However, Fesch's drawings for Smith's work were tiny, and their main importance lies in the influence they had on the work of the early Bell artists such as Roberts, Ramberg, and Parkinson, rather than on the collections of plates produced over 50 years later. The other collection published before Terry's *British Theatrical Gallery* was *Cooke's Illustrations to the British Theatre* (1821). It was merely a re-issue of 56 of the plates from the 1791–97 edition of Bell's *British Theatre*.[20]

Three of the most distinguished collections of plates were the work of Richard James Lane, who had a distinctive style that owed a great deal to Wageman. His first collection, eight portraits of John Philip Kemble in character published in 1826, was based on portraits by John Boaden, but the other two collections were entirely his own work. Sixteen portraits of Charles Kemble (J.P. Kemble's brother) were published in 1840, as was Lane's most important theatrical work, his *Theatrical Sketches*, which consisted of 49 subjects. Lane executed all his plates in lithograph and the resultant limited print runs probably made the collections rather expensive.[21]

The mezzotint engravings after George Clint's theatrical scenes of the 1820s, in fact, show that there was a renewed attempt afoot to attract the modestly well-off patron, a market somewhat ignored since the late 18th century. John Hayter produced a line-engraved operatic series, with nine plates of *Mad^{me} Pasta in the Opera of Medea* (1827), and E.H. Wehnert brought out a series of plates showing Malibran in *Fidelio*, published in 1836.[22] In 1836 A.E. Chalon produced a series of seven theatrical caricatures in lithograph, *Recollections of the Italian Opera*.[23] These three series confirm that there was a growing interest in theatrical portraiture at the top end of the print-buying market; opera was, then as always, an interest that required money as well as imagination.

The most surprising collections of theatrical portraits were the three series of plates showing W.C. Macready: Ellen Wallace's *12 Sketches of Macready's attitudes in Ion* (1836), Martha Sarah Rolls's 15 plates in *Dramatic Recollections of the years 1838–9* (1839), and George Scharf's 43 plates in *Recollections of the scenic effects of Covent Garden during the season 1838–39* (1839).[24] It is possible that Macready himself engineered their publication; in his financially disastrous season at Covent Garden he needed all the help he could summon. However, the extreme rarity of the engravings perhaps suggests that their popularity was restricted. Although historically important, the aesthetic impact of the engravings of Macready cannot have been great and they fall well short of the impressive series by Lane, Hayter and Chalon. They are, in fact, closer to the simple costume plates, mostly by George Scharf, in J.R. Planché's volumes describing his own productions at Covent Garden from 1823 to 1830.[25]

Although the publishers of theatrical prints were concerned primarily with the market for printed material, they did occasionally offer exhibitions of the original works painted by their artists. In 1838 George Cumberland exhibited *The Cumberland Gallery* at the Colosseum, Regent's Park. Of the 190 pictures the first 138 were genre subjects and 'old masters' with fanciful attributions. The remaining 52 pictures were all theatrical paintings, 37 of them engraved for Cumberland's two later series of plays, his *British Theatre* and his *Minor Theatre*. Evidently, Cumberland was combining picture-dealing activities with a public promotion of the artistic worth of his publishing ventures. In fact, his artists, in particular Robert William Buss and Thomas Charles Wageman, were extremely badly served by their engravers and the pictures must have come as something of a pleasant surprise to the members of the public familiar only with the engraved frontispieces.[26]

John Bell, much more fortunate than Cumberland in his choice of engravers, seems to have made a permanent feature of Samuel De Wilde's pictures, which were exhibited at the British Library in the Strand.[27] Taking his cue and advertising vocabulary from John Boydell's Shakespeare Gallery, Bell used the British Library, the well publicised centre of his publishing empire, as a gallery to show the work of his artists. Not only were De Wilde's theatrical portraits exhibited, but also the original paintings for the genre scenes in the *British Theatre*, including pictures by 20 Royal Academicians among whom were William Hamilton, Robert Smirke and Fuseli. Bell provided De Wilde with a studio at the British Library, although the artist probably had to cope with numbers of curious visitors attracted by Bell's claims that his artist was not merely Zoffany's successor and equal but in fact his superior.[28]

De Wilde seems to have been in a particularly precarious position during the early 1790s because he was apparently entirely reliant for his livelihood on the increasingly unreliable Bell. Other artists were given commissions but only De Wilde was a permanent member of the staff. Bell took his position as a semi-public art patron very seriously (although probably not quite so seriously as John Boydell took his), and insisted that De Wilde paint his theatrical portraits in oil rather than watercolour. Bell's previous publications had been illustrated with portraits engraved after watercolours by James Roberts and others, but the 1791–97 edition of his *British Theatre* was illustrated with engravings taken from oil paintings. There was no technical need for this added expense: indeed the artists might have provided the engravers with drawings based on the paintings in order to facilitate their work. The only reason for commissioning oil paintings would have been Bell's wish to exhibit the pictures, and it was perhaps, in part, this ill-advised attempt to compete with John Boydell that caused his bankruptcy in the 1790s. His problems had begun in 1793, when De Wilde's annual output of over 30 theatrical portraits for Bell fell to a mere 12 and when Bell had to sell the original drawings for the illustrations to his previous publications.[29]

In 1795 the *British Theatre* was taken over by George Cawthorn, and Samuel De Wilde probably made the transition to a new master fairly easily. Twenty years later, De Wilde's only surviving letter (now in the Garrick Club, acquired in 1981) indicates that professional relations between publisher and artist had been firmly established in the 1790s. The letter, to an unknown correspondent, shows that De Wilde had achieved a degree of independence in the intervening period.

June 28th 1815

Sir

I understand you did me the favour of call[ing] at Mr Cawthorn's on Monday. I suppose you wish to know if I had any Drawings ready for you. I have only one, of Miss Kelly in the Woodman's Hut which I flatter myself will meet with your approbation as it has with many. I should have calld at your house with it along time back but not hearing from you since I left the Drawing of Mr Dowton, I concluded you where out of Town. I have not been able to make any more it being the Benefit Season with the Actors etc. … If you will have the goodness to let me know what Day will be agreeable, I will meet you at Mr Cawthorn's and I hope I shall be able to shew you a drawing. As affluence and Artists are not synonymous terms I be[g] leave to subjoin my little account etc. …

I Remain your V H S

Saml DeWilde

Viz:	Mr Mathews as Buskin	3.0.0
	Mr Liston as Lubin Log	3.0.0
	Mr Fawcett as Cornflower	3.0.0
	Mr Mathews as Old Wiggins	3.0.0
	A sketch of Mrs Powell and a fancy Drawing	3.0.0
	Mr Dowton, as Dr Cantwell	3.0.0
	Miss Kelly in the Woodman's Hut	3.0.0
		21.0.0

De Wilde's letter contains several interesting pieces of information. It shows that the artist was still closely involved with Cawthorn the publisher and that the involvement had not made him a rich man. It implies that actors were much too busy during the benefit season, at the end of the annual theatre season, to bother themselves with sitting for their portraits. It also provides evidence that De Wilde made a habit of producing repetitions of his work when commissioned to produce a portrait of an actor rather than paint or draw a fresh portrait. At least two of the seven completed portraits mentioned in the list at the end of the letter were copies of earlier works; the earliest version of Charles Mathews as Buskin is signed and dated 1809; the version mentioned in the letter is probably the one, signed and dated 20 April 1815, that is now in the Royal Shakespeare Theatre Picture Gallery.[30] Also, there are at least three earlier versions of William Dowton as Dr Cantwell, signed and dated 1812.[31]

The diary kept by De Wilde from 1 January 1810 to 30 June 1811 (also now in the Garrick Club Library) is an even more useful source of information on the quantity and type of his work.[32] It is largely a working diary, listing his sittings and describing progress on pictures, but it also mentions social visits and visits to the theatre and gives details of picture prices, framing costs and so on. Watercolour portraits were completed in a day, the sitters coming to De Wilde's studio in Tavistock Row, which was only 50 yards from both Covent Garden and Drury Lane theatres.[33] Oil paintings took longer to complete, and it seems that De Wilde occasionally took his canvas to the sitter for repeated sittings. De Wilde's patrons, apart from theatrical publishers like Cawthorn, were mostly the sitters themselves. However, Charles Mathews often bought portraits of other actors and actresses, and the diary includes mentions of sales of pictures to several amateurs of the theatre.

Although De Wilde's diary is invaluable in describing the bare bones of his practice, there is no discussion or even mention of the particular problems of painting theatrical portraits. In fact, John O'Keeffe's description of Gainsborough Dupont working on his portrait of J.G. Holman as Edgar in *King Lear* is a unique acknowledgement that such problems existed:

> *About this time [1793] my old friend Quick brought me to see Gainsborough Dupont, the portrait-painter, at his house in London-street. Mr Harris had employed him to paint for himself, the principal performers of Covent Garden theatre, in their most distinguished characters. In the front room were many portraits in different states of forwardness. The Right Hon. William Pitt was on the easel; Governor Hastings standing on the floor; and against the wall Quick in Spado, with his little pistol, which he calls his barrel-organ, in his hand. On the door of the back drawing-room opening, I was surprised, and a little shocked, to see the room darkened, and lighted by a large lamp hanging from the centre of the ceiling: there stood a man half naked, a ghastly figure, with a blanket round him, staring wildly, holding a pole in his stretched-out hand. This was Holman, in the character of Edgar, mad Tom; Gainsborough Dupont was painting him. I heard it was the custom of the latter to paint much by lamp-light.*[34]

O'Keeffe's remarks could also serve to describe De Wilde's method of painting theatrical portraits, the point being that there was no direct contact between the performance on the stage and the work produced by the artist. De Wilde's diary shows that he, like most of his artist contemporaries, was a frequent visitor to the theatre but because the paintings were conceived entirely in the studio they were always an indication rather than a reproduction of what happened on stage.

Thomas Harris, referred to in O'Keeffe's description, was the manager of Covent Garden who commissioned Gainsborough Dupont's series of theatrical portraits. He was the major patron of theatrical paintings in the late 18th century. With the exceptions of Garrick, who mostly collected portraits of himself, and the distant prototype of the early 17th-century theatre manager and actor William Cartwright, Thomas Harris was the first patron systematically to build up a collection of theatrical portraits. The pictures by Gainsborough Dupont formed the backbone of his collection and portrayed many of the principal members of his company at Covent Garden. At least 24 portraits were painted in the series, although only 16 are known to survive.[35] Of 17 that appeared in the Harris sale in 1819, the majority were purchased by Charles Mathews.[36]

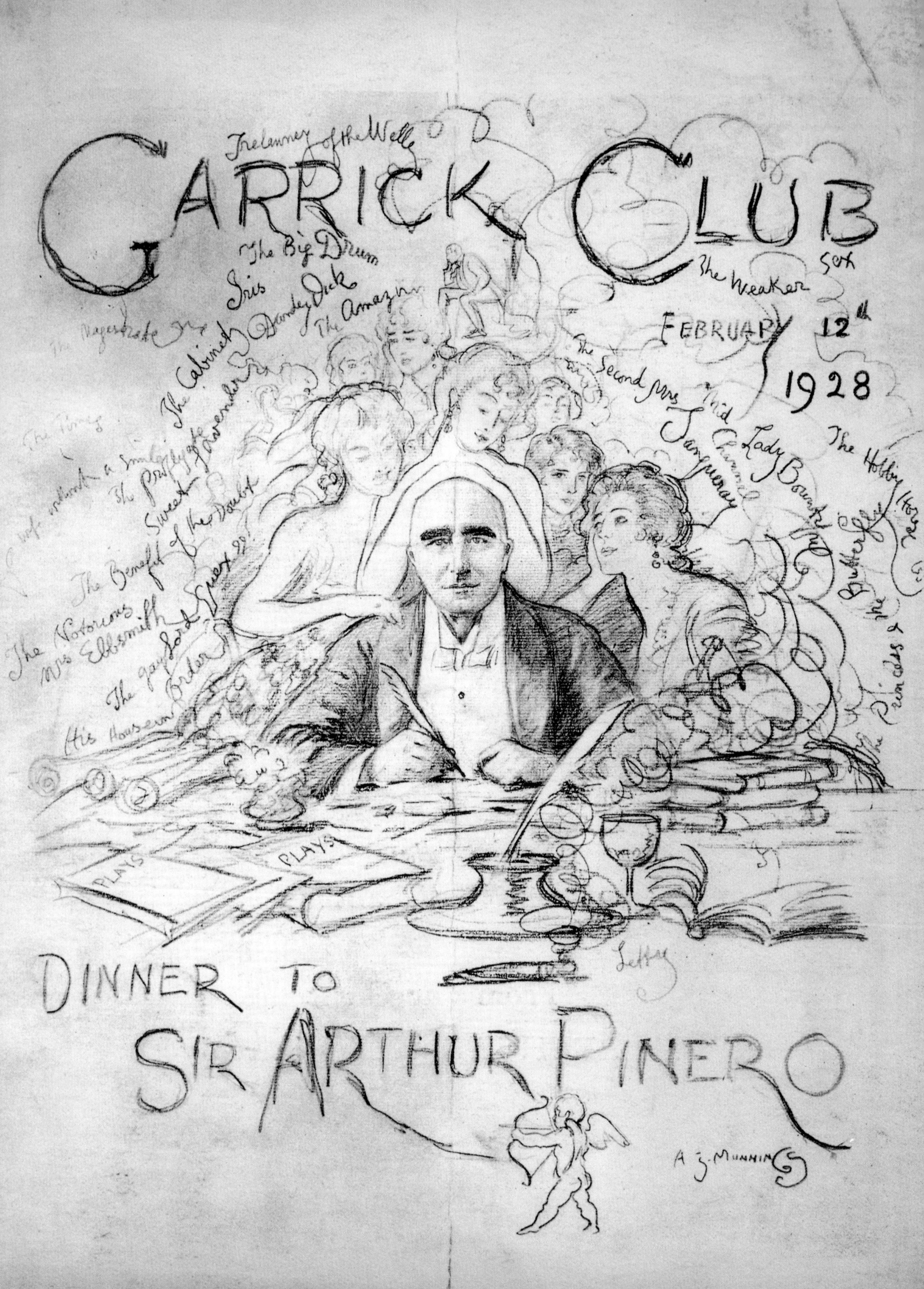
GARRICK CLUB
FEBRUARY 12th
1928
The Big Drum
Iris
Dandy Dick
The Weaker Sex
The Second Mrs Tanqueray
Lady Bountiful
The Benefit of the Doubt
The Notorious Mrs Ebbsmith
The Gay Lord Quex
PLAYS
PLAYS
DINNER TO
SIR ARTHUR PINERO
A. J. MUNNINGS

4 · CHARLES MATHEWS'S GALLERY OF THEATRICAL PORTRAITS

Charles Mathews was one of the most remarkable figures of the early 19th-century stage.[1] Apart from being funny to look at and delightful to know, he was also one of the most original and inspired comic geniuses of the British theatre. His uncompromising figure, which reminded Tate Wilkinson of a maypole, and tiny mouth that seemed to float all over his face were unexpected assets to a man who, in one of his 'At Home' entertainments, could play 30 or 40 roles in an evening.[2] He was an extremely popular performer and earned a great deal of money, which he spent on making his son a gentleman, on providing his wife with luxurious domestic bliss whilst he was away performing in the provinces, and on building up his collection of theatrical portraits, easily the largest put together by one man. It forms the basis and the major part of the Garrick Club collection.

Mathews accumulated nearly 400 paintings and drawings and saw his collection as a permanent record of the glorious but transient history of the British stage. The whole collection was shown at the Queen's Bazaar in 1833, when the aim was twofold: to give the general public an opportunity to see the famous names of the British stage tricked out in their favourite roles, and, more importantly perhaps, to find a buyer. A series of rash investments had left Mathews almost destitute and he was obliged to abandon his plan to leave his collection to the National Gallery. As we shall see, the exhibition at the Queen's Bazaar merely added to Mathews's existing troubles. The story, however, has a relatively happy ending.

Charles Mathews was born in Richmond, Surrey, on 28 June 1776, the son of a sectarian bookseller of strong opinions and strong prejudices, some of them directed against the stage. The huge and interminable four-volume biography of Mathews, edited by his second wife Anne, weaves a web of romantic adventure around his early career, but it seems clear that his first professional engagement was in Dublin in 1794. The following year he moved to Swansea, where he married his first wife, Eliza Kirkham Strong, on 19 September 1797 and performed for two years before joining Tate Wilkinson's company in York.[3] There he replaced John Emery as the company's leading comedian and (his first wife having died of consumption on 25 March 1802) married Anne Jackson on 8 March 1803.[4] Tate Wilkinson's company was the natural stepping stone to a London engagement and Mathews opened at the Haymarket Theatre on 16 May 1803 in a double bill, playing Jabal in Richard Cumberland's *The Jew* and Lingo in O'Keeffe's *An Agreeable Surprise.* In the summer of 1804 he signed up for five years with Drury Lane, making his first appearance on 18 September as Don Manuel in *She Would and She Would Not.* Mathews's contract also included his wife Anne, who was evidently an actress of limited inspiration; however, her name appears exceedingly rarely on the playbills and she probably spent most of her time taking notes from her current reading. Their son Charles James Mathews, born in 1803, later recorded that at her death Anne left six quarto volumes of such notes, attesting to her 'taste and industry'.[5] Mathews moved to Covent Garden from 1812 to 1816 and thereafter – apart from a single season at Drury Lane in the late 1820s – concerned himself entirely with his one-man shows.[6]

His first one-man show was given at Hull on 12 April 1808 under the title *The Mail Coach Adventure; or, Rambles in Yorkshire.* It was merely an amalgam of character sketches Mathews had put together, mostly while he was with Tate Wilkinson's company. Much of the material was written by James Smith. It was a popular evening's entertainment, and Mathews continued to embellish and enlarge upon the original material for almost 10 years. This is the entertainment captured in Harlow's quintuple portrait of Mathews, a picture painted to commemorate a private performance of the piece in front of Queen Charlotte in 1814.[7] In the autumn of 1817 Mathews gave a series of performances of *The Mail Coach Adventure*, whose huge success prompted S. J. Arnold to offer Mathews a seven-year contract to give one-man performances at the English Opera House each spring. The 'At Homes' were given in April and May in London then taken on tour. Mathews gave 'At Homes' almost every year in London until 1834 – he was in America in 1823 and there was no 'At Home' in 1828 – and dominated this increasingly popular theatrical genre. From 1829 the 'At Homes' were given under his own management at the Adelphi Theatre.[8]

The initial theme for an 'At Home' was often suggested by a well-known contemporary dramatist such as W.T. Moncrieff or R.B. Peake. Their ideas were developed by Mathews into his own surreal performance of impersonations, transformations, ventriloquism and patter. The culmination of the evening was a 'monopolylogue', in which all his extraordinary talents and feats were demonstrated during a rambling commentary. The 'monopolylogue' was probably largely impromptu, although numerous editions of Mathews's entertainments were published, each claiming to reproduce the actual text of the 'monopolylogue'. Mathews initially tried to stop their publication but no doubt changed his mind and decided that the publicity they brought could do him no harm. He gave 15 'At Homes' and although the pirated texts read somewhat drearily we must assume that the spark of theatrical magic was there. Their most evocative feature is often the foldout illustration showing Mathews in some of the characters introduced into the entertainment. Indeed, it is evident from the texts, however distorted they may be, that Mathews was a visual rather than a literary performer.

The visual stimulation for Mathews's 'At Homes' is made perfectly clear in only one of the entertainments, the *Home Circuit; or, Cockney Gleanings* of 1827. Two texts of this were published, one by J. Limbird and the other by John Duncombe, the former being much the more complete. The section of the entertainment entitled *Mathews' Dream* is described as follows:

> *The Scene represents the interior of Mr. Mathews' Theatrical Picture Gallery, Ivy Cottage, Kentish Town, of which it is a most beautiful and finished view, by that extraordinary artist Roberts, now attached to the establishment of Covent Garden Theatre; and who is, perhaps, the most promising scene painter of the day. Mr. Mathews enters in his morning gown soliloquizing on the difficulty of finding anything new in the shape of a monopolylogue, and almost cursing the hour he ever introduced that species of entertainment to the public, in which a man is obliged to become a sort of dramatic harlequin, wearing his own rue, with this difference, that instead of changing others he has to change himself, become his own double several times removed. He says he has hit upon a hundred admirable jokes over night, every one of which he has invariably found the next morning in Joe Millar, and has invented innumerable excellent plots only none of them, unfortunately, happened to be practicable. His Gallery, he says, he has collected for the purpose of catching inspiration from the mimic semblances of the mighty masters of his art, an art declared by Colley Cibber and Garrick, whose words he quotes, to perish with the artist; this Mr. Mathews denies, he says imitation, which has grown into disrepute of late days from having been made the instrument of personality, can perpetuate both the art and the artist; we all know, he continues, how much even the commonest portrait of our beloved Shakespeare would fetch. Now, he says, had imitation been encouraged, we might at this moment have had his living semblance, with all his peculiarities and manner before us. I knew Tate Wilkinson, who knew Garrick; Garrick knew Betterton; Betterton knew Booth; Booth knew Davenant, who was Shakespeare's godson; Davenant knew Ben Jonson, and Ben Jonson was Shakespeare's friend. Now had they possessed the power of handing down imitation from each other, I might this evening put Shakespeare before you. Ah, (he continues) if any stretch of fancy could animate these gifted shades – wearing the habits they were wont to wear, and speaking the language they were wont to speak – what an entertainment they might furnish, but that, says he, is impossible. After giving an imitation of John Palmer's plausible manner of wheedling an audience; vindicating the character of Cooke from the charge of habitual drunkenness, and reading an eulogy on Dickey Suett, from Charles Lamb's Elia's Essays, Mr. Mathews goes to sleep. Five whole length portraits of Suett, in Dickey Gossip; Kemble, in Penruddock; Incledon, as the Sailor in the Storm; Cooke, as Sir Pertinax McSycophant, and King, as Sir Peter Teazle, then become successively animated. Dickey Suett gives a scene out of My Grandmother, between himself and Bannister; Kemble presents an imitation of Garrick, in the opening soliloquy of Richard the Third; and relates a curious anecdote of Joe Millar, never having uttered a jest in his life. Cooke vindicates himself from the character of a sot. Incledon sings the Storm: and King presents an animated picture of the old school of acting; and the monopolylogue ends with Mr. Mathews awaking and requesting leave to dream again another evening.*[9]

All the actors Mathews impersonated were dead, and, although some of his audience would have remembered their performances, a large section of Mathews's public could have known them only through prints and through Mathews's collection of paintings, part of which was evidently displayed on stage in the 1827 'At Home'.

There are three prints depicting Mathews on stage with his collection of theatrical portraits during his *Home Circuit* entertainment of 1827. A. Ducote's lithograph, after a drawing by Auguste Herrieu, is included as a folding plate in volume three of Anne Mathews's biography of her husband.[10] In it he is shown in 16 characters with texts below, and displayed on the walls are 18 paintings, with the Harlow quintuple portrait hung left of centre. Thomas Jones's etching, dated 26 March 1827, also shows Mathews in 16 roles with texts below.[11] This time 22 paintings are shown, including the Harlow portrait in the centre below J.P. Kemble as Rolla by Lawrence. The third print is by Henry Heath, dated March 1827.[12] Here Mathews is shown in 13 characters with text below; five full-length paintings are covered with curtains to be drawn back as Mathews impersonates each of the historic actors, and 22 portraits are shown, but not the Harlow. The two printed texts published by Limbird and Duncombe had smaller foldout illustrations.[13]

The fact that Mathews was able to introduce his collection of portraits into his performance is an indication of the popular interest the pictures excited in the early 19th century. There was, of course, a huge market in theatrical prints, and the Royal Academy annual exhibitions included 15 to 30 theatrical portraits every year between 1795 and 1835.[14] It is unlikely that Mathews started his collection of theatrical portraits with the sole aim of using them in performance, or even simply as models for poses and costumes. It is evident, however, that the pictures were a continuous inspiration, a debt that Mathews acknowledged in the 1827 'At Home'.

Mathews's collection was much larger and more wide-ranging than the collections of Garrick and Thomas Harris. He probably started collecting soon after he moved back to London in 1803, when it seems he lost little time in making the acquaintance of Samuel De Wilde, the most prolific of all theatrical artists. De Wilde was working for George Cawthorn, who had taken over John Bell's stock of theatrical plates, and he was happy to paint versions of existing theatrical portraits for Mathews as well as providing new ones. Mathews was also able to add to his collection by taking advantage of several major sales. In 1818 the possessions of James Grant Raymond, who had been stage manager at Drury Lane, were sold.[15] The Raymond sale included 40 theatrical pictures. John Philip Kemble's sale in 1821 included a number of theatrical pictures, and the Garrick sales of 1823 have already been mentioned.[16] The most important sale took place on 12 July 1819, when the major part of Thomas Harris's collection was sold. It included 71 theatrical portraits, of which two-thirds were bought by Charles Mathews.

Thomas Harris had added a gallery to Belmont, his house on Uxbridge Common, in which to display his collection of theatrical portraits. Charles Mathews did the same when he moved to Ivy Cottage in May 1819. Ivy Cottage was on the edge of Lord Mansfield's estate of Kenwood, then known as Caen Wood, and consisted of a mock Tudor house by Peter Frederick Robinson, the architect of the Egyptian Hall in Piccadilly, and a generous garden of about seven acres. According to Anne Mathews, the new gallery was designed by Augustus Pugin, to whom Charles James Mathews had just been articled as a pupil for four years. However, according to Mathews junior he had designed the building himself – his 'first essay as an architect' – along with a 'small Gothic library'.[17]

The picture gallery is visible to the left of the house in G.E. Nadsley's lithograph of 1841, although the Gothic library (also visible in C.J. Mathews's own lithograph of the house) looks more like a Gothic conservatory.[18] The picture gallery was 30 feet long by 17 feet wide and just under 15 feet high, and had a slightly coved ceiling. The entrance was through a small ante-gallery, nine feet wide by 14 feet long and 10 feet high. The pictures were hung floor-to-ceiling and the larger gallery seems to have contained six presses for drawings. There is a detailed wall-plan of the gallery, published after the pictures had been purchased by the Garrick Club in 1835, showing 148 numbered items.[19] When Charles Mathews's pictures were shown at the Queen's Bazaar in 1833 the exhibition consisted of 388 paintings and drawings – the catalogue does not mention the medium. It is not impossible that the six presses in the gallery contained 240 drawings. It is unlikely, however, and it seems probable that Mathews's collection flowed out of the gallery and over the rustic walls of Ivy Cottage.

Mathews was extremely proud of his gallery and encouraged the serious to visit. Charles Lamb was overwhelmed by the experience and published his impressions in the *London Magazine* in October 1822. His article, entitled 'The Old Actors', was used as a preface to the Queen's Bazaar exhibition catalogue. He called Mathews's gallery 'the matchless Highgate Collection' and indulged in a somewhat purple series of theatrical recollections.

Another enthusiastic visitor was P.G. Patmore, who included in his *British Galleries of Art* (1824) a description of the gallery along with nine other major collections of Old Masters. He devoted two chapters to the Mathews gallery, the first describing some of the pictures, the second discussing other items such as busts and Garrickiana. After an enthusiastic description of Mathews's garden, Patmore related 'entering the Gallery, which is a detached building erected for the purpose', and finding himself 'in the midst of an assemblage unique in its kind – an audience of actors'.

Unfortunately, what had been a privileged private view at Ivy Cottage became something less exciting as a public exhibition at the Queen's Bazaar. The awaited wealthy prospective buyer of the entire collection did not turn up, and even the expense of renting the exhibition gallery became a liability when the general public stayed away in droves. There was also the added expense of the catalogue, which identified artist, sitter, part and play, sometimes with quite extensive biographical details. It seems to have been a joint effort by father and son, with Charles James probably doing most of the writing and his father most of the remembering.[20]

The exhibition opened in May 1833 and aroused limited enthusiasm. In her biography of her husband (4: 163), Anne Mathews reproduces the best review she could find (although she does not cite the source):

As a collection of pictures it is not, generally speaking, of the first – of the very first class; but, as an illustration of Britain's histrionic history during, perhaps, one of the brightest periods that ever beamed upon the land, it is unexampled, and utterly impossible to be excelled. The pictures, as works of art, painted by various artists, and at different times, must of necessity be unequal; they are so. But, then it is not as works of art that we go to gloat over them: it is to revive the recollections, mayhap of experience, mayhap of reading, and to live in the excellencies of the past, unheeding and uncaring for the present. The portraits by Zoffany are certainly the best, though there are many by the veteran De Wilde, full of character and identity. It is curious to contrast the peculiarities of the olden actors with the general common-place air of contemporary players.

There is a resounding lack of documentary material on Charles Mathews's collection. Even the Mathews family papers at Princeton University have little to offer to explain his buying habits, the prices he paid or the commissions he gave. However, the failure of the Queen's Bazaar spawned a number of documents now in the Princeton papers and in a volume of manuscript material in the Garrick Club library. A letter (now at Princeton) from Mathews to his wife, dated Worcester 18 October 1833, discusses plans after the failure of the exhibition:

You have felled me by summing up such a conclusion to the Exhibition. I wish I had been spared that. What induced you to advertise if this is the case? G. Robins of course – who gets a good return for his – and can't lose – I really had hopes it was mending by seeing the Post of Monday with the Advert. It is a wretched business but they had better all be piled in my drapery Room than pay for the Rooms at the Bazaar. I hope you do not wish me to take less than £3000 for them. The plan I went on with the Club – was to put a price against every one – either original cost or fair legitimate value of Picture according to the Artist's reputation. Broderip thought it perfectly fair – and under the mark. On your principle of asking more I should say that they had cost £3500 – and that was what I asked. I would take 3000 but I hope neither you or Charles would let me take less if you can possibly help it. D[uke] of B[edford] would advise it I've no doubt. I have long intended to offer them to the Government if I see the National Gallery once advancing. It will be advisable to say that some have been borrowed – (including Cobbler of yours sc.) and to prevent misunderstanding. I don't quite like the view for sale. It would not bring anybody that did not wish to purchase and how few if any would be found.

The exhibition at the Queen's Bazaar had coincided with the forced move from Ivy Cottage, which was purchased by a Mr Shoolbred, who later decided to sell it on the expiry of Mathews's lease in 1841.[21] At the new house – No. 101 Great Russell Street – there was room only for the much smaller collection of pictures eventually sold in August 1835, after Mathews's death. An earlier plan had been to sell the pictures to the Garrick Club, but negotiations seem to have fallen through because the Club could not match Mathews's asking price. Both Charles and his son were original members of the Garrick, and in his diary Charles James Mathews mentions his attendance at the opening dinner on 15 February 1832. After the Queen's Bazaar exhibition at least some of the pictures appear to have been on loan to the Garrick and were hung in the original club house in King Street, Covent Garden.[22]

The plan of putting a price against each picture was carried out, at least in part, and the Garrick Club library has no less than four priced inventories of the pictures.[23] One, in Charles Mathews's own hand, lists 235 pictures and is headed 'Catalogue of Pictures with their cost'. Most items are priced at between £5 and £50, although the small De Wilde full-lengths are all listed at £3. The most expensive items were the small version of Lawrence's portrait of J. P. Kemble as Cato and Clint's scene from *Lock and Key*, both at £100. Two more scenes by Clint and the full-length portrait of Eliza O'Neill as the Tragic Muse by Joseph are next at £80. Joseph's picture had been the centre-piece of the Ivy Cottage gallery. The great Zoffany of *The Clandestine Marriage* is listed at only £50 and his scenes from *Macbeth* and *Venice Preserv'd* both at a mere £30. The prices, as Mathews claimed, do seem to reproduce purchase cost rather than current value. The future Earl of Durham paid about 30 guineas each for his theatrical Zoffanys at the Garrick sale in 1823; £100 would have been the price charged by Lawrence for a small replica of one of his large full-lengths; and in 1813 Samuel De Wilde was charging £3 each for small full-lengths (although in watercolour, not oil).[24]

The other three inventories at the Garrick Club reproduce the prices of Charles Mathews's own list, two of them giving the prices in code. All three appear to be in the same round hand, possibly that of Anne Mathews. All three more or less follow the numbering of the engraved plan of the Ivy Cottage gallery up to No. 148, at which point things become rather confused. Three of the lists have 235 or more items and one of them, chronologically probably the second, goes as far as listing the engravers of some of the pictures, adding now and again a second price to the coded listing of the inventory. (For instance, the Gainsborough Dupont portraits of Mrs Mattocks and John Quick are priced at *E* or £10 and the added note indicates the actual price of £5.15s.6d given for each of them at the Thomas Harris sale.) The details of the inventories are endlessly fascinating but their conclusive and four-fold evidence did not impress the committee of the Garrick Club. The pictures remained the property of Charles Mathews despite the fact that many of them were hanging on the walls of the Garrick.

Eventually, though not until shortly after Mathews's death, the Garrick Club did buy the pictures. The committee met on 14 August 1835 and decided to offer a derisory £1,000 for them. James Winston, the secretary of the Club, communicated the offer to Charles James Mathews on 22 August, and he and his mother were forced to agree to what she called 'a sad sacrifice'.[25] They had little choice; the three-day sale of Charles Mathews's property had raised less than £700.[26] According to Charles James Mathews's diary, the pictures were all transferred to the Garrick on 25 August 1835 and the cheque finally arrived on 29 March 1836.[27] Although the diary makes no mention of the fact, the credit for providing the £1,000 is given by the Garrick Club to John Rowland Durrant, who was a friend of Charles James Mathews but had not been held in high regard by Mathews senior. A letter from Charles Mathews to his wife Anne, dated

Boston (Lincs.) 21 November 1831, suggests that he harboured some doubt over Durrant's credentials as a businessman:

> ... *Durrant is a nice man of business – I sent him an order for £630 – on a Banker in London – having paid that sum into a Bank in Hull – and he has suffered me to be a week in suspense – torturing myself if I pleased by alarms that they had not been faithful. I have written to twit him. I will not believe that he is a rich man. I have long suspected he is not a strict man of business. I would not bank with a man as careless as he is.*

[Despite Mathews's reservations, Durrant, a stockbroker and an original member of the Garrick Club, proved to be a worthy benefactor. Having bought the pictures and loaned them to the Club, he donated the entire collection when it was found that the Club could not afford to purchase it from him. In his *The Garrick Club* (1896), the Rev. R.H. Barham described Durrant as 'one of the kindest and most upright men I ever met ... In early life he was an amateur actor and was always passionately fond of the drama.' An inscription on a wall of the Club's entrance hall gratefully acknowledges Durrant's great gift.]

Once behind the closed doors of the Garrick, the pictures once again became a sight reserved for the curious and fashionable. James Winston had admission tickets printed, carefully restricting both the times of viewing and the numbers of visitors. This situation still prevails, thanks to the disastrous free-for-all of the Queen's Bazaar exhibition of 1833.

NOTES

1 · The Garrick Collection

1 *Catalogue raisonné of Mr Mathews's Gallery of Theatrical Portraits*, now exhibited for the first time, and forming a nearly complete dramatic record from the year 1659 down to the present time. Queen's Bazaar, Oxford Street. London: printed by W. Clowes, 14 Charing Cross, 1833. Price: one shilling.

2 *Catalogue of the Pictures and Miniatures in the Possession of the Garrick Club* (London: Eyre & Spottiswoode, 1909, revised edition). Walters' 'Introduction' is dated June 1908.

3 Clarkson Stanfield's view of Ancona was listed as No. 128 in the 1936 C.K. Adams catalogue; this picture was given to the Theatre Museum in 1976.

4 Louis Hague, 'Interior of a Flemish Inn', C.K. Adams catalogue No. 127, sold 1965; Louis Hague, 'Exterior of a Flemish Inn', C.K. Adams No. 129, sold 1965; Sir John Gilbert, *The Standard Bearer*, No. 891.

5 'Order in which the pictures are Catalogued. Coffee Room, Corridor, Visitors' Coffee Room, Lobby, Visitors' Smoking Room, Members' Smoking Room, Private Room, Members' Back Staircase, Billiard Room, Card Room, Library, Morning Room, Landing (including Miniatures), Grand Staircase, Lounge, Bath Room, East Dressing-Rooms (2), Landing Outside, West Dressing-Room.' There is no indication where the contents of one room end and those of the next begin.

6 *A Catalogue of the Pictures in the Garrick Club. Published by the Club* (London, 1936).

7 Samuel De Wilde: Adams Nos. 45 (A–F), 46 (A–F), 58 (A–F), 59 (A-F), 60 (A–F), 61 (A–F); 63 (A–F), 65 (A–F), 66 (A–F), 68 (A–F), 69 (A–C).

8 Jack Gilroy, see Index of Artists.

2 · The Golden Age of British Theatrical Portraiture

1 For instance the portraits of David Garrick at Chatsworth (by Liotard), Burghley (Angelica Kauffmann) and Althorp (Vandergucht and Nollekens), and the three theatrical scenes by Zoffany at Castle Howard: David Garrick, John Palmer and William Burton in *The Alchymist*; Samuel Foote and Robert Baddeley in *The Mayor of Garratt*; and Samuel Foote and Thomas Weston in *The Devil Upon Two Sticks*.

2 Geoffrey Ashton, 'A Catalogue of British Theatrical Portraits *c.* 1600–1843', unpublished. The 'Catalogue' consists of 8,216 entries. There was a fairly steady stream of exhibited theatrical portraits over the period; viz: R.A. 1795 – 15 theatrical portraits; 1796 – 16; 1797 – 15; 1798 – 29; 1799 – 32; 1800 – 25; 1801 – 16; 1802 – 18; 1803 – 22; 1804 – 28; 1805 – 19; 1806 – 22; 1807 – 10; 1808 – 18; 1809 – 17; 1810 – 14; 1811 – 18; 1812 – 19; 1813 – 20; 1814 – 15; 1815 – 16; 1816 – 16; 1817 – 19; 1818 – 17; 1819 – 22; 1820 – 14; 1821 – 18; 1822 – 23; 1823 – 14; 1824 – 17; 1825 – 22; 1826 – 15; 1827 – 20; 1828 – 18; 1829 – 15; 1830 – 26; 1831 – 16; 1832 – 16; 1833 – 12; 1834 – 12; 1835 – 15; 1836 – 10; 1837 – 6.

3 For instance: Charles Bannister by Thomas Pye (Garrick Club 31); Charles Bannister by Thomas Rowlandson (Yale Center for British Art); and Benjamin Charles Incledon by Thomas Charles Wageman (private collection, London).

4 Johan Zoffany: Garrick as the Farmer and Mrs Bradshaw as his wife in *The Farmer's Return*. Oil on canvas 101.6 x 127, exh: S.A. 1762 (138), coll: Lord Lambton. There are two subsequent versions, both apparently by Zoffany: oil on canvas 101.5 x 127, coll: Yale Center for British Art (B1981.25.731); and oil on canvas 101.6 x 127, Christie's, 20 November 1981 (lot 123).

5 Johan Zoffany: Garrick as Jaffeir and Mrs Cibber as Belvidera in *Venice Preserv'd*, oil on canvas 101.6 x 127, exh: S.A. 1763 (137), coll: Lord Lambton. There are three other versions, all largely by Zoffany: oil on canvas 115 x 145.5, coll: Somerset Maugham Collection, Royal National Theatre; oil on canvas

92.7 x 125.7, coll: Garrick Club (252); and oil on canvas 71 x 91, coll: Museum of Fine Arts, Budapest.

6 Johan Zoffany: Garrick as Sir John Brute, with Henry Vaughan, Thomas Hull (not Hullet as sometimes stated), Thomas Clough, William Parsons, Thomas Phillips and Watkins as watchmen in *The Provok'd Wife.* Oil on canvas 99.1 x 124.5, exh: S.A. 1765 (167), coll: Wolverhampton Art Gallery. The first version was rejected by Garrick so Zoffany repainted the head: oil on canvas 99.1 x 124.5, coll: Marquess of Normanby. A painting of the single figure of Garrick probably marks an interim stage between the two versions of the scene: oil on canvas 74.9 x 62.2, coll: Somerset Maugham Collection, Royal National Theatre (2).

7 [Upon his return from his Grand Tour in 1765, Garrick introduced oil lamps and made other significant advances in lighting techniques at Drury Lane. See K.A. Burnim, *David Garrick: Director* (1961), pp. 78–82.]

8 Francis Hayman: Garrick as Richard III, oil on canvas 89.5 x 64.1, s.& d. F.H. 1760, exh: S.A. 1760 (25), coll: Somerset Maugham Collection, Royal National Theatre (2); and Nathaniel Dance: Garrick as Richard III, oil on canvas 243.8 x 152.4, exh: R.A. 1771 (54), coll: Stratford-upon-Avon Town Council.

9 Covent Garden finally lost its forestage in 1819 and Drury Lane in 1822, although the Covent Garden forestage had been drastically cut back in Henry Holland's alterations of 1792 and Drury Lane's had largely disappeared in the same architect's rebuilding of the theatre in 1794.

10 Clint exhibited 10 theatrical groups at the Royal Academy between 1819 and 1831 as well as a number of single figures. The groups are as follows:

(i) William Farren as Lord Ogleby, Charles Farley as Canton and Richard Jones as Brush in *The Clandestine Marriage*, oil on canvas 151.1 x 125.7, R.A. 1819 (48), coll: Garrick Club (216);

(ii) Edmund Kean as Sir Giles Overreach with 13 others in *A New Way to Pay Old Debts*, oil on canvas 165.1 x 234.9, R.A. 1820 (311), coll: Garrick Club (355);

(iii) Joseph Munden as Old Brummagen, Edward Knight as Ralph, Mrs Orger as Fanny and Miss Cubitt as Laura in *Lock and Key*, oil on canvas 125.1 x 99.7, R.A. 1821 (273), coll: Garrick Club (630);

(iv) Scene in *The Beggar's Opera* – Mrs Peachum (with the aid of strong cordial) recovers from fits occasioned by the discovery of Polly's marriage with Captain Macheath; the portraits are of Mary Ann Davenport, Maria Tree and William Blanchard. R.A. 1822 (272), present location unknown;

(v) Mrs Harlowe as Miss Pickle, John Tayleure as Tag and Miss Clara Fisher as Little Pickle in *The Spoiled Child*, oil on canvas 90.2 x 73.65, R.A. 1823 (13), coll: Garrick Club (787);

(vi) Colonel Berkeley as Brutus, Captain Augustus Berkeley as Mark Antony and Captain Austin as Cassius in *Julius Caesar*, oil on canvas 165 x 235, R.A. 1823 (263), Royal Shakespeare Theatre Memorial Gallery, Stratford-upon-Avon;

(vii) Charles Kemble as Charles II and John Fawcett as Captain Copp in *Charles the Second; or, The Merry Monarch*, oil on canvas 111.8 x 82.55, R.A. 1825 (302), coll: Garrick Club (224);

(viii) John Liston as Paul Pry with Mme Vestris, Miss P. Glover and Mr Williams in *Paul Pry*, oil on canvas 121.9 x 96.5, R.A. 1827 (222), coll: Theatre Museum (25);

(ix) John Liston as Lubin Log, Charles Mathews as Flexible, William Blanchard as Dr Camphor and John Emery as Andrew in *Love, Law and Physic*, oil on canvas 121.9 x 96.5, R.A. 1830 (238), coll: Garrick Club (477);

(x) Charles Mayne Young as Hamlet and Miss P. Glover as Ophelia in *Hamlet*, oil on canvas 121.9 x 96.5, R.A. 1831 (281), coll: Theatre Museum (28).

Clint also exhibited scenes at the British Institution in 1830 and 1831: B.I. 1830 (338), Scene in the Play of *Charles XII* (untraced); and B.I. 1831 (95), Falstaff's Assignation with Mrs Ford – *Merry Wives of Windsor* (William Dowton as Falstaff, Miss Pearson as Mistress Ford and Miss Byfield as Mistress Page), oil on canvas 73.2 x 61, coll: Tate Gallery (377).

11 A sketch for the head of Edmund Kean as Sir Giles Overreach [note 10 (ii) above] is in the Theatre Museum (23). There are two sketches in the Mander and Mitchenson Theatre Collection: one sketch, of two full-length figures, is a study for one of the series of three theatrical groups now at Petworth (R.A. 1833, Nos. 59, 78 and 232); the other, of two half-length figures, is a preparatory sketch for the scene in *The Merry Wives of Windsor*, now in the Tate Gallery [note 10 (x) above]. For a discussion of these sketches and the finished works, see Geoffrey Ashton, 'Paintings in the Mander and Mitchenson Theatre Collection', *Apollo* (August 1981), No. 234 (New Series), 114: 88–92.

12 Johan Zoffany: Studies of Garrick as Abel Drugger in *The Alchymist.* Oil on canvas 33 x 38, coll:

Ashmolean Museum, Oxford (A196). There are two oil sketches on the canvas, and the one on the right relates most nearly to the finished picture at Castle Howard (R.A. 1770, No. 212).

13 For instance, Garrick as Lord Chalkstone in *Lethe*:
(i) Oil on canvas 74.9 x 62.2, Garrick Club (124);
(ii) Oil on canvas 76.2 x 62.2, private collection, New York (the single figure is taken from the scene with three figures exhibited at the Society of Artists, 1766 [No. 198] now in the Birmingham City Art Gallery), and John Beard as Hawthorn in *Love in a Village*, oil on canvas 75 x 62, Christie's, 4 June 1923 (23). The single figure of Beard is taken from the scene with three figures (S.A. 1767, No. 194) now in the Detroit Institute of Fine Arts (47.398). Other versions are in the Royal National Theatre, Somerset Maugham Collection (4), oil on canvas 101.5 x 127; and in the Yale Center for British Art, oil on canvas 101.5 x 127.

14 Francis Wheatley: Elizabeth Young as Viola, James Love as Sir Toby Belch, James William Dodd as Sir Andrew Aguecheek and Francis Waldron as Fabian in *Twelfth Night*, oil on canvas 101.6 x 127, S.A. 1772 (374), coll: City of Manchester Art Galleries (1953.4).

15 Samuel De Wilde: John Liston as Moll Flagon, Richard Jones as Young Contrast and Hamerton as Sergeant Crimp in *The Lord of the Manor*, oil on canvas 48.25 x 59, R.A. 1814 (516), coll: Garrick Club (438). There is a watercolour drawing by De Wilde of Richard Jones as Young Contrast in the Somerset Maugham Collection, Royal National Theatre (46), without a background and possibly preparatory for the finished oil. The three characters appear together in a watercolour in the Yale Center for British Art (1975-4-1991), s. & d. 1812, also without a background.

16 Benjamin Wilson: Garrick as Romeo and George Anne Bellamy as Juliet in *Romeo and Juliet*. Oil on canvas 63.5 x 76.2 (1753), Theatre Museum (8). For a discussion of the accuracy of the representation of the theatrical scene see Kalman A. Burnim, *David Garrick, Director*, pp. 127–40. The version in London is much closer to S.F. Ravenet's engraving of 1753, on which Burnim bases his thesis, than to the larger painting generally thought to be Wilson's original version now in the Yale Center for British Art (B.1975-5-29), oil on canvas 137.2 x 190.5, s. & d. 1753. A third version of the picture, painted in 1757, is at Stourhead; see Geoffrey Ashton, *Shakespeare and British Art* (Yale Center for British Art, 1981), No. 162.

17 Clair Hughes, 'Zoffany's trial scene from *The Merchant of Venice*', *Burlington Magazine* (May 1981), 123: 290–95.

18 See Marvin Karlson, 'A Fresh Look at Hogarth's *Beggar's Opera*', *Educational Theatre Journal* (1975), 27: 30–39, for a discussion of changes Hogarth made in the portraits of the audience on stage from the early 1728 versions of the scene to the later, more elaborate, versions of 1729–30.

19 Mary Dorothy George, *Catalogue of Political and Personal Satires in the British Museum (1870–1954)*. Nos. 4329, 6534, 6535, 7380, 7937 and 9244, for example, all show political characters in Shakespearean scenes.

20 *Political and Personal Satires*, Nos. 15787, 15880, 15899 and 16037.

21 *Political and Personal Satires*, Nos. 15382 and 15746.

22 The production was researched and designed by J.R. Planché. See James Robinson Planché, *Costume of Shakespeare's historical tragedy of King John, selected and arranged from the best authorities expressly for the proprietors of the Theatre Royal, Covent Garden; with biographical, critical, and explanatory notices, by J.R. Planché. The figures designed and executed on stone, by J.K. Meadows (Dramatic Costume No. 1)*, 1823. Subsequently, Planché provided Charles Kemble with the same vigorous research for productions of *Henry IV Pt. 1 & Pt. 2* (1824), *As You Like It* (1825), *Hamlet* (1825), *Othello* (1825), *The Merchant of Venice* (1825) and *Richard III* (1830). A. & R. Nos. 3418–3423.

23 Anonymous engraving: James Quin as Coriolanus (and probably George Anne Bellamy as Volumnia and Peg Woffington as Veturia) in James Thomson's adaptation of *Coriolanus*. Etching 20.3 x 23.2 (B.M.C.7). [A pen and grey ink wash drawing by an unknown artist, with the engraver's red chalk on the reverse, was sold at Christie's on 15 November 1982, was bought by Carter, and is now owned by Richard Jeffree, Richmond, Surrey.] The shape relates closely to the tonnelet, worn by male dancers in the 18th century, which had been developed, it seems, from the undergarments of medieval knights.

24 Diana de Marly, *Costume on the Stage 1600–1940* (B.T. Batsford, 1982), pp. 25–63.

25 For instance: Henry Harris as Cardinal Wolsey. Pastel 39.4 x 32.4, s. & d: JG del: 1664, coll: Magdalen College, Oxford; and Thomas Betterton as Bajazet. Pastel 47.65 x 36.2, s. & d: JG / 1663, coll: National Trust, Kingston Lacy.

26 Lawrence Gowing, *Hogarth* Exhibition catalogue, Tate Gallery (1971–72), Nos. 44–47; and Gabriele Baldini, *L'opera completa di Hogarth pittore* (Milan, 1967), Nos. 9 A–F.

27 See Geoffrey Ashton & Ian Mackintosh, *The Georgian Playhouse* Exhibition catalogue (Arts Council, 1975), Nos. 1–4.

28 William Hogarth: Garrick as Richard III, oil on canvas 190.5 x 250.8, 1745, coll: Walker Art Gallery, Liverpool; for Dance's picture, see note 8; William Hamilton: John Philip Kemble as Richard III, oil on canvas 218 x 155, R.A. 1788 (22), coll: Mander & Mitchenson Theatre Collection.

29 Sir Thomas Lawrence: John Philip Kemble as Coriolanus, oil on canvas 287 x 179.1, R.A. 1798 (255), coll: Guildhall Art Gallery; J.P. Kemble as Rolla in *Pizarro*, oil on canvas 335.2 x 223.5, R.A. 1800 (193), coll: Kansas City Art Institute; J.P. Kemble as Hamlet, oil on canvas 306.1 x 198, R.A. 1801 (187), coll: Tate Gallery (142); J.P. Kemble as Cato in *Cato*, oil on canvas 254 x 177.8, R.A. 1812 (57), coll: A.B.C. Philips. For a discussion of the four pictures see Geoffrey Ashton, *Royal Opera House Retrospectives 1732–1982*, Royal Academy 1982–83, Introduction to Nos. 136–39. A replica of the Cato picture is in the Garrick Club (385). For information about the provenances and further details on these pictures, see Philip H. Highfill, Jr., Kalman A. Burnim & Edward A. Langhans, *A Biographical Dictionary of Actors, Actresses, Musicians, Dancers, Managers and Other Stage Personnel in London 1660–1800* (hereafter called BD), 8: 377–87.

30 The first was *The Farmer's Return* (see note 4 above), commissioned in 1762, quickly followed by *Venice Preserv'd* (see note 5), which was commissioned the following year. In 1762 Garrick also commissioned from Zoffany a series of pastoral conversation pieces, set in the grounds of his villa at Hampton, two of which now belong to Lord Lambton, and a third to Lord Egremont. For a discussion of these pictures and other commissions given by Garrick to Zoffany, see Martyn Anglesea, 'David Garrick and the Visual Arts', unpublished MA thesis, Edinburgh University, 1965.

31 Garrick as Romeo and George Anne Bellamy as Juliet (1753, see note 16 above), and Garrick as Hamlet (1754), a mezzotint by James MacArdell (1754). The mezzotint of Garrick as Hamlet appears to relate to a scene in the Folger Shakespeare Library, attributed to Zoffany but possibly by Wilson, oil on canvas 125.7 x 115.7. The picture was in Sir Henry Irving's sale at Christie's, 16 December 1905 (lot 103). James MacArdell's mezzotint of 1761 is the best record of Wilson's lost painting of Garrick as King Lear, with Edgar and Kent, on the heath. The mezzotint was shown at the Society of Artists in 1761 (174): *Mr. Garrick in the character of Lear; drawn upon with Indian ink, by Mr. Wilson, from whose original picture it was taken.* The exhibited work seems to have been a proof corrected by the artist. The picture was evidently one of Garrick's favourite images of himself; a reproduction of it was carved by Thomas Davies on the Mulberry Wood Casket made to contain Garrick's Freedom of Stratford-upon-Avon (see *The Georgian Playhouse*, Nos. 48–62, especially No. 49). For further information on all these pictures see BD, Garrick iconography, 6: 81–103.

3 · Theatrical Prints

1 David M. Little and George M. Kahrl, *The Letters of David Garrick* (1963), vol. 2, letter No. 400. 'Many thanks to you for the Print – it will do & do again – the Bookseller here has sent for a Cargo, & I am told that it is the fashionable thing at present in London – I rejoice to hear it for many reasons...' The print was probably the 1765 re-issue of François Simon Ravenet's engraving of 1753. The letter is dated only 'Bath Wednesday' but the editors have assigned it to Garrick's stay in Bath from 9 March to the beginning of May 1766.

2 Johan Zoffany: Samuel Foote as Major Sturgeon and Robert Baddeley as Sir Jacob Jollup in *The Mayor of Garratt*, oil on canvas 101.6 x 127, S.A. 1764 (140), coll: Castle Howard.

3 Kean made his mature début at Drury Lane on 26 January 1814 as Shylock in *The Merchant of Venice*, and at the same theatre on 12 February 1814 he played Richard III, the part with which he became particularly associated. Within two years of his début at least 34 dated portraits of him had appeared. No doubt many works were also produced without the retrospective convenience of a date.

4 Bell's 1773–74 'acting' edition of *Shakespeare* was originally illustrated with scenes from the plays, in the tradition of Rowe's edition of 1709 and subsequent editions. It was the first edition to appear with new plates since the considerably more lavish Hanmer edition of 1744. All the rather stiff plates are dated between 1 February 1773 and 8 November 1774, and most of them (32) are by Edward Edwards. The plate to *Othello* is by Isaac Taylor, the plate to *Richard III* is anonymous, and the plates to *The Taming of the Shrew* and *Titus Andronicus* are by John Keyse Sherwin. The plays were published with cast lists from productions at Covent Garden and Drury Lane and plays that had not been performed were prefaced by a Dramatis Personæ. In 1775–76 character plates were added. The plates are dated from 25 September 1775 to 16 March 1776 and are by James Roberts (21), Thomas Parkinson (9) and Robert Dighton (4). The plate to *The Taming of the Shrew* is taken from Benjamin Vandergucht's portrait of Henry Woodward as Petruchio in Garrick's *Catherine and Petruchio*. Vandergucht's three-quarter-length portrait is given a pair of unconvincing legs. Charles Grignion engraved 17 of the plates and most of the others were engraved anonymously.

From the number of surviving examples it is evident that the character plates were popular. Many copies were bound up with the character plates alone, but the editors have not come across a copy with both character and scene plates. A contemporary advertisement suggests that the first series of character plates was not necessarily seen as an integral part of the edition and that it was the success of this series that led Bell to add character plates to his later publications: 'Complete sets of Dramatic Characters. Bell's Edition of Shakespeare's Works, Being now finished, The Prints will be sold at 12s. per Set, neatly sewed in Marble Paper; or at 10s.6d. each Set, in loose Prints, for ornamental Furniture, or to bind up with any Edition of Shakespeare. On Common Paper, 6d. each Number. On fine Royal Paper, with Proof Impressions of the Characters only, at 1s. each Number. On fine Royal Paper, with Proof Impressions of the Characters, and also Proof Impressions of the Historical Scenes, which were originally engraved for this Work, at 1s.3d. each Number.'

The earliest plate to the 'literary' edition of Bell's *Shakespeare* is dated 12 January 1784 and the latest 20 March 1788. The edition itself was published 1785–88. The main contributor to the scene plates was P.J. de Loutherbourg, whilst Johann Heinrich Ramberg produced 19 of the 36 character plates. The others are by Edward Francis Burney (10), Mather Brown (5), John Sanders (1) and William Hamilton (1). The engravers included Charles Grignion (4) and Francesco Bartolozzi (5), but most prolific was J. Thornthwaite with 20 plates. J. Hall contributed 13 plates and John Keyse Sherwin 6.

5 The 1776–77 edition of Bell's *British Theatre* (20 vols.) consisted of 105 plays, each with a portrait by James Roberts. The earliest plate is dated 10 April 1776 and the latest 7 April 1778. Roberts also produced five extra plates, four of ballet dancers and one of an opera singer. There are five folding plates, each showing two performers; 23 plates were engraved anonymously, and J. Thornthwaite, with 54, engraved most of the rest. The other engravers included Burnet Reading (6), J.Page (5) and Robert Pollard (6). Roberts engraved at least 10 of his own plates.

The 1797 edition of Bell's *British Theatre* ran to 102 plays before production was stopped. De Wilde produced 83 plates for this edition. The scene plates in this edition were produced by the same group of artists who provided similar plates for Bell's 'literary' edition of *Shakespeare* 1785–88, although Richard Westall (2) and William Hamilton (4) also provided character plates. Thornthwaite engraved 31 character plates, as did Philippe Audinet. William Leney engraved 19 plates.

The first edition of Bell's *British Theatre* was quickly followed by *The New English Theatre*, published by a number of booksellers, the principal one being T. Lowndes. A general frontispiece of Thalia is followed by 70 plays with portrait frontispieces. The earliest is dated 3 June 1776, less than two months after Bell's first *British Theatre* plate, and the plays and their plates were published regularly until the end of 1777, by which time 60 plays had appeared. Evidently production difficulties, such as those later experienced by Bell, beset the project. Three plays eventually appeared in 1782, four more in 1786, one in 1787 and the final two in 1788. The major contributor to the edition was Daniel Dodd with 27 plates; Isaac Taylor produced 11, Edward Edwards 9, Thomas Parkinson 4, Robert Dighton 4 and T.T. Barralet 7. Thomas Stothard contributed 5 of the later plates. The main engravers were Walker (21 plates), Collyer (14) and Golder (9).

Bell's 'acting' *Shakespeare*, 1775–78, and the first editions of *British Theatre* have character plates set in a spatial void, the chief interest being the gestures and costumes of the actors and actresses. The figures in the plates to *The New English Theatre* are stylistically very similar to those in the earlier Bell editions, but they are placed in a theatrical setting with other characters sometimes glimpsed in the background. Although the settings, sometimes overly complex like many painted theatrical scenes, perhaps detract from the theatrical immediacy of the plates, they do add a certain veneer of sophistication, and Bell's later character plates all have scenic backgrounds.

6 The plates to *Henry VI*, for instance. The only 18th century production of any part of the play on the London stage was a single performance of Part I at Covent Garden on 13 March 1738. *Antony and Cleopatra* was given only 10 performances at Drury Lane in 1759. *Richard II* was not performed after 1739 and only intermittently before, *Troilus and Cressida* was not seen after 1734, and the last performance of *Titus Andronicus* in the 18th century was in 1724.

7 Cumberland's *British Theatre* was published in monthly parts from 1823 and was still being produced in 1841 when it had been taken over by another publisher, Davison. The title was inherited by Lacy and eventually taken over by French. The *British Theatre* was reprinted as a set in 1850. Cumberland's *Minor Theatre*, another part-work, was published in the early 1830s and was collected in an edition of 16 volumes. The plates to the Cumberland series were badly engraved, although the original works, especially those by Robert William Buss, are extremely lively and compare favourably with De Wilde's small full-length portraits. The myriad sets of plays published in London in the second quarter of the 19th century make it difficult to distinguish one series from the next. There is, however, a progressive cheapening of production throughout the century. The illustrations become rare and, when they are included, start to depict small theatrical scenes – at their best by Robert and George Cruikshank – rather than the individual characters that had been traditional since the first edition of Bell's *British Theatre*.

8 Raymond Mander and Joe Mitchenson thought that some of the scenes contributed by William Hamilton to the third edition of Bell's *British Theatre* depicted Sarah Siddons in various roles. See Raymond Mander & Joe Mitchenson, *Guide to the Maugham Collection of Theatrical Paintings* (1980), No. 13.

9 The 27 oval portraits in Parson's *Minor Theatre* are dated between 1793 and 20 December 1794 and were all engraved by William Ridley. The artists include Edridge, Reynolds, Colson, Barry, Shee and De Wilde. The portraits were evidently not produced especially for the publication, unlike the scenes, which are mostly by Charles Reuben Ryley and Henry Richter.

10 *The Thespian Dictionary: or, Dramatic Biography of the present age: containing sketches of the lives, lists of the productions, various merits, &c. &c. of all the principal dramatists, composers, commentators, actors and actresses, of the United Kingdom: Interspersed with numerous original anecdotes, Forming a Complete Modern History of The English Stage.* The 1802 edition, published in London by T. Hurst (A. & R. 42) has 7 illustrations, and the 1805 edition, published in London by James Cundee (A. & R. 43) has 22 illustrations. The 20 oval bust portraits in the text are slight things, mostly engraved by Mackenzie from portraits by Robert Dighton.

11 Oxberry's *Dramatic Biography, and Histrionic Anecdotes* (1825–27), 8 vols. (A.& R. 4139), 125 weekly issues, each accompanied by a steel portrait engraving. The engravings, which are only occasionally of any quality, are all small rectangular half-lengths within a decorative border. Most of the engravings are by J. Rogers (86), including all those in vols. 1–4.

Other engravers include J. Kennerley (13) and R. Page (12). The principal artists are T. Wageman (30) and J. Kennerley (22), with contributions from a number of others such as T.O. Steeden (5), S. De Wilde (6) and G.H. Harlow (4). Harlow's work was used posthumously, as it was throughout the 1820s. All the portraits are in character, apart from that of Joseph Grimaldi. Generally, the portraits of actors and actresses appeared alternately in the weekly issues.

Oxberry's Dramatic Mirror, containing the biography ... of ... Eminent Performers, 1827 (A. & R. 2229), reprinted 1828 (A. & R. 2230). This work is no more than a selection of 23 plates from *Oxberry's Dramatic Biography* (12 from vol. 1, 8 from vol. 2, 2 from vol. 3, and 1 from vol. 4), with an additional plate (J.P. Kemble as Rolla, engraved by J. Rogers after G.H. Harlow, dated 6 August 1825).

12 *Oxberry's New English Drama* (1818–21), pub. W. Simpkin & R. Marshall and C. Chapple. The 71 plays are accompanied by frontispiece portraits engraved in line and stipple. Forty-one portraits are by T.C. Wageman, and other artists include S. De Wilde (7) and G. Clint (4). The principal engravers are J. Thomson (21), T. Wright (16), T. Woolnoth (14) and H.R. Cook (8). Wageman engraved 5 of his own plates. Considering the restrictive format, the portraits are extremely inventive. For example, Wageman's portrait of Mrs Faucit as Lady Racket in Arthur Murphy's *Three Weeks After Marriage*, in which the right hand of the actress breaks through the frame, is one of the most refreshing and striking small-scale portraits of the early 19th century.

13 *The Macaroni and theatrical magazine (or monthly register, of the fashions and diversions of the times conducted upon a much more elegant and liberal plan, than any other work of the kind hitherto published*, October 1772 to March 1773; then *The macaroni savoir vivre, and theatrical magazine* April–June 1773; then *The Macaroni, savoir vivre, and theatrical magazine* July–September 1773; vol. 2, October 1773–September 1774; vol. 3, October 1774. The first volume is supposed to have 25 plates, according to the directions to the binder. The copy cited by A. & R. (4082) in the V&A Library, has 19 plates. The V&A set has been missing for some years and I have not been able to find another copy of the periodical. It is likely that only some of the plates were of a theatrical nature.

14 *Actors by Daylight; or Pencilings in the Pit. Containing the correct memoirs of upwards of forty of the most celebrated London performers: Original Tales, Poetry and Criticisms: the whole forming a faithful account of the London stage for the last twelve months*: vol. 1, Nos. 1–43, 3 March–22 December 1838; then *Actors by Daylight; and miscellany of the drama, music, and literature. Containing correct memoirs of the most celebrated London performers; original tales, poetry, and criticisms*: vol. 2, Nos. 44–55, 27 December 1838–16 March 1839 (A. & R. 4170). Most of the 55 title pages take the form of full-length theatrical portraits with some letterpress above. (Nos. 30, 32 and 48 have half-length portraits.) The wood-engraved portraits are drawn and engraved anonymously; they are often as witty as the accompanying theatrical memoirs. No. 10, for instance, shows John Pritt Harley looking into the window of a print shop – a direct crib from William Heath's caricature of the Duke of Wellington (*Political and Personal Satires*, 1829, BM No. 15859).

15 *The Monthly Mirror: reflecting men and manners. With strictures on their epitome, the stage* (1795–1811): vols. 1–22, December 1795–December 1806; new series vol. 1–9, January 1807–February 1811 (A. & R. 4090). All 184 issues have portrait frontispieces. There are extra portrait plates in the September 1797 and May 1799 issues. The format is usually that of a small oval containing a stipple portrait, although there are some rectangular portraits and a few vignettes. Most of the portraits depict actors and actresses, although very few of them are in character. Other portraits depict writers as well as a number of doctors and political figures. The portraits in vols. 1–20 were all engraved by W. Ridley and he shared the plates of vols. 21 and 22 with W. Holl and A. Cardon. The plates in the new series, vols. 1–9, were engraved by S. Freeman, apart from the first plate, which was engraved by Ridley and Blood. The artists were many and various but included S. De Wilde (20) and C.A. Allingham (6).

16 *The Theatrical Inquisitor: or, literary mirror* (1812–13): vol. 1, September 1812–January 1813; then *The Theatrical Inquisitor, and Monthly Mirror* (1813), vols. 2–11, February 1813–June 1819; then *The Theatrical Inquisitor* (1819–20), vols. 15–16, July 1819–June 1820 (A. & R. 4104). The 94 issues have 92 portrait frontispieces. The May 1816 issue has 2 portraits, and there were frontispieces in the issues for March, May and June 1820. The portraits are all full-length and in character. From September 1812 to December 1814 and from April 1815 to February 1816 the portraits are contained within simple and uniform rectangular borders, although the figures themselves vary in size. The other plates are vignettes with figures on a larger scale. Principal amongst the 13 engravers were J. Thomson (22 plates), H.R. Cooke (13), Carver (12) and Scriven (7). S. De Wilde (36 plates) was much the most prolific of the 21 artists, who also include J. Partridge (11), J. Boaden (5), T. Wageman (4) and H. Singleton (4). Although the plates after De Wilde are based on drawings, other artists, such as Singleton and Boaden, seem to have provided oil paintings.

17 See note 11.

18 *Roach's Authentic Memoirs of the green room, containing the lives of all the performers of the Theatres Royal, Drury Lane, Covent Garden and Haymarket, with poetic criticisms to each and characters of the patentees, the whole being entirely new* (1796) (A. & R. 2214). The only illustration is the engraved frontispiece. [Wally Chamberlain Oulton], *Authentic Memoirs* of the *Green-Room; involving sketches, biographical, critical, & characteristic, of the performers of the Theatres Royal, Drury-Lane, Covent-Garden, and the Hay-Market. In two volumes. Embellished with seven portraits of eminent performers* (1806) (A. & R. 2221).

W.C. Oulton published his rather scurrilous *Memoirs of the Green-Room* annually from 1799 to 1804 (A. & R. 2215–2220). The 1806 edition combines the 1802, 1803 and 1804 editions with a new section. The portraits are simple and small oval bust portraits engraved in stipple by Alais after Linsell (2), Foster (1), Barry (1), H. Bone (1) and Anonymous (2). Five of the seven portraits are in character.

19 Daniel Terry, *British Theatrical Gallery. A Collection of Whole Length Portraits, with Biographical Notices by D. Terry Esq.* (1825) (A. & R. 2228). The 20 plates were all engraved by Robert Cooper and are dated between 1 March 1822 and 23 September 1822. The artists were M.W. Sharp (5), F. Waldeck (6), S. De Wilde (4), G. Clint (4) and G.H. Harlow (1). *Dramatic Characters, or different portraits of the English stage. In the days of Garrick &c.* (A. & R. 2204): 24 plates engraved by John Smith after Jean Louis Fesch – all small full-lengths taken from paintings by Johan Zoffany and Benjamin Wilson. *Dramatic characters or different portraits of the English stage. In the days of Garrick &c.* (1773) (A. & R. 2205) 38 plates. Re-issue of A. & R. 2204 with 14 extra plates.

20 In fact the 56 plates were produced for a collection of 56 plays published by Richard Cumberland in 14 vols. *The British Drama, A Collection of the most Esteemed Dramatic Productions, with Biography of the Respective Authors; and critique on Each Play, by R. Cumberland, Esq.* (1817). The Bell plates were re-engraved and given heavily decorated borders which frequently interfere with the figures and their settings.

21 *Illustrations of the late John Philip Kemble. Drawn on stone by Richard J. Lane from pictures painted in his lifetime by John Boaden, exhibiting that great actor in the characters of Coriolanus, Hamlet, Hotspur, Macbeth, King John, Cato, The Stranger, Penruddock.* All plates are dated 1 October 1826 (A. & R. 3207); Richard James Lane, *Sixteen portraits of Charles Kemble Esq.* (1840), (A. & R. 3177); and *Richard James Lane, Theatrical sketches, drawn from life, by R.J. Lane, Lithographer in ordinary to Her Majesty, and to His Royal Highness the Prince Albert, A.R.A.* (1840), (A. & R. 2235).

22 [John Hayter], *Sketches of Mad*[me.] *Pasta in the Opera of Medea with Portraits of Mad*[me.] *Pasta, Mad*[me.] *Caradori and Sign*[r.] *Curioni* (1827 and A. & R. 3403); and E.H. Wehnert, *Reminiscences of Madame Malibran De Bleriot in a Series of Illustrations of Her Principal Characters. No. 1, Containing Ten Illustrations of Fidelio, and a portrait of Malibran Designed and Drawn on Stone by* E.H.WEHNERT (1836). The plates closely resemble Retszch's *Shakespeare Outlines.*

23 Alfred Edward Chalon, *Recollections of the Italian Opera 1835* (1836), (A. & R. 2081).

24 Ellen Wallace, *Twelve sketches of Macready's attitudes in Ion. by Ellen Wallace.* All the plates are dated 15 October 1836 (A. & R. 3275); Martha Sarah Rolls, *Dramatic recollections of the years 1838–9 drawn and etched from memory* (1839), (A. & R. 3277); and Sir George Scharf, *Recollections of the scenic effects of Covent Garden Theatre during the season 1838–9. Dedicated (by permission) to W.C. Macready Esqr. by G.S.* (1839), (A.& R. 1307).

25 See note 22 on page XLIX.

26 *A Catalogue of The Cumberland Gallery of Pictures Containing a Choice Selection of the Ancient Masters, with a Sprinkling of the Modern Exhibiting at the Colosseum, Regent's Park* (1838). Cumberland's exhibition included 21 theatrical portraits by Wageman and 16 by Buss. The other artists represented in the theatrical section of the exhibition were George Morland (2), De Wilde (1), Zoffany (1), Singleton (1), Vandergucht (1) and Hoppner (1).

27 See Ian Mayes, 'John Bell, *The British Theatre* and Samuel De Wilde', *Apollo* (February 1981), pp. 100–103. Mayes discusses the connections between publisher and artist and suggests that Bell was responsible for Samuel De Wilde taking to theatrical portraiture as his particular specialised genre.

28 'Zoffani has hitherto been considered as the most celebrated Painter of small whole lengths, but comparison now gives De Wilde a place as his superior.' *The Oracle* (8 April 1791). Cited by Mayes.

29 John Bell's career is described and discussed in Stanley Morison's *John Bell 1745–1831* (1930). The sale of Bell's collection of drawings was held at Christie's on 27 March 1793: *A Catalogue of the Original Drawings which have distinguished Bell's Various Editions of the British Classics, and others of his Miscellaneous Publications forming together a Complete School of Arts.* Many of the drawings were bought by Charles Burney and are now in the Burney Collection in the British Museum; see J. F. Kerslake, *Catalogue of Theatrical Portraits in London Public Collections* (1961).

30 Charles Mathews as Buskin in *Killing No Murder.* A: watercolour 35.4 x 22.2, s.&d. 15 September 1809, coll: Garrick Club (464); B: watercolour 37.3 x 23.35, s. & d. 1809, coll: Somerset Maugham Collection, Royal National Theatre (43); and C: watercolour 37.3 x 23.35, s. & d. 20 April 1815, coll: Royal Shakespeare Theatre Memorial Gallery, Stratford-upon-Avon. Mathews first played the part at the Haymarket on 21 August 1809.

31 William Dowton as Dr Cantwell in *The Hypocrite.* A: watercolour 37.1 x 24.4, s. & d. May 1809, coll: Ian Mayes; B: watercolour 37.15 x 24.8, s. & d. May 1809, coll: Somerset Maugham Collection, Royal National Theatre; and C: watercolour 35.9 x 22.6, s. & d. May 1809, coll: British Museum (M.32–35). Dowton first played the part at Drury Lane in 1804. In 1812 he acted the role at the Lyceum Theatre (with the Drury Lane Company) on 12 and 19 March and 8 April. A different version of De Wilde's portrait of Dowton as Dr Cantwell was engraved for Terry's *British Theatrical Gallery*. This may have been the drawing listed in De Wilde's letter of 28 June 1815.

32 The diary was given to the Garrick Club by the De Wilde Holding family in 1965. Edward De Wilde Holding planned an edition of it in the 1930s, but this was never completed. His material is now with Ian Mayes. An analysis of the diary was published by Sybil Rosenfeld, 'A Diary by Samuel De Wilde', *Theatre Notebook* (1965–66), 20: 35–36.

33 The inside front cover of the diary is inscribed 'January 1st 1810 N.9 Tavistock Row, Covent Garden. Sam De Wilde'. Tavistock Row joined the Piazza, Covent Garden, with Tavistock Street which still runs parallel to the Piazza on the south side, between the Piazza and the Strand. De Wilde's address during the years he exhibited at the Royal Academy between 1804 and 1815 was Tavistock Place.

34 John O'Keeffe, *Recollections of the life of John O'Keeffe, written by himself* (1826), 2: 326–27.

35 See John Hayes, 'Thomas Harris, Gainsborough Dupont and the Theatrical Gallery at Belmont', *The Connoisseur* (1968), 169: 221–27, and Geoffrey Ashton, *Royal Opera House Retrospective* Exhibition Catalogue, Royal Academy 1982–83, Intro. and Nos. 123–35. Thirteen of the surviving 16 portraits were shown in this exhibition.

36 *A Catalogue of The Valuable Collection of Original Theatrical Portraits … The Genuine Property of T. Harris, Esq.* Messrs. Robbins, 12 July 1819, 71 lots (with 31 additional lots of non-theatrical paintings and drawings) (Lugt 9630). Some of the pictures not bought by Charles Mathews appeared in a later sale, *A Catalogue of a collection of theatrical portraits of a gentleman, deceased, formerly forming part of the gallery of the late Thomas Harris, Esq.* Messrs. Robbins, 13 June 1848 (A. & R. 90).

4 · Charles Mathews's Gallery of Theatrical Portraits

1 See Anne Mathews, *Memoirs of Charles Mathews, Comedian* 4 vols. (Richard Bentley: 1838–39). This lumbering compendium of Mathews's papers, Mathews anecdotes and his wife's opinions is the best biographical source. The 'Mathews Family Papers' are at Princeton University and the Garrick Club has a quantity of material, including an extra-illustrated copy of the biography.

2 Richard L. Klepac, *Mr. Mathews at Home* (Society for Theatre Research, 1979). This introduction to the subject should be supplemented with a study of the material in the Garrick Club and elsewhere.

3 Princeton University, Mathews Papers AM 18790. Marriage certificate of Charles Mathews and Eliza Kirkham Strong, at Swansea Parish Church, 19 September 1797. Curate John Jones; witnesses Eva Francis and John Wyroose (?).

4 Princeton University, Mathews Papers AM 18790. Marriage certificate of Charles Mathews and Anne Jackson, at St. Helen's, York, 8 March 1803. Vicar John Parker; witnesses Adelaide Decamp and Eliza Desiman.

5 The best biographical source for Charles James Mathews is: Charles Dickens the Younger (ed.), *The Life of Charles James Mathews chiefly autobiographical with selections from his correspondence and speeches*, 2 vols. (Macmillan & Co, 1879). There are many important C.J. Mathews documents, including diaries, at Princeton.

6 His first appearance at Covent Garden as a regular performer was on 12 October 1812, as Buskin in *Killing No Murder.* He returned to Drury Lane on 31 December 1827 as Buskin and Sir Fretful Plagiary in *The Critic* and stayed until the end of the season on 28 June 1828.

7 George Henry Harlow: Charles Mathews 'in private and in various characters', oil on canvas 74.29 x 61.59, coll: Garrick Club (103), exh: Royal Academy 1814 (159).

8 See James Ellis's review in *Theatre Notebook* (1982) 36: 40–44, of R.L. Klepac's *Mr. Mathews at Home* (note 2, above). Ellis lists the 15 'At Homes' and provides a comprehensive bibliography, adding 19 titles to the 28 given by Klepac.

9 *Mr. Mathews' Celebrated Lecture on Character, Manners, and Peculiarities, entitled the HOME CIRCUIT; or, Cockney Gleanings: Performed with the most distinguished success at the Theatre Royal English Opera House including all the Laughable Tales, Anecdotes, and original comic songs: among which are Royal Exchange, Medley of Melodists, Short Stages, Things That Were Not! Royal Academy, The Epping Hunt and the Farewell Finale &c, &c. Also a Monopolylogue, called MATHEWS' DREAM: or, The Theatrical Gallery: In which is introduced Imitations of Suett, Cooke, Incledon, King, and Kemble* (J. Limbird: 1827). The passage quoted is from *Mathews' Dream*, which is part 3 of the entertainment. The edition of *Home Circuit* published by John Duncombe is much less complete.

10 Anne Mathews, vol. 2 between pp. 572 and 573. Title: *The MATHEW ORAMA for 1827 or Cockney Gleaning Aint that a good un now?*

11 *The Mathews-orama for 1827 – or Cockney Gleanings – Aint that a good un Now?*, drawn and etched by Thomas Jones, published 26 March 1827 by G. Humphrey.

12 *MATHEWS-ORAMA for 1827 being The Home Circuit or Cockney Gleanings 'Look at Home' – 'Look abroad' – 'Look everywhere'*, drawn and engraved by Henry Heath, published March 1827 by J. McLean.

13 On the Limbird edition foldout are five whole-length vignettes of Mathews playing the five actors in *Mathews' Dream.* On the Duncombe edition foldout the portion above shows Mathews seated behind a table with two full-length figures on either side of him. The portion below shows Mathews seated centre with five picture frames behind showing full-lengths of the five actors in *Mathews' Dream.* Both etchings are coloured and anonymous.

14 A total of 778 theatrical portraits were shown between 1795 and 1835. The most prolific years were 1798 (29), 1799 (32), 1800 (25), 1804 (28), 1819 (22), 1822 (23) and 1830 (26).

15 *A Catalogue of the library of books, more particularly as relates to theatricals, and about forty very fine original pictures*… Messrs. Robbins, 25 May 1818.

16 *A Catalogue of the valuable and extensive miscellaneous library, choice prints, and theatrical portraits of John Philip Kemble, Esq.* … Evans, 26 January [1821] and the following nine days.

17 Dickens the younger, 1: 43.

18 *Mr. Shoolbred's Villa on the Rise of Highgate Hill. For Sale by Auction by Mr. Geo. Robins at the Auction Mart, on Thursday July 29th 1841*, drawn and lithog. by G.E. Nadsley; and *Mr. Mathews's Cottage Highgate Hill* (n.d.), drawn by C.J. Mathews.

19 *Plan of the particular disposition of the Histrionic Portraits at Ivy Cottage, Kentish Town, Collected by the late Mr. Charles Mathews and now in the Possession of the Garrick Club. Engraved from a Drawing in the possession of James Winston Esqr.* The plan was engraved for George Daniel's *View of Ivy Cottage, Kentish Town: With some account of the life and genius of the late Charles Mathews. Contributed by George Daniel, Esq. of Islington.* It was printed (25 copies) as an extract from *Historical and Literary Curiosities* (1840), selected and engraved by Charles James Smith.

20 Anne Mathews, 4: 163; and Charles Dickens the younger, 2: 61 (for a more general reference to the collapse of Charles Mathews's finances).

21 Anne Mathews, 4: 159; and *Mr. Mathews' admired Villa and Grounds called Ivy Cottage, With immediate Possession, and held on Leases expiring at the distant period of 1911. ... It will be sold by Mr. Geo. Robins, At the Auction Mart, opposite the Bank on Tuesday, April the 16th 1833*. The house is lavishly described, including: 'The Spacious Picture Gallery ... (which would make a superb Ball Room).' It was bought by a Mr Shoolbred, who in turn sold it through George Robins in 1841.

22 Percy Fitzgerald, *The Garrick Club* (Elliot Stock: 1904), pp. 122–24, 127–28; and Guy Boas, *The Garrick Club 1831–1947* (The Garrick Club: 1948), p. 91.

23 List A: 'A List of Mathews Picture Portraits of Performers 1833', 6pp., 207 items. Based on the Ivy Cottage Plan. Priced in code; List B: 'List of Mr Mathews portraits &c', 8pp., 240 items. Differs from A after No. 148. Priced in code; List C: 'Mathews', 10pp., 235 items. Corresponds with A and B to 148 with minor changes; and List D: 'Catalogue of Pictures with their Cost' (in Mathews's hand), 12pp., 235 items.

24 See letter from Samuel De Wilde to an unknown client, dated 28 June 1815, transcribed on page xxxv.

25 Princeton University. Mathews Papers, misc. papers file. C.J. Mathews's diary, 15 August 1835: 'My mother informed me that yesterday's decision was favourable. The Gallery is to be purchased by the Garrick Club for £1000, "a sad sacrifice" as she says.'

26 *Catalogue of the miscellaneous and dramatic library, engraved theatrical portraits, dramatic and literary autograph letters, and a collection of theatrical relics, the property of Charles Mathews, Esq, ...* Sotheby & Son, 19 August 1835 and three following days. Princeton University. Mathews Papers, misc. papers file. C.J. Mathews's diary 19 (&c) August 1835: 'First day's sale of Books and Engravings at Sotheby's. The 3 days only realized between £600 and £700 – however, as not a soul was left in town to attend, perhaps it was as much as could be expected – certainly not a fifth of their value.'

27 Princeton University. Mathews Papers, misc. papers file. C.J. Mathews's diary, 29 March 1836: 'Received cheque from Garrick Club for pictures.'

ORGANISATION OF THE CATALOGUE

The catalogue is arranged alphabetically by sitter, or under the name of the main sitter where a works depicts more than one person. Other works in which subsidiary sitters appear may be found under their own alphabetical listings. (To locate all the entries in which a particular sitter appears, readers should consult the Index of Sitters, where cross-references for name variants are also given.) Following the alphabetical entries, portraits of anonymous sitters begin at No. 873, and subjects other than portraits (such as landscapes, caricatures and other illustrations) at No. 885. Recent acquisitions (since 1988) are then catalogued, from No. 941. Sculptures are listed in a separate section, again with additions and recent acquisitions placed at the end.

Some works catalogued by C.K. Adams in 1936 were not traced by Geoffrey Ashton in 1988, while others are known to have left the collection at some point. Almost all such items are included in the present catalogue as a matter of record and their present whereabouts given, if known.

Entries are organised in the following manner:

CATALOGUE NUMBER (an asterisk indicates that the picture is also reproduced as a colour plate – see list on page LXII)

SITTER (birth and death dates are given in the separate Index of Sitters)

ARTIST (birth and death dates are given in the separate Index of Artists)

MEDIUM & MEASUREMENTS in centimetres

INSCR: Inscriptions

INV: Previous Garrick Club inventory and catalogue numbers (RW: Robert Walters's checklist, 1900; CKA: C.K. Adams catalogue, 1936)

PROV: Provenance (previous owners are listed in the separate Index of Former Owners)

EXH: Exhibition history (a full list of exhibitions is given in a separate index)

REL: Related works

LIT: Literature relevant to the entry

COMMENTARY AND INFORMATION (the editors' comments and/or additional information usually appear in square brackets)

The list of abbreviations on the following page also constitutes the bibliography of sources cited in the catalogue (with the unfortunate exception of some which the editors have been unable to identify, such as: BS, GRB, TAM). Additional sources are given within individual entries and in the Index of Sitters.

Thanks largely to Geoffrey Ashton, the history of the art of the British theatre has become a lively new object of study. It is recognised that this catalogue, unfinished as it was at Dr Ashton's death, represents only a starting point. The information it contains will itself be amplified and corrected by future research and it is hoped that others will be stimulated to continue the work.

Mr Henry McGee is compiling biographies of sitters which the Club hopes to publish in a companion volume to the catalogue in the not-too-distant future.

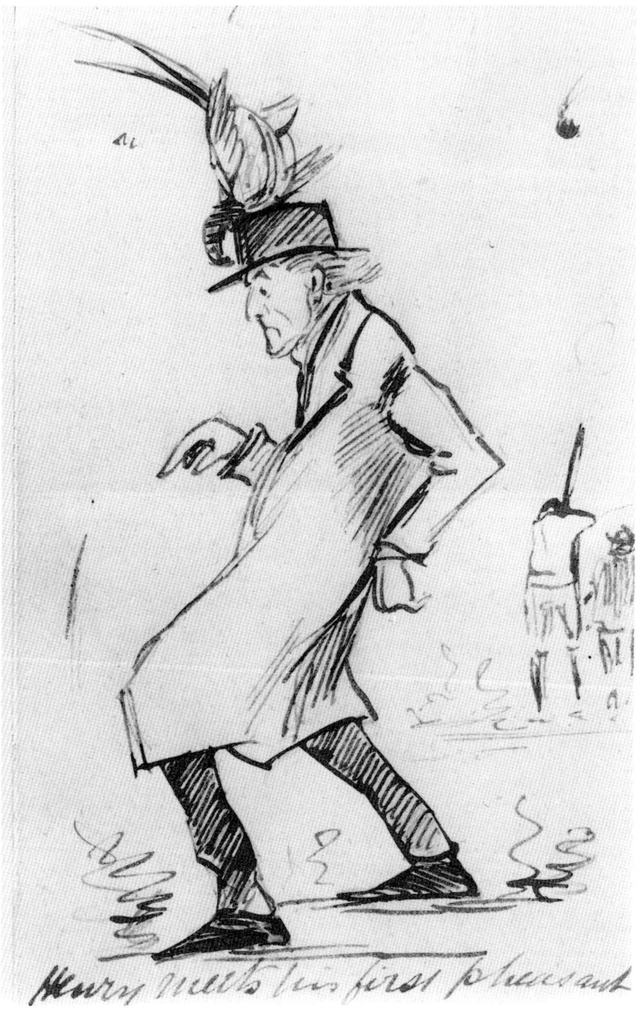

320
SIR HENRY IRVING

ABBREVIATIONS

A&R: *English Theatrical Literature 1500–1900, A Bibliography*. Edited by James Arnott & John Robinson (London, 1970).

Baker 1764: David Erskine Baker, *The Companion to the Play-House*, 2 vols (London, 1764).

BD: Philip H. Highfill, Jr, Kalman A. Burnim & Edward A. Langhans, *A Biographical Dictionary of Actors, Actresses, Musicians, Dancers, Managers and Other Stage Personnel in London 1660–1800*. Southern Illinois University Press (1968–94), 16 vols.

Bebb: Richard Bebb, *Great Actors and Singers* (privately printed catalogue of his collection of figurines, 1994).

BMC: *Catalogue of Engraved British Portraits in the British Museum*. Freeman O'Donohue (London, 1908), 6 vols.

CB: *Current Biography*.

CKA: C.K. Adams, *A Catalogue of the Pictures in the Garrick Club* (London, 1936), 1 vol. + supplement.

CM: Charles Mathews.

DAB: *Dictionary of American Biography*.

Davenport Adams: William Davenport Adams, *Essays on Literature and the Stage* (London, 1891).

DM: William Oxberry, *Dramatic Mirror* (London, 1827 & 1828).

DNB: *Dictionary of National Biography*.

DP: *Daily Post*.

ES: *Enciclopedia dello Spettacolo*.

Griffiths: Arthur Griffiths, 'The Pictures in the Garrick Club', *Fortnightly Review* (1886), 39: 350–70.

Hayes 1968: John Hayes, 'Thomas Harris, Gainsborough Dupont and the Theatrical Gallery at Belmont', *The Connoisseur* (1968), 169: 221–27.

JC: John Cavanaugh, *British Theatre: a bibliography 1901–1985* (Mottisfont, Hants, 1989).

Jones 1812: Stephen Jones, *Biographica Dramatica* (1812).

Mathews: *Catalogue Raisonné of Mr. Mathews's Gallery of Theatrical Portraits, Now exhibited for the first time, And Forming a Nearly Complete Dramatic Record From the Year 1659 Down to the Present Time. Queen's Bazaar, Oxford Street* (London, 1833).

NT: Somerset Maugham Collection, Royal National Theatre.

OC: *Oxford Companion to the Theatre*.

Oxberry: William Oxberry, *Oxberry's Dramatic Biography, and his Histrionic Anecdotes* (London, 1825–27), 8 vols.

Pascoe: Charles Eyre Pascoe, *The Dramatic List: a record of the principal performances of living actors and actresses of the British stage* (London, 1879).

Patmore: Peter George Patmore, *British Galleries of Art* (London, 1824).

Pressly: William L. Pressly, *A Catalogue of Paintings in the Folger Shakespeare Library* (Yale UP, 1993).

R.A.: Royal Academy.

Reed: Isaac Reed, *Biographia Dramatica* (London, 1782 & 1812).

R.S.P.P.: Royal Society of Portrait Painters.

RW: Robert Walters, *Catalogue of the Pictures and Miniatures in the Possession of the Garrick Club* (London, 1909).

S.A.: Society of Artists.

TD: *The Thespian Dictionary: or, Dramatic Biography of the present age* … (London, 1802 & 1805).

TM: *Theatrical Monitor* (London, 1767–68).

V&A: Victoria & Albert Museum.

WCR: William Clark Russell, *Representative Actors* (London, 1872).

WWT: *Who's Who in the Theatre*.

LIST OF COLOUR PLATES

Johan Zoffany:
Sophia Baddeley, Robert Baddeley & Thomas King (No. 23)

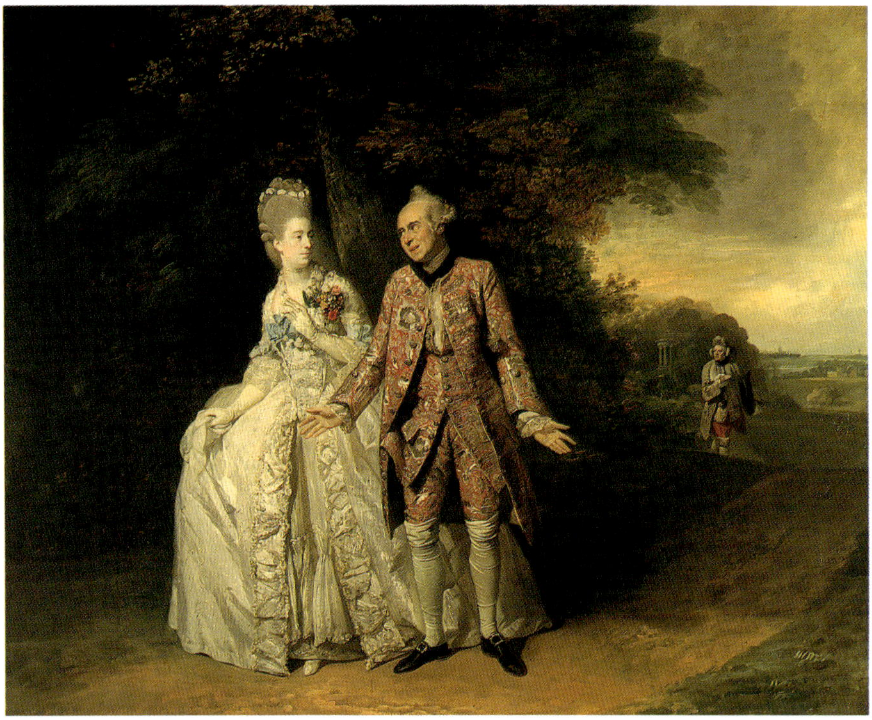

James Roberts:
Frances Abington, Thomas King, John Palmer & William Smith (No. 3)

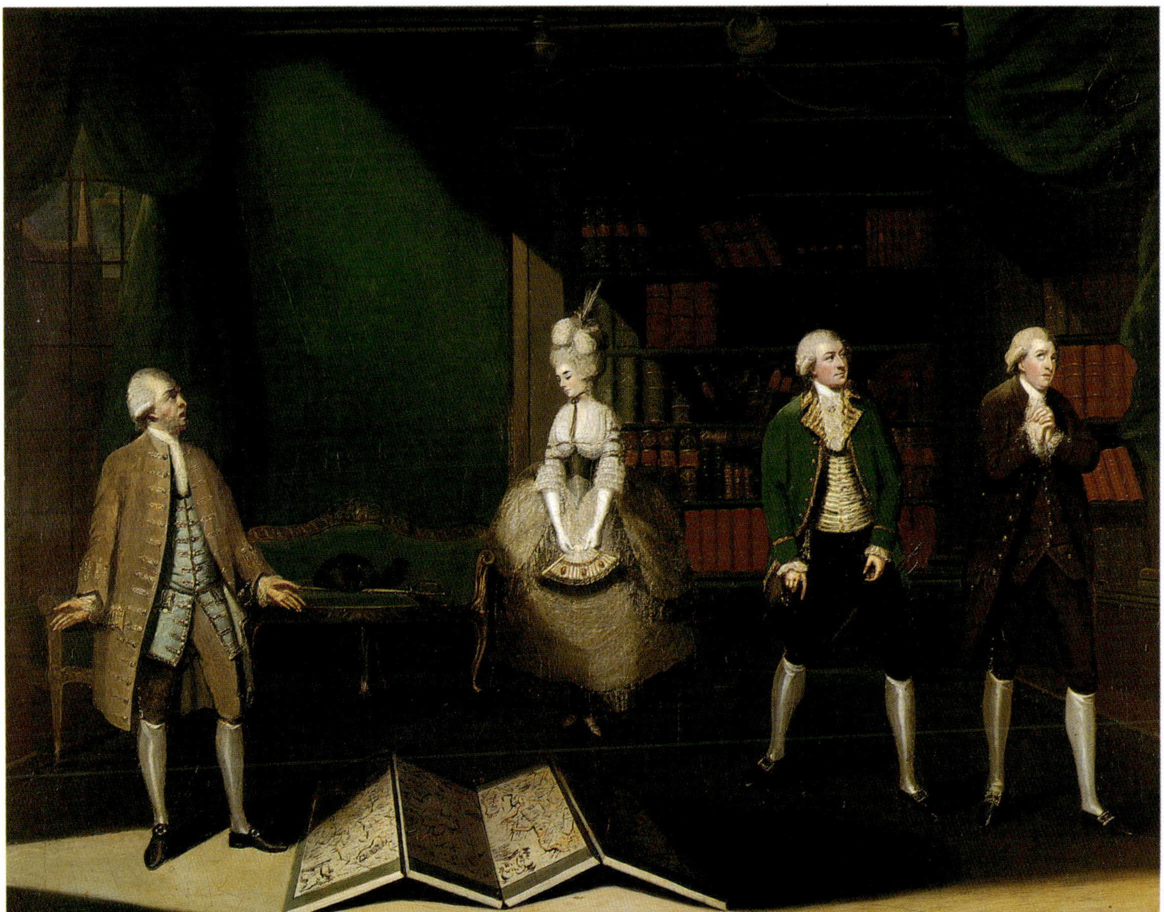

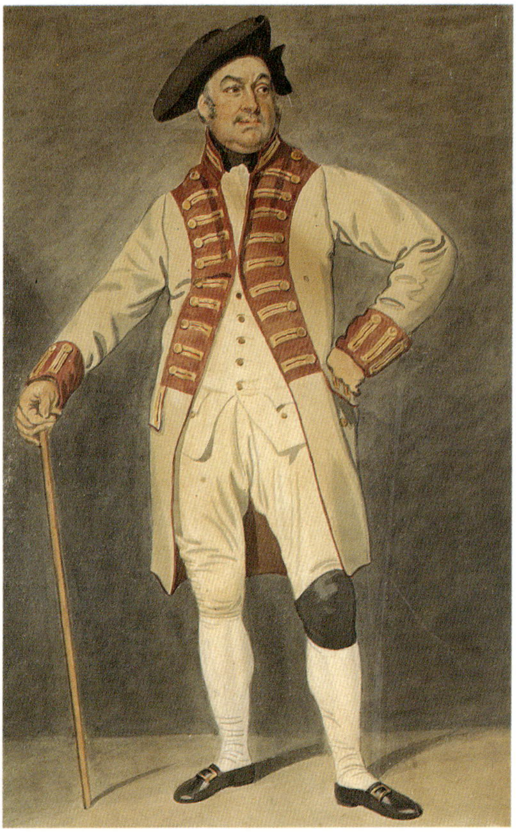

Samuel De Wilde: *John Bannister* (No. 35)

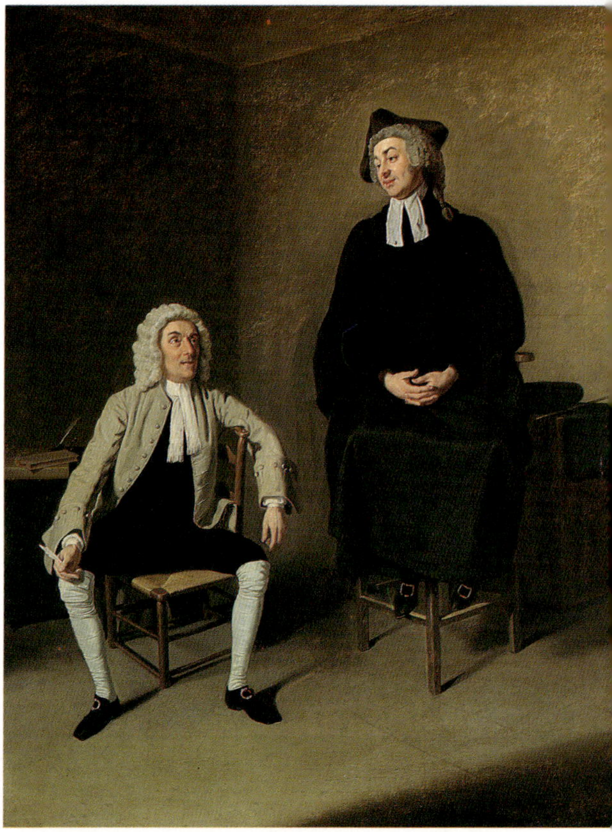

John Bannister & William Parsons (No. 39)

John Bannister & William Parsons (No. 40)

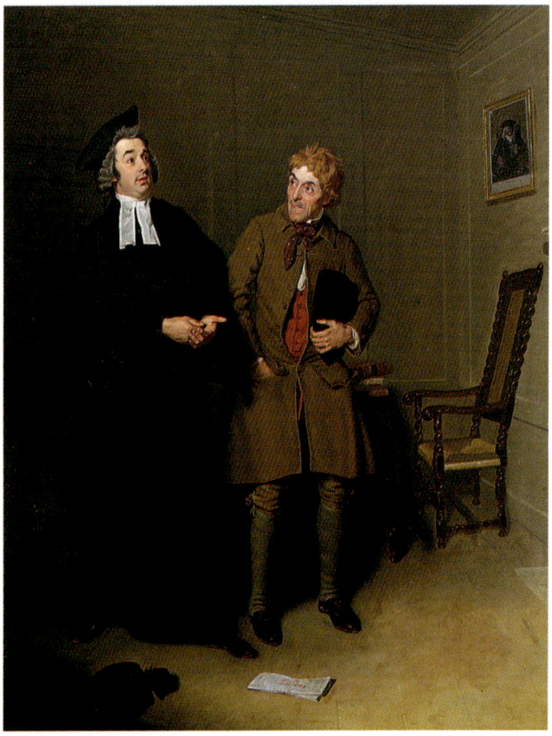

John Bannister & Richard Suett (No. 42)

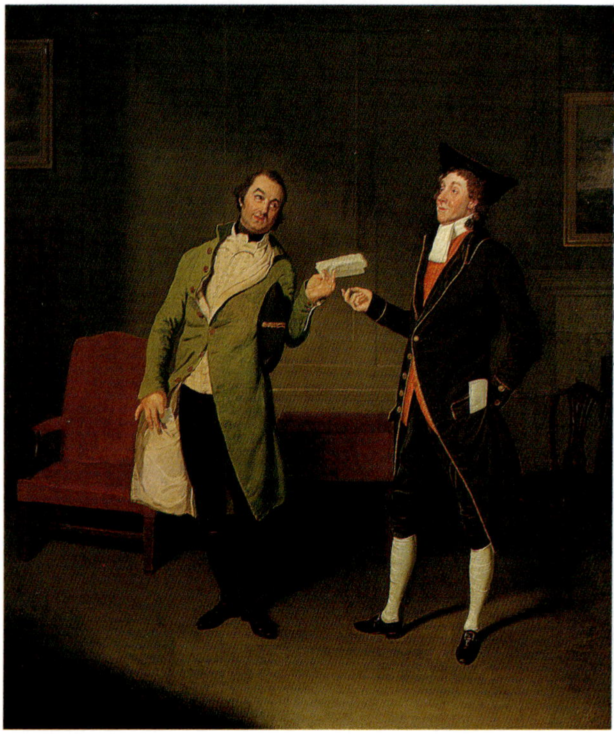

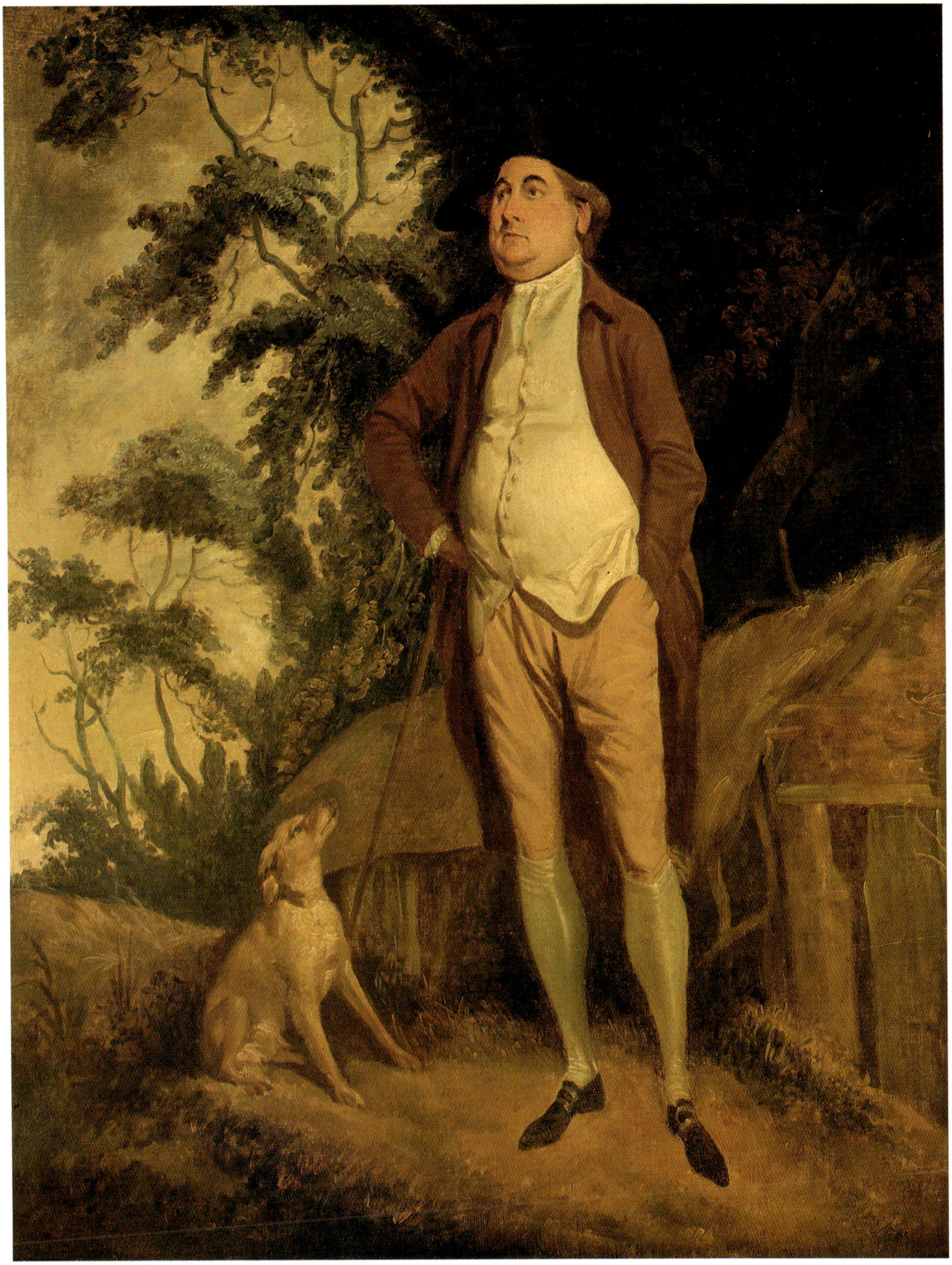

Johan Zoffany (attr.): *Charles Bannister* (No. 33)

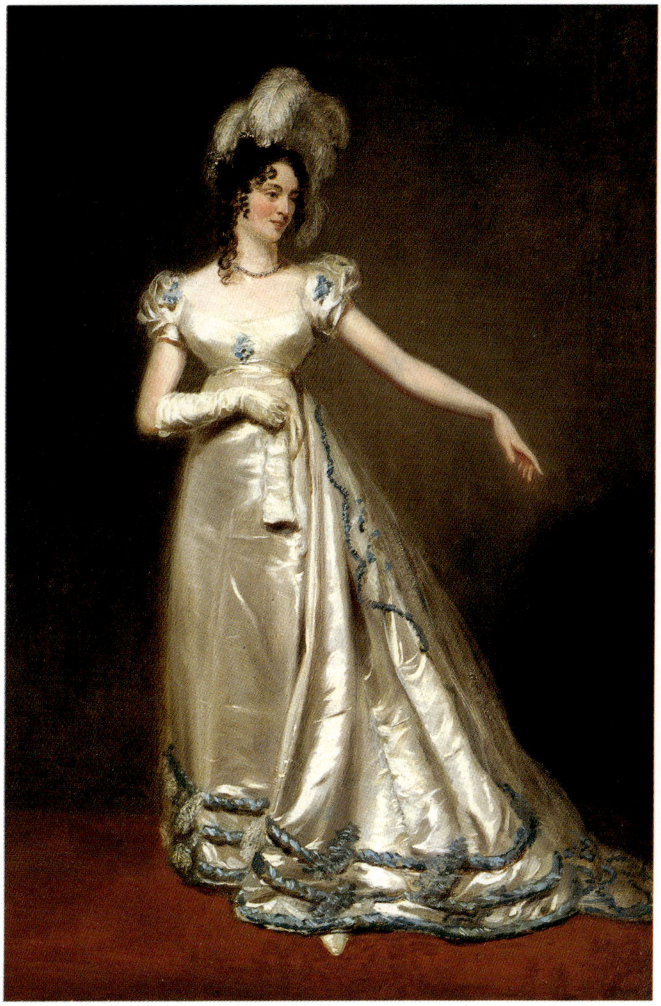

George Clint: *Louisa Chatterley* (No. 111)

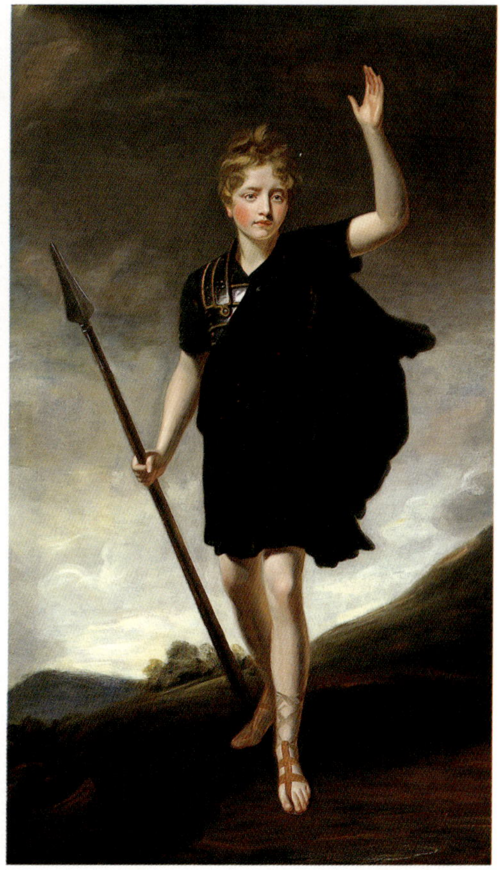

John Opie: *William Betty* (No. 67)

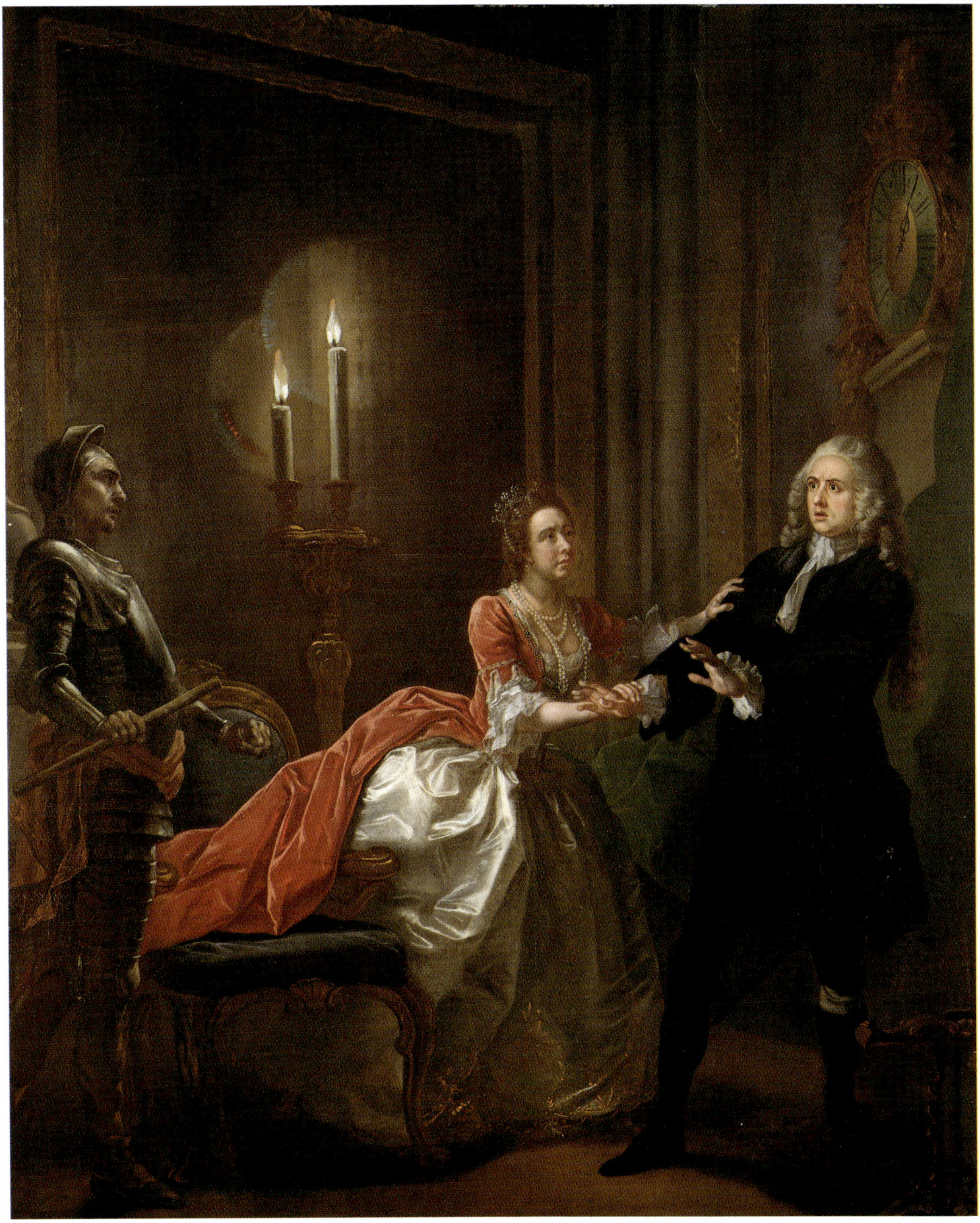

Francis Hayman: *Spranger Barry, Mary Elmy & Lacy Ryan* (No. 49)

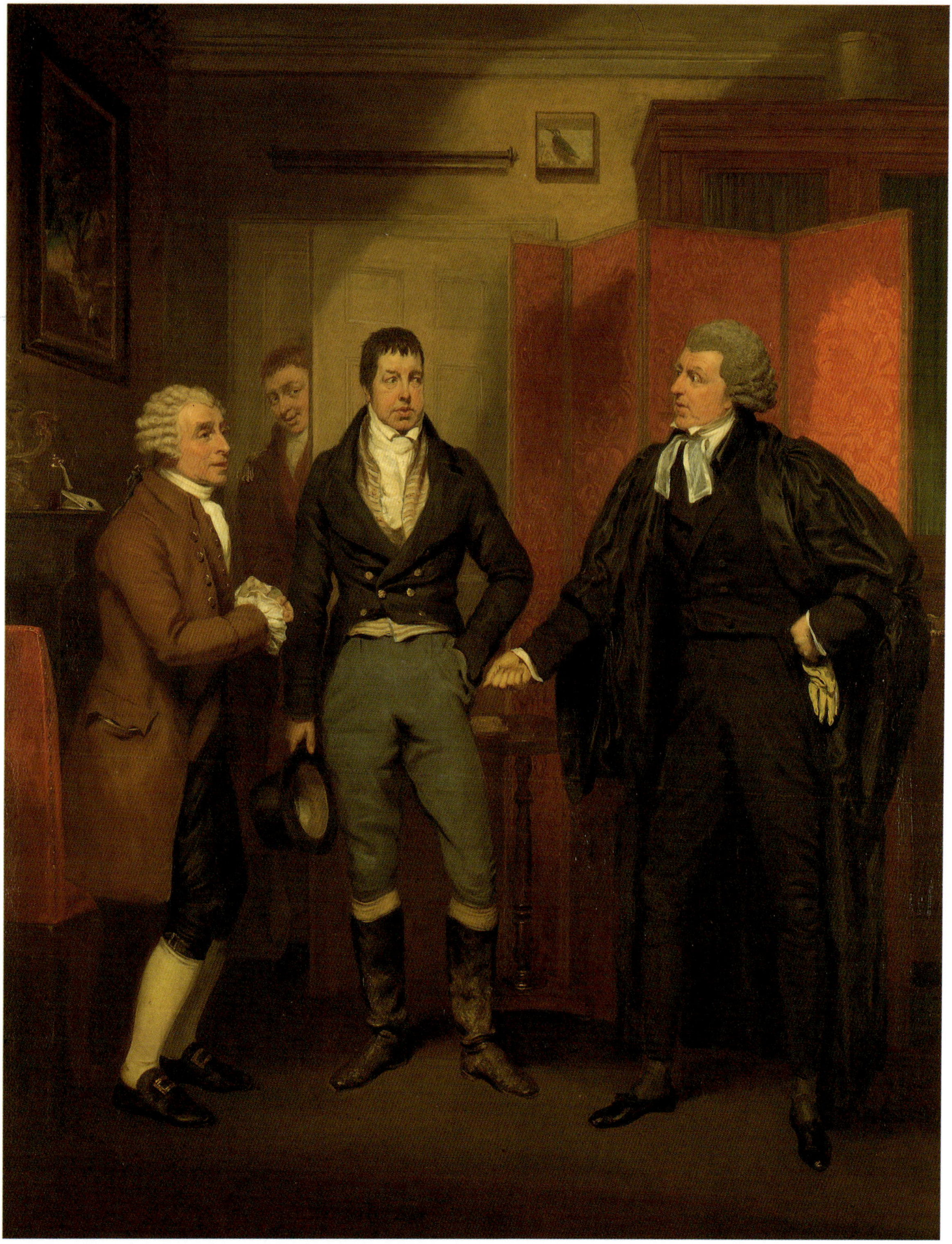

George Clint: *Charles Mathews, William Blanchard, John Emery & John Liston* (No. 477)

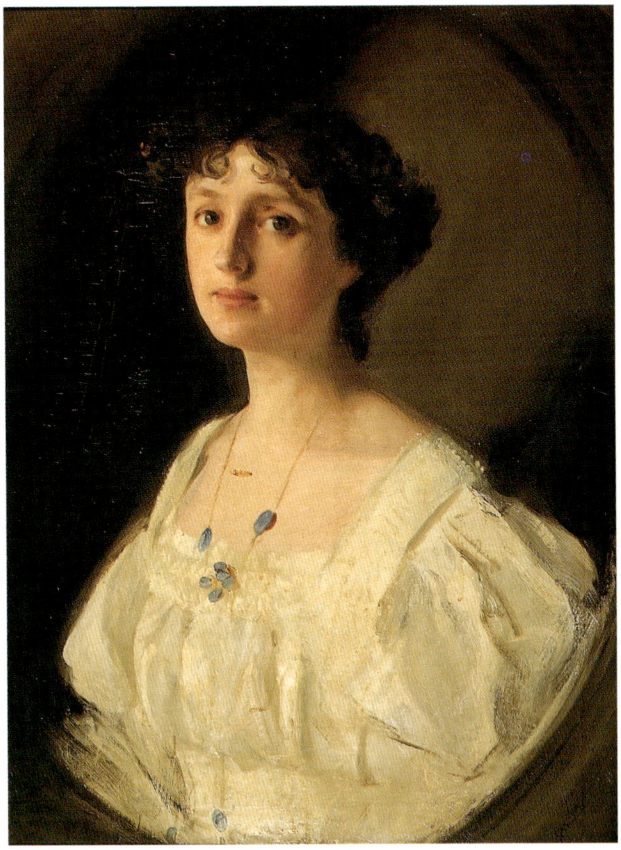

Charles Sims: *Dame Lilian Braithwaite* (No. 91)

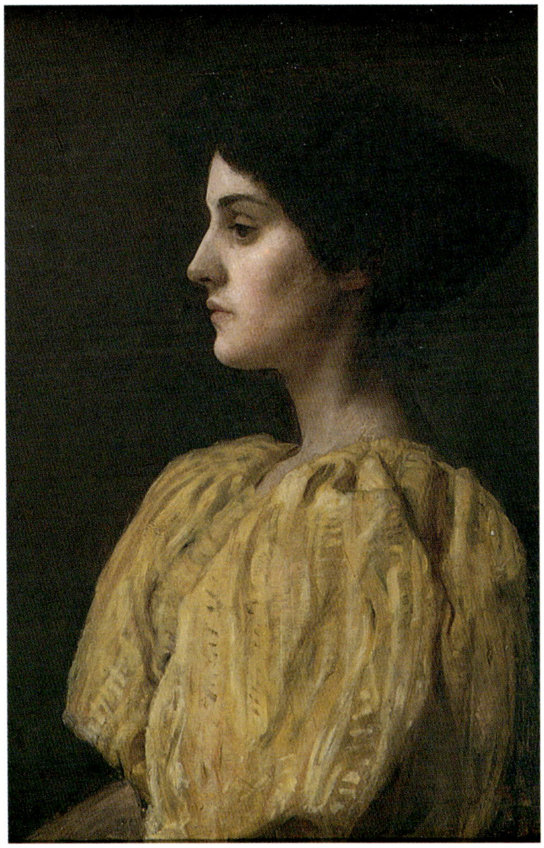

J.S. Eland: *Mrs Patrick Campbell* (No. 101)

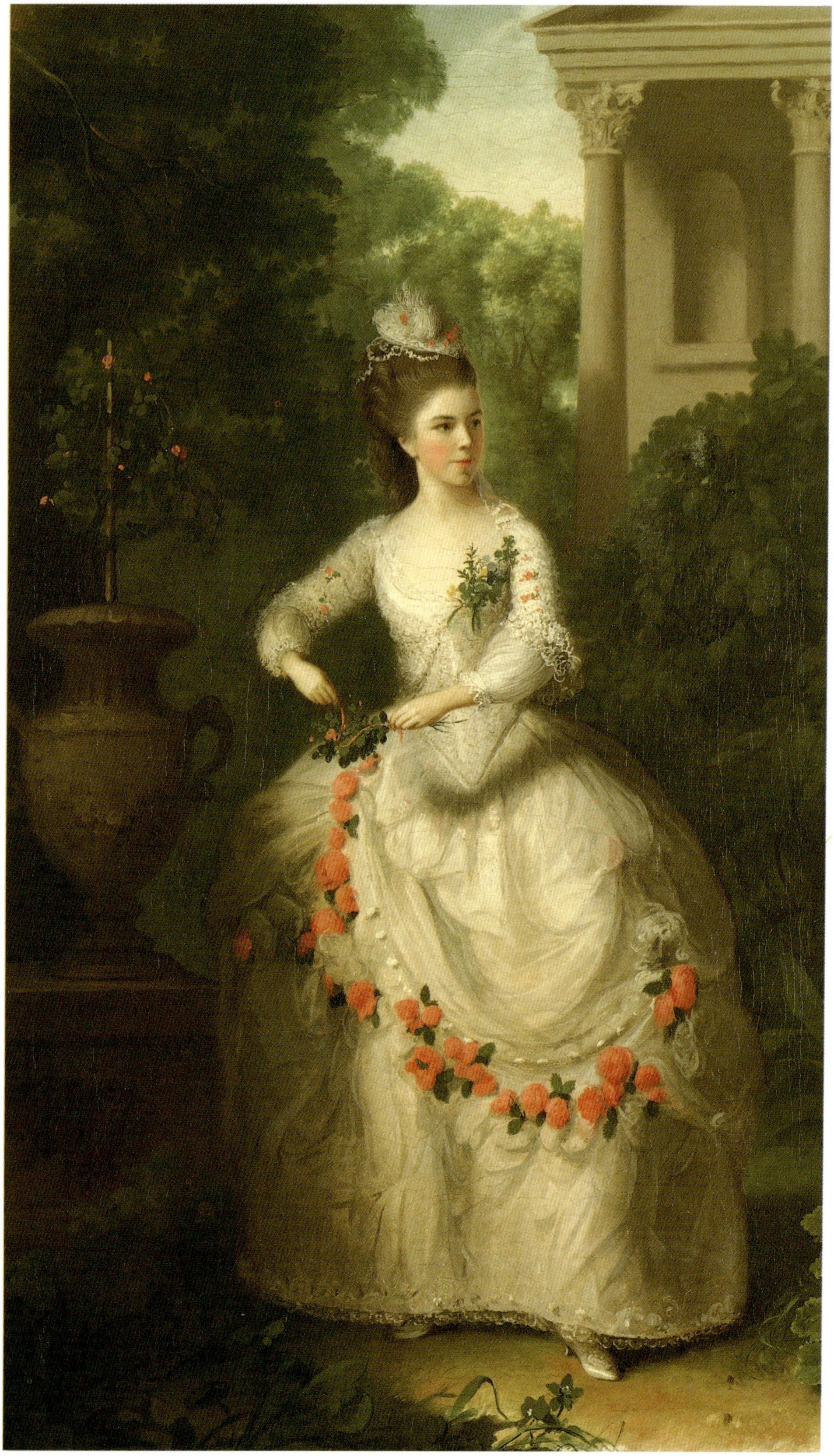

PLATE 8

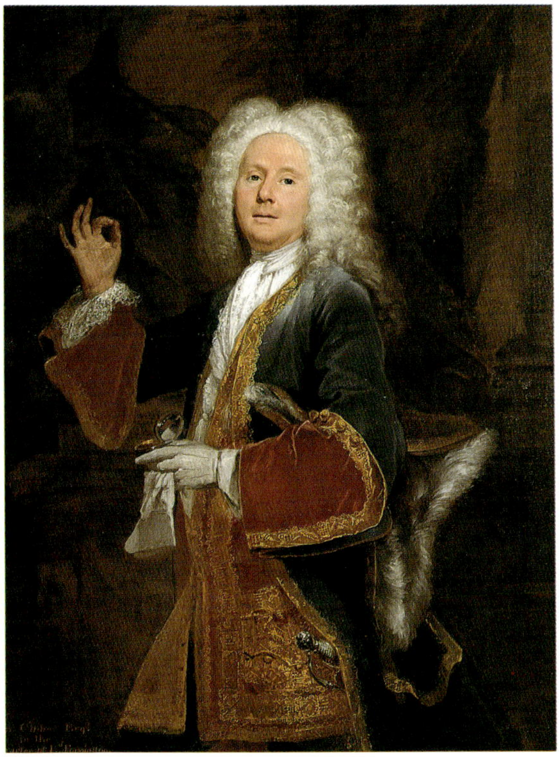
Giuseppe Grisoni: *Colley Cibber* (No. 116)

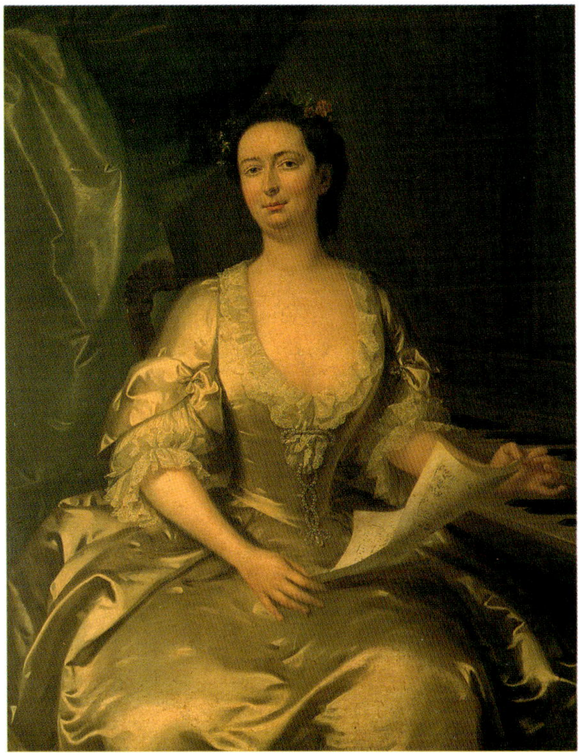
William Verelst: *Catherine Clive* (No. 122)

OPPOSITE
Thomas Hickey: *Frances Abington* (No. 1)

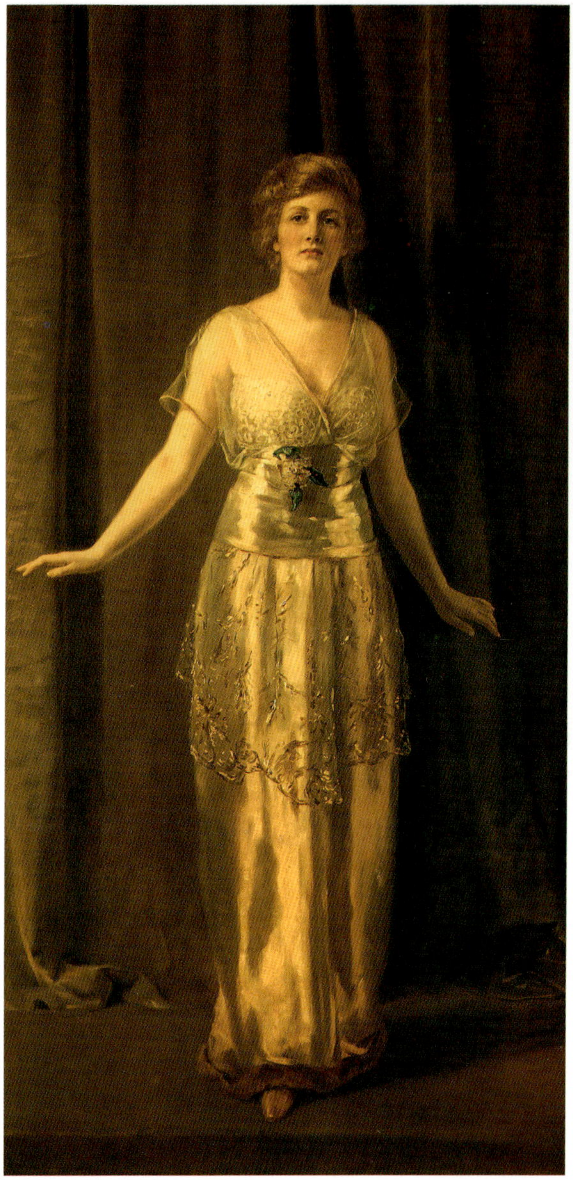

The Hon. John Collier: *Dame Gladys Cooper* (No. 138)

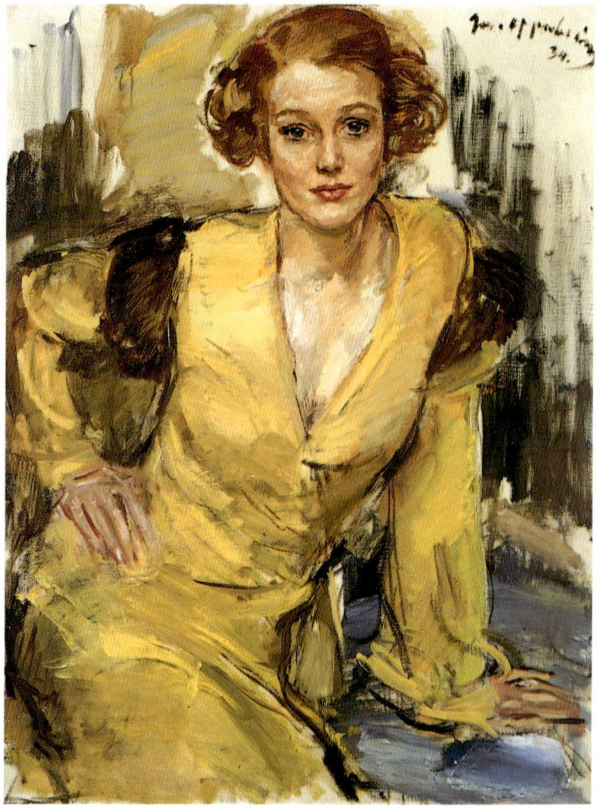

James Oppenheim: *Constance Cummings* (No. 143)

Edward Seago: *Sir Noel Coward* (No. 139)

John Gilroy: *Frederick Barker* (No. 43)

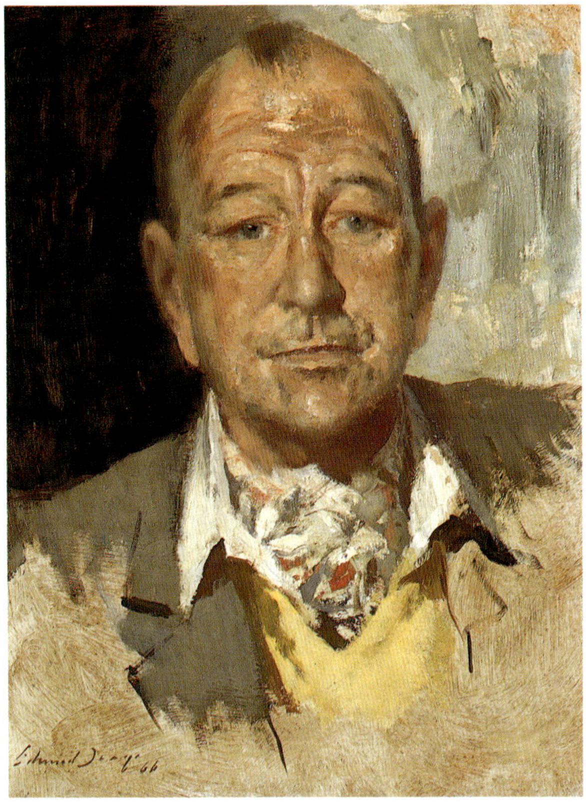

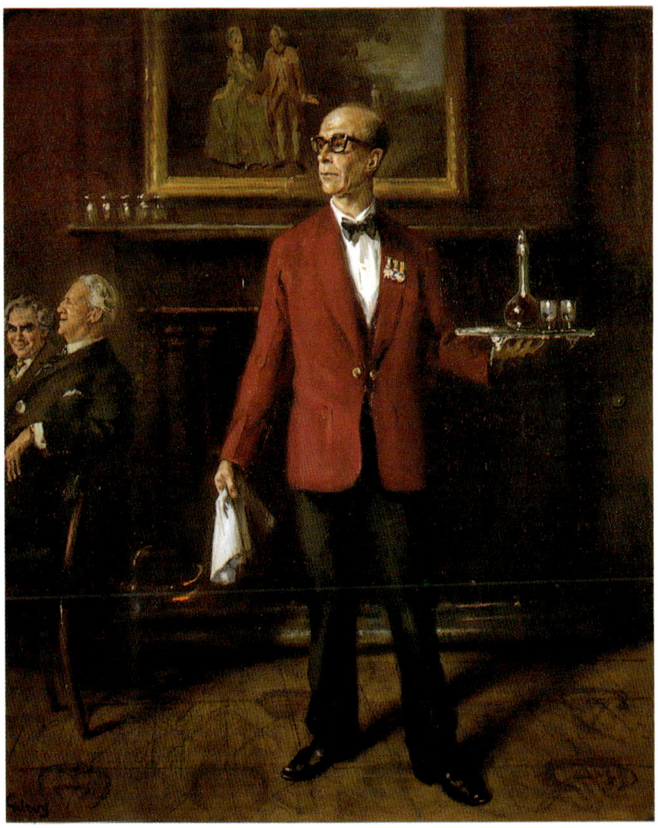

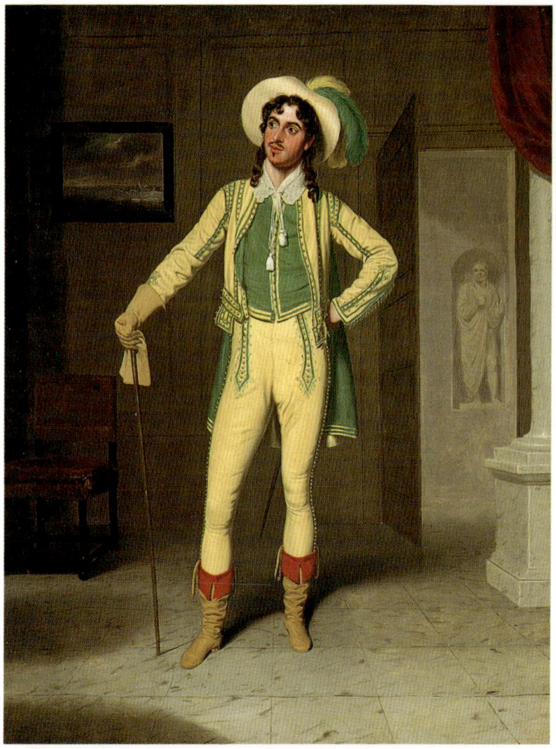

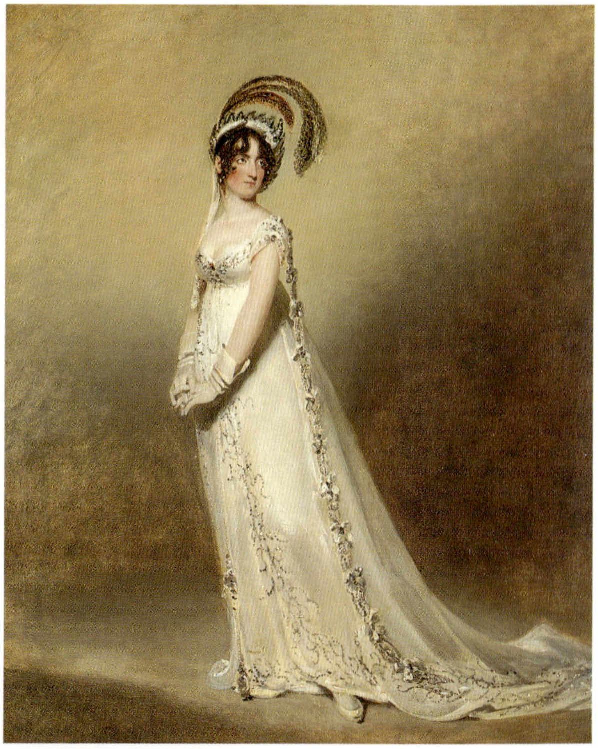

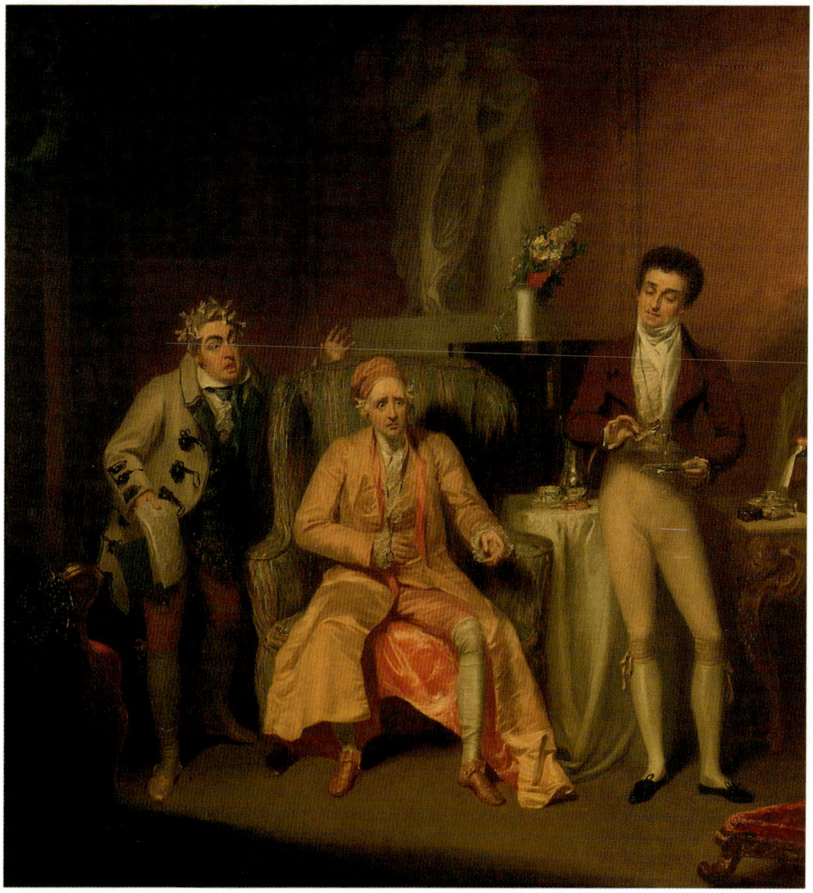

Samuel De Wilde:
Vincent De Camp (No. 151)

Henry Singleton:
Maria Davison (No. 147)

George Clint: *William Farren the Younger, Charles Farley & Richard Jones* (No. 216)

OPPOSITE

George Clint: *John Fawcett & Charles Kemble* (No. 224)

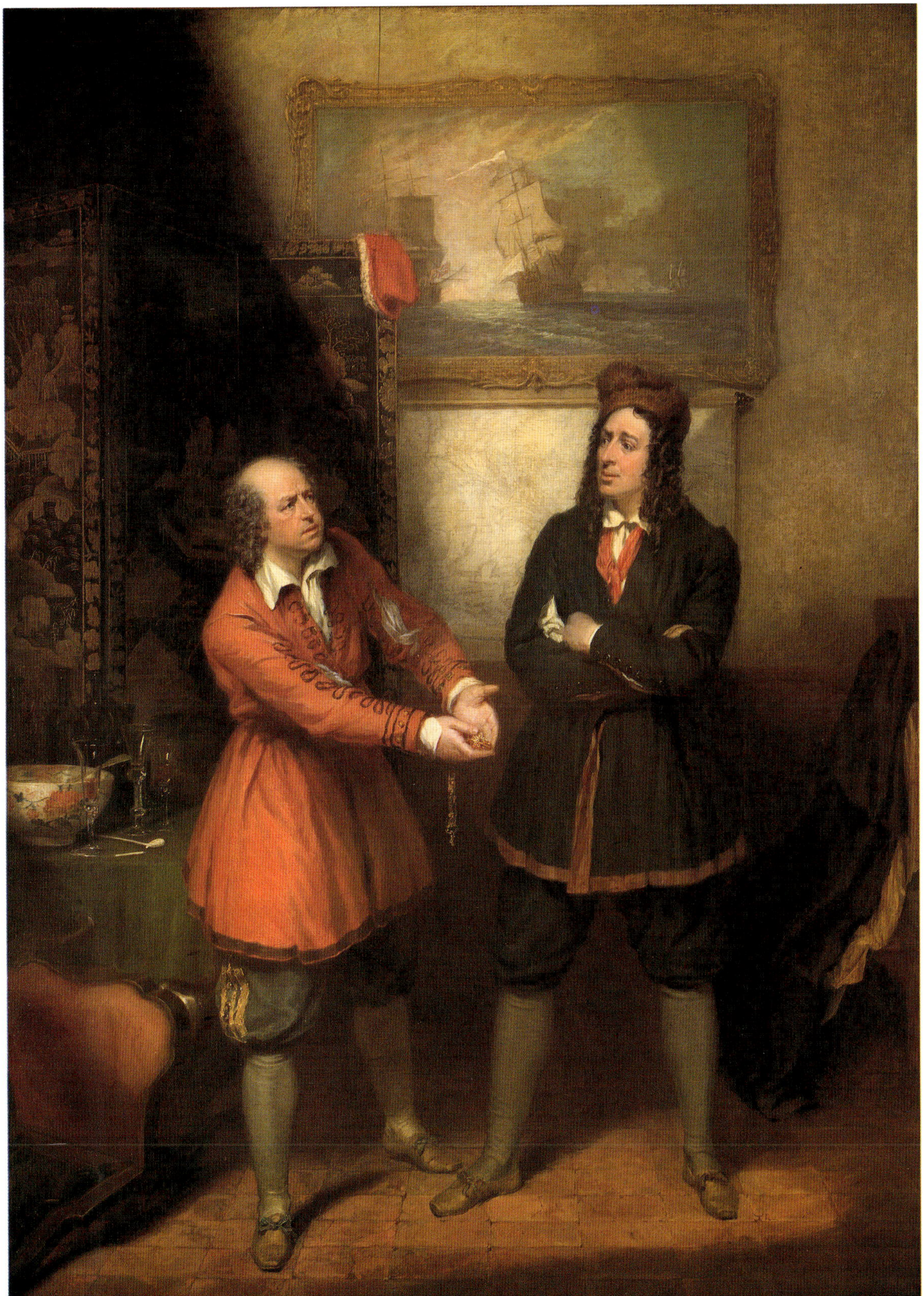

PLATE 13

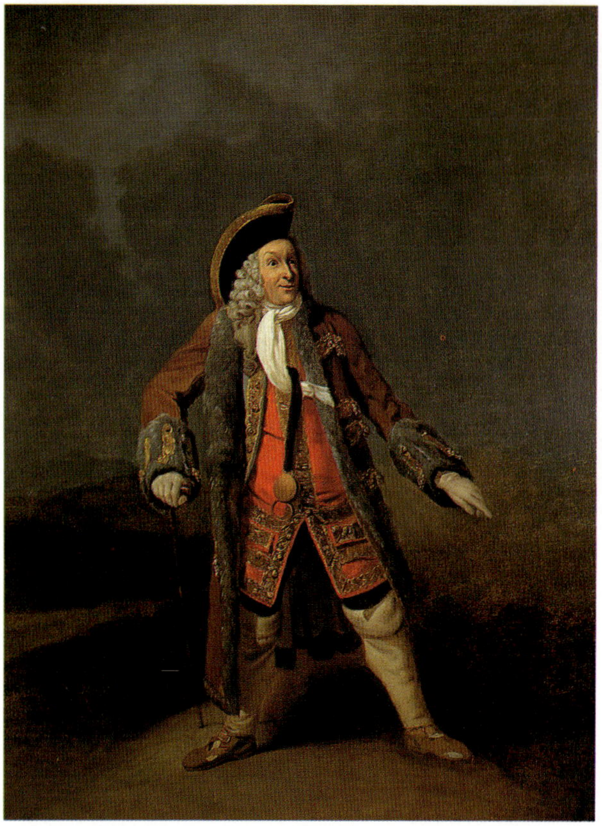

Johan Zoffany: *David Garrick* (No. 250)

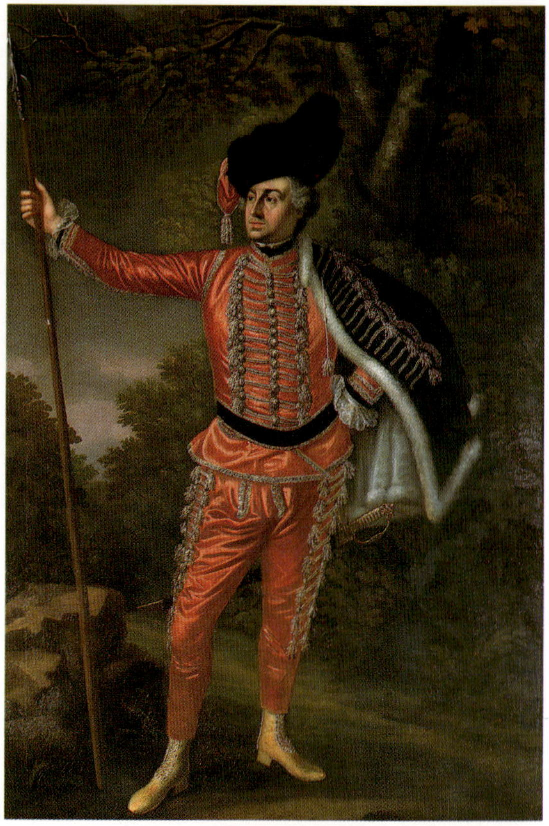

Thomas Worlidge: *David Garrick* (No. 247)

OPPOSITE

Johan Zoffany: *David Garrick* (No. 249)

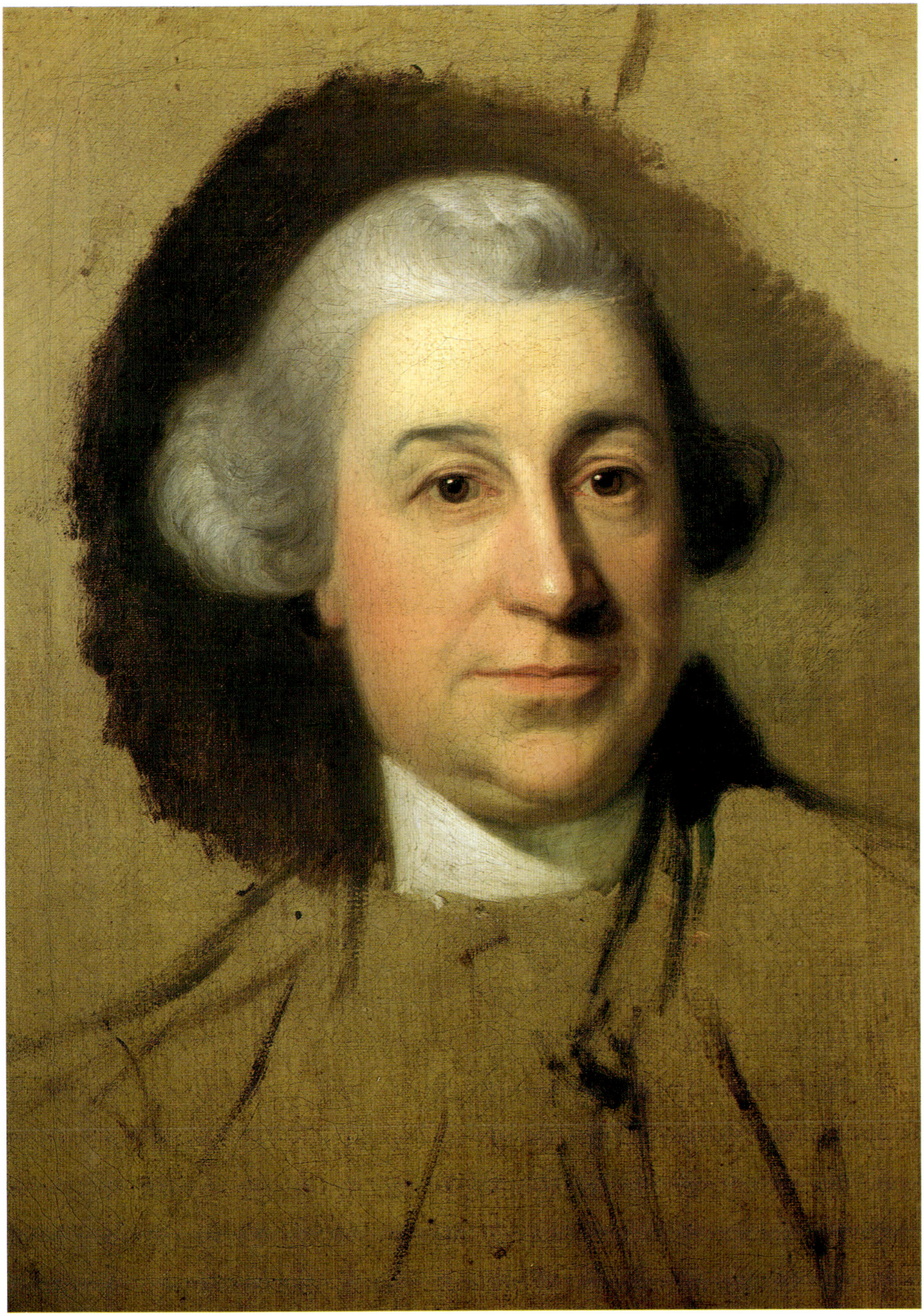

PLATE 15

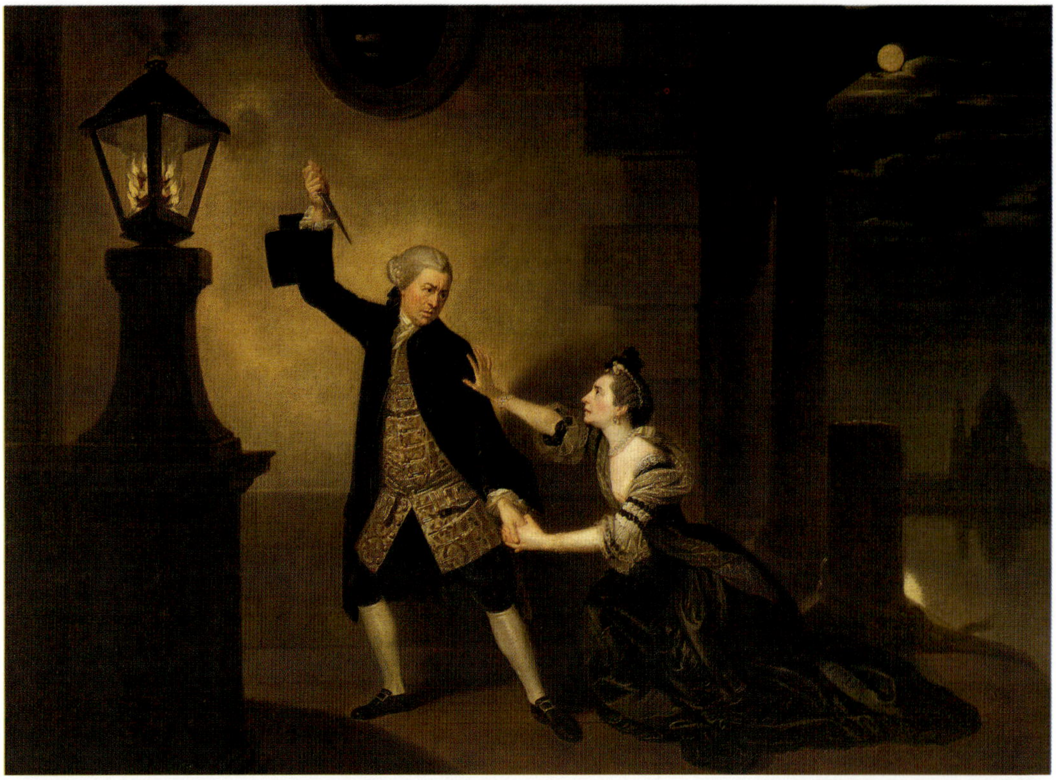

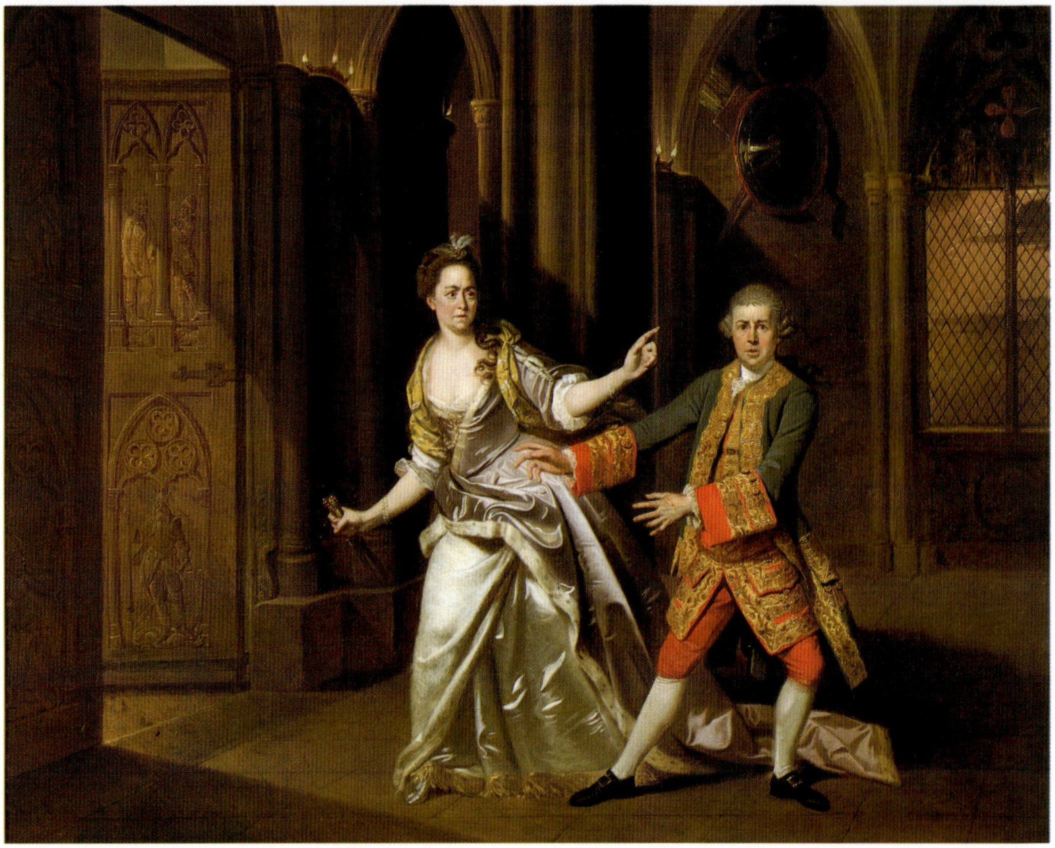

PLATE 16

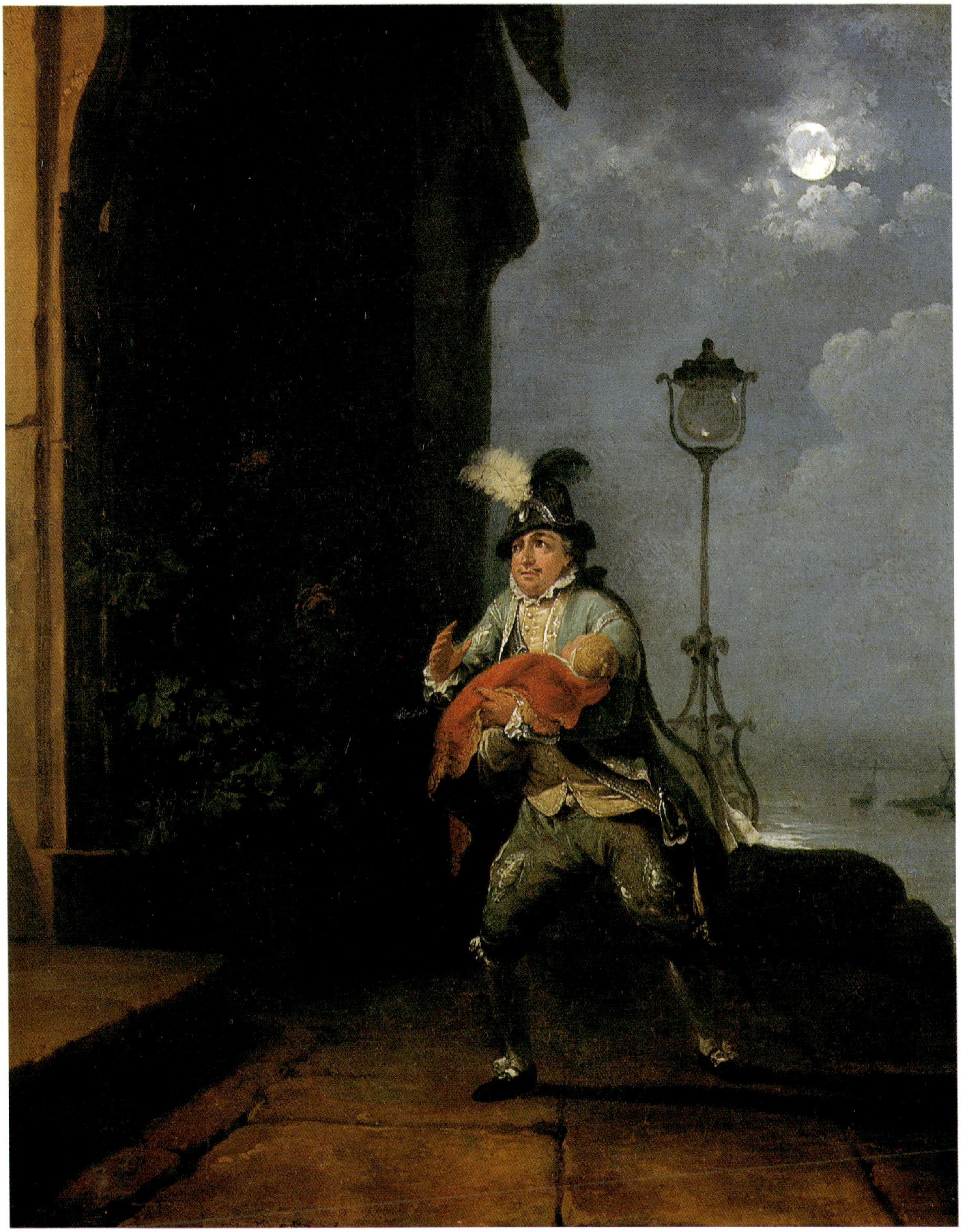

Philippe Jacques de Loutherbourg: *David Garrick* (No. 236)

OPPOSITE

Johan Zoffany: *David Garrick & Susanna Cibber* (No. 252)

Johan Zoffany: *David Garrick & Hannah Pritchard* (No. 253)

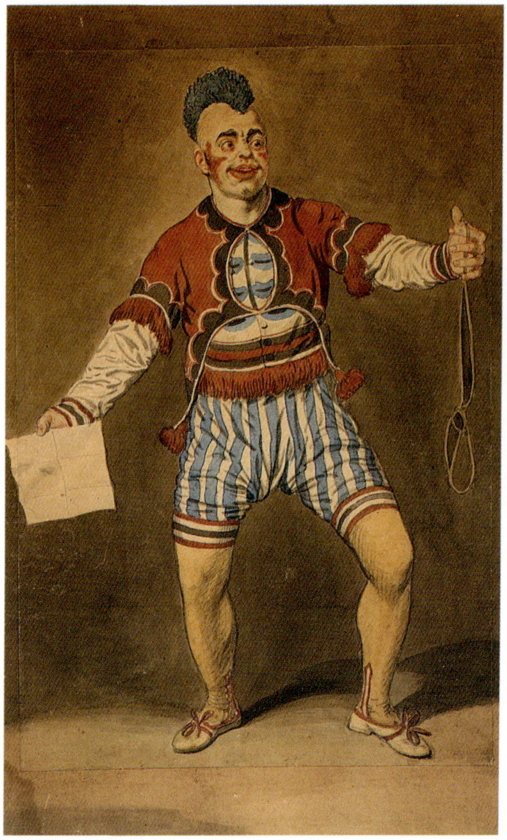

Samuel De Wilde: *Joseph Grimaldi* (No. 272)

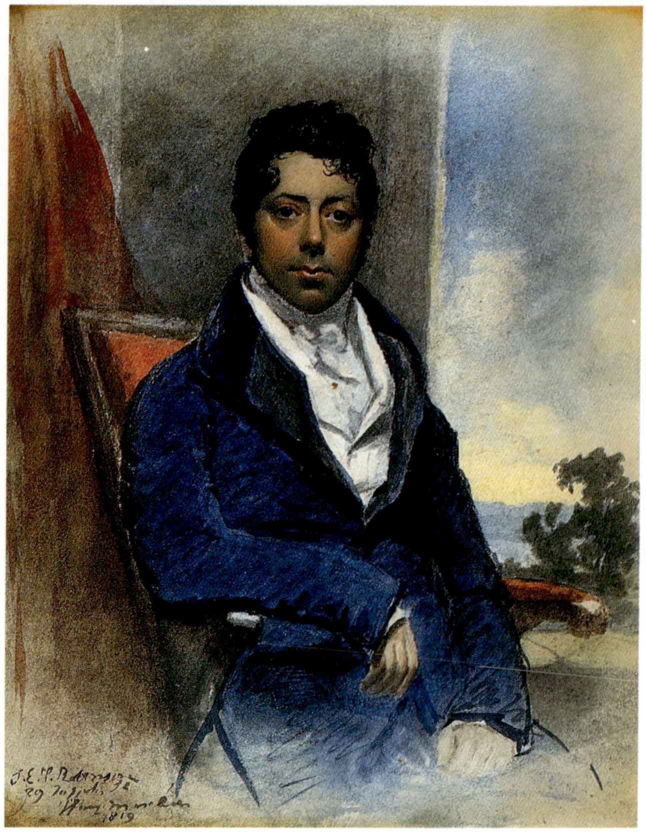

J.E.T. Robinson: *Joseph Grimaldi* (No. 273)

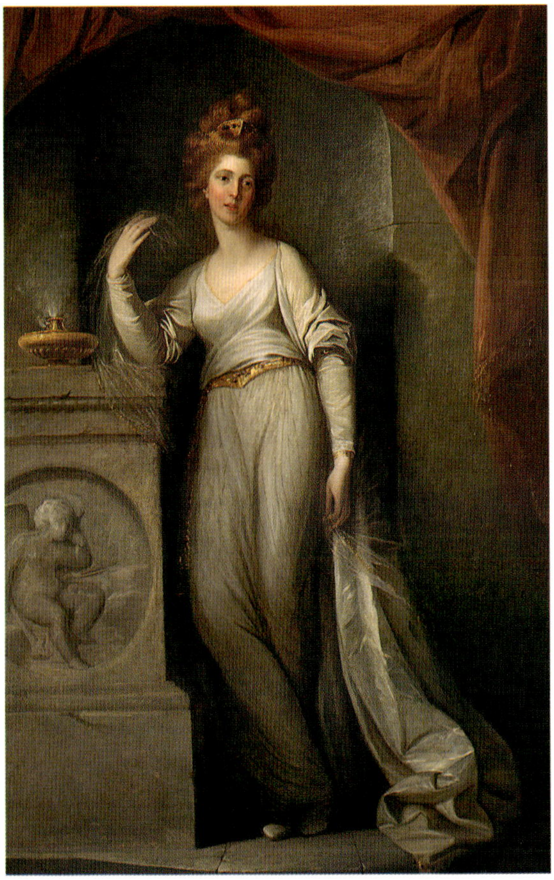

Angelica Kauffmann: *Elizabeth Hartley* (No. 291)

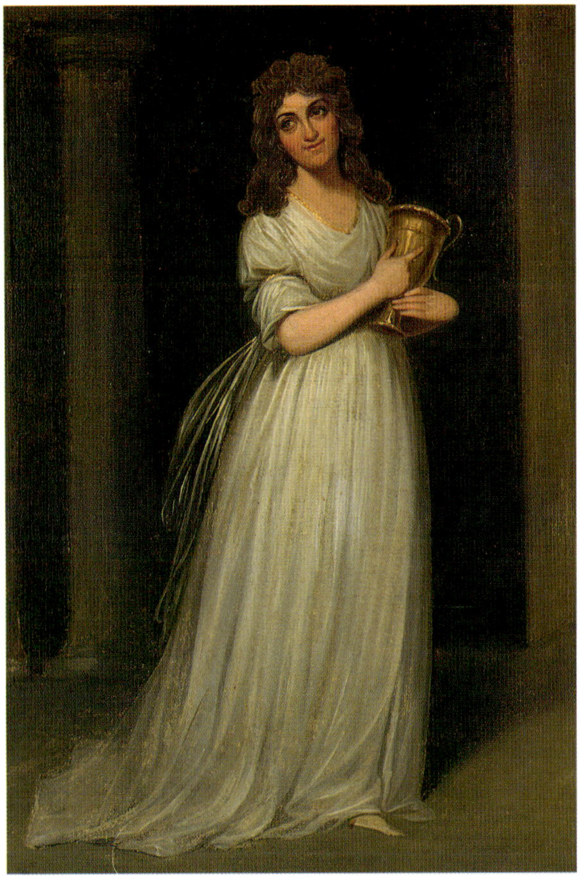

Samuel De Wilde: *Dorothy Jordan* (No. 343)

OPPOSITE

Thomas Charles Wageman (attr.): *Edmund Kean* (No. 352)

George Clint: *Edmund Kean, George Clint, Mr Carr, John Pritt Harley, Mr Holland, Mrs Edward Knight, Thomas Goff Lupton (?), Joseph Shepherd Munden, Mrs Orger, William Oxberry & Sampson Penley* (No. 355)

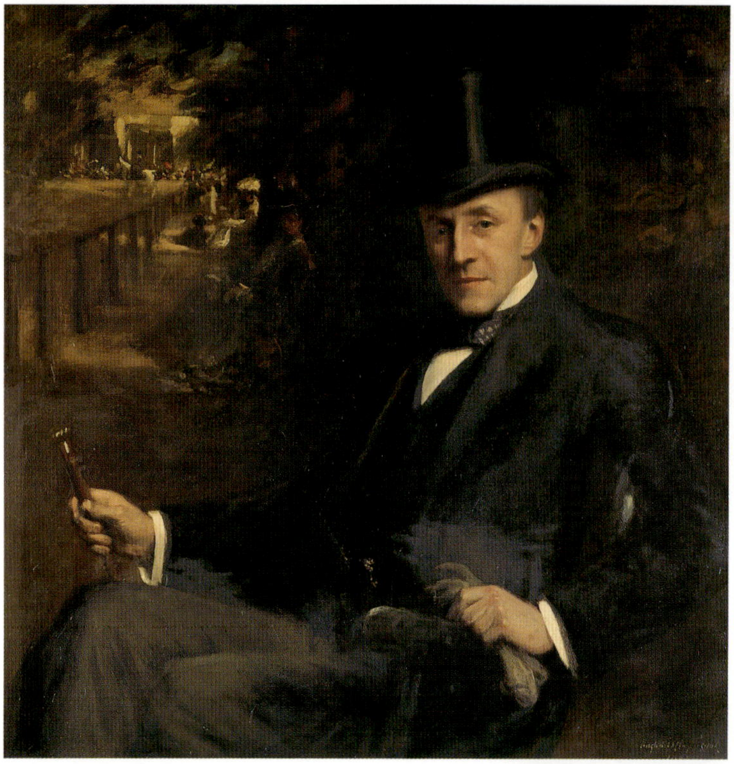

Henry Glazebrook: *Anthony Hope* (No. 307)

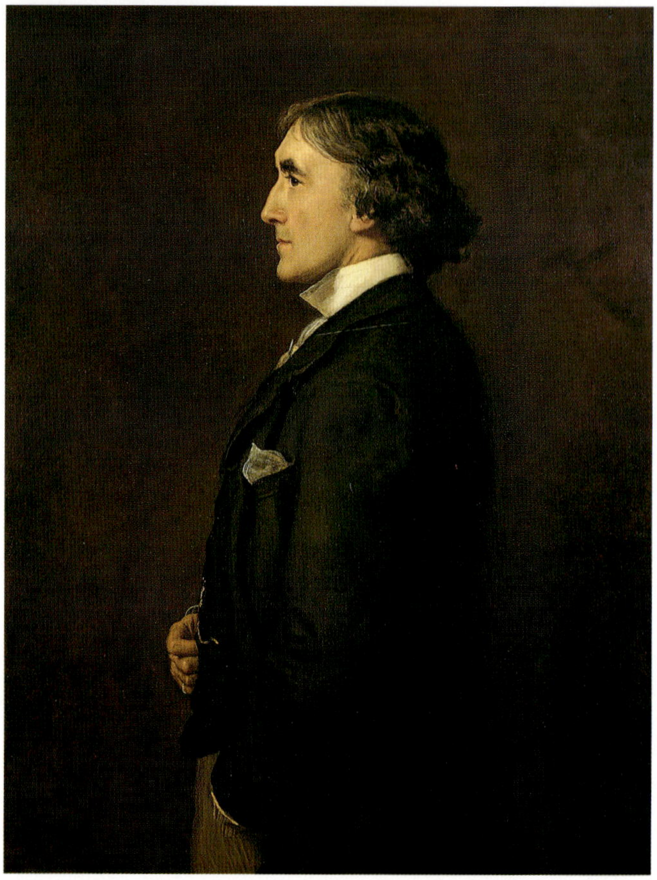

Sir John Everett Millais: *Sir Henry Irving* (No. 323)

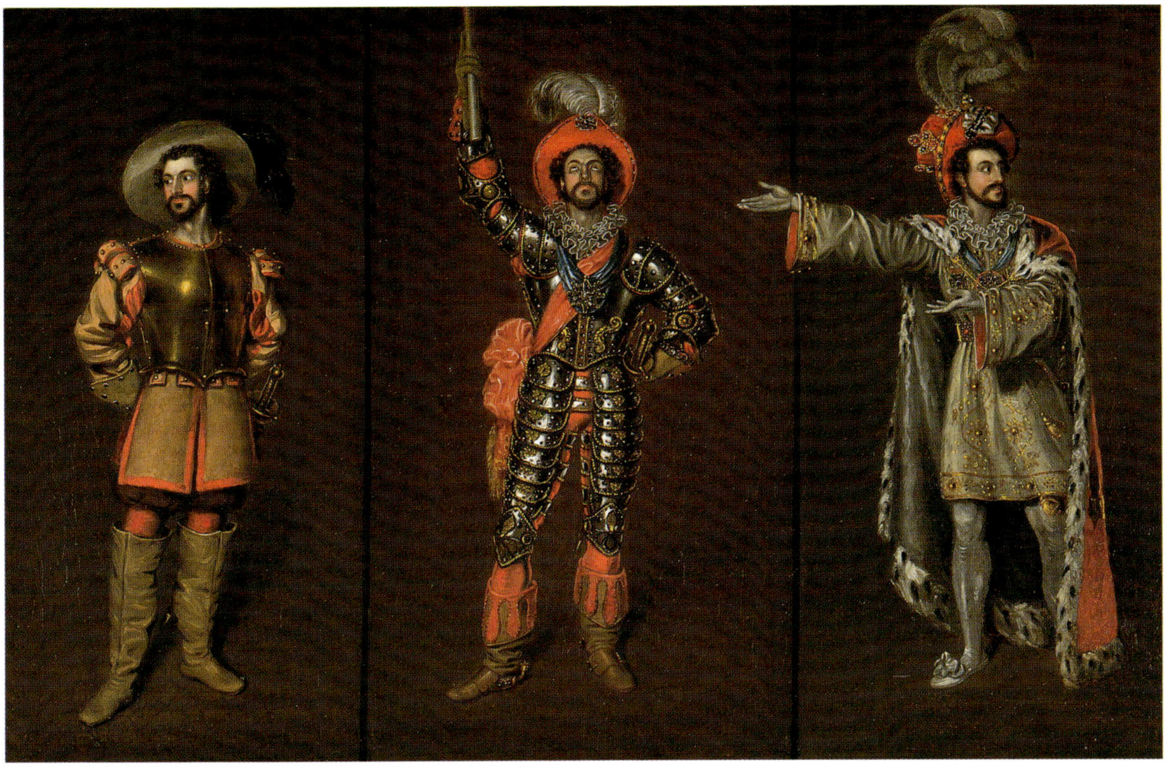

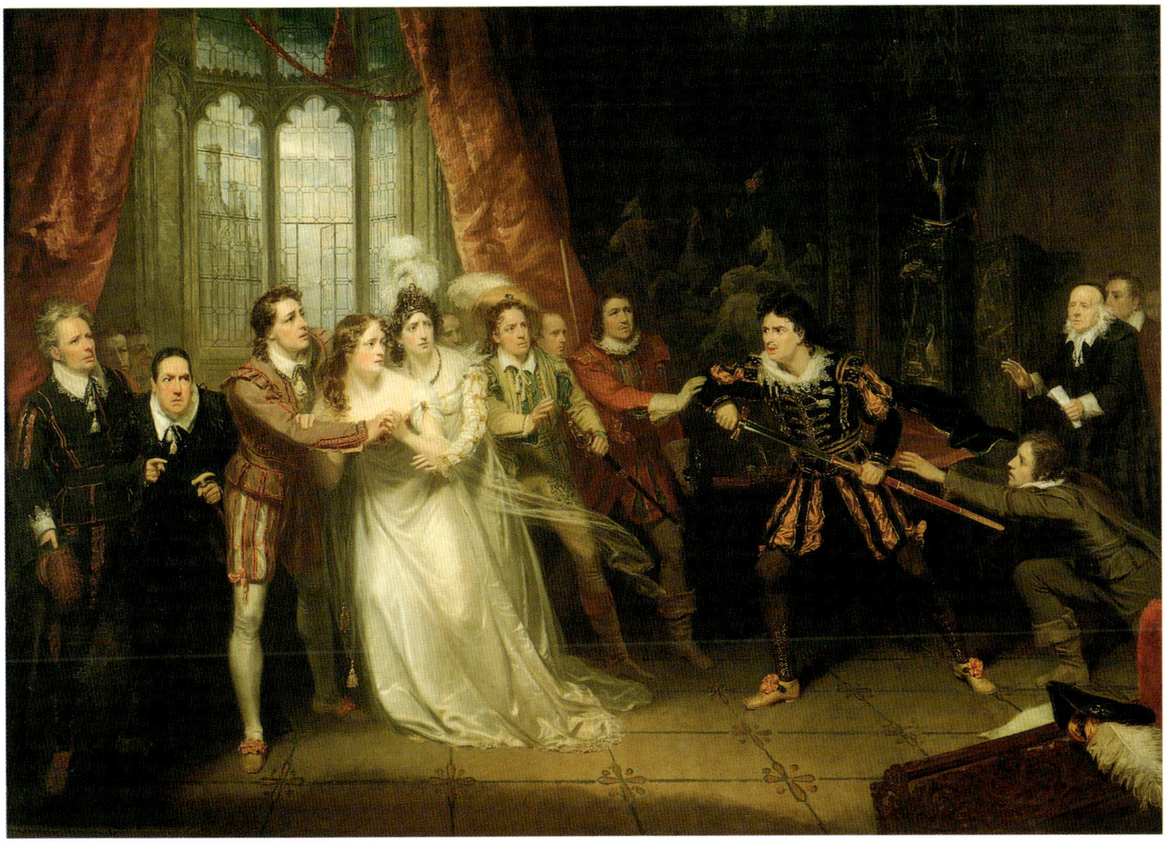

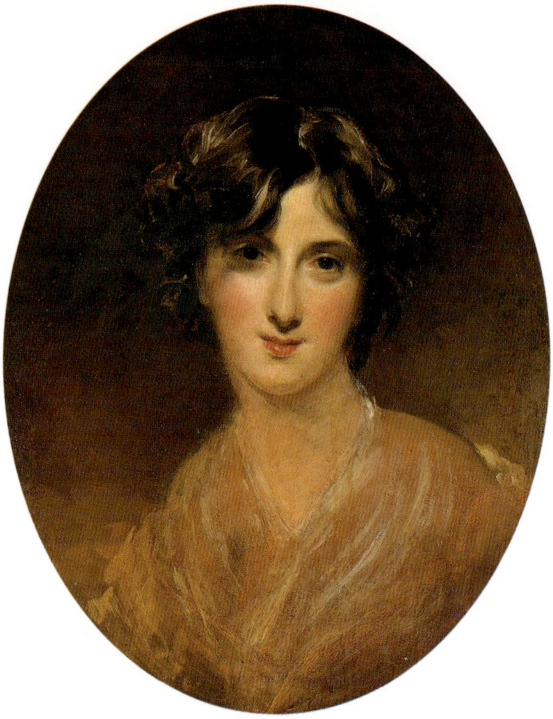

George Henry Harlow: *Lydia Kelly* (No. 363)

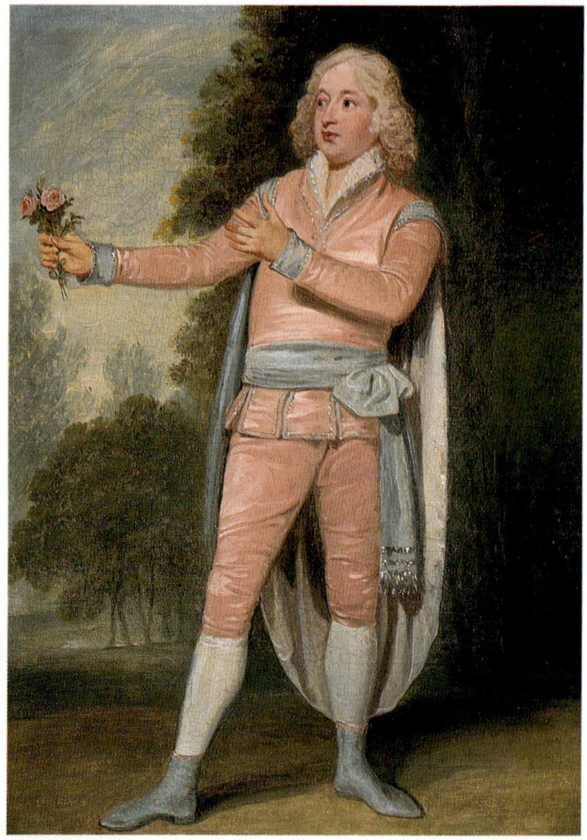

Samuel De Wilde: *Michael Kelly* (No. 364)

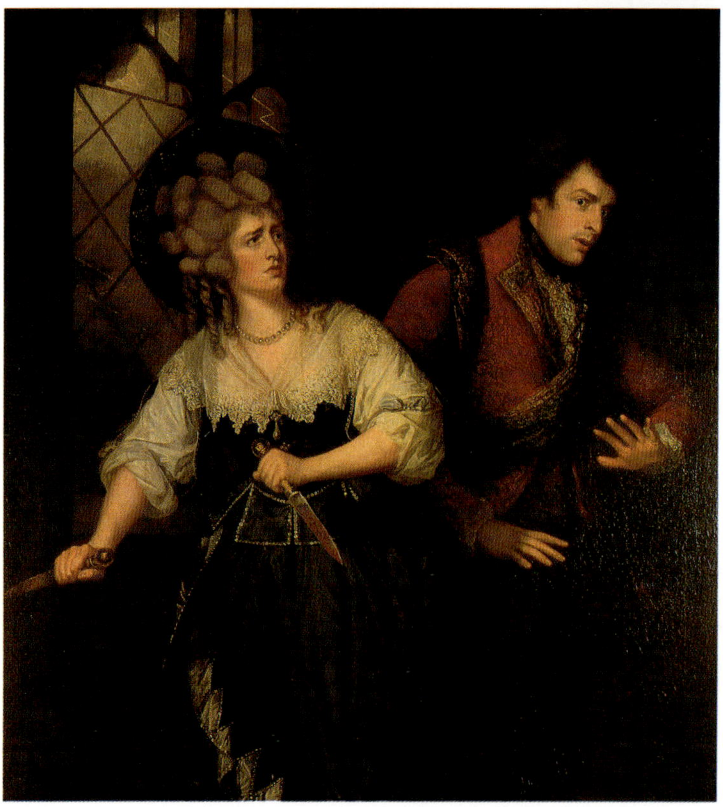

Thomas Beach: *John Philip Kemble & Sarah Siddons* (No. 390)

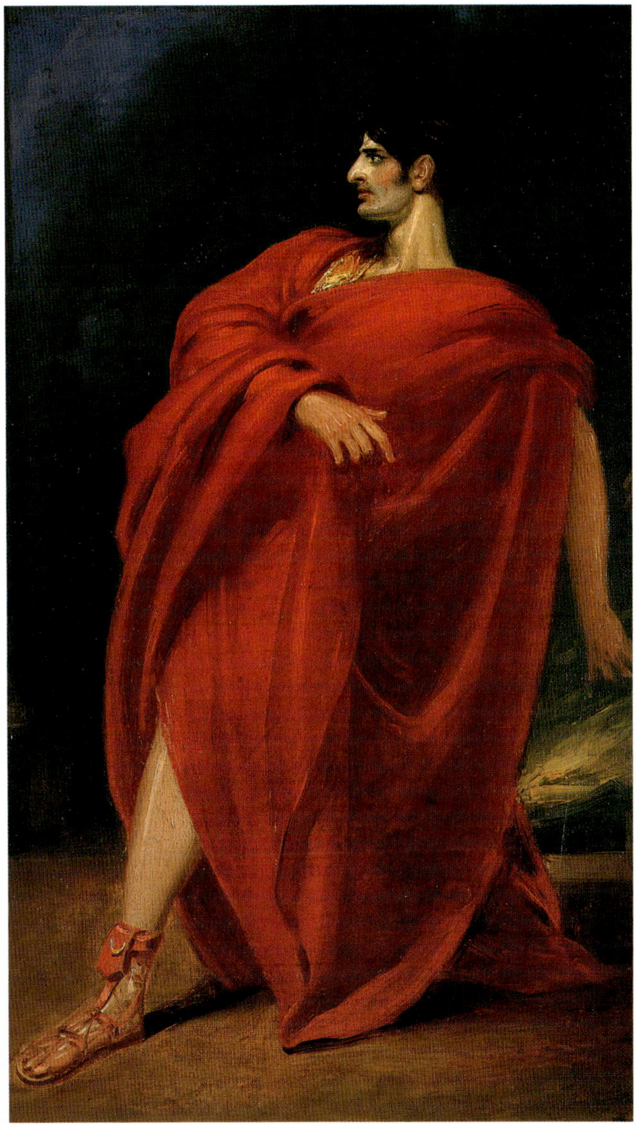

George Henry Harlow: *John Philip Kemble* (No. 381)

Sir Thomas Lawrence:
John Philip Kemble (No. 385)

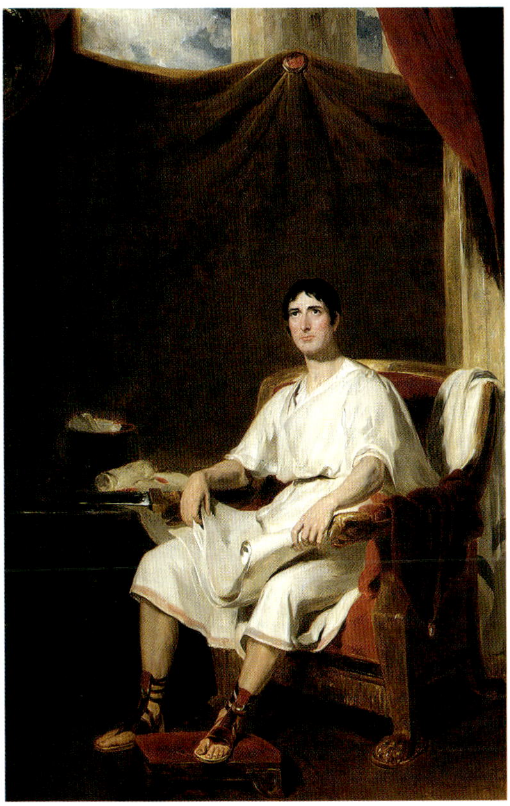

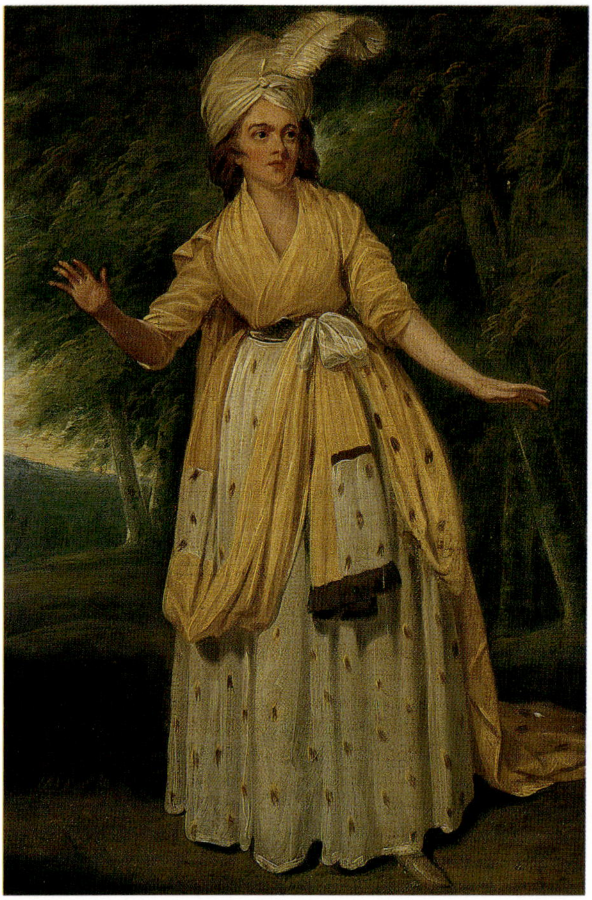

Samuel De Wilde: *Elizabeth Kemble* (No. 371)

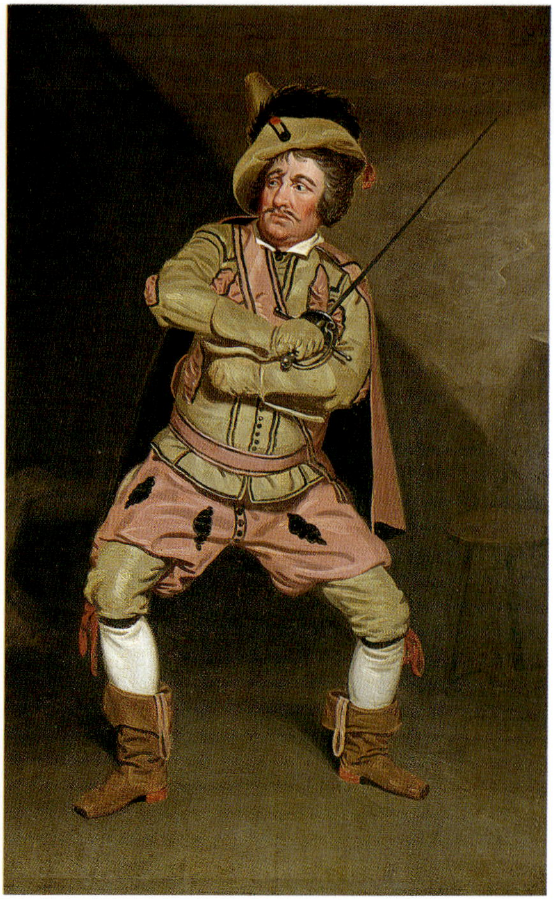

Samuel De Wilde: *Charles Lee Lewes* (No. 421)

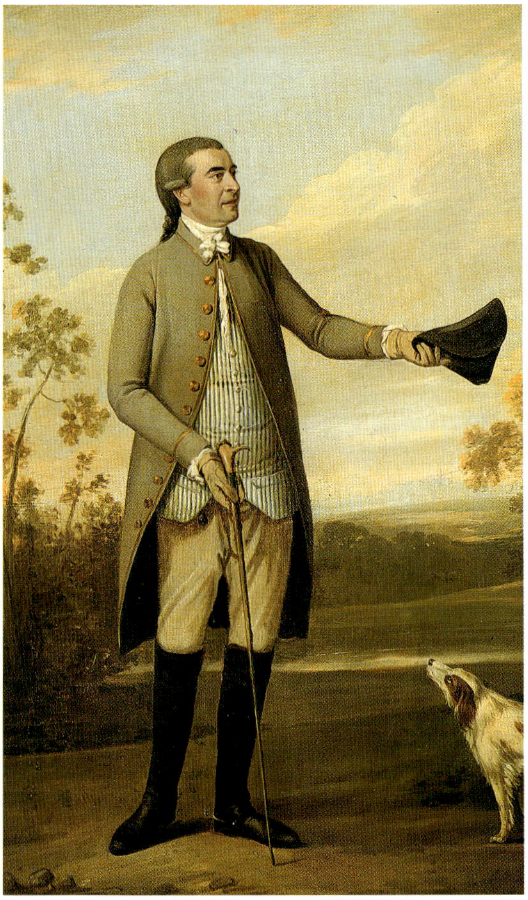

TOP LEFT
Henry Walton (attr.): *Thomas King* (No. 399)

BOTTOM LEFT
Benjamin Wilson (?): *Thomas King* (No. 400)

BELOW
Johan Zoffany: *Thomas King* (No. 401)

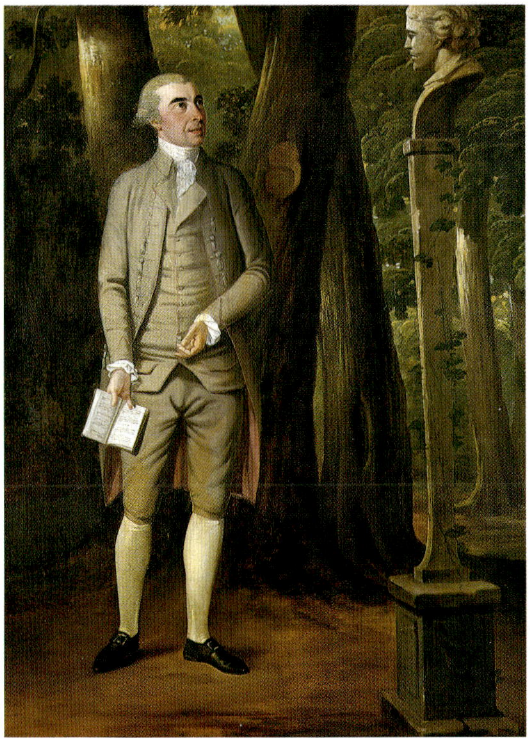

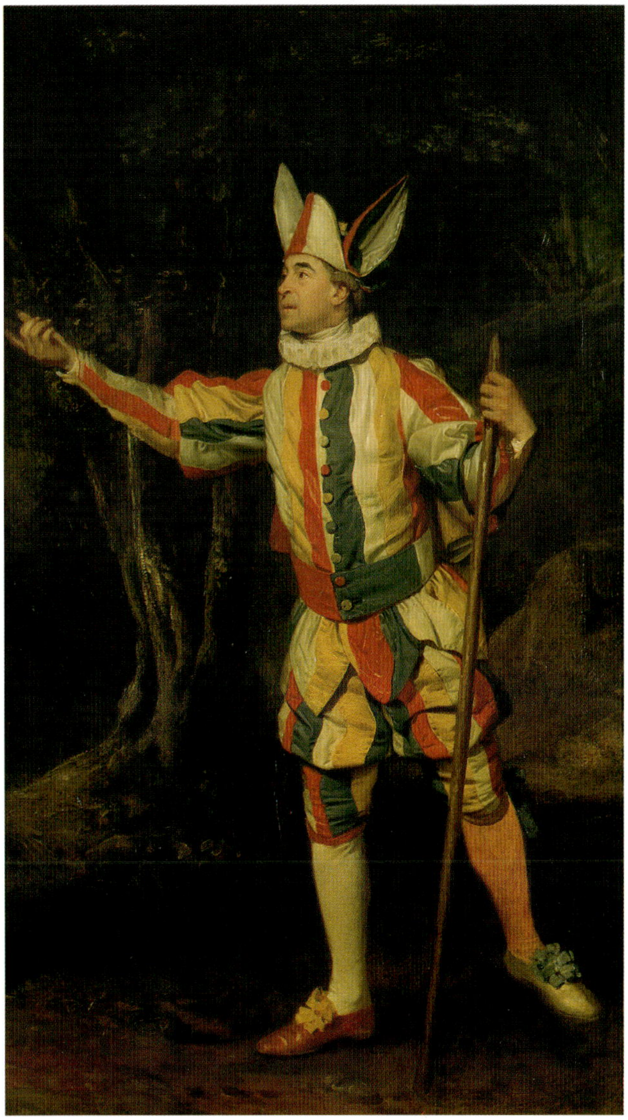

William Dobson (attr.): *Nathaniel Lee (called)* (No. 415)

Johan Zoffany: *William Thomas Lewis, Joseph Shepherd Munden & John Quick* (No. 429)

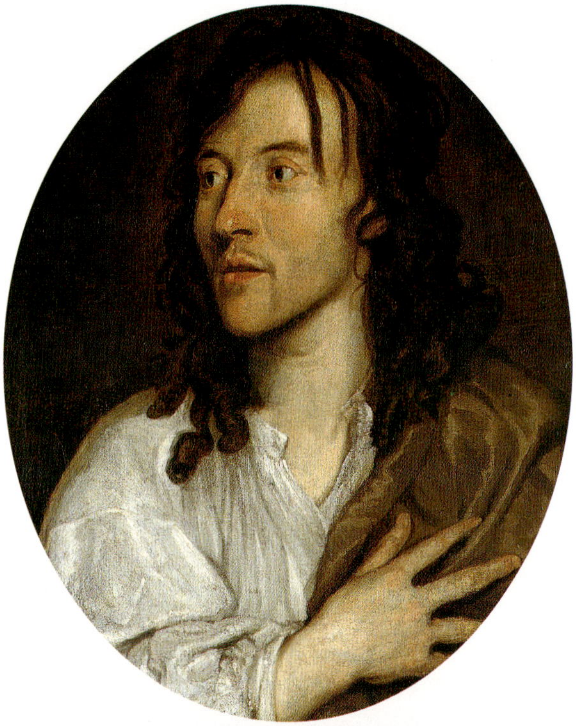

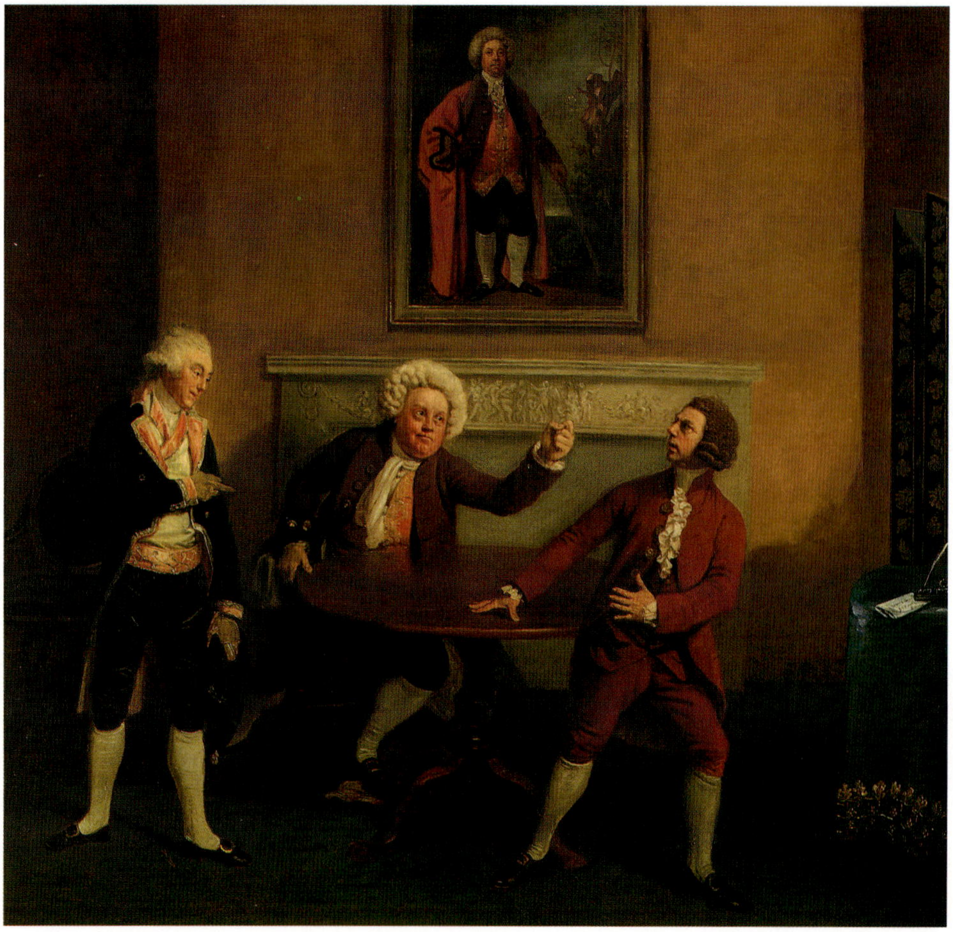

John Opie: *Charles Macklin* (No. 449)

Samuel De Wilde: *John Liston, Richard Jones & Mr Hamerton* (No. 438)

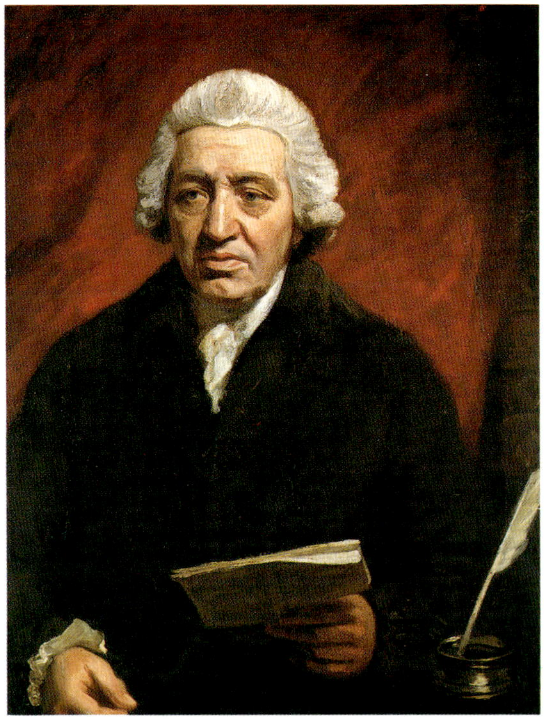

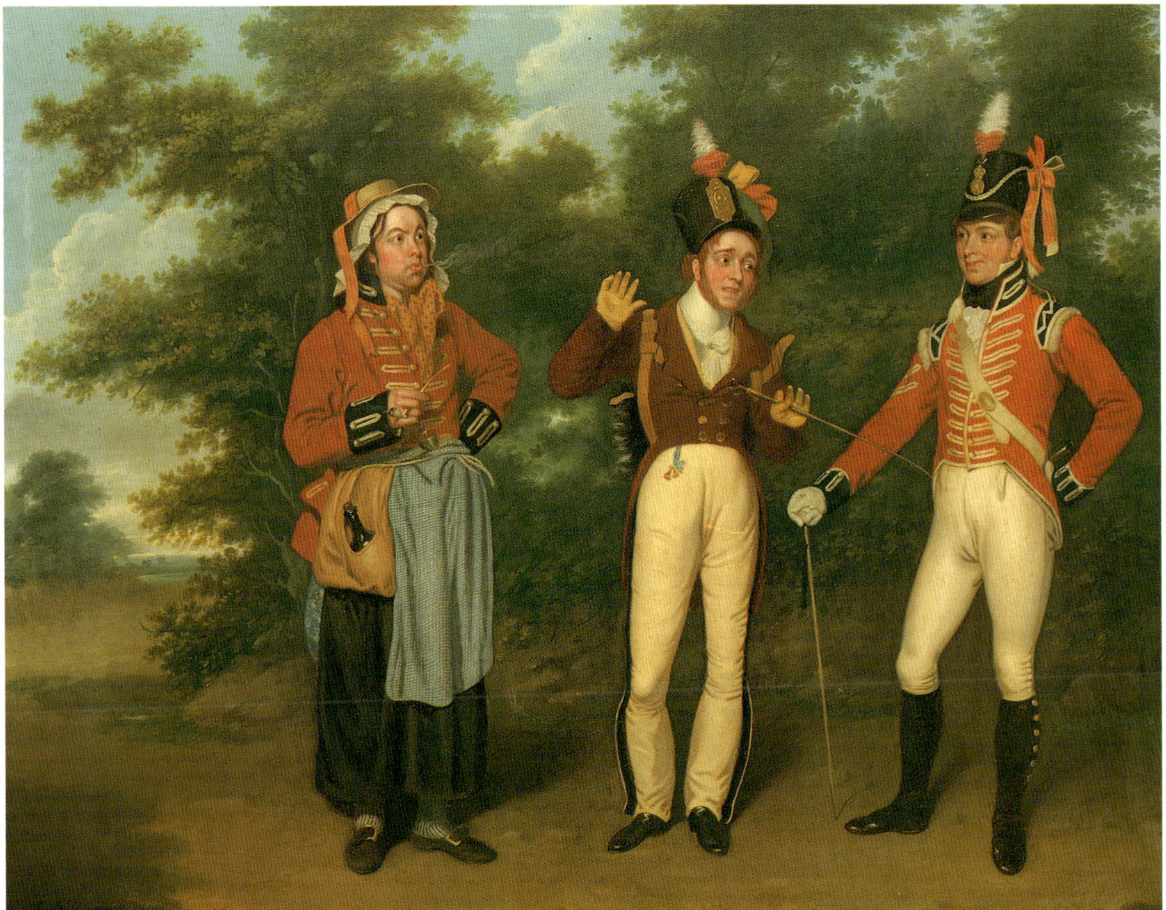

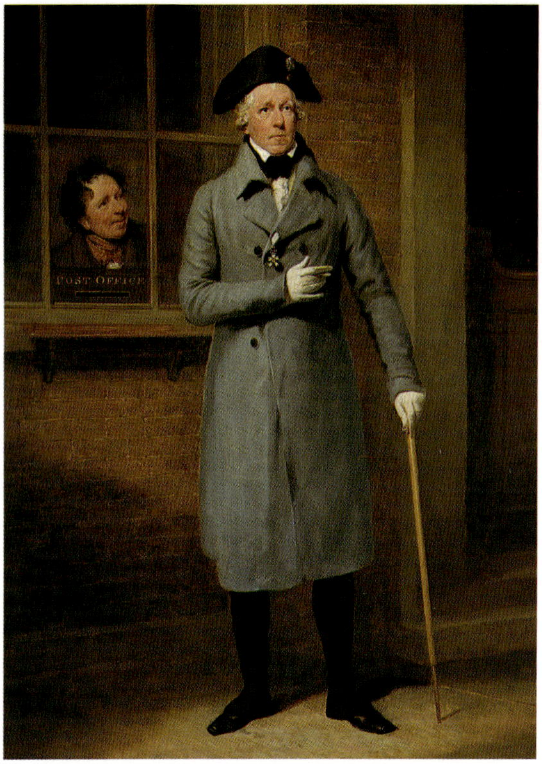

George Clint: *Charles Mathews* (No. 463)

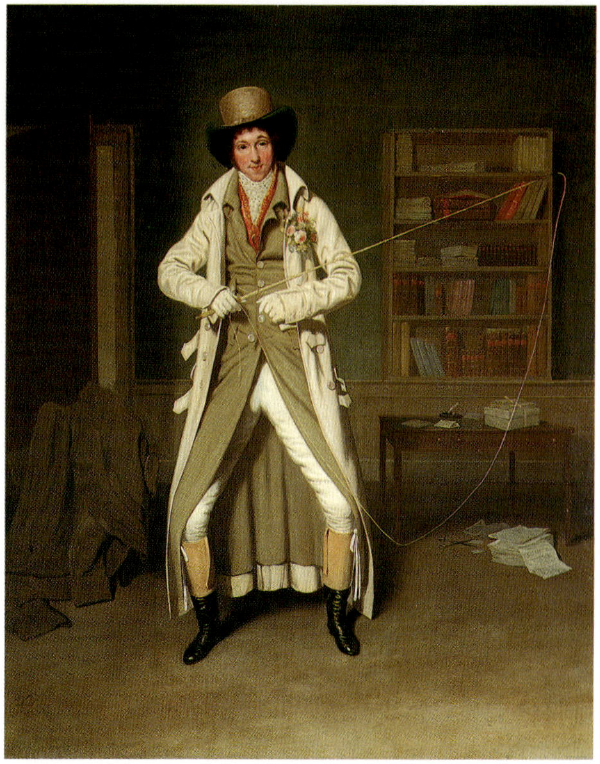

Samuel De Wilde: *Charles Mathews* (No. 465)

James Warren Childe: *Charles Mathews* (No. 486)

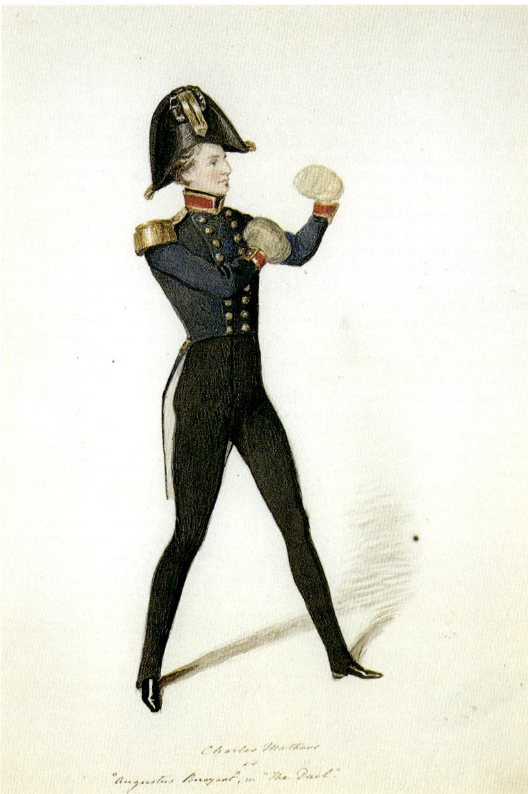

Samuel De Wilde: *Charles Mathews* (No. 469)

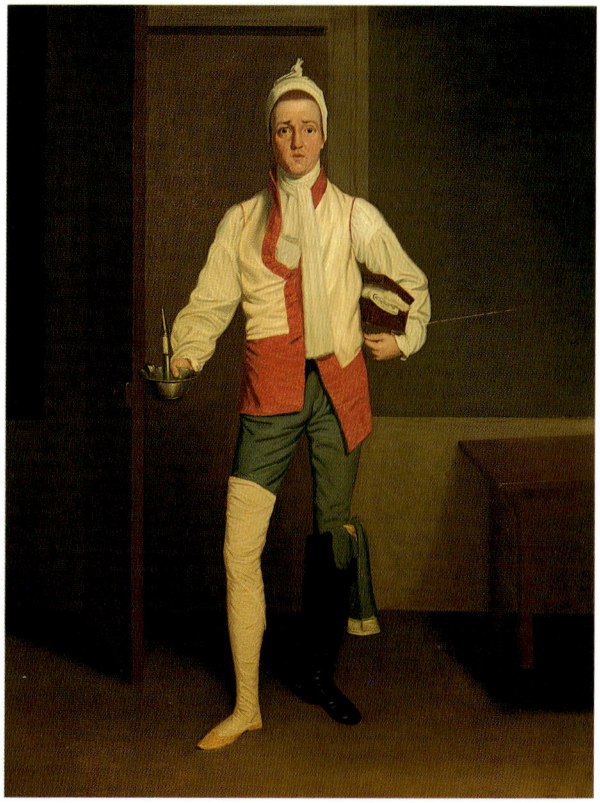

James Lonsdale:
Charles Mathews (No. 472)

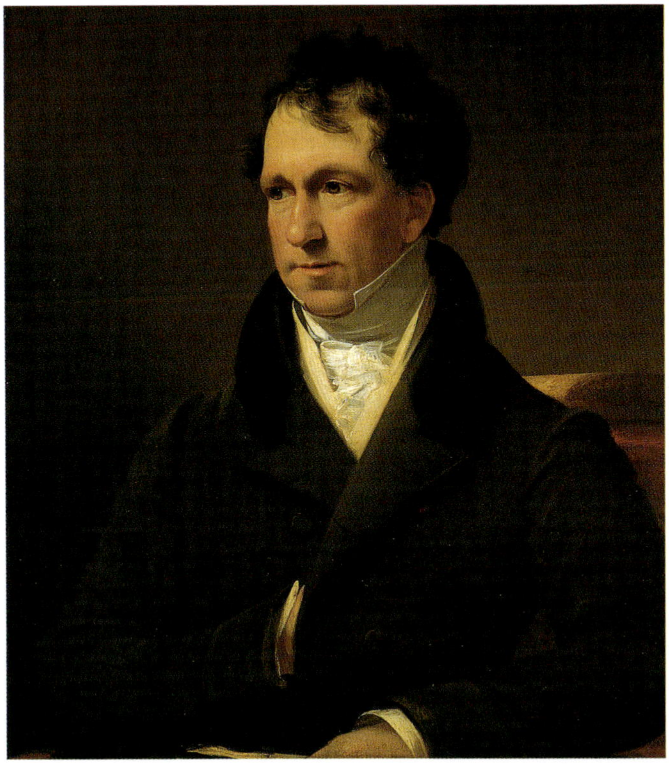

George Henry Harlow:
Charles Mathews (No. 471)

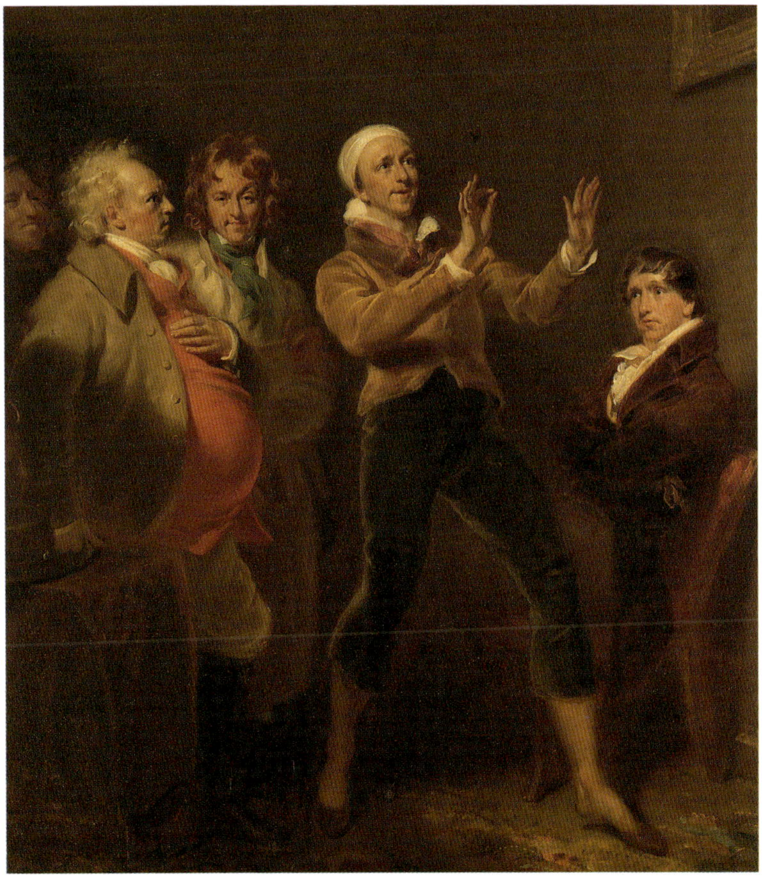

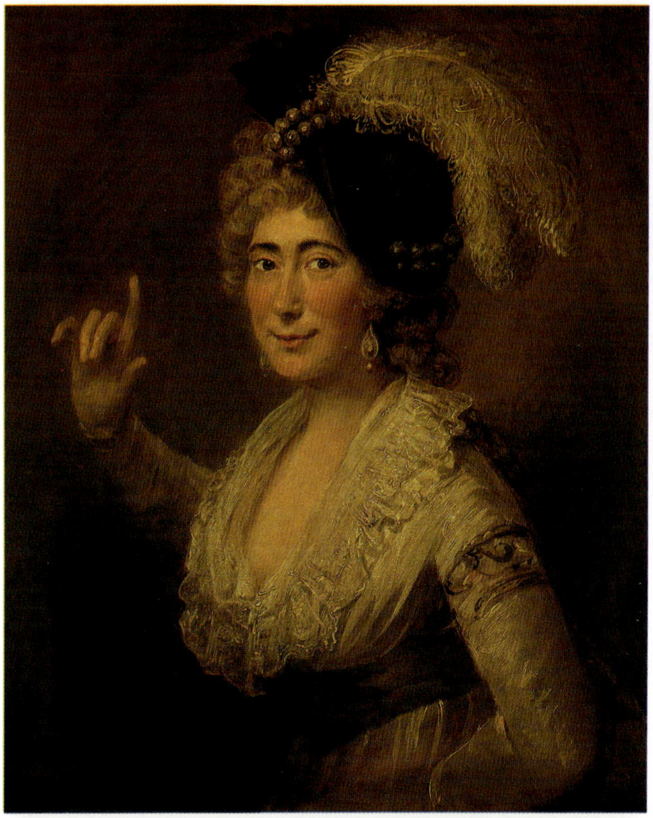

Gainsborough Dupont:
Isabella Mattocks (No. 597)

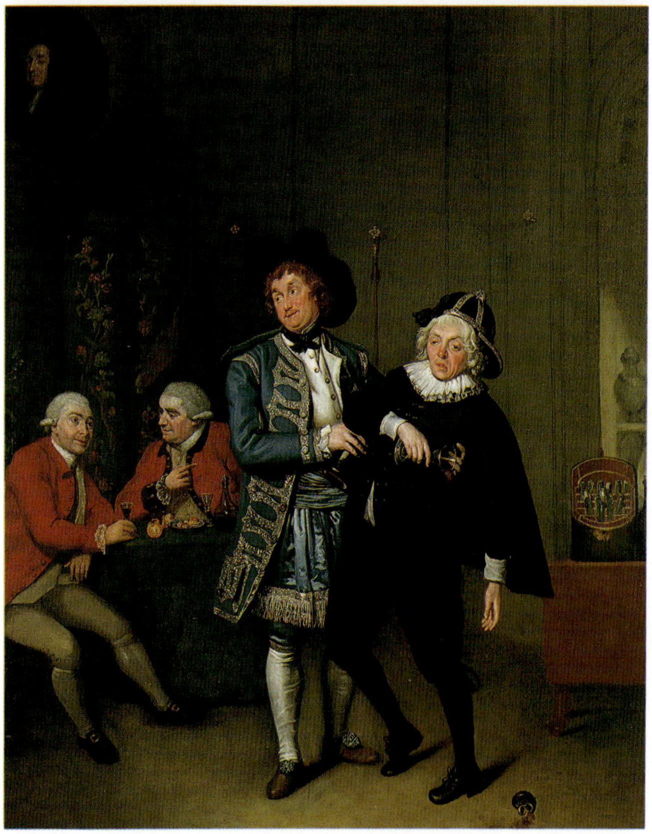

Benjamin Vandergucht:
John Moody, William Parsons, Thomas Jefferson & James Aickin (No. 613)

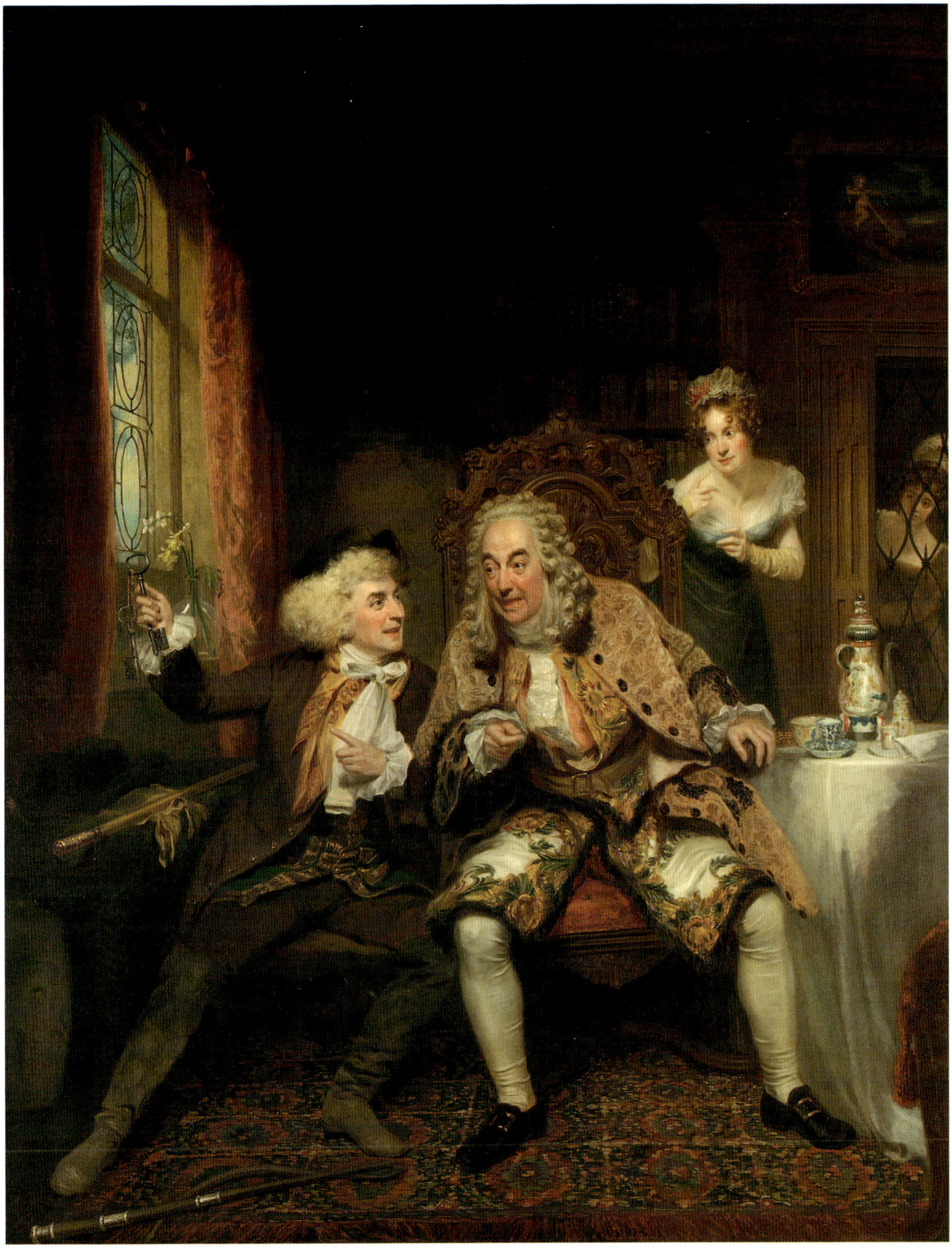
George Clint: *Joseph Munden, Marie Cubitt, Edward Knight & Mary Orger* (No. 630)

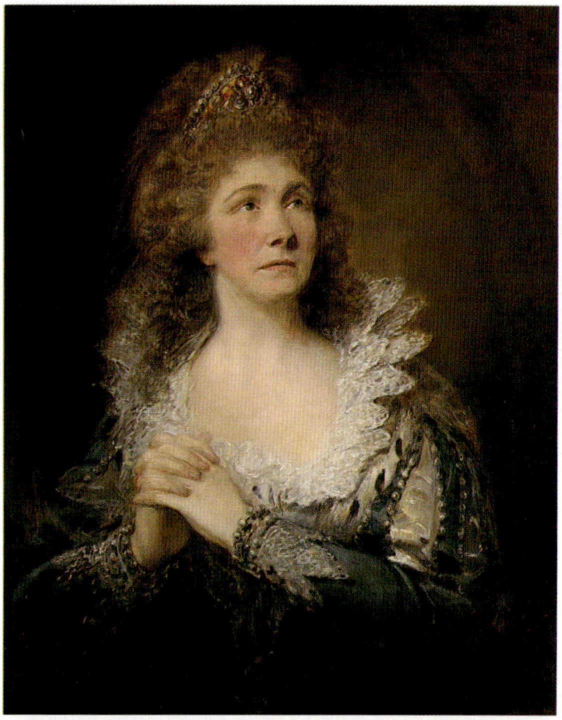

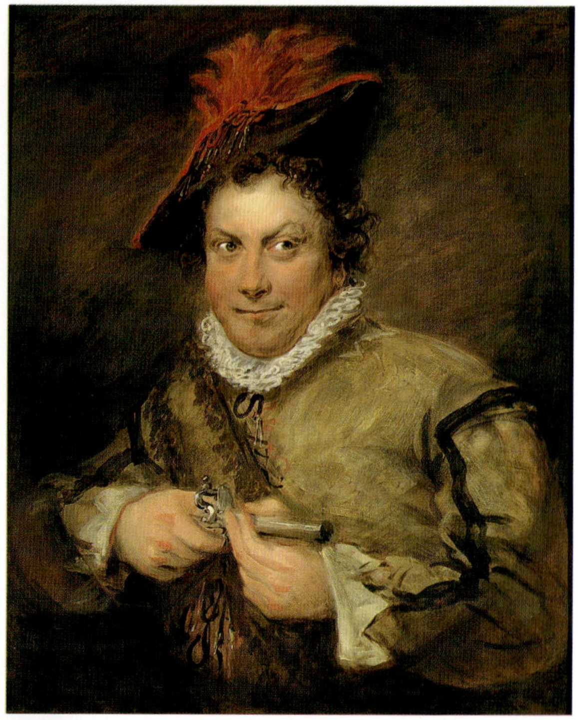

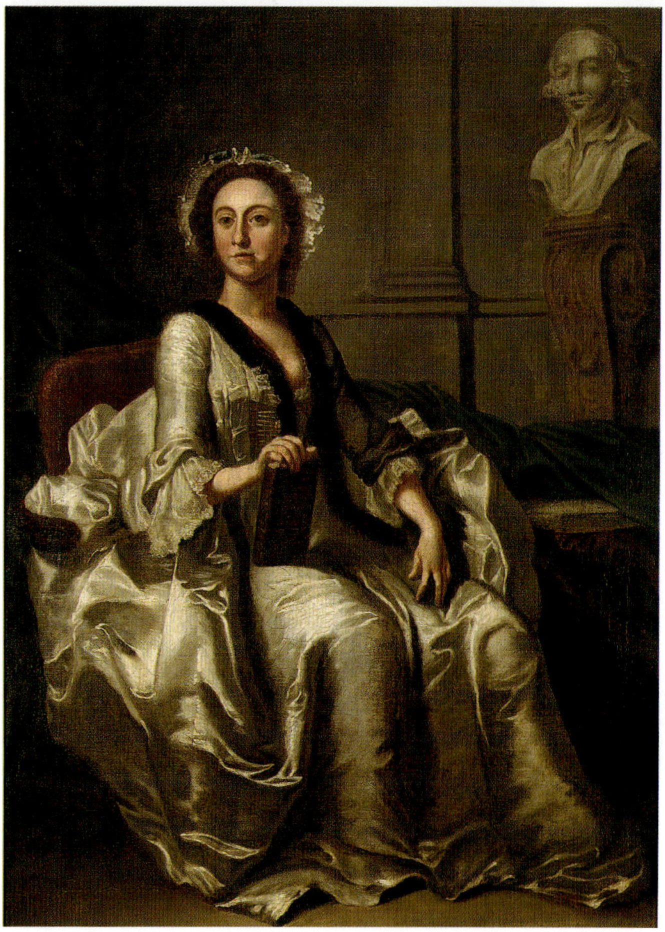

Gainsborough Dupont:
Elizabeth Pope (No. 683)

Gainsborough Dupont:
John Quick (No. 701)

Francis Hayman:
Hannah Pritchard (No. 696)

OPPOSITE

John Hamilton Mortimer:
William Powell with his wife Elizabeth & daughters Ann & Elizabeth Mary (No. 695)

Mather Brown: *Alexander Pope, Elizabeth Pope, Mary Wells, William Farren, Thomas Hull & George Inchbald* (No. 682)

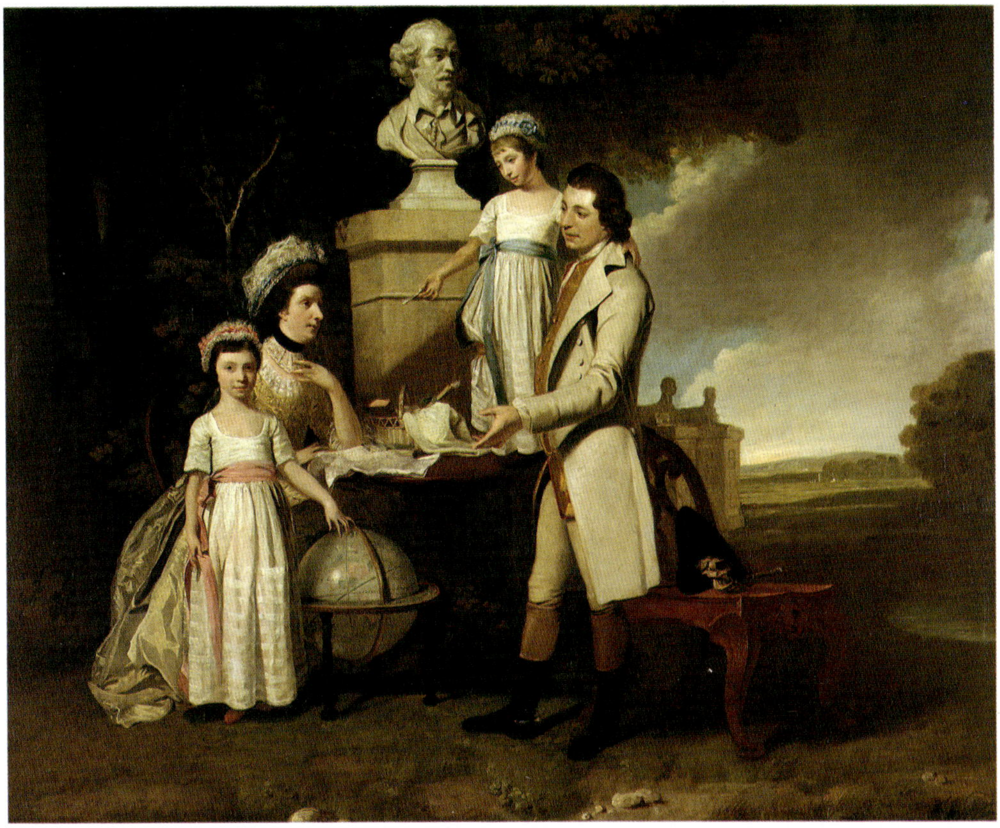

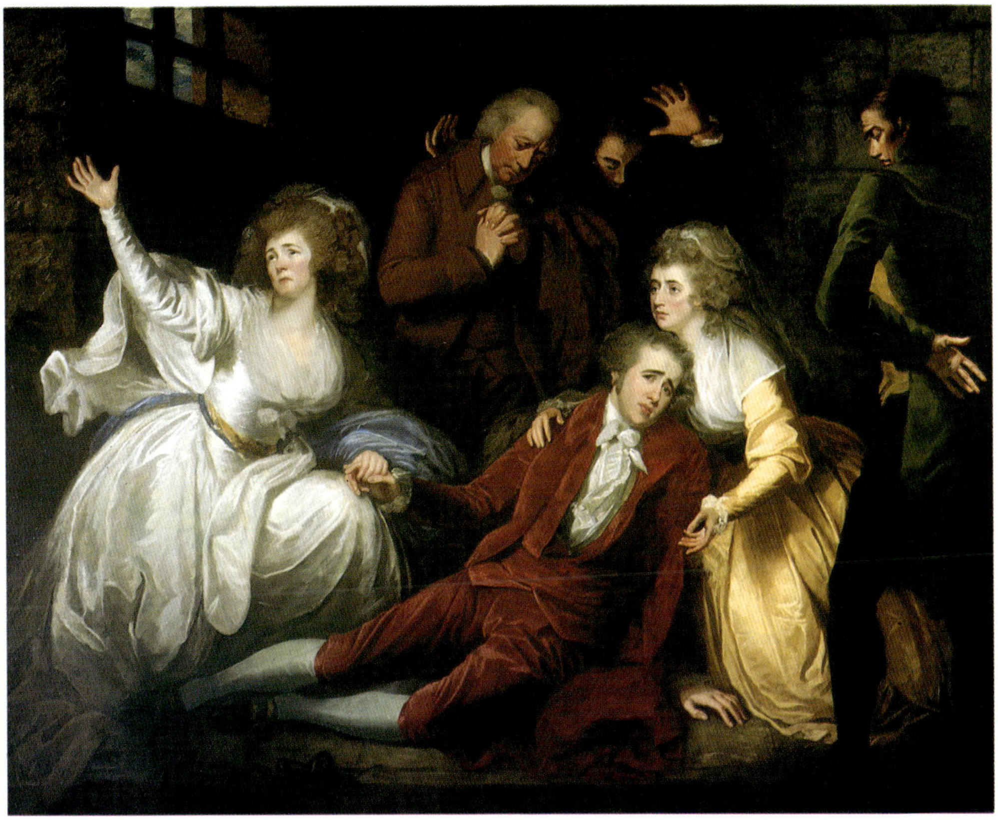

PLATE 33

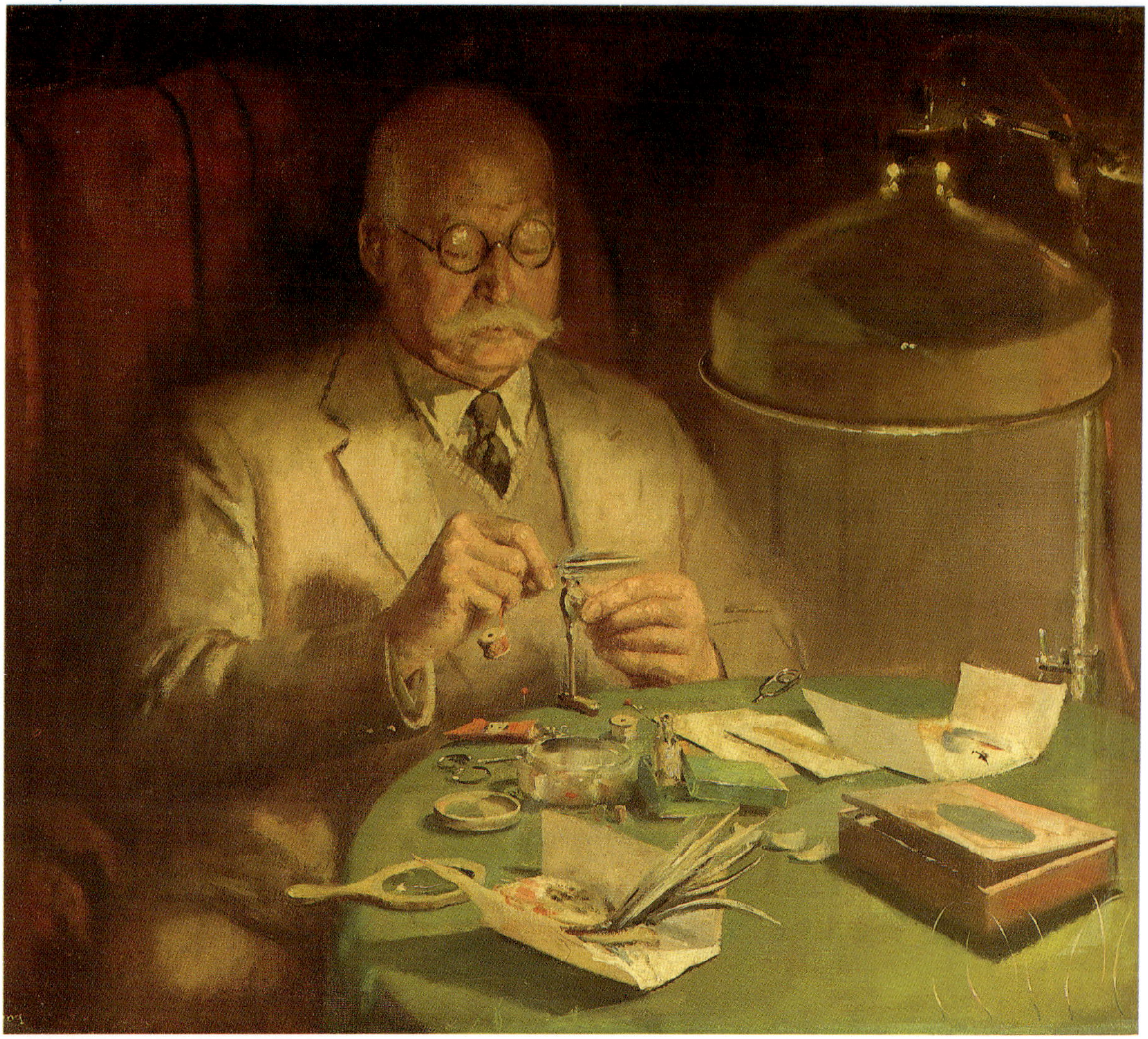

John Gilroy: *Arthur Ransome* (No. 711)

Johan Zoffany:
Frederick Charles Reinhold (No. 715)

Joseph Highmore:
John Rich & family (called) (No. 717)

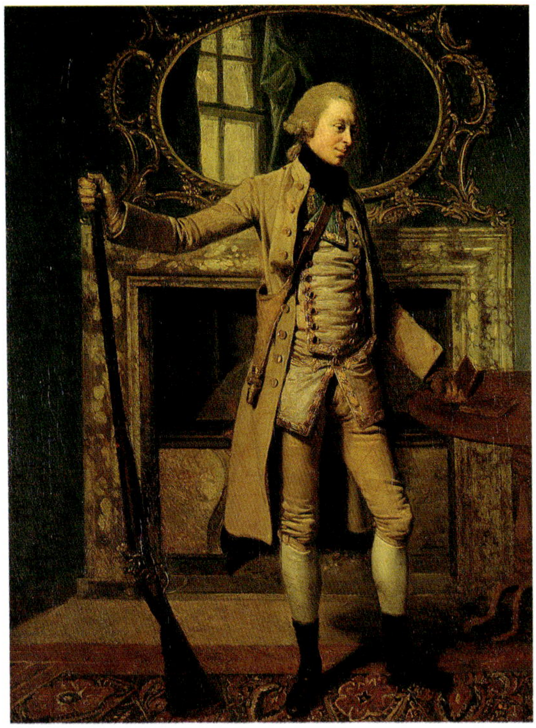

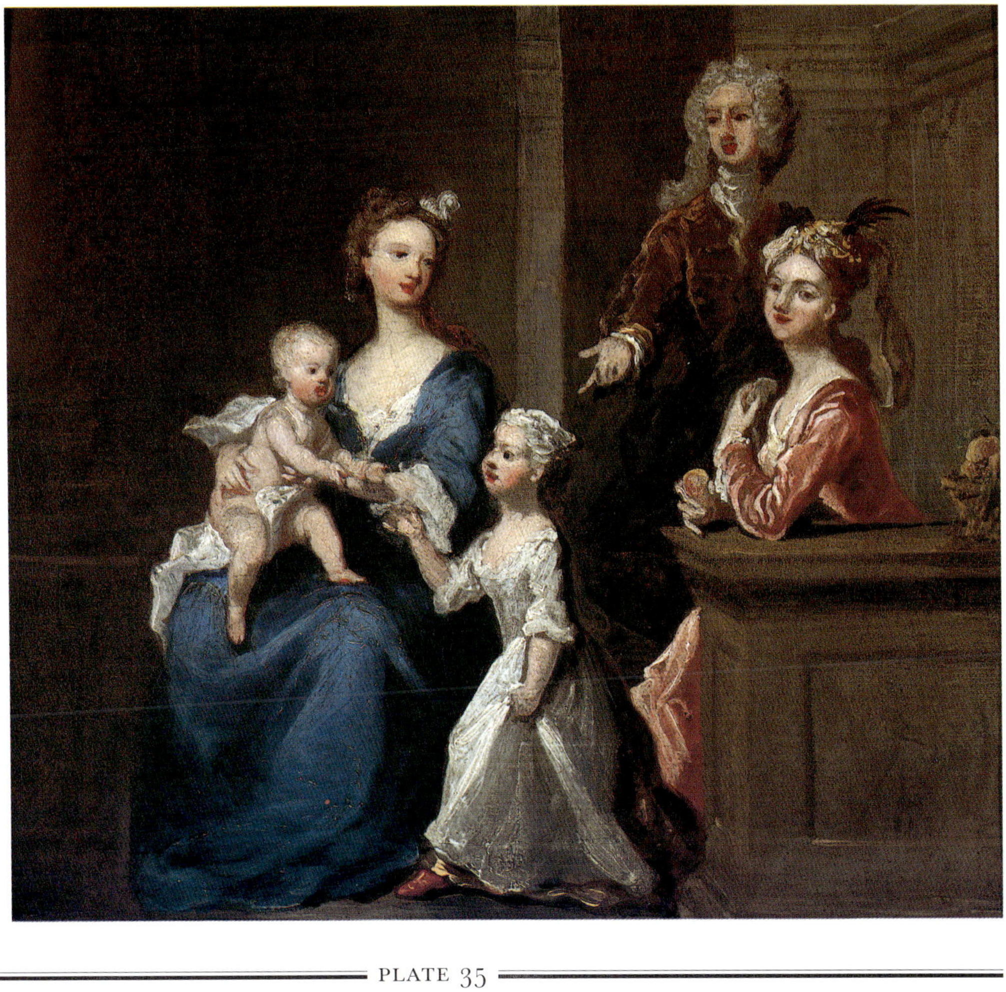

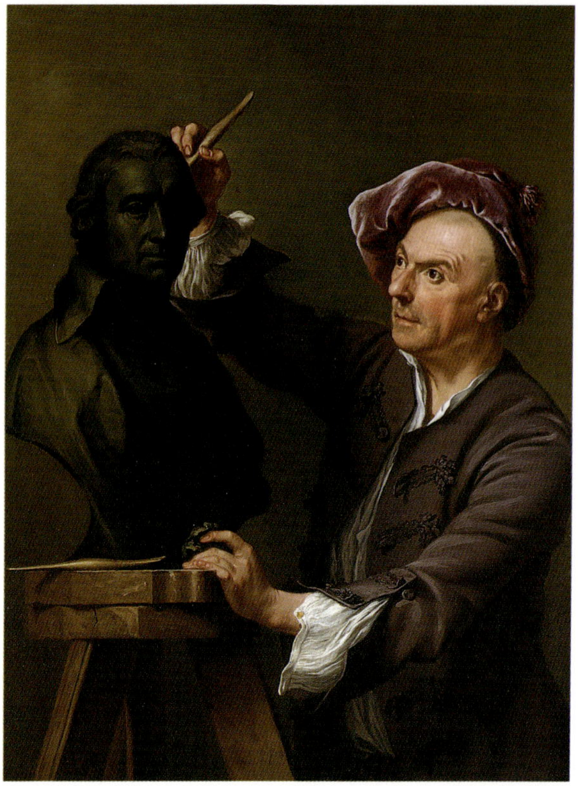

Andrea Soldi: *Louis François Roubiliac* (No. 727)

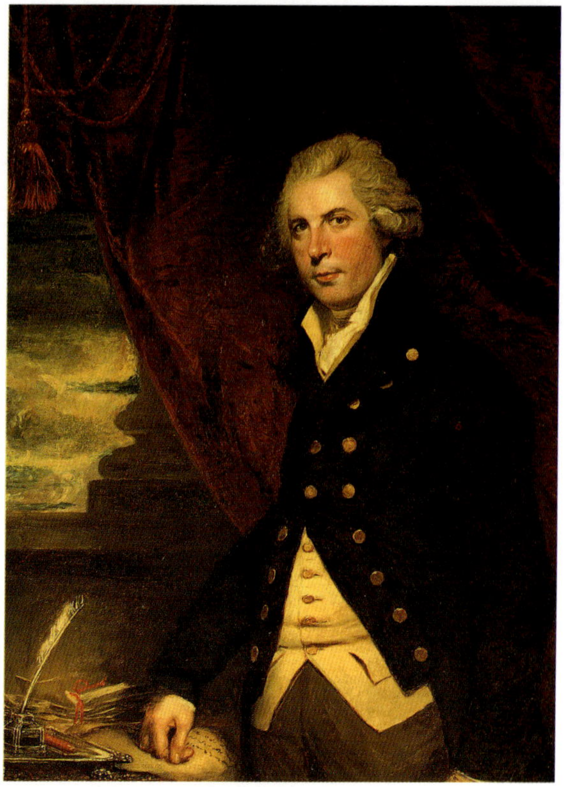

Sir Joshua Reynolds (studio): *Richard Brinsley Sheridan* (No. 738)

Sir Thomas Lawrence: *John Philip Kemble* (No. 383)

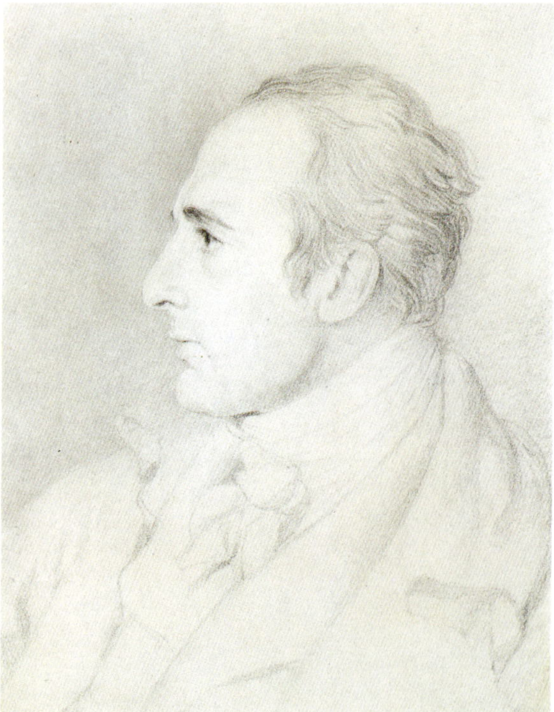

OPPOSITE
Sarah Siddons

TOP LEFT: John Raphael Smith (?), after Lawrence (No. 747)

TOP RIGHT: Sir Thomas Lawrence (No. 744)

BELOW: George Henry Harlow (Nos. 742 & 743)

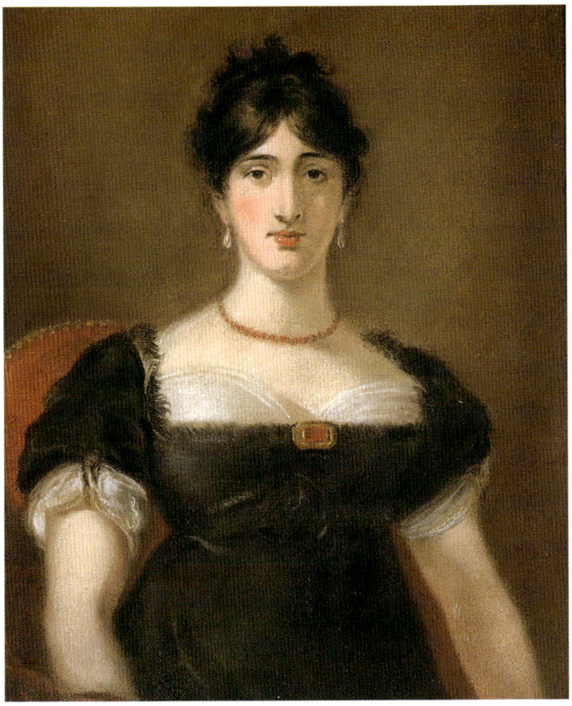
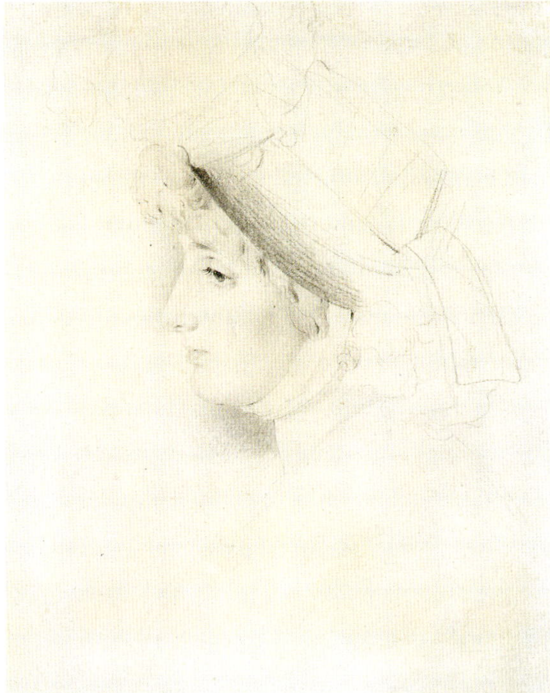
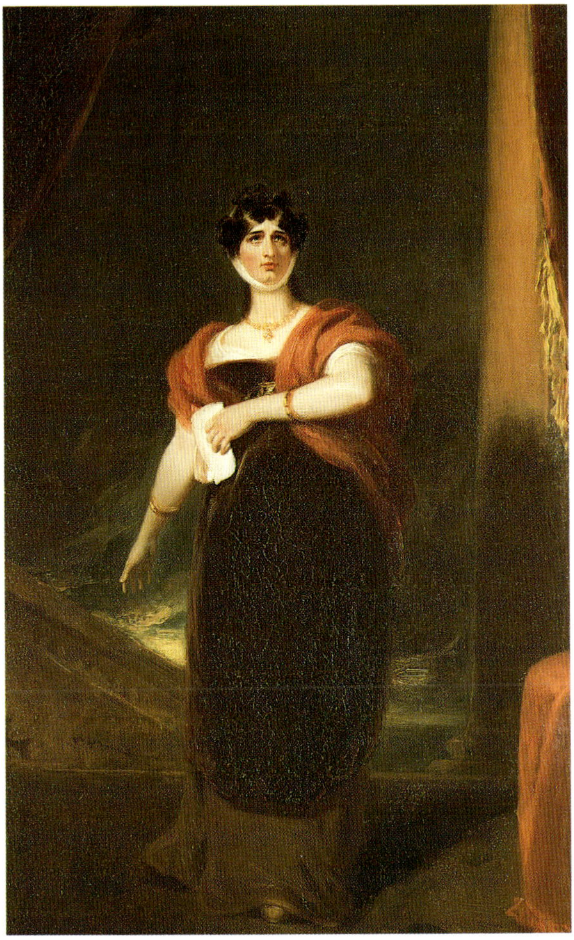
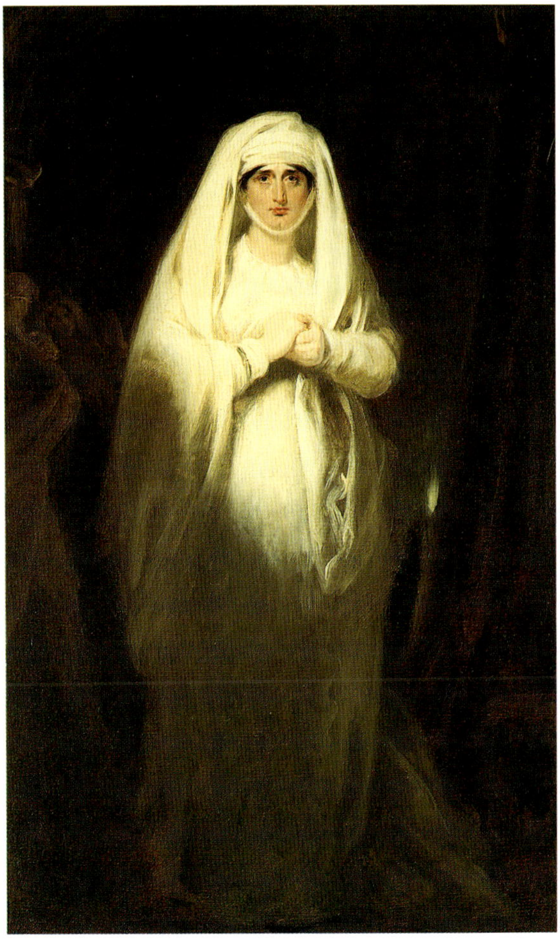

PLATE 37

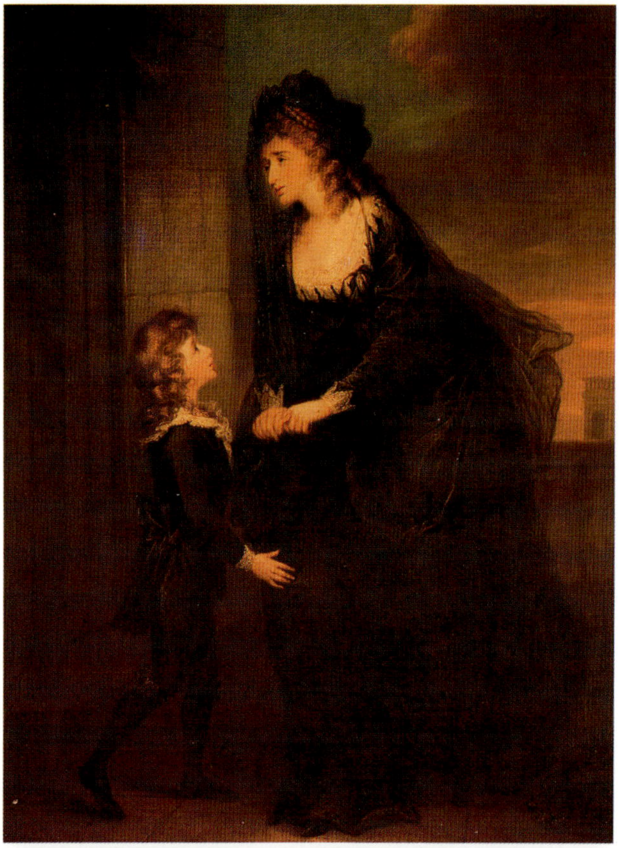

William Hamilton:
Sarah Siddons & Henry Siddons (No. 749)

Michael William Sharp: *Anna Storace* (No. 780)

G.W. Baldry: *Dame Ellen Terry* (No. 800)

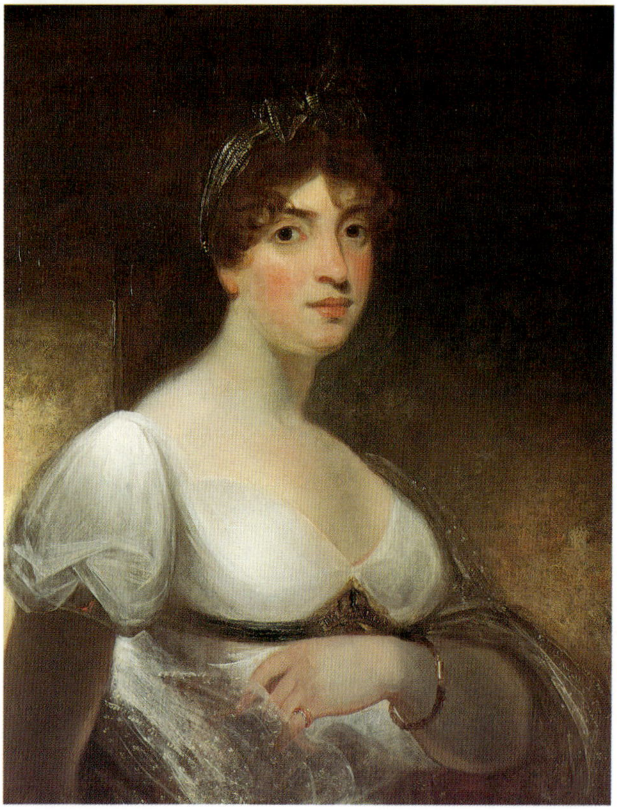

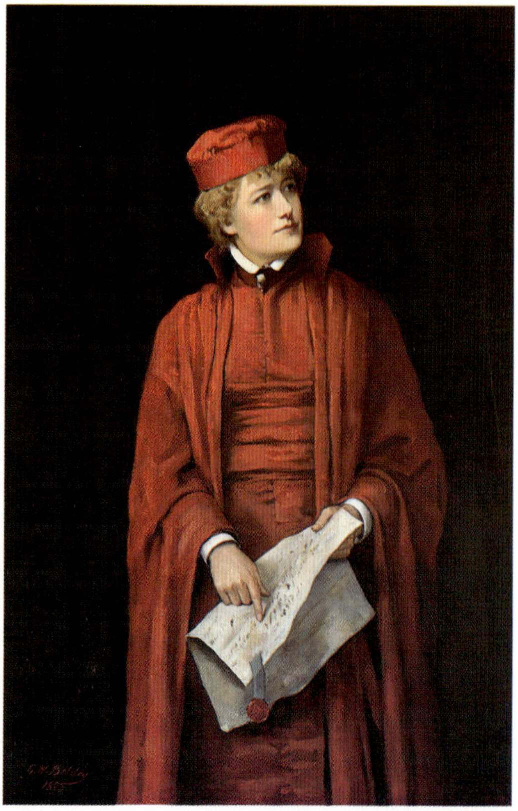

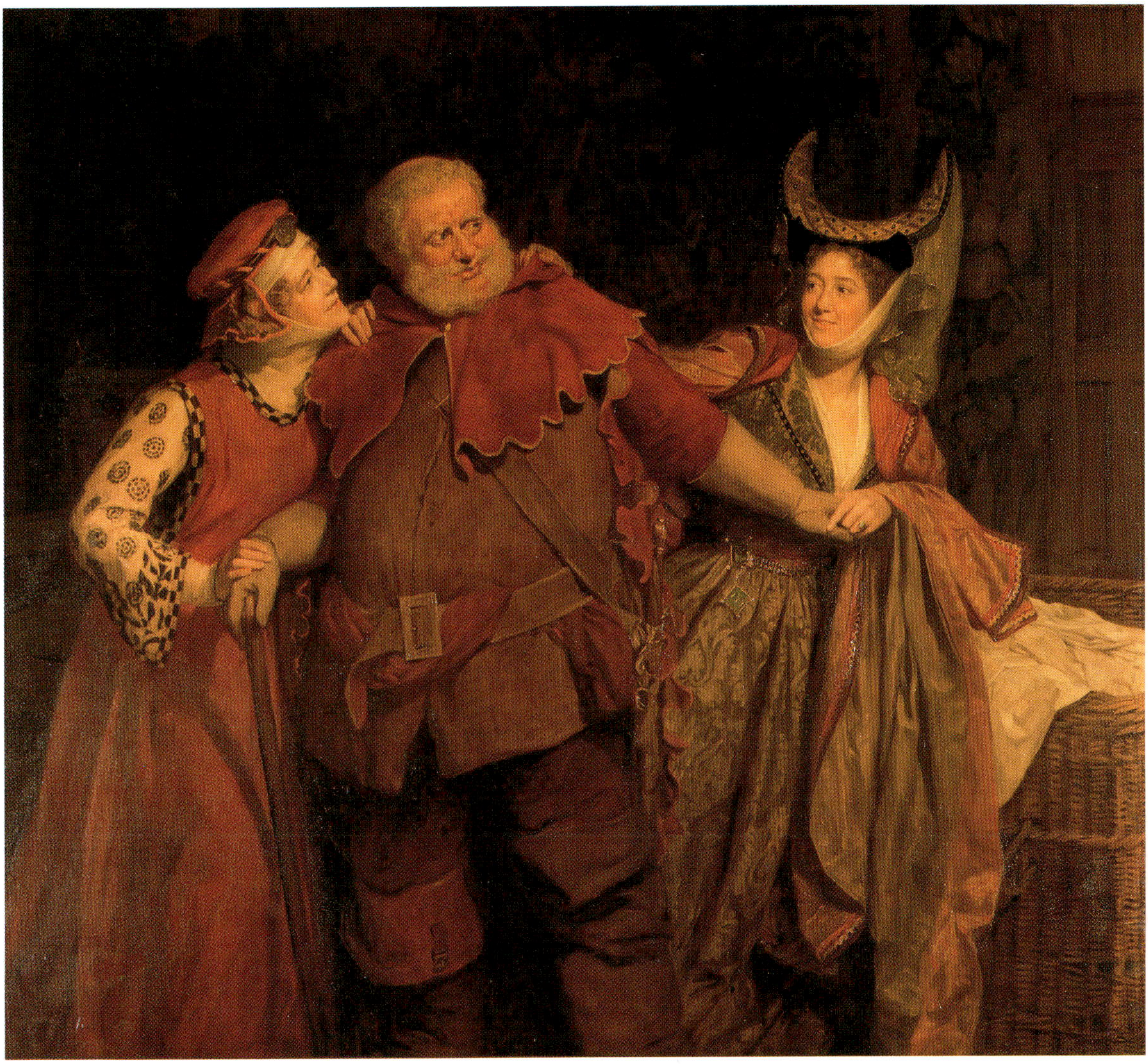

The Hon. John Collier: *Sir Herbert Beerbohm Tree, Dame Ellen Terry & Dame Madge Kendal* (No. 820)

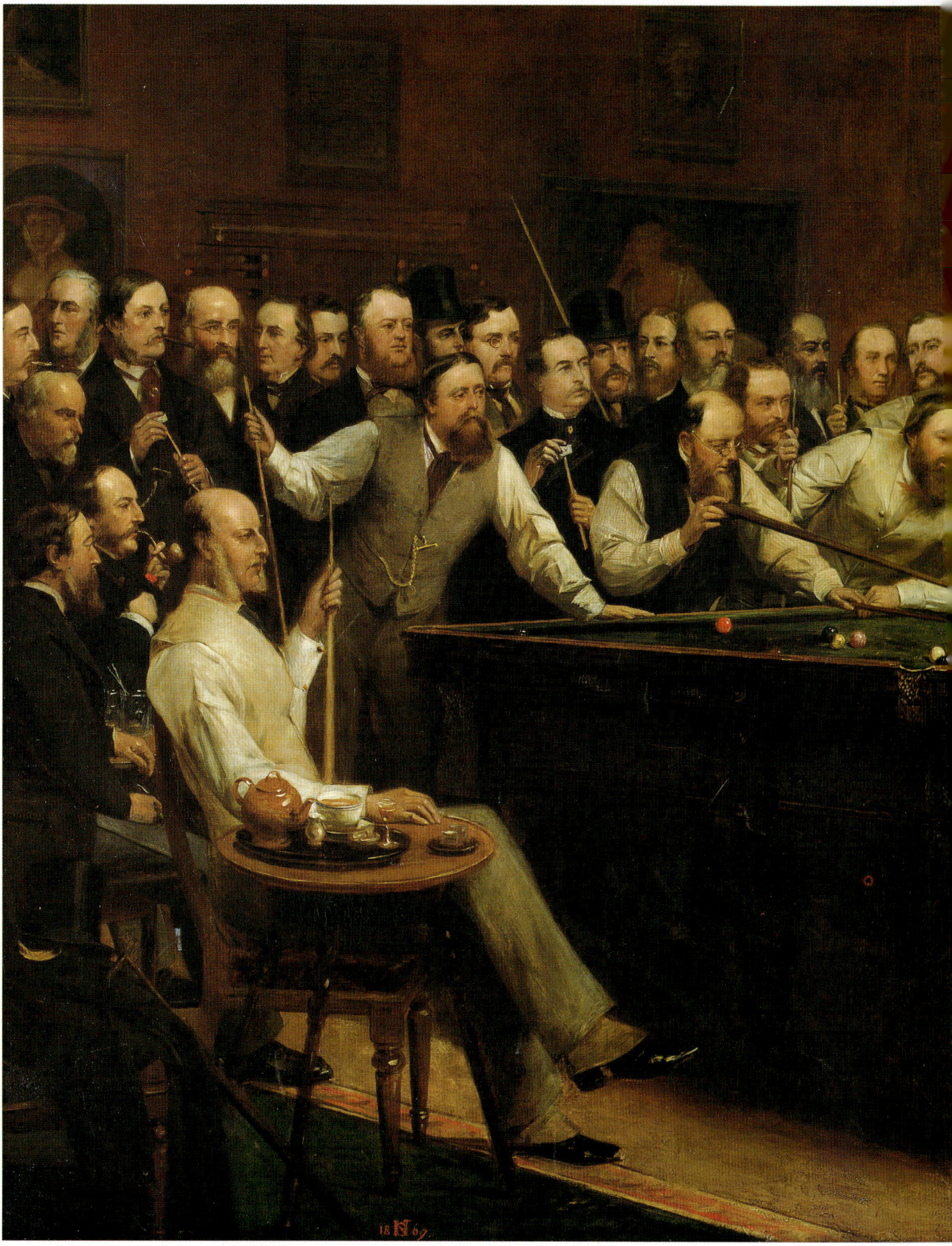

Henry O'Neil: *Sir Charles Taylor & others (Forty-three members in the Billiard Room of the Garrick Club)* (No. 793)

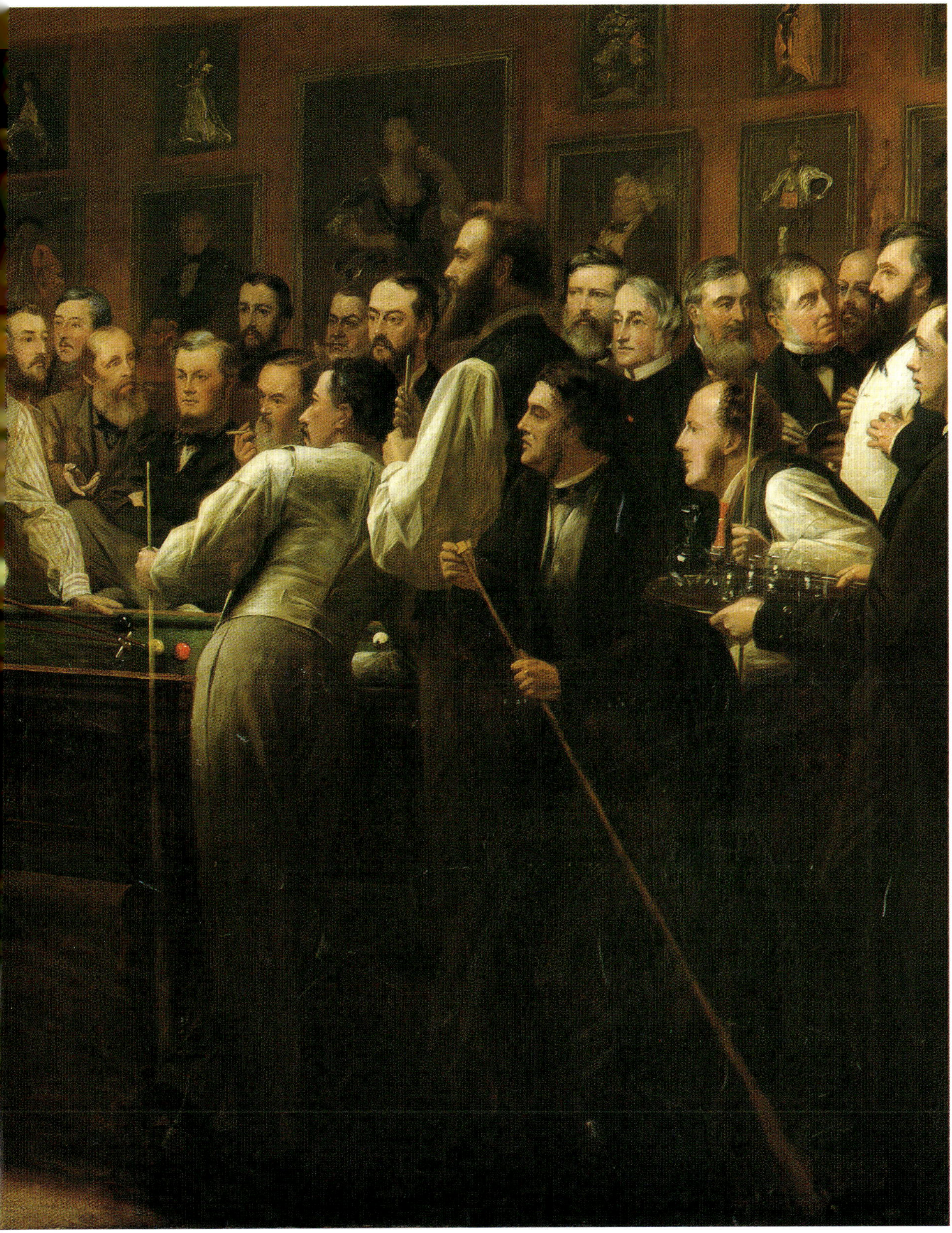

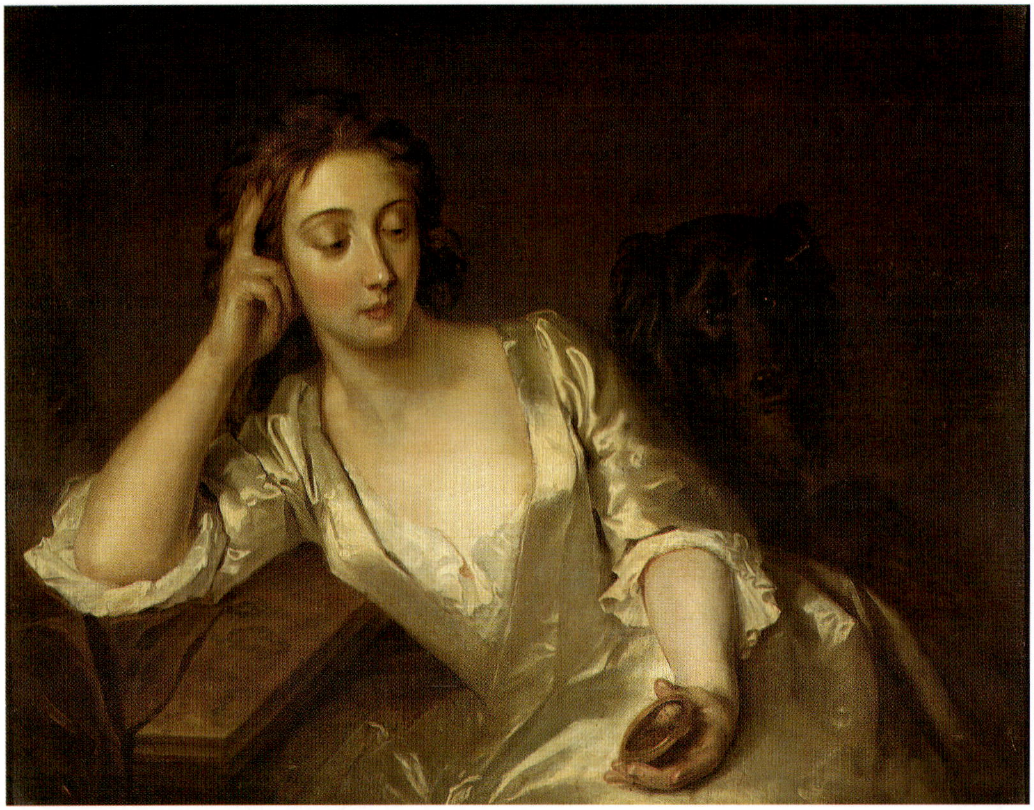

Philip Mercier: *Margaret ['Peg'] Woffington (called)* (No. 847)

Henry O'Neil: *Anthony Trollope* (No. 821)

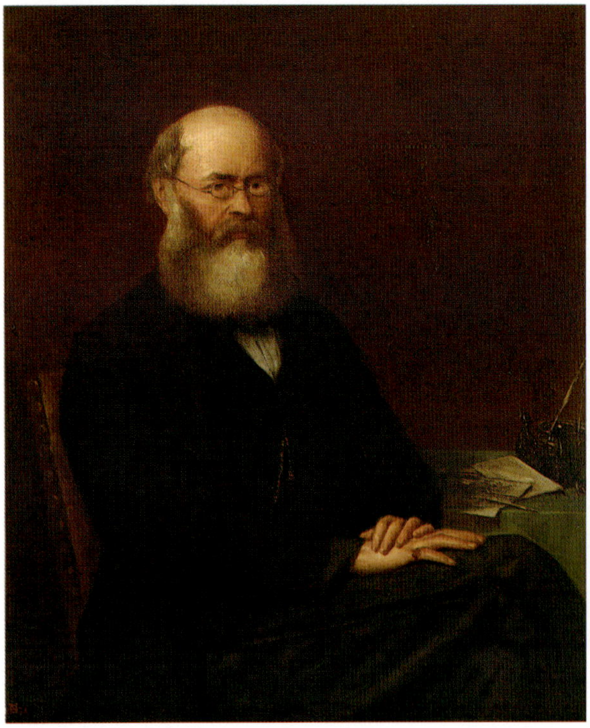

Benjamin Vandergucht: *Henry Woodward* (No. 853)

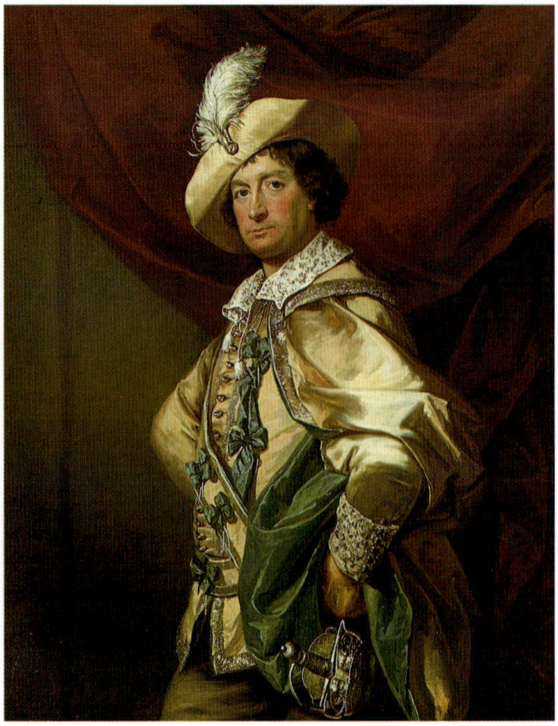

Sir Arthur Stockdale Cope:
Arthur Wontner (No. 851)

Unknown artist: *The Banqueting Scene from Macbeth* (No. 924)

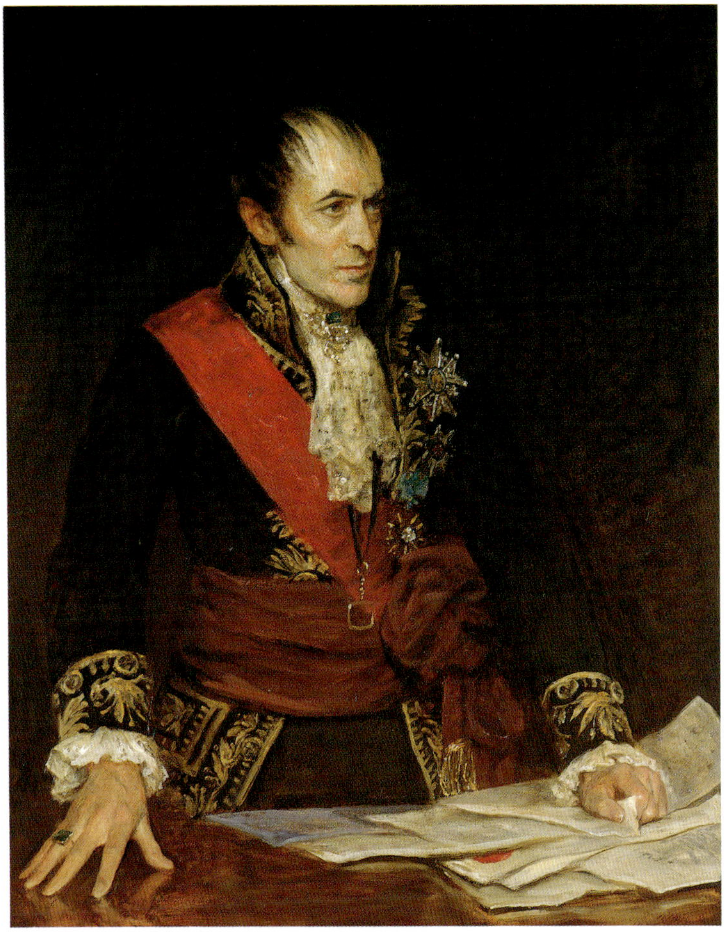

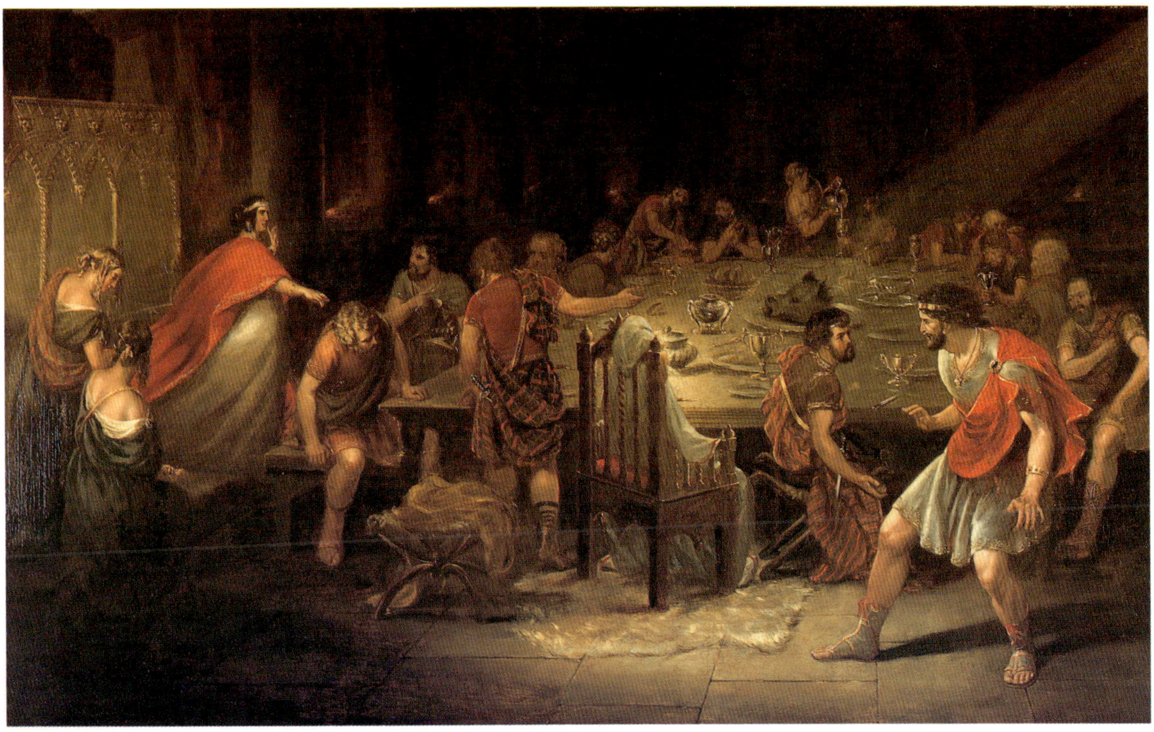

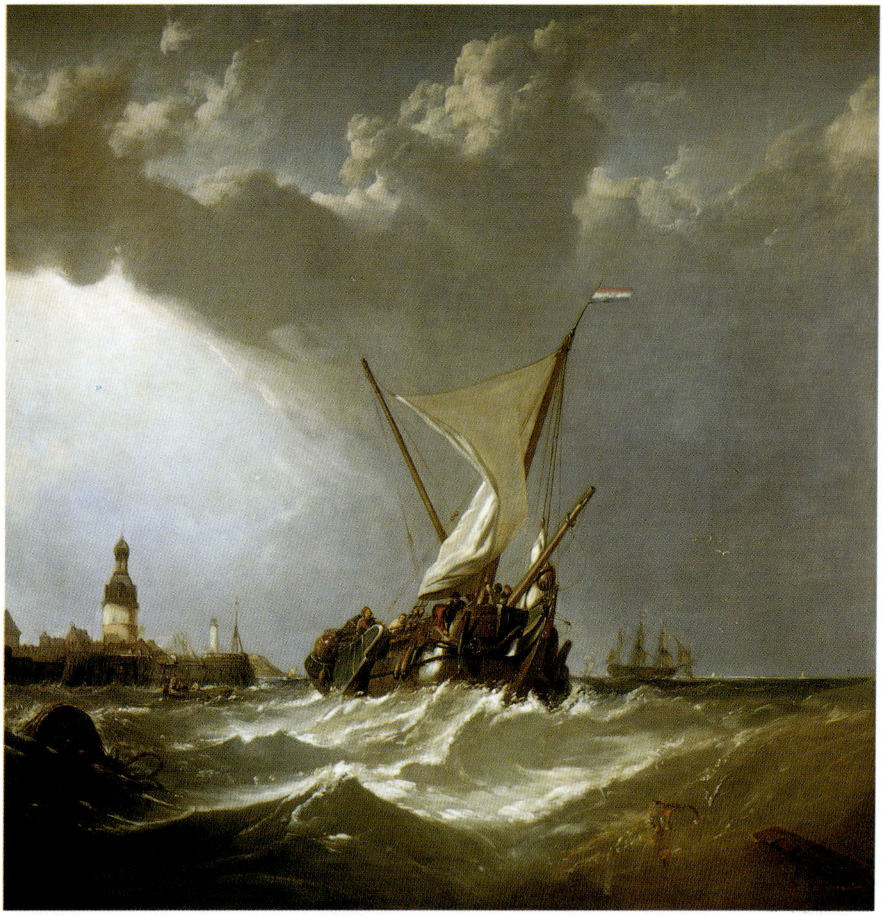

Clarkson Stanfield:
A Dutch Blazer Coming out of Monnickendam, Zuyder Zee (No. 935)

David Roberts:
View of the Temple of the Sun at Baalbec (No. 932)

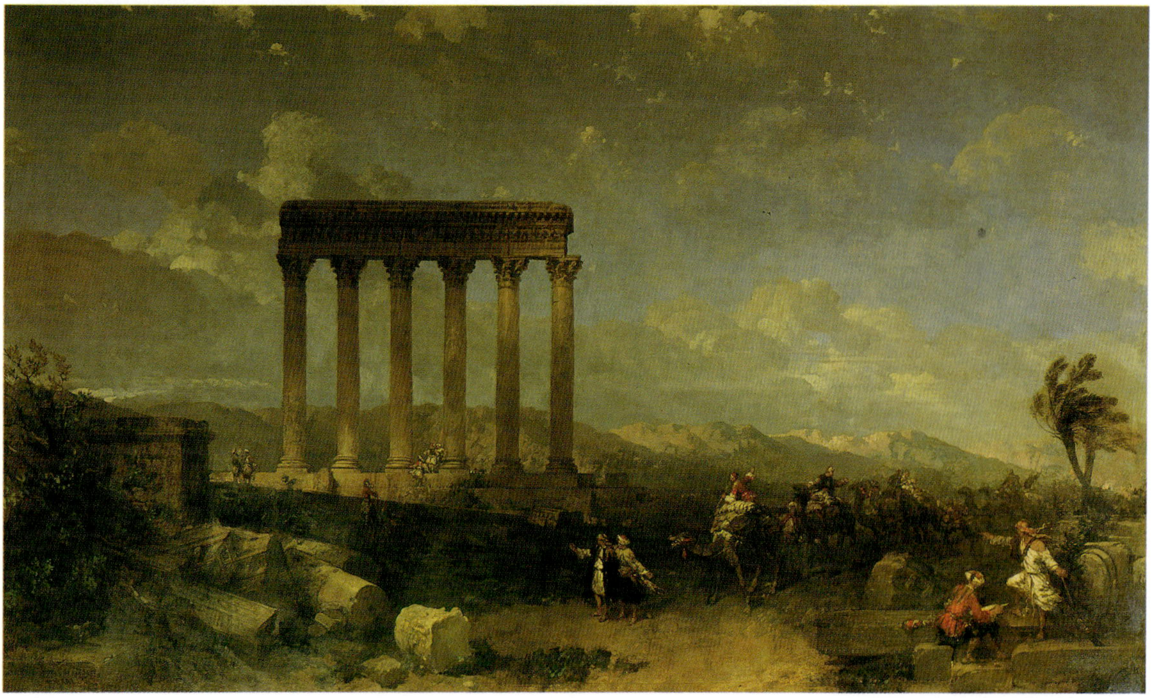

Louis François Roubiliac: *David Garrick* (S15)

Christian Frederick Zincke
(after Benjamin Wilson *c.*1765):
David Garrick & George Ann Bellamy
(No. 967)

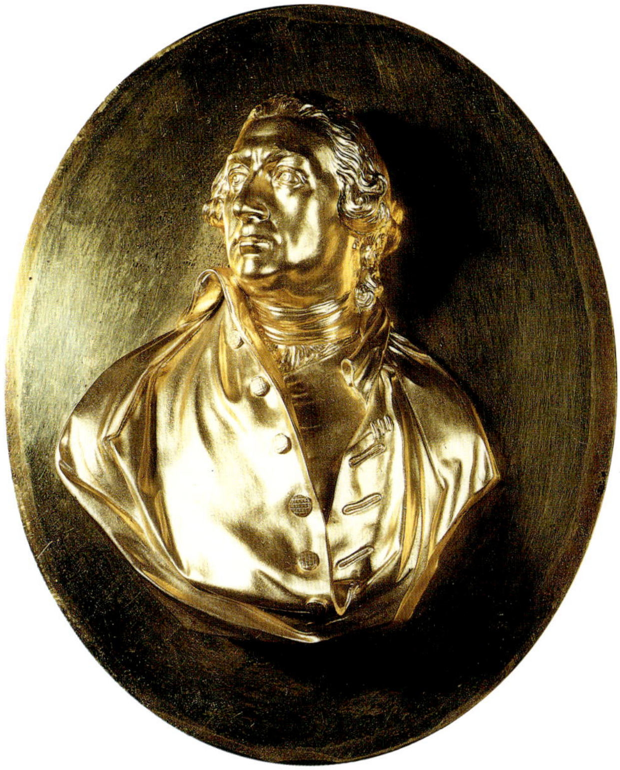

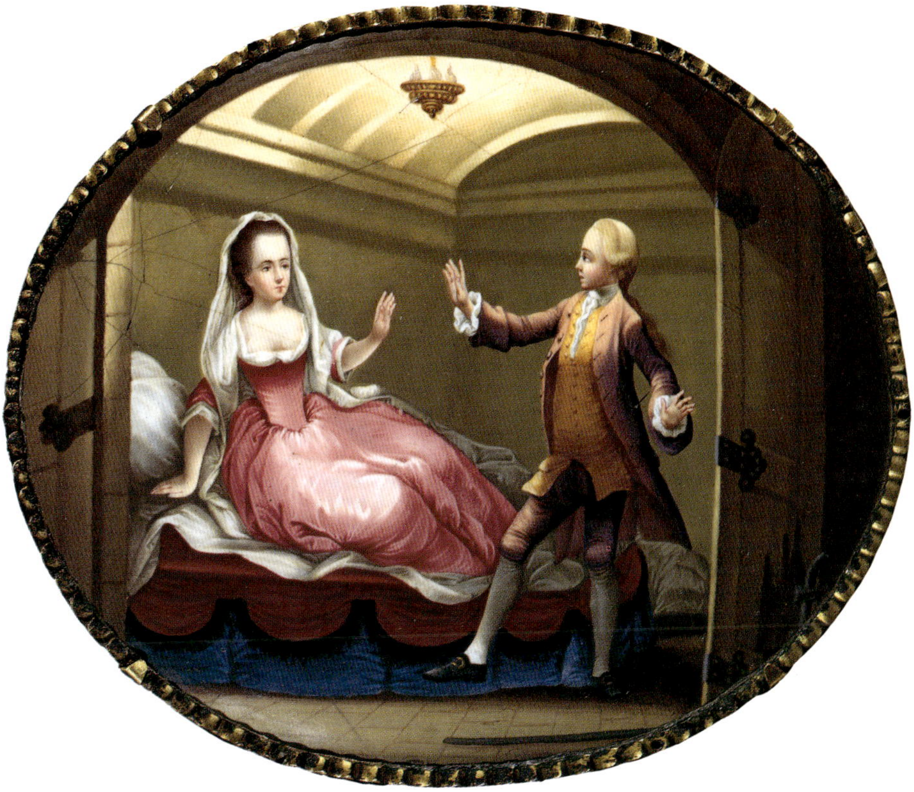

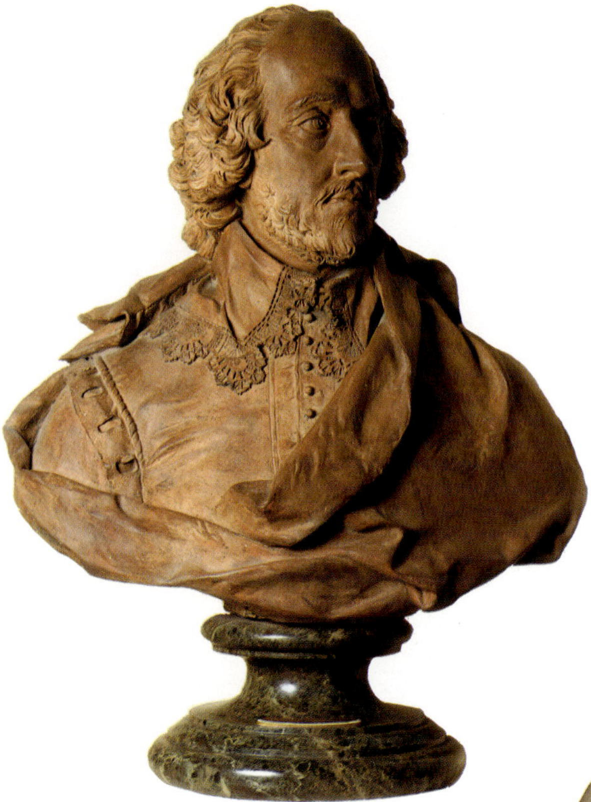

Louis François Roubiliac:
William Shakespeare (S29)

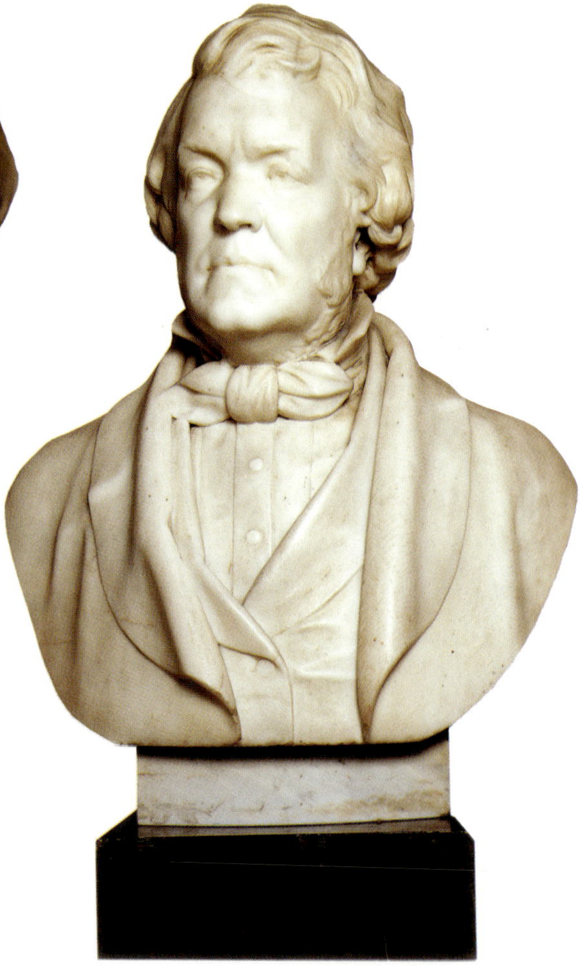

Joseph Durham: *William Makepeace Thackeray* (S35)

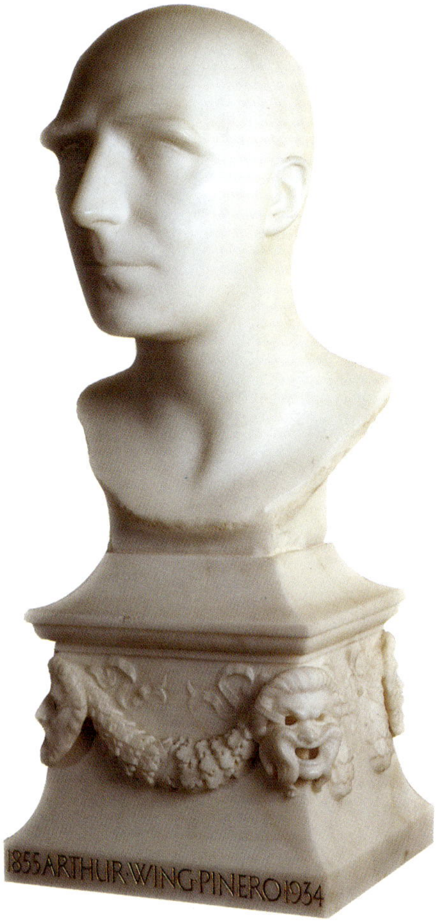

Emil Fuchs:
Sir Arthur Wing Pinero (S27)

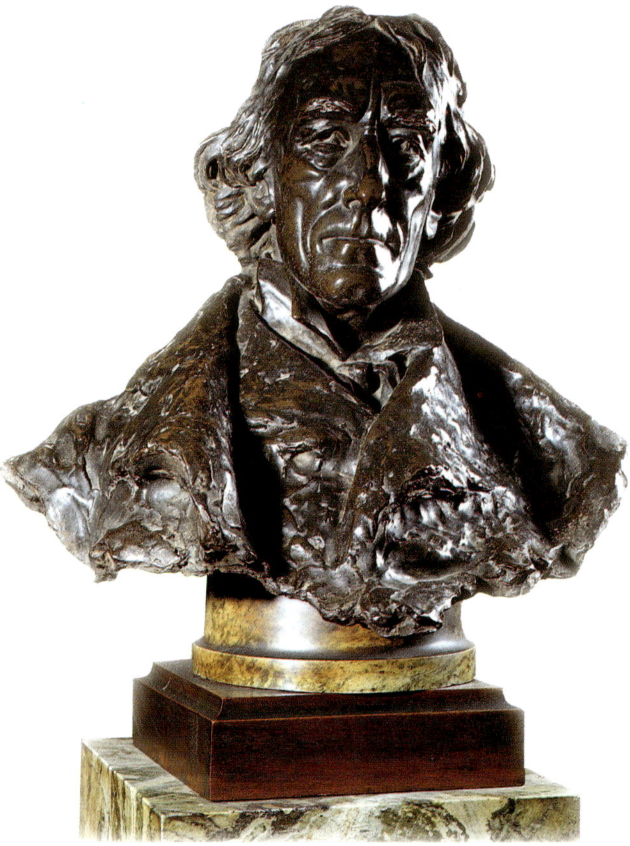

Courtney Edward Maxwell Pollock: *Sir Henry Irving* (S22)

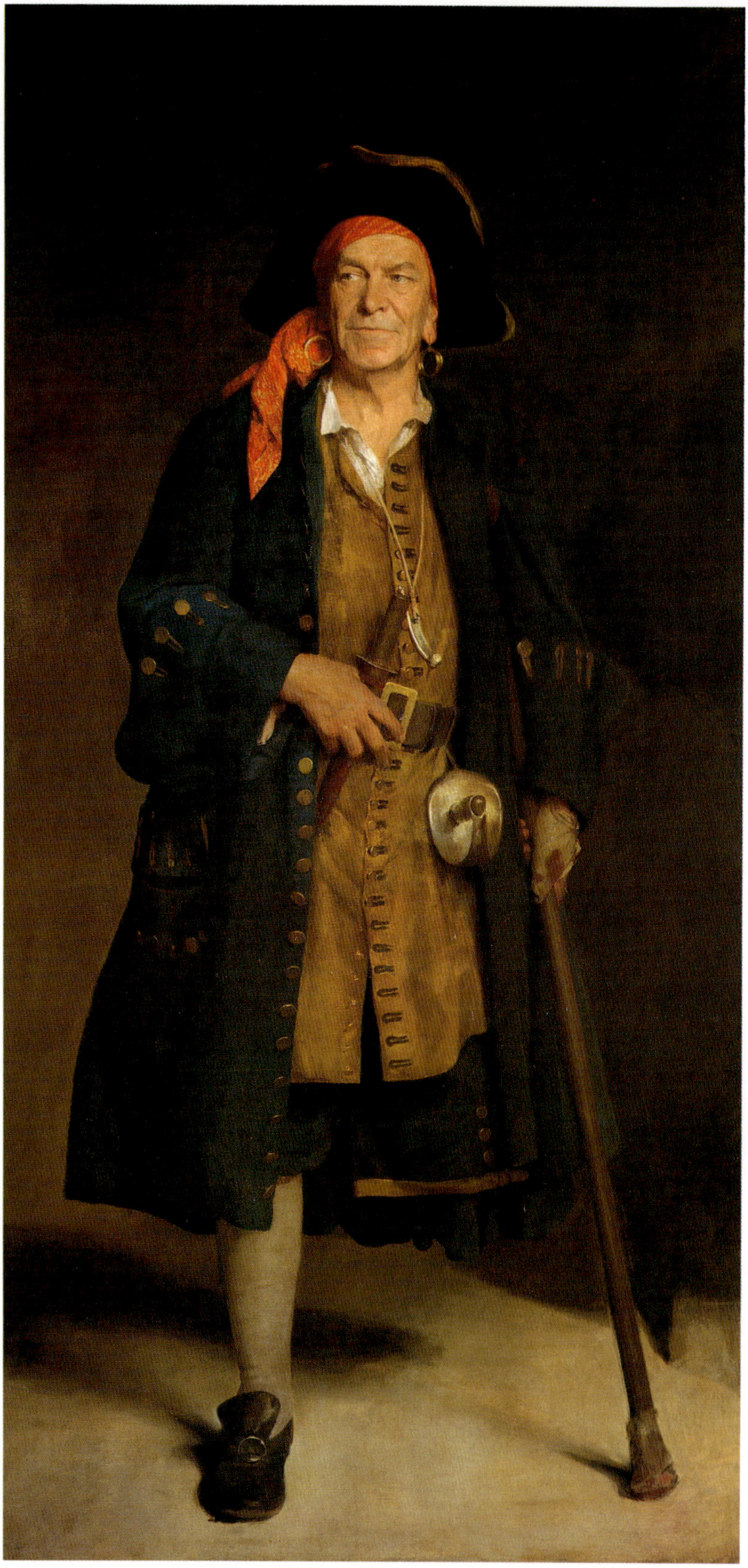

Sir Gerald Kelly:
Arthur Bourchier (No. 86)

PORTRAITS

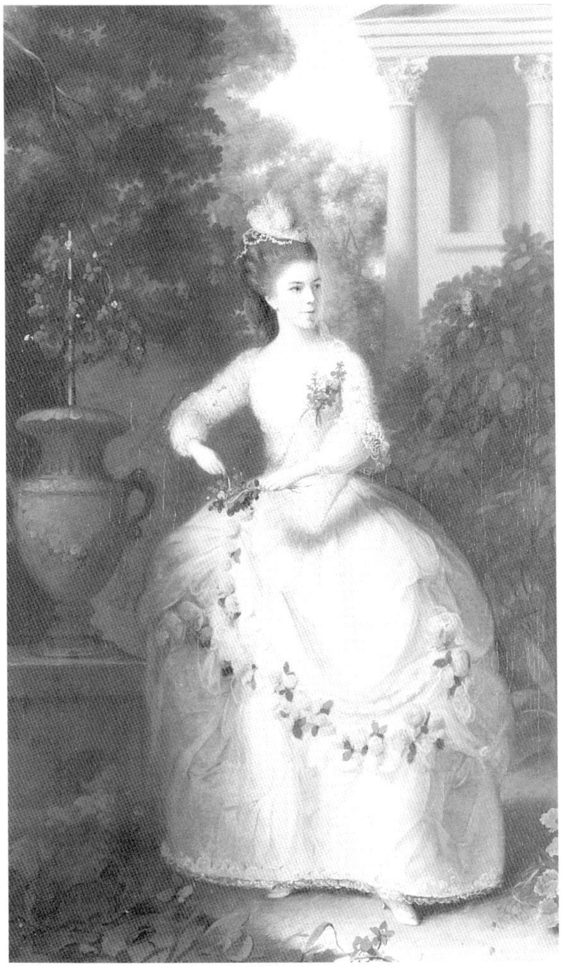

1*

FRANCES ABINGTON

as Lady Bab Lardoon in *The Maid of the Oaks*
by Lieutenant-General John Burgoyne

Thomas Hickey

Oil on canvas 88.2 x 52
INSCR: on pedestal at left: 'T. Hickey/1775'
INV: Mathews 14; RW/CKA 380
PROV: Charles Mathews
EXH: 1833 London (14); 1934 London (238); 1951 London (23)

Lady Bab Lardoon is a guest of Mr Oldworth, owner of 'The Oaks', who is holding a *fête champêtre* to celebrate the marriage of his daughter Maria, the 'Maid of the Oaks', to Sir Harry Groveby. Oldworth describes Lady Bab as 'the Princess of dissipation – for though she has been but three days out of London, she is as uneasy as a mole in sunshine'. Another guest, Charles Dupeley, has a low opinion of women, and Lady Bab, to teach him a lesson, seduces him in the garden. Hickey depicts the moment when Lady Bab, dressed for the fête as a shepherdess, unpins her nosegay and gives it to Dupeley. Wishing to know her name, Dupeley asks to whom he is obliged. She avoids identifying herself by saying: 'To the garden man to be sure.' Mathews attached her next lines to the picture: 'He has made flowers grow all over the garden, and they smell so sweet; pray smell them (Act II).' The reference is a mistake for Act III, scene 3. The garden setting includes a stone urn on a pedestal, containing a plant supported by a cane and possibly concealing Oldworth, who watches from behind 'a stump of shrubs', and a temple-like building behind on the right. Mrs Abington's small cap is adorned with white plumes and red flowers. Her white panniered frock has a white overskirt with large pink roses.

Mrs Abington was the original Lady Bab in Burgoyne's 'Dramatick Entertainment', which was first produced at Drury Lane on 5 November 1774. It had an overture and music between the acts by F. H. Barthélemon. De Loutherbourg designed the scenery and is mentioned in the play as 'Mr Lanterbug'. The reviewer in the *Westminster Magazine* of November 1774 mentions the 'superb exhibitions of transparent scenery' whilst damning the play itself.

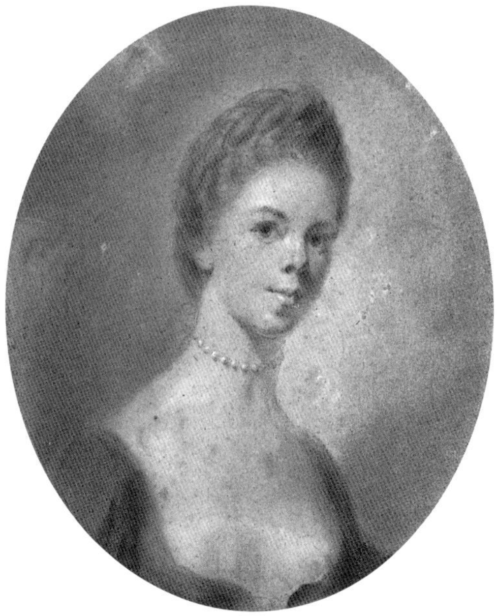

2

FRANCES ABINGTON

Robert West

Black and white chalks on buff laid paper 24 x 20 (oval)
INSCR: 'R West delt'
INV: Mathews 340; RW 548B (unknown sitter by unknown artist); CKA 548B
PROV: Charles Mathews
EXH: 1833 London (340)

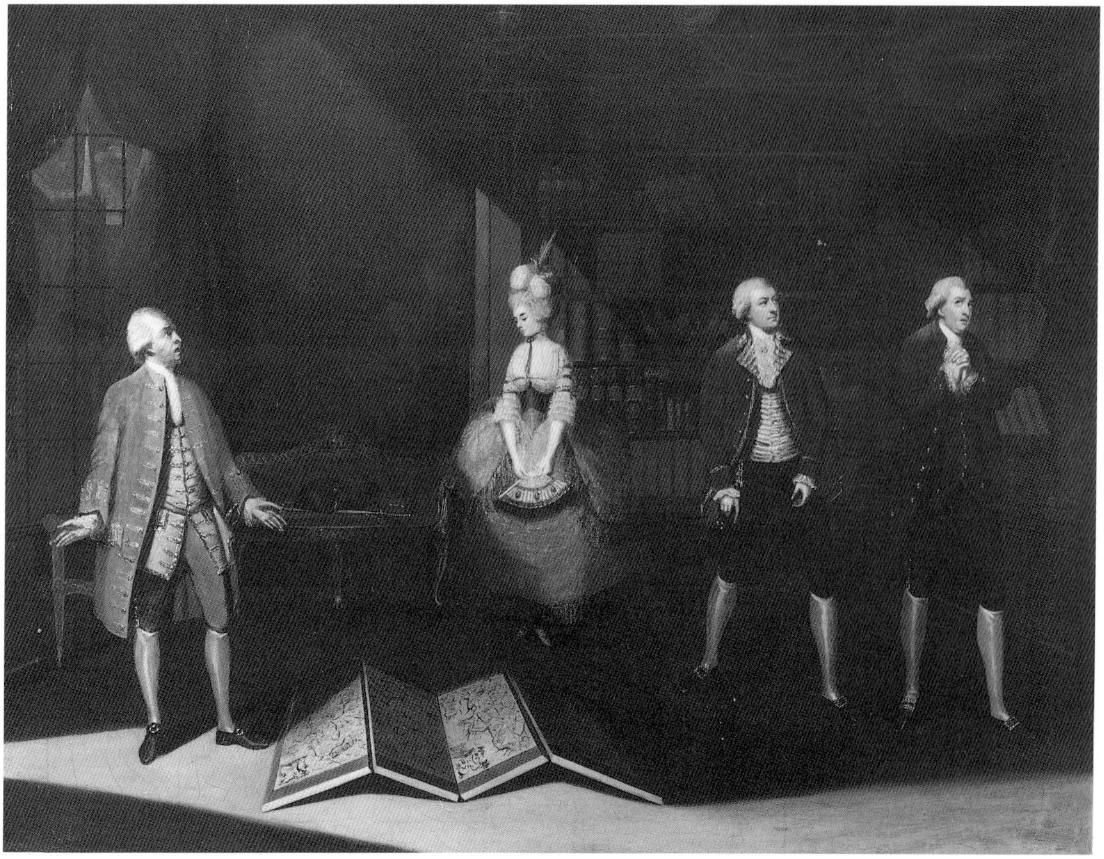

3*

FRANCES ABINGTON as Lady Teazle,
THOMAS KING as Sir Peter Teazle,
JOHN PALMER as Joseph Surface and
WILLIAM SMITH as Charles Surface
in *The School for Scandal*
by Richard Brinsley Sheridan

James Roberts

Oil on canvas 100 x 126
INV: Mathews 15; RW/CKA 15
PROV: Thomas Harris; Harris sale, Robins
12 July 1819 (52); Charles Mathews
EXH: 1779 R.A. (268); 1833 London (15);
1975 London (37)
LIT: Patmore, p. 265; Griffiths, pp. 317–18,
TAM 1935, reproduced

The scene is the library in Joseph Surface's house, Act IV, scene 3. Surface's brother Charles has just thrown down the screen to reveal Lady Teazle. Mathews's caption to the picture cites the reactions of Charles Surface and Lady Teazle's husband, Sir Peter Teazle – 'CHARLES: Lady Teazle, by all that's wonderful! SIR PETER: Lady Teazle, by all that's damnable.' The hypocritical Joseph is thus revealed to be her lover, and Charles, previously thought by Sir Peter to be the guilty party, is vindicated.

King as Sir Peter Teazle on the left shows his amazement at the unexpected appearance of his wife. He wears grey breeches and a matching coat with gold frogging over a pale blue waistcoat trimmed with silver. Mrs Abington as Lady Teazle wears a grey panniered dress trimmed with black and white lace. Smith as Charles Surface wears black breeches, a green coat trimmed with gold, and a blue and white striped short waistcoat with revers. Palmer as Joseph Surface, clasping his hands in guilty consternation, wears a dark brown suit with shiny buttons.

Sheridan's comedy was first performed at Drury Lane on 8 May 1777. The sitters in Roberts's painting were the original performers. King spoke Garrick's prologue and Mrs Abington spoke the elder Colman's epilogue. The review in the *Gazetteer* of 9 May was typical of the enthusiastic response that greeted the play: 'No modern theatrical piece ever met with a fuller success, nor deserved it more. ... The performers deserve every sort of commendation for their spirited exertion in supporting the respective characters, especially Smith, King and the incomparable Mrs Abington.'

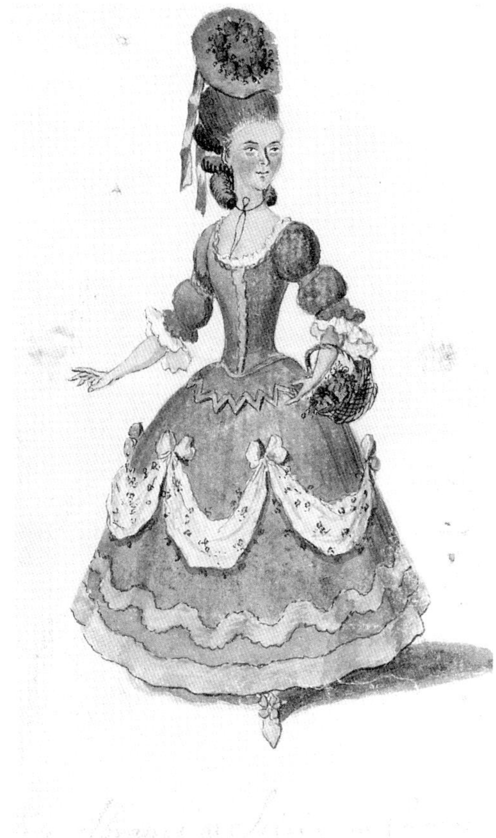

4
HARRIET ABRAMS
as Sylvia in *Cymon* by David Garrick

Unknown Artist

Pen and black ink with watercolour
on laid paper 10.8 x 6.5
INSCR: 'Miss Abrams as Silvia in Cymon' (pencil b.c. CM?)
INV: Not listed
PROV: Charles Mathews (Print Collection Vol. III f.56)
ENGR: Anon. pub. J. Bew 1 August 1778, line (vignette), with caption: 'Oh, why should we sorrow who never knew sin', which is the title of the song Miss Abrams sang in Act III, scene 3

Miss Abrams, as the innocent shepherdess Sylvia, wears a blue frock. Below the waist, falling from bows, there are flounces of white material with a floral pattern.

Garrick's dramatic romance was first performed at Drury Lane on 2 January 1767, with Elizabeth Arne as Sylvia. The piece was revived at Drury Lane on 17 January 1778, with Miss Simson making her stage début as Sylvia. Miss Abrams, who was the sister of the great tenor John Braham, appeared as Sylvia for the first time at Drury Lane on 9 May 1778, her only performance in the role that year.

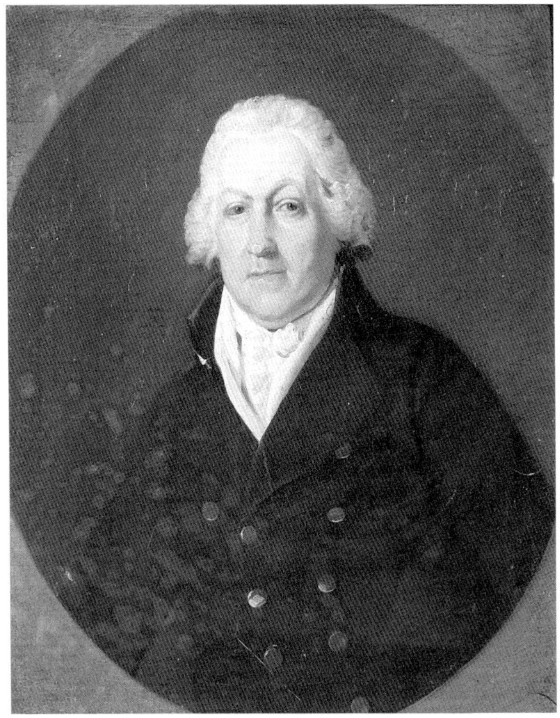

5
JAMES AICKIN

Samuel De Wilde (?)

Oil on canvas 35.5 x 29.5
INV: Mathews 379 (artist unknown); RW/CKA 260
PROV: Charles Mathews
EXH: 1833 London (379)

Half-length in a feigned oval. Aickin wears a dark blue jacket with brass buttons.

A stipple engraving by J. Heath, after a half-length portrait of Aickin by Anthony Devis, was published by J. Heath and J.P. Thompson in 1800.

James Aickin made his début on 6 November 1767 at Drury Lane, as Young Belmont in *The Foundling*. He was an active player at that theatre during Garrick's management and throughout the 1799–1800 season. He was one of the committee of actors appointed in 1776 to set up the Drury Lane Theatrical Fund.

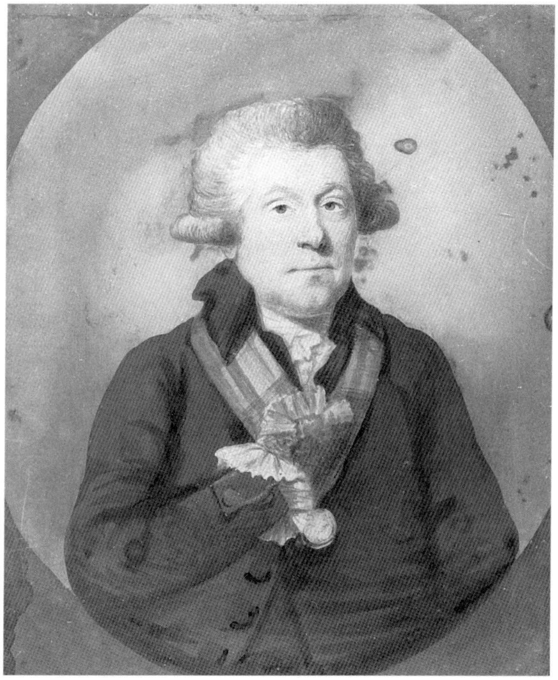

6

JAMES AICKIN

'School of Garrick'

Henry Spicer

Pencil and watercolour on laid paper 26.5 x 21
INV: Mathews 267 (artist unknown);
RW/CKA 50A (artist unknown)
PROV: Charles Mathews
EXH: 1833 London (267)
LIT: Patmore, p. 273

Aickin wears a blue jacket with collar turned down over his Shakespeare Ribband, from which hangs a Shakespeare favour. The background is pale blue.

The 13 portraits of the 'School of Garrick' were drawn in the early 1790s by either Robert Dighton or Henry Spicer (Nos. 6, 21, 22, 32, 37, 100, 166, 211, 612, 650, 655, 661 and 858). Evidence for the authorship of each drawing is discussed under its own entry where there is secondary evidence, but the balance is in favour of Spicer. Several of his engraved portraits are extremely close to the drawings. However, the large mezzotint of Charles Bannister, probably by James Laurie after Robert Dighton, was almost certainly Spicer's main point of reference when drawing the portraits of the entire group. The 'School of Garrick', a club founded by several of Garrick's contemporaries, dined together once a week during the theatrical season. The club faded out in the early years of the 19th century. (See Michael Kelly, *Reminiscences* [1826] 2: 42–44; also Folger Library Art vol. d. 94: 'Garrick & his contemporaries / Collected by / George Daniel', p. 104 – 'Theatre Royal, Drury Lane / London Novr 23 1805 / The inclosed print which is the only proof / before the letter – was etched & designed by / Rowlandson – for the notice of meetings / of a Society of Performers in honour of the / Memory of the late David Garrick Esq / and called "The School of Garrick"– / Every Member must have been engaged / by & have acted under the management / of the "British Roscius" Consisting of the / Following Gentlemen. / Messrs. John Palmer Francis Aickin / William Parsons Robert Palmer / Robert Baddeley John Moody / James Aickin William Farren [erased] James Dodd / John Burton James Wrighten / William Farren Francis Waldron / Wm. Powell Prompter.'

Charles and John Bannister replace Francis Aickin and Waldron in Spicer's drawings. The members of the 'School of Garrick' are all shown wearing the Shakespeare Ribband, first manufactured for Garrick's 1769 Shakespeare Jubilee at Stratford upon Avon, and a Shakespeare favour. All those who attended the Shakespeare Jubilee were requested to wear 'Shakespeare Favours', small medallions of copper gilt, silver or gold with an image of Shakespeare on the recto with the inscription 'We shall not look upon his like again', and on the verso the inscription 'Jubilee at Stratford in Honour and to the Memory of Shakespeare September 1769 David Garrick Steward'. The image of Shakespeare was similar to that on the larger medal worn by Garrick as Steward of the Jubilee. The multi-coloured ribbon was 'made on purpose at Coventry [and] call'd The Shakespeare Ribband: it is in imitation of the Rainbow, which uniting the colours of all Parties, is likewise an emblem of the Great Variety of his Genius'.

7

SIR GEORGE ALEXANDER

as Rudolf Rassendyll in *The Prisoner of Zenda*
by Edward Rose, after the novel by Anthony Hope

Robert Brough

Oil on canvas 228 x 129.5
INSCR: 'Robert Brough 1901'
INV: CKA 650; Gift 658
PROV: Bequeathed by the sitter, subject to the life interest of his widow; received 1947
EXH: 1902 R.A. (212); 1909 R.S.P.P. (112)
REL: Aberdeen Art Gallery oil on canvas 92 x 71.3, inscr: 'Sketch for George Alexander in "The Prisoner of Zenda" by Robert Brough ARSA.'
LIT: Derek Hudson, 'A "new look" for the Garrick Club Pictures', *The Connoisseur* (June 1969), 171: 82, No. 9

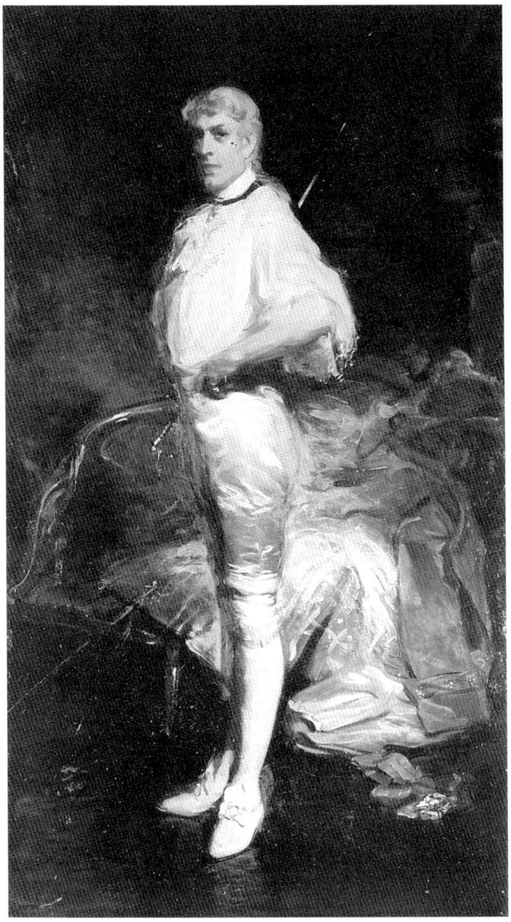

7 *Sir George Alexander as Rudolf Rassendyll*

In Brough's evocation of the well turned-out romantic hero, Alexander wears white hose, creamy breeches and a white shirt. Around his neck is a blue ribbon with an order.

Edward Rose's romantic drama played in New York in 1895, with Richard Southern as Rudolph. It was given its first London production at the St James's on 7 January 1896, ran until 18 July, disappeared for the summer, reopened on 20 October, and ran again until 28 November 1896. There were 255 performances in all. George Alexander played the triple role of Prince Rudolf / Rudolf the Fifth / Rudolf Rassendyll, with H.B. Irving as Captain Hentzau / Lawrence Cautley, Allan Aynesworth as Bertram Bertrand, and Evelyn Millard and Julia Neilson both playing Princess Flavia. The scenery was by H.P. Hall, Walter Hann and William Telbin, and the costumes by Mmes Savage and Purdue with L. & H. Nathan. When the St James's acquired a telegraphic address in 1897, Alexander chose the name 'Ruritania', a constant reminder of the 'Romantic Play in a Prologue and Four Acts'.

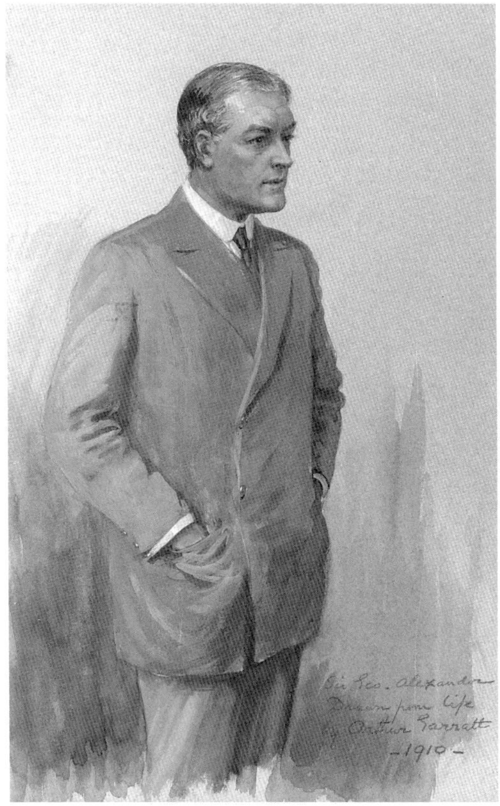

8

SIR GEORGE ALEXANDER

Arthur Garratt

Pencil with watercolour and body colour
on blue wove paper 53.3 x 36.8
INSCR: 'Sir Geo. Alexander / Drawn from life /
by Arthur Garratt / – 1910 – '
INV: CKA 643; Gift 625
PROV: Presented by the artist, 1945

Alexander wears a grey double-breasted suit and waistcoat and a blue tie.

A letter from the artist to the Club Secretary, dated 21 March 1945, describes the circumstances of creation: 'This drawing (19 x 15) was done by myself when I worked for the old weekly *Graphic* & allied weeklies from 1900 onwards. Sir Geo. Alexander gave me a special sitting at St. James's & was very pleased about it – It was, I think, considered a good likeness & it seems a pity that the drawing is not hung somewhere he was known. I did a good many portraits of various important people of the time & I have given some of them to relatives, clubs & institutions. If the Club would like to have the drawing, please let me know & I will send it to you.'

Sir George became a member of the Garrick Club in 1886.

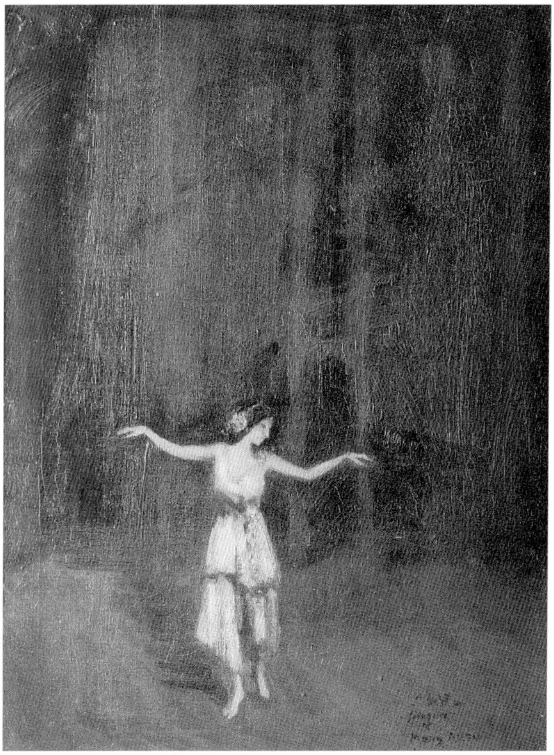

9
Souvenir of
MAUD ALLEN

Reginald Howard Wilenski

Oil on canvas 62 x 46.5
INSCR: 'R. H. W. / Souvenir / of / Maud Allen / London / '08'; 'Rowley Gallery' (label on verso)
INV: CKA 634; Gift 582
PROV: Presented by C. B. Andrews, 1939

A dancing Maud Allen wears a ragged white dress in two layers, which has a swathe of roses tumbling from the waist.

On her first visit to England, in March 1908, Maud Allen brought her extraordinary repertoire to the Palace Theatre, London. She created a sensation with her *Vision of Salome*, which had had its first performance in Vienna in 1903, and also appeared in a number of less controversial classical dances.

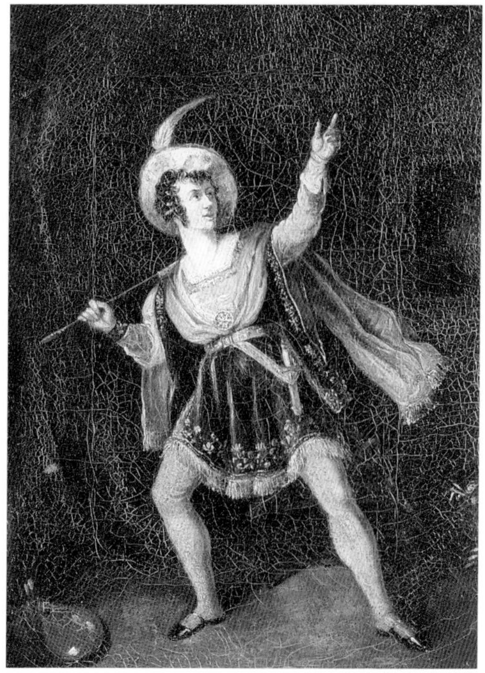

10
GEORGE ALMAR
as Carnaby Cutpurse in *The Cedar Chest or The Lord Mayor's Daughter* by George Almar

Robert William Buss (copy after?)

Oil on panel 28 x 20.3
INSCR: Supplier's stamp (verso): 'PREPARED BY / ROBERSON & MILLER / 31 LONG ACRE LONDON'
INV: RW/CKA 271; Gift 250
PROV: Presented by Sir Edward Feetham Coates, 1896
ENGR: George Hollis for Cumberland's *Minor Theatre*, 4 August 1834, stipple 10.8 x 7
REL: Coll: David Macdonald, oil on canvas 53.3 x 40.6 (original); Mander & Mitchenson Theatre Collection 1, oil on canvas 48 x 36

Carnaby Cutpurse's first dress in *The Cedar Chest* is described in the preamble to the text in Cumberland's *Minor Theatre* as: 'Rich puce-coloured velvet shirt, fringed and braided with gold–orange-coloured satin arms and vest – leno [cotton gauze] characteristic sleeves – rose-coloured scarf – red leggings with embroidered clocks – broad brim white satin hat, and heron feathers – black sandal shoes – broad belt – gold buckle – dagger.' The costume in the painting generally follows this stage direction; added are brown gauntlets and the sword over his right shoulder. The wild attitude is called for in the text. In Act 1, scene 1, the painter Hans Holbein is using Carnaby Cutpurse as a model. Carnaby asks how he should stand. Holbein replies: 'As yesterday. [taking a sword and gauntlet off the table] Here, put on this gauntlet, and take this sword in thy hand; suppose in thy mind thou hadst a falcon on thy wrist, think there's a heron in the sky, and you cast the falcon off. Pause ye yet? – consider thou art poaching.' CARNABY: 'Poaching – now I comprehend! Fly, falcon, fly! Hellish bird! [Chord – Casting off the bird in supposition, and seeming to follow its career through the air] Will that do for thee?' HOLBEIN: [in rapture] 'Good! Be still and stir not.'

Almar's melodrama was first given at Sadler's Wells on 14 July 1834.

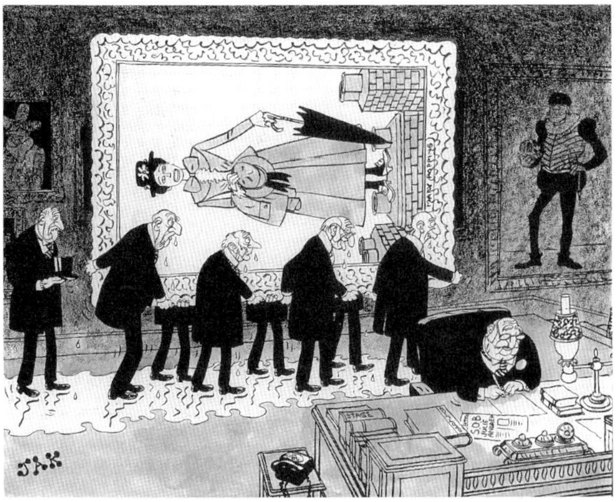

11

JULIE ANDREWS

as Mary Poppins in *Mary Poppins* by Bill Walsh (Screenplay by Eustace Lycett, Peter Ellenshaw and Robert A. Mattey)

Raymond Jackson (JAK)

Pen and ink and blue wash 43 x 54.5 (sheet 54 x 61)
INSCR: 'MARY POPPINS' (on frame of picture c.r.); 'JAK' (b.l.); 'STAGE' (on spine of book b.r.); 'SPOTLIGHT' (on front of book b.r.); 'S.O.B. / JULIE /ANDREWS' (on newspaper b.r.) (all pen and black ink); 'DEAR MISS ANDREWS, IT IS WITH MUCH REGRET I HAVE TO INFORM YOU, THAT FOLLOWING/AN EXTRAORDINARY GENERAL MEETING THE COMMITTEE HAS REMOVED YOUR PORTRAIT FROM / THE GARRICK CLUB!' / x 4 Col FRI 3RD JULY 1981 40% TINT 20% ON PORTRAIT. FLOWER' (pencil, under)
INV: Not listed; Gift 891
PROV: Presented by Mr P. Fone, 1981
ENGR: 3 July 1981

Julie Andrews, popular as a nanny and singing nun, in 1981 surprised some members of the establishment by appearing immodestly in a film called *S.O.B.*, produced and directed by her husband, Blake Edwards.

The cartoon and cartoonist's note refer, of course, to a fictitious event. The pictures shown in the drawing are also invented.

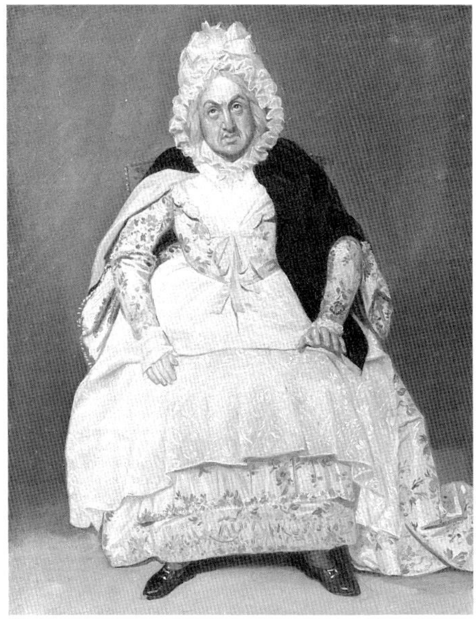

12

HENRY ANGELO

as Mrs Cole in *The Minor* by Samuel Foote

Samuel De Wilde

Oil on canvas 36.5 x 28
INV: Mathews 367; RW/CKA 253
PROV: John Bell; Charles Mathews
EXH: 1833 London (367); 1951 London (10); 1971 Northampton (9)
ENGR: William S. Leney for Bell's British Library 29 September 1792, line 10.2 x 7.6, pub. Bell's *British Theatre* (1797), vol 2, with the inscription 'All shall have their call as Mr Squintum says sooner or later'; Anon. printed for C. Cooke 23 January 1809

Mrs Cole is an inebriated brothel-keeper who suffers from gout and lives in Covent Garden Piazza. Mr Squintum (mentioned in the quotation printed on the engraving) is an imaginary character whom Mrs Cole evokes as the source of her more philosophical comments. Mrs Cole wears black shoes, an enormous long-sleeved light blue dress embroidered with flowers, a black cloak lined in pink, and a large frilled cap with a pink bow on top.

Foote's comedy was originally performed in a two-act version at the Crow Street Theatre, Dublin, on 28 January 1760. The first London performance followed shortly afterwards, in a three-act version, at the Haymarket Theatre on 28 June 1760, with Foote as Mrs Cole. Henry Angelo's 'first and only appearance' as Mrs Cole was at the King's Theatre on 29 March 1792. The Drury Lane company was temporarily established in the opera house and the occasion was John Bannister's benefit. See Henry Angelo's *Reminiscences* (1828), I: 331–32.

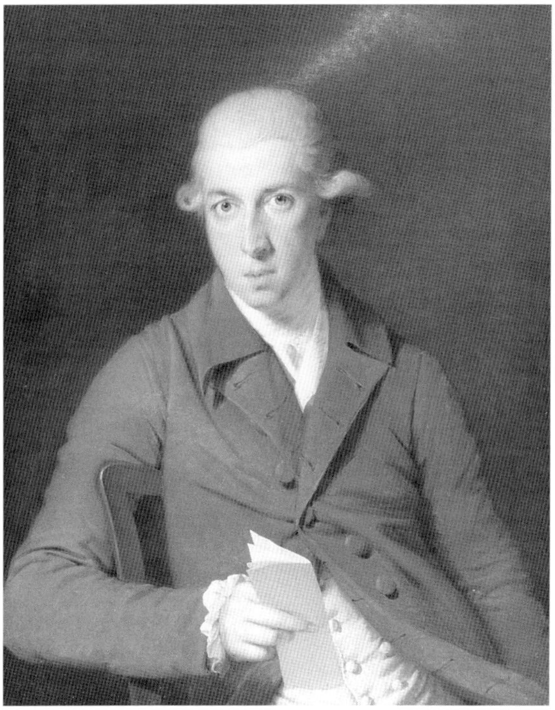

13

CHARLES ARMSTRONG (?)

Nathaniel Dance

Oil on canvas 72.4 x 59
INV: CKA 619 (Dr John Armstrong); Gift 525
PROV: Bequeathed by Captain Cecil F. Armstrong, 1935

The sitter wears a brown coat and a white waistcoat, and holds a folded paper in his right hand. The picture was bequeathed as a portrait of Dr John Armstrong, the poet and physician who lived from 1709 to 1779. The sitter wears a costume of circa 1780 and seems to be aged about 30. If the picture is an Armstrong family portrait, perhaps the most likely candidate is Charles Armstrong, whose portrait was also drawn by Nathaniel Dance's brother, George (engraving published 8 February 1803, when the sitter appears to be about 50). The attribution to Nathaniel Dance is convincing and the picture would be one of his later portraits; he gave up portrait painting in 1782.

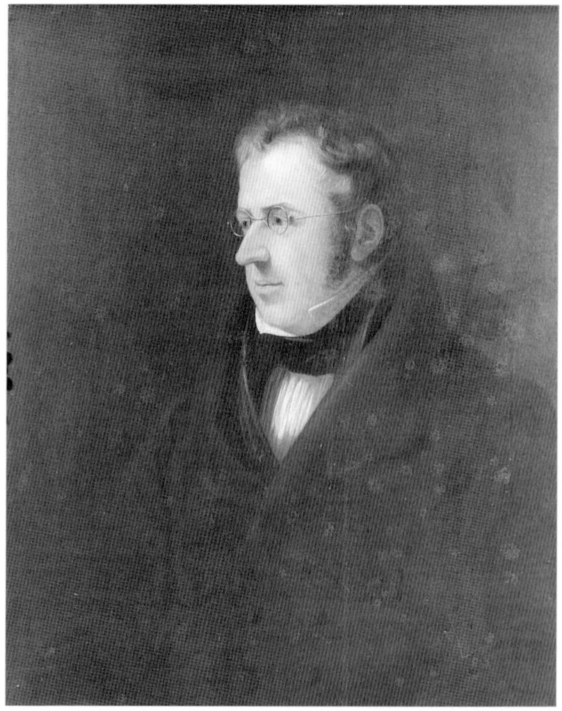

14

SAMUEL JAMES ARNOLD

James Lonsdale

Oil on canvas 74.9 x 62.2
INV: RW/CKA 327; Gift 141
PROV: Presented by the sitter's son A.W. Arnold, 1856
REL: Coll: F.H.A. Engleheart, oil on canvas
(this version was probably that loaned to the 1868
3rd National Portrait Exhibition [374])

The sitter wears wire spectacles, a dark wraparound coat, reddish waistcoat, white shirt with high collar, and a dark cravat. This picture, in damaged condition, was in storage in 1994.

15

HANNAH ASTLEY

James Saxon

Oil on canvas 76 x 62.5
INV: RW/CKA 360; Gift 130
PROV: Presented by Mr Robinson of Bond Street, 1855
EXH: ? 1809 R.A. (138)

Hannah Astley, the equestrienne and wife of the equestrian manager John Philip Conway Astley, wears a dark low-cut dress, edged in yellow. The fact that Nos. 15 and 16 are clearly a pair perhaps throws some doubt on the suggestion that No. 15 is to be identified as the picture shown, apparently independently, at the R.A. in 1809. Saxon exhibited several theatrical and other portraits at the Academy between 1795 and 1816.

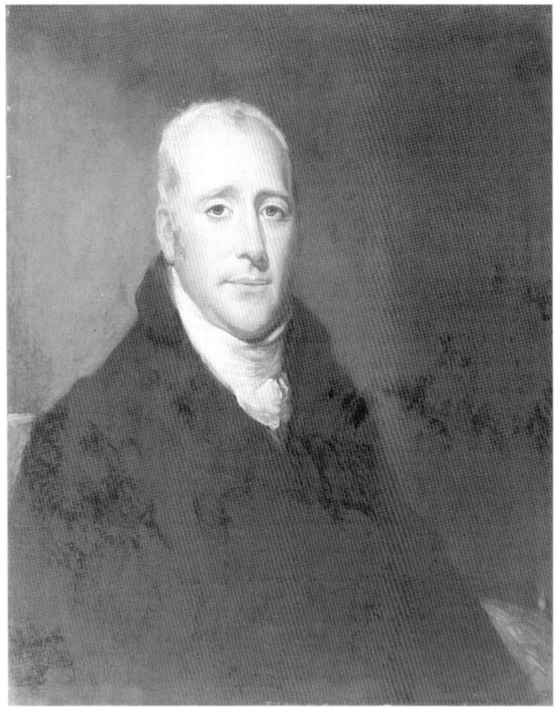

16

JOHN PHILIP CONWAY ASTLEY

James Saxon

Oil on canvas 77 x 63
INV: RW/CKA 359; Gift 130
PROV: Presented by Mr Robinson of Bond Street, 1855

Astley wears a dark jacket with high collar, and a high white stock and collar. The padded armchair is upholstered in red.

One of the greatest showmen of his time, Astley managed the Amphitheatre at St George's Fields, Lambeth, from about 1784 until his death in 1821. He also had enterprises in Dublin, Paris and elsewhere. Though regarded as coarse and indolent, he was talented in riding, dancing and music.

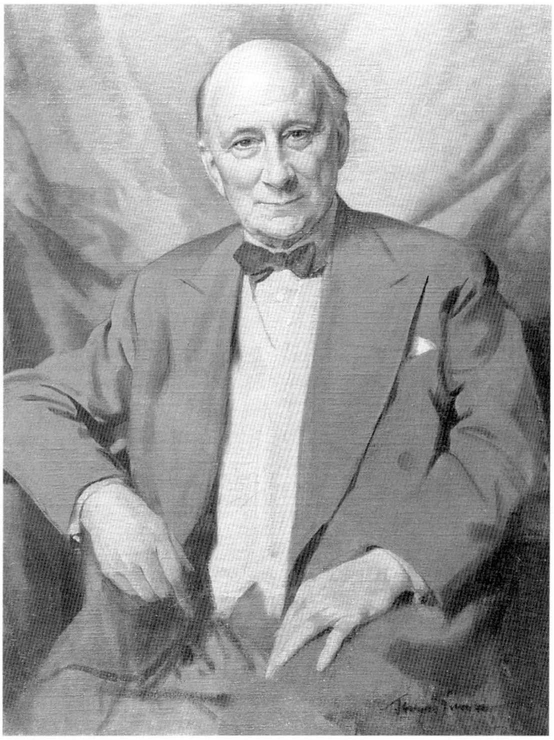

17

SIR FELIX AYLMER

James Gunn

Oil on canvas 48.2 x 38.1
INSCR: 'James Gunn'
INV: GCL 703; Gift 788
PROV: Presented by the artist, 1962

The sitter wears a grey suit, pale blue pullover, pale blue shirt, and purple bow tie.

Sir Felix made his first appearance at the Coliseum in March 1911 as the Italian in *The Cook's Man* and subsequently appeared in numerous productions until his death in 1979. He became a member of the Garrick Club in 1937.

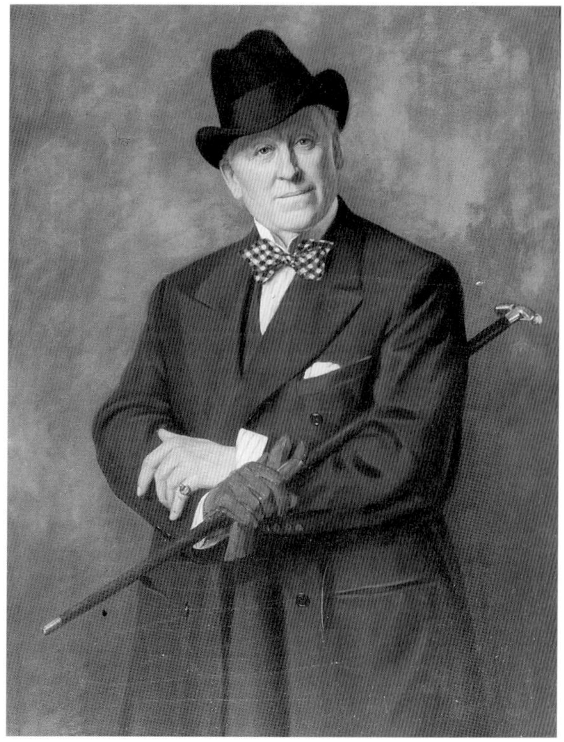

18

ALLAN AYNESWORTH

Maurice Codner

Oil on canvas 85.1 x 74.3
INSCR: 'Maurice Codner'
INV: CKA 632; Gift 546
PROV: Presented by a number of members, 1937
EXH: 1935 R.A. (615)

The actor Allan Aynesworth, who became a member of the Garrick Club in 1895, wears a black hat and a long grey coat over a grey suit and white shirt with a black and white checked bow tie. On his little finger is a ring with a blue stone.

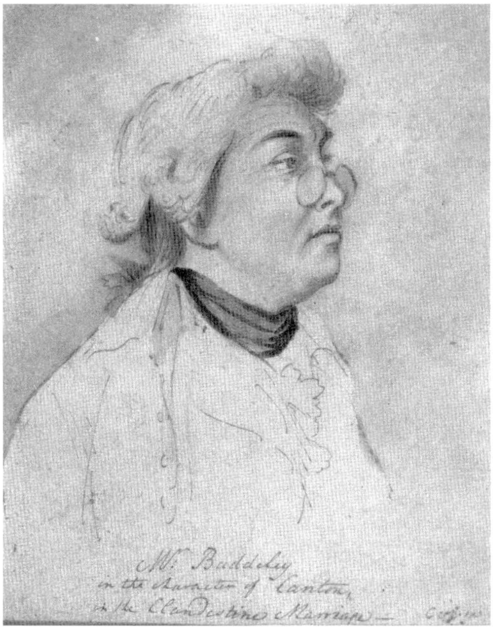

19

ROBERT BADDELEY

as Canton in *The Clandestine Marriage*
by David Garrick and George Colman the Elder

Richard Cosway (attr.)

Pen and brown ink with watercolour
on wove paper 11.2 x 9 (SIGHT)
INSCR: 'Mr Baddeley / in the character of Canton, /
in the Clandestine Marriage –' (pen and brown ink, b.c.);
'cosway' (pencil, b.r.)
INV: RW/CKA 427J
PROV: Acquired before 1888
ENGR: Similar to a portrait drawn, etched and published
by Sylvester Harding 1 September 1794, in which the
sitter is shown t.q.l. seated to r., looking down at a paper
REL: NPG 2541, watercolour on paper 38.1 x 25.4,
by Sylvester Harding h.l. in oval to l., holding up
and reading a book, wearing the same black neckband
but also a velvet jacket with large turned-back cuff
LIT: Fitzgerald, pp. 160–61

The quality of this miniature is too high to be attributed to Sylvester Harding. The drawing in the NPG is much more typical of Harding, with its harsh lines and unsubtle colouring. It is likely that this miniature, the drawing in the NPG and the etching are all based on a lost original, perhaps by Richard Cosway.

Baddeley played Canton in the first production of *The Clandestine Marriage* at Drury Lane on 20 February 1766. His last performance in the part was at Drury Lane on 30 September 1794. He was taken ill in his dressing-room on 19 November 1794 and died early the following day.

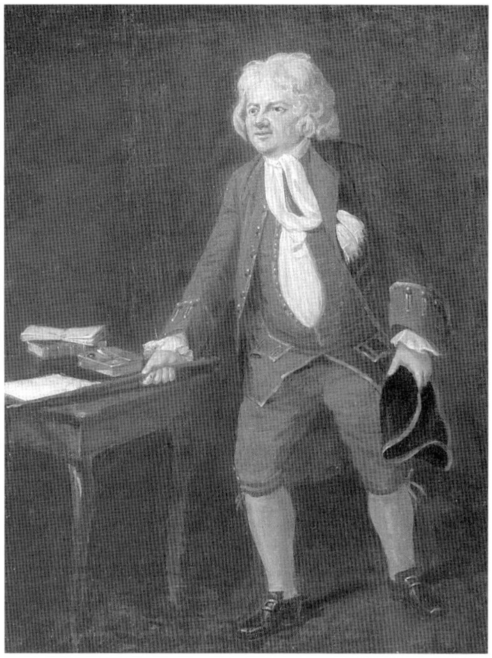

20

ROBERT BADDELEY

as Sir Harry Gubbin in *The Tender Husband*
or The Accomplished Fools by Sir Richard Steele

Samuel De Wilde

Oil on canvas 34.3 x 26.3
INV: Mathews 177; RW/CKA 264
PROV: John Bell; Charles Mathews
EXH: 1833 London (177)
ENGR: Philippe Audinet for Bell's British Library
28 July 1791, line 11.75 x 7.9 (inscr: 'De Wilde del
ad vivam'), published Bell's *British Theatre* (1797), vol 20,
with the line quotation, 'Come, come, I wont be us'd thus';
Anon. printed for C. Cooke 24 January 1807, line 12.2 x 7.6
(with the line quotation, 'Don't disgrace me, sirrah! /
you grim, graceless rogue. / Vide Act 1 Scene 1')
LIT: *Illustrated Sporting and Dramatic News* 15 July 1919, wood
engr., inscr: 'Mr Baddeley as Sir Harry Gubbin / in / "The
Tender Husband" / after a Drawing by / DE WILDE / (1790)'

The quotation inscribed under the Audinet 1792 engraving and used by Mathews is inappropriate. The action in Act V, scene 2 requires Sir Harry to draw a sword against Mr Tipkin, whose niece he thinks is going to marry his son Humphrey. The 1807 engraving has the correct quotation from Act I, scene I, where Sir Harry threatens his son with a 'crab-stick' to show Mr Tipkin what authority he has over the boy. Baddeley bangs his 'crab-stick' on the table. In his other hand he holds a black tricorn hat. He wears black shoes, white hose, purple breeches, coat and waistcoat, and a white shirt with the loose stock in his left lapel.

Steele's comedy was originally performed at Drury Lane on 23 April 1705. Baddeley acted Sir Harry Gubbin for the first time on 6 April 1772, at Drury Lane. His performance on 17 April 1789 was the last one given before De Wilde painted this picture. The inscription 'De Wilde del ad vivam' on the engraving suggests that the plate was taken from a drawing rather than a painting. Three other plates in the 1797 edition of Bell's *British Theatre* seem to have been engraved from drawings rather than paintings. There are oil versions of all of them in the Garrick Club: Nos. 71, 140 and 657.

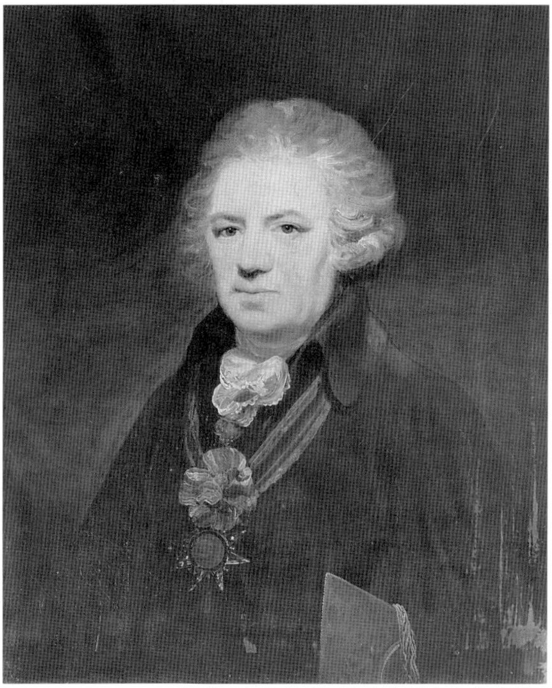

21

ROBERT BADDELEY

'School of Garrick'

Thomas Hardy (?)

Oil on canvas 74.9 x 62.2
INV: Mathews 193 (artist unknown);
RW 424 (artist unknown); CKA 424
PROV: Charles Mathews
EXH: 1792 R.A. (162); 1833 London (193)
ENGR: William Ridley for Parsons's *Minor Theatre*
December 1793, stipple 6.9 x 5.6

Baddeley, shown half-length, has a red mortarboard with a gold tassel under his left arm. He wears a dark green coat, a white stock and a Shakespeare Ribband with a rosette and a Shakespeare favour (see No. 6).

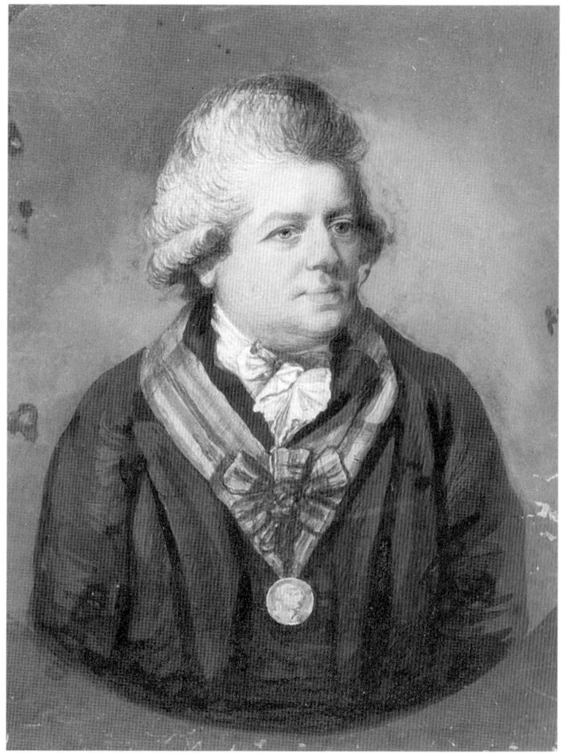

22

ROBERT BADDELEY

'School of Garrick'

Henry Spicer

Black chalk and watercolour on laid paper 26.5 x 21
INV: Mathews 265 (artist unknown);
RW/CKA 48D (artist unknown)
PROV: Charles Mathews
EXH: 1833 London (265)

The sitter wears a blue jacket and has a Shakespeare Ribband with a rosette and a Shakespeare favour (see No. 6).

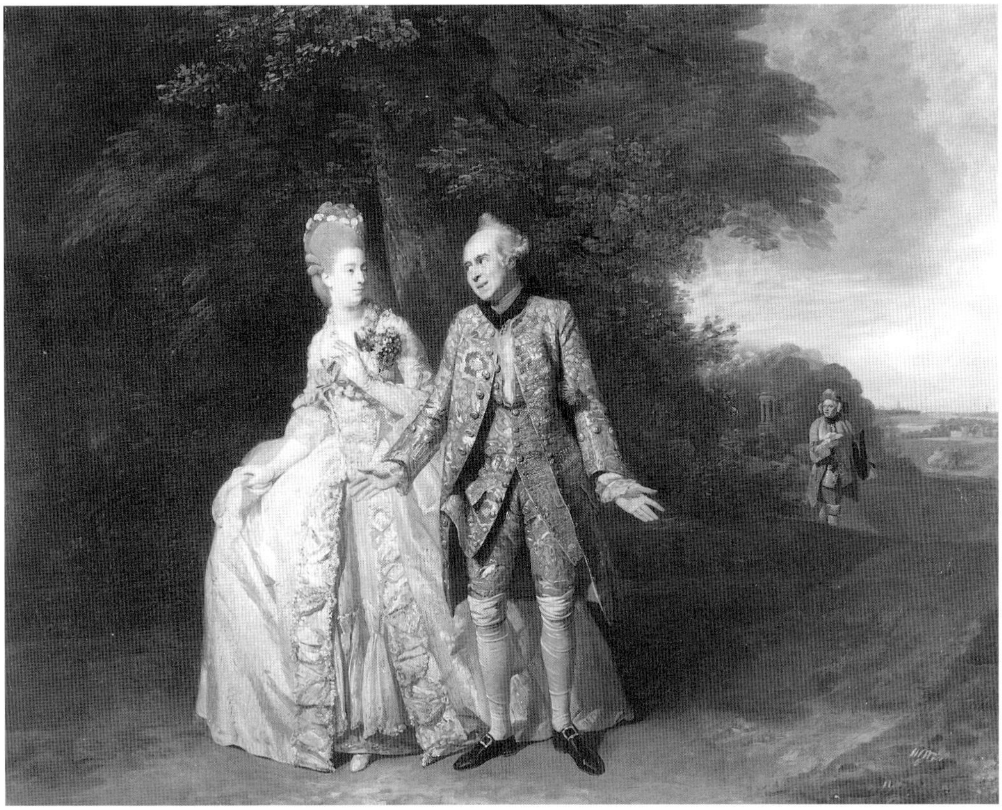

23*

SOPHIA BADDELEY as Fanny Sterling, *ROBERT BADDELEY* as Canton and *THOMAS KING* as Lord Ogleby in *The Clandestine Marriage* by David Garrick and George Colman the Elder

Johan Zoffany

Oil on canvas 102 x 128
INV: Mathews 35; RW/CKA 23
PROV: Charles Mathews
EXH: 1833 London (35); 1934 London (238); 1949 Birmingham (199); 1949 Port Sunlight (276); 1951 London (39); 1954–55 London (125); 1977 London (57)
ENGR: Richard Earlom 1772, mezzotint 42.5 x 55.5; R. Laurie pub. Robert Sayer 1 September 1772, mezzotint 35.6 x 27.8 (head of Sophia Baddeley only)
LIT: Elizabeth Steele, *The Memoirs of Sophia Baddeley* (1787), pp. 13–16; Patmore, p. 262; Fitzgerald, pp. 157–60; Griffiths, p. 322; Lady Victoria Manners & Dr G.C. Williamson, *John Zoffany* (1920), pp. 143–44; TAM (1935), reproduced; David Mannings, 'Gainsborough's Duke and Duchess of Cumberland', *The Connoisseur* (1973), 183: 92–93

Fanny, the pretty younger daughter of a rich and vulgar merchant, hopes to have Lord Ogleby protect her from the attentions of Sir John Melvil and help to forward her affair with Lovewell. Misunderstanding, Lord Ogleby thinks she is making a declaration of love. Canton, Lord Ogleby's Swiss valet de chambre, interrupts at a strategic moment.

Lord Ogleby, centre, wears black shoes with silver buckles, white stockings, silver knee-breeches with a red floral pattern, a long jacket, and a waistcoat of the same elaborate material. He carries a tricorn hat with a feathered brim. Fanny's white silk panniered frock is decorated with blue bows, and her extravagant corsage includes pink flowers and daffodils. Canton, in the distance, wears red knee-breeches and a grey coat lined in red over a grey embroidered waistcoat.

Garrick and Colman's comedy was first performed at Drury Lane on 20 February 1766, with King as Lord Ogleby and Baddeley as Canton, but with Mrs Palmer as Fanny Sterling. The Royal Command performance which Zoffany's picture is traditionally supposed to commemorate occurred on 12 October 1769. Elizabeth Steele states that the picture was painted at the express command of George III, but as the picture never seems to have been anywhere near the Royal Collection there is no reason to take the claim seriously. In 1824 Patmore wrote: 'This picture is in excellent condition, which is rarely the case in Zoffany's works.'

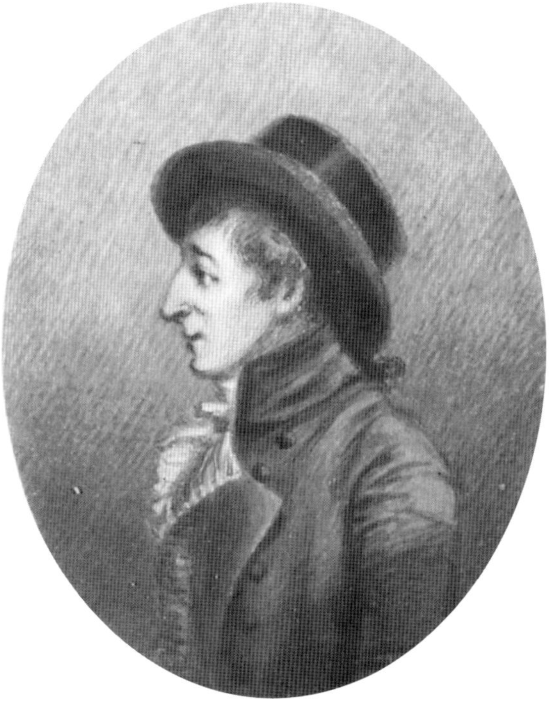

24
WILLIAM BAILEY

James Dowling Herbert

Black chalk with watercolour on buff wove paper
10.1 x 8.2 (oval)
INSCR: 'Herbert fecit' (pen and brown ink on mount b.l. CM);
'O'Reilly Comedian Dublin /died 1791'
(pen and brown ink on mount b.c. CM)
INV: RW 560B (artist unknown); CKA 560B
PROV: Charles Mathews (not in catalogue)

The sitter is shown in profile, wearing a top hat on the back of the head.

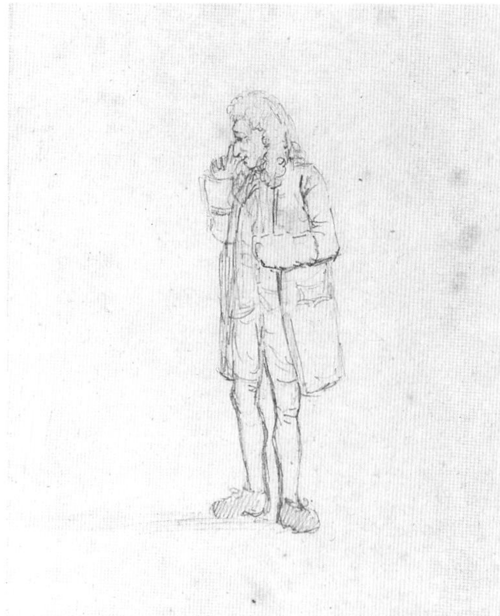

25
WILLIAM BAILEY
as Justice Woodcock in *Love in a Village*
by Isaac Bickerstaffe

Unknown Artist

Pencil on wove paper 21.2 x 17
INSCR: by Charles Mathews: 'Mr O. Riley
as Justice Woodcock. / Dublin 1790'
(pen and brown ink on mount b.c.)
INV: CKA 501
PROV: Charles Mathews (not in catalogue)

An amateur drawing. In May and June 1778 Bailey operated a summer theatre in China Hall, Rotherhithe, but he did not play Justice Woodcock at that time. He probably acted the role in Dublin, however; he made his début at the Smock Alley Theatre in Dublin on 2 November 1782, and remained there for most of the rest of his life.

26
LOCATION UNKNOWN
SIR SQUIRE BANCROFT

David Ingles

Charcoal on wove paper 74.9 x 54.6
INSCR: 'D.N. Ingles, ARHA'
INV: CKA 526; Gift 463 (not located 1988, previously disposed of because it was so badly damaged)
PROV: Presented by Sir Arthur Wing Pinero, 1926

CKA describes as: 'Head and shoulders, slightly to left, looking at spectator; eyeglass in his right eye.'

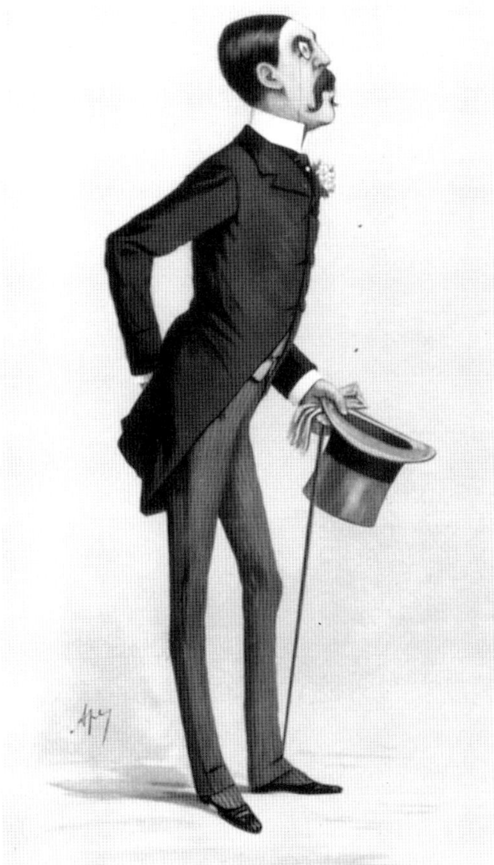

27

SIR SQUIRE BANCROFT

Carlo Pellegrini ('Ape')

Pen and black ink, watercolour and body colour
on grey-blue wove paper 28 x 50.4
INSCR: 'Ape' (pen and brown ink b.l.); 'To my friend
J.L. Toole / Carlo Pellegrini /August 83'
(pen and brown ink on mount b.r.)
INV: Not listed; Gift 538
PROV: Given by the artist to J.L. Toole;
John H. Harris, by whom presented, 1936

Bancroft wears black shoes with brown stripes, grey spats, brown trousers with vertical grey stripes, a grey jacket with tails, a white shirt, and a black cravat with a pearl stick pin. He has a large blue flower in his buttonhole.

There is another caricature portrait of Bancroft by Pellegrini in the National Portrait Gallery (5072 watercolour 56.2 x 34.3) signed *Ape*. It dates from about 1880 and shows Bancroft as Captain Hawtree in T.W. Robertson's *Caste*.

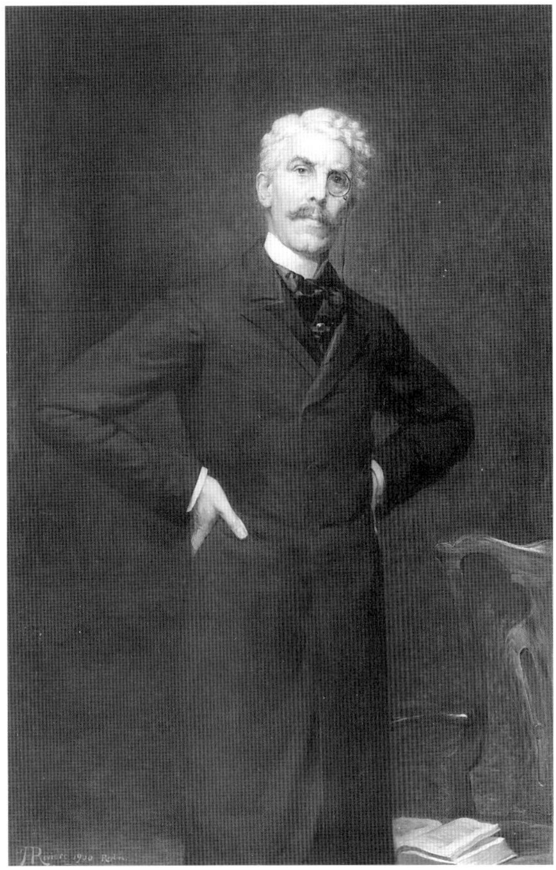

28

SIR SQUIRE BANCROFT

Hugh Goldwin Riviere

Oil on canvas 149.8 x 96.5
INSCR: 'H Riviere. 1900. Replica.' (red paint b.l.)
INV: RW/CKA 324
PROV: Presented by 104 members, 1900
REL: Original: NPG 2121, oil on canvas 149.9 x 99.1,
bequeathed by the sitter, 1926,
exh: R.A. 1900 (568)

Bancroft, standing almost full-length, with his hands on his hips, wears a long grey coat with white satin shirt cuffs. He became a member of the Garrick Club in 1869.

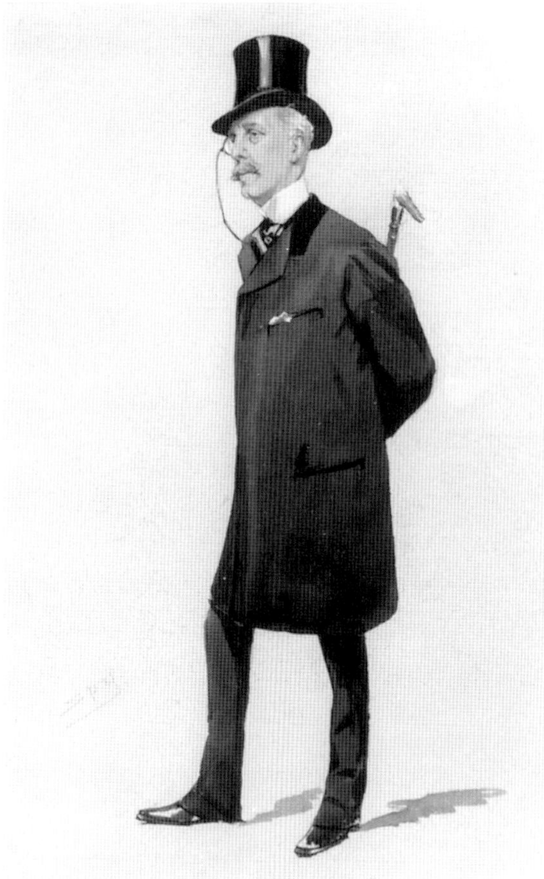

29

SIR SQUIRE BANCROFT

Sir Leslie Ward ('Spy')

Pencil with pen and black ink, watercolour and body colour on pale blue-grey wove paper
35.5 x 22.5
INSCR: 'SPY' (pencil b.l.)
INV: CKA 589; Gift 377
PROV: Presented by the sitter, 1917
LIT: *Vanity Fair* 13 June 1891, inscr: 'B'

Bancroft is dressed entirely in black, with a long coat and top hat – a typical 'Spy' caricature.

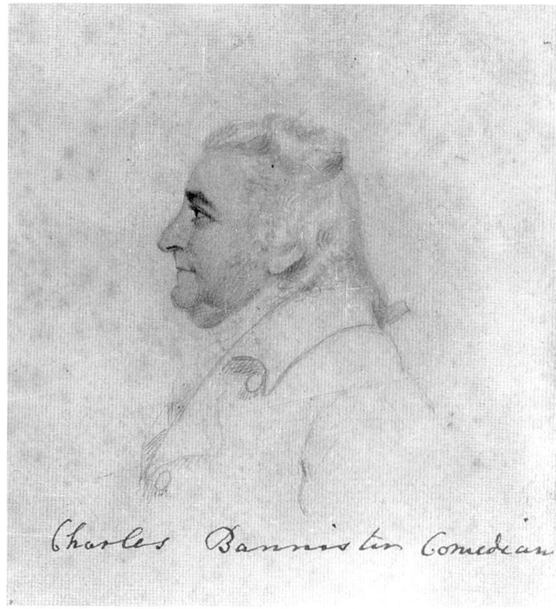

30

CHARLES BANNISTER

Miss Bannister

Pencil and watercolour on wove paper 11.7 x 10.8
INSCR: 'Charles Bannister Comedian'
'Miss Bannister Fecit'
(pen and brown ink on mount b.l. CM)
INV: Mathews 269; RW/CKA 491B
PROV: Charles Mathews
EXH: 1833 London (269)
ENGR: Anon. pub. for E. Scott by E. Walker
1 November 1804, etching 10.2 x 9.2 (bust in oval to r.)

Bannister is shown in profile to left, head and shoulders only.

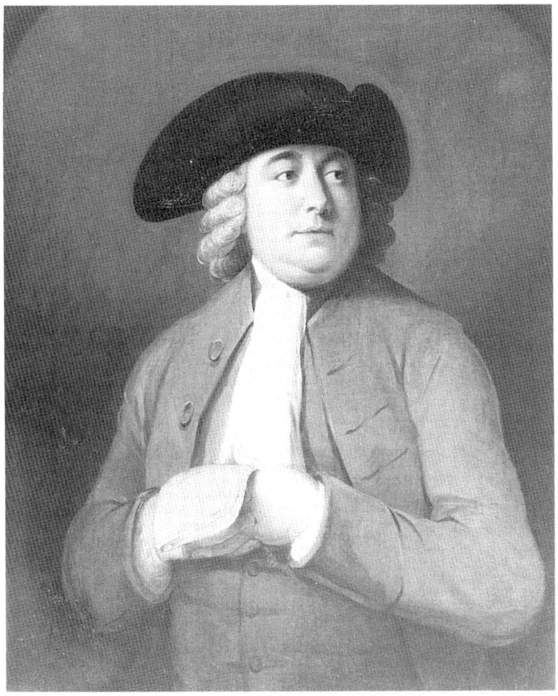

31

CHARLES BANNISTER

as Steady in *The Quaker* by Charles Dibdin

Thomas Pye

Oil on canvas 90.2 x 69.8
INV: Mathews 8; RW/CKA 470
PROV: Charles Mathews
EXH: 1833 London (8)
ENGR: Anon. for the *European Magazine* pub. J. Asperne
1 December 1804, stipple 9.2 x 7.9
LIT: Fitzgerald, p. 238

Bannister wears a brown Quaker suit. His curly wig is largely hidden by a black tricorn hat. He holds his hands in front of him with fingers intertwined and thumbs together; the attitude of the hands was particular to the part of Steady. Wageman's 1820 drawing of Incledon in the part shows exactly the same pose. That drawing was sold at Christie's on 15 March 1977 (lot 83); it was engraved by Woolnorth for Oxberry's *New English Drama*, 1820.

The Quaker was first performed at Drury Lane on 7 October 1777, with Bannister as the original Steady. He was still playing the part 20 years later; his last performance of the role was at Drury Lane on 12 February 1798.

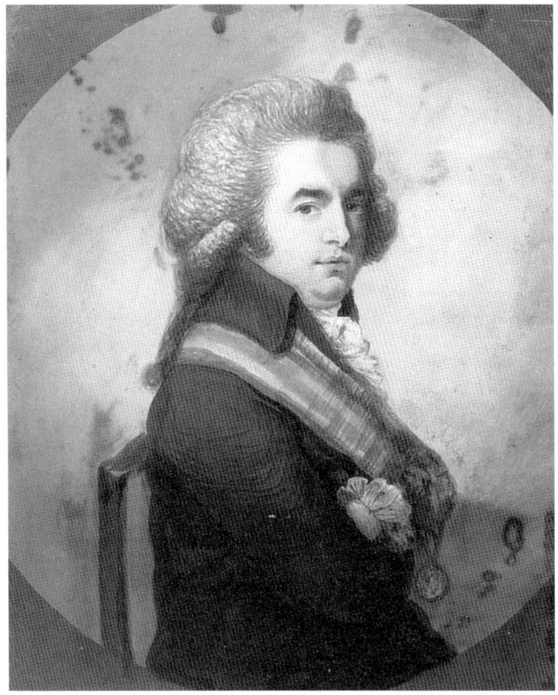

32

CHARLES BANNISTER

'School of Garrick'

Henry Spicer

Black chalk and watercolour on laid paper 26.5 x 21
INV: Mathews 268 (artist unknown);
RW/CKA 48C (artist unknown)
PROV: Charles Mathews
EXH: 1833 London (268)
ENGR: William Ridley for Parsons's *Minor Theatre*
28 June 1794, stipple 7 x 5.5 (to l.)

Bannister wears a blue jacket and a Shakespeare Ribband with a rosette and Shakespeare favour (see also No. 6).

The engravings of Nos. 32 and 37 are the principal pieces of evidence for assigning the School of Garrick drawings to Henry Spicer. His portrait of Charles Bannister evidently owes something to Laurie's mezzotint, published 15 November 1787, after a similar portrait by Robert Dighton.

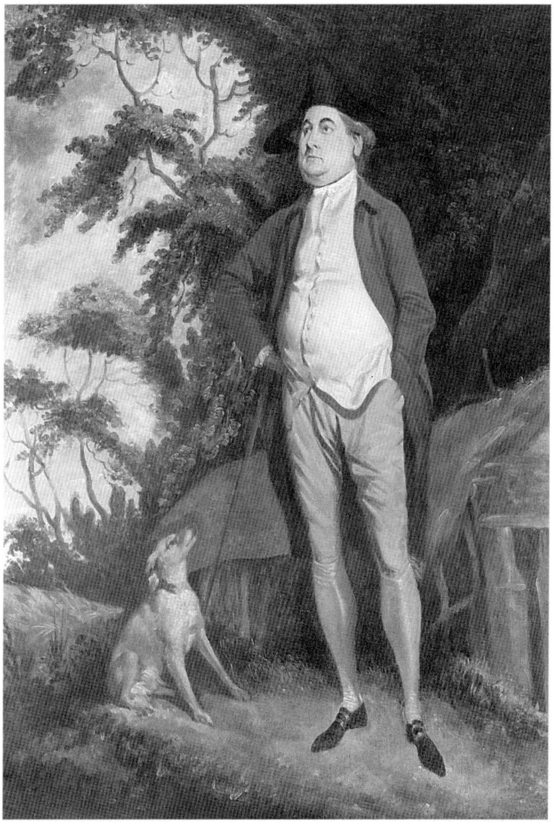

33*
CHARLES BANNISTER
as Launce in *The Two Gentlemen of Verona*
by William Shakespeare

Johan Zoffany (attr.)

Oil on canvas 88.9 x 69.2
INV: RW 447 (by J. Zoffany);
CKA 447 (attributed to J. Zoffany); Gift 239
PROV: Presented by William Banting
between 1846 and 1888
EXH: 1951 London (48)
LIT: Lady Victoria Manners & Dr G.C. Williamson,
John Zoffany (1920), reproduced p. 148;
Griffiths, p. 333; TAM (1935), reproduced

Bannister is shown full-length, standing outdoors. He wears a black tricorn hat, silver hose, pink breeches, a purplish-brown coat, a white waistcoat, and a white stock. A brown dog with brown eyes looks up at him.

A comparison with documented or engraved portraits of Charles Bannister suggests that he is the subject of No. 33, although he did not play this role in London. The portrait also bears a passing resemblance to James William Dodd, who did play Launce at Drury Lane on 15 and 20 January and 3 June 1790. The attribution of the work to Zoffany is uncertain, but the artist had returned from his stay in India in August 1789 and would have been in London to see these performances. The play, rarely performed in the 18th century, had not been seen at Drury Lane since 1763, although there were performances at Covent Garden on 13 and 28 April 1790 with John Quick as Launce. It is possible that Bannister performed the amusing scene with the incontinent and smelly dog Crab as an entr'acte diversion or as part of a benefit performance. See also No. 652.

[The style of this picture seems close to that of William Hodges (1744–1797), who is not, however, known to have produced theatrical portraits.]

34
JOHN BANNISTER
as Gradus in *Who's the Dupe?*
by Hannah Cowley

Samuel De Wilde

Oil on canvas 74.5 x 56.5
(relining canvas 77.5 x 57.5)
INSCR: 'S De Wilde/ft 1795' (brown paint b.l.);
'From your very grateful friend / Seymour Hicks'
(pen and brown ink on frame b.r.)
INV: GCL 661
PROV: Seymour Hicks; Francis Tufton,
by whom presented, 1987
ENGR: Edward Bell pub. E. Bell 1794,
mezzotint 53.3 x 40.6; Charles Picart
for the *Theatrical Inquisitor* pub. C. Chapple
1 February 1820, stipple 23.4 x 14.4 (plate);
Thomas Wright after a drawing
by Thomas Charles Wageman
for Oxberry's *New English Drama*
pub. Simpkin & Marshall 1821, stipple 10.2 x 7.4
(head and shoulders only)

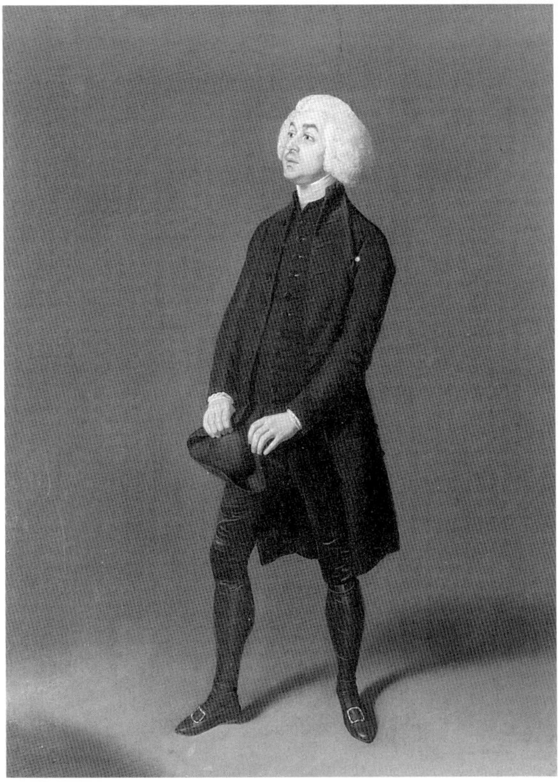

34 *John Bannister as Gradus*

In the first act we see the scholarly Gradus standing full-length, wearing a black suit and an old-fashioned powdered wig, and holding a black tricorn hat. In the next act, in order to woo Miss Elizabeth Doiley, who is bored by his loquacity, he dresses in the height of fashion. However, the change dismays Elizabeth's father, Old Doiley, who is duped into allowing the suit of her lover, Granger, disguised himself in black and talking nonsense.

Mrs Cowley's comedy was first performed at Drury Lane on 10 April 1779, with Thomas King as the original Gradus and William Parsons as Doiley. John Bannister played Gradus for the first time at Drury Lane on 22 October 1782. Bannister's last Drury Lane performance in the part before De Wilde produced his portrait took place on 1 January 1793, although later he played the part 10 times at the Haymarket, between 15 June and 19 November 1793. The play was rehearsed at Drury Lane on 1 January 1795 but the following day's performance was cancelled because of Parsons's illness. Bannister resumed the part of Gradus at Drury Lane on 13 October 1796.

If the date on the mezzotint (1794) is correct, then it is probable that No. 34 (dated 1795) is not the original version of the composition.

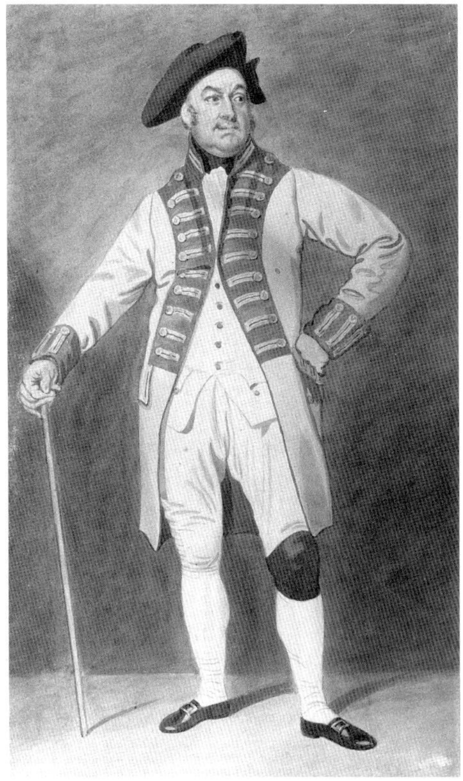

35*

JOHN BANNISTER

as Storm in *Ella Rosenberg* by James Kenney

Samuel De Wilde

Pencil and watercolour on wove paper 37 x 23.5
INV: Mathews 334; RW/CKA 65B
PROV: Charles Mathews
EXH: 1833 London (334); 1975 London (150)

Captain Storm is visited in his 'plainly furnished' apartment by Flutterman, the Burgomaster of Molwitz, 'A Province of Prussia', who asks him to join a deputation to the Elector Alberto. Storm is morose, saying that his grey hairs and crippled limb, indicated by his leg bandage, used to remind him of 'years of hard and glorious service' but now remind him only of his poverty.

Storm has a black tricorn hat with a black cockade over his left ear. He wears yellow gloves, black shoes, white stockings with a black bandage around his left knee, white breeches, a cream coat lined and trimmed in red with red cuffs, and a white waistcoat and high black stock.

Kenney's two-act melodrama with music by M.P. King was first performed at Drury Lane on 19 November 1807, with Bannister as the original Storm. There were 37 performances during the first season, the last on 6 June 1808.

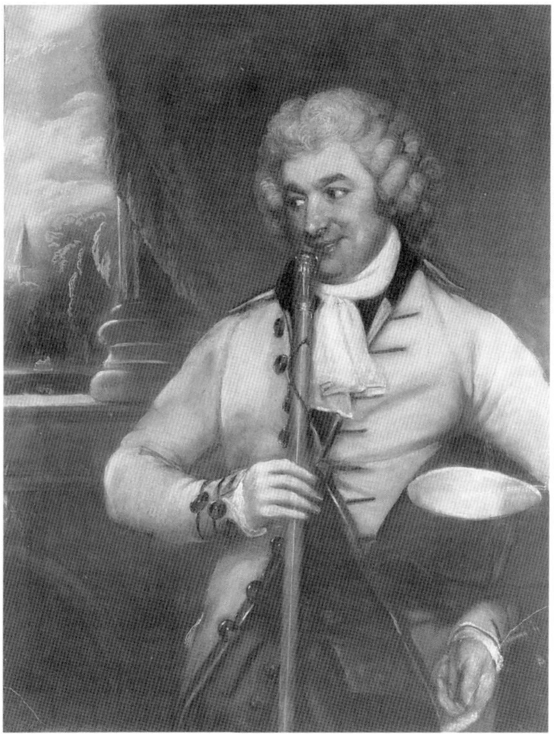

36

JOHN BANNISTER

as Lenitive in *The Prize*
or 2, 3, 5, 8 by Prince Hoare

John Russell

Pastel on paper 97.8 x 76.2
INSCR: 'J. Russell R.A. pinxit. 1802' (red chalk b.l.)
INV: Mathews 306; RW/CKA 309
PROV: The artist; his sale, Christie's 1807 (81);
Charles Mathews
EXH: 1802 R.A. (405); 1833 London (306)
ENGR: W. Greatbach after a drawing by
George Perfect Harding pub. Richard Bentley
1839, stipple and line 11.4 x 8.9
LIT: TAM 1935, reproduced; Griffiths, p. 374

Lenitive, a doctor who talks pseudo-medical nonsense, is visiting his patient Heartwell. Lenitive's servant brings news of a £10,000 prize with the lottery number 2538. Lenitive decides to drop his profession and go off to woo Caroline. At the end of the play Lenitive hears that he has been misinformed about the lucky number.

Lenitive wears a wig with large curls at the sides (to which Caroline objects). In the Cumberland edition stage instructions the wig is described as 'large and bushy' and the rest of the first act costume as 'Gray coat and buff waistcoat, trimmed with black binding, and large black horn buttons – gray breeches and stockings – little cocked hat – cane – shoes and paste buckles'.

In Russell's drawing Lenitive has a gold-topped cane and a black tricorn hat with a white lining. He wears a white coat with black buttons over a dark garment. Despite the fact that the scene is set inside Heartwell's house, there is a landscape view with a church spire.

Prince Hoare's musical farce, with music by Stephen Storace, was first performed by the Drury Lane company at the King's Theatre on 11 March 1793, with Bannister as the original Lenitive. He also played the part in the first performance at the Haymarket on 30 August 1793. Bannister remained popular in the role at both theatres until well into the 19th century.

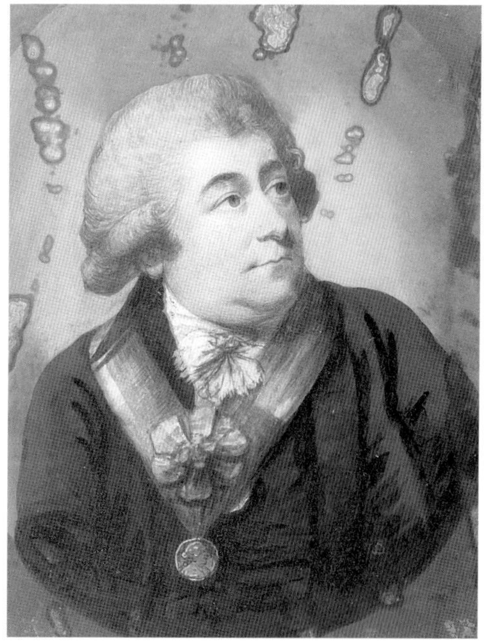

37

JOHN BANNISTER

'School of Garrick'

Henry Spicer

Pencil and watercolour on laid paper 26.5 x 21
INV: Mathews 259 (artist unknown);
RW/CKA 48F (artist unknown)
PROV: Charles Mathews
EXH: 1833 London (259)

The sitter wears a blue jacket and a Shakespeare Ribband (see No. 6).

This drawing is similar in pose and concept to the portrait by Henry Edridge engraved by William Ridley for Parsons's *Minor Theatre*, April 1794, a publication that appears to be closely associated with the School of Garrick portraits.

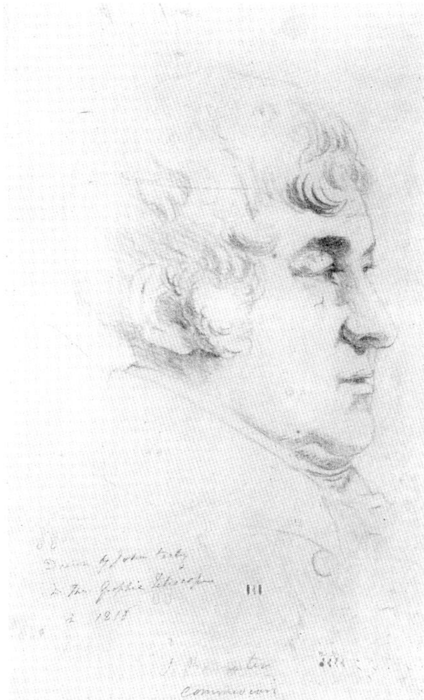

38

JOHN BANNISTER

John Varley

Pencil on wove paper 29.8 x 17.8
INSCR: 'Drawn by John Varley/in the Graphic Telescope/ in 1816' (pencil b.l.); 'J. Bannister/Commedian' (pencil b.c.)
INV: RW/CKA 134
PROV: Presented by an unknown donor between 1888 and 1909
LIT: *Walpole Society* 21, pl. XLV; for the 'Graphic Telescope' see *Burlington Magazine* (1972), 114: 72

Head only, facing to right. There is another drawing by Varley of John Bannister in the V&A (E.1139–1927), pencil on pink wove paper 33.6 x 23.5. It was also drawn with the aid of the graphic telescope, one of a collection of 109 similarly produced drawings by a number of artists, contained in two volumes, from the collection of Dawson Turner. On 4 June 1811, John Varley's brother Cornelius registered a 'Patent of a New Construction of a Telescope or Optical Instrument for Viewing Distant Objects & for other Useful Purposes, with a suitable Table or Stand for the same' (Patent No. 3430). It was a portable variant on the *camera obscura*, and by a system of mirrors projected the image onto a flat table so that it could be traced on paper. It was widely used for landscape drawings by John Sell Cotman and others, but John Varley seems to have been the first to use it for portraits. See C.M. Kauffmann, *John Varley 1778–1842* (1984), pp. 132–35 (cat. 34–35).

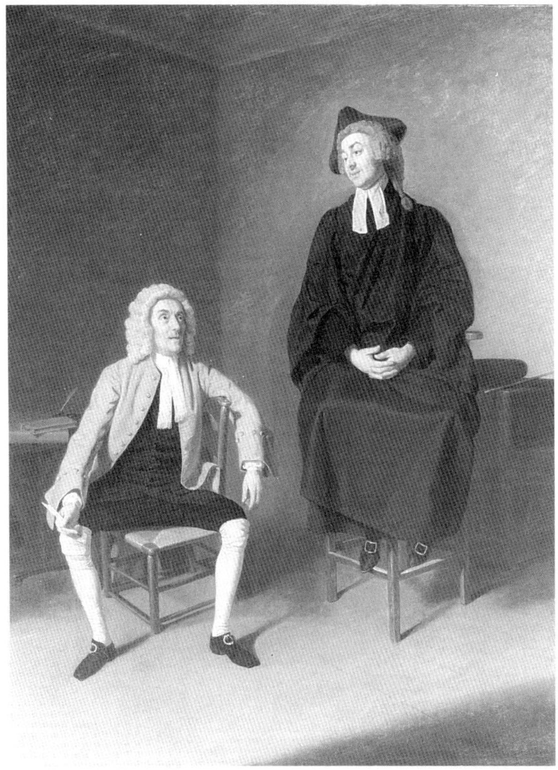

39*

JOHN BANNISTER as Scout and *WILLIAM PARSONS* as Snarl in *The Village Lawyer* by George Colman the Elder

Samuel De Wilde

Oil on canvas 92 x 71.5
INV: RW/CKA 449 (by J. Zoffany. Parsons as Sheepface); Gift 239
PROV: Presented by William Banting between 1846 and 1888
[This is possibly the painting described as 'life-size', attributed to Gainsborough and called 'Bannister Jnr and Parsons' in *The Citizen*, that was sold for £31 10s. in the Royal Dramatic College sale at Fairbrother, Lye and Palmer on 24 February 1881 (lot 46)]
EXH: 1951 London (49); 1956–57 London
LIT: Lady Victoria Manners & Dr G.C. Williamson, *John Zoffany* (1920), p. 145 reproduced p. 144; Griffiths, p. 334

The setting is as described in Lacy's edition of the play: 'Snarl's Shop. A counter; several pieces of flannel, baize &c., four yards of iron-grey broadcloth; tailor's pattern-book, shears, yard measure; table right, a chair right side of counter, shop stool left.' Scout, a down-at-heel lawyer, is visiting Snarl in the hope of getting a length of cloth for a new suit. Scout, perched on a high stool, wears a black tricorn hat and a long black gown with white bands. There are pentimenti all round the upper part of his body. Snarl, seated and looking up at Scout, wears a grey wig, black breeches and waistcoat, and a pale grey coat.

The elder Colman's farce, based on *L'Avocat Patelin* by David Augustin de Brueys, was first performed at the Haymarket on 28 August 1787, with Bannister as Scout and Parsons as Snarl. This picture has been attributed to Zoffany from the time it was given to the Garrick Club in the mid-19th century, and the attribution has been generally accepted. However, Zoffany was in India from 1783 to 1789 and could not have seen Parsons perform Snarl (Baddeley took over the role in the 1789 summer season). Although the picture would be rather early for a large-scale work by De Wilde, it becomes his first major painting; it bears considerable stylistic resemblance to No. 40, which is well documented.

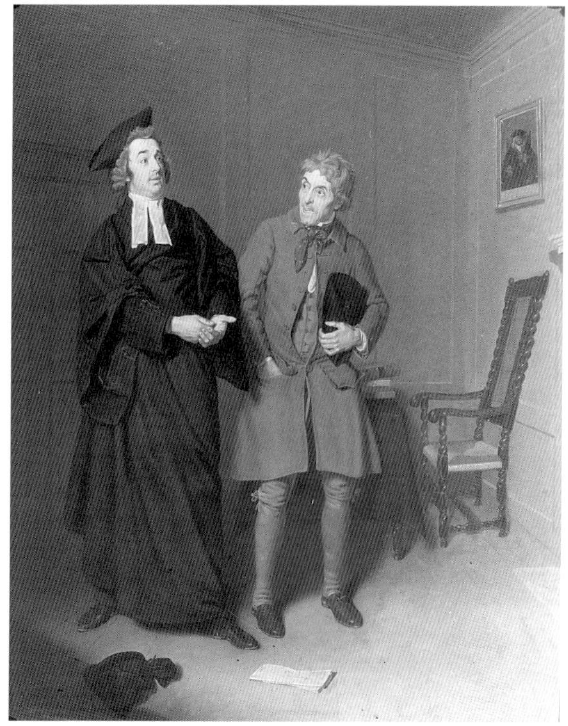

40 *John Bannister as Scout and William Parsons as Sheepface*

40*

JOHN BANNISTER as Scout
and *WILLIAM PARSONS* as Sheepface
in *The Village Lawyer*
by George Colman the Elder

Samuel De Wilde

Oil on canvas 77 x 63
INSCR: 'S De Wilde ft 1793' (dark brown paint b.l.)
INV: Mathews 133; RW/CKA 114
PROV: Charles Mathews
EXH: 1793 R.A. (285); 1833 London (133);
1950–51 London (248); 1951 London (8);
1951–52 London (107); 1965 Kenwood (15);
1975 Milan (106)
ENGR: John Raphael Smith 1796, mezzotint, possibly from the smaller version at Leicester which is therefore likely to have been the version shown at the R.A. in 1795 (201)
REL: Leicester 51, oil on canvas 61.6 x 51.1
[Prov: Spinks 1941; John A. Lewis & Son, oil, 1965
Prov: Sabin Galleries, Mrs Basil Ionides, Sotheby's
29 March 1963; see Mander & Mitchenson,
Theatre Notebook, 20 (1965)]
LIT: Patmore, p. 267, where described as the companion to No. 42; Fitzgerald, pp. 145–46

The scene is a courtroom. Scout has just brought off Sheepface on a charge of sheep-stealing by getting him to reply 'Ba-a-a' to all the Justice's questions. Sheepface cannot pay the fee and continues to bleat. Scout (Bannister), on the left, wears a long black gown over a dark brown coat. He has a tricorn hat on the back of his head. Sheepface (Parsons) wears grey stockings, light brown breeches and matching coat over a red waistcoat, and a spotted purple neckerchief. Hanging on the wall to the right is a mezzotint of Lord Mansfield.

The elder Colman's farce was first performed at the Haymarket on 28 August 1787 (see No. 39). John Edwin was the original Sheepface; Parsons's first appearance in the part was at the Haymarket on 10 June 1791. Parsons played the role 12 times during the season, including his benefit performance on 2 August. During the 1792 summer season Parsons played Sheepface eight times; his last performance before De Wilde's picture was painted occurred on 1 September 1792. For another study by De Wilde of Parsons in this role, see No. 658.

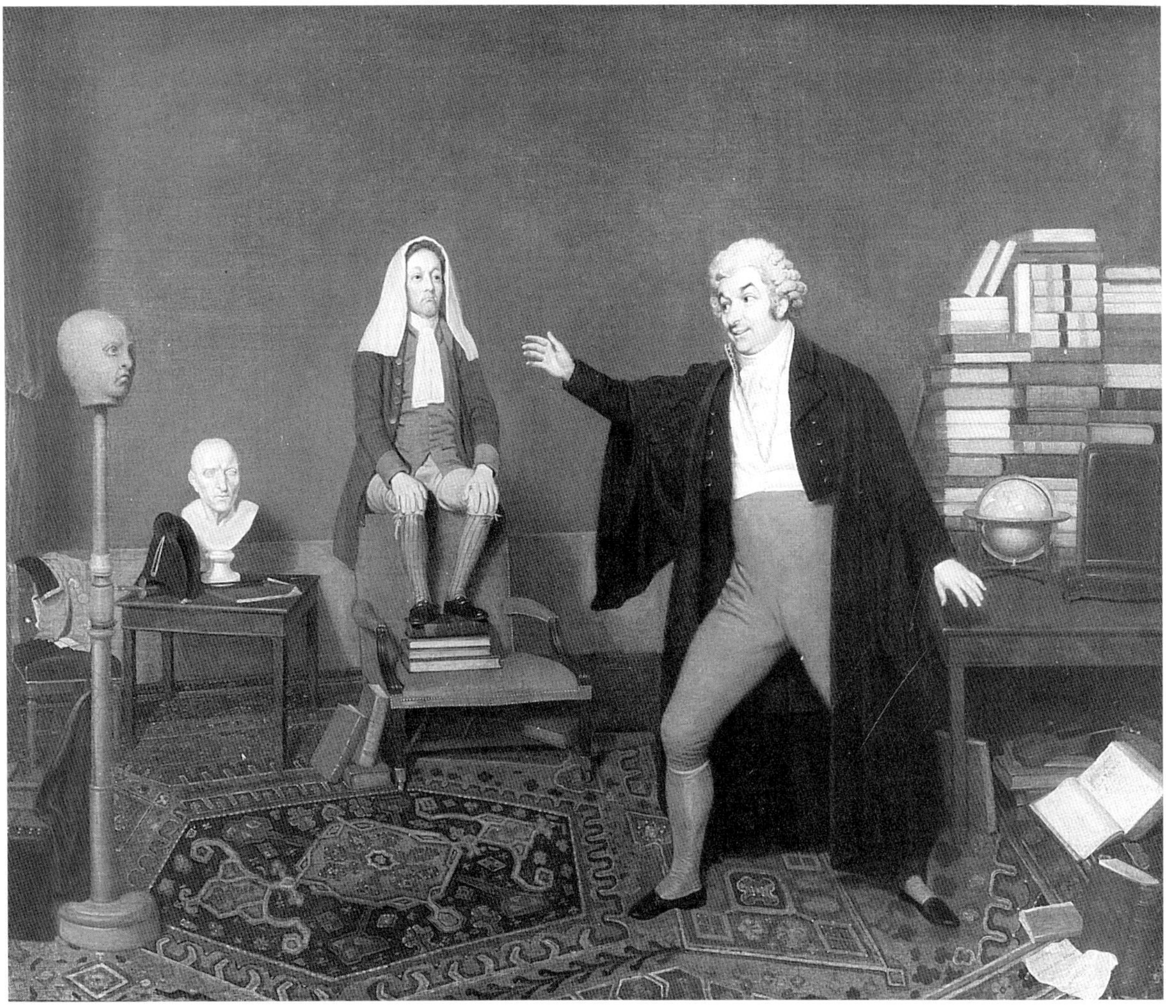

41

JOHN BANNISTER as Tristram Fickle
and *JOHN PURSER* as Sneer
in *The Weathercock* by John Till Allingham

Samuel De Wilde

Oil on canvas 121.9 x 101.6
INSCR: 'PLATONIS' (black paint on page of open book b.r.);
'Theatre Royal Covent G... / Romeo & Juliet / ... /
WEATH...' (black paint on playbill b.r.)
INV: GCL 672; Gift 725
PROV: Presented by Mrs Basil Ionides, 1953
EXH: 1808 R.A. (518)

Fickle by name and fickle by nature, Tristram Fickle cannot decide on a career. The room in De Wilde's picture is filled with the relics of previous passions. The stage direction for Act I, scene 2 lists the furnishings of Tristram's apartment, most of which are included in the painting: 'Tristram Fickle's apartment. Musical Instruments, Books, a Telescope, an electrifying Machine, a Quadrant, Globes &c., all about the Room in disorder. A Bust of Cicero on the Table, a Lawyer's Wig on Block and Gown, and a regimental Coat and Hat.' Tristram has donned the wig and gown to act as a Barrister and argue a case against the use of coal. The wig-block is his opponent and his servant Sneer is the judge, wearing a white handkerchief as a wig. The books are some of the 'twelve square foot of books' ordered by Tristram when he 'first thought of embracing the arduous profession of the law'. Towards the end of the scene Tristram decides to drop the law for the stage, and then for a military career. He puts on the military jacket draped over the chair to the left and smashes the bust of Cicero with his sword.

Tristram (Bannister) wears brown breeches with a high waist, a very dark green coat, a white waistcoat, and a high collar lined in blue. Over his costume is a black legal gown. Sneer (Purser) wears brown shoes, striped blue stockings, brown breeches, a brown jacket with red cuffs, and a red waistcoat.

Allingham's farce in two acts, with music by M.P. King, was first performed at Drury Lane on 18 November 1805, with Bannister as the original Tristram Fickle and Purser the original Sneer. A popular production, it was given almost 30 times during its first season. There were two performances during the 1807–8 season, on 16 December and 6 February, before De Wilde's picture was exhibited. De Wilde's drawing of the figure of Purser, signed and dated 1808, is in the Garrick Club collection (No. 698).

For his group portraits, De Wilde seems to have prepared separate drawings of the individual actors involved. There is no equivalent study of Bannister for this picture, but the extremely uncomfortable perspective, most notable in the patterned Turkey carpet and the curious midget-like figure of Purser, confirms that the figures were conceived separately and only subsequently combined as a group composition. The same process is evident with the drawing of Richard Jones as Young Contrast in the Somerset Maugham Collection (No. 46) and the group portrait with John Liston and Mr Hamerton in the Garrick Club Collection (No. 438).

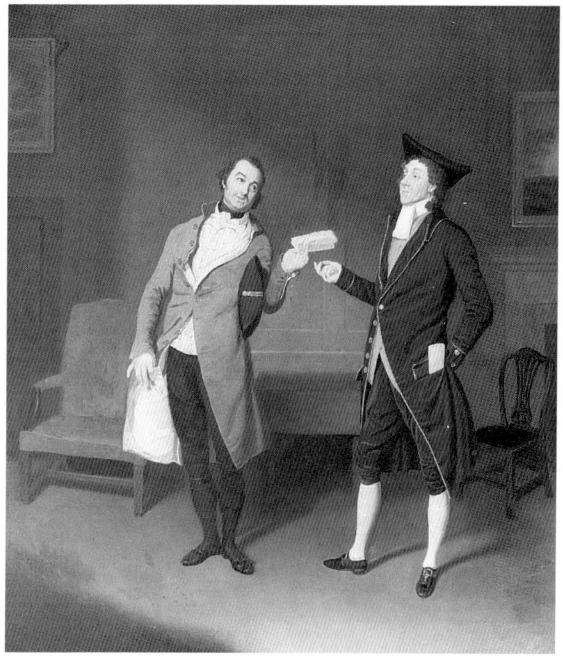

42*

JOHN BANNISTER as Sylvester Daggerwood
and *RICHARD SUETT* as Fustian
in *New Hay at the Old Market (or Sylvester Daggerwood)*
by George Colman the Younger

Samuel De Wilde

Oil on canvas 85 x 74
INSCR: 'S. De Wilde Pinxt 1797'
(dark brown paint b.l.)
INV: Mathews 132; RW/CKA 401
PROV: Charles Mathews
EXH: 1798 R.A. (159); 1833 London (132);
1934 London (263); 1951 London (13)
REL: NT 27, oil on canvas 83 x 72,
inscr: 'S. De Wilde pinxt, 1798'
LIT: Patmore, p. 267, where described as the
companion to No. 40; TAM 1935, reproduced

Sylvester Daggerwood and Fustian are provincial actors waiting for an audition in the antechamber in a manager's house. In De Wilde's picture, Fustian (on the right) has just woken Daggerwood, who hands him a playbill. The furled paper in Fustian's pocket is his tragedy, 'The Humane Footpad', which he later attempts to read to Daggerwood. The scene ends with the news that the manager has left without seeing them, having gone to discuss 'particular business' with Mr Bannister Jnr and Mr Suett.

De Wilde seems to have tidied up the original costumes, described by 'D.G.' in the introduction to the Samuel French edition of the sketch: 'Bannister fluttered in a miscellany of tawdry tatters that the loosening of a single button would have indecorously discomposed. His coat was a lattice, party-coloured – a patch-work quilt, his continuations [breeches], the sign of the chequers – an escutcheon, quartering all the colours of the rainbow; and his linen, the colour of an old hat, while the little that remained of it was hanging out, like bulrushes at the bottom of an old chair. … Then Suett, with snuff-coloured suit, every thread of which might have been accurately counted; long, lank visage; blue, gooseberry eye; gorgon wig, in eternal buckle.'

In his desire to capture theatrical elegance, De Wilde has clearly missed much of the humour of the scene. Daggerwood (Bannister) stands on the left, with a black tricorn hat under his left arm. He wears black shoes with bows, black stockings and breeches, a long green coat with a white lining and large brass buttons, a white waistcoat and a black stock. Suett has a black tricorn hat, black shoes, white stockings, black breeches, a brown coat and a red waistcoat.

The younger Colman's *New Hay at the Old Market; An Occasional Drama* was first performed at the Haymarket on 9 June 1795, with John Bannister as Daggerwood and Suett as Fustian. The cast also included Thomas Caulfield as Apewell – who lived up to his name and delivered a series of imitations. The piece was given 32 performances during its first summer season. Bannister borrowed the first scene for his benefit at Drury Lane on 13 April 1796, and played it with Suett and Caulfield. Colman seems to have liked Bannister's idea of reducing the piece to a single scene, and in that form it was given as *Sylvester Daggerwood* on 7 July 1796. Bannister played the title role, Suett was Fustian and Caulfield appeared again as Apewell with his imitations. The *Monthly Mirror* for July 1796 (p.185) reported: 'Caulfield's imitations of Aickin, Suett, King and Dignum are exact even to astonishment – of the rest we do not think much.' The new version of the piece did not prove as popular as the longer version and was only given 10 performances during the summer season. In several subsequent seasons it was occasionally performed, usually for Bannister's or Suett's benefit.

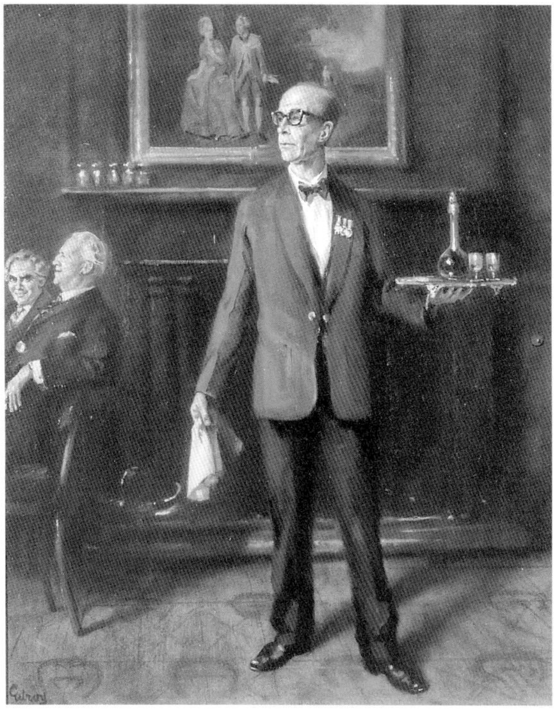

43*

FREDERICK BARKER

John Gilroy

Oil on canvas 66 x 50.8
INSCR: 'Gilroy' (black paint b.l.)
INV: GCL 714; Gift 817
PROV: Presented by the artist, 1967

Frederick Barker, the Club's wine waiter from 1936 to 1966, wears black shoes, dark trousers, black bow tie, and a claret Garrick Club jacket with medals on the left lapel. He is serving in the Coffee Room in front of the fireplace at the west end, over which hangs Zoffany's *Clandestine Marriage*. To the left, Sebastian Earl is seated in profile and Donald Wolfit looks out of the picture. See also No. 892.

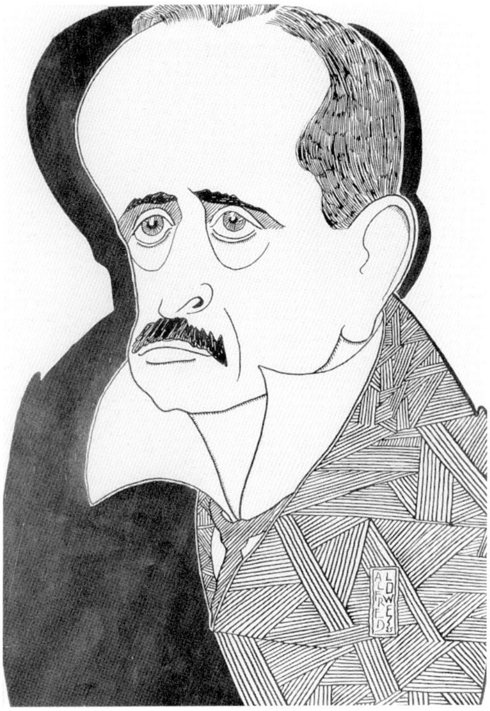

44

SIR JAMES MATTHEW BARRIE

Alfred Lowe

Pen and black ink with black wash
on wove paper 36.3 x 26.3 (sight)
INSCR: 'ALFRED LOWE 25'
(in two vertical lines, pen and black ink b.r.)
INV: GCL 682; Gift 566
PROV: Presented by Sir John Simon, 1938
REL: Lord Kennet, copy by GAL (NPG neg. 27983);
another portrait of the same sitter by the same
artist is in an English private collection

Half-length caricature, wearing a coat half black, half black and white stripes, and a white shirt with large lapels.

A typed letter attached to the back-board of the drawing – from John Simon to Colonel Plimpton, the Club Secretary, dated 5 May 1938 – reads: 'Dear Colonel Plimpton, Do you think the Garrick Club would care to have a framed caricature of Sir James Barrie drawn many years ago by Alfred Lowe? I bought it because I was a friend of Barrie and because it was rather an amusing treatment of him as a younger man. I don't suppose it is of any great merit or value but as I do not intend to take it to 11 Downing Street, and if the Committee care to have it and put it in a corner somewhere, I should be glad to give it to the Club. Yours sincerely...'

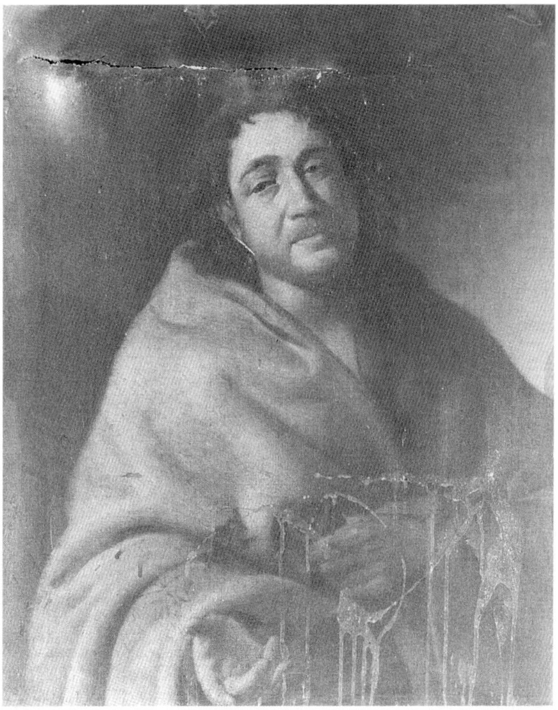

45

JOHN BARRINGTON
as Teague in *The Committee*
by Sir Robert Howard

Unknown Artist

Oil on canvas 74.3 x 61.6
INV: Mathews 189; RW/CKA 352
PROV: Thomas Harris; Harris sale, Robins
12 July 1819 (31), as by Sir Godfrey Kneller;
Charles Mathews
EXH: 1833 London (189)
REL: See No. 46

Teague is an itinerant Irishman and his first lines are those cited by Mathews: 'I am a poor Irishman, Heaven save me, and save all your three faces! Give me a thirteen.' A 'thirteen' was an Irish term for a silver shilling, it being worth 13 rather than 12 Irish pennies. Head and shoulders to front, his right hand extended towards the spectator, his left hand clasping a grey drapery to his breast. This picture, in much deteriorated condition, was in storage in 1994.

Howard's comedy was first given at the Theatre Royal, Vere Street, on 27 November 1662. Barrington played Teague for the first time at Covent Garden on 11 October 1749. It was one of the most popular plays in the repertory during the first half of the 18th century, but received only intermittent performances from 1760. See also Nos. 46 and 613.

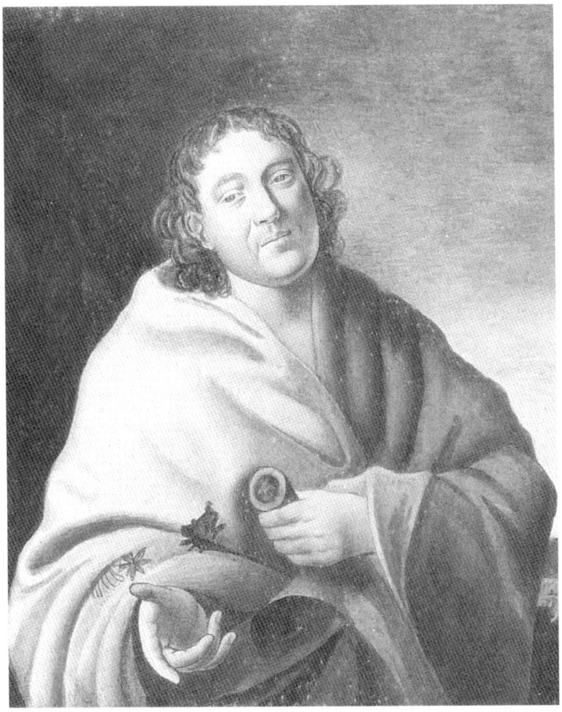

46

JOHN BARRINGTON

as Teague in *The Committee*

by Sir Robert Howard

Sylvester Harding

Pen and grey ink with watercolour
on wove paper 17 x 14.6
INSCR: 'Mr Barrington, as Teague in the Committee – Drawn by S. Harding, 1791'
(pen and brown ink, on mount below)
INV: Not listed; Gift 683
PROV: Presented by Miss F.L. Rudston Brown, 1949

Copied from No. 45, possibly preparatory to an engraving that was never made.

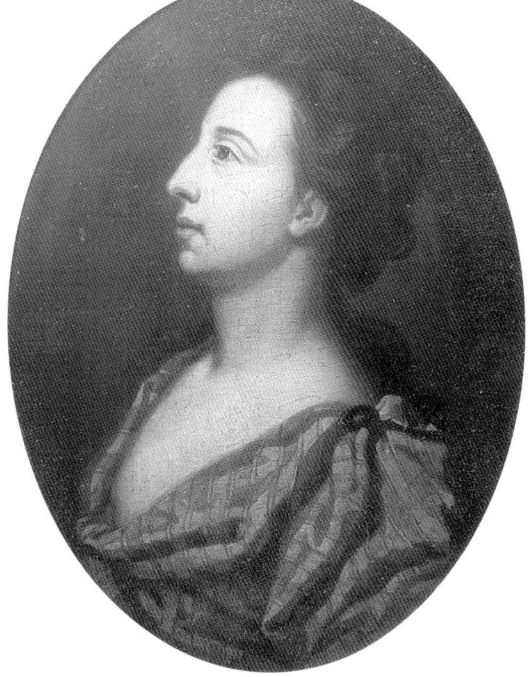

47

ELIZABETH BARRY

Sir Godfrey Kneller (copy after)

Oil on panel 21.9 x 16.8
INV: Mathews 138 (artist unknown); RW 284 (artist unknown); CKA 284
PROV: Charles Mathews
EXH: 1833 London (138)
ENGR: Charles Knight for Harding's *Biographical Mirrour* pub. E. & S. Harding 17 December 1792, stipple 12.9 x 10.2, inscr: 'From an original picture by Sr Godfrey Kneller / in the Collection of the Rt. Hon the Earl of Orford at Strawberry Hill'; Anon., mezzotint 10.8 x 8.2; Anon., stipple 9.8 x 7.6
REL: The Strawberry Hill portrait, described as head and shoulder in profile 30″ x 25″, was sold at Sotheby's on 3 May 1972 (128), seller and buyer unknown

The sitter wears a brown and blue striped dress caught up on left shoulder with a pale blue knot.

No. 47 may have been copied from Charles Knight's engraving, after the Kneller original.

Recognised as the first great English actress, Elizabeth Barry probably made her début on the London stage as Draxilla in Otway's *Alcibiade* at Covent Garden in late September 1675. She retired after the season 1709–10. Her magnetic intensity was at its best in such roles as Roxalana in *The Rival Queens*, Calista in *The Fair Penitent*, and Lady Macbeth.

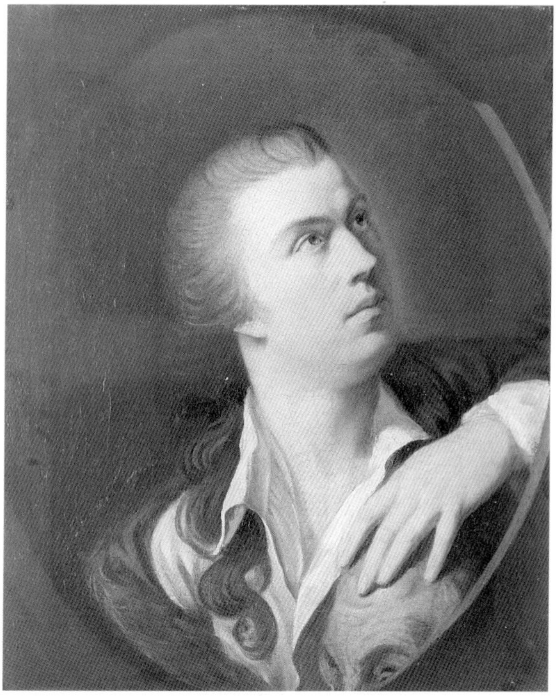

48
SPRANGER BARRY

Unknown Artist

Oil on canvas 62.5 x 52.5
INV: Mathews 25; RW/CKA 361
PROV: Charles Mathews
EXH: 1833 London (25)

The bust on which Barry rests his left hand appears to be of Shakespeare. He wears a red garment, with brown fur trimming over his shoulders, and a white shirt.

The handsome Irishman Spranger Barry, who 'was less comfortable on stage in a modern dress than in a Roman shape or a regimental uniform' (BD), rivalled Garrick as Romeo and excelled in such roles as Othello, Douglas, and Evander in *The Grecian Daughter*.

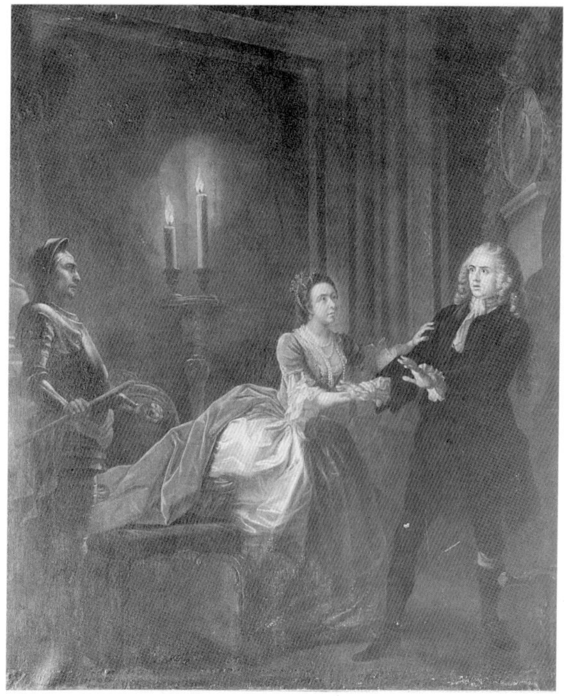

49*
SPRANGER BARRY as Hamlet,
MARY ELMY as Gertrude
and *LACY RYAN* as the Ghost
in *Hamlet* by William Shakespeare

Francis Hayman

Oil on canvas 127 x 108
INV: Mathews 168 (Betterton as Hamlet and Mrs Barry as the Queen, artist unknown);
RW 115 (Betterton and Mrs Barry); CKA 115
PROV: Thomas Harris; Harris sale, Robins 12 July 1819 (32), with date 1757; Charles Mathews
EXH: 1833 London (168); 1947 London (3); 1951 London (21); 1960 Kenwood (18); 1964 London [1] (13); 1987 Yale and London (41)
REL: Folger Shakespeare Library, sketch in pencil, grey wash, pen and black ink, heightened with white 17.8 x 17.3
ENGR: Grignion for Charles Jennens's edition of *Hamlet* 1773, line 13.8 x 9.8 (David Garrick's features are substituted for those of Spranger Barry); see Brian Allen *Hayman* catalogue No. 41 and check-list No. 311
LIT: Fitzgerald, pp. 212–13; Griffiths, pp. 296–98

The Ghost, on the left, wears half-armour over long brown leather trousers. A broad orange sash is draped around his waist. Gertrude wears a very full red velvet panniered dress over a white silk petticoat, embroidered in gold with a deep floral pattern around the hem, and strands of pearls round her neck. Hamlet is dressed in black, with his left stocking ungartered.

It is unlikely that the interior reflects an actual production. The drawing in the Folger Library, probably a preliminary sketch for the painting, shows a large wardrobe, topped with vases, and a large platter in place of the looking glass. The composition extends further to the right, and the overturned chair is more conspicuous. The figures are more dramatically conceived, with the Ghost holding his baton in an extended right hand and Gertrude and Hamlet grappling with each other.

The Garrick Club painting is more sedate, and the memory of the performance is clearly tempered by the artistic prototype, Boitard's drawing, engraved by Kirkall for Rowe's 1709 edition of Shakespeare. Rowe's was the first illustrated edition, and it monopolised Shakespeare imagery until the mid-18th century. The Hamlet and Gertrude in the 1709 engraving are traditionally supposed to be Thomas Betterton and Elizabeth Barry, and those identifications no doubt persuaded Mathews to identify Hayman's sitters as the great Restoration actors, both of whom were dead before the artist was five years old. Perhaps the engraving influenced performances, as well as illustrations, of *Hamlet.*

Hamlet's attitude was that adopted by all 18th-century Hamlets when seeing the Ghost. Perhaps the most celebrated example is Benjamin Wilson's portrait of Garrick, known only through the mezzotint by James McArdell of 1754. Garrick's pose is graphically described by Henry Fielding in *Tom Jones.* See also K.A. Burnim, *David Garrick: Director* (1961), pp. 159–61.

The identification of the Hamlet here as Spranger Barry is convincing. He played Hamlet at Covent Garden three times during 1757, the date mentioned in the Harris sale catalogue. However, he played opposite Peg Woffington on all three occasions, and the Gertrude in Hayman's picture does not show her. There is no comparative iconography for Mary Elmy, but she played Gertrude to Barry's Hamlet between 1751 and 1754. She returned to the role for the 1758–59 season, but David Ross was then her Hamlet. Ryan played the Ghost throughout the 1750s and gave his last performance in the role on 18 March 1760. Brian Allen dates the picture stylistically about 1755–60.

Also in the Garrick Club is a scene from *Hamlet* by James Roberts, once thought to show Barry as Hamlet and Mrs Barry as Gertrude. But the figures seem to be William Smith and Elizabeth Hopkins; see No. 769.

50

WILLIAM BARRYMORE

as Hubert in *King John*

by William Shakespeare

Samuel De Wilde

Black chalk and watercolour on discoloured wove paper 19.2 x 17.8

INSCR: 'De Wilde / Sunday / N 20th / 1803' (black chalk b.l.); 'Mr Barrymore' (pen and brown ink on mount b.c. CM)

INV: Mathews 296 (no part); RW/CKA 564 (no part)

PROV: Charles Mathews

EXH: 1833 London (296)

ENGR: James Parker after Edward Francis Burney for the Manley Wood edition of Shakespeare printed for George Kearsley 31 March 1804, line 8.1 x 7.7 (f.l. scene with Prince Arthur)

De Wilde's drawing of Barrymore's head, with his hand to his chin, is clearly a sketch prepared for Burney; Barrymore's name is printed over the top of the illustration. Most of the illustrations in the Manley Wood edition are of imaginary subjects.

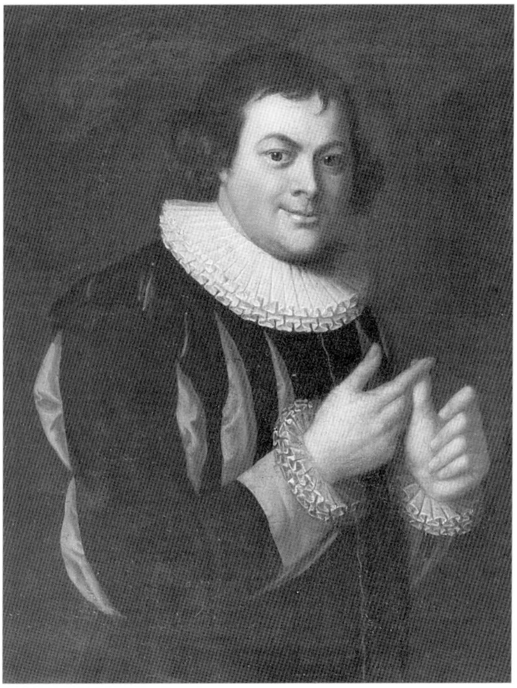

51

GEORGE BARTLEY

as Hamlet in *Hamlet*

by William Shakespeare

Isaac Pocock

Oil on canvas 77 x 64

INV: Mathews 157; RW/CKA 415

PROV: Charles Mathews

EXH: 1833 London (157)

Half-length, facing front. Bartley, with curly brown hair, wears an open white collar, a grey cloak wrapped round his shoulders, and under that a black leather jerkin with silver studs.

Bartley does not seem to have played Hamlet in London. It is possible that he played the role in the provinces, however, where he was better known as a comedian. Pocock must have painted the picture before Bartley's retirement in 1819.

Mathews's choice of quote is particularly apt, if obvious: 'To be or not to be, that is the question.' See also No. 447.

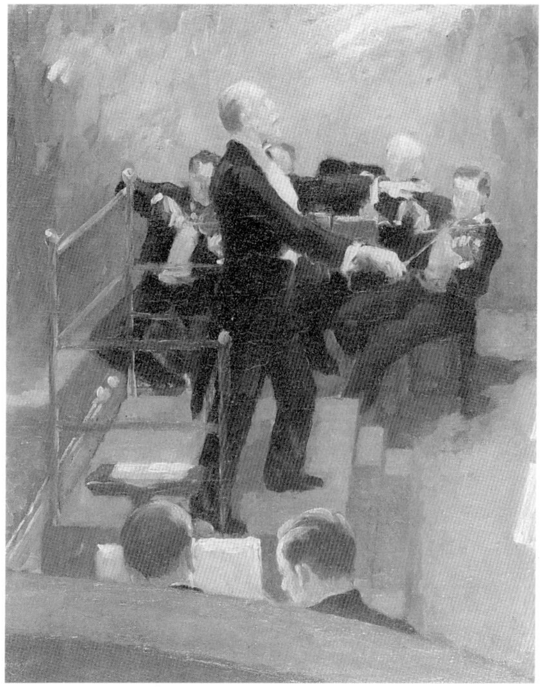

52

SIR THOMAS BEECHAM

Conducting in Queen's Hall

John Aubrey

Oil on canvas 50.5 x 39.8

INSCR: 'Aubrey' (red paint b.l.)

INV: GCL 730; Gift 870

PROV: Presented by Sir Thomas Armstrong, 1976

Sir Thomas, in evening dress, stands conducting before four musicians. Two other performers are seen in the foreground, beyond the parapet of a box.

Queen's Hall opened in 1893 and was destroyed during the Second World War. Apart from the Albert Hall, it was the major London concert hall, the forerunner of the Royal Festival Hall, which was built to replace it.

Sir Thomas became a member of the Garrick Club in 1938.

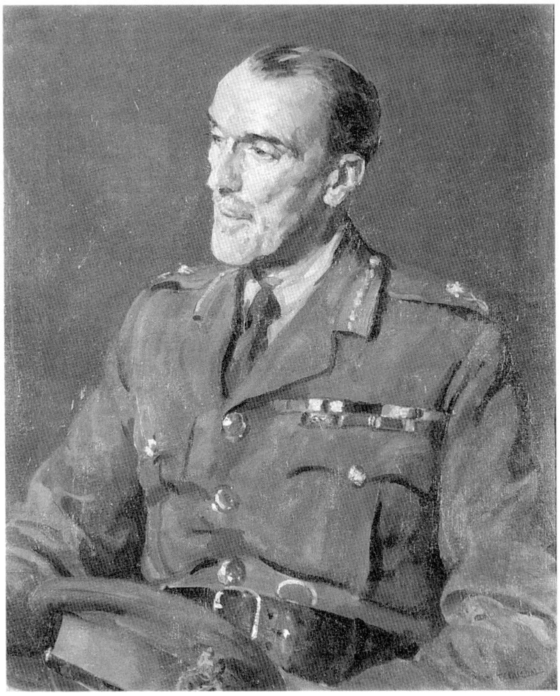

53
MAJOR-GENERAL JOHN HAY BEITH

T.C. Dugdale

Oil on canvas 76.2 x 63.5
INSCR: T C DUGDALE (brown paint b.r.)
INV: GCL 671; Gift 724
PROV: Bequeathed by the artist, 1953
EXH: 1940 R.A. (207); 1962 (530) R.S.P.P.

The general is dressed in his uniform. He became a member of the Garrick Club in 1919.

After service in World War I, Beith took up writing and the theatre. Writing under the pseudonym of Ian Hay, he adapted several of his novels into plays, including *The Safety Match* (1921), *Housemaker* (1936) and *Tilly of Bloomsbury* (1919). He also collaborated with such authors as Guy Bolton, Sir Seymour Hicks and P.G. Wodehouse. He was Chairman of the Society of Authors (1921–24 and 1935–39) and President of the Damatists Club from 1939. During World War II he rose to the rank of Major-General as Director of the War Office public relations.

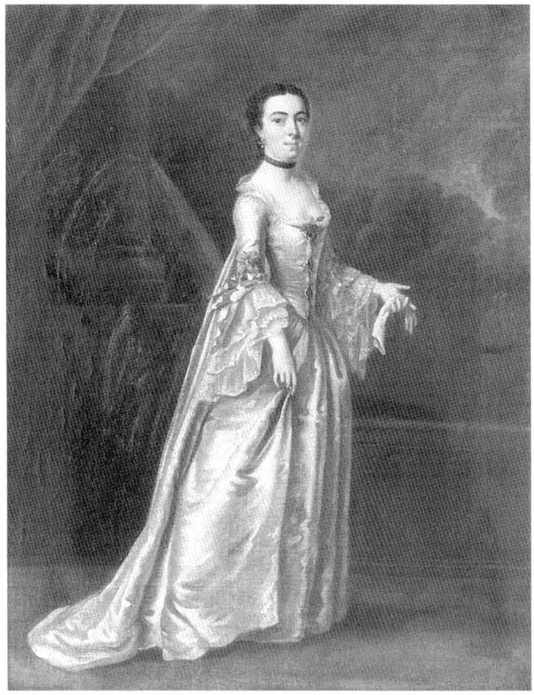

54
GEORGE ANN BELLAMY

F. Lindo

Oil on canvas 69.2 x 54
INV: Mathews 24; RW 108 (artist unknown); CKA 108
PROV: Charles Mathews
EXH: 1833 London (24)

Mrs Bellamy, standing full-length, wears a silvery-white silk dress trimmed with lace. She has a dark blue riband collier.

Lindo, probably a pupil of Francis Hayman, was active 1755–65. All his known signed works were painted in Scotland from 1760 to 1762, in the Lowlands and Aberdeenshire. Brian Allen supports the attribution, and believes that the picture was probably painted in the mid-1750s.

After her début at Covent Garden in 1744, Mrs Bellamy acted some 96 roles in London until her retirement in May 1785. 'Her face and figure gave great delight' (BD) and her best roles included Juliet, Estifania in *Rule a Wife*, Jane Shore, and Cordelia. She died destitute in 1788.

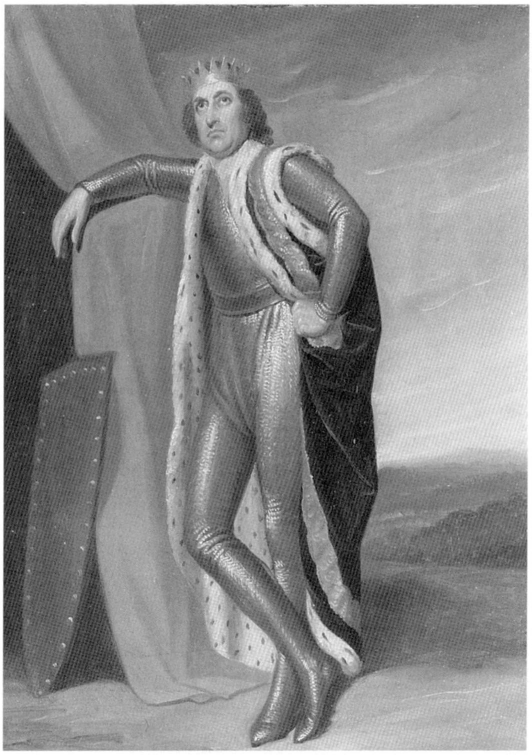

55
ROBERT BENSLEY
as Harold in *The Battle of Hastings*
by Richard Cumberland

Samuel De Wilde

Oil on canvas 36.8 x 28.3
INV: Mathews 181; RW/CKA 251
PROV: John Bell; Charles Mathews
EXH: 1833 London (181); 1975 Brighton (J14)
ENGR: Philippe Audinet for Bell's British Library
23 February 1793, line 11.5 x 8.2, published
Bell's *British Theatre* (1797), vol 6, with the quotation:
'– disastrous Signs! / What shall I do?'

The scene is 'The English Camp. The royal Tent with the Banners of Harold unfurled.' Harold wears a complete suit of chain mail with a red belt edged in gold, and a dark green mantle edged in gold and lined and trimmed with ermine. He leans contemplatively at the entrance to his tent.

Cumberland's tragedy was first performed at Drury Lane on 24 January 1778, with Bensley as the original Harold. The play was given 13 times during the season. After a single performance the following season, on 1 October 1778, the play was dropped from the repertory.

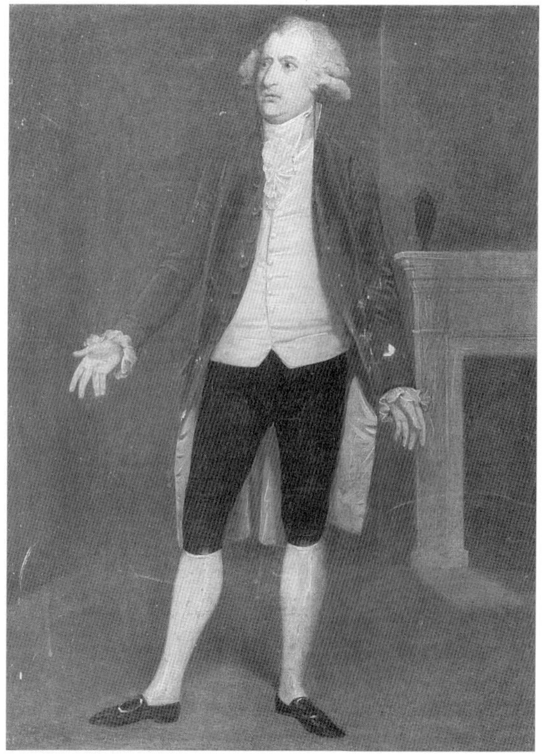

56
ROBERT BENSLEY
as Oakly in *The Jealous Wife*
by George Colman the Elder

Samuel De Wilde

Oil on canvas 36 x 27.2 (on relining canvas 36.8 x 28.4)
INV: Mathews 174; RW/CKA 432
PROV: John Bell; Charles Mathews
EXH: 1833 London (174)
ENGR: Philippe Audinet for Bell's British Library
27 October 1792, line 11.5 x 8.2, published Bell's *British Theatre* (1797), vol 20, with the quotation: 'Lord this is the strangest Misapprehension! I am quite astonished.';
Ferguson pub. W. Jones, Dublin, n.d.;
Anon. for C. Cooke 2 April 1807, line 12.2 x 7.4

The scene is set in a room in Oakly's house, in Act II, scene 2. Oakly, standing full-length, wears black shoes with silver buckles, white stockings, black breeches, a crimson velvet jacket, a white waistcoat, and a high white stock with rosette. There is a marble 'Adam' fireplace on the right.

The elder George Colman's comedy was first performed at Drury Lane on 12 February 1761, with Garrick as Oakly. Bensley's first performance in the role was at Drury Lane on 25 September 1788, and his last performance of it before De Wilde painted his picture was on 29 September 1789.

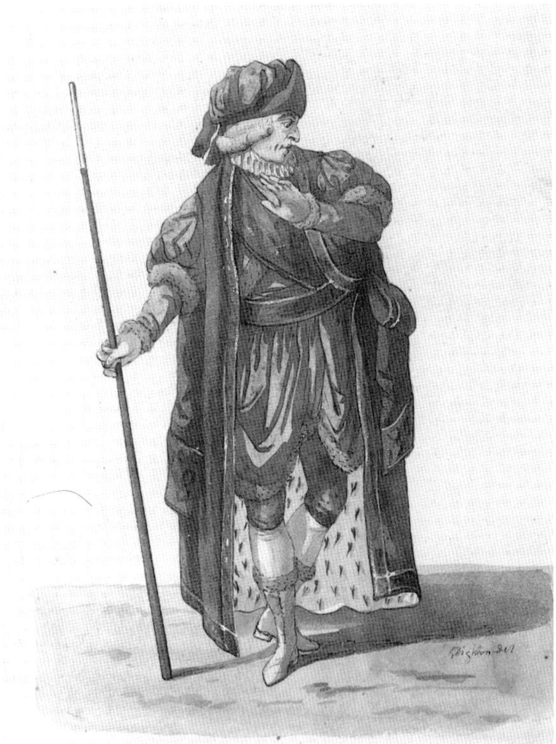

57
ROBERT BENSLEY
as Prospero in *The Tempest*
by William Shakespeare

Robert Dighton

Pen and brown ink with watercolour and some blue body colour on discoloured wove paper 21.6 x 15.2
INSCR: 'R. Dighton del.' (pen and brown ink b.r.); 'Mr Bensley as Prospero in the Tempest.' (pen and brown ink on mount b. CM)
INV: RW 555A (artist unknown); CKA 555A
PROV: Charles Mathews (not in catalogue)
REL: Folger Library (similar, but cruder), inscr: 'R Dighton del' (b.r.); 'Moody in Prospero' (b.c.)

Bensley wears yellow boots with fur tops, white stockings, red breeches, a red fur-trimmed costume over which is a long black sleeveless coat lined with ermine, and a belt and sash decorated with cabalistic signs. His headgear is red and black.

Bensley played Prospero for the first time in a revival at Drury Lane on 4 January 1777. It was an extravagant venture, with an opening shipwreck designed by De Loutherbourg and new music by the younger Thomas Linley. Charles Bannister received most praise for his Caliban (with songs), but Bensley's Prospero became one of his most distinguished roles. This production had just been pipped at the post by the first-ever performance of the play at Covent Garden on 27 December 1776, with Hull as Prospero. However, this seems to have been cobbled together in a hurry and it faded away, whilst the Drury Lane production remained a popular part of the repertory.

The Folger Library drawing is presumably a copy. Also in the Folger is a watercolour by W. Loftis of Bensley as Prospero.

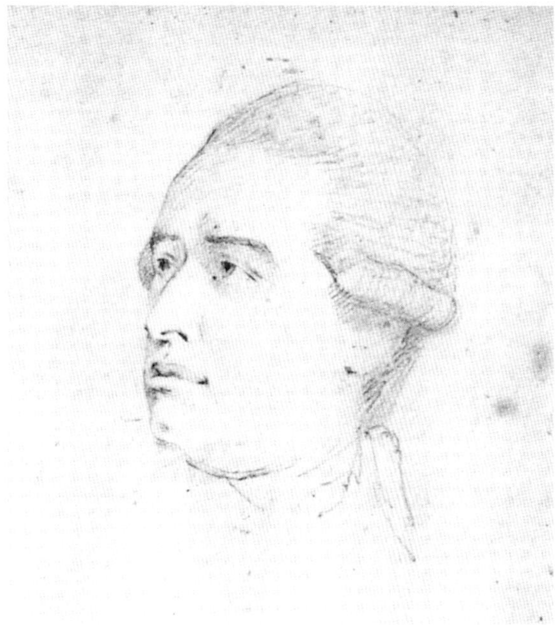

58
ROBERT BENSLEY

James Roberts

Pencil on laid paper 8.2 x 7.6
INSCR: 'Bensley' (pen and brown ink on mount b. CM)
INV: RW/CKA 493B
PROV: Charles Mathews (not in catalogue)
REL: See Harvard 76M–66 6Ms Thr30

Head only, looking up to left.

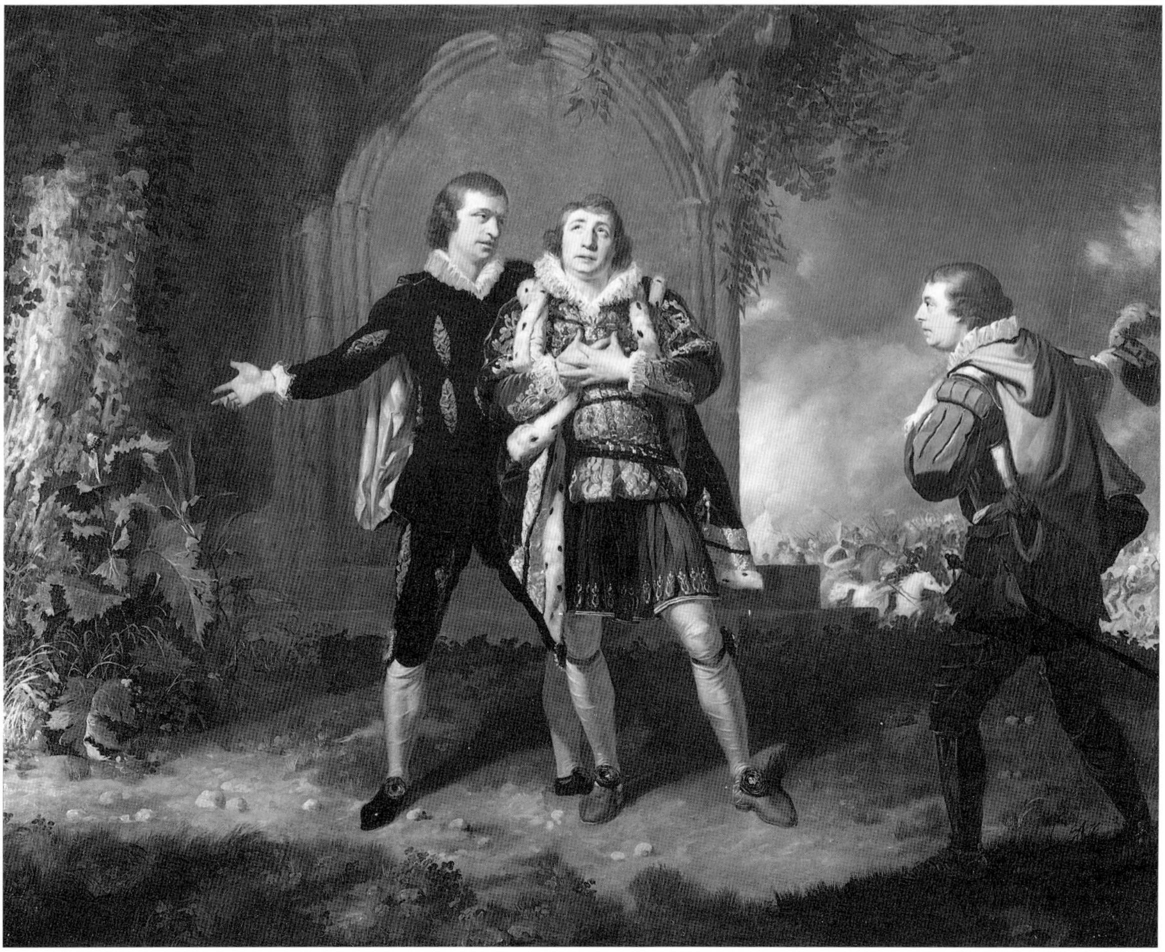

59

ROBERT BENSLEY as Hubert,
WILLIAM POWELL as King John
and *R. SMITH* as a Messenger
in *King John* by William Shakespeare

John Hamilton Mortimer

Oil on canvas 101 x 127
INV: Mathews 16; RW/CKA 17 (William Smith as Bastard?)
PROV: William Powell; Charles Mathews
EXH: 1768 S.A. (107) ('A scene in King John, act the fifth, scene the fifth'); S.A. Special Exh. (74); 1833 London (16); 1968 Eastbourne & Kenwood (80); 1982–83 London (192)
ENGR: Valentine Green, 1769, pub. Wynne Ryland 9 January 1771, mezzotint 42.2 x 55.3; and Ryland 26 March 1771, mezzotint 42.2 x 55.3, inscr: 'William Powell and Robert Bensley as King John and Hubert, with William Smith as a Messenger'
LIT: Patmore, p. 262; Fitzgerald, pp. 225–27; reproduced Mander & Mitchenson (1957), figure 123; M. Webster, *Francis Wheatly* (1970), p. 18; *LS* pt 4, 1156, 1219, 1278, 1301; John Sunderland, 'John Hamilton Mortimer', *The Walpole Society* (1936) 52: 125–26, reproduced figure 31

Hubert (Bensley) stands left of centre. He wears black shoes with blue rosettes, silver hose, black breeches, a black doublet, a black belt, and a dark cloak with a white lining. King John (Powell) stands in the centre, wearing brown shoes with blue rosettes, silver hose, blue garters with rosettes, a red tunic trimmed with silver, a red velvet doublet heavily decorated with silver braid, embroidery and buttons, and a lace ruff. Over the doublet he has a purple velvet coat embroidered in silver and trimmed with ermine and silver braid. He has a sword in his blue sash. The Messenger (Smith) gestures towards the distant battle with his blue-plumed brown hat. He wears brown leggings with armour over feet, shins, and thighs, a doublet, a white shirt, brown leather shoulder pads, breastplate and armour over shoulders, brown leather belt with sword, and a short red cloak.

The play was given a newly-dressed revival at Covent Garden on 23 September 1767, with Powell as King John (a role he had acted for the first time in London on 20 March 1766 at Drury Lane) and Bensley playing

Hubert for the first time. Richard Smith, who played the King's Messenger, has been confused in the past with William Smith, the more considerable actor who played Philip the Bastard. *King John* was given a second performance on 22 December 1767, a third on 3 May 1769, and then disappeared from the Covent Garden repertory until 1 December 1775.

The scene depicted is Act V, scene 3, rather than Act V, scene 5, as suggested on the mezzotint, or Act IV, as indicated by Mathews.

Sunderland (p. 32) points out Mortimer's close dependence on Zoffany in this picture, especially in relation to Zoffany's 1766 canvas showing Garrick and others in *Lethe* (Birmingham City Museums and Art Gallery).

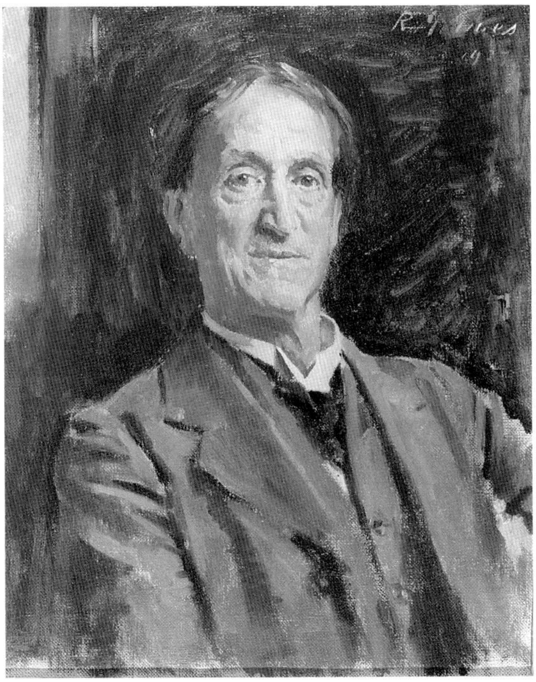

60

SIR FRANK BENSON

Reginald Grenville Eves

Oil on canvas 55.9 x 50.8
INSCR: 'R G Eves / 1927' (pink-white paint t.r.)
INV: GCL 660
PROV: Unknown
EXH: 1928 R.A. (62)
REL: Theatre Museum (TM88), sketch in oil on canvas 39.2 x 33, head and shoulders to l., looking to front; preparatory drawing, black chalk 53.2 x 40 s. & d: 'R.G. Eves / 1927,' head and shoulders to l., head turned to front, looking to r., Sotheby's 23–30 April 1986 (lot 465, 11 in lot)

Benson wears a grey jacket and waistcoat, high wing collar, and brown cravat.

There is another portrait by Eves of Benson, half-length, seated to right, in the NPG (3777), oil on canvas 74.3 x 62.2, signed and dated 1924. A third portrait, oil on canvas 75 x 62.2, was sold at Phillips, 30 November 1973 (lot 39) and is owned by Richard Bebb.

Sir Frank became a member of the Garrick Club in 1893. Knighted by King George V in 1916, he was a successful manager and is best remembered for the Shakespearean company with which 'he toured the provinces, keeping the plays of Shakespeare always before the public, and ... providing a fine training for countless young actors and actresses' (OCT).

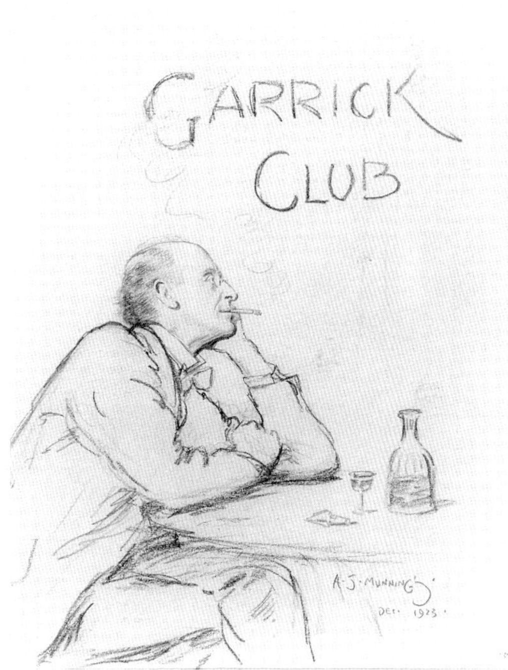

61

ROWLAND BERKELEY

Sir Alfred Munnings

Pencil on wove paper 35.6 x 27.6
INSCR: GARRICK / CLUB (black chalk t.c.); 'A. J. Munnings. / DEC. 1923.' (black chalk b.r.)
INV: CKA 529 (in 528 frame); Gift 418
PROV: Presented by the artist, 1924

This sketch was drawn for the front cover of the menu of a dinner given for Rowland Berkeley on 16 December 1923. Berkeley was a member of the Garrick Club from 1904 until his death in 1924. See also Nos. 62 and 63.

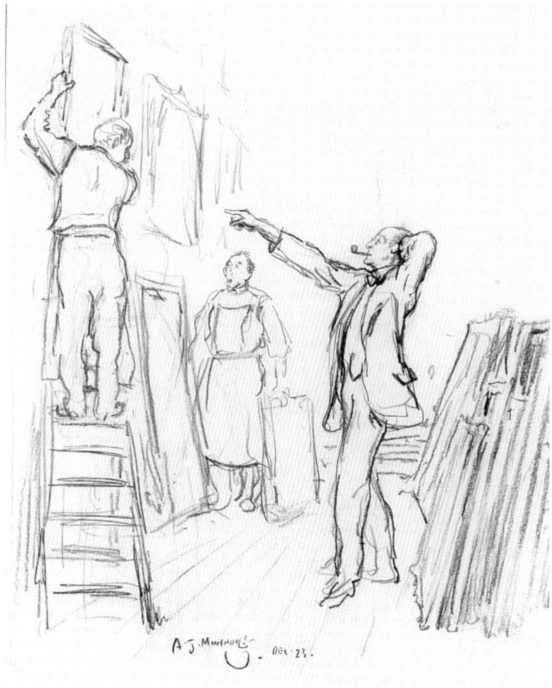

62

ROWLAND BERKELEY

Sir Alfred Munnings

Black chalk and pencil on wove paper 37.5 x 29.8
INSCR: 'A. J. Munnings. DEC. 23.' (black chalk b.c.)
INV: CKA 528 (in 529 frame); Gift 418
PROV: Presented by the artist, 1924
REL: See No. 63 (sketch for this drawing)

Design for the back cover of the menu of a dinner given on 16 December 1923 for Rowland Berkeley, Chairman of the Picture Committee, seen here directing a hang.

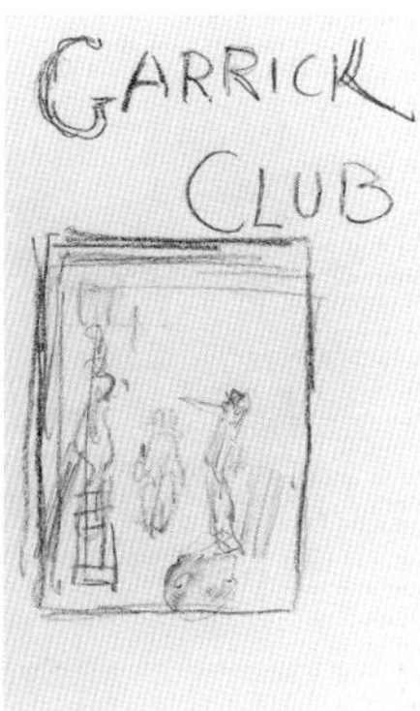

63

ROWLAND BERKELEY

Sir Alfred Munnings

Black chalk and pencil
on wove paper 27 x 16.3 (sight)
INSCR: 'GARRICK/CLUB'
(black chalk t.c.)
INV: Not listed
PROV: Unknown
REL: See No. 62

First sketch for No. 62 above, showing the placing of the three figures. There is a head of Berkeley in pencil to the left (inverted).

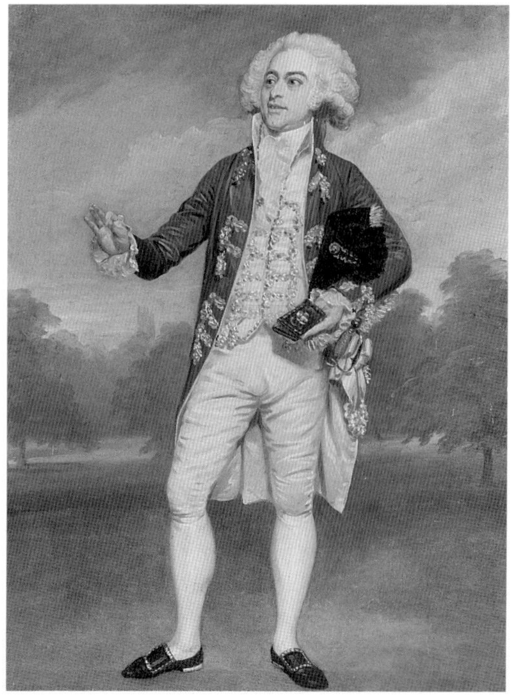

64

JOHN BERNARD

as Jack Meggot in *The Suspicious Husband*
by Benjamin Hoadley

Samuel De Wilde

Oil on canvas 36.2 x 26.7
INV: Mathews 386; RW/CKA 235
PROV: John Bell; Charles Mathews
EXH: 1833 London (386)
ENGR: John Corner for Bell's British Library
12 November 1791, line 11.5 x 8, pub. Bell's *British Theatre* (1797), vol 4, with quotation: Bel. "Dead, pray who was the gentleman?" J. Meg. "This gentleman was my monkey Sir."'; Maguire for Jones's *British Theatre* pub. Wm. Jones, Dublin, 1794, line 11.1 x 7.6; Anon. printed for C. Cooke 20 January 1808, pl. to *British Drama* (1817), line 12 x 7.5

The scene is set in St James's Park, Act 1, scene 3. In the left distance are the west towers of Westminster Abbey. Frankly and Bellamy, in amorous pursuit of Clarinda and Jacintha, meet Frankly's friend Jack Meggot, a dilettante who has just returned from Rome. One of his Roman prizes was the monkey Otho, who has died after breaking a great deal of china and gnawing Meggot's Spanish leather shoes. Meggot wears black shoes, white hose, pink breeches, a green coat lined in pink, a pink waistcoat, and a white stock with frills.

Benjamin Hoadley's comedy was first performed at Covent Garden on 12 February 1747, with Garrick (in his only season at that theatre) as Ranger and Mrs Pritchard as Clorinda. Bernard's first performance as Jack Meggot was at Covent Garden on 2 January 1788, and he had played the role 10 times by 8 June 1791. But at the performance closest to the date of the engraving after De Wilde's painting, at Covent Garden on 16 September 1791, the part was taken by Thomas Marshall.

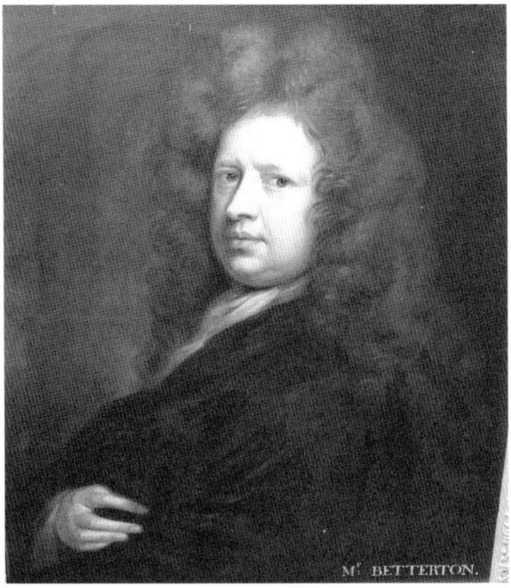

65
THOMAS BETTERTON

Sir Godfrey Kneller

Oil on canvas 74.3 x 61
INSCR: 'MR: BETTERTON' (yellow paint b.r.)
INV: RW/CKA 474; Gift 327
PROV: Presented by 10 members, 1907
ENGR: R. Williams pub. E. Cooper, mezzotint 28.6 x 23.8 (oval); Michael Vandergucht as frontispiece to Betterton's *Life* pub. Robert Goshing 1710, line 16.8 x 10.1 (and in oval frame on pedestal); approximately 10 others of later date
REL: Knole 165, oil on canvas 76.2 x 63.5; NPG 752, oil on canvas 76.2 x 64.8 (studio); Theatre Museum (TM3), oil on canvas 29 x 23; Scone Palace, oil on canvas 76.2 x 63.5 (copy by Alexander Pope)

Of the two types of portrait of Thomas Betterton attributed to Sir Godfrey Kneller, the first is known only in a single example, at Knole. This picture, which Oliver Millar has attributed to Charles Jervas, is inscribed and dated 1708. The second type is known in several versions; the best is at Knole, but No. 65 is also of high quality. The version in the NPG is definitely a studio copy; that in the Theatre Museum is probably copied from Williams's mezzotint; and the Mansfield version is a late 18th-century copy by the actor–painter Alexander Pope.

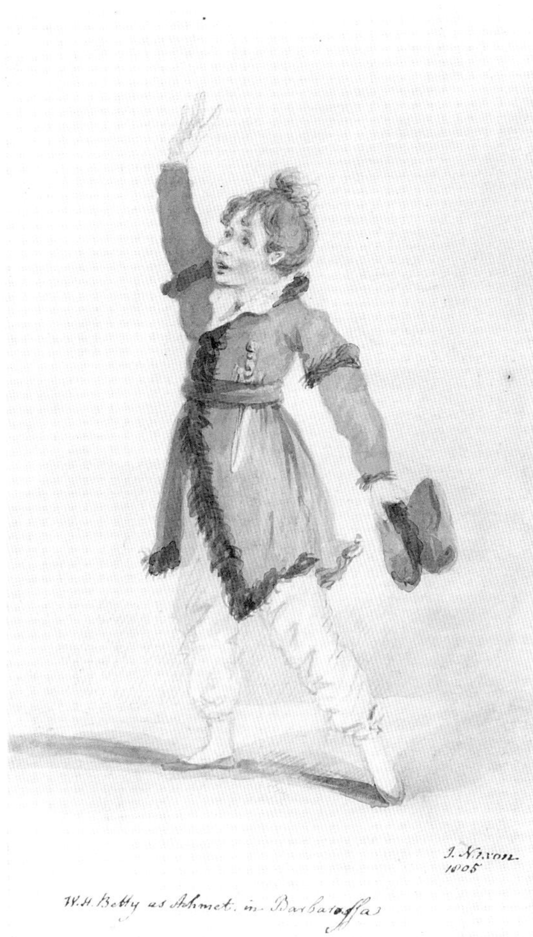

66
WILLIAM BETTY as Achmet
in *Barbarossa or The Freedom of Algiers*
by Dr John Brown

John Nixon

Pencil and watercolour on wove paper 19.4 x 11.5
INSCR: 'J. Nixon/1805' (pen and black ink b.r.); 'W. H. Betty as Achmet in Barbarossa' (pen and black ink b.c.)
INV: Not listed
PROV: John Nixon, *Dramatic Annals*, 2: 440a

Master Betty wears red slippers, white pantaloons, and a long brown tunic edged in fur, with a gold-hilted dagger in his belt.

Dr Brown's tragedy was first performed at Drury Lane on 17 December 1754. The 14-year-old Master Betty played Achmet for his first London performance, at Covent Garden on 1 December 1804.

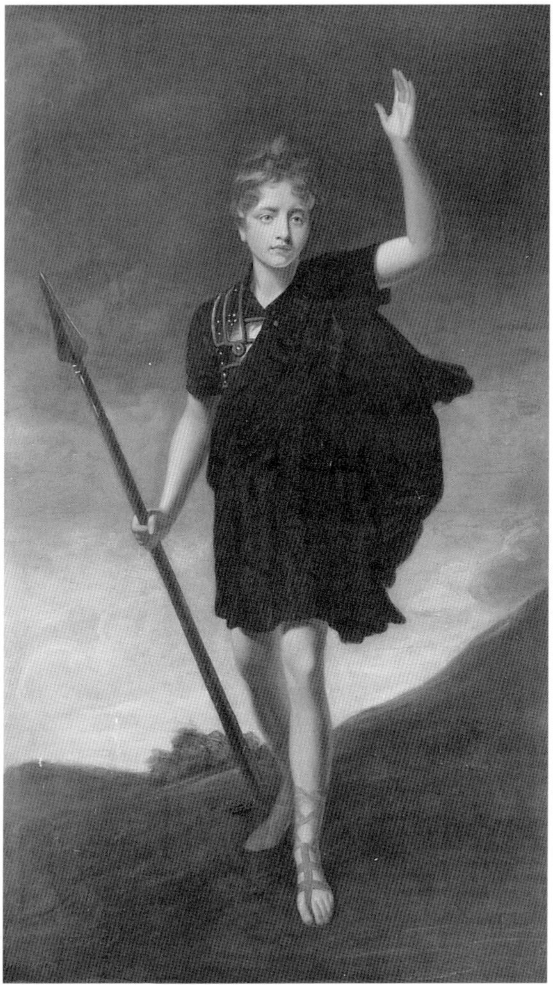

67*

WILLIAM BETTY

as Young Norval

in *Douglas*

by John Home

John Opie

Oil on canvas 204.4 x 129.5
INV: Mathews 77; RW/CKA 431
PROV: Thomas Harris; Harris sale, Robins 12 July 1819 (30) 'Betty, the Young Roscius, as Norval, original, Northcote'; Charles Mathews
EXH: 1833 London (77)
ENGR: James Heath pub. W.H. Betty &c. 1807, line 50.8 x 33; Kennerley, stipple (h.l.)
REL: NPG 1392, oil on canvas 198.1 x 149 (bequeathed by the sitter's son, 1905); probably the version shown at the R.A. and the version from which the engraving was done
LIT: Patmore, pp. 257–58; Fitzgerald, pp. 144–45; Griffiths, pp. 331–32

Mathews chose for his citation, in Act II, scene I, the most famous speech from one of the most popular plays of the 18th century: 'My name is Norval; / on the Grampian hills / My father feeds his flocks; a frugal swain, / Whose constant cares were to increase his store. / And keep his only son, myself, at home.' The young man has just saved the life of Lord Randolph who is married to Norval's real mother, Lady Randolph. She has not seen her son since the day of his birth. Master Betty, holding a spear in his right hand, strides over the Scottish moors in sandals, a green kilt, silver body armour edged in gold, and a billowing blue cloak.

In some ways, Master Betty, the 14-year-old prodigy, was a particularly apt choice for Young Norval. His pubescent looks matched the description given by Glenalvon, the villain of the play, in Act III: 'Norval, I'm told, has that alluring look, / 'Twixt man and woman, which I have observ'd / To charm the nicer and fantastic dames, / Who are, like Lady Randolph, full of virtue.'

Home's tragedy was first played in Edinburgh on 14 December 1756 and received its first London performance at Covent Garden on 14 March 1757, when Spranger Barry played Douglas or Young Norval. Master Betty's first London appearance in the role was at Covent Garden on 4 December 1804, and he acted it for his début at Drury Lane on 10 December 1804. The NPG picture was probably the original version, commissioned by Thomas Parker, of Browsholme Hall in Lancashire, who also commissioned the Northcote full-length portrait of Master Betty as Hamlet, now at Stratford-upon-Avon.

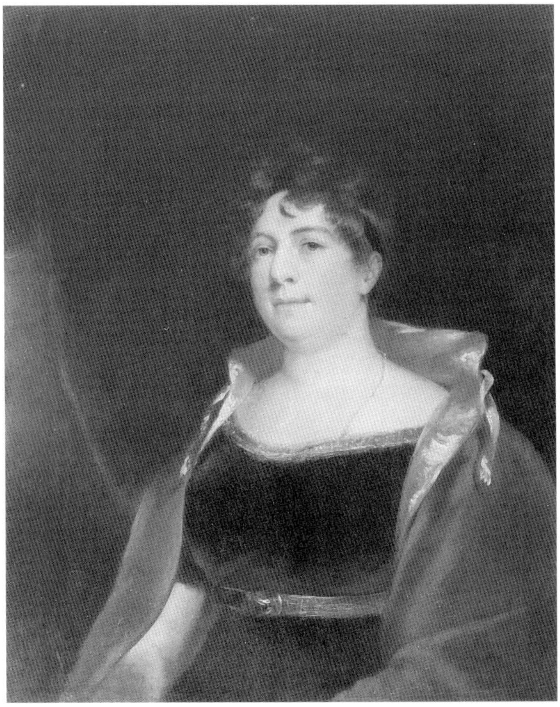

68

ELIZABETH BILLINGTON

John James Masquerier

Oil on canvas 76.5 x 63
INV: Mathews 162; RW/CKA 345
PROV: Charles Mathews
EXH: 1813 R.A. (723); 1833 London (162)
LIT: Fitzgerald, p. 218; R.M. See, *Masquerier and his Circle* (1922), pp. 85, 134, 181, pl. XXIV (t.r.)

Mrs Billington wears a dark blue velvet frock with a gold band around the bustline, a gold belt, and a gold chain round her neck. Her red velvet cloak is lined in white satin.

Masquerier produced three portraits of Mrs Billington; the other two were in pastel, drawn in 1801 and 1802. R.M. See claims that the first of these, owned by M. Jaselman in 1922, is in costume, but there seems to be little evidence for this.

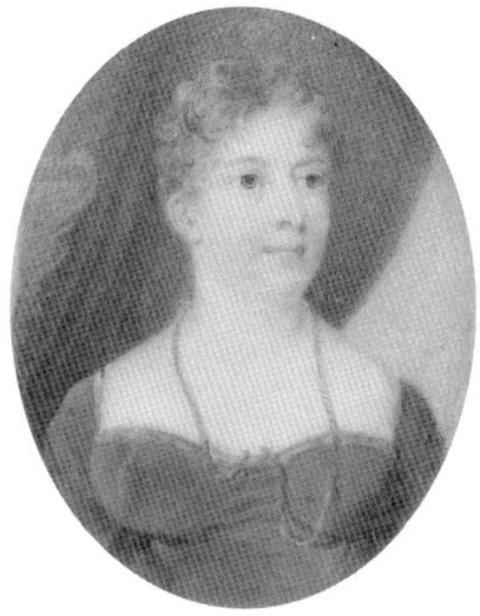

69

ELIZABETH BILLINGTON

Alexander Pope

Miniature watercolour on ivory 6.4 x 4.8 (oval)
INV: Mathews 319 (artist unknown); RW 427M (Elizabeth Farren); CKA 427M (Unknown Lady and artist unknown)
PROV: Charles Mathews
EXH: 1833 London (319)
ENGR: M. Greatbach, after a drawing by George Perfect Harding pub. Richard Bentley 1838, stipple and line 6.7 x 4.5, inscr: 'From a Miniature by Pope in the possession of the Garrick Club'

The sitter wears a crimson velvet dress trimmed with gold. The drapery is green.

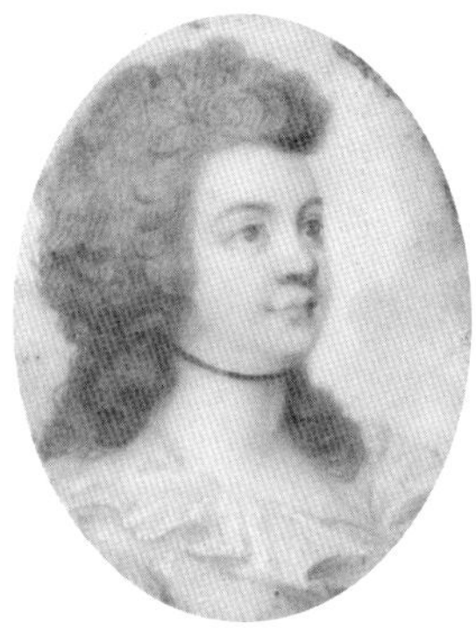

70

CHRISTINA ANN BIRCH

Richard Cosway (?)

Miniature watercolour on ivory 4.3 x 3.3 (oval)
INV: GCL 743; Gift 899
PROV: Bequeathed by Mrs Lisa Puckle in memory of her father, Sir Nevil Macready, 1983

Christina Ann Birch was the mother of William Charles Macready. She married William Macready Snr (1755–1829) in June 1786.

Eds: The attribution to Cosway is perhaps less likely than one to Nathaniel Plimer (1757–1822) or Samuel Shelley (1750/6–1808).

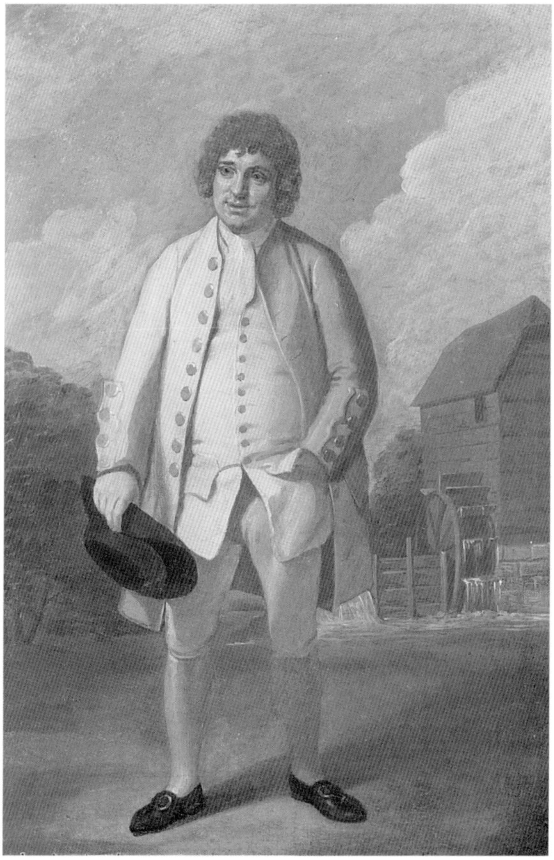

71
THOMAS BLANCHARD
as Ralph
in *The Maid of the Mill*
by Isaac Bickerstaffe

Samuel De Wilde

Oil on canvas 36.5 x 28.2
INV: Mathews 374; RW/CKA 258
PROV: John Bell; Charles Mathews
EXH: 1833 London (3); 1951 London (11); 1971 Northampton (5)
ENGR: J. Thornthwaite for Bell's British Library 4 January 1791, line 10.8 x 8 ('De Wilde del ad vivam'), pub. Bell's *British Theatre* (1797), vol 8; William S. Leney, printed for J. Bell, 29 May 1792, stipple 22.8 x 17.8 (inscr: 'Engraved by Leney, from the original Picture which was painted from life by De Wilde, / from the Maid of the Mill by Bickerstaffe, / in the Celebrated Edition of Bell's British Theatre, which is now publishing Periodically'), with quotation 'There's no harm in putting a civil question be there? Why you look as cross and ill-natured –'
REL: See No. 72

The quotation on the 1792 engraving is from Act II, scene 10, in which Ralph talks to Fanny, the gypsy girl who hopes to marry him. She has been assisting Mervin in his amorous pursuit of Theodosia, and Ralph asks where he is. However, this scene takes place in front of 'a view of Lord Aimworth's house, and improvements; a seat under a tree, part of the garden wall, with a Chinese pavilion over it'. John Inigo Richards, who created the original scenery for *The Maid of the Mill*, painted a scene with the mill (versions: Yale Center for British Art and Sotheby's, 27 June 1973, lot 33). The original version by Richards is probably the larger picture at Frampton Court, Gloucestershire. The text for Act I, scenes 1 to 5 calls for a rural prospect, with a mill at work. A house on one side of the stage and the barn on the other side are visible in Richards's painting but not in De Wilde's, which shows only the mill with the waterwheel and mill-pond. Blanchard as Ralph wears black shoes with gold buckles, white hose, yellowish breeches, a cream coat and waistcoat, and a white stock with flaps. At his side he holds a hat in his right hand.

Bickerstaffe's comic opera, with music selected by the author in collaboration with Samuel Arnold, was first performed at Covent Garden on 31 January 1765, when Charles Dibdin created the part of Ralph. Blanchard was playing Ralph at Covent Garden when De Wilde painted his picture. He first acted the role on 12 December 1789 and his fifth and final performance was on 17 April 1790.

The inscription on the original engraving suggests that the plate was taken from a drawing rather than the present painting. It is one of only four plates similarly inscribed in the second edition of Bell's *British Theatre*. There are also oil versions of the other three in the Garrick Club: Nos. 20, 140 and 657. The drawing may have been No. 72 below.

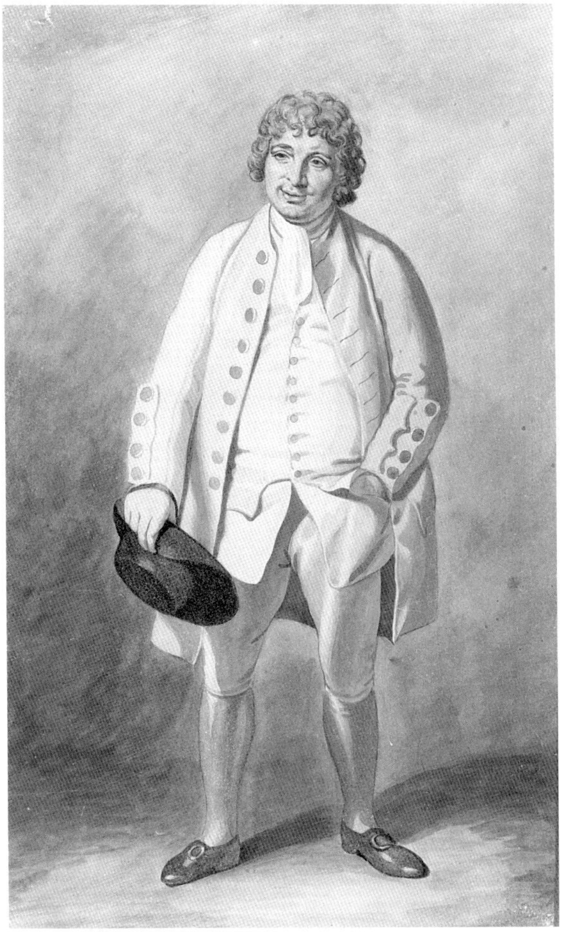

72
THOMAS BLANCHARD
as Ralph in *The Maid of the Mill*
by Isaac Bickerstaffe

Samuel De Wilde

Pencil and watercolour
on wove paper 37 x 23.5
INV: Mathews 211; RW/CKA 45E
PROV: Charles Mathews
EXH: 1833 London (211); 1975 London (141)
REL: See No. 71

Ralph, in a red wig, wears black shoes, blue stockings, yellowish breeches and coat, a waistcoat in faded pink, and a white stock.

There is a possibility that this drawing was preparatory to Thornthwaite's engraving rather than the painting, No. 71. This is the only De Wilde drawing that can be associated with the 1797 edition of Bell's *British Theatre*. There are oil versions for all four plates inscribed 'De Wilde del...' They are all in the Garrick Club: Nos. 20, 71, 140 and 657.

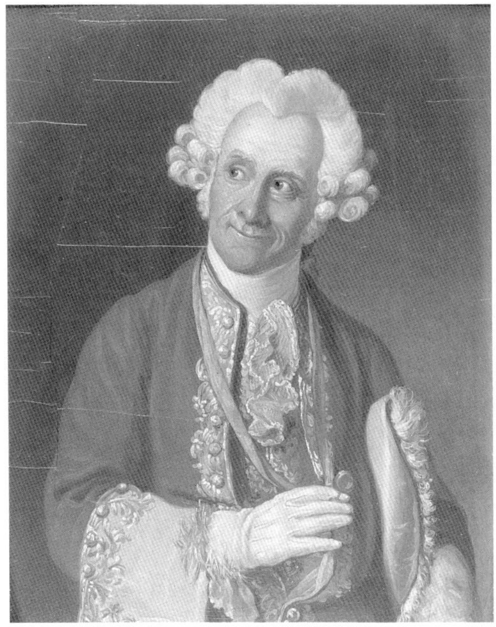

73
WILLIAM BLANCHARD
as the Marquis de Grand Château
in *The Cabinet* by Thomas John Dibdin

Samuel De Wilde

Oil on panel 25.3 x 20.8
INV: Mathews 139; RW/CKA 234
PROV: Charles Mathews
EXH: 1833 London (139)
ENGR: William Ridley for the *Monthly Mirror*
pub. Vernor & Hood 30 April 1805,
stipple 8.6 x 7.2 (bust in oval)

The scene is Act I, scene 2, the Grand Saloon of the Castle of Count Curvoso, who wishes to marry his daughter to the Marquis, 'a rich old nobleman'. The marquis enters 'most elegantly drest' preceded by Mannikin, his Italian page, and followed by six 'Gentlemen in splendid liveries'. The marquis wears a brown jacket lined in pink, with pink cuffs to match. Under his left arm is a pink tricorn hat trimmed with feathers and silver lace. He has a curiously mannered wig and white gloves trimmed with fur. Whereas he is shown here about to view his prospective bride through his eyeglass, in the oval bust engraved by Ridley the eyeglass rests on his waistcoat.

Dibdin's three-act comic opera was based on an old ballad called 'The Golden Bull' and was given for the first time at Covent Garden on 9 February 1802, with Blanchard as the original Marquis de Grand Château. The production was given 30 times in its first season. See also Nos. 477 and 750.

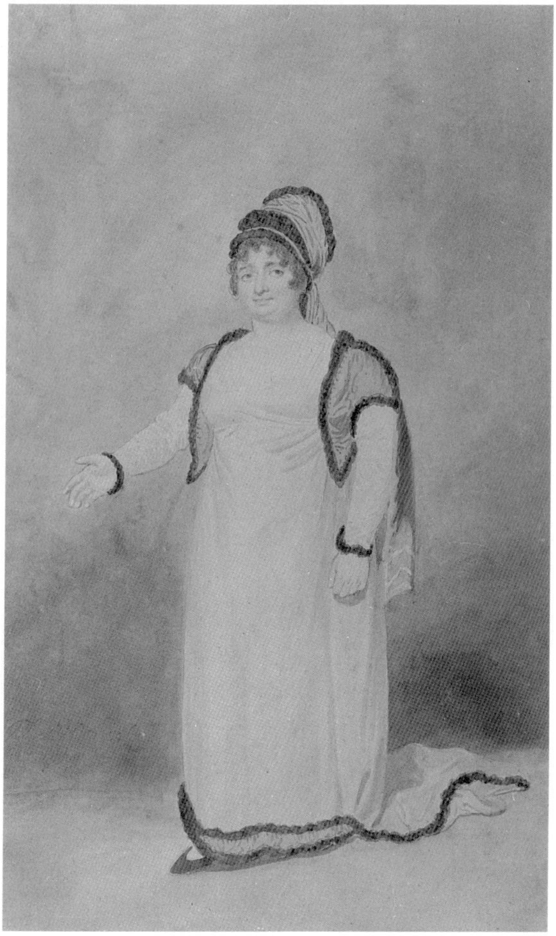

74
MARIA BLAND
as Christine in *Tekeli or The Siege of Montgatz*
by Theodore Edward Hook

Samuel De Wilde

Pencil and watercolour on wove paper 37 x 23.5
INSCR: 'S De Wilde delin / Feby 1808' (pencil b.l.)
INV: RW/CKA 58B
PROV: Charles Mathews (?) (not in catalogue).
[Possibly the portrait of Maria Bland by De Wilde, signed and dated, that was in the Royal Dramatic College sale at Fairbrother, Lye and Palmer on 24 February 1881 (lot 100C)]

Christine is probably shown at her big moment at the beginning of Act II, when she waits for her fiancé Isidore and sings the air 'How sweet are the flowers that grow by yon fountain'. Her fur-trimmed costume is supposed to be Hungarian. It consists of a long-sleeved cream dress with dark brown fur trimming, a little blue short-sleeved jacket edged in fur, and a blue hat with a drape decorated with bands of brown fur.

T.E. Hook's melodrama in three acts, with music by James Hook, was based on Pixérécourt's *Tekeli; ou, le siège de Montgatz*, first seen in Paris on 29 December 1803. The English version opened at Drury Lane on 24 November 1806. The scenery, designed by Thomas Greenwood, in front of which Christine sings, is described in unusual detail in the stage directions: 'An interior view of the Mill of Kebe – in front a Barn filled with the implements of husbandry, beyond is a court-yard bounded by a brick wall two feet high, behind which runs the river Torza, on the left in the third wing a water mill, beyond the mill a low wooden bridge runs from the second wing on the right to the last wing on the left, before the termination of the bridge on the right a windmill with a storehouse beneath, in the back at the supposed distance of three miles is the fortress of Montgatz on a rock, the mills are both discovered in motion and continue during the scene – In the front two or three barrels.'

Mrs Bland was the original Christine (the Miller's Daughter), with Wroughton as her father, Elliston as Count Tekeli, Miss Duncan as Alexina (the Heroine of Montgatz) and Charles Mathews as Bras-de-fer. The piece was popular, receiving over 50 performances in its first season.

This watercolour and No. 109 were assumed by Walters and Adams to have come from Mathews's collection because they had been framed with groups of watercolours that were certainly from that source. The accepted identification comes from the labelling given to the drawings at some point in the 19th century. The sitter in No. 74 is certainly Mrs Bland, and the 'Hungarian' costume suggests that the identification of the part is also correct.

75
MARIA BLAND
as Madame Belgarde in *Monsieur Tonson*
by William Thomas Moncrieff

Samuel De Wilde

Pencil and watercolour on wove paper
37 x 23.5
INV: Mathews 310; RW/CKA 59C
PROV: Charles Mathews
EXH: 1833 London (310)
ENGR: Robert Cooper for Terry's *British Theatrical Gallery* pub. H. Berthoud Jnr. 20 April 1822, stipple 19.5 x 14.3

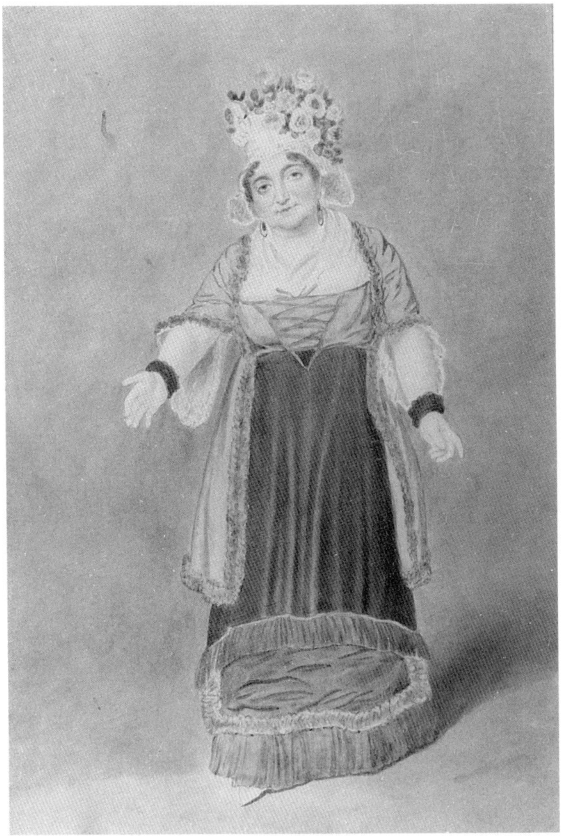

75 *Maria Bland as Madame Belgarde*

Mme Belgarde plays a minor role in *Monsieur Tonson*, as housekeeper to M. Morbleu, a French perruquier who lives in Seven Dials. Mathews has chosen to identify Mme Belgarde's first entrance in Act I, scene 2: 'Exterior of Monsieur Marbleu's House and Shop in the Seven Dials – A Watch Box at one corner. Night.' Morbleu enters and knocks at the door of his shop. The door is opened by Mme Belgarde, and Morbleu tells her: 'Que tu es charmante ma chère Mme Belgarde.' She replies coyly. A more likely moment is perhaps the opening of Act II, scene I, in which Mme Belgarde is discovered alone on stage in Marbleu's shop and sings an air, 'Partant pour la Syria', which begins 'Oh France, beloved native land'.

Mme Belgarde's costume consists of a grey, green-fringed skirt over a paler green dress with green fringes and pink frills. The yellow bodice has yellow strapwork and the yellow jacket is edged in pink frills and lined in white. Her flowerpot hat is trimmed with pink roses.

Moncrieff's farce was first performed at Drury Lane on 20 September 1821, with Mrs Bland as Mme Belgarde. There were 44 performances during the first season.

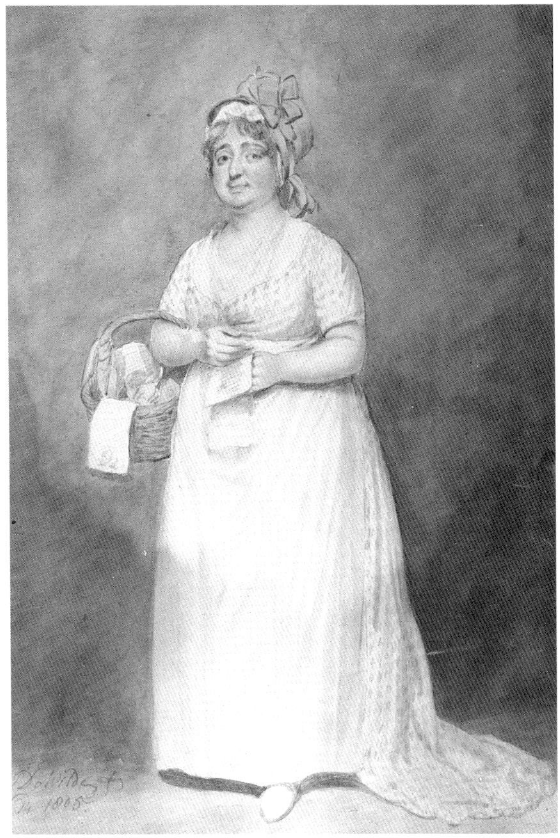

76

MARIA BLAND

as Sally Shamrock in *The Shipwreck*

by Samuel James Arnold

Samuel De Wilde

Pencil and watercolour on wove paper 37 x 23.5

INSCR: 'S De Wilde f / Nr 14 1805' (black chalk b.l.)

INV: Mathews 235; RW/CKA 69C

PROV: Charles Mathews

EXH: 1833 London (235)

ENGR: Richard Cooper for Cawthorn's *Minor British Theatre* pub. John Cawthorn 31 January 1807, stipple 12 x 7.6 (with landscape background)

The scene is Act I, scene 4, with a view of the beach. Sally Shamrock, 'an Irish Girl, with a basket of various articles on her Arm', enters and talks about the previous night's shipwreck. She thinks her lover is drowned but determines to marry 'as soon as I can get any body to have me'. According to Oxberry's 1820 edition of the play, Sally's costume should consist of a 'Coloured open gown, stiff petticoat, apron and straw hat'. In the drawing (which has a plain grey background) she has a dress of blue and white check, with a long white apron, and a straw bonnet with a blue ribbon.

Arnold's comic opera, with music by his father, Dr Samuel Arnold, was first performed at Drury Lane on 10 December 1796 with Mrs Bland as Sally Shamrock. The first performance at the Haymarket, on 23 August 1798, was given as part of Mrs Bland's benefit, when she added extra variety to the evening by singing 'There stood Jones'.

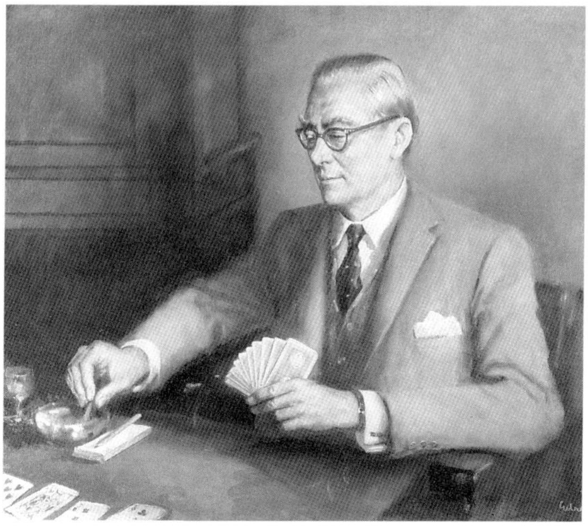

77
VISCOUNT BLEDISLOE

John Gilroy

Oil on canvas 63.2 x 76
INSCR: 'Gilroy' (grey paint b.r.)
INV: GCL 718; Gift 834
PROV: Presented by the artist, 1969

Viscount Bledisloe was a member of the Garrick from 1959 until his death in September 1979. Wearing a grey suit, he is seated at one of the Club's card tables, stubbing out a cigarette before taking a sip of his Beaumes de Venise.

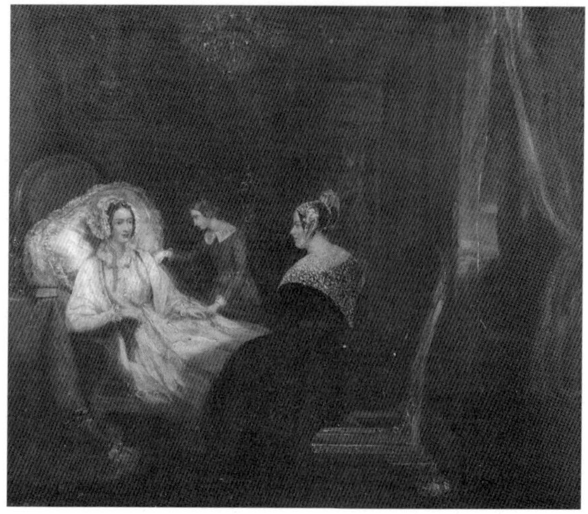

78
LADY BLESSINGTON
and her niece

Alfred Count D'Orsay (attr.)

Oil on canvas 49.5 x 59.7
INSCR: 'HOLY BIBLE' (on book on table at l.)
INV: CKA 653; Gift 670
PROV: Presented by Michael Sadleir, 1948

Adams records: 'This painting was found in a shop in Hertfordshire, and named as above when offered to the donor, whose great knowledge of both Lady Blessington and Count D'Orsay leads him to believe it is correctly named.'

The attribution of the work to D'Orsay is indeed convincing. Lady Blessington was a close friend of Charles James Mathews, the son of Charles Mathews, who spent some time with her and the Comte D'Orsay in Florence. (See introduction to Nos. 479–594.)

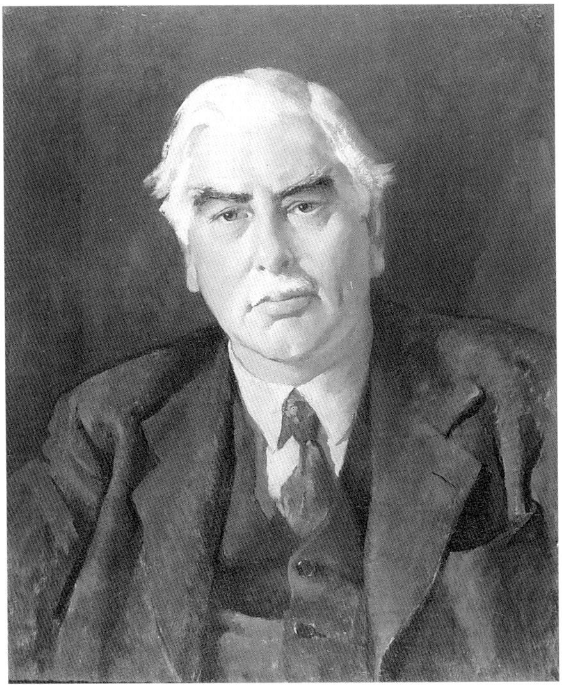

79
GUY BOAS

Elsa Ayres

Oil on panel 59.5 x 49
INSCR: 'ELSA AYRES / '55'
(purple paint tinged with pink t.r.)
INV: GCL 669; Gift 851
PROV: Presented by the sitter's son, 1973

The sitter has white hair and wears a green jacket and waistcoat. Guy Boas was Hon. Librarian of the Garrick Club from 1952 to 1960 and a member from 1943 until his death in 1966. He wrote *The Garrick Club (1831–1947)*, published by the Club in 1948.

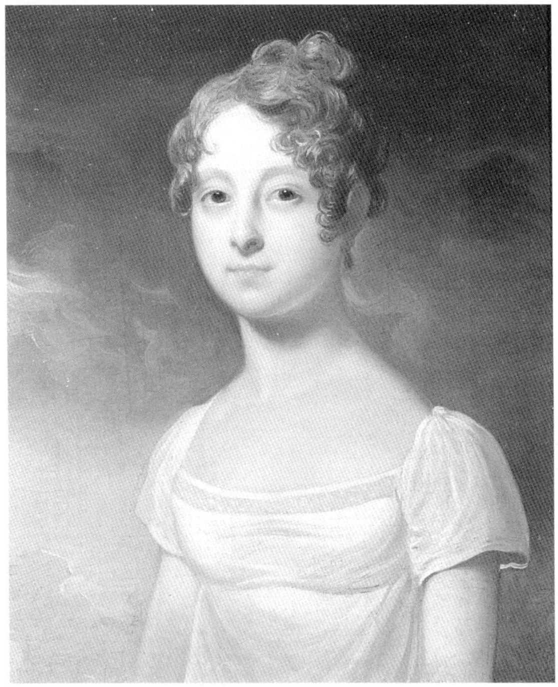

80
MARY CATHERINE BOLTON

Samuel De Wilde

Oil on panel 23 x 18.2
INV: Mathews 350; RW/CKA 204
PROV: Charles Mathews
EXH: 1833 London (350); 1971 Northampton (21)
ENGR: H.R. Cook pub. H.R. Cook 20 September 1813, stipple and line 11.3 x 9.5
INSCR: 'MISS BOLTON / Engraved by H.R. Cook from the original Picture by De Wilde / in the possession of Charles Mathews Esq.'
The same plate was issued 10 December 1813 with the title altered to 'Lady Thurlow'; a reissue with a different title, 'Countess Thurlow, late Miss Bolton', was published by I.W.H. Payne, 1814.

The sitter wears a short-sleeved white dress decorated with a band of pink across the bustline.

A popular actress in the first two decades of the 19th century, she married Edward, 2nd Baron of Thurlow.

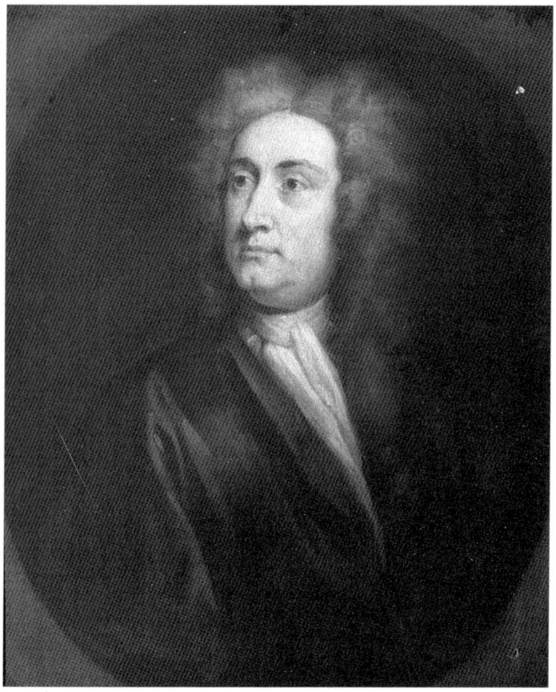

81
BARTON BOOTH

John Vanderbank

Oil on canvas 77 x 64
INV: Mathews 87 or 118 (artist unknown); RW/CKA 36
PROV: Charles Mathews
EXH: 1833 London (87 or 118)
ENGR: Gerard Vandergucht as frontispiece to Booth's *Life and Poems* (1733), line 15.6 x 8.9 (to r., oval on pedestal); Anon. for the *Universal Magazine* pub. J. Hinton, line 15.9 x 9.5
LIT: Patmore, p. 272 (as by Vanderbank)

Booth, shown half-length in oval, wears a brown coat, a white shirt and stock, and a grey wig.

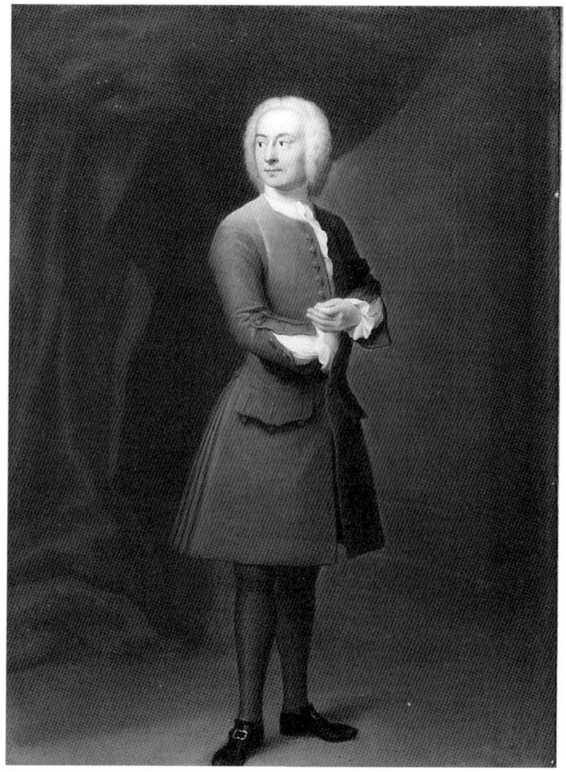

82
BARTON BOOTH (?)

Unknown Artist

Oil on copper 34.3 x 24.8
INV: Mathews 87 or 118; RW/CKA 430
PROV: Charles Mathews
EXH: 1833 London (87 or 118)
ENGR: E. Smith from a drawing by George Clint pub. W. Walker 1 September 1822, line 10.1 x 7.6 (h. l.)

The sitter appears to be quite young, and the costume dates from the mid-18th century. Barton Booth, therefore, is an extremely unlikely candidate for this portrait. Compare to No. 81.

The sitter, standing full-length, wears black shoes and purple-grey hose, breeches and coat.

One of the foremost actors of his day, Booth had a majestic style, but 'seemed afraid of putting into his acting ... humanity' (BD). Among his best roles were Castalio in *The Orphan*, Brutus in *Julius Caesar*, and Valentine in *Love for Love*.

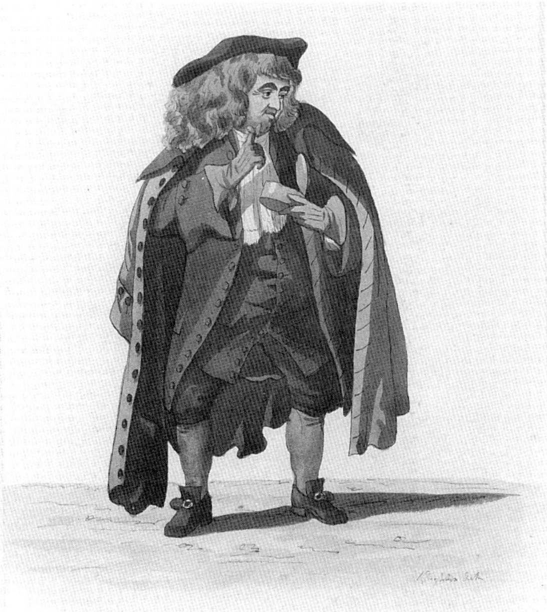

83

COCKRAN JOSEPH BOOTH

as Father Luke in *The Poor Soldier* by John O'Keeffe

Robert Dighton

Pen and grey ink with watercolour
on wove paper 22.2 x 16.5
INSCR: 'R Dighton. del' (pen and grey ink b.r.);
'Pub. Novr–6–1790– by R Dighton Charing Cross'
(pen and grey ink b.c.); 'Mr Booth as Father Luke in the
Poor Soldier.' (pen and brown ink on mount b.c. CM)
INV: RW 554A (artist unknown); CKA 554A
PROV: Charles Mathews (not in catalogue)
ENGR: There is no trace of a print of this subject
published 6 November 1790 or any other date.
If there was one, it is likely to have been similar to the
etching of Dodd as Lord Foppington; see No. 162.
REL: Folger Library (W.b.473, p.85), pen and brown ink
and watercolour, inscr: 'R Dighton del' (b.r.);
'Booth in the Poor Soldier.'

Booth wears grey square-toed shoes, blue stockings, grey breeches, and a grey coat and jacket.

O'Keeffe's comic opera with music by William Shield was first performed at Covent Garden on 4 November 1783. It was an alteration of the same author's comedy *The Shamrock; or, St Patrick's Day*, first given at the Crow Street Theatre, Dublin, on 15 April 1777 and at Covent Garden on 7 April 1783. It was licensed as *The Shamrock; or, The Anniversary of St Patrick, A Pastoral Romance*. Richard Wilson was the original Father Luke, and he kept the part until 25 November 1785, when Booth played it for the first time. Booth acted the role 24 times – all at Covent Garden – the last time being 16 March 1789.

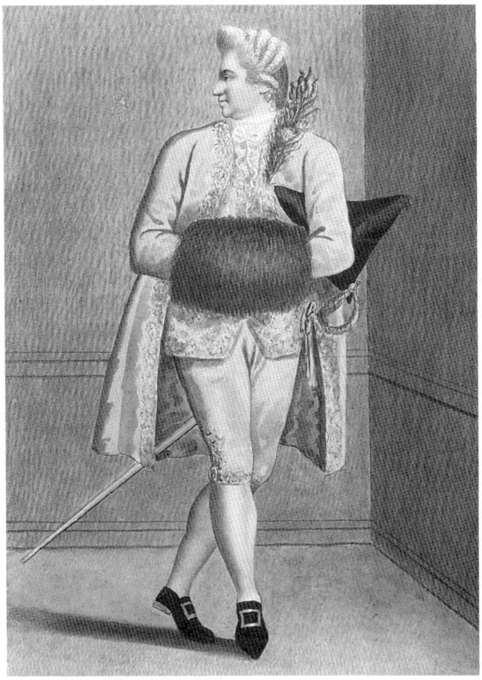

84

COCKRAN JOSEPH BOOTH

as Lord Froth in *The Double Dealer*
by William Congreve

Sylvester Harding (after James Roberts)

Pencil and watercolour with some black ink
on wove paper 24.3 x 15.8
INV: Not listed
PROV: Charles Mathews (Print Collection Vol. IV f.64)
ENGR: D. Reading for Bell's *British Theatre*
1 July 1777, line 13 x 9.2

Lord Froth, 'a solemn coxcomb', is shown in Act III, scene 1, singing the song 'Ancient Phillis has young graces'. There is no reference in the text to either the muff – in which his hands are placed at his waist – or the corsage of pink flowers worn by Booth as Lord Froth. He also wears black shoes, white stockings, pink breeches, a pink-lined blue coat, and a pink waistcoat.

Congreve's comedy was originally performed at Drury Lane in October 1693. It was revived at Covent Garden on 5 January 1776, with Booth as Lord Froth. He repeated the performance on 17 December 1776 then gave three more performances in 1782, on 19 March, 16 April and 25 May. These were the last performances of *The Double Dealer* at Covent Garden in the 18th century.

This is an enlarged and not very good copy of Roberts's drawing. Roberts's drawing was bought by Cooke in the Bell sale at Christie's on 27 March 1793 (lot 3), but its present location is unknown. See also No. 297.

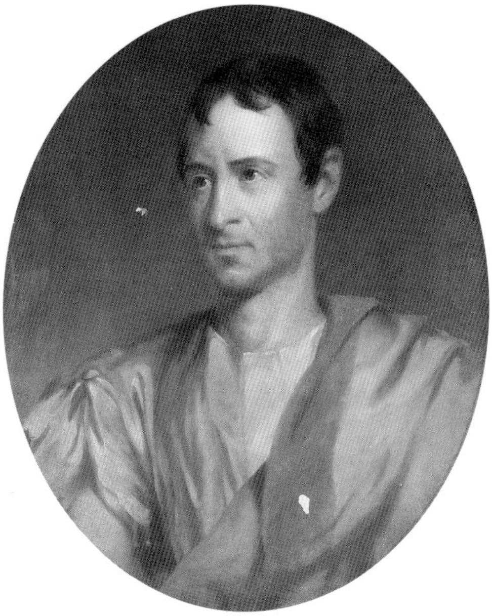

85
JUNIUS BRUTUS BOOTH
as Lucius Junius Brutus in *Brutus or The Fall of Tarquin* by John Howard Payne

Thomas Le Clear (after John Neagle)

Oil on canvas 62.9 x 52.7 (framed in oval)
INV: RW/CKA 89 (as Brutus in 'The Fall of Tarquin; or, The Distressed Lovers' by William Hunt)
PROV: Presented by the sitter's son, Edwin Booth, 1867

A favourite subject with neo-classical painters, Brutus is the noblest of Romans, who puts the honour of Rome before the life of his children. Payne's play ends with the death of his son, Titus.

Brutus is alone on stage on a number of occasions, any one of which might be that evoked in Neagle's portrait. The original, which is in the Museum of the City of New York, is signed and dated 1827 (oil on canvas 66 x 40). Le Clear, who came from New York, exhibited two portraits at the Royal Academy in 1873, one of them (18) being a portrait of Booth's son, Edwin, 'American Tragedian'. Head and shoulders. Junius Brutus Booth wears a buff toga edged with a broad band of red.

Edmund Kean played Brutus in the first production of Payne's tragedy at Drury Lane on 3 December 1818. Booth's first appearance in the part seems to have been at the Royal Coburg early in 1820, when the play was performed on five consecutive nights. Booth's brief engagement at Drury Lane after his first trip to America opened with his Brutus on 8 October 1825. The only other parts he played were Richard III, on 13 October, and Othello, on 17 October.

William Hunt's tragedy was originally given by the Duke of Norfolk's Men in the Merchant Taylors' Hall, York, in 1713. There were no performances in London in the 18th or early 19th centuries.

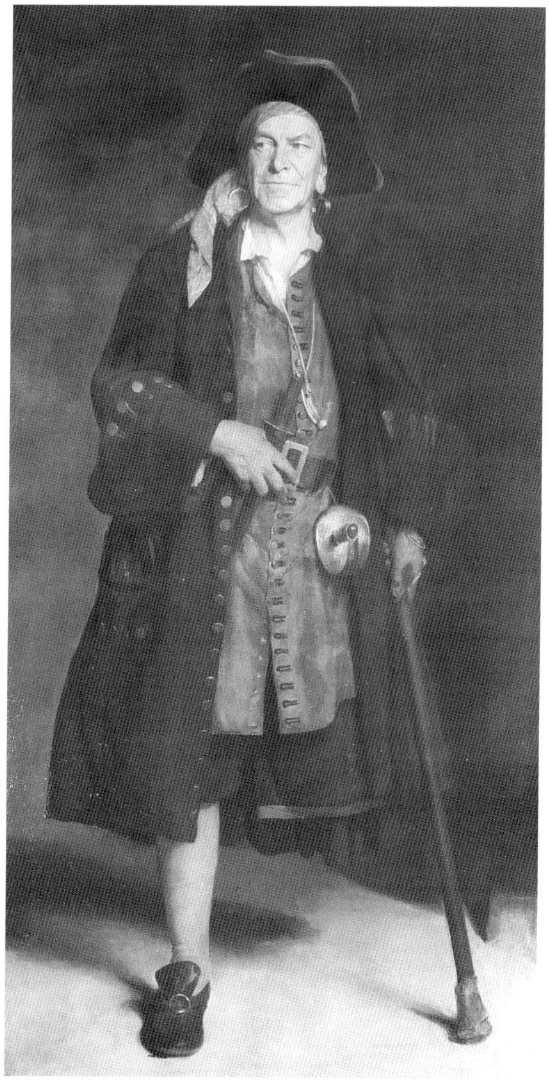

86*
ARTHUR BOURCHIER
as Long John Silver in *Treasure Island* by James Bernard Fagan, after Robert Louis Stevenson

Sir Gerald Kelly

Oil on canvas 200 x 101.6
INV: CKA 649; Gift 650
PROV: Presented by the sitter's widow, 1946
EXH: 1924 R.A. (230)
REL: Private coll., London, oil on canvas 196 x 97.2, inscr: 'Kelly. Aug. 1923' (brown paint b.l.)

Bourchier's costume includes a black tricorn hat, dark blue breeches and coat, a leather jerkin with gold buttons, and a brown belt with a gold buckle. He is armed with a dagger and a sword, and has a boatswain's whistle on a band around his neck. A red and yellow handkerchief is tied around his head under a black tricorn hat. He leans on a crutch, to support himself standing on his one leg.

The other version of the picture, which has been left unfinished in the bottom right corner, is clearly the original. However, despite being much more forceful, the somewhat demonic glare given to the character seems not to have appealed to the sitter, and the more subdued Garrick Club version was the one accepted by Bourchier and shown at the Royal Academy.

Fagan's adaptation of Stevenson's romance of 1883 was first given at the Strand Theatre (which was managed by Arthur Bourchier) on 23 December 1922, with Bourchier as Long John Silver. The Christmas run was extended to 7 April 1923 and the play was revived the following Christmas and again in 1925 and 1926. Bourchier retained his original part in all the revivals.

Arthur Bourchier became a member of the Garrick Club in 1885.

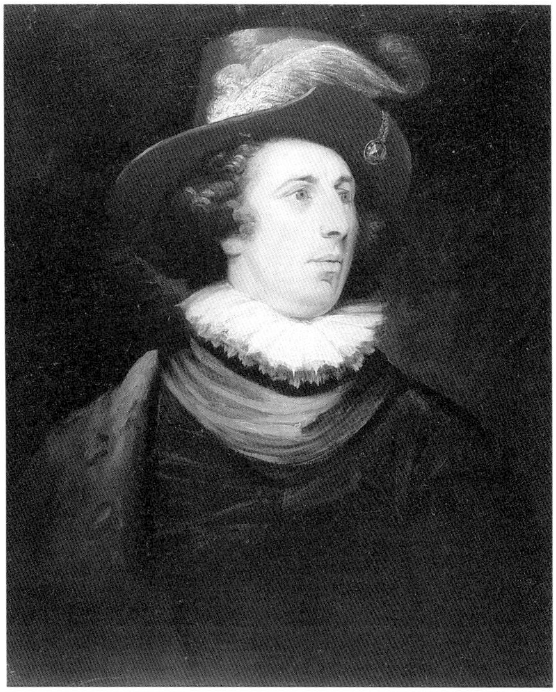

87 *Wright Bowden as Robin Hood*

87

WRIGHT BOWDEN

as Robin Hood

in *Robin Hood or Sherwood Forest*

by Leonard Macnally

Gainsborough Dupont (?)

Oil on canvas 76 x 63.5

INV: Mathews 33; RW/CKA 245

PROV: Charles Mathews

EXH: 1833 London (33); 1982–83 London (132)

LIT: Hayes 1968

Robin Hood is betrothed to Clorinda, the 'Huntress of Titbury'. In Act II, Clorinda tells Robin to stop 'consuming life and reputation within the sequestered shades of a forest' and fight for his king. Robin replies with the line cited by Mathews, 'You know all the wrongs I have suffered' – at having been banished on a false accusation, and having had Clorinda forced from his arms. Bowden wears a brown doublet, a fur-trimmed cloak with a red band round his neck, and a brown hat with a white plume.

Macnally's comic opera, with music mostly by William Shield, was first performed at Covent Garden on 17 April 1784, with Charles Bannister in the title role. Wright Bowden made his début at Covent Garden in the role on 18 October 1787, and repeated it several times during the season. If this picture relates to the series commissioned by Thomas Harris from Gainsborough Dupont, about 1793, it is likely that it was inspired by the performance on 2 May 1794 (for Incledon's benefit), which marked Bowden's return to London after six years in the provinces.

In his catalogue Mathews attributed the picture to Dupont, but stylistically it differs from the other works by him in the collection, and the attribution must be doubtful. The identity of the sitter is secure, and the picture relates closely to John Raphael Smith's mezzotint of Bowden as Robin Hood, published in 1787.

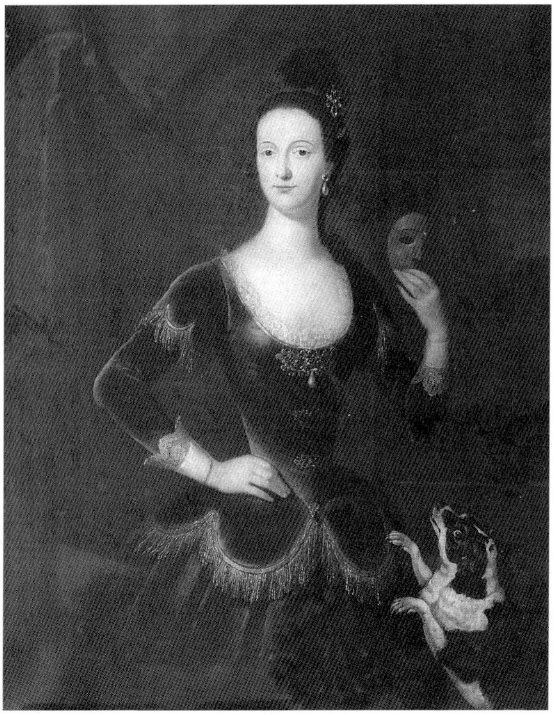

88
Called
ANNE BRACEGIRDLE

Unknown Artist

Oil on canvas 126 x 101 (127 x 103 lining canvas)
INV: Mathews 47; RW 400 (artist unknown); CKA 400 (called Anne Bracegirdle, perhaps by Thomas Bardwell)
PROV: Charles Mathews
EXH: 1833 London (47)
LIT: Fitzgerald, p. 223; Griffiths, pp. 229–30

The sitter wears a blue velvet panniered dress with separate bodice and long sleeves with scalloped lace cuffs. She has a jewel in her hair, from which spouts a black plume.

It is unclear why Mathews should have thought that this was a portrait of Anne Bracegirdle. It shows a lady in masquerade costume and dates from about 1750. This crude piece of work is not really good enough for Thomas Bardwell, who painted a good portrait of David Garrick as Richard III in 1742 (in the Russell-Cotes Art Gallery, Bournemouth).

One of the most splendid tragic actresses of her day, Anne Bracegirdle was regarded as a handsome and tantalising woman, who excelled as Statira in Lee's *The Rival Queens*, Lady Anne in *Richard III*, Desdemona and Ophelia. She also played such comic roles as Araminta in Congreve's *The Old Bachelor* and Millamant in *The Way of the World*.

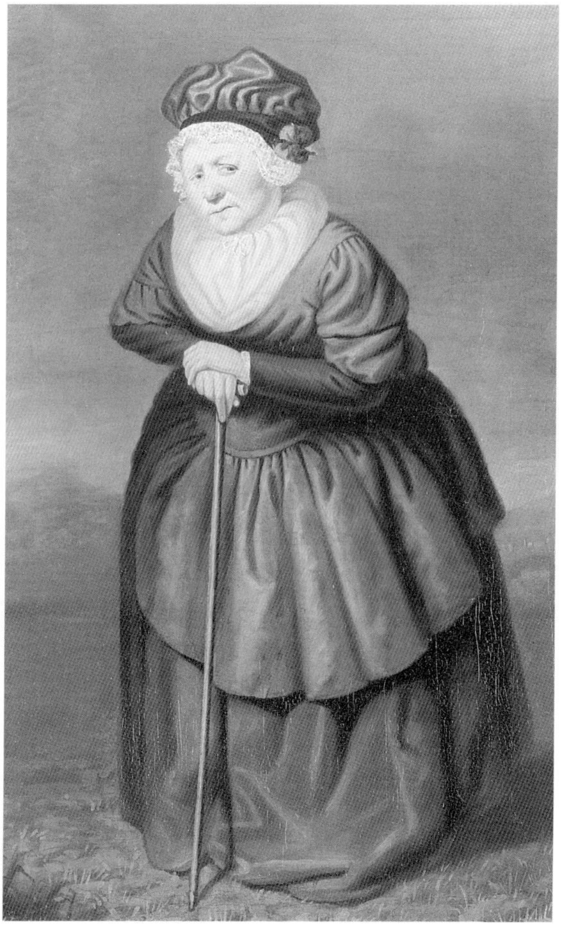

89
MARY BRADSHAW
as Dorcas in *Cymon*
by David Garrick

Thomas Parkinson

Oil on canvas 64.1 x 41.9
INSCR: '...nson Pinxt' (brown paint b.l.)
INV: Mathews 105; RW/CKA 119
PROV: Charles Mathews
EXH: 1833 London (105); 1983 Buxton (19)

Dorcas is a deaf old woman who looks after Sylvia, the heroine of *Cymon*. She appears only in Act III, scene 3. Dorcas sings an air, the burden of which, cited by Mathews, is 'I tremble at seventy-two'. She wears a blue shift over a long-sleeved blue dress, and a blue cap over grey hair.

David Garrick's dramatic romance was based on Dryden's *Cymon and Iphigenia* and had music by Michael Arne. The first performance took place at Drury Lane on 2 January 1767, with Mary Bradshaw as the original Dorcas.

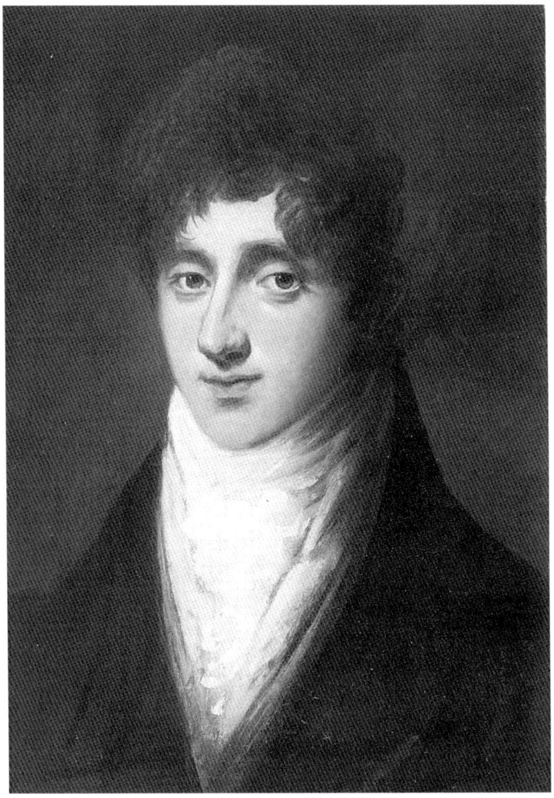

90
JOHN BRAHAM
as Lord Aimworth (?)
in *The Maid of the Mill* by Isaac Bickerstaffe (?)

Thomas Foster (attr.)

Oil on canvas 49.5 x 35.5
INV: Mathews 322 (artist unknown, no part);
RW/CKA 91 (artist unknown, no part)
PROV: Charles Mathews
EXH: 1833 London (322)

There is no doubt about the identity of the sitter for this bust, but the attributions of the artist and role are suggestions based on Thomson's stipple engraving after Thomas Foster's drawing of Braham as Lord Aimworth, published in 1818. The costume is exactly the same in both portraits – a dark coat and a white shirt with ruffs – although this could be seen simply as somewhat elegant everyday dress. Foster, only just entering the R.A. schools in 1818, might easily be the author of this portrait that is so similar to the published drawing.

The flattering juvenile image in the portrait would have pleased the 44-year-old sitter, who was one of the greatest tenors of his time. See also No. 652.

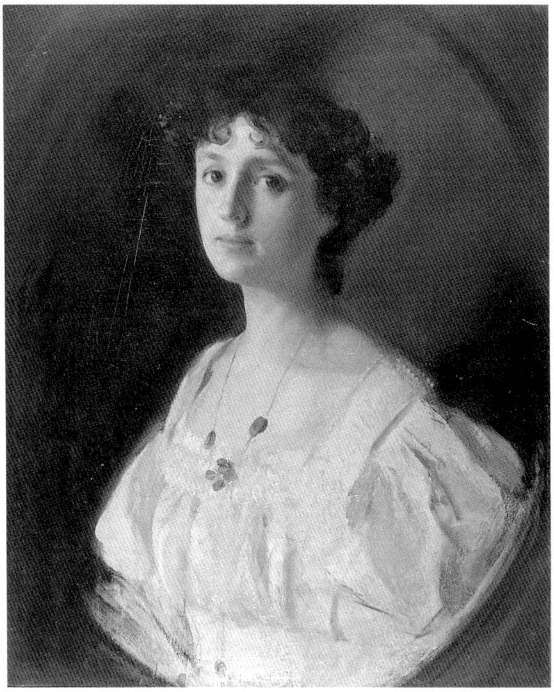

91*
DAME LILIAN BRAITHWAITE

Charles Sims

Oil on canvas 76.5 x 61
INSCR: Handwritten label on verso: 'The Secretary/ The Garrick Club / from James Gunn / frame for portrait of / Lillian Braithwaite'
INV: GCL 677; Gift 737A
PROV: Presented by Joyce Carey, 1954
EXH: 1902 R.A. (489)

Dame Lilian wears a white dress with flounced sleeves and a selection of gold and turquoise jewellery. She is shown in a feigned oval, imitating 17th and 18th century portrait practice.

Made a DBE in 1943, Lilian Braithwaite appeared in numerous new plays and revivals of the classics. She played Abby Brewster in the first London production of *Arsenic and Old Lace*, which opened in 1942 and ran for three years. She was the first wife of the actor Gerald Lawrence (1873–1957); their daughter, the actress Joyce Carey, gave this portrait to the Club.

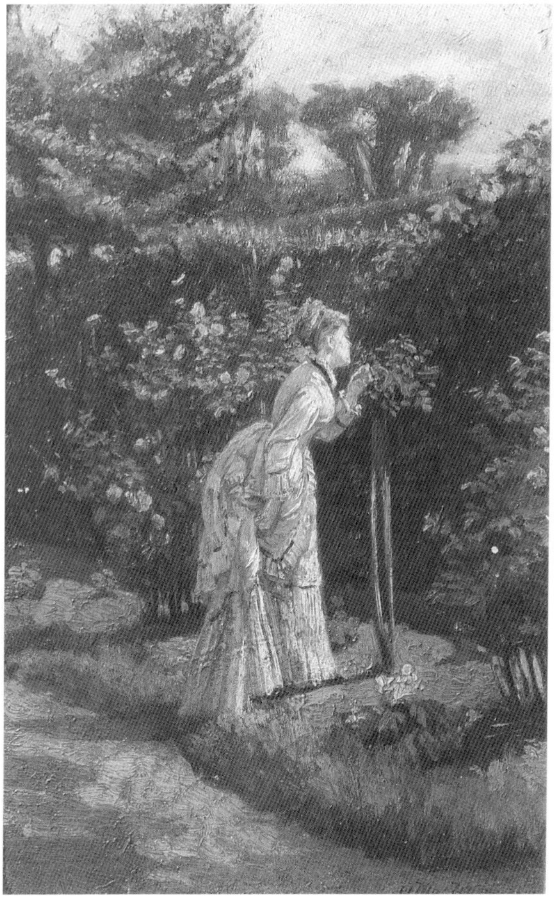

92

MAUD BRANSCOMBE

Alex MacLean

Oil on panel 25.4 x 16.5
INSCR: 'A MacLean 1892' (? brown paint b.r.)
INV: GCL 691; Gift 767
PROV: Bequeathed by William Edward Goodair, 1959

W.E. Goodair bequeathed two oil paintings of Maud Branscombe. The other has disappeared from the Club.

Maud Branscombe, standing full-length and sniffing a rose in a garden, is dressed rather frigidly in a long white dress with bustle and frills at the hem. Her light brown hair is tied back with a blue ribbon.

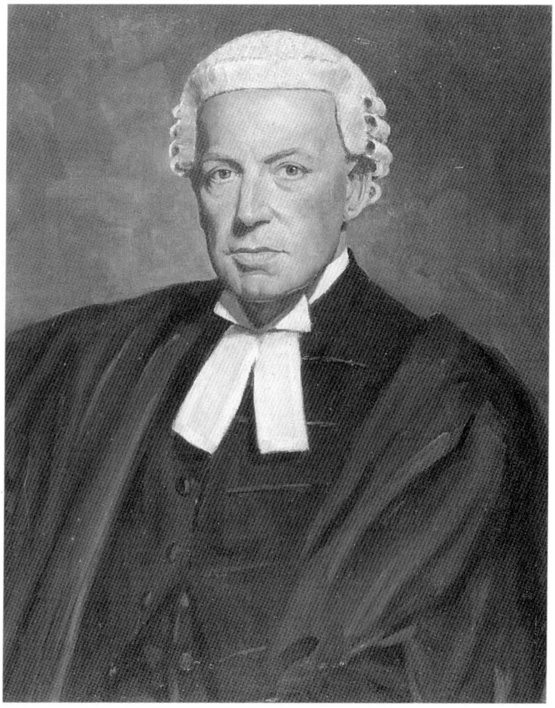

93

CLIVE BROOK

as Sir Walter Gaskany in *The Judge's Story*
by Diana Morgan and Clive Brook,
after Charles Morgan

Maurice Codner

Oil on canvas 66 x 52.5
INSCR: 'CLIVE BROOK 13 / 8 8 53'
(stamped on label on verso)
INV: GCL 731; Gift 869
PROV: Presented by the sitter's widow, 1976

Clive Brook wears a barrister's wig, a grey gown and coat, and a legal collar.

Diana Morgan and Clive Brook's adaptation of Charles Morgan's novel was presented by Clement Scott Gilbert on behalf of New Pembroke Theatre Ltd at the Ashcroft Theatre, Croydon, on 4 May 1964. The production was designed by Jeanette Campbell and directed by Royston Marley. The leading part of the retired judge, Sir Walter Gaskony, was played by Walter Fitzgerald. Clive Brook did not appear in the play, although the picture was presented as 'Portrait of Clive Brook as the Judge in "The Judge's Story" by Maurice Codner R.A.'. Codner died in March 1958, some six years before the play opened.

Brook became a member of the Garrick Club in 1946.

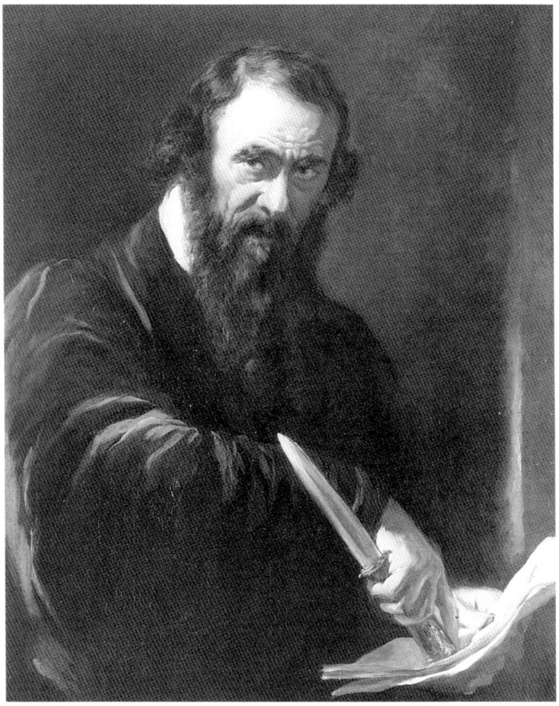

94
GUSTAVUS BROOKE
as Shylock in *The Merchant of Venice*
by William Shakespeare

Unknown Artist

Oil on canvas 87.6 x 67.3
INV: RW/CKA 90; Gift 184
PROV: Presented by Edward Greaves, 1865
EXH: 1964 London [2] (4)

Brooke wears a puce mantle over a black coat. He appears to be portrayed saying: 'I'll have my bond' (Act 3, scene 3).

Brooke gave his first performances of Shylock at the Olympic in 1848. His engagement at that theatre marked his début as a major actor; he also played Hamlet, Richard III, Virginius, Brutus and Sir Giles Overreach.

A bust of Brooke by Watkin D. Jones was shown at the R.A. in 1854 (1405), and another bust by F.B. Tussaud was shown there in 1857 (1285).

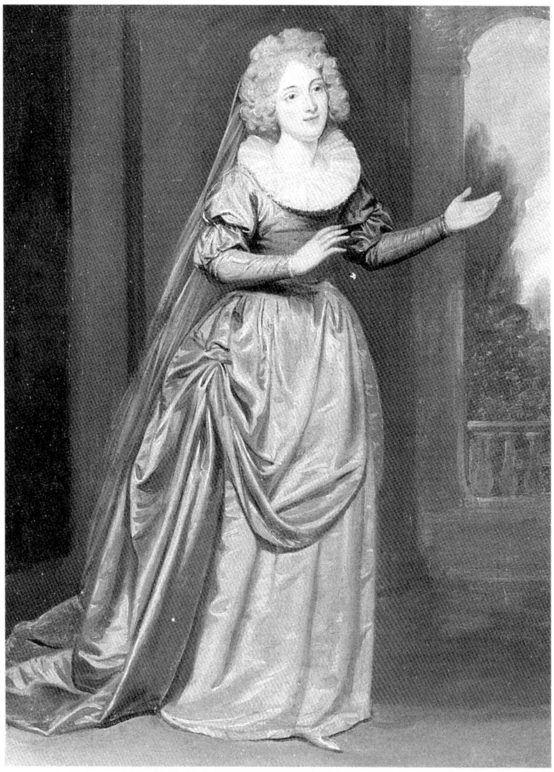

95
MRS BROOKS
as Leonora in *The Revenge*
by Edward Young

Samuel De Wilde

Oil on canvas 37.7 x 28.4
INV: Mathews 80; RW/CKA 241
PROV: John Bell; Charles Mathews Exh: 1833 London (80)
ENGR: J. Chapman for Bell's British Library 9 March 1793, line 10.8 x 8, pub. Bell's *British Theatre* (1797), vol 8, with quotation: 'Your sighs are mine, my Lord, and I shall feel them all' (Act IV)

Mrs Brooks wears a pale blue full-skirted dress with a low ruff and a long gauze veil. Described as tall, with an elegant figure and a beautiful face, Mrs Brooks acted at the Haymarket Theatre from 1786 to 1794, playing innocent young ladies such as Miss Richland in *The Good-Natured Man* and Cecilia in *The Chapter of Accidents*.

Young's tragedy was first performed at Drury Lane on 18 April 1721. Mrs Brooks never played Leonora in London.

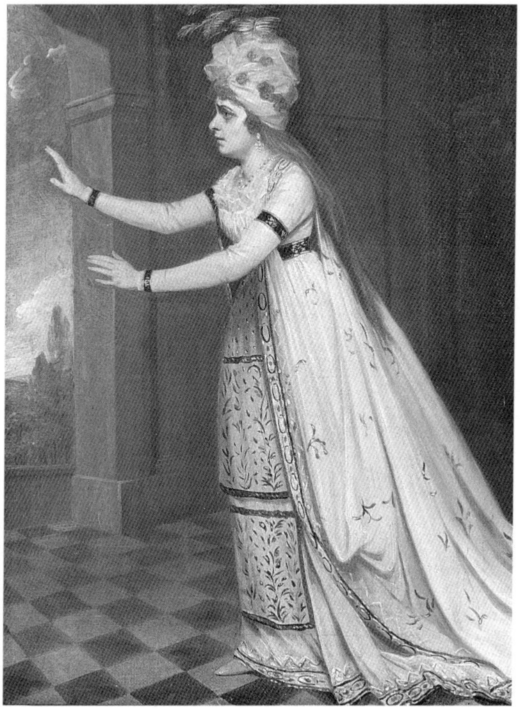

96
ANNE BRUNTON
as Alzira in *Alzira or The Spanish Insult Repented*
by Aaron Hill

Samuel De Wilde

Oil on canvas 35.5 x 27.3
INV: Mathews 91; RW/CKA 457
PROV: John Bell; Thomas Harris; Harris sale, Robins 12 July 1819 (67); Charles Mathews
EXH: 1833 London (457)
ENGR: William S. Leney for Bell's British Library 7 January 1792, line 10.8 x 7.6, pub. Bell's *British Theatre* (1797), vol 7, with the quotation 'By heaven, if 'tis death, I'll follow thee' (Act IV)

The play is set in the city of Lima. Alzira is the daughter of Ezmont, the Indian king of a part of Peru conquered by the Spaniards. She was betrothed to Zamor, another Peruvian king, but believes him dead and has married Don Carlos, the cruel Spanish governor. Alzira stands full-length with her arms outstretched towards an arch that leads outdoors. She wears a white dress, the hem decorated with green circles and red spots, with a panel below the knees embroidered with green foliage and red flowers. On her head is a high eccentric turban with feathers.

Hill's tragedy was first performed at Lincoln's Inn Fields on 18 June 1736. Anne Brunton never essayed the role, and the play was not performed in London after 1759.

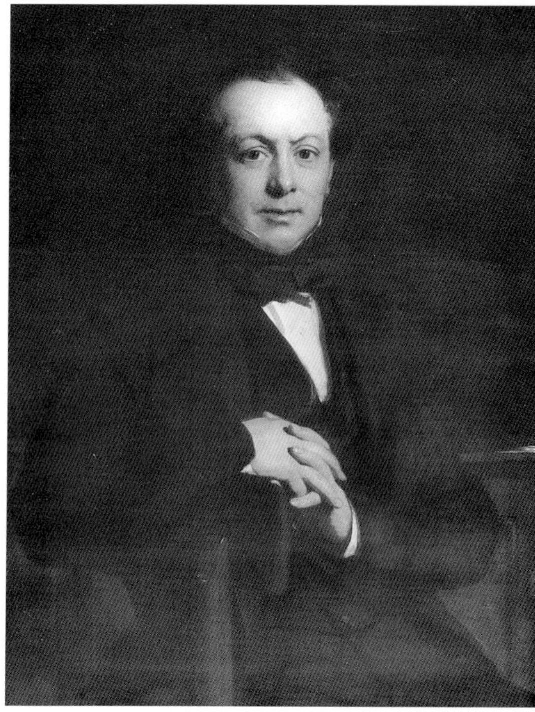

97
JOHN BALDWIN BUCKSTONE

John Prescott Knight

Oil on canvas 88.9 x 68.6
INV: RW/CKA 341; Gift 155
PROV: Presented by the sitter, 1859
EXH: ?1850 R.A. (59) 'John Baldwin Buckstone, Esq, TR, Haymarket'
LIT: *Illustrated Sporting and Dramatic News* 17 June 1876; Herman Dyson, *John Prescott Knight R.A., a catalogue* (1971), No. 132

Buckstone, seated with his hands folded over the back of a chair, wears dark grey trousers and a jacket over a mulberry waistcoat.

This is almost certainly the picture exhibited by Knight at the Royal Academy in 1850.

Buckstone became a member of the Garrick Club in 1854.

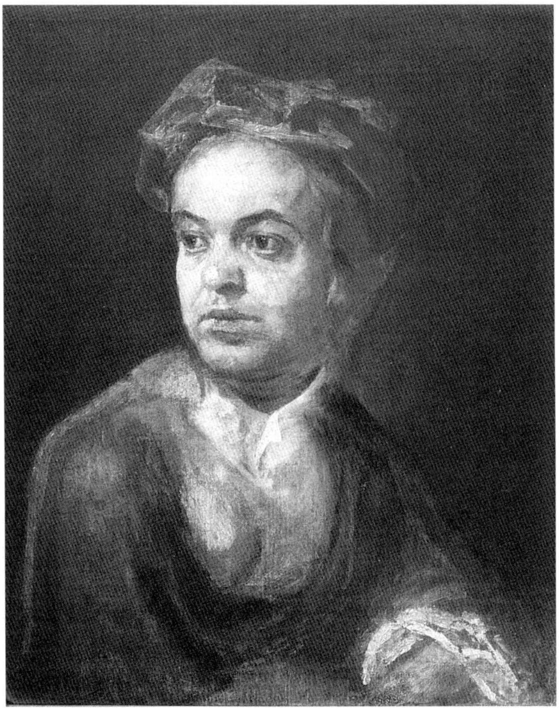

98
CHRISTOPHER BULLOCK

Unknown Artist

Oil on canvas 62 x 52
INV: Mathews 190; RW 383 (by William Hogarth); CKA 383
PROV: H.R. Willett; Charles Mathews
EXH: 1833 London (190); 1951 London (24); 1957 London
ENGR: Charles Hall pub. J. Thane 1781, 10.5 x 8.6
LIT: Austin Dobson, *Hogarth* (1902), p.176

[The head of a man in a smoking cap, whom Mathews thought to be Bullock, has been painted over another portrait, apparently showing a woman in a low-cut bodice, her sleeves having lace flounces at the elbows. It is tempting to believe that Hall's engraving, with its attribution to Hogarth, was taken from a more resolved work than this curious palimpsest.]

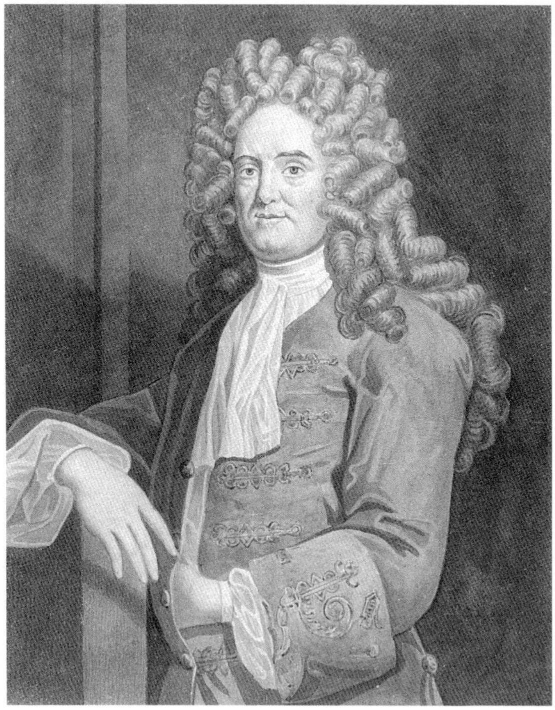

99
WILLIAM BULLOCK

Sylvester Harding (after Thomas Johnson)

Watercolour on wove paper 20 x 15.9
INSCR: 'Mr. Wm. Bullock.'
(pen and brown ink on mount b.c. CM)
INV: RW/CKA 551A
PROV: Charles Mathews (not in catalogue)
ENGR: By Harding and Thomas Johnson, mezzotint 32.4 x 25.1; Anon., stipple 16.5 x 14 (bust in oval)
REL: NPG 2540, watercolour 20.3 x 16.5, also by Sylvester Harding after Thomas Johnson and dated *c.* 1710–20; Harvard Theatre Collection, pen and grey ink copy of the stipple engraving by A. Toedteberg

Bullock, shown half-length, wears a pink coat with gold embroidery and an ample full-bottomed wig.

The patriarch of a family of performers, Bullock acted on the London stage for some 40 years. He also managed the largest booth at Bartholomew Fair in the 1730s.

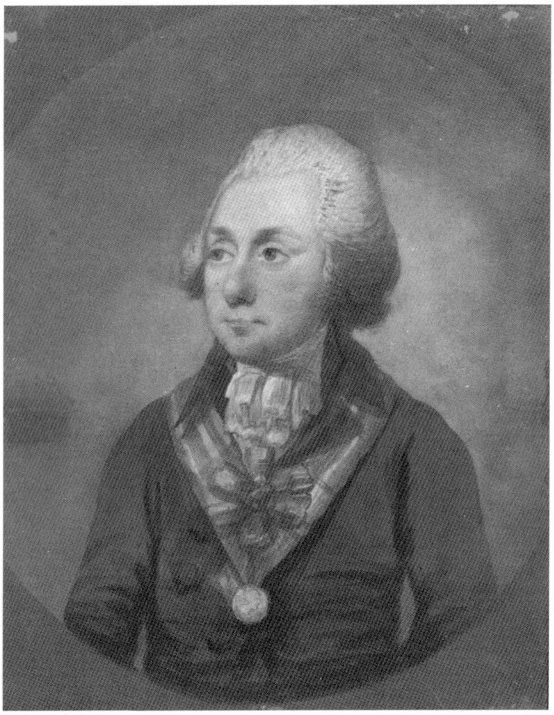

100

JOHN BURTON

'School of Garrick'

Henry Spicer

Black chalk and watercolour
on laid paper 26.5 x 21
INV: Mathews 263 (William Burton, artist unknown);
RW/CKA 50B (William Burton, artist unknown)
PROV: Charles Mathews
EXH: 1833 London (263)

Burton wears a blue jacket with a Shakespeare Ribband, rosette and Shakespeare favour. See No. 6.

When still a child, John Burton made his first appearance on the London stage, at Drury Lane on 28 October 1762, as a page in *Love Makes a Man*. He continued as a modestly useful actor until 1795–96, playing such roles as Thomas in *The Irish Widow*, Daniel in *The Conscious Lovers*, a witch in *Macbeth*, and a watchman in *Much Ado About Nothing*.

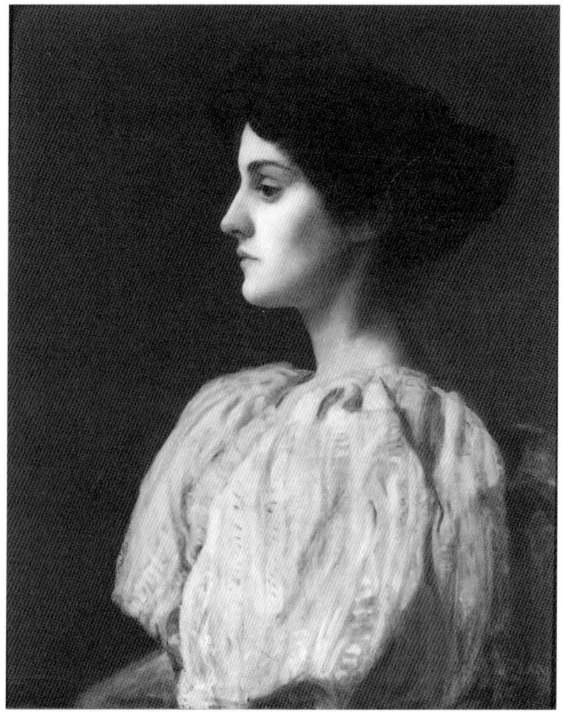

101*

MRS PATRICK CAMPBELL

as Rita Allmers in *Little Eyolf*
by Henrik Ibsen

J.S. Eland

Oil on canvas 61 x 40.6
INSCR: 'J.S. Eland /96' (brown paint b.r.)
INV: GCL 690
PROV: Unknown

Mrs Patrick Campbell's most enterprising venture of 1896 was her introduction to Ibsen in the unlikely part of the Ratwife in *Little Eyolf*, in a matinée performance at the Avenue Theatre on 23 November. The presence of Mrs Campbell made the production financially successful, and commercial managements began to take an interest. Mrs Campbell immediately ousted Janet Achurch from the much more important role of Rita Allmers by offering her services for a reduced fee. The production ran for 25 performances – a long run for an Ibsen play – although George Bernard Shaw objected to Mrs Campbell's turning Ibsen into 'a full-blown fashionable theatrical spectacle'.

A wood-engraving of Janet Achurch in the part shows her wearing a dress identical to that in Eland's portrait of Mrs Campbell, with leg-of-mutton sleeves and a similar collar. Mrs Campbell's dress is yellow, and her hair is tied back in a chignon.

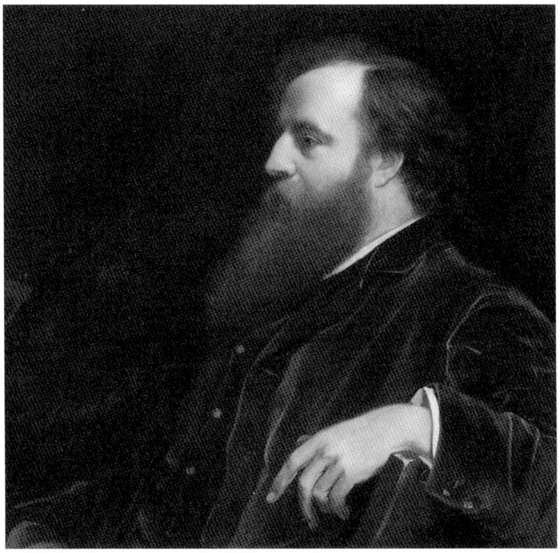

102

J. COMYNS CARR

Charles Edward Hallé

Oil on canvas 69.2 x 71.7
INV: CKA 587
PROV: Presented by the sitter's widow, 1917
EXH: 1881 Grosvenor Gallery Summer Exhibition (154)
'J. Comyns Carr – A Study'

Carr, with a red beard, sits with his left arm over the back of a chair and wears a mulberry velvet jacket with gold buttons.

The artist and sitter were joint assistant directors of the Grosvenor Gallery 1879–86.

Carr became a member of the Garrick Club in 1886.

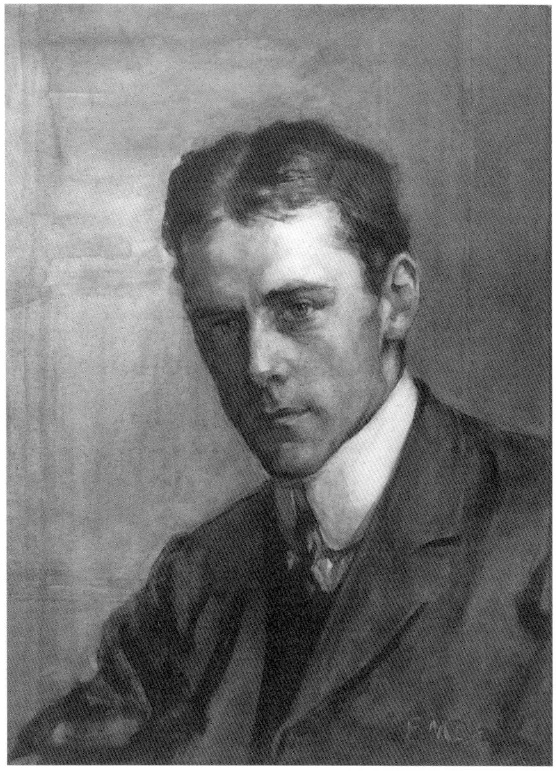

103

SIR LEWIS CASSON

W. Mear

Watercolour on wove paper 58.4 x 45.7
INSCR: 'E. Mear / 1906' (white body colour b.l.)
INV: GCL 725; Gift 855
PROV: Presented by Dame Sybil Thorndike, 1974

Sir Lewis wears a grey jacket with a white shirt and patterned tie. Casson had a fine speaking voice and beautiful diction. He acted in a number of Shaw's plays under Granville-Barker's management from 1904 to 1907. After marrying Sybil Thorndike in 1908, he toured with her to Australia, South Africa and throughout Britain. He became a member of the Garrick Club in 1954. See also No. 785.

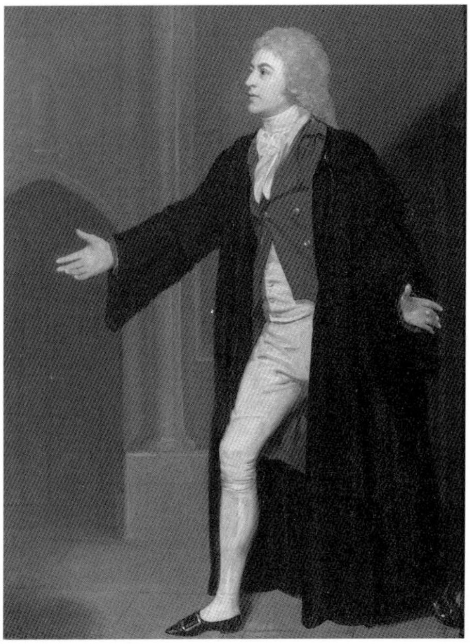

104

THOMAS CAULFIELD

as Mirabel in *The Inconstant or The Way to Win Him*
by George Farquhar

Samuel De Wilde

Oil on canvas 37 x 28.5
INV: Mathews 388; RW/CKA 209
PROV: John Bell (Bell sale at Leigh & Sotheby's 25 May 1805, lot 284); Charles Mathews
EXH: 1833 London (388)
ENGR: William S. Leney for Cawthorn's British Library 26 September 1795, line II.I x 7.6, pub. Bell's *British Theatre* (1797), vol 32

Mirabel is contracted to Oriana. She loves him but he apparently rejects her. In order to get her man she pretends to have taken the veil. Act IV, scene 2 is set in a monastery, with Oriana dressed in a nun's habit. Mirabel enters wearing a friar's habit and, convinced that he is going to lose Oriana, reveals his identity on the line 'No, my fair Angel, but let me repent' (given on the engraving) and pleads with her to fulfil the contract. Mirabel wears a long black habit, open to reveal pale buff breeches and waistcoat and a green coat.

Farquhar's comedy was first performed at Drury Lane on 28 November 1698. Caulfield did not play Young Mirabel in London. At the start of the 1791–92 season he joined the Drury Lane, where the part of Young Mirabel was always taken by Richard Wroughton until the end of the 1797–98 season, when it was taken over by Montague Talbot. The Bell text gives a Covent Garden cast, with Alexander Pope as Young Mirabel.

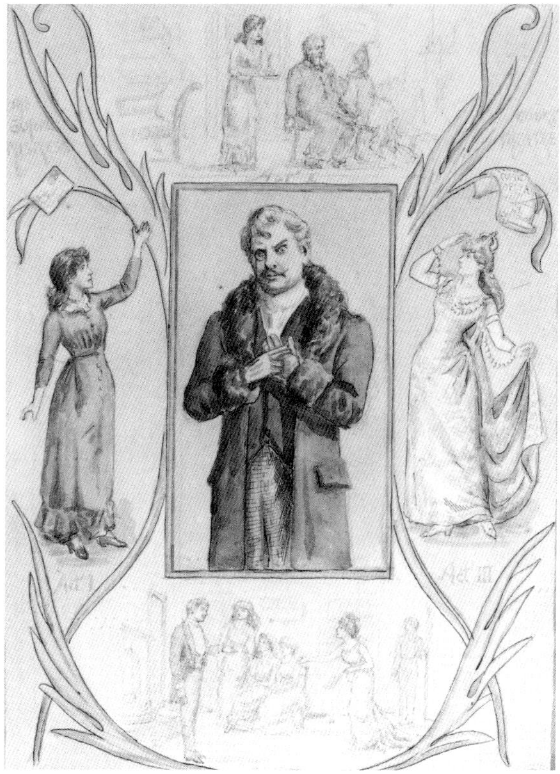

105

ARTHUR CECIL

as the Hon. Vere Queckett in *The Schoolmistress*
by Sir Arthur Wing Pinero

Graham Robertson

Pencil, pen and brown ink with watercolour 25 x 18.4
INSCR: 'GR' (b.r.); 'THE / SCHOOL / MISTRESS' (u.l.); 'ACT I' (u.c.); 'COURT / THEATRE' (c.r.); 'Act I' (l.l.); 'Act II' (b.c.); 'Act III' (l.r.); 'Miss / M. Haselrigg / Volumnia / House' (t.l.); new/comic/opera/.../ appearance/of / Miss / CONSTANCE / D(YOTT)' (t.r.)
INV: RW/CKA 533A
PROV: Presented by G.F.W. Blunt, 1896

The central panel shows Arthur Cecil dressed for his Act I entry as the Hon. Vere Queckett. The stage directions describe him: 'He is a fresh, breezy, dapper little gentleman of about forty-five with fair curly hair, a small waxed moustache, and a simple boyish manner.' He is dressed in the height of fashion in a blue overcoat with fur collar and cuffs, a blue jacket, brown tweed trousers and buff suede gloves, and he wears an eyeglass. To the left is the figure of Peggy Hesslerigge, an articled pupil. According to the stage directions she is 'a shabbily dressed, untidy girl with wild hair and inky fingers; her voice is rather shrewish and her actions are jerky; altogether she has the appearance of an overwise and neglected child'. Her 'shabby' dress is reddish brown, as is her hair. The letter above her head is addressed to her at 'Volumnia House'. To the right is the figure of Miss Dyott dressed in her burlesque queen costume for her entry in Act III. As she is not carrying the broken bust called for in the text, the artist may have been trying to evoke her performance on the stage earlier in the evening.

The scene at the top shows Mrs Rankling kneeling at the feet of her husband, Admiral Rankling. Peggy Hesselrigge 'advances with cake and wine'. In the scene at the bottom, Queckett 'in a perfectly fitting evening dress' is on the left, formally greeting Peggy at the party she has organised. The other three girls at Volumnia College are seen beyond: Dinah in the middle, Gwendoline and Ermyntrude on either side. Tyler, the servant, stands at the door, having just announced Peggy.

Pinero's farce was first given at the Court Theatre on 27 March 1886, with Arthur Cecil as the original Hon. Vere Queckett. Miss Norreys played Peggy Hesslerigge and Mrs John Wood played Miss Dyott, alias Mrs Queckett, but the small full-length figures of these two female characters cannot be seen as theatrical portraits.

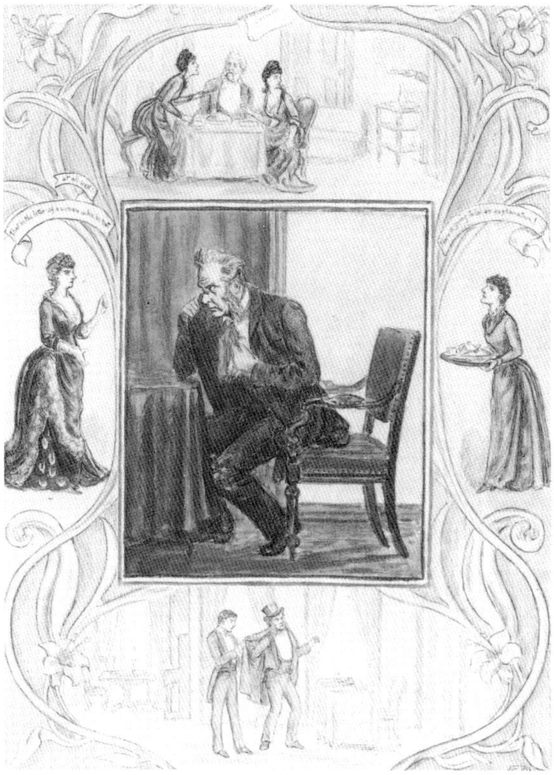

106 *Arthur Cecil as Mr Poskett*

106

ARTHUR CECIL

as Mr Poskett in *The Magistrate*

by Sir Arthur Wing Pinero

Graham Robertson

Pencil, pen and brown ink with watercolour 24.7 x 18.5

INSCR: 'GR' (grey wash b.r.); 'THE MAGISTRATE / COURT THEATRE' (pen and brown ink t.c.); 'at all well / That is the letter of a woman who is not' (pen and brown ink t.l.); 'There is going to be an explanation' (pen and brown ink t.r.)

INV: RW/CKA 533B

PROV: Presented by G.F.W. Blunt, 1896

The central scene shows Arthur Cecil as Mr Poskett in Act III, scene I, sitting in the magistrate's room at Mulberry Street Police Court. He has a bandage over an injury on his nose sustained the previous night, and wears a red necktie loaned by Mr Warrington, the Chief Clerk. His jacket is brown and his trousers are black.

The figure on the left, in a green dress trimmed with fur, is Agatha Poskett in Act I, which is set in Mr Poskett's drawing-room in Bloomsbury. She has just received a letter from Lady Jenkins and says: 'This is the letter of a woman who is not at all well.'

In the bottom scene we are still in Act I and see Cis helping his stepfather, Mr Poskett, into his coat on the line: 'Mind your arm, Guv. You've got your hand in a pocket. No, no – that's a tear in the lining.' The 19-year-old, thought by Poskett to be a mere 14, is taking the older man out for an evening at the disorderly Hôtel des Princes.

The top scene shows the Supper Room at the Hôtel des Princes in Act II. Agatha Poskett, with her sister Charlotte, has traced Colonel Lukyn to the hotel. He sits at the table with Agatha on the left and Charlotte on the right. Charlotte spies a hand appearing from behind the curtain, taking a dish of lemons. It belongs to Captain Vale, who hid on the arrival of the ladies. (Captain Vale was engaged to Charlotte and had that evening broken it off by letter.) Both ladies are about to scream.

The figure on the right is Charlotte who, in Act III, scene 2, the final scene of the play, 'takes the tray and everything on it and goes towards the door', speaking the line inscribed above.

Pinero's farce was first given at the Court on 21 March 1885, with Arthur Cecil as the original Mr Poskett.

See No. 105.

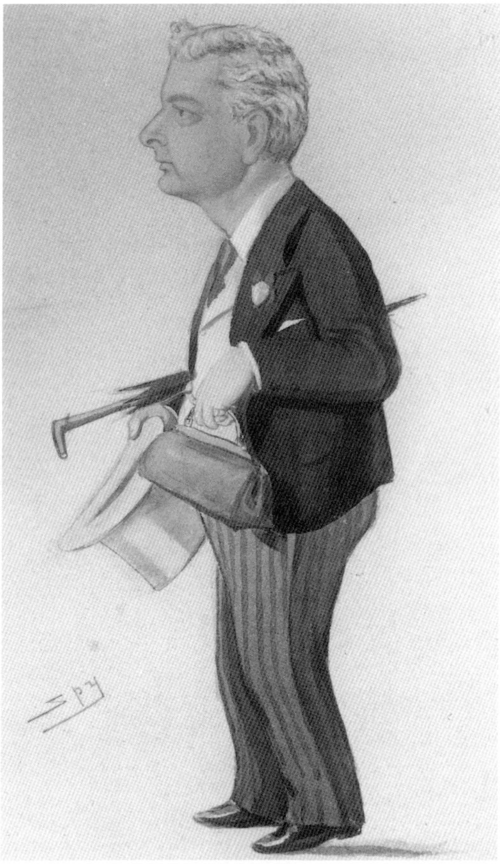

107
ARTHUR CECIL

Sir Leslie Ward ('Spy')

Pencil with watercolour and body colour
on blue-grey wove paper 28.6 x 17.1
INSCR: 'SPY' (pencil b.l.)
INV: CKA 581; Gift 366
PROV: Presented by Theobald Mathew, 1913
LIT: *Vanity Fair* 28 December 1889,
inscr: 'Mr Arthur Cecil'; Frederic Whyte,
Actors of the Century (1898), p. 122

Cecil wears a red tie, a white shirt, a black coat and grey striped trousers. He carries a brown bag, a black umbrella and a grey top hat.

Cecil became a member of the Garrick Club in 1867.

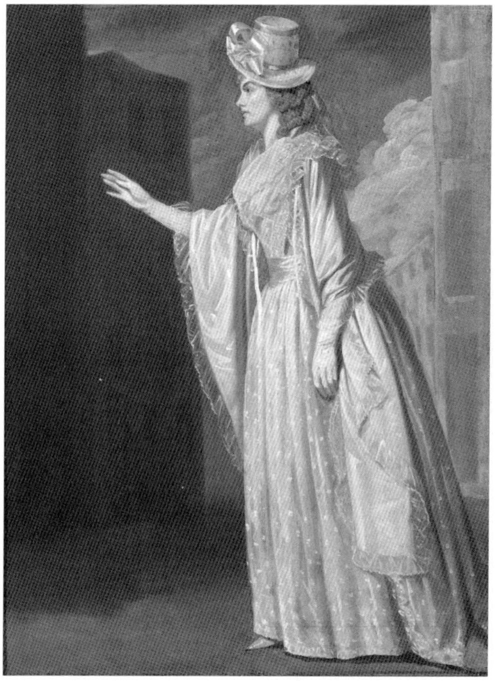

108
CHARLOTTE CHAPMAN
as Augusta Aubrey in *The Fashionable Lover*
by Richard Cumberland

Samuel De Wilde

Oil on canvas 36.5 x 28
INV: Mathews 88; RW/CKA 207
PROV: John Bell; Charles Mathews
EXH: 1833 London (88)
ENGR: J. Thornthwaite for Bell's British Library 19 January 1793, line 11.7 x 8, pub. Bell's *British Theatre* (1797), vol 18

The scene designated on the engraving (Act I, scene 3) is a misprint for Act III, scene I. In the latter scene, 'The Street, with a distant view of a square', Augusta wanders disconsolate with no roof over her head and hesitates outside the house of her lover, Tyrrel. She meets Colin Macleod, a Scot in the service of Lord Abberville, and tells him of her troubles, 'I have no Friend or Refuge in this World', the line given on the engraving. Augusta wears long white gloves, a white sprig muslin dress and underskirt with a white sash, a white shawl trimmed with lace and a lace-edged fichu. Her yellow straw hat is trimmed with white ribbons.

Cumberland's comedy was first performed at Drury Lane on 20 January 1772, with Ann Barry as the first Augusta Aubrey. Charlotte Chapman never played the role in London, but De Wilde probably chose to depict her in it because she was a fairly prominent actress at Covent Garden in the early 1790s.

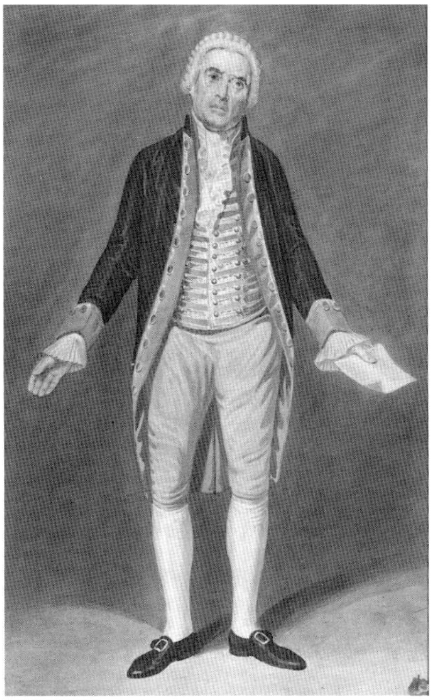

109

WILLIAM CHAPMAN
in character

Samuel De Wilde

Pencil and watercolour on wove paper 37 x 23.5
INSCR: 'S De Wilde delin /________' (pencil b.r.)
INV: RW/CKA 46c (John Chapman)
PROV: Charles Mathews? (not in catalogue)

The sitter is shown wearing black shoes with silver buckles, pink breeches, a grey silk jacket lined in pink, a dark grey collar lined with pink and trimmed with silver braid, and a pink waistcoat.

The identity of the actor is a problem. The De Wilde watercolours in the Garrick Club were framed in groups some time between the purchase of the Mathews collection in 1835 and Robert Walters's catalogue of 1908. They were presumably labelled when they were framed. C. K. Adams's assumption that No. 109 is from Mathews's collection springs from the fact that it is framed with five other watercolours by De Wilde that certainly were (Nos. 316, 340, 346, 439 and 760). If the actor's name is Chapman, then William, who was engaged by George Colman the Younger at Covent Garden to replace Murray, is a much more likely candidate than the all-but-untraceable John, whose name is given on the label to the watercolour. Walters says that John Chapman 'played old men', something that William Chapman certainly did; the *Thespian Dictionary* for 1804 states that he had lately 'applied himself to the study of old sentimental gentlemen'.

110

LOCATION UNKNOWN

CHARLOTTE CHARKE

Unknown Artist

Brown wash on laid paper 25.6 x 19.8
INSCR: 'Mrs Charlotte Charke' (pen and black ink b.l.);
'Mrs Chark daughter of C. Cibber'
(pen and brown ink on mount b.c. CM)
INV: CKA 625
PROV: Unknown

A young girl, standing full-length with her right hand to her breast, wears a long dress dating from about 1725 (CKA).

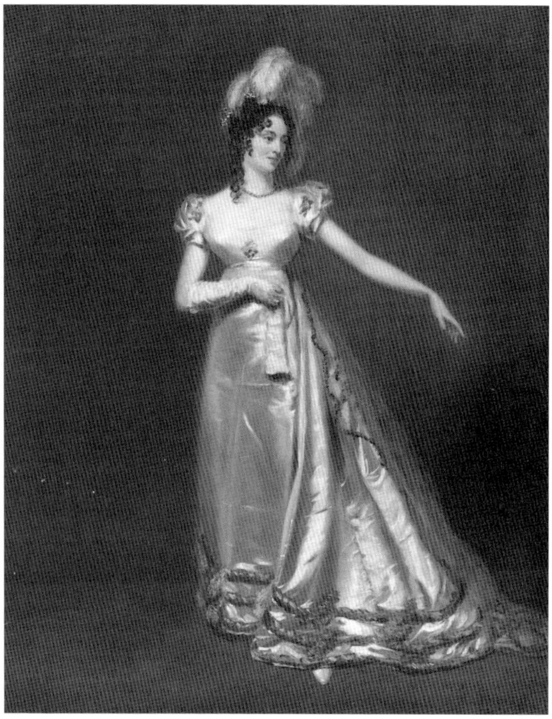

111*

LOUISA CHATTERLEY
as Lady Teazle in *The School for Scandal*
by Richard Brinsley Sheridan

George Clint

Oil on canvas 51.5 x 41.2
INV: RW/CKA 456; Gift 160
PROV: Presented by Sir William de Bathe Bt, 1860

Louisa Chatterley wears a white silk dress. The gauze over the train has blue scalloped edges. The extravagant headdress is a feast of feathers and jewels.

After a career at Drury Lane and the Haymarket, Louisa Chatterley appeared at Covent Garden for the first time on 6 November 1821, as Miss Hardcastle in *She Stoops to Conquer*. Davenport Adams suggests that she played Lady Teazle at Covent Garden in 1822, which is borne out by No. 112, but all performances of the part that year (19 March, 19 & 26 April and 5 June) were given by Maria Davison. Louisa Chatterley played Lady Teazle at Covent Garden on 8 January 1823, but the part was given to Miss Chester thereafter. The costume would confirm a date for the picture in the early 1820s.

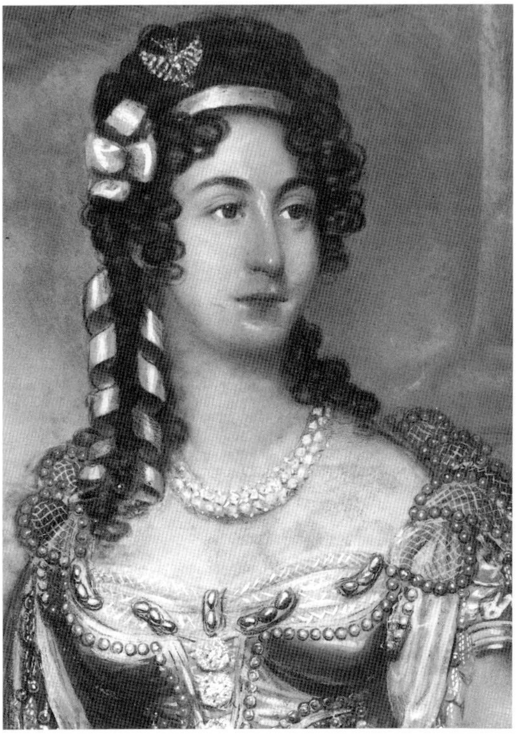

112

LOUISA CHATTERLEY

as Lady Teazle in *The School for Scandal*

by Richard Brinsley Sheridan

Rose Emma Drummond

Pastel on paper 54.6 x 41.9

INV: RW 304 (unknown sitter by unknown artist);

CKA 304 (by S. Drummond)

PROV: Unknown

ENGR: Anon. for *La Belle Assemblée* 1822, stipple (vignette, more of bodice visible at b.); J. Rogers for Oxberry's *Dramatic Biography* (1826), stipple 6.6 x 5.1

The sitter has pink ribbons in her hair and wears a pink dress trimmed with lace. She is awash with pearls and diamonds. See No. 111.

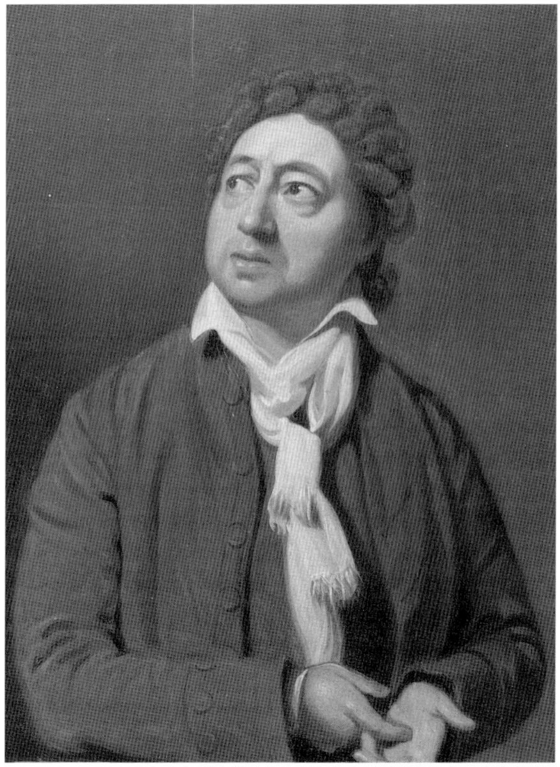

113

ANDREW CHERRY

as Item in *The Deserted Daughter*

by Thomas Holcroft

Samuel De Wilde

Oil on panel 23.5 x 19.3

INV: Mathews 140; RW/CKA 228

PROV: Charles Mathews

EXH: 1833 London (140)

In Act v, scene 12, Item, a dishonest steward, attempts to recover his account book from his nephew, Clement, who has found it on a table. The account book chronicles Item's dirty dealings, and he pleads with Clement, 'My dear nephew! my good boy! My kind Clement! I'll supply all your wants! I'll pay your debts! I'll never deny anything you want!' Item wears a brown coat and waistcoat and a curly brown wig. He scratches the palm of his left hand in a cambistic manner.

Holcroft's comedy was first performed at Covent Garden on 2 May 1795. It was based partly on Richard Cumberland's comedy, *The Fashionable Lover*. Quick was the original Item. Cherry did not act the role in London during the 18th century. See No. 114.

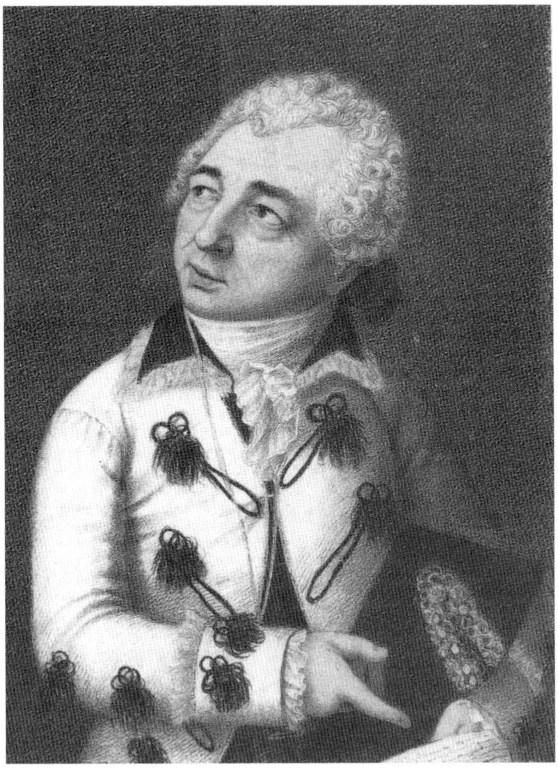

114

ANDREW CHERRY

in character

Sylvester Harding

Black chalk and watercolour
on wove paper 19.4 x 16.2
INSCR: 'Harding Fecit' (pen and brown ink
on mount b.l. CM); 'Andrew Cherry'
(pen and brown ink on mount b.c. CM)
INV: Mathews 287; RW/CKA 551B
PROV: Charles Mathews
EXH: 1833 London (287)

The pose – down to the pointing forefinger – is copied quite brazenly from De Wilde's portrait (No. 113). However, the striking costume cannot be associated with the role of Item. Cherry wears a distinctive white coat with black frogging and fringed rosettes, the cuffs and black collar trimmed with pink frills.

For Cherry as playwright, see No. 124.

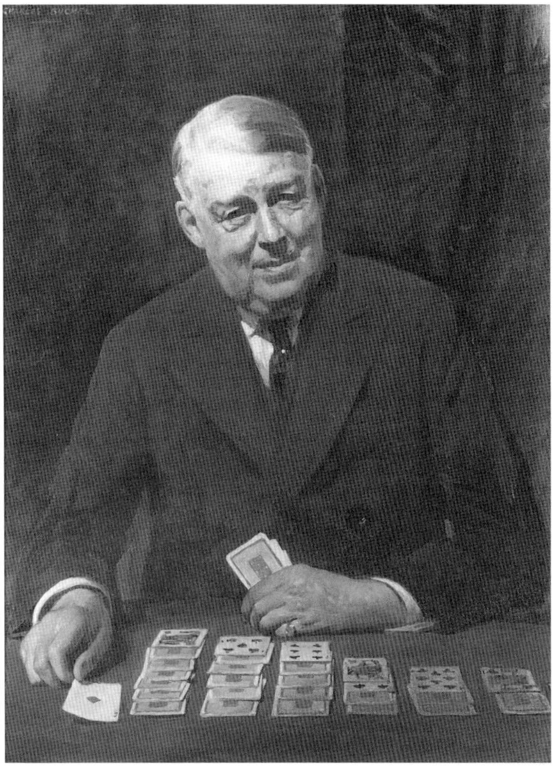

115

ARTHUR CHUDLEIGH-LILLIES

Charles Buchel

Oil on canvas 88.9 x 68.6
INSCR: 'CHARLES BUCHEL'
(cream yellow paint t.l.)
INV: CKA 586
PROV: Presented by a number of members, 1932

Chudleigh is playing a game of patience and holds an Ace of Diamonds. Seated against a red drape, he wears an ill-fitting dark brown jacket, waistcoat, white shirt, and purplish tie with a pearl stick pin.

CKA states that the portrait was painted after the sitter's death in 1932.

Chudleigh became a member of the Garrick Club in 1891.

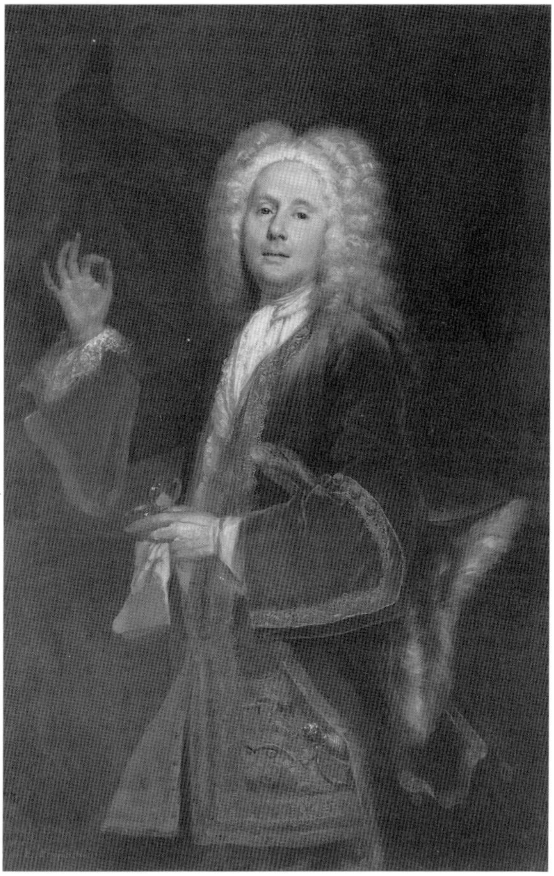

116*

COLLEY CIBBER

as Lord Foppington

in *The Relapse or Virtue in Danger*

by Sir John Vanbrugh

Giuseppe Grisoni

Oil on canvas 127 x 102

INSCR: 'Colley Cibber Esqr./in the/Character of Ld. Foppington' (brown paint b.l.)

INV: Mathews 46; RW/CKA 11

PROV: Joseph Addison?; Mr Ireland?; Thomas Harris; Harris sale, Robins 12 July 1819 (46); Charles Mathews

EXH: 1833 London (46); 1949 Birmingham (53); 1949 Port Sunlight (69); 1951 London (20); 1958 Liverpool; 1975 London (18); 1992 London, Tate Gallery, *The Swagger Portraits* (23)

ENGR: Jean Simon, mezzotint 31.7 x 24.7; J.H. Robinson from a drawing by George Clint for *Effigies Poeticæ* pub. W. Walker 1 November 1822, line 9.5 x 8.2 (h.l. only, inscr: 'From a Picture by Grisoni in the Collection /of Charles Mathews Esq.')

Sir Novelty Fashion, newly created Lord Foppington, is proud of his extravagant appearance and his prowess with the ladies. Cibber is shown in one of his greatest roles, probably speaking the epilogue to the play: 'Gentlemen and ladies, / These people have regal'd you here to-day / (In my opinion) with a saucy play.' Later on he says: 'Did ever highway-man yet bid you stand / With a sweet bawdy snuff-box in his hand?' The reference fits the pose. On the other hand, Lord Foppington may be shown on the completion of his toilet in Act 1, scene 3. He objects to the height of the pocket in his coat to the tailor, to the tightness of his shoes to the cobbler and to the padding in his stockings to the hosier. His wig, into which the perruquier has 'cramm'd twenty ounces of hair' does not suit him because it reveals too much of his face. The one thing he likes is his steenkirk, or neckcloth. In fact, he is 'in love with it, stap my vitals'.

Lord Foppington wears a blue velvet frock-coat with red velvet cuffs trimmed with gold braid and gold buttons, and a rust-red waistcoat richly embroidered in gold and trimmed with gold braid. Under his left arm is a dark tricorn hat with extreme points, edged in gold braid, the brim stuffed with feathers.

Cibber created the role of Lord Foppington in Vanbrugh's comedy at Drury Lane on 21 November 1696 and played it with extreme success for the rest of his career. Grisoni arrived in London with John Talman in 1715 and stayed until 1728, so he could have painted the portrait at any point over this 13-year-period. However, if there is any basis for P.G. Patmore's statement in *British Galleries of Art* (1824) that the picture belonged to Joseph Addison, then it must have been painted before Addison's death in 1719.

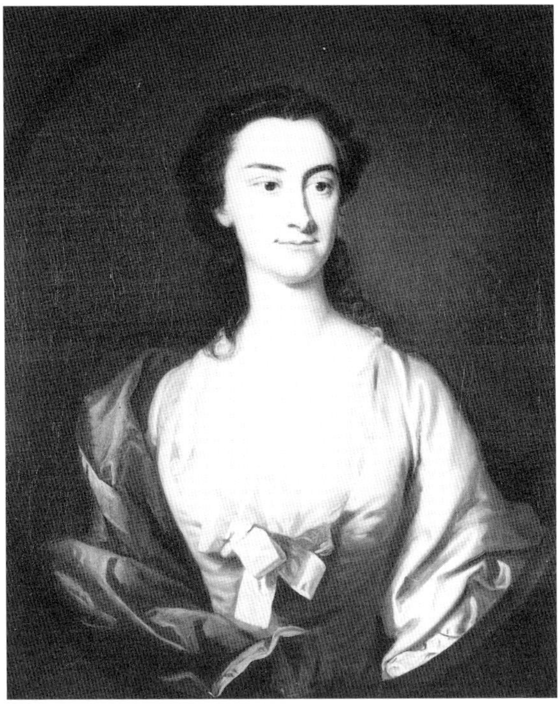

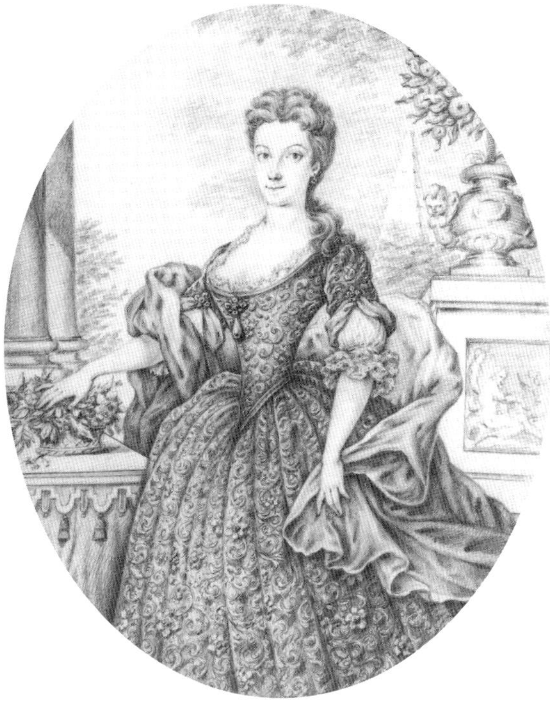

117

SUSANNA CIBBER

Thomas Hudson

Oil on canvas 74.3 x 61.6
INV: Mathews 13; RW/CKA 18
PROV: Charles Mathews
EXH: 1833 London (13); 1951 London (18)
ENGR: Anon. for *The Comforts of Matrimony* (1739), line 9.5 x 7.3 (oval); John Faber fecit 1748 pub. J. Faber, mezzotint 27 x 22.5; Anon., mezzotint 9.2 x 7.3
LIT: Julian Herbage, *Messiah* (1948), p. 20 (reproduced)

Mrs Cibber wears a white silk dress with a pink bow at the front and a blue drapery over her right shoulder. A similar but later portrait of Susanna Cibber (NPG 4526) was engraved by J. Marchand and published in 1749.

Mrs Cibber, who had the ability to wring tears from an audience, excelled as Juliet (to Barry's Romeo) and as Monimia in *The Orphan* (to Garrick's Chamont). She sang in the first performance of Handel's *Messiah* in Dublin on 13 April 1742.

118

SUSANNA CIBBER

Thomas Worlidge

Plumbago on vellum 27.5 x 22.2 (oval)
INSCR: 'Worlidge Fecit'
(pen and brown ink on mount b.l. CM)
INV: Mathews 276; (not in RW); CKA 596
PROV: Charles Mathews
EXH: 1833 London (276)

There are several drawings on vellum of members of the Cibber family in the collection of the late Robert Eddison, but none of them approaches the sophistication of this portrait of Susanna Cibber, who stands full-length in an embroidered dress with a low neckline against a background of columns, urn and pyramid. See also No. 252.

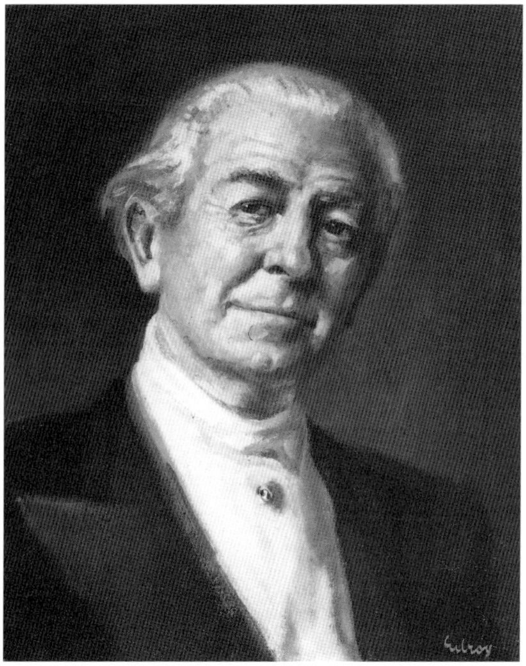

119

SIR JOHN SELBY CLEMENTS

John Gilroy

Oil on canvas 50.7 x 40.6
INSCR: 'Gilroy' (yellow paint b.r.)
INV: GCL 728; Gift 862
PROV: Presented by the artist, 1975

Sir John Clements became a member of the Garrick Club in 1943. He was a Life Member from 1978. He is shown half-length, wearing a black coat and a white shirt.

In 1935 Clements founded the Intimate Theatre in Palmers Green, where he eventually offered over 200 plays. He acted in a number of West End productions, and sometimes managed the St James's, the Phoenix and the Saville theatres. In 1966 he became Director of the Chichester Festival, a post he held until 1973. At Chichester he also appeared in many plays, his roles including those of Shotover in *Heartbreak House*, Antony in *Antony and Cleopatra*, Prospero in *The Tempest*, and Macbeth.

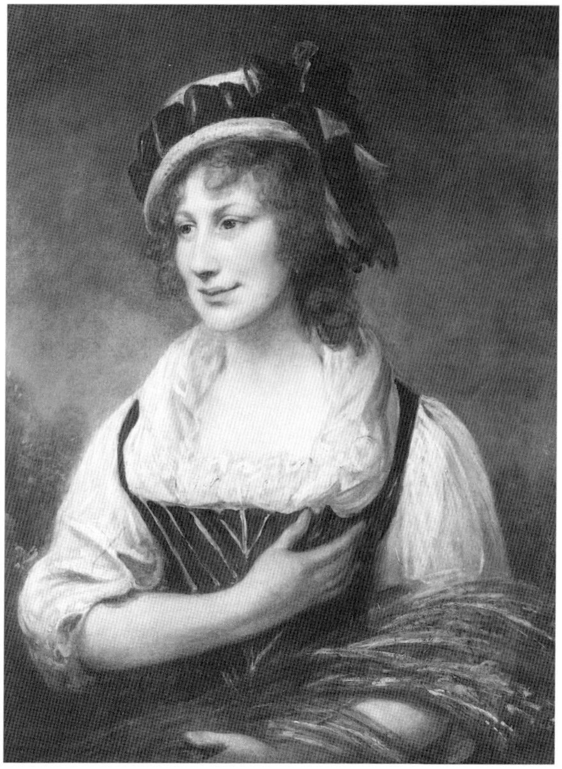

120

ELIZABETH CLENDINING
as Rosina
in *Rosina* by Frances Brooke

Gainsborough Dupont

Oil on canvas 74.9 x 61
INV: RW 370 (Mrs Jordan attr. to Romney);
CKA 370 (Mrs Jordan); Gift 211
PROV: Thomas Harris; Harris sale, Robins 12 July 1819 (12); Presented in 1887 by Mrs Fitzgerald of Sharlestone Manor, Bucks, in memory of her son, Captain K. Fitzgerald, a member of the Club
EXH: 1982–83 London (134)
LIT: *The Morning Herald* 23 April 1795; TAM 1935, reproduced, as Mrs Jordan; Hayes, 1968 (illus.)

The scene is Act I, scene I: 'A rural prospect: on the left side a little hill with trees at the top; a spring of water rushes from the side, and falls into a natural basin below: on the right side a cottage, at the door of which is a bench of stone. At a distance a chain of mountains. The manor-house in view: A field of corn fills up the scene.' Clearly the production went to great lengths to create verisimilitude. Rosina is scolded by Rustic, the bad-tempered steward, who is struck by Rosina's beauty. Rustic says: 'Keep back; wait till the reapers are off the field; do like the other reapers.' Rosina replies timidly: 'If I have done wrong, Sir, I will put what I have gleaned down again,' and drops the corn. In the 1820 Oxberry edition of the play, Rosina's costume is given as 'Buff stay-bodice, white petticoat and apron, trimmed with buff and green'. In Dupont's half-length portrait, she wears a yellow straw hat with blue ribbons, and a green bodice ribbed in yellow over a white chemise.

Mrs Clendining acted Rosina for the first time on 13 December 1792 at Covent Garden. Dupont's picture commemorates her performance in the role at Covent Garden on 19 March 1795.

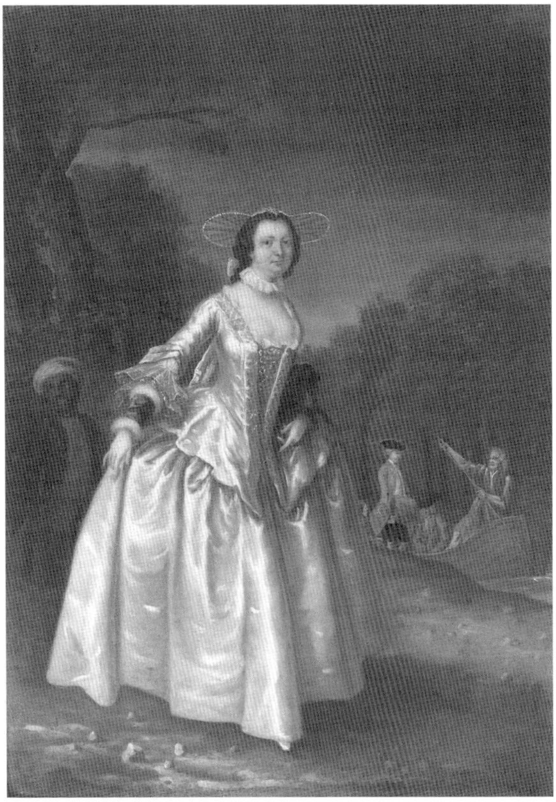

121 *Catherine Clive as Mrs Riot, the Fine Lady*

121

CATHERINE CLIVE

as Mrs Riot, the Fine Lady

in *Lethe or Aesop in the Shades*

by David Garrick

Pieter Van Bleeck

Oil on canvas 60 x 44

INV: Mathews 94 (by Hogarth); RW 376 (by Hogarth); CKA 376 (artist uncertain)

PROV: Charles Mathews (bt. 1822)

EXH: 1833 London (94); 1962 Chichester (15); 1974 Twickenham (11)

ENGR: Charles Mosley 1750, line 29.8 x 22.2 (in reverse; there is no black boy behind Mrs Riot, her dress has a decorated hem, and the boat is placed further away, with the passengers arranged somewhat differently) [the engraving was used by the Bow factory to manufacture one of the first four portrait figures in English porcelain]; Anon., line 4.5 diam. (watch paper)

The scene is 'a grove, with a view of the River Lethe'. Mrs Riot has already arrived in Elysium, the seventh visitor of the day after the Poet, the Old Man, a Fine Gentleman, Mr and Mrs Tatoo, and a Frenchman. She thinks Aesop very ugly and demands the pump-room, thinking Elysium a fashionable watering place: 'Show me to the pump-room, then, fellow – where's the Company? I die in solitude.' Aesop tries to philosophise with her, but she gives him a receipt for the vapours and sings a song: 'The card invites, in crowds we fly / To join the jovial rout full cry.'

She wears a full silver panniered dress with a separate silver silk bodice. She has a blue muff trimmed with white fur on her right arm and holds a little black dog under her left arm. The black boy on the left wears a red jacket and blue waistcoat. A man and a boatman are seen in the background on the left.

This dramatic satire by Garrick, his first success as a playwright, was originally produced at Drury Lane on 15 April 1740, with Henry Woodward as the Fine Gentleman and Mrs Clive as Mrs Riot. Mrs Clive chose *Lethe* for her final benefit at Drury Lane on 24 April 1769, when Thomas King played Lord Chalkstone for the first time, and James Dodd took the part of the Fine Gentleman.

This vivacious comedienne was one of England's celebrated personages in the middle years of the 18th century. An amusing actress and a good comic singer, 'Kitty' Clive was lavishly lauded by the critics and by adoring members of society.

In his *Dramatic Censor* (1770), Francis Gentleman described the role of Mrs Heidelberg in *The Clandestine Marriage* as having been 'lost to the public when Mrs Clive retired'.

A phosphatic porcelain figure of her as the 'Fine Lady' was made at Bow *c.*1750–55. A companion figure of Henry Woodward as the 'Fine Gentleman' was fired at the same time.

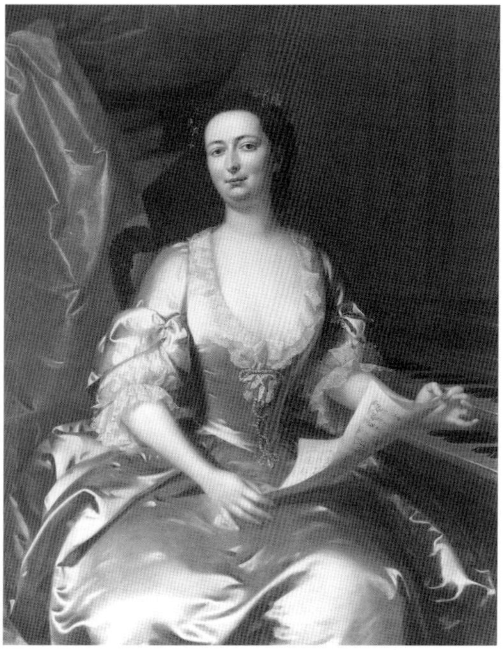

122*

CATHERINE CLIVE

William Verelst

Oil on canvas 124.5 x 99
INSCR: 'Wm. Verelst Pinxit 1740' (c.r.)
INV: Mathews 48; RW 25 (by Joseph Van Haaken or J. Davison); CKA 25; Gift 230
PROV: Charles Mathews;
Francis Fladgate, by whom presented, 1854
EXH: 1833 London (48)
LIT: Fitzgerald, p. 224; Griffiths, p. 306

Mrs Clive is shown three-quarter length, seated at a harpsichord and holding a sheet of music on which are written the words 'Sweet Bird'. She wears a grey silk dress trimmed with lace and pearls.

A portrait of Kitty Clive by Jeremiah Davison, once owned by her neighbour at Strawberry Hill, Horace Walpole, and now at Longleat, shows her similarly posed with an open book of music.

123

ROBERT COATES

as Romeo in *Romeo and Juliet*
by William Shakespeare

Samuel De Wilde

Pencil and watercolour on wove paper 36.8 x 19.7
INSCR: (Illeg. b.l.?)
INV: Mathews 250; (not in RW); CKA 523
PROV: Charles Mathews

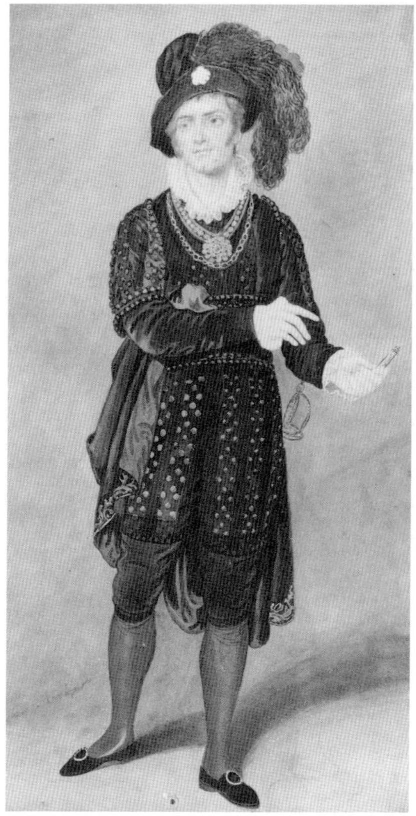

123 *Robert Coates as Romeo*

EXH: 1833 London (250); 1964 London [2] (29); 1986 Montgomery (18)
ENGR: Samuel De Wilde pub. S. De Wilde & J. Cawthorn 22 May 1812, soft ground etching 36.8 x 22.6, inscr: 'Drawn from the life and etcht de S. De Wilde', with the line from Act V, scene I: 'Doing more murders in this loathsome world/ Than these poor compounds that thou mayst not sell.'
REL: A portrait by De Wilde, signed and dated, of Coates as Romeo was in the Dramatic College sale at Fairbrother, Lye and Palmer on 24 February 1881 (lot 97)

Coates wears black shoes with paste buckles, grey stockings, black breeches, and blue-studded doublet and coat. His black coat has blue embroidery along the border. One of two gold chains round his neck supports a large jewel. His hat is also black, with black ostrich feathers. There is a slight study of his left foot in the bottom right-hand corner of the sheet.

Coates, a native of Antigua, made his English début as Romeo at the Theatre Royal, Bath, in February 1809. He appeared in London in December 1811, and his dreadful acting – especially as Romeo – helped to earn him considerable notoriety. At Covent Garden on 25 February 1813 Charles Mathews played Romeo Rantall, a caricature based on Coates's histrionics, in the anonymous farce, *At Home*.

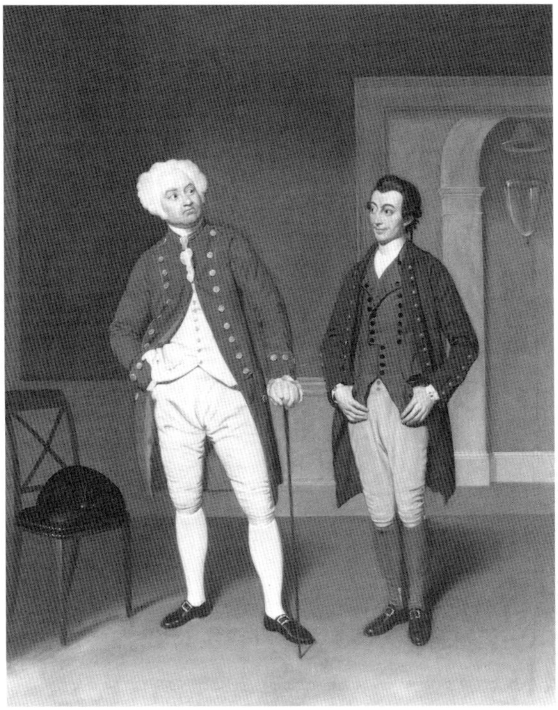

124

THOMAS COLLINS as Timothy Quaint and *WILLIAM DOWTON* as Governor Heartall in *The Soldier's Daughter* by Andrew Cherry

Samuel De Wilde

Oil on canvas 83.5 x 70.5
INV: Mathews 131; RW/CKA 393
PROV: Charles Mathews
EXH: 1805 R.A. (568); 1833 London (131); 1950–51 London; 1951 London (12); 1951–52 London (110)

In an era of mediocre plays, Andrew Cherry's seemingly endless piece is one of the worst. It is full of motiveless acts of extreme generosity and evil by uninteresting cardboard figures. De Wilde, however, has managed to capture the dramatic characters of the sitters most successfully. The scene is Act IV, scene 3, the house of Governor Heartall. The Soldier's Daughter of the title is the widow Cheerley, pursued and won by Frank Heartall. Governor Heartall (Dowton) stands on the left wearing white stockings, buff breeches, and a paler buff waistcoat under a green coat lined in red. Timothy (Collins), on the right, wears blue-green stockings and waistcoat, buff breeches and a greenish-brown coat.

Cherry's comedy was first performed at Drury Lane on 7 February 1804, with Dowton as the original Governor Heartall and Collins the original Timothy Quaint. There were 35 performances during the first season.

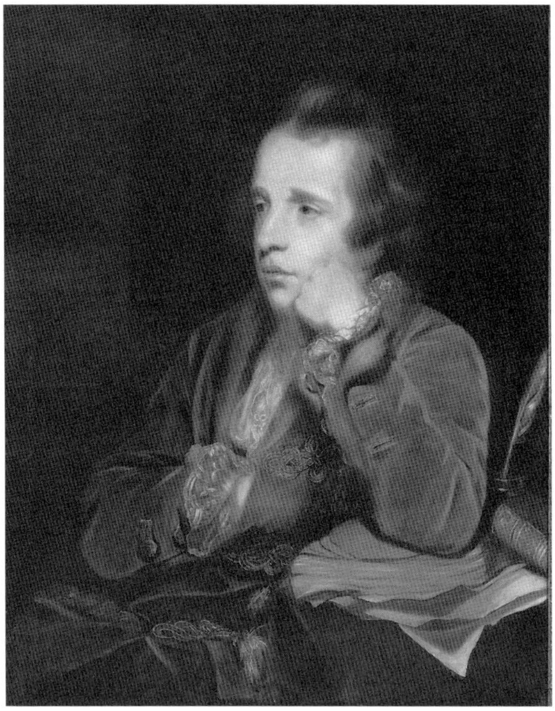

125

GEORGE COLMAN THE ELDER

Sir Joshua Reynolds (studio)

Oil on canvas 74.9 x 61
INV: RW 40 (after Sir Joshua Reynolds); CKA 40
PROV: Unknown; Garrick Club by 1909
EXH: 1973 York; 1974 Twickenham (34)
ENGR: Giuseppe Marchi pub. Marchi 1773, mezzotint 40 x 33.3; Niccolo Schiavonetti pub. 7 March 1807, line and stipple 7.1 x 5.4; Edward Scriven after a drawing by John Jackson, as a plate to *Contemporary Portraits* pub. Cadell & Davies 8 March 1813, stipple 21.5 x 18 (h.l. only); S. Fisher pub. R. Bentley 1841, line and stipple 10.8 x 8.6
REL: Original painted for Lord Musgrave 1767 (unlocated), exh: R.A. 1770 (150); Buscot Park, oil on canvas 76.2 x 63.5 (studio); NPG 1364, oil on canvas 73.7 x 62.2 (studio); Gow sale, Christie's 28 May 1937 (106) bt. Vicars (studio)

Colman, seated with his left elbow resting upon a book on a table, wears a red velvet jacket with tassels, buttons and fur trimming.

Colman, who managed Covent Garden from 1767 to 1774 and the Haymarket from 1777 to 1786, was also a leading playwright (he wrote and translated or collaborated on some 49 dramatic works), journalist and essayist.

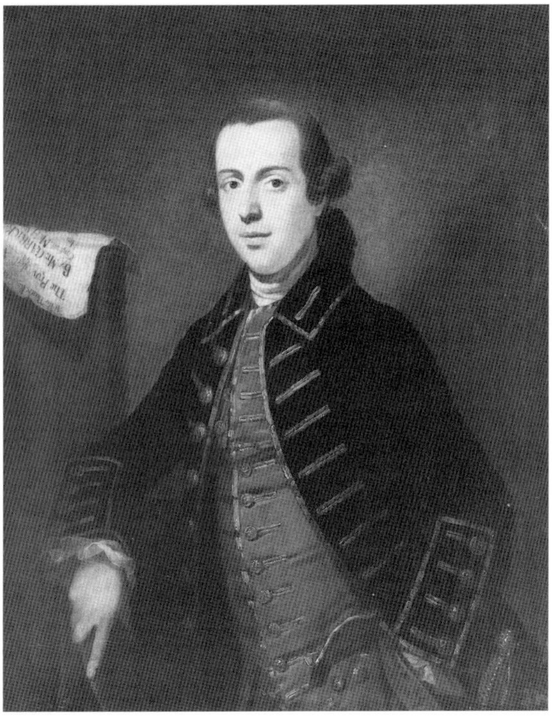

126

GEORGE COLMAN THE ELDER

Johan Zoffany (after)

Oil on canvas 91 x 71
INSCR: 'COKE/ON/LITERATURE' (on spine of book at l.);
'At the Theatre Royal Dr./ The Provoked W.../
JOHN BRUTE – / By Mr GARRICK / Constant
Mr H_______ /_______'
(black paint on playbill draped over book)
INV: RW 385 (artist unknown); CKA 385
PROV: Unknown; Garrick Club by 1909
ENGR: Edward Smith after a drawing by John Thurston,
as a plate to *Effigies Poeticæ* pub. W. Walker 1 January 1822,
line 10.1 x 8, inscr: 'From a picture by Zoffany
in the possession of the publisher'
REL: Original at Sotheby's 10 (& 17?) July 1985 (51),
withdrawn. Prov: Thomas Harris: Harris sale,
Robins 12 July 1819 (33); W. Walker; Lord O'Hagan;
sold as the property of a Lady

Colman wears a dark coat and red waistcoat. In his right hand is a dark tricorn hat.

The original engraved version is cut off on the left by the coat cuff, and along the bottom just below the pommel of the sword.

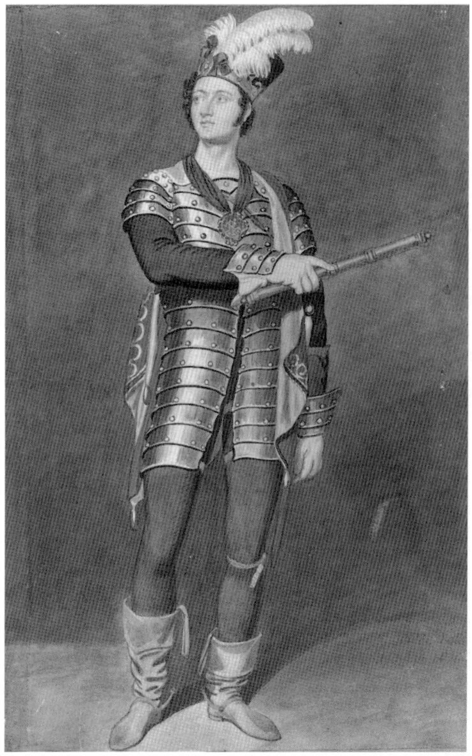

127

WILLIAM CONWAY

as Henry in *Henry V* by William Shakespeare

Samuel De Wilde

Pencil and watercolour on wove paper 38.1 x 24.1
INSCR: 'S De Wilde delin / April 16 1814' (pencil b.r.)
INV: Mathews 244 (as Richmond); RW/CKA 55 (as Richmond)
PROV: Charles Mathews
EXH: 1833 London (244)
ENGR: Rivers for the *The Theatrical Inquisitor* pub. C. Chapple
1 June 1814, line 17.8 x 11.7 (same costume without the hat,
holds sceptre or baton at side in l.h., gesture to r.
with r.h., low mountainous horizon)

The romantic Conway wears brown boots with gilt spurs, blue stockings with a white and gold garter, and an armadillo-like body armour over a jerkin with blue sleeves. His red cloak is lined in white and his silver crown has a blue cap with red bows and ostrich feathers.

Conway made his London début at Covent Garden on 4 October 1810 as Alexander in *Alexander the Great.* His first Shakespearean role was Othello, on 7 October, and he followed this with Romeo on 25 October. On 1 November 1813 he played Henry V for the first time, and on 14 March 1814 he replaced Mr Abbott as Richmond. He acted Henry six times and Richmond three times during this season. The caption on the 1814 engraving identifies the character as the King. See also No. 750.

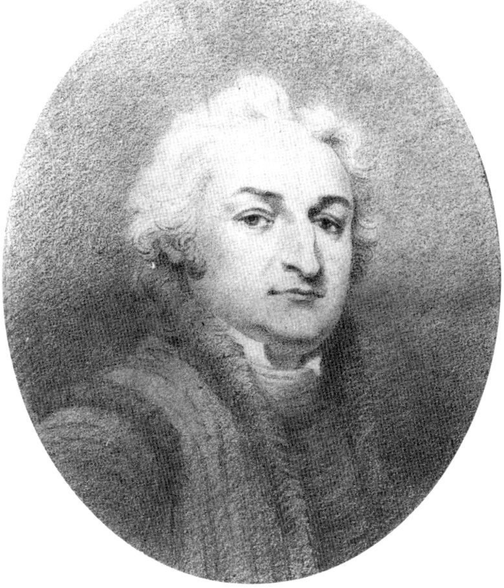

128

GEORGE FREDERICK COOKE

as Richard in *Richard III* by William Shakespeare

J. Corbett

Black chalk on wove paper 14.3 x 11.7 (oval)
INV: Mathews 273 (artist unknown, no character);
RW/CKA 491C (artist unknown, no character)
PROV: Charles Mathews
EXH: 1833 London (273)
ENGR: John Whessell pub. T. Simpson & Thompson
6 April 1801, stipple 14.7 x 11.7;
reissued pub. John P. Thompson 4 June 1804

Cooke wears the fur-trimmed sleeveless jacket associated with his Richard III. See No. 130.

Cooke played Tressel in *Richard III* at China Hall, Rotherhithe on 26 June 1778, apparently his first appearance in the play. His first performance as Richard seems to have been given in Newcastle early in 1788, when he played the part for his own benefit. It was one of his principal roles by the time he played his first Dublin season, 1794–95, and he returned to the London stage in the role on 31 October 1800. He had been away from London for 22 years, and his Covent Garden début was an enormous success. He was immediately proclaimed to be the best Richard since Garrick, and acknowledged as the most exciting actor on the London stage. He played Richard 44 times during his first Covent Garden season. Cooke was due to open the 1801–2 Covent Garden season on 14 September with his Richard, but his inebriation caused the performance to be postponed until 19 October, when he made a public apology.

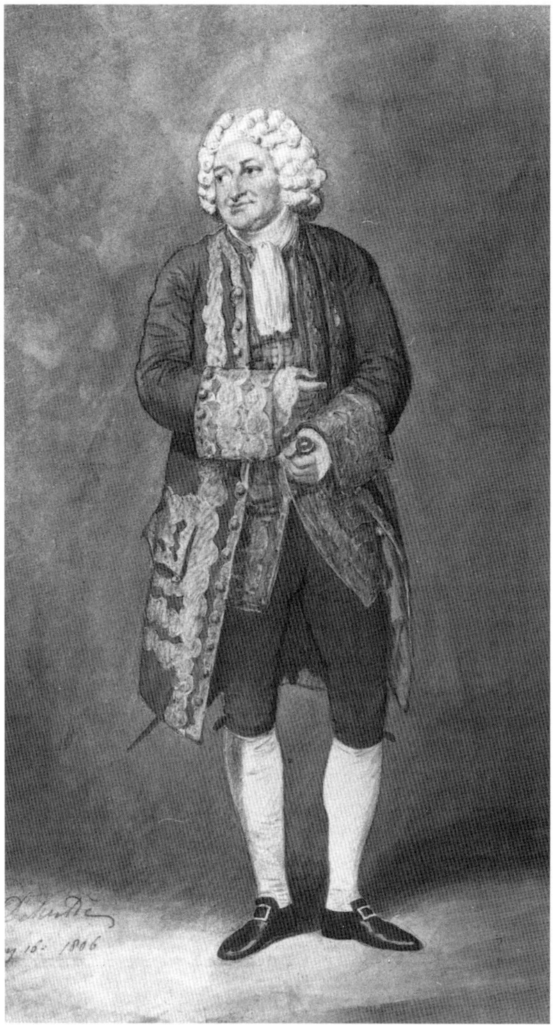

129

GEORGE FREDERICK COOKE

as Sir Archy MacSarcasm in *Love à la Mode*
by Charles Macklin

Samuel De Wilde

Pencil and watercolour on wove paper 37 x 23.5
INSCR: 'S De Wilde / May 16 1806' (black chalk b.l.)
INV: Mathews 209; RW/CKA 61E
PROV: Charles Mathews
EXH: 1833 London (209)
ENGR: Richard Woodman pub. John Cawthorn 1808,
stipple 41.9 x 28.2; same plate with title 'Mr Cooke as
Sir Pertinax Macsycophant'; Anthony Cardon for
Cawthorn's *Minor British Theatre* pub. John Cawthorn
4 October 1806, stipple 12 x 7.6; Anon., stipple 16 x 12
(h.l. to below hands); Kennerley for Oxberry's
Dramatic Biography pub. J. Duncombe 1826, stipple and line
7.1 x 5 (h.l.); Anon. pub. Oliver & Boyd, Edinburgh, 1811,
line 10.2 x 7.1 (crude adaptation with r.h. to l.,
holding a pinch of snuff)

Sir Archy is described by Beau Mordecai as 'almost buried in snuff, the roll of his eyes, and twist of his mouth, his strange inhuman laugh, his tremendous periwig, and his manner altogether ... [I] always take him for a mountebank-doctor at a Dutch fair'.

Sir Archy, holding a snuffbox and with a powdered curly wig, wears black shoes, grey breeches, a grey coat decorated with gold braid, and a blue waistcoat trimmed with gold braid.

Cooke played Sir Archy for the first time in London at Covent Garden on 13 November 1800. It became his most popular comic role and, like his Shylock (seee No. 133), was compared favourably with Macklin's famous interpretation. During a performance of *Love à la Mode* in the spring of 1803, Cooke was hooted off the stage for being drunk.

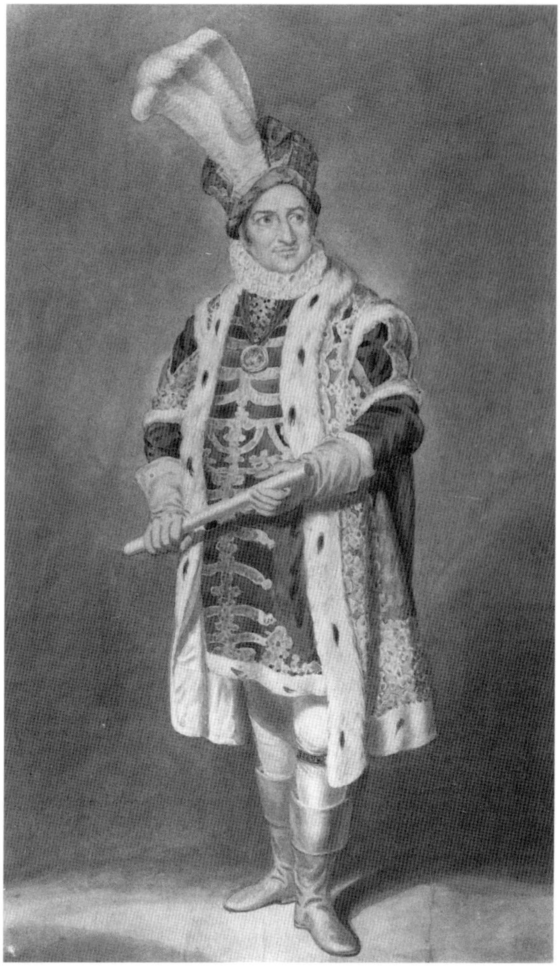

130

GEORGE FREDERICK COOKE

as Richard in *Richard III* by William Shakespeare

Samuel De Wilde

Pencil and watercolour on wove paper 37 x 23.5
INSCR: 'S De Wilde delin. / Jany 19 1809' (pencil b.l.)
INV: Mathews 246; RW/CKA 65C
PROV: Charles Mathews
EXH: 1809 R.A. (510) 'A drawing of Mr Cook, in the character of Richard III'; 1833 London (246); 1975 London (151)
ENGR: Thomas Cheesman for the *Theatrical Inquisitor* pub. C. Chapple 1 September 1813, stipple and line 15.3 x 9.1; same plate used for *Le Beau Monde & Monthly Register* pub. W. Read
LIT: Griffiths, p. 331

Cooke wears white gauntlets, brown boots, white stockings with a blue garter, a red coat with a white lining, embroidered in gold and trimmed with ermine, a blue tunic with gold embroidery and ermine trim, and a blue jerkin. He has a blue and gold George around his neck.

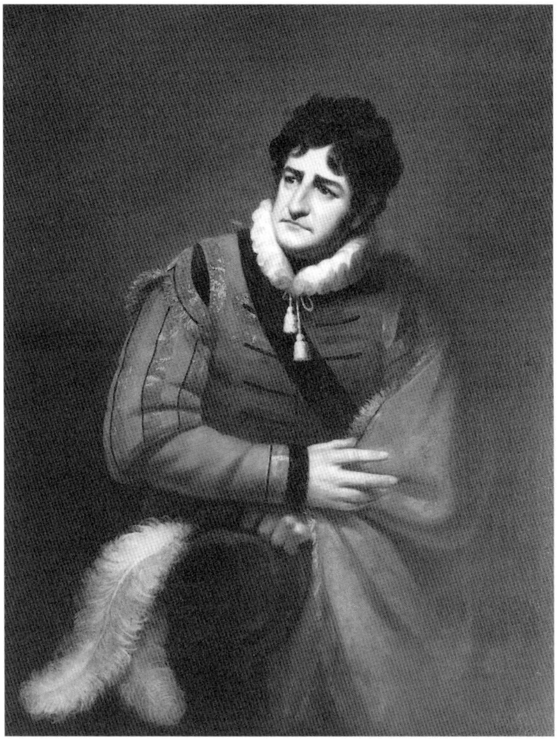

131
GEORGE FREDERICK COOKE
as Iago in *Othello* by William Shakespeare

James Green

Oil on canvas 127.5 x 101
INSCR: 'Jas. Green 1801'
INV: Mathews 108; RW/CKA 4
PROV: Charles Mathews
EXH: 1801 R.A. (127); 1833 London (108);
possibly the painting by Green of Cooke
as Iago at British Institution 1807
ENGR: James Ward pub. Ward & Co. 21 April 1801,
mezzotint 47.6 x 33.7; Anon., etching 16.2 x 10.8,
with quotation 'O beware, my Lord, of jealousy'
REL: Folger Library (after Green), oil 77.8 x 63.7;
Sotheby's 29 November 1971 (44) bt. Limner Antiques,
watercolour on card 10.8 x 8.3
LIT: Patmore, p. 268; Pressly, *Folger*, 111

Cooke wears a military jacket in red with black decoration, and a red cloak with a gold fringe. There is a plumed grey hat in his left hand.

Cooke was a successful Othello at Newcastle in 1788 and played the part for his début at the Crow Street Theatre, Dublin, on 19 November 1794. However, by the time he reached London in 1800, he had decided that the role of Iago suited him better. He gave his first performance in that role in London at Covent Garden on 20 December 1800, with Alexander Pope as Othello.

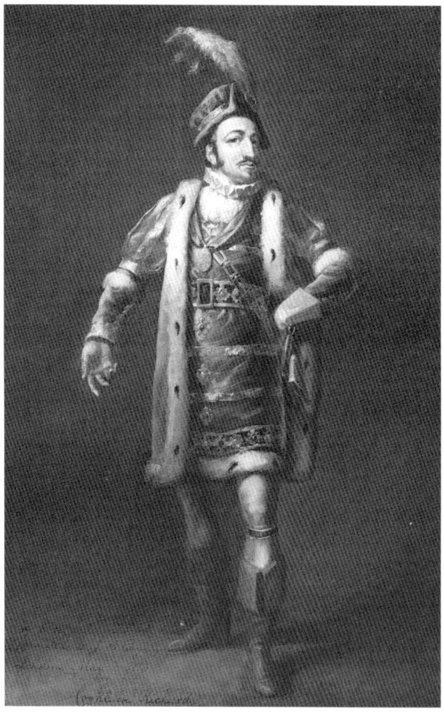

132
GEORGE FREDERICK COOKE
as Richard in *Richard III* by William Shakespeare

Charles Robert Leslie

Oil on canvas 44.5 x 29.2
INSCR: 'by C.R. Leslie and by him / presented to
J.H. Payne / London May 7 1813 / Cooke in Richard' (b.l.)
INV: RW/CKA 363; Gift 8
PROV: John Howard Payne; T. Longman Jnr,
by whom presented, 1838
EXH: 1982–83 London (144)
ENGR: Thomson for Oxberry's *New English Drama*
pub. Simpkin & Marshall 1818, stipple 11.7 x 8,
inscr: '...from an original Painting by C.R. Leslie /
in the Possession of John Howard Payne, Esqr.'
REL: Watercolour by C.R. Leslie, 1811, untraced (?)

Cooke wears brown boots, white hose with a blue garter, a purple tunic trimmed with ermine and horizontal bands of gold with jewels, and a red coat trimmed with ermine. His gold George hangs from a blue ribbon, and his plumed purple hat has a gold band with a jewel.

Leslie evidently painted the portrait of Cooke as a gift whilst another picture (of J.H. Payne as Douglas) was in progress. It is copied from a print of Cooke as Richard, engraved by D. Edwin for the *Mirror of Taste and Dramatic Censor*, March 1811, from a watercolour by Leslie. This watercolour recorded a performance given by Cooke in Philadelphia on 25 March 1811 and was one of a series of drawings by Leslie showing the actor in various roles.

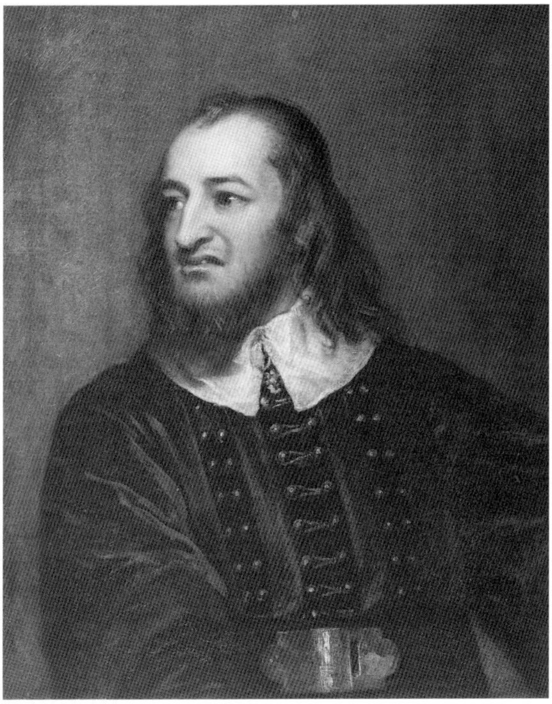

133
GEORGE FREDERICK COOKE
as Shylock in *The Merchant of Venice*
by William Shakespeare

Thomas Phillips

Oil on canvas 76 x 63
INV: Mathews 1; RW/CKA 460
PROV: Charles Mathews
EXH: 1833 London (1)
LIT: Griffiths, p. 331

Cooke, with long hair, wears a dark blue velvet tunic trimmed with fur. His black belt has a gold buckle.

In his record of sitters, on 6 April 1803 Phillips entered: 'Mr Cooke in "Shylock", w.l.' Cooke's first recorded performance as Shylock was at Sheffield in 1790. When he played the part in Manchester on 2 April 1794, the *Monthly Mirror* said that the performance was 'not to be equalled by any other actor in the kingdom'. Shylock was the second role played by Cooke on his return to London in 1800, and his performance on 10 November 1800 was compared favourably to Macklin's famous interpretation. Shylock was the last role Cooke played on the London stage, when he appeared for Mrs Clarke's benefit on 22 June 1810.

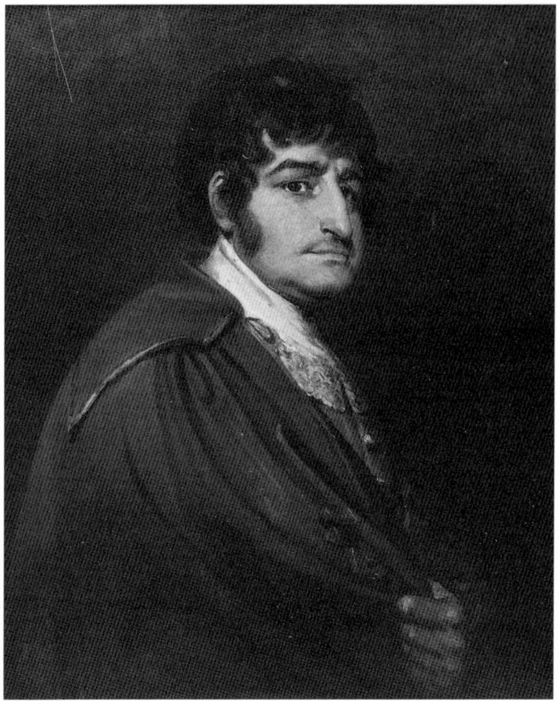

134
GEORGE FREDERICK COOKE
as Kitely in *Every Man in His Humour* by Ben Jonson

Henry Singleton

Oil on canvas 73.7 x 61
INV: Mathews 3; RW/CKA 462
PROV: Charles Mathews
EXH: 1833 London (3)
REL: Sarah Singleton exhibited a portrait of Cooke as Kitely, R.A. 1802 (728), probably a miniature copy of her brother's picture
LIT: Patmore, p. 268; Griffiths, p. 331

Kitely talks to his servant Thomas Cash in his warehouse. He has an appointment at the exchange, but feels that his absence may test his wife's constancy. Kitely wears a cloak in several scenes, but in Act III, scene 2 he puts his cloak on, takes it off, and puts it on again before going out. In the picture he has a green-grey cloak edged in blue, and a brown jacket.

Kitely was one of the first roles that Cooke played on his return to the London stage in 1800; his first performance of it was on 17 December 1800.

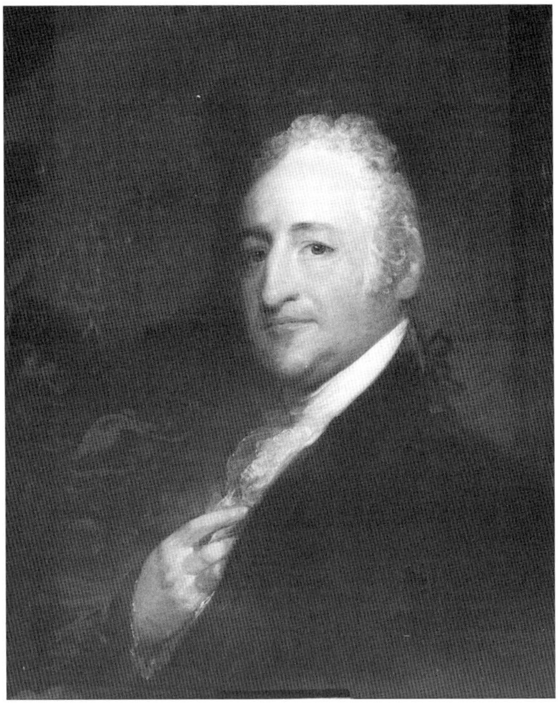

135
GEORGE FREDERICK COOKE

Gilbert Stuart

Oil on panel 68.6 x 55.9
INV: Mathews 49; RW 372 (by J. Stewart); CKA 372
PROV: Price; Charles Mathews
EXH: 1833 London (49)
LIT: William Dunlap, *Memoirs of Cooke* (1813), II, 185–86; Laurence Park, *Gilbert Stuart* (1926), I, 236–37

A mature Cooke wears a dark blue velvet jacket with traces of powder on the shoulders.

This portrait was painted in Boston for Price, the New York theatre manager, and was completed on 6 January 1811. Patmore calls it 'the last portrait for which he ever sat, painted in America'.

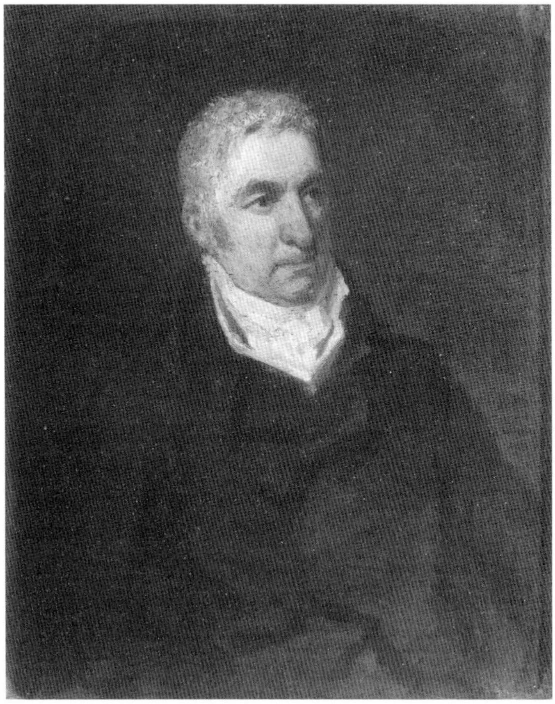

136
GEORGE FREDERICK COOKE

Unknown Artist

Oil on panel 19.7 x 16.2
INV: RW/CKA 283
PROV: Unknown; Garrick Club by 1909

Cooke wears a dark brown jacket and trousers, white waistcoat with red decoration, and a high white stock.

No. 136 is similar to S. J. Stump's portrait, engraved in stipple and line by James Hopwood and published on 1 October 1807.

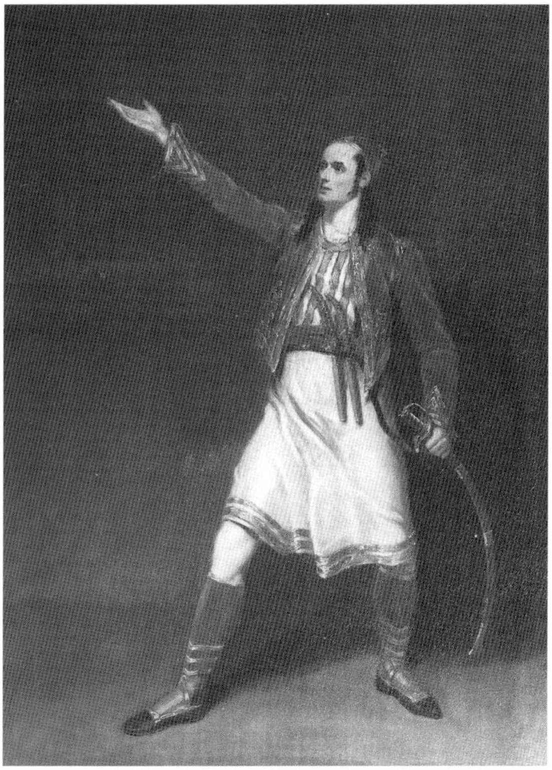

137
THOMAS P. COOKE
as Zenocles in *Ali Pacha or The Signet Ring*
by John Howard Payne and James Robinson Planché

George Clint

Oil on canvas 52.1 x 40.6
INV: RW/CKA 451; Gift 160
PROV: Presented by Sir William de Bathe Bt, 1860

Zenocles wears black slippers trimmed in gold, blue stockings, red leggings with horizontal gold bands, a white tunic trimmed with gold, and a gold cummerbund with a belt in which are two pistols. His red velvet jacket is trimmed with gold and his gold velvet hat has a red band and gold frills.

Payne and Planché's melodrama was first performed at Covent Garden on 19 October 1822. It was licensed as *The Pacha* and billed as 'A New Grand Serious Melo-Drama'. T.P. Cooke was the original Zenocles and William Farren the original Ali Pacha. There were 16 performances to 28 November 1822.

Cooke was an original member of the Garrick Club in 1831.

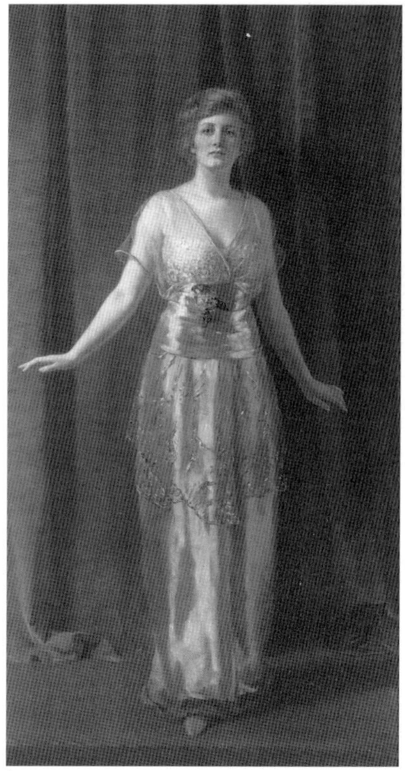

138*
DAME GLADYS COOPER
in *My Lady's Dress* by Edward G. Knoblauch

The Hon. John Collier

Oil on canvas 217.8 x 116.8
INSCR: 'John Collier' (brown paint b.r.)
INV: GCL 706; Gift 804
PROV: Presented by the sitter, 1965
EXH: 1915 R.A. (627); 1958 Liverpool

The sitter wears a long white silk dress with short sleeves and red fur trimming, and a broad silk sash with a rose tucked into it. She stands in front of a dark yellow curtain, possibly taking a curtain call.

Knoblauch's epic play, following the history of a dress, was first given at the Royalty on 21 April 1914 and ran until 8 August, when all London theatres were disrupted by war nerves. It re-opened on 7 September, but failed to attract much of an audience and closed on 24 October 1914 after an aggregate of 176 performances. Gladys Cooper played the leading multi-role of Anna/Nina/Annette/Antze/Annie/Anna/Anita opposite Dennis Eadie as John/Gioann/Joanny/Jonkheer Ian Van de Bom/Jack/Ivan/Jacquelin. Edith Evans was also in the cast. The play's provocative title stimulated a revue with Alice Delysia at the Ambassadors called *My Lady's Undress*, which opened on 17 October 1914.

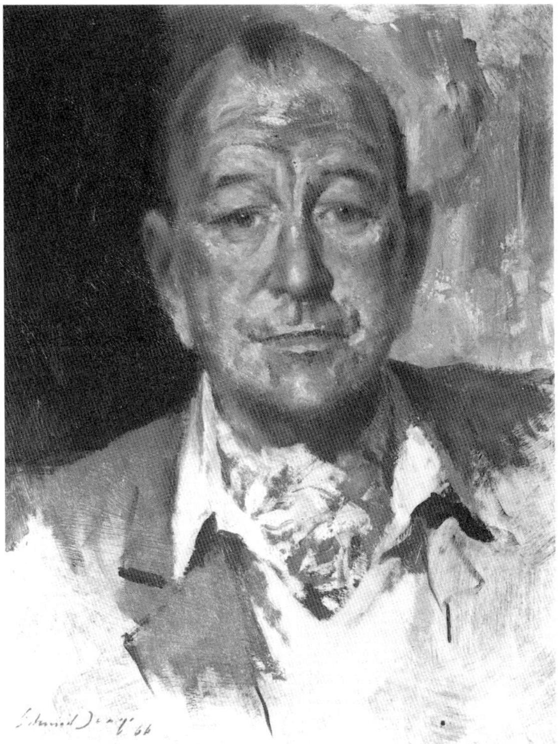

139*

SIR NOEL COWARD

Edward Seago

Oil on canvas 53.3 x 40.6
INSCR: 'Edward Seago /' 66' (brown paint b.l.)
INV: GCL 715; Gift 818
PROV: Presented by the artist, 1966
EXH: 1974 London
REL: Noel Coward Estate, oil on canvas 53 x 40.5;
Phoenix Theatre, Noel Coward Bar,
oil on canvas 53 x 40.5
LIT: Jean Goodman, *Edward Seago – the Other Side of the Canvas* (1978), p. 231, illus. between pp. 200 and 201; reproduced in *Barbara Cartland's Book of Personalities* (1979)

The sitter wears a grey coat, a yellow pullover, and a cravat in white, red and grey.

Artist and sitter met at a Sandringham house party in 1965. When Coward was elected to the Garrick Club the following year, Seago celebrated the overdue event by painting him. The sitter was pleased with the result, and Seago painted him a copy, which Coward had reproduced for use as a Christmas card. When the Phoenix Theatre opened its Coward Bar in 1969 to celebrate the 70th birthday of 'The Master', Seago painted another copy.

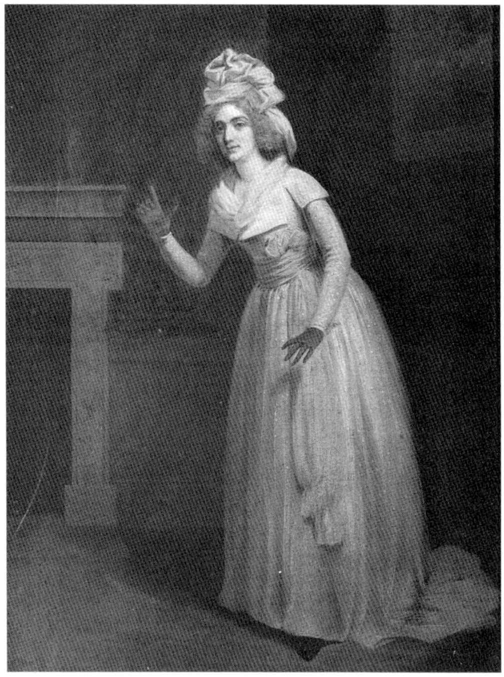

140

ANNA MARIA CROUCH

as Polly in *The Beggar's Opera* by John Gay

Samuel De Wilde

Oil on canvas 43 x 28.5
INV: Mathews 179; RW/CKA 482
PROV: John Bell; Charles Mathews
EXH: 1833 London (179)
ENGR: J. Thornthwaite for Bell's British Library 2 February 1791, line 10.8 x 8 (inscr: 'De Wilde del'), pub. Bell's *British Theatre* (1797), vol 11; W. Esdall for Jones's *British Theatre* pub. Wm. Jones, Dublin, 1791, line 10.8 x 8 (reversed)
REL: Watercolour by De Wilde (untraced), the probable original for the 1791 engraving

Polly wears a white spotted muslin dress with a pale green sash, which matches the ribbon on her muslin cap.

Gay's comic opera, first performed at Lincoln's Inn Fields on 29 January 1728, was one of the most popular pieces of the 18th century, staged several times at all three Patent theatres almost every year. When still Miss Phillips, Mrs Crouch first played Polly at Drury Lane on 16 April 1784 (she had acted the role in her début at Liverpool on 11 June 1781), and she was the Polly at the last Drury Lane performance (16 April 1790) before De Wilde's picture was painted.

The inscription on the original plate suggests that the source was a drawing rather than a painting. There are four such plates in the 1797 edition of Bell's *British Theatre*. There are oil versions of all four in the Garrick Club: Nos. 20, 71, 140 and 657.

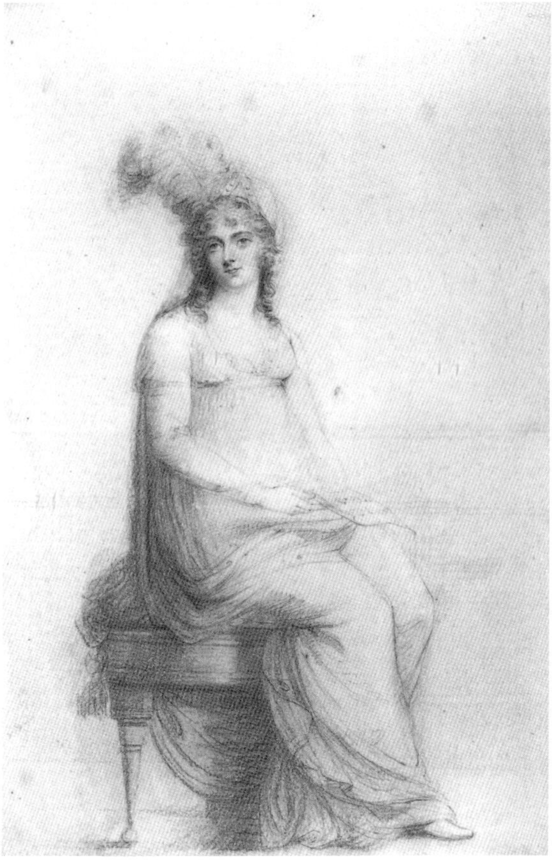

141
ANNA MARIA CROUCH

Rev. Mr Thomas

Pencil and watercolour on wove paper 26.5 x 17.9
INSCR: 'Revd. Mr Thomas Fecit.'
(pen and brown ink b.l.)
INV: Mathews 275; RW/CKA 490
PROV: Charles Mathews
EXH: 1833 London (490)

Mrs Crouch is presented in high neo-classical style, seated on a circular stool, wearing an ostrich feather headdress and holding a sheet of music. She is shown wearing a similar headdress, but a different gown, in John Raphael Smith's engraving after a miniature by J. Barry. In that composition she holds up a rose, as Selima in Collier's *Selima and Azar*, a role she acted for the first time at Drury Lane on 28 January 1788 and for the last time on 21 April 1792. The date of the drawing is perhaps nearer 1800.

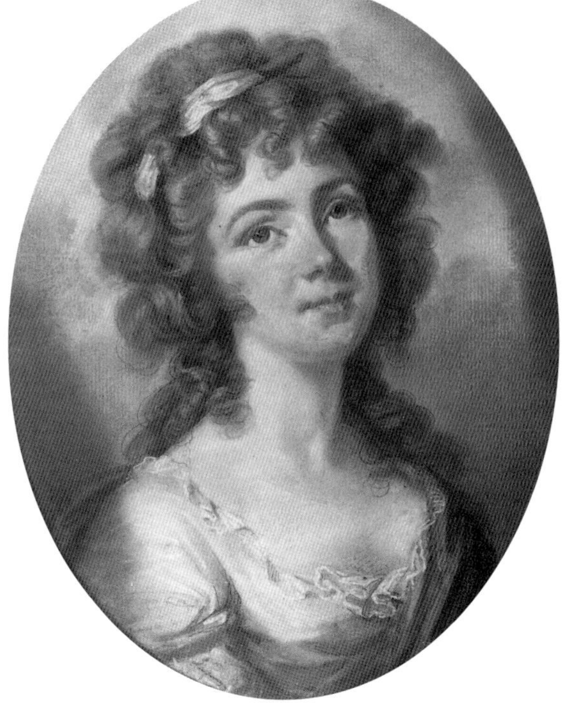

142
ANNA MARIA CROUCH (?)

Unknown Artist

Pencil and pastel on laid paper 25.4 x 20.3
INSCR: (illegible l.c.)
INV: RW 305 (sitter and artist unknown); CKA 305
(unknown, possibly by J.R. Smith)
PROV: Unknown; Garrick Club by 1909

The sitter has a white ribbon in her hair, and wears a white dress.

This drawing dates from the early 1790s and is similar to the series that Condé drew for the *Thespian Magazine* in 1792. It is more substantial, however, and he is not the artist. The identification of the sitter as Anna Maria Crouch is based entirely on the similarity of this drawing to other portraits of her, particularly that by Condé, which is dated 1792.

'At the peak of her powers Anna Maria Crouch combined extraordinary beauty and grace of person very effectively with a good stage presence and a fine singing voice to seize the affections of a large public. She was not a powerful actress, but most of the parts she sustained required no great power' (BD).

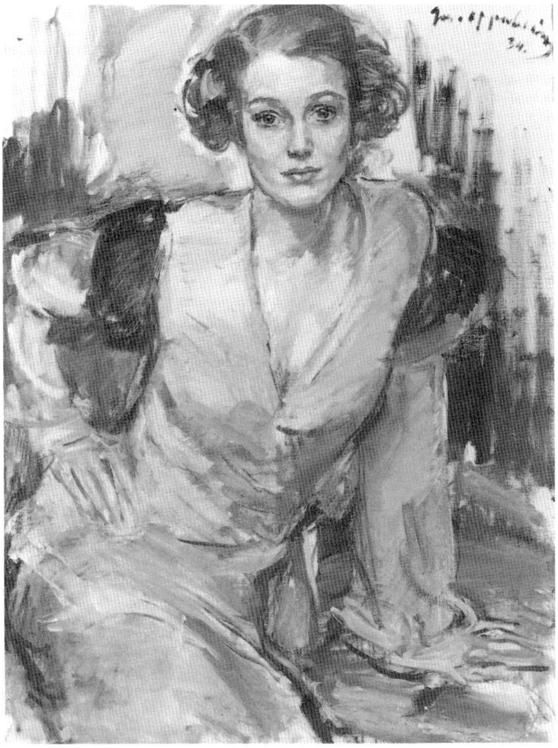

143*
CONSTANCE CUMMINGS

James Oppenheim
Oil on canvas 92 x 71.5
INSCR: 'Jas. Oppenheim /34' (dark brown paint t.r.)
INV: GCL 733; Gift 876
PROV: Presented by the sitter, 1977

The sitter wears a yellow fur-trimmed dress. Her left hand is leaning on a blue cushion bottom right.

Constance Cummings made her London début on 22 July 1934, as Alice Overton in *Sour Grapes*, by Vincent Lawrence. The play was produced by her husband, Ben W. Levy, and was transferred to the Apollo on 9 August 1934.

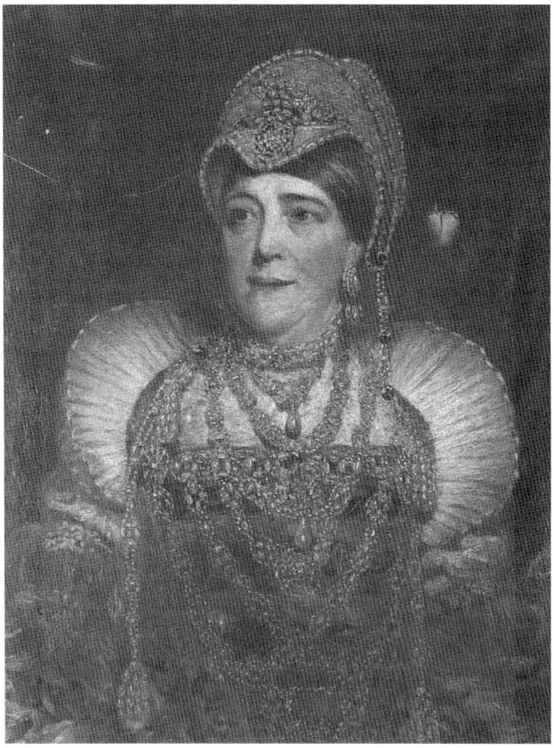

144
MARY ANN DAVENPORT
as Lady Denny in *Henry VIII*
by William Shakespeare

Benjamin Burnell
Oil on canvas 73.7 x 61.6
INV: Mathews 54 (by Blundell);
RW 419 (by Blundell?); CKA 419
PROV: Thomas Harris; Harris sale,
Robins 12 July 1819 (58); Charles Mathews
EXH: 1818 R.A. (495), with lines quoted in the catalogue:
'King: "Is the Queen delivered?/Say Ay – and of a boy."/
Lady: "Ay, Ay, my Liege." '; 1833 London (54)

Half-length. Lady Denny wears a gold cap encrusted with jewels and many jewelled necklaces over a red-striped stomacher. There are ruffs on her shoulders.

Mrs Davenport played Lady Denny in the new production of *Henry VIII* that opened at Covent Garden on 23 April 1806. The cast also included Sarah Siddons as Queen Katherine, John Philip Kemble as Cardinal Wolsey, Charles Kemble as Cromwell, and Alexander Pope as King Henry. The play was given 'New Scenes, Dresses and Decorations', and presumably Lady Denny's extravagant costume was created at that time. Mrs Davenport's last performances as Lady Denny before the picture was painted were on 27 May and 2 and 17 June 1817.

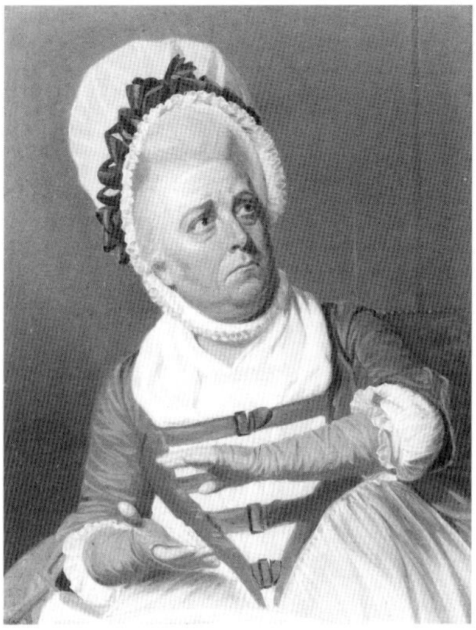

145
MARY ANN DAVENPORT
as Dame Ashfield in *Speed the Plough*
by Thomas Morton (?)

Samuel De Wilde

Oil on panel 24.5 x 20
INV: Mathews 150 (as Mrs Moral in 'The Birth-Day');
RW 220 (as Mrs Moral); CKA 220
PROV: Charles Mathews
EXH: 1833 London (150)
ENGR: William Ridley for the *The Monthly Mirror*
pub. Vernor & Hood 28 February 1805,
9.2 x 7.6 (as Mrs Grundy)
REL: V&A D.34, black chalk and wash 23.5 x 17.8 s. & d.
'De Wilde / delin 1802' (black chalk u.l.) [Possibly the portrait of Mrs Davenport by De Wilde, signed and dated, that was in the Royal Dramatic College sale at Fairbrother, Lye and Palmer on 24 February 1881 (lot 100A)]

The quotation supplied by Mathews ('What, drinking again! I'll tell you it's both immoral and genteel!') is not from *Speed the Plough*, nor is it from *The Birth-day*, in which the only female members of the cast are two young ladies of the languid kind, not Mrs Davenport's type of character at all. The costume seems to be rather grand for the rustic farmer's wife in *Speed the Plough* (see No. 194). The engraving called the character Mrs Grundy, who does not appear in *Speed the Plough* but to whom Dame Ashfield constantly refers. Mrs Davenport is dressed in white and brown, and sits on a red padded chair.

Morton's comedy, with incidental music by John March and and scenery by John Inigo Richards, was first performed at Covent Garden on 8 February 1800. There were 41 performances of the popular piece during its first season. Mrs Davenport was the original Dame Ashfield.

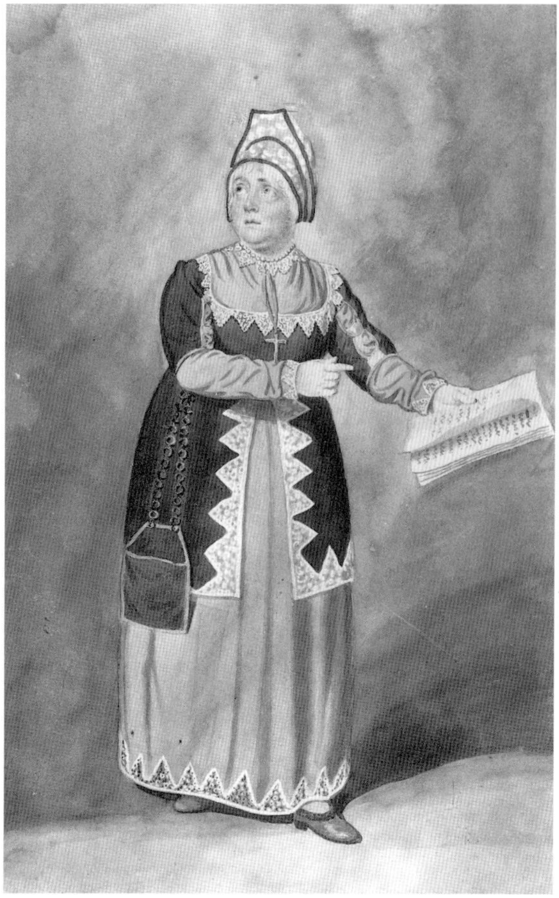

146
MARY ANN DAVENPORT
as Fiametta in *The Tale of Mystery* by Thomas Holcroft

Samuel De Wilde

Pencil and watercolour on wove paper 37 x 23.5
INSCR: 'De Wilde 1809' (pencil b.r.)
INV: Mathews 292; RW/CKA 63D
PROV: Charles Mathews
EXH: 1833 London (292); 1975 London (146)

Fiametta is the faithful servant with a heart of gold, who has worked for Bonamo for 23 years. In the second act she defends the dumb and abused Francesco in the face of her master's wrath – a moment that De Wilde no doubt hoped to evoke here. Fiametta wears brown shoes with fur edging, a long-sleeved brown dress with white hem, a dark green overfrock open at the front to the knees, and a headdress with three bands of decoration.

Holcroft's melodrama was first given at Covent Garden on 13 November 1802, with Isabella Mattocks as Fiametta. Mrs Davenport played Fiametta at the Haymarket four times over the summer of 1809, first on 9 June and for the last time on 8 August.

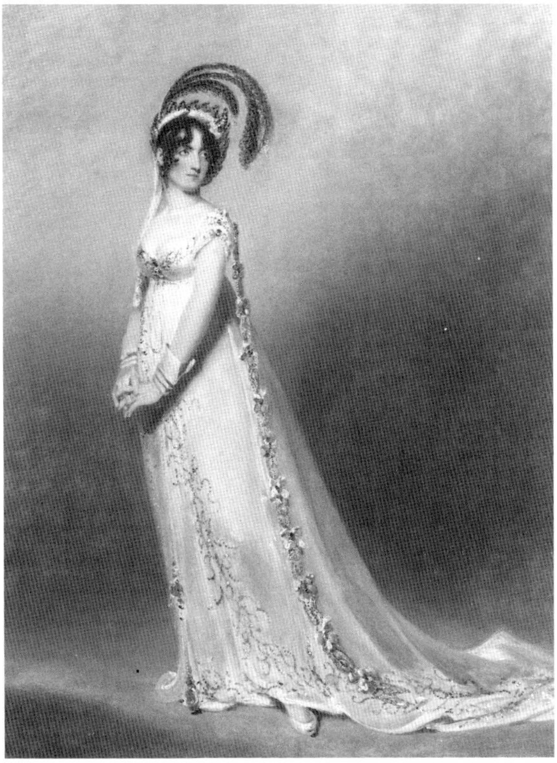

147*

MARIA DAVISON

as Juliana in *The Honey Moon*

by John Tobin

Henry Singleton

Oil on canvas 76.5 x 63.5

INV: Mathews 23; RW/CKA 142

PROV: Charles Mathews

EXH: 1805 R.A. (280); 1833 London (23);
1934 London (319); 1951 London (35)

ENGR: H.R. Cook for the *Theatrical Inquisitor*
1 February 1812, stipple 15 x 9.7;
H.R. Cook pub. Sherwood & Co. 1813, stipple 16.2 x 11.1
(indications of skirting board visible)

The scene is a room in Balthazar's house. Juliana, his daughter, has just entered wearing the wedding dress in which she is to marry Duke Aranza. She is a vain shrew, whom the Duke sets about taming during the rest of the play. Juliana's wedding dress is trimmed with silver sequins and looped beads. There is a red jewel at her breast, and from her shoulders hangs a long gauze drape edged in flower embroidery of stiff gauze and sequins. Her striking headdress is white, with a jagged profile edged with dark sequins and with three plumes.

Tobin's comedy was first performed at Drury Lane on 31 January 1805. It was seen 29 times that season, with Miss Duncan (Mrs Davison) as the original Juliana.

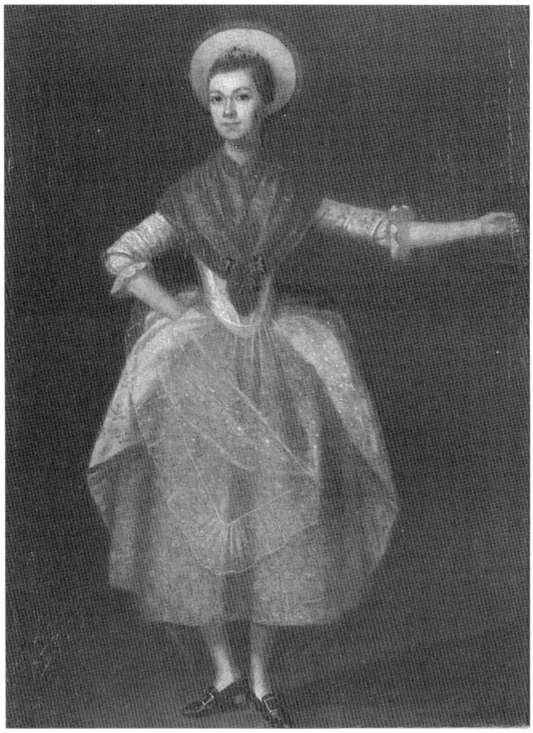

148

NANCY DAWSON

Samuel De Wilde
(copy by De Wilde after Unknown Artist?)

Oil on canvas 37 x 29

INV: Mathews 183 (artist unknown); RW/CKA 272

PROV: Thomas Harris?; Harris sale,
Robins 12 July 1819 (7)?; Charles Mathews

EXH: 1833 London (183)

ENGR: M. Jackson after Anon. pub. M. Jackson,
mezzotint 33 x 25.1; same plate printed for R. Sayer

Nancy is shown dancing her celebrated hornpipe. She wears green shoes with paste buckles, a round yellow straw hat edged with blue ribbon, and a short white dress open at the front to reveal a pink underskirt, over which she has a spotted muslin apron. Her fichu is bronze-coloured with red stripes and tied with a blue bow. She has a choker consisting of three rows of pearls.

De Wilde was CKA's tentative attribution, and the picture does seem to relate technically to his other small full-length portraits. It is a copy after the anonymous mezzotint, and may have been the picture in the Thomas Harris collection. The original artist of this design might have been Edward Penny (1714–1791).

For details on the novelty and popularity of Nancy Dawson's hornpipe – a tune written by Thomas Arne and still sung as 'Here we go round the Mulberry Bush' – see the BD 4: 237–43.

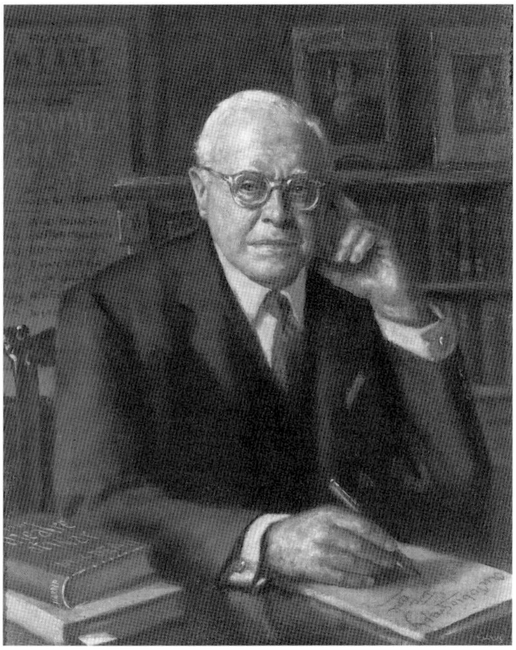

149

BASIL DEAN

John Gilroy

Oil on canvas 66 x 71

INSCR: 'Gilroy' (white paint b.r.) 'The / Theatre / at War / BASIL DEAN' (on book jacket b.l.); 'Autobiography / Chapter / one' (on sheet of paper b.r.); '[MI]DSUMMER / [N]IGHT'S / DREAM / BALLETS BY FOKINE / MILES MALLESON / CLIFFORD MOLLISON / H.O. NICHOLSON / [MAG]GIE TEYTE / WISON OULE / ATHEN[E SEYLER] / WILF[RED WALTER]' (on playbill t.l.)

INV: GCL 713; Gift 816/828

PROV: Presented by the artist, 1967

The sitter wears a grey suit and green tie.

The playbill is for Basil Dean's production of *A Midsummer Night's Dream*, which opened at Drury Lane on 26 December 1924. The cast included Miles Malleson as Snout, Clifford Mollison as Flute, H.O. Nicholson as Starveling, and Wilfred Walter as Bottom. Athene Seyler was Hermia, and Edith Evans was Helena, with Leon Quartermaine as Lysander and Frank Vosper as Demetrius. Gwen Ffrangcon Davies was Titania. Michel Fokine was responsible for the ballet. Maggie Teyte, mentioned in the inscription, is not recorded as having been in the production.

Dean, an actor, dramatist and director, had a long and extensive career; among his key productions were *Johnson Over Jordan* (1939), *An Inspector Calls* (1946), and *The Aspern Papers* (1959). In 1947 he was awarded the CBE. He became a member of the Garrick Club in 1939.

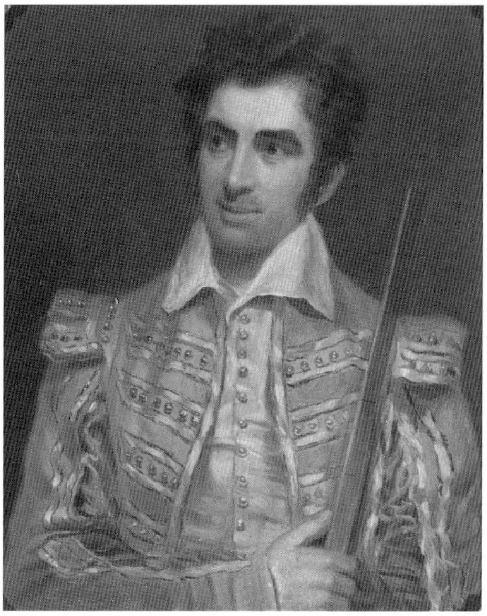

150

VINCENT DE CAMP

as Figaro in *Follies of a Day or The Marriage of Figaro* by Thomas Holcroft

George Clint

Oil on panel 29.2 x 24.1

INV: CKA 602; Gift 339

PROV: G.P. Harding, by whom presented to the Garrick Club, 1909

ENGR: Cooke for Oxberry's *New English Drama* pub. Simpkin & Marshall June 1822, stipple 10 x 7.7

Figaro is shown at the beginning of Act I, scene I, in a room in Count Almaviva's castle. He is measuring the room with his 'wand' to see if the bed given to him and his wife Susan by the Count will fit in. The Oxberry edition stage directions give Figaro's costume as 'Light blue Spanish dress of kerseymere [cashmere] trimmed with pink bordering'. In the portrait, which was engraved for the same edition, he is shown in a pink doublet elaborately decorated in blue and white with blue slashing and pearls, and a white shirt with pearl buttons.

Holcroft's comedy, taken from Beaumarchais, was first performed at Covent Garden on 14 December 1784, with incidental music by William Shield. The play was licensed as *The Marriage of Figaro*. The author was himself the first Figaro, and by the end of the century Charles Farley had played the part at Covent Garden and Robert Palmer at Drury Lane. Figaro does not appear in the manuscript list of De Camp's parts in the Folger Library. That list dates from about 1814, when De Camp left London for the provinces and later the United States.

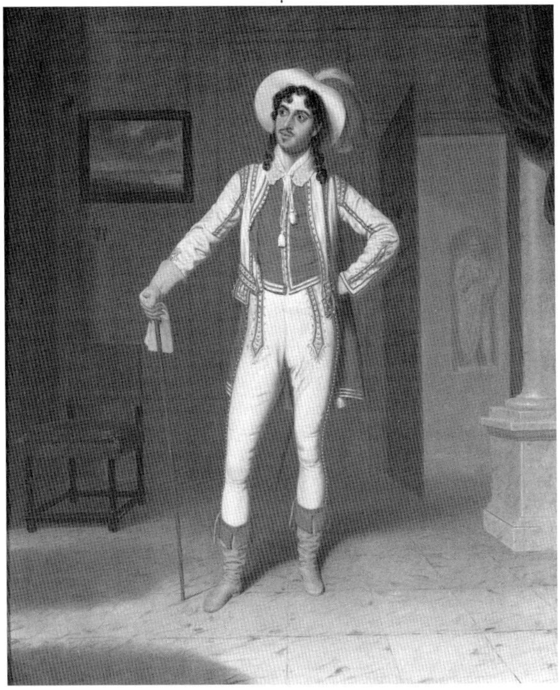

151*

VINCENT DE CAMP

as Master Heartwell in *Riches or The Wife and Brother* by Sir James Bland Burges

Samuel De Wilde

Oil on canvas 76 x 63

INV: Mathews 129 (as Edward Lacey); RW/CKA 113

PROV: Charles Mathews

EXH: 1811 R.A. (538); 1833 London (129); 1951 London (7); 1950–51 London (247); 1951–52 London (127)

Heartwell is 'a rich country gentleman', 'A Glostershire esquire, whose lands return him Three thousand pounds a year'. He wears brown boots with red tops, cream stockings, a cream suit trimmed with green, and a green waistcoat and cloak with cream trim. His wide-brimmed white hat has white and green ostrich feathers.

Burges's drama, an adaptation of Massinger's *The City Madam*, was first performed by the Drury Lane company at the Lyceum on 3 February 1810. It was licensed on 25 January as 'The Mind's Magnet; or, The School of Arrogance'. Vincent De Camp was the original Master Heartwell. De Wilde's diary for November 1810 mentions two sittings for De Camp as Heartwell.

See also No. 180.

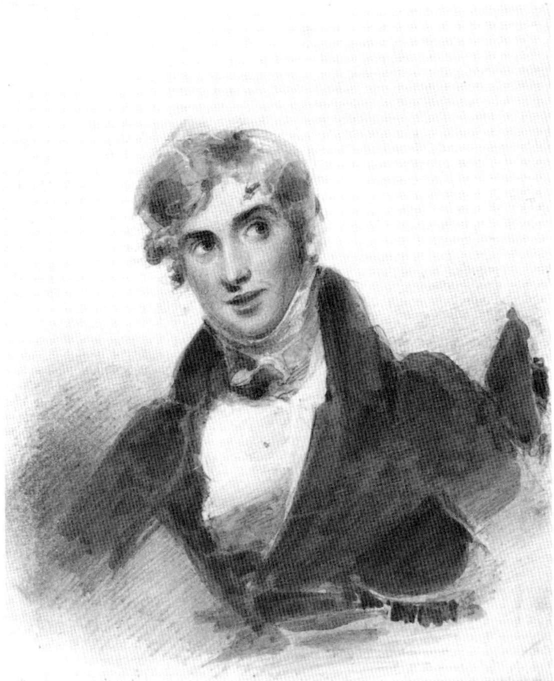

152

VINCENT DE CAMP

William Foster

Black chalk and watercolour on wove paper 20.8 x 16.5

INSCR: 'Foster Fecit' (pen and brown ink on mount b.l. CM); 'Mr De Camp' (pen and brown ink on mount b.c. CM)

INV: Mathews 281; RW/CKA 547A

PROV: Charles Mathews

EXH: 1833 London (281)

The sitter wears a black coat and a high blue stock.

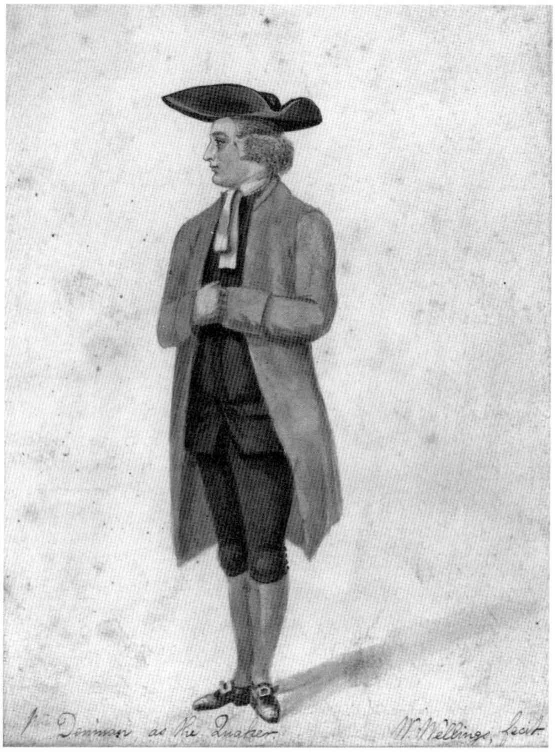

153
WILLIAM DENMAN
as Solomon in *The Quaker* by Charles Dibdin

William Wellings

Pencil and watercolour on wove paper 23.6 x 17.8
INSCR: 'Wm Denman as the Quaker'
(pen and brown ink b.l. CM);
'W. Wellings, fecit' (pen and brown ink b.r. CM)
INV: CKA 522
PROV: Charles Mathews (not in catalogue)

Denman wears a Quaker's suit – a drab coat, brown waistcoat and breeches, and a tricorn hat.

Dibdin's comic opera, with music by the author, was first performed at Drury Lane on 7 October 1777. William Parsons was the original Solomon. Suett appears to have had the part at Drury Lane for the whole of Denman's career there. There was an exception on 20 December 1797, when the part was taken by Hollingsworth. Perhaps Wellings was recording a provincial performance.

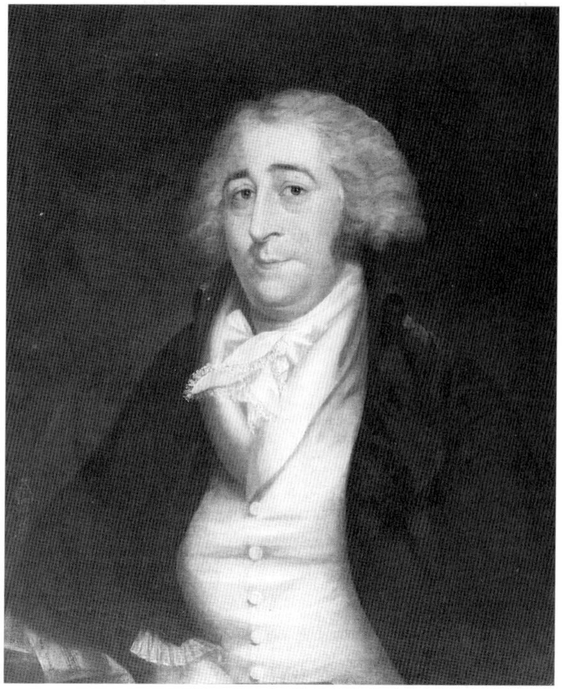

154
CHARLES DIBDIN

Samuel James Arnold

Oil on canvas 77 x 64
INSCR: 'Lovely Nan' (on paper on table b.l.)
INV: RW 381 (artist unknown); CKA 381; Gift 77
PROV: Presented by James Goding, 1842
EXH: 1958 London

Dibdin wears a dark green jacket and a white waistcoat.

The epitome of the popular showman, Dibdin was an indefatigable actor, singer, composer and manager. Perhaps his most famous role was that of Mungo in Bickerstaffe's *The Padlock*, for which he also wrote the music. He worked for almost all the London theatres in the latter half of the 18th century, and managed some of them, including the Royal Circus and the Sans Souci.

According to the *London Stage* calendars, 'Lovely Nan', one of the numerous songs written by Dibdin, seems to have been sung for the first time at the Haymarket on 1 September 1796, by George Wathen.

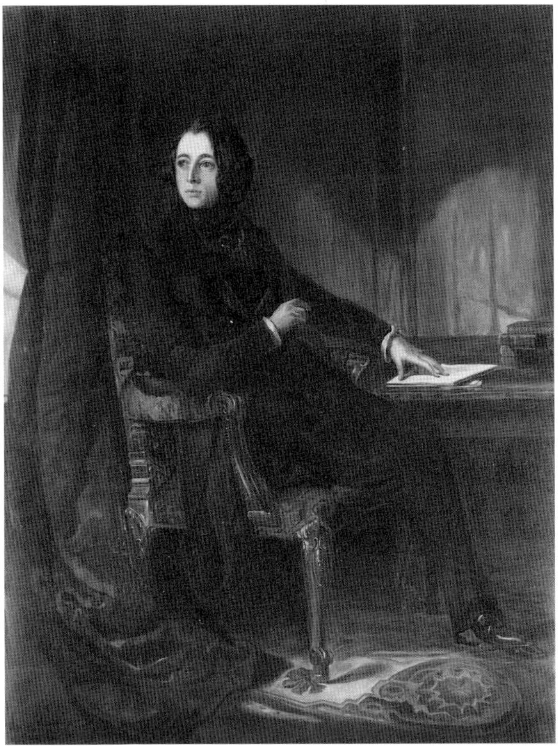

155

CHARLES DICKENS

Charles Fullwood (after Daniel Maclise)

Oil on canvas 90.2 x 69.8
INSCR: 'Charles Fullwood / D Maclise' (black paint b.l.)
INV: RW/CKA 349; Gift 292
PROV: Presented by Sir Herbert Beerbohm Tree, 1905
REL: Original: NPG 1172, oil on canvas 91.4 x 71.4 s.&d. 1839; engr: Finden as frontispiece to *Nicholas Nickelby* (1839), stipple 12.7 x 9.8 (tql); reissued pub. Chapman & Hall 1839; C.H. Jeens for Forster's *Life of Charles Dickens* (1872), stipple 11.7 x 8.9

Dickens wears black shoes, dark green trousers, a grey day coat, a brownish waistcoat, and a high black cravat. He sits in a chair which is upholstered in red velvet with a floral pattern. There is a long green curtain over the window on the left. Dickens became a member of the Garrick Club in 1837.

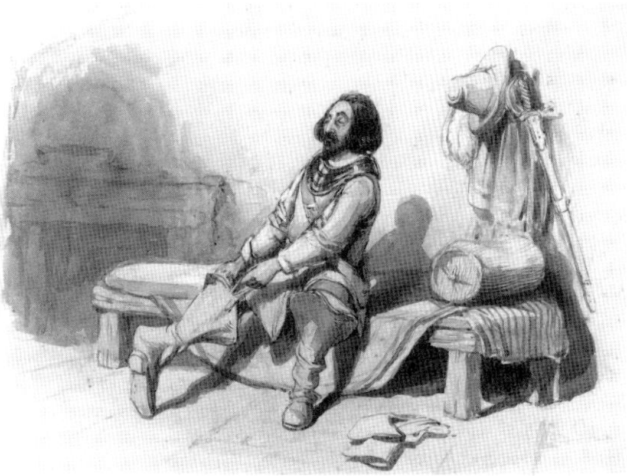

156

CHARLES DICKENS

as Bobadil in *Every Man in his Humour* by Ben Jonson

Clarkson Stanfield

Pencil, pen and brown ink, brown and grey wash with white body colour on wove paper 27.3 x 35
INV: (not in RW); CKA 499
PROV: Mrs Stanfield; her sale, Christie's 23 March 1876 (7) bt. Johnson 5 guineas; presented to the Club before 1888
EXH: 1979 Bonn & Sunderland (288)

Bobadil is shown on his first appearance, 'discovered upon a Bench' in his lodgings at the house of Cob, the water-bearer. Stanfield's drawing perhaps relates to a painting by C.R. Leslie showing Dickens at the same moment in the play, with the addition of the Hostess arriving through a door on the right. It was shown at the R.A. in 1846 (355) and is now in an American private collection. Both painting and drawing have a curious source in Taylor's frontispiece to Thomas Lowndes's edition of the play, engraved by Goldar and published on 2 November 1776. In Leslie's picture Bobadil is shown pulling on his boot, and even the articles hanging from the hook on the wall are similar.

In their *Recollections of Writers* (1878), Charles and Mary Cowden-Clarke recalled Dickens's performance as Bobadil thus: 'The way in which Charles Dickens impersonated that arch braggart Captain Bobadil, was a veritable piece of genius; from the moment when he is discovered lolling at full length on a bench in his lodging calling for a "cup o' small beer" to cool down the remnants of excitement from last night's carouse with a set of roaring gallants, till his final boast of "having not so much as once offered to resist" the "coarse fellow" who set upon him in the open streets, he was capital.'

The drawing is executed in the style of the Sketching Club, to which Stanfield belonged in the 1840s. See Jean Hamilton, *The Sketching Society 1799–1851*, exh. cat. V&A, 1971.

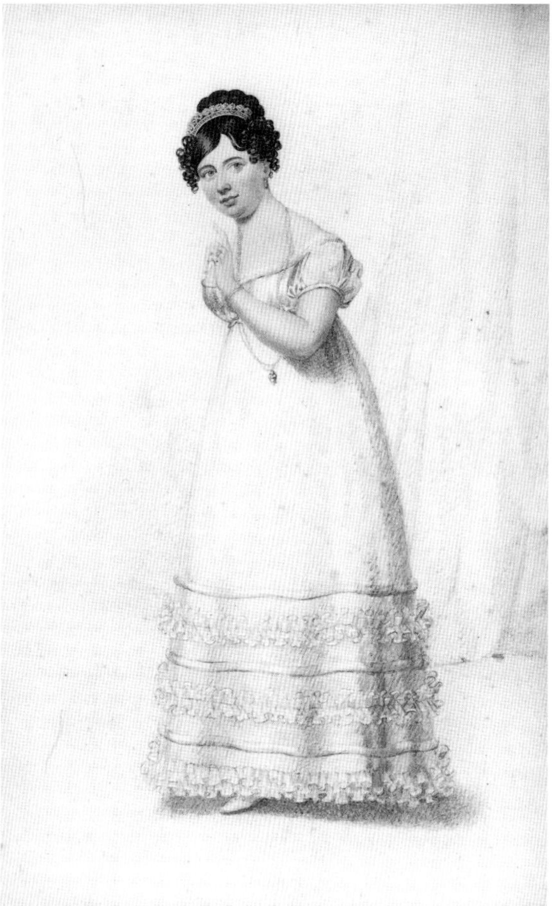

157
MARIA DICKONS
as Rosina
in *The Barber of Seville*
by John Fawcett and Daniel Terry

William Bradley

Pencil with watercolour and body colour
on wove paper 30.5 x 21
INV: CM 302; RW 563 (sitter and
artist unknown); CKA 563
PROV: Charles Mathews
EXH: 1833 London (302)
ENGR: Kennerley for the *Theatrical Inquisitor*
pub. C. Chapple 1819, stipple;
C. Penry pub. J. Bradley 1 May 1819,
stipple (h.l. only)

Fawcett and Terry's comic opera follows Beaumarchais's plot, with Count Almaviva stealing Rosina from under the nose of her guardian, Don Bartolo. Rosina's gesture possibly relates to the moment in Act 1, scene 2, Rosina's apartment, where Figaro tells Rosina that the music master – the Count in disguise – is in love with a lovely girl. Figaro says that the name of the girl must not pass his lips so 'he makes the letters of her name with his fingers, and she repeats them with the signs'. *Rosina:* 'R. O. S. I. N. A. – Rosina!'

Rosina wears white slippers and a white high-waisted dress decorated with a triple row of flounces at the hem.

John Fawcett and Daniel Terry's comic opera, with much of its music by Henry Bishop, was first performed at Covent Garden on 13 October 1818. It was described in the playbill as a 'Comick opera (in two acts) called The Barber of Seville (Founded on the Opera of that name) – In which will be introduced part of Rossini and Paisiello's celebrated music from "Il Barbiere di Siviglia"; the Overture and Music composed, and the whole adapted to the English Stage by Mr Bishop'.

Mrs Dickons played Rosina, her first appearance since her return from the Continent, where she had been working since 1816. She had been a child prodigy who, at the age of six, played Handel concertos on the harpsichord. As Miss Poole, she first appeared on the London stage on 1 May 1787, singing in *La Vestale*, an opera by her teacher, Rauzzini. She made numerous concert appearances in London and the provinces in the 1790s, and in August 1800 married Peter Dickons, a businessman who soon became a bankrupt. As Mrs Dickons she performed until her retirement in March 1819 and died in 1833, at the age of 59.

158
CHARLES DIGNUM
as Tom Tug
in *The Waterman or The First of August*
by Charles Dibdin

Samuel De Wilde

Black chalk and watercolour on wove paper 37.5 x 23.5
INSCR: 'S De Wilde ft / October / 8 1801'
(black chalk b.l.)
INV: Mathews 241; RW/CKA 597
PROV: Charles Mathews
EXH: 1833 London (241)
ENGR: William Bond for Cawthorn's *Minor British Theatre*,
pub. John Cawthorn 26 July 1806, stipple 11.5 x 76
(landscape background)

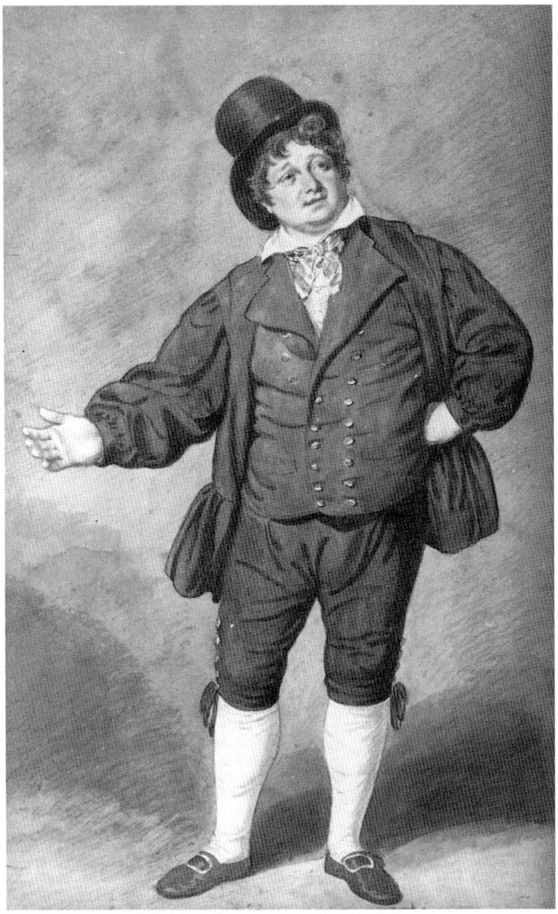

158 *Charles Dignum as Tom Tug*

Tom wears grey shoes, white stockings, blue breeches, a baggy blue waterman's jacket, a red waistcoat, a white shirt, and a white neckerchief with a blue pattern.

Wilhelmina, the daughter of Mr Bundle the gardener, has a choice of two suitors: Robin, 'who dresses so smart', favoured by her mother, and Tom Tug, 'who makes plainness his plan', favoured by her father. Tug overhears Wilhelmina sing a song in Act I, when she tries to decide between the two, and tells her to choose him. He then sings an air, 'And did you not hear of a jolly young waterman?' – probably the moment illustrated. Wilhelmina flirts with both, but eventually takes Tom when he wins the Coat and Badge, the annual race for watermen on the Thames.

Charles Dibdin's ballad opera, with music composed and selected by the author, was first performed at the Haymarket on 8 August 1774, with Charles Bannister as Tom Tug. In the late 1790s it was a Covent Garden piece, with Incledon the first choice as Tom Tug. Dignum does not seem to have played the role in London.

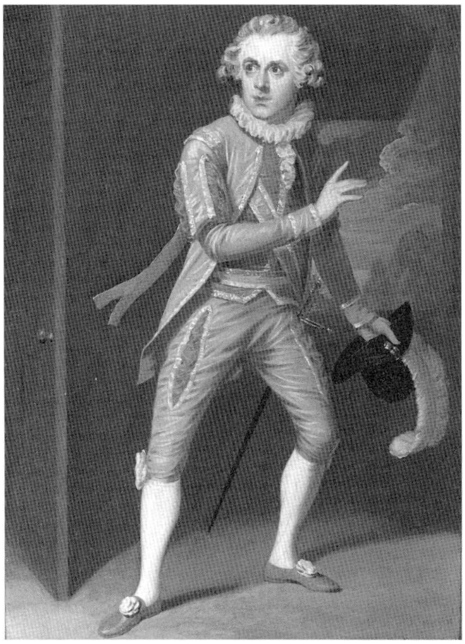

159

WILLIAM WYATT DIMOND

as Don Felix in *The Wonder, a Woman Keeps a Secret* by Susannah Centlivre

Samuel De Wilde

Oil on canvas 36.2 x 26.7
INV: Mathews 382; RW/CKA 252
PROV: John Bell; Thomas Harris; Harris sale, Robins 12 July 1819 (10); Charles Mathews
EXH: 1833 London (382)
ENGR: Philippe Audinet for Bell's British Library 21 July 1792, line 11.4 x 8.2, pl. to Bell's *British Theatre* (1797), vol 21; Anon. printed for C. Cooke 1809, pl. to *British Drama* 1817, line

Donna Violante has been advising Colonel Brittan on his affair with Donna Isabella. In Act IV, Don Felix, Violante's lover, arrives unexpectedly, and Violante tells the Colonel to hide in her bedchamber. Violante's father then arrives and, wishing to avoid him, Felix says: 'Let me step into your Bed-chamber, he won't look under the bed.' He pushes open the door, thinks he sees a man, and says the line cited by Mathews and quoted on the engraving: 'Either my eyes deceive me or I saw a man within.' Don Felix wears brown shoes, white stockings, pink breeches, a pink coat with green lining and gold trim, a green waistcoat trimmed with gold, a pink and gold belt and scabbard band, and a ruff. In his left hand he holds a black hat with a white plume.

Susannah Centlivre's comedy was first performed at Drury Lane on 27 April 1714. A popular play, it was included by both Kitty Clive and David Garrick in their final farewell performances. Dimond does not seem to have played the part in London.

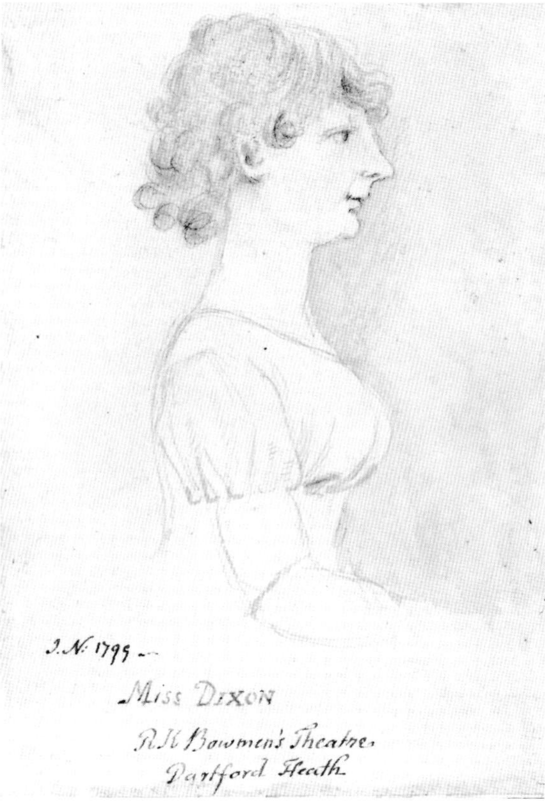

160

CLARA ANN DIXON

John Nixon

Pencil and watercolour on wove paper 11.5 x 8.6
INSCR: 'J.N. 1799' (pen and grey ink b.l.);
'MISS DIXON / R.K. Bowman's Theatre / Dartford Heath'
(pen and grey ink b.c.)
INV: Not listed
PROV: John Nixon *Dramatic Annals*, 3: 229
LIT: Sybil Rosenfeld, 'Private Theatricals at Bowman's Lodge, Dartford', *Theatre Notebook* (1961–62), 16: 125–26, pl. 2

Half-length in profile to right, wearing a high-waisted white dress. See also No. 600.

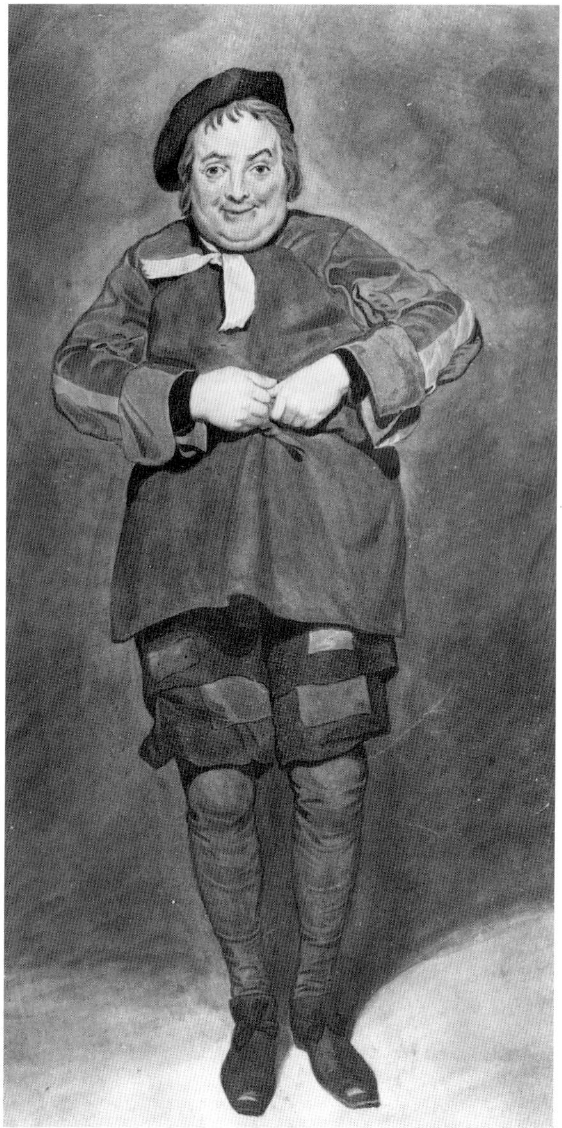

161

JAMES WILLIAM DODD
as Abel Drugger
in *The Alchymist* by Ben Jonson

Samuel De Wilde

Pencil and watercolour on wove paper 37 x 23.5
INV: Mathews 315; RW/CKA 66A
PROV: Charles Mathews
EXH: 1833 London (315)
ENGR: J. Thornthwaite for Bell's British Library
10 May 1791, line 11.5 x 7.6,
pl. to Bell's *British Theatre* (1797), vol I

In Act IV, scene 3, Abel Drugger, the gullible tobacconist, is being duped by the charlatan Subtle and his assistant, Face. Face asks Drugger to borrow a Spanish suit, saying 'Hast thou no credit with the players?', to which Drugger replies 'Yes Sir. Did you never see me play the fool?' (lines quoted on the engraving).

Drugger wears brown shoes, loose red stockings, grey breeches with red, white, orange and blue patches, a red jerkin with blue cuffs, a green apron, and a white stock.

Garrick's adaptation helped to popularise Jonson's play in the mid-18th century, but there were few performances after Garrick's last appearance as Abel Drugger on 11 April 1776, at Drury Lane. The next performance was on 21 March 1782, when Dodd played Abel Drugger at the same theatre. The last performance before De Wilde painted his picture, and the last performance of the century in London, took place at Drury Lane on 10 April 1787, when Dodd played Abel Drugger as part of his benefit night.

Dodd, who specialised in the roles of fops, was at Drury Lane from October 1765 until his death in 1796. He acted dozens of parts, and James Boaden in his *Memories of the Life of John Philip Kemble* (1825) described him as: 'one of the most perfect actors that I have ever seen. ... He was, to be sure, the prince of pink heels, and the soul of empty eminence.'

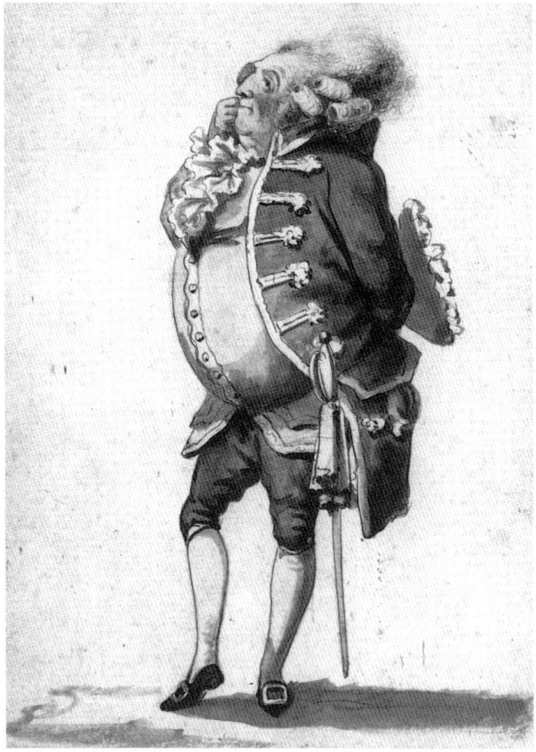

162

JAMES WILLIAM DODD

as Lord Foppington in *The Trip to Scarborough*

by Richard Brinsley Sheridan

Robert Dighton

Pencil, pen and grey ink with watercolour
on laid paper 19.4 x 13.3
INSCR: 'Mr Dodd as Lord Foppington'
(pen and brown ink on mount b.c. CM)
INV: Mathews 272; RW/CKA 550A
PROV: Charles Mathews
EXH: 1833 London (272)
ENGR: Anon., etching 19.7 x 12.9 (NPG copy has watermark
'WM. / WHATMAN / 1794' and inscr. in pen and brown ink:
'Mr Dodd in the Character of Jack Meggot')

Dodd wears black shoes with gold buckles, white stockings, blue breeches and coat with large frogs, and a pink waistcoat over his ample stomach.

Sheridan's adaptation of Vanbrugh's *The Relapse* was first performed at Drury Lane on 24 February 1777, when Dodd played Lord Foppington. He had previously played Foppington in Vanbrugh's original and rather better version of the play. Dodd's last performance in the play before the print was issued was at Drury Lane on 22 May 1793.

Dighton's caricature does not appear to be a particularly accurate account of Dodd's appearance.

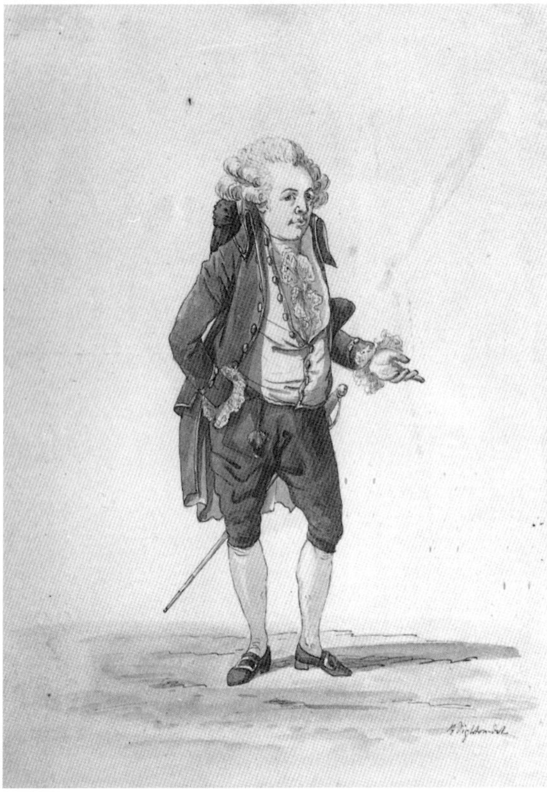

163

JAMES WILLIAM DODD

as Sparkish in *The Country Girl*

by David Garrick

Robert Dighton

Pen and black ink with watercolour
on wove paper 21 x 15.2

INSCR: 'R. Dighton del' (pen and brown ink b.r.);
'Mr Dodd as Sparkish – Country Girl.'
inscription in Mathews's hand,
pen and brown ink on mount b.c.

INV: RW 555B (artist unknown); CKA 555B

PROV: Charles Mathews (not in catalogue)

Dodd wears black shoes, white stockings, black breeches, a blue jacket, and a white waistcoat with gold buttons.

Garrick's comedy, an adaptation of Wycherley's *The Country Wife*, was first performed at Drury Lane on 25 October 1766, with Dodd as the original Sparkish.

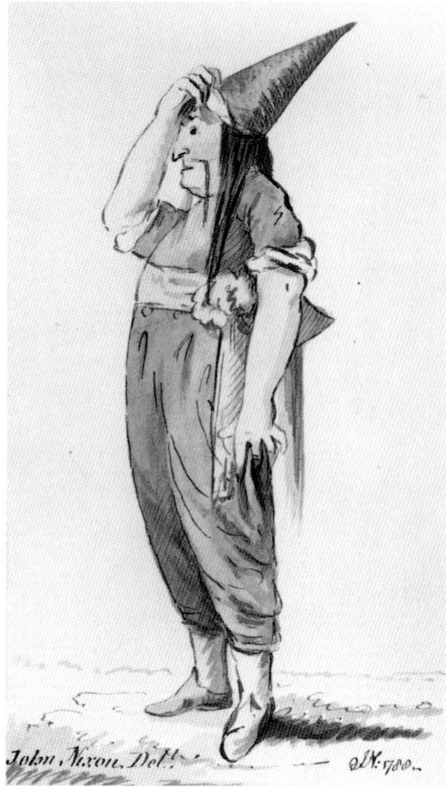

164

JAMES WILLIAM DODD

as Ali in *Selima and Azar*

by Sir George Collier

John Nixon

Pencil, grey wash and watercolour on wove paper
14.9 x 8.2 (sheet 18.9 x 10.2)

INSCR: 'John Nixon Del.t' (pen and brown ink b.l.);
'JN: 1788' (pen and black ink b.r.);
'Dodd in the Character of Ali / Selima & Azar'
(pen and black ink below)

INV: Not listed

PROV: John Nixon, *Dramatic Annals*, 1: 260

Dodd wears yellow slippers, green pantaloons and short-sleeved tunic, a yellow sash, and a conical red hat.

Collier's musical play, based on Marmontel's *Zemère and Azor*, and with music by Thomas Linley Snr., was first performed at Drury Lane on 23 October 1777 with Dodd as the original Ali.

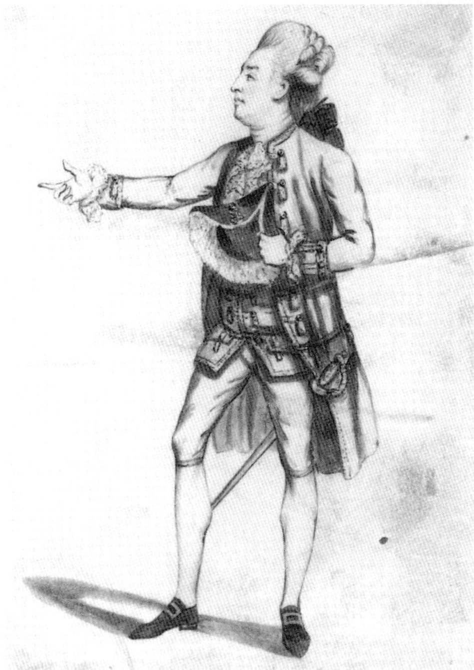

165
JAMES WILLIAM DODD
as Lord Foppington in *The Careless Husband*
by Colley Cibber

James Roberts

Brush and black ink with a little watercolour
on vellum 9.8 x 7
INV: RW 560D (sitter and artist unknown);
CKA 560D (Unknown Man by J. Roberts?)
PROV: Unknown, but acquired by the Club before 1888
ENGR: J. Thornthwaite for Bell's *British Theatre*
1 January 1776, line 13.3 x 9.2; reissued 1 January 1778

In Act II, scene 3, Lord Foppington has just arrived in Windsor and is visiting Sir Charles Easy in his lodgings. Sir Charles asks him 'What really brought you to Windsor?', to which Lord Foppington replies with the line printed on the engraving: 'Why two hours, and Six of the best Nags in Christendom, or the Devil drive me.'

Lord Foppington is dressed in the height of fashion of the mid-1770s, with a high powdered wig. He holds a black tricorn hat trimmed with feathers, and his suit is tinted pale pink.

Cibber's comedy, written as a vehicle for himself as a sequel to Vanbrugh's *The Relapse* (see No. 116), was first performed at Drury Lane on 7 December 1704. Dodd played Lord Foppington for the first time at Drury Lane on 16 May 1767, repeating the role on 25 and 31 January and 6 October 1770, and on 26 November 1771, the last performance before the date of the engraving.

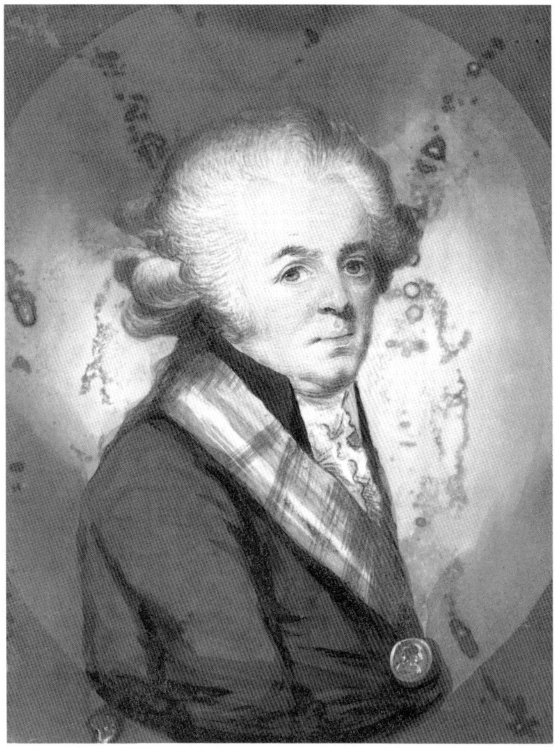

166
JAMES WILLIAM DODD
'School of Garrick'

Henry Spicer

Pencil and watercolour on laid paper 26.5 x 21
INV: Mathews 266 (artist unknown);
RW/CKA 48A (artist unknown)
PROV: Charles Mathews
EXH: 1833 London (266)
REL: Similar to Laurie's small mezzotint
after Dighton, published 10 July 1779

Dodd wears a blue jacket, white stock, and a Rainbow Ribband with a Shakespeare Favour.

Dodd and Garrick seem to have been good friends, despite the embarrassment caused by Dodd's extra-marital adventures. In September 1774 Garrick sent him money so that he could return from Dublin.

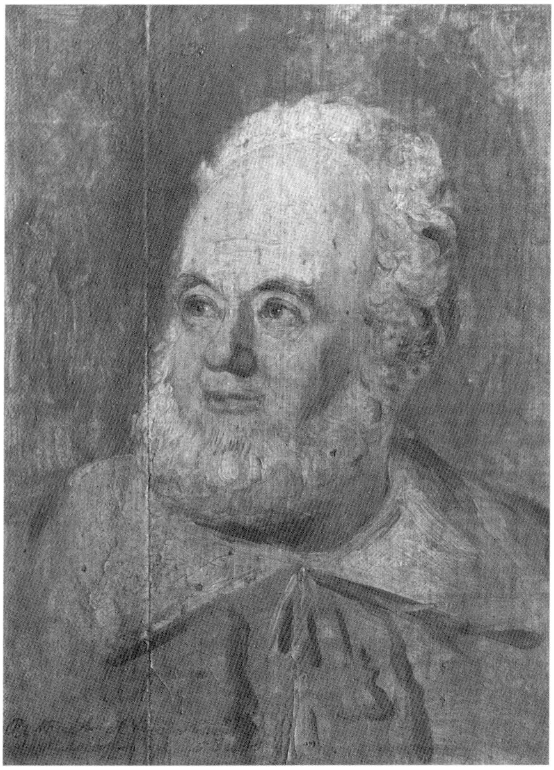

167
WILLIAM DOWTON
as Falstaff in *2 Henry IV*
by William Shakespeare

Robert William Buss

Oil on panel 21.9 x 16.5
INSCR: 'Portrait of Dowton / as Falstaff R.W. Buss'
(brown paint b.l.)
INV: RW/CKA 198
PROV: Presented by Lord Burnham, 1905

Falstaff wears a red doublet with white collar.

The two sketches by Buss (this one and No. 168) may relate to a picture in the Harvard Theatre Collection, bought from Child's Gallery in Boston, 1956, which Mander & Mitchenson attributed to Clint for no very good reason. It appears to have little in common with the style of that artist, although the scene and the actors are the same as in Clint's R.A. 1833 exhibit (232): 'Falstaff relating his valiant exploits at the Boar's Head, Eastcheap' (Petworth House, Sussex, commissioned by the 3rd Earl of Egremont as one of a trio of Shakespeare compositions with William Dowton as Falstaff and, in the other two pictures, as Sir Toby Belch). The other actors shown in the Harvard picture are John Cooper as Prince Hal and John Balls as Poins. All three actors appeared in the revival of *2 Henry IV* at Drury Lane on 1 December 1832. Dowton was also portrayed as Falstaff by Wageman in a plate published in 1831 for Cumberland's *British Theatre*, a work for which Buss painted a number of portraits.

Dowton seems to have enjoyed some success as Falstaff towards the end of his career, although his début in the role on the American stage, at the Park Theater, New York, on 21 June 1836, was not especially memorable.

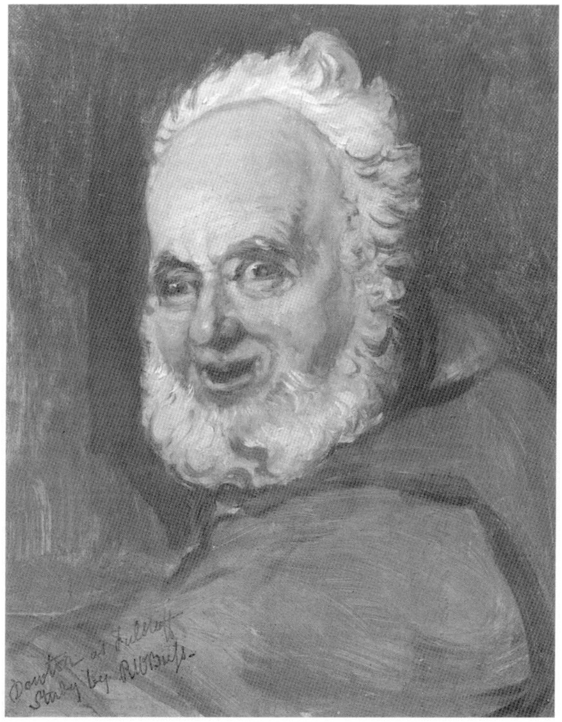

168
WILLIAM DOWTON
as Falstaff in *2 Henry IV*
by William Shakespeare

Robert William Buss

Oil on panel 23.5 x 18.5
INSCR: 'Dowton as Falstaff / Study by R W Buss.'
(brown paint b.l.)
INV: RW/CKA 199
PROV: Presented by Lord Burnham, 1905

As in No. 167, Dowton is dressed in red. His expression is considerably more animated.

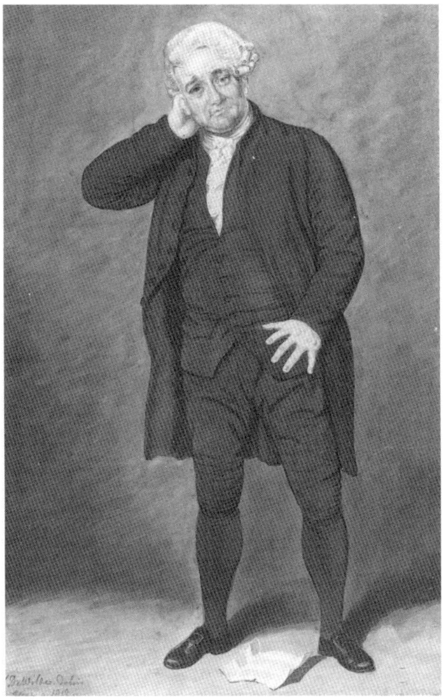

169

WILLIAM DOWTON

as Sir Oliver Cypress in *Grieving's a Folly*

by Richard Leigh

Samuel De Wilde

Pencil and watercolour on wove paper 37 x 23.5
INSCR: 'S De Wilde. delin / June 9 1812.' (pencil b.l.)
INV: Mathews 219; RW/CKA 60A
PROV: Charles Mathews
EXH: 1833 London (219)

Sir Oliver Cypress affects melancholy for the death of his wife, and mourns extravagantly in front of her portrait. Whilst doing this, he sees the delightful Ellen and decides to write her a love letter. Her lover, Charles Sedly, sees the letter and sends Sir Oliver a challenge (the paper on the ground between Sir Oliver's feet). Sir Oliver is distressed, and after some confusion agrees to retire in the face of youth. He wears black shoes, black stockings, black breeches, a black coat and waistcoat, and a white stock.

Leigh's comedy was first performed by the Drury Lane company at the Lyceum on 21 April 1809, with Dowton as the original Sir Oliver Cypress. The play was not a great success. The profits of the only performance the following season, on 20 October 1809, were 'offered in aid of the contributions for the liberation of imprisoned Debtors'.

There were no performances of the piece in 1811–12, the season in which De Wilde made his watercolour.

170

LOCATION UNKNOWN

WILLIAM DOWTON

as Dr Cantwell in *The Hypocrite*

by Isaac Bickerstaffe

Samuel De Wilde

Pencil on wove paper with incised squaring-up 19.6 x 14.9
INV: Not listed
PROV: Charles Mathews (Print Collection Vol. IV f. 108)
ENGR: R. Cooper for Terry's *Theatrical Gallery*,
pub. H. Berthould 16 September 1822
REL: BM L.B.7, pencil and watercolour on wove paper 36.5 x 22.5; NT 45, pencil and watercolour on wove paper 37.1 x 24.8; ex. coll. Ian Mayes, pencil and watercolour on wove paper 37.1 x 24.4, inscr: 'S De Wilde delin / May 1812.'
[Possibly the picture by De Wilde, signed and dated, of Dowton as Cantwell that was in the Royal Dramatic College sale at Fairbrother, Lye and Palmer on 24 February 1881 (lot 100A)]

Dr Cantwell, the Hypocrite of the title, pretends piety whilst harbouring fleshly desires. De Wilde's drawing probably shows him soon after his first entrance in Act I, impressing the gullible Lady Lambet, whose daughter he later tries to seduce – 'Alas madam! I am not a good man: I am a guilty wicked sinner, full of iniquity...' His sin was inciting the little dog Minxy to such a passion that it bit him. Dr Cantwell wears striped stockings, breeches, coat, waistcoat and stock.

The squares are 0.7 cm across and are scored into the paper rather than drawn. They may indicate part of the preparation for Cooper's engraving, and the drawing may have been prepared by Cooper from one of the versions of De Wilde's portrait.

Bickerstaffe's play was adapted from Colley Cibber's *The Non Juror* (based on Molière's *Tartuffe*), which was first performed at Drury Lane in 1717. Dowton first played Dr Cantwell at Drury Lane on 16 April 1804, for Mrs Jordan's benefit, and it quickly became one of his best-known roles. He acted the part in a revival at the Lyceum on 12 March 1812 (with the Drury Lane company), and repeated it on 19 March and 8 April 1812, a month before De Wilde made the May version of this subject. See also No. 124.

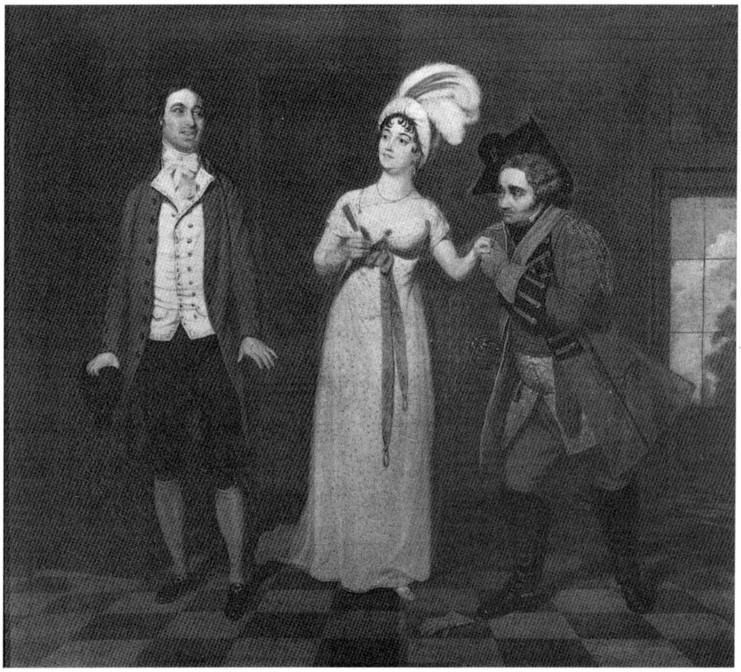

171

WILLIAM DOWTON as Major Sturgeon,
SARAH HARLOWE as Mrs Sneak and
SAMUEL THOMAS RUSSELL as Jerry Sneak
in *The Mayor of Garratt* by Samuel Foote

Samuel De Wilde

Oil on canvas 67 x 78.5
INV: Mathews 172; RW/CKA 367
PROV: Charles Mathews
EXH: 1810 R.A. (447); 1833 London (172);
1950–51 London (248A); 1951–52 London (138)

The scene is Act I, scene I, Sir Jacob Jollop's house at Garratt. Sneak (Russell) stands on the left holding a black tricorn hat. He wears black shoes with gold buckles, grey stockings, black knee-breeches, a red jacket with brown buttons, a white waistcoat trimmed with gold and with gold buttons, and a high white stock. Mrs Sneak (Harlowe) wears a finely plumed hat with a white brim. Her white frock is decorated with a red band, gold tassels and a blue ribbon. The Major (Dowton) wears a black tricorn hat with a cockade, black boots, red knee-breeches, a red military jacket with black panels, and a red waistcoat. He has a broad leather shoulder band, possibly for a powder horn. The 1820 Oxberry edition of the play gives slightly different costume directions. Sneak is given a 'crimson coat, bordered white waist-coat and black breeches', Mrs Sneak a 'blue sarsnet gown trimmed with crimson ribbon, crimson silk scarf', and the Major a 'scarlet regimental coat, flowered waist-coat, scarlet breeches, black boots and gold laced hat'. Patmore wrote: 'The likeness and characteristic expression of Dowton are perfect; but the other two are not so good in this respect.'

Garratt was a village in Surrey, near Wandsworth, where the villagers in the latter part of the 18th century made a practice of electing a 'mayor' when a general election took place. He acted as a sort of chairman of a local body for the defence of their rights. In the play, Sneak, surprisingly, wins the election. An election in both Garratt and Britain generally would have just taken place when Foote wrote his play in 1763, as Pitt had gone to the country because George III would not accept some of the leading Whigs. The Wilkes affair was attracting great interest. Wilkes was first arrested and released in 1763. The military references that permeate the play refer to the Seven Years War, which ended with the Treaty of Paris signed by Britain, France and Spain on 10 February 1763. Major Sturgeon is an officer in the Middlesex militia, the butt of much humour throughout the play.

Foote's comedy was originally performed at the Haymarket on 20 June 1763, with the author as Major Sturgeon, Weston as Jerry Sneak, and Mrs Daily as Mrs Sneak. It was revived at Drury Lane on 2 February 1808, the first time for five years according to the playbill, with the cast as shown in the picture. There were 12 performances before the end of the season, the last on 16 June 1808.

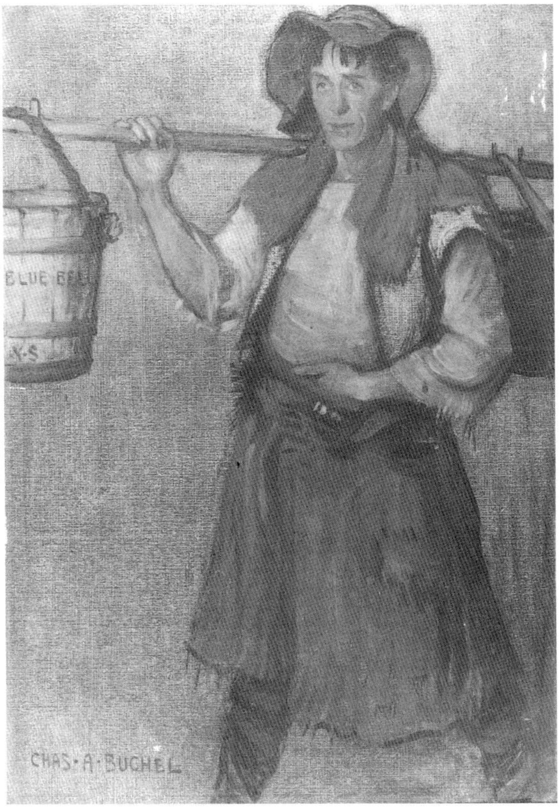

172
SIR GERALD DU MAURIER
as Hon. Ernest Woolley in *The Admirable Crichton*
by J.M. Barrie

Charles A. Buchel

Oil on board 46.2 x 32.5
INSCR: 'CHAS. A. BUCHEL' (brown paint b.l.);
'BLUEBELL / N. S' (blue paint on pail t.l.);
'4 (circled) / Gerald Du Maurier'
(pen and blue-black ink verso)
INV: CKA 645; Gift 630
PROV: Presented by Capt. C. Riddell Williams, 1945

Du Maurier, carrying two pails on a pole, is dressed in rustic red-brown with a ragged whitish jacket, for the second act on the desert island.

Barrie's play opened at the Duke of York's on 4 November 1902 and ran for 326 performances, until 28 August 1903. Gerald Du Maurier was the original Hon. Ernest Woolley; he also appeared in the revival, which ran for 117 performances, from 2 March to 12 June 1908. The manager in both productions was Charles Frohman and the director Dion G. Boucicault.

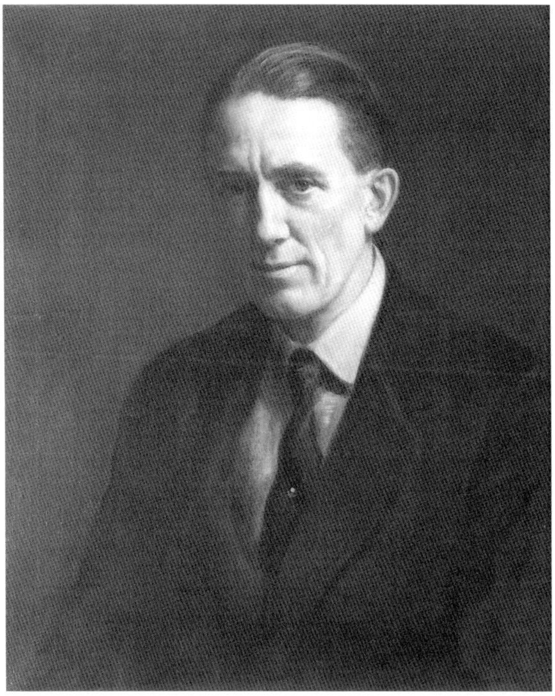

173
SIR GERALD DU MAURIER

The Hon. John Collier

Oil on canvas 61.5 x 51
INV: GCL 666; Gift 706
PROV: Presented by Lt. Col. R.R. Gibson, 1951
EXH: 1923 R.S.P.P. (9)

Du Maurier wears a dark blue coat, pale blue shirt, and a dark blue tie with pearl stick pin.

Collier exhibited a more spectacular full-length portrait of Du Maurier at the R.A. in 1922 (59). Given the title 'The Producer', it shows the sitter directing a play on stage, with the auditorium behind him. That picture now hangs in Hampstead Town Hall, Haverstock Hill.

In 1910, with Frank Curzon, Du Maurier became manager of Wyndham's Theatre, where he remained until 1925, producing and acting in such plays as Barrie's *Dear Brutus*, Sandon's *The Diplomacy*, and Bancroft's *The Ware Case*. He later managed at the St James's Theatre.

Du Maurier became a member of the Garrick Club in 1903.

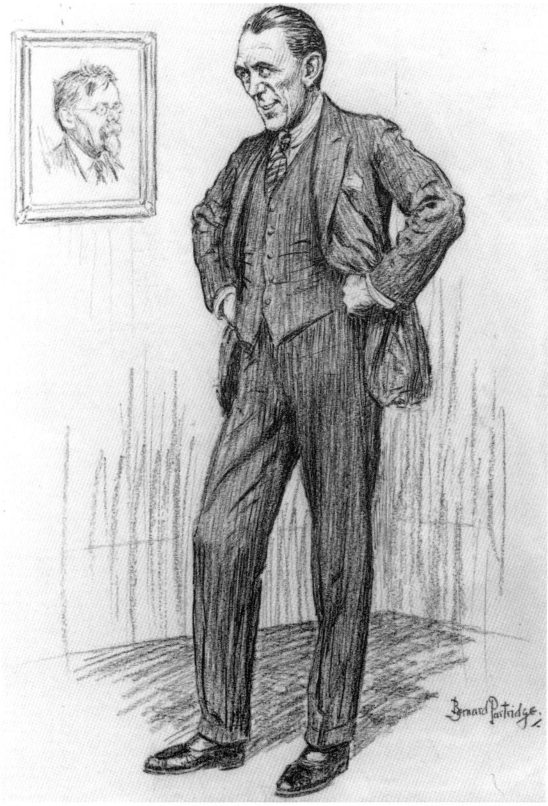

174
SIR GERALD DU MAURIER

Sir J. Bernard Partridge

Black chalk on wove paper 50.8 x 45.7
INSCR: 'Bernard Partridge' (black chalk b.r.);
'SIR GERALD DU MAURIER / L'artiste du "Punch",
feu du Maurier, / Moissant un beau tas de lauriers; /
Et de nos jours son fils / Dans les rangs de Thespis /
S'est établi au front – et encore y est!'
(pen and black ink on mount b.c.);
'Punch 2.2.1927' (pen and black ink on mount b.r.)
INV: GCL 655; Gift 680
PROV: Presented by D.P. Whitley, 1948
LIT: *Punch*, 2 February 1927

Du Maurier is shown looking at a portrait of his father, the novelist and cartoonist George Du Maurier.

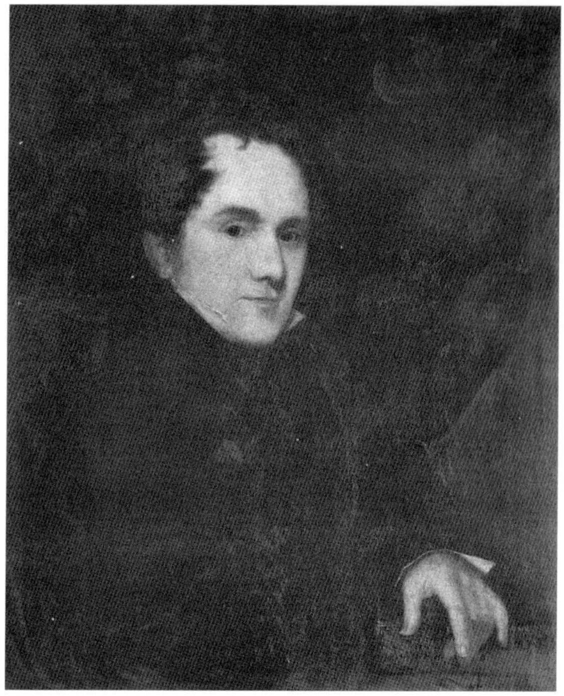

175
WILLIAM DUNN

Unknown Artist

Oil on canvas 72.4 x 59.7
INSCR: 'Isaac Walton' (on book)
INV: RW/CKA 321; Gift 169
PROV: Presented by J.R. Anderson, 1862
[plate on frame: 'Presented by T. ANDERTON.']

Dunn is shown seated, half-length, with his left hand resting on a book on a table at left. He was chief clerk and deputy treasurer at Drury Lane Theatre between 1798 and 1817.

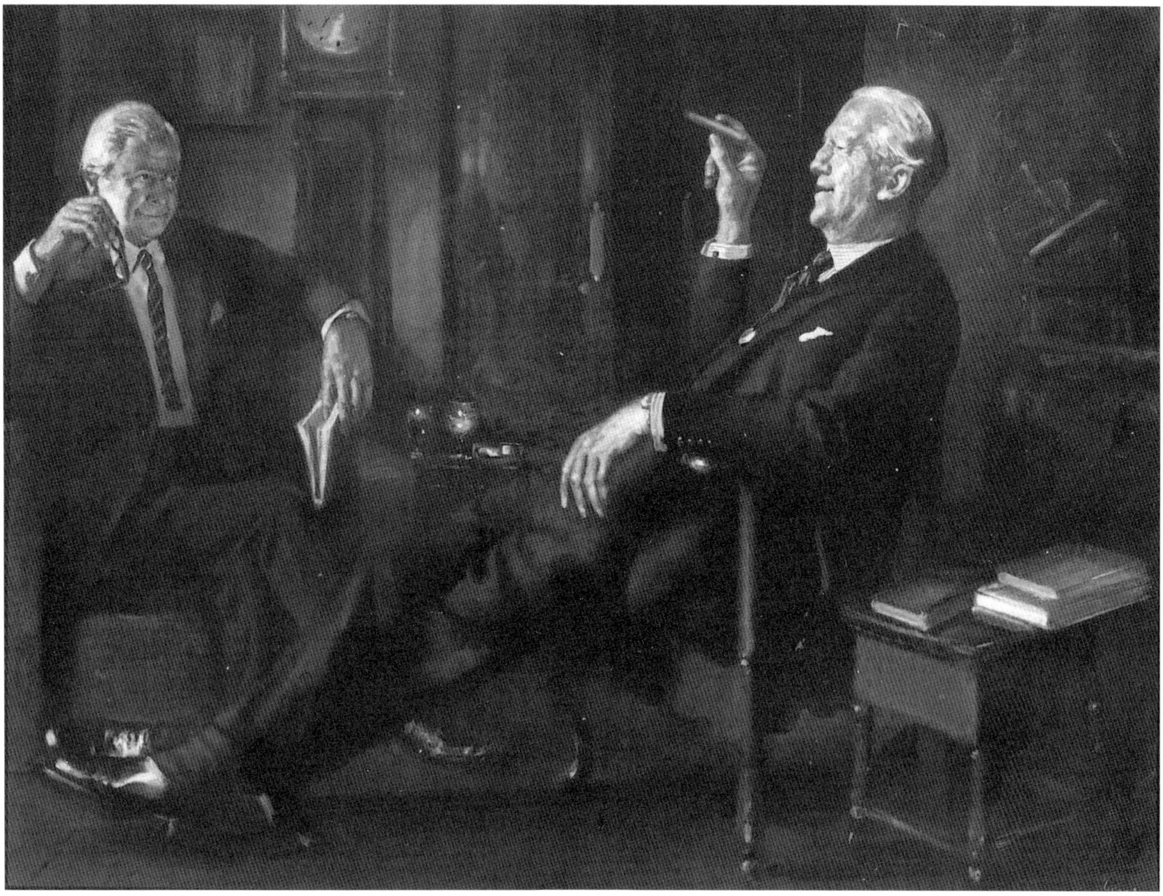

176
SEBASTIAN EARL
and *TREVOR FENWICK*

John Gilroy

Oil on canvas 70 x 100
INSCR: 'Gilroy' (white paint b.r.)
INV: Not listed
PROV: Presented by the artist

Trevor Fenwick, wearing a grey suit, is seated on the left on a red upholstered sofa. Sebastian Earl, seated in a chair at the right, also wears a grey suit, with a blue tie. The 'ghost' in the middle is a self-portrait by Jack Gilroy, subsequently painted out. As the paint settles, this figure is becoming more visible.

Earl and Fenwick were members of the Garrick from 1946 and 1955, respectively, until their deaths. See also No. 892.

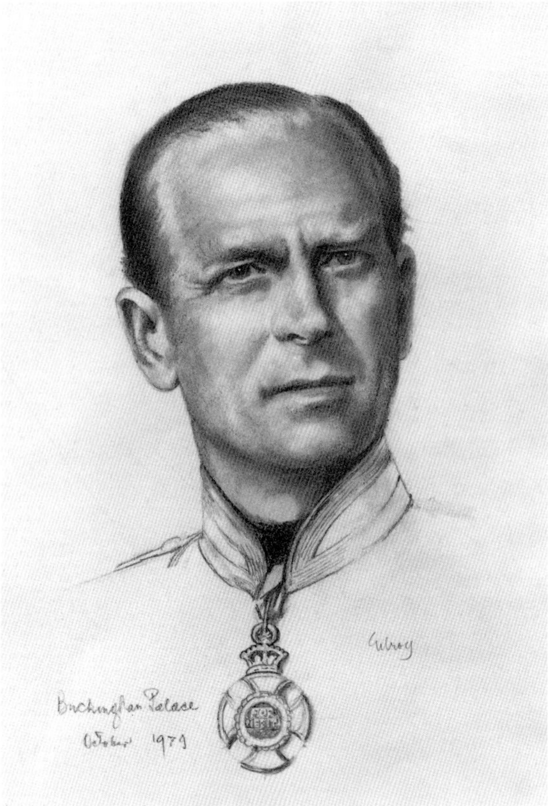

177

H.R.H. THE DUKE OF EDINBURGH

John Gilroy

Black and red chalk on wove paper 43.5 x 31.4 (sight)
INSCR: 'Gilroy' (pencil b.r.);
'Buckingham Palace / October 1979' (pencil b.l.)
INV: GCL 741; Gift 893
PROV: Presented by the artist, 1981
REL: Christie's South Kensington 15 May 1986 (50)
There were 15 drawings in the lot, all of members of the Royal Family, including the Queen, the Duke of Edinburgh, the Queen Mother, the Princess Royal, Princess Margaret, Princess Alexandra and Earl Louis Mountbatten

The Duke of Edinburgh wears the Order of Merit over a military coat. Unfinished.

H.R.H. Prince Philip, Duke of Edinburgh is Patron of the Garrick Club.

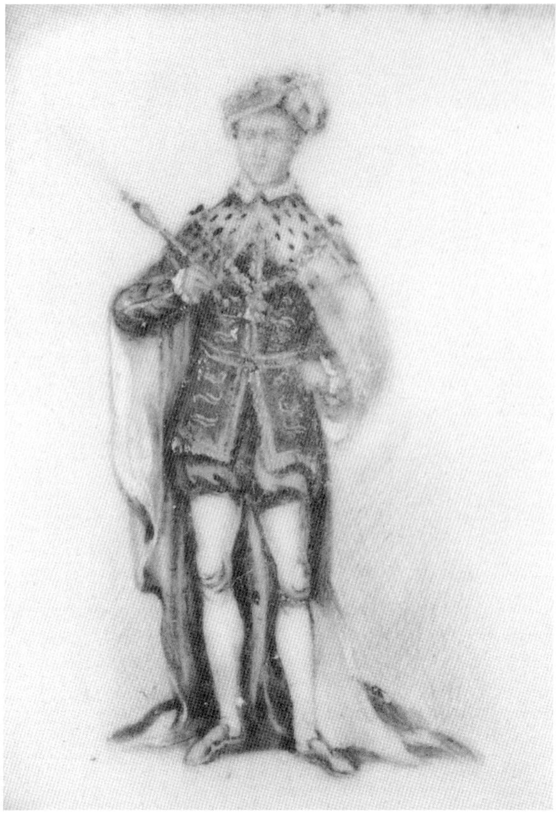

178

EDWARD VI

Unknown Artist, late 18th century

Miniature, watercolour on ivory 6.5 x 5.2
INV: CKA 538; Gift 422
PROV: Presented by H.G. Rooth & Miss M.A. Rooth, 1924

The boy king wears white stockings, blue trunk-hose and tunic decorated in gold, a red hat with a feather, and a large red cloak decorated in gold and lined in white. He has a gold George round his shoulders.

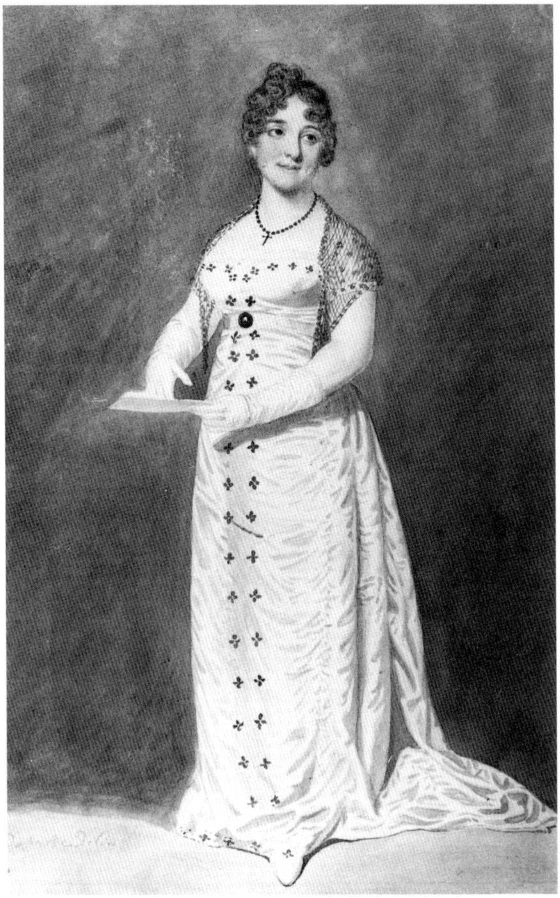

179

ELIZABETH EDWIN

as Albina Mandeville in *The Will*

by Frederick Reynolds

Samuel De Wilde

Pencil and watercolour on wove paper 37 x 23.5
INSCR: 'S De Wilde. delin' (pencil b.l.)
INV: Mathews 206; RW/CKA 61C
PROV: Charles Mathews
EXH: 1833 London (206)

The scene is Act v, scene 2, in the Baron's chamber, at the climax of the play. Albina Mandeville, rather than her father, has inherited her grandfather's fortune. Albina, who is supposed to be 18 years of age, wears white gloves and shoes, and a white silk dress. Over her shoulders she has a black net shawl. With her right hand she gestures to the will in her left hand.

Reynolds's comedy was first performed at Drury Lane on 19 April 1797, with Mrs Jordan as the original Albina Mandeville. Mrs Edwin played the part during her season in Edinburgh, from 3 December 1808.

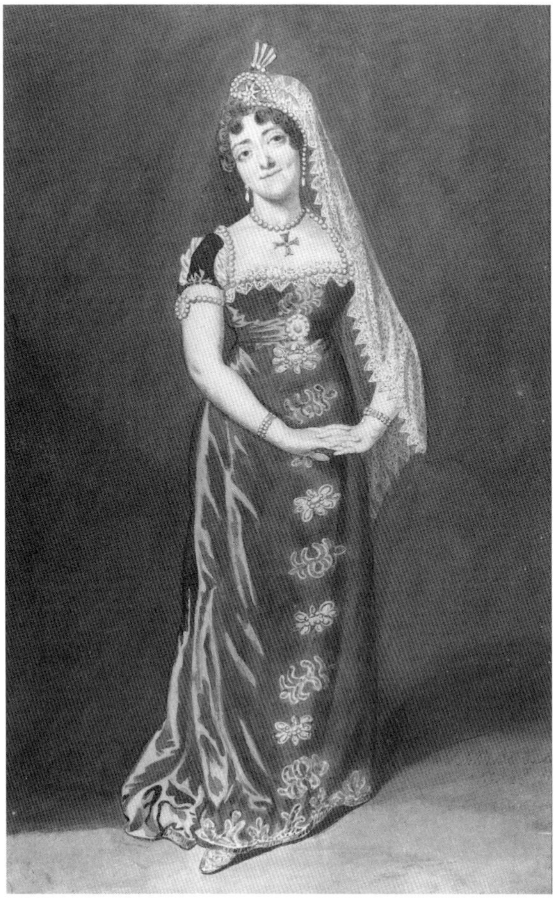

180

ELIZABETH EDWIN

as Lady Traffic in *Riches or The Wife and Brother*

by Sir James Bland Burges

Samuel De Wilde

Pencil and watercolour on wove paper 37 x 23.5
INSCR: 'S. De Wilde delin / October 22nd 181[0].' (pencil b.r.)
INV: Mathews 205 (as Eliza); RW/CKA 60B
PROV: Charles Mathews
EXH: 1833 London (205)

Lady Traffic is the vain, bad-tempered wife of Sir John Traffic. She has two grown-up daughters, Maria and Eliza, whom she treats badly because they 'strive to vie with me in fashion's walk'. Lady Traffic's tinsel trappings consist of quantities of pearls including a pearl necklace with a Maltese Cross and a pearl tiara with star and aigrette. She has a green belt with a large jewelled buckle, and wears green and gold slippers. Her green velvet dress has a gold hem and gold embroidery.

Mrs Edwin was the original Lady Traffic when Burges's play opened at the Lyceum on 3 February 1810. See No. 151.

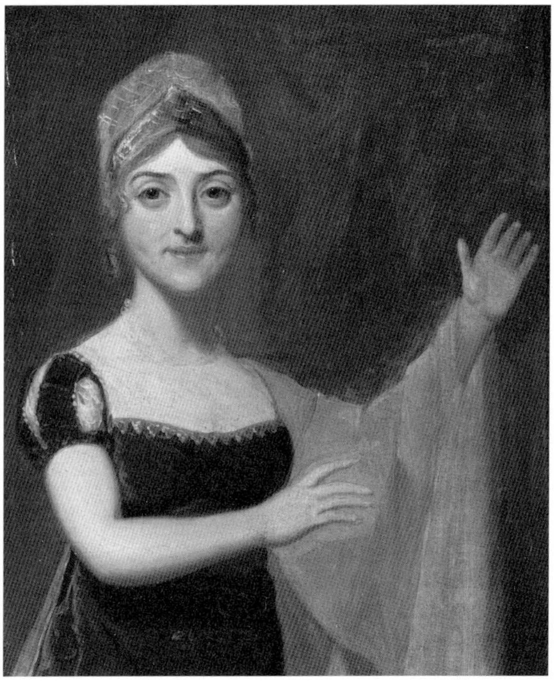

181

ELIZABETH EDWIN

as Lady Traffic in *Riches or The Wife and Brother*
by Sir James Bland Burges

Samuel De Wilde

Oil on panel 22.7 x 19
INV: RW/CKA 292 (as Eliza)
PROV: Unknown

Lady Traffic is shown half-length. Her headdress consists of a kind of helmet of yellow fabric and silver. Her green velvet dress has slashed puff sleeves that reveal a white lining, and zigzag decoration in gold braid round the square neck. She has a grey muslin shawl over her left arm. There are pentimenti around the fingers of her right hand. See No. 180.

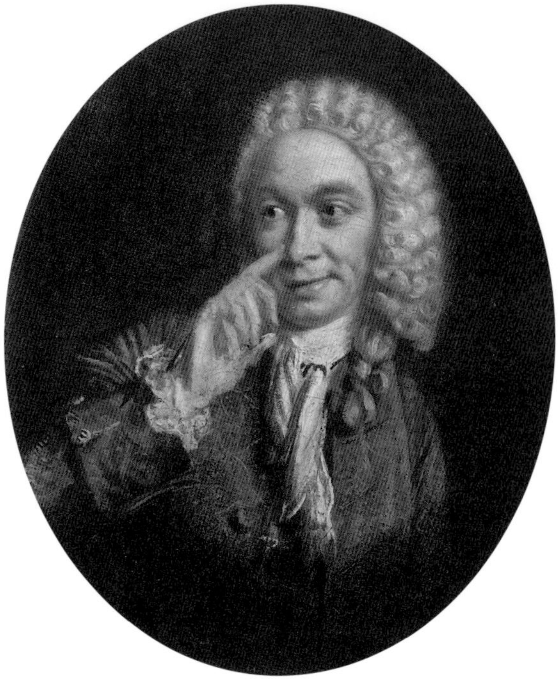

182

JOHN EDWIN

as Justice Woodcock in *Love in a Village*
by Isaac Bickerstaffe

Thomas Beach

Oil on canvas 34.3 x 29.2
INV: Mathews 38; RW/CKA 288
PROV: Charles Mathews
EXH: 1833 London (38)
LIT: Patmore, p. 268 (No. 183);
E.S. Beach, *Thomas Beach* (1934), p. 59 (No. 82)

Justice Woodcock, half-length, holds his right forefinger to his nose. He wears a green jacket with paler linear pattern, and a curly wig.

Bickerstaffe's comic opera was first performed at Covent Garden on 8 December 1762, with Shuter as Justice Woodcock. Edwin played the part for the first time at the Haymarket on 12 August 1777.

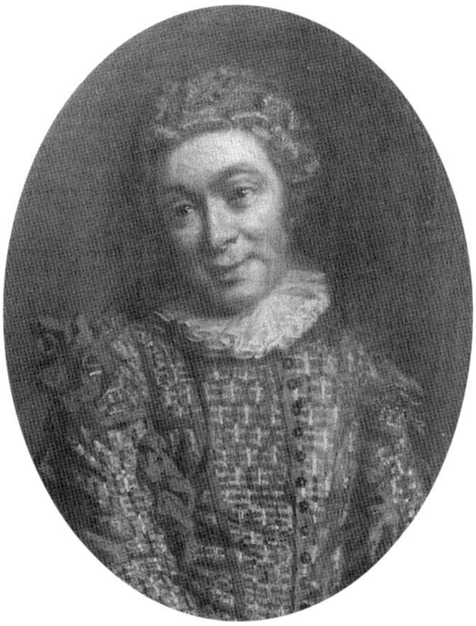

183
JOHN EDWIN
as Peeping Tom in *Peeping Tom of Coventry*
by John O'Keeffe

Thomas Beach

Oil on canvas 35.5 x 28
INV: Mathews 27; RW/CKA 297
PROV: Charles Mathews
EXH: 1833 London (27)
LIT: Patmore, p. 268 (No. 182);
E.S. Beach, *Thomas Beach* (1934), p. 59 (No. 81)

The Earl of Mercia has put a tax of a thousand marks on the city. The citizens send a deputation to the Earl and his wife, Godiva, and she pleads their cause. He agrees to waive the tax if Godiva rides naked through the city, an idea intended as a joke but taken up by the lady. Tom is excited: 'Talk of a Coronation! – 'tis no more to this – lady Godiva is a procession in herself. I must go in time to procure a good place.' The mayor demands that all stay indoors during the ride, but Tom peeps and is condemned to death – a sentence later commuted.

There is no reference in the text to Tom's extravagant costume. He wears a pink doublet with a pattern of red and white vertical lines and green horizontal lines under vertical bands of green ribbon. The doublet is trimmed with black buttons and green ribbons.

O'Keeffe's comic opera, with music by Dr Samuel Arnold, was first performed at the Haymarket on 6 September 1784, with Edwin as the original Tom. He was also the first Tom at Covent Garden, where he played the part for his own benefit on 20 April 1789.

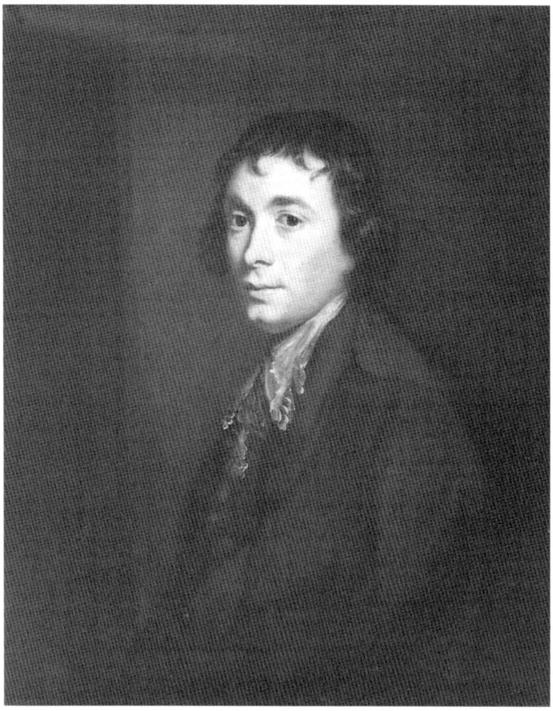

184
JOHN EDWIN

Thomas Beach (attr.)

Oil on canvas 76 x 63
INV: Mathews 192 (by Gainsborough);
RW 195 (by Gainsborough);
CKA 195 (attributed to Thomas Gainsborough)
PROV: Charles Mathews
EXH: 1833 London (192); 1951 London (195)

Edwin, shown half-length in a feigned oval, wears a brown jacket and a loose lace collar.

This picture does not appear in the Gainsborough literature (although Patmore gave the picture to him and described it as 'a capital specimen'). A letter from Michael Harvard, dated 22 July 1952, argues strongly for the attribution to Gainsborough, citing Fulcher: 'Edwin – a face full of expression; the colouring beautiful. Half-length. Possession – Garrick Club House.'

The picture seems to have more in common with Beach's somewhat plodding Reynoldsian style. Beach, like many of his contemporaries, often painted bust portraits in false ovals.

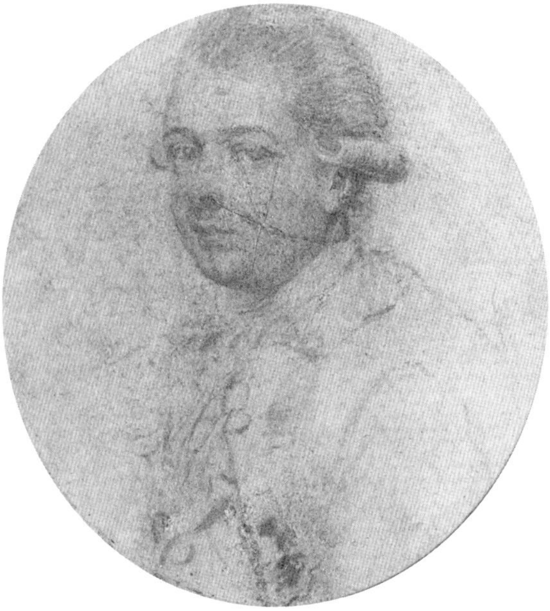

185

JOHN EDWIN

Henry Edridge

Pencil with watercolour and white body colour
on laid paper 5.7 x 5 (oval)
INSCR: 'Mr Ibbetson' in pencil on back (CKA)
INV: Mathews 317; CKA 627
PROV: Charles Mathews
EXH: 1833 London (317)
ENGR: William Ridley for the *Monthly Mirror*, 1805,
stipple 7.3 x 6 (oval)

Head and shoulders, three-quarters to left, with head completed and coat outlined.

A talented comic actor, the elder John Edwin was considered by George Colman to be the best burletta singer the theatre had ever seen: 'While he sung in a style which produced roars of laughter, there was a melody in some of the upper tones of his voice that was beautiful.' Edwin was as celebrated for his occasional songs 'in character' as for his acting. His son, the younger John Edwin (1769?–1805) also became a popular and successful performer.

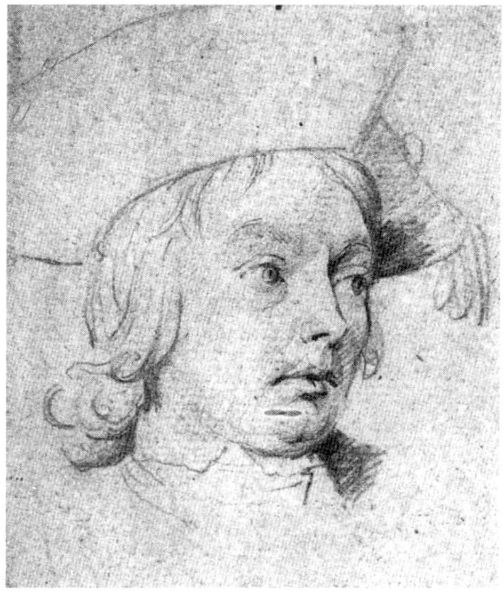

186

JOHN EDWIN

James Roberts

Pencil on discoloured laid paper 10 x 8.7
INSCR: 'Edwin' (pen and brown ink on mount b.c. CM)
INV: RW/CKA 493C
PROV: Charles Mathews (not in catalogue)

The actor's head looking to right, wearing a tricorn hat.

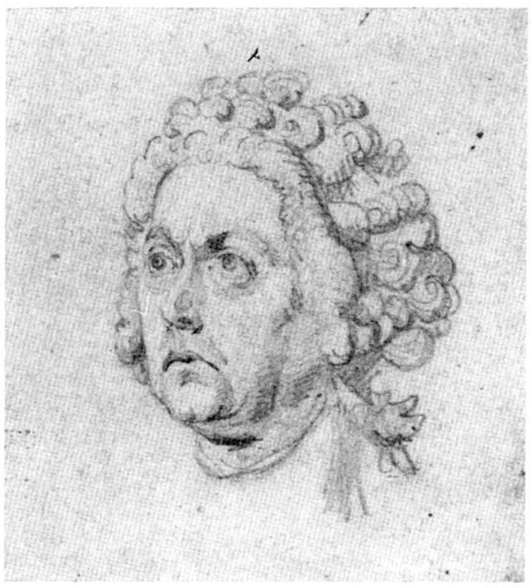

187

JOHN EDWIN

James Roberts

Pencil on discoloured laid paper 8 x 7.4
INSCR: 'Edwin' (pen and brown ink on mount b.c. CM)
INV: RW/CKA 493E
PROV: Charles Mathews (not in catalogue)

Head only, looking to left, in a curled wig.

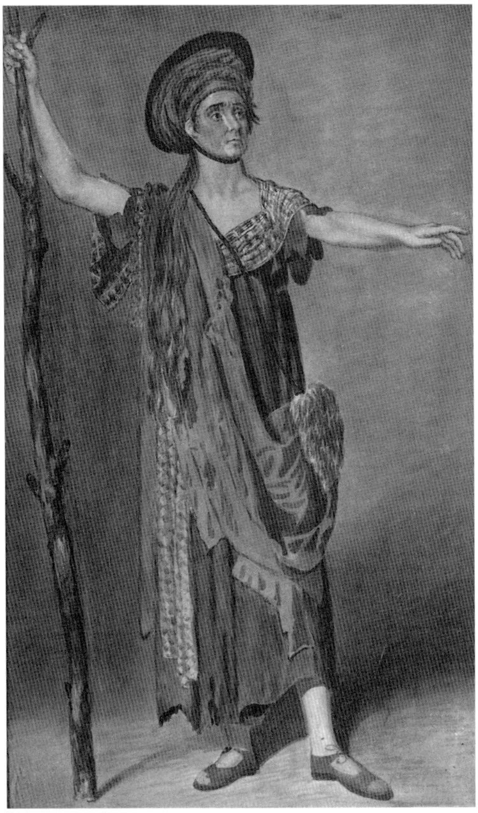

188

SARAH EGERTON

as Meg Merrilies in *Guy Mannering*
or The Gipsey's Prophecy by Daniel Terry

Samuel De Wilde

Pencil and watercolour on wove paper 38.1 x 24.1
INSCR: 'S De Wilde / delin 1816' (pencil b.l.)
INV: Mathews 253; RW/CKA 54
PROV: Charles Mathews
EXH: 1833 London (253)
ENGR: J. Thomson for the *Theatrical Inquisitor* pub. C. Chapple 1 April 1817, stipple (appears to be based on the watercolour, although there are slight differences, notably the branch resting against the left arm rather than being held in the right hand)
REL: Harvard Theatre Collection TS 990.1.3F Vol. II (14), pencil and watercolour on wove paper n.d.; BM L.B.4, red chalk and watercolour on wove paper 37.5 x 22.8, inscr: 'De Wilde delin / 1816'

Meg Merrilies is the 'ruler and terror of the gipseys' and 'renown'd for her sorceries'. She foresees her own death, which takes place in the glen in Act II, scene I; the quotation on the engraving is her line: 'If ever the dead come back among the living I'll be seen in that glen many a night.' In the costume notes to the 1820 Oxberry edition, Meg Merrilies is given a 'brown cloth petticoat and body, torn old red cloak, torn pieces of plaid, and old russet shoes'. In De Wilde's drawing she wears rough sandals tied over her instep and a long, ragged short-sleeved brown dress, with plaid around the bust and a red drape around the shoulders to her left hip. Under her black cap is a red band. She holds a rude staff in her right hand.

Terry's musical play was written in collaboration with Sir Walter Scott, whose novel *Guy Mannering* had been published anonymously in 1815. *The Gipsey's Prophecy* was licensed on 26 February 1816 as 'Right and Might; or, The Castle of Ellangowan'. It opened at Covent Garden on 12 March 1816, with Mrs Egerton as the original Meg Merrilies. There were 18 performances of the piece during its first season.

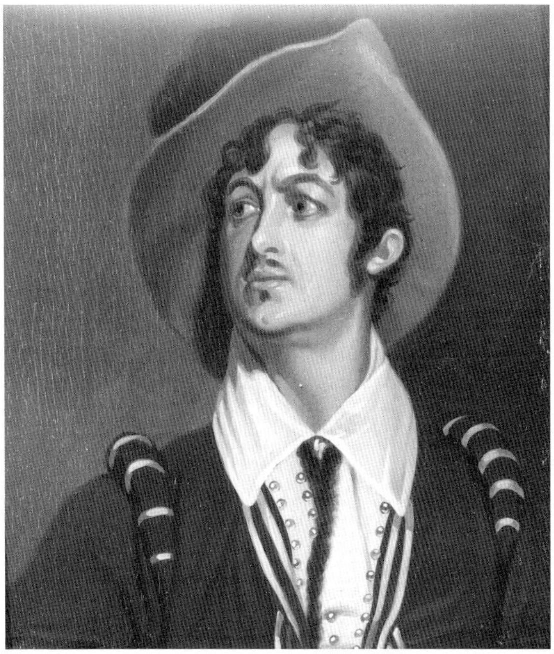

189

ROBERT ELLISTON

as Duke Aranza in *The Honey Moon* by John Tobin

Samuel De Wilde

Oil on panel 23.1 x 19.1
INV: Mathews 353; RW/CKA 230
PROV: Charles Mathews
EXH: 1833 London (353)
ENGR: James Hopwood for *The Cabinet* pub. Mathews & Leigh 1 March 1807, stipple & line 14.6 x 9.5
REL: Harvard Theatre Collection TS 990.1.3F Vol. I (30), pencil and watercolour on wove paper 36.9 x 22.5, inscr: 'Sam De Wilde delin / Dr 1807' (pencil b.l.); BM L.B.10, pencil and watercolour on wove paper 36.2 x 22.8, inscr: 'De Wilde delin / July 1808' (pencil)

One of these full-length copies of the Garrick Club picture was engraved by Edward Scriven pub. Bell & DeCamp 1 November 1808, stipple 15 x 10.1, and by Edward Scriven pub. Thomas Tegg 1810, stipple 12.7 x 7.6.
There is a copy in the Theatre Museum, pencil and grey wash on wove paper 35.5 x 22.8, dated 1808.

Elliston is shown in Act III, scene 2. Duke Aranza has pretended to his new wife Juliana that he is a lowly rustic rather than the Duke she thought she had married. She takes her complaint to Jacquez, one of the Duke's servants, who is playing the part of his master whilst he is away. The Duke 'in a peasant dress' joins Juliana and is reprimanded by Jacquez. The Duke is amused by the servant's performance, and says, according to the quotation printed on the engraving, 'How well the fellow reproves me' (actually in the text 'The rogue reproves me well'). His peasant costume, rather lacking in rusticity, consists of a wide-brimmed felt hat with black plumes, dark brown doublet with buff trim over a fur-trimmed buff jerkin and plain white turn-down collar. There is a brown and buff striped ribbon round his neck.

Tobin's comedy was first performed at Drury Lane on 31 January 1805, with Elliston playing the part of Duke Aranza. See also No. 147.

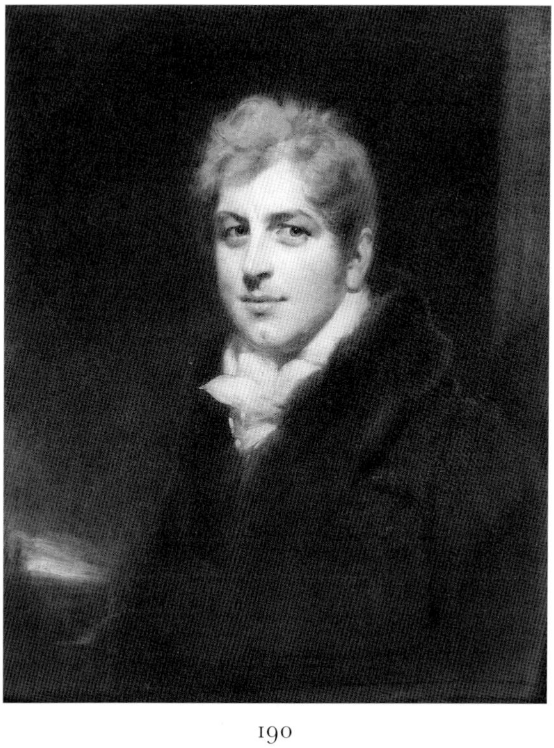

190
ROBERT ELLISTON

George Henry Harlow

Oil on canvas 76.5 x 63.5
INV: Mathews 159; RW/CKA 373
PROV: Charles Mathews
EXH: 1833 London (159)
ENGR: Charles Turner pub. John P. Thompson 9 July 1808, mezzotint 27 x 22.8
REL: NPG 2136 oil on canvas 78.1 x 64.8, bequeathed by the sitter's daughter, Miss Mary Anne Elliston, in 1926, and possibly the engraved version; Art Gallery, Tasmanian Museum, Hobart, oil on canvas n.s.

Elliston wears a dark brown jacket with a high fur collar, and a high white stock. There is a view of a sunset landscape to the bottom left.

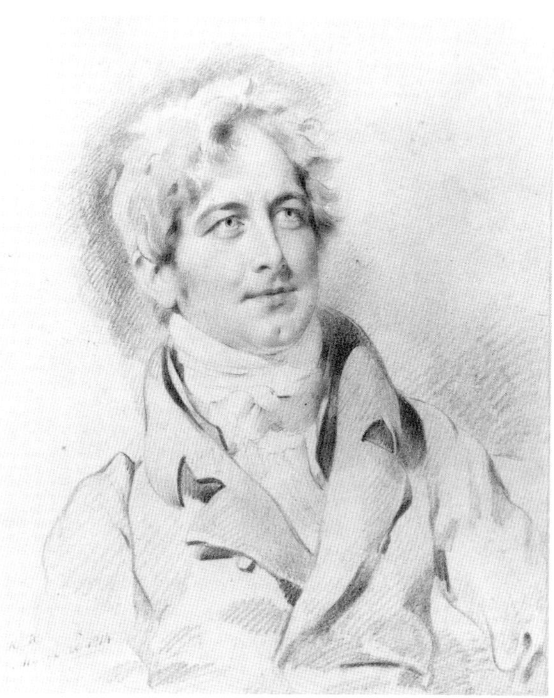

191
ROBERT ELLISTON

George Henry Harlow

Red and black chalk on rough wove paper 26.6 x 17.8
INSCR: 'G.H.H. / March 20th. 1814' (black chalk b.l.); 'Elliston' (pencil b.c.); 'G.H. Harlowe Fecit' (pen and brown ink on mount b.l. CM)
INV: Mathews 300; RW/CKA 489
PROV: Charles Mathews
EXH: 1833 London (300)
ENGR: J.J. Penstone pub. Cunningham & Mortimer 1843, stipple, inscr: '...from an Original Drawing by George Henry Harlowe / in the Possession of the Garrick Club'
LIT: Fitzgerald, pp. 196–97

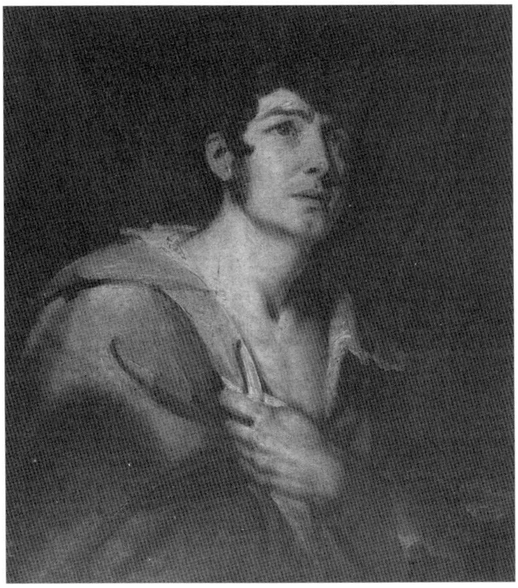

192
ROBERT ELLISTON
as Octavian in *The Mountaineers*
by George Colman the Younger

Henry Singleton

Oil on canvas 74.3 x 61.6
INV: Mathews 2; RW/CKA 20
PROV: Charles Mathews
EXH: 1804 R.A. (68); 1833 London (2)
ENGR: H.R. Cook for the *Theatrical Inquisitor*
pub. C. Chapple 1 April 1813, stipple 16.2 x 11.1 (full-length with right hand raised, but evidently based on No. 192)

Don Octavian, who is in love with Floranthe, wounds a rival preferred by Floranthe's father and takes to living in a cave on the Sierra de Ronda. He has been there for a year and is unaware that the rival has survived and married someone else or that Floranthe still loves him. Dressed as a cavalier, and accompanied by Roque, Floranthe searches for Octavian and finds him inside a goatherd's cottage. She exclaims: 'Oh! what hast thou endur'd! Wand'ring, exposed, unshelter'd!' Octavian shrugs off his hardships, which include having been struck by lightning. He clutches his breast and says: ''Tis here – only here I am vulnerable.' Elliston, half-length, wears a jerkin made of animal skins, and a buff mantle.

The younger Colman's melodrama, with music by Dr Samuel Arnold and scenery by Michelangelo Rooker, was first performed at the Haymarket on 3 August 1793. John Philip Kemble was the original Octavian, and later became the first Octavian at Drury Lane, on 31 October 1794. Singleton's painting was inspired by Elliston's performances at the Haymarket over the summer season of 1803, when he played the part 19 times.

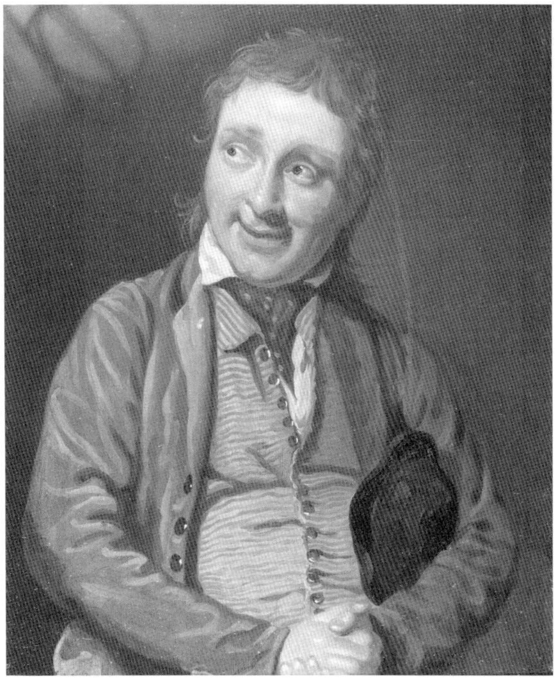

193
JOHN EMERY
as Dan in *John Bull or The Englishman's Fireside*
by George Colman the Younger

Samuel De Wilde

Oil on panel 24.2 x 19
INV: Mathews 32; RW/CKA 206
PROV: Charles Mathews
EXH: 1833 London (32)
ENGR: William Ridley for the *Monthly Mirror*
pub. Vernor & Hood 26 May 1803, stipple 8.9 x 7.6 (bust in oval)
REL: Sir Henry Irving sale, Christie's 16 December 1905 (152), oil on panel 35.6 x 28

Dan works as a waiter at Denis Brulgruddery's Inn, The Red Cow. Custom is very occasional, and Dan commiserates with the landlord. He is shown half-length, wearing a rustic brown jacket, a buff waistcoat with narrow horizontal red stripes, and a spotted red neckerchief.

The younger Colman's comedy was first performed at Covent Garden on 5 March 1803, with Emery as Dan. There were 48 performances during its first season. See Nos. 220 and 334.

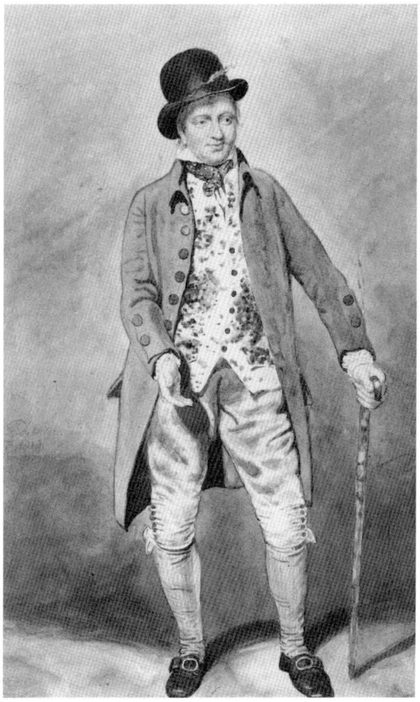

194
JOHN EMERY
as Farmer Ashfield in *Speed the Plough*
by Thomas Morton

Samuel De Wilde

Pencil and watercolour on wove paper 37 x 23.5
INSCR: 'S De Wilde delin / Fr 1809' (pencil b.l.)
INV: Mathews 213; RW/CKA 68C
PROV: Charles Mathews
EXH: 1833 London (213)

In Act III, scene 3, an apartment in Sir Philip Blandford's castle, Sir Philip asks Farmer Ashfield to evict the virtuous young man Henry from his cottage, which is on the Blandford estate. The moment pictured, according to Mathews's quotation, is when the farmer makes a long speech beginning 'Well zur, I'll argufy the topic' and ends by refusing. Farmer Ashfield shows his bluff, rustic nature with the ear of corn in the brim of his tall black hat. He wears black shoes, pale blue stockings with darker blue vertical stripes, pinkish moleskin breeches, a long brown coat, brown waistcoat and brown scarf.

Morton's comedy was first performed at Covent Garden on 8 February 1800, with Thomas Knight as Farmer Ashfield. Emery played the role for his own benefit on 9 June 1812, although the part was usually taken by Knight. The performances nearest in date to De Wilde's portrait were on 6 January and 21 March 1809, when Emery played Farmer Ashfield with the Covent Garden company at the Haymarket.

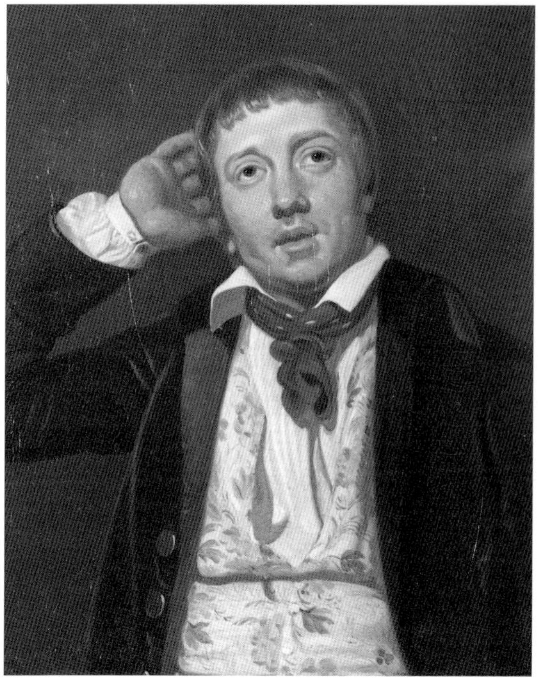

195
JOHN EMERY
as John Lump
in *The Review or The Wags of Windsor*
by George Colman the Younger

Samuel De Wilde

Oil on panel 23.7 x 19.3
INV: Mathews 151; RW/CKA 226
PROV: Charles Mathews
EXH: 1833 London (151)
ENGR: Richard Woodman pub. M. Emery 1815, stipple and line 13.7 x 11.5
REL: Mander & Mitchenson II, oil on canvas 76 x 59
This full-length version was probably exhibited R.A. 1802 (108). It is in a rubbed and damaged state.

Half-length. John Lump is a dense but canny Yorkshireman. In the second scene, an apartment in the house of Mr Deputy Bull of Windsor, he seeks and receives a job as a servant. He wears a green velvet jacket with brass buttons and a paler green lining, a white waistcoat embroidered with pink flowers and green leaves, a white shirt with gold cuff links, and a brown neckerchief with white spots.

The younger Colman's operatic farce, with a military overture and new music by Dr Samuel Arnold, was first given at the Haymarket on 1 September 1800, with John Emery as the original John Lump.

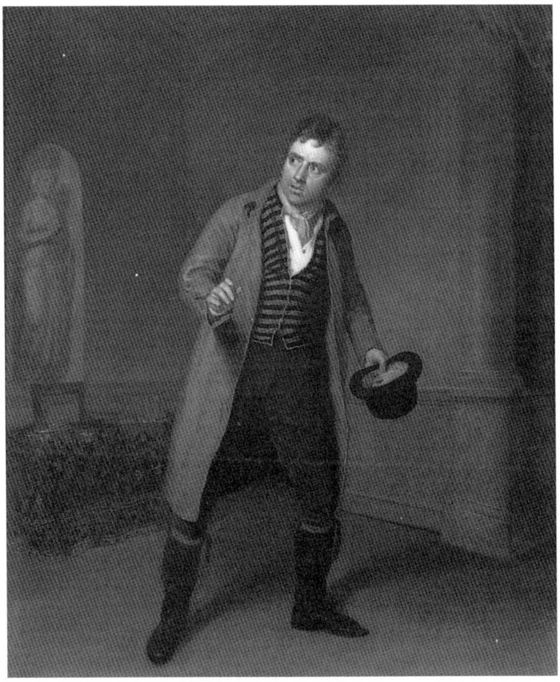

196
JOHN EMERY
as Tyke in *The School of Reform or How to Rule a Husband*
by Thomas Morton

Samuel De Wilde

Oil on canvas 71.7 x 55.2
INV: Mathews 67; RW/CKA 290
PROV: Charles Mathews
EXH: 1806 R.A. (282); 1833 London (67);
1951–52 London (136)
ENGR: Charles Turner pub. C. Turner 14 June 1808,
mezzotint 50.5 x 40; Richard Woodman for
The Cabinet pub. Mathews & Leigh 1 February 1808,
stipple and line 14.3 x 9.5
REL: NT 32, oil on canvas 74 x 56.5 (Mander & Mitchenson believed this to be the version engraved and shown at the R.A.); Priv. coll., USA, oil on canvas n.s.; NT 38, pencil and watercolour on wove paper 37.3 x 23.6 (paper watermarked 1815; perhaps a copy after Turner's mezzotint)
[Possibly one of the above was the picture by De Wilde, signed and dated, of Emery as Tyke that was in the Royal Dramatic College sale at Fairbrother, Lye and Palmer on 24 February 1881 (lot 100B)]
LIT: Griffiths, p. 336

Tyke has been arrested for trying to rob Lord Avondale's guests, General Tarragon and his daughter Julia. He is brought before Lord Avondale for his punishment. However, Avondale recognises Tyke as the son of the man to whom he entrusted his child, the product of a secret marriage. Tyke recognises the guilty lord and sees that he will not be punished for the attempted robbery. Tyke, shown full-length standing, holds a black hat and wears brown boots, light stockings, brown breeches, a grey coat, a waistcoat of dark green and gold horizontal bands, a loose white shirt, and a pink neckerchief with white spots.

Morton's comedy was first performed at Covent Garden on 15 January 1805, with Emery as Robert Tyke. The 12th performance, on 29 January 1805, was by Royal Command, and the play was given 26 times over the season.

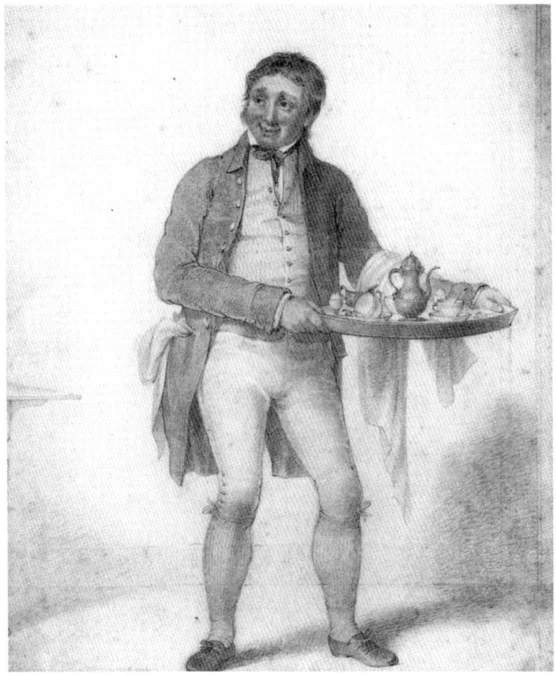

197
JOHN EMERY
as Sam in *Raising the Wind* by James Kenney

C. Linsell

Pencil on wove paper 33.6 x 26
INSCR: 'C. Linsell / delt. 1815' (pencil c.l.)
INV: Mathews 293; CKA 505
PROV: Charles Mathews
EXH: 1833 London (293)

Sam is a Yorkshireman who has just procured a position waiting at tables at an inn. He carries a breakfast tray, and has a cloth over his left arm.

Kenney's two-act farce was first performed at Covent Garden on 5 November 1803, with Emery as the original Sam. His only performance as Sam in 1815, the date on the drawing, was at Covent Garden on 20 July, the last night of the 1814–15 season. See No. 339.

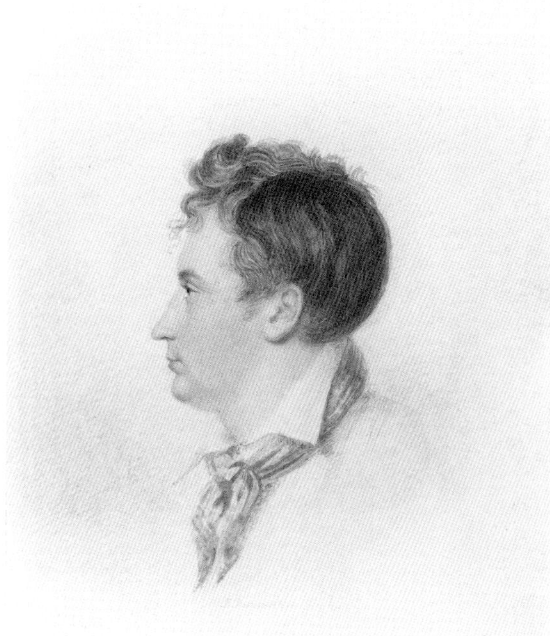

198
JOHN EMERY

John Turmeau

Pencil and watercolour on wove paper 16.5 x 14.6
INSCR: 'J Turmeau del.' (pencil b.c.);
'Turmeau Fecit.' (pen and brown ink on mount b.l.);
'Mr Emery' (pen and brown ink on mount b.c.)
INV: Mathews 343; RW 546 (artist unknown); CKA 546
PROV: Charles Mathews
EXH: 1833 London (343)

Head in profile to left, wearing a light red neckerchief.

Emery performed on the London stage for some 24 years, mostly at Covent Garden, where he made his début in September 1798. He excelled in the line of old men and country rustics. The *New Monthly Mirror* in October 1821 called him 'one of the most real, hearty, and fervid of actors'. Hazlitt wrote of his acting: 'It is impossible to praise it sufficiently because there is never any opportunity of finding fault with it.'

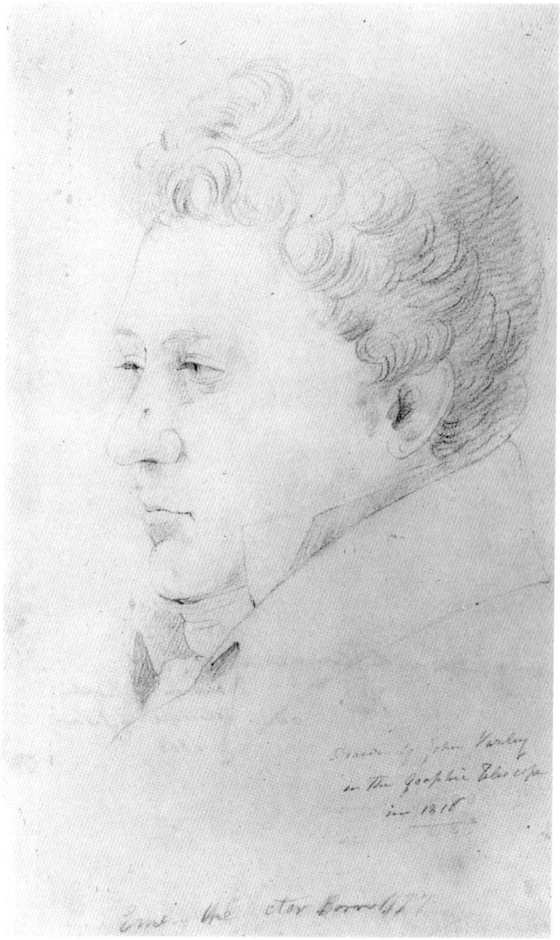

199
JOHN EMERY

John Varley

Pencil on wove paper 45.1 x 33
INSCR: 'Drawn by John Varley / in the Graphic Telescope / in 1816' (pencil b.r.);
'Emery the Actor Born 1777'
(pencil b.c. in another hand)
INV: RW/CKA 136
PROV: Unknown, seemingly acquired between 1888 and 1909
LIT: For the 'Graphic Telescope' see *Burlington Magazine* (1972), 114: 72

Head only, facing to left. See No. 38.

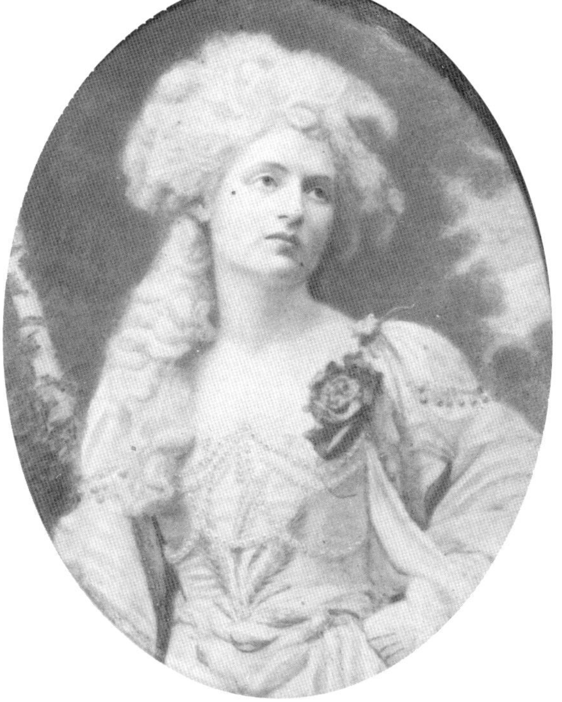

200
WINIFRED EMERY
as Lady Teazle in *The School for Scandal*
by Richard Brinsley Sheridan

W. Graham Simpson

Watercolour on card 15.2 x 12 (oval)
INV: GCL 673; Gift 430
PROV: Presented by Cyril Maude, 1924
LIT: Cyril Maude, *The Haymarket Theatre. Some Records and Reminiscences* (1903), pl. XVII (as 'From the miniature by Mr Simpson'); Cyril Maude, *Behind the Scenes with Cyril Maude* (1927) reproduced opposite p.150 (as 'Winifred Emery as Elizabeth Linley. From a miniature in the Garrick Club')

Miss Emery wears a great bluish powdered wig with big curls falling over her right shoulder. Her blue-white dress has strands of pearls at the breast and is decorated with ears of corn at the front. This miniature seems to have been copied from a photograph.

A protracted illness kept Winifred Emery from the stage between 1902 and 1905. Her only performances as Lady Teazle appear to have been at the Vaudeville in 1890, when *The School for Scandal* was performed 27 times from 11 January. Cyril Maude, Winifred Emery's husband, played Joseph Surface.

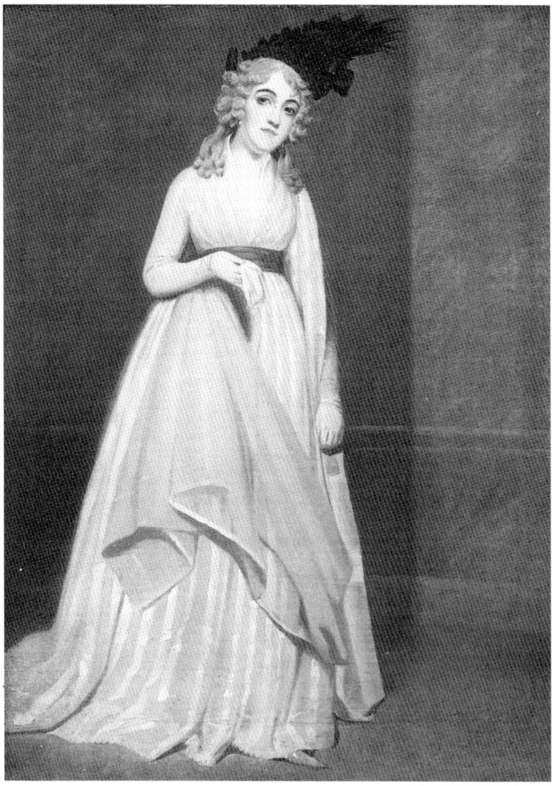

201
HARRIET PYE ESTEN
as Lady Flutter in *The Discovery*
by Frances Sheridan

Samuel De Wilde

Oil on canvas 36.2 x 28
INV: Mathews 89; RW/CKA 441
PROV: Charles Mathews
EXH: 1833 London (98); 1974 Twickenham (47)
ENGR: William Leney for Bell's British Library 30 March 1793, line 11.1 x 8.2, published Bell's *British Theatre* (1797), vol 5

The scene is Act II, scene I, Sir Henry Flutter's dressing room. He has called for his wife, and she enters 'with Knetting in her hand'. They quarrel and Sir Henry tells her to 'retire with your trumpery work – I choose to be alone'. But Lady Flutter decides to stay: 'Then I'll stay to vex you' (quotation on the engraving). Lady Flutter wears a white dress trimmed with vertical lines, a blue sash, and a black hat with feathers and ribbons. In her right hand she holds her 'knetting'.

Mrs Sheridan's comedy was first performed at Drury Lane on 3 February 1763, with Jane Pope as Lady Flutter. Mrs Esten never played the role in London.

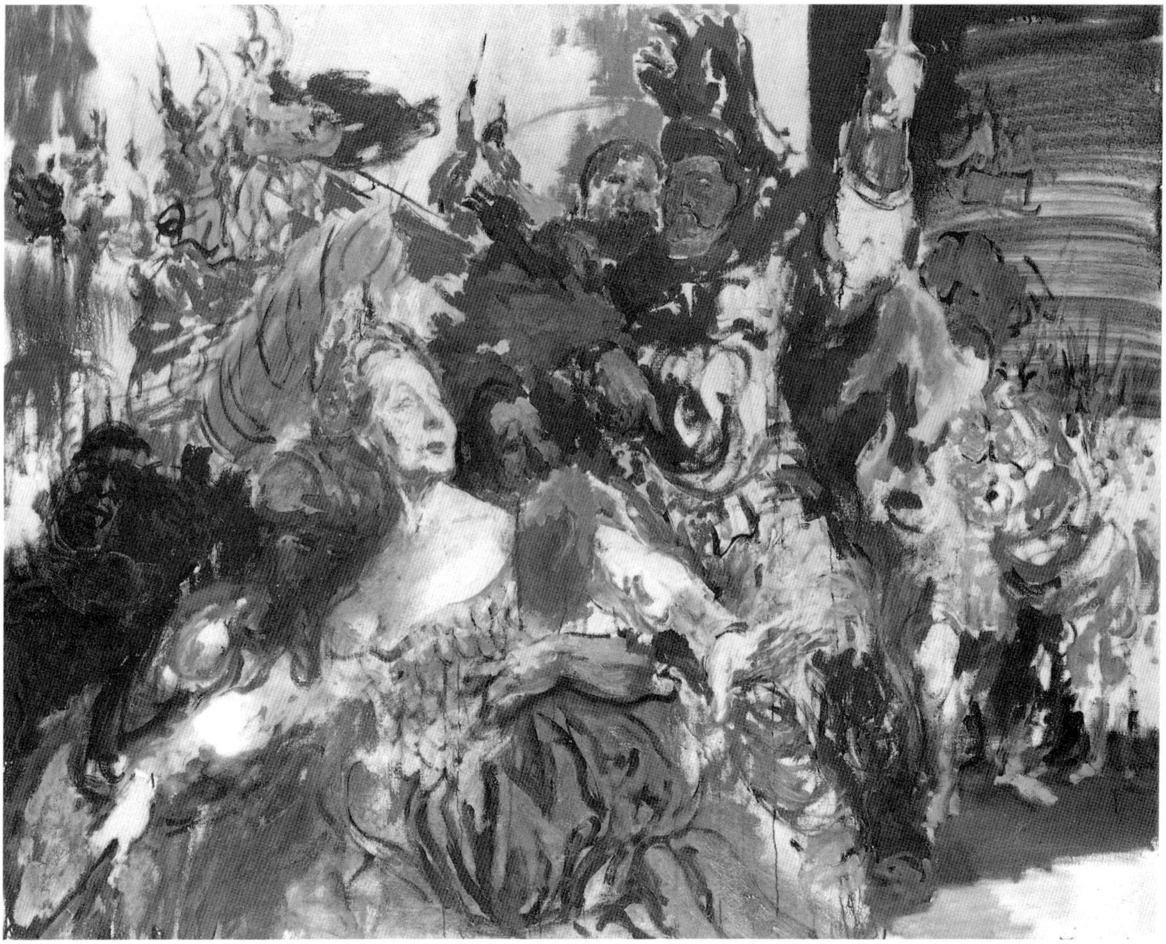

202

DAME EDITH EVANS as Cleopatra
and *SIR GODFREY TEARLE* as Antony
in *Antony and Cleopatra* by William Shakespeare

Feliks Topolski

Oil on canvas 109.2 x 137.1
INSCR: 'Feliks Topolski '47' (brown paint b.r.)
INV: GCL 734; Gift 877
PROV: Edith Evans; bequeathed to Margaret Rawlings, by whom presented to the Garrick Club, 1977
EXH: 1962 Chichester (64)

This evocation of Shakespeare's tragedy is loosely painted on a white ground with the artist's characteristic thick impasto on the faces. The striking figure of Cleopatra holds a fan, and wears gold-scaled body armour and a red frock. Antony wears greenish body armour and a helmet with plumes.

Edith Evans played Cleopatra rather late in life, in a revival at the Piccadilly Theatre in December 1946. The production was directed by Glen Byam Shaw, designed by Motley, and had music by Anthony Hopkins. Anthony Quayle played Enobarbus. According to Muriel St Clare Byrne: 'The costumes represented a free treatment of the Renaissance style, with some suggestions of Roman and Egyptian, and were so designed in order to bear the same kind of relationship to early 17th-century theatrical practice as the setting bore to the Shakespeare stage.'

At a meeting of the Picture Committee on 18 April 1945, it was suggested by Christopher Hussey that the Garrick Club might commission a portrait of Edith Evans as Lady Bracknell from Laura Knight. Correspondence on the matter between Colonel Plimpton and Sir Alfred Munnings ensued, but nothing seems to have come of the idea.

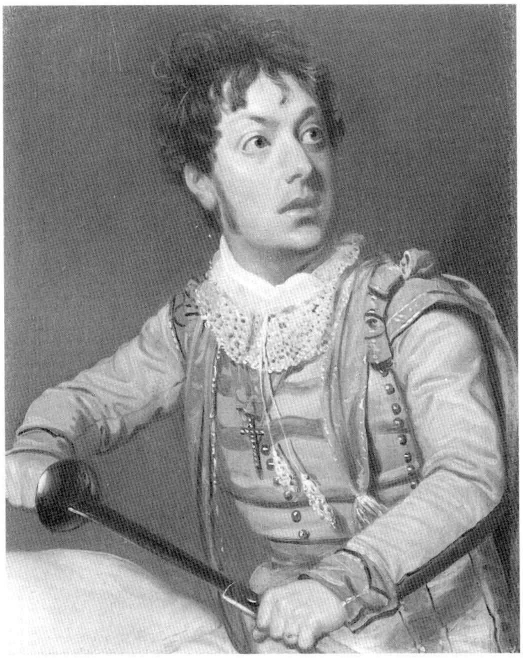

203
CHARLES FARLEY
as Francisco in *The Tale of Mystery* by Thomas Holcroft

Samuel De Wilde

Oil on panel 22.2 x 18.4 (identified on the plate bottom front of frame as 'Farren')
INV: Mathews 351; RW/CKA 218
PROV: Charles Mathews
EXH: 1833 London (351)

At no point in *The Tale of Mystery* does the text indicate that Francisco unsheathes a sword. Towards the end of Act I, Francisco is attacked by Romaldi (alias Bianchi, his wicked brother) and his servant Malvoglio. They brandish daggers, and Francisco defends himself with two pistols. The costume is not the same as that worn by Farley in De Wilde's full-length portrait of him in the same part (Somerset Maugham Collection, Royal National Theatre, 16), which shows him in Act I. It is possible that he had a costume change for his daughter's wedding in Act II, and that in his attempts to defend his brother at the end of the play he drew his sword. In the Garrick Club picture Farley wears a yellow-brown doublet decorated with horizontal brown stripes, a cloak, and a lace collar.

Holcroft's melodrama was adapted from Pixérécourt's *Coelina; ou, l'enfant du mystère*, performed in Paris in 1800. The English version opened at Covent Garden on 13 November 1802, with Farley as Francisco. See Nos. 146, 259 and 709.

Farley became a member of the Garrick Club in 1831.

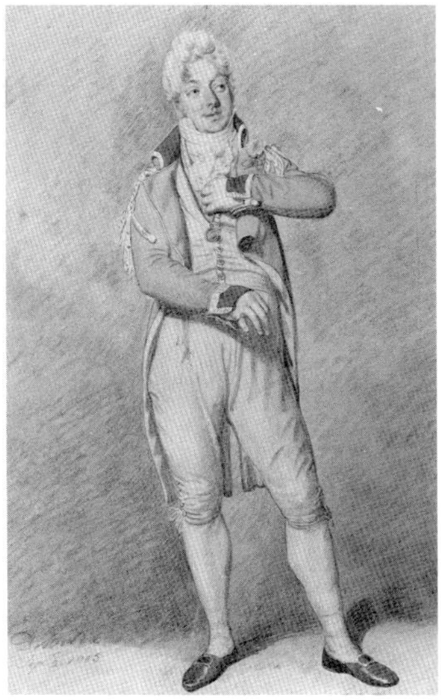

204
CHARLES FARLEY
as Jessamy in *Bon Ton or High Life Above Stairs*
by David Garrick

Samuel De Wilde

Black chalk, pencil and watercolour on wove paper 37 x 23.5
INSCR: 'De Wilde / Sepr 20 1805' (black chalk b.l.)
INV: Mathews 252; RW/CKA 59A
PROV: Charles Mathews
EXH: 1833 London (252)
ENGR: Cooke for Cawthorn's *Minor Theatre*, pub. John Cawthorn 1 January 1806, stipple 12 x 7.6 ('De Wilde pinxt.' with pillar behind at left, dado rail behind thighs)

In Act II, scene I, Jessamy tells Sir John Trotley of a masked ball he attended, where, by accident, he came across his own wife, who recognised him from the diamond ring he was wearing. The line quoted on the engraving – 'You see, Sir John, it is a very pretty Diamond Ring' – does not appear in Garrick's text. Jessamy, one of Lord Minikin's rather grand servants, wears black shoes with gold buckles, faded white stockings, creamy breeches, a blue cutaway coat lined in white, a high turned collar in black with white edging, a creamy waistcoat, a monocle on a black band around his neck, and a very high stock. There is a pink flower on his left shoulder. He displays the diamond ring on the little finger of his right hand.

Garrick's farce was first given at Drury Lane on 18 March 1775, with Philip Lamash as the original Jessamy. The only London performances of *Bon Ton* during the 1805–6 season (in which De Wilde drew the picture) were given at Drury Lane, the first on 16 December 1805, with Vincent De Camp as Jessamy.

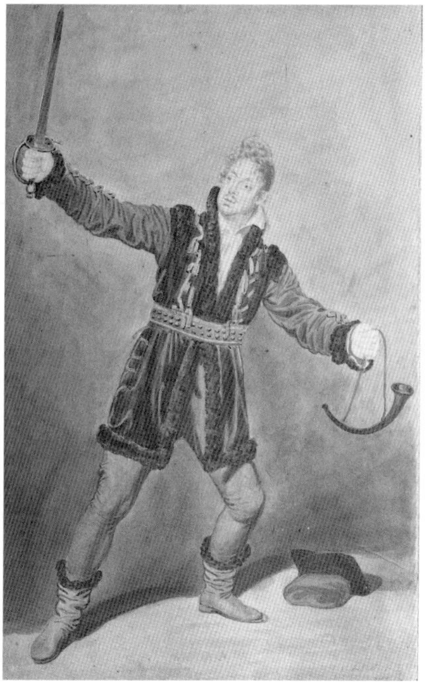

205
CHARLES FARLEY
as Kalig in *The Blind Boy* by James Kenney

Samuel De Wilde

Pencil and watercolour on wove paper 37.5 x 23.5
INSCR: 'S. De Wilde' in pencil b.l.
INV: RW 64 (sitter and artist unknown); CKA 64; Gift 153
PROV: Bequeathed by the sitter, 1859
ENGR: William Bond pub. Bell & De Camp 1809, stipple 15 x 10.1

Kalig, 'a reduced Gentleman', is shown at the climax of the play, fighting the villainous Starow to save the life of Edmond, the Blind Boy and long-lost heir to the throne of Sarmatia. Act II, scene 2 is set on the banks of the Vistula, where Edmond is to be drowned. Starow is dragging Edmond to the boat when Kalig accosts him. The stage direction reads: 'Kalig leaves the Prince, and goes round to Starow, takes hold of the horn that hangs on his neck, and throws him from the Prince round to R[ight]. – the chain of the horn breaks, and Kalig draws his sabre – they stand for a moment, gazing at each other.' Kalig's line is printed on the engraving: 'I am no Traitor, – but while this arm can wield a sword it shall protect its lawful Prince.' Edmond is saved, and, for some reason, Kalig is made heir to the throne.

Kalig wears fur-trimmed soft leather boots, red hose, a fur-trimmed blue coat with red sleeves and gold frogging, a broad red belt with gold studs, and a white shirt with loose collar. A red and black hat lies on the ground.

Kenney's two-act melodrama was first performed at Covent Garden on 1 December 1807. According to the playbills, it was a 'Grand Historical Melo-Drama ... the Musick, Scenery, Machinery, Dresses & Decorations entirely new'. The action, and everything else, was under the direction of Charles Farley, who also played Kalig.

206
ELIZABETH FARREN
as Clarinda in *The Suspicious Husband*
by Benjamin Hoadley

Richard Cosway (attr.)

Oil on canvas 90.2 x 71.7 (oval)
INV: RW/CKA 448; Gift 124
PROV: Presented to the Garrick Club by William A. Commerell, 1854 (as by Gainsborough)

Miss Farren holds a black mask with ribbons. Her dress has long white sleeves and a pink silk bodice trimmed with lace and pink bows. Her cloak is lined in pink.

The character has been identified by Susan Bloxham, who cites the stipple engraving of Elizabeth Farren as Clarinda by J. Phillips after an anonymous artist, published by E. Hedges in 1785.

[The attribution to Cosway given by Adams is most unlikely, though the picture is accomplished and charming. It is apparently by a Continental hand, perhaps French or Scandinavian, and on grounds of costume seems to date from about 1790.]

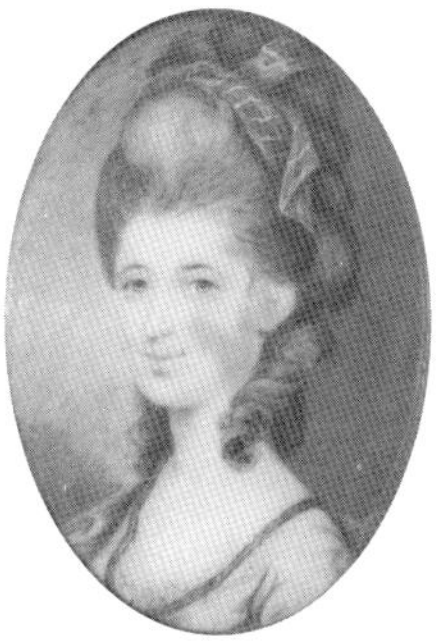

207
ELIZABETH FARREN (?)

Unknown Artist

Watercolour on ivory 5 x 3.7 (oval)
INSCR: 'Miss Farren now Countess of Derby' (on back)
INV: Mathews 329?; RW 427R (unknown sitter by Horace Hone); CKA 427R (attr. Horace Hone)
PROV: Charles Mathews
EXH: 1833 London (329)

The sitter wears a pink dress and has an elaborate coiffure typical of the late 1770s. Despite the inscription, her identity is not secure. Mathews 329 appears amidst a group of miniatures and might easily be this small and doubtful work.

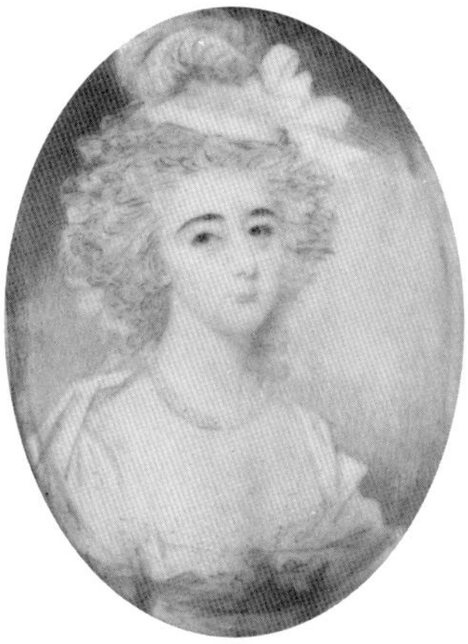

208
ELIZABETH FARREN (?)

Unknown Artist

Watercolour on ivory 6.7 x 6 (oval)
INV: RW 427Q (by Horace Hone); CKA 427Q
PROV: Unknown, but acquired before 1909

The sitter has powdered hair with feathers and a big pink ribbon. Her identity is uncertain, but there are similarities to Downman's 1787 portrait of Elizabeth Farren in the National Portrait Gallery and a miniature of her by Cosway in the collection of the Earl of Derby, exh: R.A. 1956–57 (274), watercolour on ivory 6.7 x 5.7.

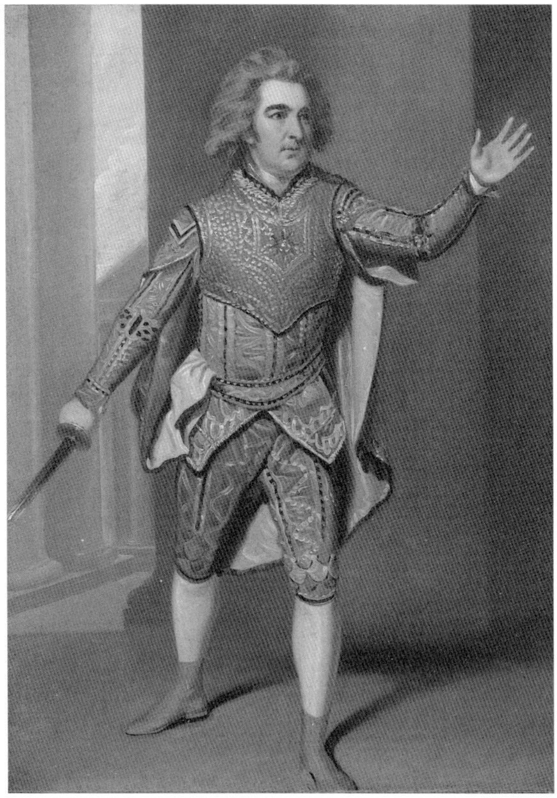

209
WILLIAM FARREN THE ELDER
as Orestes in *The Distressed Mother*
by Ambrose Philips

Samuel De Wilde

Oil on canvas 37.5 x 28.3
INV: Mathews 100; RW/CKA 231
PROV: John Bell; Charles Mathews
EXH: 1833 London (231); 1962 Chichester (20)
ENGR: J. Thornthwaite for Bell's British Library 19 August 1791, line 10.5 x 7.4, published Bell's *British Theatre* (1797), vol 6
LIT: Fitzgerald, pp. 209–10

Orestes enters in Act V, scene I, to tell his cousin Hermione, the daughter of Menelaus and Helen of Troy, that he has killed Pyrrhus, the son of Achilles. His line is quoted on the engraving: 'Madam, tis done; your orders are obeyd. The Tyrant lies expiring at the altar.' Farren's costume consists of short scarlet boots, white stockings and pale blue doublet and breeches decorated in black and silver, with red embroidered tabs and belt. He has a scarlet mantle lined in white and decorated in black and silver, and an elaborately chased steel breastplate. Philips's tragedy was originally performed at Drury Lane on 17 March 1712. Farren seems not to have played the role in London.

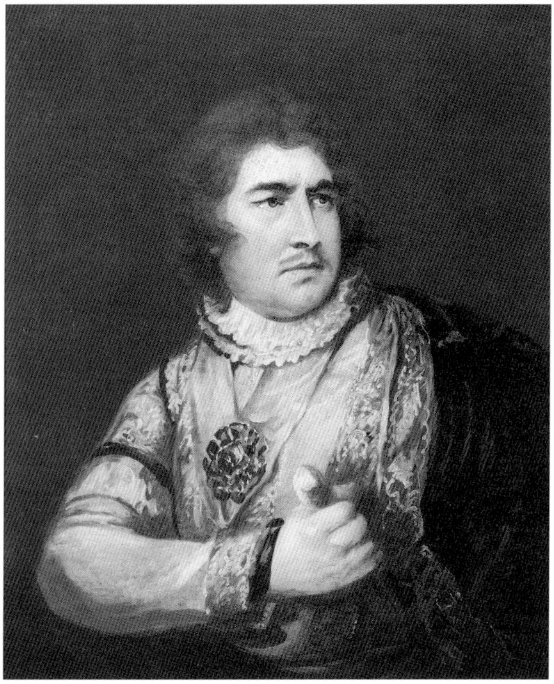

210

WILLIAM FARREN THE ELDER
as The Earl of Chester (?) in *England Preserv'd*
by George Watson

Gainsborough Dupont

Oil on canvas 77 x 63.5
INV: CKA 182 (no character); Gift 398
PROV: Thomas Harris (?); Farren family;
bequeathed to the Garrick Club by
Miss Florence Helen Farren, 1921
(as a portrait of William Farren by Zoffany)
EXH: 1951 London (16); 1982–83 London (133)
LIT: *The Morning Herald* 23 April 1795;
Hayes, 1968 (reproduced)

Farren seems to be holding a pistol to his chest. He wears a yellow tunic. Around his neck is a pale green ribbon with a jewel and he has a dark blue cloak.

This picture was not in the Harris sale of 1819. There seems to be no doubt about the identity of the sitter, but the character is a problem. It was incorrectly identified as Carlos in Colley Cibber's *Love Makes a Man; or, The Fop's Fortune* for the 1982–83 Royal Opera House exhibition; the costume in that play would not have been historical. Farren played two new parts in the final months of his career in the spring of 1795, shortly before this picture was mentioned in the *Morning Herald*: the Earl of Chester in George Watson's *England Preserv'd* and Edward III in *Windsor Castle*. The Earl of Chester seems a likely subject for this painting.

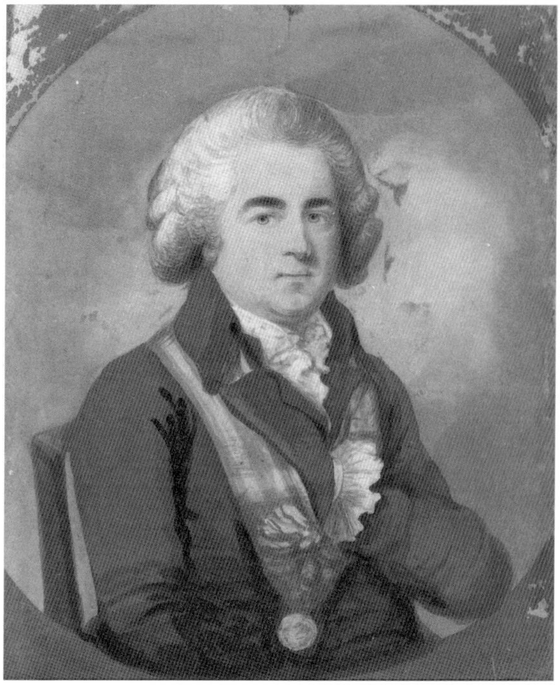

211

WILLIAM FARREN THE ELDER
'School of Garrick'

Henry Spicer

Pencil and watercolour on laid paper 26.5 x 21
INV: Mathews 261 (artist unknown);
RW/CKA 50D (artist unknown)
PROV: Charles Mathews
EXH: 1833 London (216)
ENGR: Similar to William Ridley after Anon.
for Parsons's *Minor Theatre* 1793, stipple 7.3 x 6
(no ribbon or medal and no hand in breast)

Farren wears a blue-grey jacket with collar turned down over his Rainbow Ribband, which has a rosette and supports a Shakespeare Favour. See No. 6.

Farren acted only one full season (1775–76) under Garrick's management, at Drury Lane, but he remained on the London stage until 1795. 'Though not an actor of the first rank or quality,' he served in supporting roles 'with evident sense and reliability' (BD). His son, William Farren (1786–1861), became a leading actor of his day and a successful manager.

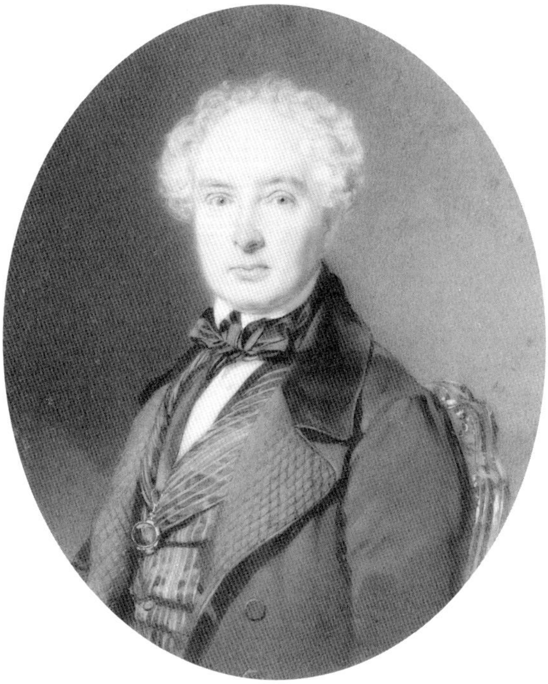

212

WILLIAM FARREN THE YOUNGER

Thomas Carrick

Watercolour on ivory 20 x 17 (oval)
INSCR: 'The Subject, The late Wm. Farren Esqr / Exhibited in the Royal Academy / Painted by Thos Carrick / 32 Regent Street Piccadilly Circus / London – / The Property of Wm. Farren Esq' (pen and ink on label on verso); 'MR' (blue crayon on verso)
INV: CKA 193; Gift 398
PROV: Bequeathed to the Garrick Club by Miss Florence Helen Farren, 1921
EXH: 1845 R.A. (775)
ENGR: H. Robinson pub. E. Gambart 1846, stipple and line 24.8 x 21

Farren wears a grey coat with quilted lapels, a red waistcoat with vertical gold stripes, white collar, and grey silk bow tie. An eyeglass hangs from a grey ribbon.

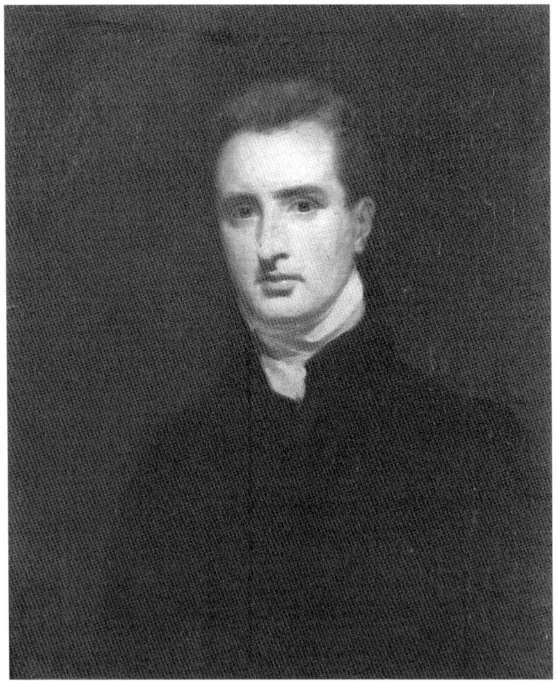

213

WILLIAM FARREN THE YOUNGER

George Clint

Oil on canvas 74.9 x 61
INV: CKA 568; Gift 398
PROV: Bequeathed to the Garrick Club by Miss Florence Helen Farren, 1921
ENGR: James Thomson for the *European Magazine* pub. J. Asperne 1822, stipple 10.1 x 8.2

Half-length, looking out at spectator.

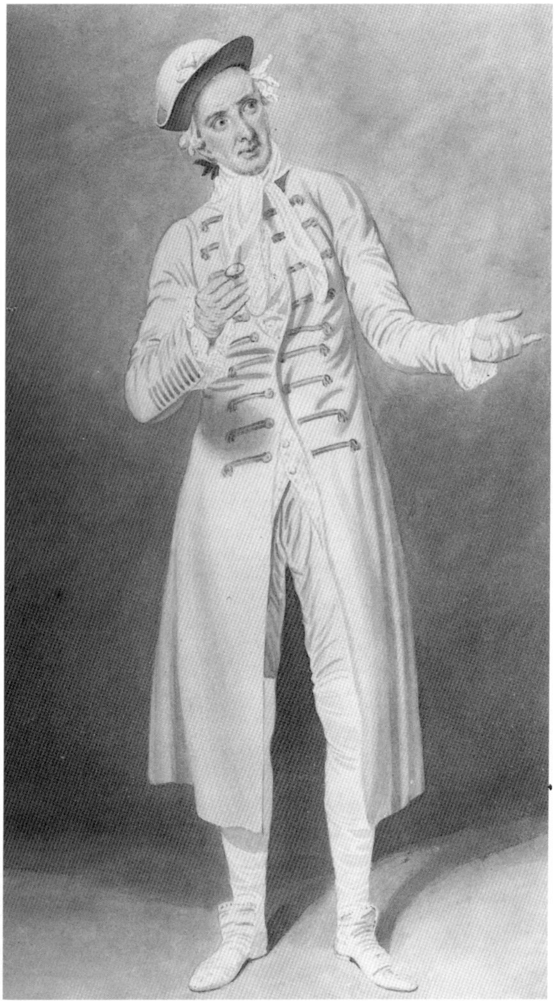

214

WILLIAM FARREN THE YOUNGER

as Lord Ogleby

in *The Clandestine Marriage*

by David Garrick and George Colman the Elder

Samuel De Wilde

Pencil and watercolour on wove paper 37 x 23.5
INV: Mathews 233; RW/CKA 68A; Gift 398
PROV: Charles Mathews
EXH: 1833 London (233)
REL: NT 56 pencil and watercolour on wove paper 37.5 x 23.5 s. & d: 'S De Wilde / 5 January 1819' (pencil b.l.); Theatre Museum (TM22) oil on canvas 29.2 x 24.1 s. & d: 'DeWilde Pinx / 1818'.
The small Theatre Museum picture shows the sitter slightly more than half-length to right, looking to front, holding a rose in his right hand; it was engraved by James Hopwood for Oxberry's *New English Drama* pub. Simpkin & Marshall 1818, stipple and line 11.5 x 7.6; Coll: Cyril Maude 1933, s. & d: 'S de Wilde delin Nr. 1828'? exh: 1933 London *Theatre Exhibition* (183)

[One of the above was probably the picture by De Wilde, signed and dated, of Farren as Lord 'Ogelvie' that was in the Royal Dramatic College sale at Fairbrother, Lye and Palmer on 24 February 1881 (lot 67), bought by J. L. Toole for £4 16*s*.]

The version of the picture in the Theatre Museum can be assigned to Act III, scene 2 because of the rose that Lord Ogleby is holding. He has just been presented with it by Miss Sterling, to replace her younger sister's nosegay. The scene is Mr Sterling's garden, where Lord Ogleby is being shown the improvements.

In No. 214 Ogleby wears a white cap with a bow, yellow gloves, pink shoes with high tongues edged in white, loose white stockings over pink knee-breeches, a long white coat, a pink waistcoat embroidered in gold, lace cuffs, and a loose white scarf. The long white coat would have been associated by the audience with the usual costume of a running footman, an amusingly inappropriate garment for a fashion-conscious lord.

Garrick and Colman's comedy was originally performed at Drury Lane on 20 February 1766, with Thomas King as Lord Ogleby. William Farren played the part for the first time, at Covent Garden, on 18 September 1818. See Nos. 19, 23, 226, 398 and 445.

215

WILLIAM FARREN THE YOUNGER (?)

as Sir Peter Teazle (?)

in *The School for Scandal*

by Richard Brinsley Sheridan

Henry Meyer (attr.)

Oil on canvas 41.9 x 33
INV: RW/CKA 289 (sitter, artist and play unknown)
PROV: Unknown

The sitter wears black shoes, white stockings with gold garters below the knee, grey knee-breeches, a grey jacket trimmed with gold braid, a white waistcoat decorated in gold, and a high white stock. A red handkerchief decorated in gold protrudes from the lower left pocket of his jacket.

The screen and library setting suggest that this is the 'screen scene' in *The School for Scandal* (see No. 3). The screen, however, does not appear to be painted with maps, and Lady Teazle would have considerable difficulty in concealing herself behind a screen folded so tightly. The desk appears to date from the 1820s, and the ugly chairs are probably later. The curious habit of wearing stockings over knee-breeches seems to be more

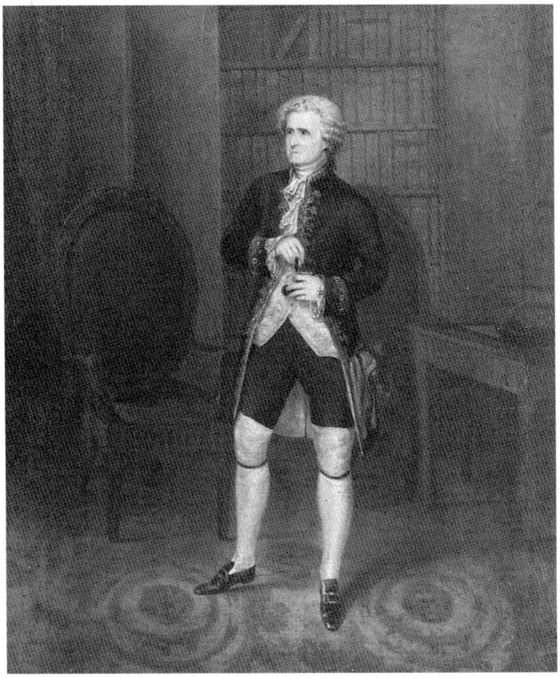

215 *William Farren the Younger (?) as Sir Peter Teazle (?)*

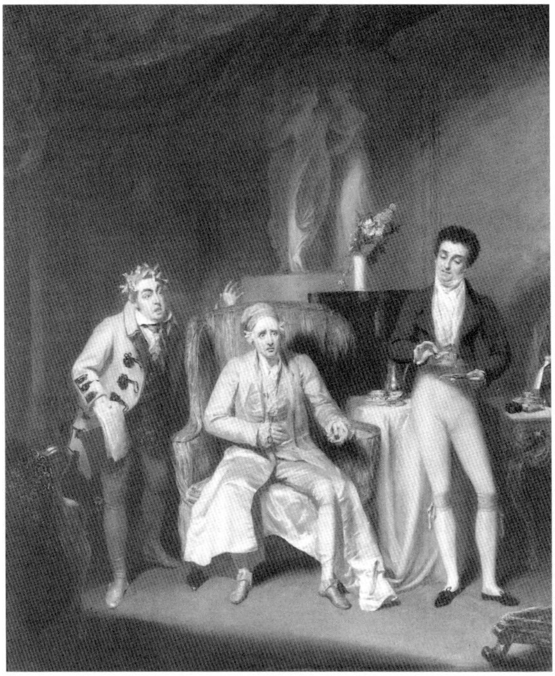

216 *William Farren as Lord Ogleby, Charles Farley as Canton & Richard Jones as Brush*

of an early Victorian stage costume convention than actual 18th-century practice.

The identity of the sitter is not secure, but William Farren was the most considerable Sir Peter Teazle between 1825 and 1845, dates that would match the attribution to Meyer. There may be some connection with C.J. Mathews's first Charles Surface (see Nos. 500 and 501) at Covent Garden on 10 October 1839.

216*

WILLIAM FARREN as Lord Ogleby,
CHARLES FARLEY as Canton
and *RICHARD JONES* as Brush
in *The Clandestine Marriage*
by David Garrick and George Colman the Elder

George Clint

Oil on canvas 155.5 x 134
INV: RW/CKA 37
PROV: Thomas Welch; purchased by the Garrick Club, 1850
EXH: 1819 R.A. (48)
ENGR: Henry Meyer 1821 pub. Hurst, Robinson & Co. (late Boydells) 16 March 1821, line 24.9 x 20.8
LIT: Fitzgerald, p. 163

The scene (II, I) is the antechamber to Lord Ogleby's bedroom in Mr Sterling's house, where Lord Ogleby is a guest. He has been helped to his chair by his two servants and served his chocolate by Brush. Ogleby's palsy drops being administered by Brush are eau d'arquibusade, according to Canton, who is about to read out an advertisement for the Cosmétique Royale from the paper he holds in his hand. On the engraving are quoted the lines: 'Where are the palsy drops, Brush?' 'Here, my lord!'

Lord Ogleby (Farren) wears pink shoes trimmed with silver, white stockings drawn over pink breeches, a peach silk day-coat lined with pink silk, and a matching waistcoat and pink cap. An eyeglass hangs from a blue ribbon around his neck. His chair is upholstered in pale blue with pink stripes. Canton (Farley), on the left, has his hair in curl-papers. He wears gold slippers, white stockings, red breeches, a richly embroidered waistcoat, and a white coat lined in green and with black trim and elaborate frogging. He has a blue neckerchief. Brush (Jones) wears black pumps, pale buff breeches, and a brown cutaway coat. The neo-classical group of the three Graces behind Lord Ogleby presumably represents the aggressive good taste of Mr Sterling's house.

Colman and Garrick's comedy was originally performed at Drury Lane on 20 February 1766, with Thomas King as Lord Ogleby, Robert Baddeley as Canton, and John Palmer as Brush. William Farren, Charles Farley and Richard Jones played these parts at Covent Garden on 18 September 1818. See Nos. 19, 23, 214, 398 and 445.

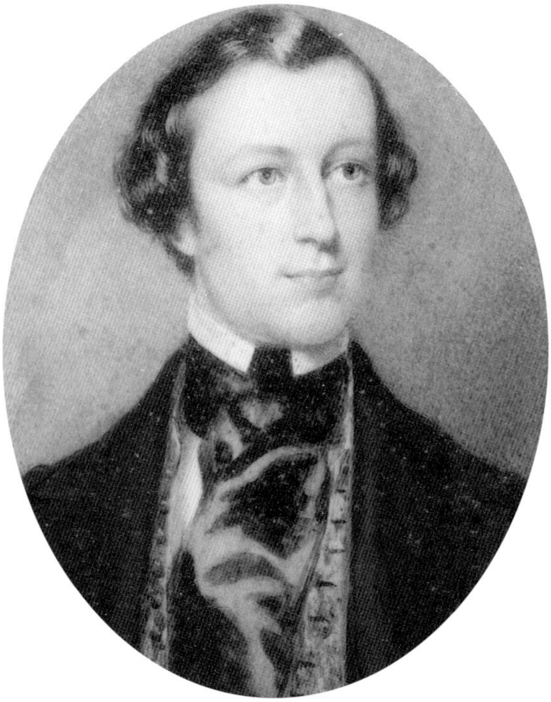

217
WILLIAM FARREN

Unknown Artist

Watercolour on ivory 8.5 x 6.5 (oval)
INSCR: 'For Miss Stallard / William Farren / in 1846'
(pen and ink on back-board)
INV: GCL 675; Gift 656
PROV: Bequeathed to the Garrick Club
by Miss A.H.I. Stallard, 1947

Farren wears a black coat and a waistcoat embroidered in blue, green and red. This William Farren, the third of that name and the son of William Farren (1786–1861), also acted in London.

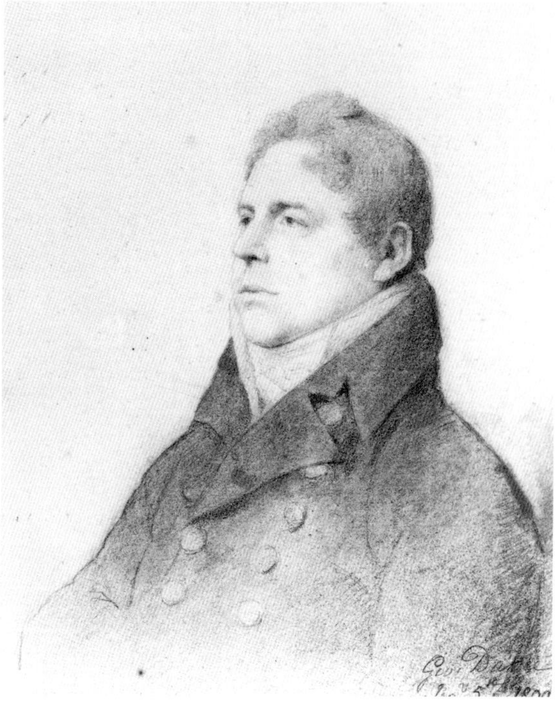

218
JOHN FAWCETT

George Dance

Pencil on wove paper 22.8 x 17.8
INSCR: 'Geo. Dance / Jany 5th. 1809' (pencil b.r.)
INV: CKA 194; Gift 353
PROV: J.L. Rutley, by whom presented
to the Garrick Club, 1911

[Dance's pencil portraits of contemporary celebrities constitute a particularly vivid record of the personalities of the day. They are typically profiles, and this three-quarter likeness represents a type that seems to have entered Dance's repertory after the turn of the century. His interest in the theatre is apparent in the many caricature drawings he made showing imaginary actors, dancers, acrobats, singers and musicians.]

John Fawcett the Younger was the son of the comic actor John Fawcett (d. 1793). He spent most of his long acting career at Covent Garden and in 1808 became treasurer and trustee of that theatre. For nearly 40 years he 'was one of the leading portrayers of low comedy, rustic, and eccentric characters, especially those which required singing' (BD).

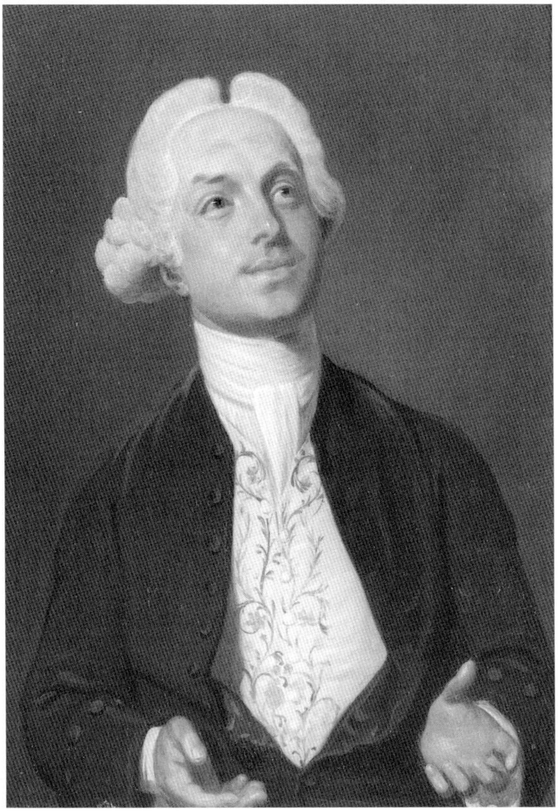

219
JOHN FAWCETT
as Caleb Quotem
in *The Review or The Wags of Windsor*
by George Colman the Younger

Samuel De Wilde

Oil on panel 23.8 x 19.3
INV: Mathews 30; RW/CKA 208
PROV: Charles Mathews
EXH: 1833 London (30)
ENGR: Thomas Cheesman pub. C. Chapple
1 October 1807, stipple 8.2 x 6.7 (bust in oval)

Caleb Quotem has little to do with the scant plot of *The Review*. He is introduced in the third scene, 'A Street in Windsor, with a view of Windsor Castle – Quotem's house R.; a wall with door L.; over the door of Quotem's house is a board inscribed – CALEB QUOTEM / Auctioneer, Plumber, Glazier, Engraver, Apothecary, School / master, Watch maker. Sign Painter &c. &c...'. He boasts that he has a different wig for each profession. In the picture he is presumably wearing a holiday wig, as he is off to see the Review. He sends his servant Dubbs to the Widow Thumpkin to tell her that he cannot bury her husband until tomorrow because of the Review, and because he doesn't feel like it.

Quotem, shown half-length, wears a dark grey velvet coat with a white waistcoat embroidered in green and yellow.

The younger Colman's operatic farce, with music by Dr Samuel Arnold, was first performed at the Haymarket on 1 September 1800, with Fawcett as the original Caleb Quotem. The character was taken from Henry Lee's *Throw Physick to the Dogs!*, first acted at the Haymarket on 6 July 1798, with Fawcett as Quotem and Mrs Hale as Mrs Quotem. The farce was published in 1809 as *Caleb Quotem and his Wife; or, Paint, Poetry, and Putty*. The popular character was used by Charles Williams in his *Parish Characters by Paul Pry*; plate 9 (of 10), published 12 June 1829, depicts the Duke of Wellington as Caleb Quotem, expressing his willingness to undertake any task.

220
JOHN FAWCETT
as Job Thornberry
in *John Bull or The Englishman's Fireside*
by George Colman the Younger

Samuel De Wilde

Pencil and watercolour on wove paper 37 x 23.5
INSCR: 'S De Wilde / Or 1807' (pencil b.r.)
INV: Mathews 222; RW/CKA 45F
PROV: Charles Mathews
EXH: 1833 London (222); 1975 London (14241)
ENGR: Richard Woodman for *The Cabinet*
pub. Mathews & Leigh 1 March 1808,
stipple & line 14.3 x 9.5
(bust half-length, back of chair visible)
REL: NT 40 pencil and watercolour on wove paper
36.8 x 23.5 s. & d: 'S De Wilde delin / O 1807'
(pencil b.r.) (standing); HTC TS 990.1.3F Vol. II (21)
pencil and watercolour on wove paper 37.2 x 22.6
s. & d: 'S DeWilde delin / 1819' (pencil)
[One of the above may have been the portrait of Fawcett
in character by De Wilde, signed and dated, that was
in the Royal Dramatic College sale at Fairbrother,
Lye and Palmer on 24 February 1881 (lot 100F)]

Job Thornberry is an honest brazier of Penzance. His daughter Mary has been seduced by Frank Rochdale, and in Act V, scene 2 he takes his daughter to Hollyhock House to confront Sir Simon Rochdale with his son's misdemeanour. Sir Simon is a Justice, and Job describes

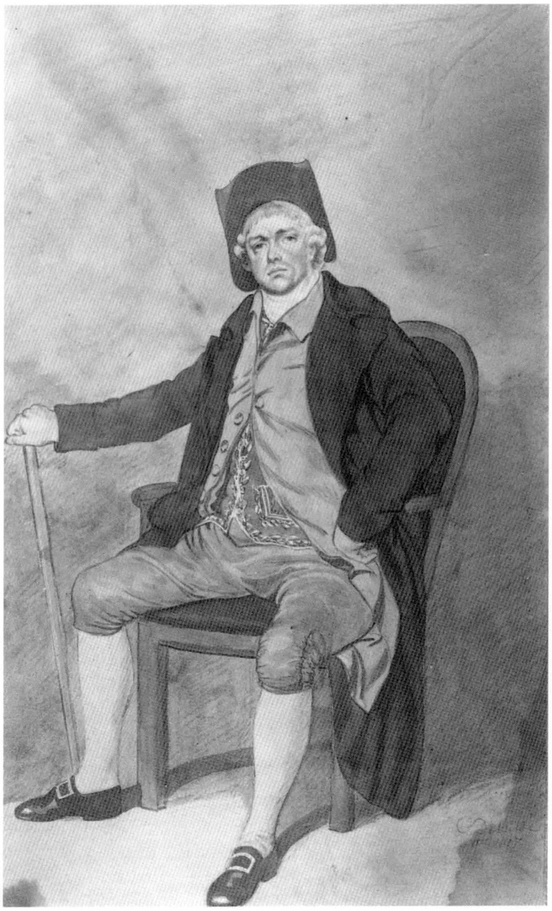

220 *John Fawcett as Job Thornberry*

the facts of Mary's seduction without giving the name of the seducer. Sir Simon agrees that the young man must marry the girl, but changes his mind when he hears that the culprit is his son, and tries to persuade Job to hush up the matter. Outraged, Job sits on the magistrate's chair, after slamming it down in the middle of the room. The cudgel we see in Job's right hand had been used in the previous scene to threaten one of Sir Simon's cheeky servants.

Job wears the waistcoat worked by his daughter for his birthday, five years before her seduction. It is red, embroidered with a floral pattern. He also wears black shoes with gold buckles, brownish or faded white stockings, green breeches, a long brown coat over a paler brown coat, and a grey hat.

The younger Colman's comedy was first performed at Covent Garden on 5 March 1803, with Fawcett as Job Thornberry. The first performance of the 1807–8 season at Covent Garden was on 4 November 1807 (about the time De Wilde drew the picture), when Fawcett played Job Thornberry as usual.

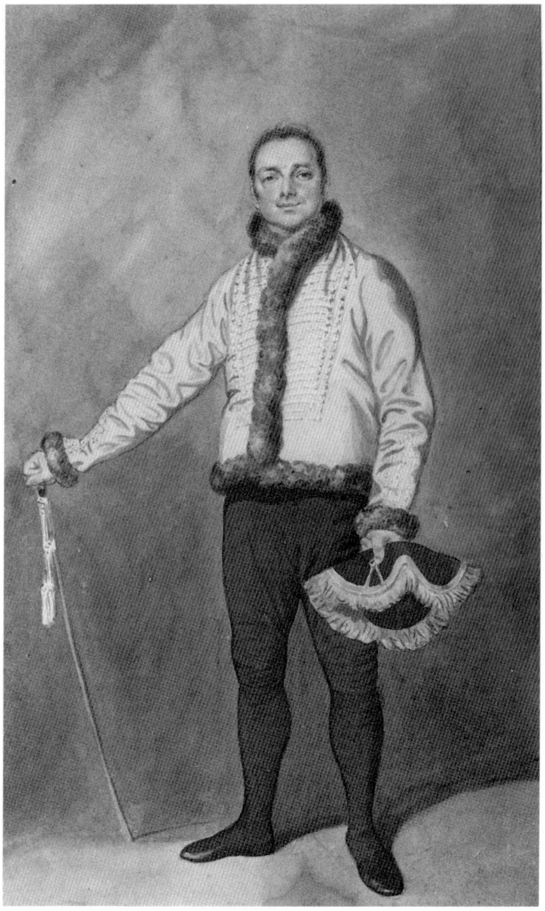

221

JOHN FAWCETT

as Servitz in *The Exile or The Deserts of Siberia*
by Frederick Reynolds

Samuel De Wilde

Pencil and watercolour on wove paper 37 x 23.5
INV: Mathews 223; RW/CKA 58A
PROV: Charles Mathews
EXH: 1833 London (223)
ENGR: Edward Scriven pub. Bell & DeCamp 2 January 1809, stipple and line 14.6 x 9.8; unknown engraver pub. Tagg 1810

Petroff Servitz is valet to Count Calmar. His 'Russian' costume consists of black slippers, black stockings and breeches, and a padded yellowish tunic trimmed with pale brown fur. In his left hand he holds a tricorn hat trimmed with gold braid and fringes.

Reynolds's 'New Grand Melo-Dramatick Opera in 3 Acts', with music by Mazzinghi and Henry Bishop, was first performed at Covent Garden on 10 November 1808, with John Fawcett as the original Servitz. He appears to have played all 42 performances during the first season.

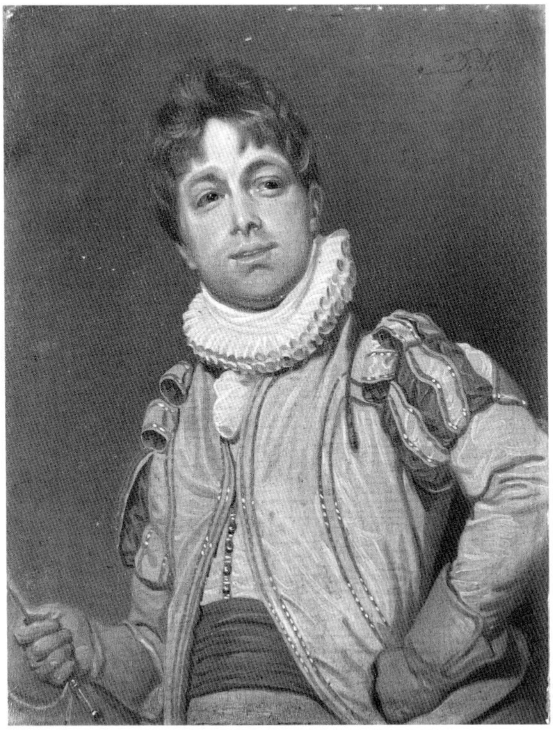

222

JOHN FAWCETT

as Whimsiculo in *The Cabinet*

by Thomas John Dibdin

Samuel De Wilde

Oil on panel 23.5 x 19
INSCR: 'S De Wilde / ft.' (dark brown paint t.r.)
INV: Mathews 42; RW/CKA 216
PROV: Charles Mathews
EXH: 1833 London (42)
REL: NT 41, pencil and watercolour on wove paper 37 x 23.3 s. & d: 'S De Wilde / 20 May 1808' (pencil b.r.), full-length Engr: Thomas Charles Wageman pub. I. Clark 1808, stipple 36.5 x 24.5; Anon. for the *Theatrical Inquisitor* pub. C. Chapple 1 January 1814, stipple and line 15.9 x 12; Anon., stipple and line (vignette, inscr: 'But what, my valiant tail of a lion?'); Folger Library (Art Box K.29 No.1), pencil with pen and black ink and watercolour on wove paper 36.5 x 26.3, inscr: Kelly 1814 (copy by Kelly of NT 41) [One of the above may have been the portrait of Fawcett in character by De Wilde, signed and dated, that was in the Royal Dramatic College sale at Fairbrother, Lye and Palmer on 24 February 1881 (lot 100F)]

Whimsiculo is the confidential valet to Orlando, who is in love with Constantia. Constantia's father, Count Curvoso, is determined to marry her to the very rich and old Marquis de Grand Château (see No. 73), whom he greets in the grand saloon of his castle in Act 1, scene 2. Whimsiculo gets in amongst the guests, dressed in the livery of the Marquis, and is noticed by the angry Count Curvoso. The livery of the Marquis worn by Whimsiculo consists of blue breeches with a broad red band around the waist, a blue doublet edged in red, with long blue sleeves, the flounced upper sleeves slashed to reveal a red lining. This rather spectacular costume is completed by a yellow waistcoat with red band down the front and little pearl buttons.

Dibdin's comic opera was first performed at Covent Garden on 9 February 1802, with Fawcett as Whimsiculo.

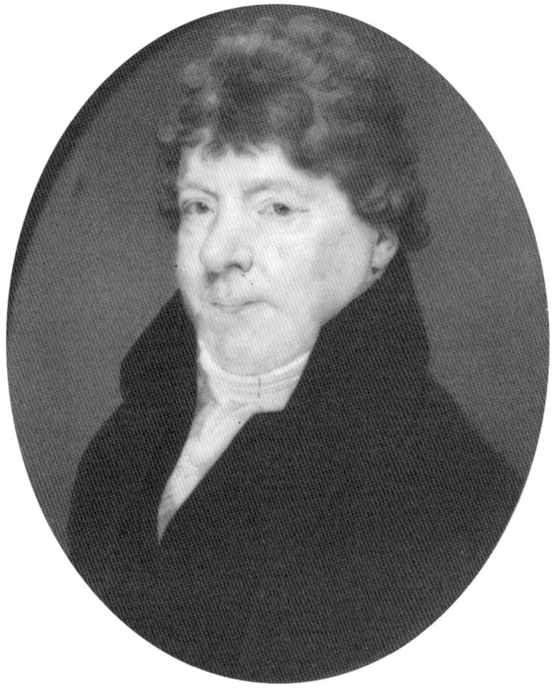

223

JOHN FAWCETT

Charles Jagger (?)

Watercolour on ivory 7 x 5.3 (oval)
INV: RW 427P (by R. Cosway);
CKA 427P (Called John Fawcett); Gift 108/110
PROV: Presented to the Garrick Club by Mrs Bartley (Barclay?) through Mr Meadows, 1850

Fawcett wears a brown jacket and waistcoat, both with high collar.

Comparison with other portraits confirms that No. 223 depicts John Fawcett. CKA suggested that the artist, previously thought to be Cosway, is Charles Jagger.

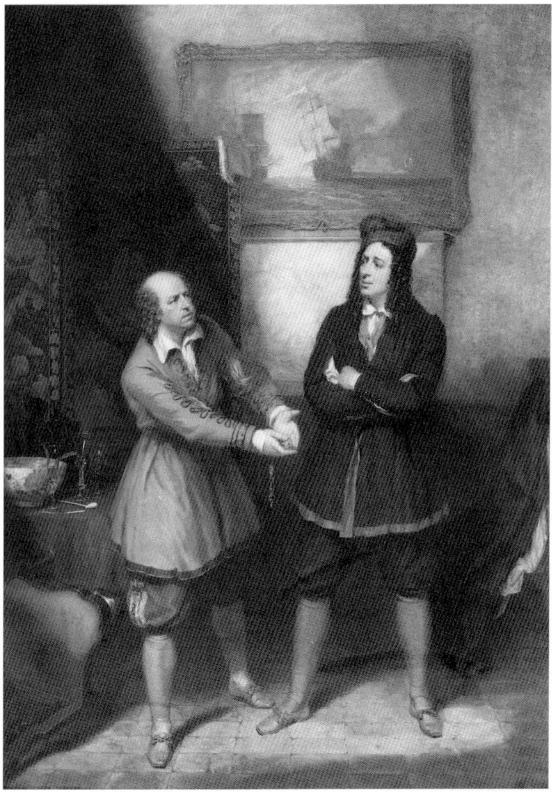

224*

JOHN FAWCETT as Captain Copp
and *CHARLES KEMBLE* as Charles II
in *Charles the Second or The Merry Monarch*
by John Howard Payne

George Clint

Oil on canvas 115 x 85
INV: Mathews 128; RW/CKA 9
PROV: Charles Mathews
EXH: 1825 R.A. (302); 1833 London (128);
1982–83 London (150)
ENGR: Thomas Lupton pub. T. Lupton 1 August 1826,
mezzotint 48.3 x 35.2, inscr: 'The original picture
in the possession of Charles Mathews'
LIT: Griffiths, p. 329

The scene is Act II, scene 2, 'A Room in Copp's House'. Charles II and Lord Rochester have disguised themselves as sailors in order to investigate the lovely Mary, niece of Captain Copp, the proprietor of the Grand Admiral Tavern, Wapping. In an attempt to reform the King's loose ways, Rochester has disappeared, taking the money needed to pay the bill. Charles offers his watch instead. Captain Copp, believing that he must have stolen it as it is studded with diamonds, speaks the line given with the title in the 1825 R.A. catalogue and quoted on the engraving: 'How came you by this watch?'

Charles (Kemble) stands on the right in his sailor's costume: brown shoes, grey stockings, black breeches, a dark green jacket edged in brown, a white shirt, a loose red neckerchief, and a brown wool cap. Captain Copp (Fawcett) holds the watch with chain and key. He wears pale brown shoes, grey stockings, black breeches with gold braid, and a red tunic with brown frogging and hem.

John Howard Payne's comedy was first performed at Covent Garden on 27 May 1824, with music by Henry Bishop and scenery by 'Mr Grieve and his two sons', and with Kemble as the original King Charles and Fawcett as the original Captain Copp. Fawcett's role, particularly, was associated with his final years on the stage; he played Captain Copp for his farewell performance at Covent Garden on 20 May 1830. The first edition of the play (1824) was dedicated to Charles Kemble and included a tribute to Fawcett in the introduction: 'The part of Captain Copp, in the hands of Mr Fawcett is one of those rich and racy pieces of acting that can only be furnished by the veteran artist in whom vigorous original talent has been refined and mellowed by time and experience. It has all the spirit of youthful days with the generous flavour of maturer age. I may speak almost impartially on this subject, for, in fact, Mr Fawcett has made the character his own by his inimitable acting.'

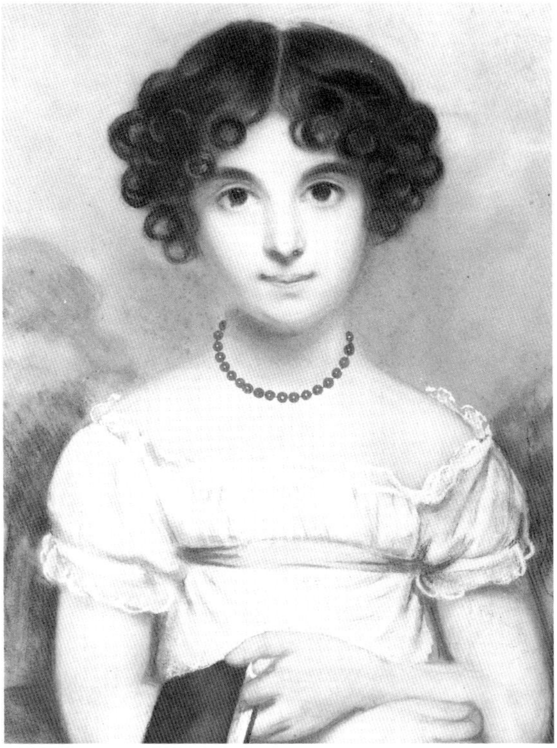

225

CLARA FISHER

Rose Emma Drummond

Pastel with watercolour and body colour on paper 50.1 x 40

INV: RW 315 ('believed to be Clara Fisher', artist unknown); CKA 315 (probably by S. Drummond)

PROV: Unknown

ENGR: Similar to J. Alais for *La Belle Assemblée* pub. John Bell 1818, stipple (vignette, full-length, seated, slightly to left, looking to front, hands folded in lap, two strings of coral beads); re-issued plate pub. D. Rymer with inscr: 'Miss Clara Fisher / The Lilliputian Performer who acquired great celebrity at / Drury Lane Theatre in 1818 / Engraved by J. Alais from "an Original Painting by Rose Emma Drummond"'

Miss Fisher wears a white frock with a yellow bow, and a dainty strand of coral beads. She holds a red book in her left hand. See also No. 787.

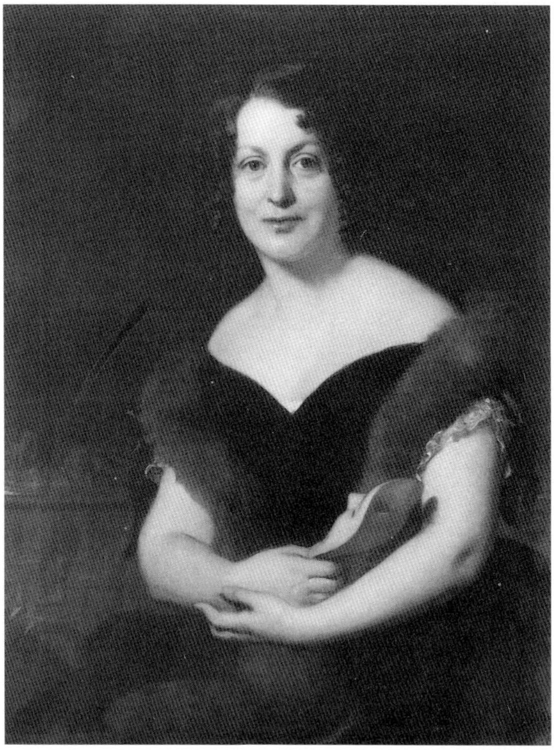

226

FANNY ELIZABETH FITZWILLIAM

John Prescott Knight

Oil on canvas 91.5 x 71

INV: RW/CKA 94

PROV: Bequeathed to the Garrick Club by the sitter's son, Edward Francis Fitzwilliam, 1859

EXH: 1850 R.A. (500 Portrait of Mrs Fitzwilliam, of the Theatre Royal, Haymarket)

LIT: Herman Dyson, *John Prescott Knight R.A., a catalogue* (1971), No. 139

Mrs Fitzwilliam wears a dark green off-the-shoulder dress and a fur wrap. She holds a white mask in her right hand.

Wife of the actor Edward Fitzwilliam (1788–1852), Mrs Fitzwilliam acted with great success over more than 40 years at the Olympic and Surrey under Thomas John Dibdin, and at Drury Lane, the Haymarket and the Adelphi. Her son, Edward Francis Fitzwilliam, was musical director at the Lyceum under Madame Vestris and at the Haymarket in the 1840s.

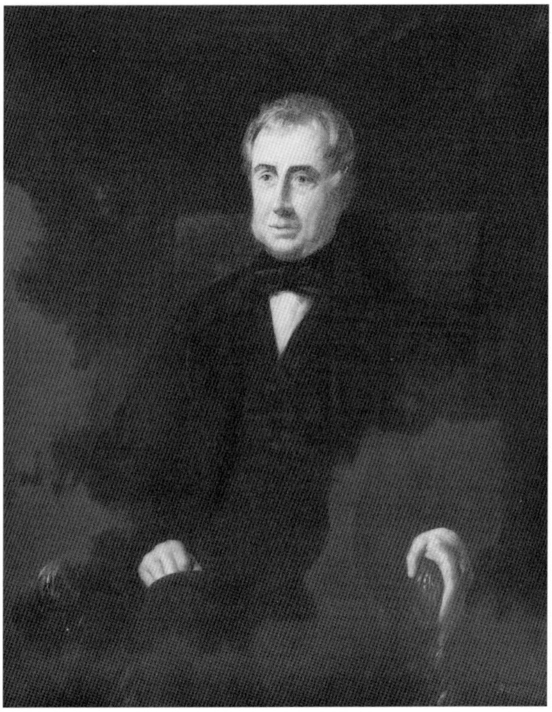

227

FRANCIS FLADGATE

Henry O'Neil

Oil on canvas 59.7 x 48.2
INSCR: 'H. O'Neil 1876' (b.r.)
INV: RW/CKA 328
PROV: Presented to the Garrick Club by the artist between 1876 and 1880

Fladgate, a barrister, seated in a chair, is dressed in black, wearing a blue bow tie. See also No. 793.

He became a member of the Garrick Club in 1832.

228

NOT ILLUSTRATED

SIR WILLIAM FRANCIS FLADGATE

Frank Moss Bennett

Oil on canvas 116.8 x 92.7
INSCR: 'F.M. Bennett, Feb. 1912' (red paint b.r.)
INV: CKA 651; Gift 661
PROV: Bequeathed to the Garrick Club by Sir Francis Fladgate subject to the life interest of Lady Fladgate and received, 1947 (on long-term loan to Messrs Fladgate & Co.)

Sir William wears a brown-grey suit and blue tie, and holds a pince-nez in his right hand and a book in his left.

He became a member of the Garrick Club in 1878.

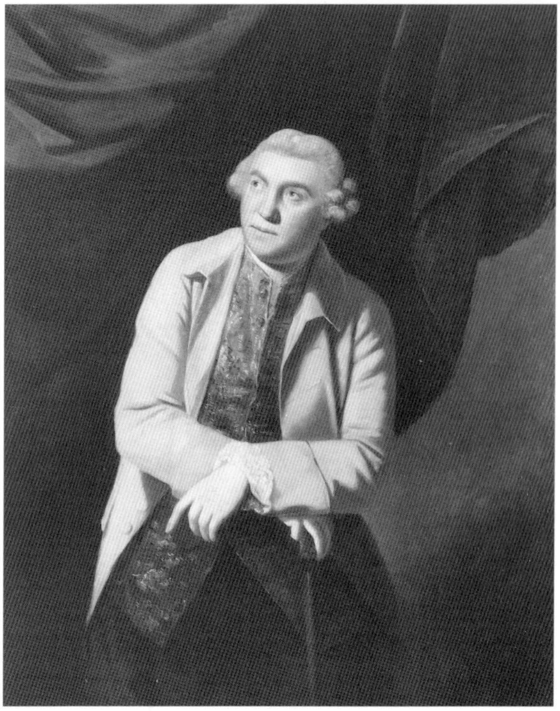

229

SAMUEL FOOTE

Sir Joshua Reynolds (studio)

Oil on canvas 125.7 x 99.7
INV: Mathews 45; RW/CKA 35
PROV: Caleb Whiteford?; his sale, Christie's 5 May 1810 (170) bt. Lockyer; Penny; his sale, Christie's 15 March 1822 (5) bt. in; Charles Mathews
EXH: 1833 London (45); 1951 London (33)
REL: Original: coll: Lady Burton; Engr: T. Blackmore mezzotint 41.3 x 33 pub. W.W. Ryland 1771; Cooper, as a plate to *Biographical Magazine* pub. Harrison 1785; unknown engraver as a plate to *Universal Magazine*, printed for J. Hinton, n.d.
LIT: Patmore, p. 272 'Foote by Reynolds'; Percy Fitzgerald, *Life of Samuel Foote*; Griffiths, p. 324

Three-quarter length, leaning on a stick. Foote wears a fawn coat and a long brown waistcoat embroidered in gold and red.

The original picture in the collection of Lady Burton was painted about 1767. There are several copies and several engraved versions. A copy by Romney, after Reynolds, is at Knole; it was bought by the 3rd Duke of Dorset in 1779. The Harvard Theatre Collection has an etching by T. Priscott, published by C. Dyer, which is a full-length adaptation of Reynolds's picture. The Harvard catalogue is incorrect in stating that this full-length picture is in the Garrick Club collection.

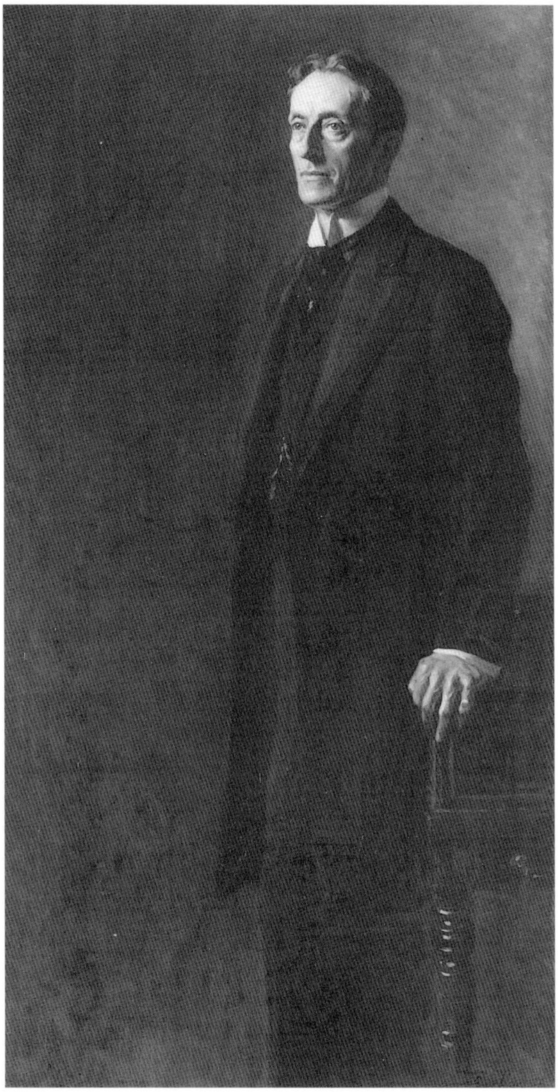

230

SIR JOHNSTON FORBES-ROBERTSON

George Harcourt

Oil on canvas 171 x 88
INSCR: 'George Harcourt' (black paint b.r.)
INV: GCL 700
PROV: Purchased for 100 gns. from the artist's daughters, 1950
EXH: 1913 R.A. (880); 1919 R.S.P.P. (93) [possibly another picture?]; 1950 London, 'George Harcourt Memorial Exhibition'
LIT: Reproduced in the Souvenir for Forbes-Robertson's Farewell Performance at Drury Lane, 1913

Forbes-Robertson, standing almost full-length, wears a dark grey morning suit, with a waistcoat and a grey cravat. He became a member of the Garrick Club in 1888.

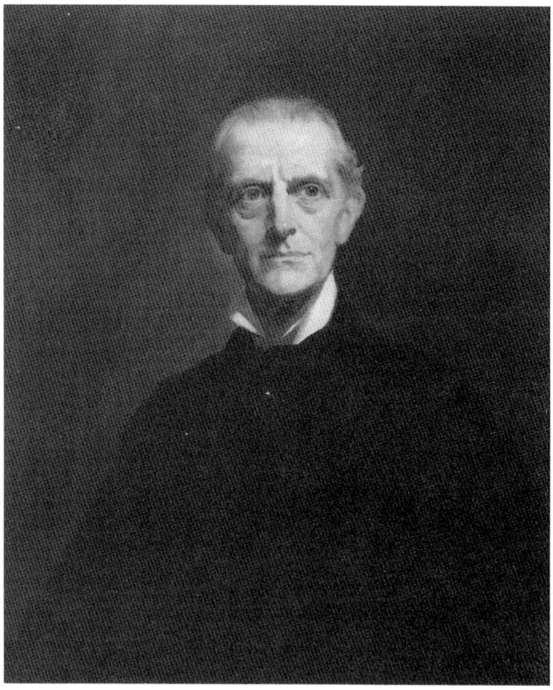

231

NORMAN FORBES-ROBERTSON

Edmund Brock

Oil on canvas 75 x 62.2
INV: CKA 247; Gift 508
PROV: Presented by the sitter's widow, 1932

The sitter, half-length, wears a dark suit, wing collar, and dark green cravat with pearl pin.

The younger brother of Sir Johnston, Norman Forbes-Robertson was an actor and sometime manager of the Globe Theatre. He wrote several plays, including dramatic versions of *The Scarlet Letter* and *The Man in the Iron Mask*, and became a member of the Garrick Club in 1902.

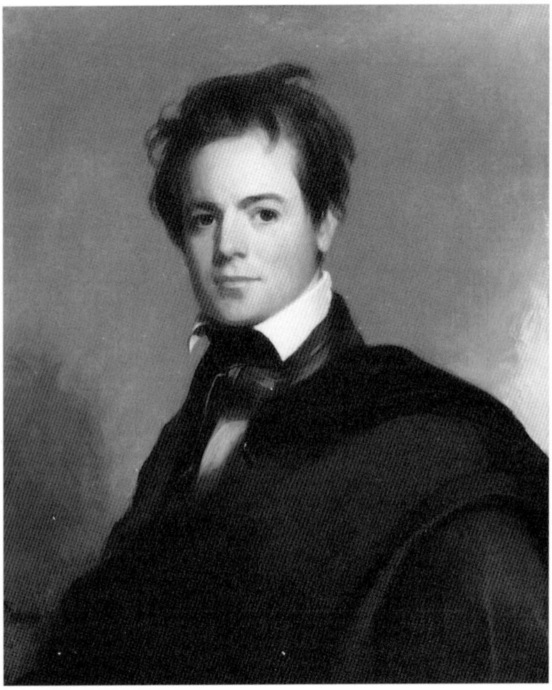

232
EDWIN FORREST

Thomas Sully

Oil on canvas 74.9 x 62.2
INV: RW/CKA 74; Gift 56
PROV: Presented by the artist, 1840
ENGR: A. Newsam pub. C. Alexander, Philadelphia 1836
printed by Duval, lithograph
LIT: Edward Biddle & Mantle Fielding,
Life and Works of Thomas Sully (1921), p. 154 (No. 599)

Forrest wears a grey jacket and, over his left shoulder, a black cloak, and a white shirt and stock.

According to Sully's register, this picture was begun on 19 September 1836 and finished on 26 October 1839.

Forrest, a great American tragic actor of the 19th century, played in London in 1836 and in 1845. He was received on the latter visit with hostility, which he attributed to W.C. Macready. Their antipathy culminated in the Astor Place riot in New York in 1848, when Mc-ready's life was put in jeopardy.

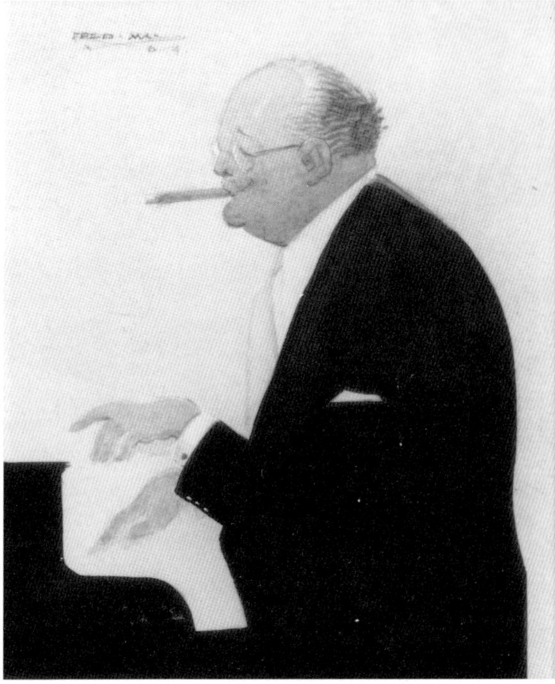

233
ALFRED FRANCIS

Fred Mex

Caricature, pencil, pen and red ink, brush and black ink and watercolour 15.7 x 10.8 (sight)
INSCR: 'LIVERPOOL'S ALFRED THE GREAT' (pen and red ink b.); 'Fred Mex 9 64' (pen and red ink t.l.); 'PRESENTED BY / THE DIRECTORS OF / OLD VIC TRUST / TO THEIR CHAIRMAN / ALFRED FRANCIS / IN RECOGNITION OF / HIS GREAT SERVICES / TO THE OLD VIC' (inscr. brass plaque on verso)
INV: Not listed; Gift 913
PROV: Presented by Tessa Neal, 1985

The sitter wiggles his fingers at the piano. His well-padded figure is clothed in a black jacket, white shirt, and pink tie.

Alfred Francis, O.B.E. was a member of the Garrick from 1959 until his death in 1985. He held a number of important posts, among them those of Administrator of the Old Vic and Chairman of the Old Vic Trust, and Governor of the Royal Victoria Hall Foundation.

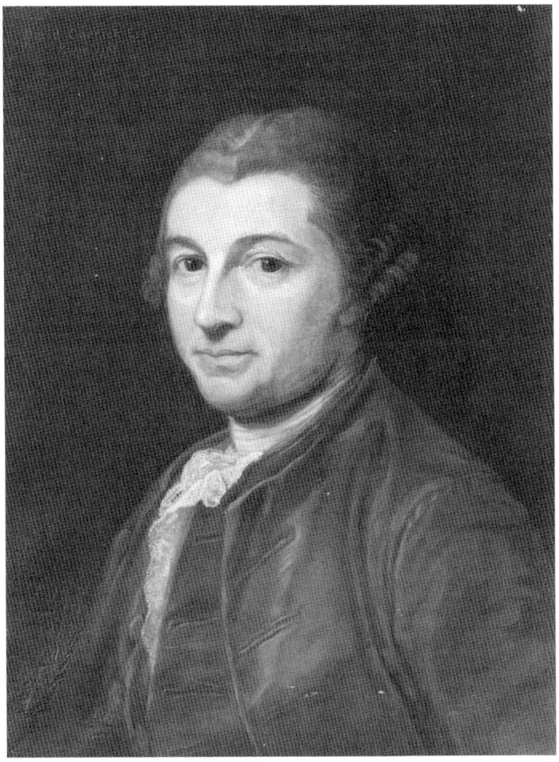

234
DAVID GARRICK

Pompeo Batoni (after)

Oil on canvas 54 x 40.6
INSCR: 'David Garrick Esq / Rome 1764' (t.l.)
INV: CKA 571 (artist unknown); Gift 436
PROV: Green; sold, Christie's 22 July 1871 (109)?; presented anonymously to the Garrick Club in memory of Rowland Berkeley, 1926
REL: Original: Oxford Ashmolean 52 (Clark 266) oil on canvas 76 x 63, probably given by Garrick to Richard Kaye, Dean of Lincoln
LIT: Anthony M. Clark, *Pompeo Batoni: A Complete Catalogue of his Works with an Introductory Text*, ed. Edgar Peters Bowran (Oxford 1985)

Garrick wears a mulberry-coloured velvet jacket, a waistcoat of the same material, and a lace-edged white stock.

Garrick sat for the original version of this picture in Rome in 1764. In it, he points at an edition of Terence, an allusion, perhaps, to Garrick's prowess as a comic dramatist and to the blank verse translations by George Colman published in 1765, each play dedicated to a friend – *Phormio* to Garrick.

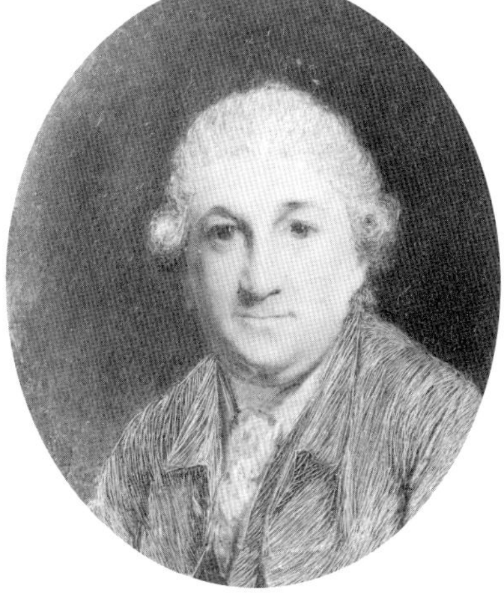

235
DAVID GARRICK

Anne Louisa Lane

Miniature, watercolour with hair on card 18.4 x 18.4 (oval)
INV: GCL 689; Gift 641 or 763
PROV: Presented to the Garrick Club by Gerald Lawrence, 1946, or A. Darnborough, 1958 (see below)
EXH: 1975 London (65); 1981 Buxton (13)
REL: Another hair portrait of Garrick was engraved by J. Heath pub. J. White 1819. The sitter is shown in profile to right, without a wig. Beneath inscr: 'MR GARRICK sat for the last time and afterwards sent a lock of his hair to MISS LANE, inclosed in a note, for the purpose of her completing the miniature for Mrs Garrick, a few months before his decease.' [This portrait or the Garrick Club version was owned by the artist's brother, the Rev. Theophilus Lane, Rector of St Michael's, Crooked Lane, and then was in the possession of the Rev. Trevor Garrick (a descendant of George Garrick) until his death in the 1940s. See Mander & Mitchenson, *The Artist and the Theatre*, p. 68.]
LIT: Little & Kahrl, 3: 1261–62 (No. 1221)

Garrick's wig is made of hair, and hair is applied to his brown jacket. He wears a brown waistcoat and a white stock.

Garrick wrote to Anne Louisa Lane just before his death, in January 1779: 'Mr Garrick presents his Compts to Miss Lane – He has sent a little of Mrs Garrick & his own hair – He has but one lock behind or he wd have sent more – Mr Garrick is much Oblig'd to Miss Lane for her politeness about his Picture.' The composition is based on Reynolds's Thrale portrait (see No. 241). In 1778 Garrick had commissioned from Miss Lane a copy in hair of Reynolds's portrait of John Campbell, later Lord Cawdor. He also ordered portraits of himself and Shakespeare done in the hair of Lady Spencer and the Duchess of Devonshire.

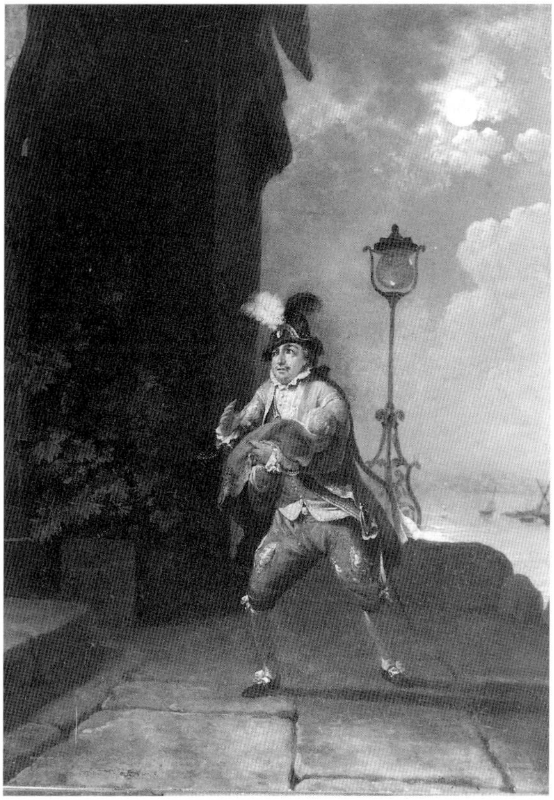

236*

DAVID GARRICK

as Don John in *The Chances*

by Francis Beaumont and John Fletcher,

adapted by David Garrick

Philippe Jacques de Loutherbourg

Oil on canvas 35 x 28

INV: Mathews 95; RW/CKA 280

PROV: Charles Mathews

EXH: 1833 London (95)

ENGR: Hall after Edwards for Lowndes's *New English Theatre* pub. T. Lowndes & Partners 16 September 1777, line 13 x 8.9

REL: Theatre Museum (TM9), oil on panel 46 x 68.6, inscr: 'P.I. de Loutherbourg' (b.r.), exh: 1774 R.A. (163) 'Mr Garrick, in the character of Don John, with a view of Naples, by moon-light' (Engr: Charles Phillips 1775, etching, a version that shows Garrick in a ruined building; also by Phillips 1776); M&M 12, oil on canvas 46 x 68.5; V&A P.46–1935, pencil and watercolour on laid paper 29.7 x 40.9, inscr: 'P.I. de Loutherbourg 1774'; BM E.e.3–87, pencil on laid paper 25.1 x 20, perhaps a tracing of the Phillips engraving

LIT: Patmore, p. 268

Don John has just been presented, surprisingly and mistakenly, with an unknown baby whilst wandering through the streets of Naples. He rushes across the stage with the baby, wrapped in a red shawl, on his left arm. He wears a plumed black hat, black shoes with silver bows, silver hose, blue-grey breeches slashed over the thighs to reveal white, a blue jacket with upper sleeves slashed to reveal white, and a yellow waistcoat, buttoned up the front with silver buttons and edged with silver braid. The moonlit marine scene has boats to the right and a wrought-iron lamp. Light streams out of an open door on the left, not visible in this version of the picture. Quoted on the engraving is Don John's line: 'What have I got by this now? – a Child.'

Garrick's adaptation of *The Chances* was first given at Drury Lane on 7 November 1754, with Garrick as Don John. His last performance of the part took place on 13 April 1758 although the play was revived for a single performance on 22 April 1772, when Cautherley played the role for his benefit. De Loutherbourg had joined the Drury Lane staff at the end of 1772, and may have been involved in the designing of scenery for the play. The emphasis on the view of Naples in the R.A. catalogue entry for his portrait of Garrick as Don John suggests that the scenery was as important a consideration as the actor.

The portrait was exhibited with a pendant, showing Garrick as Richard III in a similar moonlit setting (R.A. 1774 [166], oil on panel 43.2 x 64.8, Christie's 20 February 1925 [73]). The Garrick Club version of the single figure may relate to the Lowndes engraving, but it seems more likely that both derive from the original work.

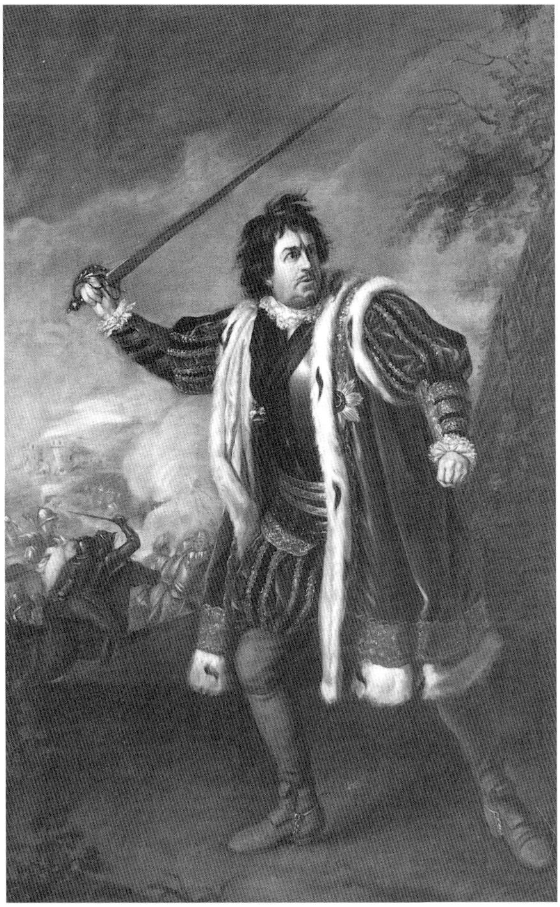

237
DAVID GARRICK
as Richard
in *Richard III* by William Shakespeare

Henry Robert Morland
(after Nathaniel Dance)

Oil on canvas 87 x 58.4
INV: Mathews 61; RW/CKA 107
PROV: Charles Mathews
EXH: 1833 London (61); 1975 Brighton (J13); 1981 Buxton (5.2)
REL: Original: Stratford-upon-Avon Town Council oil on canvas 243.8 x 152.4, exh: 1771 R.A. (54); Engr: John Dixon pub. J. Boydell 28 April 1772, mezzotint 62.2 x 39.7
There are many copies after Dance's original picture, including those in the Folger Library; Hurst House, Carmarthenshire; Royal National Theatre, London (Somerset Maugham Collection); and the collections of several private owners. The figure was also moulded into perpetuity by the potters of Derby and Staffordshire. For details of the various versions, see BD, 6: 98–99, Nos. 206 & 214, and William L. Pressly, *A Catalogue of Paintings in the Folger Shakespeare Library* (Yale U.P., 1993), No. 107.

Richard wears high brown boots with flaps at the front and gold spurs, brown knee-breeches, hose of red velvet under blue strips, a breastplate over doublet with upper sleeves of red velvet under vertical blue bands edged in gold, a broad red belt with three horizontal gold bands, and a long, sleeveless red jacket edged in ermine and gold braid. An order is on his chest, and a George hangs from a blue ribbon around his neck. A battle is in progress to the left. Mathews cites the familiar line: 'A horse, a horse, my Kingdom for a horse!'

Morland's picture is the best of the copies of the large picture by Dance. The original hung in the drawing room of Sir Watkin Williams Wynn's house at 20, St James's Square in the late 18th century. Morland may have copied his picture from Dixon's mezzotint.

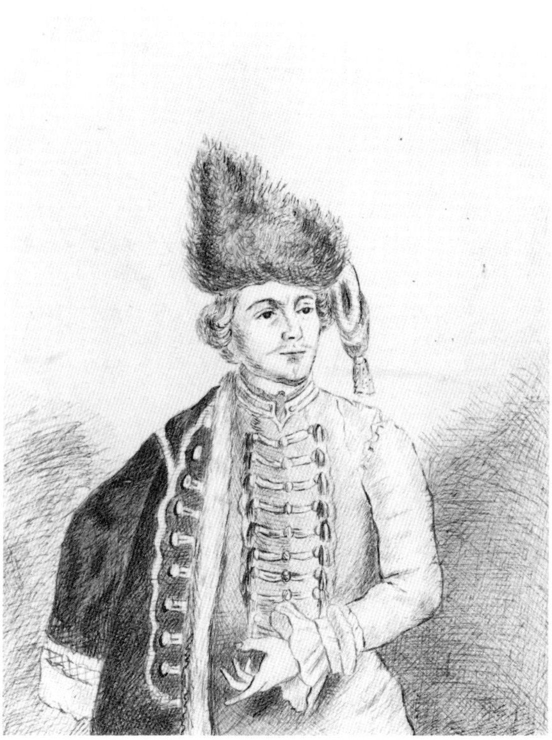

238

DAVID GARRICK

as Tancred in *Tancred and Sigismunda*

by James Thomson

John Nixon (after Thomas Worlidge)

Pencil, pen and black ink and wash on laid paper
16.4 x 12.9 (sheet 19.4 x 12.9)
INSCR: 'John Nixon fecit 1773' (pen and grey ink b.l.);
'Mr. GARRICK / in the Character of TANCRED'
(pen and grey ink b.c.);
'1745 / TANCRED AND SIGISMUNDA'
(pen and brown ink b.c.)
INV: Not listed
PROV: John Nixon, *Dramatic Annals* I: 190

This is a copy of the half-length version of Worlidge's etching after his own painting (see No. 247).

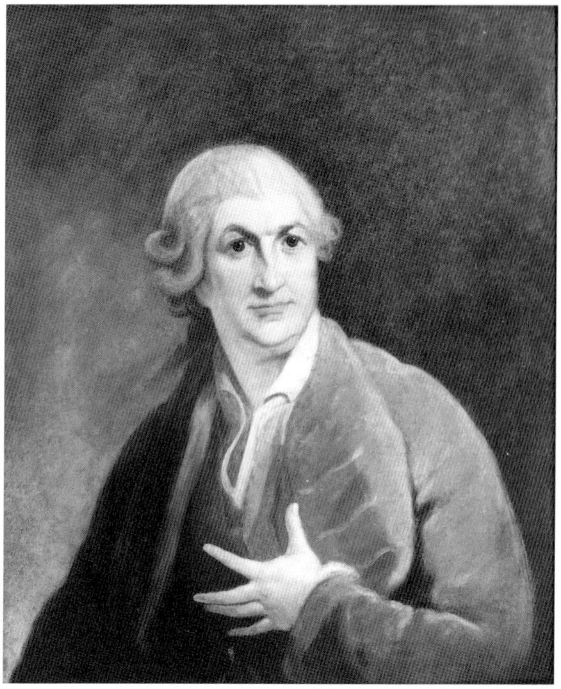

239

DAVID GARRICK

Robert Edge Pine

Oil on canvas 76 x 63.5
INV: Mathews 110; RW/CKA 478
PROV: Charles Mathews
EXH: 1833 London (110); 1973 York;
1975 London (90); 1981 Buxton (20)
REL: Original: NPG 82 oil on canvas 88.9 x 71.1
Engr: William Dickinson pub. Pine & Dickinson 1778
(proof in HTC dated 1 December 1776), mezzotint 34 x 28

Garrick wears a red velvet collarless coat, a pink and blue waistcoat, and a white open-necked shirt.

This picture is one of the better derivatives of NPG 82. The catalogues of the 1975 London and 1981 Buxton exhibitions suggest that it shows Garrick as Don Felix in Mrs Centlivre's *The Wonder*. This does not seem to be the case.

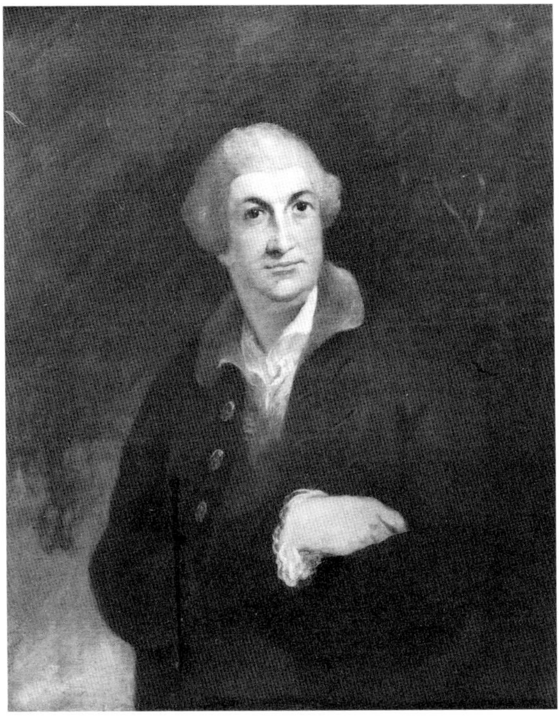

240

DAVID GARRICK

Robert Edge Pine

Oil on canvas 88.9 x 71.7
INV: CKA 186; Gift 380
PROV: Presented to the Garrick Club
by Lockett Agnew, 1918
EXH: 1951 London (32)

Garrick wears a blue coat with gold buttons and loose red collar, and a yellowish waistcoat.

There are several types of portraits of Garrick by Pine. NPG 82 is the prototype for most, including No. 239 (see BD 6: 85 No. 39). In the original three-quarter-length version, Garrick is shown reading from *Macbeth*, and the dramatic gestures in the derivative versions, often showing Garrick without the book, have inspired a number of imaginative interpretations. The second major engraved type was probably that exhibited at the R.A. in 1780 (82), which in 1818 belonged to the widow of 'the late George Wilson'. Garrick is shown three-quarter length, seated with face to front, left elbow resting on table at right, with book in left hand, right hand resting in lap. No. 240 relates to neither of the two major prototypes, but must date from about the same time, 1776–80. Pine also produced a mezzotint of Garrick's death mask, 'with eyes added', that was published in 1779. A wood carving of Garrick's death mask is in the Club. See also Pressly, *Folger*, 120.

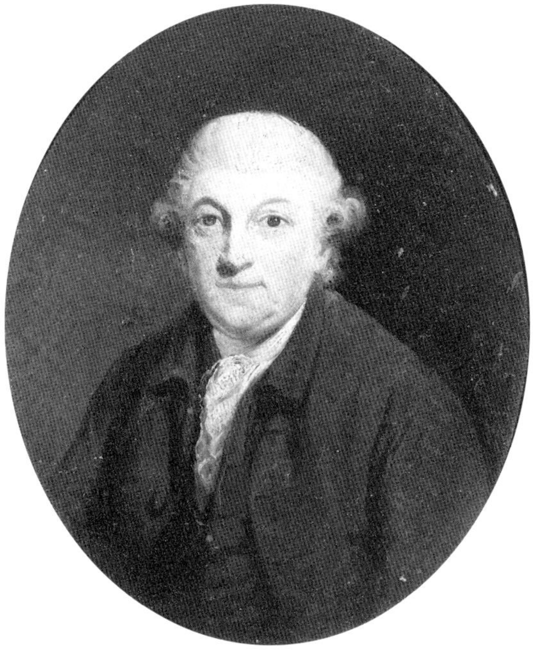

241

DAVID GARRICK

Sir Joshua Reynolds (after)

Oil on panel 16 x 13.4 (oval)
INV: RW 202 (artist unknown); CKA 202
PROV: Unknown
REL: Original: Christie's 24 November 1972 (140, bt. by Lawson), oil on canvas 73.7 x 61 (commissioned by Mrs Thrale 1776), exh: 1776 R.A. (241) Engr: Robert Laurie pub. J. Stevens 1779, mezzotint 31.7 x 25.4; Thomas Watson pub. Watson & Dickinson 1779, mezzotint 33.7 x 28
There is a replica by Reynolds at Knole 75 oil on canvas 76.2 x 63.5 (bt. by the 3rd Duke of Dorset, 1778); other versions are at the National Portrait Gallery and the Folger Library, and a crude 19th-century copy is also at the Folger (see Pressly, *Folger*, 121)

Garrick is shown half-length, facing the spectator, wearing a mulberry coat and waistcoat.

This version is a poor copy distantly related to Reynolds's Thrale portrait of Garrick, of which there are numerous copies, almost all of them better than this one (see BD 5: 85–86 No. 42). The oval and reduced format suggest that the picture may relate to one of the engravings produced in the late 18th and early 19th century showing the sitter without hands and table, viz: William Ridley for Parsons's *Minor Theatre* 1793, stipple 7.6 x 6; William Bromley for the *Biographical Magazine* pub. Harrison & Co., line 4.8 x 3.8; W. Evans as frontispiece to Thomas Davies's *Life of David Garrick*, Longman & Co. 1806, stipple 10.1 x 7.

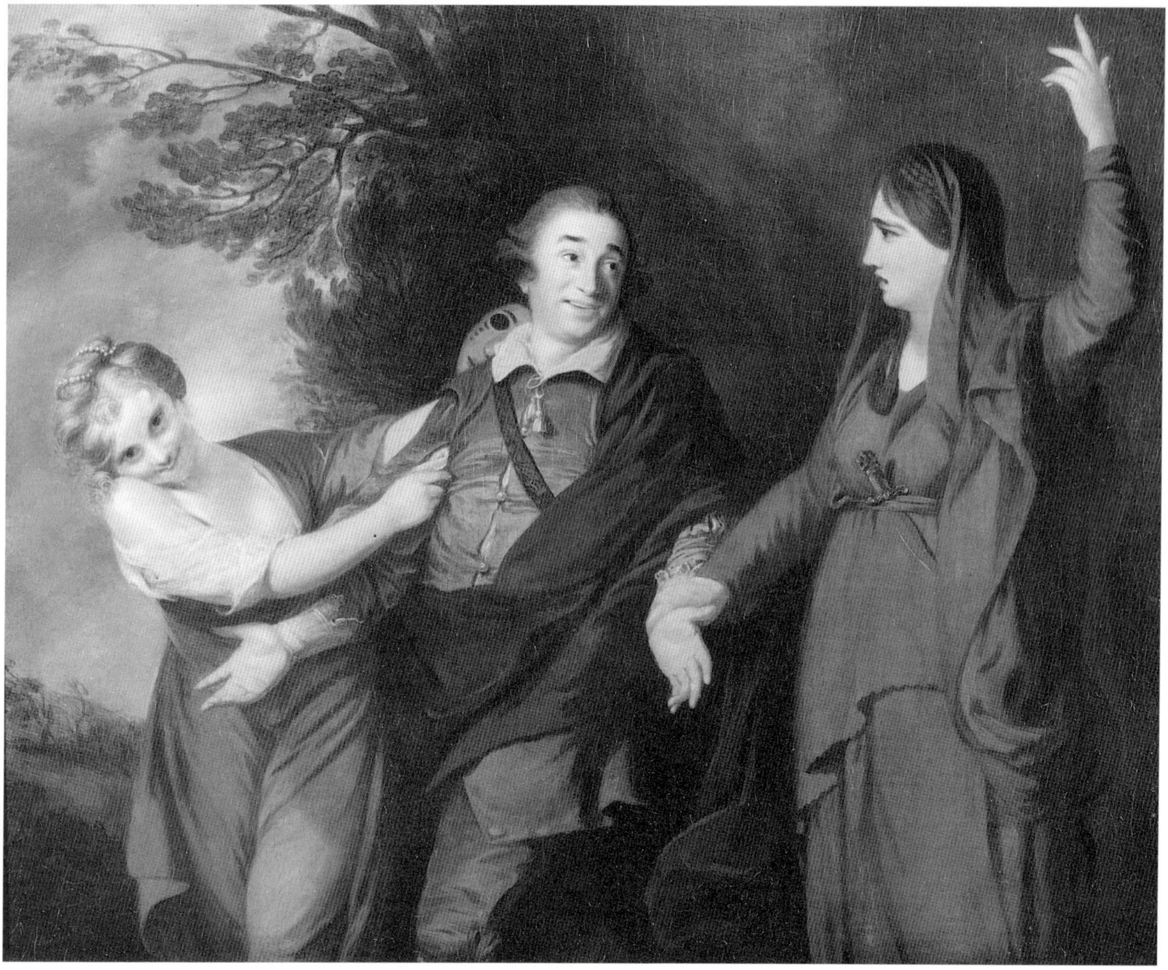

242
DAVID GARRICK
Between the Muses of Comedy and Tragedy

Sir Joshua Reynolds (after)

Oil on canvas 31.7 x 40
INV: Mathews 119; RW/CKA 2
PROV: Charles Mathews
EXH: 1833 London (119); 1972 Tunbridge Wells
REL: Original: Jacob Rothschild, oil on canvas 148 x 183, exh: 1762 S.A. (88); Engr: Edward Fisher pub. E. Fisher, J. Boydell, E. Bakewell & H. Parker 1762, mezzotint 2.7 x 50.2

LIT: David Mannings's entry (42) in the Reynolds exhibition catalogue R.A. 1986, which has a full bibliography

Garrick, in brown breeches and doublet, stands between Comedy, on the left, and Tragedy on the right. Comedy is draped in red and Tragedy in blue. Tragedy carries a dagger at her waist.

This is a good reduced copy of Reynolds's picture. See BD 5: 86–87, No. 44 for details and provenances of various versions and their engravings.

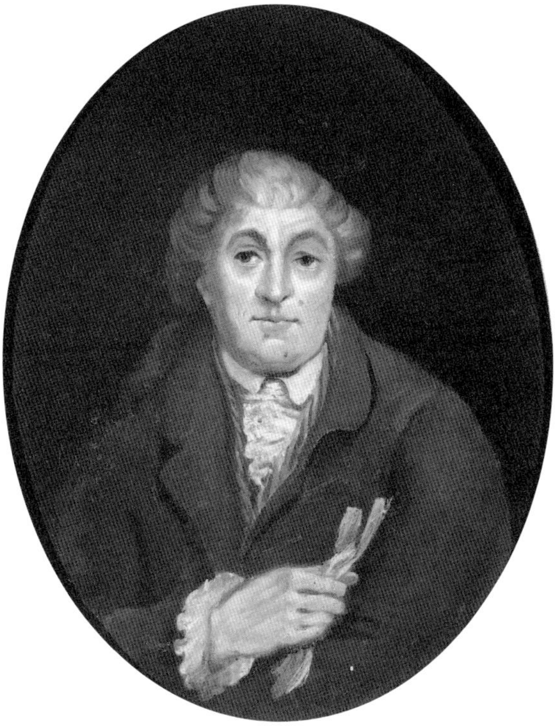

243
DAVID GARRICK

Benjamin Vandergucht (after)

Oil on canvas 69.8 x 54.6
INV: RW 469 (artist unknown); CKA 469; Gift 273
PROV: Henry Harrison; sold, Foster's 13 May 1896 (127)?; presented to the Garrick Club by Sir Squire Bancroft, 1900
REL: Original: Spencer Coll., Althorp Estate, Northampton, oil on canvas 76.2 x 63.5, exh: 1779 R.A. (334) 'A head of the late Mr Garrick, being the last picture he sat for.'

Garrick wears a brown jacket. The portrait is said by CKA to have been painted for Hannah More, though there is no evidence to support this statement.

[A reduced version of the Althorp picture, after Vandergucht, was once at Nantlys, Bodfari, Wales, the property of D.H. Pennant. Perhaps that is the version that eventually found its way to the Garrick Club?]

No. 243 had been on loan to the Bristol Old Vic for some time, but was returned to the Club in 1994. In bad condition, it was in storage until August 1994, then was hung on the back staircase to the basement.

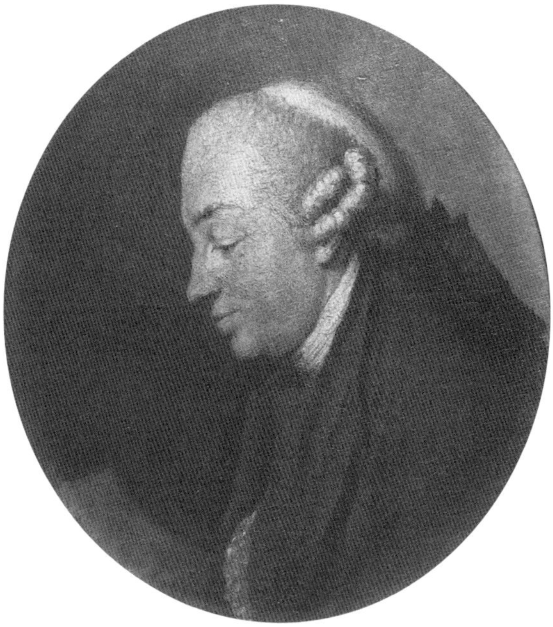

244
DAVID GARRICK
Steward of the Stratford Jubilee

Benjamin Vandergucht (by or after)

Oil on canvas 20.3 x 17.8 (bust in oval)
INSCR: 'Prologue / ... the ... / ... / D Garrick' (black paint on paper b.l.)
INV: Mathews 29 (artist unknown); RW/CKA 371
PROV: Charles Mathews
EXH: 1833 London (29); 1974 Twickenham (1); 1981 Tokyo (FJ18)
REL: Original: Parham Park, oil on canvas 75 x 61, exh: 1776 R.A. (309)? 'The steward of the Stratford Jubilee, ditto (tql)' Engr: J. Saunders pub. J. Saunders 1773, mezzotint 33.3 x 29.8

Garrick wears a green jacket and waistcoat.

This small picture is copied from the portrait now at Parham Park, which was engraved by J. Saunders in 1773.

It seems unlikely that a picture engraved and published three years earlier would be exhibited at the R.A. in 1776. This observation, combined with the fact that the exhibited picture was a three-quarter-length and not a half-length picture like that at Parham, suggests that there was a second Vandergucht of Garrick as the Steward of his Shakespeare Jubilee at Stratford in 1769.

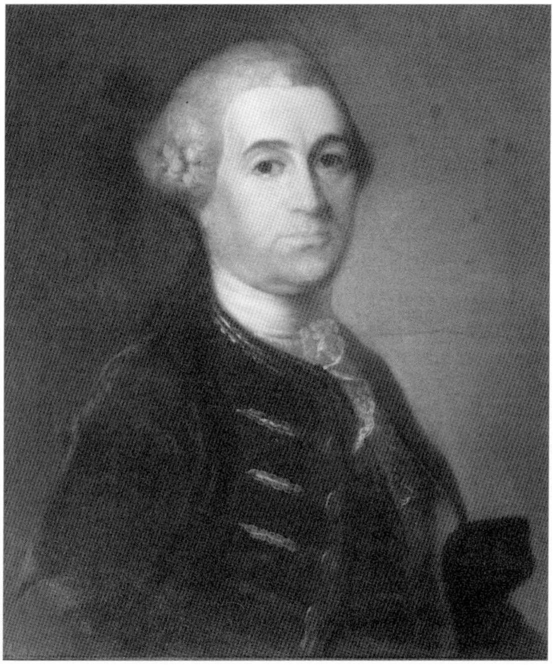

245
DAVID GARRICK

François Xavier Vispré

Pastel on paper 57.2 x 48.2
INSCR: 'Vispré' (b.l.)
INV: CKA 570; Gift 421
PROV: Presented to the Garrick Club
by Major R. Woodhouse, 1924
EXH: 1981 Buxton (27)
REL: Sotheby's 11 June 1947 (3), pastel on paper
57.2 x 49.5, inscr: 'Vispré' (c.l.) from the collection
of Sir W. Bromley-Davenport

Garrick has a black tricorn hat under his left arm. He wears a blue velvet jacket with gold buttons and silver embroidery down the front, and a blue waistcoat.

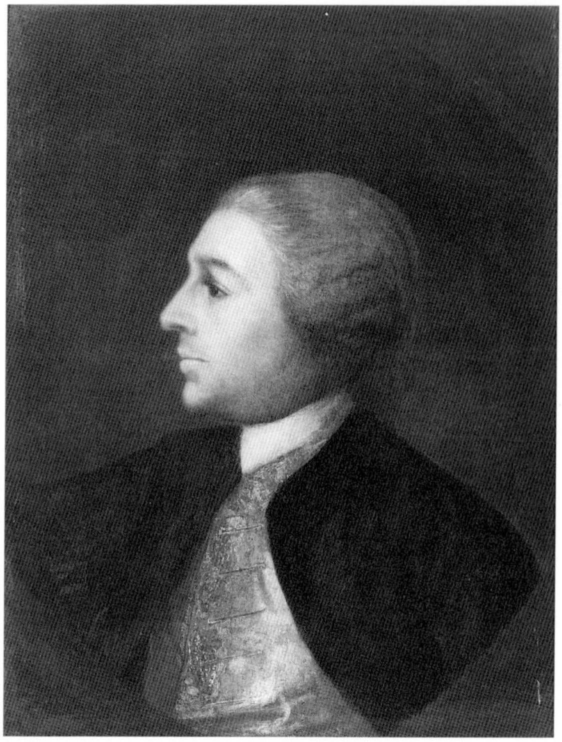

246
DAVID GARRICK
as Romeo (?) in *Romeo and Juliet*
by William Shakespeare

Benjamin Wilson (after)

Oil on canvas 60 x 47
INV: Mathews 348 (artist unknown);
RW 440 (by Samuel De Wilde); CKA 440
PROV: Charles Mathews 348
EXH: 1833 London (348); 1964 London [2] (37)
ENGR: Benjamin Wilson, etching (vignette)
This engraving was printed in reverse for
T. Purland 1851 in an edition of 20.
The image was also etched anonymously
for Billie Wright in an edition of two
LIT: Patmore (p. 271) says that Mathews owned
several portraits of Garrick: 'One of these portraits
of him is curious and valuable, as having been
painted by Wilson, the landscape-painter.'
He has presumably mistaken Benjamin for
Richard Wilson, although Mathews's catalogue
gives no artist at all for this picture.

Garrick wears a dark blue coat and an embroidered orange silk waistcoat.

There is a passing similarity to the figure of Garrick as Romeo in Benjamin Wilson's scene, with George Anne Bellamy as Juliet, engraved by François Simon Ravenet in 1753 and 1765. See also No. 967.

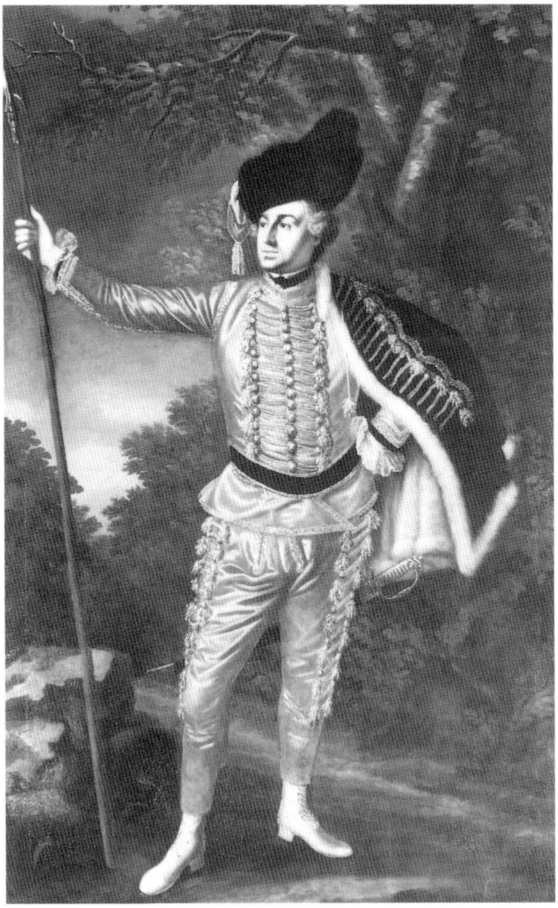

There is only one outdoor scene in *Tancred and Sigismunda*, Act IV, scene I, which is set in the garden of Siffredi's house. Tancred is never on stage on his own in this scene. He is shown standing full-length, holding a spear in his right hand and wearing yellow shoes laced in silver, long pink trousers with gold braid, a pink tunic trimmed with silver braid around the neckband, shoulder, sleeve, wrist and peplum, a blue band at the neck with a little white collar, a dark blue silver-edged belt, a dark blue cloak, lined and trimmed in fur, over the left shoulder, and a large, dark fur hat with a tassel. The costume is a type often used as masquerade dress in the mid-18th century.

James Thomson's play was first performed at Drury Lane on 18 March 1745, with Garrick as Tancred. Worlidge evidently was depicting Garrick in one of the five performances given in the spring of 1752.

247*

DAVID GARRICK

as Tancred in *Tancred and Sigismunda*

by James Thomson

Thomas Worlidge

Oil on canvas 221 x 147

INV: Not listed

PROV: Wynne Morgan 1920; F. J. Nettlefield, by whom presented to the Garrick Club, 1940

ENGR: Thomas Worlidge, printed for E. Jackson 1752, etching 29.7 x 19.3; Thomas Worlidge sold by T. Worlidge, etching 14.6 x 11.4 (half length), 2nd state with added hatching on belt and elsewhere on wove paper watermarked '1794' under Fleur de Lys; Thomas Worlidge, etching 14.8 x 11.3 (h.l.), inscr: '3' t.l. in border and '79' t.r. out of border (this size without the inscr. is called by HTC a reprint of 1850); Anon. printed for John Bowles, etching 15.2 x 11.2, inscr: 'Etched in the manner of Rembrandt'

REL: Priv. coll., London, oil on canvas 101.1 x 72.5; Theatre Musem (TM7), oil on canvas 62.9 x 52 (bust only); see Nos. 238 & 248

LIT: C. Reginald Grundy, *Catalogue of the Pictures and Drawings in the Collection of Frederick John Nettlefold*, 4: 184

248

LOCATION UNKNOWN

DAVID GARRICK

as Tancred in *Tancred and Sigismunda*

by James Thomson

Thomas Worlidge

Black chalk on laid paper 12.7 x 10.1

INSCR: 'J W / 1752' (black chalk b.r.)

INV: Not listed

PROV: John Baskett

EXH: 1979 London (2) (32)

Garrick wears the costume seen in No. 247.

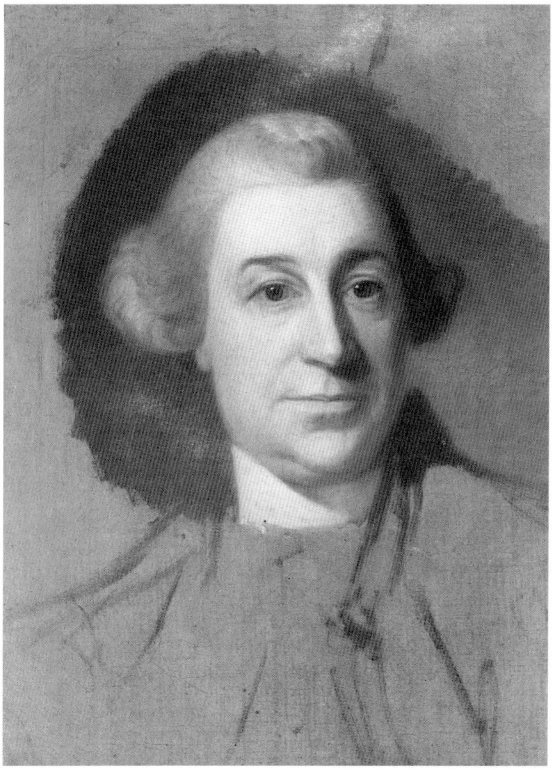

249*
DAVID GARRICK

Johan Zoffany

Oil on canvas 47 x 35
INV: Mathews 123 (by Hogarth); RW/CKA 135
PROV: Robert Baddeley [Supposedly Baddeley left the portrait to the Drury Lane Theatrical Fund, but that institution never received it; in his will Baddeley left his pictures to Mrs Catherine Strickland, his executrix]; according to Fitzgerald, *The Garrick Club* (1904), Baddeley gave the portrait to Billy Dunn, who transferred it to Roland Stevenson, a banker; Stevenson sale, Christie's? 13 April 1829 (15) (as 'J. Reynolds Portrait of Garrick unfinished') bt. for £8 10s. by Charles Mathews; but a letter from E.T. Smith to *The Era* on 29 January 1854 states that Baddeley did give the picture to Dunn, who gave it to Roland 'Stephenson'; at Stevenson's sale after his death it was purchased by Mathews, but at his death it was sold to John Durrant. Probably it was Durrant who gave it to the Garrick Club.
EXH: 1833 London (123); 1948 Paris; 1951 London (44); 1975 London (89)
LIT: Percy Fitzgerald, *The History of the Garrick Club*, p. 154; *The Era* 29 January 1854; Lady Victoria Manners & Dr G.C. Williamson, *John Zoffany* (1920), p. 140

Only the head of this portrait is finished; the canvas has possibly been cut down from a larger intended work.

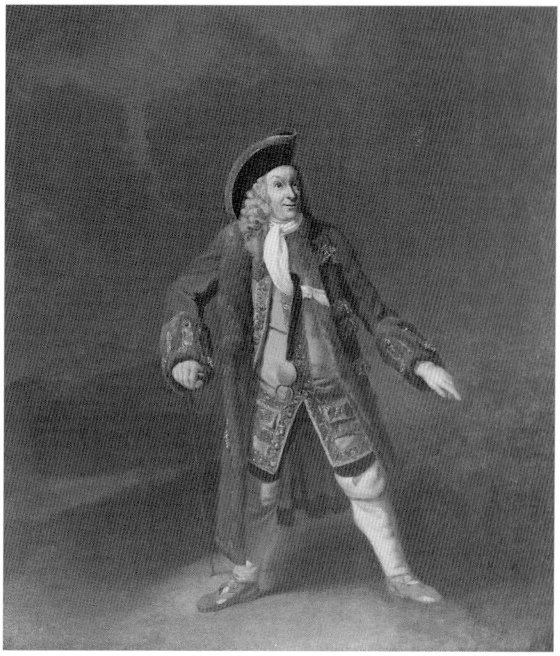

250*
DAVID GARRICK
as Lord Chalkstone in *Lethe or Aesop in the Shades* by David Garrick

Johan Zoffany

Oil on canvas 76 x 63.5
INV: Mathews 63; RW/CKA 124
PROV: Berry; Berry sale, Christie's 8 July 1814 bt. in, 10 March 1815 (33) bt. Davis; Charles Mathews
EXH: 1833 London (63); 1951 London (43)
ENGR: John Smith after a drawing by Jean Louis Fesch pub. J. Smith & R. Sayer 1770, line (vignette), from one of the three versions of the painting
REL: Coll: William Randolph Hearst (1951), oil on canvas 76.2 x 62.2, prov: Garrick sale 1823, bt. by Wamsey; Christie's 13 July 1951, bt. by Messrs Mallet, agents for W.R. Hearst; Babette Craven, oil on canvas 75 x 62
LIT: Patmore, p. 268

Lord Chalkstone has arrived in Elysium with some difficulty because of his gout and rheumatism (see No. 121). He is a merry soul and is described by his companion Bowman as 'always the best company, and the merriest of his family'. His gout is reflected in his rickety pose and his stick, and his jollity by his smiling face. He wears grey gloves, brown shoes, leggings over blue knee-breeches, a long brown coat with green fur lining and cuffs, trimmed with gold braid, and a red patterned waistcoat.

Garrick's dramatic satire was first performed at Drury Lane on 15 April 1740. The part of Lord Chalkstone was later written in and was first seen at Kitty Clive's benefit on 27 March 1756. This picture is one of a series painted in 1766, perhaps to celebrate the Royal Command performance of 23 January 1766. Zoffany exhibited two scenes at the S.A. in 1766: No. 198, depicting Garrick as Lord Chalkstone, Ellis Ackman as Bowman, and Astley Bransby as Aesop; and No. 199, depicting William Parsons as the Old Man, Astley Bransby again as Aesop, and Watkins as the Servant. Both these pictures are now in the Birmingham City Art Gallery. The single figures of Garrick were taken from the first scene, which was never engraved.

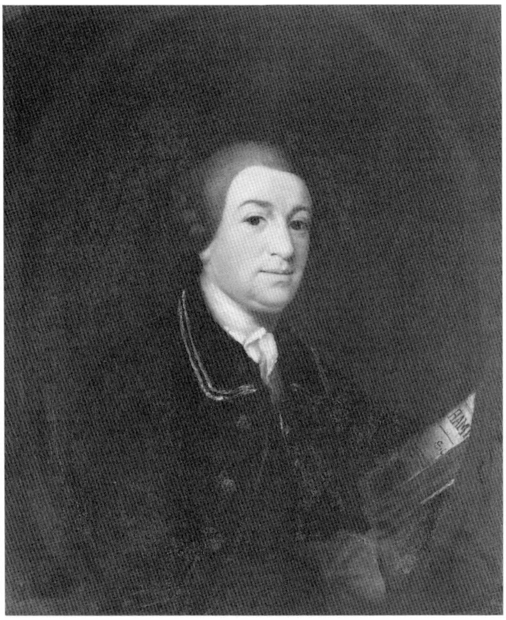

251
DAVID GARRICK

Unknown Artist

Oil on canvas 74.9 x 62.2
INSCR: 'Haml ...' (black paint on book b.r.)
INV: RW 7 (by Reynolds); CKA 7; Gift 216
PROV: Presented by the Duke of Fife, 1888

Garrick is shown half-length, in a feigned oval, holding a book which is open at *Hamlet*. He wears a dark blue jacket, the collar edged with double band of gold and with gold buttons, and a blue waistcoat.

According to CKA: 'Formerly at Duff House. It was stated to be by Reynolds and to have been acquired by James, Earl of Fife, a friend of Reynolds.' The statement appeared in the list of gifts: 'Collected by James Earl of Fife an intimate friend of the great Painter & has remained in the family since the death of Garrick.' This portrait type has nothing to do with any surviving or known portraits of Garrick by Reynolds, and it does not conform in style to Reynolds's work.

252*
DAVID GARRICK as Jaffeir
and *SUSANNA CIBBER* as Belvidera
in *Venice Preserv'd* by Thomas Otway

Johan Zoffany

Oil on canvas 101.5 x 126
INV: Mathews 17; RW/CKA 378
PROV: Charles Mathews
EXH: 1833 London (17); 1951 London (45); 1959 Lichfield
REL: Lord Lambton oil on canvas 101.6 x 127, exh: 1763 S.A. (137); Engr: James MacArdell 25 March 1764, mezzotint 43.2 x 52.7 (commissioned and owned by Garrick), also engravings by Stayner, published by C. Shepherd, and by Wilson, published by R. Sayer; Garrick sale, Christie's 23 June 1823, lot 612, bt. Lambton; Somerset Maugham Collection, Royal National Theatre, oil on canvas 101.5 x 127; Szepmuveszeti Museum (Budapest) 5880, oil on canvas 71 x 91
LIT: Patmore, p. 263; Fitzgerald, pp. 164–65; Griffiths, pp. 309–11; BD, 6: 96 (No. 169); Mander & Mitchenson, pp. 5–11

Belvidera is seen as she kneels on the line 'Oh! Mercy!' She has made Jaffeir reveal to the Senate a conspiracy against the state. Jaffeir had expected the lives of the conspirators, including his friend Pierre, to be saved as a result of his honesty, but earlier in the scene they are condemned to death. Jaffeir then threatens to kill Belvidera unless she secures a pardon from her father Priuli, one of the senators. In the text, Act IV, scene 2 is an interior scene: 'The Senate-House, where appear sitting the Duke of Venice, Priuli, Antonio, and eight other Senators.' Jaffeir is alone when Belvidera enters, and they begin their passionate scene. The text calls for no change of venue from the senate-house, which must have enough seats for 11 actors. [Probably not all the actors sat; 18th-century actors spent a lot of time standing on stage.] Either Garrick added a scene, perhaps closing the senate-house scene with an evening view of Venice, or Zoffany's setting is entirely imaginary. It seems unlikely that the street lamp would have been trundled on in the middle of a scene, although the moon (made of a conical tin containing a lamp and reflector, with the larger end covered with transparent coloured cloth) could have been flown in. More likely, Zoffany was merely providing a suitably Venetian setting for the stage action. The Salute is seen from across the Grand Canal, but the architecture behind the figures does not relate to any specific Venetian building (although there is a passing resemblance to the Dogana, which is on the same side of the Grand Canal as the Salute). The bars across the window suggest that the

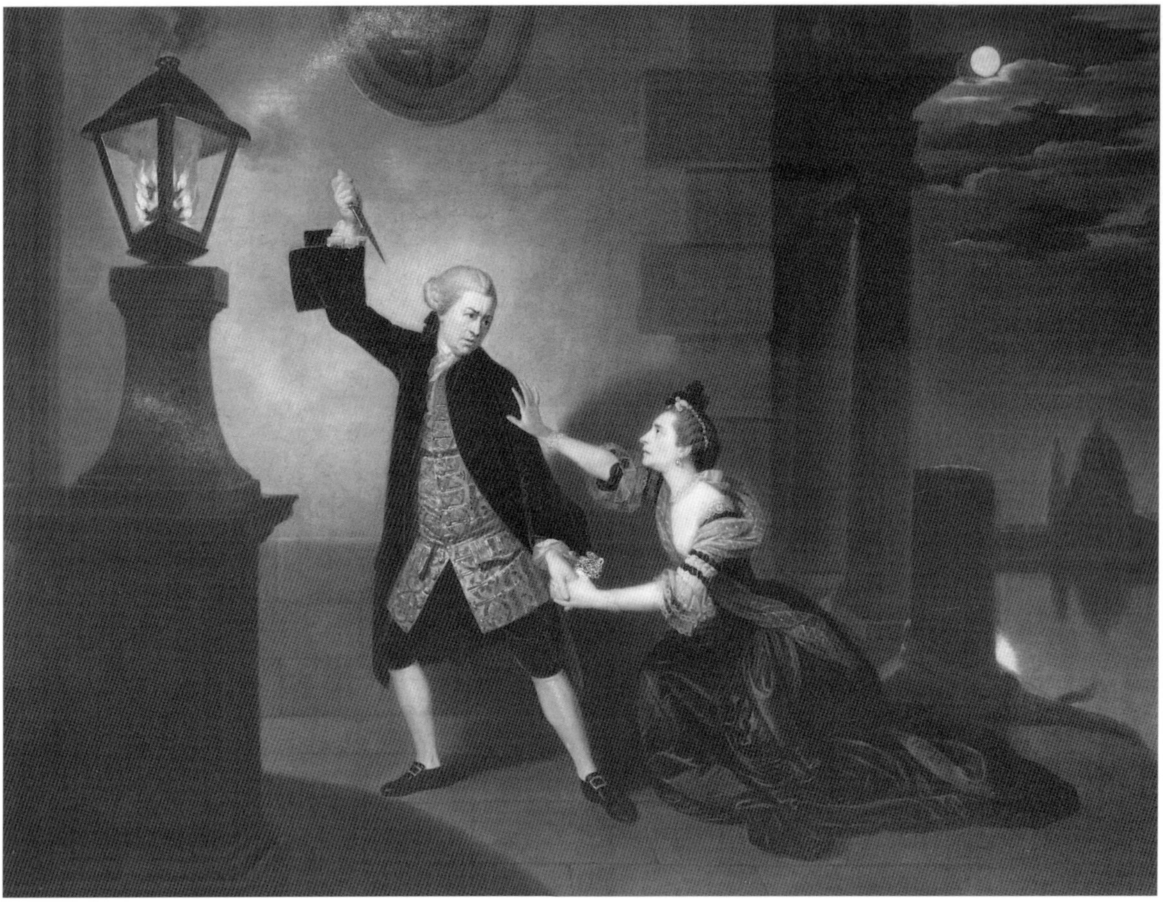

252 *David Garrick as Jaffeir and Susanna Cibber as Belvidera*

building is supposed to be the prison to which the conspirators have just been taken. The building is architecturally quite dissimilar to the state prisons across the Bridge of Sighs from the Ducal Palace (and the 'senate-house'). The broken column is a pictorial conceit to denote tragedy. John Graham's frontispiece to the 1791 Bell edition of the play, which describes itself as 'Adapted for Theatrical Representation, as performed at the Theatres-Royal Drury Lane and Covent Garden, regulated from the prompt book', shows the same scene as No. 252 but a few moments later, when Jaffeir has flung down his dagger. The setting is an interior with a table and chair visible on the left.

While on the Grand Tour, Garrick wrote from Venice on 12 June 1764 to George Colman, referring to *Venice Preserv'd*: 'I have taken my Evening walks of Meditation on the Rialto, and have fancy'd myself waiting for my friend Pierre.'

In *David Garrick, Director*, Kalman Burnim refers to a comment in the *Royal Female Magazine* (December 1760) on the costumes in the Drury Lane production of *Venice Preserv'd*. The writer complained that rather than suiting 'the dress to the character, with the most minute exactness to complete the deception of the scene', the actors chose the richest suit of clothes available in the wardrobe, without considering the nature of their roles. It seems unlikely that Garrick and Mrs Cibber joined in this free-for-all, although their clothes are very splendid. Jaffeir is dressed in black, with a white silk waistcoat elaborately embroidered in gold, with foliage and flowers in green and pink. Belvidera is also in black, with a white gauze stole round her shoulders.

Otway's tragedy was probably first performed at Dorset Garden Theatre on 9 February 1682 with Thomas Betterton as Jaffeir and Elizabeth Barry as Belvidera. Garrick first acted Jaffeir at Drury Lane on 8 February 1748 (having played the other main protagonist, Pierre, since his first season at Goodman's Fields in 1742); Mrs Cibber was his Belvidera. The play was equally popular at Drury Lane and Covent Garden.

The Drury Lane performances closest to Zoffany's painting were given on 20 October and 16 November 1762 and 26 March 1763, when Garrick and Mrs Cibber played their familiar roles.

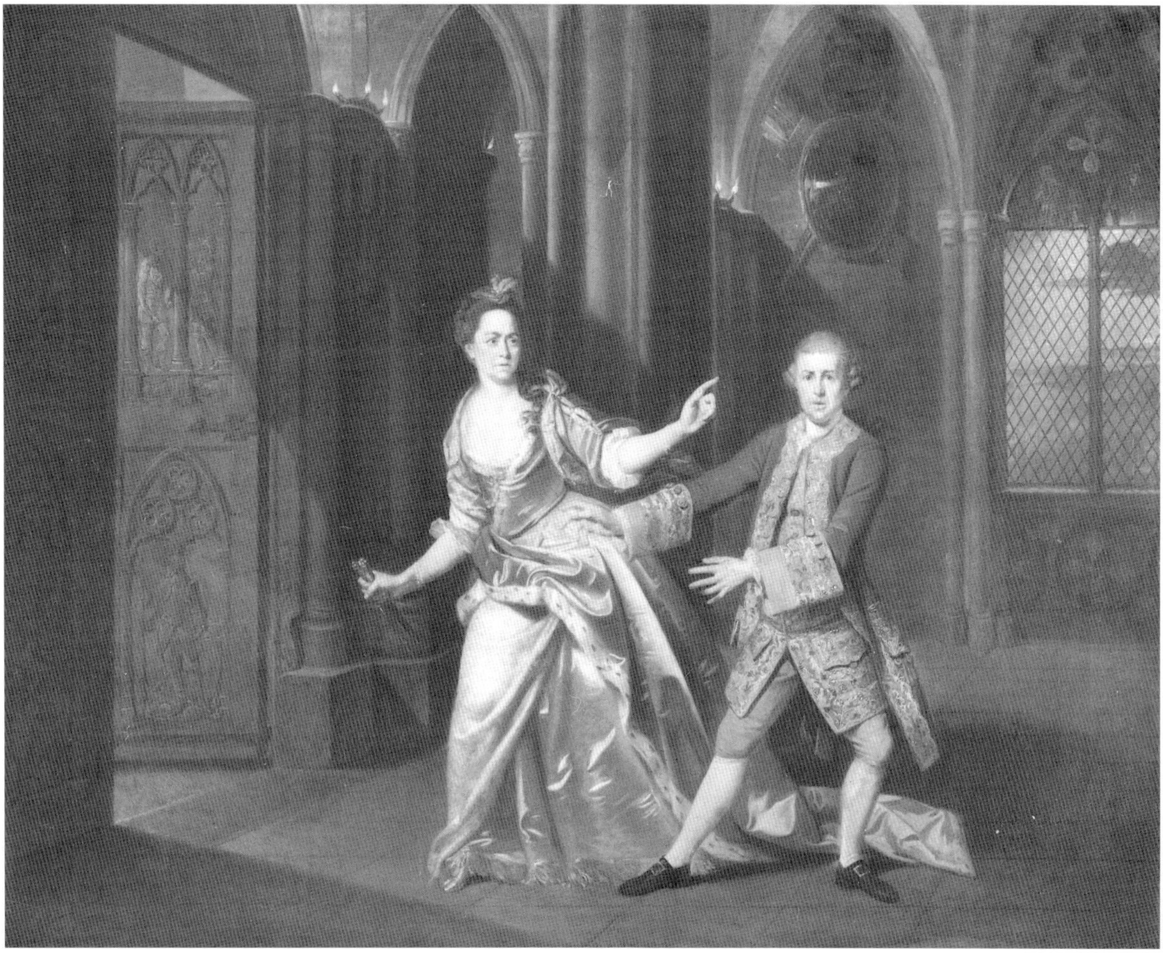

253*

DAVID GARRICK as Macbeth and
HANNAH PRITCHARD as Lady Macbeth
in *Macbeth* by William Shakespeare

Johan Zoffany

Oil on canvas 102 x 127.5
INV: Mathews 57; RW/CKA 386
PROV: Charles Mathews
EXH: 1833 London (57); 1951 London (47);
1961 Nottingham (16), in catalogue but not loaned;
1964 London [1] (15)
REL: Baroda Museum, oil on canvas 101.6 x 127
Engr: Valentine Green pub. J. Boydell 30 March 1776,
mezzotint 42.5 x 55.4, when owned by George Keate
LIT: Patmore, p. 263; Anthony Vaughan *Born to Please* (1979),
p. 50; Fitzgerald, pp. 154–57; Griffiths, pp. 209–11

Mathews identifies the moment of Zoffany's picture at the point (Act II, scene 2) when Macbeth says 'Look out again, I dare not', and Lady Macbeth replies 'Infirm of purpose!/Give me the daggers'. Macbeth's hands are stained with blood. He wears black shoes, white stockings, red breeches, a blue-green collarless coat edged with a broad band of gold braid and gold buttons, and a red waistcoat trimmed with gold braid. The costume for Macbeth in the 18th century was traditionally a Windsor uniform, but Garrick's costume seems rather lavish for military garb. Lady Macbeth, holding the daggers, wears a purple silk dress trimmed with ermine over a white silk petticoat, a purple silk bodice, and a yellow shawl with silver stripes.

According to Arthur Murphy in *The Life of David Garrick* (1801), Garrick returned from the murder of Duncan looking 'like a ghastly spectacle, and his complexion grew whiter every moment'. The *Connoisseur* of 1 September 1754 suggested that this effect was achieved by the actor wiping off his make-up before he reappeared on stage after the murder. The first time Garrick played Macbeth he returned from the murder with his coat and waistcoat unbuttoned. He is supposed never to have repeated this device, although his jacket is certainly unbuttoned in Zoffany's picture. In his *Dramatic Miscellanies* (1784), Thomas Davies gave a good description of the moment depicted by Zoffany:

> The representation of this terrible part of the play, by Garrick and Mrs Pritchard, can no more be described than I believe it can be equalled. I will not separate these performers, for the merits of both were transcendent. His distraction of mind, and agonizing horrors were finely contrasted by her seeming apathy, tranquillity, and confidence. The beginning of the scene ... was conducted in terrifying whispers. Their looks and actions supplied the place of words. You heard what they spoke, but you learned more from the agitation of the mind displayed in their action and deportment. The dark colouring given by the actor to these abrupt speeches, makes the scene awful and tremendous to the auditors. The wonderful expression of heartful terror, which Garrick felt when he shewed his bloody hands, can only be conceived and described by those who saw him!

See also K. A. Burnim, *David Garrick, Director*, pp. 113–16.

Garrick played Macbeth for the first time at Drury Lane on 7 January 1744. He restored a great deal more of the original text than is found in the version by William Davenant then in general use. Hannah Pritchard played Lady Macbeth for the first time on 13 April 1744, but in Davenant's version and at Covent Garden. She finally played opposite Garrick in his version on 19 March 1748, and their joint performance continued to be one of the glories of the London stage for the next 20 years. Mrs Pritchard played the part for her farewell performance on 24 April 1768.

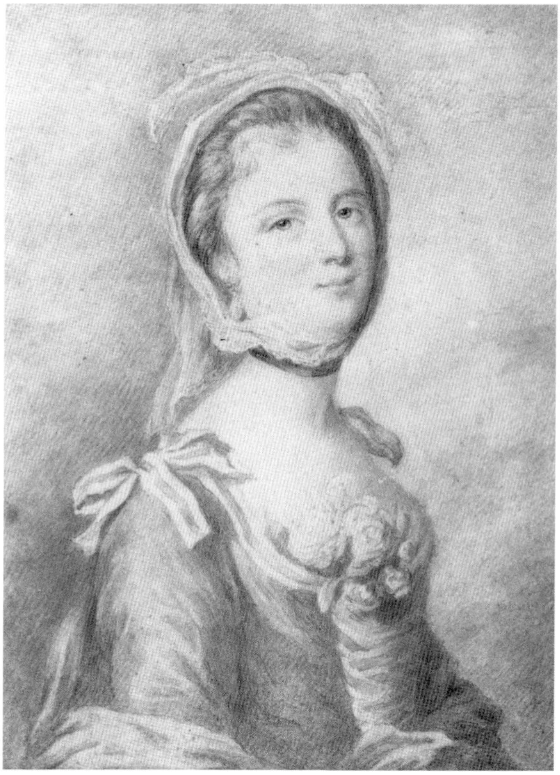

254

EVA MARIA GARRICK

Catherine Read (after)

Watercolour on wove paper 13.4 x 10 (sight)
INV: Mathews 312 (by Cipriani);
RW 427 I (by Cipriani); CKA 427 I
PROV: Charles Mathews
EXH: 1833 London (312)
REL: Original: V&A P.11–1963, pastel on paper 58.8 x 48.3 *c.*1755 Engr: William P. Sherlock pub. Anthony Molteno 1802, stipple 14.3 x 11.1, when the original was owned by S. Edwards; Anon., stipple 9.8 x 7.3
LIT: Fitzgerald, p. 224

Mrs Garrick (who before her marriage had appeared on the stage as 'Violetti') wears a purplish dress with blue and white bows and white lacing against a blue bodice.

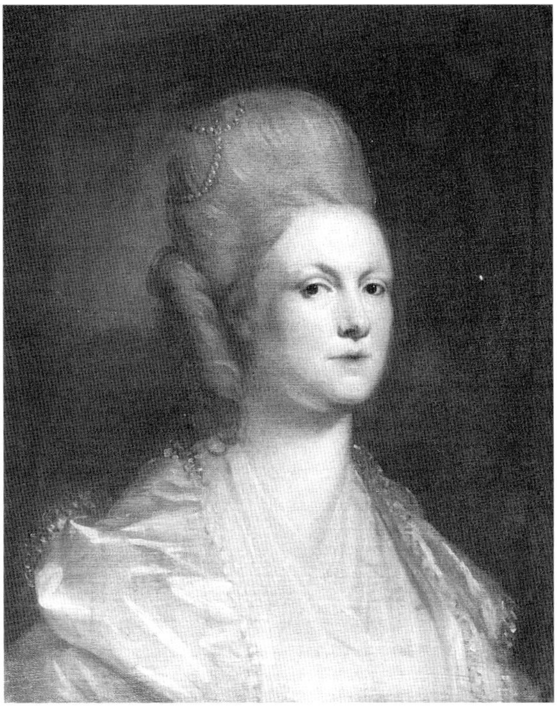

255
EVA MARIA GARRICK

Unknown Artist

Oil on canvas 60 x 49
INV: RW 387 (by Thomas Gainsborough);
CKA 387 (by Rev. Matthew William Peters)
PROV: William Commerell, by whom presented
to the Garrick Club, *c.*1854

The sitter, shown half-length, wears a white silk dress and a grey wig.

[The identity of both sitter and artist is exceedingly uncertain. The picture is neither by Gainsborough nor Peters, but may possibly be from the circle of Ozias Humphry (1742–1810). It was presented by William Commerell along with his equally dubious portrait of Elizabeth Farren (No. 206).]

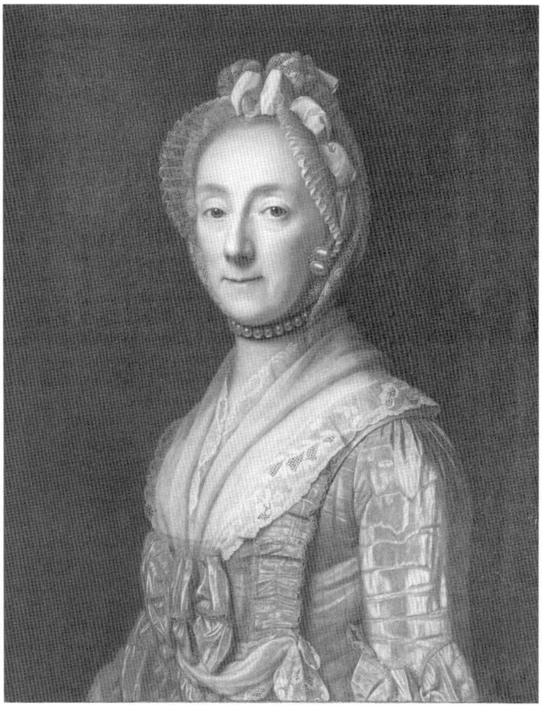

256
EVA MARIA GARRICK (?)

Unknown Artist

Oil on canvas 55 x 43
INV: CKA 628; Gift 543
PROV: Sir Henry Irving; Irving sale, Christie's
16 December 1905 (157); bequeathed to the
Garrick Club by Harry Graham, 1936
EXH: 1951 London (51)

The sitter wears a ruched lace cap with white satin ribbons, pearl earrings and a pearl choker. Her dress is of oyster-coloured watered silk.

[This picture was once attributed to Zoffany but does not relate stylistically to Zoffany's work, although it does appear to be Continental. A date in the 1760s is likely. The identification of the sitter as Mrs Garrick seems to have been mere wishful thinking.]

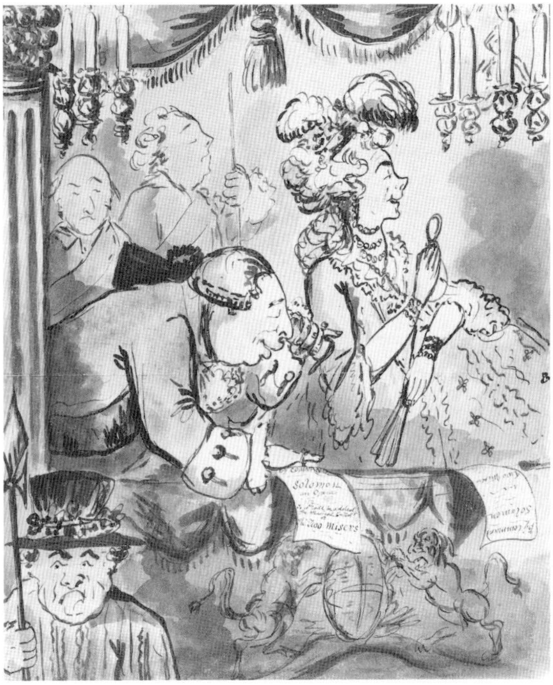

257
GEORGE III & QUEEN CHARLOTTE
'A Stage Box in London'

John Nixon

Pencil, with pen and black ink and watercolour on laid paper 26.7 x 22.2 (sheet 29.7 x 23)
INSCR: 'A Stage Box in London' (pen and black ink on mount below); 'BY / COMMAND / SOLOMON / an Opera / To wch will be added / The Musical Entert / of / The Two Misers' (pen and black ink on playbill l.c.)
INV: Not listed
PROV: Sir Henry Irving; Irving sale, Christie's 16 December 1905; from Irving's 'David Garrick A Memorial' Vol. IV f. 10

In this caricature drawing, George III and Queen Charlotte sit in the Royal Box, with the Royal Coat of Arms on the front and two playbills draped over the edge. The allusion is to the alleged meanness of the King and Queen.

There does not appear to be an occasion on which a performance of *Solomon* coincided with one of *The Two Misers*. It was not customary for a farce to follow performances of the Lenten oratorios at either of the patent theatres. Nixon's choice of programme must relate more intimately to the subject matter of his drawing.

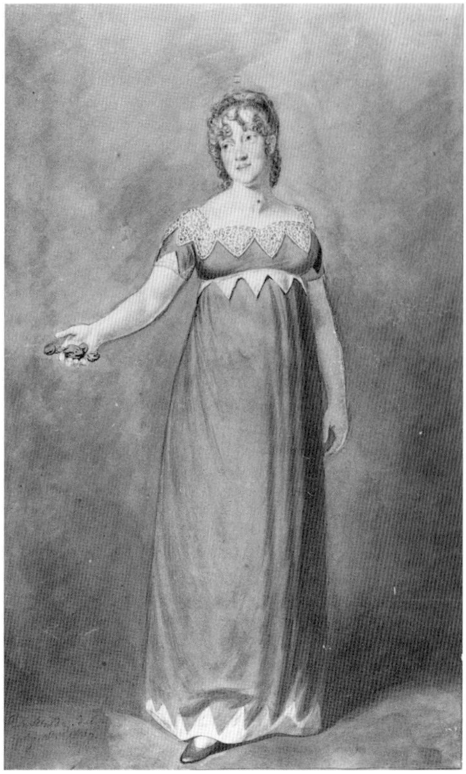

258
MARY GIBBS
as Blanch in *The Iron Chest*
by George Colman the Younger

Samuel De Wilde

Pencil and watercolour on wove paper 37 x 23.5
INSCR: 'S De Wilde. delin / July 18. 1809.' (pencil b.l.)
INV: Mathews 200; RW/CKA 45C
PROV: Charles Mathews
EXH: 1833 London (200); 1975 London (139)

Blanch, maid to Helen, has just delivered a letter to Sir Edward Mortimer from her mistress. In the hall in Sir Edward's lodge she is accosted by his brother, Captain Fitzharding. He offers her a purse (in the text he gives her two pieces of gold from the purse) which she thinks is intended for charitable purposes. Fitzharding has something else in mind, and when Blanch realises what he intends, she throws the money down. Blanch wears black slippers, white stockings, and a short-sleeved pale blue dress.

The younger George Colman's melodrama, with music by Stephen Storace, was first performed at Drury Lane on 12 March 1796, with Mrs Gibbs as the original Blanch. She also played the role at the Haymarket on 29 August 1796 and at Covent Garden, to which theatre she had moved, on 23 April 1799.

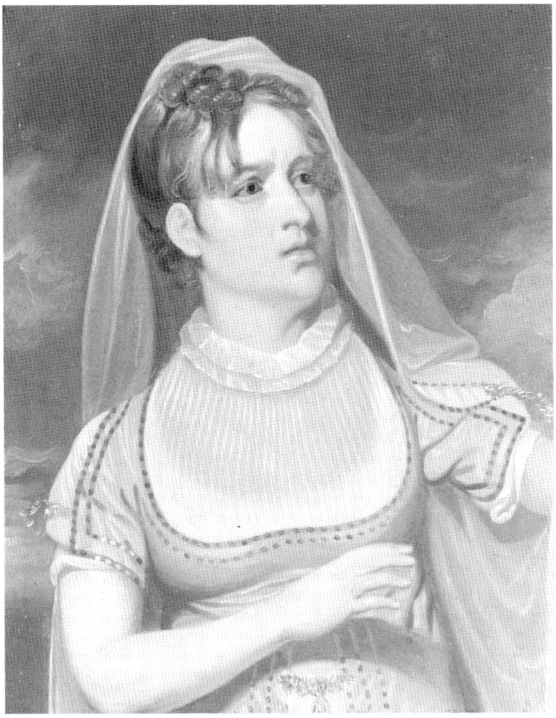

259
MARY GIBBS
in character

Samuel De Wilde

Oil on panel 23.5 x 19
INV: RW/CKA 212 (Blanch in *The Iron Chest*)
PROV: Unknown; acquired by the Club before 1888?
[Possibly the picture of Mrs Gibbs in character, signed and dated by De Wilde, that was in the Royal Dramatic College sale at Fairbrother, Lye and Palmer on 24 February 1881 (lot 100B)]

The sitter wears a pale blue dress trimmed with silver over a striped muslin chemise with double collar frill, and a long muslin veil. She could be Mrs Gibbs; there is some resemblance to documented portraits of her. The part she is playing is clearly not the servant girl Blanch in *The Iron Chest*, as indicated in the label on the frame. The costume does not match that in De Wilde's watercolour (No. 258), and the text includes no indication of a change of costume during the play. In any event, the high neckline and veil in No. 259 suggest a tragic role rather than that of a servant, and the dramatic gesture is of an elevated nature.

This half-length portrait is similar to others in the same format by De Wilde which date from 1802–4.

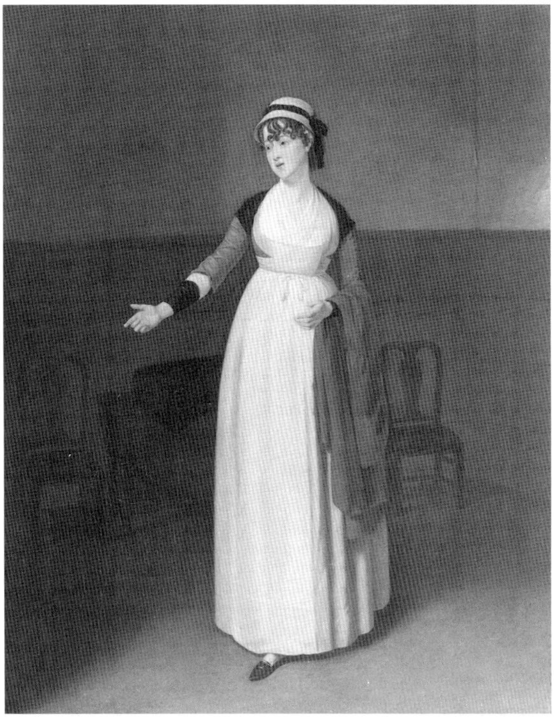

260
MARY GIBBS
as Selina in *The Tale of Mystery*
by Thomas Holcroft

Samuel De Wilde

Oil on canvas 76 x 59.5
INV: Mathews 356; RW/CKA 106
PROV: Charles Mathews
EXH: 1833 London (356); 1934 London (264)

Selina is shown in Act I, scene I, where the scene is: 'A hall in the house of Bonamo, with two side doors, and folding doors in the back scene: a table, pen, ink, and paper, chairs &c.' Upon the entrance of her servant Stephano, Selina chides him for being away so long; Mathews provides Selina's line: 'Why are you so late, Stephano? I had a thousand alarms.' De Wilde's portrait of Charles Farley as Francisco in this play (Somerset Maugham Collection, Royal National Theatre, 16) shows the same interior with more emphasis on the Strawberry Hill furniture. (See also No. 203 for Farley as Francisco.)

Selina has a red cloak over her left arm. She wears black shoes and white stockings, and a white dress which has dark blue shoulders and pale blue sleeves. Her little straw bonnet has a dark blue band and bow.

Holcroft's melodrama was first performed at Covent Garden on 13 November 1802, with Mrs Gibbs as Selina.

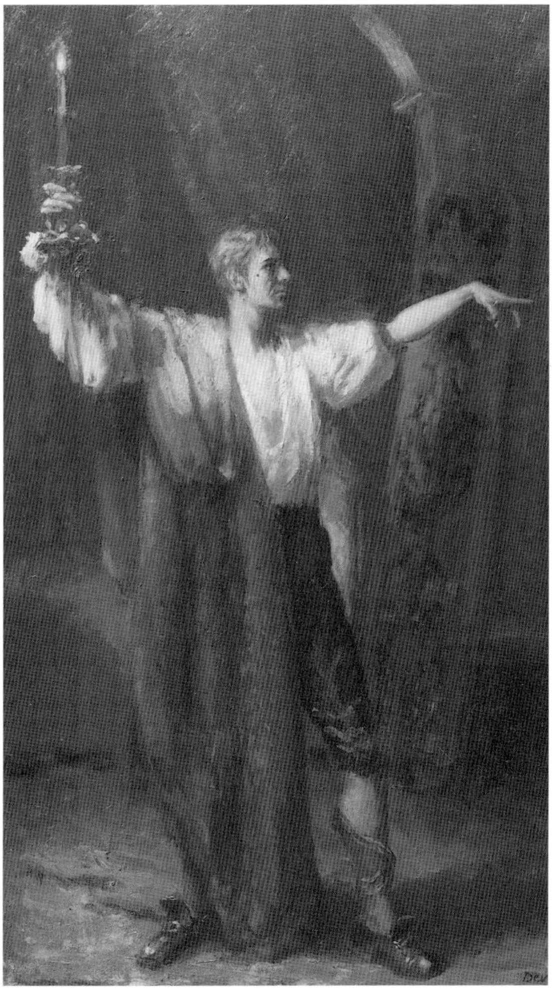

261

SIR JOHN GIELGUD

as Valentine in *Love for Love*

by William Congreve

Anthony Devas

Oil on canvas 101.5 x 63.5
INSCR: 'Devas '43' (brown paint b.r.)
INV: GCL 747
PROV: The artist's widow; Nigel Rideout; bt. by the Garrick Club for £4,000, 1986
EXH: 1949 Port Sunlight (40)
REL: There are two sketches for this picture in the Mander & Mitchenson Theatre Coll., 13A & 13B, oil on paper 49.4 x 24.5 and 49.4 x 24.8, which were bought from the artist's widow in 1982

Valentine is seen in Act IV, set in his lodging. Upon the arrival of his father, Sir Sampson Legend, Valentine is discovered 'upon a couch disorderly dressed'. His disorderly dress consists of old black shoes with gold buckles, ragged purple stockings, purplish breeches, a loose white shirt, and a swathe of purple drapery.

Gielgud directed the production, in which he also played Valentine. It opened at the Phoenix in April 1943 and enjoyed a long run. It was revived the following year in a repertory season at the Haymarket that also included *Hamlet*, *A Midsummer Night's Dream*, *The Duchess of Malfi*, and *The Circle*. Sir John sent an explanatory letter on hearing that the Club had purchased the picture:

> This portrait was painted in 1943 by Antony Devas in my favourite dressing-room at the top of the Haymarket Theatre in the character of Valentine Legend, the hero of Congreve's comedy 'Love for Love'. Valentine's father, Sir Sampson, trying to thwart his interest in the rich heiress Angelica, attempts to make him sign away his own inheritance and brings a lawyer, Buckram, to give him the necessary papers – Valentine assumes madness and drives the lawyer away, managing also to contrive a love-scene with Angelica. The success of that scene – in my own production (originally produced in 1943 at the Phoenix Theatre), which had a brilliant cast, Yvonne Arnaud, Leslie Banks, Leon Quartermaine, Miles Malleson, Cecil Trouncer, Max Adrian, Angela Baddeley, Marion Spencer and Rosalie Crutchley, lay in the fun I had in posturing as the madman in a kind of burlesque performance of my own Hamlet, which, when the production was transferred to the Haymarket, in my 1944 season there, included revivals of 'Hamlet', &c...

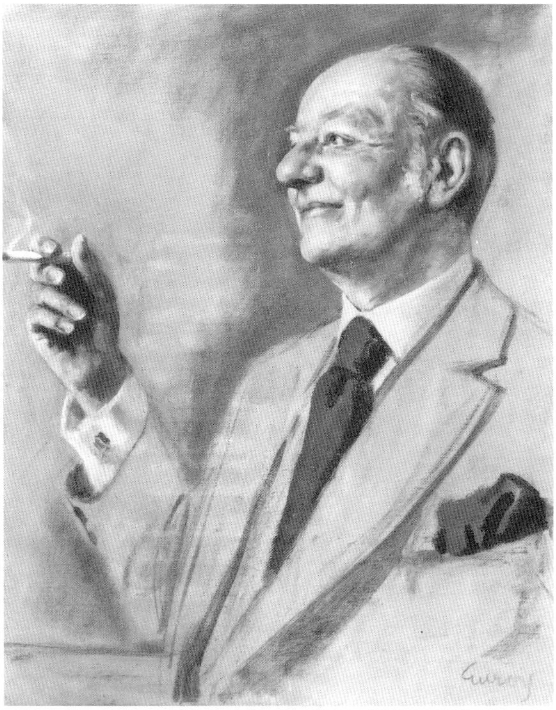

262

SIR JOHN GIELGUD

John Gilroy

Oil on canvas 76.2 x 71.1
INV: GCL 724; Gift 854
PROV: Presented by the artist, 1974
EXH: 1987–88 London
(Theatre Museum Gielgud Exhibition)

Sir John, one of the most distinguished actors of the 20th century, became a member of the Garrick Club in 1970.

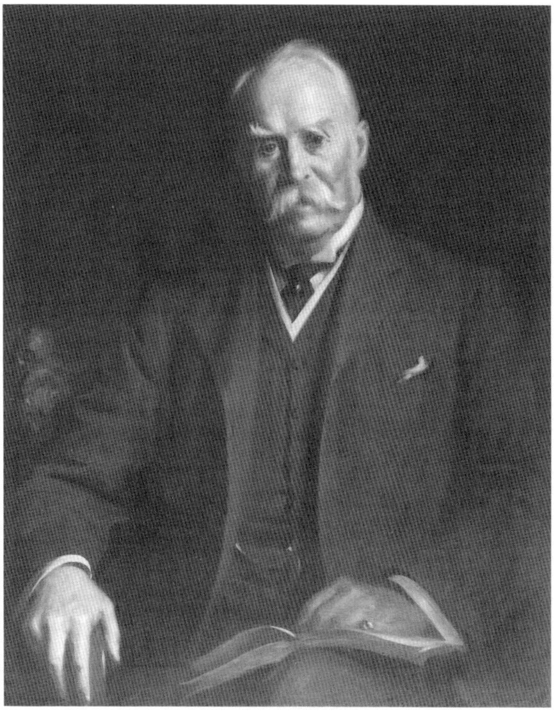

263

SIR WILLIAM SCHWENK GILBERT

Herbert Herkomer

Oil on canvas 91.5 x 83.8
INV: GCL 680; Gift 742
PROV: Bequeathed by Miss McIntosh, 1954

W.S. Gilbert, comic poet and illustrator, was librettist of the Savoy operas, for which Sir Arthur Sullivan wrote the music. Gilbert is shown seated and holding a book on his left knee. He wears a grey suit and waistcoat, with a grey tie.

Sir William became a member of the Garrick Club in 1906.

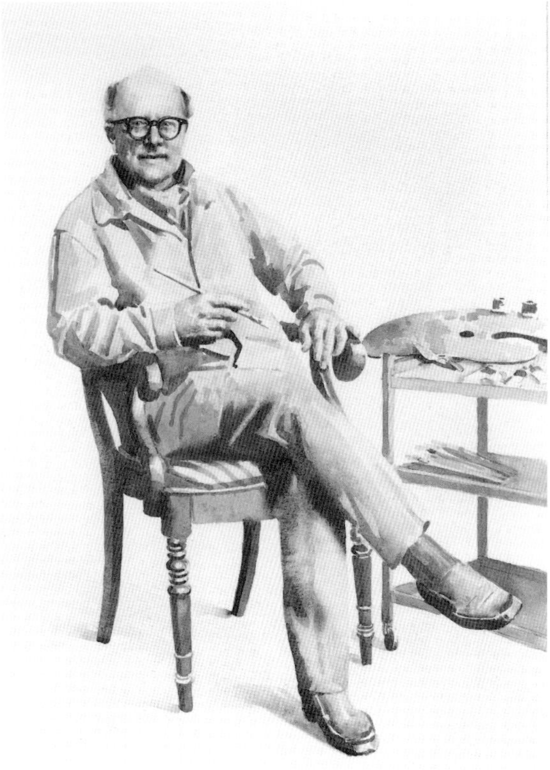

264
JOHN GILROY

John Gilroy

Pencil and watercolour on wove paper 76 x 56.5
INV: Not listed; Gift 926
PROV: Presented by the sitter's widow, 1987

The artist wears brown shoes, green socks, brown trousers, a loose green jacket, and a red cravat.

As will be seen from this catalogue, Gilroy, a life member of the Garrick Club, was responsible for a large number of the portraits in the Club's collection. He also made portraits of members of the Royal Family and of Sir Winston Churchill. See also No. 892.

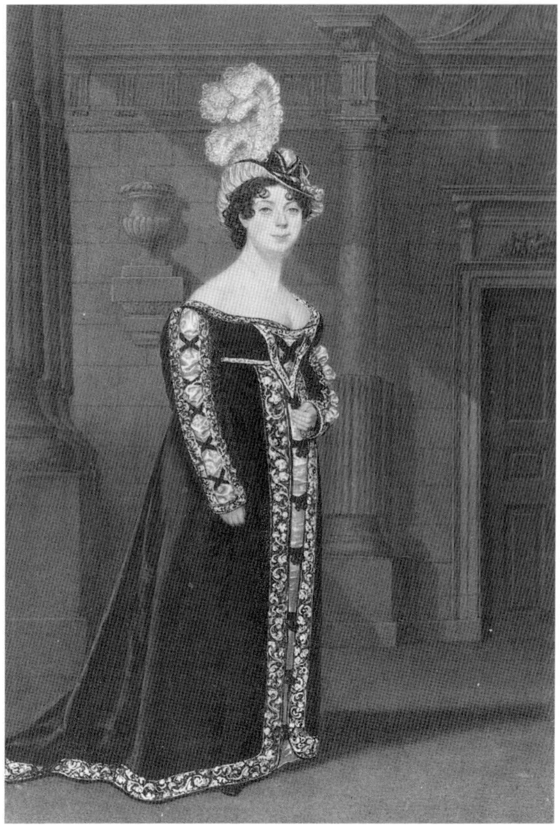

265
JULIANA GLOVER
as Lady Allworth in *A New Way to Pay Old Debts*
by Philip Massinger

Walter Stephens Lethbridge

Pencil with watercolour and body colour
on wove paper 25.6 x 18
INSCR: 'Lethbridge Fecit.' (pen and brown ink
on mount b.l. CM); 'Mrs Glover'
(pen and brown ink on mount b.c. CM)
INV: Mathews 288; RW/CKA 558
PROV: Charles Mathews
EXH: 1833 London (288)
ENGR: Thomson for the *Theatrical Inquisitor*
pub. C. Chapple 2 March 1818, stipple
(vignette; very little detail in background
compared with the drawing)
REL: A pencil drawing, artist unnamed, of Mrs Glover
was in the Dramatic College sale at Fairbrother,
Lye and Palmer on 24 February 1881 (lot 95)

The line suggested by Mathews, 'Wet [actually Sort] those silks well. / I'll take the air alone', is spoken by Lady Allworth on her first entry in Act I, scene 2, when she gives directions to her servants Tabitha and Abigail. The engraving quotes a later moment in the same scene, when Lady Allworth advises her stepson Allworth on his military career under Lord Lovell: 'These are the essential parts that make up a Soldier, Not swearing, dice, or drinking.' According to the 1818 Oxberry edition of the play, Lady Allworth's first-act costume consisted of: 'A black velvet train dress bordered with satin and point-lace; long sleeves, slashed and trimmed to correspond; high ruff; stomacher of point; black velvet hat, white feathers, and tassels.' The costume in Lethbridge's drawing corresponds exactly. The scene is set in the hall of Lady Allworth's house and is depicted as a classical interior with Tuscan pillars supporting an entablature. Lady Allworth's hall is also the setting for Clint's great picture, No. 355, but there the interior is uncompromisingly gothic. Nos. 352 and 355 show later moments in the same play.

Mrs Glover played Lady Allworth when *A New Way to Pay Old Debts* was revived on 12 January 1816 in order to give Edmund Kean a new vehicle for his demonic histrionics, and she played in all 26 performances before the end of that season.

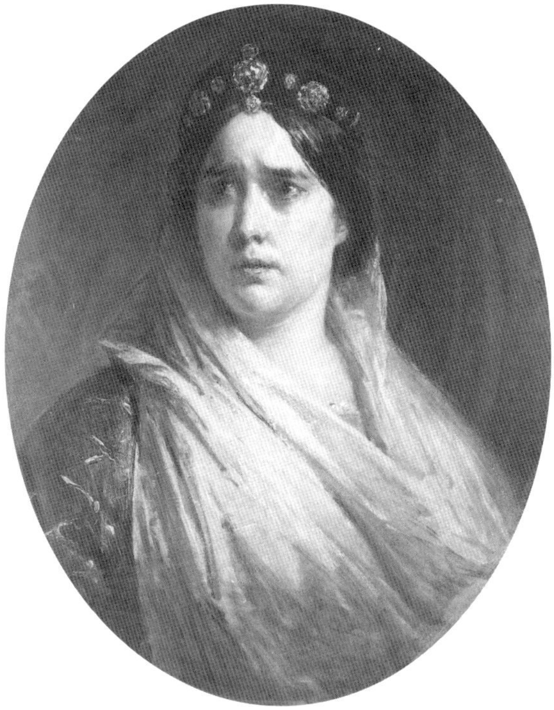

266
ISABELLA GLYN
as Constance in *King John*
by William Shakespeare

Henry Wyndham Phillips

Oil on canvas 73.7 x 61 (oval)
INV: RW/CKA 93; Gift 182
PROV: Presented by the artist, 1865
EXH: 1980 Buxton (28)

Constance wears a diamond tiara, from which a white veil hangs over her shoulders, and a blue dress with criss-cross gold design.

The picture may date from 1849, when Isabella Glyn had given her last performance as Constance as a member of Samuel Phelps's company at Sadler's Wells. But her matronly aspect and the style of the work suggest a date nearer to that of the artist's gift, 1865. Although she made a celebrated come-back as Cleopatra at the Princess's in 1867, she was spending most of her professional time in the 1860s as a Shakespeare reader rather than as a stage performer.

Farquhar's comedy was originally given at Drury Lane on 28 November 1699. Mrs Goodall's first portrayal of Sir Harry Wildair, at the Haymarket on 30 July 1789, was her first performance at that theatre. She acted the role three more times that season and took the role back with her to Drury Lane on 8 October 1789, playing it once again on 20 November before Mrs Jordan resumed her option on the role on 12 February 1790. Mrs Goodall's last performance before De Wilde's picture was painted was at Drury Lane on 10 December 1790.

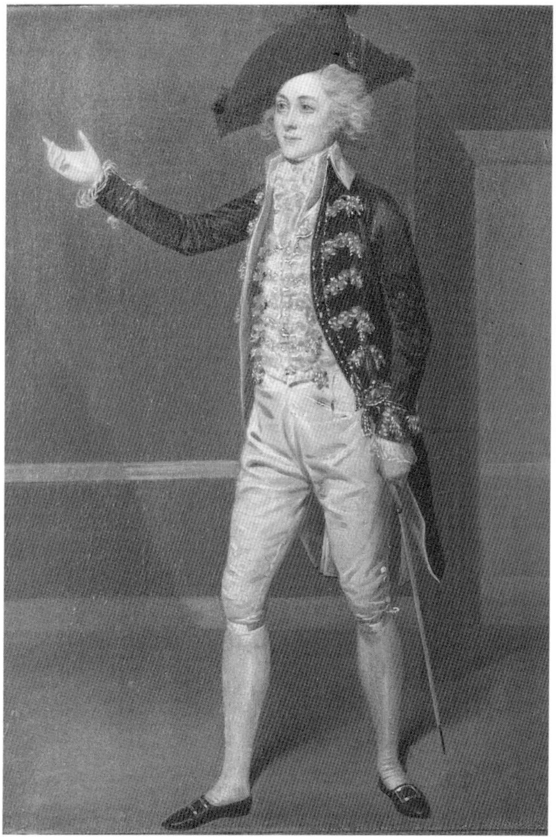

267

CHARLOTTE GOODALL

as Sir Henry Wildair in *The Constant Couple* by George Farquhar

Samuel De Wilde

Oil on canvas 36.5 x 28
INSCR: 'W' (b.r.)
INV: Mathews 92; RW/CKA 217
PROV: John Bell; Charles Mathews
EXH: 1833 London (92); 1934 London (262)
ENGR: William S. Leney for Bell's British Library 2 June 1792, line 10.5 x 7.6, pub. Bell's *British Theatre* (1797), vol 16, with the quotation 'Oh, the delights of love and burgundy!'; Anon. printed for C. Cooke 30 October 1806, pl. to *British Drama* (1817), line

Mrs Goodall is seen as Sir Harry Wildair in Act IV, scene I, when he enters drunk. Sir Harry is 'newly come from Paris' where he 'bought half a dozen new suits' and is generally admired and envied for his fashionable, debonair appearance. He wears black shoes with gold buckles, white stockings, yellow breeches and waistcoat, a green coat lined in yellow; both coat and waistcoat have silver frogging. He has a black tricorn hat, worn at a rather jaunty angle.

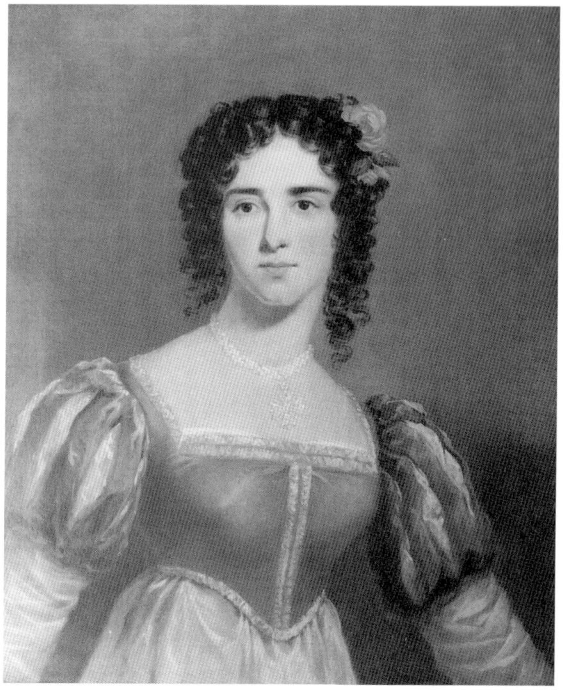

268

MISS GRADDON

as Linda in *Der Freischutz* by Carl Maria von Weber, in a version by George Soane

William Brockedon

Oil on canvas 73.7 x 61.6
INV: RW/CKA 413; Gift 36
PROV: Presented by the artist, 1836
EXH: 1825 R.A. (371); 1962 Chichester (8)

Linda must be shown in her costume for Act II, scene I, because in her other appearances she is dressed as a bride, in white. She sits with Rose, and has ominous thoughts. Left on her own, she sings a recitative, 'How gentle was my slumber, / Ere tasted love's first kiss...' and an air, 'Streams are flowing / Stars are glowing'. Miss Graddon, half-length, wears a pearl necklace with a pendant Maltese Cross, and 'Tudor' costume: a green bodice and puffed shoulders slashed to reveal pink undersleeves; her skirt is pink, and the bodice is trimmed with pink ruching.

Weber's opera, with a libretto by Johann Friedrich Kind, was first given at the Schauspielhaus, Berlin, on 18 June 1821. The first London performance was at the English Opera House on 22 July 1824, with the libretto translated into English by W. McGregor Logan and music 'adapted' by W. Hawes. The opera was performed at six London theatres during 1824. The first Drury Lane performance was given on 10 November 1824, with a text 'altered from the German' by George Soane and additional music by Sir Henry Bishop. Miss Graddon played Linda. The opera was given in Italian at Covent Garden in 1825 with recitatives by Costa to replace the original spoken dialogue.

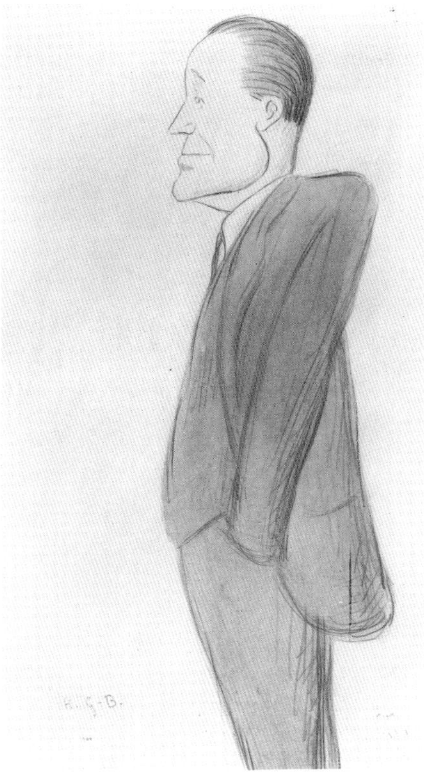

269

HARLEY GRANVILLE-BARKER

Sir Max Beerbohm

Caricature, pencil and watercolour
on discoloured laid paper 32 x 18.7
INSCR: 'max / 1923' (pencil b.r.); 'H.G.B.' (pencil b.l.)
INV: CKA 647; Gift 632
PROV: Presented by Nicholas Hannen, 1945

'In the first decade of the 20th century Granville-Barker was in the forefront of the progressive movement in England. As playwright, actor and producer, he displayed that alert intelligence which, combined with artistic taste and sound scholarship, did so much to revitalise the English theatre.' (OC)

Granville-Barker became a member of the Garrick Club in 1908.

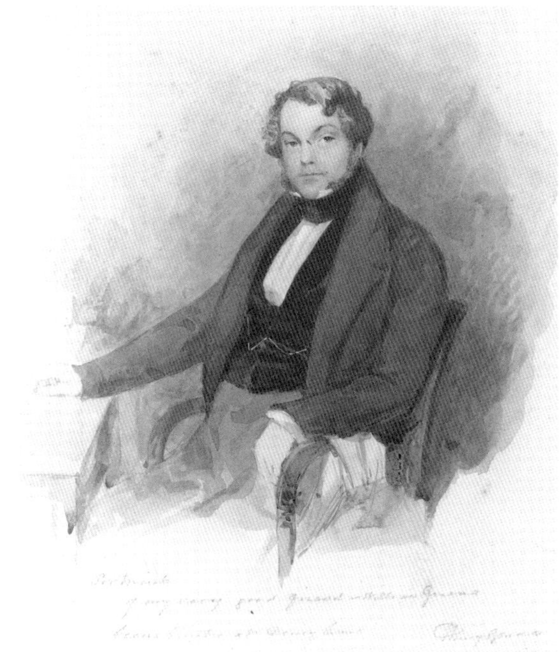

270

WILLIAM GRIEVE

William Henry Graves (?)

Pencil and watercolour on wove paper 28 x 26
INSCR: 'Portrait / of my very good friend – William Grieve / Scene Painter at Drury Lane' (pencil b.c.); 'W Henry Graves' (pen & brown ink b.r.)
INV: RW/CKA 187; Gift 261
PROV: Algernon Graves; Henry Graves by whom presented, 1898
EXH: 1897 Victorian Exhibition; 1979 Bonn & Sunderland (53)

Seated at a table, three-quarter length, facing spectator, and wearing a dark grey coat with black waistcoat and stock.

A member of a 19th-century dynasty of scene-painters, William Grieve, after the death of Stanfield, ranked as the premier scenic artist of his time.

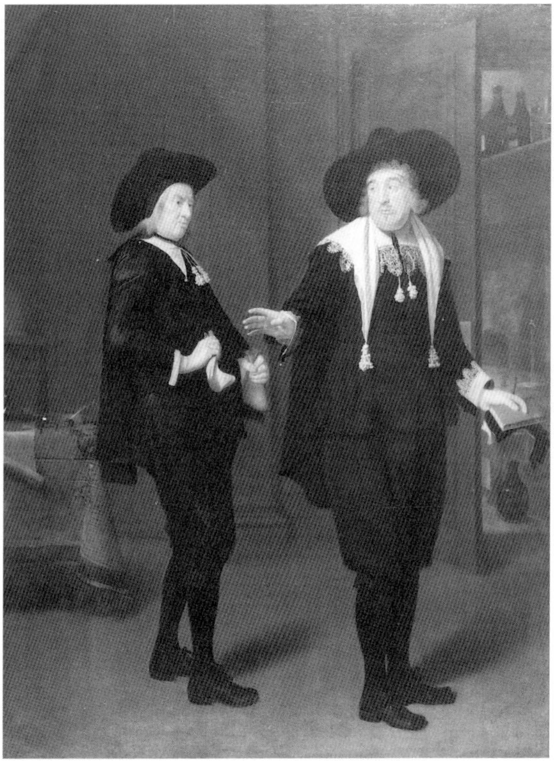

271
BENJAMIN GRIFFIN as Tribulation
and *BENJAMIN JOHNSON* as Ananias
in *The Alchymist* by Ben Jonson

Pieter Van Bleeck

Oil on canvas 237.5 x 179.1
INV: RW/CKA 464; Gift 5
PROV: Presented by George H. Robins, 1833
ENGR: Pieter Van Bleeck, mezzotint 41.3 x 30.8,
inscr: 'Peter van Bleeck pinxt 1738'
LIT: Thomas Davies, *Dramatic Miscellanies* (1784)

Ananias, a deacon of Amsterdam, and Tribulation, a zealous pastor of Amsterdam, visit Subtle, the quack alchemist, in order to have some goods they have obtained from widows and orphans turned from pewter into gold. Tribulation is anxious to get on with the job, whilst Ananias, inspired by bigotry, retains his doubts. Subtle lists all the mortifications endured by the two prelates, and suggests that with the power of the stone they will be unnecessary. He says they will no longer have to make decisions such as 'whether matrons of the holy assembly / May lay their hair out, or wear doublets, / Or have that idol starch about their linen'. Ananias interrupts with 'It is indeed an idol', and Tribulation tells Subtle 'Mind him not, sir', then addresses Ananias with the line quoted on the engraving: 'I do command thee Spirit (of Zeal, but Trouble) to Peace within him.' This scene was heavily cut in later 18th-century editions of the play because it was thought to be too critical of Christian virtues, and this exchange was always omitted. It would probably have been omitted from performances as well. Subtle's makeshift laboratory is depicted with some care but it is curious that Subtle himself is absent. Tribulation (Griffin) stands on the right in a broad-brimmed black hat, black shoes, stockings, breeches, and coat. Ananias (Johnson) is also dressed in black.

Griffin, whose career began at Lincoln's Inn Fields on 16 February 1715 and ended at the Haymarket on 25 April 1748, spent most of his life acting at Drury Lane, where he gave his first Tribulation in 1721. Benjamin Johnson was at Drury Lane from September 1695 to 12 May 1742. There were two performances of *The Alchymist* at Drury Lane during 1738 (the year of the engraving), on 21 February and 27 May, both with Griffin as Tribulation and Johnson as Ananias. They also played the parts at the two previous performances, 22 October 1736 and 15 November 1737.

According to Davies, Griffin and Johnson:

> ... were much admired for their just representations of the canting puritanical preacher and his solemn deacon and botcher; there was an affected softness in the former which was finely contrasted by the fanatical fury of the other – Griffin's features seemed ready to relax into a smile, while the stiff muscles and fierce eye of the other admitted of no suppleness or compliance. There is still to be seen a fine print of them in these characters, from a painting of Vanbleek; they are very striking resemblances of both comedians.

272*
JOSEPH GRIMALDI
as Clown in
Harlequin and Mother Goose
or The Golden Egg

Samuel De Wilde

Pencil and watercolour on wove paper,
drawn on a smaller piece of paper (30 x 20)
and stuck onto a larger one (37 x 23.5)
INV: Mathews 290; RW/CKA 63B
PROV: Charles Mathews

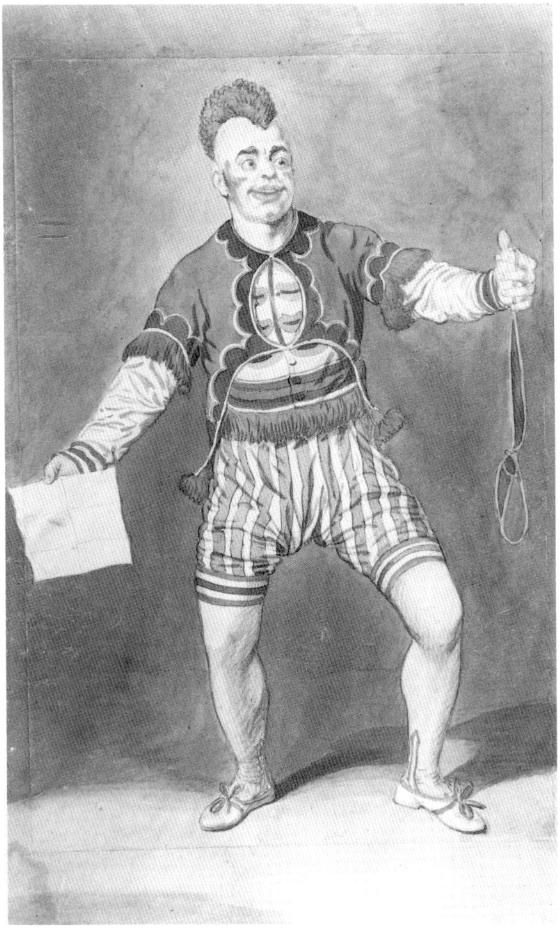

272 *Joseph Grimaldi as Clown*

EXH: 1833 London (290); 1975 London (144)
ENGR: (Samuel De Wilde) pub. S. De Wilde 14 February 1807, etching 16.5 x 11.4; (Samuel De Wilde) pub. S. De Wilde 14 February 1807, etching 29.5 x 20, inscr: 'MR. GRIMALDI AS CLOWN / In the Popular new Pantomime of MOTHER GOOSE / Price 2.6 coloured'; J. Harris for Grimaldi's *Memoirs* pub. R. Bentley 1846, aquatint and etching 12 x 8

Grimaldi has a blue Mohican-style tuft of hair, black eyebrows, and clown face-paint with red lips, stars on his cheeks and white on face and neck. He wears white slippers with red bands and bows, yellow tights with red and white flashes at the ankle, shorts of blue and white vertical stripes hemmed with bands of red, white and blue, a short collarless red jacket edged in gold, and a white shirt.

The Christmas pantomime at Covent Garden in 1806 opened, a little late, on 29 December, and ran for 73 performances before 15 April 1807. Grimaldi was Squire Bugle transformed into Clown.

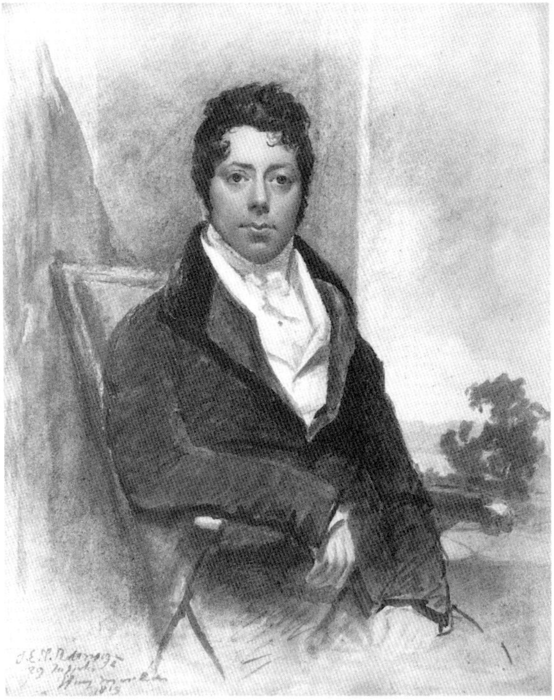

273*

JOSEPH GRIMALDI

J.E.T. Robinson

Pencil and watercolour on wove paper 29.8 x 24.5
INSCR: 'J.E.T. Robinson / 29 Suffolk St / Hay Market / 1819' (watercolour b.l.)
INV: RW 277 (artist unknown); CKA 277; Gift 189
PROV: Presented by Mrs Bryan, 1869

Grimaldi, sitting in a chair, wears a blue velvet jacket, a white waistcoat, and a white stock with a gold pin. A label on the frame reads: 'Jo Grimaldi at the age of 38.' In 1819, however, he was 41.

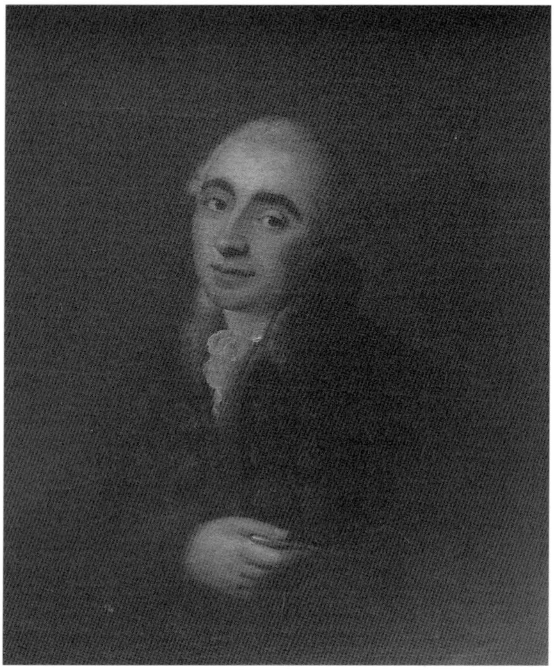

274
JOSEPH GRIMALDI

Unknown Artist

Oil on canvas 73.7 x 63.5
INV: RW/CKA 454; Gift 189
PROV: Presented by Mrs Bryan, 1869

Grimaldi wears a dark blue coat trimmed with fur and gold.

Joey – 'the King of Clowns' – performed for some 45 years at Sadler's Wells. 'If to be loved by a whole nation in his lifetime and to live in all men's fancies a hundred years after is a true sign of greatness, then Joseph Grimaldi has a right to be reckoned among our famous men.' (M. Willson Disher, *Clowns and Pantomimes*, 1925)

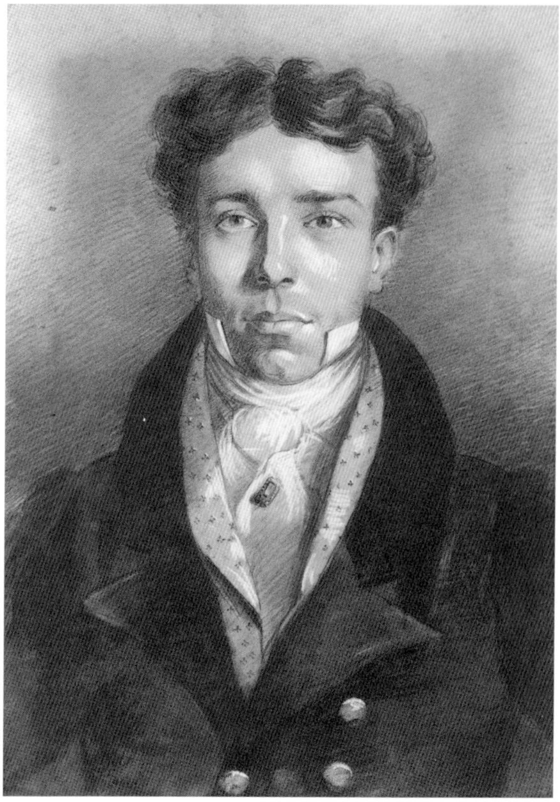

275
JOSEPH SAMUEL GRIMALDI

Unknown Artist

Black and white chalk on brown wove paper 54.6 x 40
INV: RW/CKA 310; Gift 189
PROV: Presented by Mrs Bryan, 1869

Head and shoulders, looking out at spectator.

The sitter, who was the son of the great clown Joseph Grimaldi, had some modest success in pantomimes on the London stage, but fell into a life of dissipation and died young.

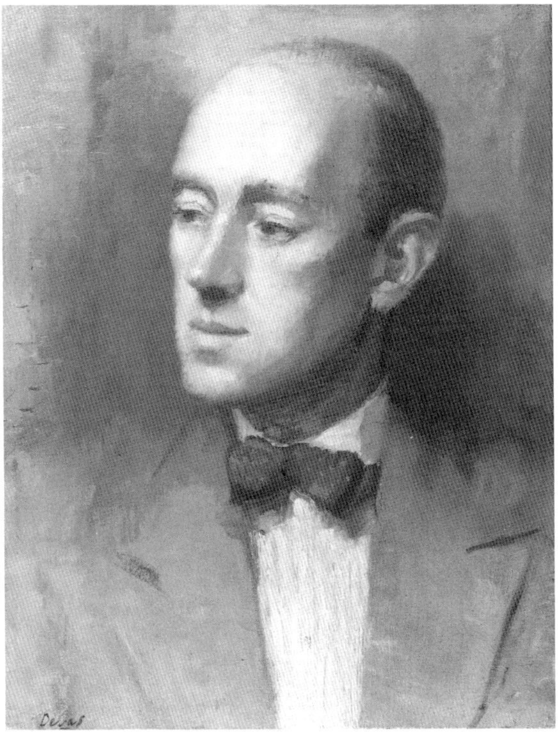

276

SIR ALEC GUINNESS

Anthony Devas

Oil on canvas 45.5 x 35
INSCR: 'Devas' (red paint b.l.)
INV: GCL 746; Gift 918
PROV: Presented by the sitter, 1985
EXH: 1949 Port Sunlight (44)?

Sir Alec wears a grey coat and a bow tie.

A portrait of Alec Guinness by Devas was included in the 1949 Port Sunlight exhibition. It is likely to have been No. 276.

Sir Alec became a member of the Garrick Club in 1948. He is one of the most creative and brilliant actors of the 20th century.

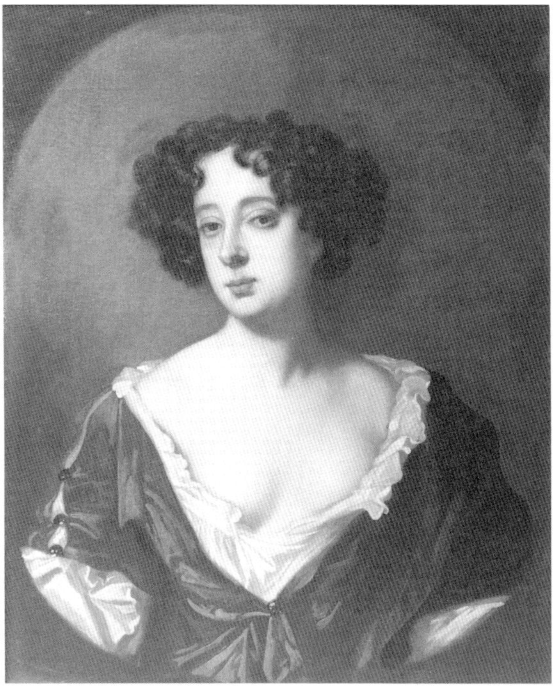

277

TRADITIONALLY CALLED

ELEANOR GWYN

Simon Verelst (?)

Oil on canvas 77 x 63
INV: Mathews 12 (by Sir Peter Lely);
RW 10 (by Sir Peter Lely?); CKA 10
PROV: Charles Mathews
EXH: 1833 London (12)
REL: NPG 2496, oil on canvas 76.2 x 63.5 s., called Nell Gwyn
LIT: Patmore, p. 272; Patmore says that there were two or three portraits of Nell Gwyn in Mathews's collection including one by Lely, presumably No.277; Griffiths, pp. 298–99

The sitter wears a loose maroon dress, with button below breasts and secured over shoulders with gold buttons. She has a loose and revealing white chemise. Her hair is brown and curly, parted in the middle. A familiar provocative image.

The National Portrait Gallery picture is signed by Verelst and has been dated by David Piper to about 1690. John Payne Collier visited Mathews's Gallery on 18 February 1832 and reported that this picture seemed 'to have been christened by Mathews, both as to person and painter'. Nell Gwyn had red hair.

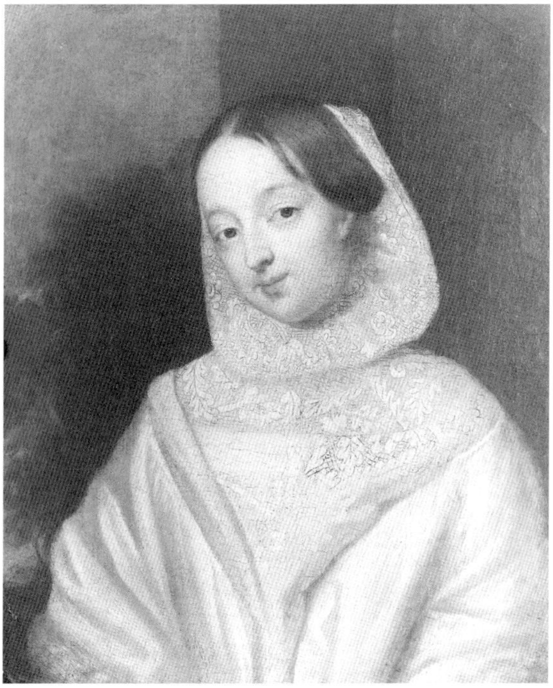

278

CALLED

NELL GWYN

Gervase Spencer (?)

Oil on canvas 33.6 x 28.6

INV: Mathews 39; RW (Marie Stuart by unknown);

CKA 299 (called Mary Queen of Scots by unknown)

PROV: Charles Mathews

EXH: 1833 London (39)

ENGR: Gervase Spencer (?) etching 7.4 x 5.7,

inscr: in plate 'GS 1753' (b.c.), 'Nell Gwyn' (b.r.)

LIT: Patmore, p. 272 (see No. 277)

The sitter wears a white, fur-trimmed jacket over a white garment. She has a white stole around her neck and over the back of her head.

There are two small etchings signed GS in the plate, said to be of Nell Gwyn and apparently by Gervase Spencer; they are both similar in feeling to Gervase Spencer's self-portrait in the British Museum. One reproduces this composition, and the other shows the sitter seated half-length to right, looking to front, hair tied back with a centre parting, pearls around the neck, and a low-cut frock with bows at breast and shoulder. There is no evidence at present that Gervase Spencer, a miniaturist working in the mid-18th century, produced oil paintings.

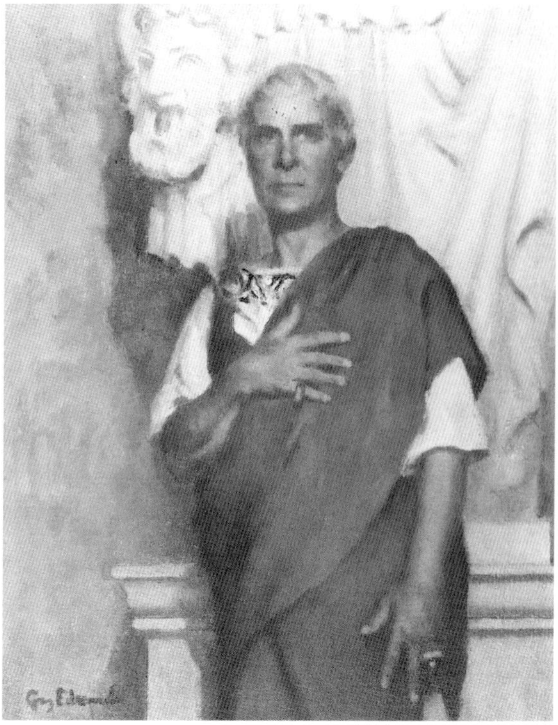

279

NICHOLAS HANNEN

as Seneca in *Quo Vadis*

by Hugh Stanislaus Stange,

after Henryk Sienkiewicz

Mrs F.M. Grey-Edwards

Oil on canvas 35.5 x 28

INSCR: 'Grey Edwards' (brown paint b.l.)

INV: GCL 696

PROV: Unknown

Seneca wears a white and red toga and two rings.

This picture presumably dates from about 1933, the probable date of its companion picture, the portrait of Athene Seyler (see No. 736). There seems to be no evidence that Nicholas Hannen played Seneca in *Quo Vadis* in 1933 or any other year. However, Hannen took a repertory of 13 plays to the Middle East in 1933, and *Quo Vadis* may have been one of them.

Hannen became a member of the Garrick Club in 1922. Probably the picture was painted from a photograph.

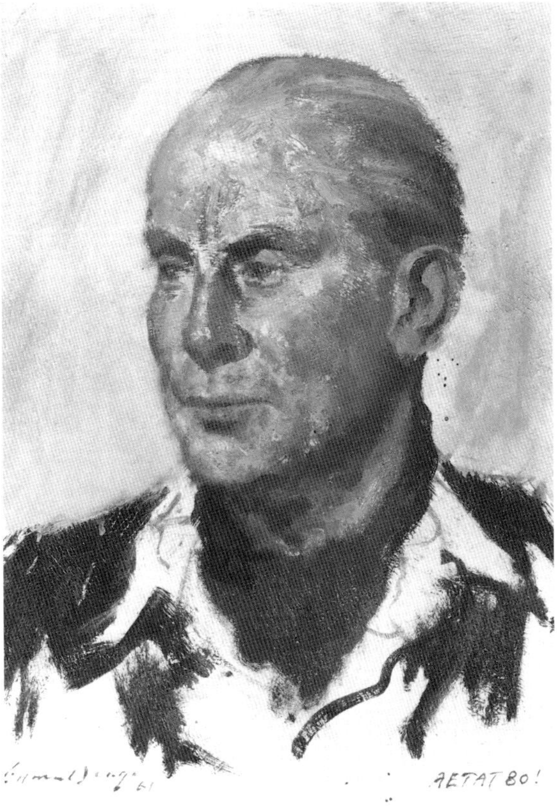

280

NICHOLAS HANNEN

Edward Seago

Oil on canvas 43.2 x 33
INSCR: 'Edward Seago. / 61' (brown paint b.l.);
'AETAT 80!' (brown paint b.r.)
INV: GCL 719; Gift 848
PROV: Presented by Athene Seyler, 1973

Hannen wears an unfinished dark jacket, an open white shirt, and a red cravat.

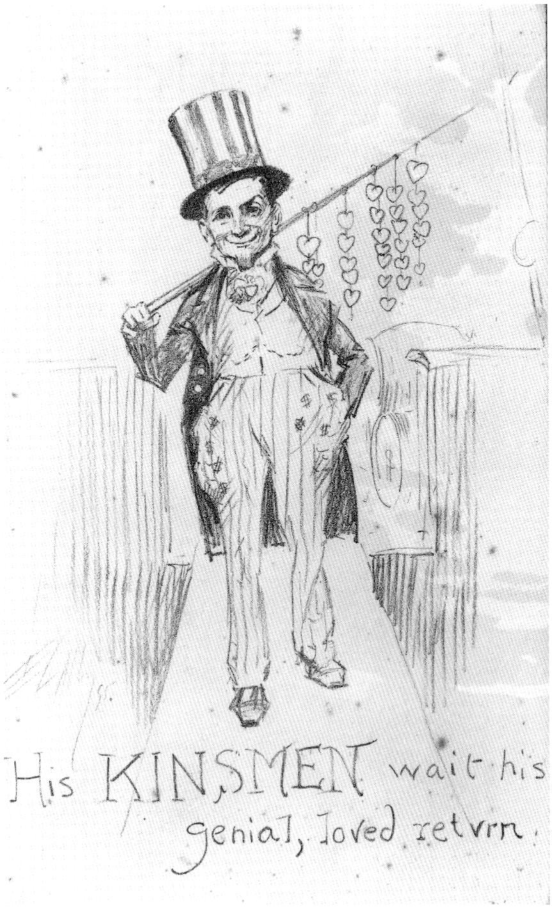

281

SIR JOHN HARE

as 'Uncle Sam'

Edward Austin Abbey

Caricature, black chalk on wove paper 43.2 x 26.7
INSCR: 'E A Abbey '95.' (black chalk b.l.);
'His KINSMEN wait his genial, loved return!'
(black chalk b.c.); 'Caricature of Sir John Hare
drawn by Edwin Abbey R.A., as frontispiece to
the Menu Cards on the occasion of the dinner
given by the Club called The Kinsmen
to welcome Hare home after his tour
in the United States' (on verso)
INV: CKA 531; Gift 434
PROV: Presented by A.R. Prideaux, 1936

Hare walks down a gangplank from a ship; over his shoulder he holds a stick on which are are six strings with dangling hearts. His striped trousers have dollar signs over the pockets.

The iconography presumably refers to the hearts Hare had won in America and to the dollars he brought back with him.

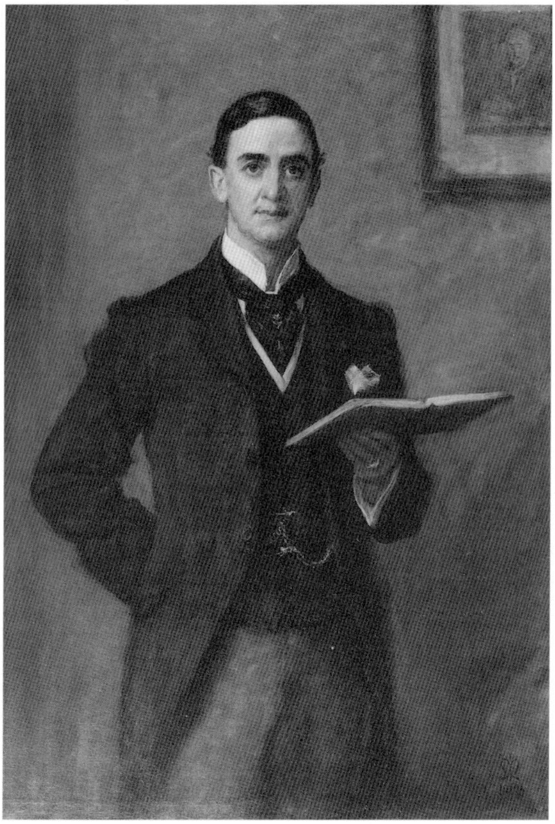

282
SIR JOHN HARE

Sir John Everett Millais
Oil on canvas 125.1 x 87
INSCR: '18 JM [monogram] 93' (dark brown paint b.r.)
INV: CKA 246
PROV: Bequeathed by the sitter, 1921
EXH: 1893 R.A. (18)

Hare, standing three-quarter length, wears a morning suit with a grey waistcoat and brownish trousers, and holds a book in his left hand. There is a framed print of Reynolds's Thrale portrait of David Garrick (see No. 241), a reference to Hare's status as one of the leaders of his profession. See also. No. 323.

Sir John became a member of the Garrick Club in 1868.

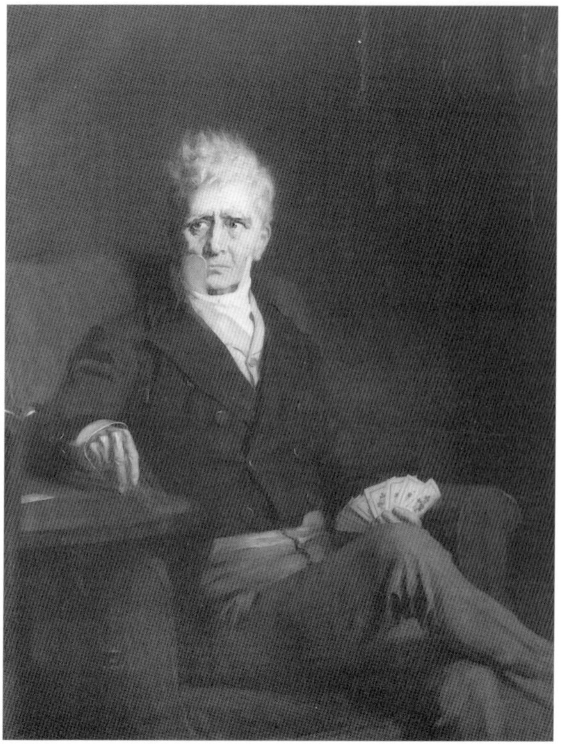

283
SIR JOHN HARE
as Lord Kildare in *A Quiet Rubber*
by Charles F. Coghlan

Hugh Goldwin Riviere
Oil on canvas 118.7 x 91.4
INSCR: 'H Riviere 1908' (black paint b.l.)
INV: CKA 598
PROV: Presented by 152 members, 1908
EXH: 1908 R.A. (898)

Hare as Lord Kildare has heavy character make-up, with white hair brushed up. He wears grey trousers with a creamy yellow band at the waist, a dark brown cut-away coat with double row of large brass buttons, and a yellow waistcoat with gold buttons. He sits in a red-brown padded armchair.

Coghlan's comedietta, adapted from a French farce, *La Partie de Picquet*, was first given at the Court Theatre on 8 January 1876, with Hare as the impecunious Lord Kildare.

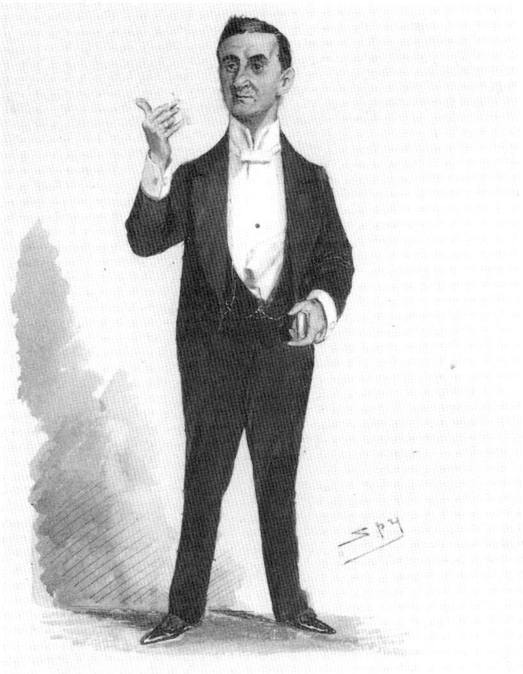

284

SIR JOHN HARE

Sir Leslie Ward ('Spy')

Caricature, pencil with pen and black ink, watercolour and white body colour on blue wove paper 35.5 x 22.5
INSCR: 'SPY' (black chalk b.r.)
INV: CKA 589; Gift 377
PROV: Presented by Sir Squire Bancroft, 1917
LIT: Pub. *Vanity Fair* 1 March 1890, inscr: 'Mr John Hare'

Hare wears evening dress, with a gold watch-chain and cuff-links. He holds a cigarette case or lucifer in his left hand and a cigarette in his right. The peculiar extension of the thumb was presumably a characteristic gesture.

285

GEORGE D. HARLEY

as Caled in *The Siege of Damascus*
by John Hughes

Samuel De Wilde

Oil on canvas 37 x 28.5
INV: Mathews 178; RW/CKA 255
PROV: John Bell; Thomas Harris; Harris sale, Robins 12 July 1819 (63); Charles Mathews
EXH: 1833 London (178); 1962 Chichester (22)
ENGR: Wilson for Bell's British Library 1 June 1793, line 11.5 x 8, pub. Bell's *British Theatre* (1797), vol 12, with the quotation 'What, dost thou frown too!'

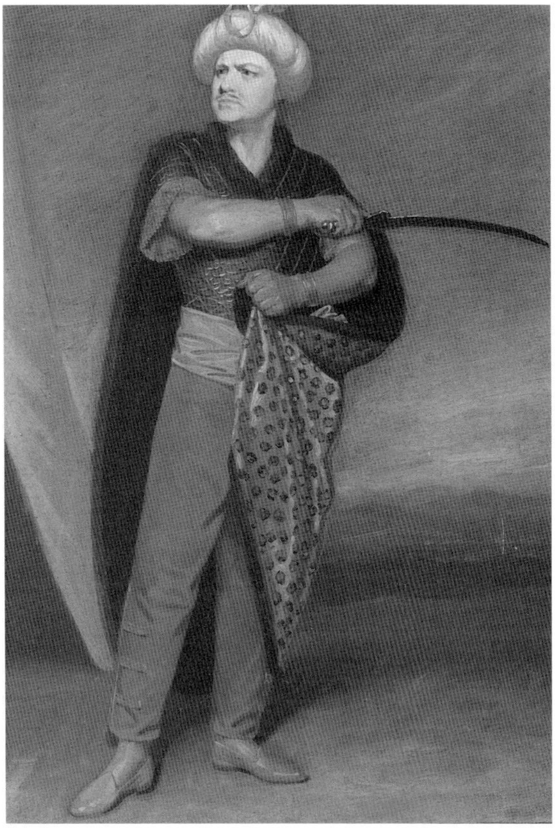

285 *George D. Harley as Caled*

Caled is the general of the Saracen army and has been laying siege to Damascus, held by the Christians under Eumenes. Act V, scene 2, shows the Christian camp outside Damascus: 'A Valley full of Tents; Baggage and Harness lying up and down amongst them. The Prospect terminating with Palm trees and Hills at a Distance.' Caled has broken his word and attacked the Christians. He is confronted by Phocyas and asks why he frowns. Phocyas tells him he has broken his promise and kills him. The text calls for Caled to carry a lance rather than a scimitar as shown by De Wilde.

Caled wears a white turban bound with gold with a crescent moon at the front, yellow slippers and sash, scarlet trousers, and fish-scale body armour decorated with diagonal scarlet stripes; this armour conceals a shirt of which we see the short scarlet and yellow sleeves, and a dark fur collar that matches the trimming of his long leopardskin cloak.

Hughes's tragedy was originally performed at Drury Lane on 17 February 1720. Harley never played Caled in London. The last performance of the play in London in the 18th century was at Covent Garden on 28 February 1785, when Henderson played Caled.

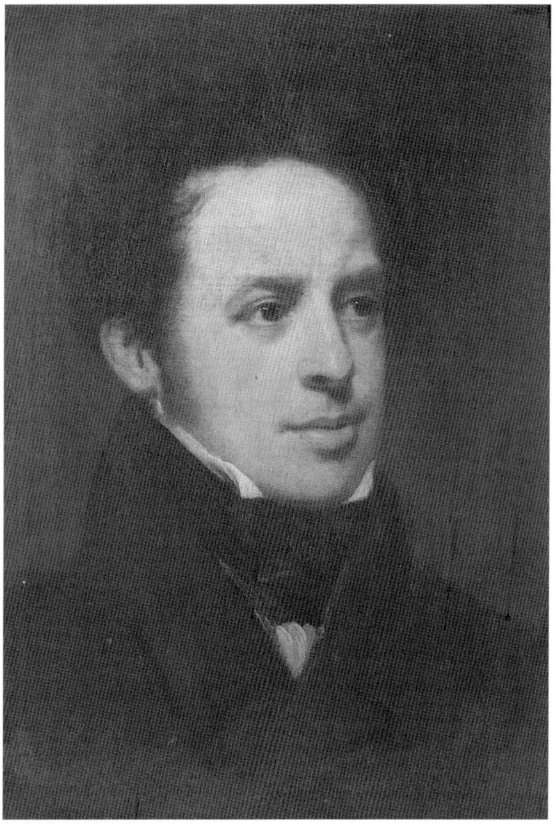

286

JOHN PRITT HARLEY

George Clint

Oil on canvas 48.9 x 34.3
INV: Mathews 121; RW/CKA 463
PROV: Charles Mathews
EXH: 1833 London (121)

Harley wears a brown jacket, white shirt, and dark stock.

Mathews describes this picture as 'a sketch' in his catalogue, so it is probably not the picture that Clint exhibited at the Royal Academy in 1832 (92), although it may be a related study. It has the appearance of having been cut down. There is a rather earlier but similar portrait by Samuel Drummond, engraved by J. Thomson and published by J. Asperne on 2 April 1821.

Harley was an original member of the Garrick Club in 1831.

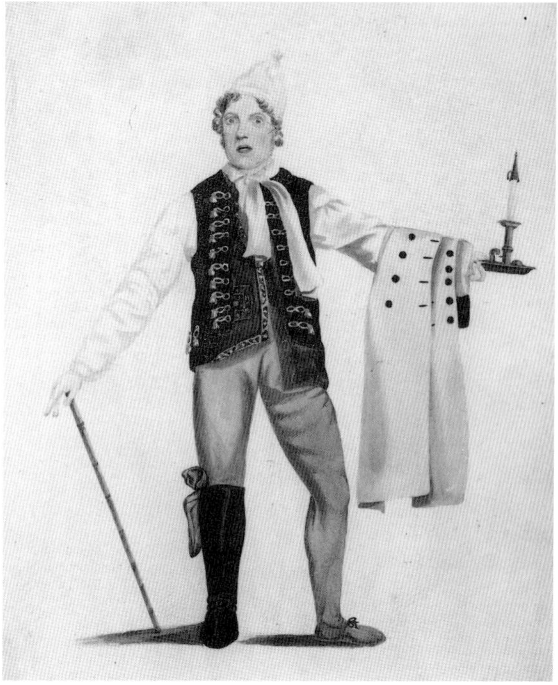

287

JOHN PRITT HARLEY

as Somno in *The Sleepwalker or Which is the Lady?* by Walley Chamberlain Oulton

Unknown Artist

Pencil and watercolour on wove paper 31.1 x 23.5
INSCR: (Pencil inscr. along bottom erased)
INV: Mathews 286; RW 189 (unknown sitter and artist); CKA 189
PROV: Charles Mathews
EXH: 1833 London (286)

In this somewhat crude drawing Somno is shown at the end of his first sleepwalking scene in Act II, scene I. Having powdered the sleeping Mr Alibi's hair, Somno exits with Alibi's coat and cane. He should also be carrying Alibi's hat and the dressing-box containing the hair powder. Somno is 'ludicrously dressed' in a white nightcap; on his left leg is a brown shoe with a black lace and a red stocking has been pulled up to the thigh over his brown breeches. On his right leg he has a high black boot with green cloth stuffed in the top. Over a white shirt he wears awry a black waistcoat with silver frogging over a green one trimmed with blue and white. No. 469 shows Somno at the beginning of the scene.

Oulton's farce was first given at the Haymarket on 15 June 1812, with Charles Mathews as Somno (see No. 469, a performance which no doubt inspired this drawing). Harley does not seem to have played the part in London.

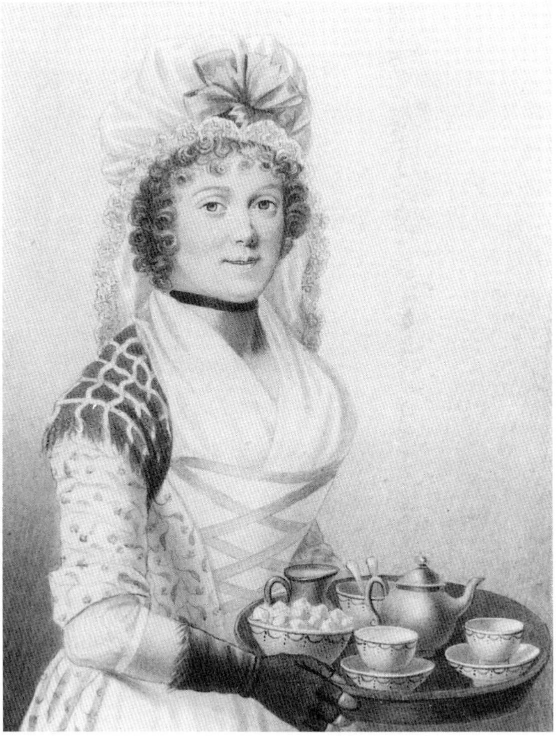

288
SARAH HARLOWE
as Dorothy in *Heigho for a Husband*
by Francis Godolphin Waldron

Sylvester Harding (after)

Pencil and pen and grey ink with watercolour
on wove paper 11.6 x 9.3
INSCR: 'MRS HARLOWE IN HEIGHO FOR A HUSBAND'
(pen and brown ink on mount b.l.);
'BY S. HARDING' (pen and brown ink on mount b.r.)
INV: RW/CKA 562; Gift 35
PROV: Presented by the sitter, 1836
ENGR: Edward Harding pub. Thos. Arrowsmith
1 November 1794, stipple and line 13.8 x 9.7
[The drawing may be copied by Edward Harding
(1776–96) from a design by his father, Sylvester Harding
(1745–1808), in preparation for the engraving, which
it resembles most precisely, down to the shading;
the inscription lower right appears to be an
acknowledgement of the original artist
rather than a signature.]

Dorothy is 'discovered setting out Tea-Things' in Act III, scene I, 'Old Rackrent's house'. Charlotte and Maria are visiting a country town hoping to find husbands. They have exchanged roles, and Maria is playing the maid. Charlotte's allure has attracted the attention of Edward, the son of Justice Rackrent, and Rackrent's housekeeper Dorothy has invited Maria to tea to pump her for information about her 'mistress'. She says that everything is ready for Maria: 'I think I ha' goyen all in apple pye order' (the line quoted on the engraving).

Dorothy holds a breakfast tray. She wears grey mittens and a white dress with a floral pattern in red and green, the stomacher laced with blue ribbon. She has a brown and white shawl and a white mob-cap with a blue bow.

Waldron's comedy was first given by the Drury Lane company at the Haymarket on 14 January 1794, with the author's wife, Sarah Harlowe, as Dorothy. She gave 13 performances as a member of the Drury Lane company and a further four during the Haymarket's own summer season. The play was an alteration of Waldron's earlier play, *Imitation; or, The Female Fortune Hunters*, first performed at Drury Lane on 12 May 1793.

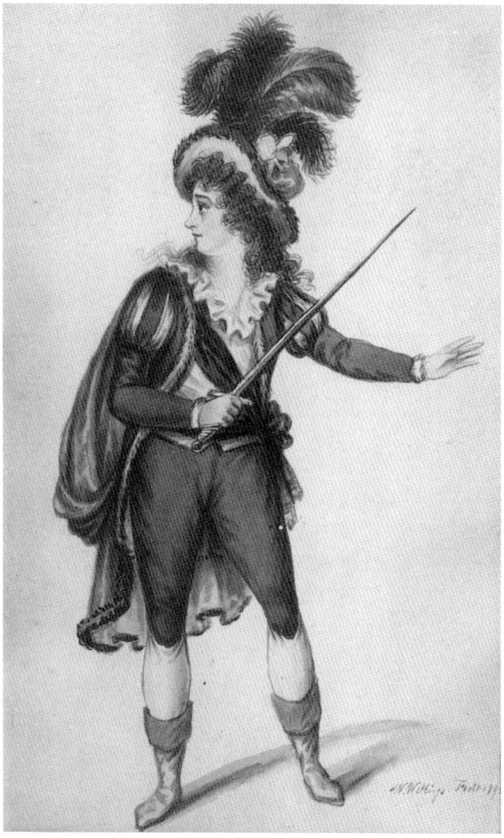

289
SARAH HARLOWE
as Adeline
in *The Battle of Hexham or The Days of Old*
by George Colman the Younger

William Wellings

Pen and grey ink with watercolour on wove paper 21 x 13.3

INSCR: 'W. Wellings. Fecit 1795' (pen and grey ink b.r.)
INV: RW/CKA 534; Gift 52
PROV: Presented by the sitter, 1839

Adeline dons 'mens cloaths' to look for her husband, a Lancastrian. She fights for Queen Margaret at the Battle of Hexham, and in the aftermath of the Yorkist victory she is detained by a group of bandits. Their leader, Gondibert, turns out to be her lost husband. Adeline wears her male garb throughout the play, but the sword and pose in Wellings's drawing suggest the flight from the Battle of Hexham in Act I, scene 4, 'The field'. Adeline is depicted in Wellings's characteristic grey monochrome with touches of pink and blue – pink for the top of her boots and blue for the lining of her cloak. The vaguely Tudor costume is crowned by a wide-brimmed hat with tall black ostrich plumes.

The younger Colman's three-act comedy, with music by Dr Samuel Arnold, was first given at the Haymarket on 11 August 1789 with Mrs Goodall as Adeline. It was a popular piece over five summer seasons. Mrs Harlowe played Adeline for the first time on 9 June 1795 at the Haymarket, repeated the performance on 18 July, and did so again on 12 occasions over the next four summer seasons. Wellings's drawing therefore celebrates one of her first two appearances in the role.

290
HENRY HARRIS
as Cardinal Wolsey in *Henry VIII*
by William Shakespeare

Unknown Artist (after John Greenhill)

Oil on canvas 35.5 x 30.6
INV: RW 295 (artist unknown);
CKA 295 (Joseph Harris); Gift 81
PROV: Earl of Orford, Strawberry Hill; Strawberry Hill sale, 1842 bt. Ralph Willett by whom presented, 1842

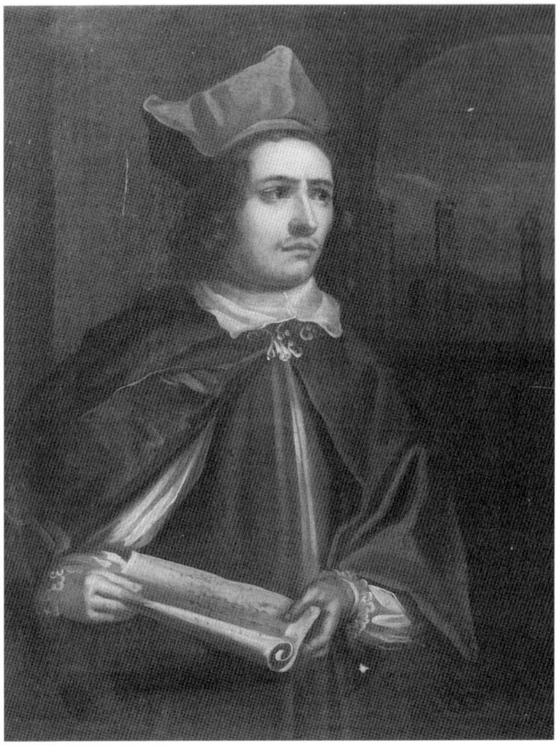

290 *Henry Harris as Cardinal Wolsey*

EXH: 1980 Twickenham
ENGR: Edward Harding after a drawing by Sylvester Harding pub. E. & S. Harding 29 August 1793, stipple and line 12.1 x 9.7; same plate used for Waldron's *Shakespearean Miscellany* (1802)
REL: Magdalen College, Oxford, chalks on laid paper 39.4 x 32.4 s. & d: 'JG del: 1664' (b.l.) (to l.); Ashmolean Museum, chalks on buff laid paper 40 x 29.5
LIT: J. Woodward, *Tudor and Stuart Drawings* (1951), p. 52; *Gentleman's Magazine* (May 1842), NS 18: 377

Harris, as Wolsey, wears the red robes of a cardinal. Towers are visible to the right. The document he holds is 'the account of all that world of wealth I have drawn together for mine own ends', which is the immediate cause of his downfall.

The Garrick Club picture was probably copied from a lost engraving either of the Magdalen or the Ashmolean version, and was commissioned by Walpole for his gallery of historical portraits at Strawberry Hill. It is much more stilted than either of the original drawings, and is reversed. The Garrick Club version has a moustache added; it also shows a view of different buildings through the arch behind the sitter.

Harris played Wolsey in a production of *Henry VIII* that opened at Lincoln's Inn Fields on 22 December 1663, with Thomas Betterton in the title role.

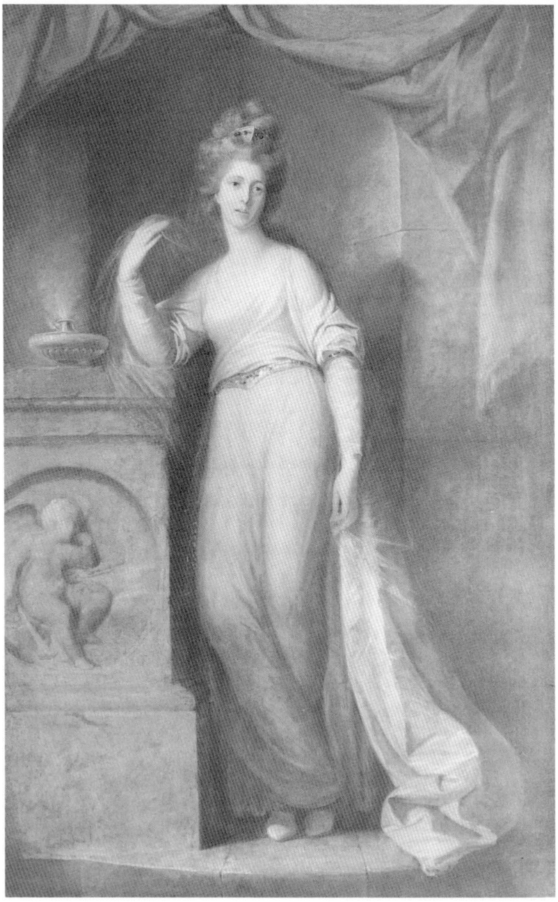

291*
ELIZABETH HARTLEY
as Hermione in *The Winter's Tale*
by William Shakespeare

Angelica Kauffmann

Oil on canvas 204.2 x 130.8
INV: Mathews 75 (no character); RW/CKA 438 (no character)
PROV: Thomas Harris; Harris sale, Robins 12 July 1819 (49)
'Mrs Hartley, as Hermione in the Statue-Scene, original by / Sir J Reynolds'; Charles Mathews
EXH: 1833 London (75)
LIT: Patmore (p. 273) mentions two portraits of Mrs Hartley. The other was No. 71 in the Mathews catalogue showing her in *The Distrest Mother*, a drawing by Sherwin. It may have been sold in 1835 and was not in the Garrick Club collection when the 1909 catalogue was compiled; Lady Victoria Manners & Dr G.C. Williamson, *Angelica Kauffmann R.A., Her Life and Her Work* (1924), p. 190

Hermione poses in neo-classical splendour, her right hand raised in an elegant gesture, her elbow resting on a pedestal. She wears a gold tiara and a long white dress of classical design, the long sleeves pulled up at the elbow with gold bands decorated with green and red stones.

Mrs Hartley played Hermione only once, at Covent Garden on 12 March 1774. There are also two prints of her in the role, in the statue scene. On 11 March 1779 at Drury Lane she recited a monody on the death of Garrick, appearing as the Tragic Muse in a repetition of the statue scene in *The Winter's Tale*. The cupid on the stone pedestal to the left is similar to another cupid by Angelica Kauffmann, engraved by C.A. Porporati in 1790.

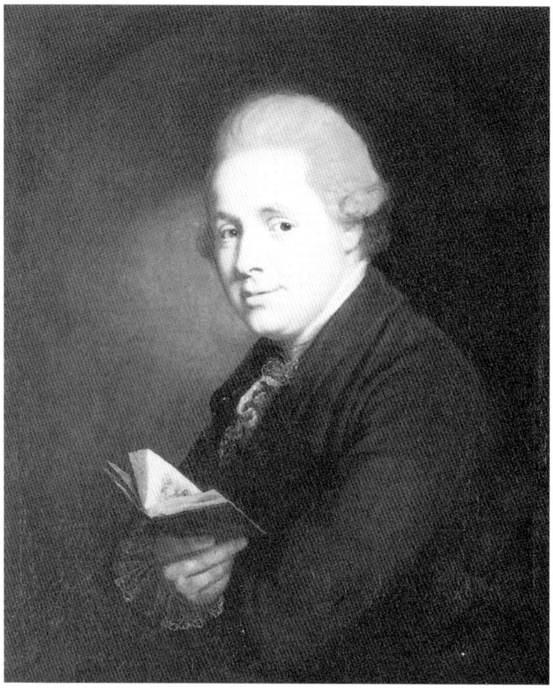

292
JOHN HENDERSON

Thomas Beach

Oil on canvas 74.3 x 61.6
INSCR: 'T Beach pt. 1773' (brown paint b.l.)
INV: RW/CKA 452; Gift 256
PROV: Presented by Sir Squire Bancroft, 1897
LIT: E.S. Beach (1934), p. 64 (No. 162); Derek Hudson, 'A "new look" for the Garrick Club Pictures', *The Connoisseur* (June 1969), 171: 78–92; Fitzgerald, p. 210

Henderson wears a brown jacket and a high white stock. He holds a book in his right hand.

Henderson made his début on the London stage as Shylock at the Haymarket on 11 June 1777 and was widely acclaimed. Regarded by his contemporaries as second only to Garrick, he died of a heart attack in the prime of his career at the age of 38.

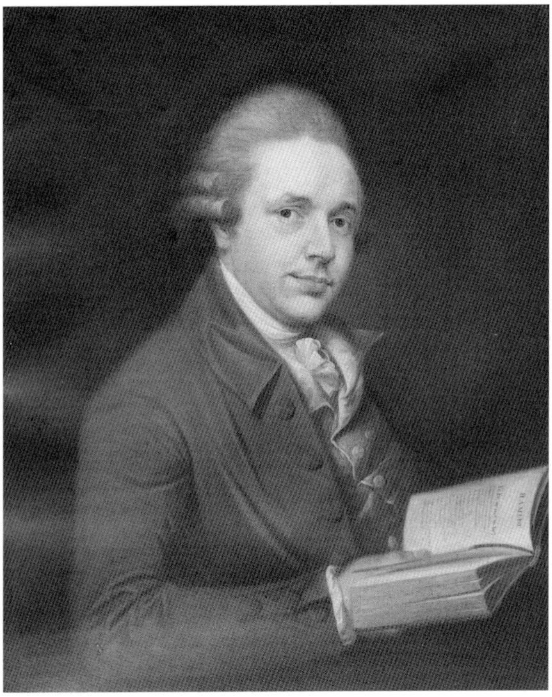

293
JOHN HENDERSON

Thomas Gainsborough (after)

Oil on canvas 77.5 x 63
INSCR: 'HAMLET / To be or not to be'
(black paint, on book b.r.)
INV: Mathews 40 (artist unknown); RW/CKA 24
PROV: Charles Mathews
EXH: 1833 London (40)
REL: Original, painted for John Ireland 1772/73 but lost.
Bust engraved by J. Jones as a plate to the
European Magazine pub. J. Sewell 1786.
There are several versions, those of the bust only
perhaps copied from the engraving (see No. 294).
A version sold at Christie's 8 July 1938 (119) has the actor
resting his left wrist on the edge of the open book.
LIT: Waterhouse, *Gainsborough* (1958), p. 73 (No. 361)

Henderson holds his book open at Hamlet's famous soliloquy in Act III, scene I. He wears an olive green coat over a cream waistcoat.

Henderson's portrayal of Hamlet, a role he first acted in London at the Haymarket on 26 June 1777, was not particularly impressive, but in other roles, such as Iago, he earned plaudits as 'a truly great actor'.

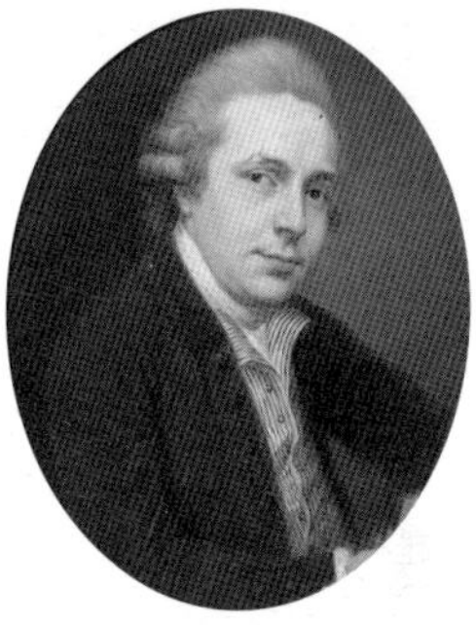

294
JOHN HENDERSON

Thomas Gainsborough (after)

Oil on panel 21 x 17 (oval)
INV: Mathews 361 (artist unknown);
RW/CKA 236 (artist unknown)
PROV: Charles Mathews
EXH: 1833 London (361)
LIT: Waterhouse, *Gainsborough* (1958), p. 73 (No. 361)

Henderson wears a brown jacket and yellow waistcoat with vertical brown stripes. This is the same portrait type as No. 293 with a different jacket and waistcoat. The corner of Henderson's book is just visible bottom right.

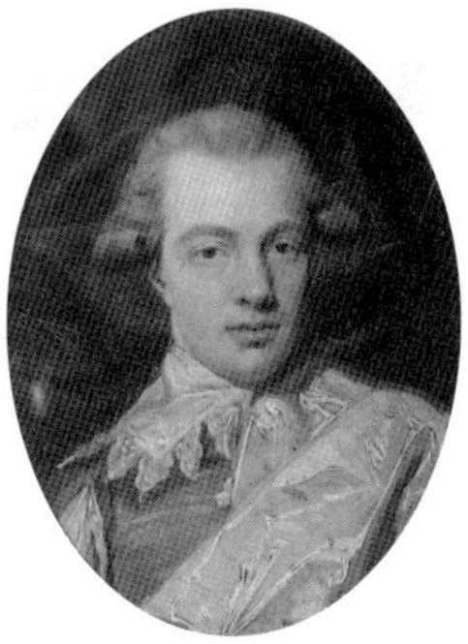

295
JOHN HENDERSON

William Hamilton (attr.)

Oil on canvas 19.5 x 15 (oval)
INV: RW/CKA 427C (artist unknown)
PROV: Presented by C. J. Welch, 1839 (possibly the
'Theatrical Portrait by Gainsborough' that is recorded as
having been given, but is not included in the list of Gifts)

Henderson is dressed in Van Dyck costume with lace collar, blue doublet, slashed at right shoulder to reveal white, and a yellowish cloak over his left shoulder. An etching by Samuel Ireland after Hamilton shows the sitter with the same flyaway hair and Van Dyck costume, half-length to right, turning head and looking to front, pulling cloak around right arm with left hand to the right.

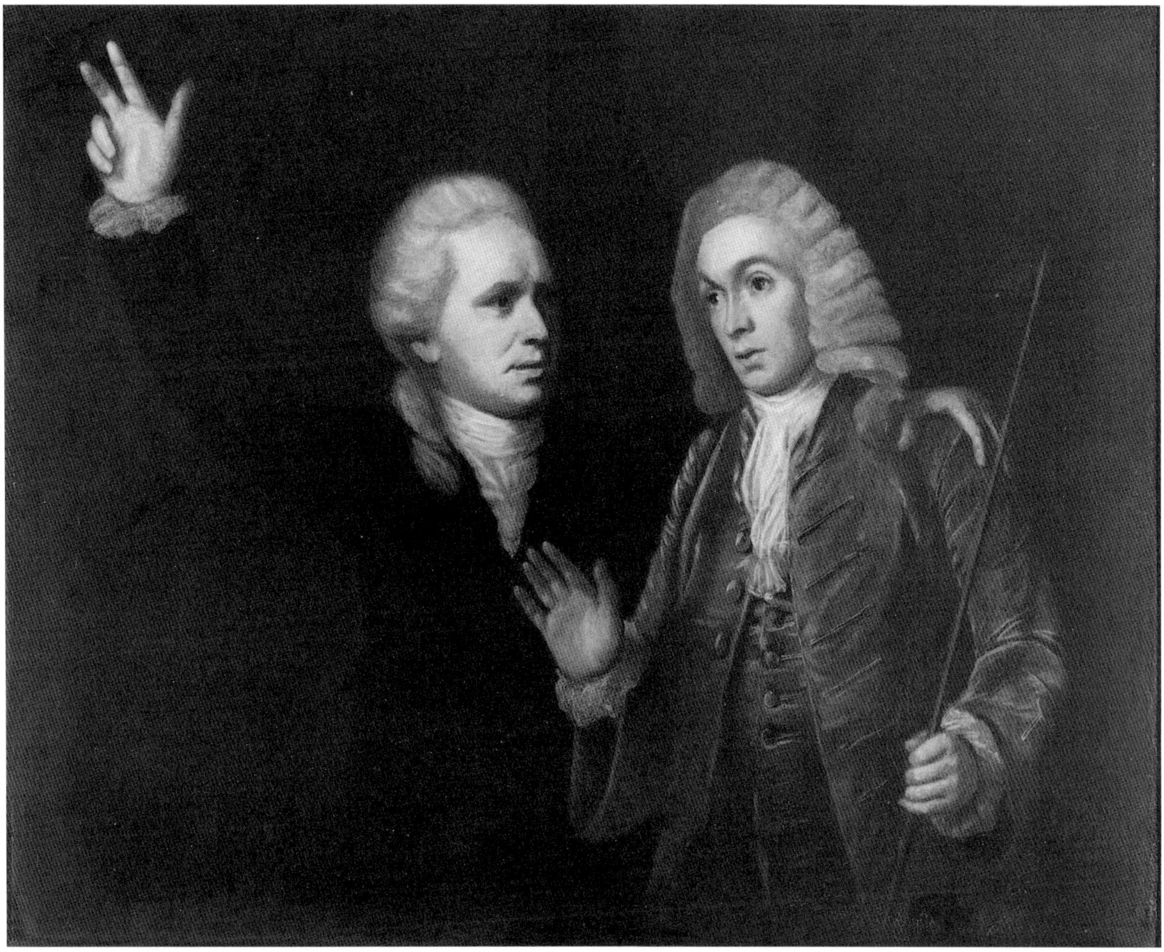

296
JOHN HENDERSON as Hamlet
and *RICHARD WILSON* as Polonius
in *Hamlet*
by William Shakespeare

Benjamin Wilson (attr.)

Oil on canvas 99 x 124.5
INV: RW/CKA 22 (attributed to George Romney); Gift 131
PROV: Presented by Andrew Archedeckne, 1855
REL: Somerset Maugham Collection,
Royal National Theatre, 16, oil on canvas 89 x 69 (f.l.)
LIT: Mander & Mitchenson, pp. 231–33

Hamlet stands on the left in black. Polonius wears a dark rust collarless jacket with turned-back cuffs and a rust velvet waistcoat.

Henderson first played Hamlet in London at the Haymarket on 22 June 1777 with Edwin as Polonius. He first acted Hamlet to Wilson's Polonius at Covent Garden on 26 April 1779.

This somewhat unsatisfactory picture has been attributed to Benjamin Wilson by Ellis Waterhouse. The Somerset Maugham version is even more inept, and has the appearance of being a copy of the Garrick Club picture, with legs added. See also No. 293.

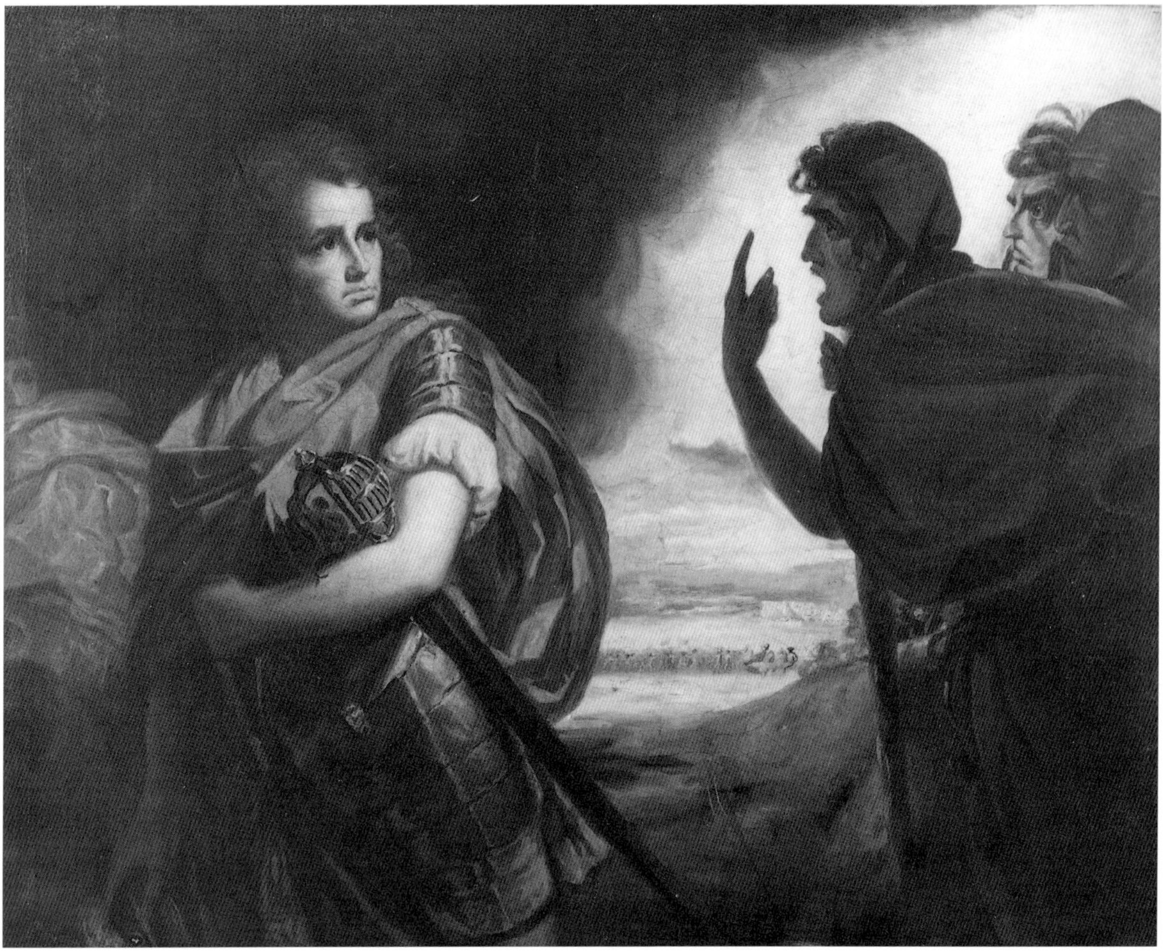

297

JOHN HENDERSON, Mr PEILE,
COCKRAN JOSEPH BOOTH,
ANN PITT and *RICHARD WEBB*
as Macbeth, Banquo and the Three Witches
in *Macbeth* by William Shakespeare

George Romney (after?)

Oil on canvas 69.2 x 87.6
INV: Mathews 52; RW 435 (by George Romney);
CKA 435 (after George Romney)
PROV: Charles Mathews
EXH: 1833 London (52); 1964 London [2] (21)
REL: Original, oil on canvas 138.5 x 163.8 lost, prov: Henderson; won in a raffle at the Unincreasables Club by W.J. Long; Long sale, Christie's 28 June 1890 (116); Folger Library, oil 42.5 x 52, prov: Montmartre Gallery 1927, Engr: John Jones pub. J. Jones 1 December 1787 (proof dated 19 May 1787), mezzotint 41 x 50.2
LIT: Fitzgerald, p. 210; Pressly, *Folger*, 124

Macbeth (Henderson) stands left of centre, his right hand holding a hat with a red feather. A flowing red mantle partly covers his armour. Banquo (Peile) has a silvery grey cloak, and the three witches wear dark red and fuscous garments. In the background a distant battle rages.

Henderson sat for Romney on 13, 18, 24 and 29 October and 23 December 1780. He played Macbeth twice in the autumn of 1780, on 23 October and on 20 November. If Romney bothered to portray the other characters accurately, he seems to have chosen the cast of 20 November, as the First Witch on 23 October was John Quick. The Witch addressing Henderson is not Quick but could be Booth. Mathews's catalogue suggests that two of the Witches were portraits of Charles Macklin and Anthony Pasquin. Henderson had first played Macbeth in London for his own benefit at Drury Lane on 31 March 1778.

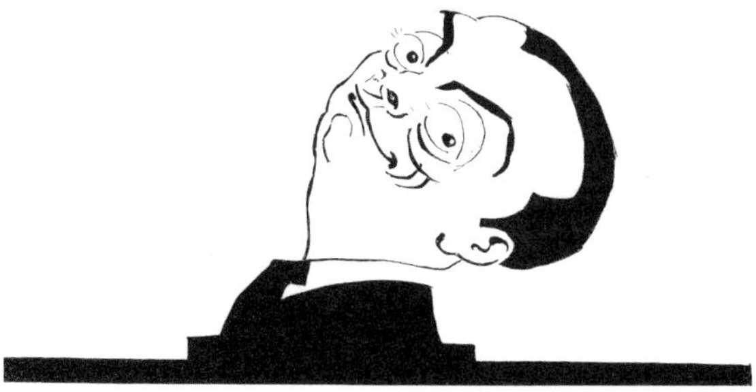

298
LESLIE HENSON

Unknown Artist

Caricature, pen and black ink on wove paper
28.2 x 21.5 (17.5 x 11.8 sight)
INV: GCL 698
PROV: Unknown

Henson, an actor and producing manager, joined the Garrick Club in 1948.

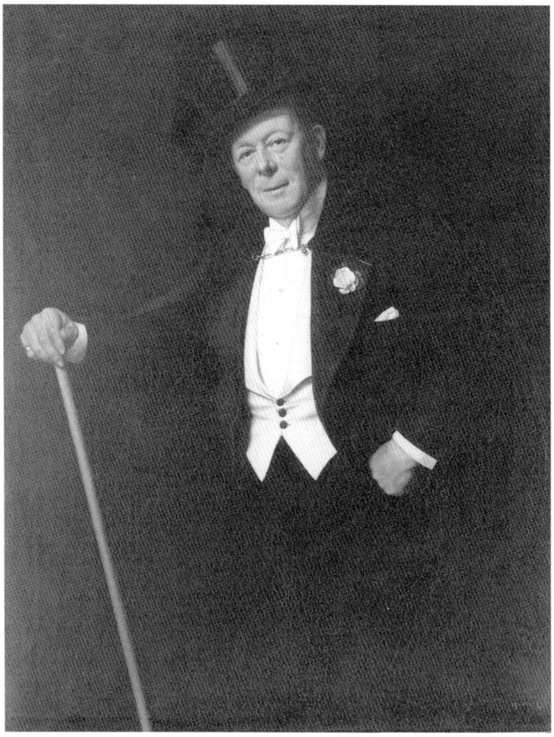

299
SIR SEYMOUR HICKS
as Lucien in *The Man in Dress Clothes*
by Seymour Hicks

Maurice Codner

Oil on canvas 129.5 x 106.7
INSCR: 'MAURICE CODNER / 1930.' (red paint b.r.)
INV: GCL 687; Gift 771
PROV: Presented by John Whitworth Codner, 1959
EXH: 1931 R.A. (585) 'Seymour Hicks as "The Man in dress clothes"'; 1959 London

Lucien wears evening dress. In his buttonhole there is a gardenia, and in his left lapel the légion d'honneur. The property gardenia was mounted and framed, and hangs below the portrait in the Garrick Club bar, having been presented by Codner in 1950. Hicks became a member of the Garrick Club in 1899.

Seymour Hicks's adaptation of André Picard and Yves Mirande's play opened at the Garrick Theatre on 22 March 1922, and ran for 232 performances, until 14 October 1922. It was presented by David Belasco and Charles B. Cochran and directed by Hicks, whose wife, Ellaline Terris, wrote and arranged the music.

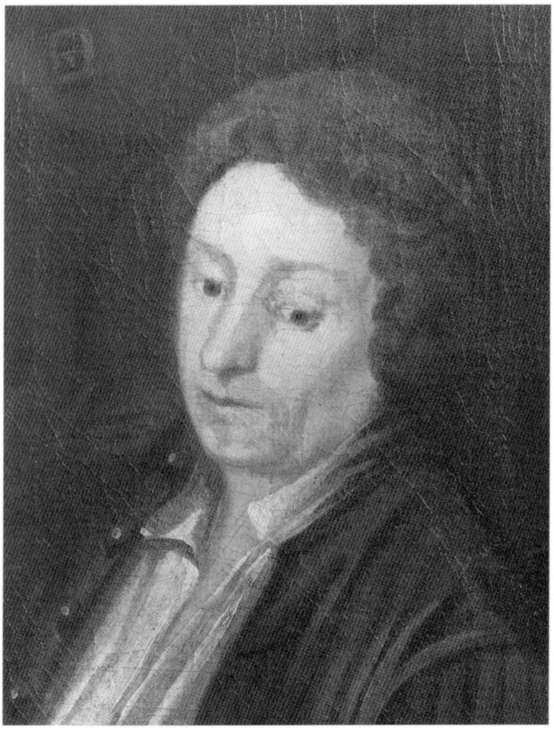

300

JOHN HIPPISLEY

Unknown Artist

Oil on canvas 48.9 x 33
INV: Mathews 134 (by Hogarth);
RW 300 (by Hogarth); CKA 300
PROV: Charles Mathews
EXH: 1833 London (134)
LIT: Fitzgerald, p. 145

Hippisley wears an ill-fitting brown curly wig, a brown jacket with gold buttons, and a loose white shirt.

This likeness bears a vague similarity to the portraits of Hippisley as Peachum in the various versions of Hogarth's scene in *The Beggar's Opera*. He was the original Peachum at Lincoln's Inn Fields on 29 January 1728.

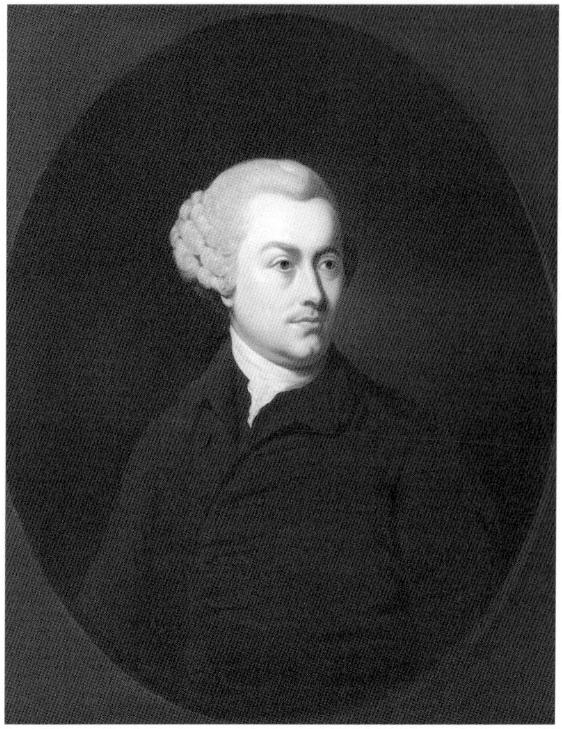

301

CHARLES HOLLAND

Hugh Barron (copy after?)

Oil on canvas 35 x 28
INV: Mathews 378 (artist unknown);
RW 263 (artist unknown); CKA 263
PROV: Charles Mathews
EXH: 1833 London (377)
ENGR: John Raphael Smith pub. J.R. Smith 1771, mezzotint 13.3 x 11.4

Holland, shown head and shoulders in a feigned oval, wears a brown jacket and waistcoat.

After his début at Drury Lane on 13 October 1755 as Oroonoko, Holland played dozens of leading and supporting roles until his death in 1769, at the age of 36. He died of smallpox, supposedly caught from a rat that ran across the stage.

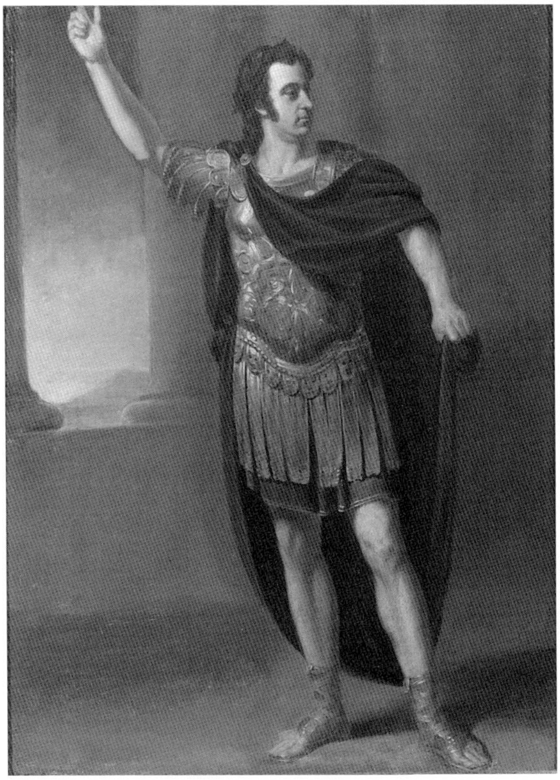

302

JOSEPH GEORGE HOLMAN

as Alexander in *The Rival Queens*

by Nathaniel Lee

Samuel De Wilde

Oil on canvas 37.3 x 28.4
INV: Mathews 180; RW/CKA 243
PROV: John Bell; Charles Mathews
EXH: 1833 London (180)
ENGR: Chapman for Bell's British Library 19 April 1793, line 10.5 x 8, pub. Bell's *British Theatre* (1797), vol I, with the quotation ''Tis False. Great Ammon gave me birth' (I, 2)

The play is set in Babylon; the scene for Act IV, scene 2 is 'The Palace with Alexander &c. discovered at a banquet'. Alexander wears the laurel wreath from Act II when, after his conquest of Babylon, he enters 'in a Triumphal Car drawn by Black Slaves' to the chorus of 'See the conq'ring hero comes', later used by Handel in *Judas Maccabæus*. Despite Alexander's insistence that his followers adopt Persian garb, he does not seem to be wearing it himself. Instead, he has blue and gold sandals, a blue tunic under a gold embossed metal cuirass with gold skirt and shoulder pieces, and a long green cloak. A row of columns stand on a raised base, and a distant hill is seen beyond.

Lee's tragedy was first performed at Drury Lane on 17 March 1677, with Hart as Alexander. Holman played the part for the first time at Covent Garden on 12 April 1792, for his benefit. The rival queens, Statira and Roxana, were played by Mrs Merry and Mrs Pope. This was evidently the performance celebrated by De Wilde, as Holman's next appearance in the role was not until 6 May 1794.

303

JOSEPH GEORGE HOLMAN

as Chamont in *The Orphan*

by Thomas Otway

Samuel De Wilde

Oil on canvas 35.5 x 27.3
INV: Mathews 93; RW/CKA 266
PROV: John Bell; Charles Mathews
EXH: 1833 London (93); 1962 Chichester (23); 1971 Northampton (4)
ENGR: J. Thornthwaite for Bell's British Library 27 May 1791, line 10.8 x 7.6, pub. Bell's *British Theatre* (1797), vol 9; Philippe Audinet for Bell's British Library 1791, line 11.1 x 8; Richard B. Godfrey pub. J. Bell June 1792, stipple 23 x 17.6, inscr: 'Mr Holman in the Character of Chamont. / Engraved by Godfrey, from the original Picture which was painted from life by De Wilde, / from the Orphan, by Otway, / in the Celebrated Edition of Bell's British Theatre, which is now Publishing, Periodically'; Anon. printed for C. Cooke 29 August 1807, line (own hair replaces wig); Anon., line 11.8 x 8 (reversed, own hair)

Chamont is an excitable young man who takes an unnatural interest in the virginity of his sister, Monimia, the Orphan. Chamont, standing full-length and drawing his rapier, wears black shoes, white stockings, fawn breeches, a long, dark green military jacket lined in red, and a white waistcoat edged in red.

The quotation on the Thornthwaite engraving reads:

> – curse on thy scandalous age,
> Which hinders me to rush upon thy throat
> And tear the root up of that cursed bramble.

Otway's tragedy was originally performed at Dorset Garden Theatre in February 1680. Holman's first performance as Chamont was at Covent Garden on 4 February 1785, when Alexander Pope played Castalio and Miss Younge Monimia. Holman acted the role 16 times over the next two seasons, and then reappeared, with William Farren as Castalio and Mrs Esten as Monimia, on 27 October, 5 November and 9 December 1790.

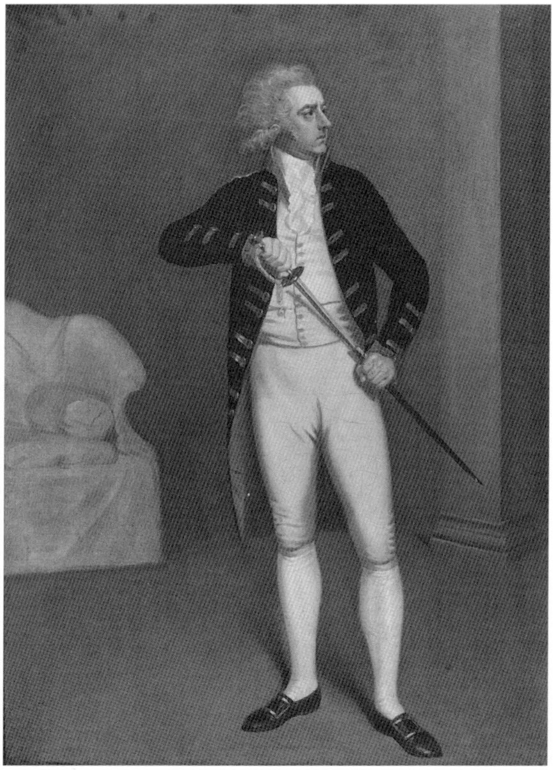

303 *Joseph George Holman as Chamont*

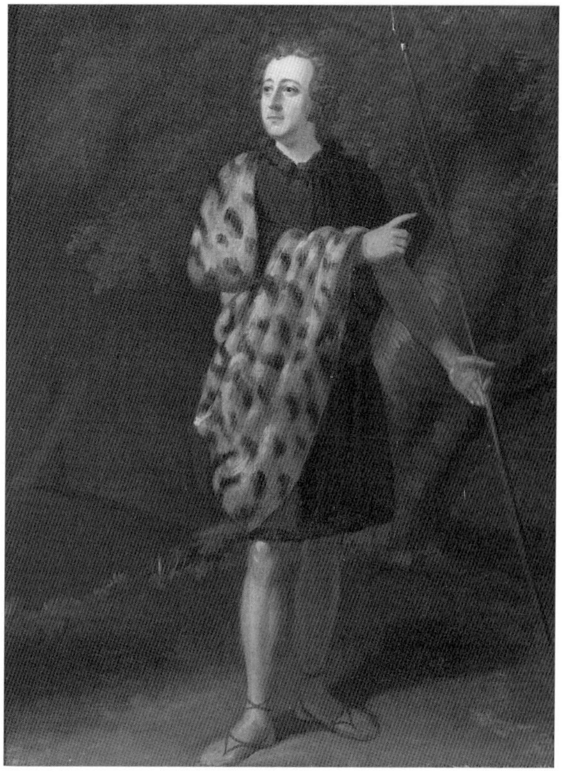

304 *Joseph George Holman as Cyrus*

These were the last performances before De Wilde painted his picture.

There is another portrait of Holman as Chamont by De Wilde in the Museum of London (A7463) oil on canvas 40.6 x 29.8 (full-length, standing, slightly to right, with right arm extended to left).

304

JOSEPH GEORGE HOLMAN

as Cyrus in *Cyrus*

by John Hoole

Samuel De Wilde

Oil on canvas 37 x 28.8

INV: Mathews 384 (by Harlow); RW/CKA 257

PROV: John Bell; Leigh & Sotheby's 25 May 1805 (280) bt. Charles Mathews

EXH: 1833 London (384)

ENGR: Philippe Audinet for Bell's British Library 30 June 1795, line 11.4 x 8.2; Wilson 30 June 1795, line 11.75 x 8.2, pub. Bell's *British Theatre* (1797), vol 24

The set for Act I, scene 2, is 'a Grove; outside of a small building of simple Architecture, representing the dwelling of Mithranes'. Cyrus enters on the line 'Can it be possible?' (quoted on the engraving). Mithranes, his supposed father, has just told him, after 20 years, that he is really Cyrus, heir to the throne of Media. He was taken from his mother, Mandane, as a baby because Astyages, the king, had a vision revealing that the child would take his throne. At the end of the play, after a series of confusions, Cyrus does become king. His appearance is described by his true father, Cambyses, also absent for 20 years, in Act IV, scene I: 'His auburn locks flow'd graceful down his back, / Quick was his piercing eye; his manly shoulders / A spotted tyger's dreadful spoils adorn'd, / Some gallant trophy of his sylvan wars.' Apart from his 'tyger' cloak, Cyrus wears a green tunic trimmed with dark fur, and strapped sandals. There is no textual reference for the gesture towards his spear; perhaps he is indicating the weapon that killed his 'tyger'.

Hoole's tragedy was first performed at Covent Garden on 3 December 1768, with William Powell as Cyrus. The only time Holman played the role was at Covent Garden on 30 May 1794, evidently the occasion commemorated by De Wilde with one of his last contributions to Bell's *British Theatre*.

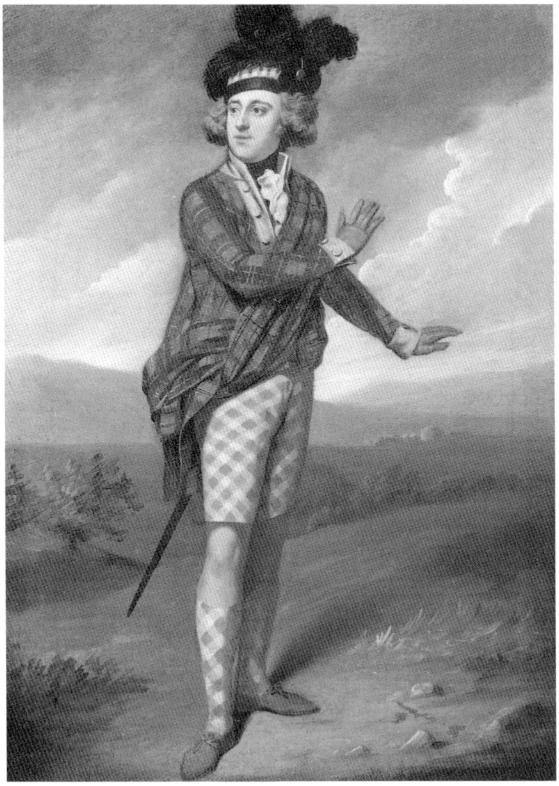

305
JOSEPH GEORGE HOLMAN
as Young Norval in *Douglas*
by John Home

Samuel De Wilde

Oil on canvas 37.2 x 28.7
INV: Mathews 175; RW/CKA 221
PROV: John Bell; Charles Mathews
EXH: 1833 London (175)
ENGR: William Bromley for Bell's British Library
7 April 1791 (De Wilde ad viv. pinxt.)
pub. Bell's *British Theatre* (1797), vol 3;
Ferguson pub. W. Jones for *British Theatre* 1792;
William Bromley printed for C. Cooke 1807
as pl. to *British Drama*

Young Norval has saved the life of Lord Randolph, whose wife, Lady Randolph, discovers from the old shepherd Norval that the young man is her long-lost son, the heir to her first husband, the brave Douglas (see No. 67). Young Norval is about to be given this startling piece of news by Lady Randolph, who will then go on to reveal herself as his mother. He asks, 'Say, who was my Father' (quoted on the engraving). He has a Scottish plumed bonnet trimmed with black fur and black feathers. He wears stockings of red and white check to below the knee, and matching short breeches cut off above the knee (there are pentimenti where the breeches were painted wider at both sides). His red and green tartan jacket has pale blue facings and cuffs, and he wears a matching plaid over his shoulder and tied round the waist.

Home's tragedy was first performed in London at Covent Garden on 14 March 1757, with Spranger Barry as Douglas. Holman's only appearance in the part was at Covent Garden on 20 December 1792. That was some time after De Wilde painted his picture – a circumstance especially interesting as the engraving bears the unusual inscription indicating that the artist painted the portrait from life.

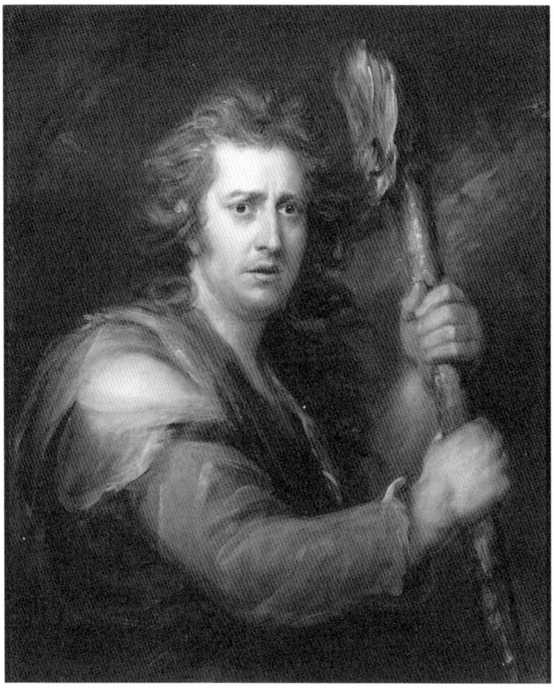

306
JOSEPH GEORGE HOLMAN
as Edgar in *King Lear*
by William Shakespeare

Gainsborough Dupont

Oil on canvas 73.7 x 62.2
INV: Mathews 154; RW/CKA 412
PROV: Thomas Harris; Harris sale, Robins 12 July 1819 (14);
Charles Mathews
EXH: 1833 London (154); 1982–83 London (127)
LIT: The *Morning Herald* 22 March 1794; Patmore, p. 272;
John O'Keeffe *Recollections* (1826), 2: 326–27;
Hayes 1968; Fitzgerald, p. 214

Edgar, wearing yellowish-brown rags, grasps a rough branch.

This picture was mentioned in the *Morning Herald* of 22 March 1794 as already finished. Holman played the part five times during the 1793–94 season to Alexander Pope's Lear; the first performance that season, on 6 January 1794, was the first time it had been played since 4 November 1791. Productions of the play became less frequent as George III's periodic bouts of madness made its subject matter awkwardly relevant.

O'Keeffe's description of Holman sitting for this picture is the only published eye-witness account of an 18th-century theatrical portrait being painted:

> About this time [1793] my old friend Quick brought me to see Gainsborough Dupont, the portrait-painter, at his house in London-street. Mr Harris had employed him to paint, for himself, the principal performers of Covent Garden theatre, in their most distinguished characters. In the front room were many portraits in different states of forwardness. The Right Hon. William Pitt was on the easel; Governor Hastings standing on the floor; and against the wall Quick, in Spado, with his little pistol, which he calls his barrel-organ, in his hand. On the door of the back drawing-room opening, I was surprised, and a little shocked, to see the room darkened, and lighted by a large lamp hanging from the centre of the ceiling: there stood a man half naked, a ghastly figure, with a blanket round him, staring wildly, holding a pole in his stretched-out hand. This was Holman, in the character of Edgar, mad Tom; Gainsborough Dupont was painting him. I heard it was the custom of the latter to paint much by lamp-light.

Mathews's notation suggests that the scene shows a moment in Act III, scene 6, when Edgar, feigning madness, speaks the line: 'Avaunt, you curs.'

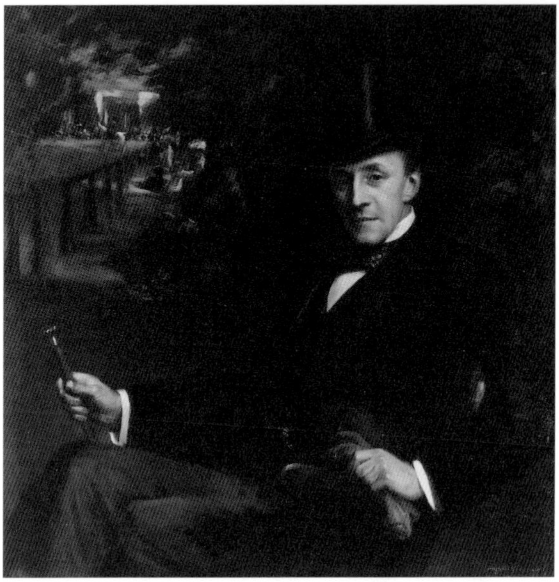

307*

ANTHONY HOPE [SIR ANTHONY HOPE HAWKINS]

Henry Glazebrook

Oil on canvas 129.5 x 129.5
INV: GCL 674; Gift 727
PROV: The sitter; by descent to his nephew Dr Anthony Fielding; presented to the Garrick Club by Fielding's daughter, Mrs B.H. Churchill, 1953

Hope, seated in an armchair, wears a black coat, a white shirt with a bow tie, and a black top hat. In his hands he holds gloves and a cane. To the left is a view of Decimus Burton's Hyde Park Corner Screen.

Under the pseudonym of Anthony Hope, the sitter wrote a number of successful novels, the most popular of which is *The Prisoner of Zenda* (1894), which was turned into a play by Edward Rose and produced successfully at the St James's Theatre in January 1896. During World War I he was with the Editorial and Public Branch Department, and was knighted for his services in 1918. He was for many years on the committee of the Society of Authors and was its chairman for four years.

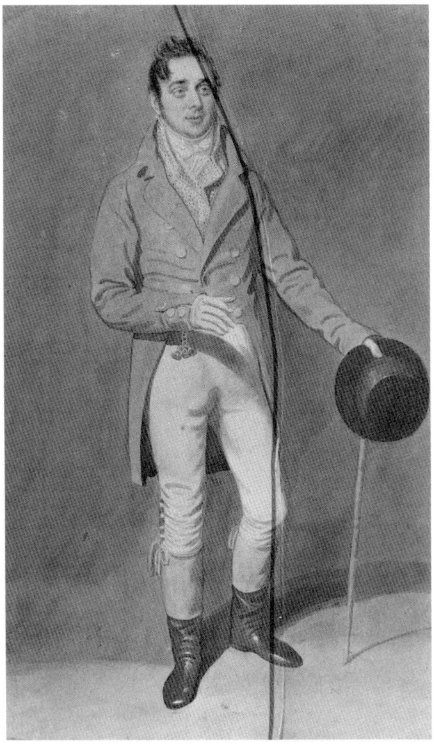

308
CHARLES EDWARD HORN
as Meddle in *Up all Night* by Samuel James Arnold

Samuel De Wilde

Pencil and watercolour on wove paper 37 x 23.5
INSCR: 'S De Wilde delin / Jany 1811.' (pencil b.l.)
INV: Mathews 243; RW/CKA 58C
PROV: Charles Mathews
EXH: 1833 London (243)

Meddle's outdoor clothes and bedraggled hair suggest that he is shown in Act III. Meddle holds a yellow glove in one hand, and a stick and tall black hat in the other. He wears black boots with tall brown tops, cream breeches with bows at the knees, a faded pink cutaway coat, and a white waistcoat embroidered in speckled green and red.

De Wilde's diary records that Horn sat for him in this character on 13 January and that he took the drawing to 'Hill' on 16 January 1811.

Arnold's three-act comic opera, with music by M.P. King, was first given at the Lyceum on 26 June 1809. Horn was the original Meddle in a popular production that was given 39 times in its first season. It was his first appearance there, and he was subjected to some withering appreciation from the *Monthly Mirror*: '...his voice is little, but pretty, and capable of improvement; his acting is incapable of deterioration.'

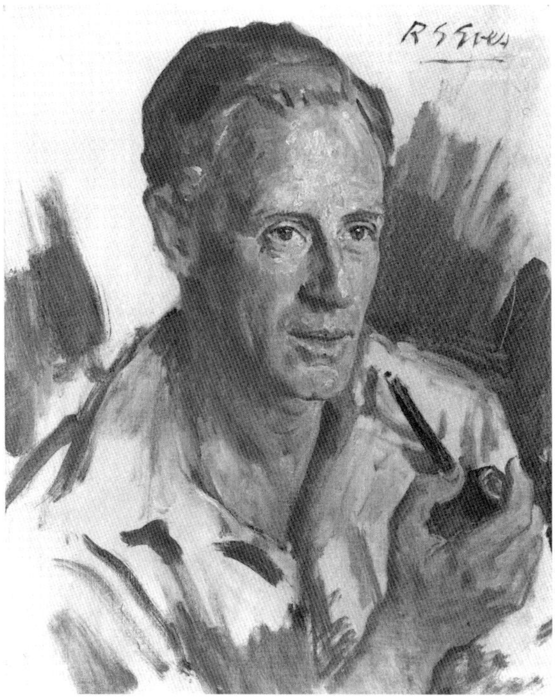

309
LESLIE HOWARD

Reginald Grenville Eves

Oil on canvas 50.5 x 40.5
INSCR: 'R G Eves' (brown paint t.r.)
INV: GCL 686
PROV: Purchased for £50 from the artist's widow, 1952
REL: R.S.P.P. 1938 (26), oil on canvas n.s., inscr: 'R.G. Eves' (b.l.), bust, to r. with pipe in r. hand, but more to r. than the Garrick Club picture; photo in NPG archive oil on canvas n.s., inscr: 'R G Eves' (t.r.) bust, head slightly to r. looking to front, pipe in r. hand; Theatre Museum (TM100), oil on canvas 50.5 x 40.5, bust with pipe in r.h., open-necked shirt and jacket

Eves painted a number of pictures of Leslie Howard and exhibited four of them. The earliest was shown R.S.P.P. 1937 (197) and reproduced in *The Times* 19 November 1937, Coll: Mrs Dale-Harris in 1982; Howard is shown half-length, wearing a suit, seated to front with fingers folded together. The second was exhibited R.A. 1938 (100) Huddersfield Art Gallery oil on canvas 76.2 x 63.5; Howard is shown half-length, seated to left, wearing a suit, cigar in his right hand, arms on arms of chair. The third, similar to the Garrick Club picture, is mentioned above; and the fourth was exhibited posthumously R.S.P.P. 1941 (92). A sketch was sold at Phillips, 30 October 1973 (70), oil on canvas 76.2 x 63.5; lots 3 and 23 in the same sale were drawings of Leslie Howard by Eves, lot 23 signed and dated 1940.

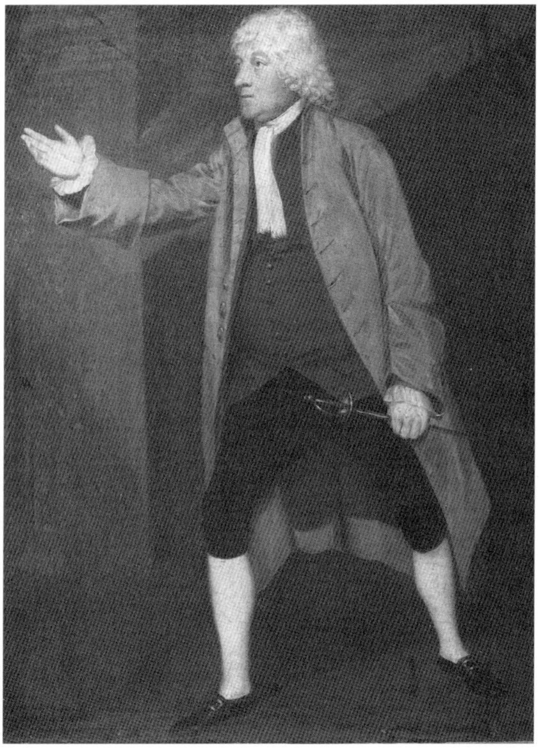

310
THOMAS HULL
as Jarvis in *The Gamester*
by Edward Moore

Samuel De Wilde

Oil on canvas 36.8 x 28.4
INV: Mathews 349 or 355; RW/CKA 261
PROV: John Bell; Charles Mathews
EXH: 1833 London (349 or 355)
ENGR: William S. Leney for Bell's British Library 4 August 1792, line 10.5 x 7.6, pub. Bell's *British Theatre* (1797), vol 10; Anon. as plate to *British Drama* (1817), line

Jarvis, Beverley's old family retainer, urges his master to return home to his long-suffering wife: 'Alas, Sir! forget your griefs and let me lead you to her' (quotation on the engraving). Jarvis wears a buff coat with brown lining over a brown waistcoat and black breeches. His white wig is uncombed.

Edward Moore's tragedy was first performed at Drury Lane on 7 February 1753. Hull last played Jarvis at Covent Garden on 25 September 1786.

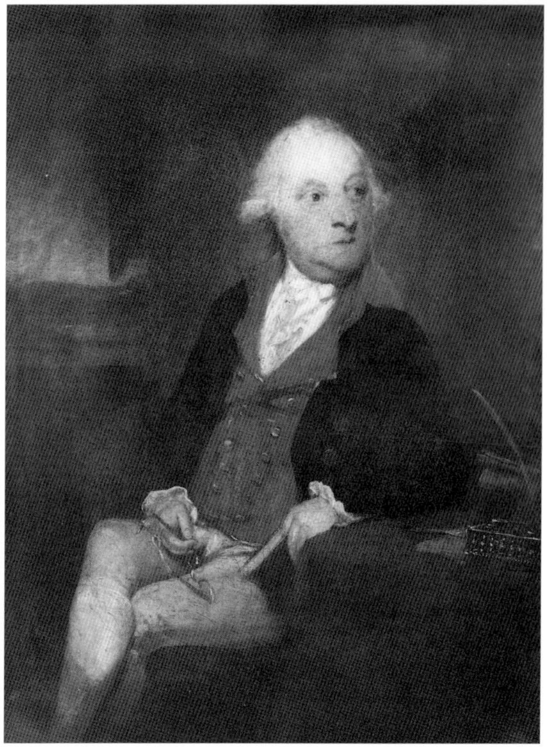

311
THOMAS HULL

John Graham

Oil on canvas 50.1 x 41.2
INV: Mathews 349 or 355 (artist unknown);
RW/CKA 121 (artist unknown)
PROV: Bell sale, Leigh & Sotheby's 25 May 1805 (279); Charles Mathews
EXH: 1833 London (349 or 355)
ENGR: William S. Leney pub. G. Cawthorn 10 January 1797, stipple 9.8 x 7.6 (oval)

Hull, seated in a chair, has a powdered wig and wears white stockings, yellow breeches, a dark blue jacket with high red collar, and a red waistcoat.

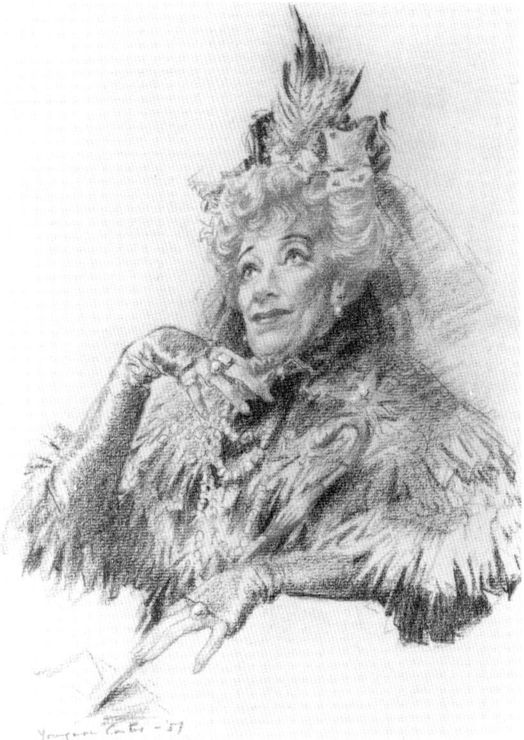

312

MARTITA HUNT

as Aurelia, The Madwoman of Chaillot
in *The Madwoman of Chaillot*
by Jean Giraudoux

Philip Youngman Carter

Black and red chalk on brown laid paper
40.6 x 30.5
INSCR: 'Youngman Carter '51'
(black chalk b.l.)
INV: GCL 711
PROV: Unknown

A half-length study. Aurelia holds her umbrella, and wears one of her extraordinary hats, mittens, and a selection of rings.

Martita Hunt made her first appearance on the American stage as the Madwoman of Chaillot, opening at the Belasco Theatre, New York, on 27 December 1948. She toured in the part during 1950 then opened at the St James's, London, on 15 February 1951.

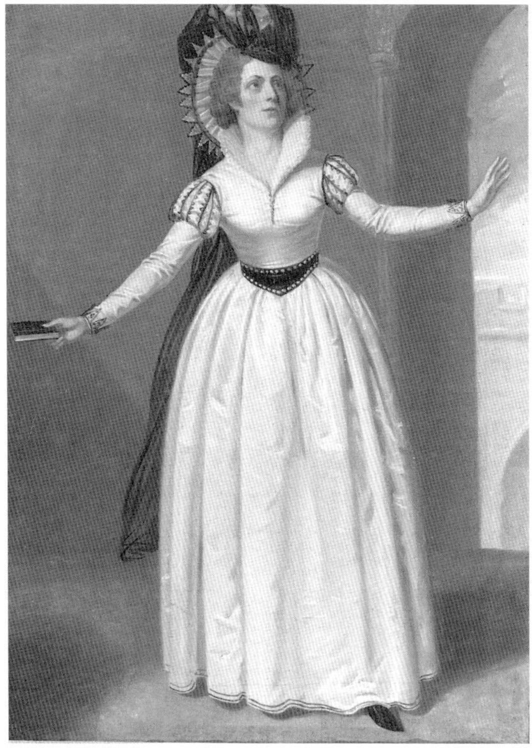

313

ELIZABETH INCHBALD

as Lady Jane Grey
in *Lady Jane Grey* by Nicholas Rowe

Samuel De Wilde

Oil on canvas 36.8 x 26.7
INV: Mathews 372; RW/CKA 233
PROV: John Bell; Charles Mathews
EXH: 1833 London (372)
ENGR: Philippe Audinet for Bell's British Library
26 November 1791, pub. Bell's *British Theatre* (1797), vol 15

Lady Jane Grey is shown just before her execution, in Act v. 'The scene draws, and discovers a scaffold hung with black, Executioner and Guards.' She gives a 'few trifles, the pledges of a dying mistress' love' to her ladies, including, to Maria, the small bible she is seen holding in De Wilde's painting, saying the lines quoted on the engraving: 'In dear remembrance of thy love, I leave thee / This book, the law of everlasting truth.'

The costume that she takes off before her execution consists of a white silk dress with lace cuffs and ruff, a black sash, and a lace cap with black ribbons. A long green sash hangs down her back. The background is presumably meant to represent the transformation from the interior of the Tower to, on the right, Tower Green, the place of execution. There is the shadow of another figure bottom left.

Rowe's tragedy was first performed at Drury Lane on 20 April 1715. Mrs Inchbald never played Lady Jane Grey in London. The last performance of the play in the 18th century was at Covent Garden on 9 December 1774, when Mrs Hartley acted the part.

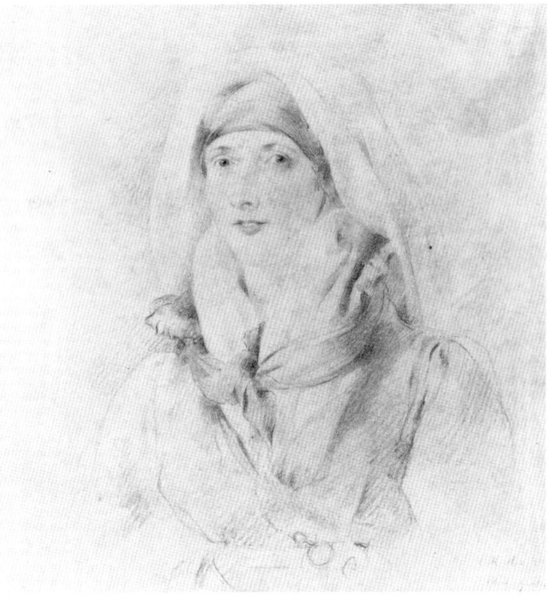

314
ELIZABETH INCHBALD

George Henry Harlow

Black, white and red chalks on wove paper 22.8 x 19
INSCR: 'G. H. H. / Aug 9. 1814' (black chalk b.r.);
'Mrs Inchbald.' (black chalk b.l.)
INV: Mathews 301; RW/CKA 492
PROV: Charles Mathews
EXH: 1833 London (301)

Mrs Inchbald retired from the stage in 1789, to become a dramatist and novelist. CKA's supposition that she is wearing a nun's habit here seems implausible.

315
BENJAMIN CHARLES INCLEDON
singing 'The Storm'

John Thomas Barber-Beaumont (copy after)

Watercolour on ivory 10.5 x 8 (oval)
INV: Mathews 325 (artist unknown); RW 427B
(by R. Cosway); CKA 427B ('Singing "The Storm"
in "Ella Rosenberg" by James Kenney')
PROV: Charles Mathews
EXH: 1833 London (325)

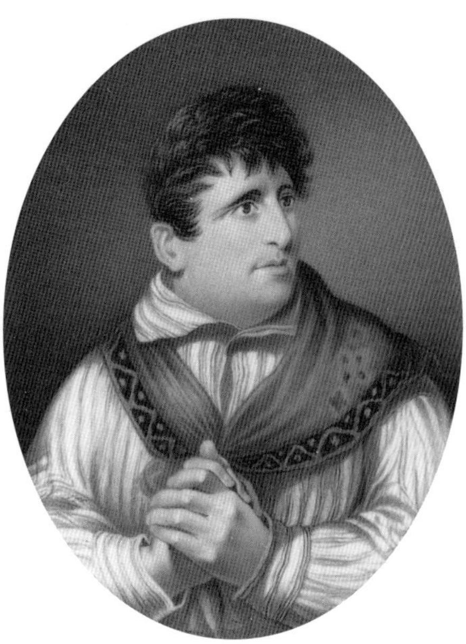

315 *Benjamin Charles Incledon singing 'The Storm'*

ENGR: John Vendramini pub. James Dunford 1812, stipple 11.5 x 9.2, with quotation 'Alas! to them there's no return'; Henry Meyer after his own drawing pub. T. & I. Elvey 1 November 1824, stipple 7.3 x 5 (storm behind, rocks on l.); G. Adcock pub. Gifford & Co. n.d., stipple 6.7 x 5, with quotation 'Cease, rude Boreas'; Page for Oxberry's *Dramatic Biography* pub. Duncombe, stipple 9.5 x 7; Reading pub. T. Williams, stipple (vignette, bust only); J. Ayton pub. August 1826, lithograph 30.5 x 26.7 (full-length with stormy background)
REL: Original, exh: 1804 R.A. (737)

Incledon wears a striped blue and white shirt; round his shoulders is a red neckerchief edged in blue and patterned in gold.

CKA confused Incledon's song with the part of Storm in Kenney's melodrama *Ella Rosenberg*, first performed at Drury Lane on 19 November 1807 with John Bannister as Storm (see No. 35); Incledon had nothing to do with it. He was singing a song called 'The Storm' by Steevens, in the 1790s; by the time he sang it at a benefit for Sedgwick at Drury Lane on 6 June 1797 it was already 'famous'. He usually reserved performances of this thrilling number for his own benefits, but also sang it for O'Keeffe's benefit at Covent Garden on 12 June 1800.

When the original picture was shown at the R.A. in 1804, the catalogue entry included lines from the song:

> While oer the ship wild waves are beating,
> We our wives and children mourn.
> Alas! from thence there's no retreating;
> Alas! to them there's no return.

See also No. 947.

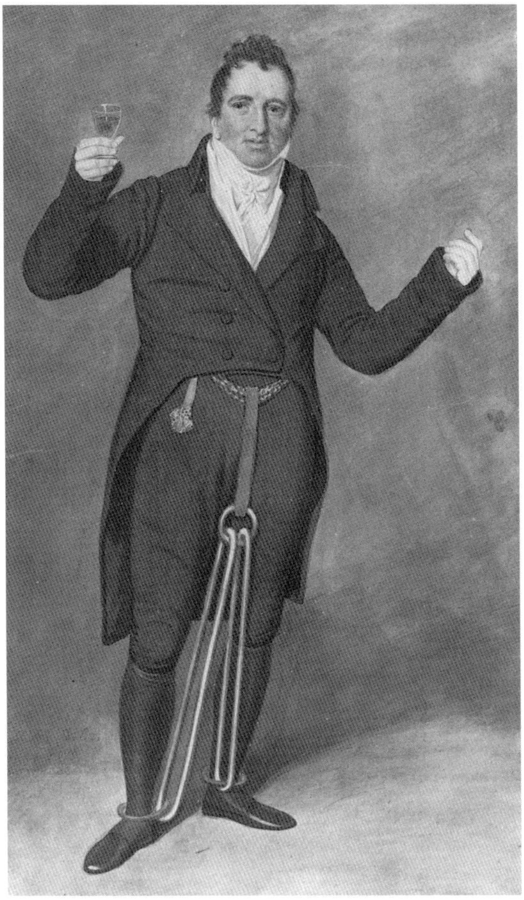

316

BENJAMIN CHARLES INCLEDON

as Captain Macheath in *The Beggar's Opera*

by John Gay

Samuel De Wilde

Pencil and watercolour on wove paper 37 x 23.5

INSCR: 'S De Wilde delin / ......l 1815' (pencil b.l.)

INV: Mathews 242; RW/CKA 46A

PROV: Charles Mathews

EXH: 1833 London (242)

ENGR: Similar to J. Thomson after Henry Singleton for the *Theatrical Inquisitor* pub. C. Chapple 1 November 1816, stipple

REL: A portrait by De Wilde of Incledon in an unnamed character that was in the Dramatic College sale at Fairbrother, Lye and Palmer on 24 February 1881 (lot 1001) may be related, and may be the other portrait by De Wilde of Incledon as Macheath that was listed in the *Mathews Collection Catalogue* (No. 130) but is not in the Garrick Club

In 'the condemn'd hold' Macheath sings a series of short airs whilst he drinks. The fourth (of 10) is 'But now again my spirits sink, I'll raise them high with wine' (the quotation on the engraving), sung to the melody 'Chevy Chase'. Macheath is encumbered with Newgate leg clamps. He has a red and gold seal on his right hip and wears black shoes and breeches, a double-breasted jacket, a waistcoat, and a high white stock with a rosette.

Incledon played Macheath for the first time at Covent Garden on 20 September 1791; the part was still in his repertory during his last season at Covent Garden, 1814–15. During the summer of 1815 he sang Macheath to Mrs Mountain's Polly at the Surrey Theatre, but the strain for the 51-year-old Incledon, according to Oxberry, was 'elephantic'.

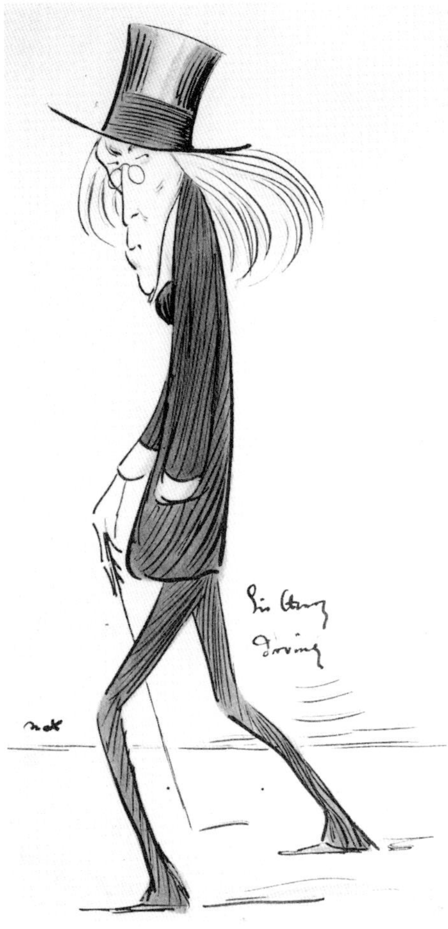

317

SIR HENRY IRVING

Max Beerbohm

Caricature pen and black ink with grey wash on wove paper 28 x 14

INSCR: 'max' (pen and black ink b.l.); 'Sir Henry / Irving' (pen and black ink b.r.)

INV: GCL 657; Gift 619

PROV: Presented by Mrs Goetze, 1943

EXH: 1951 London (1)

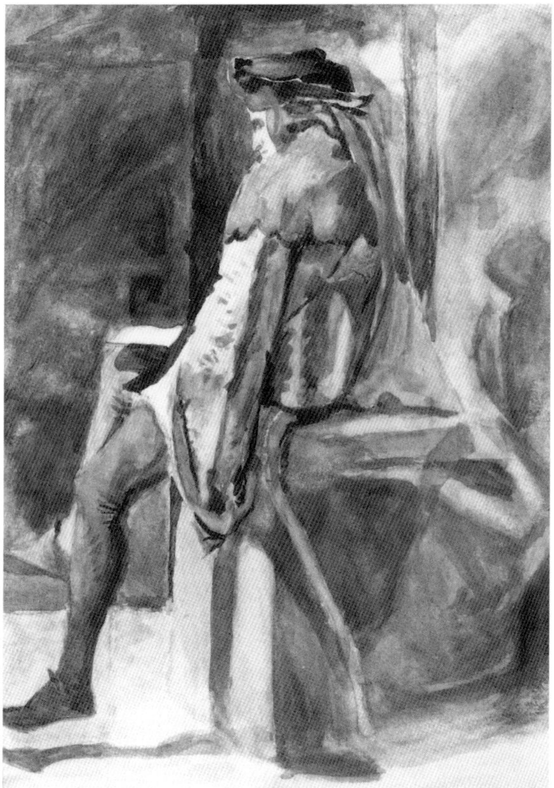

318
SIR HENRY IRVING
as Mephistopheles in *Faust*,
adapted from Goethe by W.G. Wills

[?] Collins

Pencil and watercolour on wove paper 24 x 17.5 (sight)
INSCR: 'Irving as Mephistopheles / by Collins'
(pencil on backboard)
INV: GCL 685; Gift 758
PROV: Sir Henry Irving?; Irving sale, Christie's
16 December 1905 (29)?; presented by Mrs Collins, 1958

Mephistopheles, seated on a pedestal with his back partially to front, is dressed in red and brown. He has a red tail and wears a large, grey-crowned red hat.

Lot 29 in the Irving sale was 'Sir H.I. as Mephistopheles in his dressing room'. It measured 11″ x 9″, which could be the framed measurement of No.318. The drawing has a rather intimate air, and might show Irving in costume in his dressing-room rather than on stage during a performance.

Irving's production of *Faust*, adapted by W.G. Wills from Goethe's *Faust Part 1*, opened at the Lyceum on 19 December 1885. It was one of Irving's greatest successes, and was played 792 times before its final performance in Bristol on 10 December 1902.

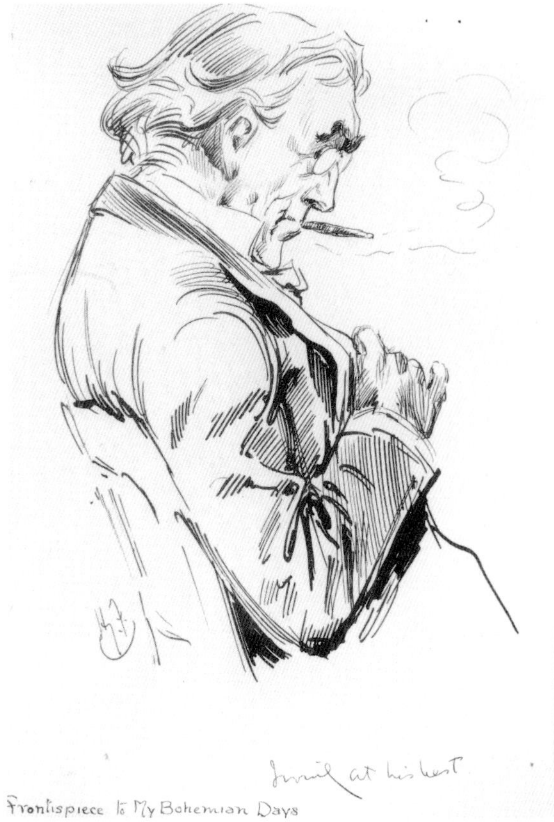

319
SIR HENRY IRVING

Harry Furniss

Pen and ink on wove paper 21.6 x 15.2
INSCR: 'Hy. F.' (pen and black ink b.l.);
'Irving at his best' (pen and black ink b.r.);
'Frontispiece to My Bohemian Days'
(pen and black ink b.c.)
INV: CKA 615; Gift 448
PROV: Presented by Miss Dorothy Furniss, 1928
LIT: Harry Furniss *My Bohemian Days* (1919), frontispiece

Sir Henry became a member of the Garrick Club in 1874.

The artist, who chose this drawing for the frontispiece to his memoirs, was a very prolific cartoonist and caricaturist who had an acquaintance with many of the famous people of his era. Furniss became a member of the Garrick Club in 1885.

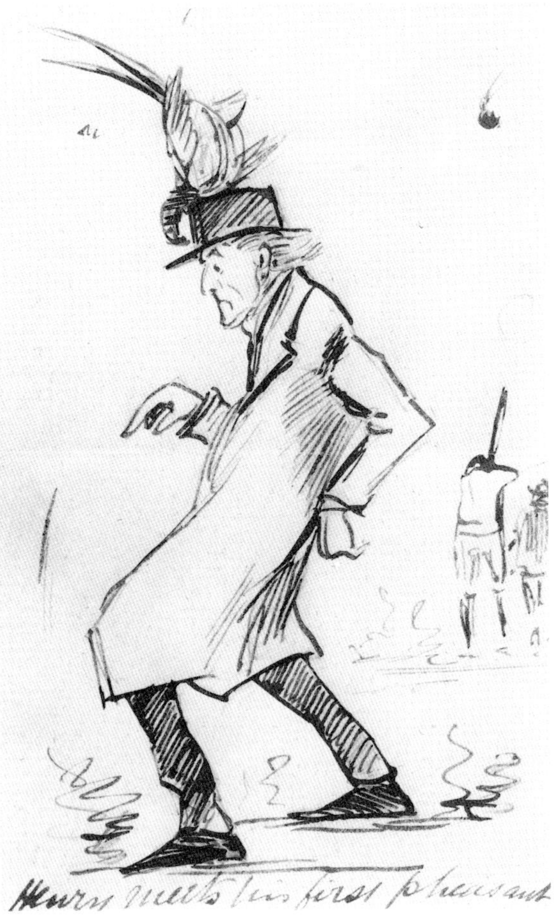

320

SIR HENRY IRVING

Sir Frank Lockwood

Pen and pencil on blue wove paper 17.1 x 10.8
INSCR: 'Henry meets his first pheasant'
INV: CKA 543; Gift 472 (not located 1988)
PROV: Presented by HM King George V, 1930

Irving walks awkwardly to the left, across wet ground. A shooting party is taking place behind him, and a pheasant has landed on his head.

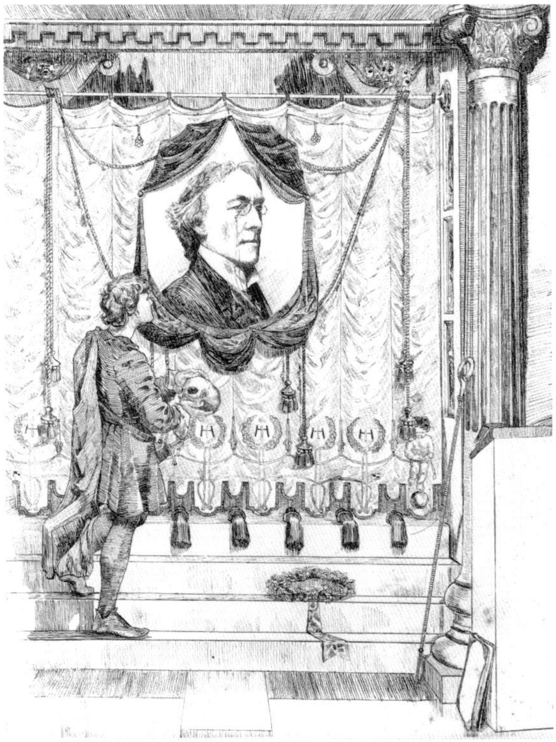

321

SIR HENRY IRVING

Andrew MacLaren

Pen and black ink on wove paper 33.5 x 27 (sight)
INSCR: 'AML / 05' (pen and black ink b.r.);
'30/12/05' (pen and black ink b.r.)
INV: GCL 664; Gift 852
PROV: Presented by Andrew MacLaren (the artist?), 1973

In this memorial drawing a young man dressed as Hamlet stands on the steps leading up to a proscenium arch. Along the bottom edge of the drop-cloth is a row of laurel wreaths, framing the initials 'HI' in monogram. Over the drop-cloth is a drapery with a picture of Irving. To the right there is a lectern with an open book and another book leaning aginst it. A laurel wreath with a ribbon is on the third step.

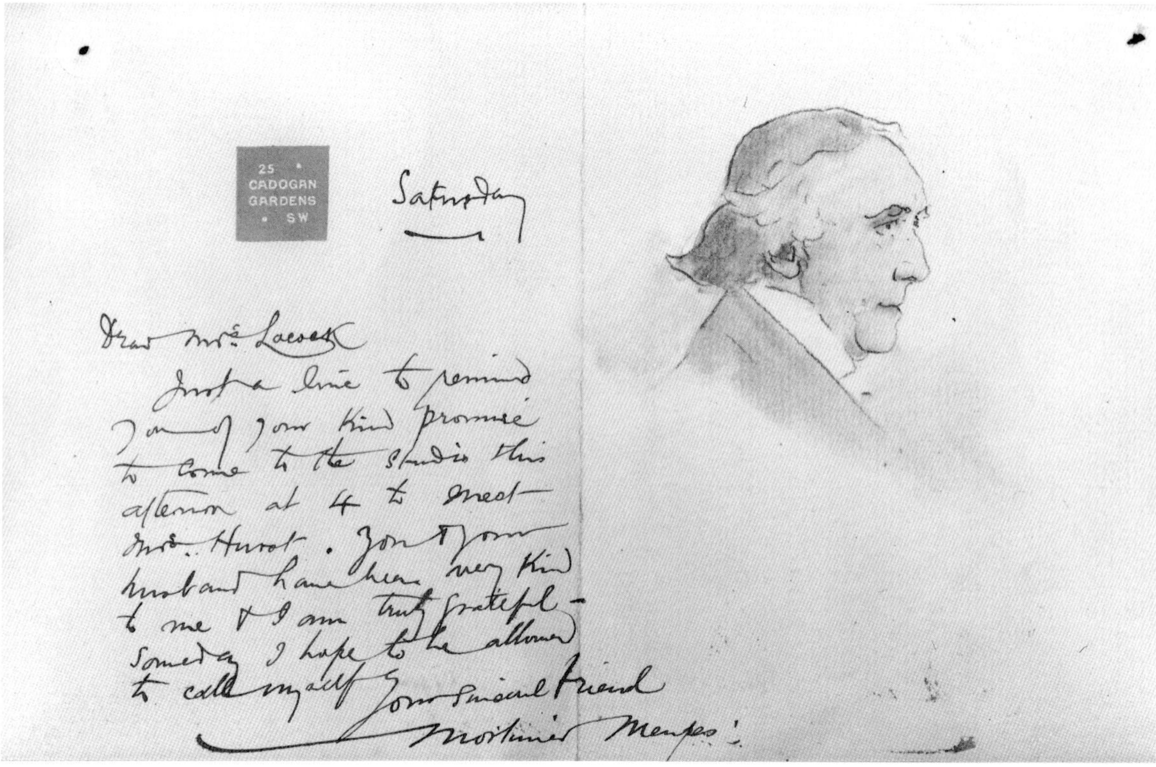
25
CADOGAN
GARDENS
SW

Saturday

Dear Mrs Lacock
Just a line to remind
you of your kind promise
to come to the studio this
afternoon at 4 to meet
Mrs Hunt. You & your
husband have been very kind
to me & I am truly grateful –
someday I hope to be allowed
to call myself Your sincere friend
Mortimer Menpes.

322
SIR HENRY IRVING

Mortimer Menpes

Pencil and watercolour on wove paper
12 x 20 (whole sheet)
INSCR: (see below)
INV: Not listed; Gift 752
PROV: Presented by Guy Knowles, 1956
LIT: Mortimer Menpes, *Henry Irving* (1906)

Menpes's *Henry Irving* consists of a short text and eight plates containing 12 watercolour drawings of Irving's head, seven of them in profile and the rest full-face. No. 322 is very similar to the left profile in plate 5. The text is a letter on writing paper headed '25, Cadogan Gardens' and written in pen and brown ink: 'Saturday / Dear Mrs. Lacock / Just a line to remind / you of your kind promise / to come to the studio this / afternoon at 4 to meet / Mrs Hunt. You and your / husband have been very kind / to me and I am truly grateful – / some day I hope to be allowed / to call myself / Your sincere friend / Mortimer Menpes.' See also No. 882.

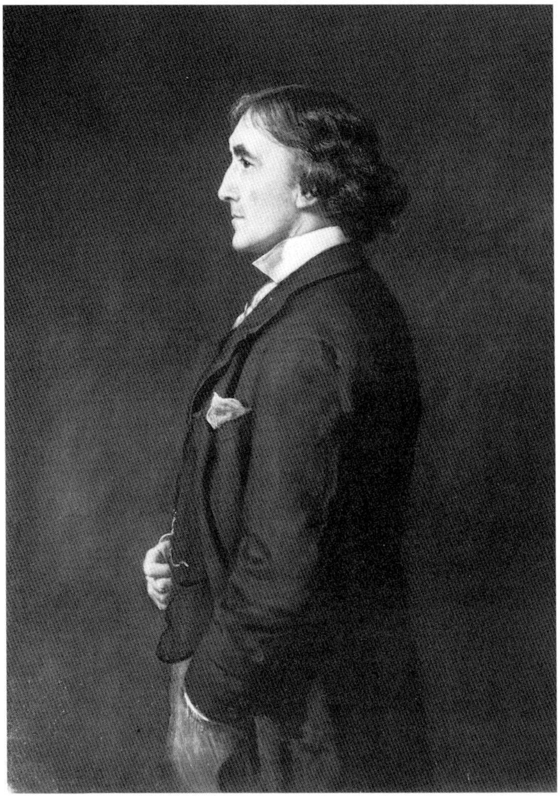

323*

SIR HENRY IRVING

Sir John Everett Millais

Oil on canvas 110.5 x 80

INSCR: '18 [Millais monogram] 83' (dark brown paint b.l.)

INV: RW/CKA 382 (repr.); Gift 196 (frame: Gift 202)

PROV: Presented by the artist, 1884 (according to the R.A. catalogue), 1886 (according to CKA); frame presented by T.O. Barlow, R.A., 1886

EXH: 1884 R.A. (372); 1886 Grosvenor Gallery; 1949 Port Sunlight (147); 1951 London (31)

REL: NPG 1453 oil on canvas 109.2 x 78.7, copy by Harry Allen, given by the Garrick Club, 1907

LIT: Fitzgerald, pp. 230–32; Griffiths, p. 341

Three-quarter length, facing left. Irving wears morning dress. He has a grey cravat with a gold pin. The carved frame includes the Garrick Club crest and motto.

Millais, himself a member of the Club, 'generally spent his evenings there', in the company of men like Irving and Hare (see No. 282). (J.G. Millais, *The Life and Work of Sir John Everett Millais* [1889], 2: 250.)

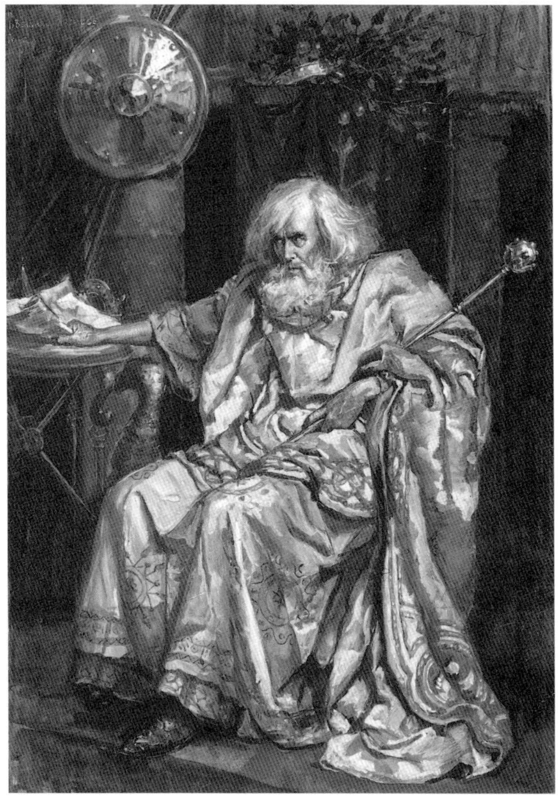

324

SIR HENRY IRVING

as Lear in *King Lear* by William Shakespeare

Sir J. Bernard Partridge

Pencil, grey wash and white body colour on card 52.2 x 37.5 (card 61 x 42)

INSCR: 'I. BERNARD. PARTRIDGE / FECIT A. D. III. IDVS / NOVEMBRES / MDCCCXCII.' (white body colour t.l.)

INV: Not listed; Gift 681

PROV: Presented by Lady Partridge, 1948

LIT: 'Souvenir of King Lear' (reproduced); Laurence Irving, *Henry Irving. The Actor and his World* (1951), reproduced opposite p. 544

Lear's voluminous costume is decorated with strapwork and circular patterns. The table to the left seems to be of classical design, and the pillars behind Lear are an approximation of J. Harker's set seen more clearly in Hawes Craven's drawing of Act I, scene I, in the Lear souvenir. Lear is probably shown at the line: 'Meantime we shall express our darker purpose – Give me the map there.' At that point, according to Irving's own pencilled note in his copy of the play in the Garrick Club Library, he looks up at Cordelia.

Partridge produced this drawing for the illustrated souvenir for Irving's production of *King Lear*. The souvenir was illustrated by Partridge and Hawes

Craven, and Partridge's contribution included another study of Irving as Lear, wearing the same costume but shown standing and holding a sword. He also provided scenes showing the reconciliation of Lear and Cordelia and Lear weeping over the dead Cordelia. The production opened at the Lyceum on 10 November 1892 and ran for a total of 76 performances until 1 February 1893. The cast included Gordon Craig as Oswald and Ellen Terry as Cordelia. Irving, we are told, looked magnificent, but his interpretation of the role was not a success; he assumed a characteristic voice and, in the opening performances at least, was completely inaudible to most of the audience.

325
LOCATION UNKNOWN
SIR HENRY IRVING
as Edgar Ravenswood in *Ravenswood*
by Herman Merivale, adapted from Sir Walter Scott

Sir J. Bernard Partridge

Pencil, grey and blue wash with white body colour
on card 35 x 24 (card 37.4 x 25.4)
INSCR: 'J. Bernard Partridge Fec.' (pen and black ink b.r.)
INV: CKA 532 (no character); Gift 439
PROV: The sitter; Irving sale, Christie's 16 December 1905 (136), bt. Lt. Col. Hugh Valdare Warrender D.S.O. by whom bequeathed, 1926
LIT: *Souvenir of Ravenswood* (repr.)

Irving is shown in Act I, having witnessed the burial of his father, Alan Ravenswood. The scene is: 'The Chapel bounds. A country landscape in the Lothians. At the back a mountainous coast, and in the distance the ruined tower of Wolf's Crag.' The play is set in the late 17th century, and Edgar is dressed informally with a long cloak.

Lot 136 in the Irving sale is described as 'Portrait of Sir Henry Irving as Ravenswood – monochrome 18 x 12½'. No. 325 is one of five monochrome drawings prepared by Bernard Partridge for the 'Ravenswood' illustrated souvenir, which included another full-length of Irving shown at the end of the play. The other illustrations were by J. Harker and Hawes Craven. The illustration taken from No. 325 is labelled 'The Master of Ravenswood'.

Merivale's play was adapted from Scott's novel *The Bride of Lammermoor*. The production opened at the Lyceum on 20 September 1890 and had had 99 performances by 3 January 1891. The cast included Gordon Craig as Henry Ashton and Ellen Terry as Lucy Ashton.

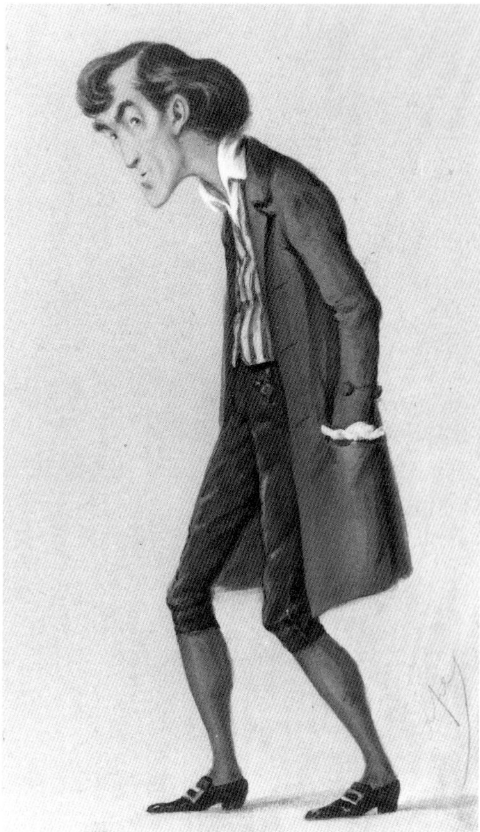

326
SIR HENRY IRVING
as Matthias in *The Bells*
by L.D. Lewis

Carlo Pellegrini ('Ape')

Pencil and watercolour on blue wove paper 30.5 x 18.1
INSCR: 'Ape' (pencil b.r.)
INV: CKA 616; Gift 359
PROV: Presented by R. Woodhouse, 1912
LIT: *Vanity Fair* 19 December 1874, inscr: 'The Bells'

Matthias wears black shoes with white buckles, red hose, green velvet breeches, a long brown coat, and a black and white striped waistcoat.

Irving first played Matthias on 25 November 1871 at the Lyceum, under the management of Hezekiah Lithicum Bateman. Like Garrick's Richard III on 19 October 1741 and Kean's Shylock on 26 January 1814, it was one of the pivotal performances in the history of the British stage, and marked Irving's elevation to the head of his profession.

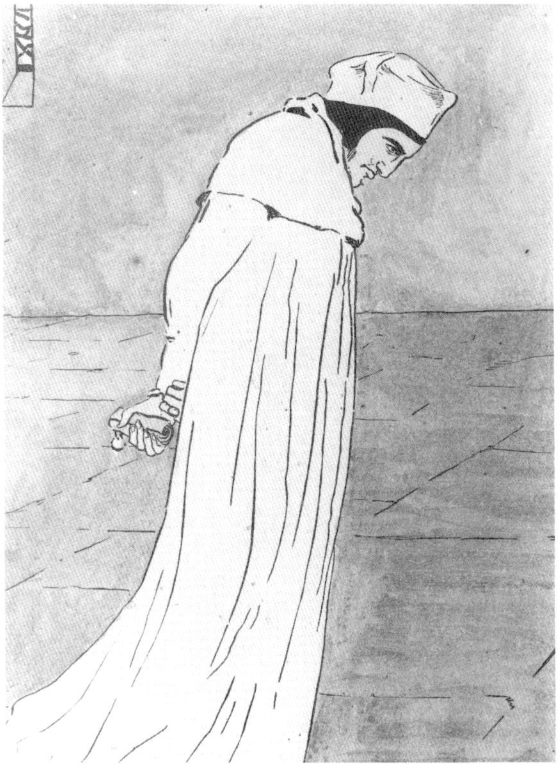

327
SIR HENRY IRVING
as Cardinal Wolsey in *Henry VIII*
by William Shakespeare

Unknown Artist

Pen and black ink and watercolour 19.7 x 15 (sight)
INSCR: (Possible signature t.l. in pen and black ink)
INV: GCL 722; Gift 850
PROV: Presented by Brigadier Cudden, 1973

Wolsey is presumably shown in Act III, scene 2, with the letter containing the catalogue of his immense riches, which is the immediate cause of his downfall.

The illustrated souvenir for Irving's production of *Henry VIII* includes a portrait of Irving by Bernard Partridge at much the same moment in the play. Along with a portrait of Ellen Terry as Queen Katherine in the Trial Scene, it was reproduced as a Doulton figurine. Irving's costume for Cardinal Wolsey is in the Mander and Mitchenson Theatre Collection. Irving's production of *Henry VIII* opened at the Lyceum on 5 January 1892 and ran until 30 July, with a shorter revival the following season, from 1 October to 5 November 1892 – a total of 204 performances. The lavish production, which cost the considerable sum of £12,000, had scenery by Joseph Harker, Hawes Craven and William Telbin, and costumes by Seymour Lucas and Mrs J.W. Comyns Carr. The production was a great critical success, as was Irving's Wolsey. The cast included William Terriss as Henry VIII, Johnston Forbes-Robertson as the Duke of Buckingham, and Gordon Craig as Cromwell. Ellen Terry as Queen Katherine attempted to recreate Harlow's image of Sarah Siddons (see No. 750). This she does in Bernard Partridge's portrait of her in the illustrated souvenir.

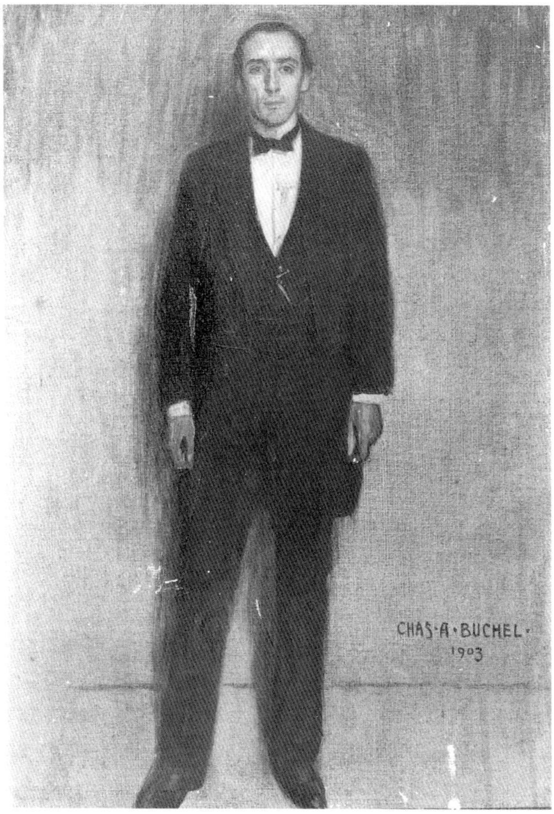

328
HENRY BRODRIBB IRVING
as Crichton in *The Admirable Crichton*
by J.M. Barrie

Charles A. Buchel

Oil on board 50.5 x 35.5
INSCR: 'CHAS. A. BUCHEL. / 1903' (brown paint b.r.);
'2 (in circle) / H.B. Irving' (pen and black ink on verso);
stamped verso: 'CHAS. H. WESTS / PREPARED BOARDS / FOR OIL PAINTING / 115, FINCHLEY ROAD / N.W.'
INV: CKA 646; Gift 630
PROV: Presented by Capt. C. Riddell Williams, 1945

Crichton is dressed as the perfect butler in a black suit. Barrie's comedy was first given at the Duke of York's on 4 November 1902, with H.B. Irving in the title role. He did not appear in the 1908 revival. See Nos. 172 and 376.

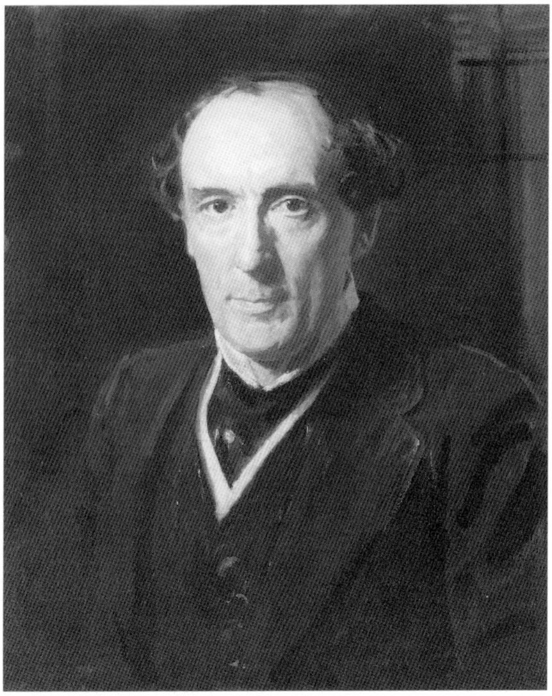

329
HENRY BRODRIBB IRVING

Reginald Grenville Eves

Oil on canvas 61 x 51
INSCR: 'R.G. Eves' (t.r.); '19..' (t.l.)
INV: CKA 569 (as Sir Henry Irving)
PROV: Purchased from the artist and presented by a number of members, 1925
EXH: 1920 R.S.P.P. (129) 'Late H.B. Irving, Esq'; 1935 Exhibition of Portraits by R.G. Eves, Knoedler & Co. (22); 1947 Eves Memorial Exhibition, Royal Society of British Artists, Suffolk Street (10)

Irving is dressed in dark grey. There is a pearl-headed pin in his dark grey cravat.

This is probably the picture shown at the R.S.P.P. in 1920. Eves exhibited a portrait of H.B. Irving as Markheim, R.A. 1908 (910), and another as 'The late H.B. Irving' at the R.S.P.P. in 1929 (134).

H.B. Irving, the son of Sir Henry Irving, became a member of the Garrick Club in 1896.

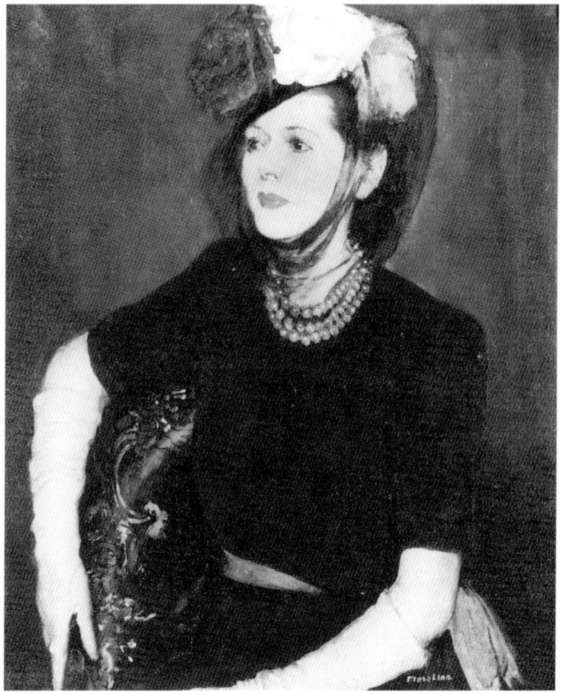

330
ISABELA JEANS

Flora Lion

Oil on canvas 86.3 x 71.1
INSCR: 'Flora Lion' (red paint b.r.)
INV: GCL 738; Gift 886
PROV: Presented by the sitter, 1978
EXH: 1947 R.A. (424)

The sitter is seated, in a simple black dress. Her black bonnet has three enormous roses, two pink and one red.

Isabela Jeans had a stage career that spanned the years from 1913 to 1968, appearing in dozens of plays, most notably in Granville-Barker's productions.

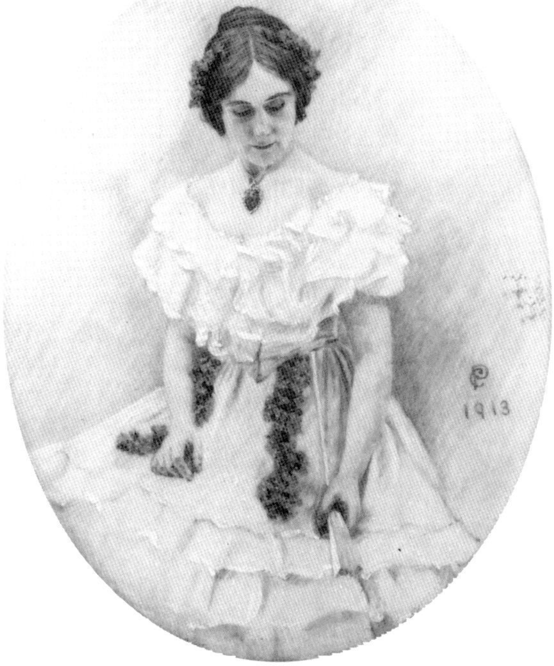

331
MARY JERROLD
as Rose Sibley, Lady Rhead
in *Milestones*
by Arnold Bennett and Edward G. Knoblauch

Cushla Parker

Watercolour on ivory 10.5 x 8.2 (oval)
INSCR: 'CP (in monogram) / 1913' (r.);
'Miss Cushla Parker / 1 Northwick Terrace / NW /
Miss Mary Jerrold / as Rose / in Milestones'
INV: GCL 679; Gift 740
PROV: Bequeathed by Alderson Burrell Horne, 1954

The sitter wears a flounced white dress.

Milestones opened at the Royalty on 5 August 1912 and ran for 608 performances until 21 August 1913, under the management of J.E. Vedrenne and Dennis Eadie.

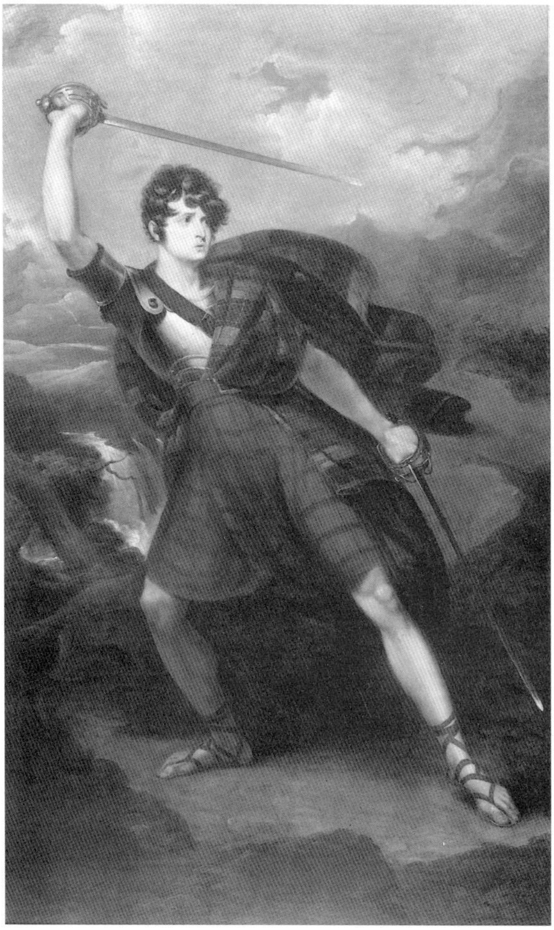

332
HENRY ERSKINE JOHNSTON
as Young Norval in *Douglas*
by John Home

Sir William Allan

Oil on canvas 235 x 143.5
INV: RW/CKA 82; Gift 165
PROV: Presented by the sitter's widow,
Mrs Magdalen Johnston, 1861

Young Norval is shown at the climax of the play in Act v, where he enters 'with a sword in each hand'. He has been mortally wounded by Lord Randolph off-stage, and staggers onto the stage to die in front of his mother, Lady Randolph. Young Norval strikes a dramatic wind-blown pose in his death throes, and wears red and green plaid over his body armour.

Johnston's first appearance in London, at Covent Garden on 23 October 1797, was as Young Norval. After three performances during the 1797–98 season, he gave the part a rest until 28 April 1800, when he played it for his benefit, shared with his wife. See also No. 333.

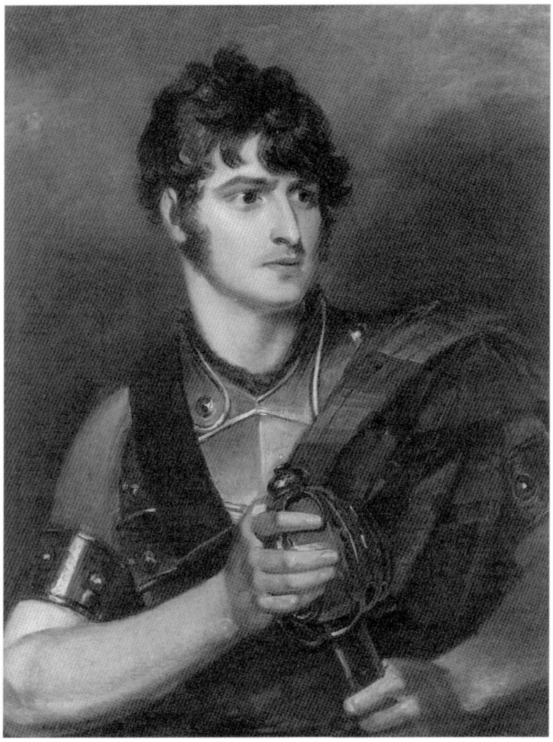

333

HENRY ERSKINE JOHNSTON

as Young Norval in *Douglas* by John Home

Henry Singleton

Oil on canvas 74.3 x 61.6
INV: Mathews 6; RW/CKA 32
PROV: Thomas Harris; Harris sale, Robins 12 July 1819 (17); Charles Mathews
EXH: 1802 R.A. (200); 1833 London (6)
ENGR: E. Mitchel, stipple and line 39.7 x 35 (full-length)
Thomas Wright for Oxberry's *New English Theatre* pub. Simpkin & Marshall 1821, stipple 10.8 x 8.2 (same composition but looking to front)
LIT: Patmore, p. 274; Griffiths, p. 335

Young Norval, the noble Douglas, has just heard from Lady Randolph the true identity of his father, Norval. He wants to know who his mother is, and Lady Randolph reveals all – for it is she, the mother he has not seen since the day he was born. He tugs at his sword to show his willingness to help her. He wears red and green plaid over steel armour. See No. 332.

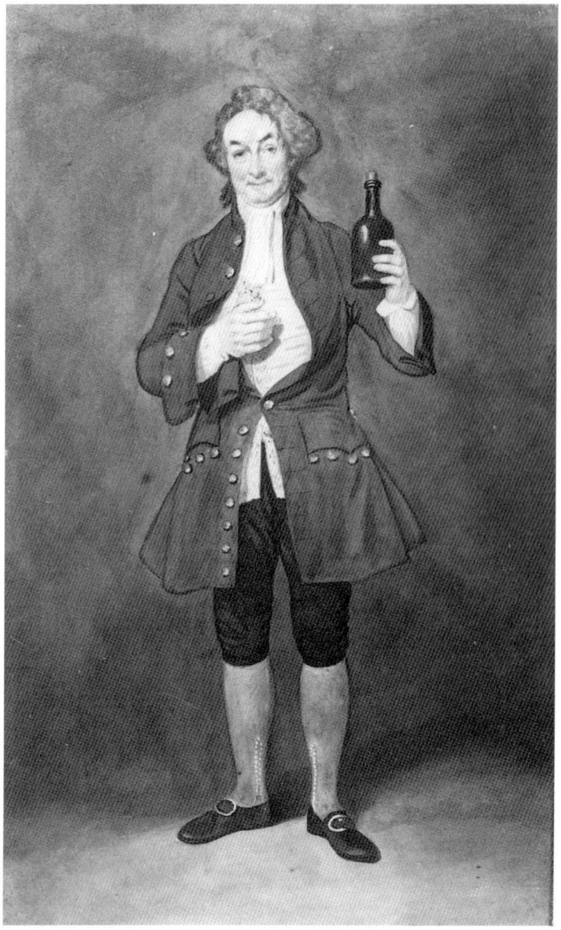

334

JOHN HENRY JOHNSTONE

as Dennis Brulgruddery
in *John Bull or The Englishman's Fireside*
by George Colman the Younger

Samuel De Wilde

Pencil and watercolour on wove paper 37 x 23.5
INV: Mathews 208; RW/CKA 45D
PROV: Charles Mathews
EXH: 1833 London (208); 1975 London (140)
ENGR: Similar to Thomson after John Partridge for the *Theatrical Inquisitor* pub. C. Chapple 1 July 1816 (same costume, and a bottle held up in l.h. but to r., looking to front)

Dennis raises his bottle of Madeira. His complexion is florid and his wig is askew. He wears black shoes, blue and white stockings, black breeches, a brown coat, and a white waistcoat with floral embroidery in green and red.

The younger Colman's comedy was first performed at Covent Garden on 5 March 1803, with Johnstone as the original Dennis Brulgruddery. See Nos. 193 and 220.

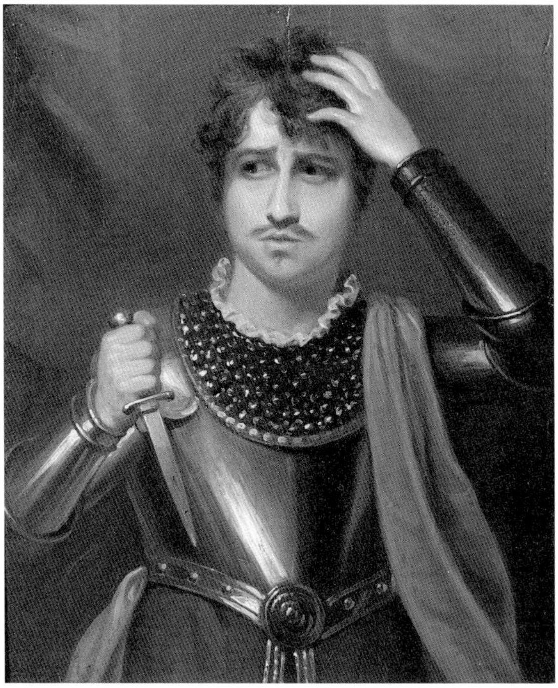

335
JOHN HENRY JOHNSTONE
in character

Samuel De Wilde
Oil on panel 23 x 18.6
INV: Mathews 357?; RW/CKA 242
(unknown man, artist unknown)
PROV: Charles Mathews
EXH: 1833 London (357)
REL: Earl of Leicester, Holkham 105, black chalk and wash on panel 25.5 x 19.7, inscr: 'S De Wilde / delin 1802' (black chalk l.r.), exh: R.A. 1802 (670)
(One of a group of seven portraits)
[This picture is possibly the one of Johnstone in character, signed and dated by De Wilde, that was in the Royal Dramatic College sale at Fairbrother, Lye and Palmer on 24 February 1881 (lot 100D)]

Johnstone wears armour with a chain-mail gorget and a red cloak. His puzzled expression as he raises a dagger and holds his hand to his head suggests a very specific moment in a play that has yet to be identified.

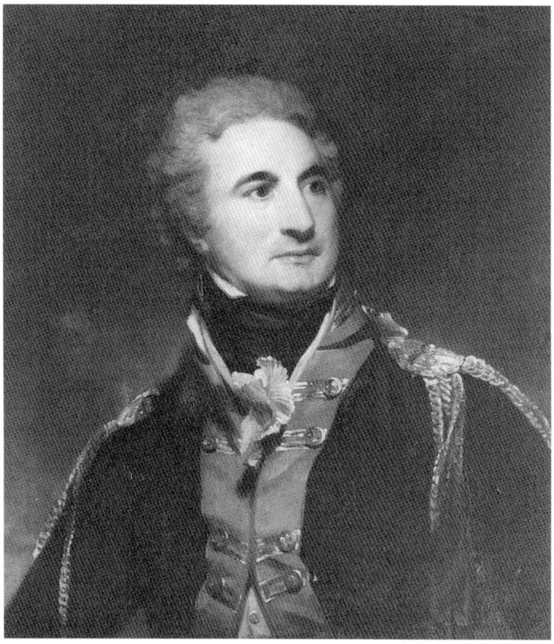

336
JOHN HENRY JOHNSTONE
as Sir Callaghan O'Brallaghan
in *Love à la Mode* by Charles Macklin

Sir Martin Archer Shee
Oil on canvas 76 x 63
INV: Mathews 117; RW/CKA 365
PROV: Thomas Harris; Harris sale, Robins 12 July 1819 (29); Charles Mathews
EXH: 1803 R.A. (92); 1833 London (117); 1934 London (357)
ENGR: William Ward pub. Messrs Ward 26 September 1803, mezzotint 26.3 x 21.2; J. Rogers for Oxberry's *New English Drama* pub. Simpkin & Marshall 1824, stipple 10.5 x 8.6; J. Rogers for Oxberry's *Dramatic Biography* pub. G. Virtue 28 January 1826, stipple 7.2 x 4.9 (M.A. Shee del.); Kennerley, stipple (vignette); Maguire for the *Cyclopaedian Magazine*, stipple and line 14.3 x 9.2
LIT: Patmore, p. 274; Griffiths, p. 335

In Act I, the bluff soldier Sir Callaghan is being made fun of by Beau Mordecai, a Jewish dandy, who speaks the line quoted on the engraving: 'You a General! faith then you will make a very pretty General. Pray, madam, look at the General!' Sir Callaghan wears a dark blue-green military jacket with pale green bands and silver braid.

Macklin's comedy was first performed at Drury Lane on 12 December 1759. John Moody was the original Sir Callaghan, with Macklin as Sir Archy MacSarcasm. Johnstone's first performance as Sir Callaghan was seen at Covent Garden on 10 November 1784, with Macklin as Sir Archy and Quick as Beau Mordecai (see Nos. 129, 752 and 753).

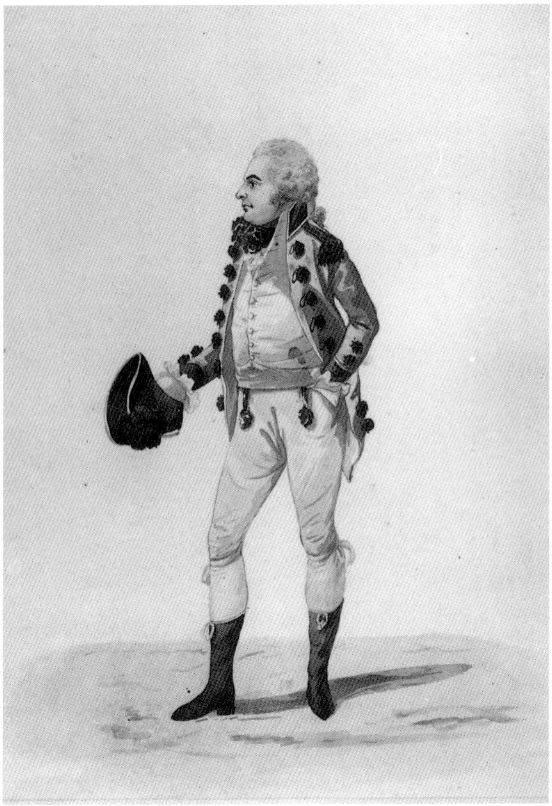

337

JOHN HENRY JOHNSTONE

as O'Whack in *Notoriety*

by Frederick Reynolds

William Wellings

Pen and grey ink with watercolour
on wove paper 22.5 x 17.5

INSCR: 'Wellings fecit' (pen and brown ink on mount b.l. CM); 'Mr John Johnstone / as / O'Whack in Notoriety' (pen and brown ink on mount b.c.)

INV: RW/CKA 549B

PROV: Charles Mathews (not in catalogue)

O'Whack is the Irish valet de chambre to Mr Nominal. He has a smattering of French which he delivers with a broad Irish brogue. His costume, singularly elegant for a valet de chambre, consists of black boots with gold bands and bows, white stockings, silvery breeches with bows, and a red military jacket with dark collar and cuffs, epaulets and frogging. Two large seals hang from beneath a pink sash, and he carries a black tricorn hat and plume.

Reynolds's comedy, based partly on Fletcher's *Monsieur Thomas*, was first performed at Covent Garden on 5 November 1791, with Johnstone as the original O'Whack.

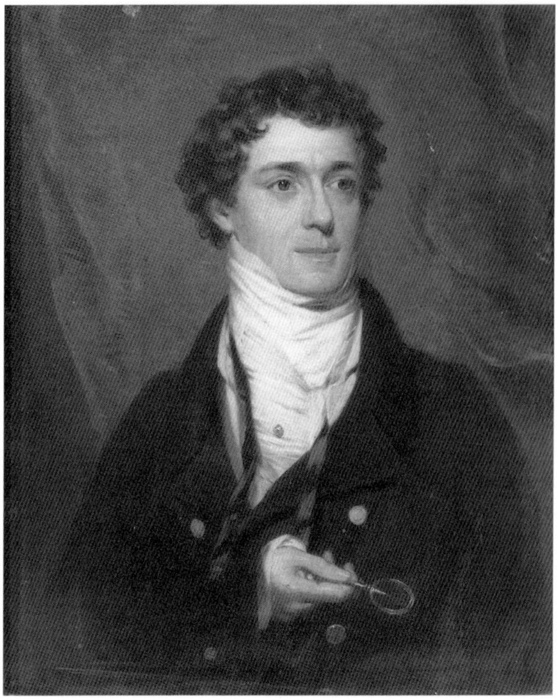

338

RICHARD JONES

Benjamin Burnell

Oil on canvas 74.3 x 61.6

INV: Mathews 116; RW 200 (by Henry Burnell); CKA 200

PROV: Charles Mathews

EXH: 1833 London (116)

Half-length, against a red curtain, holding an eyeglass on a black ribbon. Jones wears a black jacket with gold buttons over a pale buff waistcoat lined in pink.

Jones was one of the original members of the Garrick Club in 1831.

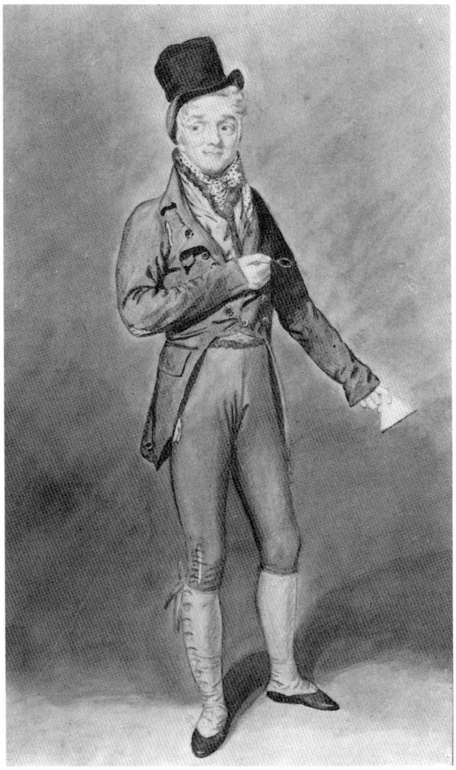

339

RICHARD JONES

as Jeremy Diddler in *Raising the Wind*

by James Kenney

Samuel De Wilde

Pencil and watercolour on wove paper 37 x 23.5

INV: Mathews 216; RW/CKA 61B (framed as 61A)

PROV: Charles Mathews

EXH: 1833 London (216)

Jeremy Diddler, a notorious scrounger, has been writing a letter to Peggy, which he has addressed to 'the beautiful Maid at the foot of the hill'. This is the paper he holds in De Wilde's drawings. Jeremy smiles under a battered black top hat with a wavy brim. He holds an eyeglass in his right hand and a folded paper in his left. He wears black shoes, brown breeches, and a shabby green cutaway coat over a pink waistcoat trimmed with brown fur.

Kenney's farce was first given at Covent Garden on 5 November 1803, with William Thomas Lewis as Jeremy Diddler. Jones played the part for the first time at the Haymarket on 6 June 1809, and for the first time at Covent Garden on 23 September 1809.

De Wilde recorded a sitting with Jones as Jeremy Diddler on 2 January 1810. The drawing was sent to Mathews on 8 January 1810.

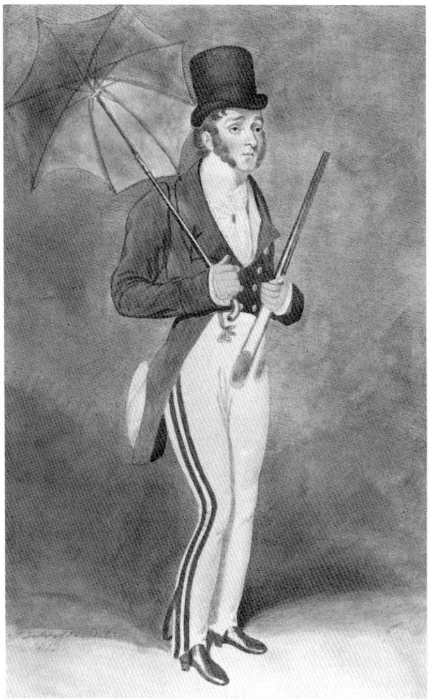

340

RICHARD JONES

as Young Contrast in *The Lord of the Manor*

by John Burgoyne

Samuel De Wilde

Black chalk, pencil and watercolour

on wove paper 37 x 23.5

INSCR: 'S De Wilde delin / 1813' (black chalk b.l.)

INV: Mathews 215; RW/CKA 46B

PROV: Charles Mathews

EXH: 1833 London (215)

ENGR: Samuel De Wilde, etching 35.9 x 22.7

REL: [A portrait of Jones as Young Contrast, signed and dated by De Wilde, was in the Royal Dramatic College sale at Fairbrother, Lye and Palmer on 24 February 1881 (lot 100E)]

Young Contrast's father has just bought Castle Manor and the youth is anxious to demonstrate his newly acquired importance by catching poachers. He enters 'attended with gamekeepers, a gun in one hand, and a silk parasol in the other'. He gives orders for all the local dogs to be hanged, and for guns, nets and snares to be seized. He is shown holding a green umbrella over his right shoulder and a gun in his left hand. He wears black shoes, faded white trousers and a brown cutaway jacket.

Burgoyne's comic opera, with music by William Jackson, was originally performed at Drury Lane on 27 December 1780, with John Palmer as Young Contrast. Jones played the part in a Covent Garden revival of 24 October 1812. See also No. 438.

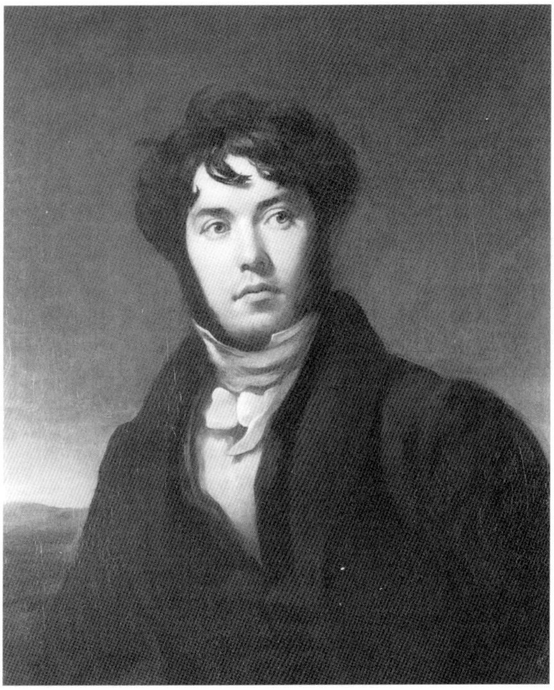

341
RICHARD JONES

Unknown Artist

Oil on canvas 75.5 x 63
INV: RW/CKA 354
PROV: Presented by Mr or Mrs Philip Birch, 1872

The sitter in this very romantic portrait wears a dark coat and a white shirt and stock. A hill can be seen in the background.

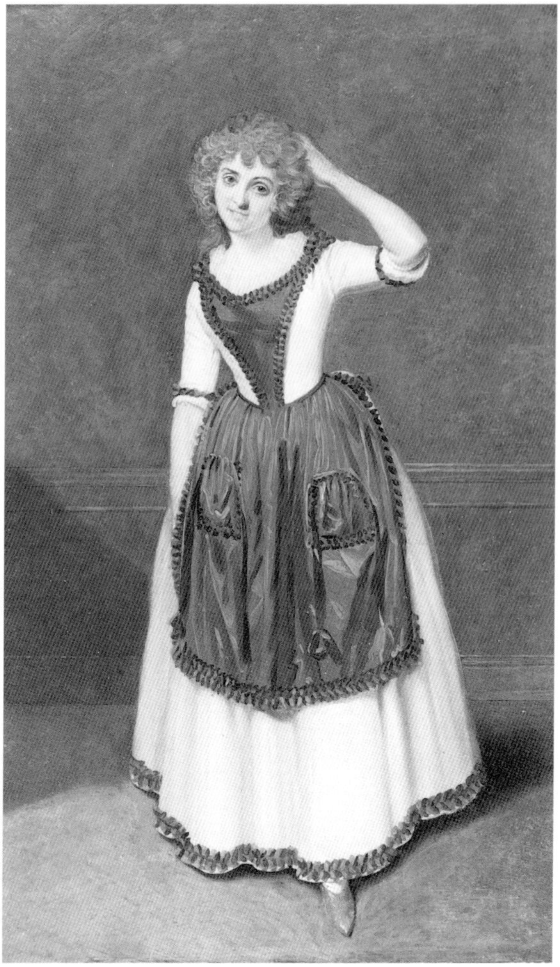

342
DOROTHY JORDAN
as Peggy in *The Country Girl*
by David Garrick

Samuel De Wilde

Oil on canvas 35.5 x 26.7
INV: Mathews 387; RW/CKA 203
PROV: John Bell; Charles Mathews
EXH: 1833 London (387)
ENGR: William Bromley for Bell's British Library
15 July 1791, line 10.5 x 8,
pub. Bell's *British Theatre* (1797), vol 13
LIT: Griffiths, p. 332

Peggy Thrift, daughter of Sir Thomas Thrift, has been brought up as a naïve country girl by her elderly guardian, Jack Moody, who has made her believe that she is married to him. Belville, her admirer, discovers that she is not married and pursues her in the face of Moody's jealousy. In Act v, scene 1, set in Moody's house, Moody interrupts Peggy whilst she is writing a love-letter to

Belville. She pretends she is writing it for Alithia, Moody's sister, and Moody proclaims that Belville is too young for his sister to marry. Peggy retorts with the line printed on the engraving: 'Why do you marry me then? tis the same thing Bud.' ('Bud' was an affectionate term for husband.) Peggy's pose is one of affected rustic puzzlement. Her simple country garb consists of a white dress trimmed with green and a green silk apron with pockets.

Garrick's adaptation of Wycherley's *The Country Wife* was first performed at Drury Lane on 25 October 1766, with Ann Reynolds as Peggy. Mrs Jordan made her very first London appearance in the part at Drury Lane on 18 October 1785. She played the role eight times during the 1790–91 season, her last performance taking place on 4 June 1791 – the final evening on which performances were given in the old Drury Lane Theatre.

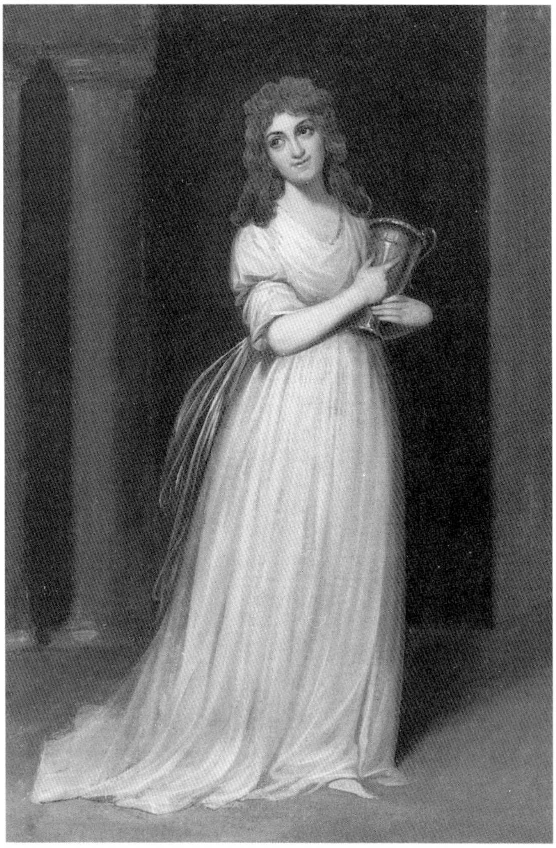

343 *Dorothy Jordan as Phaedra*

343*
DOROTHY JORDAN
as Phaedra
in *Amphitryon or The Two Socias*
by John Hawkesworth

Samuel De Wilde

Oil on canvas 36.7 x 28
INSCR: Inscr. with numbers '1' to '30' in pen and brown ink at approx. 1 cm intervals down r.h. side, and with numbers '1' to '24' in pen and brown ink at similar intervals along top edge
INV: Mathews 383; RW/CKA 223
PROV: John Bell; Charles Mathews
EXH: 1833 London (383); 1974 Twickenham (16)

ENGR: Philippe Audinet for Bell's British Library 11 August 1792, line 11.5 x 8, published in Bell's *British Theatre* (1797), vol 21

Phaedra, waiting-woman to Alcmena, is given a goblet of gold by Mercury, who intends to seduce her. She rejects him, and when Mercury asks 'Shall I come to your bedside tonight?', she replies 'No, nor tomorrow night neither', continuing with the line printed on the engraving, 'but this shall be my sweetheart in your place'. Mrs Jordan wears a simple white classical dress, in keeping with the plain column and niche that provide her background.

Hawkesworth's comedy, adapted from Dryden with memories of Plautus and a pinch of Molière, was first performed at Drury Lane on 15 December 1756, with Kitty Clive as Phaedra. Mrs Jordan never played the part, and the piece was not given in London after her arrival in the autumn of 1785. The numbers inscribed along the top and right edges of the picture are the clearest indication that the Bell engravings were taken straight from De Wilde's oil paintings, rather than from an intervening drawing.

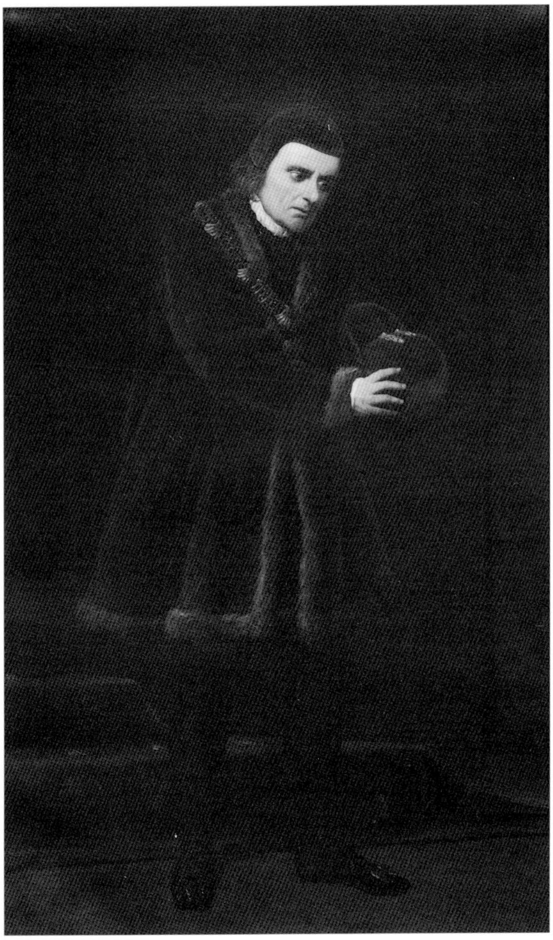

344
CHARLES JOHN KEAN
as Louis in *Louis XI, King of France* by Dion Boucicault

Henry Wyndham Phillips

Oil on canvas 208.3 x 116.8
INV: RW/CKA 72; Gift 236
PROV: Presented by the artist's widow, 1888

Louis wears a red velvet skull-cap, red shoes, red stockings and breeches, and a long red velvet jacket trimmed with fur. He has a short cloak and large gold chain. He stands on a red carpet in front of his throne. The steps are covered in a blue drape decorated with gold fleurs-de-lys and edged in gold.

Boucicault's tragedy was first given at the Princess's Theatre on 13 January 1855, with Charles Kean in the title role. 'C.S.L.' exhibited a portrait of Charles Kean as Louis XI at the R.A. in 1855 (1096), which was lithographed by R.J. Lane and published by J. Mitchell. F.B. Tussaud showed a bust of Charles Kean at the same R.A. exhibition (1471).

Kean became a member of the Garrick Club in 1833.

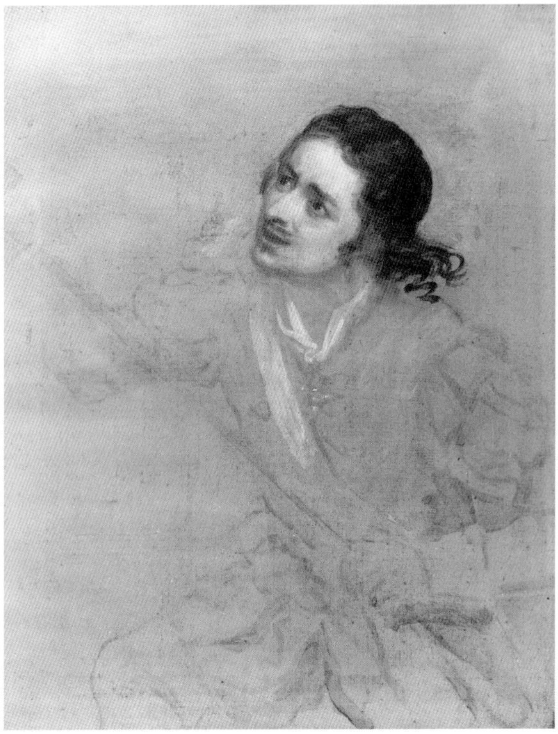

345
EDMUND KEAN
as Richard in *Richard III* by William Shakespeare

George Clint

Oil on canvas 52.5 x 41.3
INV: Mathews 146; RW 408 (sitter and artist unknown);
CKA 408 (as Sir Giles Overreach)
PROV: Charles Mathews
EXH: 1833 London (146)
ENGR: Relates to Robert Cooper for Terry's *British Theatrical Gallery* pub. H. Berthoud Jnr 1822, stipple and line 19.7 x 14.6 (full-length to l., kneeling, r.h. on chest, l.h. pointing to sword on ground)
REL: Sir Henry Irving sale, Christie's 16 December 1905 (117) 'Edmund Kean as Richard III, a sketch. Oval 13½ x 11'

Only the head has been finished by the artist. The rest of the picture is sketched in with brown underpaint over a cream ground.

Kean played Richard III at Drury Lane for the first time on 12 February 1814. His portrayal was an instant success and it remained his most popular role.

Adams's identification of the subject rests on the mistaken assumption that this study is preparatory for Clint's large scene from *A New Way to Pay Old Debts*, No. 355.

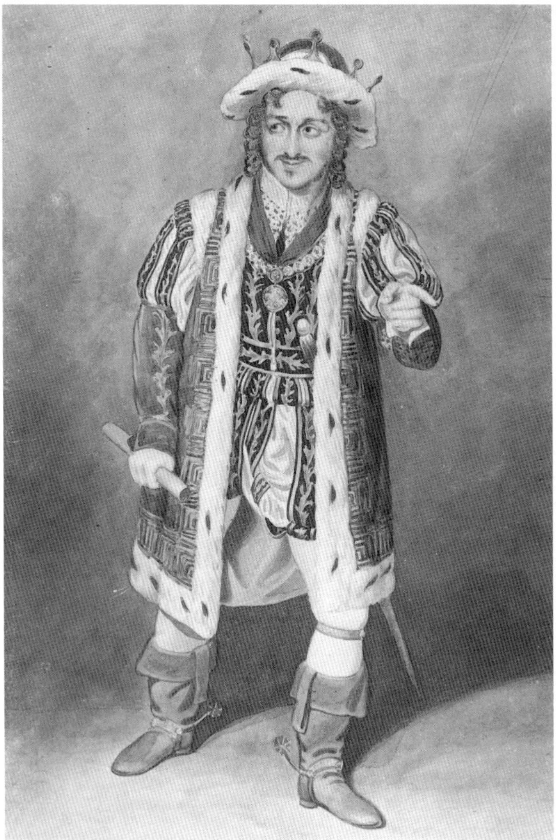

346
EDMUND KEAN
as Richard in *Richard III* by William Shakespeare

Samuel De Wilde

Pencil and watercolour on wove paper 37 x 23.5
INSCR: Illegible traces of a pencil inscr. b.l.
INV: Mathews 245; RW/CKA 46E
PROV: Charles Mathews
EXH: 1833 London (245)
ENGR: Richard Brinsley Peake for the *Theatrical Inquisitor* pub. C. Chapple 1814, stipple and line 17.5 x 11.1; James Heath pub. J. Heath 12 June 1814, stipple 11.3 x 9.2 (bust in oval without crown); Holl for the *Lady's Magazine* No. 1 January 1819, stipple 11.8 x 9.5; S.S. Jocelyn & S.B. Munson for *Unique* pub. J.P. Peaslee 1829, stipple (vignette)
REL: A portrait by an unnamed artist of Kean as Richard III that was in the Dramatic College sale at Fairbrother, Lye and Palmer on 24 February 1881 (lot 69) may possibly be related

Kean wears wide brown boots, white tights with a blue garter below the left knee, a long, sleeveless red coat trimmed with ermine, embroidered in gold and lined with white satin, and a doublet and hose of white lining under blue straps. His sleeves are red, decorated in gold, and there is an enamelled chain with a large medallion round his neck. A large blue ribbon round his neck supports a smaller medallion, and his gold crown has red jewels and a red cap.

Kean's costume as Richard III, shown in De Wilde's watercolour – and in other portraits of Kean in the part, such as John James Hall's portrait in the Theatre Museum (TM21) and Samuel Drummond's portrait on loan from the Governors of the Old Vic Theatre to the University of Bristol Theatre Collection (Georgian Playhouse catalogue No. 203) – is now in the Museum of London (53.96). The wig is also in the Museum.

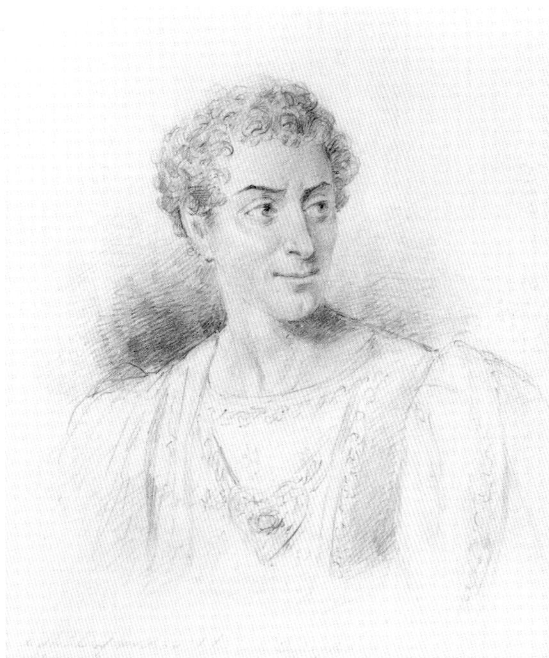

347
EDMUND KEAN
as Othello in *Othello* by William Shakespeare

E.F. Lambert

Pencil on wove paper 19.7 x 15.9
INSCR: 'A Sketch of Mr Kean, taken in his Dressing-Room / Feby 1829 by E F Lambert' (pencil b.l.)
INV: RW/CKA 509 (no character); Gift 37
PROV: Presented by Leigh & Sotheby, 1836
ENGR: 'F.W.D.' pub. Dean & Munday, coloured lithograph

Head and shoulders. Othello wears a heart-shaped medallion. The engraving bears the line: 'Oh beware my Lord of Jealousy.'

Kean's first appearance as Othello was at Drury Lane on 5 May 1814. In his last appearance on stage he played Othello to the Iago of his son Charles, at Covent Garden on 25 March 1833.

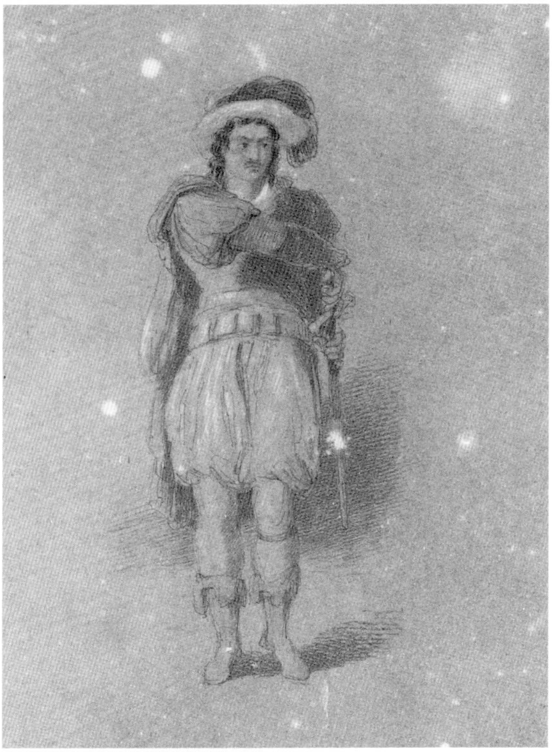

348

EDMUND KEAN

as Richard in *Richard III*

by William Shakespeare

J.S. MacAlpine

Pencil and body colour on
dark brown wove paper 21.6 x 14.6
INV: RW/CKA 535; Gift 195
PROV: Presented by Thomas Dyer Edwardes, 1885
ENGR: Relates to T. Blood after Samuel Drummond
for the *European Magazine* pub. J. Asperne 1 April 1824,
stipple (vignette, half-length to front, looking to r.);
Brocas for the *Dublin Museum Monthly*, stipple 12.4 x 9.8

A small full-length study. The hat, doublet and hose are touched in red.

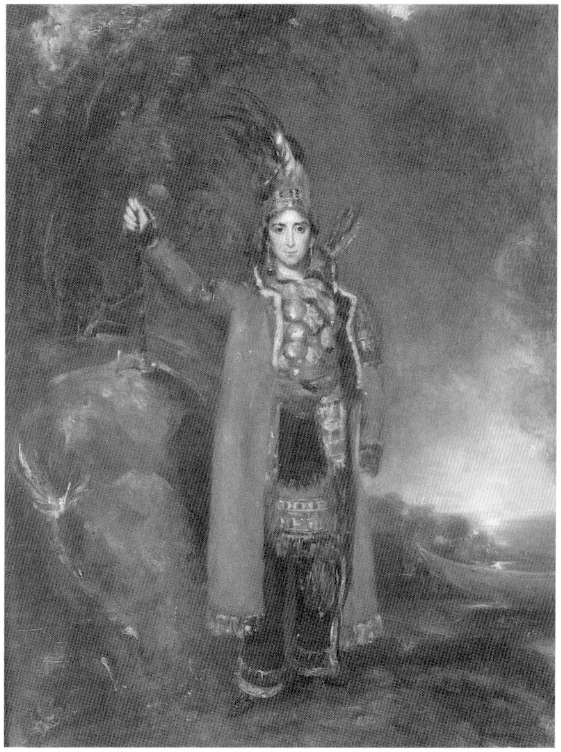

349

EDMUND KEAN

as Alanienouidet, Chief and Prince
of the Huron Tribe of Indians

Henry Meyer

Oil on canvas 57 x 42.5
INV: Mathews 171; RW/CKA 388
PROV: Charles Mathews
EXH: 1833 London (171); 1974 Twickenham (63)
ENGR: G.F. Storm pub. Wm. Kenneth 1827, stipple and line
29.2 x 21.9; same plate pub. Neal & Mackenzie,
Philadelphia 1828; Anon., etching (vignette half-length
to front, quiver full of arrows over l. shoulder – a
visiting card); Anon., line (vignette head to front,
with arrow and hatchet – a visiting card)
LIT: Griffiths, p. 339

Kean is in an extravagant American Indian costume in leather and feathers. He wears metal trophies on his chest and carries a quiver full of arrows. Meyer has attempted to suggest a North American landscape with a canoe visible bottom right.

The costume was presented to Kean when he was elected a Chief and Prince of the Hurons at Québec on 7 October 1826. He seems to have worn it with great glee on the streets of London. See also No. 350.

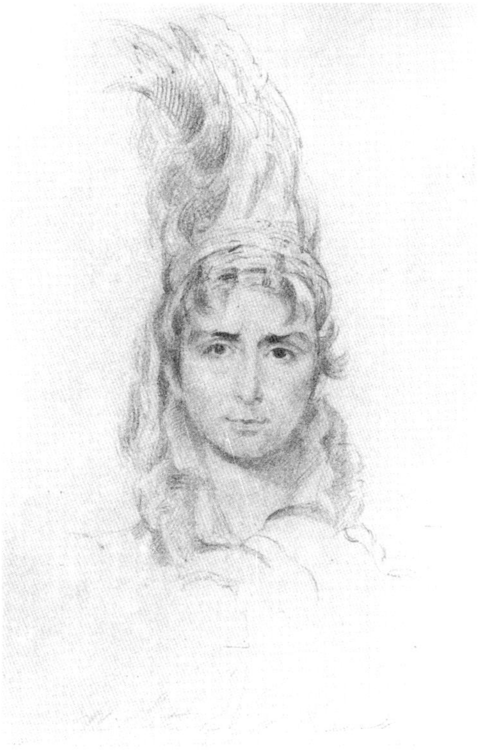

350

EDMUND KEAN

as Alanienouidet, Chief and Prince of the Huron Tribe of Indians

Henry Meyer

Pencil on brown wove paper 19 x 12.7
INSCR: 'A sketch of Mr Kean' (pencil b.c.)
INV: RW/CKA 512 (artist unknown)
PROV: Unknown but acquired by 1888

This may be a preparatory study for the painting, No. 349, but was possibly produced for one of the engraved visiting cards that Kean had made, showing him in his real-life role as an American Indian Chief.

351

EDMUND KEAN

as Sir Giles Overreach
in *A New Way to Pay Old Debts*
by Philip Massinger

William Hook Morley (after George Clint)

Oil on canvas 124.4 x 97.8
INSCR: 'Kean, / ......' (black paint b.r.); 'W. Morley pinx. 1833' (dark brown paint on paper b.c.)
INV: RW 84 (as a Huron Chief by Meyer) [This is a confusion rather than an inaccuracy, as the Meyer is correctly listed as RW 388; see No. 349]; CKA 84

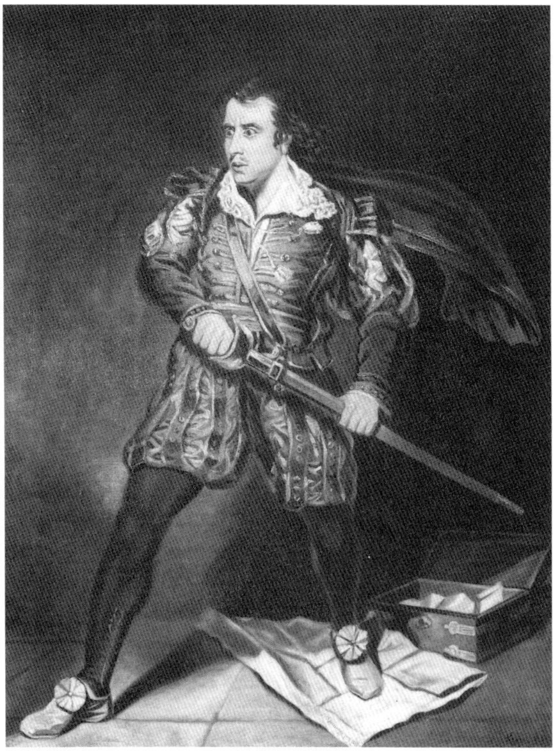

351 *Edmund Kean as Sir Giles Overreach*

PROV: Presented by Thomas F. Egan between 1846 and 1888
EXH: 1975 Brighton (J12)
ENGR: Thomas Goff Lupton after George Clint
pub. Milburn Kenneth 1833, mezzotint 46.2 x 32.5
REL: Clint's original picture has not been traced; see No. 355

The dastardly Sir Giles thinks he has gained control over the land of Wellborn, and that of Lady Allworth too, as she appears to have married Wellborn. Sir Giles claims that Wellborn signed away his property to him, and calls for the deed to prove it. His servants bring in the deed box and place it on a table – not on the floor as in this picture. Sir Giles takes out the deed and sees that it is blank and worthless. He asks his steward, Marrall, to swear that the deed was signed and sealed, but Marrall denies it and Sir Giles accuses him of betrayal. Marrall later admits to Wellborn that the writing disappeared because of 'certain minerals incorporated in the ink and wax'.

This picture is a single-figure version of Clint's scene depicting a moment slightly later in the play (No. 355), with the deed box and deed added to make theatrical sense of the single figure.

Kean, standing, legs apart and drawing his sword, wears a red Elizabethan costume decorated in gold, dark red hose and gold shoes.

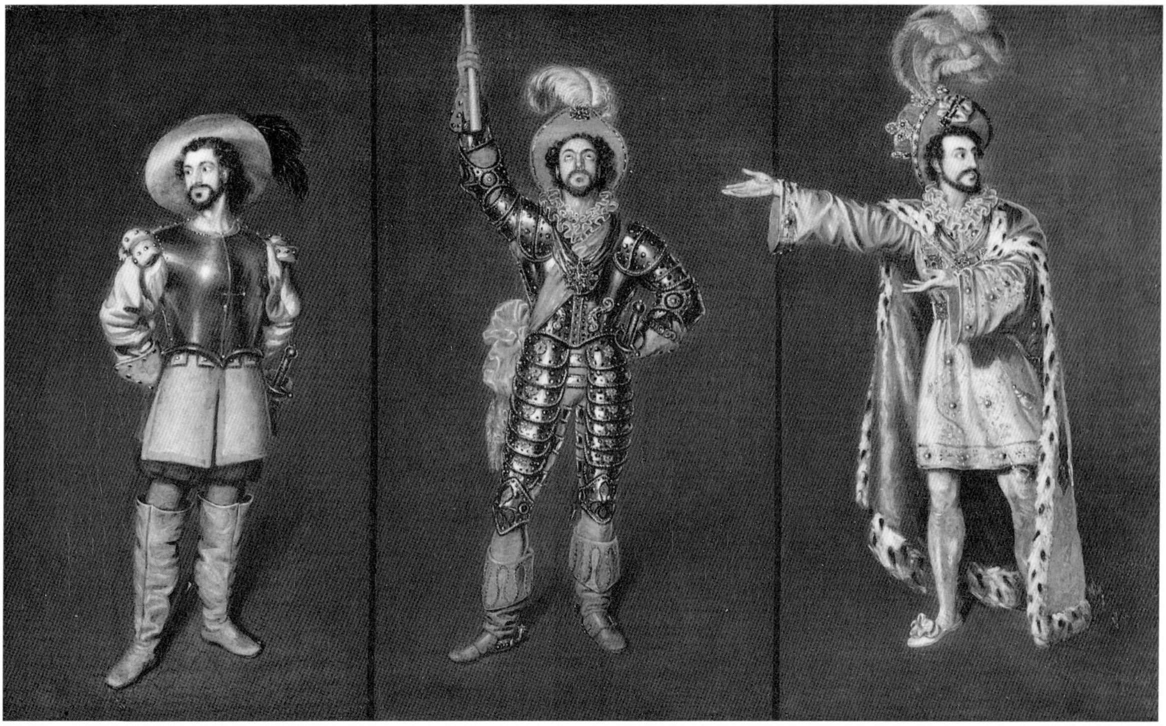

352*
EDMUND KEAN
as Richard in *Richard III*
by William Shakespeare

Thomas Charles Wageman (attr.)

Oil on canvas 45.7 x 74.9
INV: RW/CKA 125; Gift 280
PROV: Presented by Sir Squire Bancroft, 1902
EXH: 1951 London (37); 1982–83 London (147); 1984 London (108)

Richard is shown in three attitudes and three costumes, the figures divided by dark brown vertical lines. On the left, he wears thigh-length brown boots, red hose, brown gauntlets with silver studs, and a broad-brimmed silver hat with a black plume. In the middle, he has a hat with a broad red brim edged in silver sequins, with a Maltese Cross and two white plumes. He wears brown gauntlets and brown boots, red hose, and scaled armour. There is a broad pink ribbon across his chest and a silver order hanging from a blue ribbon around his neck. On the right, he wears a large red hat with a jewelled crown, white rosette, blue jewel and ostrich feathers; his regal costume consists of white slippers with rosettes, silver stockings, a grey tunic trimmed with gold and lined in red, and a red cloak lined in silver and trimmed with ermine.

The artist has neatly illustrated, in the costume, Richard's progress through the play. The attribution to Wageman is supported by a similar triple portrait exhibited by Wageman at the R.A. in 1817 (861). It shows John Pritt Harley as Jack Phantom in *Frightened to Death*. He thought highly enough of that triple portrait both to engrave and to publish it himself in the same year.

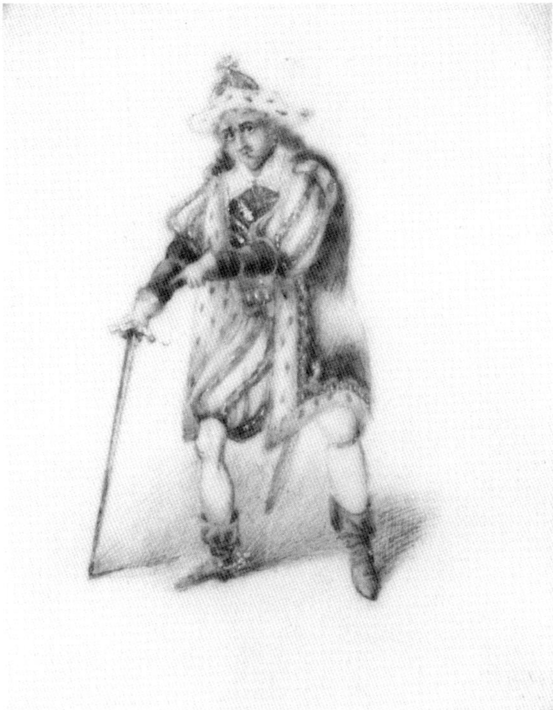

353
EDMUND KEAN
as Richard in *Richard III*
by William Shakespeare

Unknown Artist

Watercolour on ivory 6.5 x 5.2
INV: CKA 536; Gift 422
PROV: Presented by H.G. Rooth
and Miss M.A. Rooth, 1924

Richard wears red boots with gold edging, white hose with gold bands, doublet with white sleeves, and a long, sleeveless red jacket trimmed with ermine and gold. He is shown at the classic moment when he enters unhorsed at the Battle of Bosworth (Act v, scene 7).

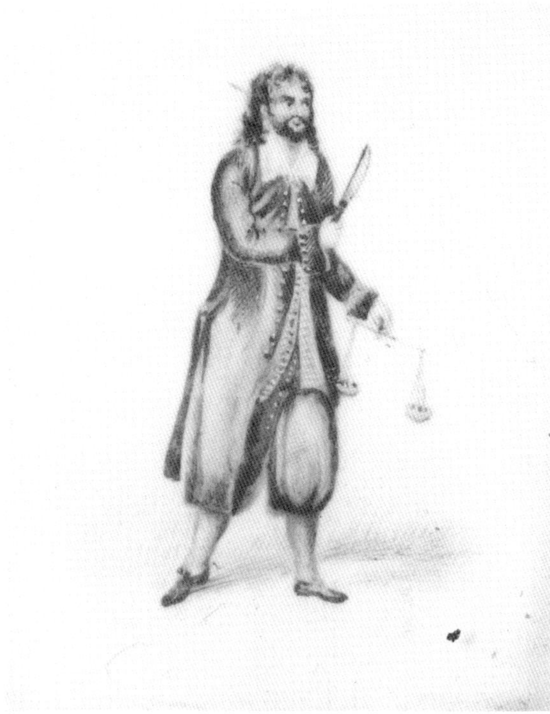

354
EDMUND KEAN
as Shylock in *The Merchant of Venice*
by William Shakespeare

Unknown Artist

Watercolour on ivory 6.5 x 5.2
INV: CKA 537; Gift 422
PROV: Presented by H.G. Rooth
and Miss M.A. Rooth, 1924

Shylock, wielding knife and scales, wears brown shoes, red stockings, long baggy purple knee-breeches, and a long purple coat with gold buttons.

Kean made his mature début at Drury Lane as Shylock on 26 January 1814. His Covent Garden début on 15 October 1817 was also as Shylock.

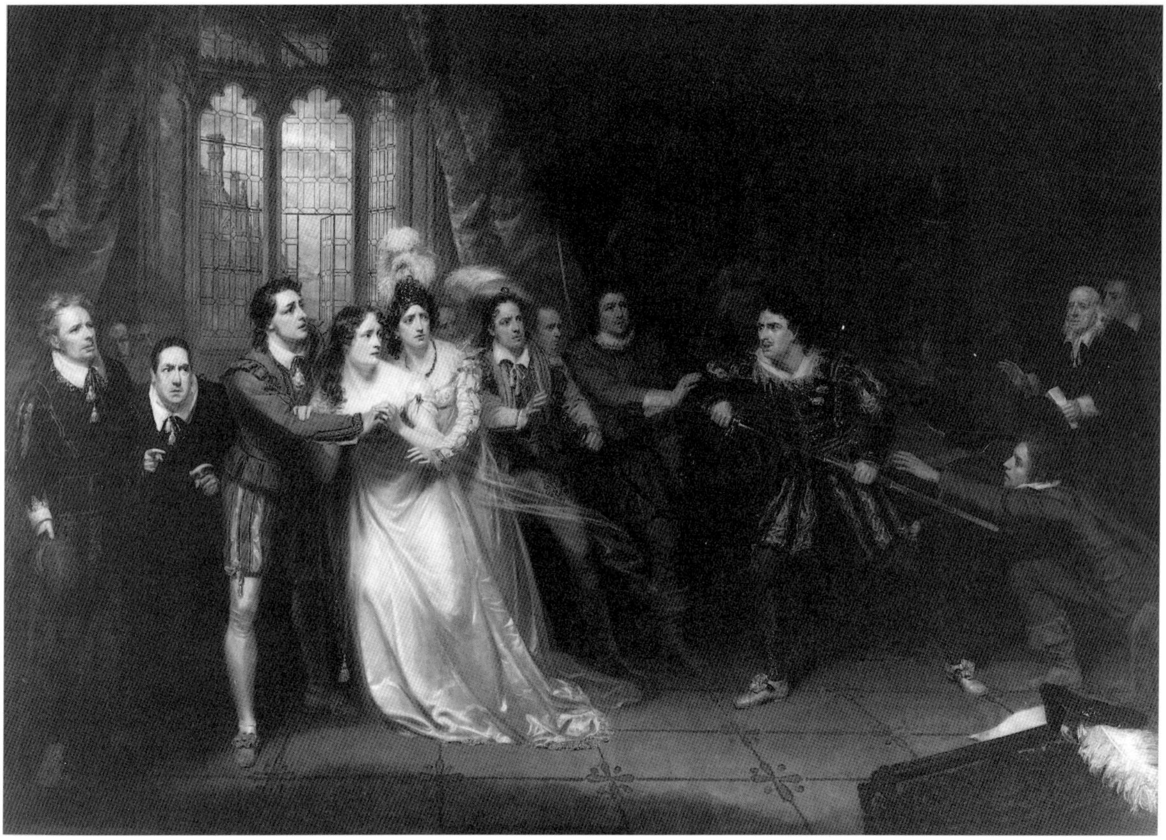

355*

EDMUND KEAN as Sir Giles Overreach with *GEORGE CLINT*, *Mr CARR* as Willdo, *JOHN PRITT HARLEY* as Wellborn, *Mr HOLLAND* as Lord Lovell, *Mrs EDWARD KNIGHT* as Lady Allworth, *THOMAS GOFF LUPTON* (?), *JOSEPH SHEPHERD MUNDEN* as Marrall, *Mrs ORGER* as Margaret, *WILLIAM OXBERRY* as Justice Greedy and *SAMPSON PENLEY* as Allworth in a scene from *A New Way to Pay Old Debts* by Philip Massinger

George Clint

Oil on canvas 165.1 x 235
INV: RW/CKA 465; Gift 218
PROV: Presented by Sir Henry Irving, 1889
EXH: 1820 R.A. (311), with the following quotation: 'Sir Giles: Village Nurses / Revenge their wrongs with curses; I'll / Not waste a syllable; but this I take / The life which, wretched, I gave to thee / (Offers to kill Margaret) Act V.' [R.A. Catalogue]
REL: Folger Library, anon., single figure (similar), oil 38.4 x 28.4 (see Pressly, *Folger*, 134); Theatre Museum (TM23), single figure by Clint, oil 30 x 22.9

Sir Giles has just discovered that his daughter Margaret has secretly married Allworth rather than Lord Lovell. Despite his plans and machinations, he has been thwarted, and 'all my hopes and labours defeated and made void'. The Royal Academy catalogue cites lines (quoted above) from a moment slightly earlier in Act V, scene I, than that depicted in Clint's picture. On hearing the news that his plan has been to no avail, according to the text Sir Giles 'offers to kill his daughter', but there is no mention of drawing his sword. After that threat, Allworth and Margaret cross over to stage right, where they stand in the painting, and Lord Lovell tells Sir Giles to stop, his extended arm clearly indicating this in the picture. After a number of virulent curses Sir Giles crosses to centre stage and 'attempts to draw his sword' but fails to do so, rushes towards his daughter, and collapses on the stage in a frenzy of madness.

Kean played Sir Giles Overreach in a revival of Massinger's comedy at Drury Lane on 12 January 1816.

Clint's picture shows the cast of the 1819–20 season, with the addition of a number of heads apparently depicting the artist and several of his friends.

Oxberry's 1818 edition of the play – 'the only edition existing which is faithfully marked with the stage business and stage directions' – has a page describing the costumes of the principal characters under the title 'Old English Costume'. These descriptions are given here with any differences in the painting noted in brackets. Kerseymere is a kind of cashmere, and galloon is a narrow silk ribbon used for trimming garments. The characters are described from left to right:

> Justice Greedy, who spends the play salivating over what he is going to eat next: 'A black kerseymere jacket; trunks and cloak trimmed with scarlet satin, galloon puffs, and black glass buttons; white square-toed shoes; black hat; gloves with high tops, and a vandyke' [the vandyke is the lace-edged linen collar; the black hat has a red feather]; unknown head wrongly called George Clint by RW and CKA; unknown head called Thomas Lupton, the engraver, by RW and CKA; Marrall, Sir Giles's evil steward who reforms and helps Wellborn recover his inheritance: 'Black cloth dress; black shoes &c.' [He seems to be holding the top of a stick for which there is no call in the text]; Allworth, in love with Margaret 'A light mixture kersey-mere jacket and trunks, trimmed with pink galloon, narrow black ribbon and plated buttons; white silk pantaloons; pink satin vest, trimmed with light blue, and plated buttons; russet shoes; lace ruff'; Margaret, Sir Giles's daughter whose secret marriage to Allworth has caused her father's violence: 'White satin dress, the sleeves and front of the petticoat ornamented with jewels; a ruff, and white satin shoes' [Clint has omitted the ruff]; Lady Allworth, the wealthy widowed step-mother of Allworth who marries the apparently destitute Wellborn: 'Second Dress. White satin train dress, with long sleeves, richly embroidered with gold; robe of white and gold; high ruff; jewel stomacher and cross; white satin hat and feathers' [the ruff is again missing and the feathered hat looks more like a jewelled tiara]; unknown head; Wellborn, ruined by his uncle Sir Giles but recovering his fortune at the end of the play: 'Second Dress. A buff kerseymere jacket and pantaloons, trimmed with green galloon, silk cord, plated buttons, and green vest, trimmed with buff; a buff hat, and white feathers; a ruff; russet boots; buff gloves, with high tops' [he does not wear the gloves and carries a sword; he has a linen collar rather than a ruff; and there is green embroidery over his thighs]; head of George Clint, the artist [identified as Kean's secretary Hughes by RW and CKA]; Lord Lovell, Allworth's commanding officer and friend and Sir Giles's choice as husband for his daughter, Margaret: 'A scarlet jacket and trunks trimmed with light blue satin, and yellow plated buttons; russet boots with red tops; scarlet mantle; a ruff; buff gloves with high tops' [he carries a sword and wears square-toed buff boots]; Sir Giles, the evil and greedy tyrant: 'Brown velvet jacket and trunks, with orange satin puffs; brown velvet cloak lined with orange satin; the dress trimmed with gold-coloured silk lace and gilt buttons; brown silk hose, the same colour as the dress, with gold embroidered clocks; square-toed shoes and jewel buckles, with orange satin roses over them; a broad Brussels point lace vandyke with two tassels; a round-crown brown hat, with orange puffs and feathers of the same colour' [the hat is on the floor bottom right]; unknown kneeling figure, presumably one of Sir Giles's unnamed servants who enter with the parson earlier in the scene (grey-green doublet and hose, buff boots); Parson Willdo [black clerical garb with lace collar; he holds the letter from Sir Giles instructing him to marry Margaret to 'this gentleman', who happens to be Allworth rather Lord Lovell]; unknown head.

The Gothic interior, 'the Hall in Lady Allworth's House', has a five-light window through which can be seen Gothic architectural details. Behind Sir Giles is a large painting, and in a niche is a gold and black armour over a coromandel screen. The cream tiled floor is decorated with a stylised floral pattern in orange and blue.

This is one of the most imposing of all theatrical paintings. It was directly inspired by George Henry Harlow's scene from *Henry VIII* (see No. 750). There are similarities in the composition, the accurate depiction of what was regarded as historical costume, and the inclusion of portraits of the artist and, presumably, some of his friends.

The moment shown in Clint's painting was the dramatic climax of Kean's career; according to Raymund Fitzsimons in *Edmund Kean: Fire from Heaven* (1976), it was 'the most powerful exhibition of human passion that has ever been witnessed on the English stage'. This hyperbole seems justified by the events of the first night. Mrs Glover, playing Margaret, collapsed into genuine hysterics, screaming women in the audience had to be led from the theatre, and Lord Byron, who was also in the audience, suffered a convulsive fit.

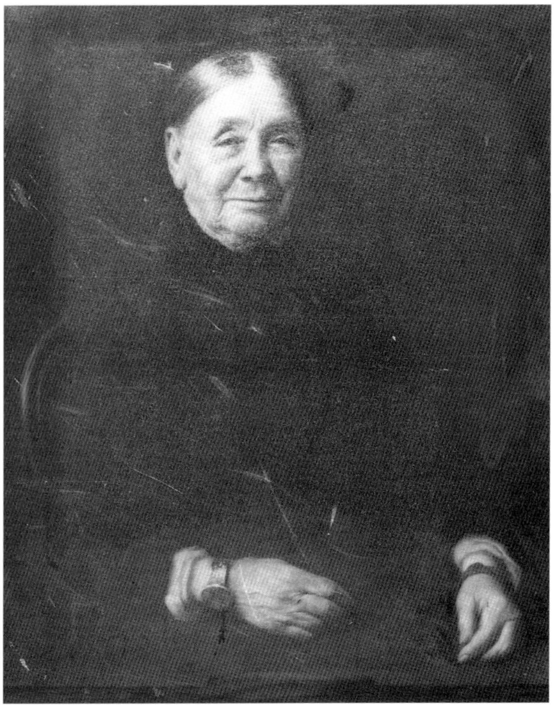

356
MARY ANN KEELEY

Walter Goodman

Oil on canvas 74.9 x 62.2
INV: RW/CKA 97; Gift 199
PROV: Presented by Spencer Brunton, 1886
EXH: 1884 R.I.
LIT: Walter Goodman, *The Keeleys on the Stage and in the Home* (1895), p. 51

Mary Ann Keeley has strikingly fair hair. She wears gold bracelets; the bracelet on her right wrist contains a miniature. Goodman began the portrait soon after 16 January 1884. He exhibited another portrait of her at the R.A. 1888 (880) called 'Mrs Keeley in her 83rd year'.

In her earlier years Mrs Keeley excelled in 'pathetic appealing parts like Nydia in *The Last Days of Pompeii* and Smirke in *Nicholas Nickleby*' (OC). Her greatest portrayal, according to the OC, was that of the title role in *Jack Sheppard*, in which the highwayman was presented as a 'wild youngster'.

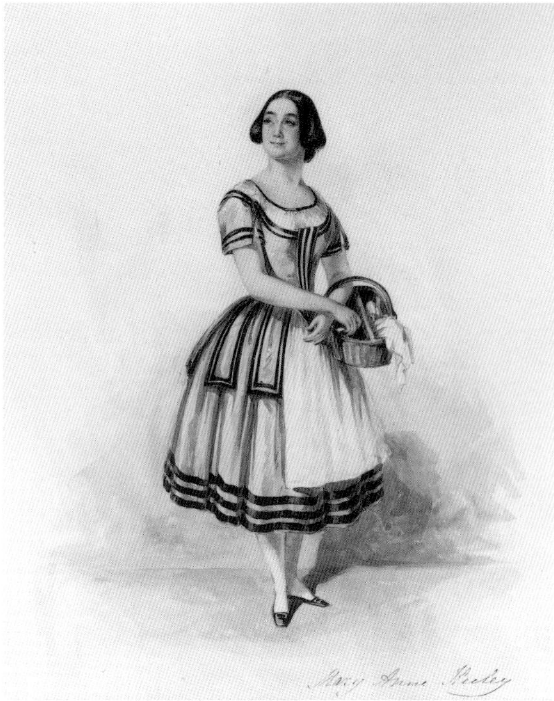

357
MARY ANN KEELEY
in character

Thomas Harrington Wilson

Pencil and watercolour on wove paper 40.6 x 30.5
INSCR: 'Mary Anne Keeley' (pen and brown ink b.r.); 'Thos. Harrington Wilson. del. 1845.' (pen and brown ink on mount b.l.)
INV: RW/CKA 192; Gift 266
PROV: Presented by Colonel Richardson, executor of Mrs Keeley's estate, 1899

The sitter wears a short-skirted silvery-grey dress edged with parallel black lines, and a white apron.

Mrs Keeley and her husband Robert took over the management of the Lyceum Theatre in 1844 and remained there until 1847, when Mrs Keeley moved to the Haymarket.

358
LOCATION UNKNOWN
ROBERT KEELEY

Henry O'Neil

Oil on canvas 52 x 41.3
INV: RW/CKA 335; Gift 171
PROV: Presented by the artist, 1863
EXH: 1863 R.A. (615) 'Robert Keeley, Esq.
Painted for the Garrick Club'

Keeley, in a black suit, holds an orange handkerchief in his lap. He became a member of the Garrick Club in 1859. This picture was not found in 1996.

359
LOCATION UNKNOWN
ROBERT KEELEY
in character

Thomas Harrington Wilson

Pencil and watercolour on wove paper 41.3 x 30.5
INSCR: 'Thos. Harrington Wilson del 1865'
(pen and brown ink on mount)
INV: RW/CKA 188 (by T.C. Wageman,
not located); Gift 266
PROV: Presented by Colonel Richardson,
executor of Mrs Keeley's estate, 1899

Keeley, who was a humorous low comedian, is dressed as a middle-aged woman in white night attire, holding a candle.

The date should probably be read as 1845, and the drawing be seen as a pendant to No. 357. This picture was not found in 1996.

360
ROBERT KEELEY
as Billy Black in *The £100 Note*
by Richard Brinsley Peake

Thomas Charles Wageman

Pencil and watercolour on wove paper 33 x 22.8
INV: RW/CKA 190 (by Thomas Harrington Wilson); Gift 266
PROV: Presented by Colonel Richardson,
executor of Mrs Keeley's estate, 1899
ENGR: Anon. pub. Wm. Kenneth 14 May 1827,
lithograph (vignette); T. Jones, aquatint 10.7 x 6.8
(J.W. Gear printed by C. Hullmandel, lithograph
[Music Sheet Inscr: 'D'ye give it up? / Written & sung
by / Mr Keeley / with the most enthusiastic Applause
at the / Theatre Royal, Covent Garden /
in the Character / Billy Black'])

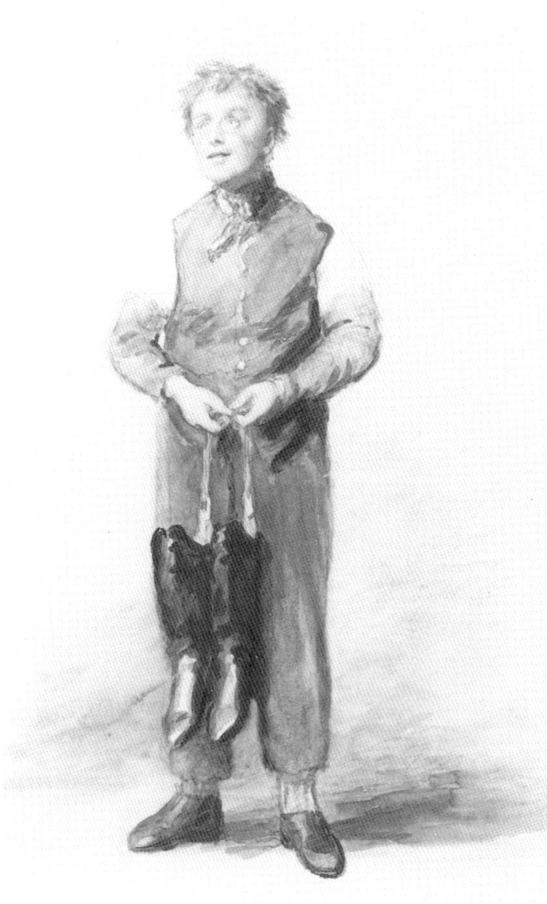

360 *Robert Keeley as Billy Black*

Billy Black is a boot-boy working for Mr Janus, the landlord of an inn. In Act 1, scene 3, he brings into an 'Apartment in the Hotel' 'a pair of clean boots, boot-hooks, brushes &c.'. He gives the boots to Montmorency, a guest at the inn, before throwing in a few conundrums. The moment is shown in Robert Cruikshank's frontispiece to the 1829 Cumberland edition of the play. Montmorency is the owner of the £100 note, the loss of which causes most of the incident of the play.

The costume for Billy Black is given in the Cumberland edition as: 'Fustian jacket – very short corderoy trousers – red waistcoat, with worsted sleeves – fur and leather cap – coloured neckerchief – worsted stockings – high-low shoes.' In Wageman's drawing Billy has ginger hair and wears black shoes, striped socks, brown trousers, a red waistcoat (unpainted down the front), a white shirt with brown cuff protectors, and a brown and green neckerchief.

Peake's farce was first performed at Covent Garden on 7 February 1827, with Keeley as the original Billy Black.

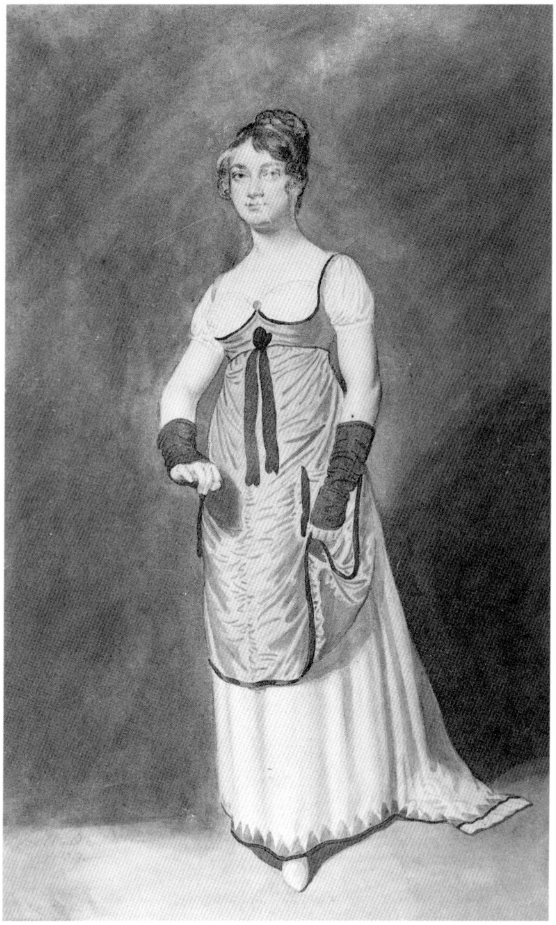

361
FRANCES KELLY
as Floretta in *The Cabinet*
by Thomas John Dibdin

Samuel De Wilde

Pencil and watercolour on wove paper 37 x 23.5
INSCR: 'S De Wilde delin / 1809' (pencil b.l.)
INV: Mathews 204; RW/CKA 68E
PROV: Charles Mathews
EXH: 1833 London (204)

Floretta wears loose grey mittens, a short-sleeved dress with a creamy-pink skirt trimmed in black and blue, and a blue bodice on which is a blue apron trimmed in grey and with grey ribbons. CKA suggests that she is speaking the line in Act I: 'I couldn't represent a princess three minutes without bringing the devil into conversation.'

Miss Kelly's first performance as Floretta in 1809 was for the Drury Lane company at the Lyceum on 13 May. Mrs Mountain had played Floretta in the four previous performances.

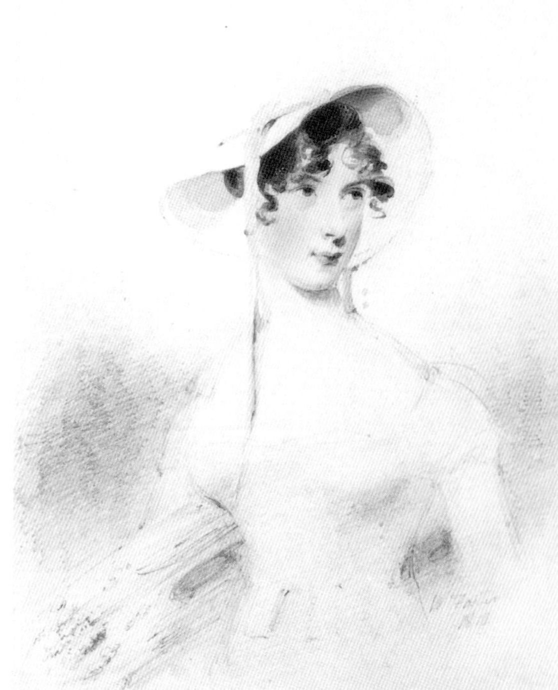

362
LYDIA KELLY
as Rosina in *Rosina* by Frances Brooke

William Foster

Pencil and watercolour on wove paper 21.6 x 17.1
INSCR: 'W Foster / 1810' (pencil b.r.)
INV: Mathews 282; RW 547B (Mrs Decamp, no character); CKA 547B (as Rosina in *The Barber of Seville*)
PROV: Charles Mathews
EXH: 1833 London (282)

In Act I, Rosina shows her aged guardian Dorcas newly harvested corn. Carrying a sheaf of corn under her right arm, Rosina wears a low-cut dress and a wide-brimmed hat with ribbons.

Lydia Kelly made her theatrical début for the Drury Lane company at the Lyceum on 11 October 1810 as Rosina. See also No. 120.

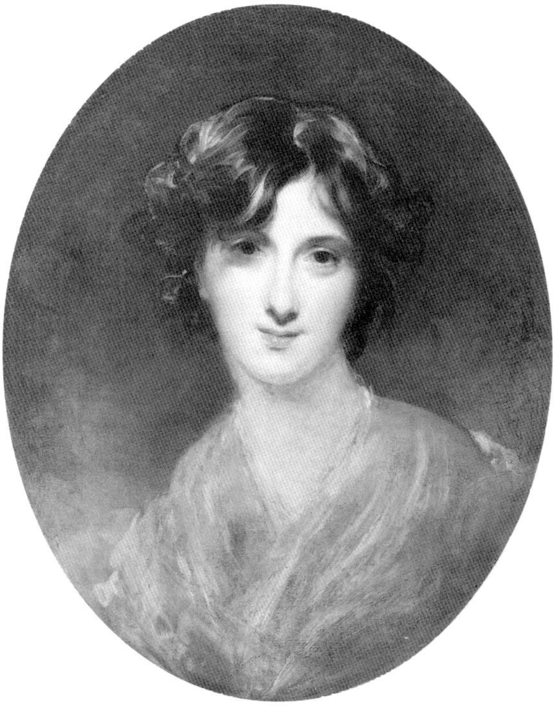

363*
LYDIA KELLY

George Henry Harlow

Oil on canvas 57.1 x 45.7 (oval)
INV: Mathews 26: RW/CKA 375
PROV: Charles Mathews
EXH: 1833 London (26)
LIT: Fitzgerald, p. 236

Head and shoulders. The pink muslin drapery around the sitter's shoulders is unfinished. However, no more finished version of the portrait is known.

364*
MICHAEL KELLY
as Cymon
in *Cymon* by David Garrick

Samuel De Wilde

Oil on canvas 37 x 29
INV: Mathews 79; RW/CKA 239
PROV: John Bell; Leigh & Sotheby's 25 May 1805 (259); Charles Mathews
EXH: 1833 London (79); 1983 Buxton (29)
ENGR: William S. Leney for Bell's British Library 15 August 1795, line 11.1 x 7.6, pub. Bell's *British Theatre* (1797), vol 23

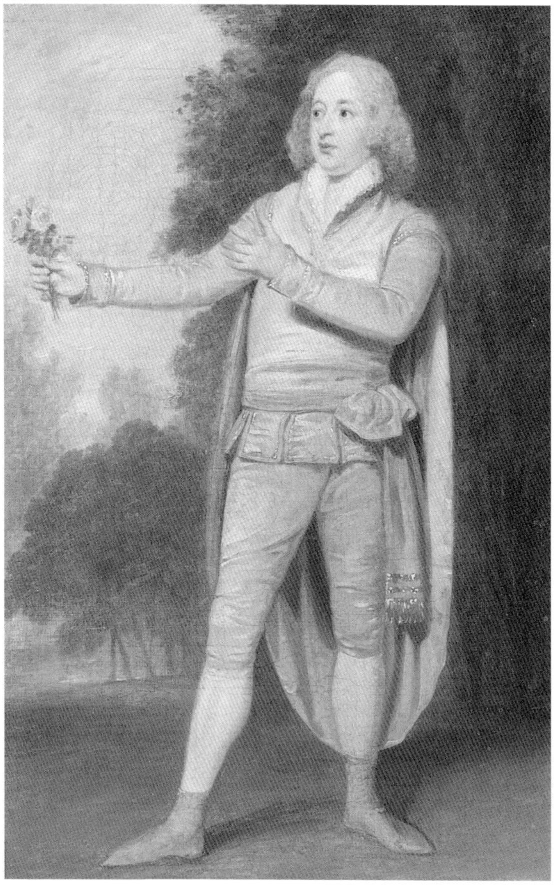

364 *Michael Kelly as Cymon*

Cymon holds the nosegay enchanted by Merlin and given to him by Sylvia, for whom he has developed a great passion. He has made an exchange with another nosegay that was given to him by Urganda, a wicked fairy and Sylvia's rival. Urganda watches him in the belief that he is in ecstasy over her own gift. The line quoted on the engraving is: 'Oh, the dear, dear Nosegay and the dear, dear giver of it.'

Cymon's bucolic costume consists of tight blue ankle boots edged in pink, a pink doublet and breeches with a pale blue sash with silver fringe, blue cuffs, and a blue cloak lined in white.

Garrick's dramatic romance, with music by Thomas Arne, was first performed at Drury Lane on 2 January 1767, with Joseph Vernon as Cymon. Kelly first played the part at the age of 15 in Dublin, at the Crow Street Theatre in June 1777. His first London performance in the role was with the Drury Lane company at the King's Theatre, in a revival on 31 December 1791. The piece was played 36 times during that season. Kelly played the role for the last time on 28 January 1793.

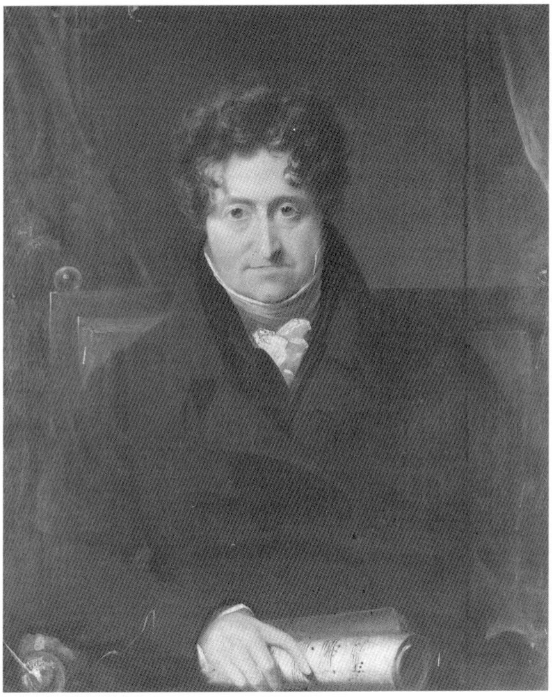

365
MICHAEL KELLY

James Lonsdale

Oil on canvas 74.9 x 61.6
INV: Mathews 102; RW/CKA 355
PROV: Rowland Stevenson; Stevenson sale, Christie's 13 April 1829 (33); Charles Mathews
EXH: 1833 London (102)
ENGR: Charles Turner pub. Mr Sams 1 June 1825, mezzotint 26 x 21

Kelly wears a brown coat and a dark green scarf over his high white cravat. In his right hand he holds a roll of music.

From his début in 1787 to his retirement in 1822, Kelly was a principal tenor in London's concerts and oratorios. He was also stage manager and leading singer at the King's Theatre in the 1790s. At the new Drury Lane Theatre, beginning in 1794, he was very popular in English operas and directed the music, much of which he composed in the vigorous tradition of English theatrical music.

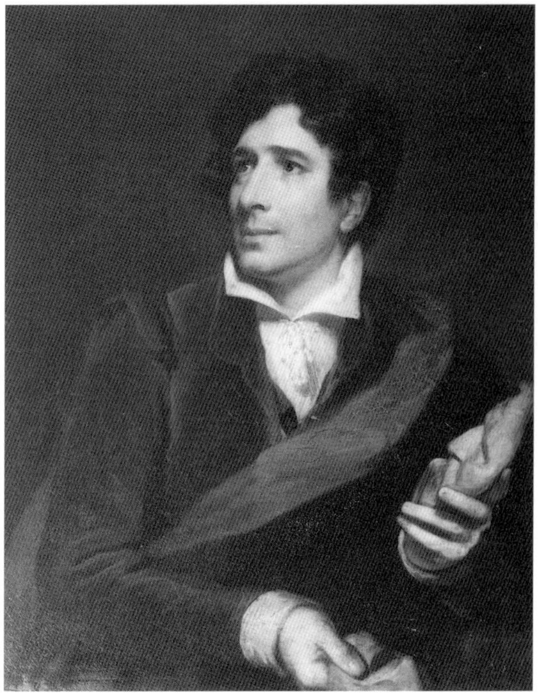

366
CHARLES KEMBLE

Henry Perronet Briggs

Oil on canvas 91 x 71
INV: RW/CKA 8; Gift 93
PROV: Bequeathed by Edward Walpole as 'Choice of Tragedy or Comedy', 1844
EXH: 1832 R.A. (477)?; 1962 Chichester (7)
REL: NG of South Africa, Capetown (331) oil on canvas 91.5 x 71 (with masks, r.h. more open, handling looser than in No. 366); this version was probably in the Irving sale at Christie's on 16 December 1905 (111); NPG 5687 oil on canvas 76.3 x 64 (smaller bust with no masks, loaned to the National Portrait Exh. 1868)

Kemble holds a mask in either hand. He wears a maroon velvet jacket. There is a red and blue drapery across his chest and over his shoulder.

There are three portrait types of Charles Kemble by Briggs. This is the finest of the second type, showing the sitter with masks. It seems likely that it is the picture shown at the R.A. in 1832, when Briggs was listed as R.A. Elect and would have been trying to impress with the historical potential of his portraiture. The earlier type (see No. 367) is simpler and probably dates from slightly before this picture. The third type is known in a single work now at Bryn Mawr, oil on canvas 91.5 x 71.1; probably that is the picture shown at the R.A. in 1835 (346).

Charles Kemble was one of the original members of the Garrick Club.

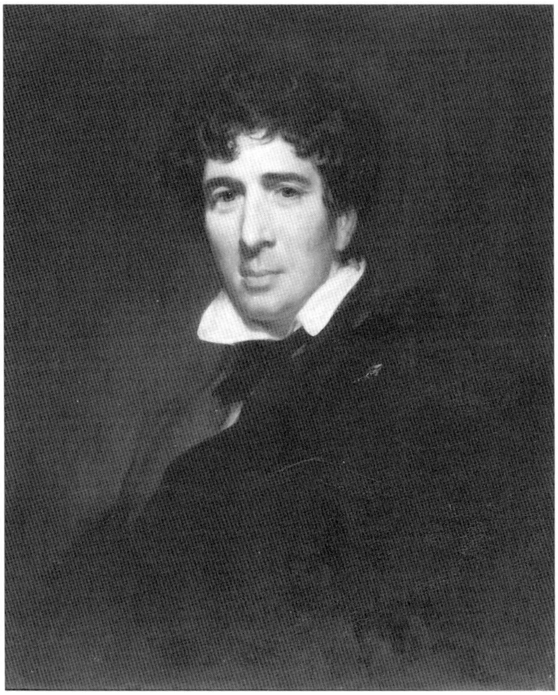

367
CHARLES KEMBLE

Henry Perronet Briggs

Oil on canvas 77.5 x 64
INV: RW/CKA 364
PROV: Unknown
REL: Dulwich 291 oil on canvas 76.5 x 63.8
(given by George Bartley, 1854);
Coll: Lady Butler 1935, oil on canvas n.s.

Kemble wears a dark cloak fastened with a gold clasp, and a white shirt with a wing collar and a black stock.

This is the best example of the earliest portrait type of Charles Kemble by Briggs. There are still memories of Harlow's portrait of the sitter as Cromwell in the group portrait of the Kemble family in *Henry VIII*, shown R.A. 1817 (17). See No. 750.

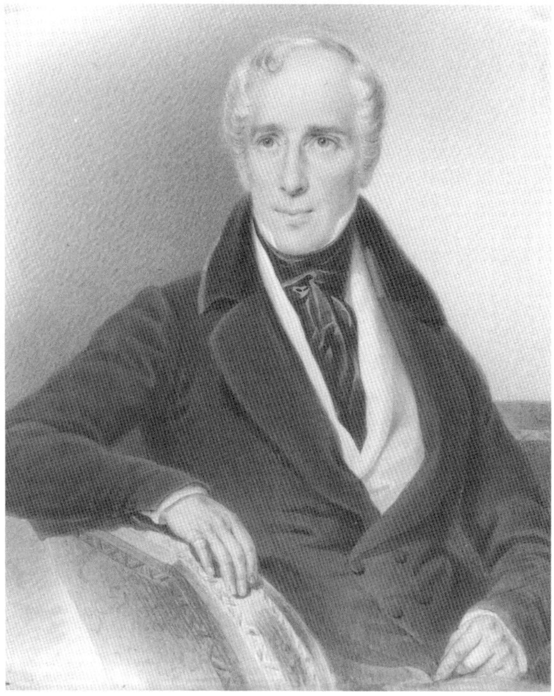

368
CHARLES KEMBLE

Richard James Lane (?)

Watercolour on wove paper 17.1 x 15.2
INV: RW/CKA 350 (artist unknown); Gift 212
PROV: Presented by Henry Kemble, 1887

Kemble is shown seated on a red sofa, wearing a black coat, white waistcoat and black cravat.

A lithograph by Lane, published by Colnaghi & Puckle in 1840, shows the sitter seated and looking to the left. He is wearing similar clothes, but with a dark waistcoat. The original is in the Folger Library (Art Box K31, No. 21). The two portraits are evidently close in date, and the Garrick Club watercolour is constructed with the hatching technique that would come more easily to one used to the resilient techniques of the engraver.

CKA noted that the donor stated the picture was drawn after Charles Kemble left the stage and before the accident that broke his nose.

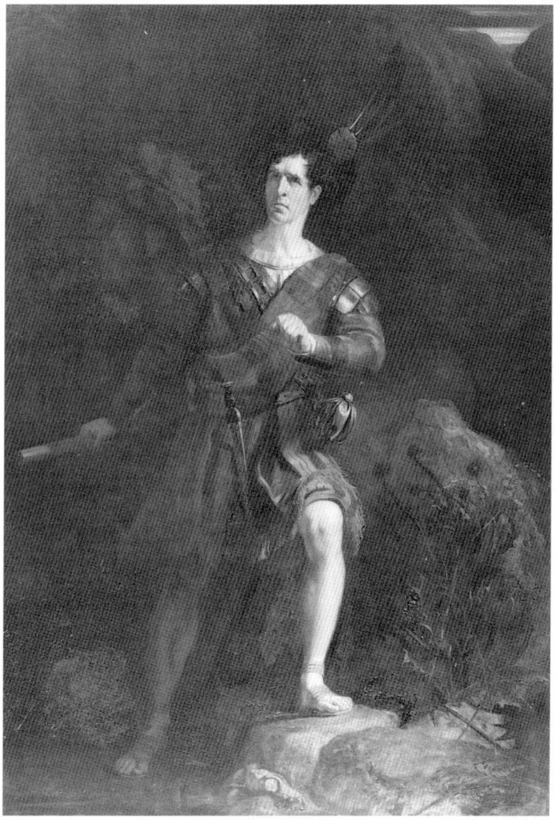

369
CHARLES KEMBLE
as Macbeth in *Macbeth* by William Shakespeare

Andrew Morton

Oil on canvas 251.5 x 176.5
INV: RW/CKA 453; Gift 234
PROV: Presented by the sitter after 1846
EXH: 1836 R.A. (221)
LIT: Fitzgerald, pp. 200–201; Griffiths, p. 329

Macbeth clenches a baton in his right hand. His costume consists of a red plaid kilt and jacket, body armour, and red and green plaid. A dirk hangs between his legs, and he wears a tam-o'-shanter with a rosette and feathers.

Kemble's Macbeth costumes were lots 22 and 23 in the sale of his wardrobe, Robins 15 June 1837. Lot 168 was 'A Magnificent Girdle of the most splendid description, decorated with large stones in imitation of diamonds, rubies, amethysts, topazes and pearls, mounted in silver, for the character of Macbeth', and lot 169 was 'The Hat with a Superb Band, to correspond with the last lot, and for the same character'. His Macbeth wig was included in lot 187.

Kemble appeared as Macbeth at Covent Garden on 13 September 1815, the first time he had acted there in three years. His interpretation was not a success, and the next performance of the play, on 17 November, had Conway in his first attempt at Macbeth. There was a famous performance of the play on 8 June 1816, when Sarah Siddons came out of retirement to play Lady Macbeth to John Philip Kemble's Macbeth. Charles played his preferred role of Macduff. The 1836–37 season was Charles's last at Covent Garden, which he chose to open with his Macbeth on 12 September 1836.

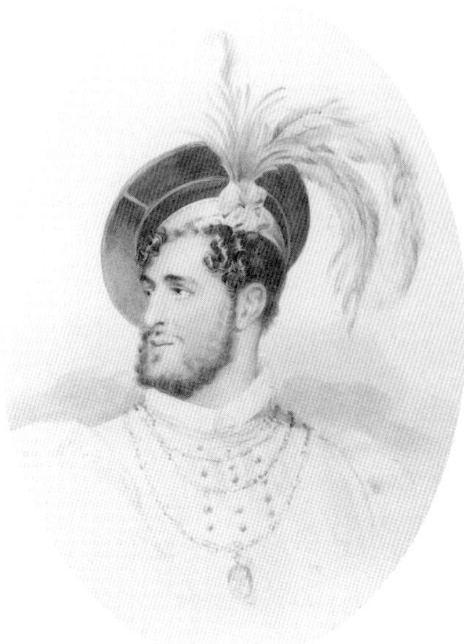

370
CHARLES KEMBLE
as Pierre in *Venice Preserv'd* by Thomas Otway

Unknown Artist (copied from a lithograph by William Sharp after John Hayter)

Pencil and watercolour on wove paper 28.6 x 21 (oval)
INSCR: 'This picture was given to me by Mr. Soper in July 1897: it was bought by him at the Sale of Mr. Thomas Turner's collection of Shakespeariana at the House now St. Mary de Crypt Vicarage in Brunswick Square. In the sale catalogue which Mr. H.W. Brunton showed me it was said to be "Charles Kemble": and without the artist's name. The sale was in 1860. Raymond W. Batten.' (on brown paper backing)
INV: CKA 608; Gift 352
PROV: Thomas Turner; Mr Soper, 1860; Raymond W. Batten, 1897; presented by L.L. Batten, K.C., 1910

Kemble is wearing a princely Renaissance costume with green plumed hat.

Adams conjectured that the role depicted is either Macbeth or Malcolm. But the drawing is apparently a copy of the lithograph by William Sharp, after J. Hayter, published by Dickinson, and seems to be by the same hand as No. 372.

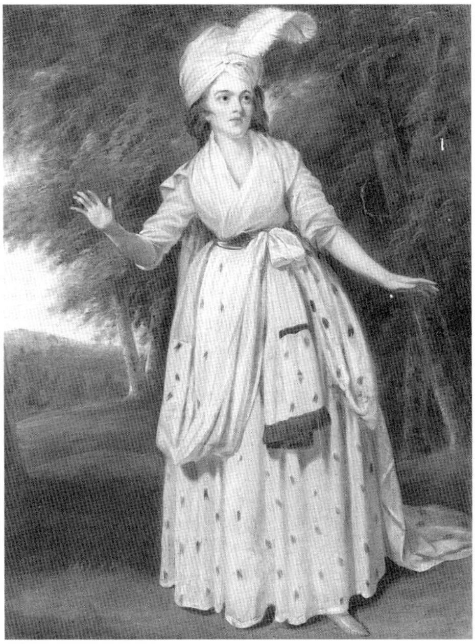

371*
ELIZABETH KEMBLE
as Imoinda in *Oroonoko or The Royal Slave*
by Thomas Southerne

Samuel De Wilde

Oil on canvas 36.5 x 28
INV: Mathews 385; RW/CKA 219
PROV: John Bell; Charles Mathews
EXH: 1833 London (385); 1962 Chichester (17)
ENGR: William S. Leney for Bell's British Library
21 October 1791, line 10.8 x 8,
pub. Bell's *British Theatre* (1797), vol 19

In Act II, scene 3, Imoinda has just recognised her long-lost husband, Oroonoko, 'son and heir to the great king of Angola', and speaks the line printed on the engraving: 'There's something in that name that voice that face – Oh if I know myself, I cannot be mistaken.' Both have been captured and taken as slaves to the British colony of Surinam in the West Indies. Imoinda is a white lady, the daughter of a stranger in the court of Angola. Though now a slave, she has retained the trappings of Angolan grandeur. She wears a white turban with an ostrich feather. Her yellow dress has a train, and a full white underskirt spotted with ermine tails, which also decorate the white panels in her long, fringed yellow sash.

Southerne's tragedy, based on the novel by Aphra Behn, was first performed at Drury Lane in November 1695, with Verbruggen as Oroonoko and Mrs Rogers as Imoinda. Elizabeth Kemble appears never to have played Imoinda, although a 'Miss Kemble' took the role on the last two occasions before De Wilde's picture was painted, on 17 March 1783 and 1 January 1784, both at Drury Lane.

Elizabeth Satchell married Stephen Kemble on 20 November 1783 and appeared on bills as Mrs Kemble from 24 November. No doubt the Miss Kemble who played Imoinda on both these occasions was Elizabeth's new sister-in-law, Frances Kemble (later Mrs Francis Twiss), who performed at Drury Lane from 1783 to 1786 and at the Haymarket during the summer of 1784. De Wilde's picture does not depict Frances Kemble. For a list of the portraits of Frances Kemble, see the BD 8: 331.

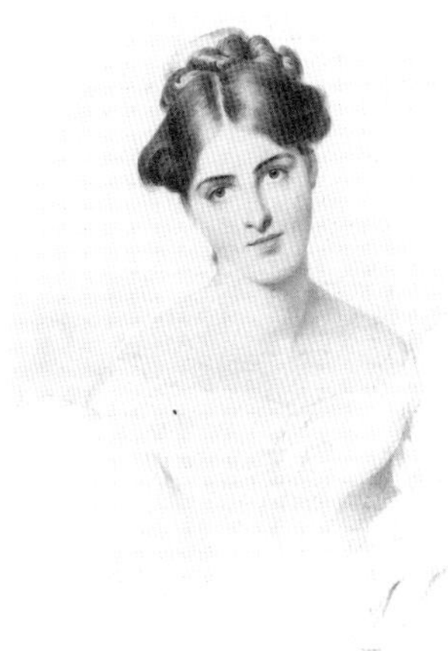

372
FANNY KEMBLE
as Juliet in *Romeo and Juliet* by William Shakespeare

Unknown Artist [copied from a lithograph by Richard James Lane after Thomas Lawrence]

Pencil and watercolour on wove paper
28.2 x 20.7 (framed in oval)
INV: CKA 609 (artist unknown); Gift 352
PROV: Presented by L.L. Batten, K.C., 1910
ENGR: (Richard James Lane pub. J. Dickinson 1830, lithograph vignette, three-quarter length, hands in lap)
REL: Lawrence's original drawing was loaned to the 'Exhibition of the Works of Sir Thomas Lawrence' at the City Art Gallery, Bristol, in 1951 (66) by Miss Evans Gordon, black, red and white chalk on wove paper 47.6 x 37.5. Many copies of this drawing exist.

Fanny Kemble's very first appearance on the stage was as Juliet at Covent Garden on 5 October 1829, the first night of the 1829–30 Covent Garden season.

Her mother, Maria Theresa Kemble, played Lady Capulet and her father, Charles Kemble, Mercutio. Romeo was acted by Mr Abbot. The enormous success of Fanny's Juliet for a time revived the fortunes of Covent Garden Theatre, managed by Charles Kemble.

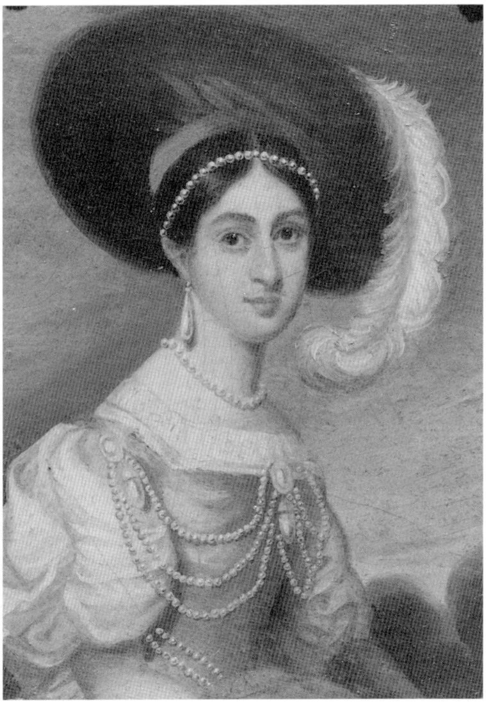

373
FANNY KEMBLE
as Portia in *The Merchant of Venice*
by William Shakespeare

Unknown Cantonese Artist
[from an engraving by Thomas Woolnoth after Charles Tayler]

Oil on card 11 x 8.5
INV: RW/CKA 4270; Gift 80
PROV: Presented by Joseph Gwilt, 1842
ENGR: Thomas Woolnoth pub. F.G. Harding 1831, stipple 12.4 x 9.5, dedicated to Mrs Siddons; J. Sartain pub. R.H. Hobson, Philadelphia, mezzotint 12.7 x 10.1

Portia wears a large black hat with a white feather, and a green dress with white sleeves. She is decked with pearls, and her hands are in a red-brown muff.

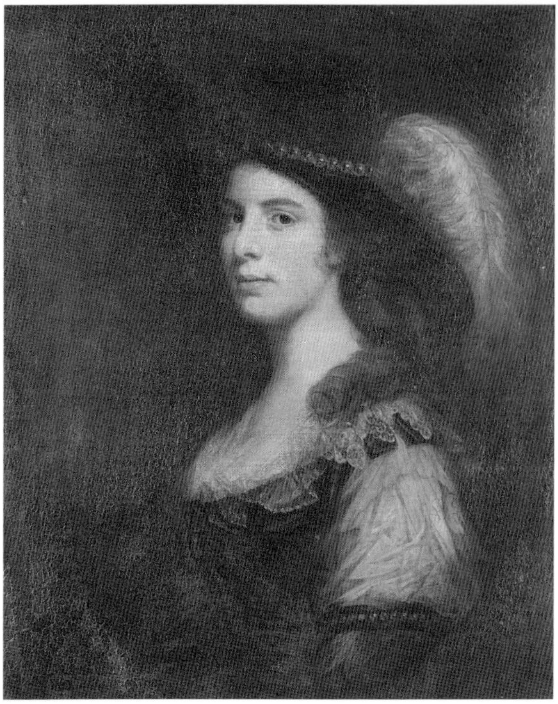

374
FRANCES KEMBLE (?)

John Downman (?)

Oil on canvas 76 x 63
INV: Mathews 103?; RW/CKA 414 (Mrs Whitlock, artist unknown)
PROV: Charles Mathews?
EXH: 1833 London (103)?

The sitter, shown half-length, wears a dress with a blue bodice and a large black hat with a band of large pearls.

CKA tentatively suggests that the sitter is Frances Kemble and the artist Downman (to correspond with Mathews's No. 103). Stylistically, however, the picture is not representative of Downman's work, and RW's identification of the sitter as Mrs Whitlock appears more likely to be correct. The BD (16: 51) attributes the picture to Thomas Beach and calls it Mrs Whitlock. See No. 841.

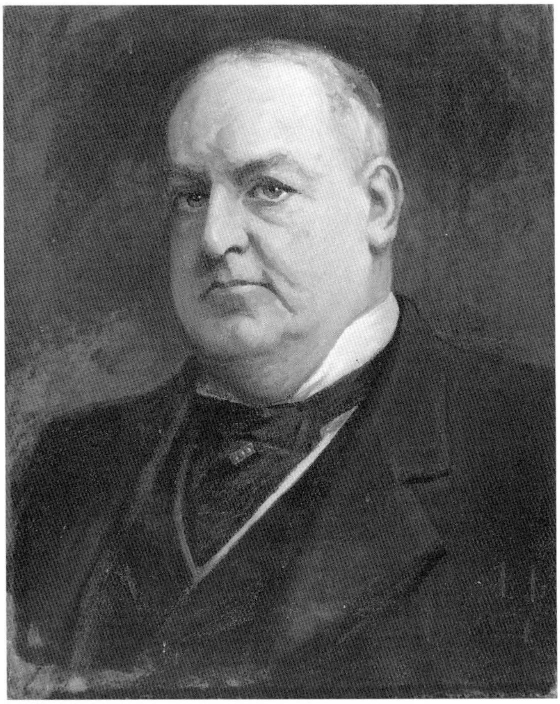

375
HENRY KEMBLE

Harry Allen

Oil on canvas 49.5 x 39.4
INSCR: 'Harry Allen / 1908.' (pale blue paint b.r.)
INV: CKA 600; Gift 336
PROV: Presented by Lady Bancroft, 1909

Head and shoulders. Henry Kemble wears a blue cravat with a pearl stick.

The sitter – nicknamed 'Harry the Beetle' – was the son of Henry James Vincent Kemble (1812–1857) and the grandson of Charles Kemble. After making his début in Dublin in 1867 and performing in the provinces, he appeared at Drury Lane in 1874. Later he was with John Hare at the Court Theatre and with the Bancrofts. He became a member of the Garrick Club in 1878.

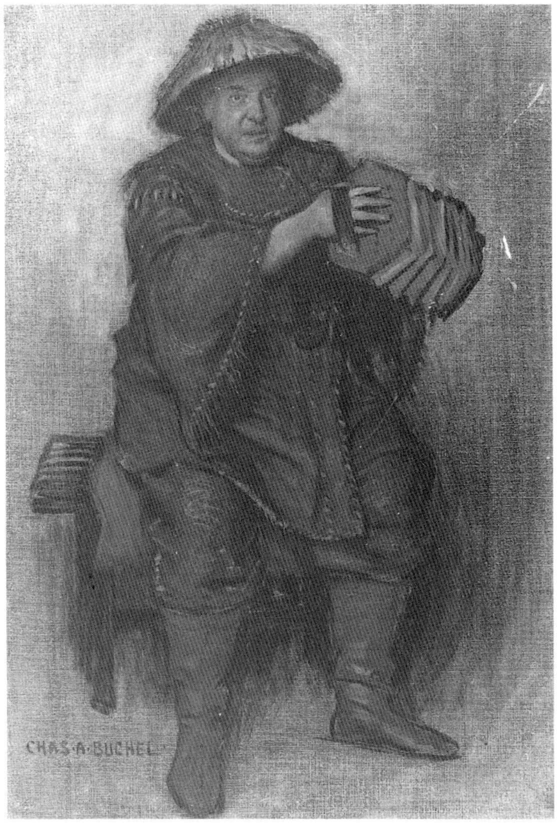

376
HENRY KEMBLE
as Lord Loam in *The Admirable Crichton*
by J.M. Barrie

Charles A. Buchel

Oil on linen-textured board 50.4 x 35.5
INSCR: 'CHAS. A. BUCHEL' (black paint b.l.);
'5 [in circle] / Henry Kemble'
(pen and black ink on verso)
INV: CKA 644; Gift 630
PROV: Presented by Capt. C. Riddell Williams, 1945

Kemble wears the costume for Lord Loam's subservient role on the desert island, in the middle act of Barrie's play. He plays a brown and red concertina with green straps and wears a straw hat, brown boots with red stripes, green trousers, and a green hide jacket with wide sleeves, fringed and sewn with leather thongs.

Kemble played the Earl of Loam when Barrie's comedy was first performed at the Duke of York's on 4 November 1902 (see Nos. 172 and 328).

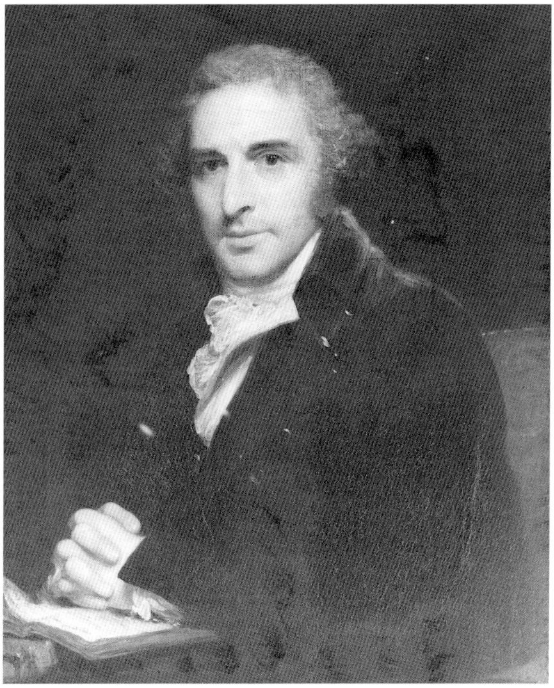

377

JOHN PHILIP KEMBLE

Sir William Beechey

Oil on canvas 75.6 x 63
INV: Mathews 164; RW/CKA 473
PROV: Charles Mathews
EXH: 1833 London (164)
ENGR: P. Roberts for the *Thespian Dictionary* 1802, stipple 8.2 x 7; same plate used for the *Thespian Dictionary* 1805; Mackenzie pub. T. Hurst 1804, stipple 8.2 x 6.7 (reversed, in oval); James Hopwood pub. H.D. Symonds 1 March 1808, stipple 7.9 x 6.6; Anon., stipple and line 11.5 x 8.9
REL: Original Dulwich III, oil on canvas 76.8 x 64.1 (commissioned by Desenfans about 1798), exh. 1799 R.A. (174)

Kemble, seated at a table with his hands folded over a book, wears a dark grey coat.

378

JOHN PHILIP KEMBLE

as Penruddock in *The Wheel of Fortune*
by Richard Cumberland

Samuel De Wilde

Pencil and watercolour on wove paper 37 x 23.5
INSCR: 'S De Wilde / 1807' (pencil b.l.)
INV: Mathews 247; RW/CKA 58E
PROV: Charles Mathews
EXH: 1833 London (247)

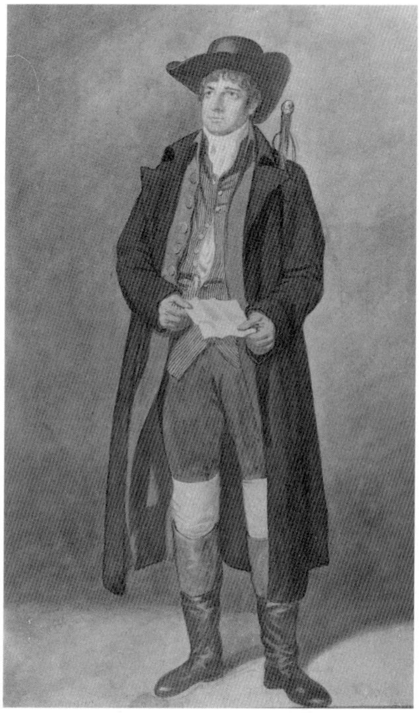

378 *John Philip Kemble as Roderick Penruddock*

ENGR: J. Hopwood for the *Cabinet* pub. Mathews & Leigh 1 May 1808, stipple and line 14 x 9.2 (bust only); Edward Scriven pub. Bell & De Camp 1 July 1809, stipple 15.1 x 9.1 (De Wilde delin.); same plate used for the *Theatrical Inquisitor* pub. C. Chapple 1 July 1814; Wright after a drawing by Wageman pub. Simpkin & Marshall 1820, stipple 11.4 x 7.6 (the costume and hat are taken from De Wilde, but the face is from the portrait that Shee exhibited R.A. 1801 [86])
REL: See No. 379

Roderick Penruddock, a scholarly recluse who lives in a cottage in the forest, inherits the fortune of his uncle, Sir George Penruddock. The inheritance includes the house of his rival, Woodville, who has ruined himself through gambling and was in debt to Sir George. Roderick is shown into one of the unfurnished rooms of the house (depicted in the oil version, No. 379, but not the watercolour original or the engravings). He has received a letter from his former paramour Arabella, asking him to take her son Henry under his protection. Eventually Roderick agrees to this request, leaving the young man his entire fortune before retiring once more to his forest cottage. Roderick holds the letter in his yellow-gloved hands and wears black boots with brown tops, white leggings over brown moleskin breeches, a long dark blue travelling coat over a brown coat, a pink waistcoat and a black hat. The first performance of Cumberland's comedy was at Drury Lane on 28 February 1795, with Kemble as Roderick Penruddock.

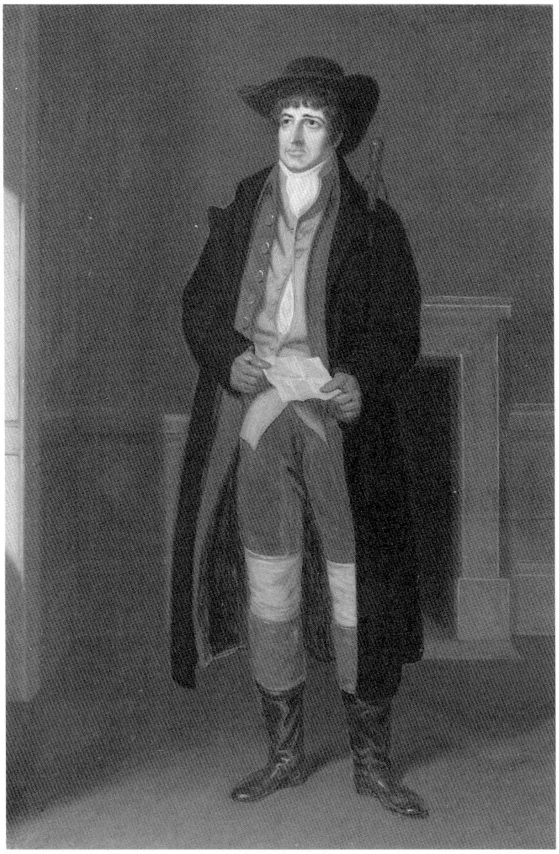

379
JOHN PHILIP KEMBLE
as Penruddock in *The Wheel of Fortune*
by Richard Cumberland

Samuel De Wilde

Oil on panel 40 x 27.3
INV: RW/CKA 248
PROV: Unknown
EXH: 1962 Chichester (19)
REL: See No. 378
LIT: Griffiths, p. 238

Penruddock's costume is the same as in No. 378, with a few differences in colour: the gloves are brown, the overcoat black, and the waistcoat pink with brown vertical stripes. The setting is the 'unfurnished room' of Act II, scene 3, which is not shown in the watercolour or the engravings. There is light from the window on the left, but the shadow of the figure is cast from an unseen light source from the spectator's left, as in the watercolour. This suggests that the watercolour is the original work and the oil painting a copy. It is cast in the format of the Bell portraits of the early 1790s.

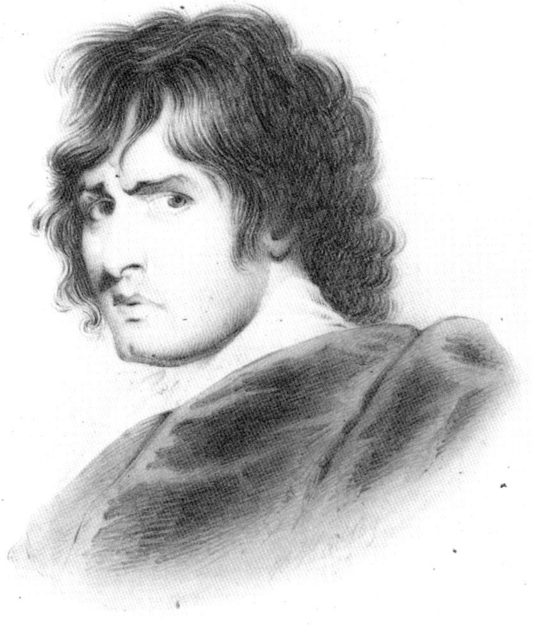

380
JOHN PHILIP KEMBLE
as Richard in *Richard III*
by William Shakespeare

H.J. Harding (after Gilbert Stuart)

Pencil and grey wash with white body colour
on wove paper 21.6 x 18.1
INSCR: 'KEMBLE AS RICHARD' and 'BY HARDING'
(pen and brown ink on mount b.);
'Bristol Paper' stamp on mount t.l.
INV: Mathews 326 or 328; RW/CKA 496
PROV: Charles Mathews
EXH: 1833 London (326 or 328)
ENGR: J. Thornthwaite (after a drawing by Mather Brown, using Stuart's portrait for the head) for Bell's *Shakespeare* 10 May 1786, line 8.9 x 6.7 (Browne del. Stewart pinxt.); George Keating pub. J. & J. Boydell 1 January 1788, mezzotint 28 x 21.6; H.H. Houston pub. Freeman & Co, Philadelphia 16 August 1796, stipple 10.5 x 8.9 (oval); Henry Meyer for *The Cabinet* pub. Mathews & Leigh 1 September 1808, stipple and line 14.3 x 9.5; J. Rogers (after a drawing by George Henry Harlow) for Oxberry's *Dramatic Biography* pub. G. Virtue 12 February 1825, stipple and line (G.H. Harlow del. 'As Hamlet')
REL: Original: Cottesloe Coll. (prov. John Pybus 1788), oil on canvas n.s., exh: 1868 V&A (82; Coll. Sir Henry Halford); 1938 Birmingham 'Midland Houses' (100)
[CKA records a signature 'H. Harding 1–28' which GA reads as '1823'. No such inscription is now visible.]

Harding's drawing is probably a copy of the Keating mezzotint done about 1810. It is likely that the attribution on the Rogers engraving to Harlow was mistaken.

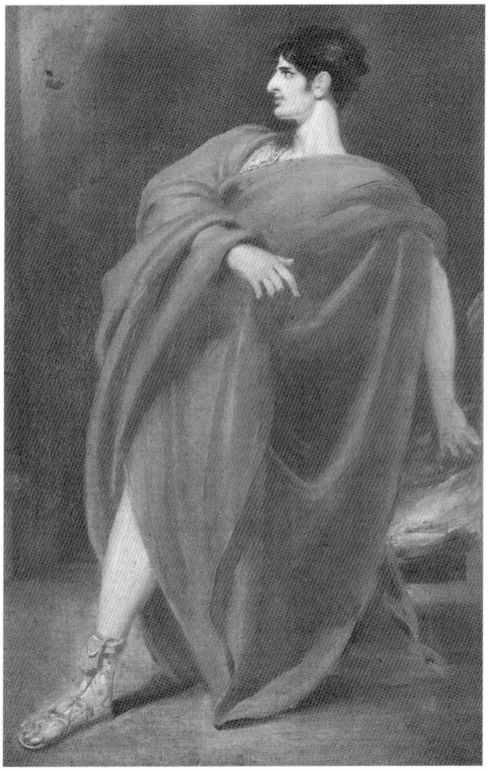

381*

JOHN PHILIP KEMBLE

as Coriolanus in *Coriolanus*
by William Shakespeare,
adapted by John Philip Kemble

George Henry Harlow

Oil on canvas 43 x 28.5
INV: Mathews 375; RW/CKA 444
PROV: Charles Mathews
EXH: 1833 London (375)

Coriolanus wears red sandals and his gold armour is just visible beneath a voluminous red cloak. There is a stormy landscape beyond the colonnaded platform on which he stands in an attitude of haughty astonishment.

Kemble's adaptation of *Coriolanus* was performed for the first time at Drury Lane on 7 February 1789, with Kemble as Coriolanus and Mrs Siddons as Volumnia.

This picture has little in common with Harlow's mature style, but it might be an early work of his dating from about 1808. The artist must have been influenced by Lawrence's vast canvas of the same subject, exhibited R.A. 1798 (225) and now in the London Guildhall Art Gallery. A drawing by Harlow of Kemble as Coriolanus is in the Folger Library (Art Box H. 286 No. 1), pencil and watercolour on wove paper 22.8 x 17.8, inscr: 'Kemble / G.H.H.'. See Pressly, *Folger*, 114.

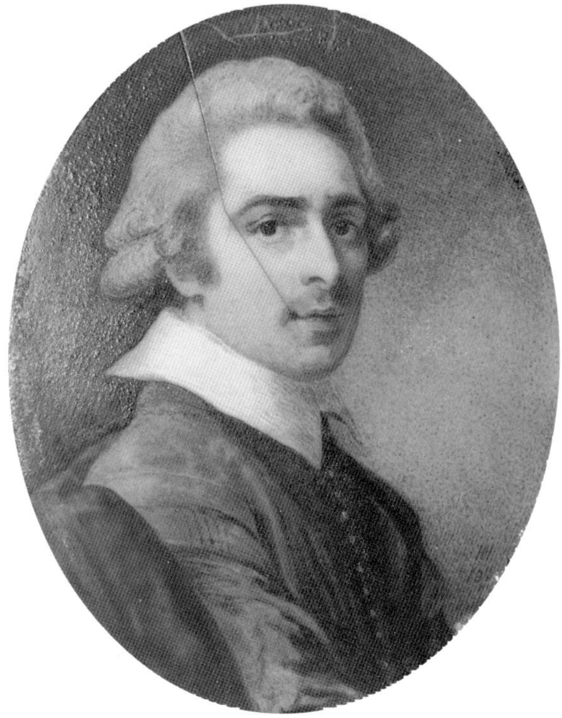

382

JOHN PHILIP KEMBLE

Horace Hone

Enamel on copper 6.2 x 5 (oval)
INSCR: 'HH / 1801 [?]' (b.r.);
'John Phil. Kemble' (enamel on verso);
'H. Hone A.R.A. Pinx / 1801 [?]' (red paint on verso)
INV: Mathews 326 or 328;
RW 427 (by Nathaniel Hone); CKA 427F
PROV: Charles Mathews
EXH: 1833 London (326 or 328)
REL: Original: Private Collection London,
watercolour on paper 11.1 x 9, initialled and dated 1786

Head and shoulders of Kemble wearing a brown doublet, a high white collar and a red cloak.

There is a 3–4 cm crack in the enamel extending from the top edge across the sitter's hair and right cheek.

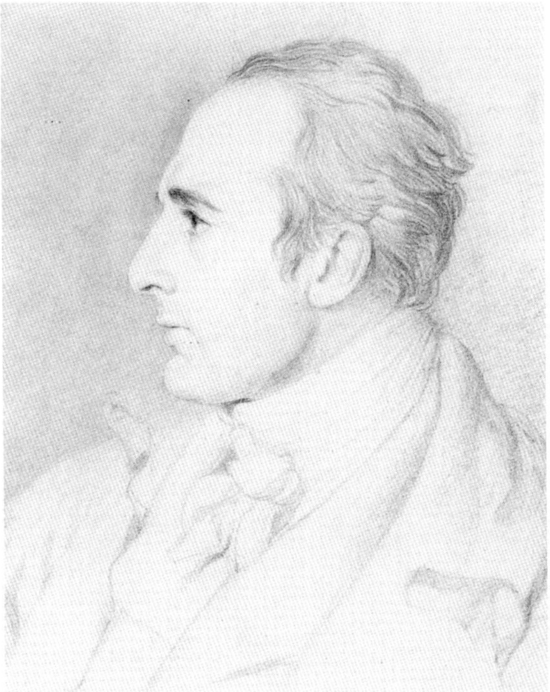

383*

JOHN PHILIP KEMBLE

Sir Thomas Lawrence

Pencil on wove paper 22.5 x 18.1
INV: Mathews 336; RW/CKA 139
PROV: Charles Mathews
EXH: 1833 London (336); 1975 London (102)
ENGR: Thomas Cheesman for *An Authentic Narrative of Mr Kemble's Retirement from the Stage* pub. J. Miller 5 August 1817, stipple 15.6 x 13 (inscr. on some later impressions of the print: 'The last likeness ever taken'); R. Cooper pub. J. Robins 1 April 1823, n.s.; Holl, stipple (vignette, bust only); Marlet, lithograph (vignette, bust only in reverse); W. Read for *Dramatic Table Talk* 1825, stipple (vignette)

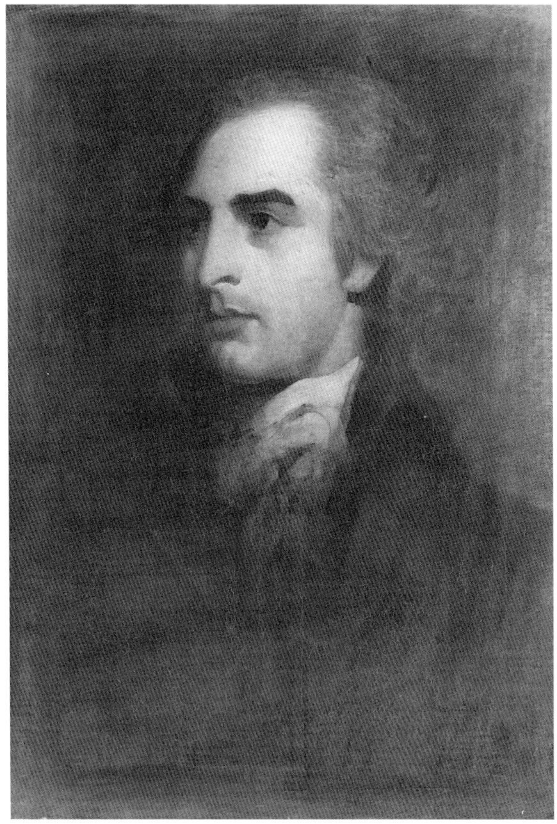

384

JOHN PHILIP KEMBLE

Sir Thomas Lawrence

Oil on canvas 65.5 x 49
INV: Mathews 161; CKA 379

Head and shoulders, head to left, wearing a dark coat and a white cravat; brown background.

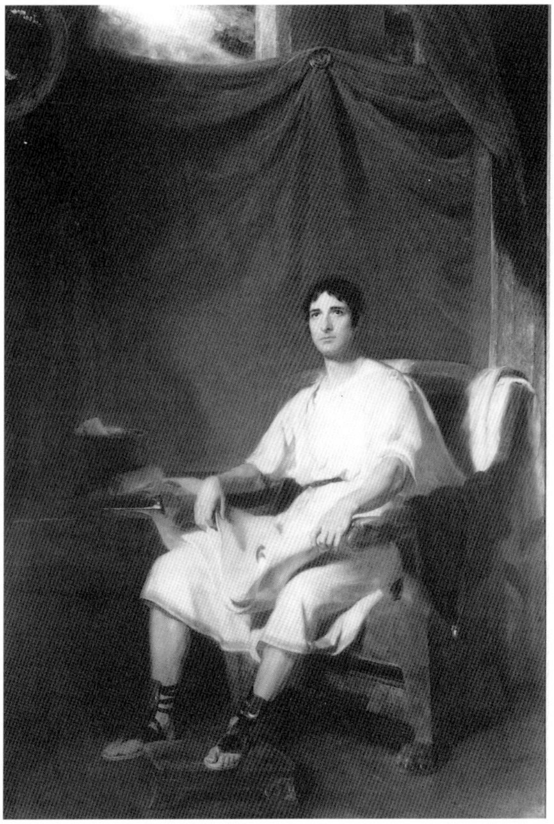

Kemble first played Cato in London at Drury Lane on 28 April 1784, in a benefit for John Bannister, the first time the role had been performed at the theatre since Thomas Sheridan acted it on 21 October 1760. Kemble played Cato again on 15 November 1784 then appears to have abandoned the role until he revived the play at Covent Garden on 26 January 1811. It was played 16 times that season and five the next, the last performance taking place on 24 June 1812.

The subject is one of four large portraits of Kemble – as Coriolanus, Rolla, Hamlet and Cato – which Lawrence produced between 1798 and 1812. See Shearer West, 'The Half-History Portraits of Thomas Lawrence', *Art History* (1991), 14: 225–49.

No. 385, on loan to the Bristol Old Vic for many years, was returned to the Club in 1994. See also No. 386.

385*
JOHN PHILIP KEMBLE
as Cato in *Cato*
by Joseph Addison

Sir Thomas Lawrence

Oil on mahogany board 109.8 x 73.7
INV: Mathews 143; RW/CKA 397
PROV: Charles Mathews
EXH: 1833 London (143); 1951 London (27)
ENGR: William Ward mezzotint 78.8 x 54.3; W. Greatback 1833; S.W. Reynolds 1841
REL: Original: Comissioned by the Earl of Blessington; then bought by John Burton Philips, Heath House, Tern; now in a private collection, London, oil on canvas. A copy, sold several times in New York, was purchased at Parke-Bernet 21–22 September 1945, buyer unknown, 254 x 177.8, exh: R.A. 1812 (57)
LIT: Anne Mathews (1835), 3: 376; Kenneth Garlick, *Sir Thomas Lawrence* (1989), p. 216

Full-length, seated. Cato wears sandals with straps and a white tunic trimmed in gold. The large gold chair and stool are upholstered in red, and a red cloak is draped over the chair. The sitter holds several papers and there are others on the table to the left.

386
JOHN PHILIP KEMBLE
as Hamlet in *Hamlet*
by William Shakespeare

Sir Thomas Lawrence (studio)

Oil on canvas 82.5 x 54.6
INV: RW/CKA 1; Gift 288
PROV: Presented by Sir Squire Bancroft, 1905
EXH: 1964 London [2] (47); 1981 Tokyo (YH24)
REL: Original: Tate Gallery 142, oil on canvas 306.1 x 198, exh: R.A. 1801 (197); Folger Library, after Lawrence, oil 76.2 x 49.3; Theatre Museum (TM17), oil 61 x 45.5
Prov: Mrs W.E. Kemble, given to TM 1988
ENGR: Samuel William Reynolds pub. Boydell & Co. 1805, mezzotint 83.2 x 54.6; see BD 8: 378 for other versions
LIT: Pressly, *Folger*, 115

Hamlet is dressed in his mourning black, and holds the skull of Yorick as in Act V, scene I. The Order of the Elephant hangs from a blue ribbon around his neck. The original at the Tate Gallery is one of Lawrence's four 'half-history' portraits of Kemble; see No. 385.

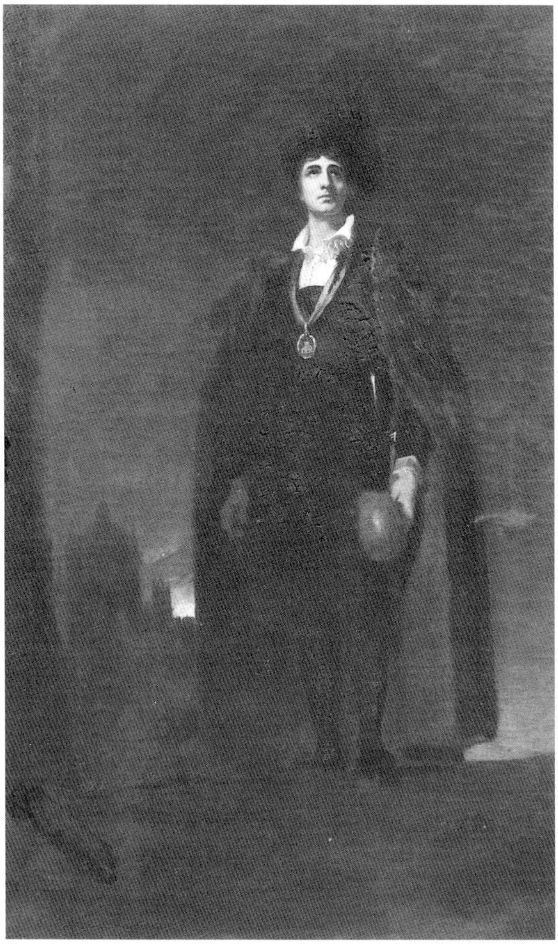

386 *John Philip Kemble as Hamlet*

Kemble made his London début as Hamlet at Drury Lane on 30 September 1783, and his first appearance upon becoming manager and proprietor at Covent Garden was again as Hamlet, on 24 September 1803, two years after the original version of Lawrence's picture was painted. He played the part frequently, and his somewhat lugubrious style of acting was seen to excellent effect in the darker sides of Hamlet's character. In 1789 Kemble's performance was praised in an anonymous publication, *A Short Criticism on the Performance of Hamlet by Mr Kemble*. It is possible that the actor produced the work himself; his essay *Macbeth Reconsidered* had been published in 1786 and had met with a surprised and favourable reception.

Kemble's more mature interpretation of the role is discussed in H. Martin's *Remarks on John Philip Kemble's Performance of Hamlet and Richard the Third* (1802). See also K.A. Burnim, 'John Philip Kemble and the Artists', *The Stage in the 18th Century*, ed. J.D. Browning (New York, 1981), and BD 8: 378.

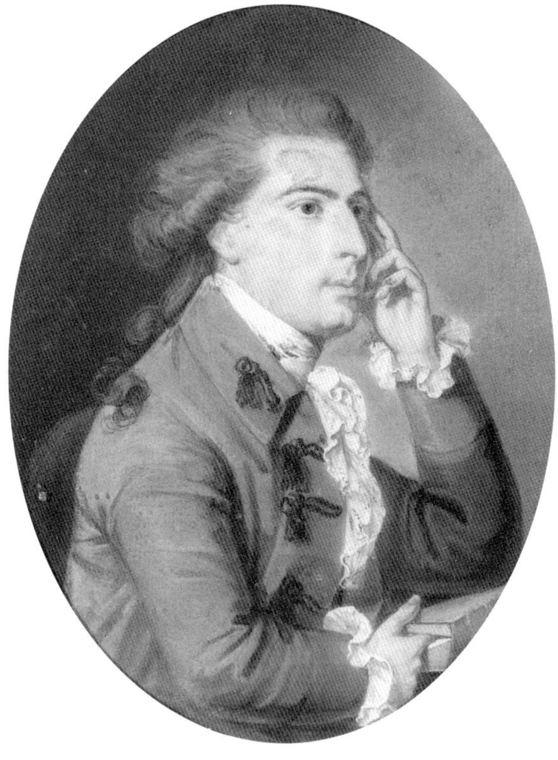

387

JOHN PHILIP KEMBLE

Alexander Pope (ascribed to)

Pastel on paper 25.4 x 20.3 (oval)
INV: Mathews 313? (artist unknown);
RW 314 (unknown by unknown);
CKA 314 (unknown man of about 1780)
PROV: Charles Mathews?
EXH: 1833 London (313)?
REL: Her Majesty The Queen, Windsor Castle (17034), pastel 27.3 x 21.5, rectangle, the name and date 1783 on label, back of frame

The sitter has his right forefinger in a book, on which he rests his left elbow. He wears a blue-grey coat, with black tasselled frogs. He resembles the young Kemble, particularly as he appears in Cook's drawing, engraved by the artist for the *Universal Magazine* pub. S.A. Cumberlege 1 November 1793, in which the sitter turns to the left, has the same style of hair, and wears a slightly simpler jacket.

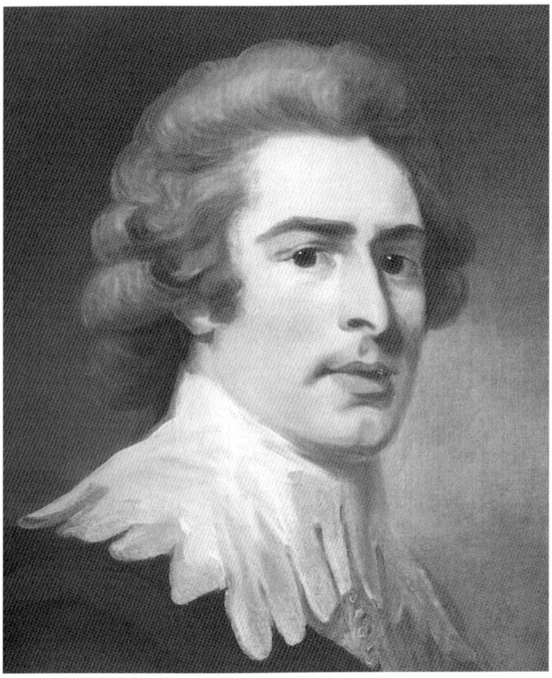

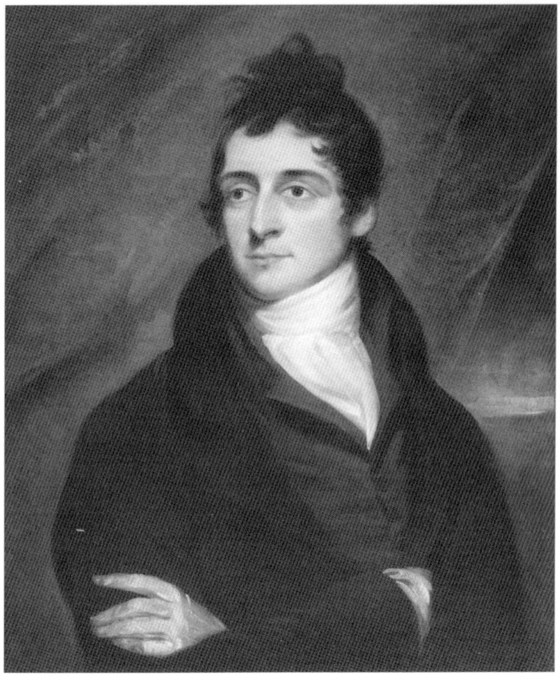

389 *John Philip Kemble*

388
JOHN PHILIP KEMBLE

Gilbert Stuart (attr.)
Oil on canvas 57 x 43
INV: Not listed
PROV: Luigi Mancini, Ile du Levant; purchased by the Garrick Club for £50 in 1950

Kemble wears a pink tunic and a vandyke collar. There is a brown cloak over his right shoulder.

The attribution is by no means certain. When the picture was purchased there seems to have been extant a certificate of authenticity (for Gilbert Stuart) from Sir Charles Holmes. [Perhaps the picture is from the studio of Mather Brown.]

389
JOHN PHILIP KEMBLE

Unknown Artist
Oil on canvas 76 x 63
INV: CKA 595 (called John Philip Kemble); Gift 381
PROV: Presented by Lt. Col. Hugh and Sir Victor Warrender, Bt, 1918

Kemble is posed in front of a dramatic red drapery with an architectural element to the right.

390*
JOHN PHILIP KEMBLE as Macbeth and *SARAH SIDDONS* as Lady Macbeth in *Macbeth* by William Shakespeare

Thomas Beach
Oil on canvas 179 x 152.4
INV: CKA 637; Gift 589
PROV: Lord Le Despencer; sale, Mereworth Castle; Christie's 9 May 1865 (138); [Possibly the picture of Kemble and Mrs Siddons in *Macbeth* sold for £4 14s. 6d. in the Royal Dramatic College sale at Fairbrother, Lye and Palmer on 24 February 1881 (lot 68)]; sold Puttick & Simpson, 13 July 1921 (159) bt. Mason 120 gns.; F.J. Nettlefold by 1933; presented by Nettlefold to the Garrick Club, 1940
EXH: 1786 R.A. (199); 1933 London (195); 1975 London (99)
LIT: C. Reginald Grundy, *A Catalogue of the Pictures and Drawings in the Collection of John Frederick Nettlefold* (1933), I: 8–10

The moment shown is Act II, scene 2. The figures are life-size, shown three-quarter length. Siddons as Lady Macbeth wears the elaborate powdered coiffure of *c.*1780 with a broad-brimmed circular hat on the back of her head. Her dress, however, is the Van Dyck style, dark green, with the bodice trimmed with sequins and the overskirt hemmed with a zigzag pattern. The sleeves of her white chemise are visible, tied with pale blue

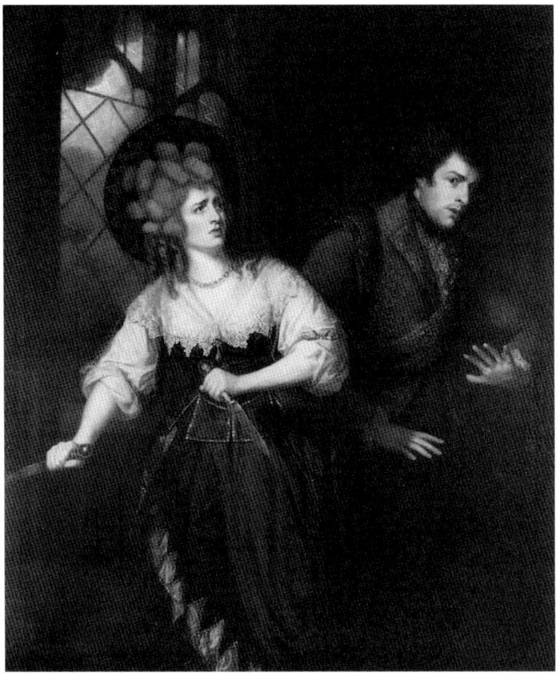

390 *John Philip Kemble as Macbeth and Sarah Siddons as Lady Macbeth*

ribbons at the elbows, and she has a wide lace collar. Kemble as Macbeth wears a late 18th-century red coat, with green lapels, and a plaid across his chest and over his shoulders. Moonlight streams through a Gothic window behind the pair.

Siddons played Lady Macbeth for the first time in London at Drury Lane on 2 February 1785 for her benefit, with William Smith as Macbeth. Kemble first played Macbeth at Hull on 30 October 1778; his first London performance of the role was at Drury Lane on 31 March 1785, for his own benefit, with his sister as Lady Macbeth. That was his only London performance of the role before Beach's picture was exhibited at the R.A., and he did not play the part again at Drury Lane until 16 October 1788, after Smith had retired. See No. 253 for comments on Garrick and Pritchard in this scene, painted by Zoffany. Their performance exerted a powerful influence on subsequent productions of the play, notably that of Siddons and Kemble depicted here. Compare also the imaginative sketch of the scene by Henry Fuseli, Tate Gallery.

Kemble's prompt copy of *Macbeth* in the Garrick Club library gives little direction for this scene, other than the fact that Macbeth enters stage right and crosses to stage left before giving the daggers to Lady Macbeth. The notes are on a 1794 edition of the play, published to mark the production for the re-opening of Drury Lane on 21 April 1794.

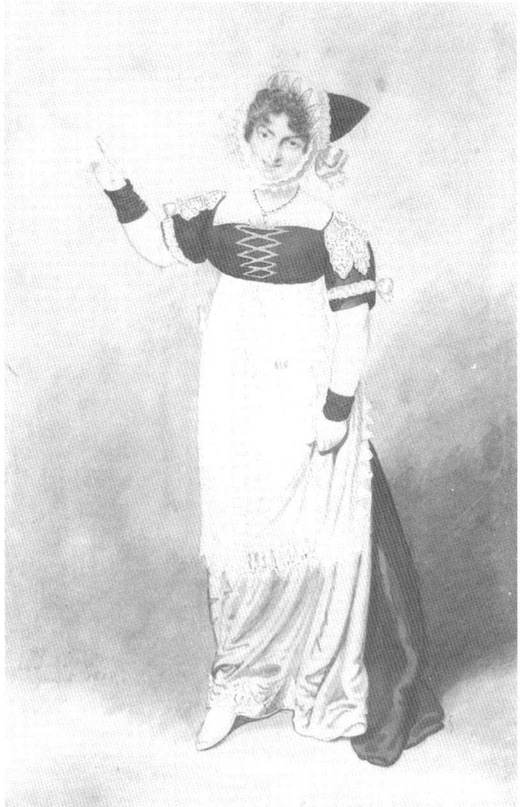

391
MARIA THERESA KEMBLE
as Mrs Ford in *The Merry Wives of Windsor*
by William Shakespeare

Samuel De Wilde

Pencil and watercolour on wove paper 37.5 x 22.8
INSCR: 'S De Wilde / Jan. 8 1808' (pencil b.l.);
Mrs C. Kemble as Mrs Ford in the Merry Wives of Windsor' (pen and brown ink on mount t.c. CM); 'We'll teach him to know turtles from jays. Act 3rd. Scene 3rd.' (pen and brown ink on mount b.c. CM)
INV: CKA 518
PROV: Charles Mathews (not in catalogue); purchased 1924
EXH: 1964 London [2] (43)

Mrs Ford wears a high-waisted black dress with a pink underskirt and pink ruched ribbons on the short sleeves, to match the decoration of her black and white cap. She has a lace apron, with matching lace decoration on the hem of her underskirt and at the shoulders. She has a high, tight 'Betsey' ruff.

The first performance of *The Merry Wives* in the 1807–8 season at Covent Garden was not until 27 April 1808, with G.F. Cooke as Falstaff, Mrs Mattocks as Mrs Page, and Maria Theresa Kemble as Mrs Ford.

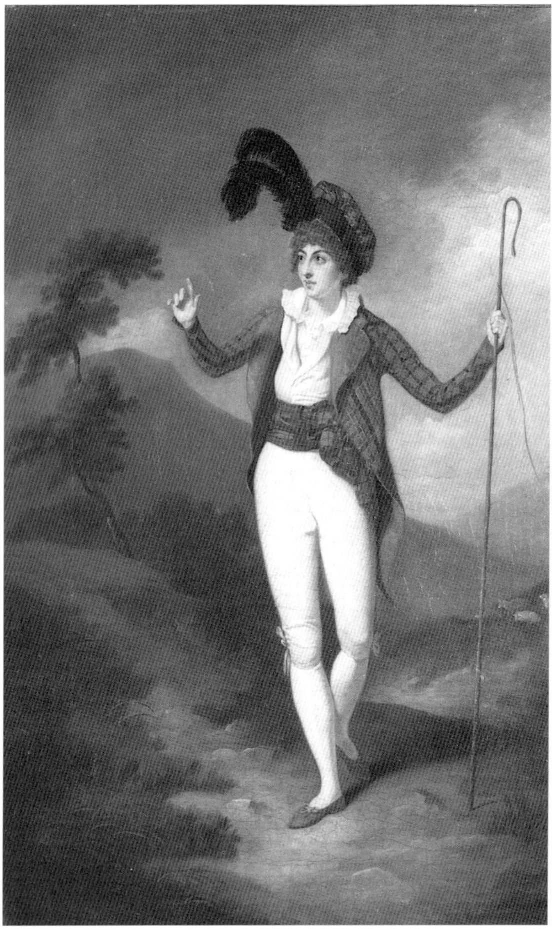

392
MARIA THERESA KEMBLE
as Patie in *The Gentle Shepherd*
by Allan Ramsay,
adapted by Richard Tickell

Samuel De Wilde

Oil on canvas 74.3 x 53.3
INV: Mathews 21; RW/CKA 403
PROV: Charles Mathews
EXH: 1833 London (21)
REL: NT 37, pencil and watercolour on wove paper
35 x 21.7 (unfinished)

Patie, a male character, is the Gentle Shepherd, in love with Peggy. 'He' holds a crook, and wears a red and green plaid tam-o'-shanter with a green band and plumes, brown shoes with pink bows, white stockings, white breeches with blue bows, a long jacket in red and green plaid with a blue lining, and a red and green plaid sash.

Allan Ramsay's pastoral poem was published in 1725. Tickell's adaptation, with music by Thomas Linley, was first performed at Drury Lane on 29 October 1781, when Ann Cargill played Patie. According to the *Universal Magazine*, November 1781:

> The above Opera, written by Allen Ramsey, has been long and justly admired, but by those only whose knowledge of the Scottish dialect has enabled them to judge of its excellencies. That an English audience might become partakers of this entertainment seems to have been the laudable design of the Dramatist, Mr Tickel, in now divesting it of its numerous provincialities, grown almost obsolete, even in Scotland, at this distant period...
>
> The characters were drest with a rustic simplicity, which tho' not exactly characteristic of the Highland manner, were perfectly Pastoral.

Maria Theresa De Camp, who married Charles Kemble, played Patie for the first time on 8 June 1796, at Drury Lane.

393
STEPHEN KEMBLE
as Bajazet in *Tamerlane* by Nicholas Rowe

Samuel De Wilde

Oil on canvas 37.1 x 28.8
INV: Mathews 184; RW/CKA 227
PROV: Charles Mathews
EXH: 1833 London (184)
ENGR: Philippe Audinet for Bell's British Library
14 April 1792, line 11.4 x 8, pub. Bell's *British Theatre* (1797),
vol 22, with the quotation '– tho' Fortune /
has stript me of the train and pomp of greatness /
Yet still my Soul is free' Act II, scene 2;
Anon. printed for C. Cooke 1808 as plate to *British Drama*,
line, octagonal, same quotation with 'Act II, scene 2'

The tyrant Bajazet has been defeated by Tamerlane, to whom he is brought in chains and scolded for causing the carnage of the battle. Bajazet is unrepentant and, despite Tamerlane's repeated acts of clemency, retains his vindictive truculence throughout the play. The setting of Act II, scene 2, in Tamerlane's camp, near Angoria in Galatria, is the 'Inside of a magnificent Tent' draped in red.

Bajazet's costume consists of gold slippers and a long gold damask robe, with cuffs edged in white fur, under a long, dark green velvet sleeveless coat, also trimmed with white fur. He wears a high white turban with a silver crescent moon and has silver manacles on his wrists.

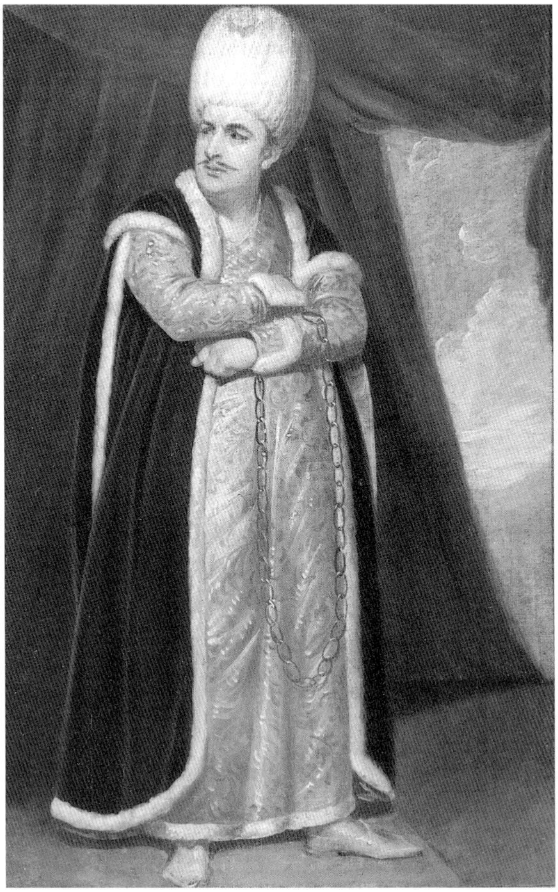

393 *Stephen Kemble as Bajazet*

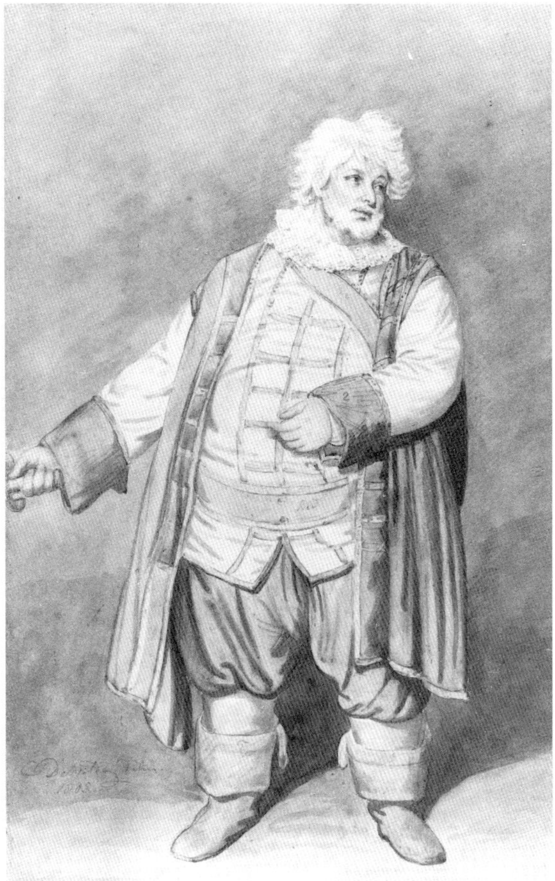

394 *Stephen Kemble as Falstaff*

Rowe's tragedy was first performed at Lincoln's Inn Fields in December 1701. Stephen Kemble played Bajazet for the first time at Covent Garden on 4 November 1783, and repeated the role the next day. He then played it nine times at Drury Lane in 1797.

394

STEPHEN KEMBLE

as Falstaff in *The Merry Wives of Windsor*

by William Shakespeare

Samuel De Wilde

Pencil and watercolour on wove paper 38.1 x 24.1

INSCR: 'S De Wilde delin / 1805' (pencil b.l.); 'Red' (pencil on belt); 'Re' (pencil on strap over chest); '2' (pencil on l. cuff); '5' (pencil on tops of boots); '4' (pencil b.r. of jacket)

INV: Mathews 337; RW/CKA 56

PROV: Charles Mathews

EXH: 1833 London (337); 1964 London [2] (42); 1971 Northampton (32)

Stephen Kemble wears a traditional Falstaff costume: wide boots, white stockings, loose knee-breeches, white doublet trimmed in yellow with red cuffs, a red belt and a red sleeveless coat also trimmed in yellow. In De Wilde's study, the reds are indicated with washes of pale pink and mauve. Kemble was to able to play the part of Falstaff without padding.

Stephen Kemble acted Falstaff in *The Merry Wives* while he was manager of the Theatre Royal, Edinburgh during the 1790s. His English début in the role was at the Theatre Royal, Bath, following his appearance as Falstaff in *1 Henry IV* in June 1804. His London début as Falstaff was not until 17 September 1806, when he played it in *1 Henry IV* at Covent Garden with his brothers John Philip as Hotspur and Charles as Prince Hal. The performance was repeated on 1 October 1806. Kemble's first London performance of the character in *The Merry Wives* was at Covent Garden on 24 September 1806.

The colour notes suggest that this is perhaps one of De Wilde's prototype drawings, the sort of popular image from which he expected a number of copies to be commissioned.

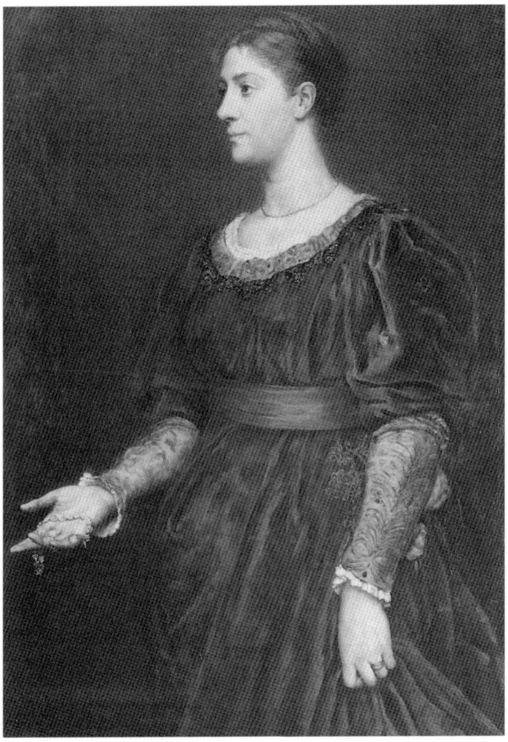

395
DAME MADGE KENDAL
as Lady Giovanna in *The Falcon*
by Alfred, Lord Tennyson

Val Prinsep

Oil on canvas 115.6 x 80
INV: RW/CKA 76; Gift 291
PROV: Presented by the artist's widow, 1905
EXH: 1883 R.A. (143); 1977 London [2] (18); 1983 Buxton (39)

The Lady Giovanna wears a dark red velvet dress; a pink damask band around the bust is decorated in gold with green jewels.

Tennyson's slow-moving symbolistic drama was performed for the first time on 18 December 1879, at the St James's Theatre. The play was privately printed for the author in 1879, and was published with *The Cup* in 1882. See also No. 820.

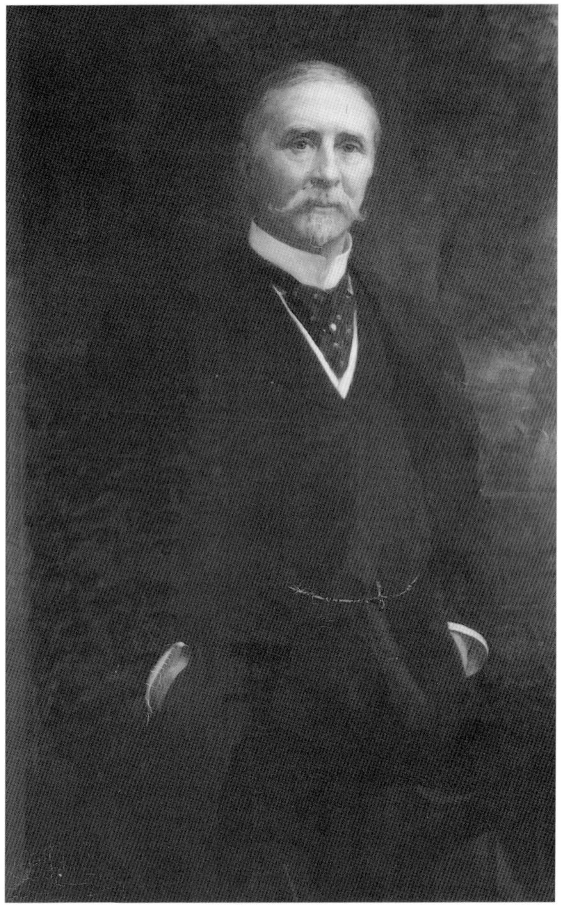

396
WILLIAM HUNTER KENDAL

Hugh Goldwin Riviere

Oil on canvas 134.6 x 102.9
INSCR: 'H Riviere 1918.' (black paint b.r.)
INV: CKA 604; Gift 486
PROV: Presented by the sitter's widow,
Dame Madge Kendal, 1931

Three-quarter length, standing in front of a balustrade with trees beyond. Kendal wears a dark blue suit and a spotted blue cravat.

On hearing that his picture had been presented to the Club, Riviere wrote in alarm to the Club Secretary on 2 June 1933:

> Dear Sir, I am horrified to hear (only today) that a Post-humous Portrait of Kendal which of course I should never have willingly exhibited anywhere, has been presented and HUNG at the Garrick Club. Had I been warned of this I think I could have put to Dame Madge Kendal what one feels about a picture painted under those circumstances & perhaps averted this unfortunate occurance. Can your Committee take it in hand

now & gently remove it to some dark passage or cellar where it can offend no one but still be at the Club if by any chance Dame Madge asked about it. Believe me yrs much concerned, Hugh G. Riviere.

The secretary replied on 6 June, saying that: 'The picture is hung in a not very conspicuous place, but as Dame Madge Kendal has been to see where it is hung the Commitee regret they cannot remove it at present for reasons they feel sure you will readily understand.'

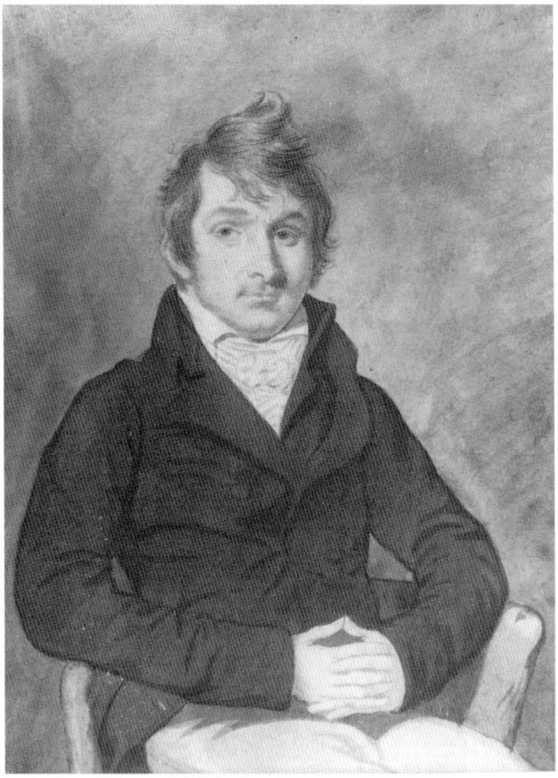

397

JAMES KENNEY

Samuel De Wilde

Pencil and watercolour
on wove paper 21.2 x 16.8
INSCR: 'Kenney' (scratched on board backing)
INV: RW 185 (unknown sitter and artist);
CKA 185 (James Kenney? by S. De Wilde?)
PROV: Presented by Owen Rees, 1835
ENGR: James Heath for *Inchbald's Collection of Farces*
pub. Longman, Hurst, Rees & Orme 1809,
stipple 9.1 x 7.4

Kenney is shown seated, three-quarter length, facing the spectator. He wears a black cutaway coat.

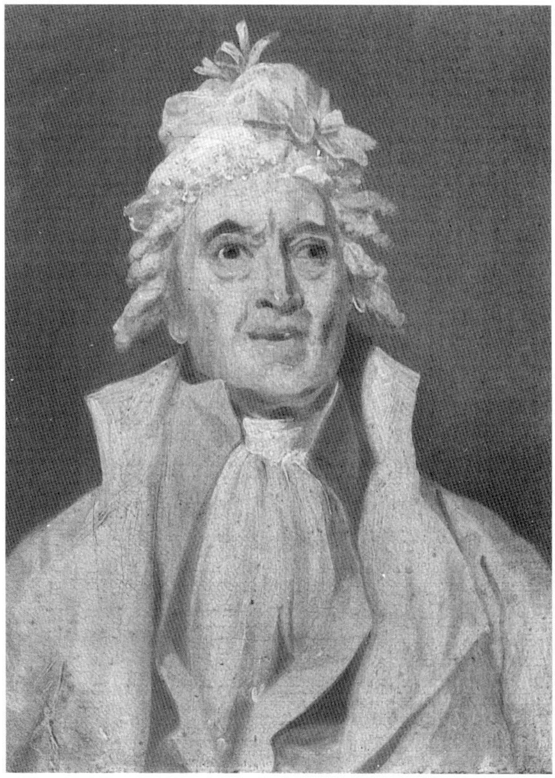

398

THOMAS KING

as Lord Ogleby
in *The Clandestine Marriage*
by David Garrick and George Colman the Elder

Samuel De Wilde

Oil on canvas 23 x 19
INV: Mathews 352; RW/CKA 285
PROV: Charles Mathews
EXH: At sale of John Bell's collections of paintings
and drawings, Christie's 25–26 March 1793;
1833 London (352)

Lord Ogleby is presumably shown in Act II, scene I, in the antechamber to his bedroom in Mr Sterling's house, where his servants are preparing him for a day of amorous adventure. See No. 216 for a more explicit depiction of the same scene, and No. 23 for another picture of King as Lord Ogleby.

Lord Ogleby's curiously curled and powdered hair sticks out underneath his little white cap, decorated with pink ribbons and bows. His white day coat has a pink lining and more pink bows, and his white waistcoat is lined in pink. See also Nos. 448 and 656.

Colman and Garrick's comedy was first performed at Drury Lane on 20 February 1766, with King as Lord Ogleby.

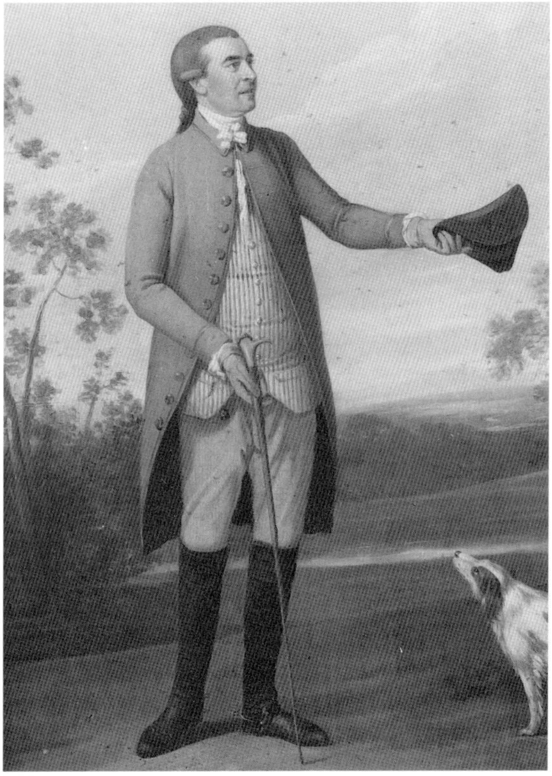

399*
THOMAS KING

Henry Walton (attr.)
Oil on canvas 74.5 x 48
INV: Mathews 68 (by Wilson R.A.);
RW/CKA 391 (by Benjamin Wilson)
PROV: Charles Mathews
EXH: 1833 London (68); 1951 London (391)

King holds a tricorn hat in his left hand. He wears black knee-length boots, buff cord breeches, and a grey coat with gold trim over a blue and white striped waistcoat. A small brown and white dog joins him in the rural setting.

[Benjamin Wilson was never a member of the Royal Academy; Mathews's attribution must be a confusion with Richard Wilson, the portrait and landscape painter, who was a member. Benjamin Wilson is certainly the artist intended by Adams, but Mathews may well have thought that the landscape background of this portrait resembled Richard Wilson's work. An attribution to John Collet (?1725–1780) could be considered.]

The technique and palette bear no resemblance whatsoever to any of Benjamin Wilson's known work. It is a much more accomplished portrait than he ever achieved, and the smooth creamy paint, exact details, surprisingly light palette and slightly stilted pose suggest the work of Henry Walton.

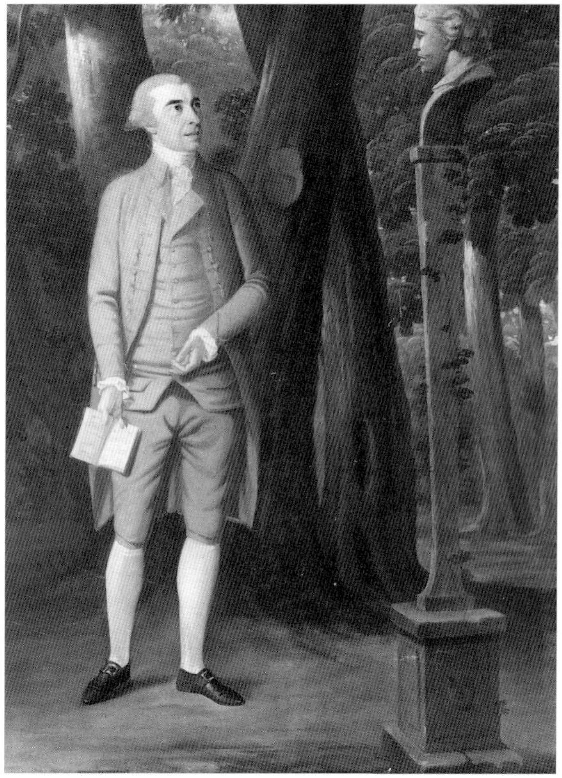

400*
THOMAS KING

Benjamin Wilson (?)
Oil on canvas 76.5 x 63.5
INV: RW 28 (artist unknown); CKA 28
PROV: Charles Mathews (not in catalogue)
LIT: Griffiths, p. 323: 'This possibly a portion of some larger work'

King, full-length, stands outdoors, holding a book in his right hand, and looks up at a bust of Shakespeare. He wears black shoes with silver buckles, white hose, light brown breeches, a light brown coat lined and trimmed in pink, and a brown waistcoat also trimmed in pink. The curiously attenuated pedestal has a relief of a mask with daggers through its eye. There is an inscription, which is illegible.

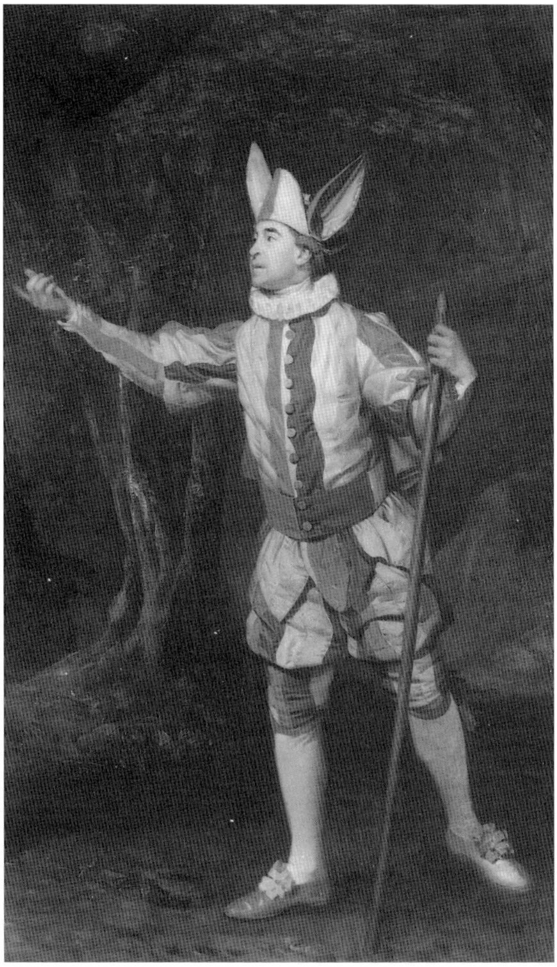

401*
THOMAS KING
as Touchstone
in *As You Like It*
by William Shakespeare

Johan Zoffany

Oil on canvas 91 x 55.5
INV: Mathews 60; RW/CKA 384
PROV: Charles Mathews
EXH: 1833 London (60); 1951 London (46);
1964 London [2] (36); 1975 Milan (102)
LIT: Lady Victoria Manners & Dr G.C. Williamson,
John Zoffany (1920), p. 148; Griffiths, p. 323

Touchstone wears the traditional and colourful 18th-century fool's costume. On his right foot is a pink shoe with a yellow rosette, on his left foot a white shoe with a blue rosette; he has a white stocking on his right leg and a pink stocking on his left. The doublet and hose have vertical yellow, red, white and blue stripes. There are blue bows at the knees. His fool's cap is lined in white. The left leg has been left unfinished from knee to foot, and probably the left hand as well. Mathews identified the moment as Act III: 'I'll rhyme you so, eight years together; dinners and suppers, and sleeping hours excepted: – It is right butter-woman's rate to market.'

King played Touchstone for the first time at Drury Lane on 22 October 1767 and it became one of his most celebrated roles. He appears in an identical costume in George Carter's 'Apotheosis of David Garrick', R.A. 1784 (336), where he and the other performers are 'all in their favourite Characters of Shakespeare' (in the Gallery of the Royal Shakespeare Theatre, Stratford-upon-Avon). During the cleaning of Zoffany's painting in 1976, an arm appeared on the left side of the picture, showing that it has been cut down from the size of his usual theatrical conversation pieces. Touchstone is addressing Rosalind, and it must be her hand that was revealed.

Between King's first performance on 22 October 1767 and Zoffany's departure for a long European absence in the summer of 1772, King played Touchstone 17 times, always with Anne Barry (earlier Mrs Dancer) as Rosalind, except for the last occasion, on 5 June 1772, when Miss Young played Rosalind. On balance, Mrs Barry is the candidate for the missing half of the picture. The figure of King is unfinished, suggesting that the rest of the painting was left unfinished and that the remaining picture was reduced to a single figure for that reason.

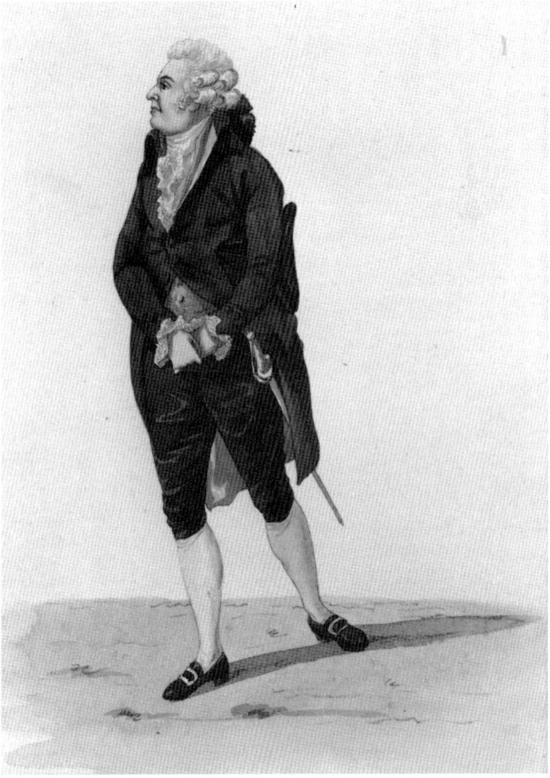

402
THOMAS KING (?)
as Sir Peter Teazle (?) in *The School for Scandal*
by Richard Brinsley Sheridan

William Wellings (?)

Pen and black ink with watercolour
on wove paper 22.8 x 16.5
(missing from Ladies' Room, April 1994)
INV: CKA 516 (as probably John Kemble by R. Dighton?)
PROV: Unknown

Full-length, walking, hands together. The sitter wears black shoes with silver buckles, white stockings, black breeches, a brown jacket and a blue waistcoat. He has a black tricorn hat under his left arm.

The style of this drawing suggests the work of William Wellings; it is certainly not by Dighton, as Adams suggested. The identity of the sitter is not secure, but it is not John Philip Kemble. The costume could be for the part of Sir Peter Teazle, and the presumed date of the drawing (*c.* 1785) suggests that the sitter is Thomas King, the most distinguished exponent of the role in the late 18th century. In its colour the costume is similar to that worn by King in Roberts's scene (No. 3), although the style of the jacket is more 'modern'. The sitter's face bears some similarity to Zoffany's portrait of King as Touchstone (No. 401).

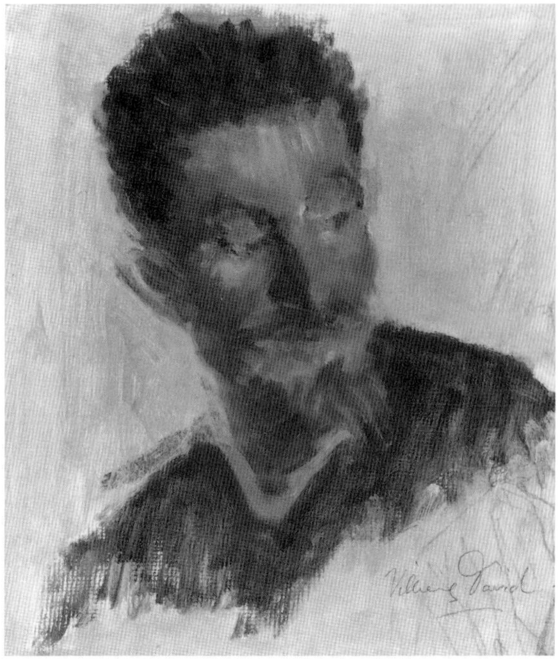

403
WILLIAM ('WILLIE') AUGUSTUS HENRY KING

Villiers David

Oil on canvas board 32.7 x 27 (sight)
INSCR: 'Villers David' (pencil b.l.);
Colnaghi label on verso inscr: 'Carlo Maratti / (From the Ettingham Park Volume)' (pen and ink)
INV: GCL 739; Gift 888
PROV: Bequeathed by the sitter's widow, 1979

'Willie' King, born on 23 February 1894, was elected to the Garrick Club in May 1937 and resigned in 1957, about a year before his death on 21 February 1958. A specialist in porcelain, King joined the staff of the British Museum in July 1926. He was deputy keeper of British and Mediæval Antiquities from 1952 until his retirement in February 1954. In this unfinished sketch he has a pointed beard.

404
EDWARD KNIGHT
as Robin Roughead in *Fortune's Frolic*
by John Till Allingham

Samuel De Wilde

Pencil and watercolour on wove paper 37 x 23.5
INSCR: 'S De Wilde delin / 1810.' (pencil b.r.)
INV: Mathews 212; RW/CKA 68D
PROV: Charles Mathews
EXH: 1833 London (212)

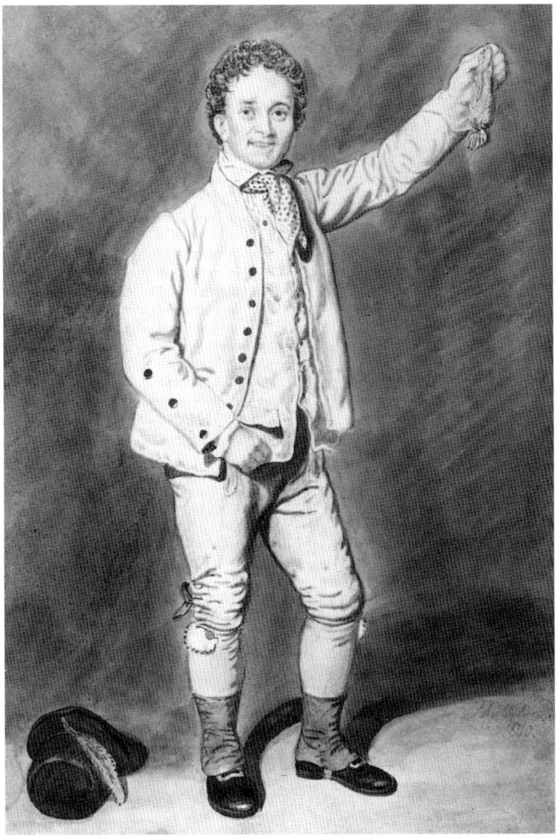

404 *Edward Knight as Robin Roughead*

Robin Roughead is a simple-minded rustic, who, to everyone's surprise, has just inherited the estate of Lord Lackwit. In Act I Robin announces his good fortune to his fellow rustics and throws them money on the line: 'Now, then, young and old, great and small, little and tall, merry men all, here's among you.' The costume notes in the 1821 Oxberry edition for Robin Roughead are 'Thickset jacket, red waistcoat, and leather breeches'. In De Wilde's drawing he wears black shoes, pale blue stockings, creamy-yellow knee-breeches with a red bow at the right knee, and a cream coat and waistcoat. His white neckerchief has blue spots, and the high-crowned, plumed hat on the ground is black. Robin holds a double-ended white purse decorated in gold.

Allingham's farce was first performed at Covent Garden on 25 May 1799, with John Fawcett as Robin Roughead and Thomas Knight as Rattle. Knight played Roughead for the first time on 14 October 1809, at the Lyceum with the Drury Lane company, and repeated the role on 17 October. These were his only appearances in the part during the 1809–10 season. According to the entries in his diary, De Wilde drew Edward Knight as Robin Roughead on 16–18 January 1810. De Wilde sold the drawing to Thomas Hill, 6–9 July 1810.

George Clint painted Knight at exactly the same moment, in a half-length picture that was probably inspired by De Wilde's watercolour; it was engraved by Thomas Woolnoth for Oxberry's *New English Drama*, and published by Simpkin & Marshall in 1821. In Clint's portrait there is an added touch of rusticity with ears of corn in Robin's buttonhole, and he wears an embroidered waistcoat.

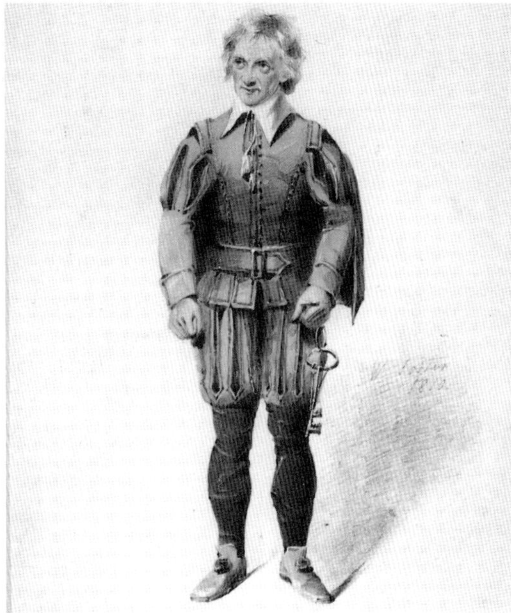

405

EDWARD KNIGHT

as Arnulf in *Plots! or The North Tower*

by Samuel James Arnold

William Foster

Pencil and watercolour on wove paper 22.5 x 16.8

INSCR: 'W Foster / 1810' (pencil c.r.);

papermaker's stamp b.l. (illeg.)

INV: Mathews 279 (as Jailor); RW 549A

(unknown sitter and artist); CKA 549A (as Jailor)

PROV: Charles Mathews

EXH: 1833 London (279)

Arnulf wears brown square-toed shoes with darker brown rosettes, loose dark brown stockings, and a grey costume.

S.J. Arnold's comic opera was first performed on 3 September 1810, during his summer season at the Lyceum. Edward Knight played Arnulf in all 12 performances. His part was described in the *Monthly Mirror* of September 1810 (p. 235) as 'a sturdy stump of domestic honesty, i.e. a servant whose honesty is chiefly displayed in blunt and insolent contradictions of his master'.

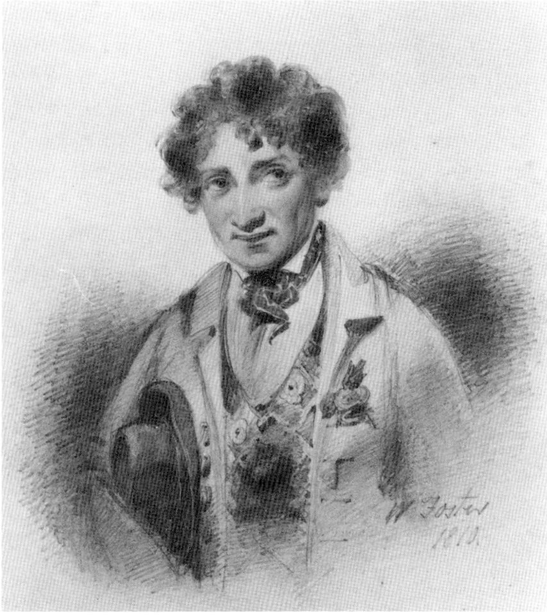

406
EDWARD KNIGHT
as Jerry Blossom
in *Hit or Miss* by Isaac Pocock

William Foster

Pencil and watercolour on wove paper 17.1 x 15.2
INSCR: 'W Foster / 1810.' (pencil b.r.);
'Foster Fecit' (pen and brown ink on mount b.l. CM);
'Mr Knight as Jerry Blossom' (pen and brown ink b.c. CM)
INV: Mathews 280; RW/CKA 544
PROV: Charles Mathews
EXH: 1833 London (280)
ENGR: Similar to: H.R. Cook for the *Theatrical Inquisitor*
pub. W. Oxberry 1 September 1812, stipple 15.4 x 10.3
(full-length with hat in left hand at side and stick in
right hand at side, inscr: 'W. Foster pinx.' &c.);
F. Waldeck for Terry's *British Theatrical Gallery*
pub. H. Berthoud 1 February 1822, lithograph
19.4 x 14.3 (inscr: 'From an Original Drawing by
Mr. W. Foster in the Possession of Mr. Knight);
H.R. Cook, line 8.9 x 7 (bust in oval, to r.,
looking to r., no hat, used as a box ticket)

Jerry Blossom (shown half-length), a retired soldier from the north, plays little part in the plot of this almost plotless piece. His costume presumably reflects that he is an honest country bumpkin. He has curly red hair and a red neckerchief.

Pocock's operatic farce was first performed by the Drury Lane company at the Lyceum on 26 February 1810, with Edward Knight as Jerry Blossom. The cast also included Charles Mathews as Dick Cypher (see No. 465).

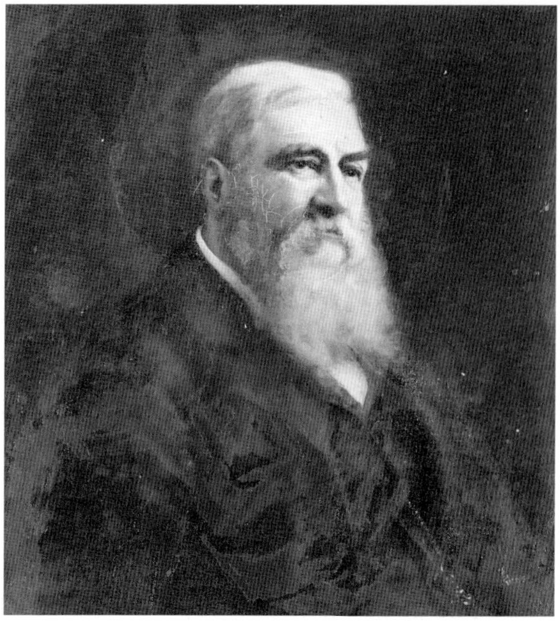

407
JOSEPH KNIGHT

Margaret Grose

Oil on canvas 59.7 x 49.5
INSCR: 'M. / Grose' (white paint b.r.)
INV: CKA 580; Gift 361
PROV: Henry B. Wheatley, by whom presented
to the Garrick Club, 1912

Head and shoulders. The sitter wears a black suit and has a grey beard and a grey hair. No. 407 seems to have been painted from a photograph. In damaged condition, this portrait was in storage in 1994. A portrait of Joseph Knight by Herkomer was exhibited R.S.P.P. 1898 (38).

Knight, who became a member of the Garrick Club in 1883, wrote many of the theatrical biographies for the DNB.

408
LOCATION UNKNOWN
JOSEPH KNIGHT

M.W.

Watercolour on ivory 10.5 x 8.2
INSCR: 'M.W. 1901'
INV: CKA 541; Gift 507 (not located 1988)
PROV: Alderson Burrell Horne, by whom presented
to the Garrick Club, 1932

This miniature, which was not located in 1988, shows the sitter bust-length, turned to the left, with grey hair and beard, and wearing a black suit.

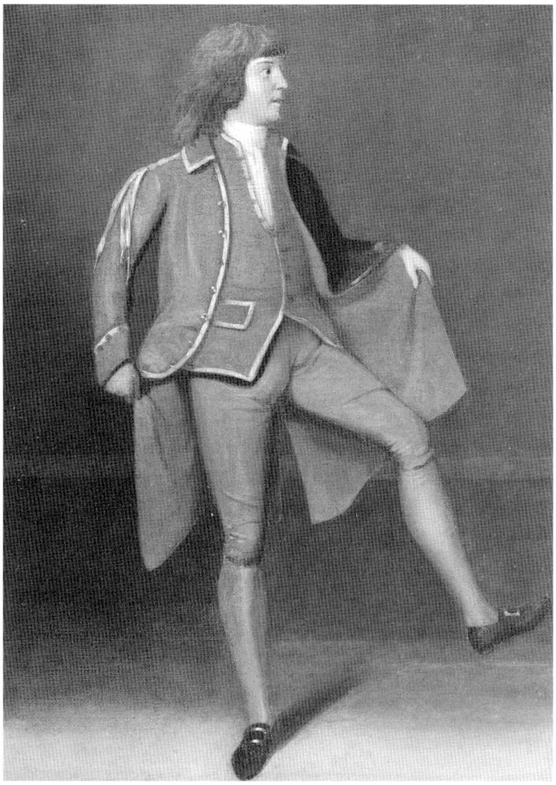

409
THOMAS KNIGHT
as Jacob Gawkey in *Chapter of Accidents*
by Sophia Lee

Samuel De Wilde

Oil on canvas 36.8 x 28.5
INV: Mathews 376; RW/CKA 205
PROV: John Bell (George Cawthorn); Charles Mathews
EXH: 1833 London (376)
ENGR: James Fittler, after a drawing by James Roberts, for the British Library, pub. G. Cawthorn 27 February 1796 line 10.8 x 7.6, pub. Bell's *British Theatre* (1797), vol 34, with the quotation '– and dancing all round the room, zoa –'

Jacob Gawkey, a tiresome bumpkin and footman, dances a minuet. He is dressed in a livery consisting of grey stockings, blue breeches, and a blue coat lined in red with red collar and cuffs and trimmed with silver braid. The red waistcoat is also trimmed in silver.

Miss Lee's confusing comedy, based partly on Diderot's *Le Père de Famille* (which in turn was based on Terence's *Adelphi*), was first performed at the Haymarket on 5 August 1780 with John Edwin as the original Jacob. Thomas Knight made his London début in the part at Covent Garden on 25 September 1795. The next day's *Morning Chronicle* applauded his rustic simplicity, which was untainted with buffoonery, and claimed that his attention was so wholly engrossed by the business of the scene as to make him appear unconscious of being before an audience. That must be the performance commemorated in De Wilde's picture, as Knight did not play the part again in London until 29 May 1800, after the issue of Fittler's print. For his first benefit at Covent Garden, on 6 May 1796, the bill included *A Ramble to Bath* (first time), with a 'descriptive "song" in the character of Jacob Gawkey by Knight'.

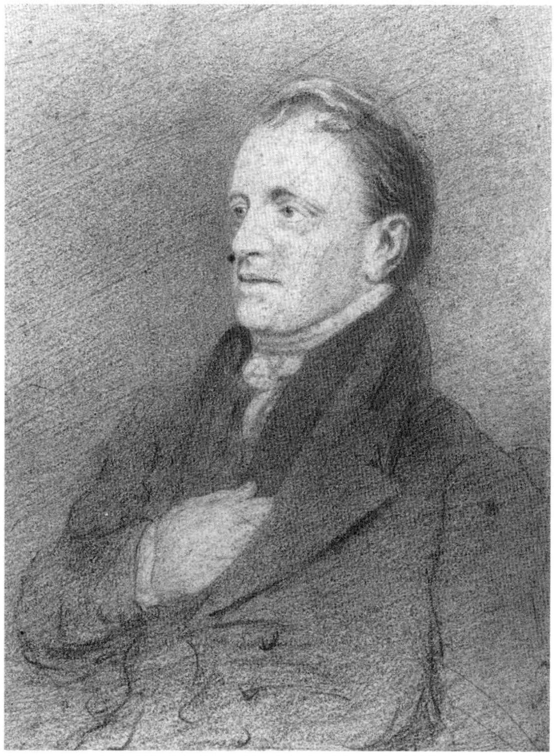

410
THOMAS KNIGHT

Thomas Charles Wageman

Black chalk on wove paper 14 x 11.5
INSCR: 'Wageman fecit' (pen and brown ink on mount b.l. CM); 'Mr Thomas Knight' (pen and brown ink on mount b.c. CM)
INV: Mathews 274; RW/CKA 491D
PROV: Charles Mathews
EXH: 1833 London (274)

Knight is shown half-length, seated facing to left, with his hand in his coat.

After withdrawing from London in 1804, Knight managed the theatre at Liverpool.

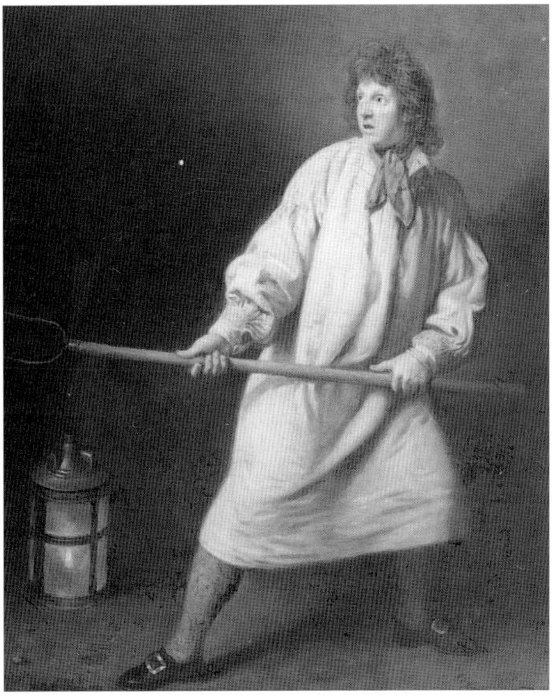

411

THOMAS KNIGHT

as Farmer Harrow in

The Ghost or The Devil to Do About Her

by an anonymous author, after Susannah Centlivre

Johan Zoffany

Oil on canvas 63 x 50.5
INV: Mathews 64 (as Roger); RW/CKA 116 (as Roger)
PROV: Artist's sale, Robins 9 May 1811 (88)
(Knight as the Countryman in 'The Ghost')
bt. Mathews for 22 gns.; Charles Mathews
EXH: 1796 R.A. (110) 'Mr Knight as the Clown in the farce of the Ghost'; 1833 London (64); 1950–51 London (257); 1951–52 London (147); 1977 London (109)
LIT: Fitzgerald, p. 169

In Act II, 'The Street before Mr Trusty's door', Farmer Harrow 'comes out of the house with a pitchfork on his shoulder, and a lanthorn in his hand'. Sir Jeffrey, whom the Farmer believes to have died, arrives to check his affairs and knocks at Trusty's door. Trusty opens it and cries out, thinking he has seen a ghost. Dolly, Trusty's maid, screams from an upstairs window that Sir Jeffrey is a ghost, whereupon the Farmer 'takes his pitchfork off his shoulder and holds it at Sir Jeffrey'. Sir Jeffrey eventually manages to prove that he is very much alive.

The Farmer is dressed as a rustic, with white smock and red neckerchief. He has black shoes with gold buckles and grey stockings. Knight's blue eyes and ginger hair offer a contrast to the white smock.

Mrs Centlivre's *The Man's Bewitched* of 1709 was adapted anonymously and given as *The Ghost; or, The Dead Man Alive* at Drury Lane on 10 April 1769, when John Moody played Roger (as the character was then called). The play was re-adapted and performed at Covent Garden on 23 April 1783 as *The Ghost; or, The Devil to Do About Her*, with John Quick playing the new part of Farmer Harrow. On 28 August 1787 another re-adaptation was given at the Haymarket, this time called *The Ghost; or, The Man Bewitch'd*, with the new part of Farmer Hodge played by John Edwin. The 1769 version was given at Drury Lane on 21 and 25 January 1793, with J. Bannister playing Roger. The performance painted by Zoffany was one of three that took place at Covent Garden in 1795–96 (19 October, and 4 & 6 January), in which Knight acted Farmer Harrow.

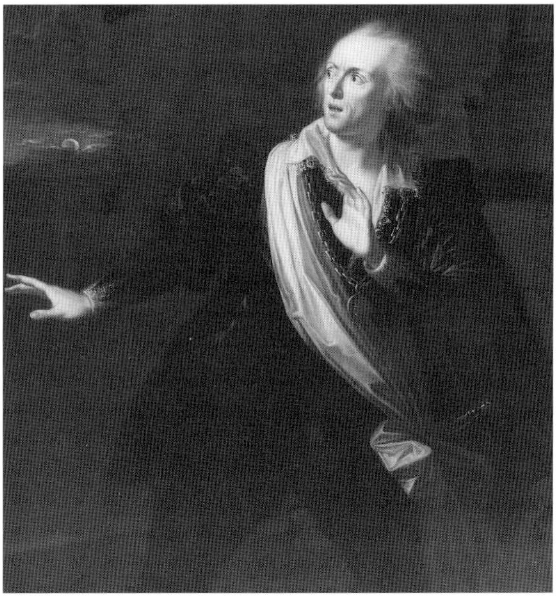

412

JOSEF LANGE

as Hamlet in *Hamlet* by William Shakespeare

Josef Hickel

Oil on canvas 81.3 x 63.5
INV: CKA 585 (Joseph George Holman);
Gift 371 (unknown actor)
PROV: Sir Edward Marshall Hall, K.C.,
by whom presented to the Garrick Club, 1915
ENGR: C. Pfeiffer after a drawing by Kininger,
stipple 9.2 x 7
REL: Vienna Burgtheater, oil on canvas n.s.

Lange is shown in black with an order hanging from a large gold chain around his neck. He also wears a silver cloak. The buildings behind him glisten in the moonlight. His pose is reminiscent of Wilson's portrait of Garrick as Hamlet, which Hickel could have seen as a mezzotint. The Vienna picture is no doubt the original version. C. Pfeiffer engraved and published a portrait of Lange by J. Wolf in 1793, in which the actor is depicted as Albrecht in *Agnes Bernauerinn*.

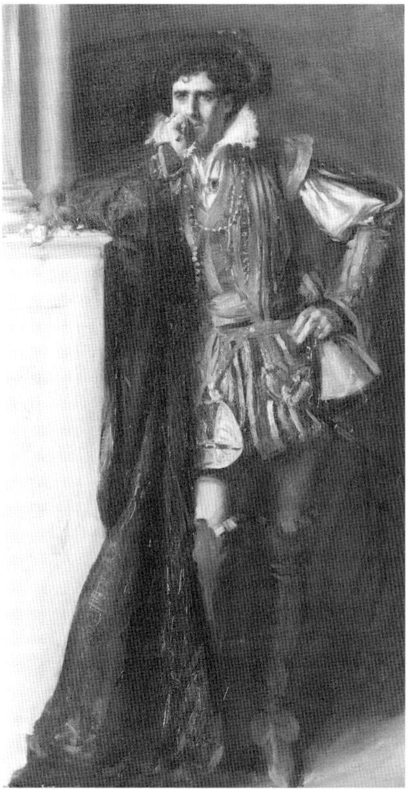

413

GERALD LAWRENCE

as Orsino in *Twelfth Night* by William Shakespeare

Charles Sims

Oil on canvas 92 x 51
INSCR: 'C SIMS' (pink paint b.l.)
INV: GCL 699
PROV: Unknown

As Orsino, Lawrence leans on a stone plinth garlanded with pink roses. He wears a hat with a purple plume, long grey boots, grey hose, a flimsy slashed grey doublet lined in grey and trimmed with gold, a red sash, gold belt and purple cloak. Lawrence played Orsino in Beerbohm Tree's production of *Twelfth Night* which opened at His Majesty's on 5 February 1901 and was particularly memorable for Tree's Malvolio. His first wife was the actress Dame Lilian Braithwaite (see No. 91). Lawrence became a member of the Garrick Club in 1944.

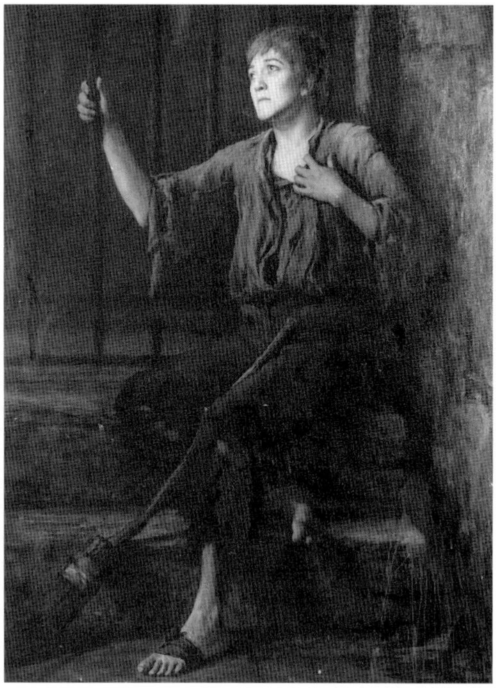

414

JENNY LEE

as Jo in *Jo* by J.P. Burnett

Henry Macbeth-Raeburn

Oil on canvas 151.1 x 104.1
INV: RW/CKA 99; Gift 207
PROV: The artist, by whom presented to the Garrick Club, 1887
EXH: 1886 R.A. (1010), 'Miss Jenny Lee as Jo' with the quotation 'He wos very good to me, he wos'

Jo, Charles Dickens's tragic juvenile road-sweeper, is dressed in shabby brown trousers and a torn purple shirt. He sits with his brush and broom in front of a grill.

Burnett's adaptation from Dickens's *Bleak House* was first performed in England at the Prince of Wales Theatre, Liverpool, on 8 November 1875. However, Jenny Lee first appeared in the play earlier that year, at the California Theatre, San Francisco. After her return to London she played at the Surrey Theatre and then leased the Globe Theatre, where she opened in *Jo* on 22 February 1876. Jo became her most celebrated role. According to the *Athenæum* of 26 February 1876, she played the part: 'with a realism and a pathos difficult to surpass. A more striking revelation of talent has seldom been made. In get-up and in acting the character was thoroughly realized; and the hoarse voice, the slouching, dejected gait, and the movement as of some hunted animal, were admirably exhibited.' J.P. Burnett, the adaptor, was Jenny Lee's husband.

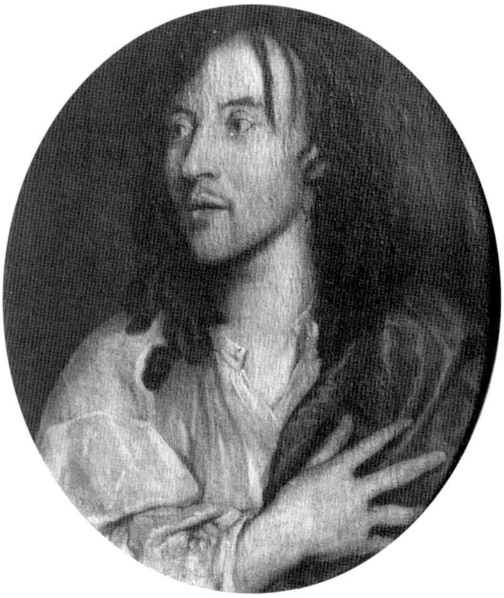

415*
CALLED
NATHANIEL LEE

William Dobson (attr.)

Oil on canvas 56.5 x 46.4
INV: Mathews 104 ('Nathaniel Lee, the Mad Poet; painted during his confinement in Bedlam' by Dobson); RW/CKA 468 (repr.)
PROV: Richard Cosway; Cosway sale, Stanley 18 May 1820 (80) 'Dobson – a capital and expressive portrait of Nat Lee the Poet, much in the style of Vandyck, particularly the making of the hand'; Charles Mathews
EXH: 1833 London (468); 1951 London (15)
ENGR: John Watts pub. J. Watts 3 September 1778, mezzotint (bust in stone oval, Dobson pinxt, picture owned by Richard Cosway)
REL: Sotheby's 28 June 1920 (313) plumbago on laid paper 25.4 x 19.7 (copy by William Faithorne)
LIT: *Notes and Queries* March 1953; Griffiths, p. 296

True to his character of a Caroline romantic, the sitter wears a loose white shirt and a distracted expression. (Nathaniel Lee was confined to Bedlam between 1684 and 1689.) Dulwich 569 (oil on canvas 62.9 x 49.5) is called 'Nathaniel Lee'. The sitter has a wandering right eye but does bear some resemblance to the sitter in the Garrick Club picture. However, the identity of the Dulwich picture is probably based on the traditional identification of the Garrick Club picture. In No. 415 the head is of an extremely high quality, and an attribution to Dobson is perfectly likely. In any event, the picture almost certainly dates from about 1640–45 rather than 1685–90. The artist died in 1646, just about the year of Lee's birth. See BD, 9: 211–14.

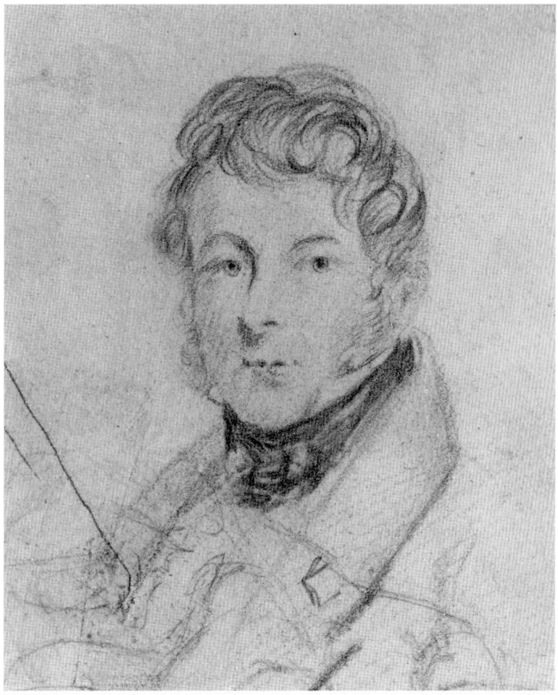

416
JOHN LEECH

John Leech

Pencil and watercolour on card 13 x 10.3
INSCR: 'John Leech by Himself' (pencil on paper below portrait)
INV: CKA 592; Gift 454
PROV: F. J. Anderson, by whom presented to the Garrick Club, 1928

This self-portrait is the earliest image of Leech. The artist became a member of the Garrick Club in 1849. See Nos. 897–922.

417
ANTHONY LEIGH
as Dominic in *The Spanish Fryar or The Double Discovery*
by John Dryden

Sir Godfrey Kneller (after)

Oil on canvas 125.7 x 100.3
INV: Mathews 107; RW/CKA 14
PROV: Thomas Harris; Harris sale, Robins 12 July 1819 (48) (?); Charles Mathews

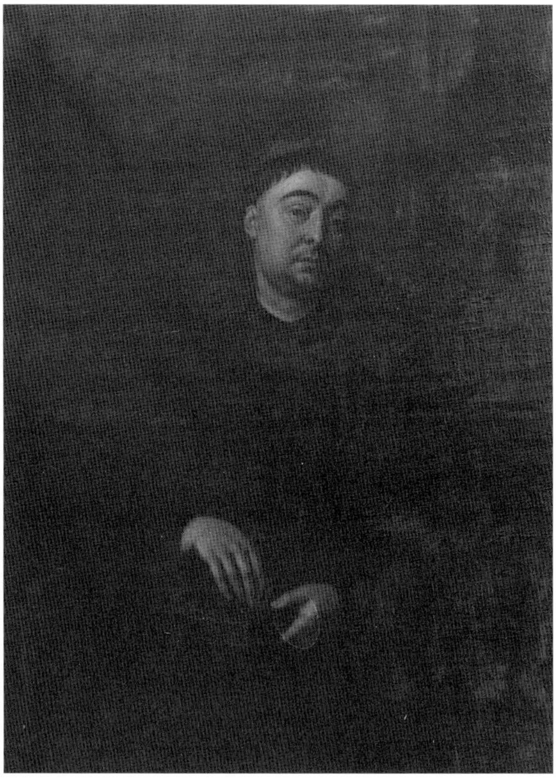

417 *Anthony Leigh as Dominic*

EXH: 1833 London (107)
ENGR: John Smith sold J. Smith, mezzotint 39.7 x 24.8
REL: Original NPG 1280, oil on canvas 231.8 x 142.2 s. & d: 1689 (full-length, holding box in left hand), prov: Earl of Dorset; Earl of Godolphin; Godolphin sale, Christie's? 1803 (63); Thomas Harris; Harris sale, Robins 12 July 1819 (48); Mrs Charles James Wylie

In Act II, scene 3, 'a Chamber with table and wine set out', Father Dominic, the Spanish friar, is offered money by Lorenzo, who claims that it is the fulfilment of a vow to St Dominic, whose spirit protected him in a recent battle. In fact, Lorenzo succeeds in bribing Father Dominic to get him into the presence of Elvira, the wife of Gomez, whom he loves. The priest is her confessor. Father Dominic wears a brown habit, and is presumably fingering Lorenzo's bribe in the silver box held in his left hand.

The NPG version is a picture of much higher quality than No. 417, which may be by Ranelagh Barret. This copy was mentioned by Vertue in his notebooks, 1746 (*Vertue Notebooks*, Walpole Society [1947], 22: 131). The Harris sale catalogue dates the picture 1689, suggesting that it was the signed and dated version now in the NPG. Dryden's comedy was first performed at the Dorset Garden Theatre on 8 March 1680.

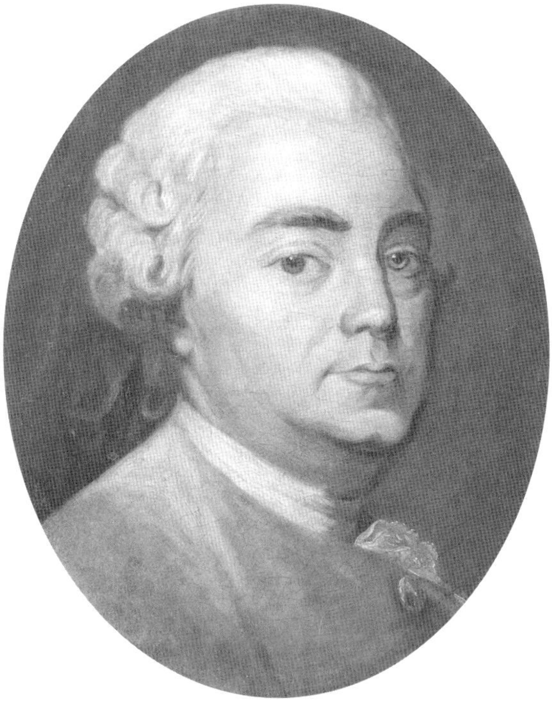

418

HENRY LOUIS CAIN LEKAIN

C.A. Littret de Montigny

Oil on canvas 33.5 x 29.2 (oval)
INV: RW/CKA 259 (artist unknown); Gift 97
PROV: Charles Kemble, by whom presented, 1846
ENGR: C.A. Littret de Montigny, line 14.5 x 11.5 (oval to left, inscr: 'C.A. Littret de Montigny ad vivum del et Sculp. / à Paris ches Buldet rue de gesures au grand Cœur' (under), 'Henry Louis LeKain Comédien Ordr Du Roy' (around oval frame at top), 'A débué par le rôle de Titus dans Brutus le 14 Septembre 1750 et a été reçu le 24 Février 1752' (around oval frame at bottom), 'Du Costume oublié été restaurateur, / C'est lui qui dans ses droits rétablit Mélopmène, / A chaque Personnage il offre un autre Acteur. / Il étonne, il impose, il subjure, il entraîne' (in tablet below portrait); Adam, line 8.8 x 6.9 (inscr: 'Gravé d'après Boucher par Adam'); Henri Lefort, line 5.2 x 4

Head only; in powdered wig and red coat.

This famous French actor made his début at the Comédie Française in 1750 as Titus in *Brutus*. He was sometimes compared to Garrick. The two great actors were friends and corresponded with each other.

419
LOCATION UNKNOWN
FANNY LESLIE
in character

Unknown Artist

Pencil on fine wove paper 30 x 21.2
INSCR: 'Fanny Leslie / (Mrs Gough)' (pencil b.c.);
'Fanny Leslie (Mrs Gough)' (pen and brown ink b.r.)
INV: Not listed
PROV: Unknown

Fanny Leslie, actress and vocalist, is elegantly dressed and has a parasol over her shoulder. This picture was not found in 1994.

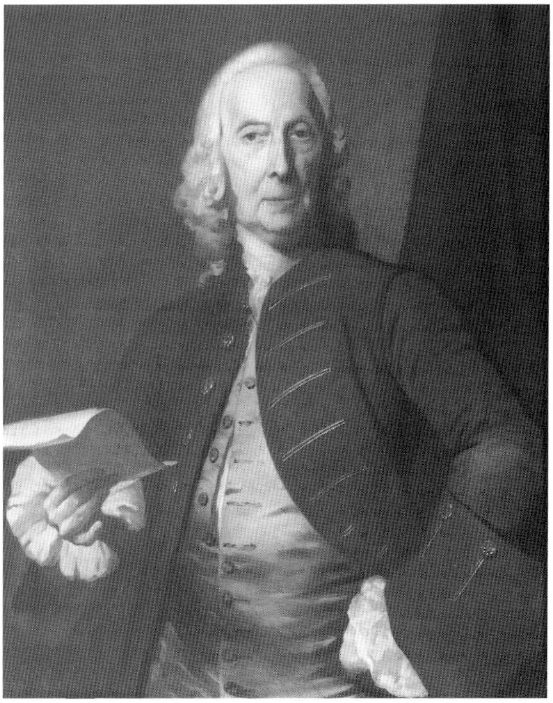

420
RICHARD LEVERIDGE

Frans Van Der Mijn

Oil on canvas 91.5 x 72.5
INV: Mathews 44 (by Frye); RW 12 (by Thomas Frye);
CKA 12 (by A.Vandermyn)
PROV: Thomas Harris; Harris sale, Robins
12 July 1819 (43) (no artist); Charles Mathews
EXH: 1833 London (44)
ENGR: A.Van Der Mijn pub. 1753, mezzotint
31.1 x 25.1 (oval in rect.), inscr:
'O the Roast Beef of Old England' (below)
LIT: Patmore, p. 272: 'Old Leveridge by Vandermyn, a most capital and characteristic head.'

Leveridge wears a dark brown coat with gold trim and a pale blue waistcoat. There is a green curtain behind him.

Patmore must have known the engraving, as he ignores Mathews's attribution to Thomas Frye.

Leveridge began his singing career in the mid-1690s and performed at various London theatres until 1751. He also composed many songs and was one of the original subscribers to the Royal Society of Musicians in 1739. He kept a coffee house at Nos. 2 & 3 Tavistock Street.

421*
CHARLES LEE LEWES
as Bobadil
in *Every Man in His Humour*
by Ben Jonson

Samuel De Wilde

Oil on canvas 43.7 x 31.2
INV: Mathews 366; RW/CKA 249
PROV: John Bell; Charles Mathews
EXH: 1833 London (366)
ENGR: William S. Leney for Bell's British Library
24 August 1791, line 10.8 x 7.6,
pub. Bell's *British Theatre* (1797), vol 4;
H. Brocas for Jones's *British Theatre*
pub. Wm. Jones, Dublin 1792, line 10.5 x 7.3
REL: See No. 422

In Act I, scene 4, Bobadil is being visited by Mr Matthew, 'the town gull', in his humble lodgings at the house of Cob, a water-bearer. Matthew complains of an insult from Squire Downright, and the belligerent Captain Bobadil tells him to challenge the Squire to a duel. He gives Matthew a lesson in swordsmanship and comments on his ineptitude, speaking the line quoted on the engraving: 'Oh, you disorder your point most irregularly.' The quotation preferred by Mathews – 'This is the most fortunate weapon ever rode on poor gentleman's thighs' – is from Act IV, scene I, 'The Stocks Market', where Bobadil brags of his exploits and praises his Toledo steel rapier. The earlier scene is more appropriate, as it is set in an interior and the text refers to Bobadil's pose: 'Hollow your body more, sir, thus. Now,

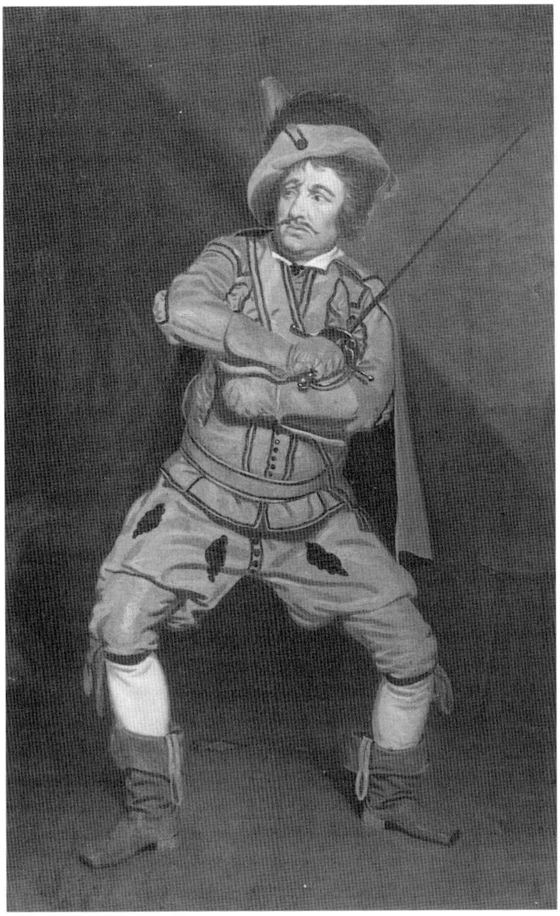

422 *Charles Lee Lewes as Bobadil*

stand fast on your left leg; note your distance; keep your due proportion of time.'

Bobadil wears a buff pointed hat with a black feather and red ribbon. He has brown boots with red heels, buff breeches tied at the knee with red bows, pink trunk hose with black, and a buff doublet slashed to reveal pink lining. His belt and baldrick are pink, as is his black-lined cloak, and his gauntlets buff.

Garrick's adaptation of Jonson's comedy was first given at Drury Lane on 29 November 1751. Charles Lee Lewes played Bobadil for the first time in London at Covent Garden on 1 October 1779. He did not play the part again in London in the 18th century.

Lewes's portrayal of Bobadil was described by one critic (cutting in the Theatre Museum) as 'totally inadequate'; it was claimed that he suffered from 'the double misfortune of entire misconception and great incapacity of execution'. In general, however, Lewes proved himself to be a good comic actor during some 43 years on the London stage. He seems to have possessed an overdeveloped sense of self-importance.

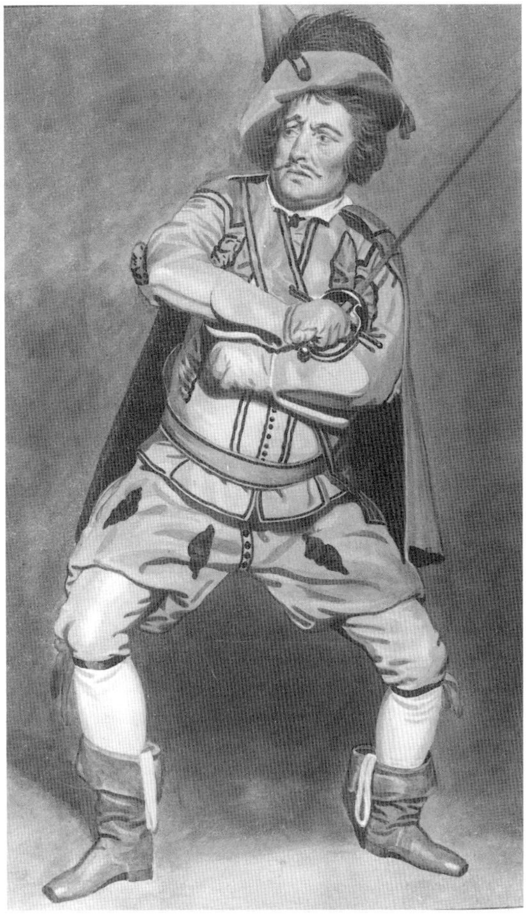

422

CHARLES LEE LEWES

as Bobadil

in *Every Man in His Humour*

by Ben Jonson

Samuel De Wilde

Pencil and watercolour 37 x 23.5
INV: Mathews 197; RW/CKA 66F
PROV: Charles Mathews
EXH: 1833 London (66F)
REL: See No. 421

Lewes wears his Bobadil hat, which is grey, with a medallion, black plume and red ribbon. His brown boots have red heels, and he also wears white stockings, grey breeches, purple hose with black flashes to resemble slashing, a tan doublet slashed with purple and trimmed with black, and a purple belt and scabbard sash, both trimmed in black. His purple cloak is lined in grey. See No. 421.

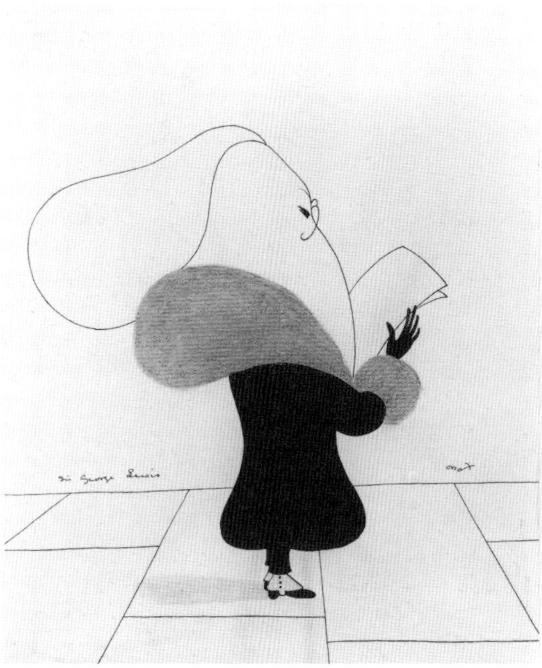

423
SIR GEORGE LEWIS

Max Beerbohm

Pencil, pen and black ink with wash
on laid paper 23.4 x 19.5
INSCR: 'max' (pen and black ink l.r.);
'Sir George Lewis' (pen and black ink l.l.)
INV: GCL 694; Gift 785
PROV: Mrs Wansborough, by whom presented
to the Garrick Club, 1961

Sir George, shown in caricature, wears a black coat with a huge brown fur collar and cuffs. He has pince-nez on his enormously long nose, and holds two sheets of paper. Sir George was a member of the Garrick Club from 1933 until his death.

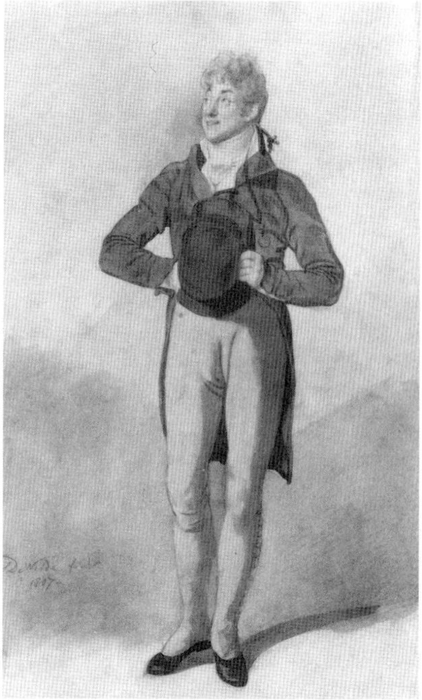

424
WILLIAM THOMAS LEWIS
as Jeremy Diddler in *Raising the Wind*
by James Kenney

Samuel De Wilde

Pencil and watercolour on wove paper 36.5 x 23
INSCR: 'S De Wilde fecit / O 1807' (pencil b.l.);
'Mr Lewis as Jeremy Diddler in Raising the Wind.'
(pen and brown ink on mount t.c. CM); 'There she is
by my hopes. Ye sylphs & cupids strengthen my sight.
Act I Scene 2nd.' (pen and brown ink on mount b. CM);
Label on verso: 'J.R. Cookson / dealer / 99, Highgate,
Kendal, No. 7604'; '209' (pen and ink on verso)
INV: GCL 670; Gift 721
PROV: Charles Mathews (not in catalogue); G.C. Rivington,
by whom presented to the Garrick Club, 1952

Act I, scene 2 is set outside Plainway's house. The short-sighted Jeremy believes the figure at the window is the delectable Peggy, whose heart he captured in Bath. But it is the frumpy Miss Duruble. A spy-glass hangs at his neck, which, had it been used, would have obviated the confusion of the scene. Jeremy wears black shoes and tight pinkish-buff trousers buttoned down the calf. His cutaway coat is dull olive green and he clasps a black hat.

Kenney's farce was first performed at Covent Garden on 5 November 1803, with Lewis as Jeremy Diddler. Lewis acted the role 36 times during the first season, to 19 June 1804, and played it for the last time in the Covent Garden company's production at the Haymarket on 6 May 1809.

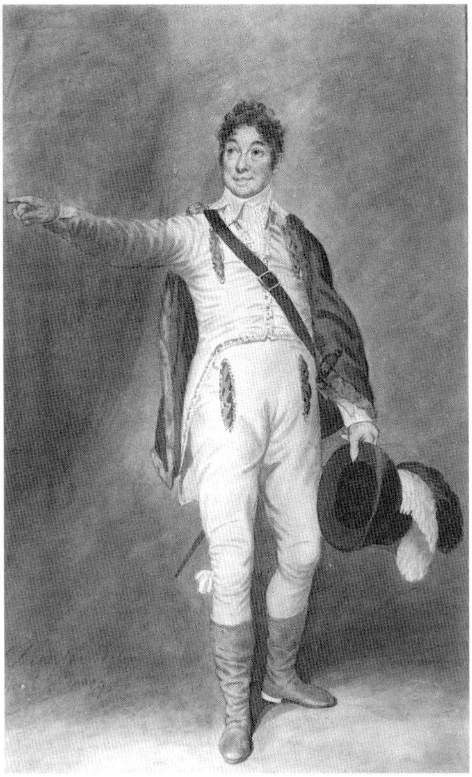

425
WILLIAM THOMAS LEWIS
as Mercutio in *Romeo and Juliet*
by William Shakespeare

Samuel De Wilde

Black chalk, pencil and watercolour
on wove paper 37 x 23.5
INSCR: 'S De Wilde delin / April 30th 1809.'
(black chalk b.l.)
INV: Mathews 214; RW/CKA 68F
PROV: Charles Mathews
EXH: 1833 London (214)

Lewis, over 60 in 1809, must have made a rather geriatric Mercutio. He holds a black hat with black and white plumes and wears yellow gloves, brown boots, white trousers slashed to reveal blue edged in gold, and a white cutaway collarless coat slashed in blue and trimmed in gold. His blue cloak is trimmed with pale brown fur.

According to Mathews, this was the last portrait ever taken of Lewis. He gave his final performance as Mercutio with the Covent Garden company at the Haymarket on 31 October 1808. His last appearance was on 29 May 1809, when he played the Copper Captain in Beaumont and Fletcher's *Rule a Wife and Have a Wife*, for his own benefit.

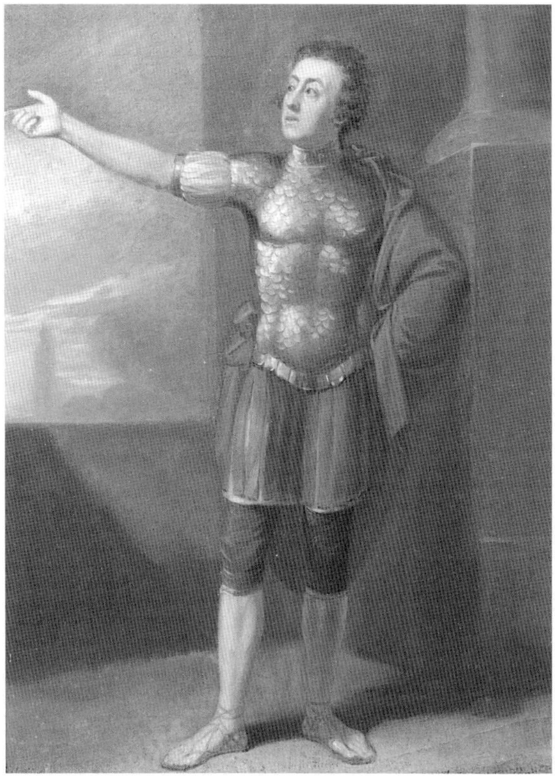

426
WILLIAM THOMAS LEWIS
as Pharnaces in *Cleonice; Princess of Bithynia*
by John Hoole

Samuel De Wilde

Oil on canvas 37.5 x 28.5
INV: Mathews 186 (as Pharnaces); RW 201?
(unknown sitter and artist); CKA 201 (as Pharnaces)
PROV: John Bell; Leigh & Sotheby's 25 May 1805 (285),
bt. Mathews; Charles Mathews
EXH: 1833 London (186)
ENGR: Philippe Audinet for Bell's British Library
6 July 1795, line 11.5 x 8.2,
pub. Bell's *British Theatre* (1797), vol 24

De Wilde shows Pharnaces in Act III, scene 2, berating Cleonice for doubting his love for her. His line 'Oh! thou most unkind' is quoted on the engraving.

Pharnaces wears a classical hero's costume consisting of brown sandals, green-grey breeches, metal scale armour with leather strips over the skirt of an undertunic, and a long red cloak.

Hoole's tragedy was first performed at Covent Garden on 2 March 1775, with Lewis as Pharnaces and Mrs Hartley as Cleonice. There were nine performances; the last, on 23 March, was a benefit for the author, before the play disappeared for ever.

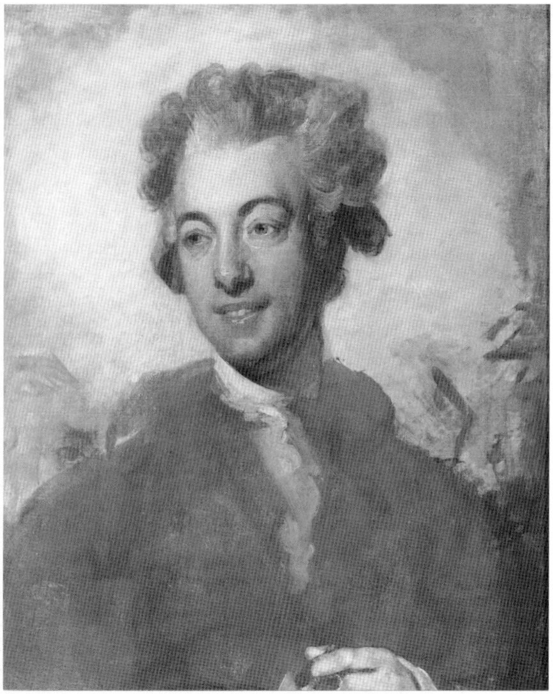

427
WILLIAM THOMAS LEWIS
as Vapid (?) in *The Dramatist*
by Frederick Reynolds

William Naish (attr.)

Oil on canvas 60.5 x 52.2
INV: RW 436 (by James Stuart); CKA 436
(by John Stewart [?], no character); Gift 21
PROV: John Dawkins, by whom presented
to the Garrick Club, 1835
ENGR: Similar to W. Hinton 'after a Picture by W. Naish'
printed W. Hinton, stipple 15.2 x 13

Vapid is the dramatist of the play's title, who finds dramatic situations in everyday events – and if he cannot find one, he creates it. The character is enthusiastic and amusing. There is no inherent iconographic reason for designating this portrait of Lewis to the role of Vapid, apart from the general jollity of both the part and the portrait. The engraved portrait by Hinton after Naish provides the strongest, if inconclusive, evidence (see below). The sitter is shown half-length, and appears to be holding a monocle in his left hand. He has wavy grey hair and wears a dark coat, which is unfinished. Three eyes have been painted over on the left, and there are various sketchy ideas all over the surface of the canvas.

Reynolds's comedy was first performed at Covent Garden on 15 May 1789, with Lewis as Vapid.

This picture is close to Hinton's engraving of William Naish's portrait of Lewis as Vapid. In that engraving, the sitter is shown half-length, slightly to the right, head turned and looking down to the left, with arms folded. It is also similar to John Corner's engraving after a portrait by Mather Brown, published by J. Sewell 1 October 1790, which shows Lewis turned to the right, holding a mask in his right hand. There is also the possibility that No. 427 is by Gilbert Stuart, the American painter who was in London between 1782 and 1787.

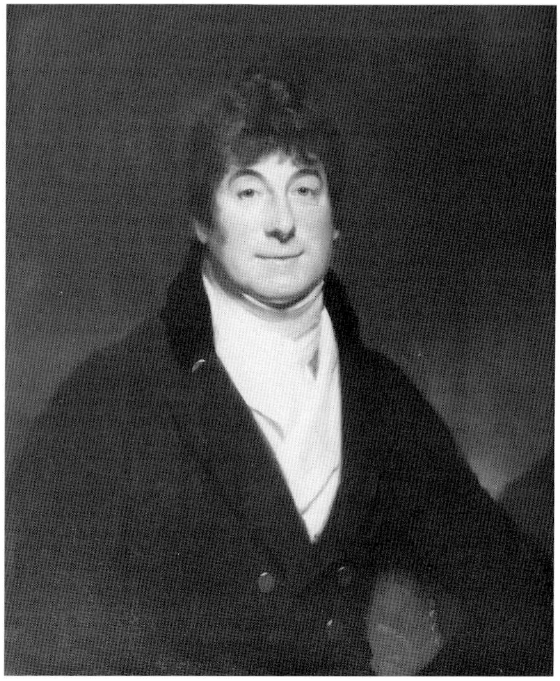

428
WILLIAM THOMAS LEWIS

Sir Martin Archer Shee

Oil on canvas 76 x 63
INV: Mathews 115; RW/CKA 389
PROV: Thomas Harris; Harris sale, Robins 12 July 1819 (40);
Charles Mathews
EXH: 1833 London (115)

Lewis wears a dark coat with gold buttons, a white waistcoat, and a white stock. Under his left arm he holds a black hat with red lining.

Shee also painted a full-length of Lewis as the Marquis in *The Midnight Hour*, which is now in the National Portrait Gallery (see BD 9:292, No. 28).

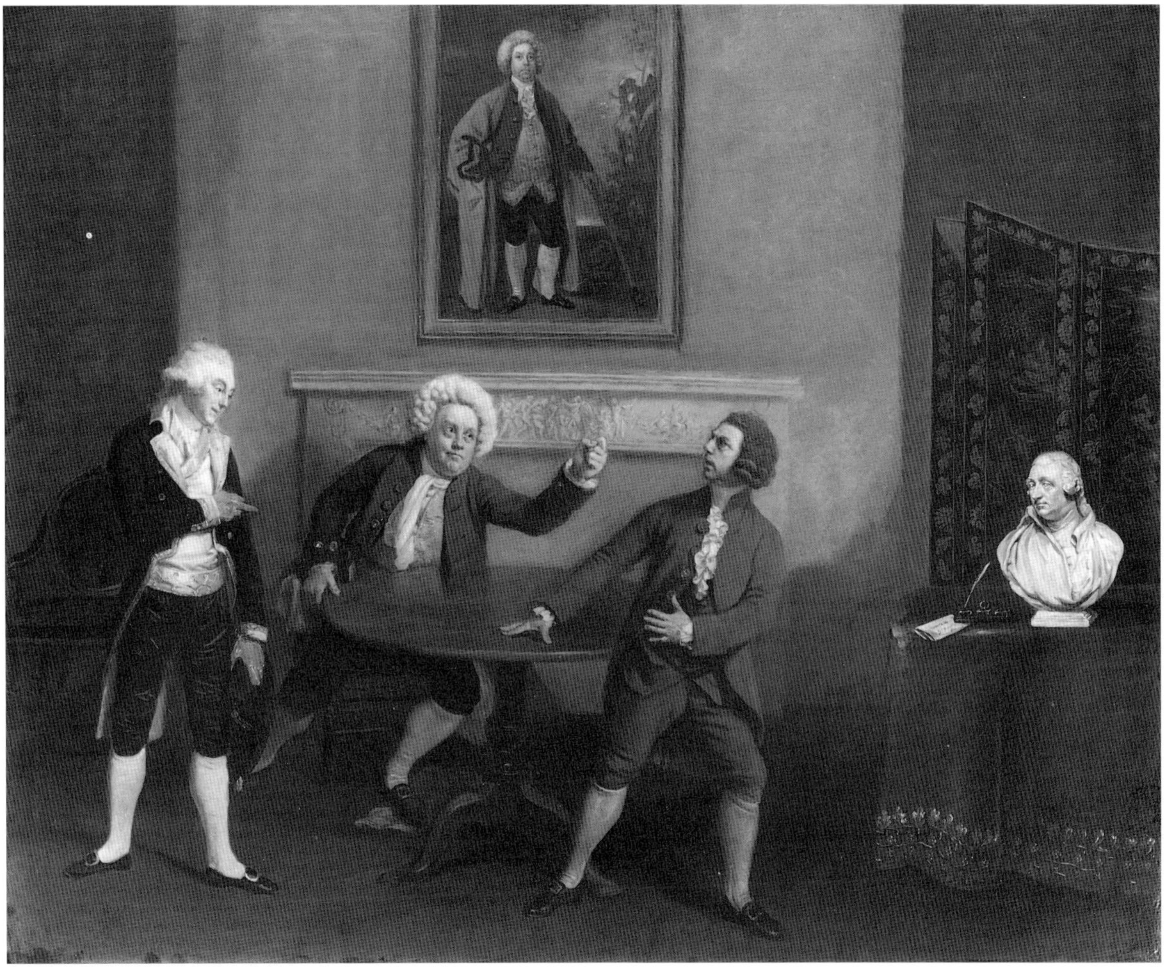

429*

WILLIAM THOMAS LEWIS as Tanjore, *JOSEPH SHEPHERD MUNDEN* as Project and *JOHN QUICK* as Alderman Arable in *Speculation* by Frederick Reynolds

Johan Zoffany

Oil on canvas 102 x 128
INV: Mathews 58; RW/CKA 104
PROV: Artist's sale, Robins 9 May 1811 (92) bt. Mathews for 31 gns.; Charles Mathews
EXH: 1833 London (58); 1951 London (41); 1960–61 London (2); 1977 London (110)
LIT: Patmore, p. 265; Lady Victoria Manners & Dr G.C. Williamson, *John Zoffany* (1920), p. 144; P.P. Howe (ed.), *The Complete Works of William Hazlitt* (1930), 17: 226; Fitzgerald, pp. 168–69; Griffiths, p. 335

The setting for Act IV, scene 2 is: 'An apartment in the Alderman's house hung with pictures, a portrait of the Alderman in his gown and full-dressed wig leaning on a Plough – A round table – Two chairs and wine on the table.' Alderman Obadiah Arable has just awakened after snoozing in his black padded chair. He shakes his fist at Project who, thinking the Alderman was asleep, has revealed to Tanjore, standing on the left, that he has speculated with and embezzled the fortune of Emmeline, the Alderman's niece. In the text, Project knocks over a chair in his surprise at seeing the Alderman awake, but this action has been painted over, along with the figure of Emmeline (see below).

Project (Munden) is plainly dressed in reddish-brown – an indication of the economies he has to make to pay for his wife's extravagances.

The Alderman (Quick), in black shoes with silver buckles, black knee-breeches and a brown jacket, also wears a red waistcoat which is the object of Tanjore's repeated disdain: 'Pray Obadiah, where did you get that curious waistcoat? – positively, it's only fit for an alderman.' The Alderman sees himself as a gentleman farmer, the image captured in the picture over the mantel, but his attempts at husbandry are hopeless and he spends all his money making his farm look 'so tasty, so neat, so clean' and has the manure transported to 'a neighbouring farmer's, for you must know I'm too cleanly to have any dust or dirt thrown on my land'.

Tanjore (Lewis) is very proud of his appearance, believing that dressing well and correctly is the principal attainment of a gentleman. He holds Project's hat, having whipped it off his head to teach him manners when he came into the room. Tanjore wears black shoes, white stockings, black knee-breeches, a black jacket with a pink collar, lined in pink and trimmed with gold, a pink cummerbund, and a white waistcoat with pink lapels. He later describes his jacket as being of 'a pretty hymeneal colour'.

There is no particular reason for the appearance of Nollekens's bust of C.J. Fox, and it may have been added, along with the lacquer screen, when the figure of Emmeline was painted over. The relief on the mantel shows the Drunkenness of Silenus, presumably a reference to the happy-go-lucky mismanagement of Alderman Arable's farm.

According to Mathews, and to Hazlitt, this picture was commissioned from Zoffany by George III. There is no evidence to support this claim, although the Zoffany sale catalogue states that the picture was painted for a 'distinguished personage'. The sale catalogue also states that the picture was unfinished and that it included a portrait of Miss Wallis as Emmeline. An X-ray examination may reveal her underneath the screen, table and bust of Fox on the right of the picture.

Reynolds's comedy was first performed at Covent Garden on 7 November 1795, with a cast that included Lewis as Tanjore, Quick as Alderman Arable, Munden as Project, Fawcett as Jack Arable, Middleton as Arable, Mrs Davenport as Lady Project, and Miss Wallis as Emmeline. The piece was played 34 times during the season, the final performance being on 13 May 1796.

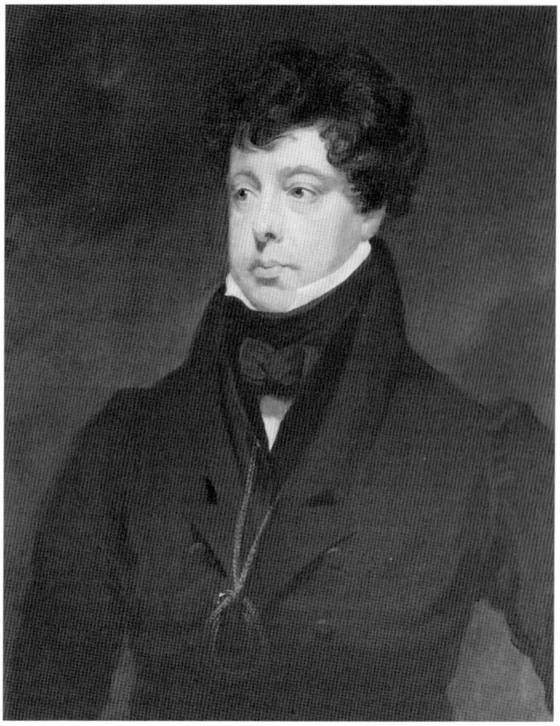

430

JOHN LISTON

George Clint

Oil on canvas 76 x 64
INV: Mathews 113; RW/CKA 480
PROV: Charles Mathews
EXH: 1827 R.A. (360); 1829 Norwich (70, for sale); 1833 London (113)
ENGR: H. Sadd pub. T. McLean, 27.3 x 22.8
REL: Christie's 30 April 1971 (144), oil on canvas n.s.; Coll: A. Guardian, Geneva, oil on canvas 60 x 50 (bust only, copy); enamel copy by W. Essex R.A. 1829 (623)

Half-length, in a black coat and stock.

During the first 30 years of the 19th century, Liston was a leading actor in London, who only had to walk on to set the audience laughing. His face, which was 'physically extraordinary', was 'his fortune' (Jim Davis, *John Liston, Comedian*, Society for Theatre Research, 1985, pp. 104–5). *The Theatrical Journal* of 13 July 1841 described him as: 'the most simple or natural actor on the stage; there is a sort of sincerity about his manner ... [that] places you at once in the presence of the identical person himself.'

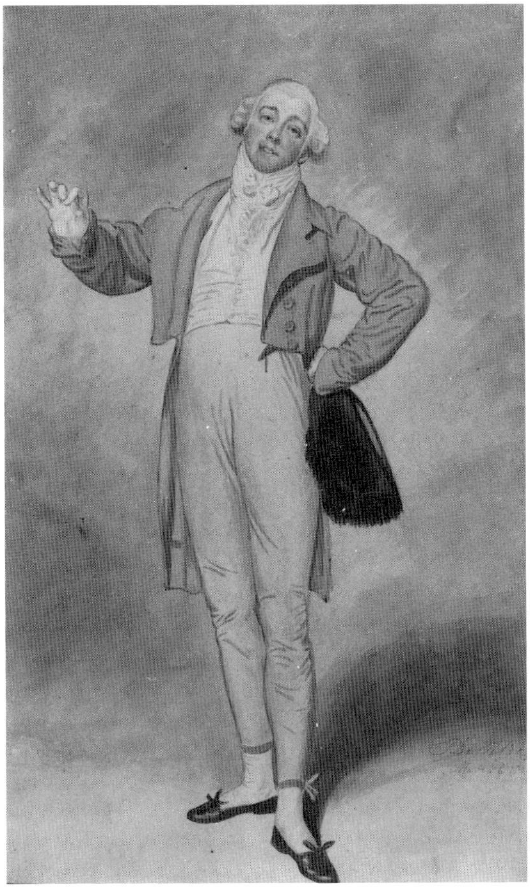

431
JOHN LISTON
as Caper in *Who Wins?* or *The Widow's Choice*
by John Till Allingham

Samuel De Wilde

Pencil and watercolour on wove paper 37 x 23.5
INSCR: 'S De Wilde / March 6 1808' (pencil b.r.)
INV: Mathews 226; RW/CKA 58F
PROV: Charles Mathews
EXH: 1833 London (226)
ENGR: Edward Scriven pub. J.B. Bell & De Camp
1 April 1808, stipple 14.6 x 9.5, with the quotation 'I have been flattered a little by the Ladies about my Dancing';
Edward Scriven pub. T. Tegg 1812, stipple 12.4 x 8

Caper adopts a flashy, dancing attitude. He has a wig with a widow's peak and curls, and he wears black slippers, white stockings, tight fawn trousers, a blue jacket, a white waistcoat with touches of blue, and a very high white stock with a big bow. In his left hand he holds a black fringed hat.

Allingham's operatic farce, with music by Condell, was first performed on 25 February 1808 at Covent Garden, with Liston as Caper.

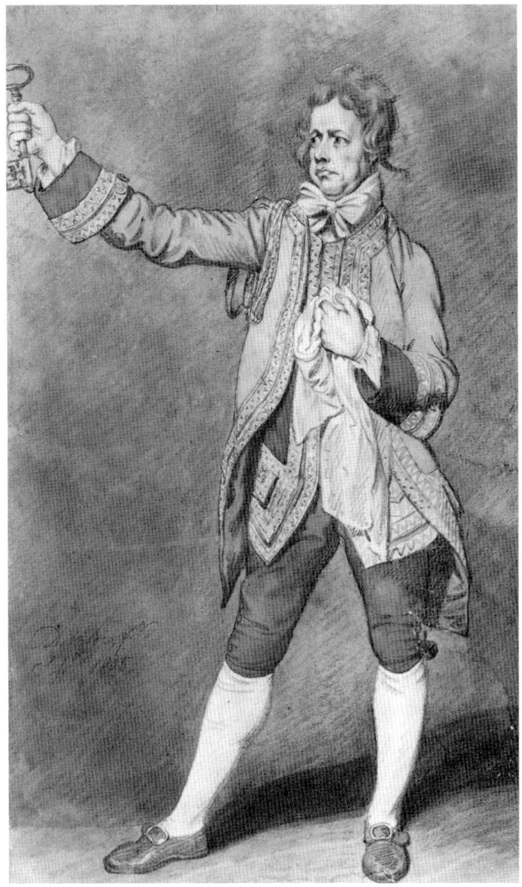

432
JOHN LISTON
as Diggery in *All the World's a Stage*
by Isaac Jackman

Samuel De Wilde

Black chalk and watercolour on wove paper 37 x 23.5
INSCR: 'S De Wilde ft / Sepr 1805' (black chalk b.l.)
INV: Mathews 225; RW/CKA 66E
PROV: Charles Mathews
EXH: 1833 London (225)
ENGR: Richard Cooper for Cawthorn's
Minor British Theatre pub. John Cawthorn 1806,
stipple 12 x 7.6

In Act II, scene I of this satire on the craze for amateur theatricals, the servants are rehearsing Nathaniel Lee's *The Rival Queens* and the butler, Diggery, practises a tragic climax by pretending to stab himself with a large key. Presumably his costume has been donned for the rehearsal, although it seems to be a comic exaggeration of everyday dress rather than an imitation of professional dramatic garb (see No. 302 for Holman's costume as Alexander; the moment shown in No. 302 is quoted by Diggery during his rehearsal of the part). Diggery has dishevelled ginger hair and wears grey shoes, white stockings, blue breeches, and a yellow coat with zigzag decoration in red and green. The coat is lined in red and trimmed with red braid. His blue waistcoat is also trimmed with a zigzag decoration.

Jackman's two-act farce was first performed at Drury Lane on 7 April 1777, with William Parsons as the original Diggery. Liston first acted the role at Covent Garden, on 28 November and again on 3 December 1805. Liston's first appearance at Covent Garden had been as Jacob Gawkey in Sophia Lee's *The Chapter of Accidents* on 15 October 1805. On 29 October, Liston wrote to Thomas Hill from the Orange Coffee House in the Haymarket, mentioning a portrait by De Wilde: 'I am writing to Mr De Wilde for a character portrait [Jacob Gawkey] which will be finished this week; should the likeness be approved the picture will be much [?] at your service' (letter in Garrick Club Library).

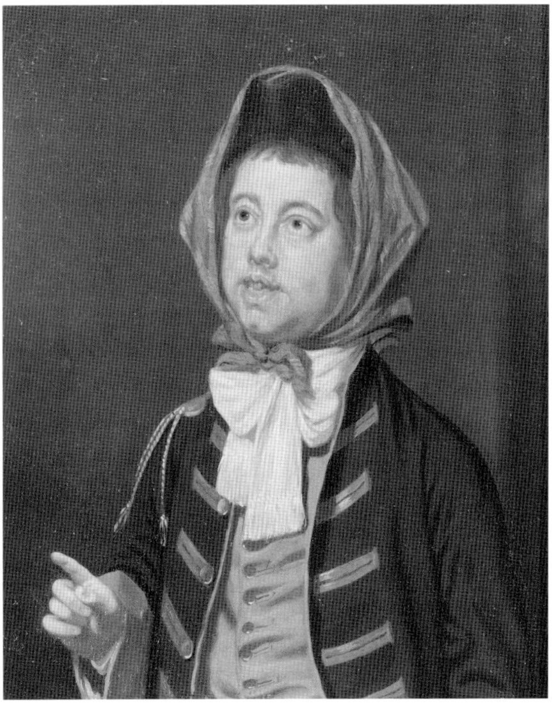

433
JOHN LISTON
as Gaby Grim in *We Fly by Night*
by George Colman the Younger

Samuel De Wilde

Oil on panel 24 x 19.3
INSCR: 'S De Wilde / Pinxt 1812' (black paint t.r.)
INV: Mathews 149; RW/CKA 210
PROV: Charles Mathews
EXH: 1833 London (149)

Gaby's ginger hair is visible under his grey tricorn hat which is tied onto his head with a grey neckerchief. He wears a dark green jacket with orange decoration and orange cuffs, an orange waistcoat, and a white scarf tied in a bow. The younger Colman's farce was first performed on 28 January 1806 at Covent Garden, with Liston as Gaby Grim.

434
JOHN LISTON
as Pompey in *Measure for Measure*
by William Shakespeare

Samuel De Wilde

Oil on panel 22.8 x 19
INSCR: 'S De Wilde 1812'
INV: CKA 567C (as Charles Mathews in character); Gift 390
PROV: Mrs Weedon Grossmith, by whom presented to the Garrick Club, 1919
EXH: 1971 Northampton (18)
ENGR: Thomas Woolnoth for Oxberry's *New English Drama* pub. Simpkin & Marshall 1822, stipple 12.1 x 8.2; Anon., stipple 19.4 x 14.6 (full-length)
REL: Theatre Museum (TM20), oil on panel 23.5 x 19, inscr: 'S DeWilde / Pinxt 1812'

In Act II, scene 2, Pompey is being led away to prison. No. 434 probably shows him on the line 'Here comes Signior Claudio, led by the provost to prison'. Pompey has a black hat on the back of his ginger hair and wears a brown doublet decorated with blue lines, a dark brown jacket trimmed with gold braid, and a blue apron. The costume worn by Pompey is not historically accurate, as the doublet is made like a waistcoat. However, there is a gesture towards 16th or 17th-century fashion that the audience would have recognised.

Liston played Pompey for the first time at Covent Garden on 30 October 1811. Hazlitt saw him in the part

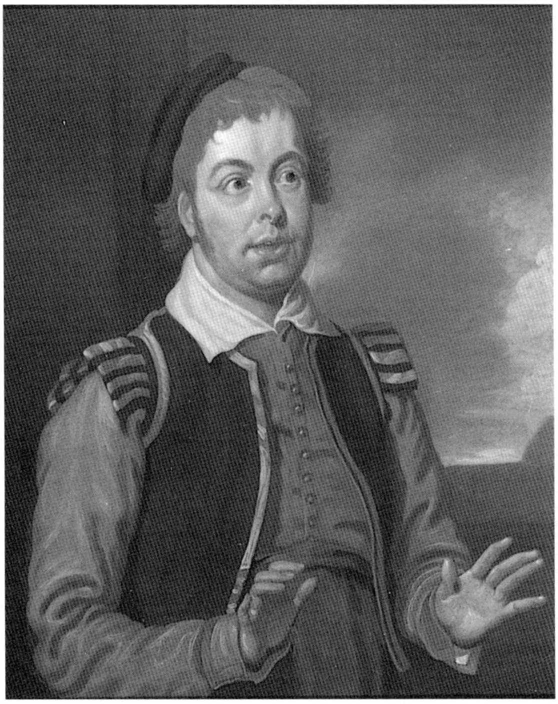

434 *John Liston as Pompey*

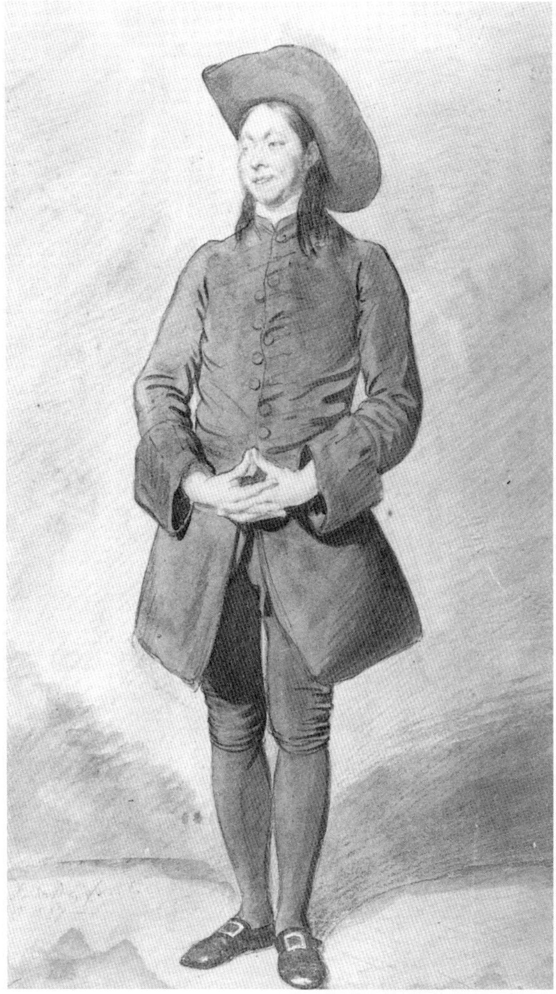

435 *John Liston as Solomon*

in 1816 and wrote: 'We cannot say that the Clown Pompey suffered in the hands of Mr Liston; on the contrary, he played it inimitably well. His manner of saying "a dish of some three-pence" was worth any thing. In the scene of his examination before the Justice, he delayed and dallied, and dangled his answers, in the true spirit of the genius of his author.' Liston was not noted as a Shakespearean actor, and he seems to have treated his audiences to a display of broad comedy when he did attempt such roles as Pompey – the part was always billed as 'Clown' – and Polonius. He was a notable Bottom in Frederick Reynolds's adaptation of *A Midsummer Night's Dream* at Covent Garden in 1816, and in 1819 he played one of the two Dromios in a musical version of *The Comedy of Errors*.

435
JOHN LISTON
as Solomon in *The Quaker*
by Charles Dibdin

Samuel De Wilde

Pencil and watercolour on wove paper 37 x 23.5
INSCR: 'S De Wilde fecit / [? 19] / 1807–' (pencil b.l.)
INV: Mathews 227; RW/CKA 63E
PROV: Charles Mathews
EXH: 1833 London (227); 1975 London (147)

Solomon is a servant in the house of Steady the Quaker. He wears a wig under a brown hat, dark brown shoes with gold buckles, brown stockings, and a Quaker's suit of drab cloth. His hands are clasped in an obsequious gesture.

Dibdin wrote both the text and the music for his comic opera, which was first performed at Drury Lane on 7 October 1777, with William Parsons as Solomon. Liston first played Solomon on 16 October 1805, at Covent Garden, his second role at that theatre.

The clasped hands with thumbs together were the hallmark of the part of Solomon. Other examples of actors depicted in exactly the same way in the role include Charles Bannister (painting by Thomas Pye, No. 31) and Benjamin Charles Incledon (drawing by Thomas Charles Wageman in a private collection, engraved by Woolnoth for Oxberry's *New English Theatre*, 1820).

Rhodes's burlesque tragic opera in one act, with music composed and selected by Ware, was first played at the Haymarket on 7 August 1810. Liston was the original Bombastes with Charles Mathews as Artaxominous, King of Utopia, and Harriet Kelly as Distaffina. There were 23 performances during the season, the last on 15 September 1810. The attribution to Lambert is suggested by the distinctive morphology of the figure. The same piggy features are present in Lambert's portrait of Liston as Apollo Belvi (NT 73), which is dated 1823, the year in which it was lithographed by W. Sheldricks.

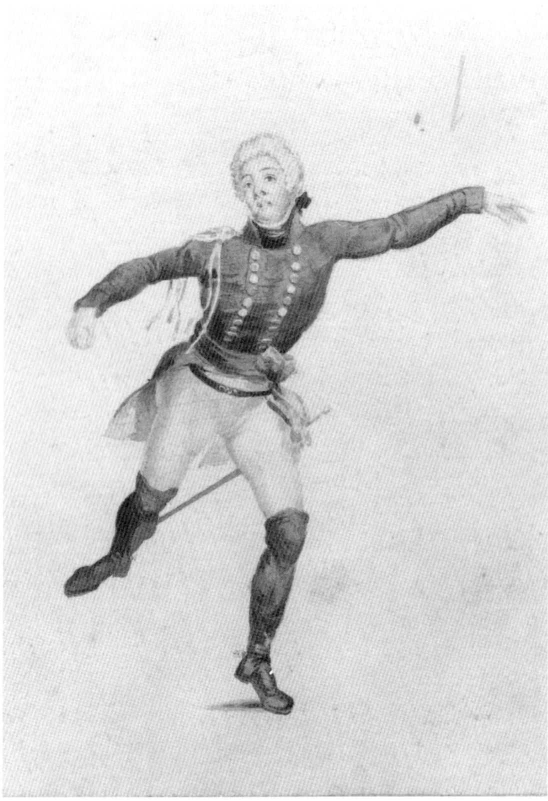

436
JOHN LISTON
as General Bombastes
in *Bombastes Furioso*
by William Barnes Rhodes

E.F. Lambert

Pencil and watercolour on laid paper 19.7 x 14.6
INSCR: 'Mr Liston as Bombastes.'
(pen and brown ink on mount b.c. CM)
INV: CKA 524 (artist unknown)
PROV: Charles Mathews (not in catalogue)

Lambert's drawing seems to show Bombastes at the end of scene 3, which is set in Distaffina's cottage. Distaffina and King Artaxominous try to stop Bombastes leaving: 'They hold him by the coat-tails, but he gradually tugs them off.' The incident is shown in one of George Cruikshank's six steel-engraved illustrations to French's edition of the burlesque in which the features of Liston can be discerned in the various depictions of Bombastes. The stage directions describe Bombastes's costume as 'A general's military suit, jack-boots, comic powdered wig and pigtail, sword and sash, general's hat and plume'. Lambert's drawing shows this costume; the jacket is red and the sash is pink, although Bombastes has lost his hat in the fracas chez Distaffina.

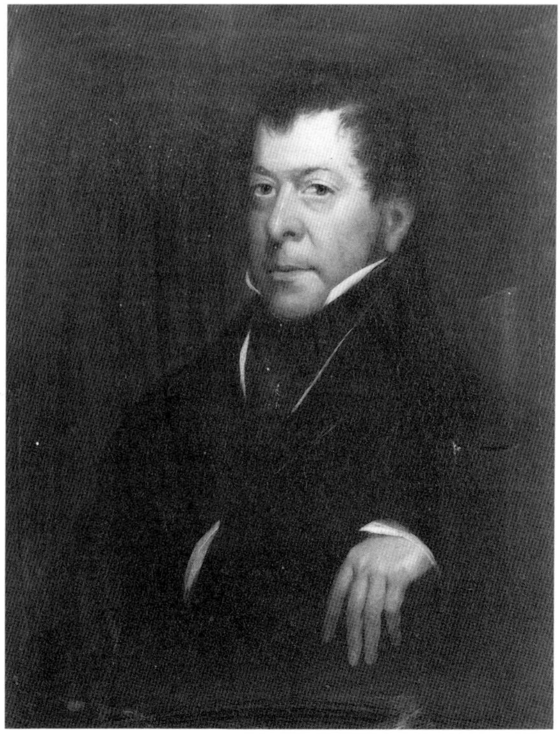

437
JOHN LISTON

Unknown Artist

Oil on canvas 73.7 x 61
INV: RW/CKA 338
PROV: Mrs M.A. Day, by whom presented
to the Garrick Club, 1895

Liston wears a dark coat lined in pink, and a green neckerchief.

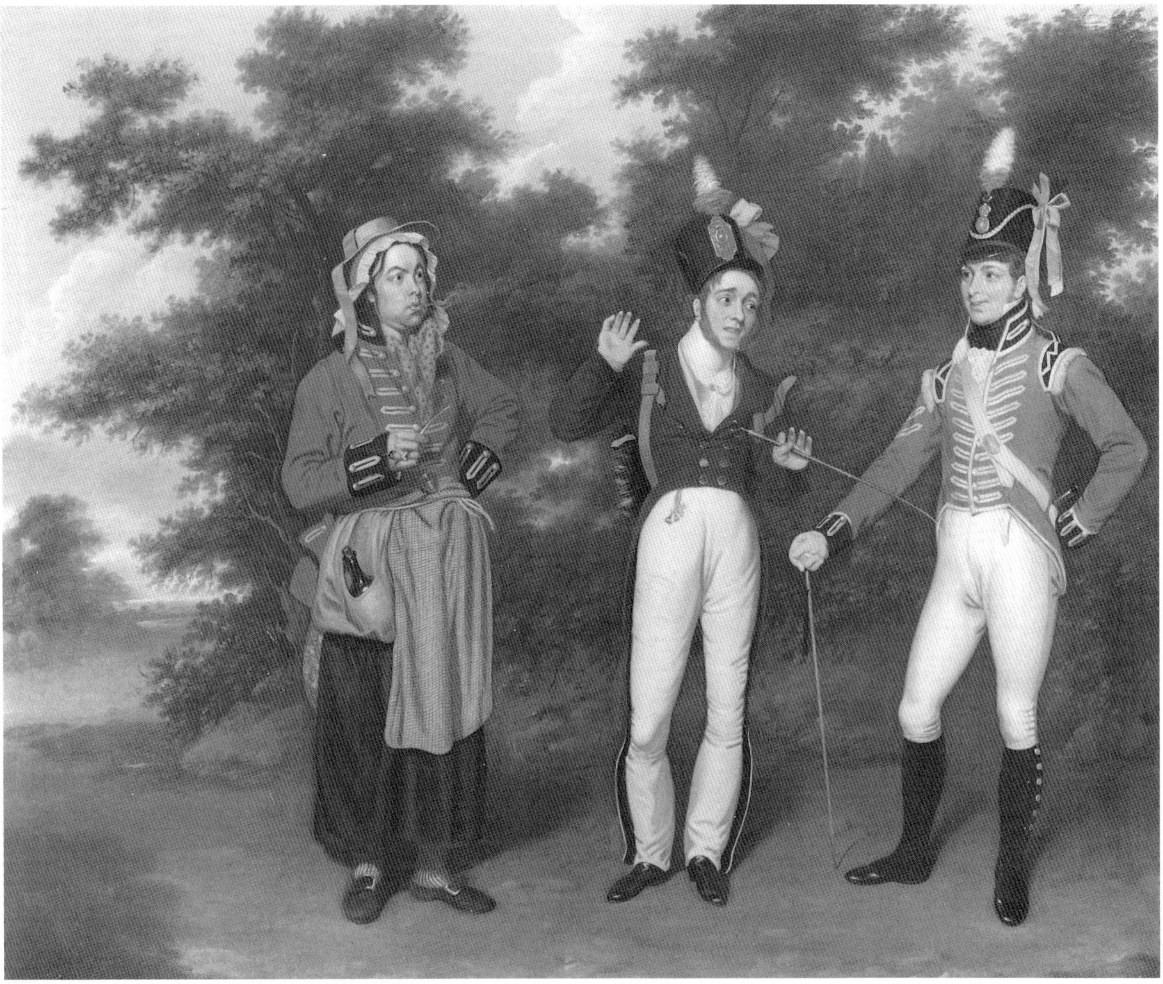

438*
JOHN LISTON as Moll Flagon,
RICHARD JONES as Young Contrast
and *Mr HAMERTON* as Sergeant Crimp
in *The Lord of the Manor*
by John Burgoyne

Samuel De Wilde

Oil on canvas 48.2 x 59
INSCR: 'De Wilde pinxt / 1814'
(brown paint b.l.)
INV: CKA 611; Gift 354
PROV: Robert Walters, by whom presented
to the Garrick Club, 1911
EXH: 1814 R.A. (516) 'A scene in the Opera
of the Lord of the Manor, with the portraits
of Mr Jones, Mr Liston, and Mr Hamerton';
1971 Northampton (20)
REL: Single figure of Moll Flagon: Christie's
24 July 1980 (144) and 13 February 1981 (76),
oil on canvas 44.5 x 35.5;
Single figure of Young Contrast:
NT 46 pencil and watercolour on wove paper
37.3 x 22.7
(this is a study for the final picture; a piece of paper
has been added along the top to accommodate
the plume of the shako, which would not have
been necessary had the drawing been a copy)

Sergeant Crimp (Hamerton) has just wrongly arrested Young Contrast (Jones) as a deserter. Moll Flagon (Liston), a camp follower, enters, 'A soldier's Coat over her Petticoat, a Gin-bottle by her Side, and a short Pipe in her mouth'. Liston (on the left) does this Brechtian prototype proud with the smoke issuing from his mouth. He has a blue and white cloth under his white straw hat with a red band over the top and down the sides. He wears brown shoes with blue buckles, white and blue striped stockings, a long baggy grey skirt, a blue and white checked apron, and a red military jacket. His orange neckerchief has brown spots, and over his right hip is his gin bottle in a brown bag. Young Contrast (in the middle) holds a riding crop in his white-gloved left hand – an indication of his gentle pursuits before he was taken into custody. He wears black shoes, white trousers with a black band at the sides, a dark red cutaway jacket with gold buttons, and a yellow waistcoat. He wears a knapsack and has a black shako with a gold badge, red, blue and white plumes, and red and yellow ribbons. Sergeant Crimp (on the right), who has ginger hair, rests his white-gloved hand on a cane. He wears black shoes with black spats and gold buttons, white trousers, and a red military jacket trimmed in gold. His black shako has a gold badge, a red and white plume, and a pink ribbon. The three characters stand before a clump of trees.

Burgoyne's comic opera, with music by William Jackson, was first performed on 27 December 1780 at Drury Lane, with Richard Suett as Moll Flagon, John Palmer as Contrast, and Robert Palmer as Sergeant Crimp. The piece was revived at Covent Garden on 24 October 1812 with Liston, Jones and Hammerton in those parts, and was performed a number of times over the next three seasons.

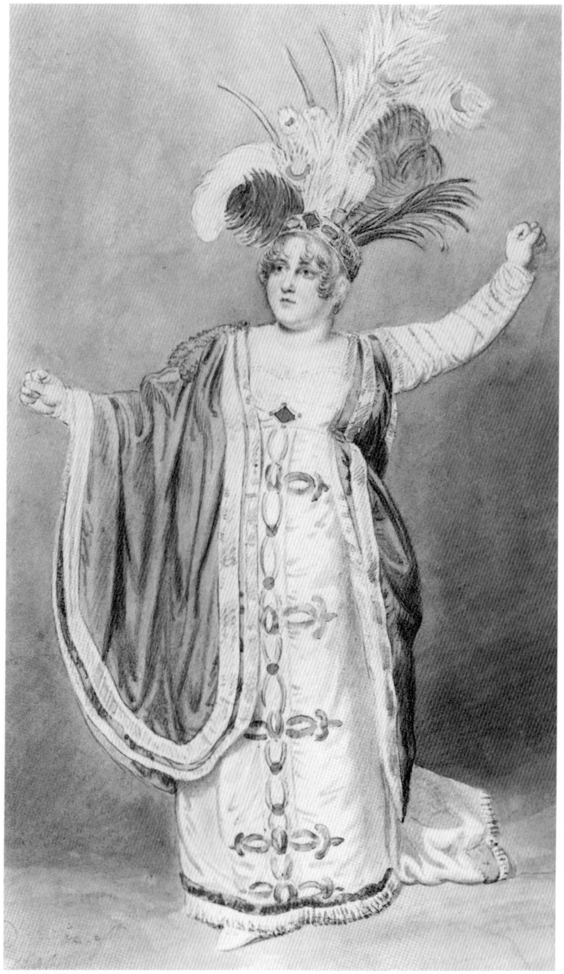

439 *Sarah Liston as Queen Dollalolla*

439

SARAH LISTON

as Queen Dollalolla

in *Tom Thumb the Great*

by Kane O'Hara,

adapted from Henry Fielding

Samuel De Wilde

Black chalk, pencil and watercolour
on wove paper 37 x 23.5
INSCR: 'De Wilde ft / 1806' (black chalk b.l.)
INV: Mathews 228; RW/CKA 46D
PROV: Charles Mathews
EXH: 1833 London (228)
ENGR: Anthony Cardon for Cawthorn's
Minor British Theatre 1805, stipple 12.4 x 8

King Arthur has just given the victorious Tom Thumb the hand of his daughter, Huncamunca, in marriage. His overweight wife, who desires the tiny hero herself, is fraught with jealousy and utters her curse as she storms out of the court with her ladies: 'Then tremble all who weddings ever made' (quoted on the engraving). The Queen wears white slippers and a white dress trimmed in brown. Her gold headdress has a blue stone at the front and red stones around the sides and, towering above, pink, blue and white ostrich feathers as well as some faded peacock feathers.

O'Hara's burletta, based on Fielding's *Tom Thumb the Great; or, The Tragedy of Tragedies* of 1730, was first played at Covent Garden on 3 October 1780, with Anne Catley as Queen Dollalolla. *Tom Thumb* was given 18 times at the Haymarket over the summer of 1806; the first performance was on 21 June, the last on 13 September. Miss Tyrer (who married John Liston at St Martin-in-the-Fields on 22 March 1807) played Dollalolla with a cast that included Fawcett as King Arthur, Liston as Grizzle, and Taylor as Noodle (see No. 790).

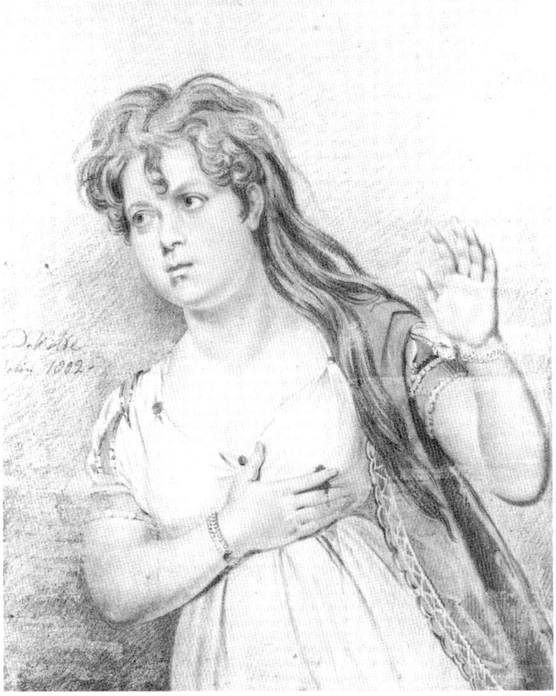

440
HARRIET LITCHFIELD
in character

Samuel De Wilde

Pencil, black chalk and watercolour
on wove paper 24 x 19.2
INSCR: 'S De Wilde / delin 1802.' (pencil c.l.)
INV: Mathews 297 (as Ophelia); (not in RW);
CKA 510 (unknown sitter)
PROV: Charles Mathews
EXH: 1802 R.A. (670), one of a group of seven portraits;
1833 London (297)

Mrs Litchfield has streaming tresses and holds her right hand to her bleeding breast. Her white dress has red trim at the shoulders, and her cloak is also red.

Four of the portraits shown at the R.A. in 1802 (670) are now at Holkham. They have a unique place in De Wilde's œuvre in their comparative monumentality, on a miniature scale, and in their restrained technique. The other three depict Mrs Litchfield, Mrs Davenport, and Mrs Mills. The drawing of Mrs Mills was the version of No. 607 sold at Christie's. Of the other two candidates, Mrs Davenport was neither comely nor tragic. This drawing is probably the one of Mrs Litchfield listed by Mathews as No. 297, and missing from RW.

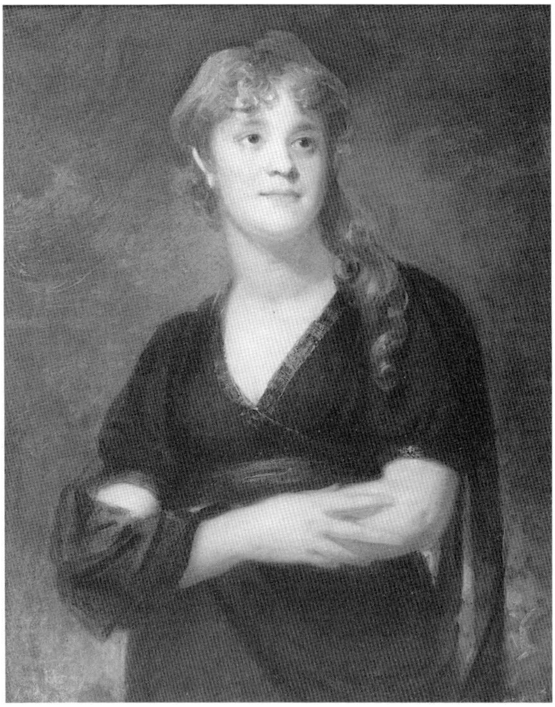

441
HARRIET LITCHFIELD

Samuel Drummond

Oil on canvas 76.5 x 63.5
INV: RW/CKA 362
PROV: John Poole, by whom presented
to the Garrick Club, 1838
EXH: 1799 R.A. (565)

Mrs Litchfield wears a dark grey dress trimmed in gold, with sleeves trimmed in gold and green. Her arms are folded at her waist.

Advertised as 'A Young Lady', the sitter made her début at Covent Garden on 27 May 1796 in the male role of Edward in *Every One Has His Fault*, at the age of 19. After her marriage a few months later to John Litchfield, a clerk to the Privy Council and sometime actor, she continued at Covent Garden until 1806 and then was at the Haymarket for several engagements. Among her best roles were Desdemona, Portia and Mrs Haller in *The Stranger*. Mrs Litchfield was reputed to have an excellent voice and good judgement, and was accounted a respectable, if not distinguished, actress. (BD)

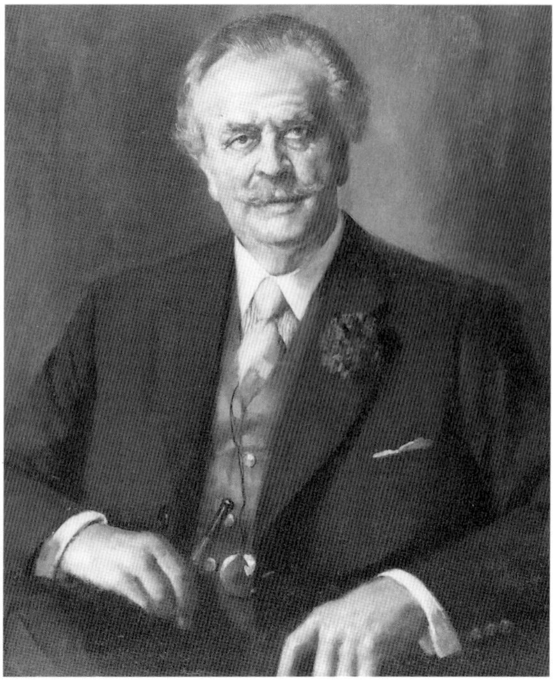

442
FREDERICK LLOYD

John Gilroy

Oil on canvas 76.2 x 63.5
INSCR: 'Gilroy' (grey paint b.l.)
INV: GCL 737; Gift 882
PROV: Presented to the Garrick Club by the artist, 1978

The sitter wears a grey suit, a blue and white striped shirt, and a Garrick Club tie.

Frederick Lloyd, who was General Manager of the D'Oyly Carte Opera Company, was a member of the Garrick Club from 1953.

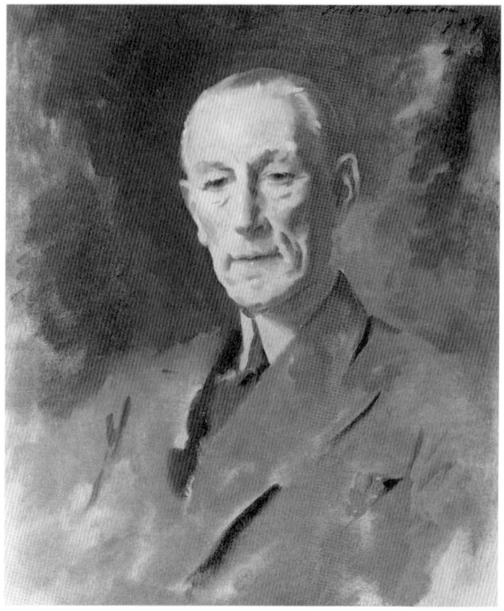

443
WILLIAM JOHN LOCKE

Gordon Stevenson

Oil on canvas 66 x 50.8
INSCR: 'Gordon Stevenson / 197' (black paint t.r.)
INV: GCL 688; Gift 770
PROV: Leslie Mitchell, by whom presented to the Garrick Club, 1959

William Locke wears a pale brown jacket, green shirt and brown tie. In his pocket is a green handkerchief.

Locke, a novelist, schoolmaster and secretary of the Royal Institute of British Architects, was a member of the Garrick Club from 1907 until his death.

444
NOT ILLUSTRATED
FREDERICK LEONARD LONSDALE

Simon Elwes

Oil on canvas 56.5 x 46
INSCR: 'Simon Elwes' (red paint b.l.)
INV: GCL 745; Gift 910
PROV: Presented by the sitter's daughter, Lady Donaldson, 1985
EXH: 1938 R.S.P.P. (63) (illustrated in catalogue)
LIT: Frances Donaldson, *Freddy Lonsdale* (1957), frontispiece

Lonsdale wears a dark blue suit, white shirt, and blue tie. He was a close friend of the artist, and used to visit him in his studio in New York, but this portrait was probably painted in London. It was transferred to the NPG at the request of Lady Donaldson. Lonsdale became a member of the Garrick Club in 1918.

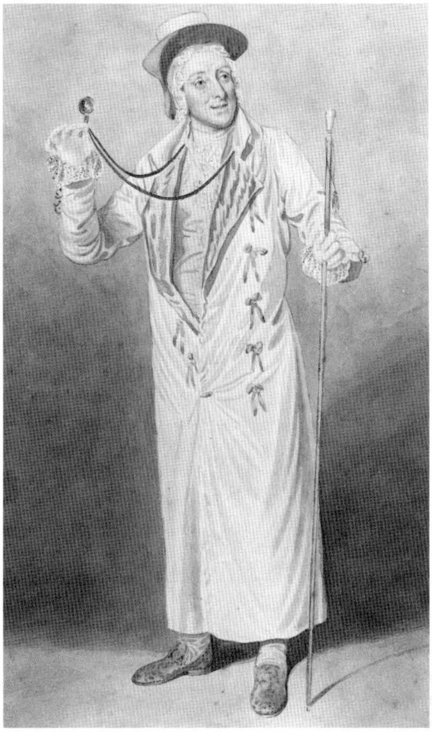

445
WILLIAM LOVEGROVE
as Lord Ogleby in *The Clandestine Marriage*
by David Garrick and George Colman the Elder

Samuel De Wilde

Pencil and watercolour 37 x 23.5
INSCR: 'S De Wilde. delin. / October 1810.' (pencil b.l.)
INV: Mathews 232; RW/CKA 59D
PROV: Charles Mathews
EXH: 1833 London (232)
REL: Another version (perhaps the original?), in watercolour, was owned by the late Robert Eddison

Lord Ogleby is shown in Act II, scene 2, the antechamber to his bedroom in Mrs Sterling's house (see No. 398). He has a cream cap and holds a monocle in his right hand and a tall cane in his left. He wears gold slippers decorated in green with pink heels, white stockings, a white coat lined in pink, and a white waistcoat with pink embroidery.

Garrick and the elder Colman's comedy was originally performed at Drury Lane on 20 February 1766, with Thomas King as Lord Ogleby (see No. 23). Lovegrove made his London début in the role with the Drury Lane company at the Lyceum on 3 October 1810. De Wilde drew him very shortly afterwards – on 23 and 24 October he recorded in his diary sittings by Lovegrove as Lord Ogleby. The finished work was loaned to Thomas Hill on 3 November 1810.

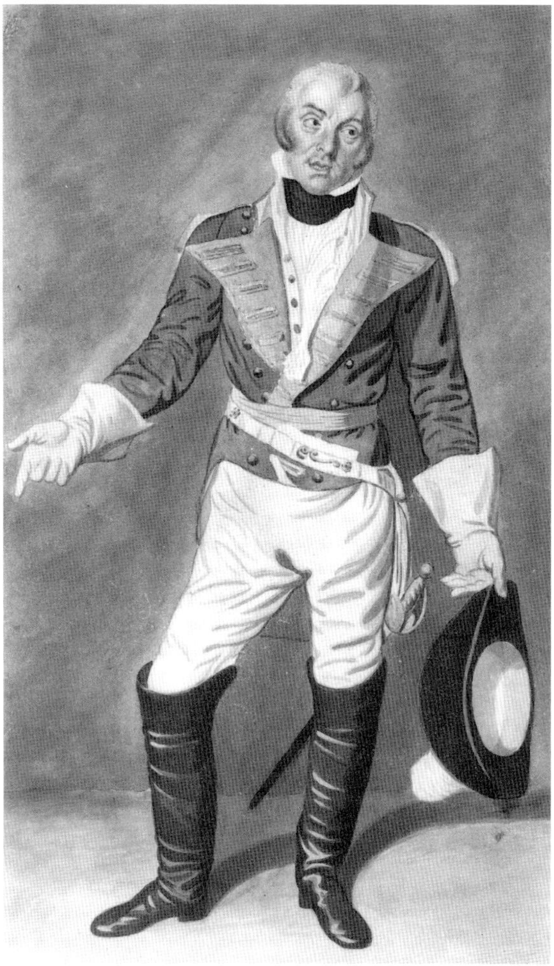

446
WILLIAM LOVEGROVE
as Captain Rattan in *The Bee Hive*
by John Gideon Millingen

Samuel De Wilde

Pencil and watercolour on wove paper 36.8 x 22.8
INV: CKA 487 (John Henry Johnstone as Major O'Flaherty in 'The West Indian'); Gift 457
PROV: Sir Arthur Wing Pinero, by whom presented to the Garrick Club, 1929;
[Possibly this portrait was one of the two pictures of Lovegrove by De Wilde that were in the Royal Dramatic College sale at Fairbrother, Lye and Palmer on 24 February 1881 (lots 100G & 100H)]
ENGR: James Thomson for the *Theatrical Inquisitor* pub. C. Chapple August 1816, stipple (vignette)

Hannibal Rattan is a bluff soldier and friend of the hero, Captain Merton, whom he impersonates to help woo the lovely heroine, Emily. He describes himself as 'born in a camp, a gun-carriage was my cradle – I fed out of a mortar-ladle'. At the end of the first act he vows not to be 'caught in the goose-step of matrimony' and sings an air, 'I, Helen's breast alone can warm'. It is the only time he has the stage to himself, and probably the moment evoked by De Wilde. 'The Bee Hive', where the play is set, is a country inn on the coast flying the yellow quarantine flag to indicate the presence of military guests from abroad sitting out their quarantine. Rattan's grey wig has rolls of fair hair at the sides. In his white gauntleted left hand he carries a half-moon hat with a white feather. He wears black riding boots, white breeches, a red military coat with gold buttons and gold epaulets, and a white waistcoat.

The Bee Hive, a musical farce in two acts with music by Charles Edward Horn, was first given by the Drury Lane company at the Lyceum on 19 January 1811; there were 48 performances during the season, the last on 11 June 1811. Lovegrove was the original Captain Grattan.

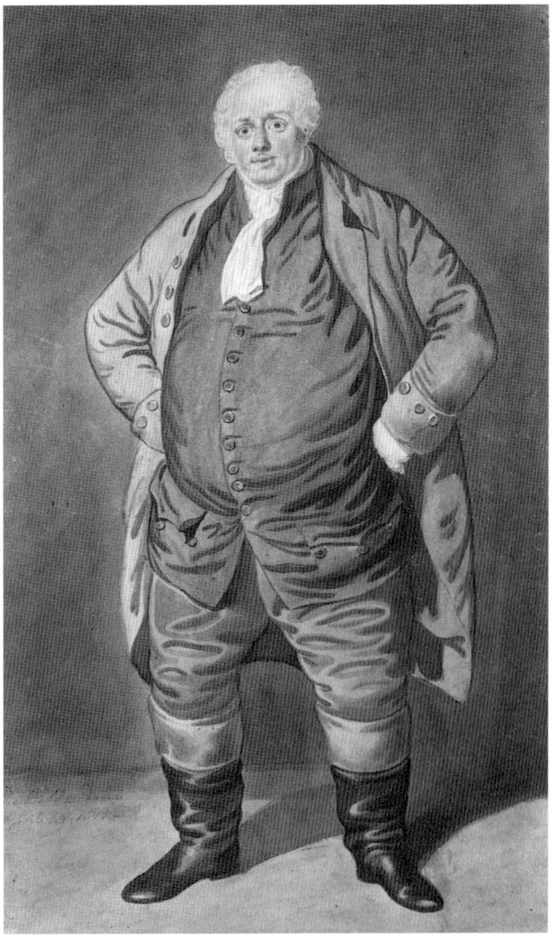

447 *William Lovegrove (?) as Realize*

447
WILLIAM LOVEGROVE (?)
as Realize in *The Will* by Frederick Reynolds

Samuel De Wilde

Pencil and watercolour on wove paper 36.8 x 22.8
INSCR: 'S De Wilde delin / April 24 1815' (pencil b.l.)
INV: CKA 488 ('in Character'); Gift 457
PROV: Sir Arthur Wing Pinero, by whom presented to the Garrick Club, 1929;
[Possibly this portrait was one of the two pictures of Lovegrove by De Wilde that were in the Royal Dramatic College sale at Fairbrother, Lye and Palmer on 24 February 1881 (lots 100G & 100H)]
ENGR: James Thomson for the *Theatrical Inquisitor* pub. C. Chapple August 1816, stipple (vignette)

The sitter is enormously fat. He wears black boots with brown tops, greenish breeches, a long greenish coat, and a red waistcoat with gold buttons.

Reynolds's play was first performed at Drury Lane on 19 April 1797, with Suett as Realize. Lovegrove's only performances in 1815–16, and the last of his career, were as Realize on 17, 18, 21 and 25 October 1815. The costume in No. 447 might be that of Realize, who is a belligerent steward, and the pose would suit the part.

There is also a possibility that the sitter is George Bartley (see No. 51), who played Falstaff in *1 Henry IV* in his first appearance at Drury Lane on 12 April 1815. He also played the part on 14, 21 and 25 April. The costume is not that usually worn by Falstaff in the early 19th century, but the huge and padded form of the actor suggests that the fat knight may be the character depicted.

448
CHARLES MACKLIN
as Sir Pertinax McSycophant
in *The Man of the World* by Charles Macklin

Samuel De Wilde

Oil on canvas 43.8 x 34.3
INSCR: 'S. De Wilde. pinxt / 1794' (brown paint b.l.)
INV: Mathews 369; RW/CKA 476
PROV: John Bell; Charles Mathews
EXH: 1833 London (369)
ENGR: Robert Hartly Cromek for Cawthorn's British Library 9 July 1795, pub. G. Cawthorn in Bell's *British Theatre* (1797), vol 17, line 11.5 x 8
REL: NG Dublin 307, oil on canvas 40 x 30

Sir Pertinax, a bad-tempered Scot, angrily addresses his son Egerton, who has changed his name from McSycophant because of the hatred of his mother's family, the

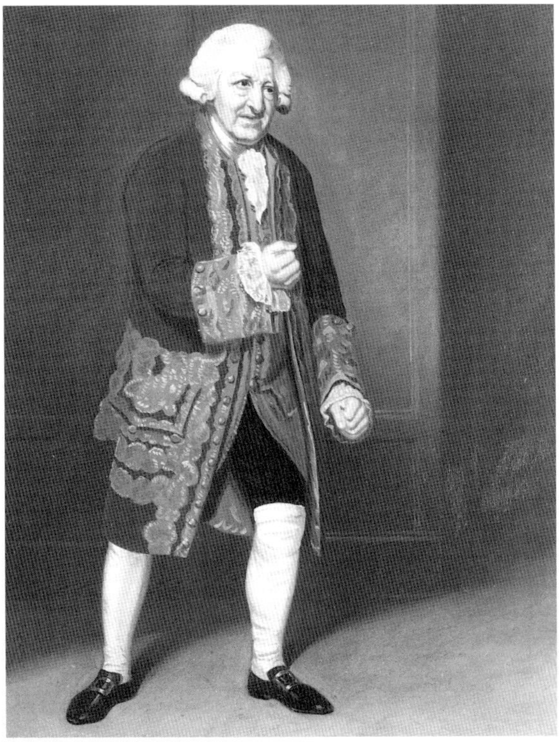

448 *Charles Macklin as Sir Pertinax McSycophant*

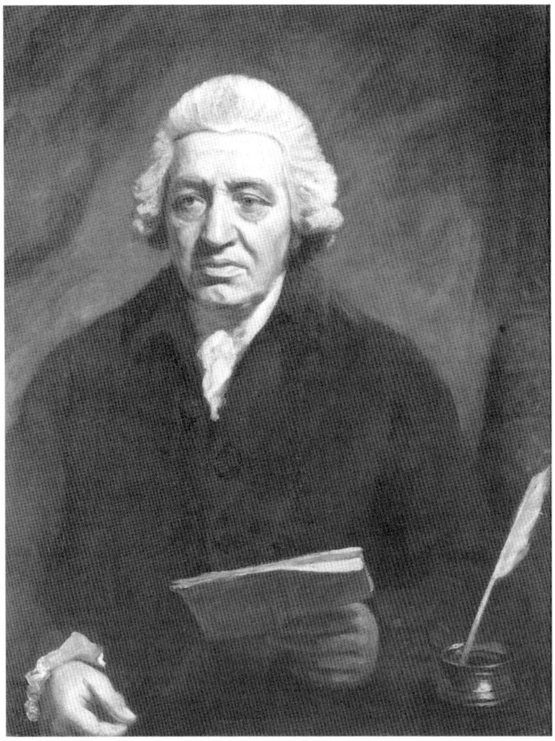

449*
CHARLES MACKLIN

John Opie

Oil on canvas 89.5 x 69.2
INV: Mathews 4; RW/CKA 16
PROV: Thomas Harris; Harris sale, Robins 12 July 1819 (35); Charles Mathews
EXH: 1833 London (4)
ENGR: J. Condé for Arthur Murphy's ed. of Macklin's *Works* pub. J. Bell July 1792, stipple and line 17.3 x 13.3 (inscr: 'Charles Macklin / Comedian / in his 93rd Year'); Samuel Freeman pub. Longman & Co. 1806, stipple 8.9 x 7.3; James Hopwood for *The Cabinet* pub. Mathews & Leigh 1 August 1808, stipple and line 9.3 x 7.2 (bust only)
REL: NPG 1319, oil on canvas 90.8 x 70.5, Prov: the Rev Edward Clarke, Christie's March 1856 bt. by Hermann for John Green, Christie's 22 July 1871, James McCulloch in 1902 when bought by the NPG
LIT: Patmore, pp. 271–72

Egertons, for Sir Pertinax – and, in particular, in order to inherit the fortune of his maternal uncle, Sir Stanley Egerton. Sir Pertinax orders his son to 'Haud your jabbering you villain, haud your jabbering' (quotation on the engraving). Macklin exhibits the clenched fists common to depictions of Sir Pertinax. He wears black shoes with gold buckles, white hose, black breeches, a brown coat lined in blue and trimmed with gold braid, and a blue waistcoat, also with copious gold braid.

Macklin's comedy was performed in London for the first time at Covent Garden on 10 May 1781, with Macklin as Sir Pertinax. It was a revised expansion of his *The True-born Scotsman*, which had been premiered at the Crow Street Theatre, Dublin, on 10 July 1764. Macklin's last appearance as Sir Pertinax was at Covent Garden on 26 November 1788.

No. 448 was one of seven paintings by De Wilde exhibited in Bell's sale at Christie's, 25–26 March 1793. It was later bought by Charles Mathews at Leigh & Sotheby's on 25 May 1805. See also Nos. 398 and 656.

Charles Macklin's career spanned almost the whole of the 18th century. When he died in 1797, at the age of 98, he had acted for nearly 70 years. He is, of course, best remembered for his electrifying and horrifying portrayal of Shylock in 1741 and for his influence – along with Garrick – in ushering onto the English stage a more naturalistic style of acting.

Macklin is depicted as an author rather than as an actor. He holds a paper in his left hand, and a white quill and silver inkwell are positioned ready for inspiration. He wears a dark coat and powdered wig.

Patmore describes this picture as an 'admirable head of Macklin, just before he died, painted with infinite force and spirit by Opie'.

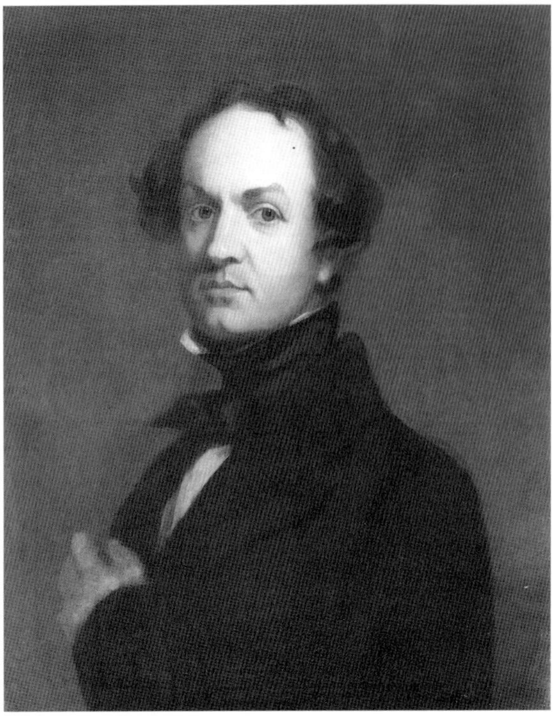

450

WILLIAM CHARLES MACREADY

Henry Perronet Briggs

Oil on canvas 68.6 x 55.9
INV: CKA 583; Gift 370
PROV: E.V. Lowne, by whom presented to the Garrick Club, 1915

Half-length. Macready wears a dark coat and high stock. His left hand is across his chest.

Macready was one of the original members of the Garrick Club in 1831.

451

WILLIAM CHARLES MACREADY

as Henry in *2 Henry IV*
by William Shakespeare

John Jackson

Oil on canvas 74.3 x 60.3
INV: Mathews 163; RW/CKA 87
PROV: Charles Mathews
EXH: 1833 London (163); 1962 Chichester (32)
ENGR: Richard James Lane pub. R. Ackermann 1823, lithograph 25.7 x 21.2; Richard James Lane pub. R. Ackermann May 1824, lithograph 20 x 16.3; C.H. Jeens for title page of Vol. 1 of Macready's *Reminiscences* (1875), stipple and line, with the quotation 'Then get thee gone, and dig my grave thyself.'

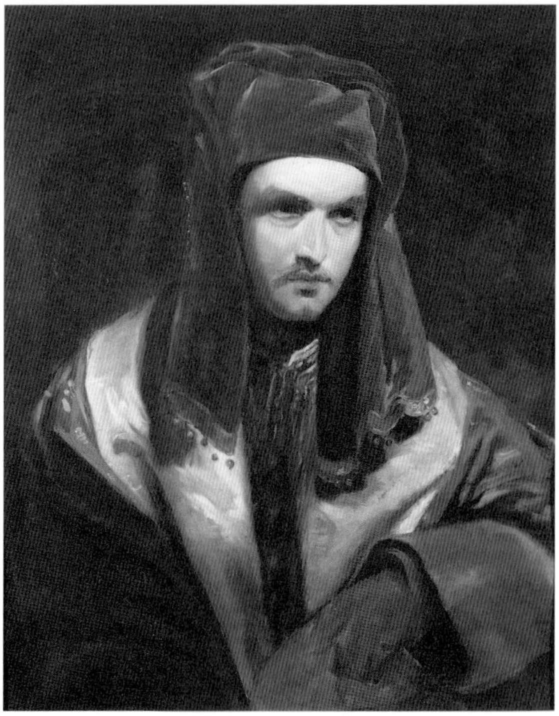

451 *William Charles Macready as Henry IV*

REL: NPG 1503, oil on canvas 91.4 x 61.6
LIT: Anne Mathews, Vol. 3: 290–91; *Macready's Reminiscences and Selections from his Diaries* ed. Sir Frederick Pollock (1875), pp. 229–30; *The Diaries of W.C. Macready 1833–1851* ed. W. Toynbee (1912), 1: 3n

Henry wears a maroon headdress and a grey and blue costume.

Macready played the King when *2 Henry IV* was performed at Covent Garden on 25 June 1821, with additional coronation scenes to mark the coronation of George IV. The original version of Jackson's picture, now in the National Portrait Gallery, was commissioned by Mathews for his gallery. However, Macready decided to keep the original, and got Jackson to paint another version for Mathews. Macready chronicles the swap in his *Reminiscences*:

> The picture had made considerable progress, when Fawcett called with me one day to see it. On coming out from Jackson's studio he exclaimed 'Why, William, you must not give that picture away – Jackson has never done anything like it!' When I reported this to Jackson, his quiet answer was, 'Well: it is very easy to paint another; you would not mind paying for the ground colours being rubbed in by another hand, would you?' My objections were vain to this proposal of my most liberal friend. His pupil made a rough copy of the picture, which Jackson, putting the first draft aside, finished at once. I sent it with a kind note to Mathews.

The note that Macready sent to Mathews, dated 29 June 1822, is published in Anne Mathews's voluminous memoirs of her husband: '... I beg leave to request your acceptance of the accompanying picture, which may derive, in your opinion, that value from the artist's genius which the subject is incapable of bestowing.' Jackson's original portrait of Macready was finished towards the end of 1821 and was exhibited at the British Institution in 1823 (201). On his death, Macready bequeathed it to the National Portrait Gallery.

No. 351 had been on loan to the Bristol Old Vic since 1973, but it was returned to the Garrick Club in 1994.

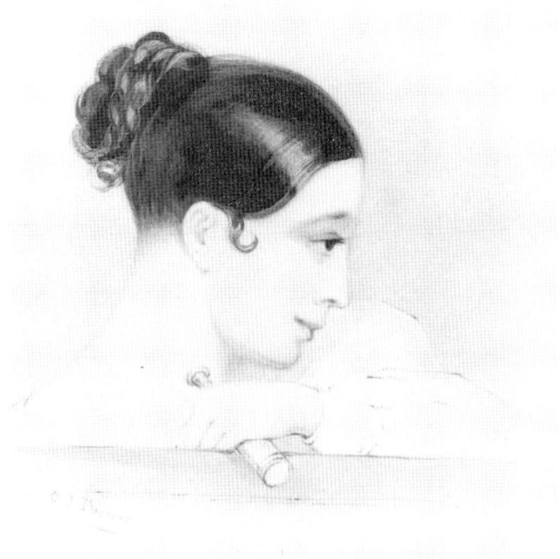

452
MARIA MALIBRAN

C.J. Fletcher (after A.E. Chalon)

Pencil with watercolour and body colour
on wove paper 18 x 15 (sight)
INSCR: 'C.J. Fletcher.' (pencil b.l.)
INV: RW 347; GCL 347A; Gift 276
PROV: Presented by Mrs Bacon (Miss Poole), 1901
ENGR: Richard James Lane, after Alfred Edward Chalon
pub. J. Mitchell 1826, lithograph
(on a sheet with full-length portrait of
Malibran as Fidelma in *Il Matrimonio Segreto*);
head only with facsimile autograph;
Anon. pub. H. Colburn 1840, lithograph
(reversed, facsimile autograph)

Malibran, looking over the edge of a theatre box, holds a small gold telescope in her left hand. The lithograph shows Malibran wearing her hair in a much more operatic manner; instead of the chignon there is a grand projection over the front of the head.

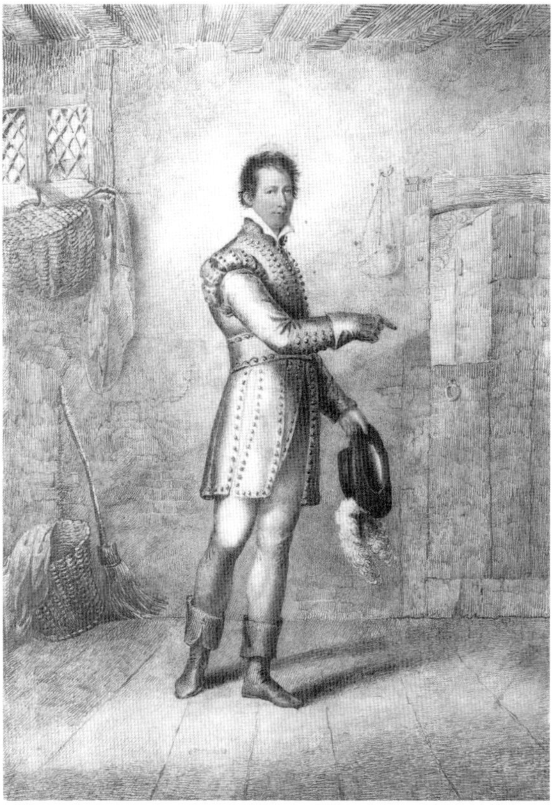

453
ROBERT MANSEL
as Duke Aranza in *The Honey Moon*
by John Tobin

Unknown Artist

Pencil and watercolour on wove paper 31.8 x 22.7
INSCR: 'Mr Mansel as the Duke in the Honey Moon'
(pen and brown ink on mount b.c. CM)
INV: Mathews 347; RW/CKA 317
PROV: Charles Mathews
EXH: 1833 London (347)

Mansel is shown as the Duke in Act II, scene I, in the rustic cottage he has prepared as a surprise for his new wife, Juliana. He is still dressed in his ducal finery, which he will soon change for 'a Peasant's Dress' (see No. 189). He wears grey stockings and a tunic trimmed with buttons. In his left hand he holds a brown hat with white plumes.

Tobin's comedy was first performed at Drury Lane on 31 January 1805, with Robert Elliston in the part of Duke Aranza. Mansel left London for the provinces in the autumn of 1800, and, according to the BD, never returned to perform in the capital. If Mathews's identification is correct, it seems that the artist – clearly very able – was recording a provincial performance.

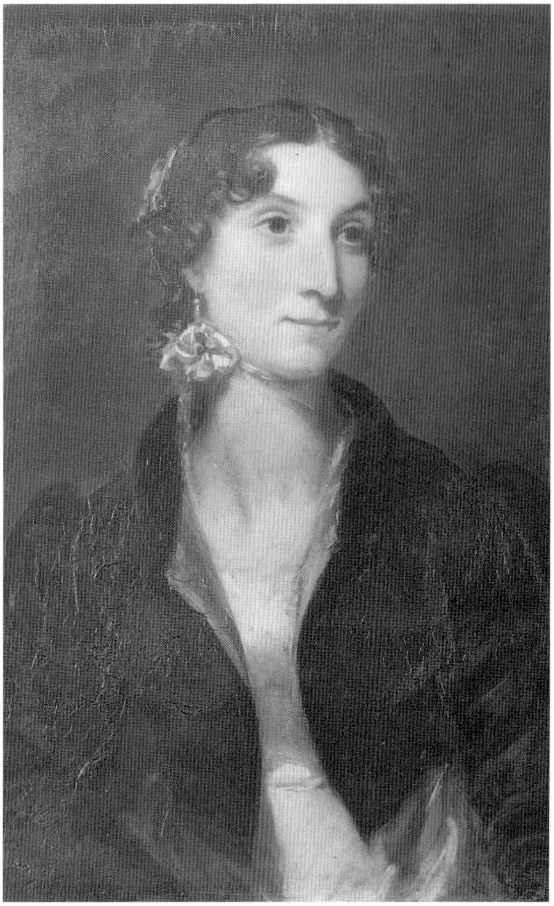

454
CHARLOTTE MARDYN

Henry William Pickersgill

Oil on panel 28.2 x 22.5
INV: RW/CKA 276; Gift 75
PROV: Presented by Captain Marryat, R.N.., 1842
ENGR: Henry Meyer pub. 1836, stipple 22.9 x 16.5
(in the engraving the sitter is not wearing a jacket, but has a scarf round her shoulders, tied at the front)

The sitter wears a blue satin cap tied under the chin with a blue ribbon. Her short black jacket, lined in matching blue, is worn over a white dress.

The artist became a member of the Garrick Club in 1832.

455
NOT ILLUSTRATED
FREDERICK MARRABLE

L. Sta...... [Richard Staigg?]

Oil on canvas 61.3 x 50.8
INSCR: 'L. Sta......' (red paint b.l.)
INV: Not listed; Gift 921
PROV: Presented on long term loan by Felicity, Lady Wakefield, 1985, but returned to her in 1994

Marrable, the architect of the Garrick Club, wears a brown jacket under a grey-brown cloak. The inscription is difficult to read, but the first three letters of the surname suggest the portraitist Richard Staigg.

Marrable was also architect of Archbishop Tenison's School in Leicester Square, the Church of St Peter at Deptford and St Mary Magdalen, St Leonards-on-Sea.

Eds: Richard Morrell Staigg (1817–1881), though born in Leeds, spent most of his artistic life in the United States. He made extended visits to Europe in 1867–69 and 1872–74, exhibiting at the Royal Academy and the Paris Salon. He may have painted the portrait of Marrable (who died in 1772) during the earlier visit.

456
SIR EDWARD MARSHALL-HALL

Sir Leslie Ward ('Spy')

Pencil with pen and black ink, watercolour and body colour on blue-grey wove paper
45 x 29.5
INSCR: 'SPY' (pencil b.l.)
INV: GCL 658; Gift 686
PROV: Bequeathed by Miss Louisa Melville, 1949
LIT: *Vanity Fair*

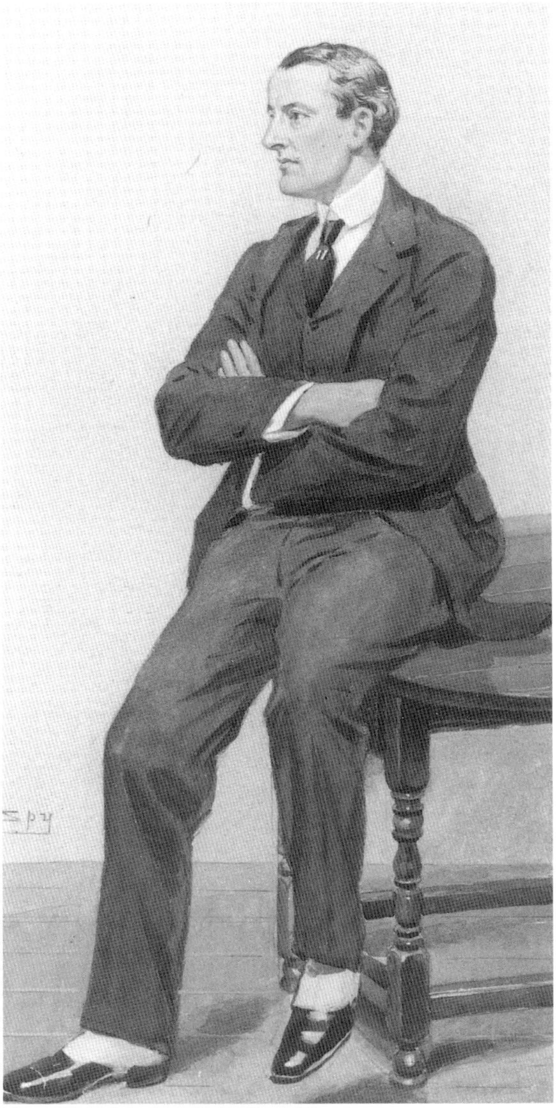

456 *Sir Edward Marshall-Hall*

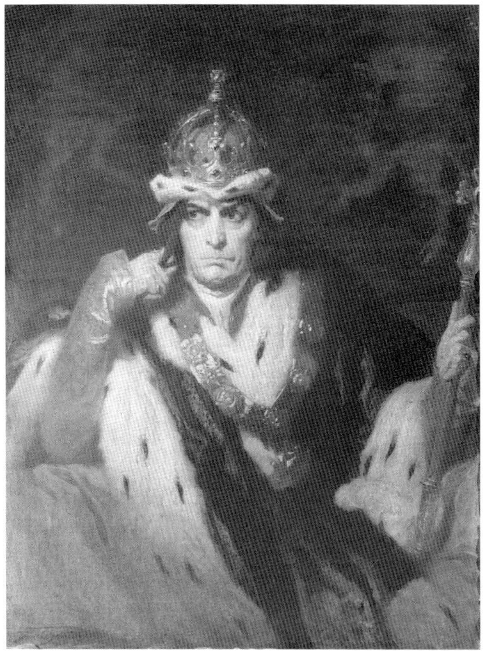

457

SIR JOHN MARTIN-HARVEY

as Richard in *Richard III* by William Shakespeare

Frank O. Salisbury

Oil on canvas 111.7 x 86.3
INSCR: 'Frank O. Salisbury' (red paint b.l.)
INV: GCL 654; Gift 678
PROV: Presented by the artist, 1948
EXH: 1925 R.A. (409)
ENGR: (mezzotint, sold Sotheby's 13 March 1978 [195]?)
REL: Coll: Jenny Walton, oil on canvas 76.2 x 64.5 (sketch for the finished painting, right hand not raised, no background), prov: the sitter, by descent, bought by the present owner in 1973
LIT: *Royal Academy Illustrated*, 1925, p. 12; B. Aquila Barber, *The Art of Frank O. Salisbury* (1936), reproduced, pp. 26–27; Sir John Martin-Harvey, *The Autobiography of Sir John Martin-Harvey* (1933), frontispiece in colour

Sir Edward, wearing a grey suit and waistcoat and a black tie, sits on the edge of a round table. Knighted in 1917, he was a distinguished and often controversial barrister. Dornford Yates recalled that he had 'the unfortunate reputation of getting across to the judge', and added that 'that reputation was not altogether undeserved. But he was a very fine advocate and he had a big success. He was tall and broad and a very handsome man; and he had the most splendid presence of anyone at the Bar' (*As Berry and I Were Saying*, 1952, p.437).

Sir Edward became a member of the Garrick Club in 1891.

Richard, shown half-length, wears a gold crown with red and green jewels, trimmed with ermine, and a red robe lined with ermine, with gold sleeves embroidered in red. A large gold band with roses hangs at his neck.

Martin-Harvey first played Richard III at the Theatre Royal, Dublin, on 13 April 1910. His first London performance was at the Lyceum on 28 May 1910. He toured widely with the production, to Canada and elsewhere, and gave his last performance as Richard in Birmingham on 31 March 1930. He became a member of the Garrick Club in 1919.

Salisbury exhibited another portrait of Martin-Harvey, R.S.P.P. 1939 (79), though not in character.

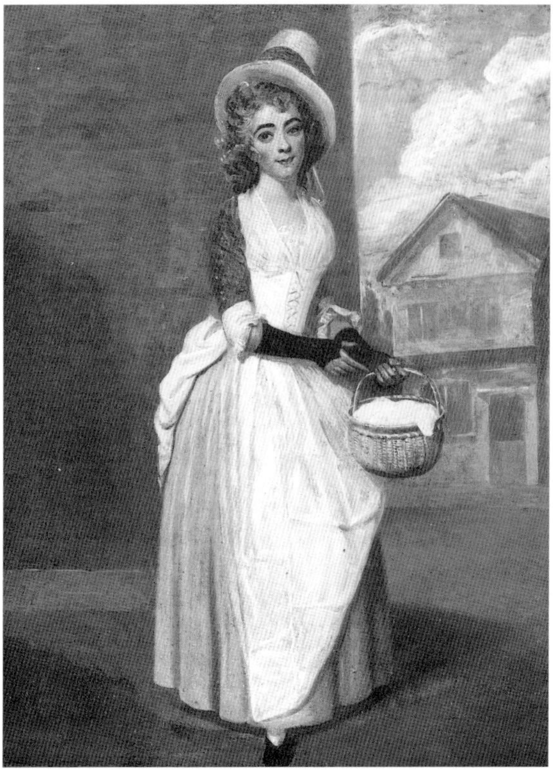

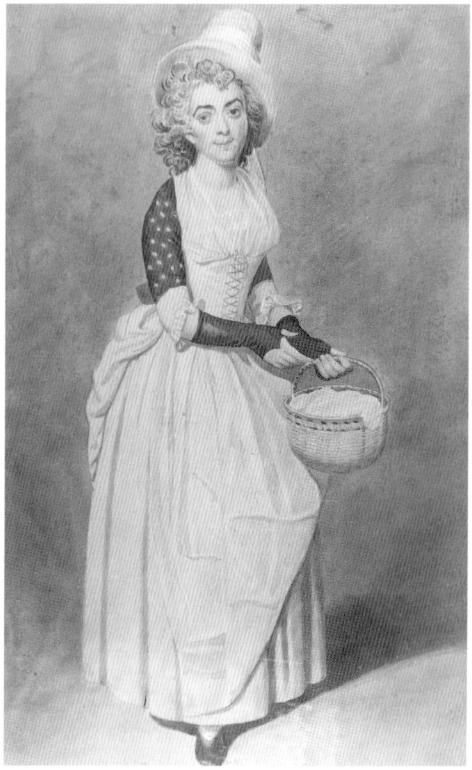

459 *Margaret Martyr as Rose*

458
MARGARET MARTYR
as Rose in *The Recruiting Officer*
by George Farquhar

Samuel De Wilde

Oil on canvas 35.5 x 26.7
INV: RW/CKA 211
PROV: Unknown
EXH: 1934 London (261)
ENGR: Philippe Audinet for Bell's British Library
12 May 1792, line 11.1 x 7.6,
pub. Bell's *British Theatre* (1797), vol 13;
Philippe Audinet printed for C. Cooke 5 July 1806, line
REL: See No. 459

Act III, scene I is set in 'The Market-Place', and Rose, a 'country wench', makes her first entry 'followed by her brother Bullock, with Chickens on her Arm, in a Basket'. She cries her wares, 'Buy chickens, young and tender chickens' (the quotation on the engraving). In the Garrick Club library is a large paper copy of Bell's edition marked up for the part of Plume. Into Rose's short list of wares is inserted 'and nosegays', an addition of which De Wilde was clearly unaware. Rose's basket is covered by a white cloth, but a single minuscule chicken-head is visible. Her rustic costume consists of black gloves, a dress with a pink skirt, brownish sleeves, and white bodice, and a white apron. Her straw hat has a red ribbon. The marketplace is visible to the right.

Farquhar's comedy was first performed at Drury Lane on 8 April 1706. It remained a popular piece in the 18th-century repertory. Mrs Martyr did not play Rose in London in the 18th century.

459
MARGARET MARTYR
as Rose in *The Recruiting Officer*
by George Farquhar

Samuel De Wilde

Pencil and watercolour on wove paper 37 x 23.5
INV: Mathews 195; RW/CKA 66C
PROV: Charles Mathews
EXH: 1833 London (195)
REL: See No. 458

Rose's costume is similar to that in No. 458, although her sleeves are red and brown with white spots, trimmed with white. Her yellow straw hat has a white ribbon.

No. 458 was presumably based on this or a similar study.

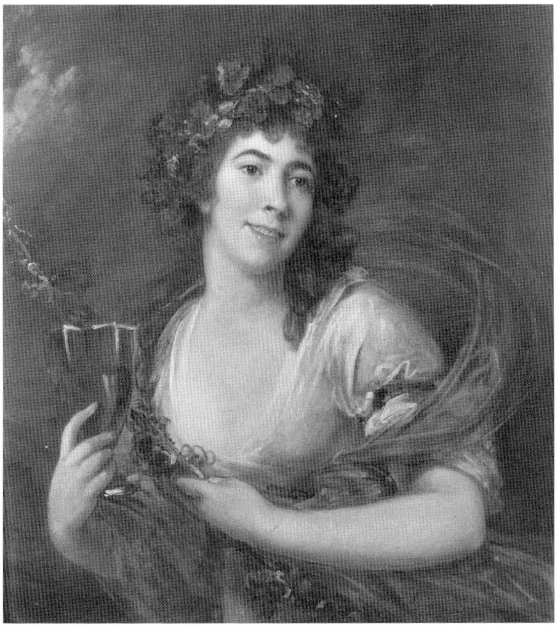

460
MARGARET MARTYR
as Euphrosyne in *Comus*
by George Colman the Elder,
altered from John Milton

Gainsborough Dupont

Oil on canvas 72.4 x 62.2
INV: Mathews 7; RW/CKA 38
PROV: Thomas Harris; Harris sale, Robins
12 July 1819 (22); Charles Mathews
EXH: 1833 London (7); 1982–83 London (131)
LIT: The *Morning Herald*, 22 March 1794;
Patmore, p. 273; Hayes 1968

Mrs Martyr, half-length in an attitude of Bacchic revelry, holds a wine glass and a thyrsus. Her high-waisted gown is white, and she wears a billowing flame-coloured bandeau.

The elder Colman's adaptation of Milton's masque, with music by Thomas Arne, was first given at Covent Garden on 16 October 1773. Mrs Martyr played the part of Euphrosyne for the first time at Covent Garden on 19 November 1780. Dupont's picture probably commemorates her performance at Covent Garden on 27 March 1794; an imminent portrait of Mrs Martyr was mentioned in the *Morning Herald*, 22 March 1794. Her next performance in the role was not until 10 June 1795.

Eds: Dupont's picture seems to allude to the famous studies of Emma, Lady Hamilton, as a Bacchante painted by Romney, Reynolds and others in the 1780s. See Ian Jenkins & Kim Sloan, *Vases and Volcanoes*, exh. cat., British Museum 1966, pp. 266–69.

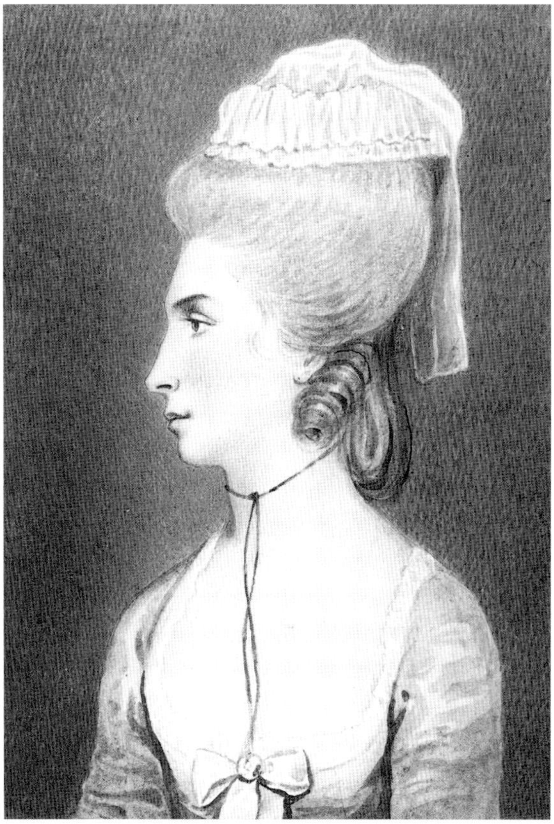

461
MRS E. MASSEY

Sylvester Harding

Pencil and watercolour on wove paper 14 x 10.2
INSCR: 'Mrs Massey' (pen and brown ink below CM)
INV: Not listed
PROV: Charles Mathews (Print Collection Vol. III f. 67)

Half-length profile left. Mrs Massey, in the high coiffure of the late 1770s, wears a lace cap and square-necked pink dress.

Representations of this actress are relatively rare. An anonymous engraver, after James Roberts, depicted her as Christina in *Gustavus Vasa* in a plate for Bell's *British Theatre*, February 1778, and an anonymous engraving of her as Albina, with William Dimond as Lord Edmond, in *Albina, Countess Raimond*, was published in the *Lady's Magazine* in November 1779.

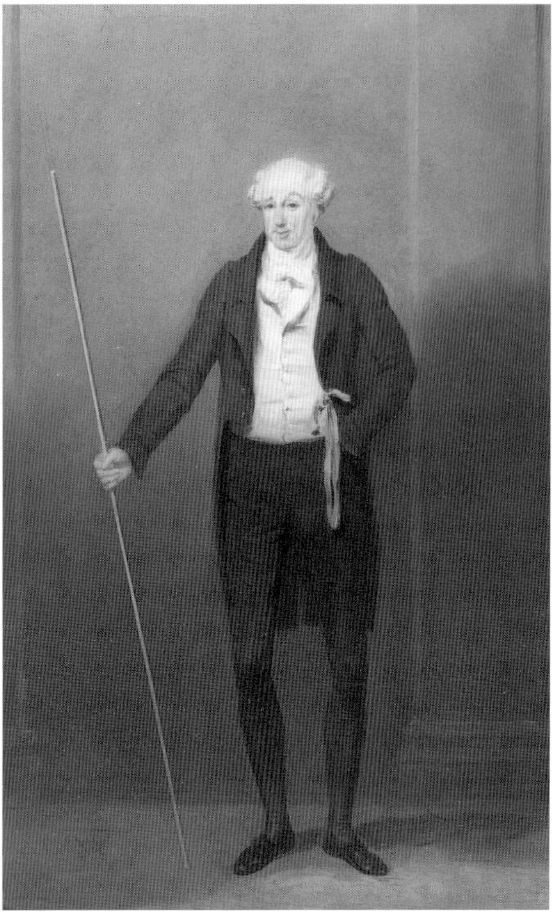

462
CHARLES MATHEWS
as Mark Magnum in *Youthful Days*
by Charles Mathews

George Clint

Oil on panel 45.7 x 33
INV: GCL 663; Gift 696
PROV: Bequeathed by Mrs George Arliss, 1950
ENGR: Anon.

Mark Magnum holds a long white wand in his right hand. He wears black hose and breeches, and a green coat with an orange ribbon tied to the front.

Mathews is shown in this part and wearing the same costume in one of a series of prints by Isaac Cruikshank entitled 'Purchase the Second', published by G. Humphrey 1 May 1822, etching 16.2 x 12.1.

Mathews was an original member of the Garrick Club in 1831.

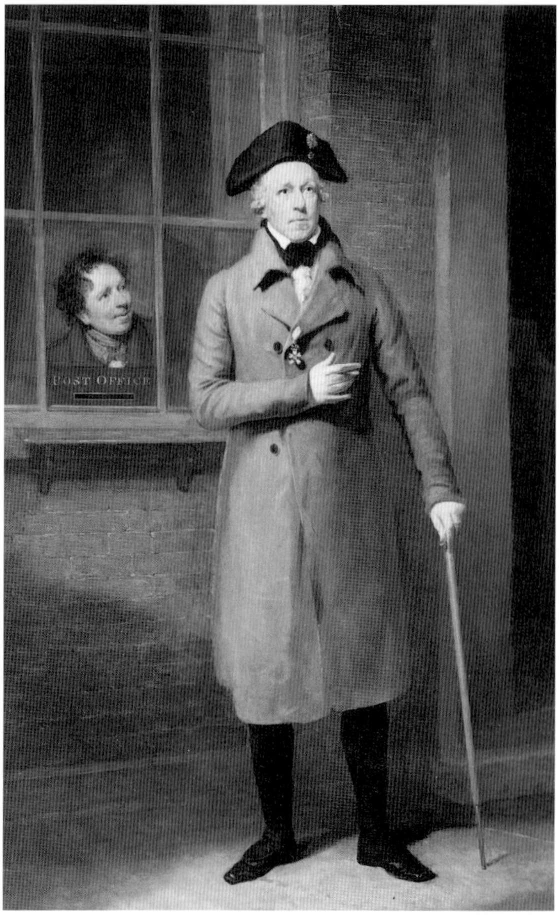

463*
CHARLES MATHEWS
as Monsieur Mallet
in *Monsieur Mallet or My Daughter's Letter*
by William Thomas Moncrieff

George Clint

Oil on canvas 82.5 x 56
INSCR: 'POST OFFICE' (yellow paint on post-office box c.l.)
INV: RW/CKA 392; Gift 13
PROV: Presented by Edward Parrott, 1833
EXH: 1832 R.A. (257) 'Mr Mathews as Monsieur Mallet, in Moncrief's drama of that name, founded on the anecdote related in "The Trip to America".'
The R.A. catalogue cites the lines 'No letter from my daughter! Can she have forgot – her poor old father?';
1950–51 London (53); 1951–52 London (121)
LIT: *Observer*, 8 December 1833

Mathews rests his left hand on a gold-topped stick. He wears a black hat, white gloves, black shoes, black trousers, and a long grey coat with an order. To his left, in the post office window, his head appears again, with dishevelled dark hair.

Moncrieff's drama, with music by J. Barnett, was first performed at the Adelphi on 22 January 1829. It was based on an anecdote related in the second part of Mathews's *Trip to America*, first given at the English Opera House on 25 March 1824. Mathews left for his first trip to America in August 1822. There are several editions of the text, the following being reproduced from that published by Hodgson in 1824:

> Our next scene is at the Boston Post-office, where a Monsieur Mallet, a French emigrant, makes repeated applications, to know if a long-expected letter from his daughter had arrived; and he attends daily with, 'Pray, Sair, have you von letter for Mr. Malley?" The man, turning over the letters always said 'No' and the poor Frenchman left the office, thinking his daughter had completely lost sight of her exiled father. Still, day after day, he repeated his visit, and was repeatedly repulsed with the familiar monosyllable 'No.' Week after week passed way, and the poor Frenchman never received the wished-for consolation. One day, however, he went to the office and while the man was sorting the letters he named several persons, and among the rest, 'Mr. Mallet; to be left till called for'. The Frenchman shrugged his shoulders, and exclaimed that it was very strange; when the Republican told him if he was not satisfied he might look over the list himself. Mr. Mallet does so; and only reflect, only conceive his astonishment, when he casts his eye upon the identical letter he had been so long searching after...

The Office-keeper's reason for not giving him the letter is: 'Why, had you said Mal-let, I should have given it to you before.' M. Mallet is furious and tears up the letter in a fit of rage. Mathews played all the parts in his one-man shows, and is seen here playing both M. Mallet and the Post Office-keeper.

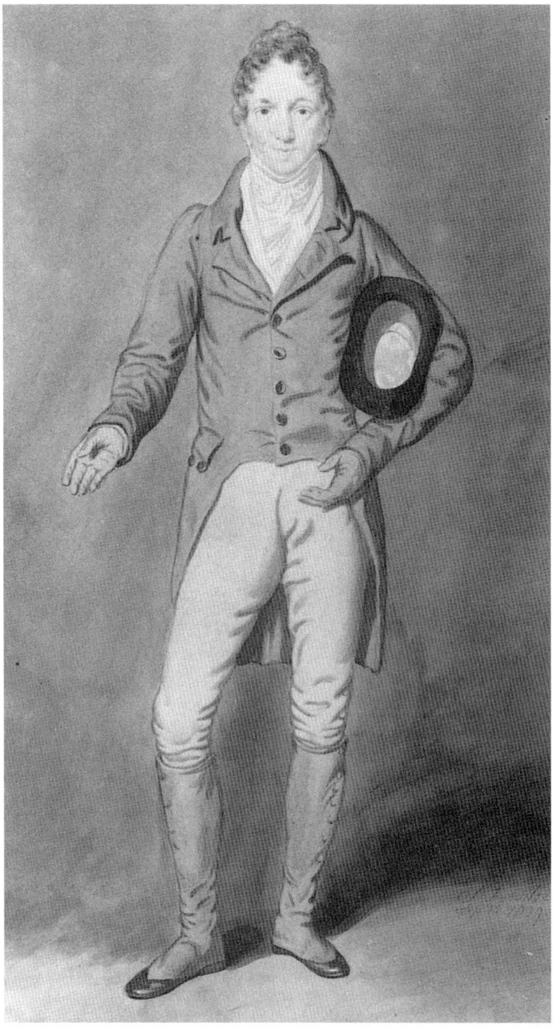

464 *Charles Mathews as Buskin*

464

CHARLES MATHEWS

as Buskin in *Killing No Murder*

by Theodore Edward Hook

Samuel De Wilde

Pencil and watercolour
on wove paper 37 x 23.5
INSCR: 'S De Wilde del / Sepr 15. 1809.' (pencil b.r.)
INV: Mathews 231; RW/CKA 59E
PROV: Charles Mathews
EXH: 1833 London (231)
REL: NT 43 pencil and watercolour on wove paper
37.3 x 23.3; RST pencil and watercolour
on wove paper, s. & d. 20 April 1815

Buskin was a part written for the quick-change talents of Charles Mathews. Buskin, a travelling actor, is staying at 'The London Inn' and hopes to marry Fanny, sister of the landlord, Tap, who believes him to be a Member of Parliament. He subsequently plays the parts of a waiter, a cook and a hairdresser, in amusing succession. Buskin's elegant costume reflects his assumption of the guise of 'a gentleman of independent fortune'. It consists of black shoes with long brown gaiters, yellowish breeches, and a reddish-brown coat with silver buttons. He holds a black hat with a white lining under his left arm and wears brown gloves.

Hook's two-act musical farce, with music by his father, James Hook, was first given at the Haymarket on 1 July 1809, with Mathews as Buskin. There were 36 performances over the summer season, the last on 15 September 1809.

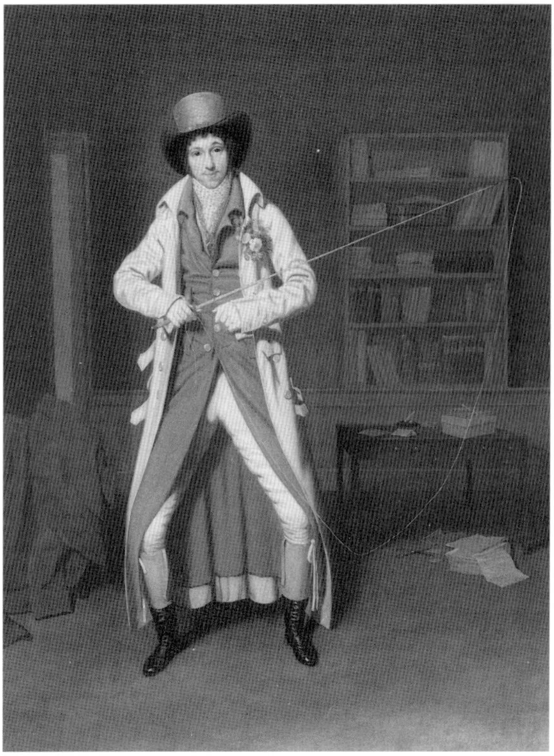

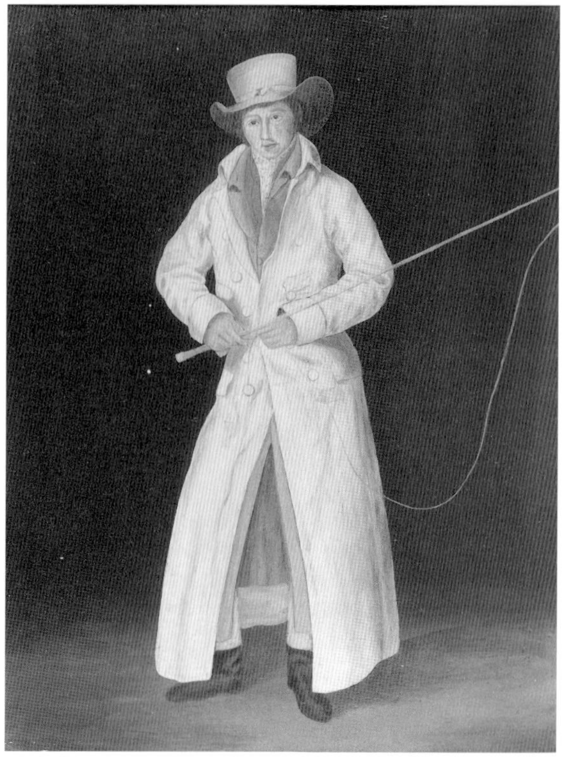

466 *Charles Mathews as Dick Cypher*

465*

CHARLES MATHEWS

as Dick Cypher in *Hit or Miss*

by Isaac Pocock

Samuel De Wilde

Oil on canvas 75.5 x 63.5
INSCR: 'S De Wilde Pinxt / 1810' (brown paint b.l.)
INV: CKA 44; Gift 393
PROV: Mr Baillie; Sir Henry Irving; Irving sale, Christie's 16 December 1905 (152); presented by Romer Williams & C. Romer Williams, 1920; possibly this picture, or No. 466, was one of the two portraits of Mathews by De Wilde that were in the Dramatic College sale at Fairbrother, Lye and Palmer on 24 February 1881 (lots 100E & 100G)
EXH: 1810 R.A. (513) 'Portrait of Mr Matthews, as Cypher, in the popular farce of "Hit or Miss"'
ENGR: Samuel De Wilde pub. De Wilde & J. Cawthorn 19 March 1810, soft ground and etching 35.5 x 24, with the quotation 'Prime! Bang up!'
REL: See No. 466

Dick Cypher does not appear until Act II, scene 3, when he arrives at the country house of Mr Jumble, a printer, having driven very dangerously down from London. His first words are 'That's prime! – that's bang up' – an enthusiastic expression of his satisfaction at having missed the china shop by driving over an old woman. He asks to be helped out of his Benjamin – his long coat – and delivers documents for Jumble which give the printer title to property he thought he had lost.

Cypher holds a long whip in his right hand. He wears black boots with high tan tops, white breeches, a long cream riding coat over a fawn coat, a red waistcoat and neckerchief, and a white stock with blue spots. There is a nosegay in his buttonhole.

Pocock's operatic farce, with music by C. Smith, was first given by the Drury Lane company at the Lyceum on 26 February 1810, with Mathews as the original Dick Cypher. There were about 35 performances over the first season.

The author included a tribute to Mathews in his preface to the play: 'To Mr Mathews I am obliged for the assistance he afforded me in heightening the character of Cypher, as well as for his extraordinary exertions in the representations of a part, which has invariably excited the most unqualified bursts of laughter and applause.' De Wilde's diary for 1810 has numerous references to Mathews sitting for a portrait as Cypher in a painting for a patron named Mr Baillie. Perhaps he was William Baillie, an amateur engraver, who was a member of the Middle Temple and Commissioner of Stamps from 1773 to 1795.

466
CHARLES MATHEWS
as Dick Cypher in *Hit or Miss*
by Isaac Pocock

Samuel De Wilde (after)

Oil on tin 37.2 x 28.2
INSCR: 'BROWN / JA...NER / PAINTER' (raised letters in tin on verso); 'C. Mathews / Bought at the sale of C. Mathews, the younger / 23 July 1878 / As Dick Cypher in "Hit or Miss" / "Prime! Bang up" / vide Memoirs III p. 114' (pen and ink on label on verso)
INV: CKA 607; Gift 349
PROV: Charles James Mathews?; H.B. Wheatley, by whom presented, 1910
REL: See No. 465

Dick, standing full-length and holding a whip, wears a costume similar to that in No. 465.

C.J. Mathews's sale was held by Robinson & Fisher on 22 July 1878. There seems to be no reference to this somewhat perfunctory study in the sale catalogue.

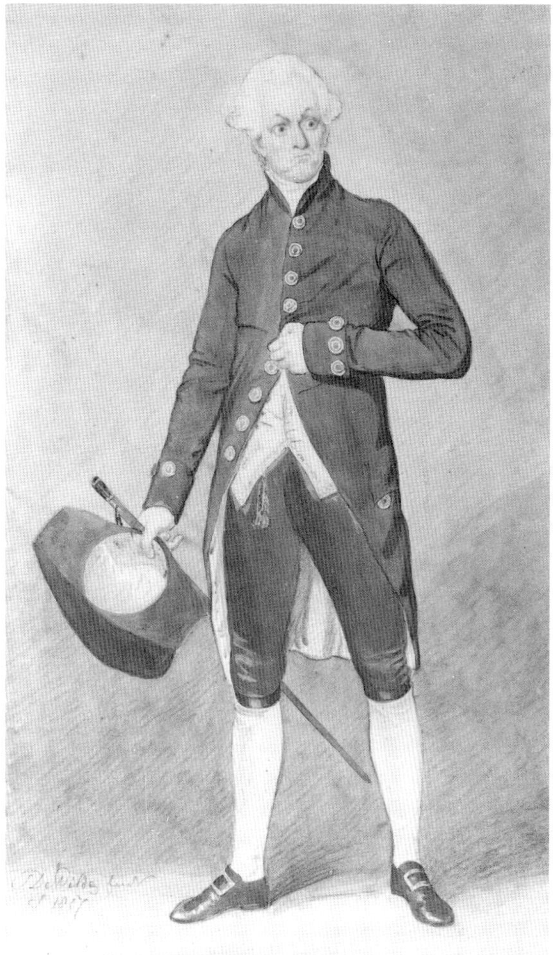

467 *Charles Mathews as Sir Fretful Plagiary*

467
CHARLES MATHEWS
as Sir Fretful Plagiary
in *The Critic*
by Richard Brinsley Sheridan

Samuel De Wilde

Black chalk, pencil and watercolour on wove paper 36.8 x 22.8
INSCR: 'S De Wilde fecit / S 1807' (pencil); 'Mr Mathews as Sir Fretful Plagiary in the Critic' (pen and brown ink on mount t.c. CM); 'I shall treat it with the same calm indifference, & philosophic contempt. Act 1st Scene 1st' (pen and brown ink on mount b.c. CM); 'Bought at the sale of Effects of his son C. Mathews the younger 23 July 1878 By Charles Wylie' (label on blackboard)
INV: Mathews 230; CKA 519
PROV: Charles Mathews; Charles James Mathews; C.J. Mathews sale, Robinson & Fisher 22 July 1878, bt. Charles Wylie for 12 gns. (with another drawing of Mathews in *Wild Oats*); purchased by the Garrick Club 1924
EXH: 1833 London (230)
ENGR: Henry Meyer pub. Mathews & Leigh 1809, stipple and line 13.7 x 8.9

In his right hand, Sir Fretful Plagiary holds a cane and a black hat with a white lining. He wears black shoes, white stockings, black breeches, a greenish-brown jacket with big white buttons, and a white waistcoat trimmed in blue.

Mathews gave 11 performances as Sir Fretful during the Haymarket 1807 summer season (when the drawing was made), the first taking place on 4 August and the last on 14 September. The cast also included John Fawcett as Puff and Robert Palmer as Sneer.

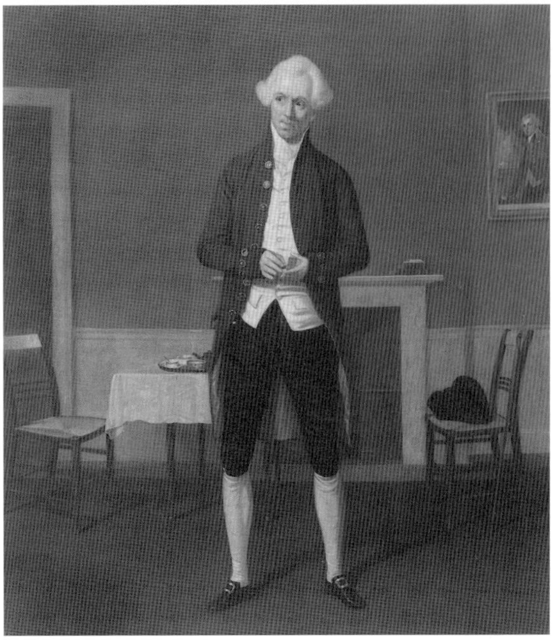

468
CHARLES MATHEWS
as Sir Fretful Plagiary in *The Critic*
by Richard Brinsley Sheridan

Samuel De Wilde

Oil on canvas 73.7 x 57.1
INSCR: 'S De Wilde pinxit / 1810' (black paint b.l.)
INV: Mathews 66; RW/CKA 110 (repr.)
PROV: Charles Mathews
EXH: 1811 R.A. (227); 1833 London (66);
1950–51 London (251); 1951 London (5);
1951–52 London (131)

Sir Fretful takes a pinch of snuff from a silver snuffbox. He wears black shoes with silver buckles, white stockings, black breeches, an olive-coloured jacket with silver buttons, and a white waistcoat. He stands on a green carpet in front of a pale green wall with a white painted dado and a wooden door with a white frame. There is a white marble fireplace behind Mathews, and on the wall to the right a framed print of Reynolds's portrait of Sheridan (see No. 738).

During the 1810 summer season (when the drawing was made), Mathews played Sir Fretful Plagiary four times, at the Haymarket on 18 and 26 June, 31 July and 8 September. Jones played Puff and Holland played Sneer.

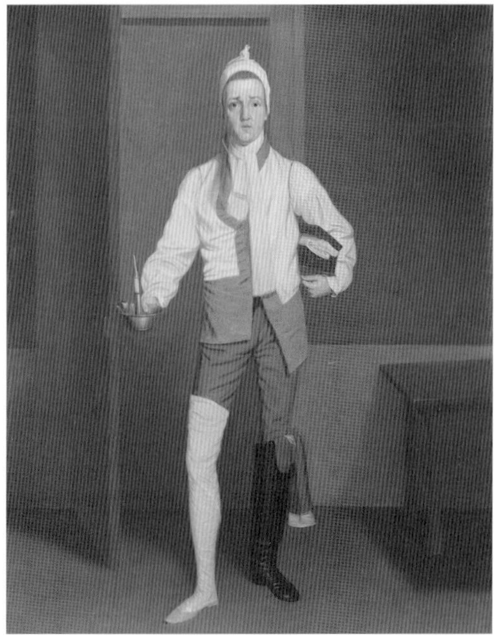

469*
CHARLES MATHEWS
as Somno in *The Sleepwalker or Which is the Lady?*
by Walley Chamberlain Oulton

Samuel De Wilde

Oil on canvas 77 x 58.3
INV: Mathews 120; RW/CKA 112
PROV: Charles Mathews
EXH: 1813 R.A. (393); 1833 London (120);
1934 London (265); 1950–51 London (246); 1951 London (6);
1951–52 London (132); 1975 London (130)
ENGR: James Thomson for the *Theatrical Inquisitor*,
pub. C. Chapple 1 August 1816, stipple (vignette)
REL: NT 48, pencil and watercolour on wove paper
36.8 x 22.6, inscr: 'S De Wilde / Sepr 20 1814' (pencil b.r.)

Somno, a servant to Sir Patrick M'Guire, has a histrionic propensity and walks in his sleep, quoting from Shakespeare and other authors. His ludicrous garb consists of a white nightcap, a yellow slipper on his right foot with a white legging, and a black boot on his left foot with a white-topped blue stocking tucked into it. His trousers are blue, his red waistcoat with white facing is fastened askew, and his stock is untied.

Oulton's farce was first given at the Haymarket on 15 June 1812, having been licensed on 13 May as *The Twin Sister; or, Forgery in Love*. In his preface to the 1817 edition of the play, Oulton thanked Mathews for 'being awake to all the eccentricities of a sleep walker', and added: 'The idea of introducing a Somnambulist in comic situations, occurred to him from Reading curious accounts of sleepwalking in "The Wonders of Nature and Art".'

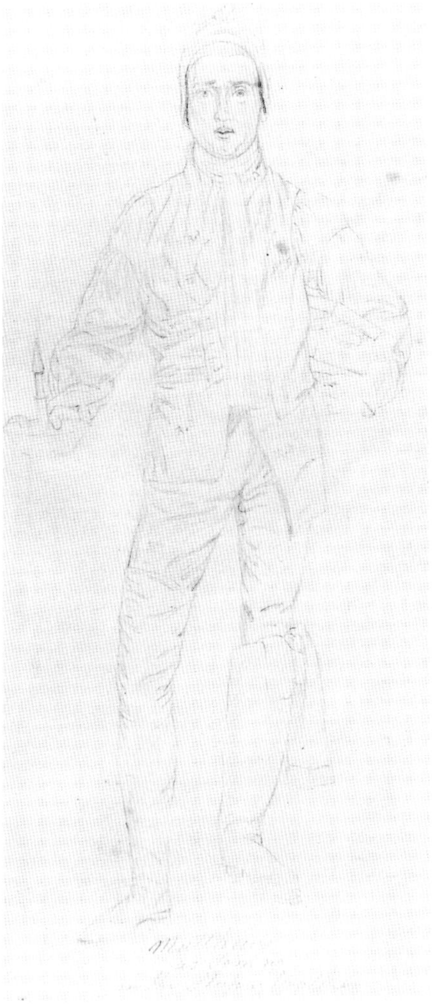

470
CHARLES MATHEWS
as Somno in *The Sleepwalker*
by Walley Chamberlain Oulton

Samuel De Wilde (?)

Pencil on very fine wove paper 33.9 x 15
INSCR: 'Mathews / as Somno / in the Sleep Walker' (pencil b.c. CM?), 'light blue' on the trousers
INV: Not listed
PROV: Charles Mathews (Print Collection Vol. v f. 45)

This is a tracing, possibly done by De Wilde for producing repetitions of the watercolour version of No. 469.

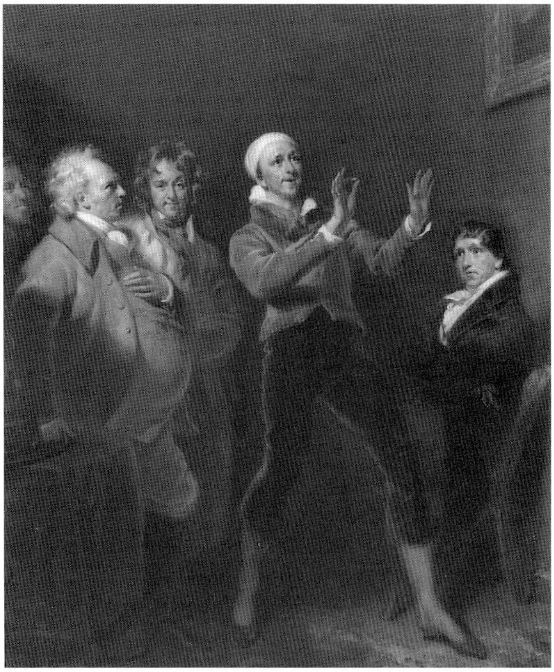

471*
CHARLES MATHEWS

George Henry Harlow

Oil on canvas 74.3 x 61.6
INV: Mathews 97; RW/CKA 103
PROV: Charles Mathews
EXH: 1814 R.A. (159) 'A group of portraits of Mr Mathews, in private, and in various characters'; 1833 London (97); 1956–57 London; 1962 Chichester (29); 1965 Kenwood (21); 1975 London (131)
ENGR: Henry Meyer pub. H. Meyer 1817, mezzotint 61 x 49.8 (inscr: see below); Henry Meyer 1819, line n.s. (inscr: see below); W. Greatbach for Mathews's *Memoirs* pub. R. Bentley 1838, stipple and line 10.1 x 8.9 (engravings of individual figures)
REL: Sotheby's 19 November 1970 (88), black and red chalk on wove paper 21.6 x 15.9, inscr: 'GHH' (b.r.) (drawing for head of seated figure); a portrait by Harlow of Mathews was in the Dramatic College Sale at Fairbrother, Lye and Palmer on 24 February 1881 (lot 48)
LIT: Fitzgerald, p. 145; Griffiths, p. 357

Mathews is shown playing four different characters and as himself. From left to right: the dirty face of Fond Barney; the rotund figure of Mr Wiggins with black boots, white breeches, a brown jacket and a red waistcoat; Buskin, the Drunken Ostler, with wavy ginger hair and a pale brown smock (see No. 464); the Idiot chasing a fly, wearing brown slippers, blue-green breeches trimmed in gold, a brown jacket, and a white shirt with a red neckerchief; and Mathews (himself) looking up in amazement from his seat at the Idiot, wearing a dark red jacket and a yellow waistcoat. The picture visible in the top right-hand corner is not identifiable.

The two prints by Meyer have the following inscription beneath them:

> That this print may not be mistaken for a collection of subjects merely Theatrical it has been deemed expedient to accompany it by a short explanation of its object. The characters introduced are all taken from life. The principal figure is an IDIOT amusing himself with a fly – the next to him a DRUNKEN OSTLER introduced in Killing No Murder. The third an extraordinary fat man whose manners and appearance suggested the idea of Mr WIGGINS in the farce of that name – and the last FOND BARNEY a character well known on the York Race Course. The intention of the artist is to present a portrait of Mr Mathews as STUDYING those characters for imitation preserving at the same time his likeness as varied in the representation of each.

Mathews gave his first one-man entertainment in York on 12 April 1808. *The Mail-Coach: or Rambles in Yorkshire* was polished up over the years and was performed as *Mail-Coach Adventures* at the English Opera House in the Strand in 1818. It was the first of his 13 *At Homes* at this theatre and at the nearby Adelphi. Prior to 1818 Charles Mathews's entertainments had tended to be part of an evening's bill of fare at whichever theatre he was playing, rather than occupying the entire programme. His performances followed a tradition in the English theatre: Charles Dibdin's one-man shows at the Sans Souci Theatre in the 1770s, for instance, and George Stevens's lectures on physiognomy in the same period. In 1818 M. Alexandre produced a one-man show in French at the Adelphi Theatre, in direct opposition to Charles Mathews, whilst John Bannister, among others, followed Mathews's lead in taking one-man shows and 'monopolylogues' into the provinces. However, Charles Mathews was the recognised master of this type of entertainment, which grew increasingly popular during the 19th century.

Three of the characters in No. 471 – the Idiot chasing the fly, the Drunken Ostler and Fond Barney – had already been invented by Mathews when he gave his first one-man entertainment in 1808. The fourth, Fat Mr Wiggins, he had created on 27 May 1803 in Allingham's *The Birthday*, during his first season at the Haymarket.

Harlow and Mathews were friends, and Harlow must have taken a special interest in Mathews's collection of theatrical portraits, which eventually included 11 of his works. Mathews must have commissioned No. 471 from Harlow and the occasion celebrated may have been his one-man performance for Queen Charlotte and the Prince Regent at Carlton House in 1813.

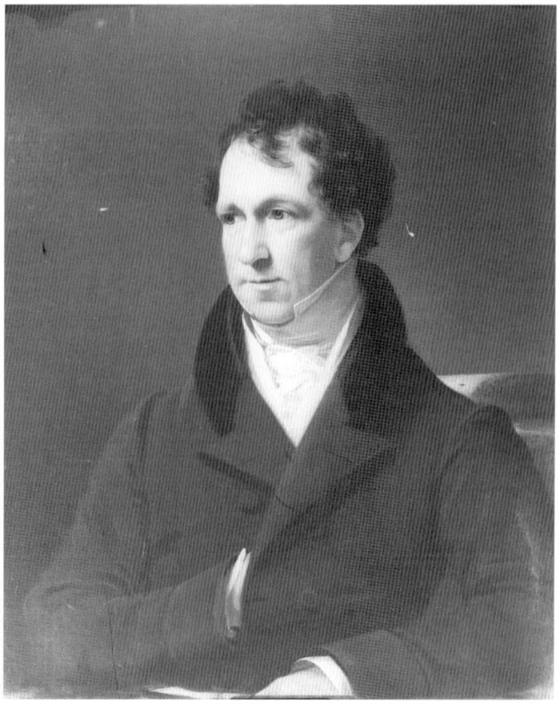

472*
CHARLES MATHEWS

James Lonsdale

Oil on canvas 74.9 x 62.2
INV: Mathews 114; RW/CKA 483
PROV: Charles Mathews
EXH: 1827 R.A. (192); 1833 London (114)
ENGR: Charles Turner pub. Paul Colnaghi & Co. 1 November 1826, mezzotint 26.7 x 21.9; W. Greatbach for Mathews's *Memoirs* pub. R. Bentley 1838, stipple and line 10.5 x 8.6

Mathews wears a grey coat with a black velvet collar, and a yellow waistcoat. He holds a paper in his left hand and his right hand is inserted in his coat.

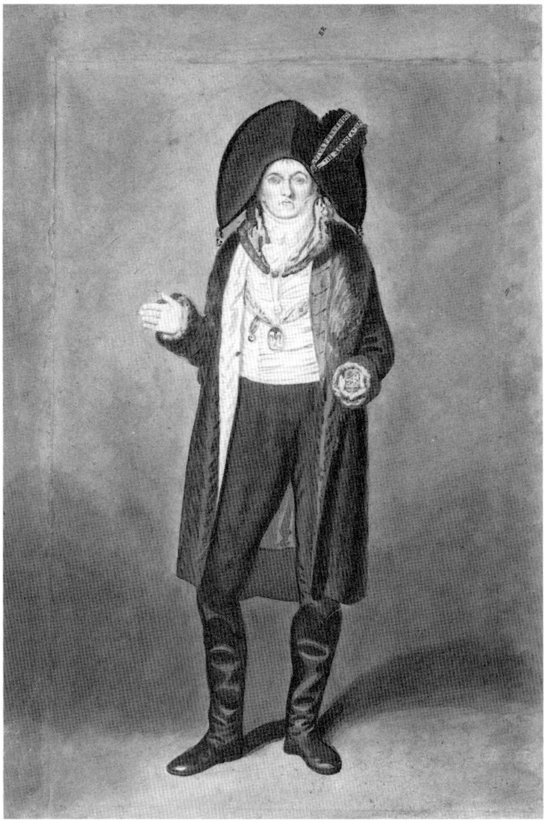

473
CHARLES MATHEWS
as the Spanish Ambassador

Unknown Artist (De Wilde?)

Pencil and watercolour on wove paper 28.6 x 19.4
(drawn on a sheet of paper stuck on to a larger one which shows 4 cm at top, 3.5 cm at left, 3 cm at right, and 1.5 cm at bottom)
INSCR: 'VIVA FERNANDO / VII V JORGE III' (on cockade);
'BR' (black stamp t.c. – collector's mark?)
INV: RW 556 (unknown sitter and artist); CKA 556
PROV: Thomas Hill; acquired by the Garrick Club at a date unknown
LIT: Anne Mathews, *Memoirs* (1838), 2: 69–77

Mathews wears small, green-tinted wire-rimmed spectacles and holds a gold, grey and red snuffbox in his left hand. He has black boots with curved tops, dark blue trousers, a dark green coat lined in white and trimmed with fur, and a white waistcoat. His large Spanish-style grey hat has tassels and a large dark grey cockade with a gold jewel sprouting two pink ribbons inscribed as above.

The story of Charles Mathews pretending to be the Spanish Ambassador on an elaborate day trip to Woolwich is told with great glee by his widow in her memoirs of her late husband. It is a story that loses in the telling.

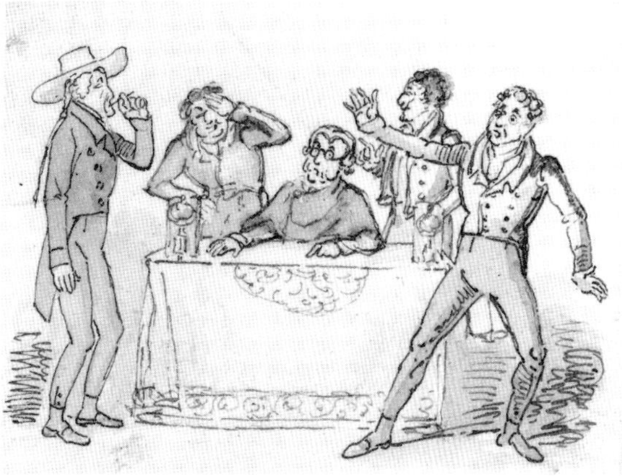

474
CHARLES MATHEWS
in Four Characters from *A Trip to America*
by Charles Mathews,
with the author out of character

Unknown Artist

Pencil, pen and brown ink with grey and pink wash on wove paper 7.4 x 9.8
INV: Not listed
PROV: 'Charles Mathews at Home' f. 60
ENGR: Anon., aquatint and etching 15.2 x 10.1,
inscr: 'MR MATHEWS in his various characters / in, / "A Trip to America"' (printed together with No. 475)

Mathews, sitting behind a table flanked by lamps, is introducing himself in the various characters of his 'At Home'.

Mathews gave his entertainment *A Trip to America*, at the English Opera House, or Lyceum, on 25 March 1824. In this 'At Home', which celebrated his recent tour in the United States, he played his usual array of odd characters. Part III was a monopolylogue entitled 'All Well at Nachitoches', in which Mathews played: Colonel Hiram Peglar, a Kentucky Shoemaker; Agamemnon, a poor runaway Negro; Jonathan W. Doubikin, a real Yankee (his master); Monsieur Capote, a French Emigrant Tailor; and Mr O'Sullivan, an Irish Improver of his Fortune. Nos. 474 and 475 relate to the characters introduced in the monopolylogue.

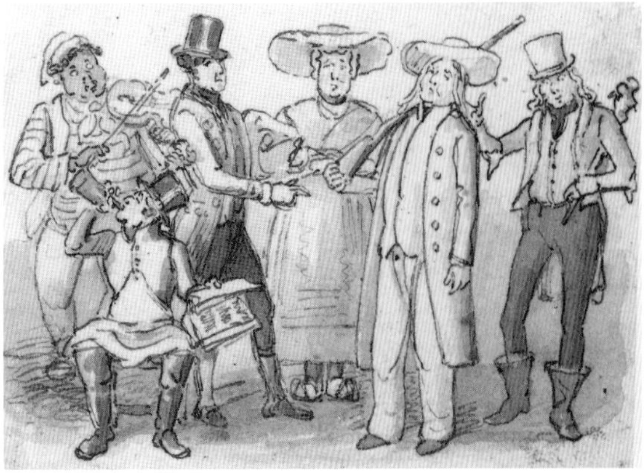

475
CHARLES MATHEWS
in Six Characters from *A Trip to America*
by Charles Mathews

Unknown Artist

Pencil, pen and brown ink with grey and pink wash
on wove paper 7.2 x 9.6
INV: Not listed
PROV: 'Charles Mathews at Home' f. 60
ENGR: Anon., aquatint and etching 15.2 x 10.1,
inscr: 'Mr MATHEWS / in, / "A Trip to America"'
(printed together with No. 474)

See No. 474.

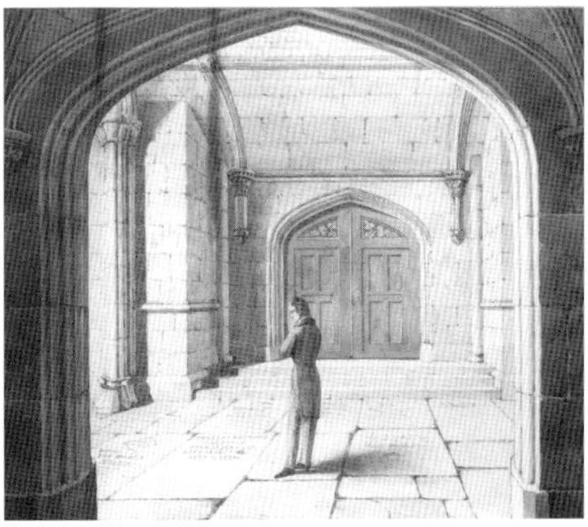

476
'TOMB OF CHARLES MATHEWS'

George Wightwick

Pencil, pen and brown ink with brown wash
on wove paper 28 x 33
INSCR: 'CHARLES MATHEWS / COMEDIAN / BORN 28 JUNE 1776 /
DIED 28 JUNE 1835 / AGED 59 YEARS'
(pen and brown ink on grave-stone lower l.);
'George Wightwick' (pen and brown ink on mount b.r.)
INV: Not listed; Gift 208
PROV: Presented by Mrs Wightwick, 1887

Mathews was interred at St Andrew's Church, Plymouth.

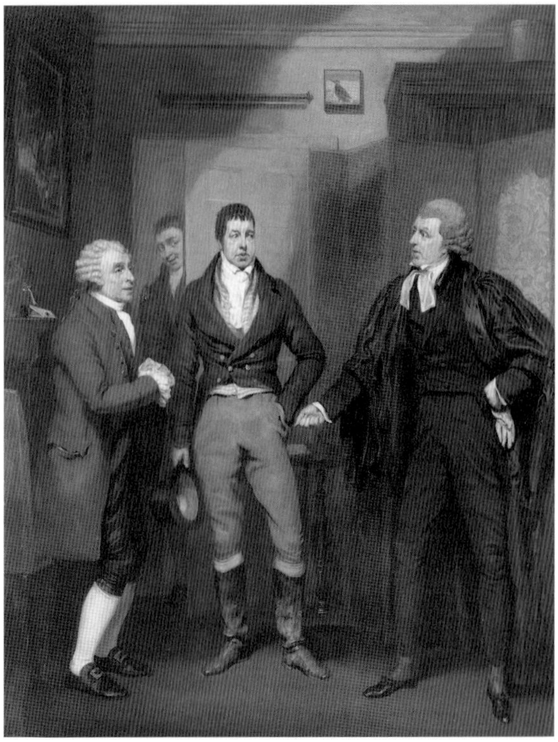

477*
CHARLES MATHEWS as Flexible,
WILLIAM BLANCHARD as Dr Camphor,
JOHN EMERY as Andrew
and *JOHN LISTON* as Lubin Log
in *Love, Law, and Physic*
by James Kenney

George Clint

Oil on canvas 127 x 101.5
INV: Mathews 166; RW/CKA 6
PROV: Charles Mathews, by whom commissioned
EXH: 1830 R.A. (238); 1833 London (166);
1951 London (3); 1950–51 London (255);
1951–52 London (137); 1982–83 London (151)
ENGR: T. Lupton pub. T. Lupton 22.4.1831,
mezzotint 44.5 x 36

Lubin Log, a somewhat simple-minded London timber merchant who was born in Tooley Street in the Borough, has inherited a large estate. He has travelled to York to marry Laura, the niece of Dr Camphor. Arriving with him in the mail coach is Flexible, 'a barrister and special pleader', who is determined to frustrate Lubin's designs on Laura on behalf of his friend Captain Danvers, who is passionately in love with her. Lubin Log admits that his uncle married a Theresina Velasco in his youth and left her and a child. Flexible determines to find them.

In Act II, scene I, 'A Room in the Doctor's House', Lubin is discussing his marriage with Dr Camphor when Flexible and 'Mr Velasco' (who is Capt. Danvers in disguise) are announced. But Captain Danvers's ruse is discovered when Andrew, Dr Camphor's servant, enters with papers stating that the Velasco child was a girl. The quotation printed on the engraving is not precisely the correct one: 'Log: "Do you mean you can prove black is white?"/ Flex: "Sir, black is white; shall a timber-merchant dare contest me in points of law?"' By this time Danvers is on stage and Andrew temporarily off. In fact we see a slightly earlier moment, after the entrance of Flexible but before that of Danvers. The stage directions give the positions of both Andrew and Flexible as stage left (right-hand side of the picture).

Lubin (Liston) wears muddy boots because he is too mean to pay a boot-boy to clean them. He carries a black top hat and wears grey-blue breeches and a dark grey cutaway coat over waistcoat striped in buff and blue. Flexible (Mathews) wears a legal grey wig and is dressed in black with a long gown and white bands. He holds a kid glove. Andrew (Emery), making his announcements through the door, wears a brown livery with gold epaulets over a red waistcoat. Dr Camphor (Blanchard), on the left, has a wig tied back with a blue ribbon, and wears black breeches and a brown jacket and waistcoat. The doctor's room contains, among other items, a red damask screen of four panels and a tall glass-fronted cabinet with green silk curtains.

Kenney's two-act farce, with music by M.P. King, was first performed at Covent Garden on 20 November 1812, with Mathews, Blanchard, Emery and Liston playing the parts shown in Clint's picture. A popular piece, it was performed 44 times during its first season. It was a significant production for Mathews, as Flexible was his first important new role at Covent Garden; he had moved from Drury Lane at the beginning of the 1812–13 season. However, the large house did not suit his style of acting any more than Drury Lane, and his appearances there became infrequent. Clint's picture, therefore, is an 18-year-old memory of one of Mathews's finest moments at Covent Garden.

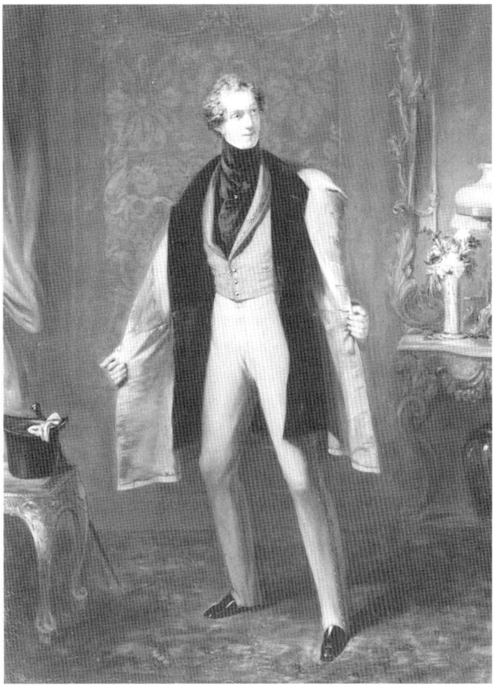

478

CHARLES JAMES MATHEWS

as George Rattleton in *The Humpback'd Lover*

by Charles James Mathews

Robert William Buss

Oil on canvas 57 x 43.5

INSCR: 'R.W. Buss 1836' (dark paint at foot of table b.r.)

INV: RW 138 (artist unknown); CKA 138; Gift 264

PROV: Presented by Sir Charles Mathews, 1899

ENGR: G. Adcock for Cumberland's *British Theatre* pub. J. Cumberland 1836, stipple and line 10.8 x 7.3

George Rattleton is pulling off a coat lined with grey silk. He wears black shoes, grey trousers with silver decoration and instep straps, a dark blue velvet jacket, and a paler blue waistcoat with three gold buttons and a large lapel embroidered in darker blue. In his huge blue-green cravat is a pearl stick. Mathews's top hat, scarf and gloves rest on the red upholstered chair and he stands in front of a blue and white floral screen in a gilt frame. The pier table to the right has on it a Chinese vase painted with a pink figure and under it a blue Chinese pot. The dark blue carpet has a brown and red floral design.

Mathews made his official début as George Rattleton at the Olympic on 7 December 1835. *The Humpback'd Lover* was the third item on a bill that consisted of four burlettas and an introductory address given by John Liston. He gave 15 performances in the role, the last on 26 December 1835. Together with his father, Mathews was an original member of the Garrick Club in 1831.

479–594
The Watercolours of
CHARLES JAMES MATHEWS

James Warren Childe

Charles James Mathews was born in Liverpool on 26 December 1803. His father, Charles Mathews, was completing a provincial engagement after his first London season – a season that initiated a 30-year career as the most successful comic actor of the early 19th century. He had started to sink most of his earnings into his collection of theatrical paintings, most notably the series of portraits of his contemporaries by Samuel De Wilde, and this obsession stretched to his son, who was portrayed by De Wilde as 'The Little Parson' on 25 July 1807. That watercolour is now in the National Theatre; No. 595 in the Garrick Club is a mediocre copy showing the three-year-old Mathews Jnr dressed in the costume in which he used to entertain his father and friends.

After an education at Merchant Taylors' and at a school in Clapham, on 4 May 1819 Mathews was articled to Augustus Pugin for four years. His first work as an architect was the Gothic picture gallery and library added to Ivy Cottage, his father's house at Highgate. In 1823 he was employed by Lord Blessington and swept off to Naples, where he met Lady Blessington and the Comte D'Orsay. With all expenses paid by his father, his life was extremely fashionable and amusing. He gained diplomas in Milan and Florence, and in the latter city helped to design a theatre for Lord Normanby in the Palazzo San Clementi. The stage was the same size as that of the Haymarket in London, and Mathews painted a drop-cloth with a view of Florence. He also took part in the theatricals, playing such parts as Tony Lumpkin and Falstaff. Back in London, he was for a while District Surveyor of Bow and Bethnal Green, but he was restless in that position, and when his father died in 1835 Mathews took up his father's profession.

The elder Mathews's one remaining asset had been a half-share in the Adelphi Theatre, and it was there that his son joined Frederick Henry Yates to begin his second career. As the son of a famous theatrical father, and with his considerable reputation in amateur productions, Mathews might have been expected to do quite well, but he still regarded himself as a gentleman and, rather than act, he decided to write. His melodrama *Mandrin*, performed on 28 September 1835, was an abject failure and Mathews retired from the Adelphi to the bosom of Mme Vestris at the Olympic. She had been one of the most considerable figures in the European theatre for 20 years, and after a career as the best known of all travesty actresses she moved into management at the Olympic in 1831. Mathews's arrival ended Mme Vestris's search for the right sort of leading man; they were married in 1838, and went on to manage Covent Garden for three seasons from September 1839 to April 1842. Unfortunately, managing a company of 684 people proved too much for the couple; Mathews went to debtors' prison then was declared a bankrupt with debts of £30,000. He ventured no more into management but spent the rest of his life as a performer.

The watercolours of James Warren Childe (*c.* 1768–1862) show Charles James Mathews in parts that he created or played for the first time between 1835 and 1845. The drawings are assumed to date from about 1845, as Mathews is not depicted in any part played exclusively after then. The first documented appearance of the drawings, however, was not until 24 July 1878 when they were sold as lot 557 in the Mathews sale. At that sale Childe was not identified as the artist. The drawings were bought by a Mr Parker, and were presented to the Garrick Club in 1879 by Robert Walters.

Childe started his professional life as a very bad miniaturist and gradually improved. He exhibited at the Royal Academy from 1815 to 1853, and at the Society of British Artists from 1827 to 1840. A large proportion of his output was theatrical, although there is no mention of him in early 19th-century theatrical memoirs. Signed examples of his work, notably two watercolours of Charles and John Mockler that were sold at Sotheby's on 17 May 1979 (lot 106), leave no doubt that he is the author of the Garrick Club drawings.

Most of the Childe drawings show Mathews in contemporary comedy, dressed immaculately in the height of current fashion. It was for the role of the dandy, endlessly and minutely varied, that he was best known. In fact, many of the drawings can be seen as fashion plates rather than theatrical portraits. To the London theatregoer of the early Victorian era, Charles Mathews was the perfect gentleman. He assumed the part with glee, and described his style, slightly tongue-in-cheek, in his autobiography, which was edited by Charles Dickens Jnr and published posthumously in 1879:

> The lighter phase of comedy, representing the more natural and less laboured school of modern life, and holding the mirror up to nature without regard to the conventionalities of the theatre, was the aim I had in view.

He was clearly the most artfully 'naturalistic' actor of his period and exuded a relaxed confidence on stage that is achieved by very few – e.g. Gerald Du Maurier earlier this century and Rex Harrison more recently.

Attired in character, Mathews clearly did not allow the part he was playing to stand in the way of his own personality; the fact that his own natural elegance was disguised became part of the joke. An early example of a heavy disguise was his role of Prince Riquet in *Riquet with the Tuft* by James Robinson Planché and Charles Dance (No. 575). This *Grand Comical, Allegorical, Magical, Musical Burlesque Burletta in One Act* was the Christmas offering at the Olympic for 1836–37; the cast included Mme Vestris as the Princess Emeralda. The entry of Prince Riquet in the third scene, which takes place in the Grand Hall of Audience, is described in some detail in the stage directions:

> The Litter is opened, and Prince Riquet comes out of it – He is hunchbacked, bow-legged, with a bump over one eye, and bald headed with the exception of one tuft of very red hair. He is richly attired and wears a miniature of Emeralda about his neck.

It is satisfying to see that Childe's watercolour agrees in all respects with the stage directions, including a rather curious interpretation of the bump over the eye.

In the following Christmas season, the Olympic presented Planché and Dance's version of a more familiar fairy-story, *Puss in Boots*, which opened on 26 December 1837. Mathews played Puss (No. 572) and his wife again donned male attire as 'Ralph (soi-disant Marquis of Carabas)'.

Mathews's Puss costume was made by Miss Glover, the best-known theatrical costumier of her day. Her account books, which are in the Garrick Club library, indicate that she provided costumes for many of the principal actors of the period, including Charles Kean, Charles Kemble and W.C. Macready. There is enough detail in the accounts to enable some sort of reconstruction of many of the costumes glimpsed in theatre portraits of, say, Charles Kean as Hamlet or Macready as Macbeth. However, in combination with the Childe watercolours of Mathews, Miss Glover's accounts become the major source for our knowledge of mid-19th-century theatre costume.

The most interesting of the Childe watercolours from the point of view of costume are the series of five drawings of Mathews as Colonel Feignwell in Mrs Centlivre's *A Bold Stroke for a Wife*, revived at the Olympic in 1836 as *The Gentleman Outwitted* (Nos. 514–18). It is an amusing play in which Colonel Feignwell, the hero, attempts to dupe the guardians of his ladylove by appearing in a variety of disguises. No. 515 shows him as the Dutchman and No. 517 as a Quaker. Miss Glover provided 'A Dutchman's Coat' at £2.10s.0d, 'One Waistcoat to match the Dutchman's Dress' at 10/– and 'A Quaker's Dress – Coat, waistcoat and Breeches' for £5 as well as '2 Leather Belts, black and brown' at 5/–, a 'Large steel buckle' at 4d, and other items. Mathews's costume bill for this production came to £14. 11s. 0d; he provided the other costumes himself, presumably having inherited a huge theatrical wardrobe from his father, but new costumes were evidently a major expense.

No. 591 shows one of Miss Glover's most lavish costumes for Mathews, as Witwoud in *The Way of the World*, which opened at the Haymarket on 17 December 1842. It cost him £8, even though he provided most of the materials. Mathews paid Miss Glover for 'Making a complete Costume Court Suit of Cut Velvet, Coat, Waistcoat and Breeches (Character Way of the World / Costume 1699) Lining of White Satin, interlining, Gold fringe trimming, frogs, Button-holes &c. (Velvet and buttons found)'. It is interesting that Miss Glover was so specific about the dating of her costume, and one wonders what sort of pattern books or visual reference she was able to use.

The texts of many of the plays in which Mathews appeared no longer exist, but a few have survived. The best known of the contemporary plays was Dion Boucicault's *London Assurance*, which opened at Covent Garden on 4 March 1841. The stage directions describe the costumes as being 'Of the day – striking and very fashionable', and the two relevant drawings, Nos. 510 & 511, show Mathews at his sartorial peak as the young ne'er-do-well Dazzle. He has a fine line in trouser legs, fastened with instep straps under his highly polished boots, elaborate waistcoats, high silken cravats, white gloves, and a curious off-the-shoulder look in jackets and coats with wide lapels and huge buttons. Perhaps there is a hint of theatrical exaggeration, but there is no doubt that this is the gentlemanly appearance that impressed his public.

There is a slight prettiness to Childe's watercolours of Mathews which makes the sitter come across as a spineless and pink-cheeked adolescent. This impression can be attributed partly to Childe's style and partly to the fact that sympathy wanes when one is confronted by 116 drawings of the same person, of exactly the same size and format. On the other hand, Childe's gentle touch manages to conjure up Mathews's charm, his debonair lack of theatrical bombast, and his casual gentlemanly insinuation. It is an aspect of the 19th-century British theatre overshadowed by the enormous interest in Shakespearean production and the development of 'realistic' drama.

Only a selection of the portraits are illustrated here. In all cases the provenance is Charles J. Mathews, Parker, R. Walters.

479
NOT ILLUSTRATED
CHARLES JAMES MATHEWS
as Algernon Bloomly in
You Can't Marry Your Grandmother
by Thomas Haynes Bayly

James Warren Childe

Pencil and watercolour on wove paper
mounted on card 36.4 x 25.4
INSCR: 'Charles Mathews / as / "Algernon"
in "You can't marry your Grandmother".'
(pen and brown ink)
INV: RW/CKA 155A (in 155B frame);
Gift 192 (Nos. 479–594)

Mathews as Algernon wears black shoes, grey trousers, and a white dressing-gown decorated with gold hexagons and red details. His waistcoat is blue with brown horizontal lines, and his extravagant cravat is black.

Bayly's burletta was first given at the Olympic on 1 March 1838, with Mathews as Algernon Bloomly and Mme Vestris as Emma Melville. It was played 24 times during the season, the last performance being given on 2 May 1838. See Nos. 480 and 481.

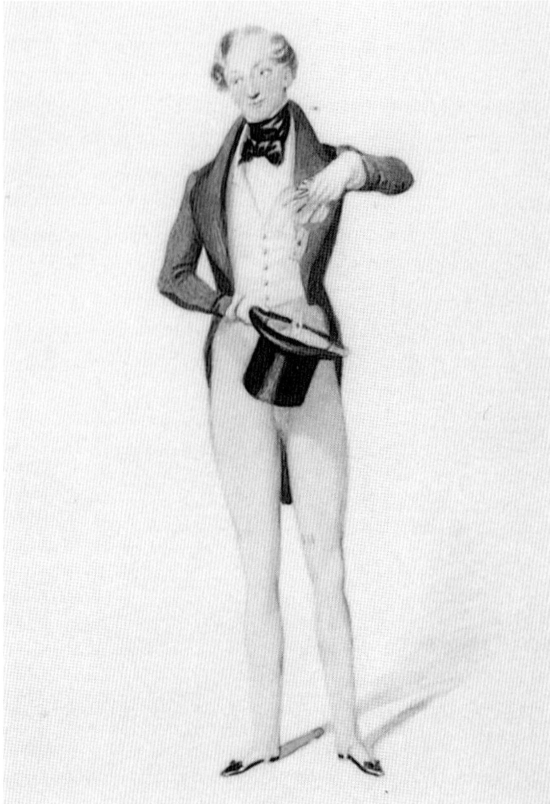

480 *Charles James Mathews as Algernon Bloomly*

480
CHARLES JAMES MATHEWS
as Algernon Bloomly in
You Can't Marry Your Grandmother
(2nd dress)

James Warren Childe

Pencil and watercolour on wove paper
mounted on card 36.4 x 25.4
INSCR: 'Charles Mathews / as / "Algernon"
in "You can't marry your Grandmother".'
(pen and brown ink b.c.)
INV: RW/CKA 161B

Algernon drops cards into a black top hat from a white-gloved left hand. He wears dainty black shoes with rosettes, white stockings, pale brown trousers with instep straps, a green cutaway jacket, a white waistcoat with silver buttons, and a black stock. See No. 479.

481
NOT ILLUSTRATED
CHARLES JAMES MATHEWS
as Algernon Bloomly in
You Can't Marry Your Grandmother
(3rd dress)

James Warren Childe

Pencil and watercolour on wove paper
mounted on card 36.4 x 25.4
INSCR: 'Charles Mathews / as / "Algernon" in "You can't
marry your Grandmother".' (pen and brown ink b.c.)
INV: RW/CKA 161

Algernon holds a black stick and top hat in his white-gloved left hand. He wears black shoes, grey trousers with instep straps, a dark grey jacket, a double-breasted waistcoat embroidered in purple and blue, and a black cravat. See No. 479.

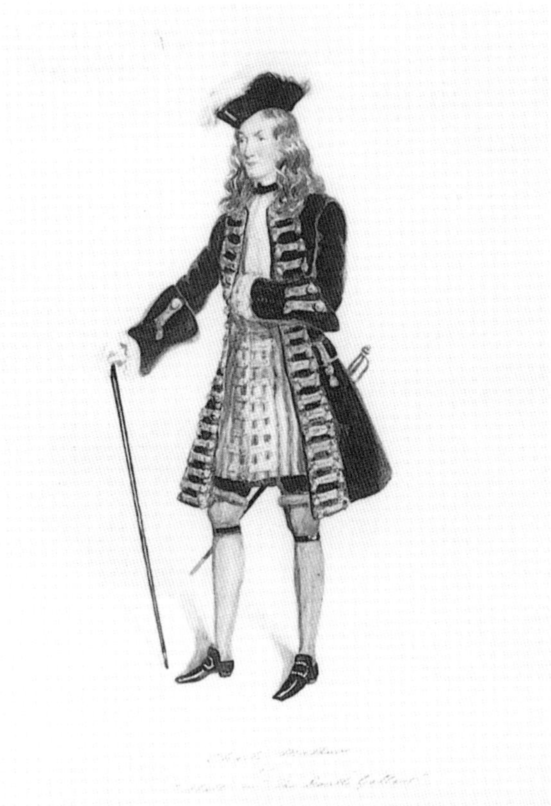

482
CHARLES JAMES MATHEWS
as Atall in *The Double Gallant*
by Colley Cibber

James Warren Childe

Pencil and watercolour on wove paper
mounted on card 36.4 x 25.4
INSCR: 'Charles Mathews / as / "Atall" in
"The Double Gallant".' (pen and brown ink b.c.)
INV: RW/CKA 178E

Atall's long fair hair tumbles from a black tricorn hat with white feathers. He rests his white-gloved right hand on a black cane and wears square-toed black shoes with paste buckles, pink stockings over black breeches with garters, a black velvet coat with gold and silver trimming, and a waistcoat of red, white and brown vertical bands with silver trimming.

Cibber's comedy was originally given at the King's Theatre on 1 November 1707. Mathews played Atall for the first time at Covent Garden on 19 March 1840 in a revival that also included William Farren as Sir Solomon Sadlife and Mme Vestris as Clarinda. See Nos. 483 and 484.

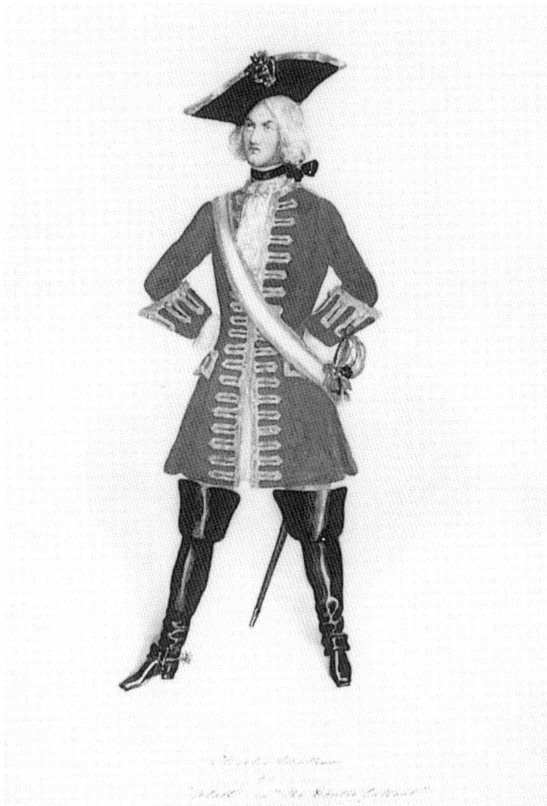

483
CHARLES JAMES MATHEWS
as Atall in *The Double Gallant*
(2nd dress)

James Warren Childe

Pencil and watercolour on wove paper
mounted on card 36.4 x 25.4
INSCR: 'Charles Mathews / as / "Atall" in
"The Double Gallant".' (pen and brown ink b.c.)
INV: RW/CKA 178F

Atall has a powdered wig under a tricorn hat with gold braid and a cockade. He wears black boots with square toes and spurs, grey breeches, and a red military coat trimmed with gold braid. See No. 482.

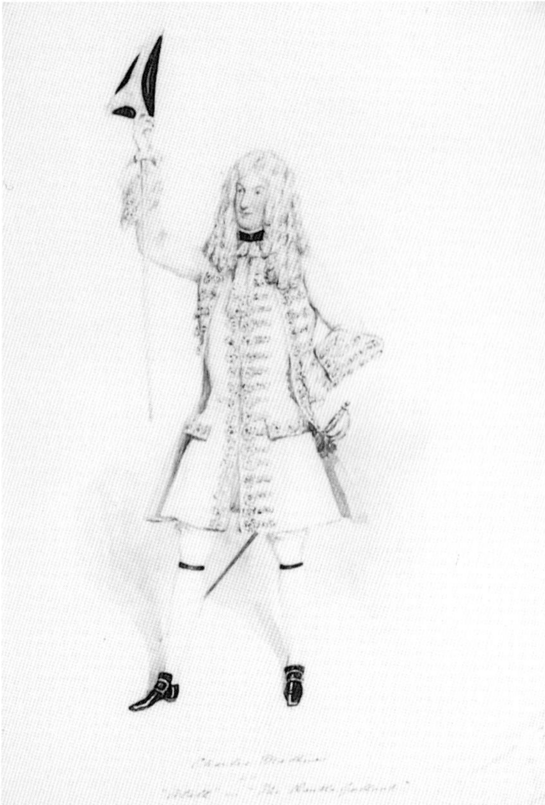

484
CHARLES JAMES MATHEWS
as Atall in *The Double Gallant*
(3rd dress)

James Warren Childe

Pencil and watercolour on wove paper
mounted on card 36.4 x 25.4
INSCR: 'Charles Mathews / as / "Atall" in "The Double Gallant".' (pen and brown ink b.c.)
INV: RW/CKA 178G

Atall wears a comic grey powdered wig with ringlets. In his white-gloved right hand he lifts a small tricorn hat with white feathers around the brim. He wears square-toed black shoes with paste buckles, white stockings over breeches with black garters, a grey coat, and a grey waistcoat with silver buttons. See No. 482.

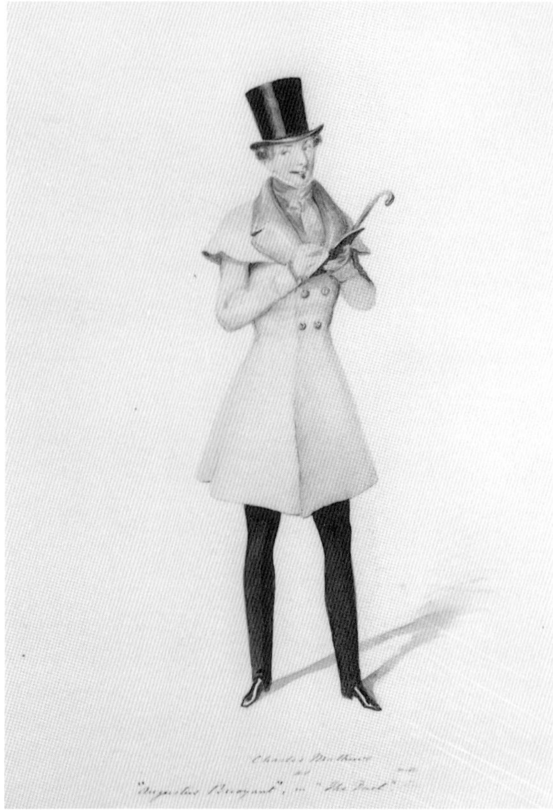

485
CHARLES JAMES MATHEWS
as Augustus Buoyant
in *The Duel or My Two Nephews*
by Richard Brinsley Peake

James Warren Childe

Pencil and watercolour on wove paper
mounted on card 36.4 x 25.4
INSCR: 'Charles Mathews / as / "Augustus Buoyant", in "The Duel".' (pen and brown ink b.c.)
INV: RW/CKA 163

Augustus Buoyant, sketching on a red-backed sketch-pad, wears black shoes, black trousers, a fawn coat, and an extravagant green cravat.

Peake's farce was first performed at Covent Garden on 18 February 1823, with Richard Jones as August Buoyant. Mathews first played the part at the Olympic on 2 November 1837. See No. 486.

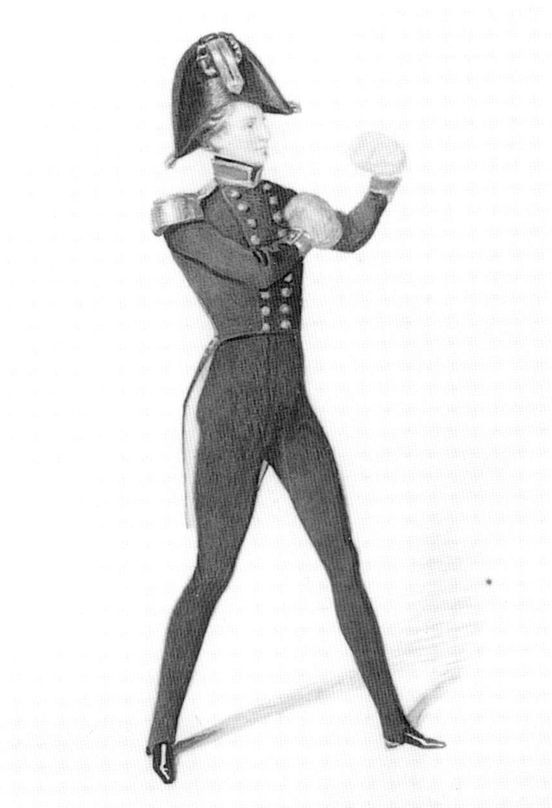

486*

CHARLES JAMES MATHEWS

as Augustus Buoyant

in *The Duel or My Two Nephews*

(2nd dress)

James Warren Childe

Pencil and watercolour on wove paper
mounted on card 36.4 x 25.4
INSCR: 'Charles Mathews / as / "Augustus Buoyant",
in "The Duel".' (pen and brown ink b.c.)
INV: RW/CKA 169

Augustus, striking a boxing attitude with boxing gloves, wears a hat with gold braid and tassel and a large black rosette, black shoes, grey trousers, a blue military jacket lined in white with gold buttons and epaulets and a red collar, and a black stock. See No. 485.

487

NOT ILLUSTRATED

CHARLES JAMES MATHEWS

as Beechwood

in *The Wrong Man*

by John Maddison Morton

James Warren Childe

Pencil and watercolour on wove paper
mounted on card 36.4 x 25.4
INSCR: 'Charles Mathews / as / "Beechwood",
in "The Wrong Man".' (pen and brown ink b.c.)
INV: RW/CKA 144E

Beechwood wears a stove-pipe hat. He wears black shoes, white trousers, a brown jacket, a white waistcoat with silver buttons, and a black cravat. He carries a gold-topped black stick in his white-gloved right hand. Morton's farce was first performed at Covent Garden on 6 November 1841, with Mathews as Beechwood.

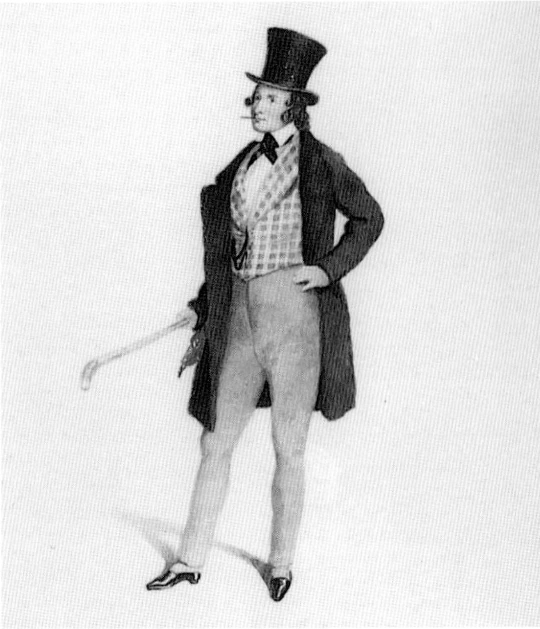

488

CHARLES JAMES MATHEWS

as Benjamin Bowles in *Brother Ben*

by John Maddison Morton

James Warren Childe

Pencil and watercolour on wove paper
mounted on card 36.4 x 25.4
INSCR: 'Charles Mathews / as / "Ben Bowles" in "Brother Ben".' (pen and brown ink b.c.)
INV: RW/CKA 157G

Benjamin Bowles wears a dark grey top hat, grey gloves, black shoes with white gaiters, grey trousers, a dark blue jacket, a waistcoat with a pattern of white horizontal lines over brown and cream vertical lines, and a black cravat.

Morton's farce was first performed at Covent Garden on 9 December 1840, with Mathews as Commodore Cutlass.

489

CHARLES JAMES MATHEWS

as Bernard in *The Barrack Room*

by Thomas Haynes Bayly

James Warren Childe

Pencil and watercolour on wove paper
mounted on card 36.4 x 25.4
INSCR: 'Charles Mathews / as / "Bernard" in "The Barrack Room".' (pen and brown ink b.c.)
INV: RW/CKA 177D

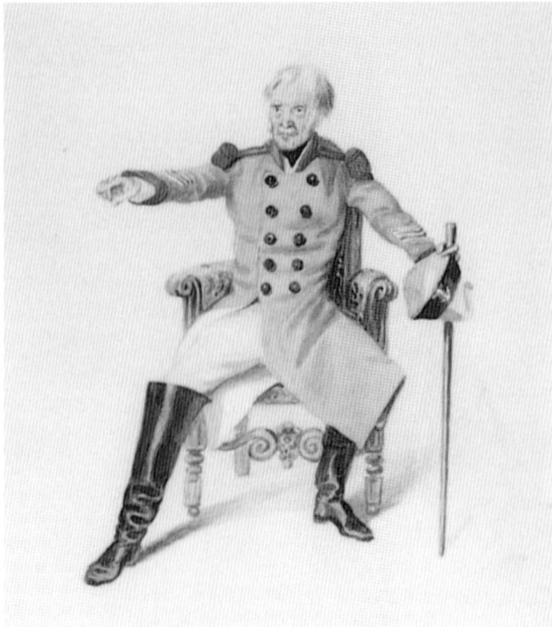

489 *Charles James Mathews as Bernard*

Bernard, with dishevelled white hair and moustache, sits in a chair upholstered in green with grotesquely carved legs and arms. He wears high black boots, white trousers, grey military coat with red cuffs, and black stock. In his extended left hand he holds a stout stick and a grey cap.

Bayly's comedietta was first given at the Olympic on 7 November 1836, with James Bland as Bernard. Mme Vestris played Clarisse de Cruzac, but Mathews did not appear in the piece at the Olympic, nor at Covent Garden or the Haymarket before 1846.

490

NOT ILLUSTRATED

CHARLES JAMES MATHEWS

as Bob Finchley in *News from China*

by John Maddison Morton

James Warren Childe

Pencil and watercolour on wove paper
mounted on card 36.4 x 25.4
INSCR: 'Charles Mathews / as / "Bob Finchley" in "News from China".' (pen and brown ink b.c.)
INV: RW/CKA 178A

Bob Finchley, his feet on a table covered with a white cloth, wears black shoes, white trousers, a green jacket, a white waistcoat, and an elaborate black cravat.

Morton's farce was first given at the Haymarket on 7 September 1843, with Charles Mathews playing Bob Finchley.

491

NOT ILLUSTRATED

CHARLES JAMES MATHEWS

as Bob Honeycombe in *Wolf and the Lamb* by Charles James Mathews or Thomas Egerton Wilks

James Warren Childe

Pencil and watercolour on wove paper mounted on card 36.4 x 25.4
INSCR: 'Charles Mathews / as / "Bob Honeycomb", in "The Wolf and the Lamb".' (pen and brown ink b.c.)
INV: RW/CKA 148C

Bob Honeycombe holds a black top hat in his left hand and a black cane in his right. He wears black shoes, white trousers, a blue jacket with large blue silk lapels and white cuffs, a yellowish waistcoat, and a high white stock.

This comedy, by Mathews or Wilks, was first given at the Haymarket on 23 June 1832.

492

NOT ILLUSTRATED

CHARLES JAMES MATHEWS

as Bolt in *A Day Well Spent* by John Oxenford

James Warren Childe

Pencil and watercolour on wove paper mounted on card 36.4 x 25.4
INSCR: 'Charles Mathews / as / "Bolt" in "A day well Spent".' (pen and brown ink b.c.)
INV: RW/CKA 168

Bolt touches the brim of his white top hat with his white-gloved right hand. He wears black shoes, grey and white striped socks, grey trousers that are a little short, a blue jacket, a white waistcoat with blue vertical and brown horizontal bands, and a blue cravat with a white pattern.

Oxenford's operatic farce was first given at the English Opera House on 4 April 1836.

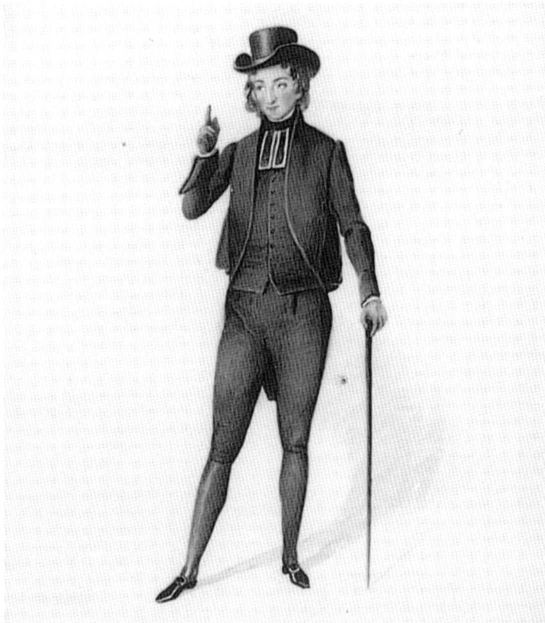

493

CHARLES JAMES MATHEWS

as Abbé le Bon in *A Hasty Conclusion* by Elizabeth Planché

James Warren Childe

Pencil and watercolour on wove paper mounted on card 36.4 x 25.4
INSCR: 'Charles Mathews / as / "The Abbé Le Bon" in "A Hasty Conclusion".' (pen and brown ink b.c.)
INV: RW/CKA 157F

Le Bon, with long fair hair under a hat with its brim turned up at the sides, rests his grey-gloved left hand on a grey stick. He wears black shoes, grey stockings, grey breeches, a grey jacket with padded shoulders, a grey waistcoat, and a black stock with grey flaps edged in white.

Elizabeth Planché's burletta was first given at the Olympic on 19 April 1838, with Mathews as the Abbé Le Bon. Mme Vestris played Marie and sang two new songs in the role. The piece was given 18 times during that season, the last on performance taking place on 10 May 1838. See No. 494.

494

NOT ILLUSTRATED

CHARLES JAMES MATHEWS

as Abbé le Bon in *A Hasty Conclusion* (2nd dress)

James Warren Childe

Pencil and watercolour on wove paper mounted on card 36.4 x 25.4

INSCR: 'Charles Mathews / as / "The Abbé Le Bon" in "A Hasty Conclusion".' (pen and brown ink b.c.)

INV: RW/CKA 177C

Le Bon's curly fair hair falls from under a black cap with red bands and a red tassel. His right arm is bandaged and his left hand is gloved in white. He wears black shoes with white spats, white trousers, a blue military jacket trimmed in red, and a white waistcoat with gold buttons. See No. 493.

495

NOT ILLUSTRATED

CHARLES JAMES MATHEWS

as Brass in *The Confederacy* by Sir John Vanbrugh

James Warren Childe

Pencil and watercolour on wove paper mounted on card 36.4 x 25.4

INSCR: 'Charles Mathews / as / "Brass" in "The Confederacy".' (pen and brown ink b.c.)

INV: RW/CKA 148B

Brass, a schoolmate of Dick Amlet, plays the part of Dick's valet when Dick goes into Society as Colonel Shapely. Mathews seems to be completely overdressed for the part. Brass staggers with his hands in his pockets. His long fair wig flows down from his tilted tricorn hat with black cockade and gold band. He wears black shoes, white stockings, green breeches, a white coat lined in green and trimmed with silver braid, a red waistcoat similarly trimmed with silver braid, and a white stock.

Vanbrugh's comedy was originally performed at the King's Theatre on 30 October 1705. Mathews played Brass for the first time in a revival at the Haymarket on 2 October 1844. Mme Vestris played Flippanta.

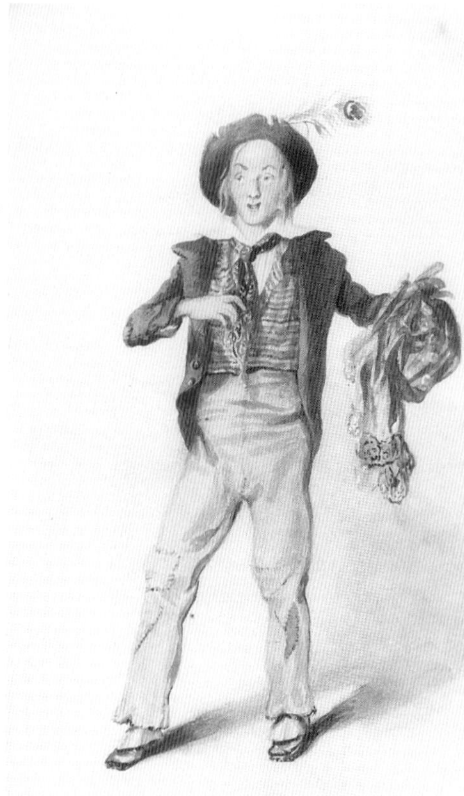

496

CHARLES JAMES MATHEWS

as Carlo in *Carlo! or The Watch Dog* by John Gideon Millingen

James Warren Childe

Pencil and watercolour on wove paper mounted on card 36.4 x 25.4

INSCR: 'Charles Mathews / as / "Carlo" in "The Watch Dog".' (pen and brown ink b.c.)

INV: RW/CKA 162B

Carlo, starting back, wears a moth-eaten grey hat with a peacock feather in the brim, grey shoes with lighter grey spats, grey trousers with patches at the knees and various repairs, a dilapidated brown jacket several sizes too small, a waistcoat with horizontal bands of white, red, yellow and green, and a brown neckerchief with a paler brown pattern.

Millingen's burletta was first given at the Olympic on 16 November 1837, with Mathews as Carlo.

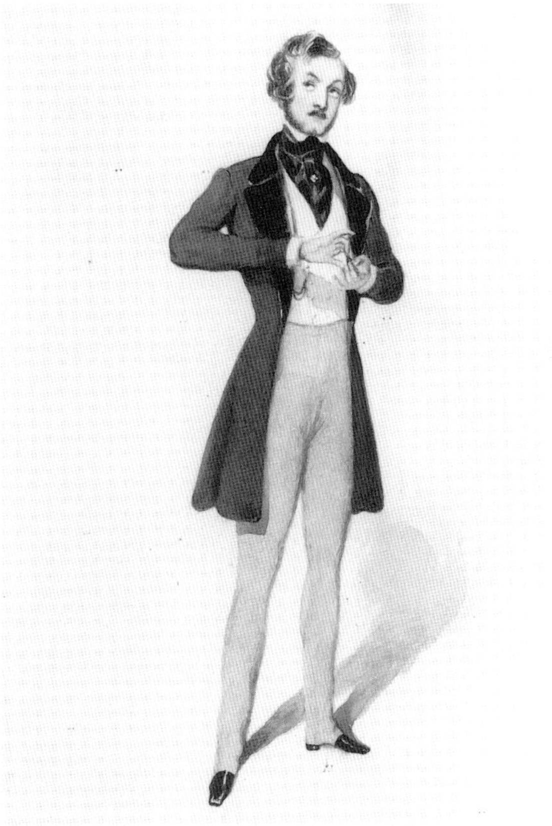

497

CHARLES JAMES MATHEWS

as Sir Charles Coldstream in *Used Up*

by Dion Boucicault and Charles James Mathews

James Warren Childe

Pencil and watercolour on wove paper
mounted on card 36.4 x 25.4
INSCR: 'Charles Mathews / as / "Sir Charles Coldstream" in "Used Up".' (pen and brown ink b.c.)
INV: RW/CKA 147A

Sir Charles sports a fair moustache and beard and considers an object held in his left hand. He wears black shoes, fawn trousers, a blue-grey jacket lined in pale blue, a double-breasted white waistcoat, and a large black cravat with a stick.

Mathews had altered the original French text of *L'homme blasé* before Boucicault adapted the play and turned it into *Used Up*. It was first given at the Haymarket on 6 February 1844, with Mathews in the part of Sir Charles Coldstream. See No. 498.

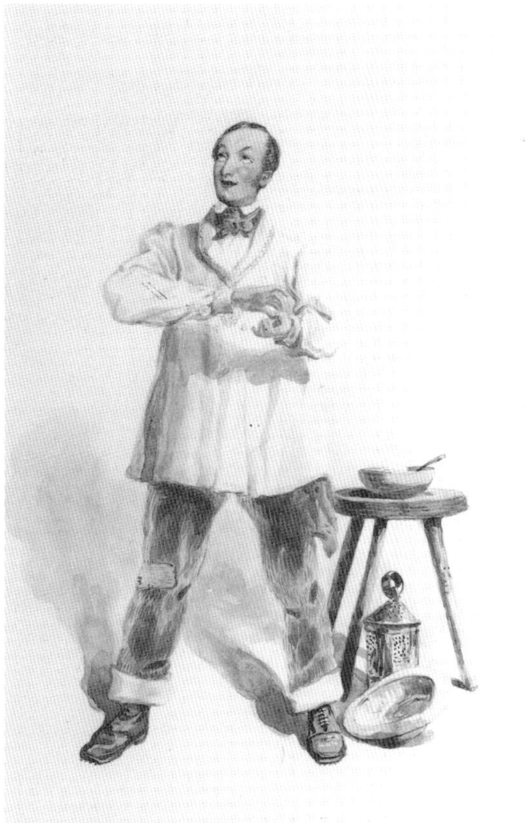

498

CHARLES JAMES MATHEWS

as Sir Charles Coldstream in *Used Up*

(2nd dress)

James Warren Childe

Pencil and watercolour on wove paper
mounted on card 36.4 x 25.4
INSCR: 'Charles Mathews / as / "Sir Charles Coldstream" in "Used Up".' (pen and brown ink b.c.)
INV: RW/CKA 147B

Mathews wears green boots, green-brown corduroy trousers with turn-ups and a patch over the right knee, a white smock and a white shirt turned down over a red neckerchief. A yellow-orange handkerchief hangs over his left hip. See No. 497.

499

NOT ILLUSTRATED

CHARLES JAMES MATHEWS

as Charles Paragon

in *Perfection or The Lady of Munster*

by Thomas Haynes Bayly

James Warren Childe

Pencil and watercolour on wove paper
mounted on card 36.4 x 25.4
INSCR: 'Charles Mathews / as / "Charles Paragon"
in "Perfection".' (pen and brown ink b.c.)
INV: RW/CKA 177A

Paragon wears white gloves, black shoes, pale grey trousers, a blue jacket, a white waistcoat embroidered in gold, green and red, a high white collar, and a full black cravat.

Bayly's farce was first performed at Drury Lane on 25 March 1830, with Richard Jones playing Paragon. Mathews first acted the role at the English Opera House on 7 September 1841.

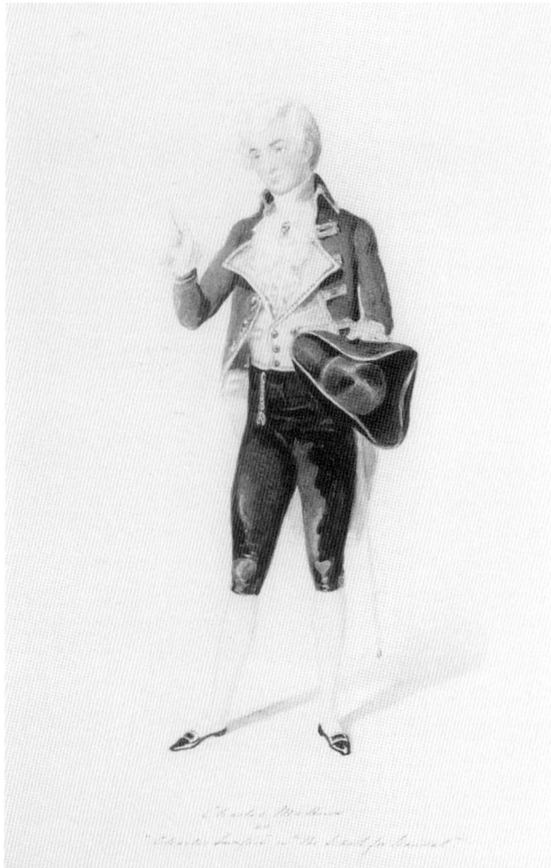

500 *Charles James Mathewsas Charles Surface*

500

CHARLES JAMES MATHEWS

as Charles Surface

in *The School for Scandal*

by Richard Brinsley Sheridan

James Warren Childe

Pencil and watercolour on wove paper
mounted on card 36.4 x 25.4
INSCR: 'Charles Mathews / as / "Charles Surface" in
"The School for Scandal".' (pen and brown ink b.c.)
INV: RW/CKA 149C

Charles raises his white-gloved right hand and in his left holds a black tricorn hat trimmed with gold. He wears black shoes, white stockings, grey breeches, a green jacket with white lining, a white double-breasted waistcoat, and a high white stock.

Sheridan's comedy was originally performed at Drury Lane on 8 May 1777, with William Smith as Charles Surface (see No. 3). Mathews first played the role for his benefit at Covent Garden on 9 June 1837, and repeated it for his wife's benefit at Drury Lane on 19 July of the following year. The couple revived the play under their own management at Covent Garden on 10 October 1839, with Mathews as Charles Surface, Mme Vestris as Lady Teazle, and William Farren as Sir Peter Teazle. See No. 501.

501

NOT ILLUSTRATED

CHARLES JAMES MATHEWS

as Charles Surface

in *The School for Scandal*

(2nd dress)

James Warren Childe

Pencil and watercolour on wove paper
mounted on card 36.4 x 25.4
INSCR: 'Charles Mathews / as / Charles Surface in
"The School for Scandal".' (pen and brown ink b.c.)
INV: RW/CKA 153C

Charles is possibly shown just after he has thrown down the screen in his brother Joseph's library, to reveal Lady Teazle (see No. 3). He holds a black hat in his white-gloved left hand and is wearing black shoes with silver buckles, white stockings, white breeches with gold buttons, a green-grey cutaway jacket with enormous lapels and collar, a silvery waistcoat with broad lapels trimmed in gold, and a very high white stock. See No. 500.

502
NOT ILLUSTRATED
CHARLES JAMES MATHEWS
as Charles Swiftly
in *One Hour or A Carnival Ball*
by Thomas Haynes Bayly

James Warren Childe

Pencil and watercolour on wove paper
mounted on card 36.4 x 25.4
INSCR: 'Charles Mathews / as / "Charles Swiftly"
in "One Hour".' (pen and brown ink b.c.)
INV: RW/CKA 150C

Charles holds a gold watch in his right hand and a white top hat in his left. He wears black shoes, white trousers, a brown jacket, a white waistcoat, and a large black cravat.

Bayly's burletta was first performed at the Olympic on 11 January 1836, with Mathews as Charles Swiftly. He introduced a 'National Air', and Mme Vestris, as Miss Dalton, sang two new songs, 'Love is the Theme of the Minstrel' and 'A Neapolitan Air'.

503
NOT ILLUSTRATED
CHARLES JAMES MATHEWS
as Charles Swiftly
in *One Hour or The Carnival Ball*
(2nd dress)

James Warren Childe

Pencil and watercolour on wove paper
mounted on card 36.4 x 25.4
INSCR: 'Charles Mathews / as / "Charles Swiftly"
in "One Hour".' (pen and brown ink b.c.)
INV: RW/CKA 150D

Mathews stands full-length in a melodramatic attitude, holding castanets. He wears black slippers with gold buckles, white stockings, green velvet breeches with gold bands down the sides, a green velvet jacket edged in gold, a red waistcoat, and a soft red cap with a red tassel over his right ear.

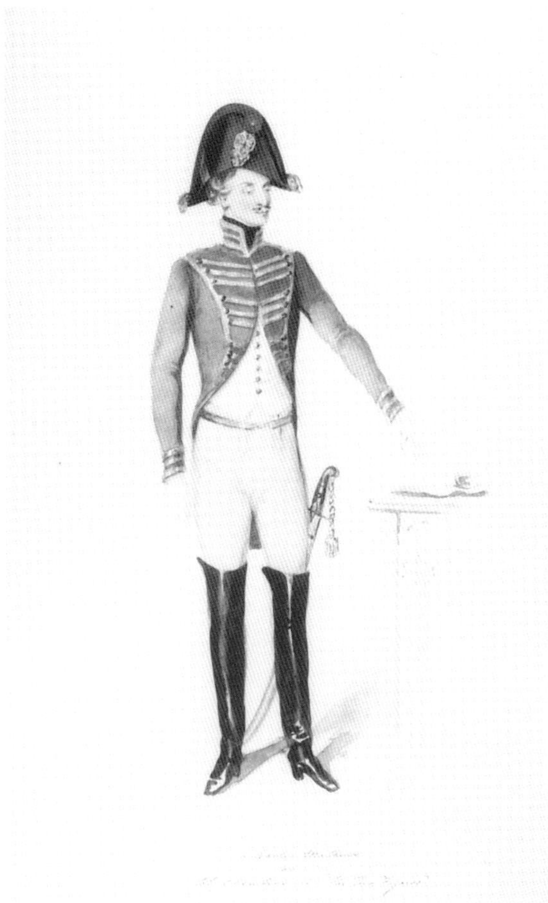

504
CHARLES JAMES MATHEWS
as Colonel Cherubino
in *The Two Figaros*
by James Robinson Planché

James Warren Childe

Pencil and watercolour on wove paper
mounted on card 36.4 x 25.4
INSCR: 'Charles Mathews / as / Col. Cherubino
in "The Two Figaros".' (pen and brown ink b.c.)
INV: RW/CKA 162A

Mathews has blue eyes, a small dark brown moustache, and curly brown hair mostly hidden by a half-moon hat. He wears white gloves, very high boots, fawn trousers, a grey-blue military cutaway jacket lined in red, a white waistcoat with gold buttons, high white collar, black stock, and a silver narrow belt below the waistcoat which supports his scabbard and sword.

Planché's burletta in two acts was first performed at the Olympic on 30 November 1836, with Mathews as Colonel Cherubino. See No. 505.

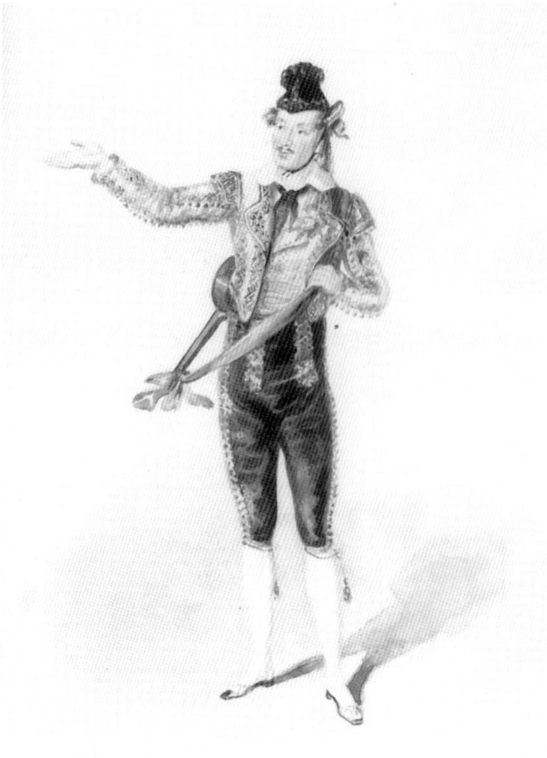

505

CHARLES JAMES MATHEWS

as Colonel Cherubino

in *The Two Figaros*

(2nd dress)

James Warren Childe

Pencil and watercolour on wove paper
mounted on card 36.4 x 25.4

INSCR: 'Charles Mathews / as / Col. Cherubino, in "The Two Figaros".' (pen and brown ink b.c.)

INV: RW/CKA 162C

Mathews has blue eyes and a small dark moustache. He wears a matador's hat with a blue bow over his left ear, black slippers with red decorations, white stockings, grey breeches with gold bands and gold tassels at knees, a broad blue cummerbund, a short pink jacket heavily embroidered with a gold criss-cross pattern, a double-breasted silk waistcoat, a white shirt with collar turned down, and a loosely-tied black neckerchief.

See also No. 504.

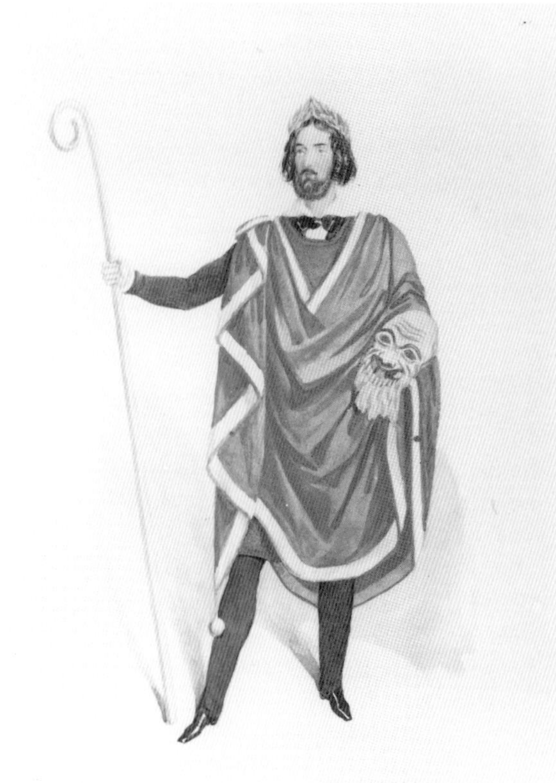

506

CHARLES JAMES MATHEWS

as the Chorus in *The Golden Fleece or Jason in Colchis and Medea in Corinth*

by James Robinson Planché

James Warren Childe

Pencil and watercolour on wove paper
mounted on card 36.4 x 25.4

INSCR: 'Charles Mathews / as / "The Chorus" in "The Golden Fleece".' (pen and brown ink b.c.)

INV: RW/CKA 147E

Mathews wears black shoes, purple trousers, and a red mantle edged in white.

Planché's 'New Grand Classical Extravaganza in Two Parts' was first performed at the Haymarket on 24 March 1845. It was an amusing spoof on classical drama and the fashion for historical reconstruction. The principals were Priscilla Horton as Jason and Mme Vestris as Medea. Mathews played 'THE WHOLE BODY OF THE CHORUS rendering at least 59 male voices perfectly unnecessary'. The scenery was by G. Morris, but what exactly he provided is unclear, as:

> The Stage, which has been constructed after the approved fashion of the revived Greek Theatre, will be partially raised, but the prices of admission remain

exactly as before. It is also requisite to observe that a frequent change of scene being contrary to the usage of the ancient Greek Drama, several of the most SPLENDID PICTORIAL EFFECTS will be left entirely to the imagination of the audience.

507

NOT ILLUSTRATED

CHARLES JAMES MATHEWS

as Dapperwit in *The Rape of the Lock*

by John Oxenford

James Warren Childe

Pencil and watercolour on wove paper mounted on card 36.4 x 25.4

INSCR: 'Charles Mathews / as / "Dapperwit" in "The Rape of the Lock".' (pen and brown ink b.c.)

INV: RW/CKA 148A

Mathews wears black shoes with silver buckles, white stockings, grey breeches, a black velvet coat with elaborate horizontal bands of gold, lace cuffs, a gold waistcoat showing at the thighs, a white stock with full lace frills, and a black bow at the neck.

Oxenford's burletta in two acts, 'Founded on Alexander Pope's celebrated poem', was first performed at the Olympic on Easter Monday, 27 March 1837, with Mathews as Dapperwit, 'a poet and Lord Moonbeam's Shadow'.

508

NOT ILLUSTRATED

CHARLES JAMES MATHEWS

as Dashwood in *Know Your Own Mind*

by Arthur Murphy

James Warren Childe

Pencil and watercolour on wove paper mounted on card 36.4 x 25.4

INSCR: 'Charles Mathews / as / "Dashwood" in "Know your own Mind".' (pen and brown ink b.c.)

INV: RW/CKA 145C

Mathews wears white gloves, grey shoes with gold buckles, cream socks, white breeches with a high waist, a brown cutaway jacket with very broad lapels, lined in white, a white waistcoat with broad collar, white shirt, and high white stock.

Murphy's comedy, based on *L'Irrésolu* by Philippe Néricault, *dit* Destouches, was first performed at Covent Garden with Charles Lee Lewes as Dashwood. Mathews first appeared in the play at the same theatre in the same role on 23 April 1840.

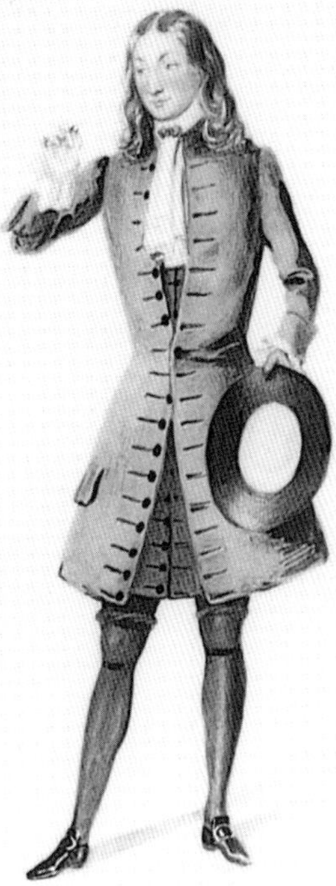

509

CHARLES JAMES MATHEWS

as David Brown in *Court Favour*

by James Robinson Planché

James Warren Childe

Pencil and watercolour on wove paper mounted on card 36.4 x 25.4

INSCR: 'Charles Mathews / as / "David Brown" in "Court Favour".' (pen and brown ink b.c.)

INV: RW/CKA 158F

Mathews wears black shoes with silver buckles and red heels, black stockings rolled over black breeches, black garters, a green coat, and a long grey waistcoat.

Planché's burletta was first performed at the Olympic on 29 September 1836, with Mathews as David Brown and Mme Vestris as Lucy Morton.

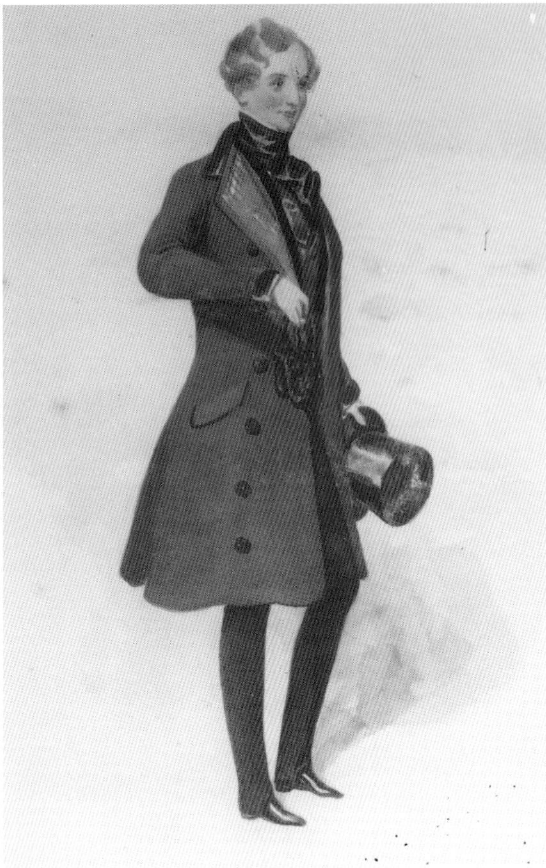

510
CHARLES JAMES MATHEWS
as Dazzle in *London Assurance*
by Dion Boucicault

James Warren Childe

Pencil and watercolour on wove paper
mounted on card 36.4 x 25.4
INSCR: 'Charles Mathews / as / "Dazzle" in
"London Assurance".' (pen and brown in b.c.)
INV: RW/CKA 147C

Mathews wears black shoes, black trousers, a long brown coat, a brown jacket, and a black cravat.

Boucicault's comedy was first performed at Covent Garden on 4 March 1841, with Mathews as Dazzle. See No. 511.

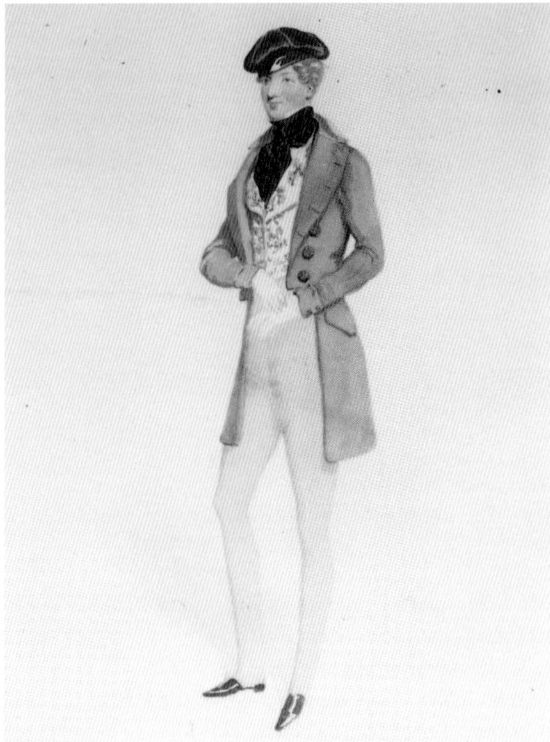

511
CHARLES JAMES MATHEWS
as Dazzle in *London Assurance*
(2nd dress)

James Warren Childe

Pencil and watercolour on wove paper
mounted on card 36.4 x 25.4
INSCR: 'Charles Mathews / as / "Dazzle" in
"London Assurance".' (pen and brown ink b.c.)
INV: RW/CKA 147D

Mathews wears a blue cap with black peak, white gloves, black shoes, grey trousers, a pale blue cutaway jacket, a white waistcoat embroidered in a purple floral design, a high white collar, and a large black cravat. See No. 510.

512
CHARLES JAMES MATHEWS
as the Chevalier Duval in *The Ladder of Love*
by Thomas Haynes Bayly

James Warren Childe

Pencil and watercolour on wove paper
mounted on card 36.4 x 25.4
INSCR: 'Charles Mathews / as / "The Chevalier" in
"The Ladder of Love".' (pen and brown ink b.c.)
INV: RW/CKA 150F

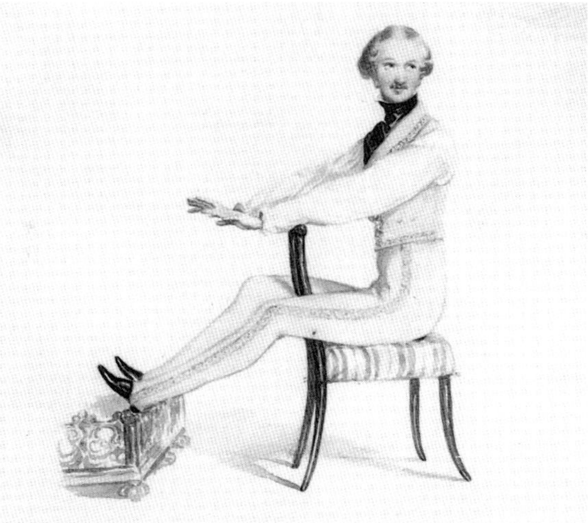

512 *Charles James Mathews as Chevalier Duval*

Mathews wears a black tricorn hat edged with gold braid, black slippers with gold buckles, white stockings, blue breeches, a blue jacket edged in gold, lace cuffs, and a white collarless waistcoat embroidered in gold and red.

Bayly's burletta was first performed at the Olympic on 16 December 1837 with Mathews as the Chevalier Duval and Mme Vestris as Suzanne.

513
NOT ILLUSTRATED
CHARLES JAMES MATHEWS
as Ernest Fitz-Flighty
in *I Will Have an Uncle*
by Charles Dance

James Warren Childe

Pencil and watercolour on wove paper
mounted on card 36.4 x 25.4
INSCR: 'Charles Mathews / as / "Ernest Fitzflighty" in "I will have an Uncle".' (pen and brown ink b.c.)
INV: RW/CKA 177B (as Ernest Fitzflighty)

Mathews has curly fair hair. He wears white gloves, black shoes, grey trousers, a blue cutaway jacket with large gold buttons down the front, a white double-breasted waistcoat, a high white collar, and an elaborate black cravat.

Dance's comic burletta was first performed at the Olympic on 29 September 1836, the first night of the season, with Mathews as Ernest Fitz-Flighty. This performance appears to have been its only one, despite the attraction of William Oxberry's first appearance at the Olympic, as Fortunatus Hunter.

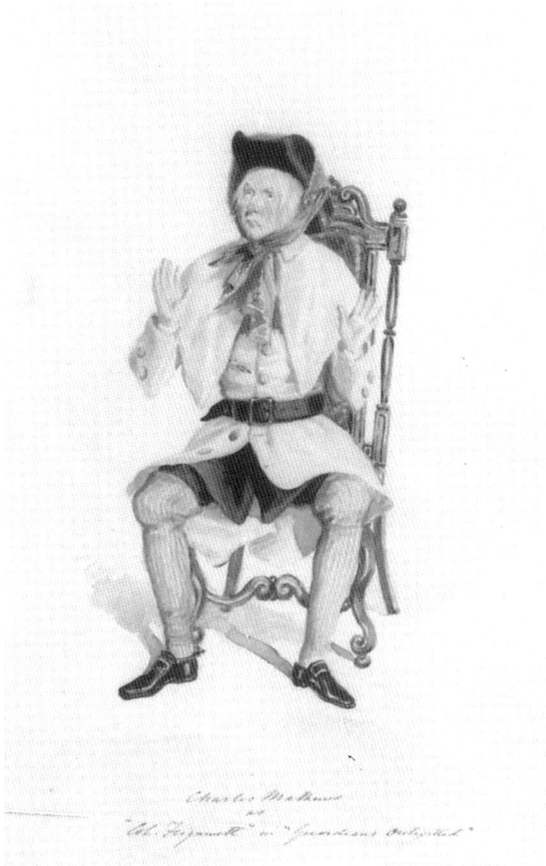

514
CHARLES JAMES MATHEWS
as Colonel Feignwell in *A Bold Stroke for a Wife*
by Susannah Centlivre

James Warren Childe

Pencil and watercolour on wove paper
mounted on card 36.4 x 25.4
INSCR: 'Charles Mathews / as / "Col. Feignwell" in "Guardians Outwitted".' (pen and brown ink b.c.)
INV: RW/CKA 151A

Mathews, seated to front in a 19th-century version of a 17th-century chair, wears black shoes with gold buckles, blue and white striped stockings over black breeches, garters below the knee, a white coat with silver buttons, a broad black belt with gold buckle, a black jacket, a pink neckerchief, and a blue neckerchief tied over a black hat and under his chin.

Mrs Centlivre's comedy was originally played at Lincoln's Inn Fields Theatre on 3 February 1718. See Nos. 515–18.

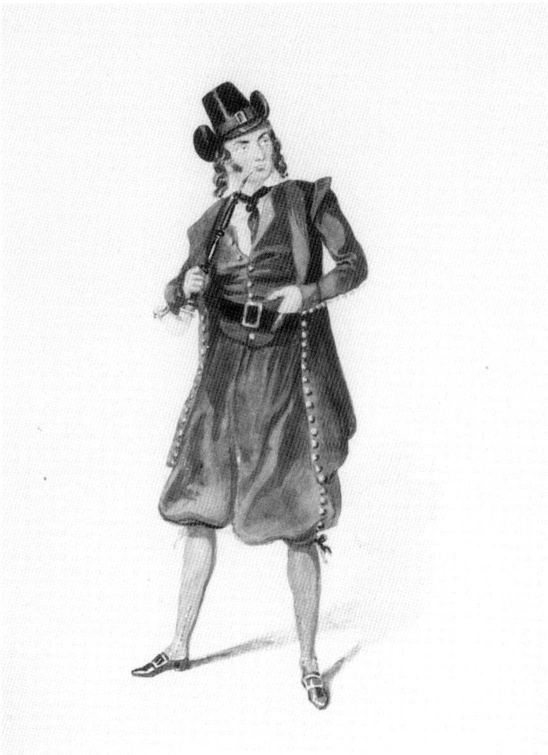

515
CHARLES JAMES MATHEWS
as Colonel Feignwell
in *A Bold Stroke for a Wife*
(2nd dress)

James Warren Childe

Pencil and watercolour on wove paper
mounted on card 36.4 x 25.4
INSCR: 'Charles Mathews/ as / "Col. Feignwell" in "Guardians Outwitted".' (pen and brown ink b.c.)
INV: RW/CKA 151B

Mathews wears a tall black hat with the brim turned up at the sides, shoes with gold buckles and red stockings, floppy brown breeches with bows at the knee, a long brown jacket, a brown waistcoat with gold buttons, a broad black belt with gold buckle, a white shirt with open neck, and a green neckerchief loosely tied. See No. 514.

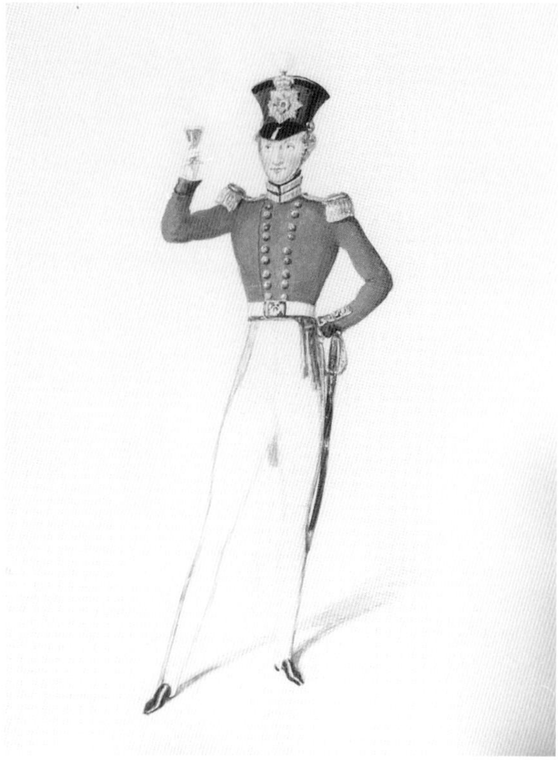

516
CHARLES JAMES MATHEWS
as Colonel Feignwell
in *A Bold Stroke for a Wife*
(3rd dress)

James Warren Childe

Pencil and watercolour on wove paper
mounted on card 36.4 x 25.4
INSCR: 'Charles Mathews / as / "Col. Feignwell" in "Guardians Outwitted".' (pen and brown ink b.c.)
INV: RW/CKA 151C

Mathews wears black shoes, white military trousers with gold braid down the side, a red military cutaway jacket, black cuffs with gold braiding, gold epaulets, and black collar with gold decoration, a white belt with a gold buckle, a red sash below belt, and a black shako on his head. See No. 514.

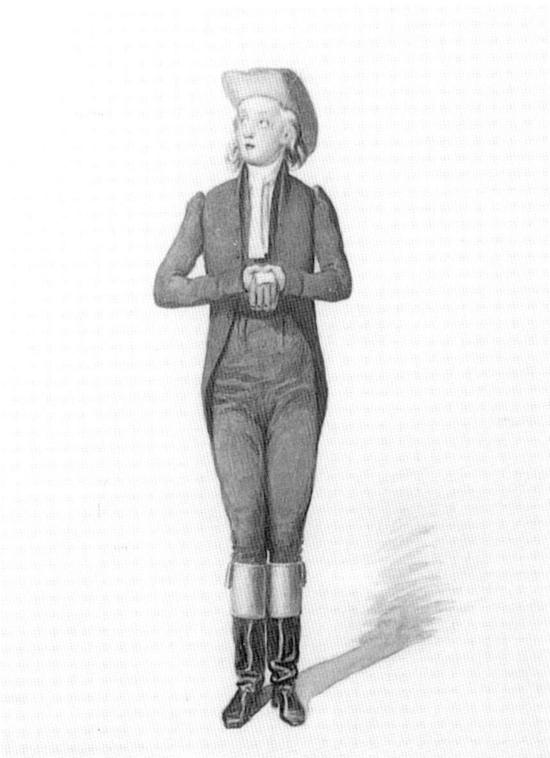

517
CHARLES JAMES MATHEWS
as Colonel Feignwell
in *A Bold Stroke for a Wife*
(4th dress)

James Warren Childe

Pencil and watercolour on wove paper
mounted on card 36.4 x 25.4
INSCR: 'Charles Mathews / as / "Col. Feignwell" in "Guardians Outwitted".' (pen and brown ink b.c.)
INV: RW/CKA 151D

Mathews has long, fair curly hair under a cap with the brim turned up at the sides. He wears tall black boots with brown tops and bands, brown trousers, a brown jerkin, a brown jacket with padded shoulders and a high collar, and a high white stock. See No. 514.

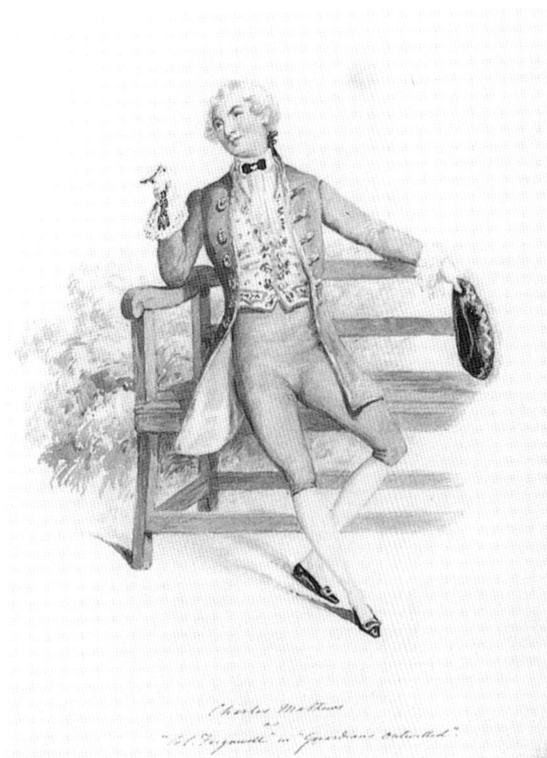

518
CHARLES JAMES MATHEWS
as Colonel Feignwell
in *A Bold Stroke for a Wife*
(5th dress)

James Warren Childe

Pencil and watercolour on wove paper
mounted on card 36.4 x 25.4
INSCR: 'Charles Mathews / as / "Col. Feignwell" in "Guardians Outwitted".' (pen and brown ink b.c.)
INV: RW/CKA 151E

Mathews, seated on a pale blue garden seat, holds a black hat with gold braid and white feathers and wears white gloves, black slippers with silver buckles, white stockings, blue breeches, a blue jacket lined in white and edged in gold, a white waistcoat edged in blue and embroidered in green, red and yellow, and a high white stock with black bow. See No. 514.

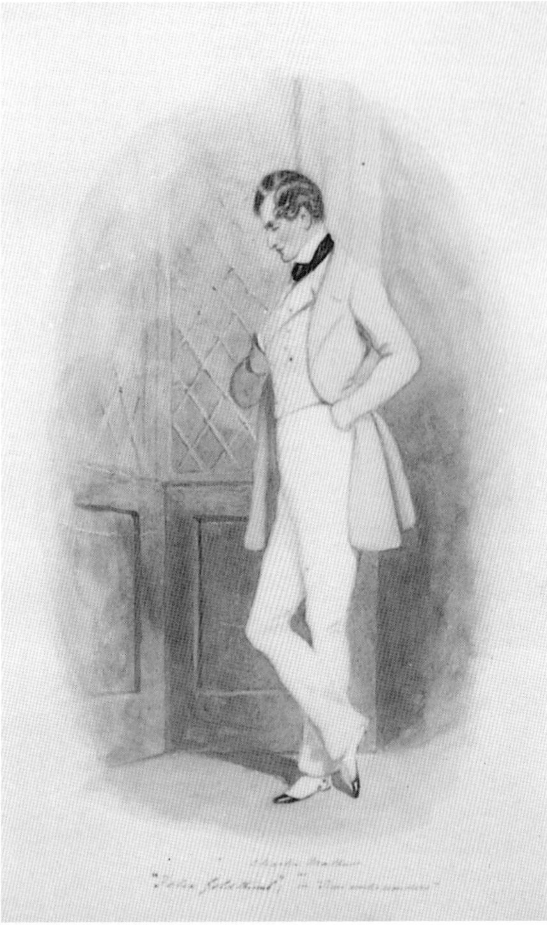

519
CHARLES JAMES MATHEWS
as Felix Goldthumb
in *Time Works Wonders*
by Douglas William Jerrold

James Warren Childe

Pencil and watercolour on wove paper
mounted on card 36.4 x 25.4
INSCR: 'Charles Mathews / as / "Felix Goldthumb", in "Time works wonders".' (pen and brown ink b.c.)
INV: RW/CKA 157D

Mathews wears black shoes with white spats, white trousers, a pale brown jacket, a cream waistcoat with two rows of pearl buttons, white collar and black cravat.

Jerrold's comedy was first performed at the Haymarket on 26 April 1845, with Mathews as Felix Goldthumb, William Farren as his father Goldthumb, and Mme Vestris as Miss Bessy Tulip. See No. 520.

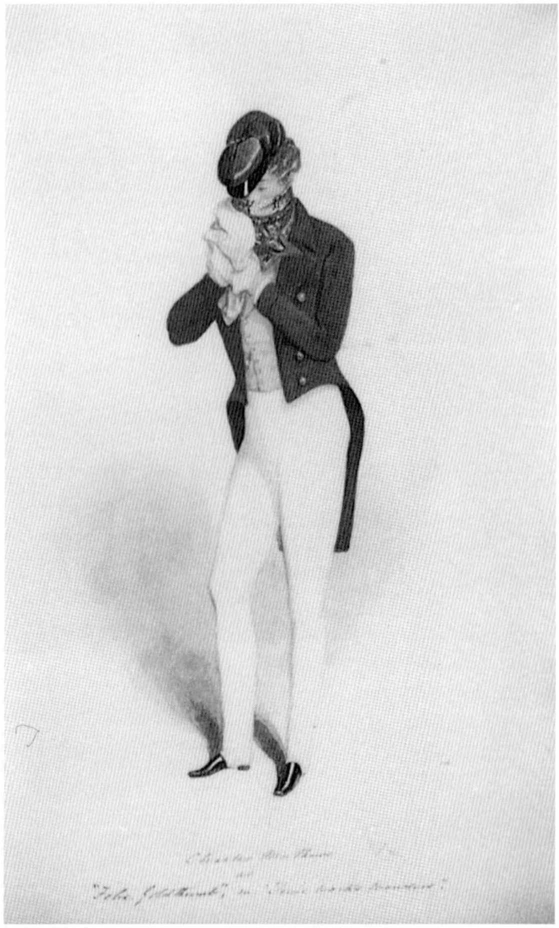

520
CHARLES JAMES MATHEWS
as Felix Goldthumb
in *Time Works Wonders*
(2nd dress)

James Warren Childe

Pencil and watercolour on wove paper
mounted on card 36.4 x 25.4
INSCR: 'Charles Mathews / as / "Felix Goldthumb", in "Time Works Wonders".' (pen and brown ink b.c.)
INV: RW/CKA 157E

Mathews's face is hidden in a red neckerchief decorated in black and white and a white cloth held up with both hands. He wears a grey cap, black shoes, white trousers, a brown cutaway jacket with gold buttons, and a pale brown waistcoat with a double row of buttons. See No. 519.

521

NOT ILLUSTRATED

CHARLES JAMES MATHEWS

as Colonel Ferrier in *The Barrack Room*

by Thomas Haynes Bayly

James Warren Childe

Pencil and watercolour on wove paper
mounted on card 36.4 x 25.4
INSCR: 'Charles Mathews / as / "Col. Ferrier", in
"The Barrack Room".' (pen and brown ink b.c.)
INV: RW/CKA 158D

Mathews holds a red shako with four gold bands round the top and wears white gloves, black shoes, red trousers, a white military tunic, and a short white cloak edged and lined in white fur.

Bayly's burletta was first performed at the Olympic on 7 November 1826, with James Vining in the part of Colonel Ferrier and James Bland as Bernard. Mme Vestris played Clarisse de Cruzac. The piece was performed 59 times during the season, the last occasion being 23 May 1837.

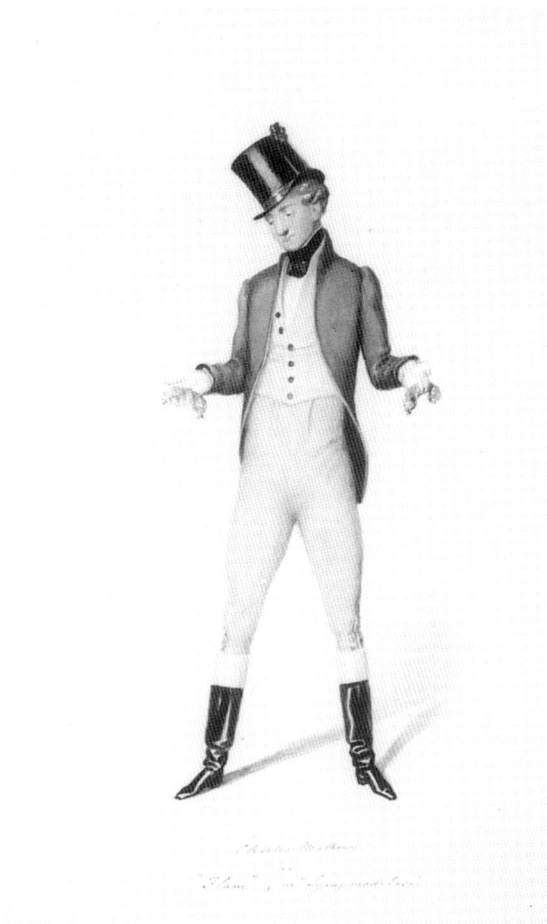

522

CHARLES JAMES MATHEWS

as Flam in *Lying Made Easy*

by an Unknown Author

James Warren Childe

Pencil and watercolour on wove paper
mounted on card 36.4 x 25.4
INSCR: 'Charles Mathews / as / "Flam", in
"Lying made Easy".' (pen and brown ink b.c.)
INV: RW/CKA 171

Mathews holds red and green purses and white gloves and wears high black boots with white tops, brown breeches, a grey cutaway jacket with red edging and padded shoulders, a cream waistcoat, a white shirt with high collar, and a black cravat.

This anonymous comic opera, with music by William Hawes, was first performed at the English Opera House on 1 August 1826.

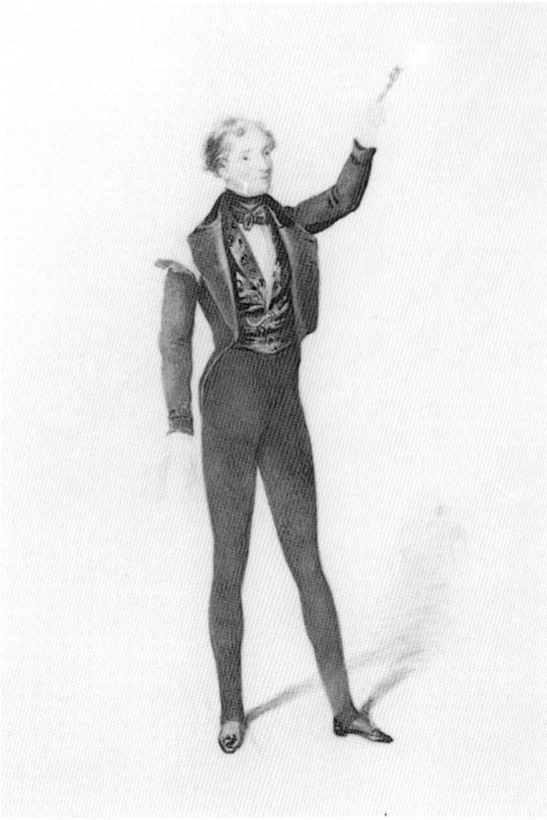

524
NOT ILLUSTRATED
CHARLES JAMES MATHEWS
as Frank Saunders
in *Alive and Merry*
by Charles Dance

James Warren Childe

Pencil and watercolour on wove paper
mounted on card 36.4 x 25.4
INSCR: 'Charles Mathews / as / "Frank Saunders" in "Alive and Merry".' (pen and brown ink b.c.)
INV: RW/CKA 160B (in 160A frame)

Mathews wears a powdered wig with curls over his ears and a black bow at the back, black shoes with gold buckles, white stockings, blue garters below the knee, white stockings over grey velvet breeches, a collarless pink jacket, and a highly embroidered pink waistcoat with buttons up the front.

Dance's farce was first performed at Covent Garden on 30 September 1839, with Mathews in the part of Frank Saunders. That night was the first of Mathews and Mme Vestris's management at Covent Garden, and the farce followed a performance of *Love's Labour's Lost.*

523
CHARLES JAMES MATHEWS
as Frank Poppleton
in *Too Late for Dinner*
by Richard Jones

James Warren Childe

Pencil and watercolour on wove paper
mounted on card 36.4 x 25.4
INSCR: 'Charles Mathews / as / "Frank Poppleton" in "Too Late for Dinner".' (pen and brown ink b.c.)
INV: RW/CKA 144A

Mathews wears white gloves, black slippers with black rosettes, grey stockings, black and grey trousers, a grey cutaway jacket with broad lapels and a black velvet collar, a grey waistcoat decorated in black, a high white collar, and a black cravat.

Jones's farce was first performed at Covent Garden on 22 February 1820, with the author as Frank Poppleton. The distinguished cast also included Liston as Mr Nicholas Twill, Blanchard as Mr Pincroft, Emery as Robert Rafte, Mrs Davenport as Mrs Thompson, and Maria Foote as Emma Somerton. Mathews first appeared in the piece, as Frank Poppleton, at the Olympic on 17 December 1835.

525
CHARLES JAMES MATHEWS
as Frederick Stanley
in *Why Did You Die?*
by Charles James Mathews

James Warren Childe

Pencil and watercolour on wove paper
mounted on card 36.4 x 25.4
INSCR: 'Charles Mathews / as / "Frederick Stanley" in "Why did you die?".' (pen and brown ink b.c.)
INV: RW/CKA 150E

Mathews wears black shoes, silver trousers, a white waistcoat decorated with silver embroidery around the lapel and hem, a high white collar, and a black cravat.

Mathews's burletta was first staged at the Olympic on 20 November 1837, with the author as Frederick Stanley. The piece was given 30 times during that season, with the last performance taking place on 23 December 1837.

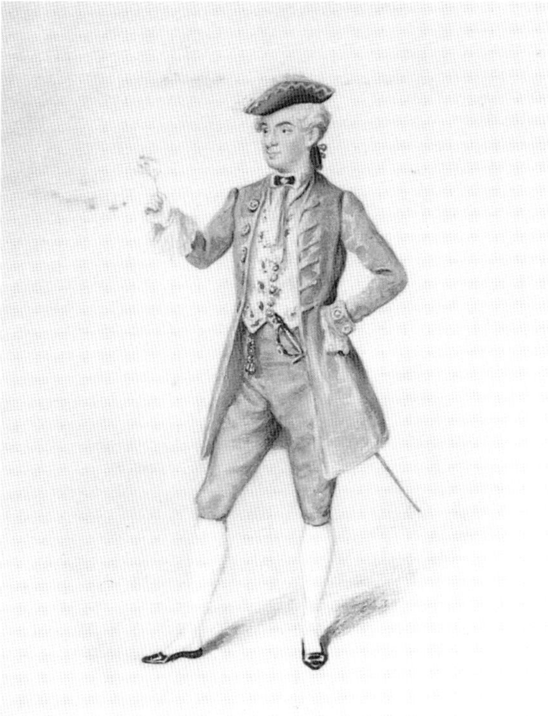

525 *Charles James Mathews as Frederick Stanley*

527

NOT ILLUSTRATED

CHARLES JAMES MATHEWS

as Giles Fairland

in *Who's Your Friend or The Queensbury Fête*

by James Robinson Planché

James Warren Childe

Pencil and watercolour on wove paper
mounted on card 36.4 x 25.4
INSCR: 'Charles Mathews / as / "Giles Fairland" in
"Who's your Friend?".' (pen and brown ink b.c.)
INV: RW/CKA 145D

Mathews wears a yellowish hat with the brim pushed back at the sides, black shoes with silver buckles, stockings with white and silver horizontal bands, brown breeches, a blue collarless coat with turned-back cuffs and silver buttons, a red waistcoat with white and creamy-brown diagonal lines, a white turned-down collar, and a blue neckerchief.

Planché's farce was first performed at the Haymarket on 22 August 1843, with Mathews in the part of Giles Fairland and Mme Vestris as the Countess of Rosedale. See No. 528.

526

NOT ILLUSTRATED

CHARLES JAMES MATHEWS

as George Rattleton

in *The Humpback'd Lover*

by Charles James Mathews

James Warren Childe

Pencil and watercolour on wove paper
mounted on card 36.4 x 25.4
INSCR: 'Charles Mathews / as / "Mr Rattleton" in
"The Humpbacked Lover".' (pen and brown ink b.c.)
INV: RW/CKA 150B

Mathews, with a hump on his back, wears white gloves, grey trousers with decoration down the sides, a fawn coat with flaps over hump and shoulders and a yellow velvet collar, a high white collar, and a black cravat.

Mathews's farce was first performed at the Olympic on 7 December 1835, with the author as George Rattleton. It was billed as his first appearance in public. There were 15 performances to 26 December 1835.

528

NOT ILLUSTRATED

CHARLES JAMES MATHEWS

as Giles Fairland

in *Who's Your Friend?*

(2nd dress)

James Warren Childe

Pencil and watercolour on wove paper
mounted on card 36.4 x 25.4
INSCR: 'Charles Mathews / as / "Giles Fairland" in
"Who's your Friend?".' (pen and brown ink b.c.)
INV: RW/CKA 145E

Mathews holds a grey tricorn hat with white plumes around the edges and wears black shoes with silver buckles, stockings with silver and white horizontal bands, grey breeches, a grey collarless coat edged in gold braid, and a long white waistcoat with vertical lines of gold braid down the front, open at the top to reveal a high white stock with frills. See No. 527.

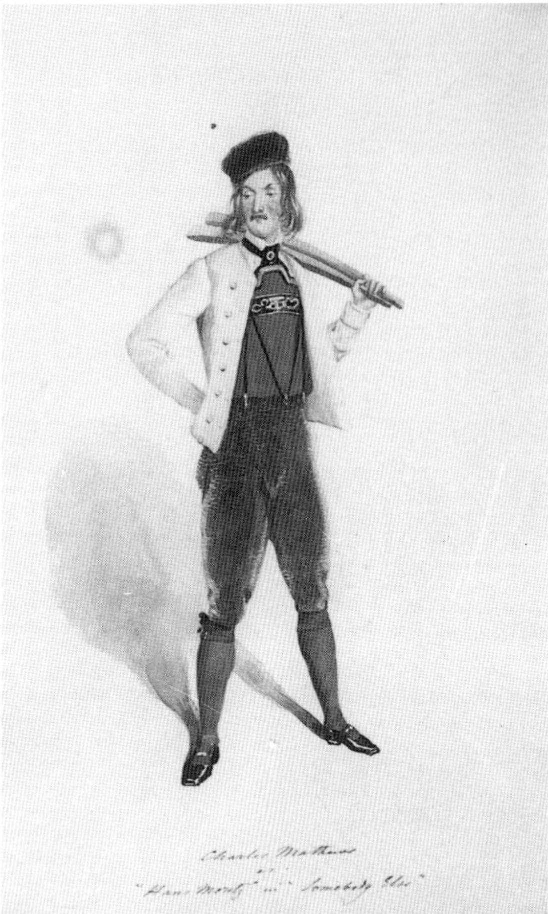

529

CHARLES JAMES MATHEWS

as Hans Moritz

in *Somebody Else*

by James Robinson Planché

James Warren Childe

Pencil and watercolour on wove paper
mounted on card 36.4 x 25.4
INSCR: 'Charles Mathews / as / "Hans Moritz" in
"Somebody Else".' (pen and brown ink b.c.)
INV: RW/CKA 144B

Mathews has long fair hair under a brown hat cocked over his right eye and wears black shoes with red panels, brown stockings with red garters, blue breeches with black braces, a white collarless jacket with buttons down the front, a red jerkin edged with a gold band at the top, and a high white collar with a black ribbon round a jewel at the front.

Planché's farce was first performed at the Haymarket on 4 December 1844, with Mathews as Hans Moritz and Mme Vestris as Minnie. See Nos. 530 and 531.

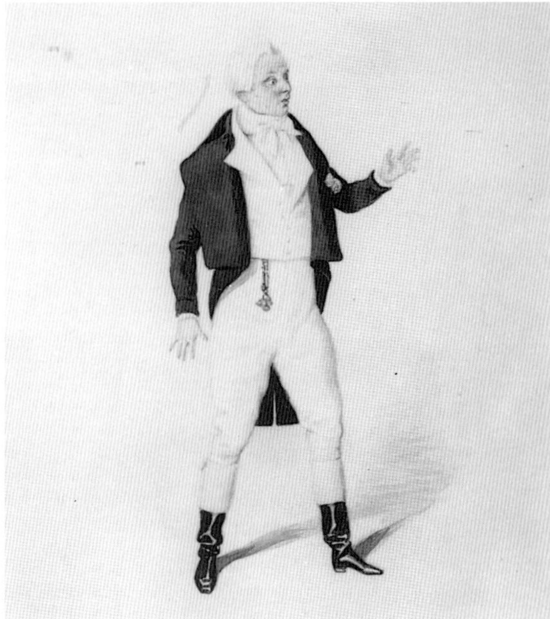

532 *Charles James Mathews as Harry Ringdove*

530

NOT ILLUSTRATED

CHARLES JAMES MATHEWS

as Hans Moritz in *Somebody Else* (2nd dress)

James Warren Childe

Pencil and watercolour on wove paper
mounted on card 36.4 x 25.4
INSCR: 'Charles Mathews / as / "Hans Moritz" in
"Somebody Else".' (pen and brown ink b.c.)
INV: RW/CKA 144C

Mathews wears a wide-brimmed grey hat and holds a gold object and a pink handkerchief. His costume is similar to No. 529, with a long grey collarless coat lined in red.

531

NOT ILLUSTRATED

CHARLES JAMES MATHEWS

as Hans Moritz in *Somebody Else* (3rd dress)

James Warren Childe

Pencil and watercolour on wove paper
mounted on card 36.4 x 25.4
INSCR: 'Charles Mathews / as / "Hans Moritz" in
"Somebody Else".' (pen and brown ink b.c.)
INV: RW/CKA 144D

Mathews wears the same costume as in No. 529, without the coat. The red tunic is sleeveless with a gold band around edge.

532

CHARLES JAMES MATHEWS

as Harry Ringdove in *The Ringdoves*

by Charles James Mathews

James Warren Childe

Pencil and watercolour on wove paper
mounted on card 36.4 x 25.4
INSCR: 'Charles Mathews / as / "Sir Harry Ringdove", in "The Ringdoves".' (pen and brown ink b.c.)
INV: RW/CKA 166 (in 165 frame; as Sir Harry Ringdove)

Mathews wears black shoes with high white tops, white trousers, a green cutaway jacket with enormous lapels from neck to waist, a white double-breasted waistcoat with broad lapels, and a high white stock tied in a bow.

Mathews's burletta was originally performed at the Olympic on 11 December 1837, with the author in the part of Harry Ringdove. There were 74 performances during the season, the last on 7 May 1838. See No. 533.

533

NOT ILLUSTRATED

CHARLES JAMES MATHEWS

as Harry Ringdove in *The Ringdoves*

(2nd dress)

James Warren Childe

Pencil and watercolour on wove paper
mounted on card 36.4 x 25.4
INSCR: 'Charles Mathews / as / "Harry Ringdove" in "The Ringdoves".' (pen and brown ink b.c.)
INV: RW/CKA 175A (as Sir Harry Ringdove)

Mathews wears black shoes, white spats, grey trousers with a high waist, a brown cutaway jacket, a white waistcoat with gold buttons, a high white collar and a dark stock. See No. 532.

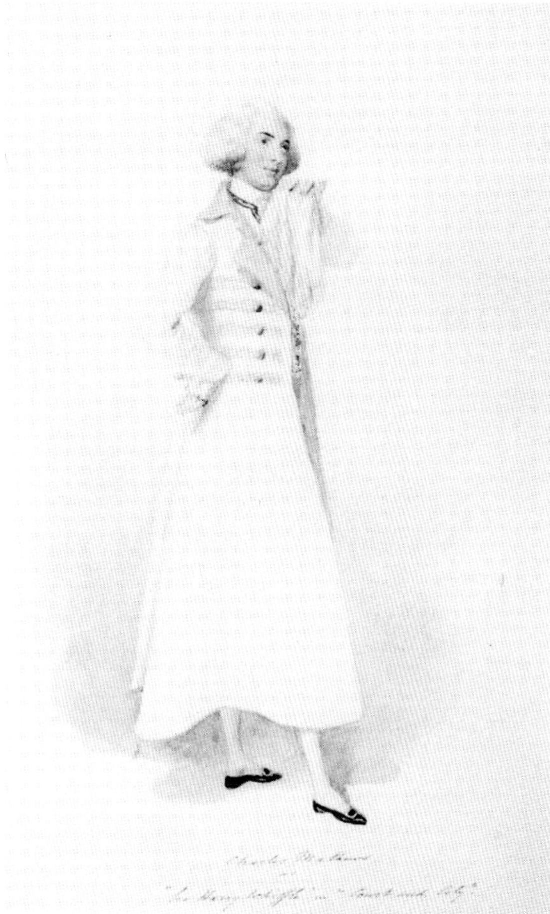

534

CHARLES JAMES MATHEWS

as Sir Harry Whiffle in *Court and City*

by Richard Brinsley Peake

James Warren Childe

Pencil and watercolour on wove paper
mounted on card 36.4 x 25.4
INSCR: 'Charles Mathews / as / "Sir Harry Whiffle" in "Court and City".' (pen and brown ink b.c.)
INV: RW/CKA 153A

Mathews holds a large white handkerchief with an elaborate lace border and wears black shoes with silver buckles, white stockings, a long white day-coat lined in pink with a broad pink collar and lapels, blue breeches just visible at the top, a white waistcoat, and a high white stock.

Peake's comedy, based on Steele's *The Tender Husband* and Mrs Sheridan's *The Discovery*, was first performed at Covent Garden on 17 November 1841, with Mathews as Sir Harry Whiffle and Mme Vestris as Lady Whiffle. See No. 535.

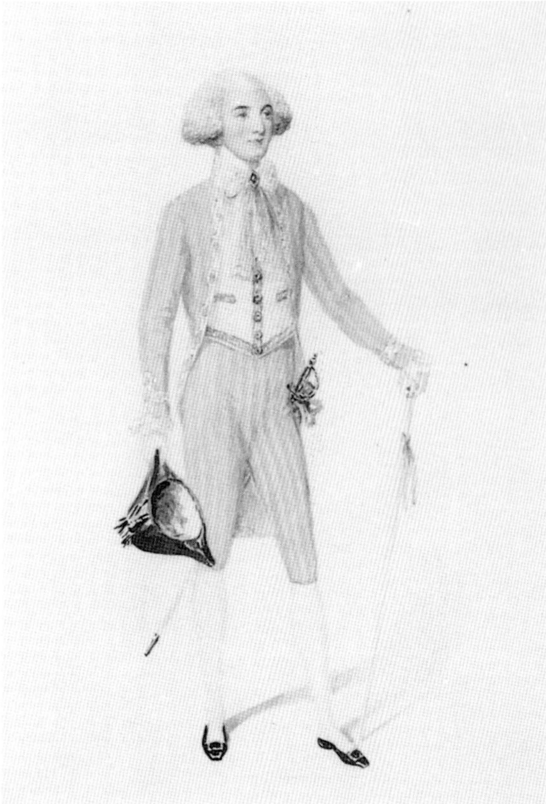

535

CHARLES JAMES MATHEWS

as Sir Harry Whiffle in *Court and City*

(2nd dress)

James Warren Childe

Pencil and watercolour on wove paper
mounted on card 36.4 x 25.4
INSCR: 'Charles Mathews / as / "Sir Harry Whiffle" in "Court and City".' (pen and brown ink b.c.)
INV: RW/CKA 153B

Mathews holds a black tricorn hat with a cockade and white gloves; he wears black shoes with silver buckles, white stockings, blue trousers with paler blue vertical lines, a jacket of the same cloth edged in a band of white embroidered in pink and blue, a white waistcoat edged in a band of green embroidery between red bands, and a high white stock. See No. 534.

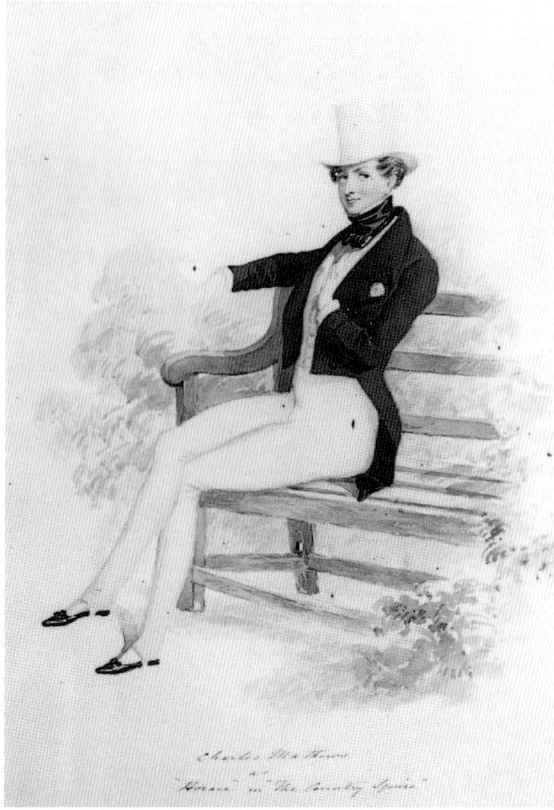

536

CHARLES JAMES MATHEWS

as Horace in *The Country Squire or Two Days at the Hall*

by Charles Dance

James Warren Childe

Pencil and watercolour on wove paper
mounted on card 36.4 x 25.4
INSCR: 'Charles Mathews / as / "Horace" in "The Country Squire".' (pen and brown ink b.c.)
INV: RW/CKA 159A (framed as 159B)

Mathews wears black shoes with black rosettes, white socks, white trousers, a blue cutaway jacket with broad lapels and high collar, a white waistcoat, a high white collar, and a black cravat.

Dance's comedy was first performed at Covent Garden on 19 January 1837, with J. Webster as Horace Aurelius Selwood. Mathews played the part for the first time on 29 September 1837, the first night of the Olympic season. See Nos. 537–39.

537

NOT ILLUSTRATED

CHARLES JAMES MATHEWS

as Horace in *The Country Squire*

(2nd dress)

James Warren Childe

Pencil and watercolour on wove paper
mounted on card 36.4 x 25.4
INSCR: 'Charles Mathews / as / "Horace" in
"The Country Squire".' (pen and brown ink b.c.)
INV: RW/CKA 175B

Mathews, with whiskers and a small moustache, has a black top hat with a wavy brim; he holds a black stick and wears black shoes, grey trousers, a green velvet double-breasted coat, and a high black cravat. See No. 536.

538

NOT ILLUSTRATED

CHARLES JAMES MATHEWS

as Horace in *The Country Squire*

(3rd dress)

James Warren Childe

Pencil and watercolour on wove paper
mounted on card 36.4 x 25.4
INSCR: 'Charles Mathews / as / "Horace" in
"The Country Squire".' (pen and brown ink b.c.)
INV: RW/CKA 175C

Mathews has a black top hat and white gloves, and wears black shoes, white trousers, a brown cutaway jacket with high collar and broad lapels, a white waistcoat edged in gold, a high white collar, and a dark cravat. See No. 536.

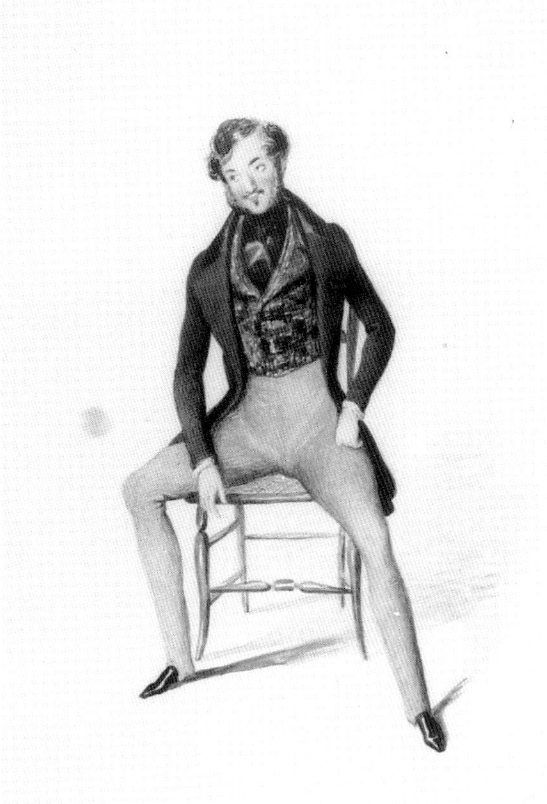

539

CHARLES JAMES MATHEWS

as Horace in *The Country Squire*

(4th dress)

James Warren Childe

Pencil and watercolour on wove paper
mounted on card 36.4 x 25.4
INSCR: 'Charles Mathews / as / "Horace" in
"The Country Squire".' (pen and brown ink b.c.)
INV: RW/CKA 176C

Mathews has a little brown moustache, hair on his lower lip, and sideburns. He wears black shoes, brownish trousers, a grey jacket, a blue silk waistcoat heavily embroidered in gold, brown and red, and a large black cravat. See No. 536.

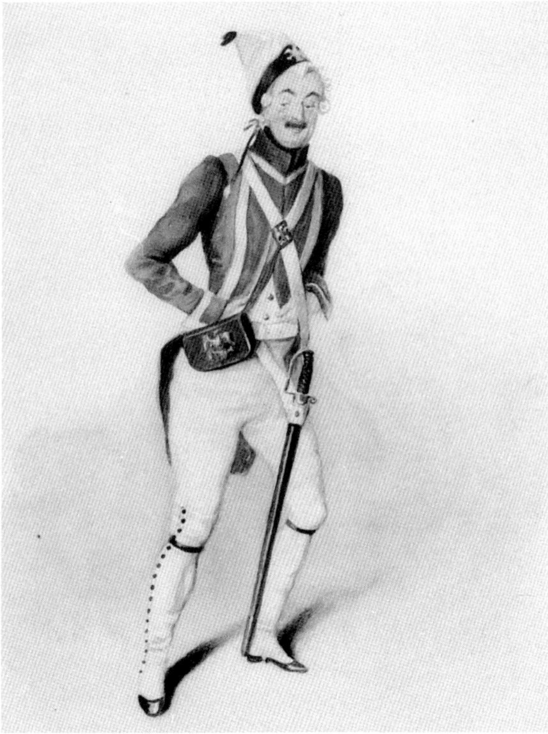

540
CHARLES JAMES MATHEWS
as Illegitimate Drama in *The Drama's Levee or A Peep at the Past, Suggested by a Dream of the Future*
by James Robinson Planché

James Warren Childe

Pencil and watercolour on wove paper
mounted on card 36.4 x 25.4
INSCR: 'Charles Mathews / as / "Melodrama"
in "The Drama's Levee".'
(pen and brown ink b.c.)
INV: RW/CKA 176B

Mathews has a black mask on the upper part of his face and a pointed clown's hat. He wears a clown body-stocking from ankle to wrist. Horizontal and vertical lines divide the costume into squares, and diagonal lines make triangles of dark green, yellow, pale blue and red. He also wears a black hat with tall crown and turned-back brim edged in gold and red plume, pointed black shoes, black tights, green hose slashed with red and edged in gold over the thigh, a green doublet, slashed at the chest, with the arms in red, and a white ruff.

Planché's review was first performed at the Olympic on 16 April 1838, with James Vining as Legitimate Drama and Mathews as Illegitimate Drama. The cast also included Mrs Orger as The Drama, Mme Vestris as Praise, and Bland as Censure.

This piece, which was acted 40 times during the season to 31 May 1838, was designed as a 'bon voyage' to Charles Mathews and Mme Vestris, who were soon to depart for North America. The 'Dream of the Future', as well as being a reference to a well-known Olympic drama, was given visual form with a 'Distant View of Liverpool' and a picture of 'An American Packet getting under weigh'. The piece was advertised as an 'entirely New Occasional, Allegorical, Valedictory Burletta'.

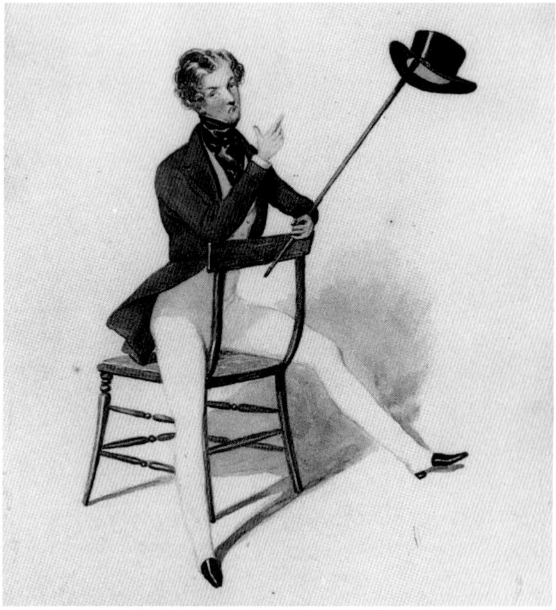

541
CHARLES JAMES MATHEWS
as Jack Bruce
in *Chaos is Come Again or The Race Ball*
by John Maddison Morton

James Warren Childe

Pencil and watercolour on wove paper
mounted on card 36.4 x 25.4
INSCR: 'Charles Mathews / as / [Jack] in
"Chaos is come again".' (pen and brown ink b.c.)
INV: RW/CKA 170

Mathews, seated with the back of a chair to the front, between his legs, wears black shoes, white trousers, a green-grey jacket, a fawn waistcoat, a high white collar, and a black cravat.

Morton's farce was first performed at Covent Garden on 9 November 1838. Mathews played Jack Bruce for the first time in a revival at the same theatre on 21 February 1840.

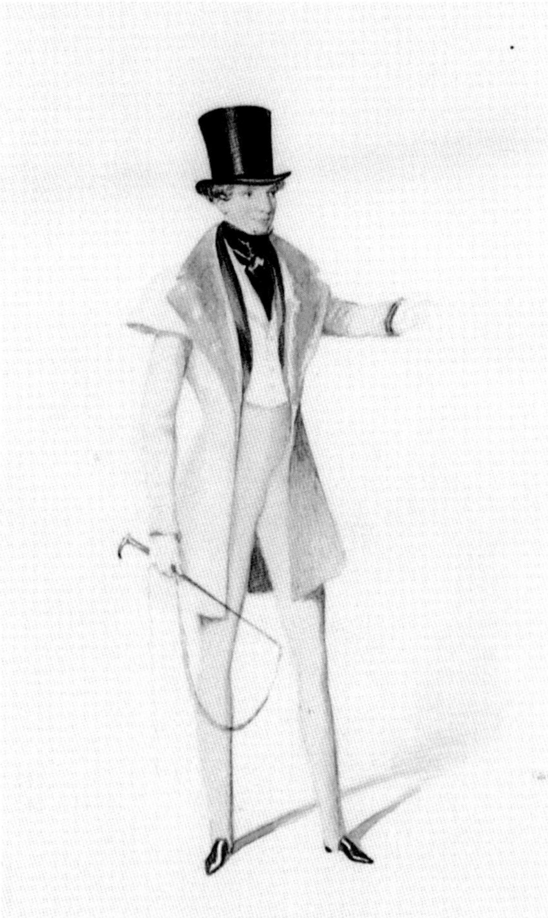

542

CHARLES JAMES MATHEWS

as Sir John Freeman in *Free and Easy*

by Samuel James Arnold

James Warren Childe

Pencil and watercolour on wove paper
mounted on card 36.4 x 25.4
INSCR: 'Charles Mathews / as / "Sir John Freeman" in "Free and Easy".' (pen and brown ink b.c.)
INV: RW/CKA 161A

Mathews holds a riding crop and wears a black top hat, white gloves, black shoes, grey trousers, a brown coat with a broad, darker brown collar, a dark jacket, a cream waistcoat with brown buttons, and a black cravat.

Arnold's comic opera, with music by Addison, was first performed at the English Opera House on 16 September 1816. It was later revived at Covent Garden, on 24 November 1841, with Mathews as Sir John Freeman, Harley as Michael, Miss Murray as Eugenia, and Mrs Orger as Gertrude.

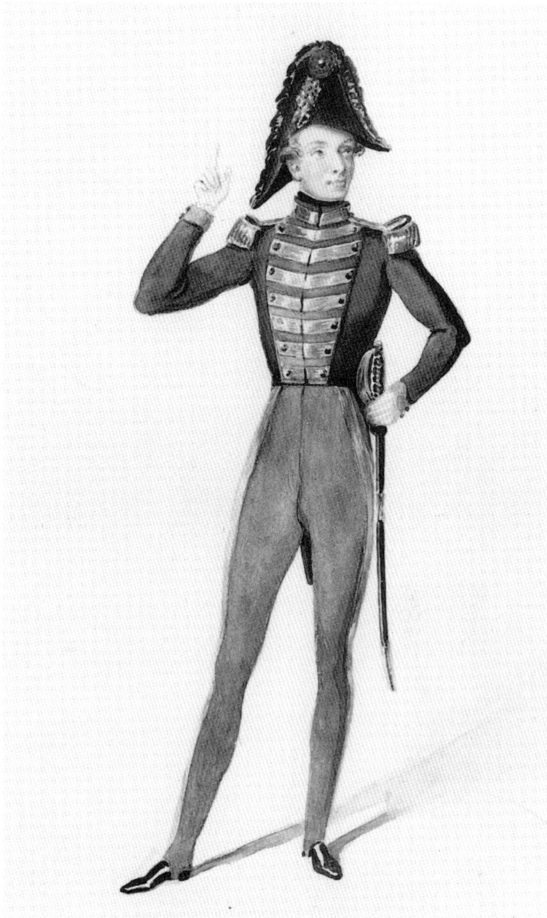

543

CHARLES JAMES MATHEWS

as Julio de Calatrava in *Black Domino*

by Charles James Mathews

James Warren Childe

Pencil and watercolour on wove paper
mounted on card 36.4 x 25.4
INSCR: 'Charles Mathews / as / "Julio", in "The Black Domino".' (pen and brown ink b.c.)
INV: RW/CKA 172

Mathews wears a black half-moon hat with black frills around the edge, black shoes, grey-green trousers, a cutaway military jacket in grey with paler grey cuffs and gold epaulets and gold braid around the collar, a white collar, and a black stock.

Mathews's burletta, adapted from Scribe's *Le domino noir*, was first performed at the Olympic on 18 January 1838, with the author in the role of Julio. The last of 25 performances that season was given on 16 February 1838.

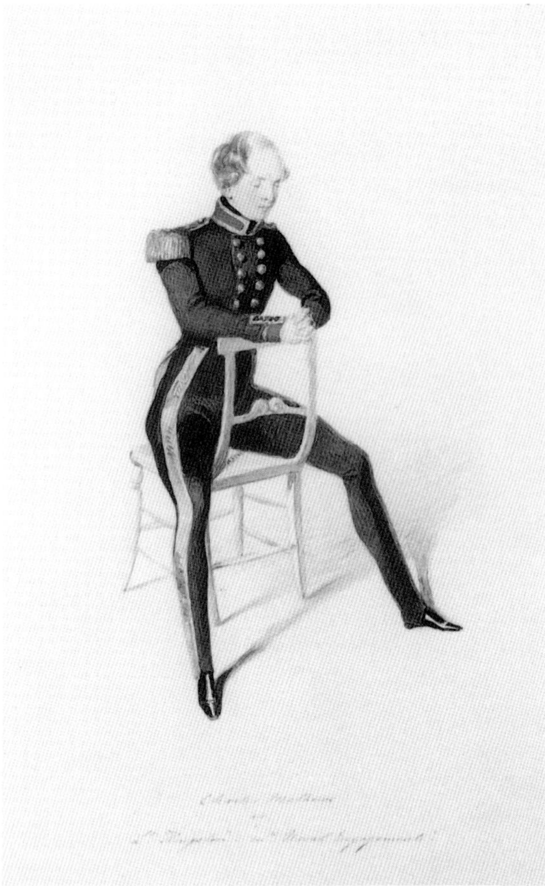

544

CHARLES JAMES MATHEWS

as Lieutenant Kingston in *Naval Engagement*
by Charles Dance

James Warren Childe

Pencil and watercolour on wove paper
mounted on card 36.4 x 25.4
INSCR: 'Charles Mathews / as / "Lt. Kingston", in "Naval Engagements".' (pen and brown ink b.c.)
INV: RW/CKA 167

Mathews, seated and leaning on the back of a flimsy chair, wears black shoes, blue military trousers with a broad gold band down the sides, and a blue cutaway military jacket with gold lapels, gold-fringed epaulets, a double row of gold buttons and red cuffs and collar edged in gold, over a white collar and black stock.

Dance's burletta was first performed on 3 May 1838, with Mathews as Lieutenant Kingston, William Farren as Admiral Kingston, and Mme Vestris as Miss Mortimer. The piece was given 25 times during the season, the last time being on 31 May 1838.

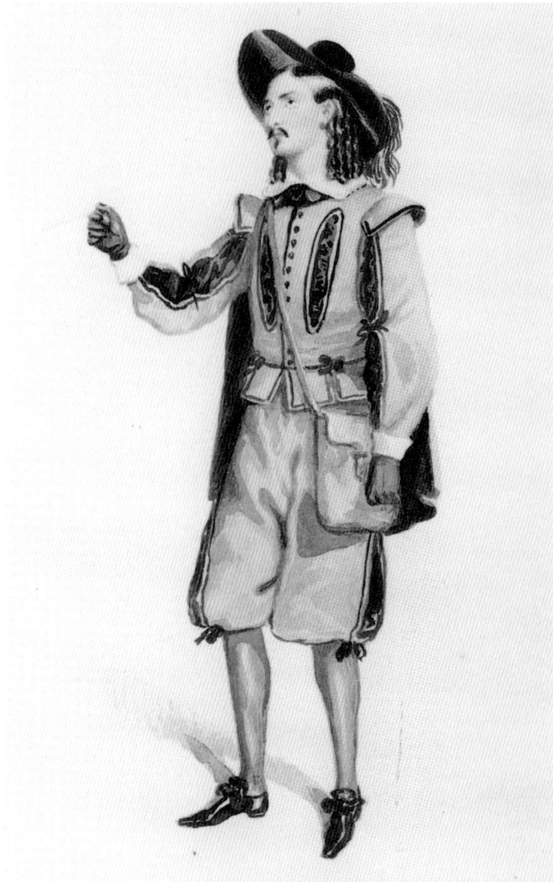

545

CHARLES JAMES MATHEWS

as Leandro in *The Spanish Curate*
by James Robinson Planché

James Warren Childe

Pencil and watercolour on wove paper
mounted on card 36.4 x 25.4
INSCR: 'Charles Mathews / as / "Leandro", in "The Spanish Curate".' (pen and brown ink b.c.)
INV: RW/CKA 165 (in 166 frame)

Mathews, with a little moustache and his dark brown hair in ringlets falling down behind his ears, wears black shoes with square toes and black bows, grey stockings, baggy grey knee-breeches with black panels up the side and black bows, a grey doublet with long sleeves, slashed in black on either side of chest and down sleeves, a turned-down collar, and a black Cavalier hat with a broad brim and a blue plume at the back.

Planché's comedy, adapted from the play by Beaumont and Fletcher, was first performed at Covent Garden on 13 October 1840, with Mathews as Leandro and Mme Vestris as Amaranta.

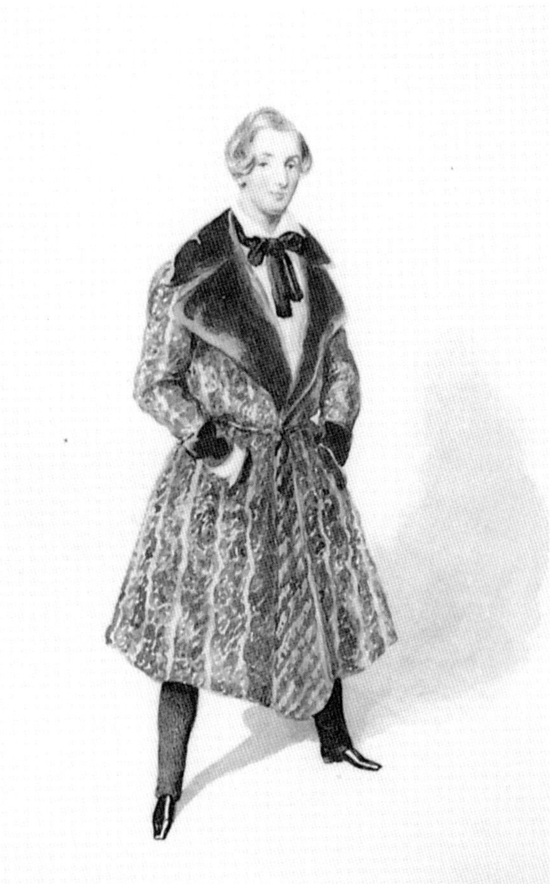

546
CHARLES JAMES MATHEWS
as Littleton Coke
in *Old Heads and Young Hearts*
by Dion Boucicault

James Warren Childe

Pencil and watercolour on wove paper
mounted on card 36.4 x 25.4
INSCR: 'Charles Mathews / as / "Lyttleton Coke" in "Old Heads and Young Hearts".' (pen and brown ink b.c.)
INV: RW/CKA 146B

Mathews, standing with his legs wide apart, wears black shoes, dark grey trousers, a long silver dressing-gown with long vertical stripes in brown and red-brown, with wide lapels and collar and cuffs in brown fur, and a white shirt with loose collar.

Boucicault's comedy was first given at the Haymarket on 18 November 1844, with Mathews as Littleton Coke and Mme Vestris as Lady Alice Hawthorn. There were 77 performances to 22 February 1845, and the play was revived after Easter. See Nos. 547 and 548.

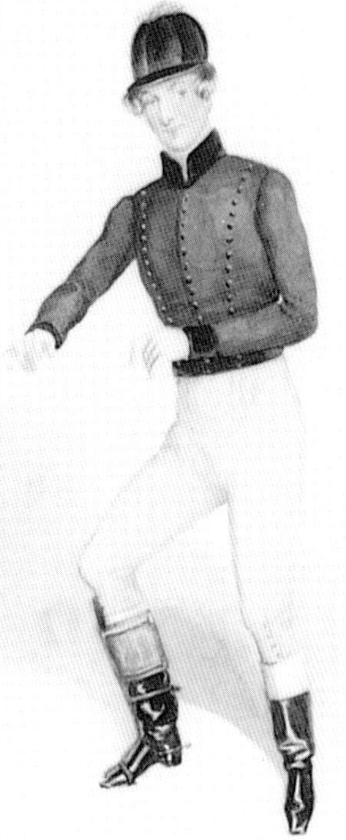

547
CHARLES JAMES MATHEWS
as Littleton Coke
in *Old Heads and Young Hearts*
(2nd dress)

James Warren Childe

Pencil and watercolour on wove paper
mounted on card 36.4 x 25.4
INSCR: 'Charles Mathews / as / "Lyttleton Coke" in "Old Heads and Young Hearts".' (pen and brown ink b.c.)
INV: RW/CKA 146C

Mathews wears white gloves, black boots with brown tops, a long leg-stirrup attached to his right leg, fawn jodhpurs with buttons at the knee, a grey-blue riding jacket with black cuffs and collar, a belt, and a white stock. See No. 546.

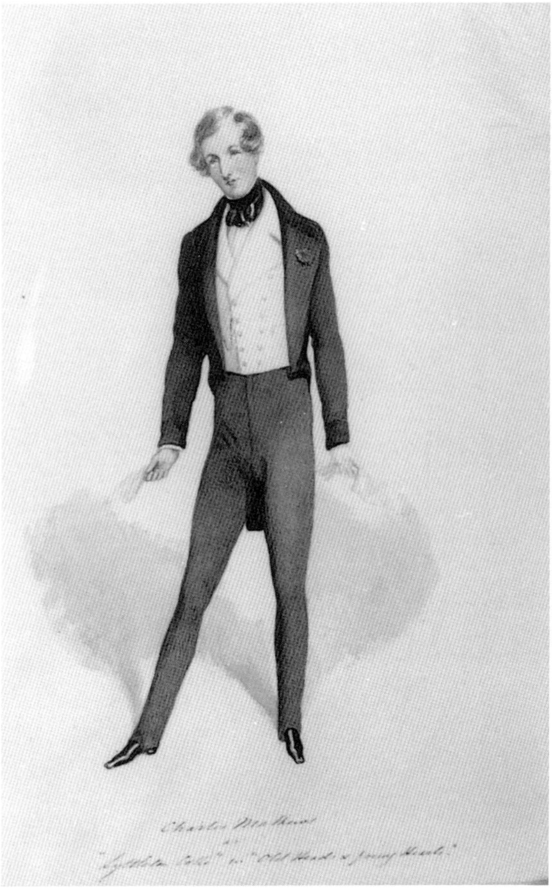

548
CHARLES JAMES MATHEWS
as Littleton Coke
in *Old Heads and Young Hearts*
(3rd dress)

James Warren Childe

Pencil and watercolour on wove paper
mounted on card 36.4 x 25.4
INSCR: 'Charles Mathews / as / "Lyttleton Coke" in "Old Heads and Young Hearts".' (pen and brown ink b.c.)
INV: RW/CKA 146D

Mathews, standing to front with hands at sides, wears grey trousers, a grey cutaway jacket with darker grey collar, broad grey lapels and darker grey cuffs, a double-breasted white waistcoat with broad lapels, a white shirt with high collar, and a black cravat with frills. See No. 546.

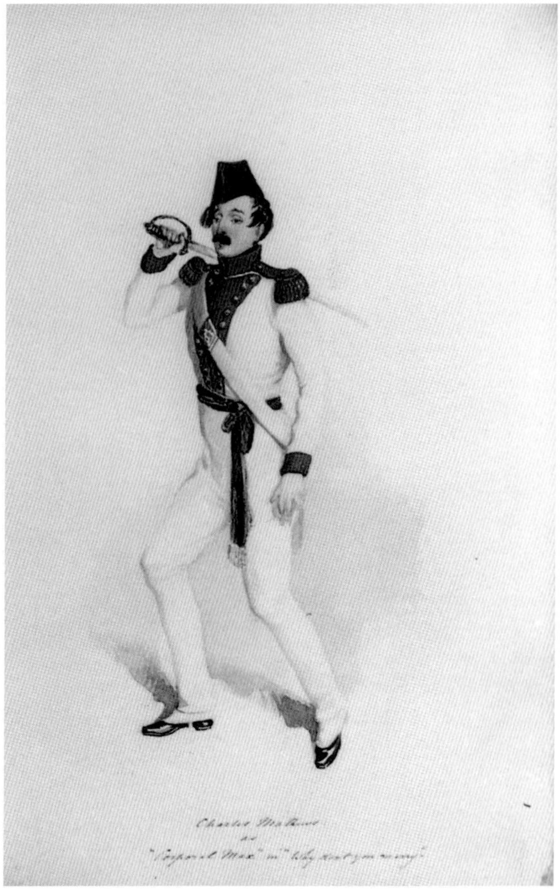

549
CHARLES JAMES MATHEWS
as Corporal Max in *The Swiss Cottage or Why Don't She Marry?*
by Thomas Haynes Bayly

James Warren Childe

Pencil and watercolour on wove paper
mounted on card 36.4 x 25.4
INSCR: 'Charles Mathews / as / "Corporal Max" in "Why don't you marry".' (pen and brown ink b.c.)
INV: RW/CKA 174

Mathews, with knees bent in a state of collapse, wears black shoes, white spats, white trousers, and a white cutaway jacket with red cuffs and large red lapels with gold buttons, a high red collar, and epaulets.

Bayly's burletta was first performed at the Olympic on 9 February 1835, with James Bland in the role of Corporal Max.

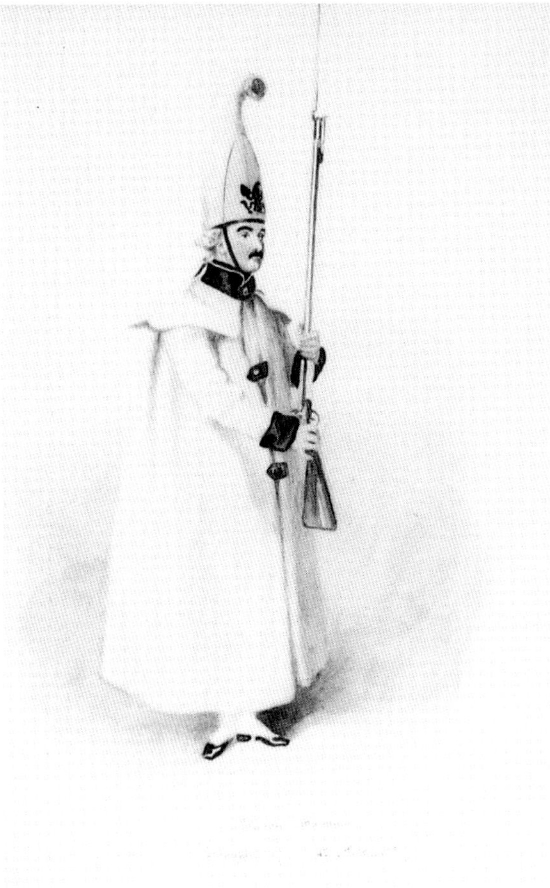

550

CHARLES JAMES MATHEWS

as Maximilian Schloppsen in *The Sentinel*

by John Maddison Morton

James Warren Childe

Pencil and watercolour on wove paper
mounted on card 36.4 x 25.4

INSCR: 'Charles Mathews / as / "Schloppsen", in "The Sentinel".' (pen and brown ink b.c.)

INV: RW/CKA 158E

Mathews, standing and holding a long rifle, has a black moustache and black eyebrows. His powdered curly hair is visible under a Grenadier's hat, brown at the front and edged with a gold band, which displays an Austrian Eagle. He wears black shoes, white spats, and a very long white coat cut extremely generously.

Morton's burletta was first performed at the Olympic Theatre on 23 February 1837, with Mathews as Maximilian Schloppsen and Mme Vestris as Linda. There were 21 performances during the season, the last taking place on 3 May 1837. See No. 551.

551

NOT ILLUSTRATED

CHARLES JAMES MATHEWS

as Maximilian Schloppsen in *The Sentinel*

(2nd dress)

James Warren Childe

Pencil and watercolour on wove paper
mounted on card 36.4 x 25.4

INSCR: 'Charles Mathews / as / "Schloppsen", in "The Sentinel".' (pen and brown ink b.c.)

INV: RW/CKA 176A

Mathews wears a powdered curly wig partly hidden by a hat cocked over his right ear, black shoes, long white gaiters to his knees, white breeches, and a grey military coat lined in red with a white panel at the front edged in red. See No. 550.

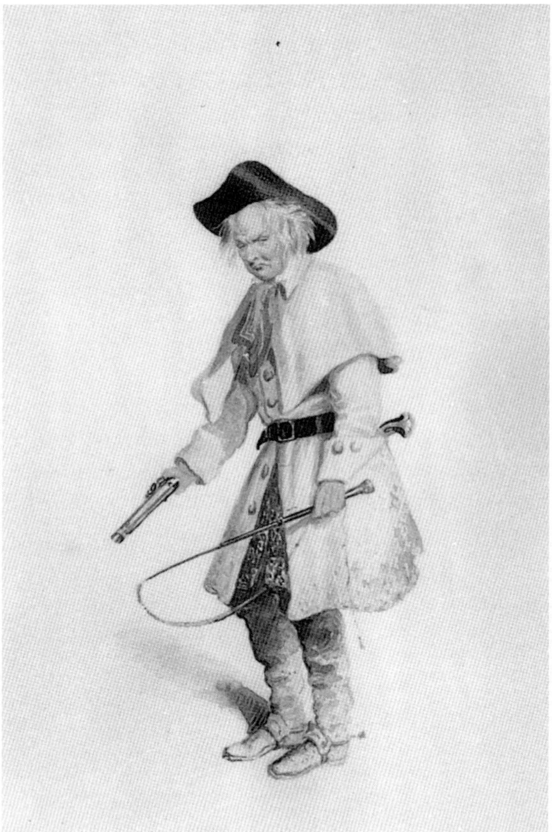

552
CHARLES JAMES MATHEWS
as Meadows in *The Deaf Lover*
by Frederick Pilon

James Warren Childe

Pencil and watercolour on wove paper
mounted on card 36.4 x 25.4
INSCR: 'Charles Mathews / as / "Meadows" in
"The Deaf Lover".' (pen and brown ink b.c.)
INV: RW/CKA 164

Mathews, with unkempt grey hair under a black hat, holds a long-barrelled silver pistol in his right hand and a riding whip in his left. He wears dirty grey boots to the knee, a fawn coat, a black belt with brass buckle, a green and gold jacket, and a white and red neckerchief.

Pilon's farce was first performed at Covent Garden on 2 February 1780, with Charles Lee Lewes playing Meadows. It was an altered version of the same author's *The Device; or, The Deaf Doctor*, which had been given an unsuccessful single performance at Covent Garden on 27 September 1779, also with Charles Lee Lewes as Meadows.

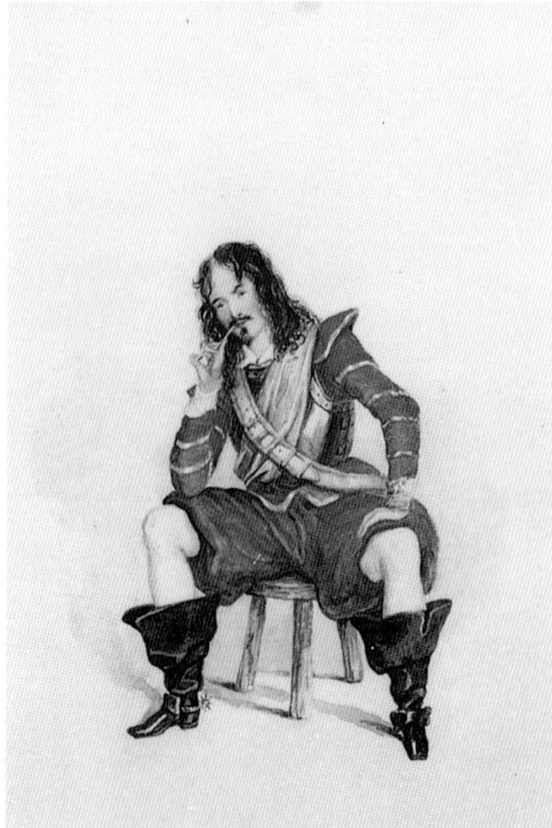

553
CHARLES JAMES MATHEWS
as Michael Perez, the Copper Captain
in *Rule a Wife and Have a Wife*
by Francis Beaumont and John Fletcher

James Warren Childe

Pencil and watercolour on wove paper
mounted on card 36.4 x 25.4
INSCR: 'Charles Mathews / as / "The Copper Captain"
in "Rule a wife and have a wife".'
(pen and brown ink b.c.)
INV: RW/CKA 173

Mathews is seated on a three-legged stool, holding a clay pipe to his mouth. He has a Caroline moustache and beard and wears black boots with silver buckles and spurs, white stockings, baggy red breeches, a long-sleeved red jerkin with gold diagonal bands and high shoulder pads edged with gold bands, body armour, a grey sash, a white belt edged in gold, and a loose white collar.

Mathews appeared as the Copper Captain in a revival of Beaumont and Fletcher's comedy at Covent Garden on 14 October 1839, with Miss Nisbett in the role of Estifania.

554

NOT ILLUSTRATED

CHARLES JAMES MATHEWS

as Millamour in *Know Your Own Mind*

by Arthur Murphy

James Warren Childe

Pencil and watercolour on wove paper
mounted on card 36.4 x 25.4
INSCR: 'Charles Mathews / as / "Millamour" in
"Know your own Mind".' (pen and brown ink b.c.)
INV: RW/CKA 145B

Mathews wears black shoes with gold buckles, cream stockings, high-waisted white breeches, a blue cutaway jacket with broad lapels and a paler blue fringe at the front, a white waistcoat with broad lapels, a white shirt, and a high white stock. See No. 508.

555

NOT ILLUSTRATED

CHARLES JAMES MATHEWS

as Motley in *He Would Be an Actor*

by Charles James Mathews

James Warren Childe

Pencil and watercolour on wove paper
mounted on card 36.4 x 25.4
INSCR: 'Charles Mathews / as / "Mottley" in
"He would be an Actor".' (pen and brown ink b.c.)
INV: RW/CKA 178B

Mathews, holding a purple-brown watering can, wears old black boots, white stockings, green breeches with bows at the knee, a black apron, a green belt, a sleeveless grey jacket, a white shirt with full sleeves, a white turned-down collar, and a brown neckerchief.

Mathews's burletta was first performed at the Olympic on 31 October 1836, with the author as Motley, Mrs Orger as Becky Morgan, and Oxberry as Dicky Darling. Motley was one of Mathews's most popular roles at the Olympic and the play was frequently revived. See Nos. 556 and 557.

556

NOT ILLUSTRATED

CHARLES JAMES MATHEWS

as Motley in *He Would Be an Actor*

(2nd dress)

James Warren Childe

Pencil and watercolour on wove paper
mounted on card 36.4 x 25.4
INSCR: 'Charles Mathews / as / "Mottley" – in –
"He would be an Actor".' (pen and ink b.c.)
INV: RW/CKA 178C

Mathews, holding a stick over his right shoulder on which is a bundle tied in a red cloth, wears a black top hat, black shoes, grey gaiters, grey trousers, a pink jacket with broad lapels, a yellow waistcoat with brass buttons, a white shirt with turned-down collar, and a black neckerchief. See No. 555.

557

NOT ILLUSTRATED

CHARLES JAMES MATHEWS

as Motley in *He Would Be an Actor*

(3rd dress)

James Warren Childe

Pencil and watercolour on wove paper
mounted on card 36.4 x 25.4
INSCR: 'Charles Mathews / as / "Mottley" in
"He would be an Actor".' (pen and ink b.c.)
INV: RW/CKA 178D

Mathews wears black shoes, a long white dressing-gown or day-coat elaborately embroidered in red trellis-work with red and blue flowers, and a white collar. See No. 555.

558
NOT ILLUSTRATED
CHARLES JAMES MATHEWS
as Lord Ortolan
in *The White Milliner*
by Douglas William Jerrold

James Warren Childe

Pencil and watercolour on wove paper
mounted on card 36.4 x 25.4
INSCR: 'Charles Mathews / as / [blank] in
"The White Milliner".' (pen and brown ink b.c.)
INV: RW/CKA 148D

Mathews wears black shoes, white stockings, grey breeches, a blue coat bordered with gold braid, a long white waistcoat copiously decorated with bands of gold braid, and a high white collar with frills down the front.

Jerrold's comedy was first performed at Covent Garden on 9 February 1841, with Mathews as Lord Ortolan, William Farren as Justice Twilight, and Mme Vestris as Albina. See No. 559.

559
NOT ILLUSTRATED
CHARLES JAMES MATHEWS
as Lord Ortolan in *The White Milliner*
(2nd dress)

James Warren Childe

Pencil and watercolour on wove paper
mounted on card 36.4 x 25.4
INSCR: 'Charles Mathews / as / [blank] in
"The White Milliner".' (pen and brown ink b.c.)
INV: RW/CKA 148E

Mathews wears a blue tricorn hat with zigzag gold braid, black shoes, white stockings, grey breeches, a long blue coat trimmed with gold braiding, a long white waistcoat with gold braid, a white stock with frills down the front and a black band round the neck, and a brown coat with thick, dark brown fur edging over his left shoulder. See No. 558.

560
NOT ILLUSTRATED
CHARLES JAMES MATHEWS
as Captain Patter in *Patter versus Clatter*
by Charles James Mathews

James Warren Childe

Pencil and watercolour on wove paper
mounted on card 36.4 x 25.4
INSCR: 'Charles Mathews / as / "Capt. Patter" in
"Patter versus Clatter".'(pen and brown ink b.c.)
INV: RW/CKA 149D

Mathews wears black shoes, long grey-green trousers, a dark grey-green braided cutaway military coat, a black belt fastened with a brass buckle at the front, a hussar's jacket over his left shoulder, dark grey and edged in fur with silver braid, and a shako with a gold star at the front.

Mathews's farce was first performed at the Olympic on 21 May 1838, with the author as Captain Patter, and was played 10 times during its first season. It was the first part that Mathews played on his return from America, on 26 December 1838, and became one of his most popular roles. His first appearance at Covent Garden as Captain Patter was on 15 September 1841. See Nos. 561–63.

561
NOT ILLUSTRATED
CHARLES JAMES MATHEWS
as Captain Patter in *Patter versus Clatter*
(2nd dress)

James Warren Childe

Pencil and watercolour on wove paper
mounted on card 36.4 x 25.4
INSCR: 'Charles Mathews / as / "Capt. Patter" in
"Patter versus Clatter".' (pen and brown ink b.c.)
INV: RW/CKA 149E

Mathews holds a white top hat in his left hand and wears black shoes, grey-green trousers, a blue cutaway jacket with dark grey collar and lining and enormous lapels from neck to waist, over an elaborately embroidered waistcoat with large collar, a high white collar, a white shirt with studs, and a large black cravat. See No. 560.

562
NOT ILLUSTRATED
CHARLES JAMES MATHEWS
as Captain Patter in *Patter versus Clatter*
(3rd dress)

James Warren Childe

Pencil and watercolour on wove paper
mounted on card 36.4 x 25.4
INSCR: 'Charles Mathews / as / "Capt. Patter" in "Patter versus Clatter".' (pen and brown ink b.c.)
INV: RW/CKA 153D

Mathews holds a yellow and pink handkerchief and wears black shoes, dark green trousers with a grey stripe down the side, a cutaway grey jacket with a double line of buttons down the front, a turned-down collar, and a high black stock. See No. 560.

563
NOT ILLUSTRATED
CHARLES JAMES MATHEWS
as Captain Patter in *Patter versus Clatter*
(4th dress)

James Warren Childe

Pencil and watercolour on wove paper
mounted on card 36.4 x 25.4
INSCR: 'Charles Mathews / as / "Capt. Patter" in "Patter versus Clatter".' (pen and brown ink b.c.)
INV: RW/CKA 153E (as Captain Clatter)

Mathews wears black shoes, grey-green trousers, a long white apron, a white jacket with white buttons, and a high white stock tied at the front. See No. 560.

564
NOT ILLUSTRATED
CHARLES JAMES MATHEWS
as Peregrine Mildmay in *A Dream of the Future*
by Charles Dance

James Warren Childe

Pencil and watercolour on wove paper
mounted on card 36.4 x 25.4
INSCR: 'Charles Mathews / as / "Peregrine Mildmay", in "A dream of the Future".' (pen and brown ink b.c.)
INV: RW/CKA 154D

Mathews, seated and holding a glass of red wine in his upraised right hand, wears black shoes, grey socks, dark grey trousers, a dark grey cutaway jacket, a dark green silk waistcoat edged in gold, a white shirt with a high collar, and a black stock.

Dance's comedy was first performed at the Olympic on 6 November 1837, with Mathews as Peregrine Mildmay, Mme Vestris as Miss Honoria Walsingham, and F. Matthews as Mr Harbottle. There were 41 performances during the season, the last on 27 February 1838. See Nos. 565 and 566.

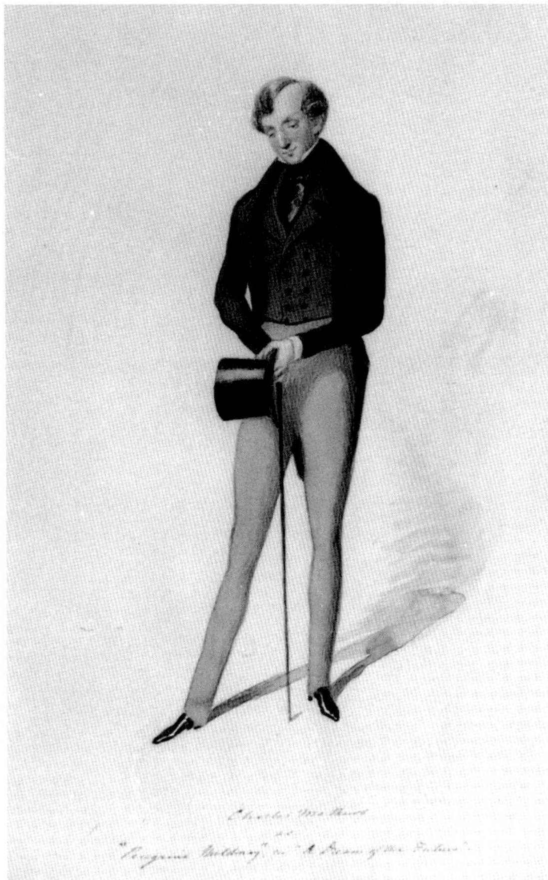

565
CHARLES JAMES MATHEWS
as Peregrine Mildmay in *A Dream of the Future*
(2nd dress)

James Warren Childe

Pencil and watercolour on wove paper
mounted on card 36.4 x 25.4
INSCR: 'Charles Mathews / as / "Peregrine Mildmay", in "A Dream of the Future".' (pen and brown ink b.c.)
INV: RW/CKA 154E

Mathews holds a black top hat and cane and wears black shoes, grey trousers, a dark grey cutaway jacket with broad lapels and collar, a dark green double-breasted waistcoat, a high white collar, and a black cravat. See No. 564.

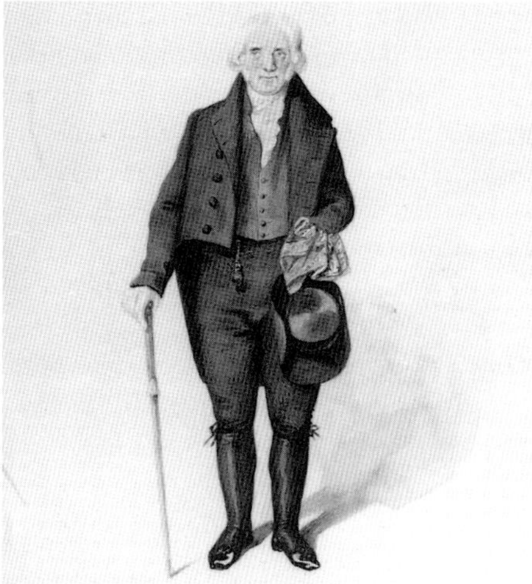

566

CHARLES JAMES MATHEWS

as Peregrine Mildmay in *A Dream of the Future*

(3rd dress)

James Warren Childe

Pencil and watercolour on wove paper
mounted on card 36.4 x 25.4
INSCR: 'Charles Mathews / as / "Peregrine Mildmay", in "A Dream of the Future".' (pen and brown ink b.c.)
INV: RW/CKA 154F

In his left hand Mathews holds a handkerchief decorated in brown and gold and a black hat. He wears black shoes, black stockings, black breeches, a black cutaway jacket, a purple waistcoat with high collar and buttons down the front, a high white collar, and a white stock. See No. 564.

567

NOT ILLUSTRATED

CHARLES JAMES MATHEWS

as Peter Spyk in *The Loan of a Lover*

by James Robinson Planché

James Warren Childe

Pencil and watercolour on wove paper
mounted on card 36.4 x 25.4
INSCR: 'Charles Mathews / as / "Peter Spyk" in "The Loan of a Lover".' (pen and brown ink b.c.)
INV: RW/CKA 145A

Mathews has a small black hat with a blue band and a small plume and wears black shoes with brass buckles, white stockings, baggy brown breeches, a cream-coloured coat with grey edging to red lapels, a greyish waistcoat, a white shirt with stiff turned-down collar, and a red and gold neckerchief.

Planché's burletta was first performed at the Olympic on 29 September 1834, with Robert Keeley as Peter Spyk. Keeley appeared in the same role in revivals at the Olympic on 29 September 1837 and Covent Garden on 5 October 1839. Mathews first played the part at the Haymarket on 22 November 1842, with Mme Vestris as Gertrude singing 'I'd Marry him Tomorrow'.

568

NOT ILLUSTRATED

CHARLES JAMES MATHEWS

as Sir Philip Brilliant in *Old Maids*

by James Sheridan Knowles

James Warren Childe

Pencil and watercolour on wove paper
mounted on card 36.4 x 25.4
INSCR: 'Charles Mathews / as / "Sir Philip Brilliant", in "Old Maids".' (pen and brown ink b.c.)
INV: RW/CKA 154B

Mathews, with dark brown hair, wears brown square-toed shoes with blue rosettes, white stockings, brown breeches slashed at sides to reveal blue with blue bows across and at the knees, a brown jacket, a white shirt with gold vertical stripes, a wide lace collar with jewel at neck, and, over his left shoulder, a brown velvet cloak lined in blue and edged with a triple band of silver braid.

Knowles's comedy was first performed at Covent Garden on 12 October 1841, with Mathews as Sir Philip Brilliant, Mme Vestris as Lady Blanche, and George Vandenhoff as Thomas Blount. There were 16 performances during the season, the last on 29 October 1841. See No. 569.

569

NOT ILLUSTRATED

CHARLES JAMES MATHEWS

as Sir Philip Brilliant in *Old Maids* (2nd dress)

James Warren Childe

Pencil and watercolour on wove paper
mounted on card 36.4 x 25.4
INSCR: 'Charles Mathews / as / "Sir Philip Brilliant", in "Old Maids".' (pen and brown ink b.c.)
INV: RW/CKA 154C

Mathews wears pale brown boots with red bows, gold spurs, brownish stockings, dark blue velvet breeches trimmed with red bows, a brown jacket which has blue sleeves with horizontal pale blue lines, red bows at the elbows and red ribbons hanging from the shoulders, white gauntlets, and a broad lace collar with hound's-tooth edging. See No. 568.

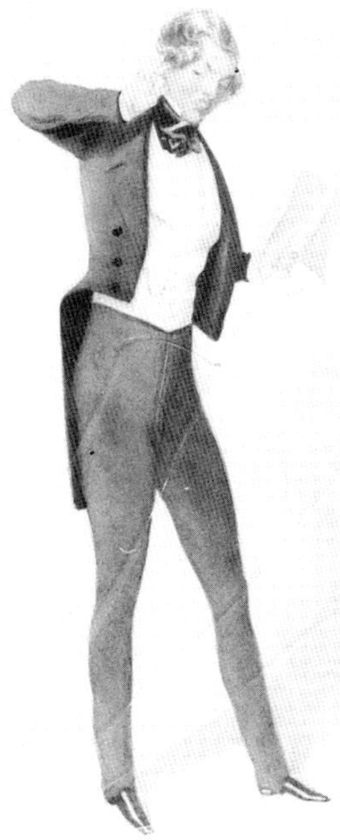

570
CHARLES JAMES MATHEWS
as Puff in *The Critic*
by Richard Brinsley Sheridan

James Warren Childe

Pencil and watercolour on wove paper
mounted on card 36.4 x 25.4
INSCR: 'Charles Mathews / as / "Puff" in "The Critic".'
(pen and brown ink b.c.)
INV: RW/CKA 149A

Mathews wears mid-19th-century evening clothes with black shoes, grey trousers, a grey cutaway jacket, a white waistcoat with broad lapels, a high white collar, and a black cravat around his neck.

Mathews first played Puff in a revival of Sheridan's burlesque at Covent Garden on 6 November 1840.

571
NOT ILLUSTRATED
CHARLES JAMES MATHEWS
as Puff in *Drama at Home or An Evening with Puff*
by James Robinson Planché

James Warren Childe

Pencil and watercolour on wove paper
mounted on card 36.4 x 25.4
INSCR: 'Charles Mathews / as / "Puff" in "The Drama at Home".' (pen and brown ink b.c.)
INV: RW/CKA 152C

Mathews holds a bunch of red flowers and a black top hat. His costume includes black shoes, white gloves, grey trousers, a grey cutaway jacket, a white waistcoat, a white shirt with high collar, and a black cravat.

Planché's 'New, original, occasional and local extravaganza' was first performed at the Haymarket on 8 April 1844. The piece opened with the sick character of 'The Drama' played by Mrs Glover and a very mad Ophelia played by Mrs Caulfield, then Mathews as Sheridan's Puff (from Sheridan's *The Critic*; see No. 570) introduced the audience to glimpses of life at Drury Lane, Covent Garden and the Haymarket.

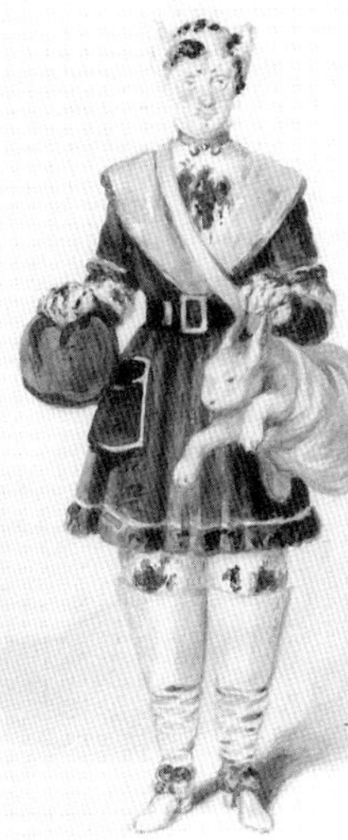

572
CHARLES JAMES MATHEWS
as Puss in *Puss in Boots*
by Charles Dance and James Robinson Planché

James Warren Childe

Pencil and watercolour on wove paper
mounted on card 36.4 x 25.4
INSCR: 'Charles Mathews / as / "Puss" in "Puss in Boots".'
(pen and brown ink b.c.)
INV: RW/CKA 156B

Mathews wears cat's whiskers and false eyebrows, and a black and white cat hat with pointed ears. In his raised left paw is a white rabbit in a pale brown bag. His costume includes high brown boots, probably a black and white feline body stocking, and a brown tunic edged in dark fur.

Dance and Planché's burletta was first performed at the Olympic on 26 December 1837, with Mathews as Puss, Mme Vestris as Ralph, and Miss Dowton as the Fairy Felina.

573

NOT ILLUSTRATED

CHARLES JAMES MATHEWS

as the Marquis de Richeville

in *Grist to the Mill*

by James Robinson Planché

James Warren Childe

Pencil and watercolour on wove paper
mounted on card 36.4 x 25.4

INSCR: 'Charles Mathews / as / "The Marquis de Richeville" in "Grist to the Mill".' (pen and brown ink b.c.)

INV: RW/CKA 158A

Mathews wears a small black tricorn hat, black square-toed shoes with silver buckles and red heels, white stockings rolled over grey, a coat horizontally striped in pink and white with white lining, a long waistcoat similarly striped, and a high white-frilled stock.

Planché's comedy was first performed at the Haymarket on 22 February 1844, with Mathews playing the Marquis de Richeville and Mme Vestris as Francine. See No. 574.

574

NOT ILLUSTRATED

CHARLES JAMES MATHEWS

as Marquis de Richeville

in *Grist to the Mill*

(2nd dress)

James Warren Childe

Pencil and watercolour on wove paper
mounted on card 36.4 x 25.4

INSCR: 'Charles Mathews / as / "The Marquis of Richeville" in "Grist to the Mill".' (pen and brown ink b.c.)

INV: RW/CKA 160A (in 160B frame)

Mathews wears black shoes, white trousers, a purple jacket, a white waistcoat, a white shirt with high collar, a wide black stock, and white gloves. See No. 573.

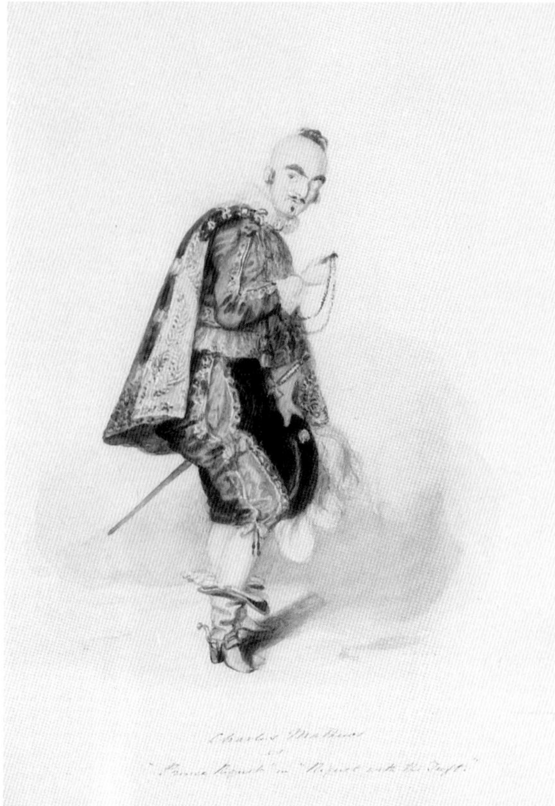

575

CHARLES JAMES MATHEWS

as Prince Riquet in *Riquet with the Tuft*

by James Robinson Planché and Charles Dance

James Warren Childe

Pencil and watercolour on wove paper
mounted on card 36.4 x 25.4

INSCR: 'Charles Mathews / as / "Prince Riquet" in "Riquet with the Tuft".' (pen and brown ink b.c.)

INV: RW/CKA 156A

Mathews is holding a broad-brimmed black hat with a red lining, a gold jewel and three large white plumes. He wears black boots with high heels, gold spurs, white stockings, purple breeches slashed down the sides to reveal blue edged in gold, a purple doublet slashed in blue down sleeves edged in gold, and a purple velvet cloak embroidered in gold and with a purple lining embroidered in gold with ears of corn. See introduction to this series, p. 271.

Planché and Dance's 'New Grand, Comical, Allegorical, Magical, Musical Burletta in one Act', based on *Riquet à la houppe*, was first performed at the Olympic on 26 December 1836 with Mathews as Prince Riquet and Mme Vestris as Princess Emeralda.

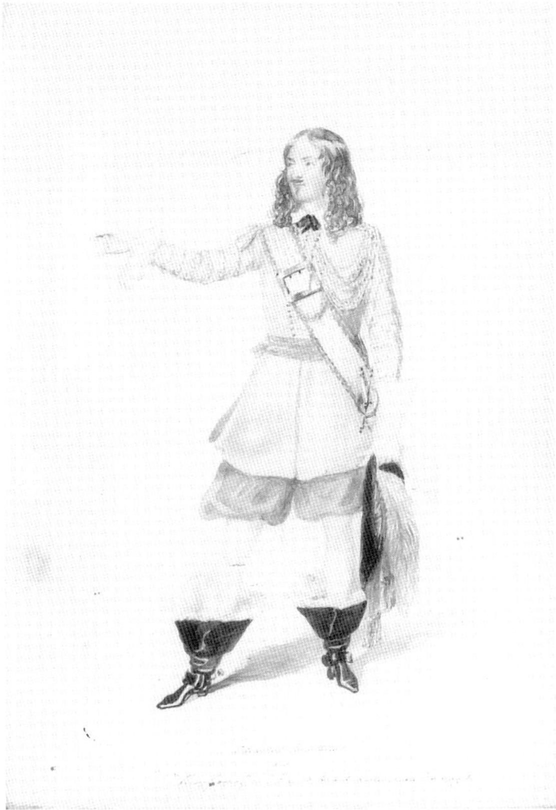

576

CHARLES JAMES MATHEWS

as Ruy Gomez in *Faint Heart Ne'er Won Fair Lady*
by James Robinson Planché

James Warren Childe

Pencil and watercolour on wove paper
mounted on card 36.4 x 25.4
INSCR: 'Charles Mathews / as / "Ruy Gomez" in "Faint Heart never won Fair Lady".' (pen and brown ink b.c.)
INV: RW/CKA 155B (in 155A frame)

In his left hand Mathews holds a red-plumed black hat with a red band with silver fringe; he wears a cream gauntlet, black boots with their wide tops lined with lace, gold spurs, white tights, baggy red breeches, a yellow-brown coat with the sleeves decorated with horizontal bands of silver braid, a turned-down white collar, and a black cravat tied in a bow.

Planché's burletta opened at the Olympic on 28 February 1839, with Mathews as Ruy Gomez. The piece was about the 15-year-old Charles II of Spain, played by Miss Lee, and was given 38 performances during the season to 27 April 1839. See No. 577.

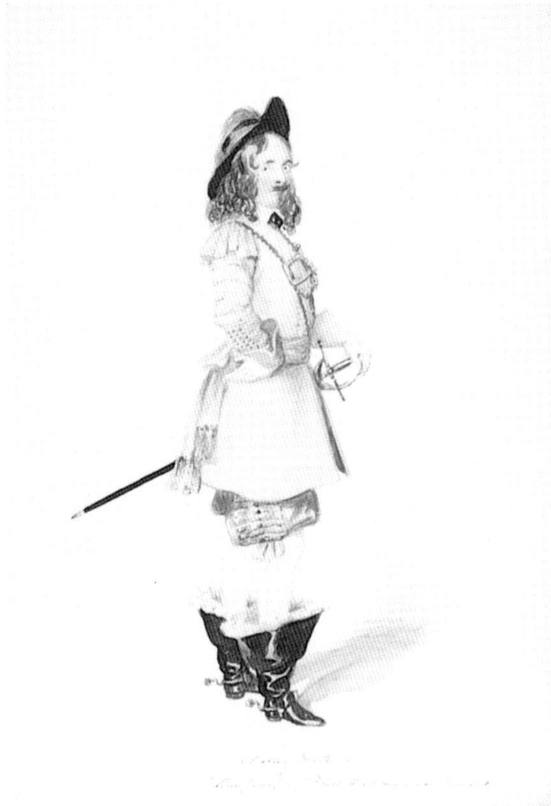

577

CHARLES JAMES MATHEWS

as Ruy Gomez in *Faint Heart Ne'er Won Fair Lady*
(2nd dress)

James Warren Childe

Pencil and watercolour on wove paper
mounted on card 36.4 x 25.4
INSCR: 'Charles Mathews / as / "Ruy Gomez" in "Faint Heart never won Fair Lady".' (pen and brown ink b.c.)
INV: RW/CKA 177E

Mathews wears yellowish gauntlets with enormously wide tops, white stockings, loose red breeches with gold braiding, a yellow coat with a broad red sash round the waist, a white collar, black neckerchief, and black hat with brim with a red band and feather. See No. 576.

578

NOT ILLUSTRATED

CHARLES JAMES MATHEWS

as Don Sebastian della Rosa

in *A Match for a King*

by Charles James Mathews

James Warren Childe

Pencil and watercolour on wove paper
mounted on card 36.4 x 25.4
INSCR: 'Charles Mathews / as / "Don Sebastian" in "A Match for a King".' (pen and brown ink b.c.)
INV: RW/CKA 152D

Mathews wears a ragged black hat, black boots with red heels, silver spurs, white stockings, baggy and torn brown breeches, a short-sleeved brownish jerkin edged in gold, open to reveal a white frilled shirt, and a white collar turned down over steel gorget.

Mathews's comedy was first performed at the Haymarket on 14 October 1844, with the author as Don Sebastian. See No. 579.

579

NOT ILLUSTRATED

CHARLES JAMES MATHEWS

as Don Sebastian della Rosa

in *A Match for a King*

(2nd dress)

James Warren Childe

Pencil and watercolour on wove paper
mounted on card 36.4 x 25.4
INSCR: 'Charles Mathews / as / "Don Sebastian" in "A Match for a King".' (pen and brown ink b.c.)
INV: RW/CKA 152E

Mathews wears a broad-brimmed hat with a white plume, brown boots with red heels and gold spurs, white stockings, baggy pale blue breeches, a brown leather sleeveless jacket and gold gorget edged in brown with a lion's head, under the brown jacket a shorter jacket with gold lines and big blue bows at the shoulder and blue ribbons, a white turned-down collar, and white gauntlets edged in gold. See No. 578.

580

NOT ILLUSTRATED

CHARLES JAMES MATHEWS

as Percival Single

in *Three and the Deuce*

by Prince Hoare

James Warren Childe

Pencil and watercolour on wove paper
mounted on card 36.4 x 25.4
INSCR: 'Charles Mathews / as / "Percival Single" in "The Three and the Deuce".' (pen and brown ink b.c.)
INV: RW/CKA 157A

Mathews, standing and looking at a puppet dressed as a clown held in his hands, wears grey gloves, black shoes, long grey trousers, a cutaway grey jacket with large lapels, a white waistcoat with brass buttons, a large white collar over the jacket, a cravat, and a round straw hat.

Prince Hoare's operatic farce, with music by Stephen Storace, was performed at the Haymarket on 2 September 1795, with John Bannister as the three Singles. There were 11 performances over the summer season then Bannister gave a single performance at Drury Lane on 8 October, the last of the 18th century. Charles James Mathews may also have appeared in this amusing triple role, but specific documentation has yet to reveal itself. See Nos. 581 and 582.

581

NOT ILLUSTRATED

CHARLES JAMES MATHEWS

as Peregrine Single

in *Three and the Deuce*

James Warren Childe

Pencil and watercolour on wove paper
mounted on card 36.4 x 25.4
INSCR: 'Charles Mathews / as / "Peregrine Single" in "The Three and the Deuce".' (pen and brown ink b.c.)
INV: RW/CKA 157B (in 157C frame)

Mathews, with fair hair brushed back under a black top hat, has a monocle in his right eye and wears black shoes, grey trousers, a grey cutaway jacket with rectangular lapels from chest to waist and pale grey lining, a red waistcoat heavily embroidered with panels of yellow and green, and a large black cravat. See No. 580.

582
NOT ILLUSTRATED
CHARLES JAMES MATHEWS
as Pertinax Single
in *Three and the Deuce*

James Warren Childe

Pencil and watercolour on wove paper
mounted on card 36.4 x 25.4
INSCR: 'Charles Mathews / as / "Pertinax Single" in "The Three and the Deuce".' (pen and brown ink b.c.)
INV: RW/CKA 157C (in 157B frame)

Mathews wears grey gloves, black shoes, grey trousers, a grey cutaway jacket, high black velvet collar, high white stock, and a black hat. See No. 580.

583
CHARLES JAMES MATHEWS
as Slender in *The Merry Wives of Windsor*
by William Shakespeare

James Warren Childe

Pencil and watercolour on wove paper
mounted on card 36.4 x 25.4
INSCR: 'Charles Mathews / as / "Master Slender" in "The Merry Wives of Windsor".' (pen and brown ink b.c.)
INV: RW/CKA 149B

Mathews wears white gloves fringed with blue feathers, yellow shoes with blue rosettes, pink stockings, yellow doublet and hose, a pink belt edged in blue with blue bows, a large white lace collar turned down, and a white hat with blue, white and pink plumes.

Mathews first played Slender in a revival of Shakespeare's comedy at Covent Garden on 30 April 1840. George Bartley was Falstaff and Mme Vestris Mrs Page.

583 *Charles James Mathews as Slender*

584
NOT ILLUSTRATED
CHARLES JAMES MATHEWS
as Captain Smoke in *Bubbles of the Day*
by Douglas William Jerrold

James Warren Childe

Pencil and watercolour on wove paper
mounted on card 36.4 x 25.4
INSCR: 'Charles Mathews / as / "Capt' Smoke" in "The Bubbles of the day".' (pen and brown ink b.c.)
INV: RW/CKA 154A

Mathews wears black shoes, blue trousers, a dark blue jacket with a high collar, a yellow waistcoat with gold buttons down the front, a white shirt with a high collar, and a black stock.

Jerrold's comedy was first performed at Covent Garden on 25 February 1842 with Mathews as Captain Smoke. An impressive cast played an array of suggestively named characters, including William Farren as Lord Skindeep, M.P., Harley as Sir Phenix Clearcake, Bartley as Mr Spreadweasel, Meadows as Malmsey Shark, and Mrs Nisbett as Pamela Spreadweasel. The piece was played on 30 April 1842, Mathews and Mme Vestris's last night at Covent Garden.

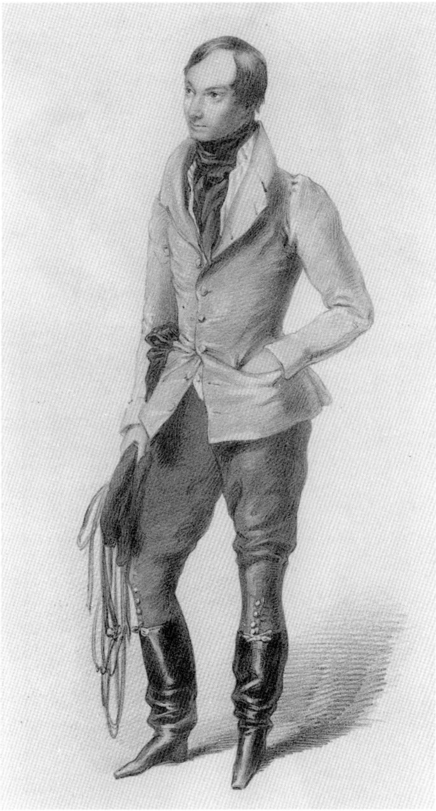

585

CHARLES JAMES MATHEWS

as Tim Topple in *The Old and Young Stager*

by William Leman Rede

James Warren Childe

Pencil and watercolour on wove paper
mounted on card 36.4 x 25.4
INSCR: 'Charles Mathews / as / "Tim" in
"The Old and Young Stager".' (pen and brown ink b.c.)
INV: RW/CKA 150A

Mathews, standing, with his left hand in his jacket pocket, wears black calf-length boots, brownish jodhpurs, a fawn riding jacket, a red and white striped waistcoat, a grey stock, and a yellow handkerchief in the left pocket of his jacket. He holds a bridle in his right hand.

Rede's burletta was first performed at the Olympic on 7 December 1835, with Mathews as Tim Topple. His father was played by Liston and Sir Pompadour Puffendale by F. Matthews. The piece was given 77 times during the season, the last time being on 26 March 1836.

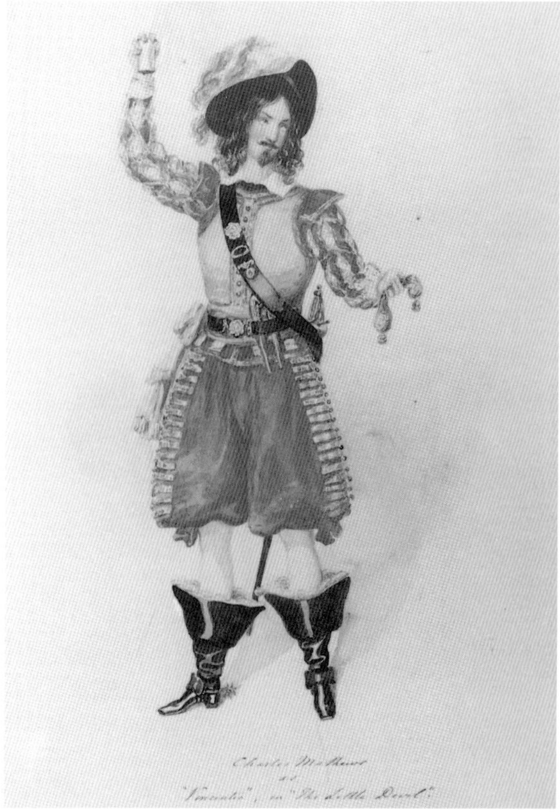

586

CHARLES JAMES MATHEWS

as Vincentio in *The Little Devil*

by Benjamin Nottingham Webster

James Warren Childe

Pencil and watercolour on wove paper
mounted on card 36.4 x 25.4
INSCR: 'Charles Mathews / as / "Vincentio", in
"The Little Devil".' (pen and brown ink b.c.)
INV: RW/CKA 152A

Mathews has a Cavalier hat with red and white plumes in the broad brim. He wears black boots with flaps at the front, gold spurs, white stockings, baggy red breeches with bows at the knee, a brown leather sleeveless jerkin edged in gold at the shoulders and with a double line of gold down the front, with gold buttons; his black belt has a white buckle in which are held two pistols.

Webster's comedy was first performed at the Haymarket on 16 May 1843 with Mathews as Vincentio d'Estella and Mme Vestris as Nicolo Angeli. It was a popular piece, given 51 performances to 2 August 1843 and played again on 14 August 1843. See No. 587.

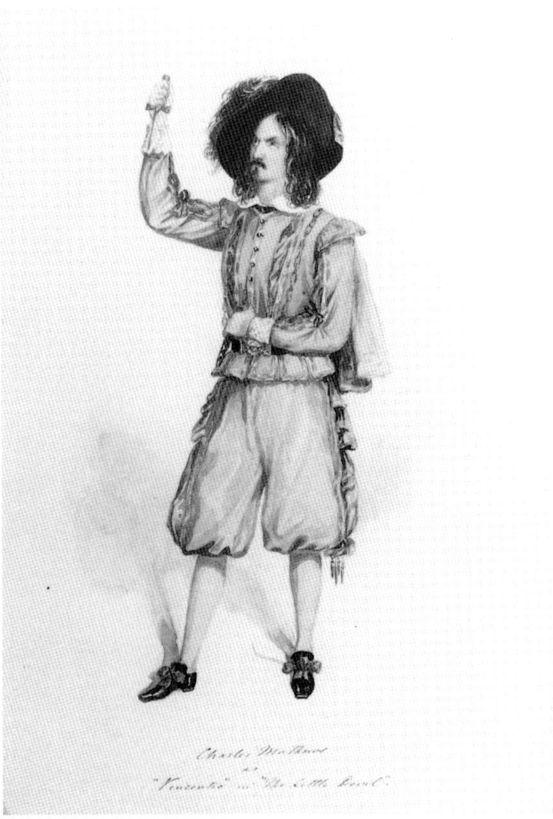

587
CHARLES JAMES MATHEWS
as Vincentio in *The Little Devil*
(2nd dress)

James Warren Childe

Pencil and watercolour on wove paper
mounted on card 36.4 x 25.4
INSCR: 'Charles Mathews / as / "Vincentio" in "The Little Devil".' (pen and brown ink b.c.)
INV: RW/CKA 152B

Mathews wears a black broad-brimmed hat with blue plumes, black shoes with blue bows, grey stockings, baggy grey-blue breeches, a grey doublet slashed down front with blue sleeves, a turned-back white collar, and a short grey cloak. See No. 586.

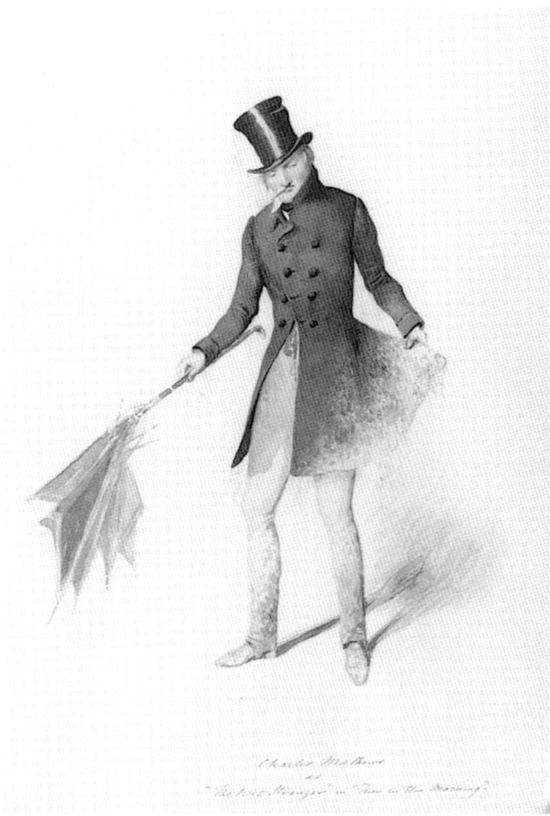

588
CHARLES JAMES MATHEWS
as The Wet Stranger in *Two in the Morning*
by Charles James Mathews

James Warren Childe

Pencil and watercolour on wove paper
mounted on card 36.4 x 25.4
INSCR: 'Charles Mathews / as / "The Wet Stranger" in "Two in the Morning".' (pen and brown ink b.c.)
INV: RW/CKA 146E

Mathews wears a tall black top hat; his extended right hand holds an umbrella that has been blown inside out, with water dripping off it. His costume includes mud-spattered brown shoes and grey trousers, a grey coat with a double line of buttons down the upper part of the front, and a white collar.

Mathews's interlude was first performed at Covent Garden on 3 October 1840, with the author playing the Wet Stranger.

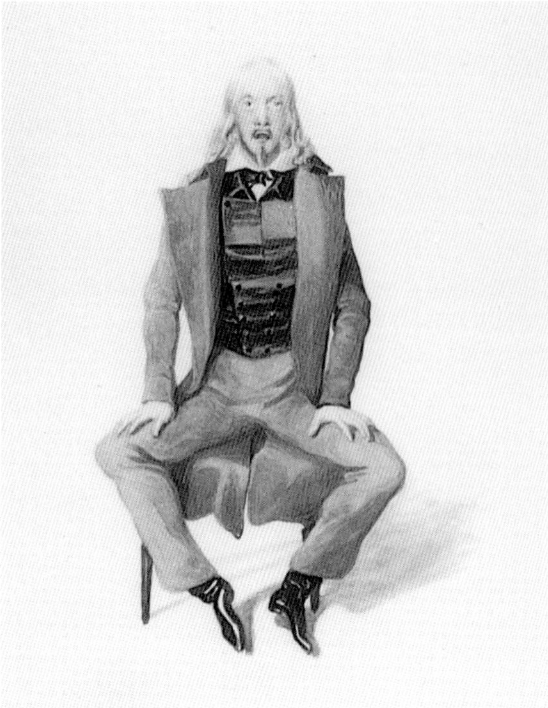

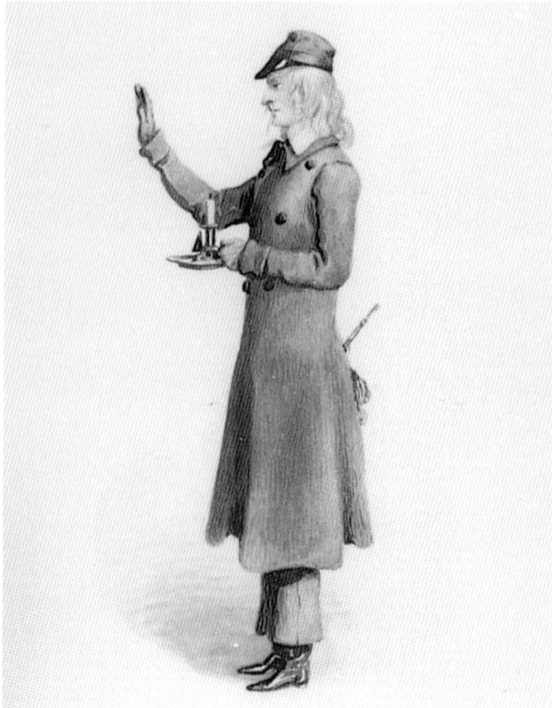

589
CHARLES JAMES MATHEWS
as Wittikind
in *Our Cousin German*
by an Unknown Author

James Warren Childe

Pencil and watercolour on wove paper
mounted on card 36.4 x 25.4
INSCR: 'Charles Mathews / as / "Wittikind", in
"A Cousin German".' (pen and brown ink b.c.)
INV: RW/CKA 177F

Mathews, seated with both hands on his knees, has a moustache and goatee beard and wears black boots, green trousers, a long green coat with enormously wide lapels, a blue double-breasted waistcoat with curious panels at the top, a white collar turned back, and a blue bow tie.

This anonymous burletta was first performed at the Olympic on 11 February 1839, with Mathews as Cousin Wittikind. There were 10 performances during the season, the last on 26 February 1839. See No. 590.

590
CHARLES JAMES MATHEWS
as Wittikind in *Our Cousin German*
(2nd dress)

James Warren Childe

Pencil and watercolour on wove paper
mounted on card 36.4 x 25.4
INSCR: 'Charles Mathews / as / "Wittikind" in
"A Cousin German".' (pen and brown ink b.c.)
INV: RW/CKA 177G

Mathews holds a candle and wears black boots, a grey cap, green trousers with wide bottoms, a long green coat, and a white shirt with turned-down collar. See No. 589.

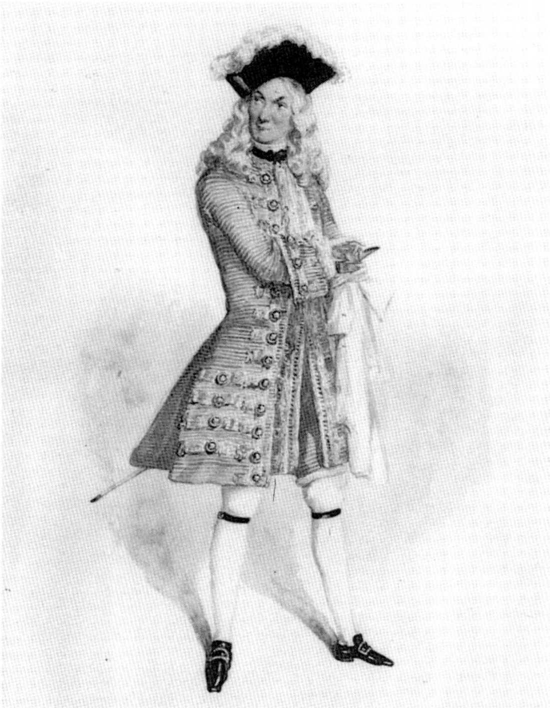

591
CHARLES JAMES MATHEWS
as Witwould in *The Way of the World*
by William Congreve,
altered by James Robinson Planché

James Warren Childe

Pencil and watercolour on wove paper
mounted on card 36.4 x 25.4
INSCR: 'Charles Mathews / as / "Witwould" in
"The Way of the World".' (pen and brown ink b.c.)
INV: RW/CKA 159B (framed as 159A)

Mathews wears an enormously long powdered wig that is tumbling over his shoulders, and a black tricorn hat with a gold band above his right eye and a brim full of white feathers. He is taking a pinch of snuff out of a gold snuffbox held in his left hand, and a white cloth hangs from his left wrist. His costume includes black shoes with silver buckles, white stockings over breeches with pink and white horizontal stripes, a pink and white striped coat, a long waistcoat of the same material, and a high frilled stock and black cravat.

Planché's alteration of Congreve's comedy was first performed at the Haymarket on 17 December 1842, with Mathews as Witwould and Mme Vestris as Millamant. The cast also included H. Holl as Mirabell, William Farren as Sir Wilfull Witwould, Buckstone as Petulent, and Mrs Glover as Lady Wishfort.

592
NOT ILLUSTRATED
CHARLES JAMES MATHEWS
as Mr Wyndham in *A Handsome Husband*
by Elizabeth Planché

James Warren Childe

Pencil and watercolour on wove paper
mounted on card 36.4 x 25.4
INSCR: 'Charles Mathews / as / "Mr Wyndham" in
"The Handsome Husband".' (pen and brown ink b.c.)
INV: RW/CKA 158B

Mathews, standing, holds a black top hat and a white cloth and wears white gloves, black shoes, grey trousers, a brown coat with grey lining and a very broad black collar and lapels, black cuffs, a grey cutaway jacket with black collar, a brown double-breasted waistcoat, a high-collared white shirt, and a curious scarf in green-blue with a pink pattern.

Mrs Planché's burletta was first performed at the Olympic on 15 February 1836, with Mathews as Mr Wyndham and Mme Vestris as Mrs Wyndham. See No. 593.

593
NOT ILLUSTRATED
CHARLES JAMES MATHEWS
as Mr Wyndham in *A Handsome Husband*
(2nd dress)

James Warren Childe

Pencil and watercolour on wove paper
mounted on card 36.4 x 25.4
INSCR: 'Charles Mathews / as / "Mr Wyndham" in
"The Handsome Husband".' (pen and brown ink b.c.)
INV: RW/CKA 158C

Mathews wears black shoes, dark grey trousers, a dark blue cutaway jacket with gold buttons down the front, a fawn waistcoat with gold buttons, a white shirt with a high white collar, and a white stock. See No. 592.

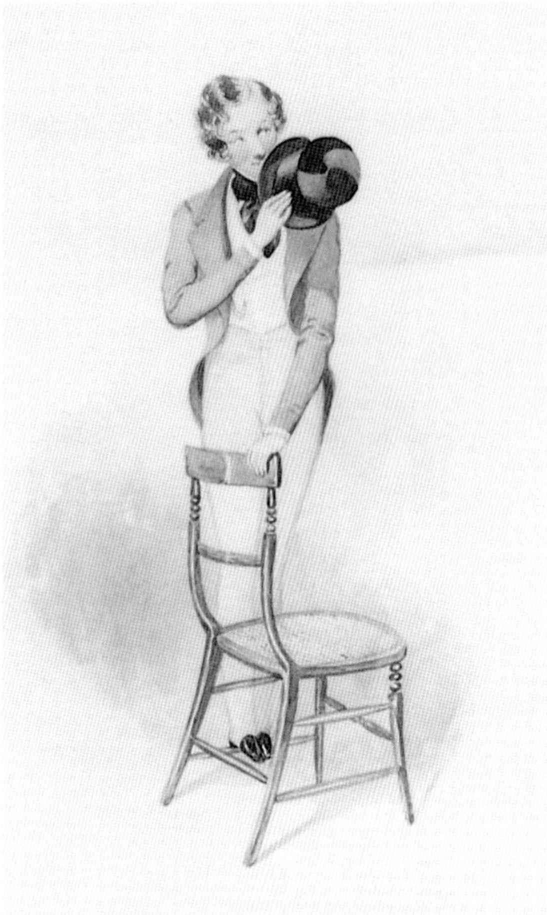

594
CHARLES JAMES MATHEWS
as Young Whimsey
in *The First Floor*
by James Cobb

James Warren Childe

Pencil and watercolour on wove paper
mounted on card 36.4 x 25.4
INSCR: 'Charles Mathews / as / "Young Whimsey"
in "The First Floor".'
(pen and brown ink b.c.)
INV: RW/CKA 146A

Mathews holds a black top hat to his mouth and rests his left hand on the back of a chair. He wears black shoes, white trousers, a green jacket, a white double-breasted waistcoat with a gold watch-chain, a white collar, and a black cravat.

Cobb's farce was first performed at Drury Lane on 13 February 1787, with Robert Palmer as Young Whimsey. Mathews's first appearance in the part was at Covent Garden on 28 November 1840.

595
LOCATION UNKNOWN
CHARLES JAMES MATHEWS
as 'The Little Parson'

Samuel De Wilde (copy after)

Oil on canvas 29.2 x 24.1, missing in 1994
INSCR: 'Portrait of C J Mathews / when a
Child, / in the Dress of a Parson'
(pen and brown ink on label on verso)
INV: CKA 605; Gift 447
PROV: Lady Mathews, by whom presented
to the Garrick Club, 1927
REL: Original: NT 39 black chalk and watercolour
on wove paper 23.8 x 18.9 s. & d:
'S De Wilde ft / July 25 1807' (black chalk b.l.)
LIT: Charles Dickens Jnr. (ed.)
The Life of Charles James Mathews (1879)

Little Master Mathews, standing, with big black eyes, raises a glass of red wine in his right hand. He described his costume in *The Life of Charles James Mathews* (I: 11–12):

> Beside the familiar sobriquet of 'Twig', I was almost generally spoken of as 'the Little Parson', and, as an appropriate birthday offering, one of our waggish friends presented to me a complete little parson's suit of black old-fashioned square-cut coat, long flapped waistcoat, knee-breeches, worsted stockings, shoes, and buckles, white bands &c. – attired in which I was lifted on the dining-room table to drink the healths of the 'tompany'. The drawing of me in my clerical costume by De Wilde bears the date of June, 1807, which would make my age at that time just three years and a half, which I fancy may be safely taken as my earliest appearance in character.

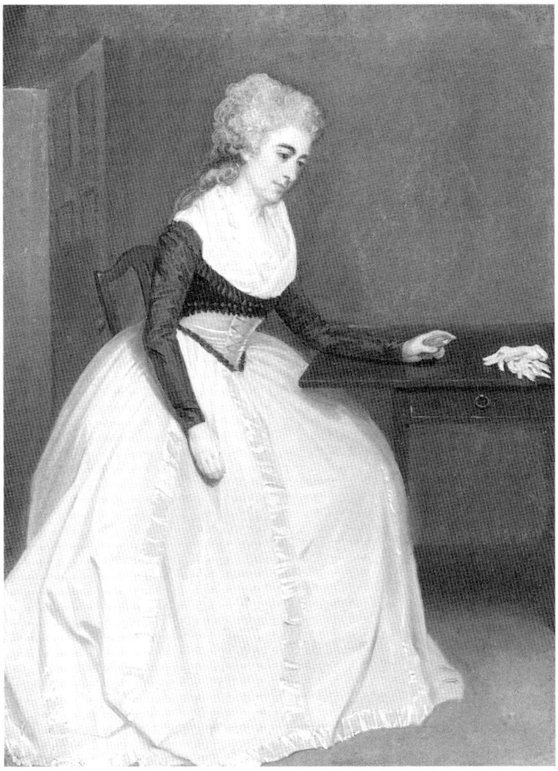

596
ISABELLA MATTOCKS
as Lady Restless in *All in the Wrong*
by Arthur Murphy

Samuel De Wilde

Oil on canvas 36.2 x 27.3
INV: Mathews 182; RW/CKA 250
PROV: John Bell; Charles Mathews
EXH: 1833 London (182)
ENGR: Philippe Audinet for Bell's British Library
5 May 1792, line II.I x 8, pub. Bell's *British Theatre* (1797),
vol 12, with the quotation from Act II, scene I:
'This really is a handsome picture:
what a charming countenance!'

Lady Restless has found a miniature of Beverly, loved by Belinda. She wears a long white dress with vertical lines of white satin and a white satin hem, a grey bodice with lozenge-shaped white stomacher, a white fichu and long grey sleeves. She sits in a chair with her left arm resting on a table, and holds the miniature.

Murphy's comedy was first performed at Drury Lane on 15 June 1761, with Miss Haughton as Lady Restless. Mrs Mattocks played the role in the first performance of the play at Covent Garden, on 26 April 1776.

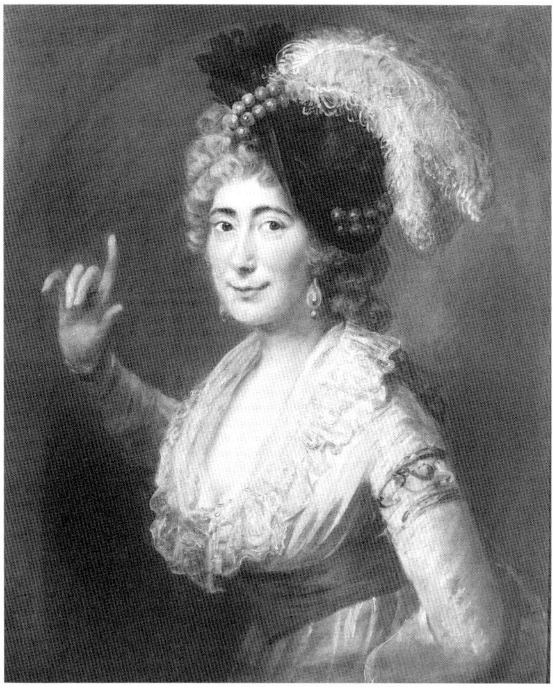

597*
ISABELLA MATTOCKS
as Catherine in *Catherine and Petruchio*
by David Garrick

Gainsborough Dupont

Oil on canvas 73.7 x 61
INV: Mathews 53 (as Louisa in 'The Duenna'
Quote: 'Is this your gallantry?' Act I);
RW/CKA 410 (as Louisa in 'The Duenna' or as Mrs Ford)
PROV: Thomas Harris; Harris sale, Robins 12 July 1819 (24)
(as Mrs Ford); Charles Mathews
EXH: 1833 London (53); 1982–83 London (129)
LIT: *Morning Herald*, 22 March 1794; Hayes, 1968

Half-length. Catherine wears a jaunty black hat with pearls and plumes over powdered hair, and a white muslin dress with a green sash.

Garrick's farce, a three-act adaptation of *The Taming of the Shrew*, was first performed at Drury Lane on 21 January 1756, with Woodward as Petruchio and Kitty Clive as Catherine. It held the stage in preference to Shakespeare's original until the late 19th century. Although the character in this picture has been identified both as Mrs Ford, a part Mrs Mattocks never played at Covent Garden, and as Louisa in *The Duenna*, there is no reason to doubt that the role is that mentioned in the *Morning Herald* of 24 March 1794, which was Catherine in *Catherine and Petruchio*. This was one of Mrs Mattocks's most popular roles, and she often appeared in it for the benefit of other members of the company.

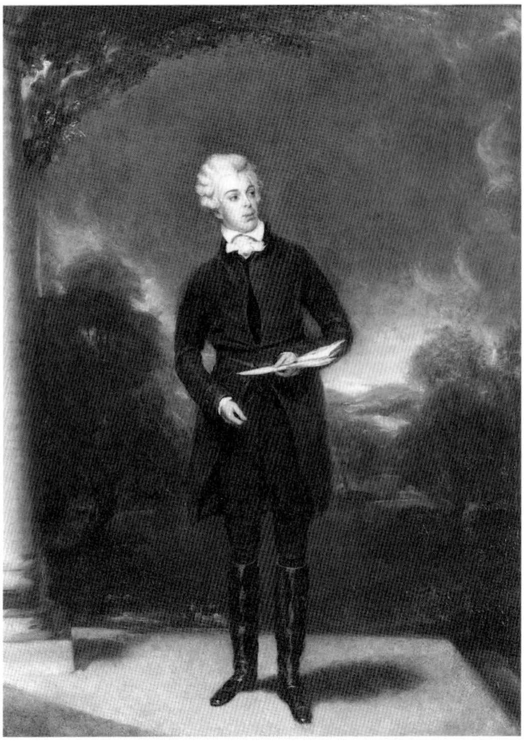

598
DRINKWATER MEADOWS
as Raubvogel in *Returned Killed*
by James Robinson Planché

Henry Meyer

Oil on canvas 58.4 x 40.6
INV: Mathews 170; RW/CKA 274
PROV: Charles Mathews
EXH: 1833 London (170)
ENGR: Anon. pub. C. Hullmandel, lithograph 15.6 x 10.9

The attorney Raubvogel has been arrested by Milligen, who believes him to be the Baron Rudolph Lindorf. Milligen has accused Raubvogel of 'charging without orders'. Raubvogel, misunderstanding the context, replies with the line quoted on the engraving: 'I shall charge what I please.'

Raubvogel, standing in a patio with a forest behind him and holding papers in his left hand, wears a very tightly fitted coat, which is black like the rest of his costume, consisting of high boots, breeches and waistcoat. He wears a short powdered wig.

Planché's farce, based on *Le mort dans l'embarras*, was first performed at Covent Garden on 31 October 1826, with Drinkwater Meadows as Raubvogel. There were 21 performances of the piece that season.

Meadows became a member of the Garrick Club in 1832 (but resigned in 1860).

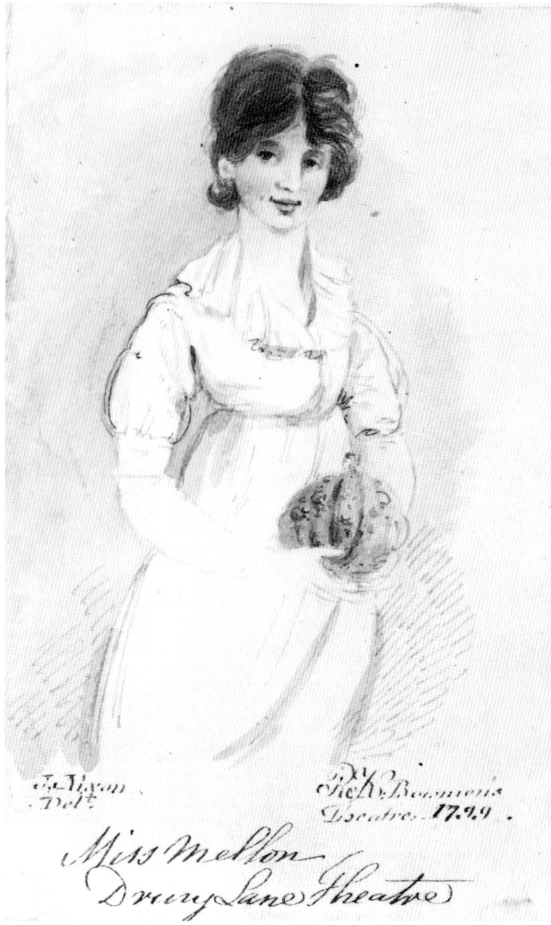

599
HARRIOT MELLON

John Nixon

Pencil and watercolour on wove paper 13.3 x 8.6
INSCR: 'J. Nixon / Delt' (pen and black ink b.l.);
'R. K. Bowman's / Theatre 1799.'
(pen and black ink b.r.);
'Miss Mellon / Drury Lane Theatre'
(pen and black ink b.c.)
INV: Not listed
PROV: John Nixon, *Dramatic Annals*, 3: 229
LIT: Sybil Rosenfeld, 'Private Theatricals at Bowman's Lodge, Dartford', *Theatre Notebook* (1961–62), 16: 125–26

The actress is shown holding a green melon.

In 1815, Harriot Mellon married her elderly patron, the banker Thomas Coutts, whose considerable fortune she inherited on his death in 1822. Five years later she married the Duke of St Albans.

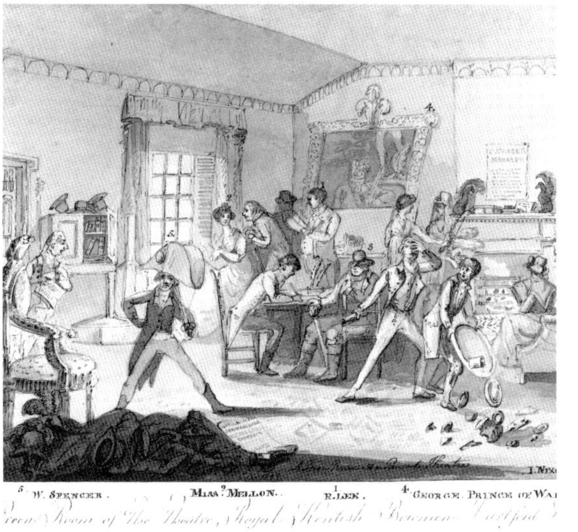

600

HARRIOT MELLON, JOE MADDOCKS, R. LEE, W. SPENCER and ten others
'Green Room of The Theatre, Royal Kentish Bowmen, Dartford Heath'

John Nixon

Black ink and wash on wove paper 16.7 x 22.1
INSCR: 'JN: 1799' (pen and brown ink b.c.);
'A Green Room at a Private Theatre'
(pen and brown ink b.c.);
'I. NIXON. 1799.' (pen and brown ink l.r.);
five figures are numbered in pen and brown ink and identified, viz: '1. R. LEE; 2. MISS MELLON; 3. JOE MADDOCKS; 4. GEORGE PRINCE OF WALES; 5. W. SPENCER; C. SPENCER / MANAGER'
(pen and brown ink over mantel at r.);
'Green Room of The Theatre, Royal Kentish Bowmen, Dartford Heath.' (pen and grey ink under)
INV: Not listed
PROV: John Nixon, *Dramatic Annals*, 3: 228
LIT: Sybil Rosenfeld, 'Private Theatricals at Bowman's Lodge, Dartford', *Theatre Notebook* (1961–62), 16: 125–26

This picture shows 14 full-length figures in an interior, four seated and the rest standing.

A man at left holds the prompt copy and points to a chair lower left. William Robert Spencer is left of centre, standing in front with his legs spread, wearing a large half-moon hat and holding a sword over his left shoulder. Miss Mellon is seated by the window behind, her head turned and looking at a man who leans on the back of her chair. On the far right, two ladies, one of them Miss Dixon, sit on a sofa by a coal fire.

A large full-length portrait of the Prince of Wales, after Hoppner, leans against the wall at the rear.

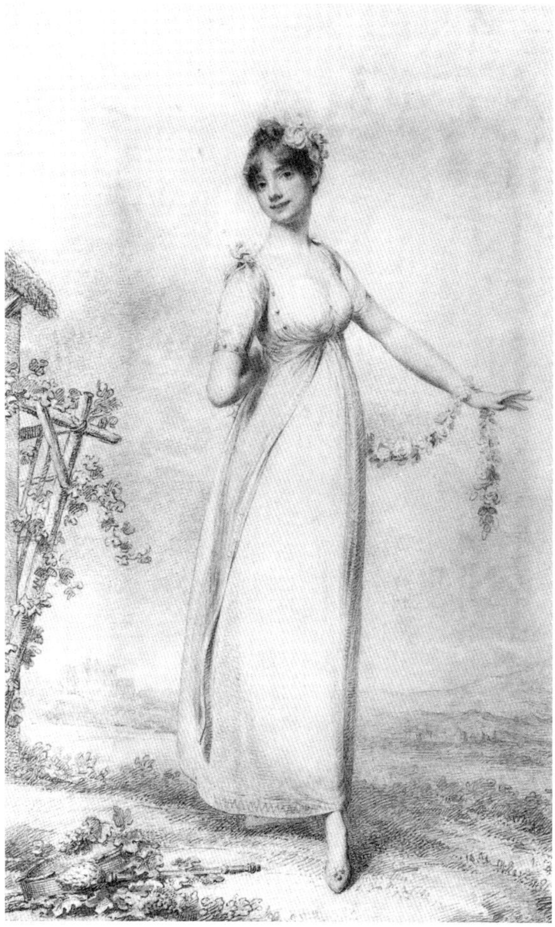

601

ARABELLA MENAGE
in character

William Wood

Pencil, pen and brown ink, and watercolour on wove paper 29.2 x 21
INV: RW/CKA 316; Gift 61
PROV: W. Abington, by whom presented to the Garrick Club, 1841

Arabella Menage wears a high-waisted white dress with a slight pink overdress, and dances with a garland. She has flowers in her hair, and a tambourine and thyrsus at her feet. These, with the Italian landscape background, including a smoking volcano, indicate that Menage is depicted in an Arcadian entertainment, though this has not been identified. The technique of the drawing is that of Cosway and Edridge, with watercolour restricted to the hair and flesh and to the pink of the dress.

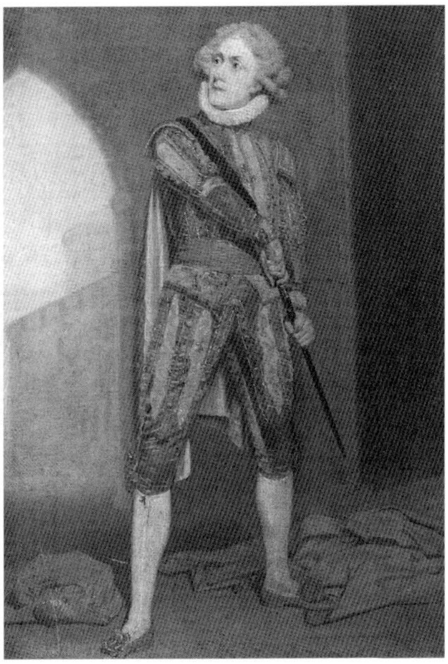

602
JAMES MIDDLETON
as Salisbury in *The Countess of Salisbury*
by Hall Hartson

Samuel De Wilde

Oil on canvas 36.2 x 26.5
INV: RW/CKA 254; Gift 88
PROV: John Bell; Mr West, by whom presented to the Garrick Club, 1843
EXH: 1962 Chichester (21)
ENGR: Philippe Audinet for Bell's British Library 9 February 1793, line 11.5 x 8.2, pub. Bell's *British Theatre* (1797), vol 18
REL: NPG Drawings Reserve D21, pencil and watercolour on laid paper 38.5 x 28 (apparently a crude copy)

In Act II, scene I, 'within a castle', Salisbury, known to most of the characters as the wandering soldier Alwin, has just flung down some of his disguise and speaks the line quoted on the engraving: 'Come on / 'Tis Salisbury, Salisbury calls thee to the Strife.' The dull pink hat with scallop shell and cloak used in his disguise are on the ground. His shoes have blue rosettes and his crimson doublet and breeches are slashed in blue and silver. His blue cloak has a white lining.

Hartson's tragedy was first performed at the Crow Street Theatre, Dublin, on 2 May 1765, and in London at the Haymarket on 21 August 1767, with Spranger Barry as Salisbury. Other actors who subsequently played the role included William Powell (CG 26 October 1768), William Smith (DL 6 March 1784), John Henderson (CG 12 January 1780) and J.P. Kemble (DL 13 April 1784), but Middleton never performed the part in London.

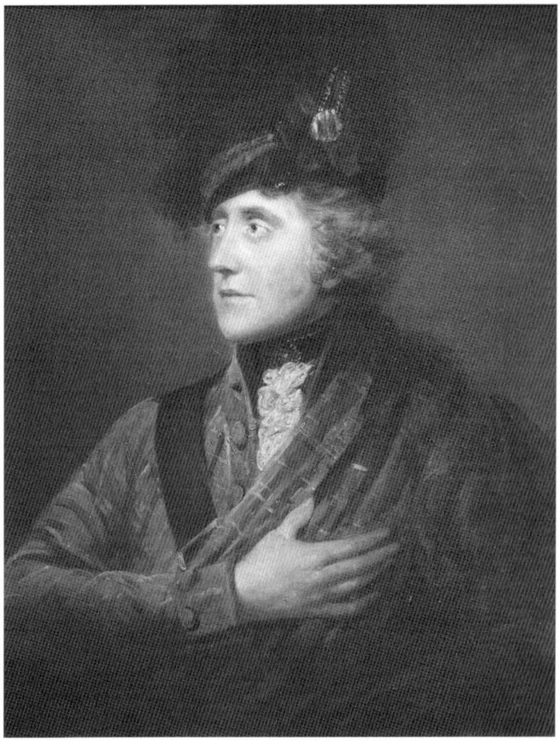

603
JAMES MIDDLETON
as Young Norval in *Douglas* by John Home

Gainsborough Dupont

Oil on canvas 78.7 x 66
INV: Mathews 156; RW/CKA 461
PROV: Thomas Harris; Harris sale, Robins 12 July 1819 (13) (no character); Charles Mathews
EXH: 1833 London (156); 1982–83 London (130)
LIT: *Morning Herald*, 22 March 1794; Hayes, 1968

Young Norval has just been told by Lady Randolph that his father was the brave and noble Douglas, and furthermore that she is his mother, parted from him on the day of his birth. The painting shows the moment just after that shown in No. 305. Young Norval wears a blue and green plaid jacket, with a red, green and yellow plaid over his left shoulder, and a tall black fur hat with a green and red plaid band around it and black feathers.

Although the *Morning Herald* of 22 March 1794 stated that Middleton had been painted as Young Norval, there is no record of his having played the part in London. His single recorded appearance in *Douglas* was as late as 26 October 1796, when he played Lord Randolph.

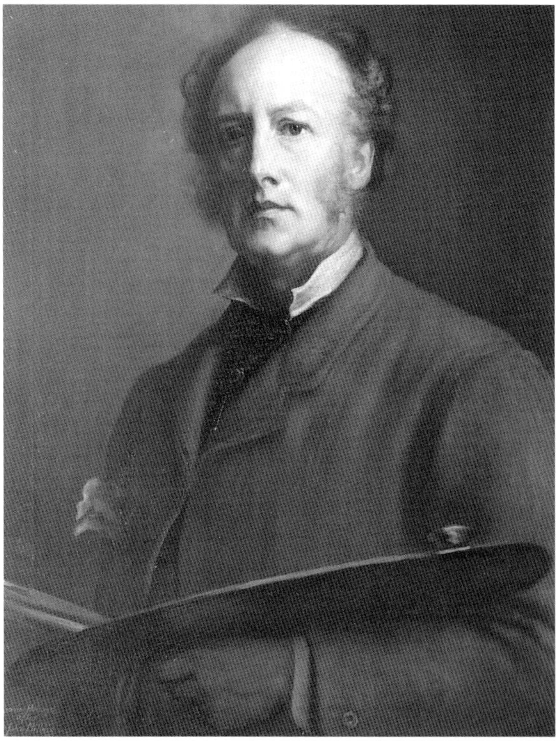

604
SIR JOHN EVERETT MILLAIS

Sir Charles Holroyd (after Millais)

Oil on canvas 84.5 x 62.2
INSCR: 'Charles Holroyd / after / Sir John Millais / of 1880.1897.' (red paint b.l.)
INV: RW/CKA 336; Gift 259A
PROV: Presented to the Garrick Club by 105 members, 1898
REL: Original: Uffizi 849, oil on canvas 86 x 65

Millais holds a palette with four brushes and a thinning pot. He wears a brown jacket, a shirt with a stand-up collar and a black tie.

Sir John, a founding member of the Pre-Raphaelite Brotherhood in 1848, became from the 1860s onward a leading society portraitist, responsible for some of the definitive images of the great men of Victorian England. Among these his likenesses of Sir John Hare and Sir Henry Irving are in the Garrick Club's collection (Nos. 282 and 323), as is a case in which are displayed a group of brushes and tubes of paint belonging to the artist. Millais was a Club member from 1855.

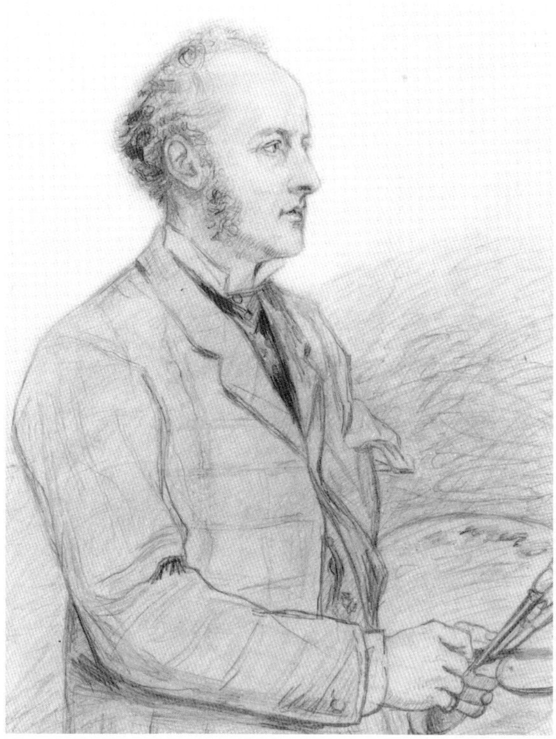

605
SIR JOHN EVERETT MILLAIS

Sir Leslie Ward ('Spy')

Pencil on wove paper with touches of brown wash 28.6 x 22.2
INSCR: 'Drawn by Leslie Ward ['Spy' of *Vanity Fair*] / for and Engraved by the / Illustrated London News. / PRESENTED BY SIR CHARLES HALL Q.C. M.P.' (pen and ink on mount b.c.)
INV: RW/CKA 584; Gift 259
PROV: Sir Charles Hall Q.C., by whom presented to the Garrick Club, 1898
LIT: *The Graphic*, 22 August 1896, p. 247

Millais hold a palette with three brushes. He wears a jacket with a large check pattern.

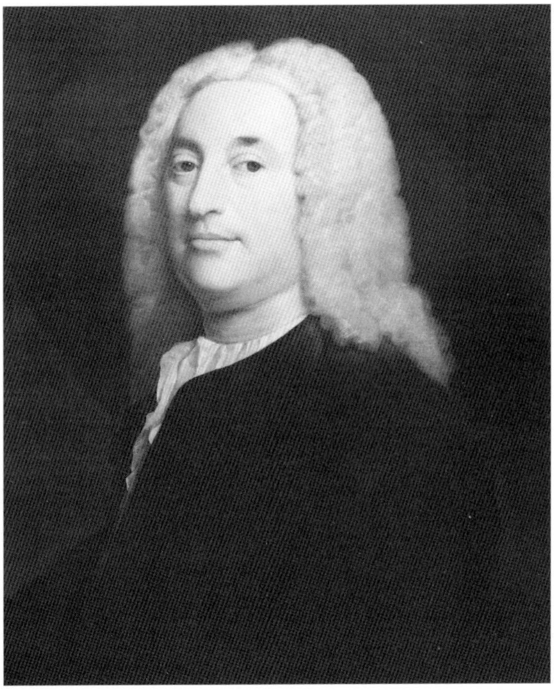

606
JOHN MILLS
as Pierre (?) in *Venice Preserv'd*
by Thomas Otway

Peter Van Bleeck

Oil on canvas 74.9 x 61.6
INV: Mathews 101 (artist unknown, no character);
RW 395 (artist unknown); CKA 395 (no character)
PROV: Jane Pope; Charles Mathews
EXH: 1833 London (101)
ENGR: Clamp after a drawing by Sylvester Harding for Harding's *Biographical Mirrour* pub. E. & S. Harding 1 December 1796, stipple 13.3 x 11.1 (inscr: 'John Mills the Elder / From an Original Picture in the collection of Miss Pope / of Drury Lane Theatre')

The sitter wears a dark jacket; his highly-coloured complexion contrasts with his full powdered wig.

The BD suggests the picture shows Mills in the role for which he was best known.

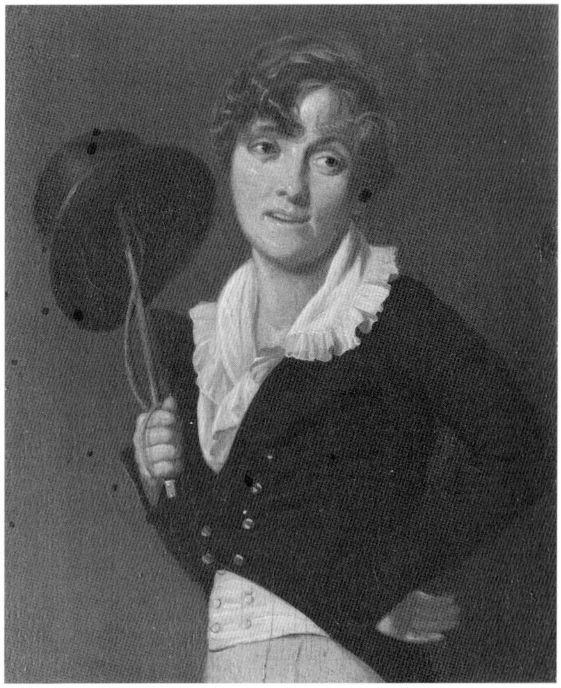

607
LOUISA MILLS
as Little Pickle in *The Spoiled Child*
by Isaac Bickerstaffe

Samuel De Wilde

Oil on panel 24 x 20.5
INV: Mathews 41; RW/CKA 222
PROV: Charles Mathews
EXH: 1833 London (41); 1971 Northampton (13)
REL: Christie's 29 March 1983 (99), black and red chalk on wove Whatman paper 24.8 x 19.3, inscr: 'S De Wilde / 1802', now owned by Ian Mayes

Little Pickle is the Spoiled Child – a boy played by an actress who looked good in breeches. Mrs Mills holds a riding crop on top of which is a black hat with a tall crown; she wears brown breeches, a grey cutaway jacket, a white waistcoat, and a wide loose white collar with frills.

Bickerstaffe's farce was first performed at the Haymarket on 22 March 1790, with Mrs Jordan as Little Pickle. Mrs Mills first played the part at Covent Garden on 3 October 1798, the night she made her début there, when she also acted Sophia in *The Road to Ruin*.

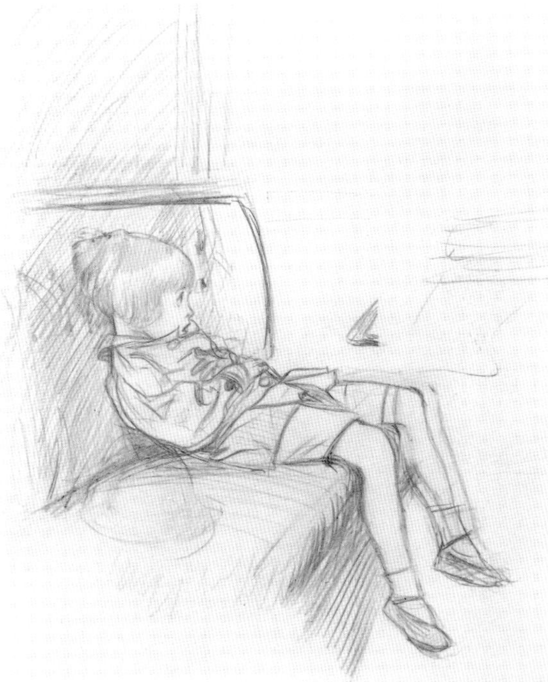

608
CHRISTOPHER ROBIN MILNE

Ernest Howard Shepard

Pencil on wove paper
INV: Not listed
PROV: Purchased 1988, for £3,000
EXH: 1988 Sotheby's Childhood Exhibition (156/1)

This drawing shows Milne as a young boy, slouching on a sofa. C.R. Milne – Christopher Robin of the Pooh stories – was a member of the Garrick Club from 1976 to 1984. The Club enjoys income from the royalties on the works of his father, A.A. Milne, who became a member of the Garrick Club in 1919.

E.H. Shepard, who worked for *Punch*, gained fame as an illustrator of children's books, notably A.A. Milne's *Winnie-The-Pooh* and Kenneth Grahame's *The Wind in the Willows.*

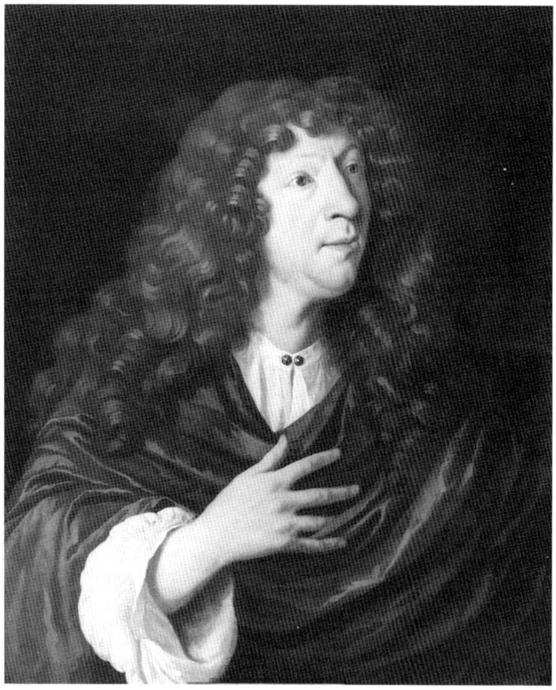

609
MOLIÈRE (?)

Abraham Cornelisz Begeijn

Oil on canvas 73.7 x 62.2
INSCR: 'A. Bega fe / 1679'
INV: RW/CKA 179; Gift 450
PROV: Francis N. Smith, by whom bequeathed to the Garrick Club, 1928

The identification of the sitter is fanciful. However, the gesture and romantic aspect of the portrait suggest he could be a poet.

The sitter, shown half-length, wears a maroon toga-like garment, a white collarless shirt, and a flowing wig.

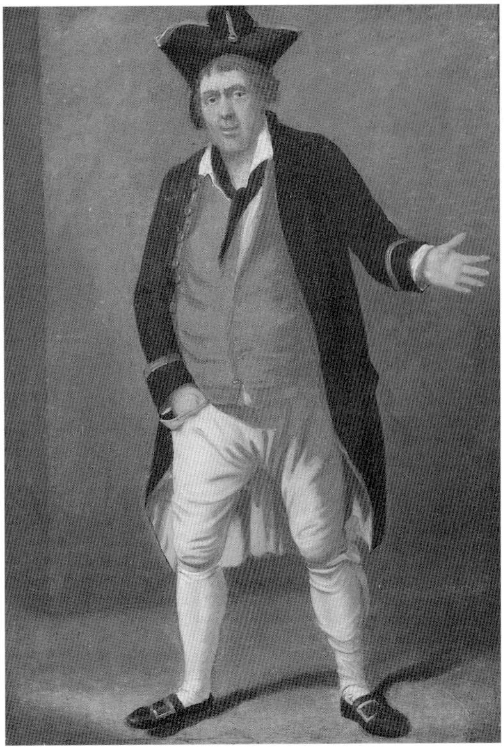

610
JOHN MOODY
as Commodore Flip in *The Fair Quaker of Deal*
by Charles Shadwell, altered by
Captain Edward Thompson

Samuel De Wilde

Oil on canvas 36.2 x 26.2
INV: RW/CKA 270; Gift 88
PROV: John Bell; Mr West, by whom presented
to the Garrick Club, 1843
ENGR: Samuel De Wilde, stipple 37.2 x 27.5; Philippe
Audinet for Bell's British Library 2 January 1792, line
11.1 x 8, pub. Bell's *British Theatre* (1797), vol 14, with the
quotation, from Act IV: 'This lady is dispos'd of, and
her inclinations (are moored to my affections).'

The Commodore prepares for his marriage by becoming inebriated. He wears black shoes, sagging white hose, loose-fitting white breeches, a long blue coat lined in white and edged in gold, a red waistcoat partly fastened with gold buttons, a white open-necked shirt, very loosely tied black stock, and black tricorn hat.

Captain Thompson's adaptation of Shadwell's 1710 comedy was first performed at Drury Lane on 9 November 1773, with Moody as Commodore Flip. The last performance before De Wilde painted his picture was at Drury Lane on 6 January 1785, with Moody in his original part.

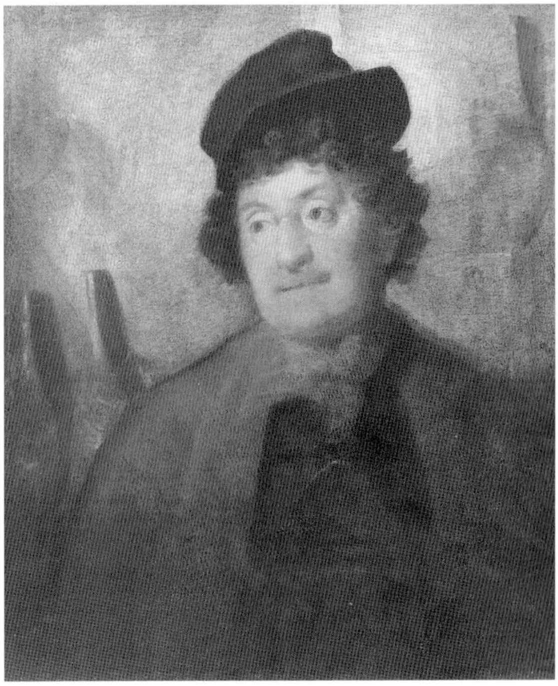

611
JOHN MOODY
as Jobson in *The Devil to Pay*
by Charles Coffey and John Mottley

Samuel Drummond

Oil on canvas 76.5 x 64.5
INV: Mathews 187; RW/CKA 455
PROV: Charles Mathews
EXH: 1833 London (187)
ENGR: William Bromley for the *European Magazine*
pub. John Sewell 1790, line 9.8 x 7.3

Zekel Jobson is the 'psalm-singing cobler' who beats his wife. His homespun costume consists of a tattered brown hat and a red garment over his shoulders.

Coffey and Mottley's ballad opera – taken from Thomas Jevon's *The Devil of a Wife* – was first performed at Drury Lane on 6 August 1731, with Harper as Jobson. Moody played Jobson for the first time on 24 November 1764, at Drury Lane.

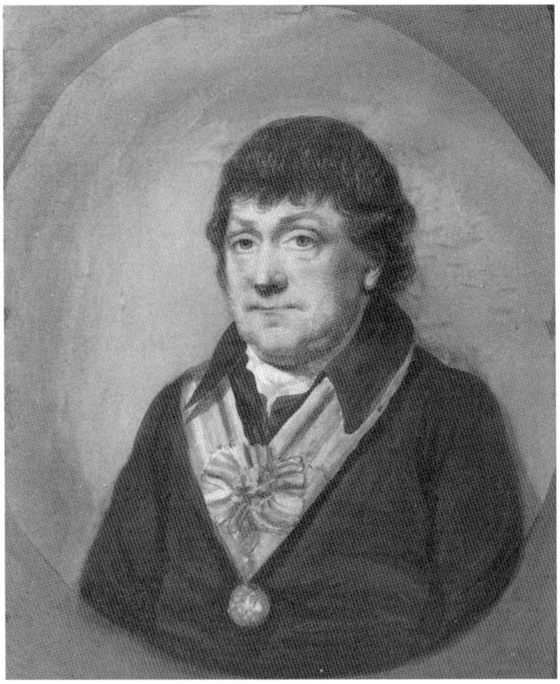

612

JOHN MOODY

'School of Garrick'

Henry Spicer

Pencil and watercolour on laid paper 26.5 x 21
INV: Mathews 257 (artist unknown);
RW/CKA 50C (artist unknown)
PROV: Charles Mathews
EXH: 1833 London (257)
ENGR: William Ridley for Parsons's *Minor Theatre*
pub. J. Parsons 18 October 1794, stipple 6.9 x 5.5
(in reverse, without ribbon and medal)

Moody is dressed in a blue jacket, with the collar turned down over his Shakespeare Ribband, from which hangs a Shakespeare Favour.

For 'School of Garrick', see No. 6. Moody acted under Garrick at Drury Lane from 1759 to 1776, and continued there under Sheridan and Kemble through 1795–96. He was a serviceable actor who excelled in the roles of comic Irishmen, notably Major O'Flaherty in *The West Indian* and Commodore Flip in *The Fair Quaker of Deal* (see No. 610).

He was one of the original committee of actors which established the rules for the Drury Lane Fund in 1774, and was the Fund's Master from 1805 to 1812. The 'Memorandum' that he kept as Master is now in the Garrick Club's library.

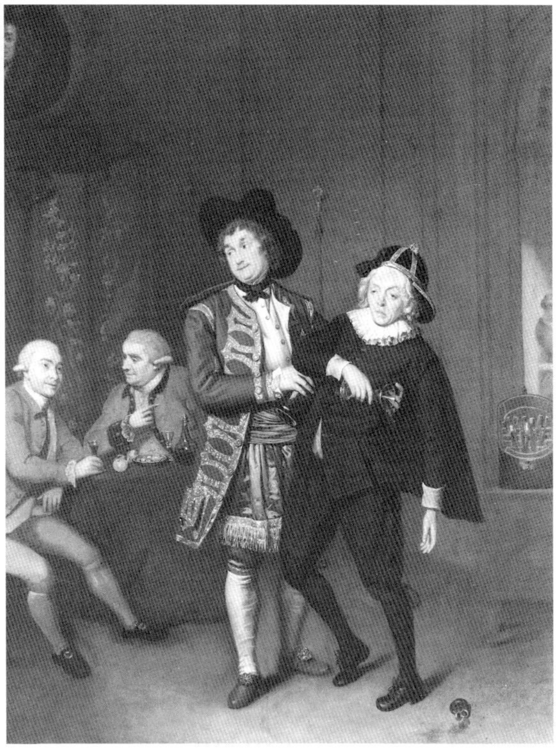

613*

JOHN MOODY as Teague,
WILLIAM PARSONS as Obadiah,
THOMAS JEFFERSON as Colonel Restless
and *JAMES AICKIN* as Colonel Blunt
in *The Committee* by Sir Robert Howard

Benjamin Vandergucht

Oil on canvas 126.5 x 100.5
INV: Mathews 127; RW/CKA 33
PROV: Charles Mathews
EXH: 1775 R.A. (321) 'A scene in the Committee, or the Faithful Irishman. Act IV Scene III';
1833 London (127); 1950–51 London (58);
1951–52 London (120)
ENGR: Joseph Collyer, after a drawing by Daniel Dodd, for Lowndes's *New English Theatre* pub. Thomas Lowndes 8 November 1776, line 13.3 x 8.6 ('Dodd ad viv. delt')
LIT: J.R. Planché, *A Cyclopædia of Costume* (1876–79), 2: 243 & 408; Griffiths, p. 324

In 1646 the Presbyterian religion was established by Parliament, the Episcopacy was abolished, the Covenant imposed, and *The Book of Common Prayer* replaced by *The Presbyterian Directory*. In Howard's play the 'Committee' is the Honourable Committee of Sequestration, which is empowered to take control of Loyalist estates and return them only on the owner's signing the Covenant. Obadiah is the clerk to the committee, and Colonel

Careless is a Royalist whose estate has been sequestered and who refuses to sign the Covenant. Teague, a blunt Irishman, has been taken on as a footman by Colonel Restless. In Act IV, scene I, Obadiah invites Careless and his friend Colonel Blunt to meet Mr Day, the chairman of the Sequestration Committee. Careless gets Teague to ply Obadiah with drink. Teague and Obadiah enter drunk and, while Restless and Blunt watch in the background, Teague offers Obadiah snuff, which spills to the ground. Obadiah says: 'I will snuff for the king no more. Good Mr Teague, give me some more sack, and sing English, for my money.' In the picture, the snuff horn lies on the floor, and Obadiah spills his wine as Teague supports him.

The text calls for a musician rather than the two seated colonels. Their incongruous late 18th-century costume and incorrect scale suggest that they were painted over the original figure of the musician. Both colonels wear red coats. Teague (Moody) has blue rosettes on his shoes, white stockings, blue breeches, a broad blue silk sash with silver fringe, a blue coat faced with silver braid, and a white waistcoat. Obadiah (Parsons) is in black, with his black and silver peaked cap awry on his head. On the back wall is a portrait, identified by CKA as Sir Robert Howard, the author of the play, but there is no support for this identification; the picture looks more like a portrait of James II, after Lely (NPG 5211).

Howard's comedy was originally performed at the Theatre Royal, Vere Street, on 27 November 1662. Moody played Teague for the first time at Drury Lane on 29 December 1760. He acted the role with Parsons as Obadiah for the first time at Drury Lane on 17 April 1771, and they appeared together five more times to 1775. The performance on 17 April 1775, when Jefferson took the part of Restless and Aickin that of Blunt, was for Moody's benefit and probably inspired Vandergucht's picture.

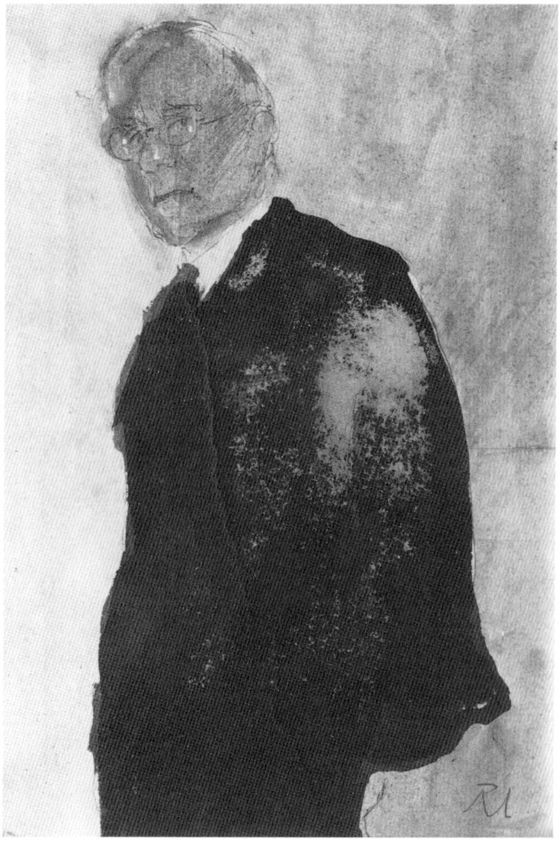

614

STANLEY ARTHUR MORISON

R. Lutyens

Pencil, watercolour and gouache
on coarse wove paper 26.8 x 20
INSCR: 'R L' (pencil b.r.);
R.W.S. Galleries label on verso, 'No. 3; 36 gns;
Sketch for the portrait of Stanley Morison Esq'
INV: GCL 717; Gift 829
PROV: J. Carter, by whom presented
to the Garrick Club, 1968

Morison wears spectacles, and a dark suit and tie. There is a large patch of rubbing in the middle of the drawing.

Stanley Morison was a member of the Garrick Club from 1931 until his death in 1967. He was an authority on typography and wrote many books and articles on that subject and on printing. His collection is in the 'Morison Room' at the Cambridge University Library. Among his publications was a study in 1930 of John Bell (1745–1831), an important printer who published various editions of Bell's *Shakespeare* and Bell's *British Theatre* with numerous engravings of actors.

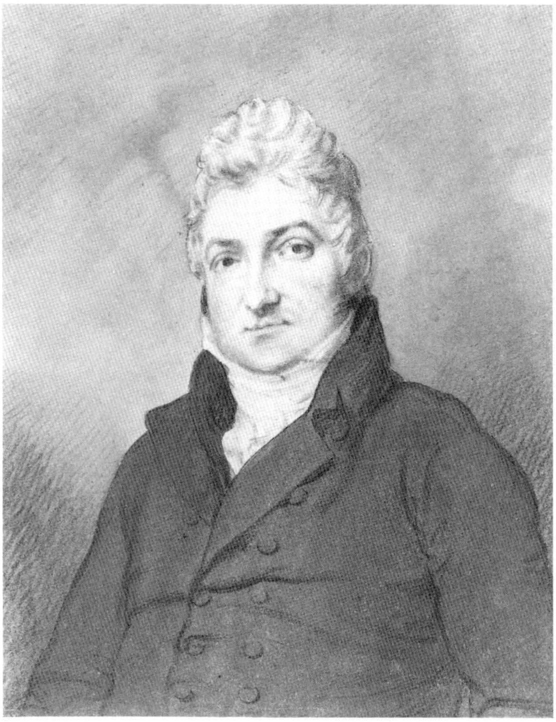

615
THOMAS MORTON

Samuel De Wilde

Pencil and watercolour on wove paper 20.3 x 16.5
INV: RW 181? (unknown by unknown);
CKA 181 (Unknown Man probably by S. De Wilde)
PROV: Unknown
EXH: 1804 R.A. (511)
ENGR: James Hopwood for Inchbald's *Farces*
pub. Longman & Co. 1806, stipple 8.9 x 7

Morton, wearing a dark grey coat, is shown half-length, facing the spectator.

He was a successful author of sentimental comedies and melodramas at the end of the 18th century. His most popular plays included *The Way to Get Married* (1796), *A Cure for the Heartache* (1797), and *Speed the Plough* (1800).

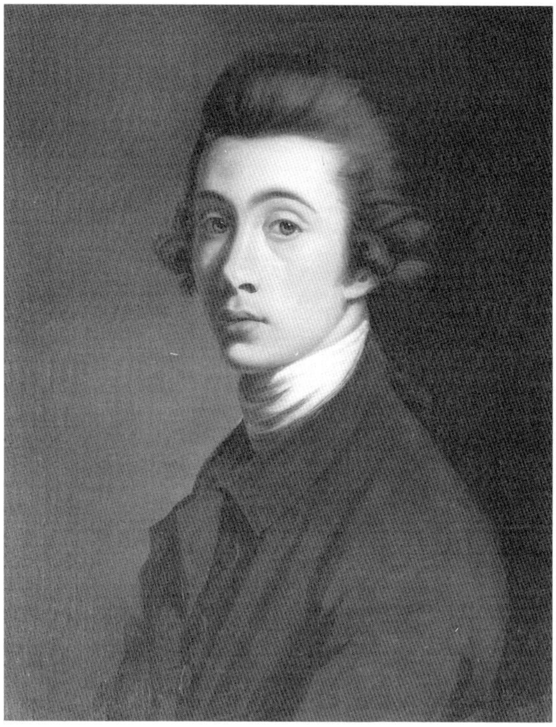

616
HENRY MOSSOP

Nathaniel Hone

Oil on canvas 61.5 x 49.5
INV: RW/CKA 42; Gift 277
PROV: Major-General John Upperton
(offered to NPG Nov 1896); Sir Squire Bancroft,
by whom presented to the Garrick Club, 1901

Head and shoulders, in a dark brown jacket.

The Irishman Mossop made his début at Drury Lane as Richard III on 26 September 1751. He left Drury Lane in 1759 and was sometime manager at the Smock Alley Theatre and Crow Street Theatre, Dublin. After becoming a bankrupt in 1772, he died in poverty in 1774. Despite his financial dilemmas, Mossop seems to have been an estimable actor at the height of his career.

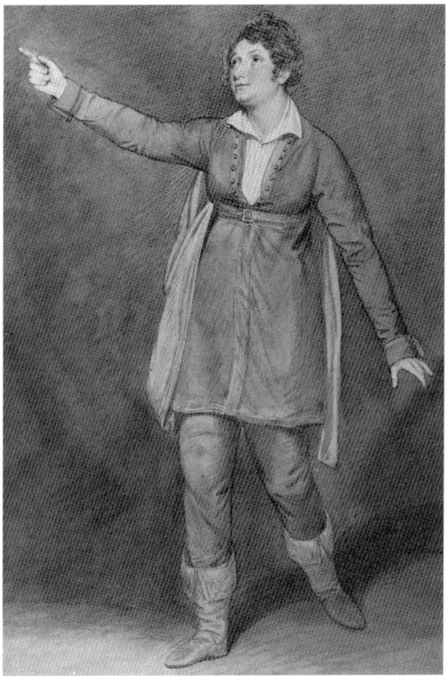

617
ROSEMOND MOUNTAIN
as Matilda in *Richard Cœur de Lion*
by John Burgoyne

Samuel De Wilde

Black chalk, pencil and watercolour
on wove paper 37 x 23.5
INV: Mathews 201; RW/CKA 61D
PROV: Charles Mathews
EXH: 1833 London (201)
ENGR: Schiavonetti for Cawthorn's *Minor British Theatre*
pub. John Cawthorn 2 August 1806, stipple 12 x 8

Matilda, disguised as a young man, is searching for her husband, Richard Cœur de Lion, who she believes is imprisoned in the castle. She is pretending to be blind, and has as her guide a 16-year-old boy called Antonio, also a cross-dressed part. Matilda wears romantic male attire: brown boots with large turnovers, green trousers, a green long-sleeved jerkin, a pink cloak edged with a green band, and a white shirt with open collar.

Burgoyne's melodrama, based on Michel Jean Sedaine's play, was first performed at Drury Lane on 23 October 1786. The music was by Grétry adapted by Thomas Linley and the scenery by Thomas Greenwood. Mrs Jordan was the original Matilda, and she kept the part until Mrs Crouch took over on 8 November 1797. Mrs Mountain first played the part at Drury Lane, on 6 October 1804, the first performance of the piece since 19 December 1797.

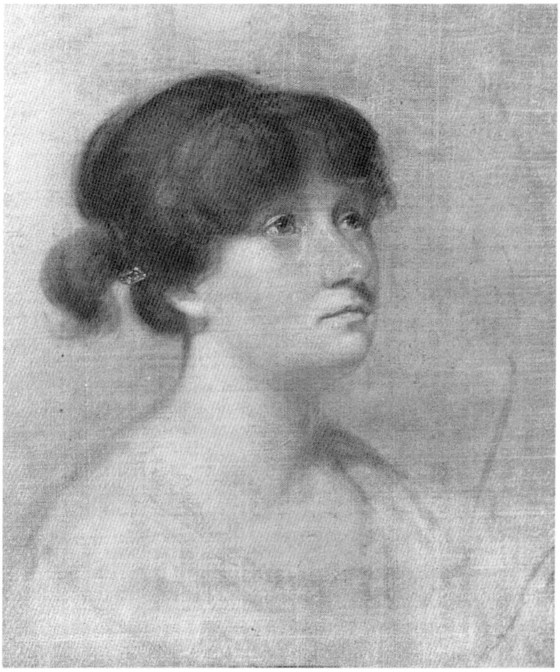

618
ROSEMOND MOUNTAIN

George Romney (?)

Oil on canvas 51.5 x 44.5
INV: Mathews 37; RW/CKA 428
PROV: Charles Mathews
EXH: 1833 London (37)

Mrs Mountain's hair is held at the back by a jewel. She wears a white dress, edged in yellow. This picture seems unfinished.

There seems no reason to doubt Mathews's identification of the sitter, and the picture dates from about 1795–1800. The attribution to Romney, however, is probably optimistic. By the time the artist retired to Kendal in 1798, he was, as Ellis Waterhouse observes, 'more or less imbecile'.

This singing actress was at Covent Garden from 1786–87 to 1797–98, and with the Drury Lane Company from 1800–1801 to 1815. Her repertoire included dozens of roles in burlettas, melodramas and other musical pieces. In his *Dramatic Biography* (1825), Oxberry praised her 'artless, elegant manners' and 'unaffected urbanity'.

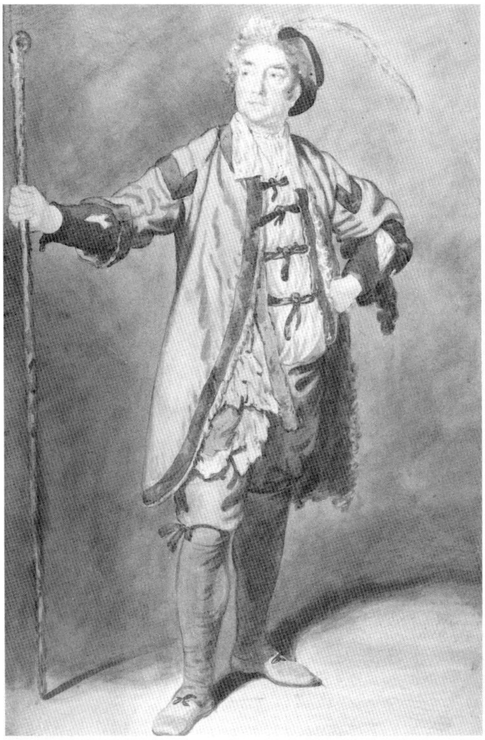

619

JOSEPH MUNDEN

as Autolycus in *The Winter's Tale*

by William Shakespeare

Samuel De Wilde

Pencil and watercolour on wove paper 37 x 23.5
INSCR: 'S De Wilde .../ 1818' (pencil b.r.)
INV: Mathews 220; RW/CKA 45B
PROV: Charles Mathews
EXH: 1833 London (220); 1975 London (138)
REL: See No. 620

The scene is Act IV, scene 2, in which Autolycus sings 'Jog on, jog on, the foot-path way', the quotation on the engraving. According to a prompt copy in the Garrick Club, Autolycus enters stage left and leaves stage right. The markings are in a copy with alterations by J.P. Kemble for his production at Drury Lane on 25 March 1802, and presumably used for his 1807 revival. A later prompt copy, with the same marking in this scene, is dated 1811. Autolycus wears brown slippers with darker brown bows, green stockings, grey breeches with bows at the knee, a long coat in faded pink, and a ragged grey jerkin torn at lower sleeves to reveal a white shirt.

Munden played Autolycus for the first time in London at Covent Garden on 11 May 1792. His only other London appearance in the role in the 18th century was at Covent Garden on 22 December 1795.

620

LOCATION UNKNOWN

JOSEPH MUNDEN

as Autolycus in *The Winter's Tale*

by William Shakespeare

Samuel De Wilde

Pencil and watercolour on wove paper 37.5 x 23.5
INSCR: 'S De Wilde del / 1822' (pencil b.l.);
'£3.3.0 De Wilde, signed 1822' (pencil on verso t.l.);
'7' (pencil on verso t.c.); '184 / 1' (white chalk on verso c.);
'Mr Munden / as / Autolycus /in the Winter's Tale'
(pen and brown ink on verso b.r.)
INV: CKA 484; Gift 457
PROV: Sir Arthur Wing Pinero, by whom
presented to the Garrick Club, 1929
EXH: 1964 London [2] (84)
ENGR: William Bond pub. Bell & De Camp 1 August 1809,
stipple 15.1 x 9; same plate for the *Theatrical Inquisitor*
pub. C. Chapple 30 June 1813
REL: See No. 619. [Two portraits of Munden in
this role, one signed and dated by De Wilde and the
other a watercolour said to be by C. Tomkins, were in
the Royal Dramatic College sale at Fairbrother, Lye
and Palmer on 24 February 1881 (lots 85 & 100K).]

Munden holds a gnarled stick and wears brown shoes with black bows, green stockings, brown breeches with dark brown bands around the knee, a long brown jacket with darker brown edging, another jacket underneath, tied with four black bows across the chest, and a white shirt. See No. 619.

This picture was not found in 1996.

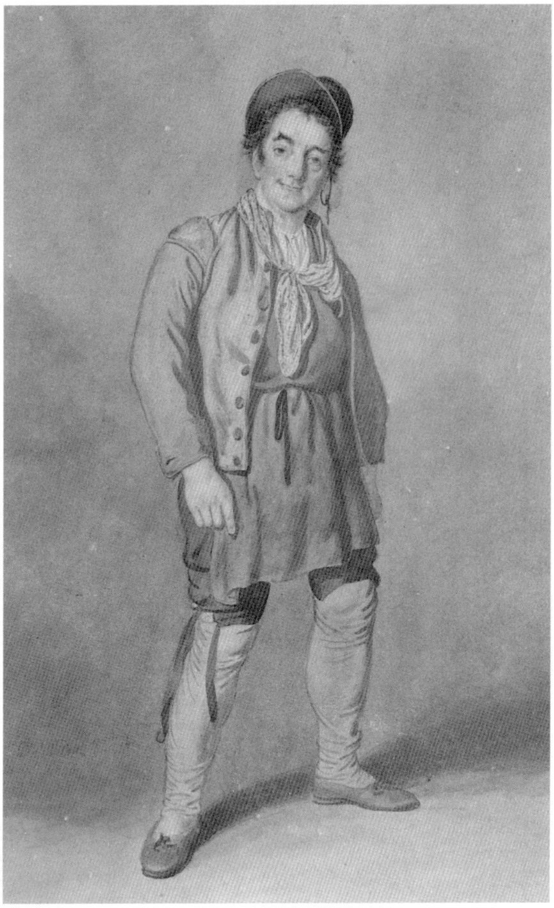

621
JOSEPH MUNDEN
as Crack in *The Turnpike Gate*
by Thomas Knight

Samuel De Wilde

Pencil and watercolour on wove paper 37 x 23.5
INSCR: 'Saml De Wilde delin / October 30th 1808' (pencil b.l.)
INV: Mathews 221; RW/CKA 60C
PROV: Charles Mathews
EXH: 1809 R.A. (399) 'A drawing of Mr Munden as Crack, in the Turnpike Gate'; 1833 London (221)

Crack is the humorous element of the play, always ready with a heavy-handed quip. He wears a grey hat on the back of his head, brown shoes, loose grey stockings, blue breeches, a brown leather apron, a brown leather jerkin with dark brown buttons down the front, and a yellow and brown neckerchief tied loosely around his neck.

Knight's comic opera, with music by J. Mazzinghi and W. Reeve and scenery by Phillips and Inigo Richards, was performed for the first time at Covent Garden on 14 November 1799, with Munden the original Crack.

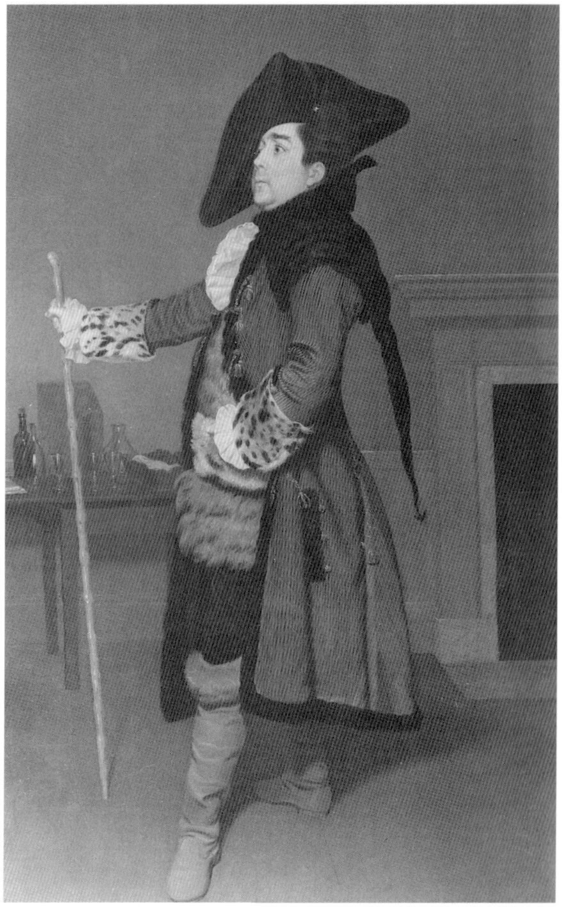

622
JOSEPH MUNDEN
as Peregrine Forester in *Hartford Bridge*
by William Pearce

Samuel De Wilde

Oil on canvas 68.5 x 42
INV: Mathews 124; RW/CKA 123
PROV: Charles Mathews
EXH: 1795 R.A. (242)? 'Scene in Hartford Bridge'; 1833 London (124); 1951 London (9)

The part of Peregrine Forester is witty, short and brilliant. He is extremely well-travelled, 'having traced the Ganges and the Whamboo to their source, wandered to the summit of the Marble Mountains, and the mountains of the moon, and toasted muffins at a volcano'.

In the Cumberland edition of the play, Peregrine's costume is described as a 'Green surtout coat, trimmed with black fur, blue plush waistcoat, black breeches'. In the painting he wears high brown boots, black breeches, a long, bright green coat edged in black fur with gold braid, black decorations and large leopardskin cuffs, a short black fur cloak, a waistcoat that appears to be made of layers of feathers, a black stock with a big white frill at the front, and a large tricorn hat.

Pearce's operatic farce, with music by William Shield, Haydn and Sacchini and scenery by Inigo Richards, was first performed at Covent Garden on 3 November 1792, with Munden as the original Peregrine Forester.

This is one of De Wilde's best pictures, and it seems likely that it is the painting exhibited at the R.A. in 1795, despite its description as a 'scene'. During the 1794–95 season, Munden played Peregrine Forester at Covent Garden on 1 October 1794 and on 10 February 1795.

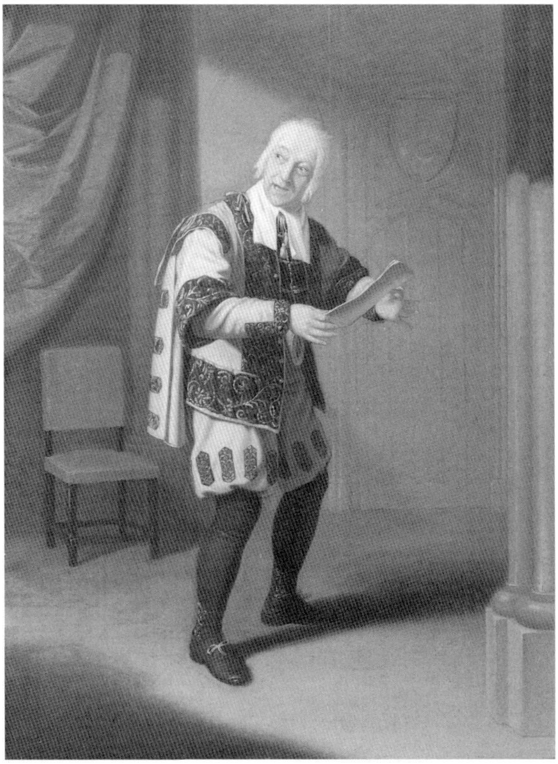

623

JOSEPH MUNDEN

as Verdun in *Lovers' Vows*

by Elizabeth Inchbald

Samuel De Wilde

Oil on canvas 73.7 x 55.9

INSCR: 'S De Wilde f / 1799' (dark brown paint b.l.)

INV: Mathews 78; RW/CKA 109

PROV: Thomas Harris; Harris sale, Robins 12 July 1819 (60); Charles Mathews

EXH: 1799 R.A. (81); 1833 London (78)

Verdun is Baron Wildenheim's butler. His elaborate livery consists of black shoes with yellow bows, black stockings with clocks, buff trunk hose with black appliqué panels embroidered in silver, buff jerkin and coat with similar decorative panels, and a white collar. A red chair and drape can be seen in the background.

Mrs Inchbald's play, adapted from Kotzebue's *Das Kind der Liebe*, was first performed at Covent Garden on 11 October 1798, with Munden as the original Verdun the Butler. It is the play which causes so much trouble at Mansfield Park in Jane Austen's novel.

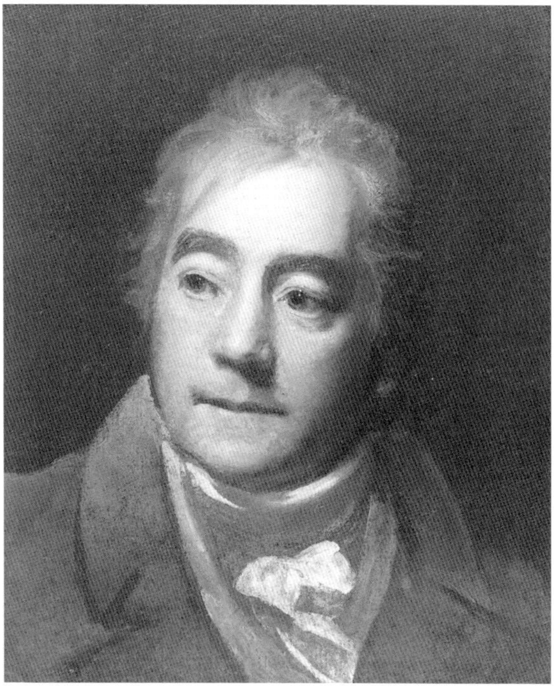

624

JOSEPH MUNDEN

Samuel Drummond

Oil on panel 41.9 x 33, possibly cut down from a larger picture

INV: RW/CKA 433; Gift 114

PROV: Apparently presented by an unknown donor, 1852

Munden has dishevelled grey hair and a florid complexion. He wears a green coat with high collar, a yellow waistcoat, and a high white stock with bow.

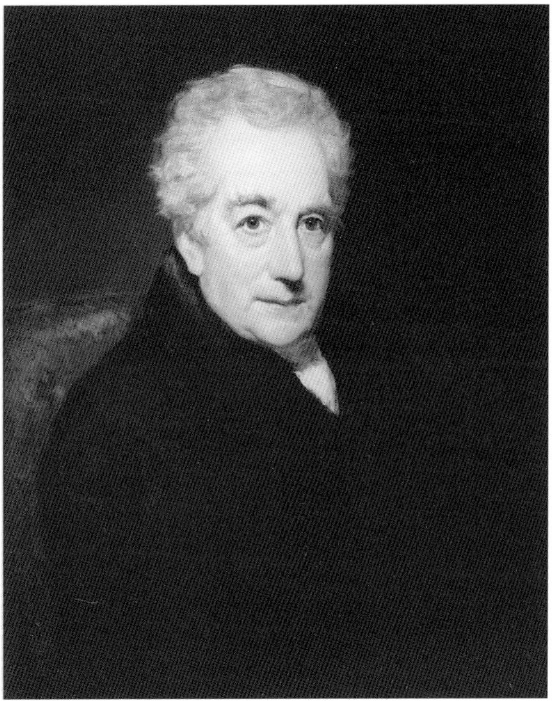

625
JOSEPH MUNDEN

John Prescott Knight

Oil on canvas 74.3 x 61.6
INV: RW/CKA 342; Gift 257
PROV: Bequeathed by Rudolph G. Glover
and received 1897
EXH: 1827 S.B.A. (89)
LIT: Herman Dyson, *John Prescott Knight, R.A., a catalogue* (1971), No. 11

The 70-year-old Munden, sitting in a padded green chair, wears a black coat and has white hair and a gnarled appearance.

626
LOCATION UNKNOWN
JOSEPH MUNDEN

James Lonsdale

Black and red chalk on wove paper 50.1 x 40
INSCR: 'Joe Munden Drawn from life by Jas. Lonsdale'
INV: (not in RW); CKA 141
PROV: Presented by the artist's son, 1852

Head and half shoulders, slightly to left, looking at the spectator.

This picture was not located in 1996.

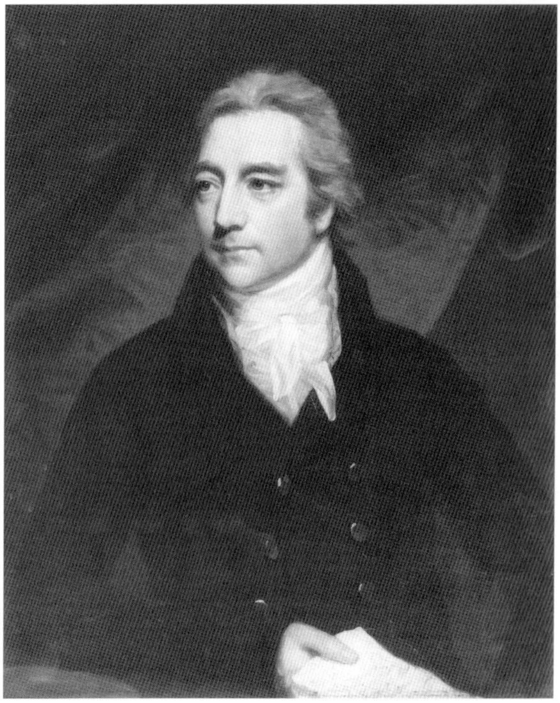

627
JOSEPH MUNDEN

John Opie

Oil on canvas 77 x 63
INV: Mathews 111; RW/CKA 405
PROV: Charles Mathews
EXH: 1833 London (111)
ENGR: Samuel William Reynolds pub. S.W. Reynolds 1804, mezzotint 28.6 x 23.9

Munden, holding a paper in his right hand, wears a dark coat with a high collar and gold buttons, a yellow waistcoat, and a high white stock with a bow.

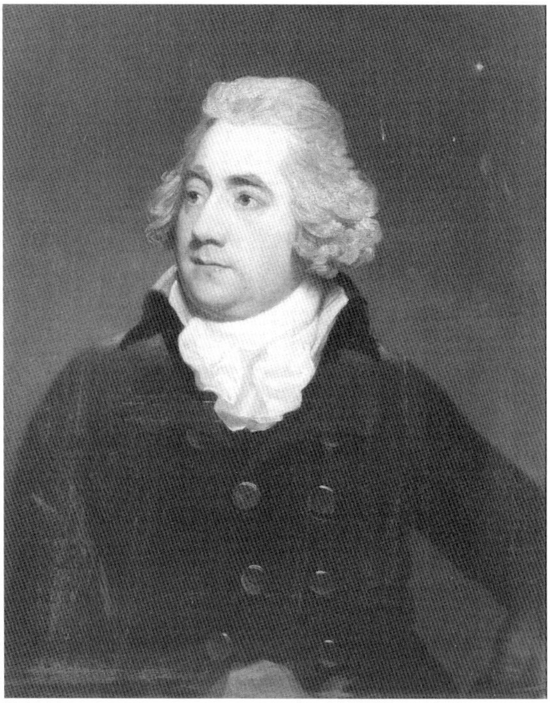

628
JOSEPH MUNDEN

Sir Martin Archer Shee

Oil on canvas 74.9 x 62.2
INV: RW/CKA 481; Gift 82
PROV: Presented by W.C. Macready, 1842
ENGR: William Ridley for Bellamy's *Picturesque Magazine*
pub. T. Bellamy 1793, stipple 9.2 x 7.9;
same plate used for the *European Magazine*
pub. J. Sewell 1 May 1796

Munden wears a dark blue coat with brass buttons, the high collar lined with yellow, and a high white stock with frills.

Munden first appeared in London at the Haymarket Theatre on 11 January 1779 as Andrew in *The Students*, but his career was spent mostly at Covent Garden from 1790–91 through 1810–11, playing in farces, light comedies and musical pieces. Though very popular with the public, he was not always praised by the critics, who accused him of mugging and caricaturing. But Lamb claimed in *Essays of Elia* that in the grotesque aspects of farce Munden stood out as single and unaccompanied as Hogarth.

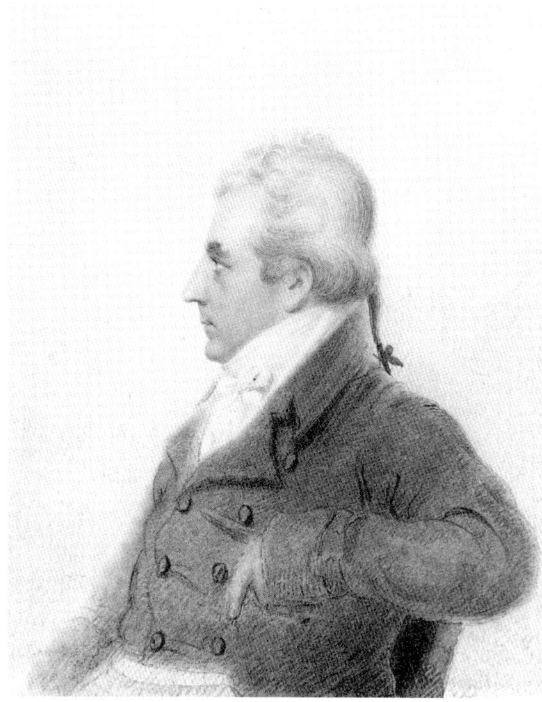

629
JOSEPH MUNDEN

John Turmeau

Black chalk with pencil and watercolour
on wove paper 17.1 x 15.2
INSCR: 'Turmeau Fecit' (pen and brown ink
on mount b.l. CM); 'Mr Munden'
(pen and brown ink on mount b.c. CM)
INV: Mathews 344; RW 559B (artist unknown);
CKA 559B (by S. De Wilde)
PROV: Charles Mathews
EXH: 1833 London (344)

Munden is shown seated in profile to left, half-length, wearing a dark cutaway coat.

Why CKA attributed the drawing to De Wilde is unclear.

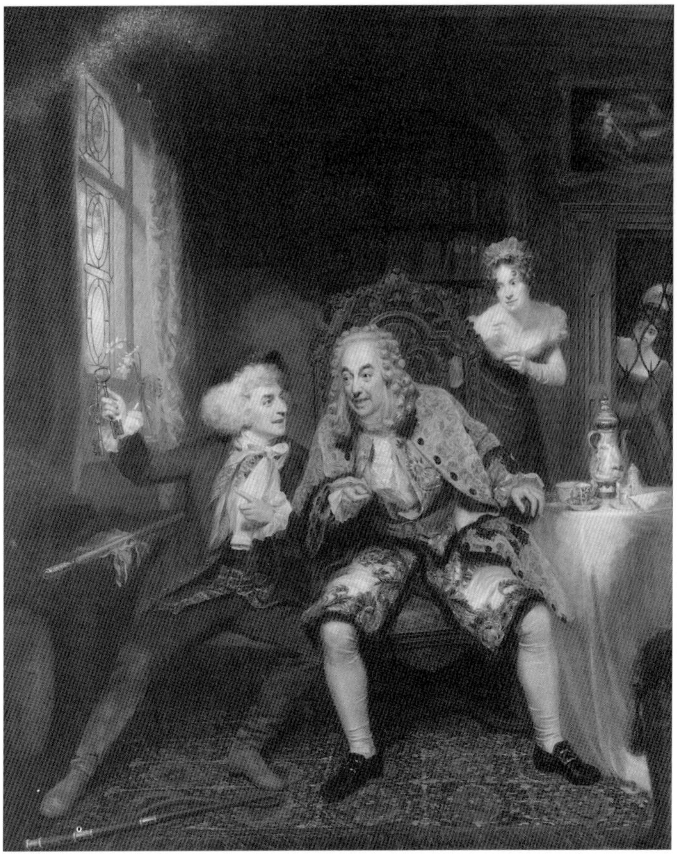

630*

JOSEPH MUNDEN as Old Brummagem,
MARIE CUBITT as Laura,
EDWARD KNIGHT as Ralph
and *MARY ORGER* as Fanny
in *Lock and Key* by Prince Hoare

George Clint

Oil on canvas 128 x 101.5
INV: Mathews 165; RW/CKA 41
PROV: Charles Mathews
EXH: 1821 R.A. (273); 1833 London (165);
1950–51 London; 1951–52 London (128)
ENGR: Thomas Lupton pub. W. Sams 1 October 1824,
mezzotint 44.6 x 35.3, inscr: 'From an original picture
in the possession of Charles Mathews'
LIT: TAM, 1935; Griffiths, p. 336

Clint's scene shows the climax of Hoare's entertainment, Act IV, scene 4, set in an apartment in Brummagem's house. Brummagem is a crusty old man who keeps his ward Laura under lock and key. She can be seen in the picture peering from behind her grille. Brummagem's man-servant, Ralph, who has conceived a plan to free Laura, sits on the left 'in a large wig, drest as a Steward'. The servant-girl Fanny stands behind the two main protagonists. The avaricious Brummagen (Munden) wears black shoes and white stockings, a fine pink damask coat with black trim over a long white waistcoat richly embroidered in a green and gold floral design (open at the top to reveal another pink waistcoat). Ralph (Knight) wears high boots, brown breeches and coat, a long green waistcoat edged in gold braid, and a red and yellow scarf under a high white stock tied in a large bow. Fanny (Mrs Orger, only partially visible behind Munden) wears blue and has a red ribbon in her cap. Laura (Miss Cubitt), behind the grille, wears yellow. Above her on the wall is a painting of Cupid riding a blindfold mastiff (?).

Hoare's entertainment, with music by William Shield, was first performed at Covent Garden on 2 February 1796. Munden was the original Brummagem; Fawcett played Ralph, Mrs Serres Laura, and Mrs Martyr Fanny. Sir Francis Chantrey wrote to Mathews on 6 May 1821 congratulating him on being the owner of a very fine picture by Clint 'in which Munden cuts a figure', saying that Lord Liverpool had wished to purchase it, but that Chantry had told him Mathews would not agree to part with it. (Letter in Ifan Kyrle Fletcher Catalogue 210 [22], Spring 1964.)

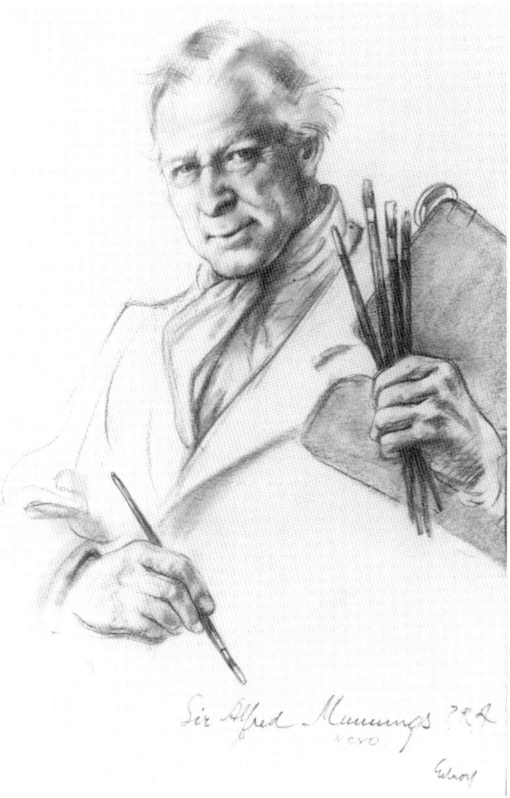

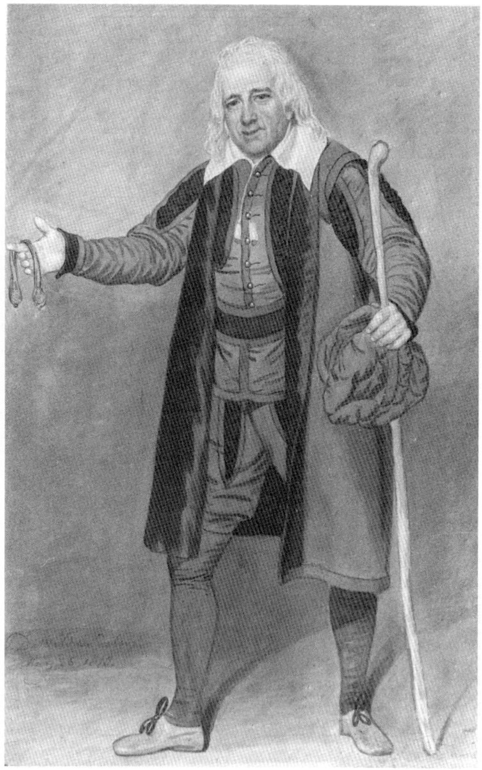

632 *Charles Murray as Tobias*

631
SIR ALFRED MUNNINGS

John Gilroy

Pencil on wove paper 61 x 43.2 (sight 39.5 x 24)
INSCR: 'Sir Alfred Munnings P.R.A / K. CVO. / Gilroy' (pencil b.r.)
INV: GCL 720
PROV: Presented by the artist

Munnings, who became President of the Royal Academy in 1944, was one of the most prominent painters of horses of his time. Here, with a brush in his right hand, he considers a picture. In his left hand he holds a palette with four more brushes. Munnings, a member of the Garrick Club, was knighted in 1944, and wrote a three-volume autobiography.

632
CHARLES MURRAY
as Tobias in *The Stranger*
by Benjamin Thompson, after Kotzebue

Samuel De Wilde

Pencil and watercolour on wove paper 37 x 23.5
INSCR: 'S De Wilde.delin / May.26.1815.' (pencil b.l.)

INV: Mathews 338; RW/CKA 65E
PROV: Charles Mathews
EXH: 1833 London (338); 1975 London (153)

Tobias is a 76-year-old countryman and relentlessly optimistic, despite having lost four of his five children. In Act IV, scene I, he receives money in a purse from the Stranger to buy his remaining son Robert out of the army. Tobias holds the purse in his right hand and a stick to support his years in his left. He wears vaguely 17th-century clothes, the remnants of his former liquidity: a soft grey cap, pale brown shoes with black bows, brown stockings, grey hose slashed over the thigh to reveal black edged in brown, a doublet in grey slashed to reveal black edged in brown either side of the chest and on thee upper arms, a black belt edged in brown, and a large loose white collar with two tassels.

Thompson's adaptation of Kotzebue's drama *Menschenhaß und die Reue* was performed for the first time at Drury Lane on 24 March 1798, with James Aicken as Tobias and J.P. Kemble as the Stranger. It was revived at Covent Garden on 4 February 1815, when Murray acted Tobias. Murray appeared in the role in all 20 performances that season, including the one on 25 May 1815, the day before De Wilde produced this picture. (See No. 868 for Young as the Stranger in the same production.)

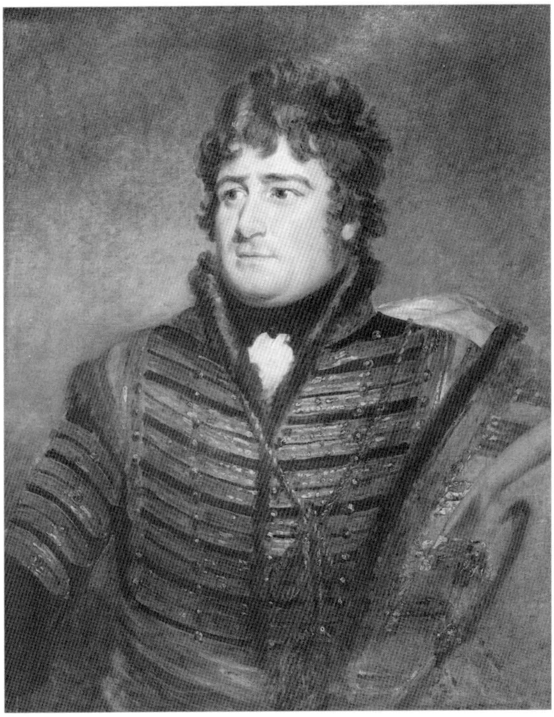

Murray is wearing a costume similar to that worn by G.F. Cooke in James Green's 1801 portrait of him as Iago (see No. 131). Murray was Cooke's predecessor as Iago at Covent Garden, having played the role on 24 October and 12 December 1796 – performances that Dupont could have been commemorating – and again on 15 October 1798 and 3 October 1799.

633

CHARLES MURRAY

possibly as Iago

in *Othello* by William Shakespeare

Gainsborough Dupont

Oil on canvas 78.7 x 66

INV: Mathews 5 (as Baron Wildenheim in 'Lovers' Vows', Quote: 'Has not Count Cassel left his chamber yet?'); RW/CKA 472 (as Baron Wildenheim)

PROV: Thomas Harris; Harris sale, Robins 12 July 1819 (16) (as Baron Wildenheim by Singleton); Charles Mathews

EXH: 1833 London (5); 1982–83 London (135)

LIT: Hayes, 1968

Murray's ornate military costume consists of a red hussar's cloak, a blue jacket trimmed with an extraordinary quantity of horizontal gold braiding, a black stock and a red sash.

Murray was the original Baron Wildenheim in Mrs Inchbald's *Lovers' Vows* at Covent Garden on 11 October 1798, a year after the death of Gainsborough Dupont. This is the part that was identified for this picture in both Mathews's catalogue and the Harris sale catalogue. In the latter, the picture is attributed to Henry Singleton, who did not die until 1839. The picture is closer stylistically to Dupont than to Singleton.

634

LOCATION UNKNOWN

HENRY MURRAY

Unknown Artist

Oil on canvas 73.7 x 62.2

INV: CKA 574; Gift 505

PROV: Miss W.E. Laycock, by whom presented to the Garrick Club, 1932

The sitter wears a dark jacket and white shirt, both with high collars, and a dark stock. [Ashton marked the painting as 'gone' in 1988.]

Henry Murray became a member of the Garrick Club in 1867.

635

LOCATION UNKNOWN

HENRY LEIGH MURRAY

Stephen Pearce

Black, red and white chalk on brown wove paper 39 x 30.1

INSCR: 'Stephen Pearce 1851' (pencil b.l.)

INV: RW 140 (artist unknown); CKA 140; missing in 1994

PROV: Presented to the Garrick Club by Mrs Leigh Murray by 1888

CKA describes this now missing picture as 'Head and shoulders, fronting spectator, head to right; black bow tie, dark coat'.

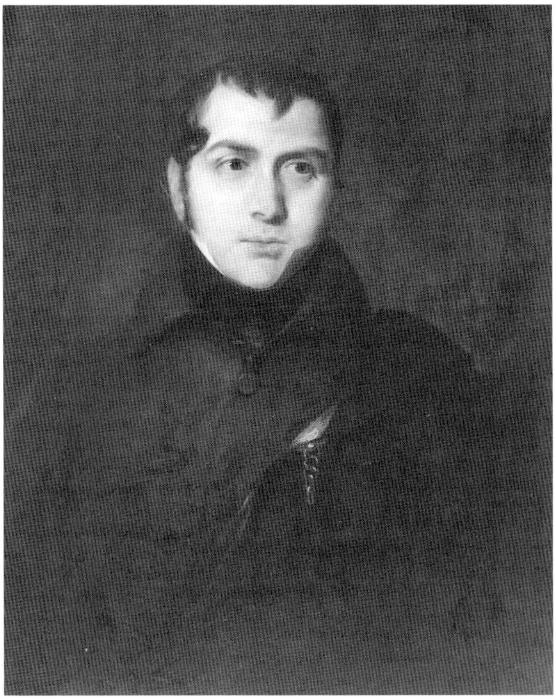

636
WILLIAM HENRY MURRAY

Sir John Watson Gordon
Oil on canvas 76 x 63
INV: RW/CKA 356
PROV: Henry Murray, son of the sitter, by whom presented to the Garrick Club, 1888
EXH: 1825 Institute for Encouragement of Fine Arts in Scotland

Murray wears a brown jacket, a white collar and stock, and over his left shoulder a dark cloak lined in white.

He became a member of the Garrick Club in 1843.

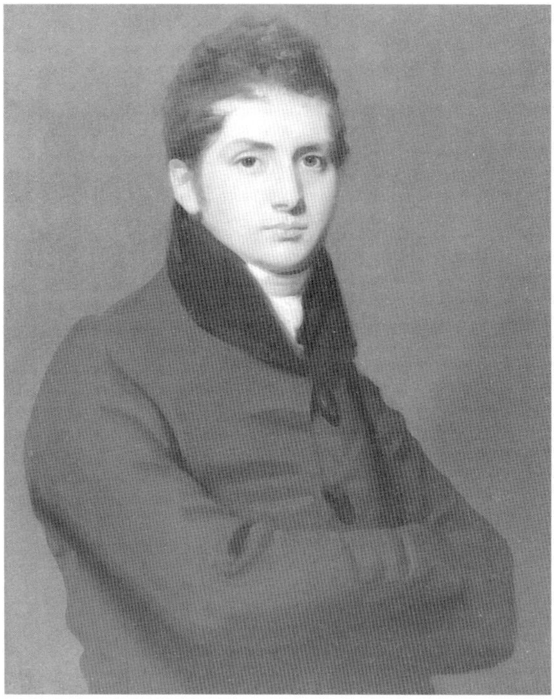

637
WILLIAM HENRY MURRAY

Unknown Artist
Oil on canvas 75 x 62.2
INV: CKA 576; Gift 505
PROV: Miss W. E. Laycock, by whom presented to the Garrick Club, 1932

The sitter wears a blue-grey jacket with black buttons and a fur collar, and a high white stock.

[This handsome picture, with its economical composition and direct presentation of the sitter, carries suggestions of Henry Raeburn (1756–1823) and might be derived from a portrait by him.]

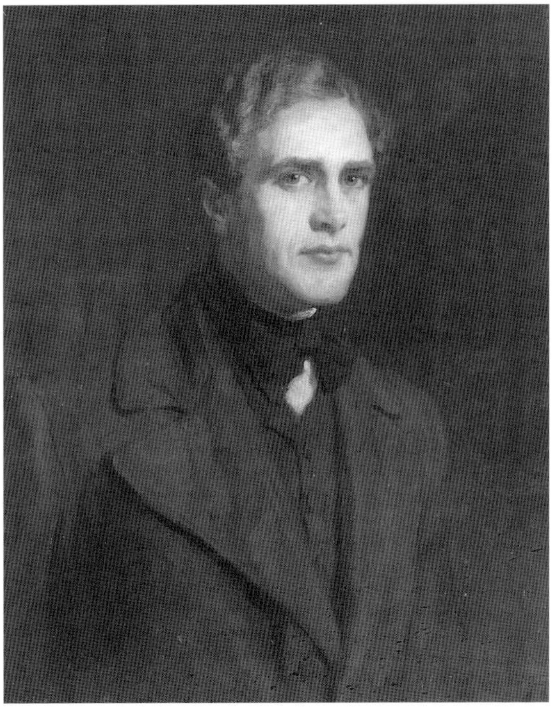

638
OWEN NARES
as David Copperfield in *David Copperfield*
by Louis N. Parker,
adapted from Charles Dickens

Hugh Goldwin Riviere

Oil on canvas 76.5 x 64
INSCR: 'HR (in monogram) / 1916' (b.r.)
INV: GCL 681
PROV: David Nares, by whom
presented to the Garrick Club
EXH: 1917 R.S.P.P. (24)

Nares is dressed in grey, with a white shirt and a dark blue cravat. He became a member of the Garrick Club in 1929.

Louis N. Parker's adaptation of Dickens's novel opened at Her Majesty's on 24 December 1914 and ran for 129 performances until 17 April 1915. The scenery was by Joseph Harker and the costumes were designed by Percy Macquoid. Owen Nares played the title role. The play had already been seen in New York's Wallack Theatre on 26 October 1914, as *The Highway of Life*.

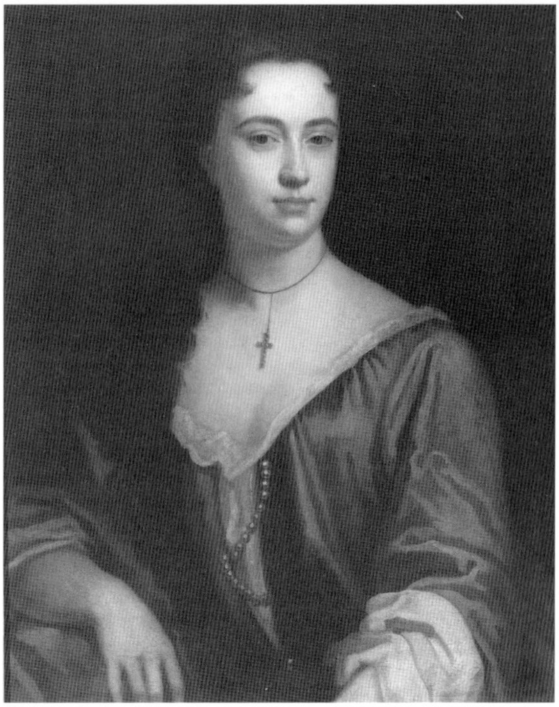

639
ANNE OLDFIELD

Sir Godfrey Kneller (after)

Oil on canvas 73.7 x 61
INV: RW/CKA 3; Gift 30
PROV: Anne Mathews, by whom
presented to the Garrick Club, 1836
EXH: 1951 London (26)

The sitter wears a loose robe in purple and white, with a red drapery over the right arm. Around her neck is a fine silver chain with a ruby cross.

She was probably the finest portrayer of ladies of quality in the first quarter of the 18th century. In his preface to *The Provok'd Husband* (in which Anne Oldfield played Lady Townly), Cibber claimed that she had the 'constant Admiration of those Spectators, who have the Pleasure of living while She is an Actress'. The prompter Chetwood eulogised her 'meridian lustre, a glow of charms not to be beheld but with a trembling eye!'.

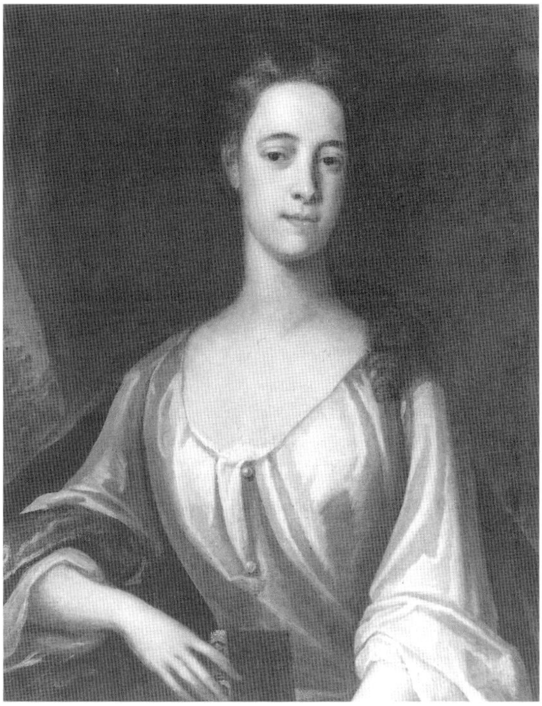

640
ANNE OLDFIELD

Jonathan Richardson (attr.)
Oil on canvas 76.8 x 61.6
INV: Mathews 50 or 73 (artist unknown); RW/CKA 34
PROV: Charles Mathews
EXH: 1833 London (50 or 73)

Mrs Oldfield wears a white dress with blue drape.

No. 640 relates somewhat distantly to the portrait by Richardson (present location unknown) that was engraved in mezzotint by E. Fisher and published by J. Spilsbury.

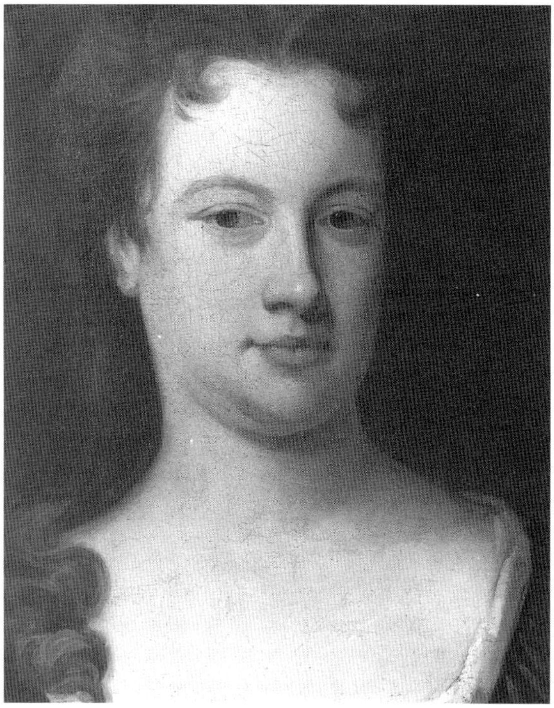

641
ANNE OLDFIELD

Unknown Artist
Oil on canvas 33.7 x 28.6
INV: Mathews 50 or 73; RW/CKA 279
PROV: Charles Mathews
EXH: 1833 London (50 or 73)

The sitter wears a low-cut blue dress edged in white. This picture, which is of high quality, has been cut down. It appears to be another variant of the type exemplified in No. 639.

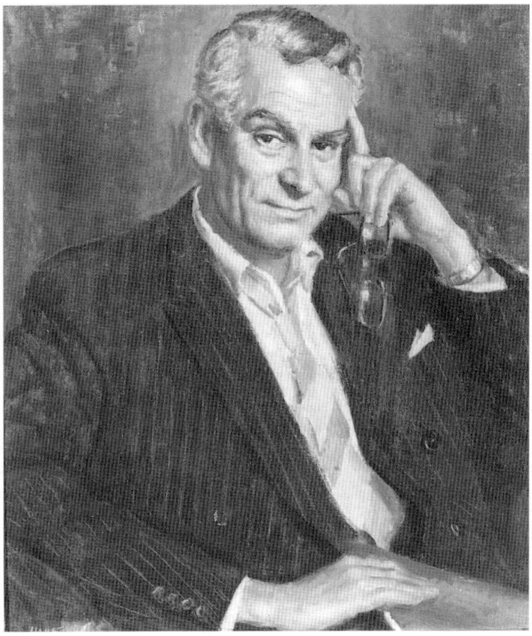

642
SIR LAURENCE OLIVIER

Bernard Hailstone

Oil on canvas 78.7 x 68.6
INSCR: 'HAILSTONE 68' (red paint b.l.)
INV: GCL 710; Gift 830
PROV: Presented anonymously, 1968
REL: Another version painted 1968 (see below)

Olivier is seated with his left hand at his face, holding a red book in his right hand. He wears a dark blue pin-striped suit, an open-necked shirt, and a loosened Garrick Club tie.

A letter from Miss Winifred Jermey (Joe Orton?) to the Club Secretary on 10 May 1968 reads:

> Dear Sir,
> In the Daily Telegraph the other day there was a photograph of Sir Laurence Olivier standing by two portraits that are being painted by Bernard Hailstone, one of which is to hang in your Club. I was shocked to see Sir Laurence looking so untidy round the neck: whoever decided to paint him with his collar undone and tie loosened? I have followed the career and life of Sir Laurence from very early days, as I am about the same age, and I am just wondering whether it is an idiosyncrasy of his to loosen his tie when he is relaxing perhaps in the Club and that is why he is being painted in this way. At the moment I am quite upset about it although I shall myself never see the finished portrait.
> I sincerely hope the finished portrait will not look so bad as Sir Laurence looked in the paper the other day.
>
> Yours faithfully,
> *Winifred Jermey* (Miss)

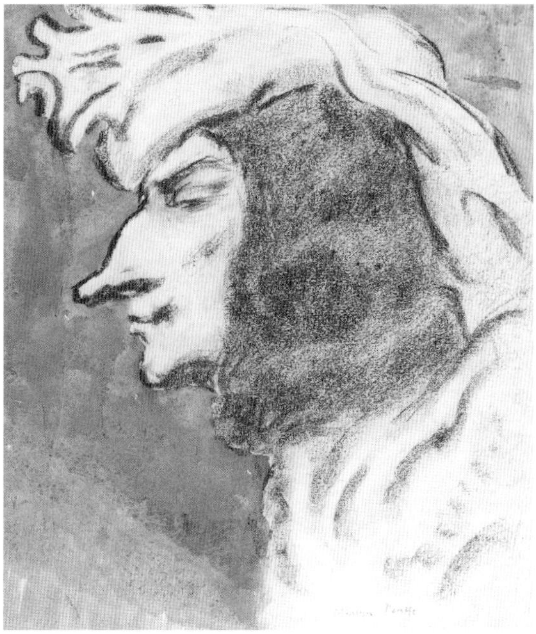

643
SIR LAURENCE OLIVIER
as Richard in *Richard III*
by William Shakespeare

Mervyn Peake

Pencil, black chalk and grey wash
on wove paper 34.5 x 28.3 (sight)
INSCR: 'Mervyn Peake' (pencil b.r.)
INV: GCL 744; Gift 908
PROV: Presented by the artist's family, 1984
REL/LIT: In Hilary Spurling, *The Drawings of Mervyn Peake* (1974), plate 50 illustrates a version of No. 643 drawn in dark green chalk and wash; the date is given as 1945

Richard is shown in Olivier's famous depiction of evil, with the meandering putty nose and 15th-century hat flopping like a deadly toadstool. Melvyn Bragg in *Olivier* (1989) writes: 'The nose in *Richard III*... became through the portrait by Salvador Dali, through the photographs, through the film and the réclame of the part almost a character in its own right with an existence of its own, a Gogolian, monstrous nose.'

At a meeting of the Garrick Club Picture Committee on 18 April 1945, Christopher Hussey proposed that a portrait of Olivier (a member since 1936) as Richard III be commissioned from A.R. Thomson. There was correspondence between Colonel Plimpton and Alfred Munnings on the suggestion, but nothing appears to have come of it.

Olivier's stage production of *Richard III* opened at the New Theatre on 13 September 1944 and his film version appeared in 1956. He became a life peer in 1970.

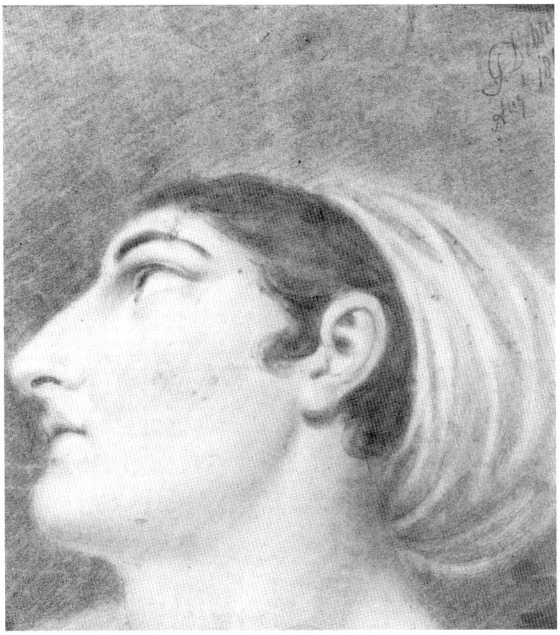

644
ELIZA O'NEILL (?)

Samuel De Wilde

Black and red chalks on wove paper 21.3 x 21.3
INSCR: 'S De Wilde / Aug 1815' (black chalk t.r.)
INV: CKA 631 (Mrs Siddons); Gift 545
PROV: George De Wilde; offered to the Club for £5.15s.0d; presumably bought and certainly presented by Mrs Ludovic G. Foster, 1937
EXH: 1971 Northampton (47)
REL: NT 52, black chalk and watercolour on wove paper 18.1 x 16.8, inscr: 'DW 1816'

The sitter's hair is wrapped in a white turban-like headdress. Her identity is uncertain. According to CKA the drawing was formerly in the possession of 'the descendants of Samuel De Wilde, and [was] said to have been drawn from the stalls', and was held by them to depict Sarah Siddons. There is some similarity to George Dawe's peculiar portrait of Miss O'Neill as Juliet, engraved and published 30 May 1816.

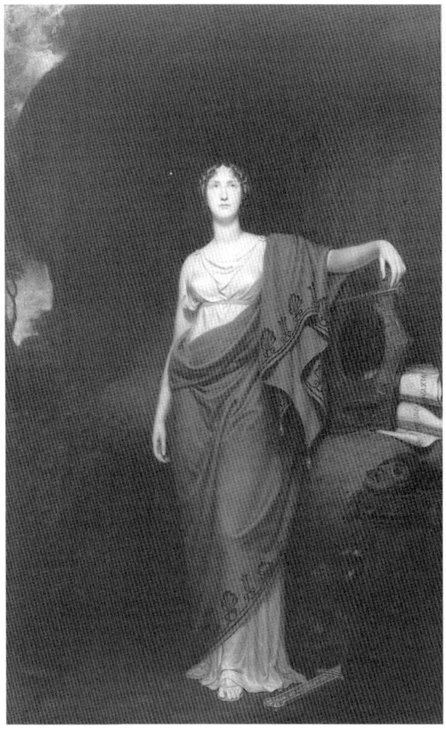

645
ELIZA O'NEILL
as 'Melpomene'

George Francis Joseph

Oil on canvas 241.3 x 147.3
INSCR: 'SOPHOCLES / AESCHYLUS / EURIPIDES' (in Greek characters on books c.l.)
INV: Mathews 76; RW/CKA 442
PROV: Charles Mathews
EXH: 1815 R.A. (39) 'Melpomene: the portrait of Miss O'Neill'; 1833 London (76)
LIT: British Galleries of Art (1825), p. 26

Melpomene, the Muse of Tragedy, stands in stately grandeur, her left arm resting on a lyre. She wears a white classical dress with a gold waistband and red sandals. The dress is largely covered by a voluminous red drapery, its border decorated with a honeysuckle motif.

The plan of Mathews's gallery locates this picture in a prominent position. It was not mentioned by Patmore in 1824, so presumably Mathews acquired it after that date.

Eliza O'Neill was considered one of the finest tragic actresses of her time, a successor to Sarah Siddons. The conception of the portrait owes much to Lawrence's 'half-history' portraits of John Philip Kemble (see BD 8: 376–82) and ultimately to Reynolds's 'Mrs Siddons as the Tragic Muse' (Huntington Art Gallery). Compare it also to Lawrence's portrait of Mrs Siddons reciting (Tate Gallery 188).

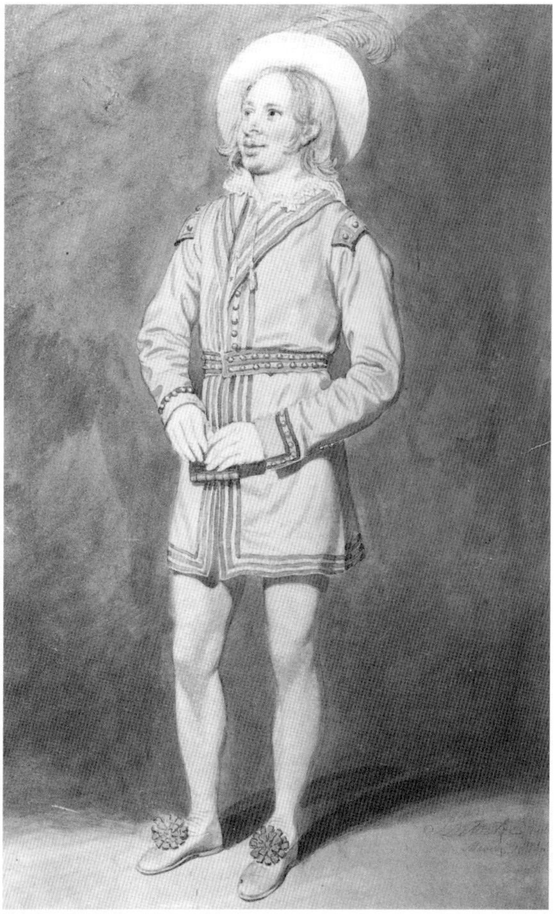

646

WILLIAM OXBERRY

as Leo Luminati in *Oh! This Love or The Masqueraders* by James Kenney

Samuel De Wilde

Pencil and watercolour on wove paper 37 x 23.5
INSCR: 'S De Wilde delin / March 1811 (8?)' (pencil b.r.)
INV: Mathews 198 (in 'The Devil's Bridge');
RW 63F (in 'The Devil's Bridge'); CKA 63F
PROV: Charles Mathews
EXH: 1833 London (198); 1975 London (148)
ENGR: Similar to H.R. Cook for the *Theatrical Inquisitor* pub. W. Oxberry (and also by Sherwood & Co.) 31 October 1812, stipple 14.6 x 9.6 (same costume, to front, looking to right, crop in left hand, dangling on ground)

Oxberry, with a blond Andrew Aguecheek wig, wears yellow shoes with blue rosettes, yellow stockings, a yellow tunic trimmed with blue bands and silver buttons, and a broad-brimmed white hat with a blue feather.

Kenney's comic opera, with music by M.P. King, was first performed at the Lyceum on 12 June 1810, with Oxberry as the original Leo Luminati.

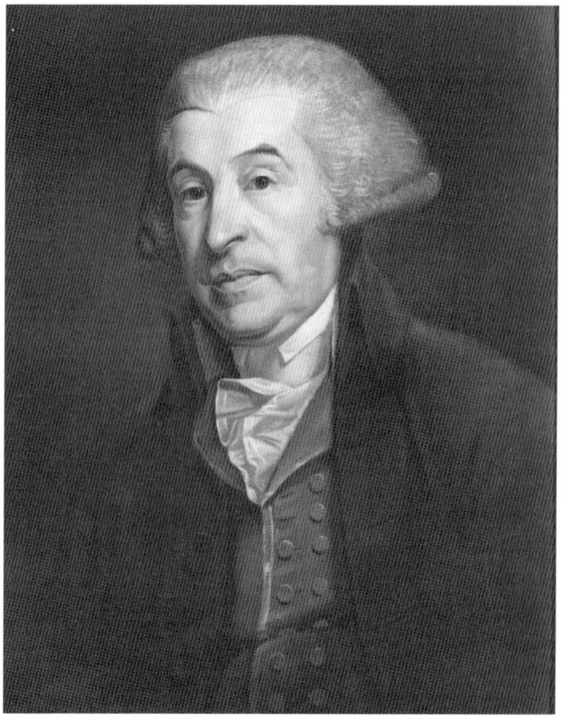

647

JOHN HAYMAN PACKER

Thomas Beach (attr.)

Oil on canvas 59 x 49.5
INV: Mathews 36 (William Packer; artist unknown); (not in RW); CKA 191 (artist unknown)
PROV: Charles Mathews
EXH: 1833 London (36)

Packer, a useful but never a fine actor, made his début at Covent Garden on 24 January 1758 as Johnson in *The Rehearsal* and that September joined the company at Drury Lane, where he remained for 46 years. He is shown half-length, wearing a brown jacket and a green waistcoat trimmed with gold.

Packer played such roles as Banquo in *Macbeth*, the Duke in *The Merchant of Venice*, Friar Laurence in *Romeo and Juliet*, and the King in *Hamlet*. He was described by Waldron, in his *Candid and Impartial Strictures on the Performers* (1795), as 'respectable in whatever he undertakes'.

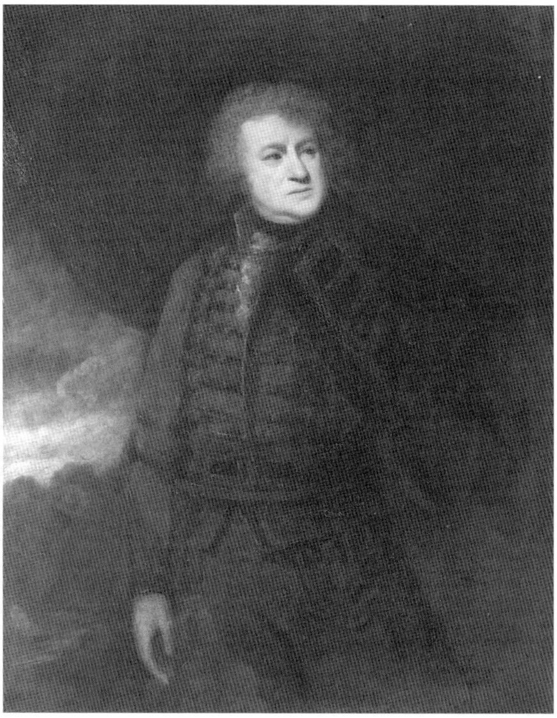

648

JOHN PALMER

as Colonel Cohenberg in *Siege of Belgrade*

by James Cobb

James Saxon (?)

Oil on canvas 127 x 100.3

INV: Mathews 109 (by Arrowsmith);

RW 19 (by James Saxon); CKA 19 (by Arrowsmith)

PROV: Charles Mathews

EXH: (1796 R.A. [465]); 1833 London (109)

LIT: Griffiths, p. 323

Colonel Cohenberg wears a red military jacket with gold braid and a dark cloak, also with gold braiding.

Cobb's comic opera, with music mainly by Stephen Storace, was first performed at Drury Lane on 1 January 1791 and became a popular piece. The previous attribution of the portrait to the deaf and dumb painter Thomas Arrowsmith is less likely than RW's attribution to James Saxon, who exhibited a portrait of Palmer as Cohenberg at the R.A. in 1796 (465).

John Palmer, a very versatile and popular actor, was known as 'Plausible Jack', a nickname he gained for his excellent delineation of the coxcomb Lord Plausible in Wycherley's *The Plain Dealer*.

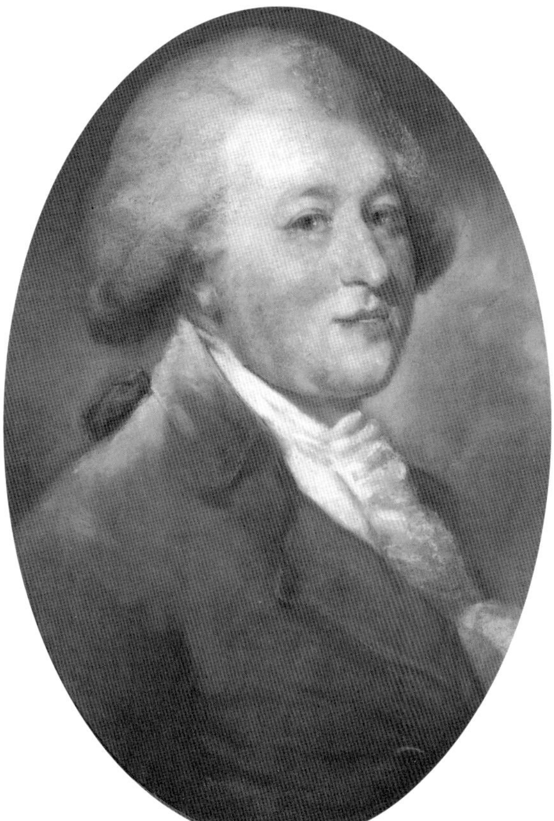

649

JOHN PALMER

John Russell

Pastel on paper 57.8 x 41.9

INSCR: 'J. Russell 1786' (red chalk l.r.)

INV: Mathews 304; RW/CKA 303

PROV: Artist's sale, Christie's 1807 (61); Charles Mathews

EXH: 1786 R.A. (152) 'Portrait of Mr Palmer, crayons'; 1833 London (304)

ENGR: Joseph Collyer pub. W. Dickenson 11 June 1787, stipple 10 x 7.7 (inscr: 'Painted by J. Russell, Crayon Painter to His Royal Highness the Prince of Wales... / Mr John Palmer / Of the Theatre Royal, Drury Lane and of the Royalty / Theatre Well-close Square / To the Lovers of the Drama This Plate Engraved from the / Original Picture is Inscr. by their Obedt humb Servt / J. Collyer')

Palmer's wig is tied with a blue ribbon. Powder from his hair is scattered over the shoulders of his red velvet jacket.

The publication of the print immediately preceded the opening of Palmer's Royalty Theatre (see No. 652).

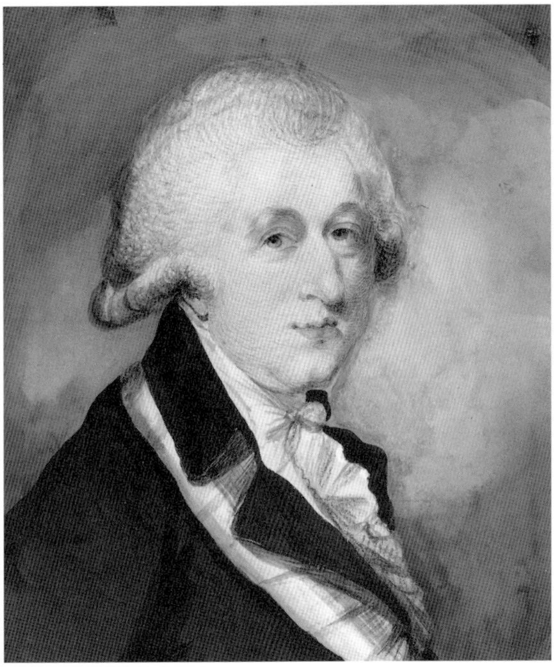

650
JOHN PALMER
'School of Garrick'

Henry Spicer

Pencil and watercolour on laid paper 26.5 x 21
INV: Mathews 262 (artist unknown);
RW/CKA 48B (artist unknown)
PROV: Charles Mathews
EXH: 1833 London (262)

Palmer wears a blue jacket and a white stock with frills. Around his neck hangs a Shakespeare Favour on a Shakespeare Ribband. See No. 6.

Palmer spent some 13 years at Drury Lane under Garrick's management and was one of the original committee members of the Drury Lane Fund.

651
JOHN PALMER as Iachimo and
SAMUEL REDDISH as Posthumus Leonatus
in *Cymbeline* by William Shakespeare,
adapted by David Garrick

Thomas Parkinson

Oil on canvas 91 x 69.5
INSCR: 'Parkinson pinx 1778' (purple paint b.r.)
INV: Mathews 70; RW/CKA 390
PROV: Charles Mathews
EXH: 1833 London (70); 1947 London (39);
1964 London [2] (15); 1975 Milan (105)
LIT: Fitzgerald, pp. 211–12

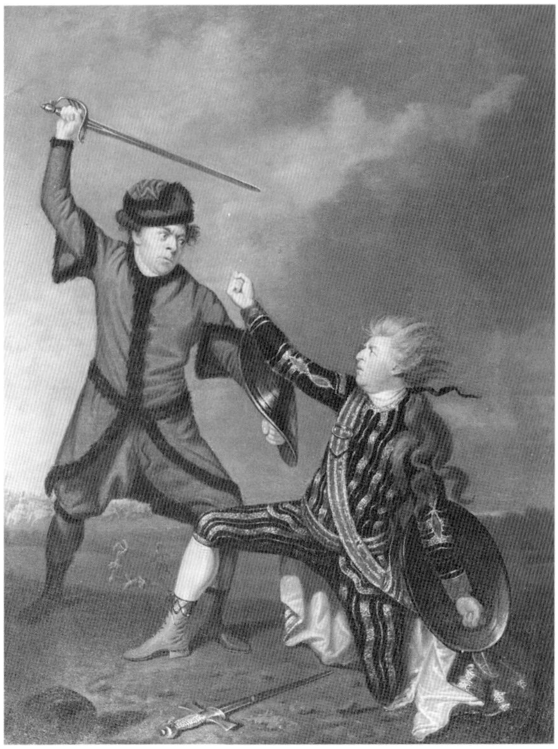

651 *John Palmer as Iachimo and Samuel Reddish as Posthumus Leonatus*

Posthumus (Reddish), on the left, strikes an aggressive attitude, his sword raised in his right hand, the strap of his round target shield clasped in his left. He wears a grey hat with black fur round the brim, grey stockings, and grey breeches and jacket, both trimmed with dark fur. Iachimo (Palmer) kneels on the right, his long, fair romantic wig blown back, with a long coif over the left shoulder. He raises a futile clenched right fist; his sword lies on the ground and his round target shield is on his left arm. Iachimo wears red boots with gold heels, white stockings, and black doublet and hose with vertical stripes of silver sequins. His black cloak is lined with white silk.

Reddish played Posthumus for the first time at Drury Lane on 10 October 1767, with Holland as Iachimo and Palmer as Arviragus. Palmer first played Iachimo at Drury Lane on 12 December 1769, and he and Reddish played opposite each other in these roles for a total of 20 performances, the last on 23 May 1774. During 1778, the year in which Parkinson signed and presumably painted his picture, neither actor appeared in the play. Palmer is shown as Iachimo in George Carter's 'The immortality of Garrick, with portraits of the principal actors', R.A. 1784 (336). Robert Edge Pine exhibited a portrait of Reddish as Posthumus at the Society of Artists in 1768 (126).

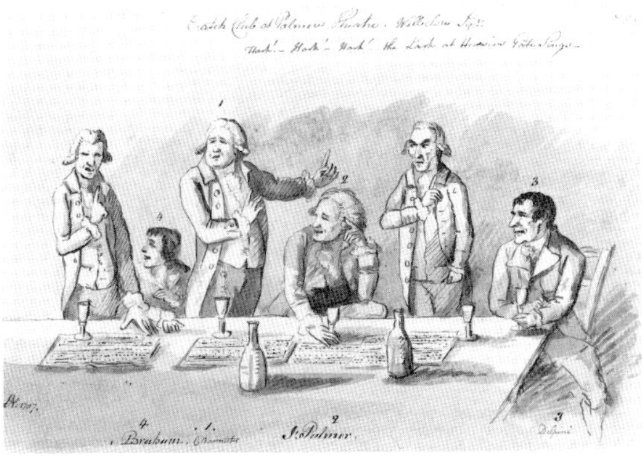

652

JOHN PALMER, CHARLES BANNISTER, JOHN BRAHAM, CARLO DELPINI and *TWO OTHERS* shown at 'The Catch Club at Palmer's Royalty Theatre, Wellclose Square'

John Nixon

Pencil, pen and brown ink with green and brown wash on laid paper 12.5 x 20.1
INSCR: '1787' (pen and grey ink b.l.);
'Catch Club at Palmers Theatre. Wellclose Sq. / Hark! – Hark! – Hark! – the Lark at Heavens Gate Sings –' (pen and grey ink t.c.);
four of the six figures identified with numbers, viz: '1. C. Bannister' (pen and grey ink), '2. J. Palmer' (pen and brown ink), '3. Delpini' (pen and grey ink), '4. Braham' (pen and brown ink)
INV: Not listed
PROV: John Nixon, *Dramatic Annals*

Palmer's Royalty Theatre opened in Wellclose Square on 20 June 1787. It was built after the model of the pre-1791 Drury Lane and sat 198 in the front boxes, 396 in the side boxes, 360 in the pit, 1000 in the first gallery, and 640 in the upper gallery. There were box lobbies and a drawing room for ladies, perhaps the room shown in Nixon's drawing. The theatre opened with *As You Like It*, in which Palmer played Jacques. The proprietors of the patent theatres soon forced the closure of Palmer's enterprise. When Palmer tried to re-open with a variety show of music, dancing and pantomime on 3 July 1787, Arrowsmith, Gaudry, Delpini, Bannister, G.L. Barrett and William Painter were charged as 'rogues, vagabonds and sturdy beggars'. Performances continued until April 1788 and then stopped. The company included Charles Bannister, Master John Braham and Carlo Antonio Delpini. John Palmer appeared on nearly every bill, acting, singing, reciting Collins's 'Ode to the Passions', or speaking prologues and epilogues.

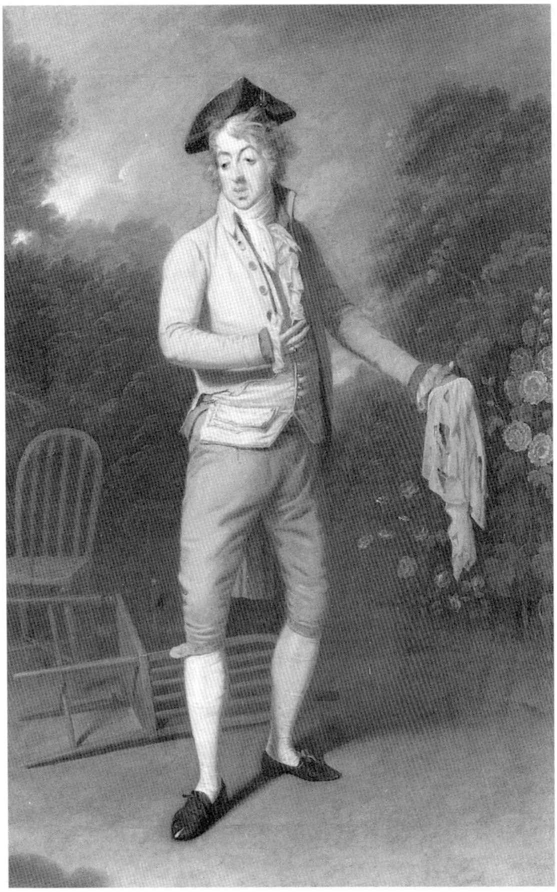

653

ROBERT PALMER
as Tag in *The Spoiled Child*
by Isaac Bickerstaffe

Samuel De Wilde

Oil on canvas 77.3 x 59.3
INV: Mathews 19; RW/CKA 105
PROV: Charles Mathews
EXH: 1797 R.A. (277); 1833 London (19); 1951–52 London (125); 1975 London (126)
ENGR: William Ridley for the *Monthly Mirror* pub. Vernor & Hood 26 October 1803, stipple 8.8 x 7.4 (bust in oval)
REL: Witt Collection, Courtauld Institute, watercolour; Sotheby's 19 November 1970 (in a volume of 28 studies by De Wilde), bt. H. Vallance, pencil and chalk [*Eds.*]

While Tag and Miss Pickle make passionate love in the garden, Little Pickle sews their clothes together. He then shouts that his father, Miss Pickle's brother, is on the way, and the lovers try to flee. The text does not call for torn clothes but they evidently added to the comic rough and tumble of the play (see No. 787 for a previous moment in the same scene). Tag holds the edge of his jacket in his right hand and the piece torn from it in his left – a tragedy indeed, considering the dapper nature of his costume. A small black tricorn hat edged in silver sits on top of his bedraggled wig with its off-centre parting. He wears black shoes with a black bow on the right foot and a red bow on the left, white stockings, red breeches, a grey jacket with red cuffs and silver buttons, and a yellow waistcoat trimmed with gold braid and buttons and possibly lined in red.

Bickerstaffe's farce was first performed at Drury Lane on 22 March 1790 with Robert Palmer as Tag. He played the part five times during the 1795–96 Drury Lane season, the last performance taking place on 7 May 1796, then again at Drury Lane on 28 April and 30 May 1797. The Little Pickle was usually played by Mrs Jordan. Palmer acted Tag four times at Drury Lane during 1803; the last occasion was 17 September, about a month before the engraving was published.

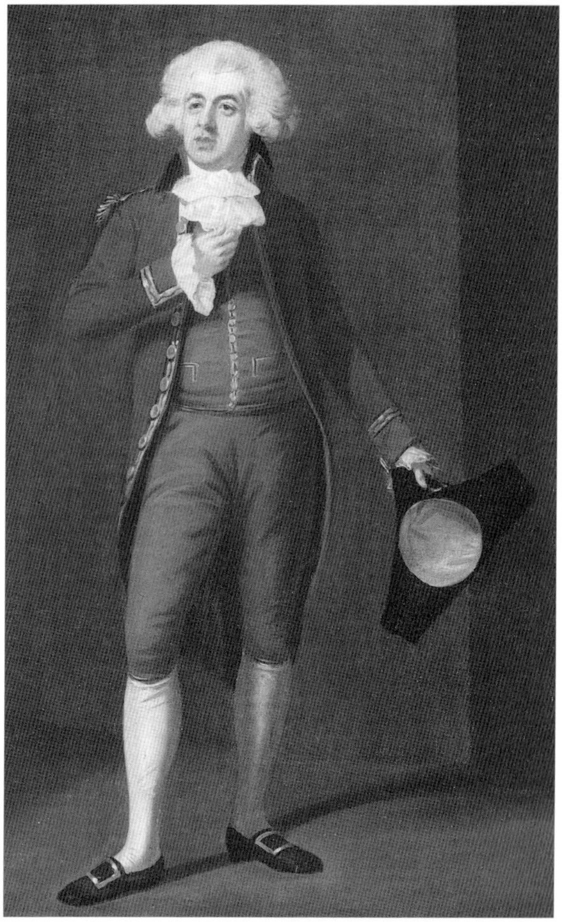

654 *Robert Palmer as Tom*

654

ROBERT PALMER

as Tom in *The Conscious Lovers*

by Sir Richard Steele

Samuel De Wilde

Oil on canvas 35.5 x 26.9
INV: Mathews 185; RW/CKA 262
PROV: John Bell; Charles Mathews
EXH: 1833 London (185)
ENGR: John Corner for Bell's British Library 16 September 1791, line 11.5 x 8, pub. Bell's *British Theatre* (1797), vol 13; Clayton for Jones's *British Theatre* pub. Wm. Jones, Dublin, line 11.7 x 8; Anon. printed C. Cooke 13 February 1807 as plate to *British Drama* 1817, line

Tom is gentleman's gentleman to Bevil Jnr, and has a rather inflated image of his station in life. In Act III, scene I he swaggers to Phillis, maid to Lucinda: 'I would not be a bit wiser, a bit richer, a bit taller, a bit shorter, than I am at this Instant' (the quotation printed on the engraving). However, Phillis has the measure of him, and replies, 'Did ever any body doubt, Master Thomas, but that you were extremely satisfied with your sweet self?' Tom is the only strong, well-rounded character in Steele's seemingly endless comedy. The Bell edition of the play indicates that at least half of the text was cut in performance.

Tom wears a pretentious wig, perhaps one belonging to Bevil. He has taken off his hat, a black tricorn lined in white, to Phillis. His costume – unduly grand for a servant – consists of black shoes, white hose, green breeches, a brown coat trimmed with gold and with green cuffs, a green waistcoat also trimmed with gold, and a high white stock with frills.

Steele's comedy was first performed at Drury Lane on 7 November 1722. Robert Palmer appears never to have played Tom in London, although his brother John took the role on two occasions: at Drury Lane on 7 October 1783 and at the Haymarket on 13 July 1786.

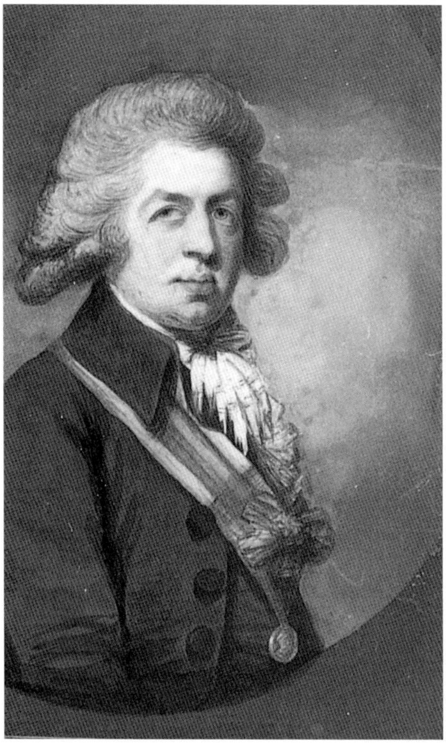

655
ROBERT PALMER
'School of Garrick'

Henry Spicer

Pencil and watercolour on laid paper 26.5 x 21
INV: Mathews 260 (artist unknown);
RW/CKA 48E (artist unknown)
PROV: Charles Mathews
EXH: 1833 London (260)

Palmer wears a blue-grey jacket, with the collar over his Shakespeare Ribband, which has a rosette and from which hangs his Shakespeare Favour. See No. 6.

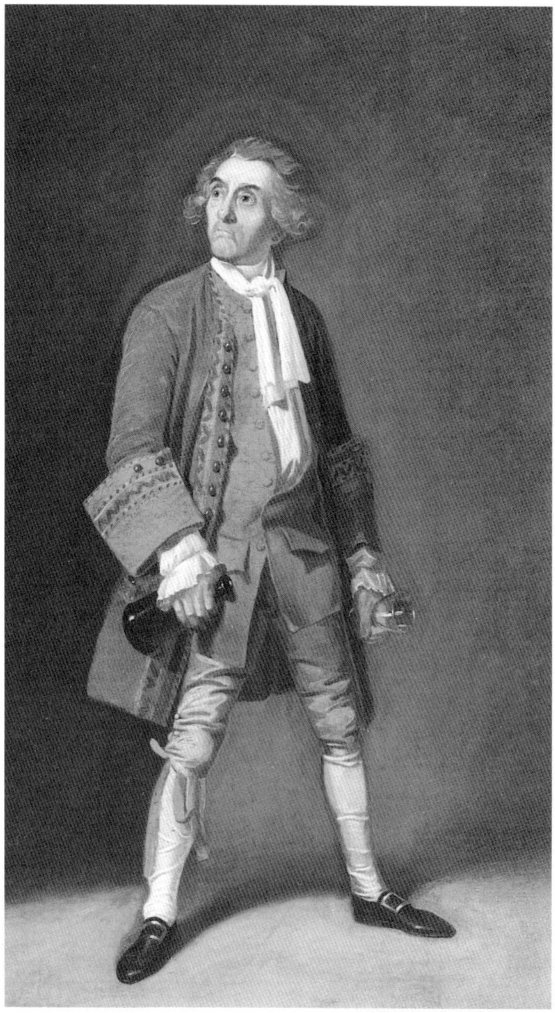

656
WILLIAM PARSONS
as Dumps in *The Natural Son*
by Richard Cumberland

Samuel De Wilde

Oil on canvas 41.3 x 32.4
INV: Mathews 368; RW/CKA 437
PROV: John Bell; Charles Mathews
EXH: 1793 London (6); 1833 London (368);
1971 Northampton (8)
ENGR: J. Thornthwaite for Bell's British Library
29 September 1792, line 11.7 x 8,
pub. Bell's *British Theatre* (1797), vol 20

Dumps, the son of a sexton, is a gruesome manservant, who supplied bodies for a surgeon for whom he worked. For five years he has been employed by Ruefull, who rightly accuses him of being drunk. Dumps turns his head with a look of defiance, his mouth firmly set, and replies with the line quoted on the engraving, 'You never gave me a chance to get tipsy in your Service' (Act III). He clutches a glass and a bottle and wears black shoes, orange breeches, a gold-trimmed blue coat with large red cuffs also trimmed with gold, a red waistcoat, incorrectly fastened, and a loose stock.

Cumberland's comedy was first performed at Drury Lane on 22 December 1784, with Parsons as the original Dumps and Moody as Major O'Flaherty. No. 656 was one of seven paintings by De Wilde exhibited at Christie's 25–26 March 1793, on the occasion of the sale of John Bell's stock of drawings (see Nos. 398 and 448).

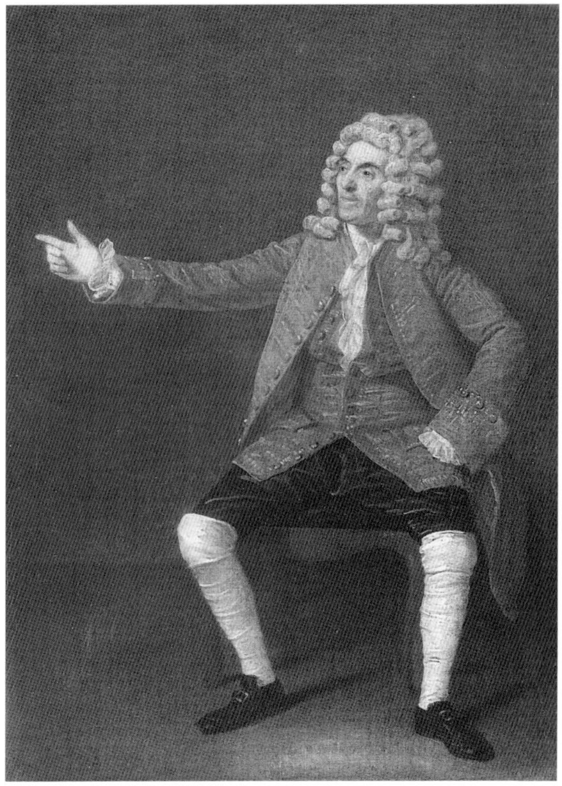

657 *William Parsons as Colonel Oldboy*

657

WILLIAM PARSONS

as Colonel Oldboy

in *The School for Fathers or Lionel and Clarissa*

by Isaac Bickerstaffe

Samuel De Wilde

Oil on canvas 36.5 x 28.5
INV: RW/CKA 267; Gift 122
PROV: John Bell; William A. Commerell, by whom presented to the Garrick Club, 1854
EXH: 1962 Chichester (24)
ENGR: John Corner for Bell's British Library 21 January 1791, line 11.7 x 8.2 (inscr. 'De Wilde del'), pub. Bell's *British Theatre* (1797), vol 21; A. Ferguson for Jones's *British Theatre* pub. Wm. Jones, Dublin, line 11.7 x 8.2; Anon. printed for C. Cooke, *British Drama* (1805), line (oval with ornaments)

Colonel Oldboy is shown shortly after the opening of the play, when he 'is discovered at breakfast'. He gestures towards his daughter Diana, whom he intends to marry off to a scion of large fortune. Parsons wears a full wig, a cherry red coat and waistcoat with gold trim, and dark green breeches. The Oxberry edition of 1818 gives Colonel Oldboy's costume as 'Blue regimental coat; with white kerseymere waistcoat and breeches, and cocked hat'.

In the engraving after De Wilde's picture of Parsons as Colonel Oldboy, the figure is set in an interior with a coal grate in a fireplace to the left and a silver jug for the breakfast milk on the mantel. The play has a frontispiece by Thomson after a painting by De Wilde showing Dowton shaking his fist as Colonel Oldboy.

Bickerstaffe's comic opera, with music by Charles Dibdin, was originally performed at Covent Garden on 25 February 1768, with Shuter as the original Colonel Oldboy, Mattocks as Lionel, and Miss Macklin as Clarissa. Parsons gave his first performance as Colonel Oldboy at Drury Lane on 8 February 1770 – the first and only performance of the play there that century – and then did not play the role again until 18 June 1785, at the Haymarket. The inscription on the original plate suggests that, like three other plates in the 1797 edition of Bell's *British Theatre*, it was taken from a drawing rather than a painting. There are oil versions of all four in the Garrick Club: Nos. 20, 71, 140 and 657.

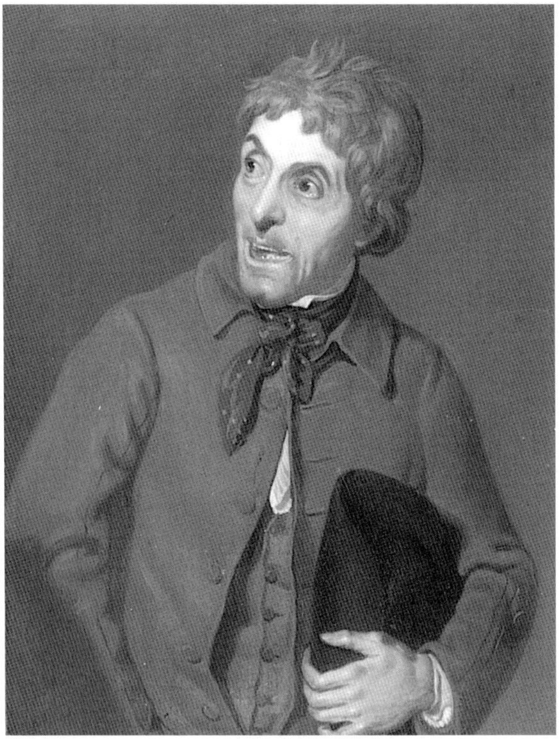

658
WILLIAM PARSONS
as Sheepface in *The Village Lawyer*
by George Colman the Younger

Samuel De Wilde

Oil on panel 22.8 x 19
INV: CKA 567A; Gift 390
PROV: Sir Henry Irving; Irving sale, Christie's 16 December 1905 (149); Mrs Weedon Grossmith, by whom presented to the Garrick Club, 1919
EXH: 1971 Northampton (18)
ENGR: Samuel De Wilde, soft ground etching 22.5 x 18.1
REL: See No. 39; V&A D.53, black chalk and watercolour on wove paper 23.5 x 17.8, inscr: 'S De Wilde / 1802'

Sheepface has ginger-brown hair. He clutches a black hat to his chest and wears a rustic brown jacket with brown buttons, a red waistcoat, white shirt and brown neckerchief.

The elder Colman's farce was first performed at the Haymarket on 28 August 1787, with John Edwin as Sheepface. Parsons gave his first performance as Sheepface at the Haymarket on 10 June 1791, and his last at the same theatre on 11 September 1794. This picture could be a study for De Wilde's large picture (see No. 39) but is more likely to relate to the V&A drawing, dated five years after Parsons's death, or to the soft ground etching probably dating from about the same time.

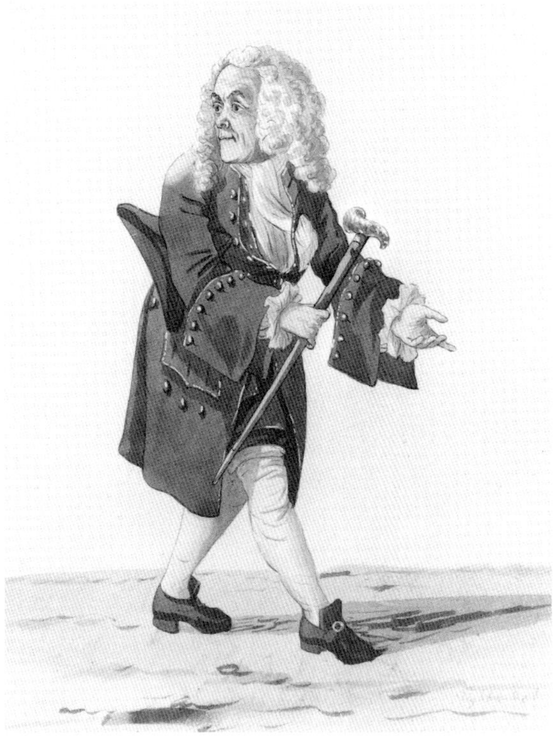

659
WILLIAM PARSONS
as Moneytrap
in *The Confederacy*
by Sir John Vanbrugh

Robert Dighton

Pencil, pen and grey ink with watercolour and touches of white body colour on wove paper 21 x 16.5
INSCR: 'Dighton del' (pen and grey ink b.r.); 'Mr Parsons as Moneytrap – Confederacy.' (pen and brown ink on mount b.c. CM)
INV: RW 554B (artist unknown); CKA 554B
PROV: Charles Mathews (not in catalogue)

Moneytrap is the wealthy husband of Araminta, whom he keeps on a short financial rein. However, he is prepared to expend large sums of money in his pursuit of Clarissa, the wife of his neighbour Gripe, who in turn has designs on Araminta. The backward glance in Dighton's drawing suggests that Moneytrap is shown in Act II, 'Mr Gripe's House', when he is parleying with Flippanta, Clarissa's maid, and they are interrupted by the sound of Gripe's voice. Moneytrap wears a dark grey coat and carries a stick.

Vanbrugh's comedy was originally performed at the King's Theatre on 30 October 1705. Parsons first played Moneytrap at Drury Lane on 8 December 1769.

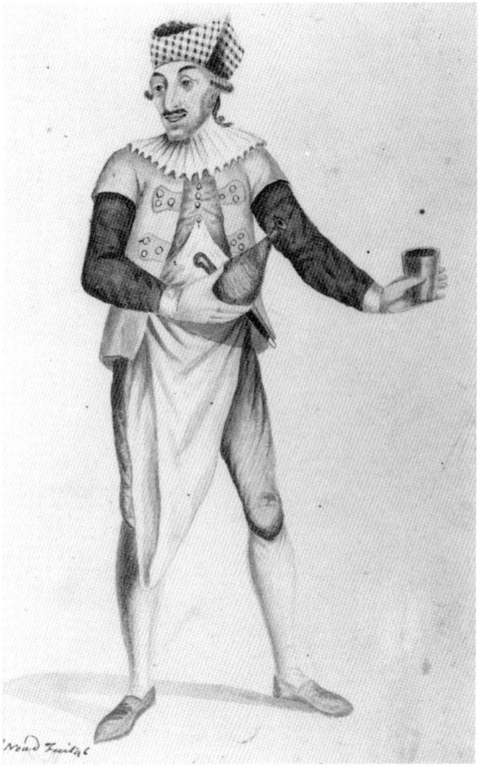

660

WILLIAM PARSONS

as Lope Tocho in *The Mountaineers*

by George Colman the Younger

Noad (?)

Pencil, pen and grey ink and watercolour on wove paper 24.1 x 14

INSCR: 'Noad Fecit 96' (pen and brown ink b.l.); 'Mr Parsons as Lope Tocho in the Mountaineers.' (pen and brown ink on mount b. CM)

INV: RW 553B (as 'Lope Tocksin', artist unknown); CKA 553B

PROV: Charles Mathews (not in catalogue)

In Act II, scene I, 'The inside of a Venta (or Spanish Inn) in Andalusia', Lope Tocho, the host of the venta, makes his first appearance. He is very swarthy and Spanish. His costume is distinguished by a curious blue and white checked cap.

The younger Colman's melodrama was first performed at the Haymarket on 3 August 1793, with Parsons as Lope Tocho. Parsons was also in the first performance at Drury Lane on 31 October 1794; Lope Tocho was the last new role he played there. This rather crude drawing was done after Parsons had died, as can be seen from the inscription, and it may relate to a series of equally crude drawings by W. Loftis in the Folger Library.

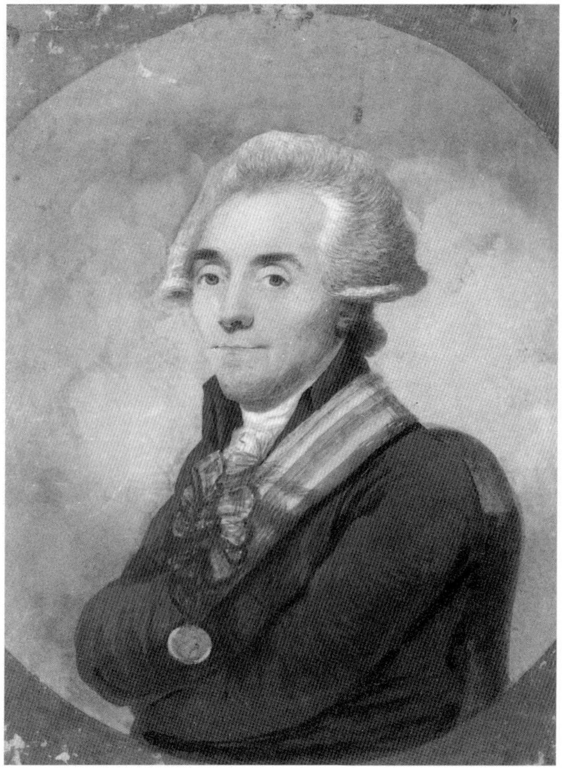

661

WILLIAM PARSONS

'School of Garrick'

William Spicer

Pencil and watercolour on laid paper 26.5 x 21

INV: Mathews 258 (artist unknown); RW/CKA 50E (artist unknown)

PROV: Charles Mathews

EXH: 1833 London (258)

Parsons's wig has a pronounced widow's peak. The collar of his blue jacket is turned down over his Shakespeare Ribband, which has a rosette and from which hangs a Shakespeare Favour.

The portrait of Parsons for Parsons's *Minor Theatre* is by De Wilde and engraved by William Ridley. De Wilde painted another portrait of Parsons, engraved in mezzotint by Edward Bell and published by P. Brown on 1 January 1796. It is inscribed 'To the School of Garrick, this Portrait of / MR PARSONS, COMEDIAN, / is respectfully dedicated, by their humble Servant / Edward Bell.' See No. 6.

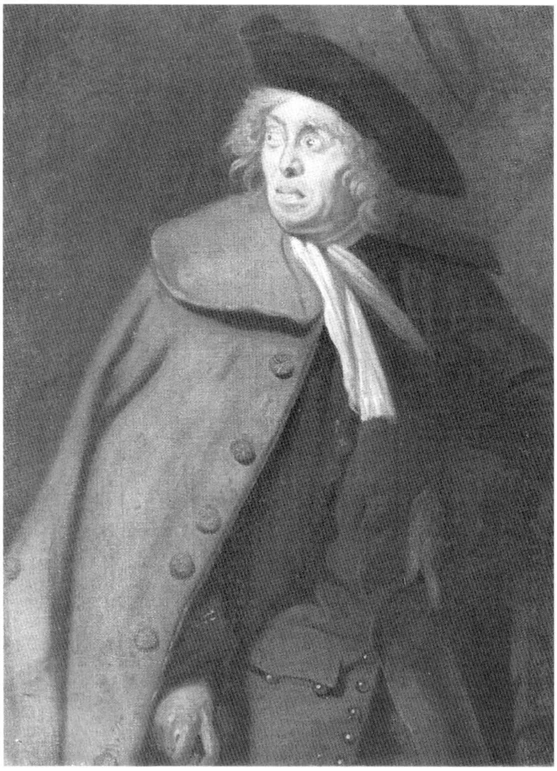

662
WILLIAM PARSONS
as the Old Man
in *Lethe or Aesop in the Shades*
by David Garrick

Johan Zoffany

Oil on canvas 37.2 x 29
INV: Mathews 82; RW/CKA 475
PROV: Charles Mathews
EXH: 1833 London (82); 1951 London (50)
REL: Birmingham City Art Gallery P.3948, oil on canvas 100.3 x 124.5, exh: S.A. 1766 (199)

The Old Man is the second visitor to Elysium to drink the waters of Lethe, on the anniversary of the Rape of Proserpine (see No. 121). Aesop tells him he has no need for the waters of forgetfulness as he has already outlived his memory. The Old Man says that it is his money that causes all his uneasiness, so Aesop offers to enable him to forget it. The Old Man, hard of hearing, asks his servant what Aesop has said. He tells him that Aesop will teach him to forget his money. The Old Man is not impressed and refuses to drink the waters. In Zoffany's picture the Old Man starts in horror at Aesop's words. He is shown three-quarter length, his hair ungroomed under a black tricorn hat, and he wears a heavy brown overcoat with large brown buttons, over a darker brown coat. The ends of his stock hang down loosely. He may be holding a stick in his right hand; the canvas has perhaps been cut down.

Garrick's farce was first performed at Drury Lane on 15 April 1740. Parsons played the Old Man for the first time at Drury Lane on 23 January 1766, a Command Performance in which Garrick played Lord Chalkstone. The Birmingham picture is the scene exhibited at the S.A. in 1766 as a pair to another scene from the play with Garrick and two others (see No. 250). It shows Astley Bransby as Aesop and Watkins as the Servant John, as well as Parsons. The Garrick Club painting is probably subsequent to that scene, painted perhaps for Parsons himself, who was at the beginning of his career at Drury Lane.

663
LOCATION UNKNOWN
WILLIAM PARSONS'S GRAVESTONE

Gosden

Pencil, pen and grey ink with watercolour on wove paper 29.2 x 21.6
INSCR: 'IN MEMORY OF / WILLIAM PARSONS, ESQR. / WHO DIED FEBRUARY 3RD 1795 / AGED 59 YEARS / "Here Parsons lies, oft on life's busy stage / With nature reader hast thou see him vie / He science knew, knew manners, knew the eye, / Respected knew to live, lamented die" ' (pen and grey ink on gravestone); 'Gosden' (pen and grey ink b.c.); 'In Lee Church Yard – Kent' (pen and grey ink b.c.)
INV: Not listed
PROV: Unknown

[Parsons was buried in St Margaret's churchyard at Lee, near Blackheath in Kent. A monument to his memory was erected there, bearing this epitaph written by the elder Charles Dibdin. The epitaph is recorded on British Library MS 11826s (v. 16), and was published (with variants) in Wewitzer's *Dramatic Chronology* (1817) and in Thomas Bellamy's *Life of William Parsons* (1795).]

This drawing was not found in 1996.

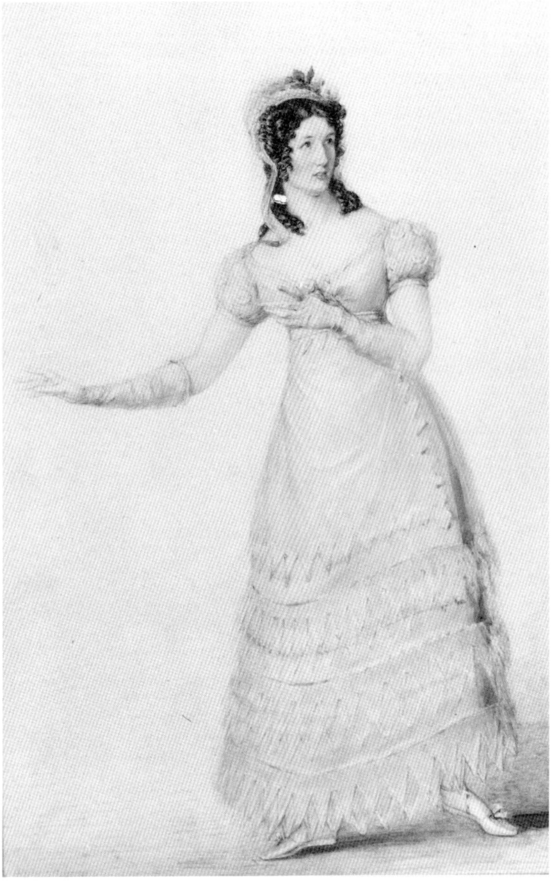

664
MARY ANN PATON
as Susanna in *The Marriage of Figaro*
by Wolfgang Amadeus Mozart and
Lorenzo Da Ponte, after P. Beaumarchais

John Stewart

Pencil with watercolour
on wove paper 29.8 x 21.9
INV: RW/CKA 319; Gift 120
PROV: W. Cribb, by whom presented
to the Garrick Club, 1854
ENGR: John Stewart pub. Colnaghi & Co.,
stipple 31.2 x 24.3

Susanna wears a high-waisted white dress with short puffed sleeves and three rows of zigzag flounces on the skirt, which has a front panel with zigzag edge. Her white cap has two white roses, and there are roses on her corsage.

Miss Paton made her first appearance on the stage at the Haymarket Theatre as Susanna on 19 October 1822, and this drawing probably dates from about that time.

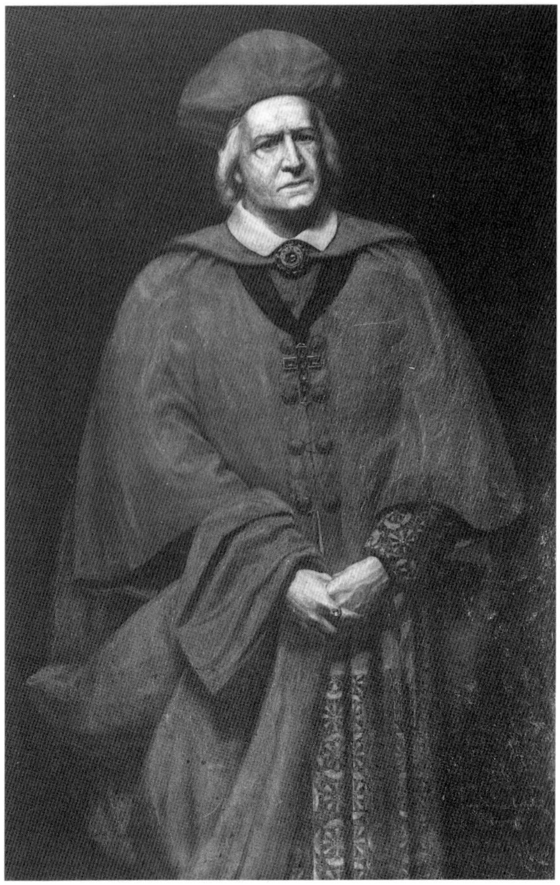

665
SAMUEL PHELPS
as Cardinal Wolsey in *Henry VIII*
by William Shakespeare

Sir Johnston Forbes-Robertson

Oil on canvas 152.5 x 100
INSCR: 'SAMUELEM PHELPS TRAGAEDUM / DISCIPULUS IN
ARTE SCENICA / JOHNSTON FORBES-ROBERTSON /
DEPINXIT / 1878' (red paint b.r.)
INV: RW/CKA 75; Gift 233
PROV: John Hollingshead; presented to the Garrick Club
by 100 members soon after the picture was painted
LIT: W. May Phelps & J. Forbes-Robertson, *Life of Samuel Phelps* (1886), p. 307, illustrated as frontispiece;
John Hollingshead, *Gaiety Chronicles* (1898), p. 281

Wolsey wears a cardinal's red costume, the surplice a design of interlocking red and white segmented circles. A ruby cross hangs from a black ribbon around his neck and above the cross is a round jewel of rubies.

Phelps told Forbes-Robertson that the character he should like best to play when he took his farewell of the stage was that of Cardinal Wolsey. On Friday 1 March 1878 his wish was fulfilled.

The dramatic end of Phelps's career is described in W. May Phelps's biography:

> In January 1877, he made up his mind to commence playing his farewell engagements at all the principal provincial theatres, but he only carried this out at three, viz. Manchester, Dublin, and Liverpool. Towards the end of 1877 he played for some time at the Aquarium Theatre several of his best characters, and agreed to act there again under Miss Litton's management early in 1878; but before this latter came off he ... agreed to recite at the Albert Hall. ... He first of all caught a cold there at rehearsal, and increased it so much at the performance that he had a bad attack of lumbago. ... This was in the middle of a week in February, and he was to appear at the Aquarium on the following Monday, which he did, although altogether unfit. He acted all that week, and five days of the next, Cardinals Richelieu and Wolsey alternately, his last part being Wolsey, on Friday 1st March. Considering his state of health, he went through the part marvellously, until he came to the last great speech, commencing, 'Farewell, a long farewell to all my greatness' into which he introduced several incongruous words; but when he reached the lines, 'O Cromwell, Cromwell! / Had I but serv'd my God with half the zeal / I serv'd my king, he would not in mine age / Have left me naked to mine enemies,' he gathered himself up with tremendous energy, as was his wont, and almost on tip-toe, for one more triumph, gave them, as far as 'zeal', with all his usual grandeur and pathos; but after muttering a word or two more, he fell on the shoulder of his Secretary, and the career of our hero was closed.

W. May Phelps also refers to Phelps's attachment to Forbes-Robertson:

> In his latter days he became much attached to young Mr J. Forbes-Robertson; indeed, so much so, that after he first played with him in Manchester in 1874, he always had him engaged to play Cromwell, Prince Henry, Egerton, Joseph Surface, and other characters. He also had a high opinion of him as an artist in oil, and sat to him for his portrait in Cardinal Wolsey, which, when finished, the Garrick Club purchased.

No. 665, therefore, celebrates Phelps's final performance on stage, a performance shared by the artist playing the part of Cromwell.

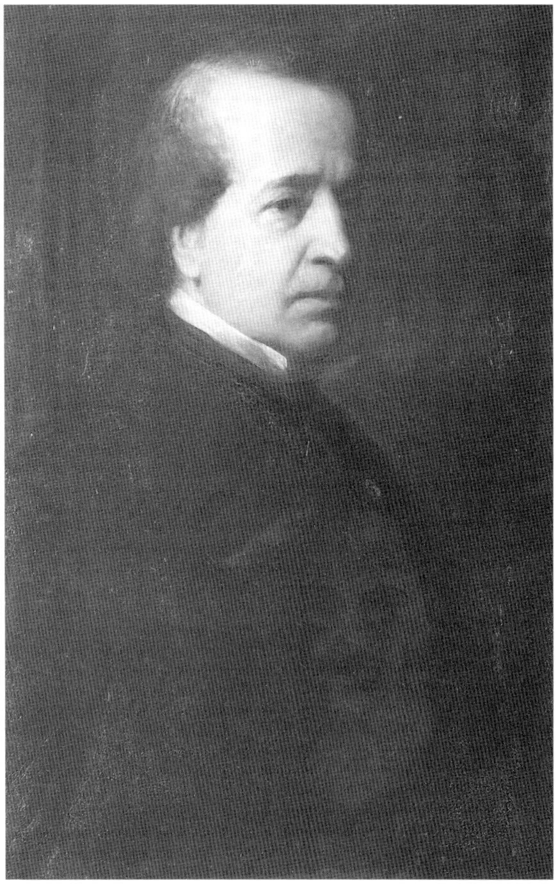

666

SAMUEL PHELPS

Richard Waller

Oil on canvas 74.9 x 62.2
INSCR: 'Richd Waller / Pinxit' (red paint b.r.)
INV: RW/CKA 323; Gift 288
PROV: Sir Squire Bancroft, by whom presented to the Garrick Club, 1905

Samuel Phelps became a member of the Garrick Club in 1874.

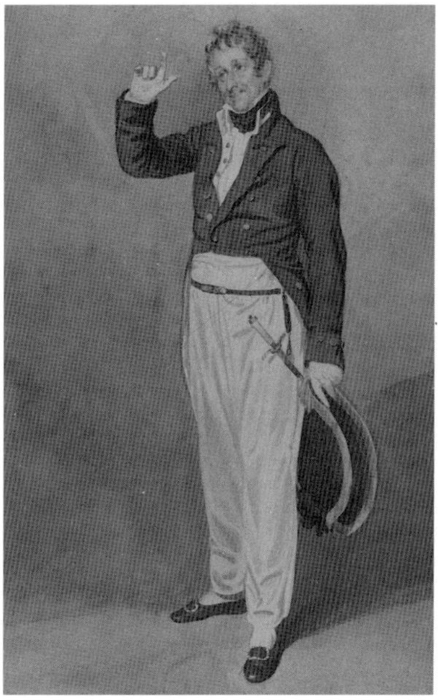

667

THOMAS PHILIPPS

as Hartwell in *Up All Night or The Smugglers' Cave*
by Samuel James Arnold

Samuel De Wilde

Pencil and watercolour on wove paper 37 x 23.5
INSCR: 'S De Wilde / July 29 1809' (pencil b.l.)
INV: Mathews 239; RW/CKA 60F
PROV: Charles Mathews
EXH: 1833 London (239)
ENGR: Stadler pub. W. Holland 1809, aquatint 35.5 x 23.5

Heartwell gestures heavenwards with his right hand, and in his left holds a black half-moon hat with gold braid and a black rosette. He wears a curious combination of military and civilian clothes: black shoes with silver buckles, black stockings, white trousers, a black belt with a gold buckle, a purplish coat with gold buttons and a high collar lined in white, a white waistcoat with gold buttons, and a black stock.

Arnold's comic opera, with music by M.P. King, was performed at the Lyceum on 26 June 1809, with Philipps as the original Young Heartwell, Charles Edward Horn as Meddle (see No. 308), and George Smith as Peter (see No. 765). The 38th and penultimate performance of the season on 16 September was for Philipps's benefit. The reviewer in the *Monthly Mirror* of July 1809 saved what kind words he had for Philipps: '...of the debutants, Mr Philipps from Dublin stands "first and foremost". He has a genteel figure and a pleasing countenance. As an actor he has much to learn ... his voice is between a tenor and a contralto.'

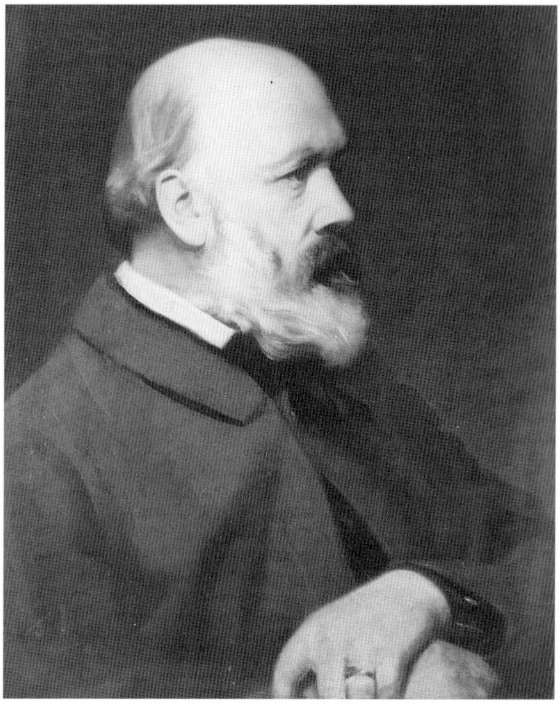

668

JOHN PHILLIP

C.E. Cundell

Oil on canvas 38.1 x 30.5
INSCR: 'C. E. C. 7' (b.r.)
INV: RW 329 (by John Phillip); CKA 329
PROV: E.J. Coleman, by whom presented
to the Garrick Club between 1864 and 1885

The artist Phillip, who was a Royal Academician, wears a dark grey coat. Possibly this portrait was painted and presented soon after the sitter's death in 1867. John Phillip became a member of the Garrick Club in 1858.

669

SIR ARTHUR WING PINERO

Max Beerbohm

Pencil with pen and black ink and watercolour 30.7 x 19.6
INSCR: 'max' (pen and black ink b.l.);
'Mr Arthur Wing Pinero' (pen and black ink b.r.)
INV: GCL 667; Gift 714
PROV: Presented to the Garrick Club by
25 subscribing members, 1952
EXH: 1949 Birmingham (107)

This is one of Max Beerbohm's finest caricatures. He gives Pinero an extremely long nose, a pea for an eye, and a thick eyebrow. The playwright's famous bald pate

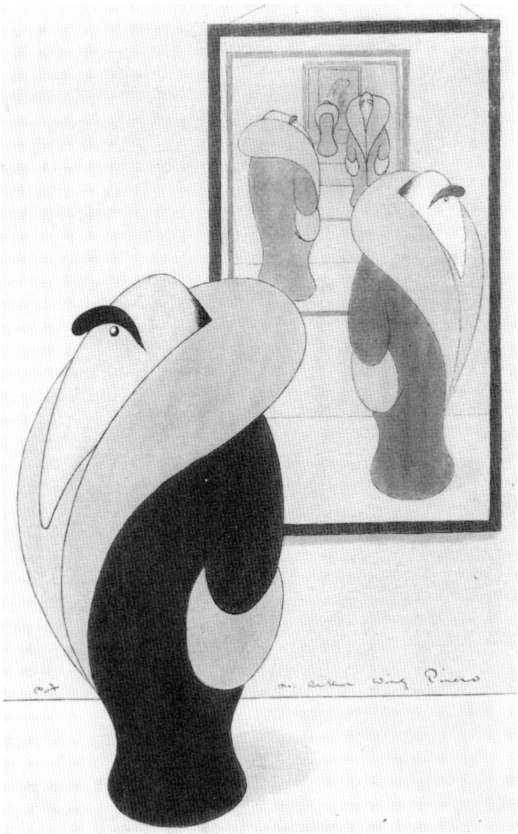

669 *Sir Arthur Wing Pinero*

(see marble bust of Pinero by Emil Fuchs, S27) is emphasised. His dark grey coat has a huge paler grey collar and cuff. A looking glass reflects the figure many times in infinite perspective, its position varying in a rotating dance of time and space.

Sir Arthur became a member of the Garrick Club in 1884.

670

LOCATION UNKNOWN

SIR ARTHUR WING PINERO

as Sir Anthony Absolute in *The Rivals*

by Richard Brinsley Sheridan

Phil May

Watercolour on wove paper 51.5 x 31.7

INSCR: 'Phil May'

INV: CKA 620; Gift 530

PROV: Pinero sale; Alderson Burrell Horne, by whom presented to the Garrick Club, 1935

Pinero wears a powdered wig with tied queue, a brown coat, a white neckcloth, a buff waistcoat, and black breeches (CKA). This picture was not found in 1988.

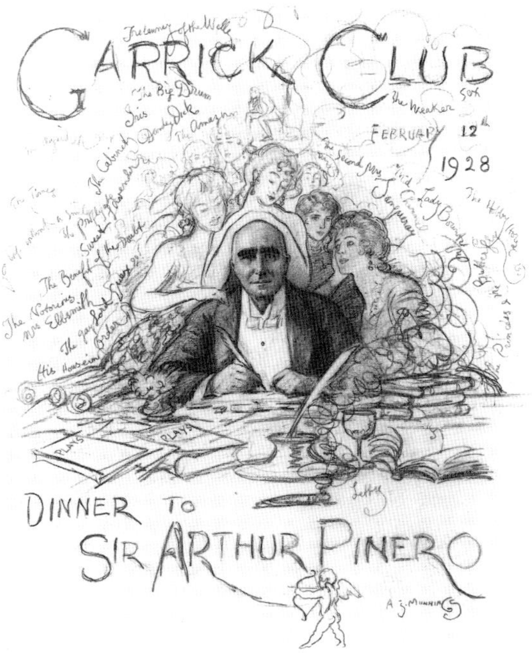

671

SIR ARTHUR WING PINERO

Sir Alfred Munnings

Pencil and black chalk on laid paper 45.7 x 39.4

INSCR: 'GARRICK CLUB / February 12 / 1928' (black chalk t.c.); 'DINNER TO / SIR ARTHUR PINERO' (pencil below); titles of plays around the head of Pinero; 'A. J. Munnings' (black chalk b.r.)

INV: CKA 527

PROV: Presented by the artist, 1929

EXH: 1949 Port Sunlight (150)

Pinero, sitting at a table with a quill in his right hand, wears a dark jacket and a high, stiff collar with a white bow tie. Behind him are a number of characters from his plays, including a young lady resting her arms upon his pate; there are six others, including a man in a pensive attitude. The names of his plays are inscribed around Pinero's figure.

This is a sketch for the front cover of the menu for a dinner that was given for Pinero on 12 February 1928. Munnings's conception is in the tradition of 19th-century illustrations of authors such as Shakespeare and Dickens in the heady act of creation, their thoughts materialising into airy characters.

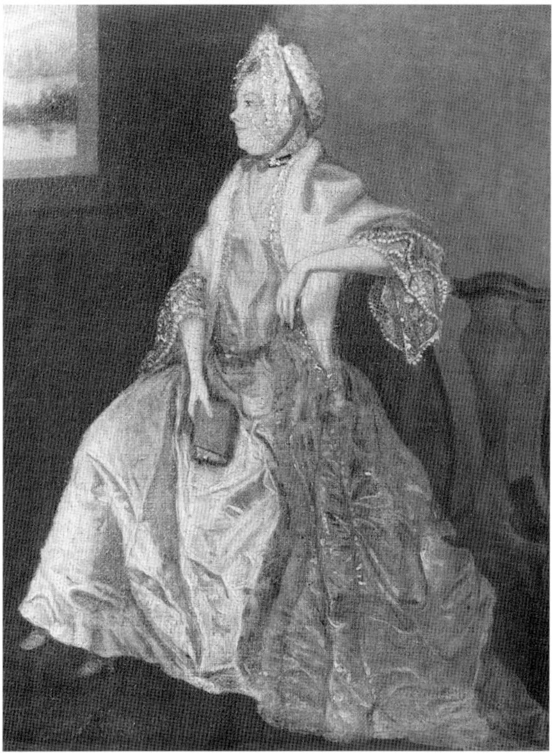

672
ANN PITT

Unknown Artist

Oil on canvas 37.3 x 29.5
INV: Mathews 28 (by Hogarth);
RW 229 (by Hogarth); CKA 229
PROV: Charles Mathews
EXH: 1833 London (28); 1951 London (38); 1957 London

The sitter, holding a book in her lap and resting her left arm on the back of her chair, wears a large panniered dress, orange-brown at the back with a train, a skirt shot green and pink, and a white lace-trimmed wrap.

If this picture could be dated to the 1720s, an attribution to Hogarth on stylistic grounds might be entertained. However, the costume is later, and the age of the sitter, presumably correctly identified by Mathews, would date the picture about 1770.

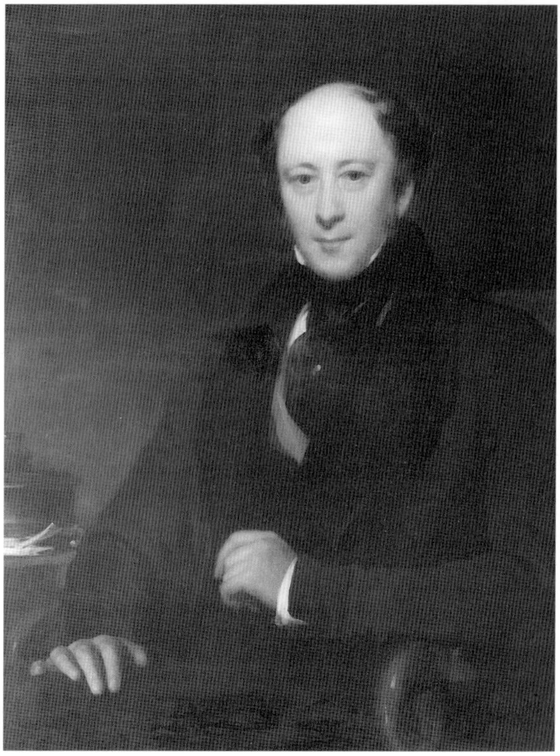

673
JAMES ROBINSON PLANCHÉ

Henry Perronet Briggs

Oil on canvas 90.2 x 69.8
INV: CKA 603; Gift 343
PROV: Captain Anthony Tucker, by whom presented to the Garrick Club, 1909
EXH: 1835 R.A. (262)
ENGR: J. Onwhyn for Webster's *Acting National Drama* (1837), vol I, line 9.2 x 7.1
LIT: David Reynolds, *Weber in London* (1976), reproduced

Planché, seated in a chair, has ginger-brown hair brushed up onto his balding pate. He wears a brown jacket with a black velvet collar, a brown waistcoat lined in red, a white shirt with a high collar, and a dark cravat with a stick.

One of the original members of the Garrick Club, Planché resigned in 1853, rejoined in 1865 and resigned again in 1869. He was a prominent dramatist and costume historian.

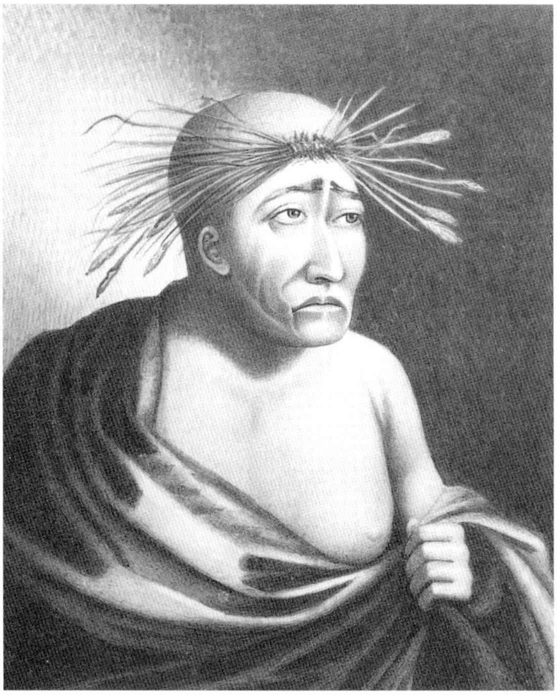

674
BARTHOLOMEW ('BATT') PLATT
as 'Mad Tom'

Sylvester Harding (after Anon.)
Pen and brown ink with watercolour
on wove paper 13.1 x 11.1
INSCR: 'Batt. Platt' (pen and brown ink below CM)
INV: Not listed
PROV: Charles Mathews (Print Collection Vol I fol 81)
ENGR: Anon. printed T. Kitchen, mezzotint 13.6 x 11.4

The sharp-featured Platt clutches a brown drapery over his right shoulder. He has corn-stalks knotted across his forehead.

This drawing is a copy from the anonymous engraving. Batt Platt is not playing in King Lear, but is singing a song at Sadler's Wells. According to Hawkins, in his *General History of Music* (1776), Platt used to sing 'Mad Tom' at Sadler's Wells 'dressed in the character of a Madman, to the great delight of all who mistook roaring for singing'.

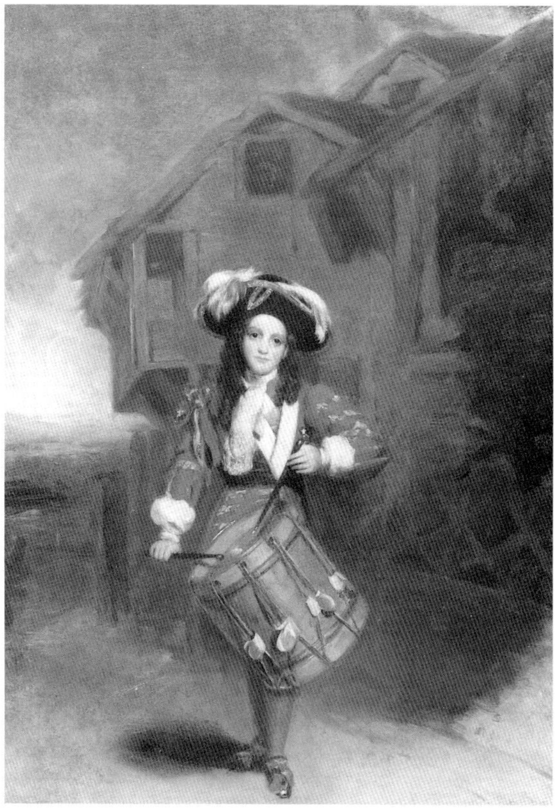

675
ELIZABETH POOLE
as the Drummer Boy in *His First Campaign*
overture and music by Adolphe Adam

Henry Meyer
Oil on board 39.4 x 28
INV: RW 443 (as Cupid Turned Drummer); CKA 443
(as Hop o'my Thumb in 'Hop o'my Thumb
and his Brothers'); Gift 153
PROV: Bequeathed by Charles Farley, 1859
EXH: 1951 London (29)
LIT: *Illustrated London News*, Christmas issue 1948
(reproduced, colour)

The diminutive Miss Poole plays an enormous drum. She wears a fanciful military costume of black shoes with red bows and decoration, red stockings, red breeches decorated with gold, and a red jacket trimmed with gold. The drum, supported by a white V-shaped band, is brown with red and yellow elements. Her black cockade hat is decorated with gold braid and white feathers.

Miss Poole played a drummer boy in Adam's *His First Campaign*, which was a great success and opened at Covent Garden on 1 October 1832. [No references have been found to either *Cupid Turned Drummer* or *Hop o'my Thumb and his Brothers.*]

676

LOCATION UNKNOWN

ELIZABETH POOLE as Jocelyn
and *WILLIAM MITCHENSON* as Tibbytight
in *Puss in Boots or Harlequin and the Miller's Son*

Henry Meyer

Oil on canvas 39.4 x 28
INV: RW 445 (as Puss in Boots);
CKA 445; Gift 153 (stolen 1983)
PROV: Bequeathed by Charles Farley, 1859
EXH: 1951 London (30)
LIT: David Mayer, *Harlequin in his Element* (1969)

This stolen picture was described by CKA as: 'Whole-length, [Miss Poole is] standing on the left, turned away from the spectator, head three-quarters to left, looking at spectator, adjusting her collar in front of mirror on dressing table in centre, a cat to right is pulling a boot on its left leg. Miss Poole wears black cocked hat with white plumes, and white dress with red ribbons on shoulders and round waist; trees to left, church to right.'

Master Mitchenson made his first stage appearance in this Covent Garden pantomime, which opened on 26 December 1832.

Unfortunately, this charming picture, the pendant to No. 675, was stolen from the Garrick Club in 1983 along with the silver helmet presented to John Philip Kemble by the citizens of Edinburgh.

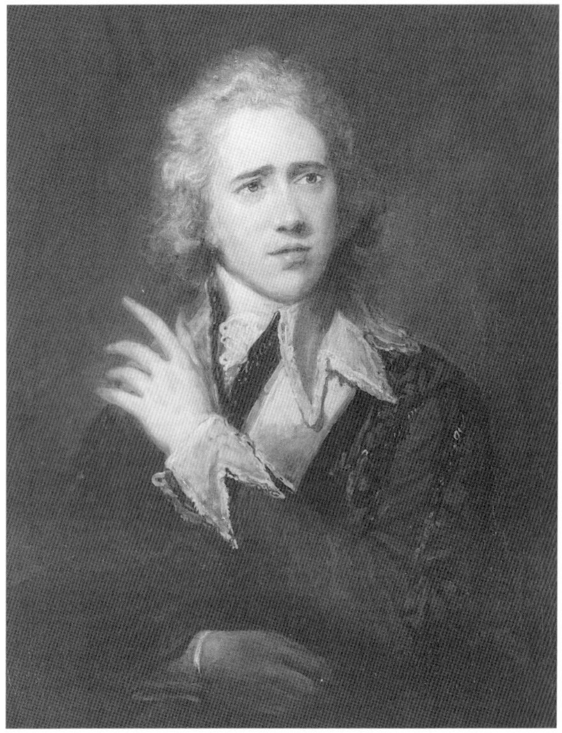

677

ALEXANDER POPE
as Hamlet in *Hamlet*
by William Shakespeare

Gainsborough Dupont

Oil on canvas 74.3 x 61.6
INV: Mathews 152; RW/CKA 422
PROV: Thomas Harris; Harris sale, 12 July 1819 (20);
Charles Mathews
EXH: 1833 London (152); 1982–83 London (125)
LIT: *Morning Herald*, 22 March 1794; Hayes, 1968

Half-length. Hamlet wears black, with a lace vandyke collar and cuffs. Across his chest there are white bands edged in red. His bedraggled powdered hair is brushed back.

Pope played Hamlet for the first time at Covent Garden on 30 October 1793, the occasion for Dupont's picture, which was finished when mentioned in the *Morning Herald* on 22 March 1794. Holman was the usual Hamlet at Covent Garden, but Pope played the part once more during the 1793–94 season, on 10 May 1794, when the playbill claimed that the play was mounted at 'the particular Desire of his Excellency the Ambassador from the Sublime Porte' (Ussuf Adijah Effendi).

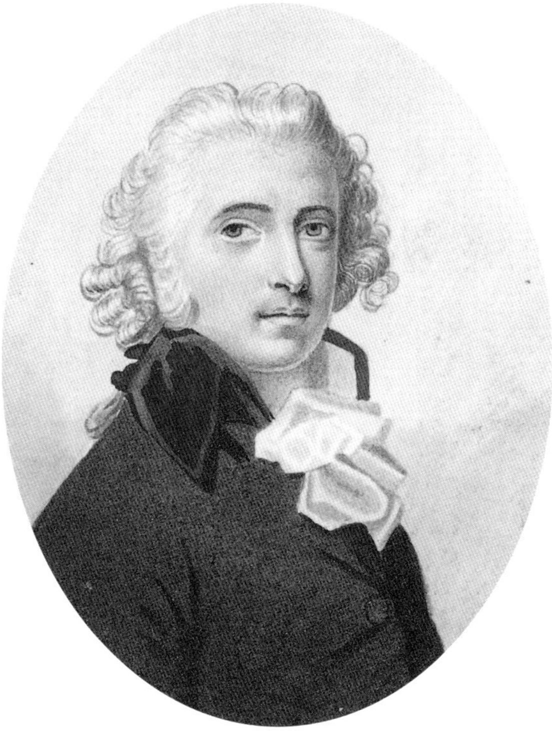

678
ALEXANDER POPE

Sylvester Harding (after Alexander Pope)

Pencil and watercolour with some black ink on wove paper 8.1 x 6.7 (oval)
INSCR: 'Mr Pope' (pen and brown ink below CM)
INV: Not listed
PROV: Charles Mathews (Print Collection Vol IV fol 46)
ENGR: William Ridley for Parsons's *Minor Theatre* 1793, stipple 7.3 x 5.7

Harding's copy of Pope's self-portrait shows Pope in a curly powdered wig and a blue jacket with a high black collar.

Pope, who was trained at the Dublin Art School and between 1777 and 1780 sent drawings to the Society of Artists in Dublin, made his début at Covent Garden on 8 January 1785 as Oroonoko. He remained on the London stage for some 44 years, playing a variety of roles. Though not an actor of exceptional quality, he earned a steady income which supported his taste for luxurious living.

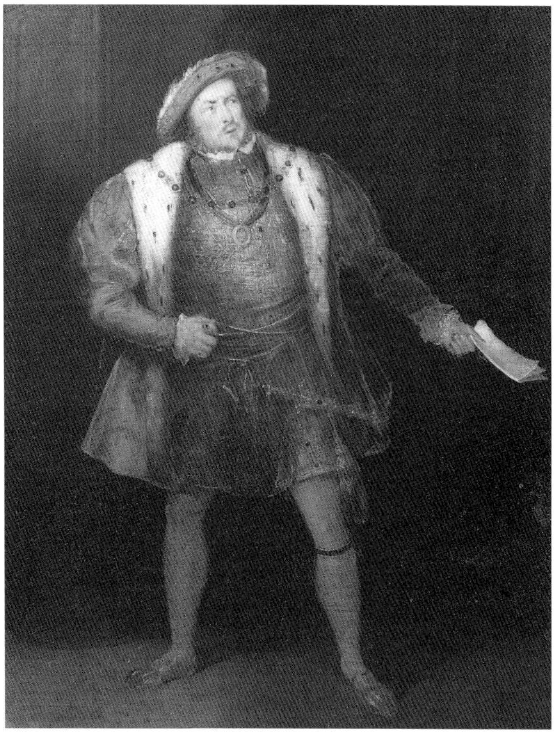

679
ALEXANDER POPE
as Henry in *Henry VIII* by William Shakespeare

Michael William Sharp

Oil on canvas 60.5 x 45.5
INV: Mathews 86; RW/CKA III
PROV: Charles Mathews
EXH: 1833 London (86)

The paper in Henry's hand suggests Act III, scene I, in which the king discovers Wolsey's great wealth: 'Enter the King, with a letter in his hand, and reading a schedule. KING: "What piles of wealth he accumulated / to his own portion!".' Henry, standing full-length, has a ginger beard and a ginger wig mostly hidden by his red hat, which is edged with gold embroidery and has white plumes in the brim. On the forefinger of his right hand is a blue ring, and on his little finger a red ring. He wears red shoes with slashed toes, red hose with a blue garter edged in gold, a gold tunic, and a red coat with flounced sleeves, which is lined with ermine and has a wide ermine collar. An order, presumably the Garter, hangs from a blue band around his neck, and a large chain over his shoulders displays the royal insignia in gold between enamelled roses.

Pope played Henry VIII for the first time at Covent Garden on 23 April 1806, with J.P. Kemble as Wolsey and Sarah Siddons as Queen Katherine.

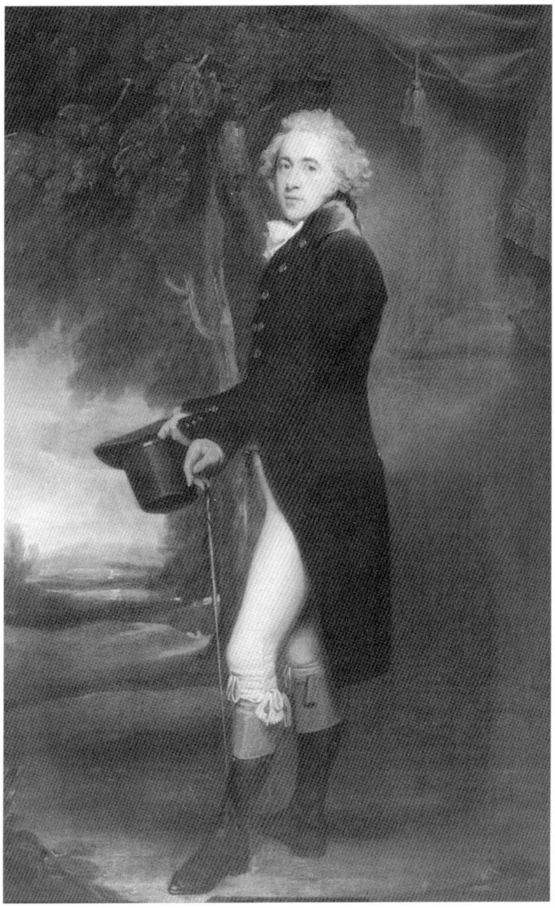

680

ALEXANDER POPE

Sir Martin Archer Shee

Oil on canvas 74 x 48
INV: RW/CKA 404; Gift 50
PROV: Bequeathed to the Garrick Club
by the sitter's widow and received 1839
EXH: 1797 R.A. (122); 1934 London (356); 1951 London (36)

Pope, standing full-length, is fashionably dressed in black boots with brown tops, tight tan breeches with buttons and bows, and a dark blue jacket with a high collar and gold buttons; there is powder on the shoulders. His grey-gloved right hand rests on a stick, and he holds a fashionable black hat with a black band.

The head is similar to a self-portrait by the sitter engraved by William Ridley for Parsons's *Minor Theatre* and published by J. Parsons December 1793. Another portrait of Pope by Shee was shown at the R.A. in 1792 (46), but its location is unknown.

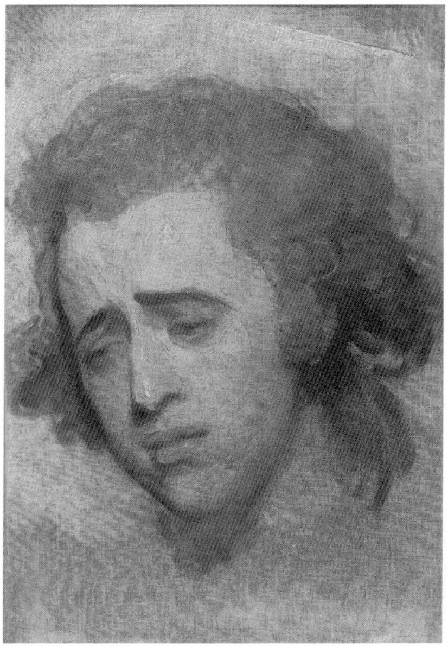

681

ALEXANDER POPE
as Posthumus in *Cymbeline*
by William Shakespeare

Gilbert Stuart

Oil on canvas 41.5 x 29
INV: Mathews 135 (no character);
RW/CKA 296 (sitter, character and artist unknown)
PROV: John Bell; Leigh & Sotheby's 25 May 1805 (258),
'Mr Pope as Posthumus in Cymbeline by Stewart',
bt. Mathews; Charles Mathews
EXH: 1833 London (135)
ENGR: J. Thornthwaite, after a drawing by Mather Brown,
28 February 1786, line 8.9 x 7, pub. Bell's *Shakespeare*,
vol 20; same plate pub. J. Cawthorn 1805

Posthumus has a pained expression and pale brown hair. This bust portrait appears to be unfinished.

This was one of Mathews's first purchases, acquired at the Bell sale at Leigh & Sotheby's on 25 May 1805, which included, as lots 258–86, 'Original Paintings, for Bell's British Theatre'. Lot 258 consisted of two portraits by Gilbert Stuart: No. 681 and a portrait of Holman as Falconbridge in *King John* (No. 145 in Mathews's 1833 catalogue but since lost). Other pictures bought in this sale by Mathews were Nos. 104, 304, 364, 426 and 448. No. 681 bears a similarity to the portrait of Alexander Pope in Mather Brown's scene from *The Gamester* and is one of four from Bell's third edition of Shakespeare, in which Mather Brown added heads by Stuart to twisted bodies. The others are: Kemble as Richard III (see No. 381), Holman as Falconbridge, and Henderson as Iago (Theatre Museum 12).

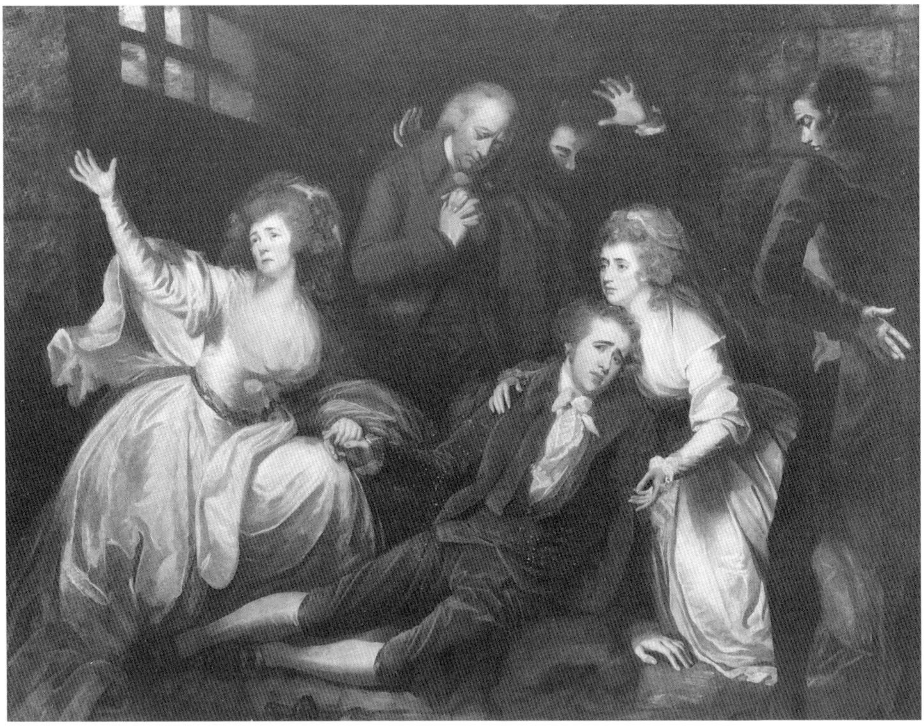

682*

ALEXANDER POPE as Beverley, *ELIZABETH POPE* as Mrs Beverley, *MARY WELLS* as Charlotte, *WILLIAM FARREN* as Lewson, *THOMAS HULL* as Jarvis and *GEORGE INCHBALD* as Stukely in *The Gamester* by Edward Moore

Mather Brown

Oil on canvas 200 x 254.6
INV: RW/CKA 446; Gift 2
PROV: Bush Hotel, Bristol; M.M. Zachary, by whom presented to the Garrick Club, 1833
EXH: 1787 R.A. (426) 'The last scene in the Tragedy of the Gamester'
LIT: *Dublin University Magazine* (1854), 43: 394; Fitzgerald, pp. 147–50

The picture shows Act V, scene 3 of Moore's tragedy, in which Beverley, imprisoned for debt, in despair has taken poison and is dying. The composition is conceived as a 'Deposition from the Cross', with Beverley (Pope) as Christ, Mrs Beverley (Mrs Pope) as the Virgin Mary, Charlotte (Wells) as Mary Magdalen, and Lewson (Farren) as St John. The looming figure of Stukely (Hull) can be read as the Roman Centurion, and Jarvis (Inchbald) perhaps as Joseph of Arimathea.

Mrs Beverley kneels on the left and is holding her husband's hand. She has a cap on her powdered brown hair and wears a white dress with gauze fichu and white drapery from the shoulders. Beverley sprawls in the pose of the Dying Gladiator or General Wolfe in Benjamin West's picture; he wears black shoes with silver buckles, white stockings, plum-coloured velvet breeches, jacket and waistcoat, a white shirt, and a loosely tied stock. His sister Charlotte wears a cap and a yellow dress with a gauze fichu. Lewson, bowing his head and clasping his hands in anguish, wears a brown coat.

Only the head of Jarvis is visible, along with his open-palmed gesture possibly taken from Caravaggio's Vatican 'Deposition'. The looming figure of Stukely looks down accusingly at the hapless figure of Beverley. He wears dark breeches, a green coat, and a yellow waistcoat. The heads and hands are painted on finer canvas than the rest of the picture, and are inserted into the larger work.

The Gamester was first performed at Drury Lane on 7 February 1753, with Garrick as Beverley, Davies as Stukely, Mossop as Lewson, Berry as Jarvis, Mrs Pritchard as Mrs Beverley and Miss Haughton as Charlotte. Mather Brown's painting depicts the Covent Garden performance of 25 September 1786, the only occasion on which the performers shown acted together in these parts. Pope was playing Beverley for the first time in London and Mrs Wells was giving her first Charlotte. Inchbald had been brought in as a last-minute stand-in for Francis Aickin, whose wife had just died.

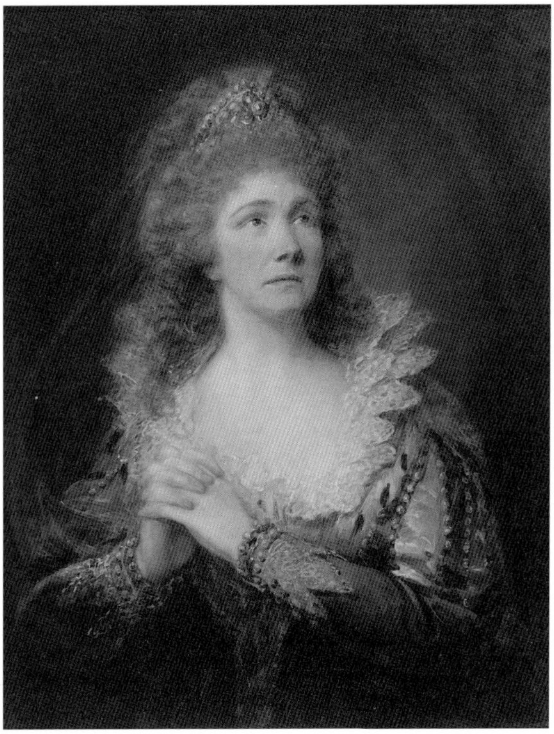

683*

ELIZABETH POPE

as Queen Elizabeth in *The Earl of Essex*

by Henry Jones

Gainsborough Dupont

Oil on canvas 76 x 63

INV: Mathews 155 (as Monimia in 'The Orphan');

RW 421 (as Monimia); CKA 421 (as Monimia or as Queen Katherine in 'Henry VIII')

PROV: Thomas Harris; Harris sale, 12 July 1819 (23) (as Queen Katherine); Charles Mathews

EXH: 1833 London (155); 1982–83 London (126)

LIT: *Morning Herald*, 22 March 1794; Hayes, 1968

Elizabeth clasps her hands yearningly. Her gold tiara has red jewels and a row of pearls; her blue dress has white slashing edged with pearls and is trimmed with lace and ermine.

Jones's tragedy was first performed at Covent Garden, on 21 February 1753, with Esther Bland as Queen Elizabeth. Despite the parts mentioned in the Harris and Mathews catalogues, Mrs Pope is almost certainly depicted playing Queen Elizabeth, the role mentioned in the *Morning Herald* of 22 March 1794.

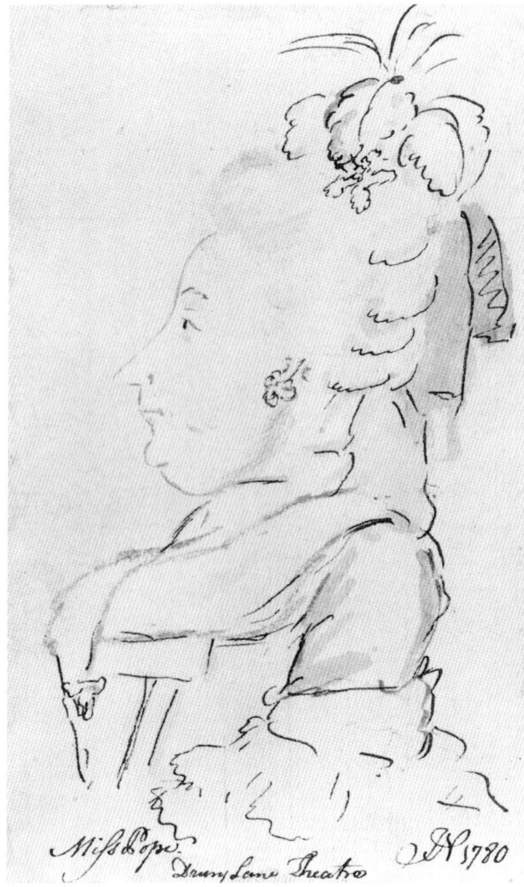

684

JANE POPE

in character

John Nixon

Pencil, pen and black ink with brown wash on laid paper 15.4 x 9.5

INSCR: 'Miss Pope.' (pen and black ink b.l.); 'JN 1780' (pen and black ink b.r.); 'Drury Lane Theatre' (pen and black ink b.c.)

INV: Not listed

PROV: John Nixon, *Dramatic Annals* I: 211

Half-length caricature, in profile to left, with a high coiffure ornamented with feathers and ribbons.

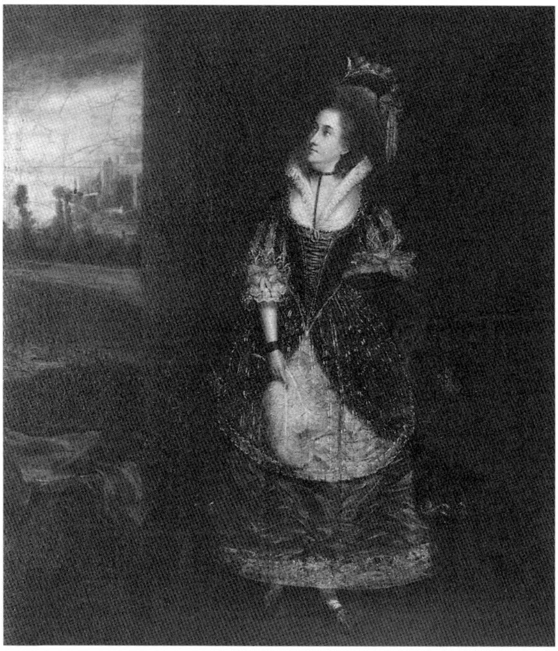

685
JANE POPE
as Mrs Page in *The Merry Wives of Windsor*
by William Shakespeare

James Roberts

Oil on canvas 89 x 68.5
INV: Mathews 59 (as Mrs Ford); RW/CKA 406
PROV: Charles Mathews
EXH: 1778 R.A. (429) 'Ditto [portrait of a lady] in the character of Mrs Page in the Merry Wives of Windsor'; 1833 London (59)

Mrs Page wears a costume of considerable richness and complexity. On her great pile of powdered hair sits a dainty tricorn hat, edged in gold with a pink ribbon inside the brim. A large pink bow and pink ribbons hang over her left shoulder, grey feathers above. She waves two feathers, perhaps by way of a fan, as she directs her servants to tip Falstaff into Datchet Mead. She wears black shoes with pink rosettes, white stockings, and a panniered grey dressed lined in red, the red hem edged in gold and the skirts pulled back with gold bows to reveal a ruched white silk underskirt with pink decoration round the hem. She has a double lace V-shaped ruff and a gauze apron trimmed in gold. The costume is a magnificent example of mid-Georgian historical fantasy.

Jane Pope performed the role of Mrs Page for the first time in London at Drury Lane on 24 February 1778, and again on 25 and 28 February, 9 March and 2 April during the 1777–78 season.

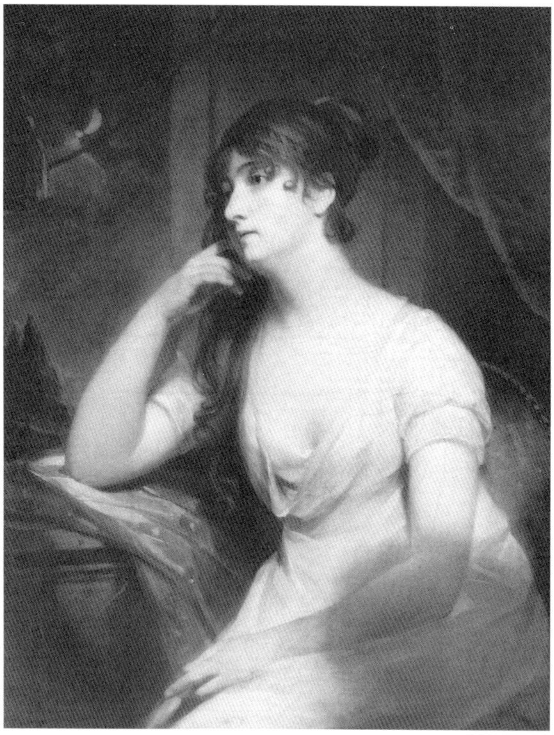

686
MARIA ANN POPE
as Juliet in *Romeo and Juliet* by William Shakespeare

Sir Martin Archer Shee

Oil on canvas 92 x 72
INV: Mathews 34 (no character); RW/CKA 377
PROV: Charles Mathews
EXH: 1803 R.A. (148); 1833 London (34)
ENGR: William Ward pub. J. Burn 1 April 1804, mezzotint 33 x 25.4, inscr: 'The late Mrs Pope as Juliet'

Juliet sits on her balcony in the moonlight. Her hair is plaited and wrapped around her head with a bun and a switch over her right shoulder. She is dressed in white. A red drapery, lined in white, hangs over the stone balcony. There are other red hangings, and the chair is upholstered in red with gold studs. Quoted on the engraving is the line: 'See how she leans her Cheek upon her hand.'

When still Miss Campion, Mrs Pope appeared as Juliet for the first time on 13 April 1795 in Belfast, where she was billed as 'the first female Ornament of the Irish Stage'. Following her Covent Garden début on 13 October 1797, as Monimia in *The Orphan*, she acted Juliet there on 2 November 1797. After marrying Alexander Pope in January 1798 she eventually moved to Drury Lane, where, on 1 February 1802, she played Juliet to her husband's Romeo.

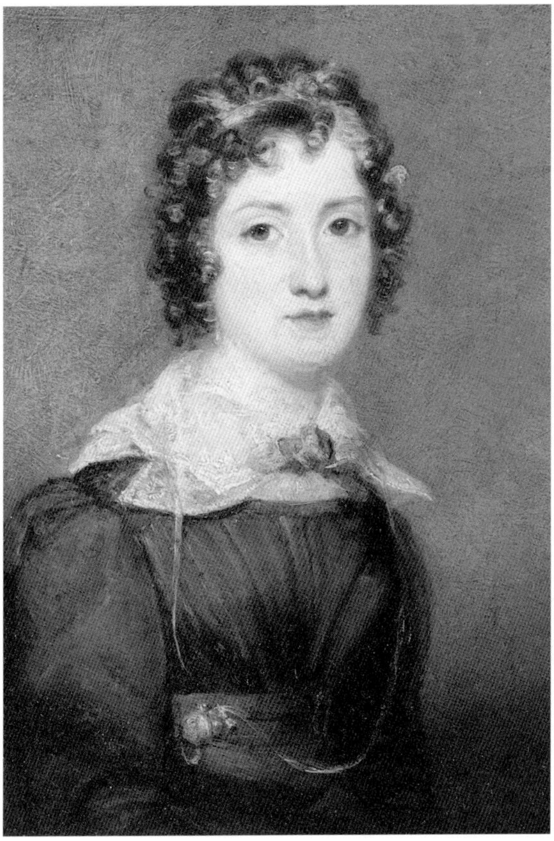

687
MARY ANN POVEY

John Prescott Knight

Oil on panel 22.3 x 17.5
INV: RW/CKA 291; Gift 167
PROV: Presented by the sitter's brother, John Povey, 1862
LIT: Herman Dyson, *John Prescott Knight R.A., a catalogue* (1971), No. 6, dated *c.*1825

Miss Povey is shown half-length, wearing a green dress with a watch-case and seals on a gold chain. A pale blue bow fastens her white muslin double collar.

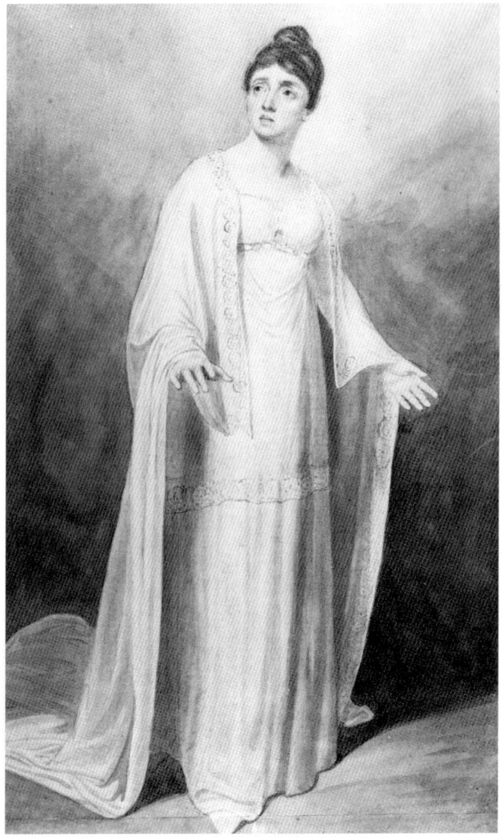

688
JANE POWELL
as Adelgitha in *Adelgitha*
by Matthew Gregory Lewis

Samuel De Wilde

Pencil and watercolour on wove paper 37 x 23.5
(piece of paper 2.5 wide added to bottom of drawing, includes part of the sitter's foot)
INSCR: 'S De Wilde / Feby 2d / 1808' (pencil b.r.)
INV: Mathews 202; RW/CKA 58D
PROV: Charles Mathews
EXH: 1833 London (202)

Adelgitha wears a loose dress in faded white, decorated in gold. A gold-embroidered white drapery hangs from her shoulders. The text calls for her to hold a scroll of paper, missing in De Wilde's drawing. The supplicatory gesture is not typical of the part; Adelgitha is a fiery lady, given to drinking blood and deft use of the dagger. She stabs herself at the end of the play, after killing Michael Ducas and revealing that the young hero, Lothair, is her son.

Lewis's tragedy, with incidental music by Michael Kelly, was first performed at Drury Lane on 30 April 1807, as a benefit for Mrs Powell, who played Adelgitha.

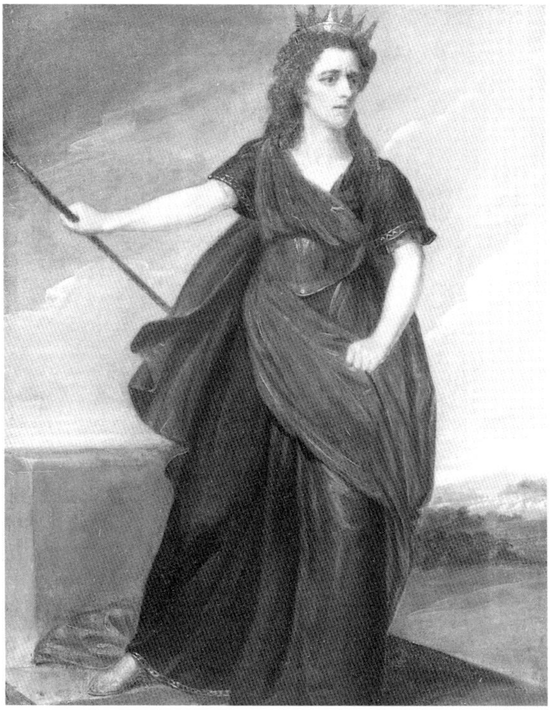

689

JANE POWELL

as Boadicea in *Boadicea* by Richard Glover

Samuel De Wilde

Oil on canvas 36.8 x 28.4
INV: Mathews 176; RW/CKA 215
PROV: John Bell; Charles Mathews
EXH: 1833 London (176)
ENGR: J. Thornthwaite for Bell's British Library
21 October 1791, line 11.5 x 7.6, pub. Bell's *British Theatre* (1797), vol 2, with the quotation: '– Not the wealth / which loads the palaces of sumptuous Rome / Shall bribe my fury' (Act I, scene I)

Boadicea descends the steps of the altar with her left fist clenched and a spear in her right hand. She wears a loose blue dress and billowing red mantle, with a gold crown and bronze stomach plate.

Glover's tragedy, with 'new pieces of music between the Acts, adapted to the Play, and composed by Dr. Boyce', was first performed at Drury Lane on 1 December 1753, with Mrs Pritchard as Boadicea. Jane Powell never played Boadicea in London.

690

JANE POWELL

as Mary, Queen of Scots in *The Albion Queens or The Death of Mary Queen of Scotland* by John Banks

Samuel De Wilde

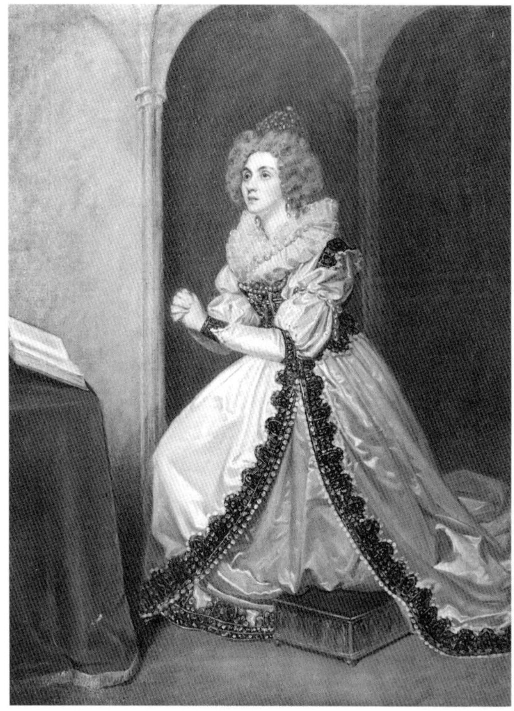

690 *Jane Powell as Mary, Queen of Scots*

Oil on canvas 35.5 x 26.5
INV: Mathews 98; RW/CKA 256
PROV: John Bell; Charles Mathews
EXH: 1833 London (98)
ENGR: William S. Leney for Bell's British Library
25 June 1791, line 10.8 x 7.6, pub. Bell's *British Theatre* (1797), vol 22, with the quotation of Douglas's line: 'Behold her kneeling' (Act V, scene 3)

In Act V, scene 3, Mary waits to be taken to the block. De Wilde has given a slightly liberal interpretation to the stage direction: 'Soft music here. A table at the upper end of the stage. Queen Mary discovered kneeling, with a book in her hand; her women kneeling by her.' The object bottom right, which looks like a footstool, appears to be her casket containing the gold and jewels that she distributes as gifts before her death.

Mary is somewhat overdressed for an execution, wearing a diadem, pendant earrings, ropes of pearls, and a silvery long-sleeved dress trimmed with black lace, split at the front to reveal a petticoat of the same colour.

Banks's tragedy was first performed at Drury Lane on 6 March 1704; it was an altered version of the same author's *The Island Queens*. The last performance in London during the 18th century took place at Covent Garden on 20 May 1779, when Mrs Hartley played Mary, Queen of Scots. Mrs Powell never acted the role in London.

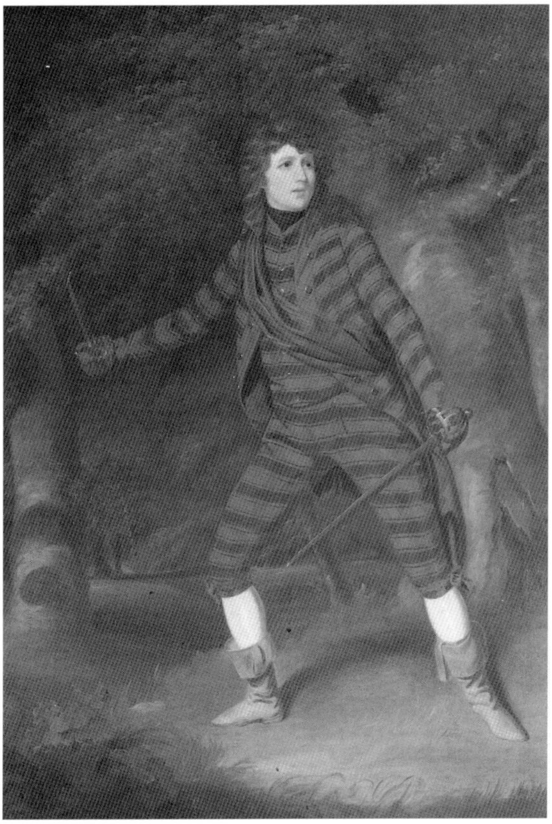

691
JANE POWELL
as Young Norval
in *Douglas* by John Home

Samuel De Wilde

Oil on canvas 76 x 55.5
INV: Mathews 18; RW/CKA 117
PROV: Charles Mathews
EXH: 1833 London (18)

Like Henry Erskine Johnston in No. 332, Mrs Powell is shown at the climax of the play in Act v, staggering onto the stage 'with a sword in each hand'. Young Norval dies in front of his mother after being mortally wounded by Lord Randolph. Mrs Powell wears brown boots, white stockings, a tight-fitting red suit with horizontal green stripes and blue facings, a blue sash, and a plain dark green stock.

Mrs Powell played Young Norval for her benefit at Drury Lane on 2 May 1795 and on several subsequent occasions.

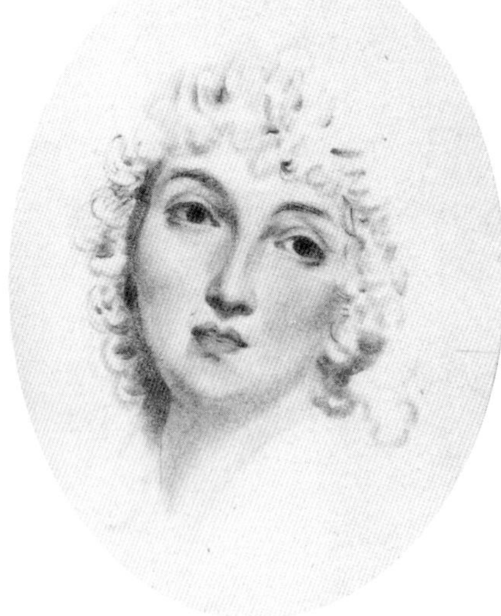

692
JANE POWELL (?)

Samuel De Wilde (?)

Black and red chalk with traces of watercolour on wove paper 12 x 18.1 (oval mount)
INV: RW 495 (sitter and artist unknown);
CKA 495 (sitter unknown)
PROV: Unknown
ENGR: Similar to: Ridley after Anon. for Parsons's *Minor Theatre* 15 November 1794, stipple 7 x 5.5 (head and shoulders to right, head turned and looking to front although head not twisted back, hat with flaps on top)

The study is of the face alone, looking out at the spectator, with indications of curled and powdered hair. The sitter may be wearing a hat.

The engraving mentioned above is extremely close to this drawing, which, however, looks like any number of pretty actresses *c.*1790–1810, and the identity of the sitter is not secure.

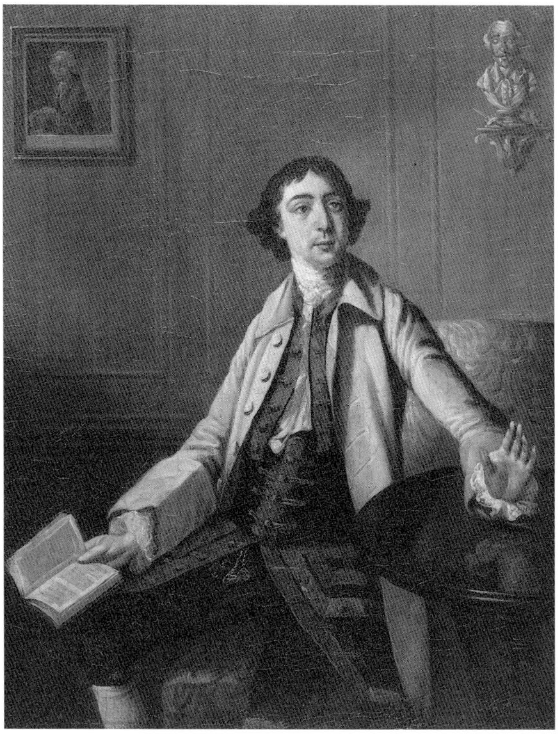

693
WILLIAM POWELL

Robert Pyle

Oil on canvas 35 x 28
INV: Mathews 378 (artist unknown);
RW 213 (by Mortimer); CKA 213
PROV: Charles Mathews
EXH: 1833 London (378)
ENGR: S. Okey Jnr pub. S. Okey Jnr,
mezzotint 31.7 x 25.4

Powell, sitting on a sofa and holding a book in his right hand, appears to be giving a dramatic reading. He wears white hose, black breeches, a cream coat, a black waistcoat with gold braiding, and a white stock. His left hand and wrist are reflected in the pedestal table. The sofa is covered with white damask. There is a bust of Shakespeare on the bracket top right and an engraving of David Garrick after Benjamin Wilson top left – references to Powell's promise as successor to Garrick as the champion of Shakespeare and British drama (see No. 695). Because of these references the picture is likely to date *c.*1767.

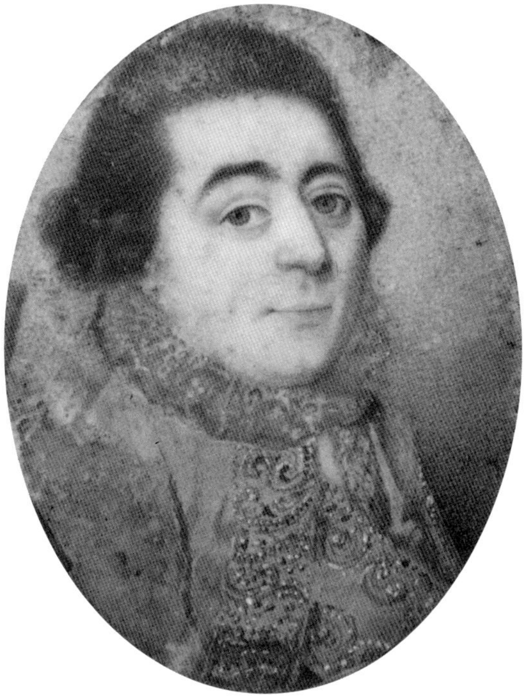

694
WILLIAM POWELL
as Posthumus in *Cymbeline*
by William Shakespeare

Henry Spicer (?)

Watercolour on paper 3.3 x 2.9
INSCR: 'the / tragedian / miniature / engd and
Miss / Pope' (?) (pen and ink on verso)
INV: RW 427X (artist unknown);
CKA 427X (artist unknown, in character)
PROV: Unknown, but acquired before 1909
EXH: ? 1768 R.A. Special (108) 'Portrait of Mr Powell:
in miniature' by Henry Spicer
REL: Christie's 26 November 1986 (34)
(three-quarter-length) seated to right, looking to front,
holding playbill for *Cymbeline* and *The Oxonian*

Powell wears a pink doublet with a ruffed collar.

The Christie's miniature celebrates the Royal Command performance at Covent Garden on 28 December 1767, when Powell played Posthumus. The elder George Colman's *The Oxonian in Town* was the afterpiece. George III and Queen Charlotte attended. It seems likely that both the Christie's miniature and No. 694 show Powell as Posthumus. The miniature (or another version of it) may have been the miniature by Henry Spicer exhibited at the Society of Artists in 1768.

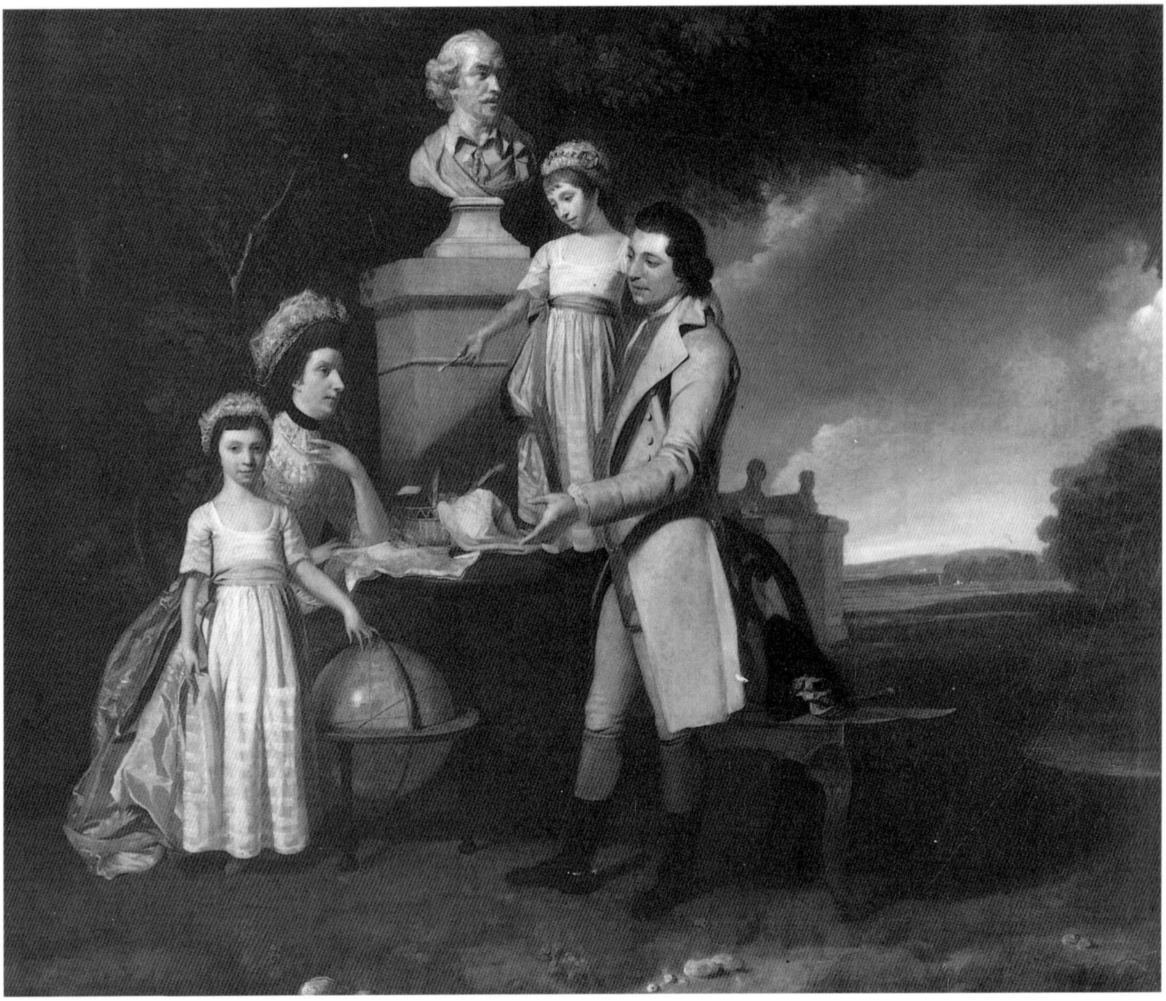

695*

WILLIAM POWELL
with his wife *ELIZABETH* and
daughters *ANN* and *ELIZABETH MARY*

John Hamilton Mortimer

Oil on canvas 98.5 x 123.5
INV: RW/CKA 13 (by Benjamin Wilson);
Gift 43 (by Richard Wilson)
PROV: William Powell; F. Mills, by whom presented
to the Garrick Club, 1837
EXH: 1768 S.A. (108) 'A family picture'; 1965 Kenwood (33)
LIT: Horace Walpole, 'Notes of Public Exhibitions',
Walpole Society (1938–39), 27: 72; (NPG) *Oh Sweet
Mr Shakespeare I'll have his Picture* (1964), p. 35 (pl. 15a);
John Sunderland, 'John Hamilton Mortimer',
The Walpole Society (1988); Fitzgerald, p. 222

Powell, depicted as a cultivated country gentleman, gestures to a paper on the table. He wears black boots with spurs and brown tops, pale buff breeches, and a silver-grey jacket over a tan waistcoat embroidered in gold and lined in red. His wife Elizabeth rests her embroidery on the table. Her oyster silk dress is trimmed with lace, as is her black velvet choker, and she wears a lace cap decorated with blue ribbon. The elder (?) daughter (Ann) shows her intellectual pretensions by touching the top of the globe at her side. She wears pink shoes, a white dress with a pink sash, and a lace cap with pink ribbon. The younger daughter (Elizabeth Mary), held on the tabletop by her father, offers a paper to her mother. She wears a white dress with a long blue sash, and a white cap with blue ribbon. There is a bust of Shakespeare on the pedestal behind the table, on which are Powell's papers and his wife's work basket. Powell's black tricorn hat, gloves and riding crop rest on the carved chair.

No. 695 was exhibited at the Society of Artists in 1768 as the pendant to Mortimer's scene from *King John*, which included a portrait of Powell as the King (No. 59).

The paintings were presumably commissioned by Powell to commemorate the most important event in his professional life, the purchase of a quarter of the Covent Garden Patent from the widow of John Rich. The scene from *King John* exemplifies his career on the stage, whereas the family group shows him as a man of substance and property; the document on the table is no doubt the Patent he had just purchased for £15,000, loaned to him by friends. As the leading actor at Covent Garden, Powell also helped George Colman as general manager and producer. Powell was generally seen as the natural successor to Garrick, and the two scenes by Mortimer amusingly ape Garrick's own patronage of Johan Zoffany. Not only did Zoffany paint Garrick in theatrical roles (Nos. 252 and 253), he also painted him as a country gentleman in his garden at Hampton.

Unfortunately, Powell's new-found glory was short-lived. In 1769 he died from pneumonia, believed to have been brought on by his stripping off and lying on the damp grass after a cricket match. His wife Elizabeth later married the musician John Abraham Fisher. His daughter Elizabeth Mary married George White, a clerk at the House of Commons, and the other daughter, Ann, married Thomas Warren, of the Inner Temple, in 1780 and John Martindale in 1795. Through their wives, White and Martindale became one-eighth shareholders in Covent Garden. Ann restored her father's tomb in Bristol Cathedral in 1811. See their several notices in the BD.

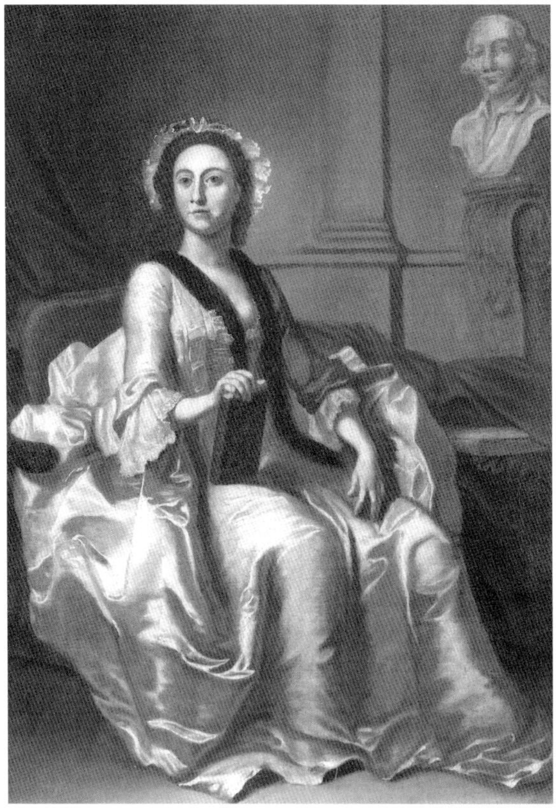

696*

HANNAH PRITCHARD

Francis Hayman

Oil on canvas 75 x 55.5
INV: RW/CKA 118; Gift 30
PROV: Presented to the Garrick Club
by Anne Mathews, 1836?
EXH: 1951 Exeter
ENGR: James McArdell pub. 25 April 1762,
mezzotint 28 x 22.8 (three-quarter length)
Inscr: 'F. Hayman pinxt 1750';
John Miller for the *London Magazine* 1768
(half-length in oval); H.R. Cook for the
Ladies Monthly Magazine 1814, stipple 9.2 x 8
LIT: Brian Allen, *Francis Hayman* (1987) (checklist No. 39)

Mrs Pritchard rests her right hand on a book on her right knee, and her left elbow on the arm of the red padded chair. She wears a white silk dress trimmed with lace and with gold strapwork on the bodice. She has a fur wrap and a lace cap with a blue ribbon. The rather imposing setting includes a bust of Shakespeare on a pedestal and a carved and gilt console table with a marble top. Behind the sitter is a green drapery.

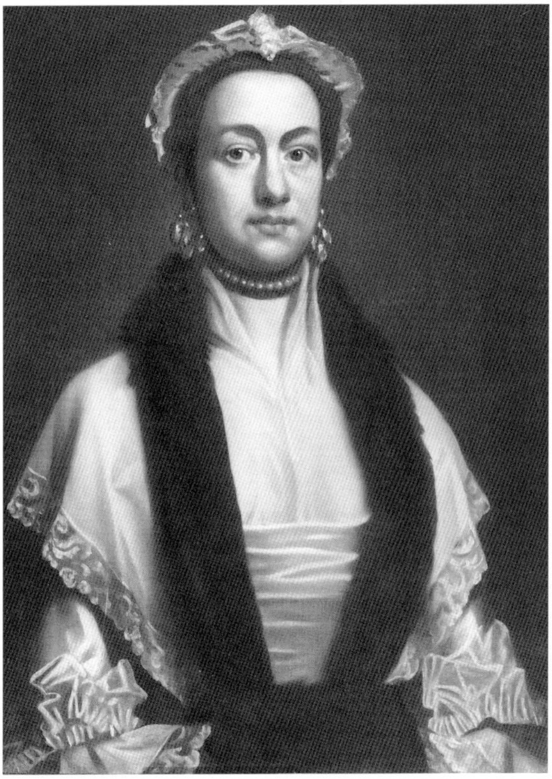

697

HANNAH PRITCHARD

Francis Hayman

Oil on canvas 75.5 x 62
(76.5 x 63.5 lining canvas)
INV: Mathews 9; RW/CKA 26
PROV: Thomas Harris; Harris sale, Robins 12 July 1819 (8); Charles Mathews
EXH: 1833 London (9)
LIT: Brian Allen, *Francis Hayman* (1987) (checklist No. 40)

Mrs Pritchard wears a white silk dress trimmed with lace, with a fur muff and tippet, a pearl choker and enormous pearl drop earrings.

Brian Allen dates this picture to the mid-1750s.

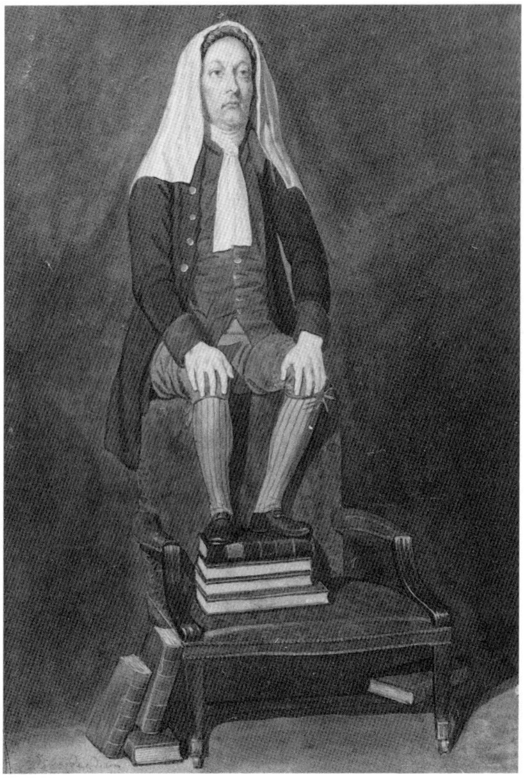

698

JOHN PURSER

as Sneer in *The Weathercock*
by John Till Allingham

Samuel De Wilde

Pencil and watercolour on wove paper 37.5 x 23.5
INSCR: 'S De Wilde delin / 1808' (pencil b.l.)
INV: Mathews 309; (not in RW); CKA 51
PROV: Charles Mathews
EXH: 1833 London (309); 1971 Northampton (40)
REL: See No. 41

Sneer, Tristram Fickle's servant, is playing the part of the judge, listening to his master's performance as a barrister deploring the use of coal (see No. 41). The cloth on Sneer's head stands in for the judge's wig. He wears black shoes with gold buckles, pale blue stockings with blue vertical lines, brown breeches, a brown jacket with silver buttons and red collar and cuffs, a red waistcoat with silver buttons, and a white stock with pseudo-legal tabs. The chair is upholstered in purple.

Allingham's farce was first performed at Drury Lane on 18 November 1805, with Purser as Sneer. He played the role twice during the 1807–8 season, on 16 December 1807 and 6 February 1808. Presumably the latter performance inspired this drawing and the subsequent oil painting shown at the Royal Academy (No. 41).

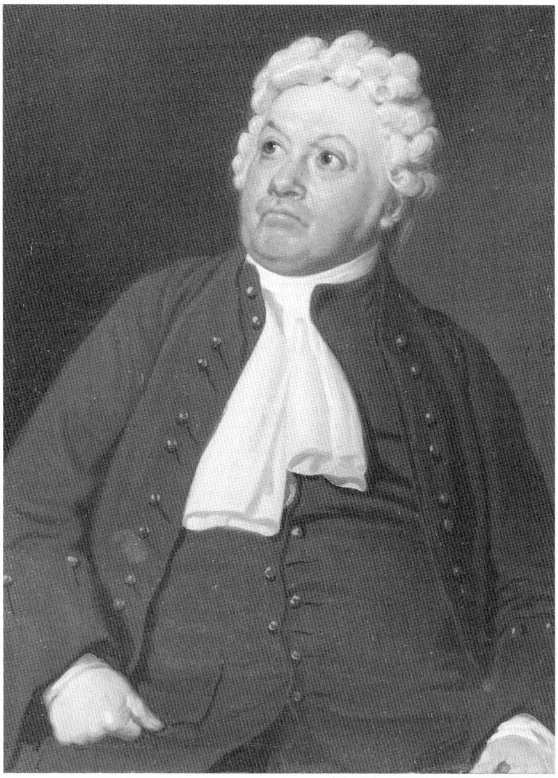

699
JOHN QUICK
as Old Doiley in *Who's the Dupe?*
by Hannah Cowley

Samuel De Wilde

Oil on panel 23.3 x 19.1
INSCR: 'S De Wilde f / 1805' (black paint c.r.)
INV: Mathews 141; RW/CKA 214
PROV: Charles Mathews
EXH: 1833 London (141)
ENGR: William Bond for Cawthorn's *Minor British Theatre* pub. John Cawthorn 4 June 1806, stipple 12 x 7.8 (full-length); James Hopwood for *The Cabinet* pub. Mathews & Leigh 1 August 1807, stipple and line 14.6 x 9.5 (half-length to elbows); Kennerley pub. Duncombe, stipple and line

Old Doiley and his daughter are at breakfast. Elizabeth has annoyed him by criticising the scholarly Gradus, his choice as her husband (see No. 34). Her father shows his anger with a clenched fist. He wears a curly white wig and a brown coat and waistcoat, both with small brass buttons.

Mrs Cowley's farce was first performed at Drury Lane on 10 April 1779, with Parsons as Old Doiley. He was followed in the role at that theatre, on 13 October 1796, by Suett. Quick did not play Old Doiley in London before 1805, or indeed any role at all for some time after the 1801–2 Drury Lane season; having played in Manchester during the summer of 1802, he disappears from the records until he turns up in Edinburgh on 25 January 1809. Possibly De Wilde depicts a provincial performance, but it is more likely that he felt Quick was the most suitable actor to be shown in the part.

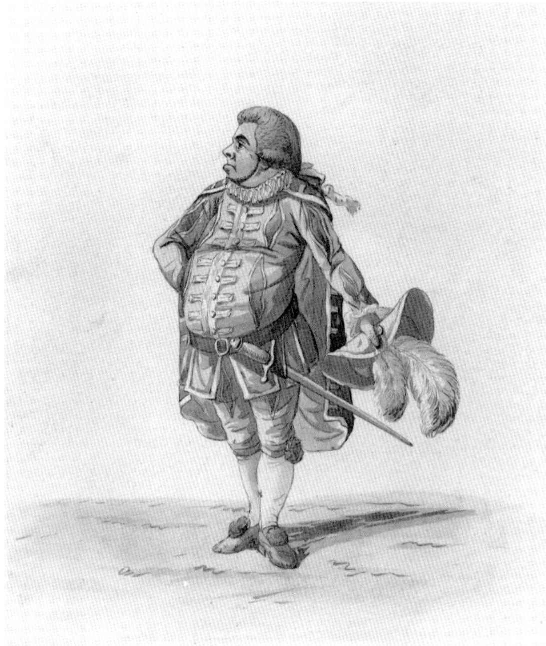

700
JOHN QUICK
as Isaac Mendoza in *The Duenna*
by Richard Brinsley Sheridan

Robert Dighton

Pen and brown ink with watercolour on faded wove paper 20 x 16.5
INSCR: 'Dighton del' (pen and grey ink b.r.); 'Mr Quick as Isaac Mendoza in the Duenna.' (pen and brown ink on mount b. CM)
INV: Mathews 270; RW/CKA 550B
PROV: Charles Mathews
EXH: 1833 London (270)

Mendoza's wig is tied with a pink bow and he holds a pink hat with two ostrich feathers. His shoes have blue rosettes, and his breeches and doublet are slashed to reveal a blue lining.

Sheridan's comic opera with 'Music partly new [by Thomas Linley] and partly selected from the most eminent composers', was first performed at Covent Garden on 21 November 1775, with Quick as the original Isaac Mendoza.

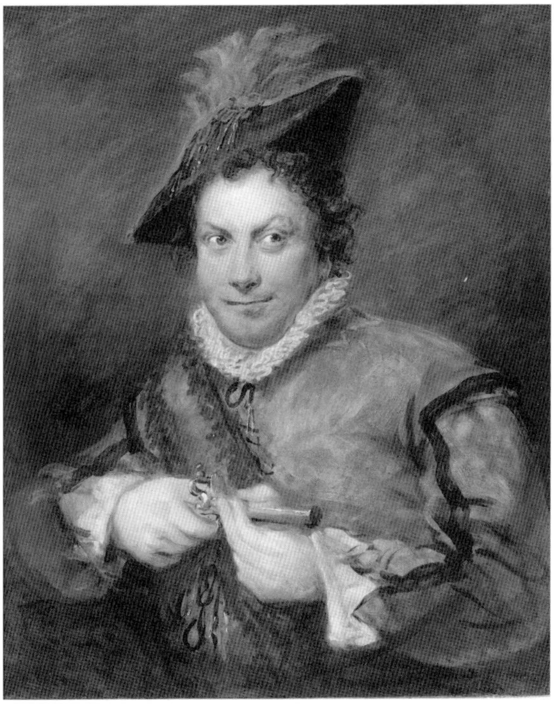

701*

JOHN QUICK

as Spado in *The Castle of Andalusia*

by John O'Keeffe

Gainsborough Dupont

Oil on canvas 76 x 63 (indications of oval frame)
INV: Mathews 153; RW/CKA 420
PROV: Thomas Harris; Harris sale, Robins 12 July 1819 (25); Charles Mathews
EXH: 1794 R.A. (268); 1833 London (153); 1982–83 London (128)
ENGR: William Ridley for the *Monthly Mirror* pub. Vernor & Hood January 1802, stipple 8.7 x 7.2 (oval)
LIT: *Morning Herald*, 22 March 1794; John O'Keeffe, *Recollections* (1826), 2: 326–27; Hayes, 1968

Spado is one of a group of bandits led by Don Caesar who plan to rob the castle of Don Scipio. Spado insinuates himself into the building, hoping to procure extra personal gain. There are many references in the text to Quick's small stature; he is known as 'little Spado', and in Act III, scene 3 sings an air, 'Tho' born to be little's my fate'. There is even a quip on Quick's name in Act III, scene 1, where Sanguino says: 'Massy plate! Quick, quick, the master key.' Spado's name relates to the small cut-and-thrust sword thought particularly Spanish in the 18th century, rather than to his being a eunuch.

Spado smiles conspiratorially under his grey hat edged in red, with red feathers. He wears a light brown tunic decorated with darker brown lines, a lace ruff and cuffs, and a broad brown band over his right shoulder, edged in darker brown and tied with brown ribbons. He holds a pistol in front of him.

O'Keeffe's three-act comic opera, with music mainly by Samuel Arnold, was first performed at Covent Garden on 2 November 1782. Quick was the original Spado but the highlight of the evening was the début on the English-speaking stage of Signora Sestini. This portrait is mentioned in the *Morning Herald* of 22 March 1794.

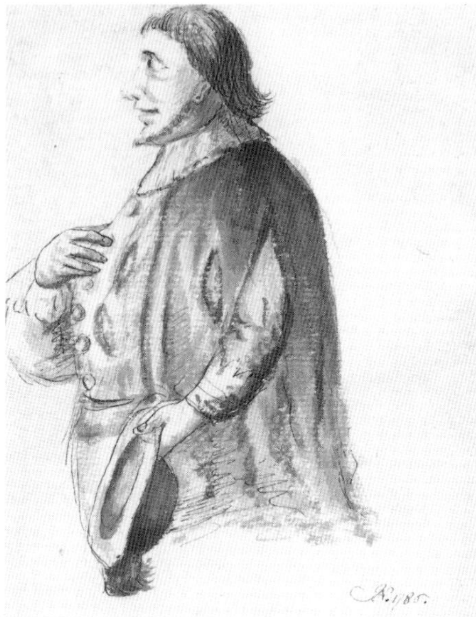

702

JOHN QUICK (?)

as Isaac Mendoza in *The Duenna*

by Richard Brinsley Sheridan

John Nixon

Pencil, pen and black ink with wash on laid paper 16.8 x 11.2
INSCR: 'JN. 1786.' (pen and black ink b.r.); 'Give Isaac the Nymphs / who no Beauty can Boast' (pen and black ink b.c.)
INV: Not listed
PROV: John Nixon, *Dramatic Annals* 1: 287

Three-quarter length in profile to left. Mendoza wears a sleeveless coat over a slashed tunic, and a flat lace collar, and holds his hat in his left hand. The line quoted at the bottom of the sheet is the opening of a song sung by Mendoza in Act II, scene 1 of *The Duenna*. Nixon transcribed all four verses on the same page of the album.

Quick played Isaac Mendoza six times at Covent Garden during 1785, the year of Nixon's drawing. As the only person to play the part in London that season, he is the most likely candidate as sitter, though in fact the identification is not entirely certain.

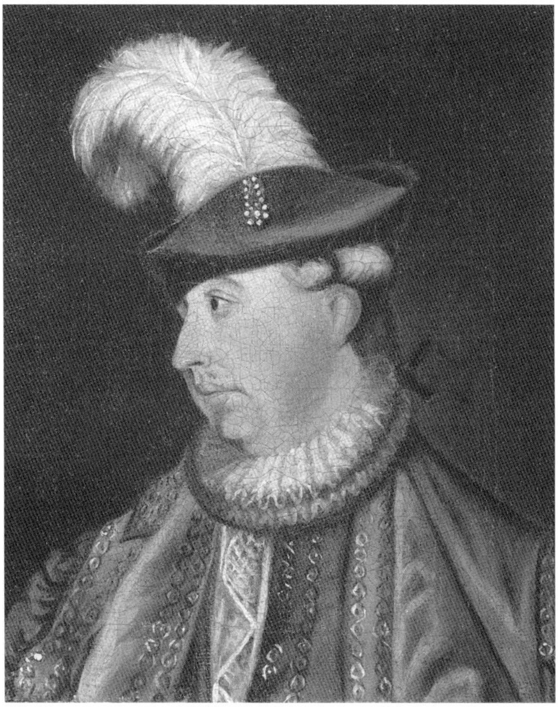

703

JOHN QUICK

as Isaac Mendoza in *The Duenna*
by Richard Brinsley Sheridan

Johan Zoffany

Oil on canvas 21.7 x 19
INV: RW 287 (sitter and artist unknown);
CKA 287 (artist unknown)
PROV: Unknown
ENGR: Anon. pub. C. Bowles 1777, mezzotint
(full-length, with George Mattocks as Don Ferdinand)

This half-length shows the head and shoulders of Isaac Mendoza. His wig is tied with a black bow and he wears a grey-green tricorn hat with a white ostrich feather and a paste brooch. He has a double ruff and a lilac jacket over a grey-green doublet with silver decoration. In Bowles's engraving Quick is shown with George Mattocks as Don Ferdinand. These two characters appear together in only one scene, set in 'The New Piazza'. Isaac goads Don Ferdinand with the news that his lady-love, Clara, is probably in the arms of another, Antonio, thanks to Mendoza's assistance.

This picture is probably cut down from Zoffany's scene, engraved and published in 1777. Sheridan's comic opera was first performed at Covent Garden on 21 November 1775, with Quick as Mendoza and Mattocks as Don Ferdinand. The two appeared together in these roles 21 times during 1777.

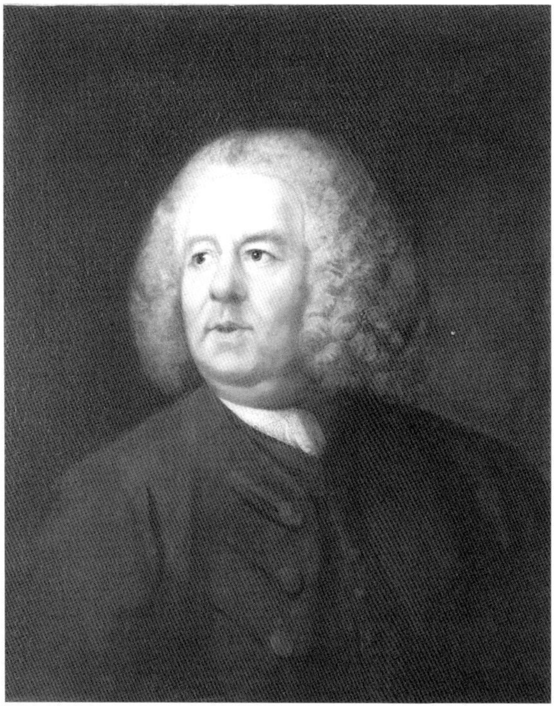

704

JAMES QUIN

Thomas Gainsborough (copy after)

Oil on canvas 74.9 x 63.5
INV: Mathews 363 (by Hogarth);
RW 399 (by W. Hogarth); CKA 399
PROV: Thomas Harris; Harris sale, Robins
12 July 1819 (39); Charles Mathews
EXH: 1833 London (363); 1951 London (18)
REL: Original: NG of Ireland 565, oil on canvas
231 x 150, exh: S.A. 1763 (41) (Waterhouse 567)
[prov: John Wiltshire until 1867, the Duke of Cleveland,
sold Christie's 8 March 1902, and Laurie (dealer)
until 1905, when bt. by NG Ireland];
Royal Collection Millar 803, oil on canvas 64.8 x 50.8,
prov: Gainsborough Dupont sale, Christie's
10 April 1797 (17) bt. by Pierce, probably for
the Prince of Wales

Quin wears a full-bottomed wig, and a red-brown coat with buttons of a similar colour.

The picture in the Royal Collection is a study of the head of Quin for the full-length portrait in Dublin. The Garrick Club picture is a copy of the study by an unidentifiable hand.

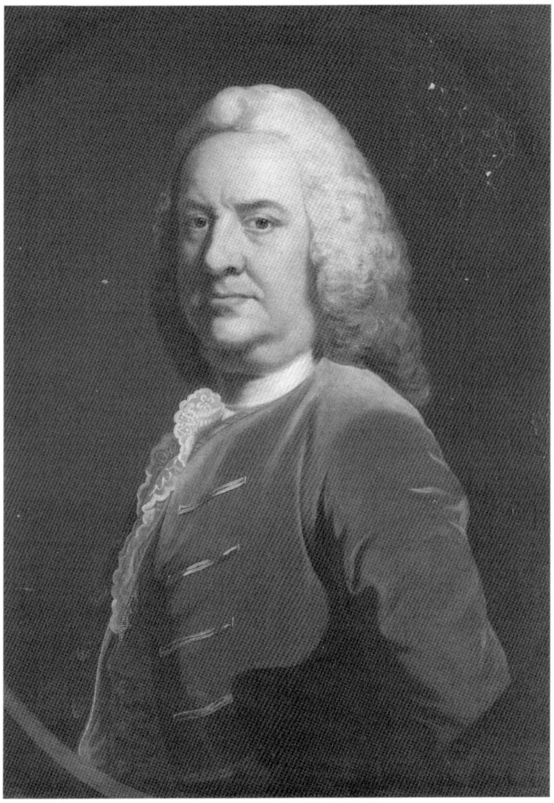

705

JAMES QUIN

Joseph Highmore (?)

Oil on canvas 74.9 x 62.2
INV: Mathews 254 (artist unknown);
RW 426 (artist unknown); CKA 426
PROV: Charles Mathews
EXH: 1833 London (254)

Quin wears a grey velvet coat trimmed with gold braid, an elaborate waistcoat embroidered in green and red, and a high white stock with a frill. He carries a black tricorn hat under his left arm.

This is a picture of high quality – Highmore at his best, if it is by him. [Hudson's portrait of 1744 is similar; that original is lost, but known by a variety of engravings, including one by J. Faber, 1744. Also, No. 705 has been attributed to Hogarth by the *Dictionary of English Portraiture*.]

It was Quin's supremacy as an actor of the old school of Betterton that was toppled by Garrick. 'With the exception of his Falstaff, which seems clearly to have been splendid, Quin may have been the best-worst really prominent actor of the first half of the eighteenth century' (BD).

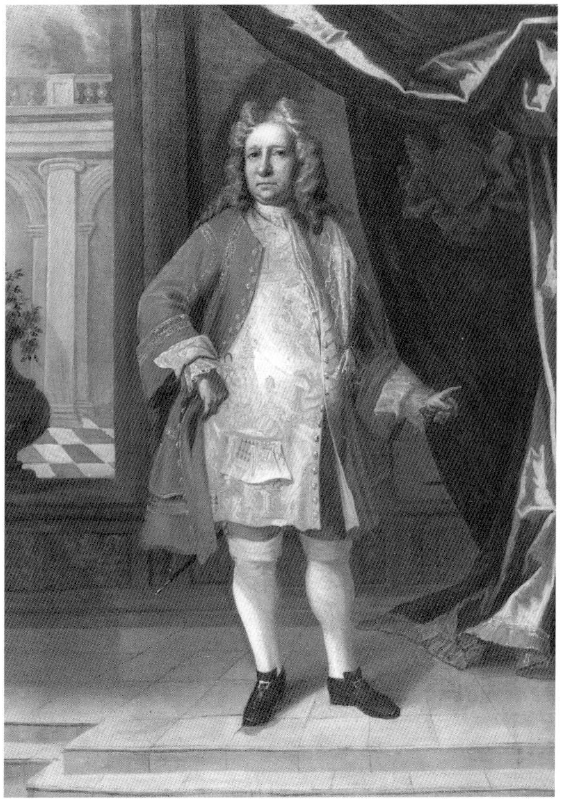

706

JAMES QUIN

Unknown Artist

Oil on canvas 53.3 x 38.1
INV: Mathews 81 (Hogarth); RW/CKA 29 (Hogarth)
PROV: Charles Mathews
EXH: 1833 London (81); 1957 London (19)
Fitzgerald, pp. 245–49; Griffiths, p. 305

Quin wears black shoes with silver buckles, white stockings pulled over brownish breeches, a red frock-coat trimmed with gold braid, and a long white waistcoat with gold buttons and pink and gold rococo embroidery. He stands in a very grand interior in an irregularly shaped area at the top of two steps; behind is a purplish wall, and to the right a green curtain pulled back to reveal, on another drapery, the Royal Coat of Arms.

The attribution to Hogarth maintained by both Mathews and CKA is entirely unconvincing. This picture is probably by an Italian artist working in London in the 1720s. The identity of the sitter appears to be secure.

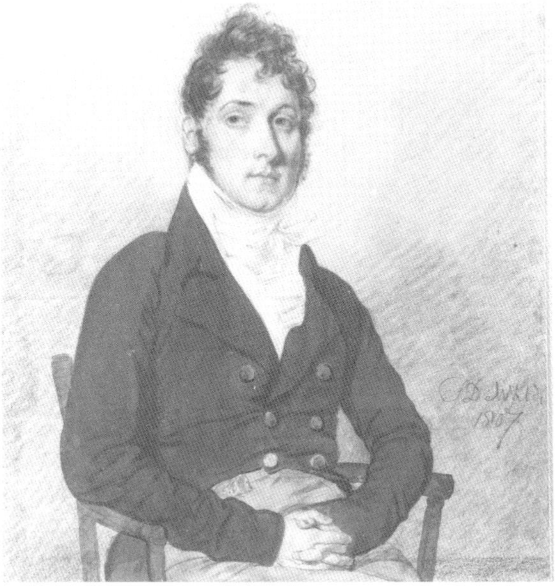

707

ALEXANDER RAE

Samuel De Wilde

Black chalk and watercolour on wove paper 26 x 22.8
INSCR: 'S De Wilde / 1807' (black chalk b.r.);
'De Wilde Fecit' (pen and brown ink on mount b.l. CM);
'Mr Rae.' (pen and brown ink b.c. CM)
INV: Mathews 283; (not in RW); CKA 521
PROV: Charles Mathews
EXH: 1833 London (283)
ENGR: Thomas Cheesman for Gilliland's *Dramatic Mirror*
pub. C. Chapple 1 June 1807, stipple 8.2 x 6.6 (bust in oval)

Rae is shown half-length, seated facing spectator. He wears a dark blue cutaway coat with brass buttons, and a high white stock.

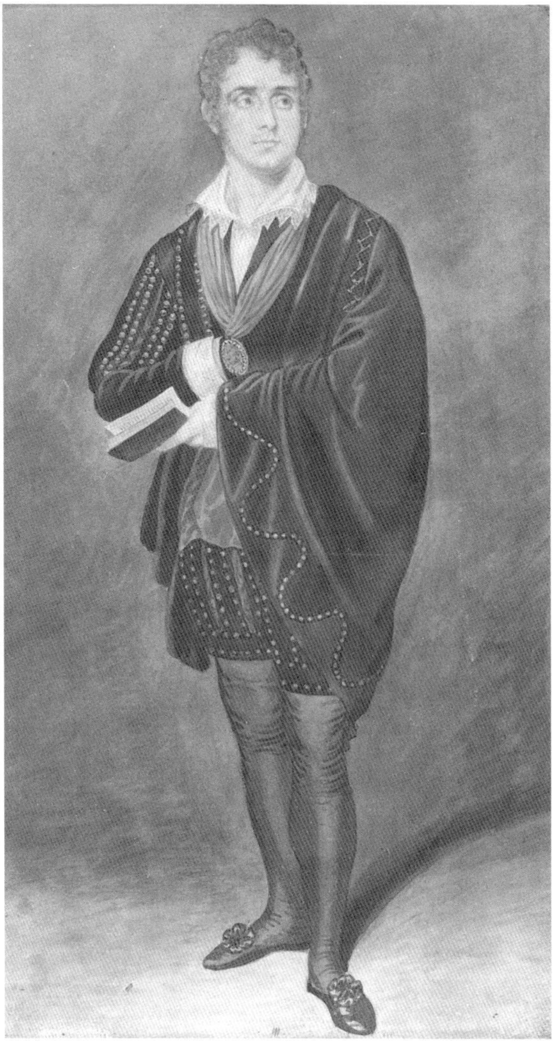

708

ALEXANDER RAE

as Hamlet in *Hamlet*
by William Shakespeare

Samuel De Wilde

Pencil and watercolour on wove paper 35.5 x 22.2
INV: Mathews 249; RW/CKA 53
PROV: Charles Mathews
EXH: 1833 London (249)

Hamlet, carrying his book in Act II, scene 2, is dressed in black, with a lace-edged vandyke collar. Blue studs decorate his doublet and trunk hose and form a serpentine pattern on his black cloak. The Order of the Elephant hangs from a blue ribbon around his neck.

Rae made his Drury Lane début in the role of Hamlet on 14 November 1812, when he was announced as 'from the Theatre Royal, Liverpool'.

709
LOCATION UNKNOWN
ALEXANDER RAE
as Romaldi in *A Tale of Mystery*
by Thomas Holcroft (?)

Samuel De Wilde

Pencil and watercolour on wove paper 36.8 x 22.8
INSCR: 'De Wilde delin / Feb 1816' (pencil)
INV: CKA 485 (Arthur Rae as Ranald);
Gift 457 (not located 1988)
PROV: Sir Arthur Wing Pinero, by whom presented to the Garrick Club, 1929 [probably the portrait of Rae as 'Rinaldo' in *A Tale of Mystery*, signed and dated by De Wilde, that was in the Royal Dramatic College sale at Fairbrother, Lye and Palmer 14 December 1881 (lot 100D)]

The figure is full-length, walking, three-quarters to right, looking at viewer, right hand in breast of coat. He has dark curly hair and bare knees, and wears a green coat, narrow ruff, green and yellow slashed trunks, and buff boots (CKA). CKA identified this now lost drawing as being of Arthur Rae as Ranald in *A Tale of Mystery*. Presumably he meant Alexander Rae and, less certainly, the part of Romaldi in Holcroft's melodrama, in which there is no character named Ranald. Rae was a member of the Drury Lane company during the 1815–16 season, when there were no performances at that theatre of *A Tale of Mystery*.

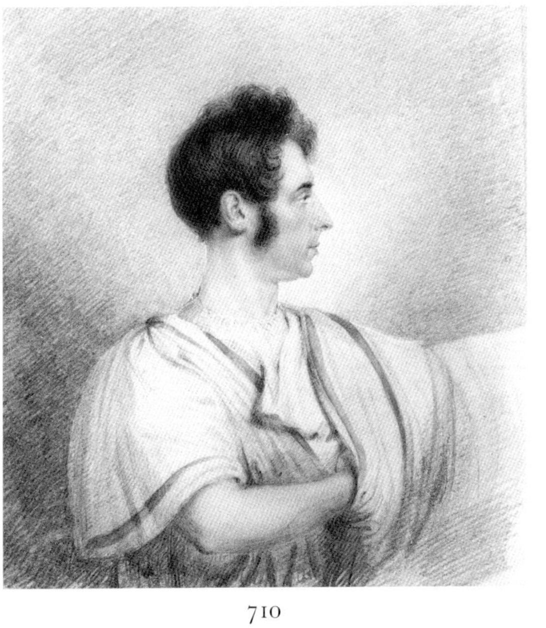

710
ALEXANDER RAE
as Cassius in *Julius Caesar* by William Shakespeare

John Turmeau

Black chalk with pencil and watercolour on wove paper 17.5 x 15.9
INSCR: 'Turmeau Fecit' (pen and brown ink on mount b.l. CM); 'Mr Rae as Cassius in Julius Caesar' (pen and brown ink on mount b.c. CM)
INV: Mathews 345; RW 559A (artist unknown); CKA 559A
PROV: Charles Mathews
EXH: 1833 London (345)

The actor is shown in profile to right, half-length. He wears a white toga with pink edging.

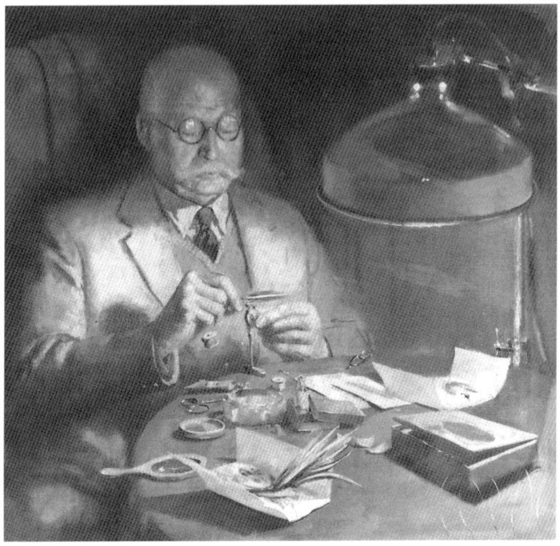

711*
ARTHUR RANSOME

John Gilroy

Oil on canvas 64 x 76
INSCR: 'Gilroy' (white paint b.l.);
'THE FLY DRESSER / DR. ARTHUR RANSOME / CBE LITT.D. / BY / JOHN GILROY / 10 HOLLAND PARK ROAD / W.14'
(white paint on back of canvas)
INV: GCL 704; Gift 805
PROV: Presented by the artist, 1964

Ransome, a keen fly-fisher, is making a fly. Sitting in a red upholstered chair, he peers through his wire-rimmed spectacles as he speculates on how to attach the feather to the body of the fly. His kit is spread out on the green baize table, lit by the brass-shaded table-lamp. He wears a pale brown tweed jacket and trousers, a brown pullover, an off-white shirt and a brown tie.

Arthur Ransome, biographer, journalist and author of the enduringly popular *Swallows and Amazons* series of children's books, became a member of the Garrick Club in 1943. He was made a C.B.E. in 1953.

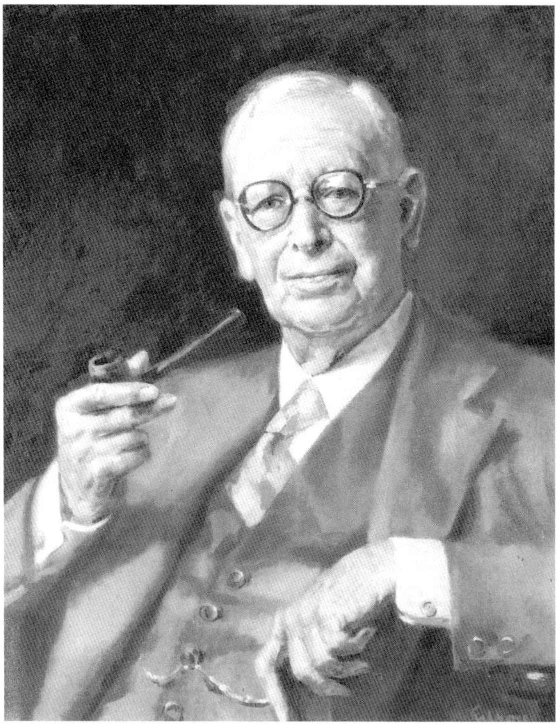

712
FRANK RATTO

John Gilroy

Oil on board 60.5 x 51
INSCR: 'Gilroy' (grey-green paint b.r.);
'Frank Ratto Mc / by his friend / J. Gilroy / 1968'
(pencil on verso)
INV: GCL 716; Gift 826
PROV: Presented by the artist, 1969

The sitter has brown-rimmed spectacles and holds a pipe in his right hand, and, possibly, a lucifer in his left. He wears a grey coat and waistcoat, a white shirt, and a Garrick Club tie. Ratto was a member of the Garrick from 1929 until his death. He held the position of Master in Lunacy, in which he had the final say as to whether or not patients needed to be detained in an asylum.

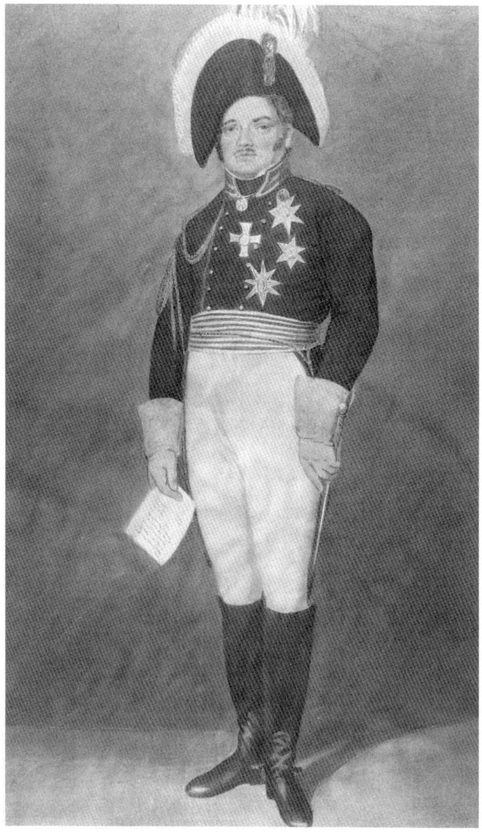

713
JAMES GRANT RAYMOND
as Frederick in *Frederick the Great or The Heart of a Soldier*
by Samuel James Arnold

Samuel De Wilde

Pencil and watercolour on wove paper 37 x 23.5
INV: Mathews 194; RW/CKA 66B
PROV: Charles Mathews
EXH: 1833 London (194)

Frederick sports that rare thing in Romantic drama, a moustache. He holds a paper in his right hand and the gold hilt of his sword in his left. His glamorous uniform consists of black boots with gold spurs, cream trousers, and a blue coat edged in red with a red collar, all generously trimmed with gold braid that hangs in loops from his right shoulder. He has white gauntlets, a red and white striped cummerbund, three large orders and a Maltese Cross on his chest, and a silver medallion hanging from his neck. He also wears a high white collar, a black military stock, a half-moon hat decorated with a gold and white fringe, and a white cockade.

Arnold's 'operatick anecdote in three acts', with music by T. Cooke, was first performed at the Lyceum on 4 August 1814, with Raymond as Frederick.

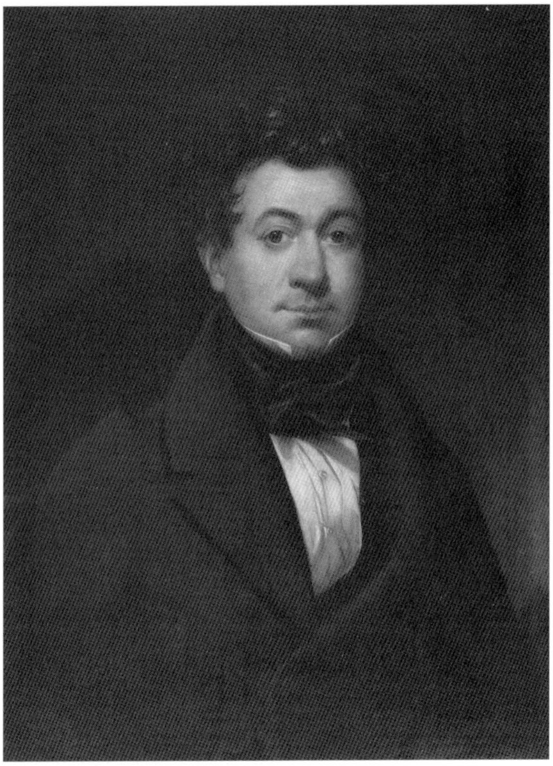

714
JOHN REEVE

C. Ambrose

Oil on canvas 76 x 63.5
INV: RW/CKA 353; Gift 87
PROV: Mrs Yates, by whom presented
to the Garrick Club, 1843

Half-length portrait in a dark brown coat and black stock. The picture presumably dates from about 1830, or a little later, and may be the source of James Warren Childe's portrait engraved by H. Barnett and presented with Part v of the *Weekly Magazine*, 1838; it was inscribed 'The Late John Reeve'.

A portrait of Reeve by an unnamed artist was in the Royal Dramatic College sale at Fairbrother, Lye and Palmer on 24 February 1881 (lot 72).

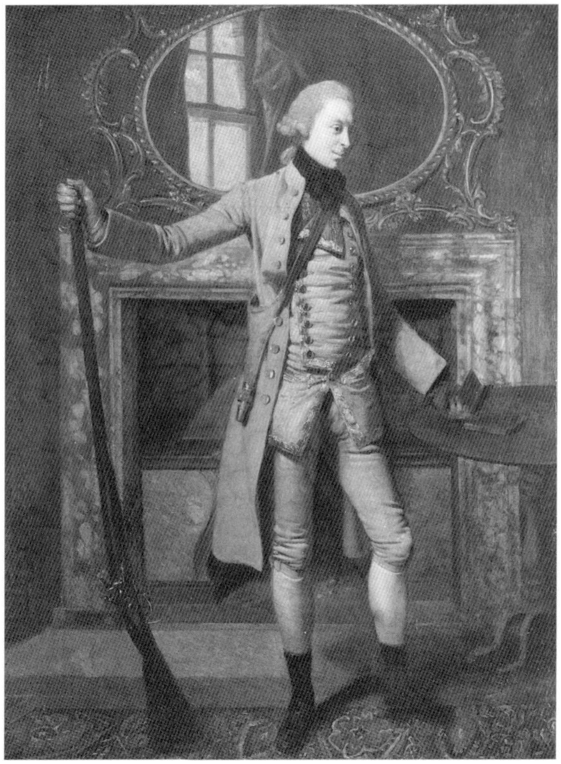

715*
FREDERICK CHARLES REINHOLD
as Hawthorn in *Love in a Village*
by Isaac Bickerstaffe

Johan Zoffany

Oil on canvas 65.5 x 50.5
INV: Mathews 65; RW 100 (by De Wilde); CKA 100
PROV: Charles Mathews
EXH: 1833 London (65); 1951 London (40);
1955–56 London (109); 1962 Chichester (80);
1975 Milan

In Act I, scene 3, a hall in Justice Woodcock's house, Hawthorn, a country squire, enters 'with a fowling-piece in his hands, and a net with birds at his girdle'. The precise moment chosen by Zoffany is not obvious, but, as Hawthorn has divested himelf of his 'net with birds', it may be after the entrance of Hodge, Justice Woodcock's bumpkin servant. The open book is not called for in the text, although in his last air, praising 'health, good-humour and competence', Hawthorn sings 'The greatness, that would make us grave, is but an empty thing', an apt moment to refer to sedentary learning, represented by the book.

Hawthorn is elegantly and sportingly dressed for his breezy life. He wears black shoes with gaiters, white stockings, fawn breeches, a long fawn jacket with large gold buttons, and a long purple-brown double-breasted waistcoat, with a green lining and with gold buttons and a thick band of gold braid. The red Eastern carpet has a floral border in blue, red, and white.

Bickerstaffe's comic opera was first performed at Covent Garden on 8 December 1762, with John Beard as Hawthorn. Reinhold played the role for the first time at Covent Garden on 17 January 1770, and for the last time at the same theatre on 22 May 1784.

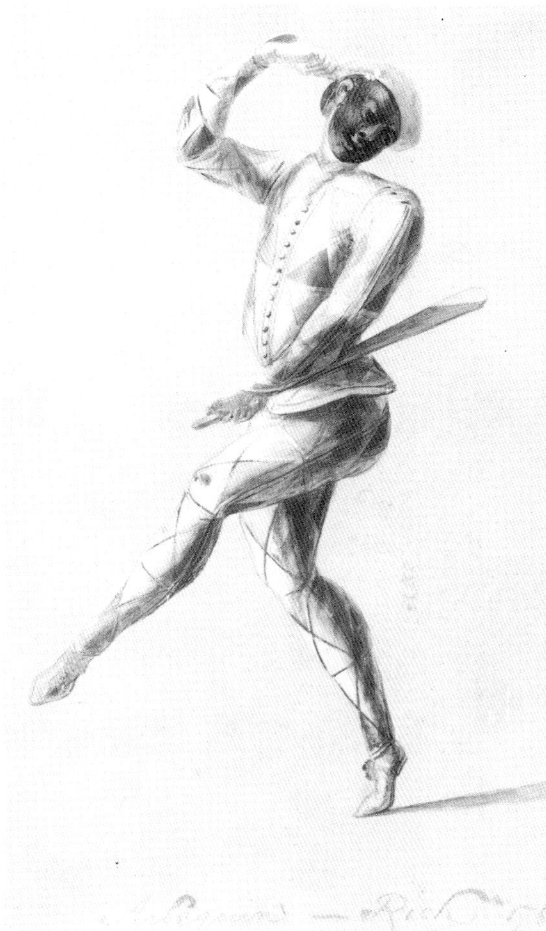

716 *John Rich as Harlequin*

716

JOHN RICH

as 'Harlequin'

Unknown Artist

Watercolour and body colour
on laid paper 22.5 x 16.5
INSCR: 'Arlequin – Rich 1753'
(pen and brown ink b.c.)
INV: Mathews 289; RW/CKA 557
PROV: Charles Mathews
EXH: 1833 London (289); 1982–83 London (185);
1987 Twickenham
ENGR: Anon. pub. R. Wilkinson 1818, line (vignette; the
mask of the drawing is replaced with a real portrait)

A dancing Rich wears a mask and holds his pantomime slapstick in his left hand. He wears a Harlequin's costume of tights and short jacket with long sleeves, divided by black lines into a pattern of blue, white and yellow triangles.

Rich devoted no great effort to producing pantomimes until the success of John Thurmond's *Harlequin Doctor Faustus* at Drury Lane in 1723 prompted him to produce his own *The Necromancer; or, Harlequin Dr Faustus* less than a month later. Although Rich's posthumous reputation is usually closely connected with the history of pantomime in England, he did not introduce the genre. He can, however, be credited with being the first to combine the earlier, grotesque *commedia dell'arte* style of Harlequin dumb-show with a more serious later style that included dialogue, recitations, songs, and a story based on mythology or a literary theme. Rich's performances as Harlequin were the principal *raisons d'être* of his pantomimes and, though much maligned in almost every department of theatrical activity, he was admired even by the most reticent of commentators. Thomas Davies, for instance, was forced to admit Rich's genius as Harlequin:

> His gesticulation was so perfectly expressive of his meaning, that every motion of his hand or head, or of any part of his body, was a kind of dumb eloquence that was readily understood by the audience. Mr Garrick's action was not more perfectly adapted to his characters than Mr Rich's attitudes and movements to the varied employments of the wooden sword magician.

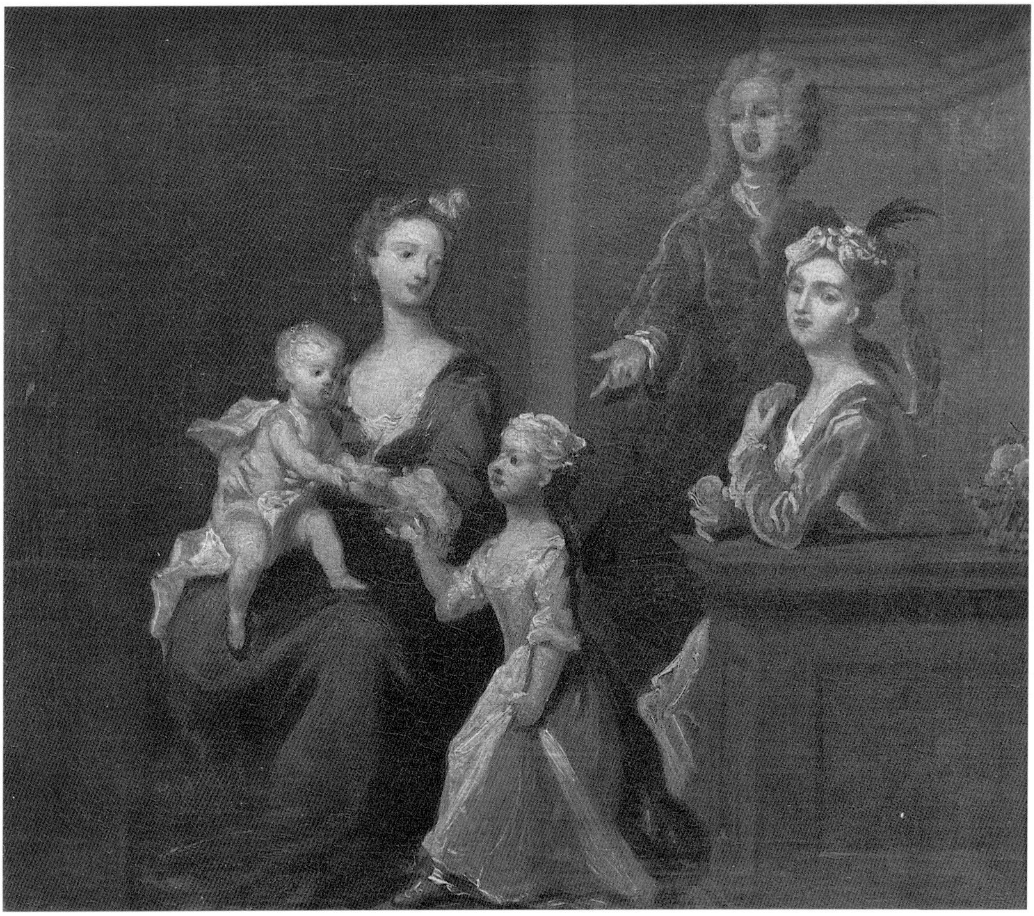

717*

JOHN RICH AND FAMILY

(called)

Joseph Highmore

Oil on canvas 29.2 x 33

INV: Mathews 90 (by Hogarth); RW/CKA 466 (by Hogarth)
PROV: Samuel Ireland; Ireland sale, Christie's 7–17 May 1801 (444) bt. Vernon for 3 gns.; John Jackson 1817; Jackson sale, Christie's 16 July 1831; Charles Mathews
EXH: 1833 London (466); 1957 London; 1958 London); 1965 Kenwood (23): 1982–83 London (185)
ENGR: Thomas Ryder for *Graphic Illustrations of Hogarth* pub. Samuel Ireland 1 May 1799, line 13.8 x 11.6 ('Hogarth delt')
LIT: John Ireland, *Hogarth Illustrated*, 3: 23 (as 'a family piece, consisting of four figures, for Mr Rich, 1728'); Austin Dobson, *Hogarth* (1909), p. 169; Ralph Edwards, 'An Attribution to Joseph Highmore', *Burlington Magazine* (July 1957), 99: 234–47, fig. 26; Alison Lewis, 'Joseph Highmore', PhD thesis, Harvard 1975

There are five figures: three adults and two children. Both women are seated; the one on the left has a baby on her knee and wears a blue dress. The other rests her left elbow on a pedestal; she wears a somewhat theatrical costume, consisting of a pink dress edged in white, and a white headdress with a yellow loop, green feathers and grey drapery. The girl responds to the baby's gesture with her right hand, and with her left pulls up her white dress to reveal a yellow petticoat. The man, standing at the back of the group and presumably the father of the family, looks down at the child. He wears a brown coat.

Ralph Edwards's attribution to Highmore is almost certainly correct; the morphology of the figures is close to the simpering figures of the 'Pamela' series, and the treatment of the group has parallels in other group portraits by Highmore. This means that the traditional connection with the reference to Hogarth's list of pictures left unfinished in 1731, 'a family piece, consisting of four figures, for Mr Rich, 1728', has been broken. Thus, there is no reason to identify the figures as John Rich and family.

[See the BD, 12: 352–53, for more information on this picture and several others by Hogarth, often called 'John Rich and Family'.]

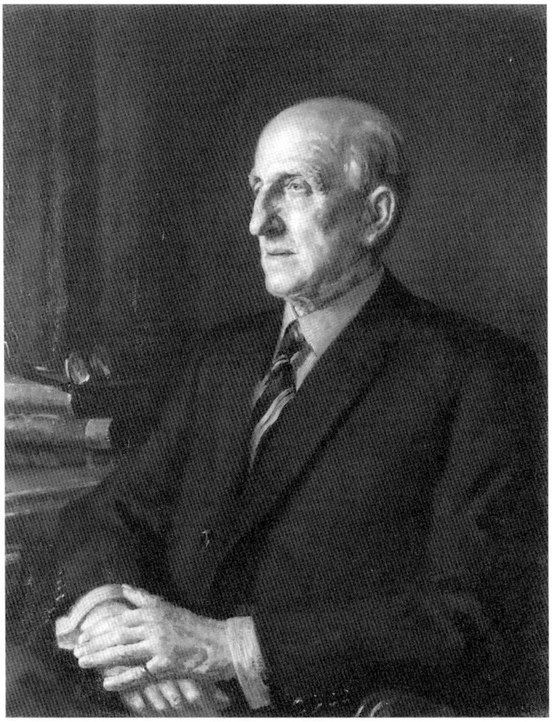

718
GERALD RIVINGTON

John Gilroy

Oil on canvas 76 x 62.5
INSCR: 'Gilroy' (orange-red paint b.r.)
INV: GCL 708
PROV: Presented by the artist, 1962
[according to the 'List of Presentations',
Sir James Gunn gave his own portrait of Rivington
to the Garrick in 1962 (Gift 788); that picture is
no longer in the Garrick Club collection]

Gerald Rivington has a gold ring on the signet finger of his left hand. He wears a dark blue double-breasted suit, a blue and white striped shirt, and a blue and white striped tie (Harrow?). There is a green curtain behind.

Rivington was a member of the Garrick from 1918 until his death in 1977.

719
THOMAS WILLIAM ROBERTSON

Unknown Artist

Pencil, pen and brown ink
with watercolour and body colour
on card 10 x 8
INSCR: 'Tom Robinson as a Child'
(pen and brown ink on verso)
INV: Not listed; Gift 756
PROV: Bequeathed by Mme Marie Monique Arkell,
the sitter's granddaughter, 1956

The sitter is a child of about five, with very curly red hair.

The drawing was bequeathed to the Club along with Robertson's gold watch. An accompanying card, dated 25 October 1956, explains the gift and describes the two objects:

> '...2. La tête en couleur cheveux roux taillés dans un cadre en cuivre ancien, sur ma cheminée du Salon grandeur environ 10 centimètres carrés. Ces objets ont pour les Anglais une valeur historique. Je tiens beaucoup à ce que ces objets demeurent au musée libre de ce club Londonien.'

[Ashton catalogued this picture as showing Madge Robertson.]

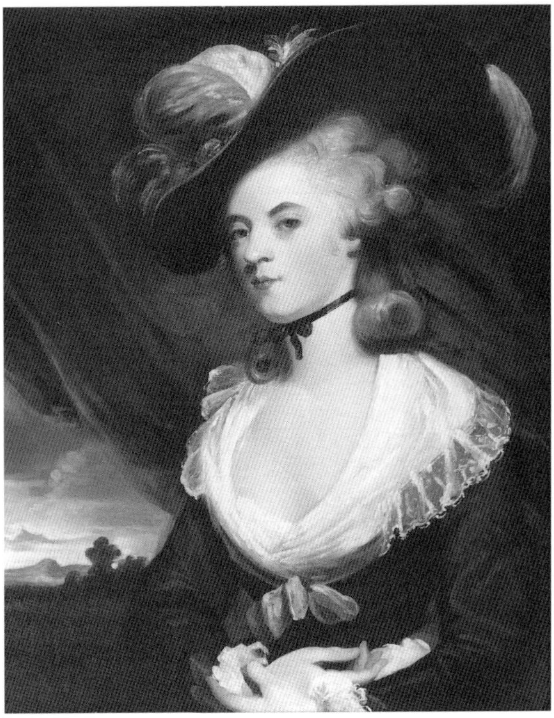

720
MARY ROBINSON

Sir Joshua Reynolds (copy after)

Oil on canvas 77 x 63.5
INV: Mathews 51; RW/CKA 423
PROV: Charles Mathews
EXH: 1833 London (51)
REL: Original: Waddesdon Manor, oil on canvas 76.2 x 63.5, exh: R.A. 1782 (22), engr: William Dickinson pub. W. Dickinson 1785, stipple 27.3 x 22.5; there are at least six copies, including No. 720 [for details of these pictures, see BD 13: 43–45]

In an archetypal image of the 1780s, Mrs Robinson wears a large black hat with blue bows and feathers, a black ribband collier tied at the front, and a dark grey dress with lace cuffs and fichu. Behind her is a red drapery.

Mary Robinson, nicknamed 'Perdita' because of her portrayal of that role in *The Winter's Tale* and as sometime mistress of the dissolute Prince of Wales, was a very beautiful woman who attracted the attention of many artists. According to the BD (13: 38), 'her talents were respectable' and she was often commended 'for her beauty, figure [especially in breeched parts], and taste in clothes'.

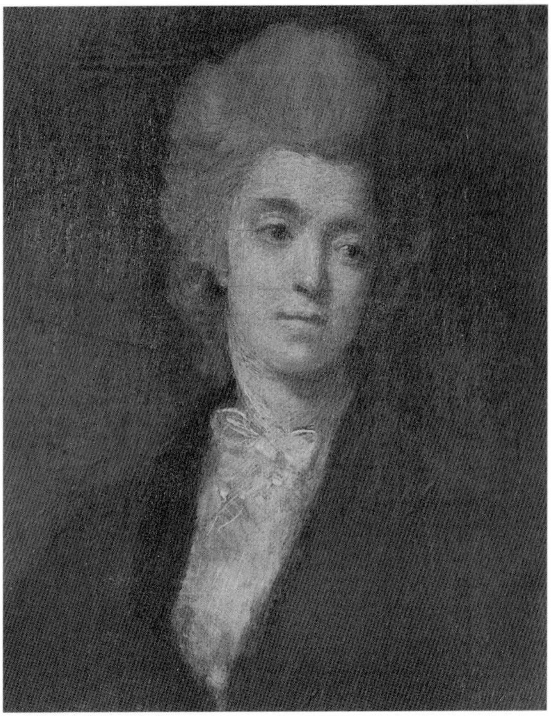

721
MARY ROBINSON
as Rosalind in *As You Like It*
by William Shakespeare

Johan Zoffany (attr.)

Oil on canvas 23.5 x 18.4
INV: Mathews 96; RW/CKA 240
PROV: Charles Mathews
EXH: 1833 London (96)
LIT: Lady Victoria Manners & Dr G.C. Williamson, *John Zoffany* (1920), p. 200

The sitter has a neat powdered coiffure. She wears a dark blue garment over her shoulders and a high white stock.

Mrs Robinson appeared as Rosalind for the first time at Drury Lane on 28 February 1780. Some doubt has been expressed over the identity, but it seems to be fairly secure.

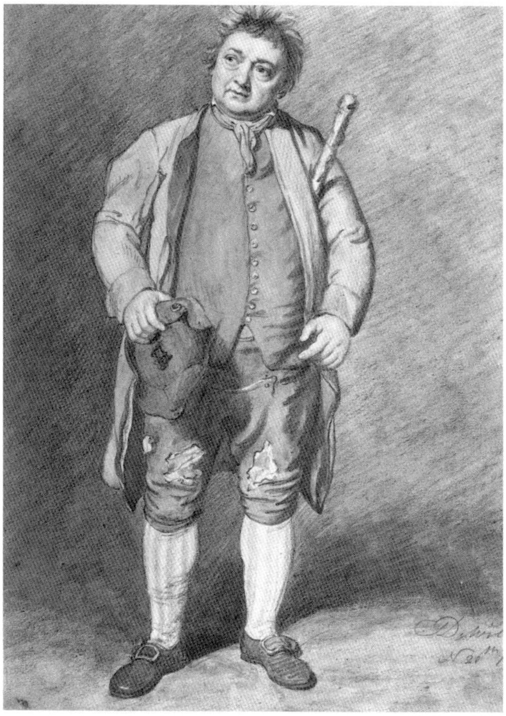

722
EDWARD ANTHONY ROCK
as the Irishman in *The Register Office*
by Joseph Reed

Samuel De Wilde

Black chalk and watercolour on wove paper 37 x 23.5
INSCR: 'S De Wilde / N 20 (6?) th 180–' (Black chalk b.r.)
INV: Mathews 207; RW/CKA 61F
PROV: Charles Mathews
EXH: 1833 London (207)
ENGR: Richard Woodman for Cawthorn's *Minor British Theatre* pub. John Cawthorn 10 April 1806, stipple 11.7 x 7.6

The Irishman has ragged ginger hair and holds a tattered grey hat and wooden cudgel. He wears grey shoes with gold buckles, white stockings with grey vertical stripes, blue breeches torn above the knee to reveal a white undergarment, an ill-fitting long grey-blue coat with a red lining, a red waistcoat with brass buttons, a white shirt, and a greyish neckerchief.

Reed's farce was first performed at Drury Lane on 25 April 1761, with John Moody as the Irishman; he was still playing the part 20 years later, giving the last performances of the century, on 28 April and 24 May 1781. The Drury Lane cast list given in the 1806 Cawthorn edition has Cherry as the Irishman. Rock was a member of the Covent Garden company during the 1805–6 season, but there were no performances of the play at that theatre.

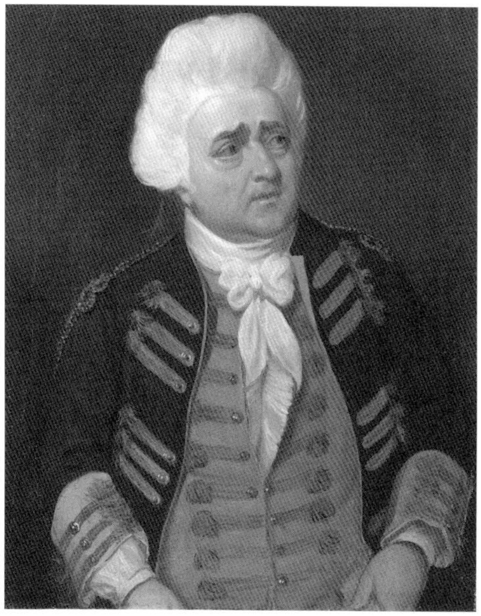

723
EDWARD ANTHONY ROCK
as Murtock Delany in *The Irishman in London*
by William Macready

Samuel De Wilde

Oil on panel 23.8 x 18.8
INV: Mathews 43; RW 244? (unknown by unknown); CKA 244
PROV: Charles Mathews
EXH: 1833 London (43)
ENGR: William Ridley for the *Monthly Mirror* pub. Vernor & Hood 31 May 1805, stipple 8.7 x 7.4 (bust in oval, cut off above cuffs)

Murtock Delany is the servant of the Irishman William Patrick O'Brien Culloony, who loves London as much as Murtock hates it. At Murtock's first entrance he is singing 'We Irishmen both high and low'. De Wilde shows him with a florid complexion and a high bouffant powdered wig. He wears a livery consisting of a green coat with buff cuffs and waistcoat; there are brass buttons with red, green and buff frogging.

Macready's farce was first staged at Covent Garden on 21 April 1792, when John Henry Johnstone played Murtock Delany as part of his benefit; he was still playing the part at Drury Lane in the early 19th century. The play was given less frequently at Covent Garden but during the 1804–5 season was seen on 21 September and 21 December 1804, on both occasions with Rock as Murtock Delany. Rock was the resident character Irishman at Covent Garden; during the 1804–5 season he also played Sir Patrick O'Neil in Garrick's *The Irish Widow* on 22 May 1805 and Parrots in John O'Keeffe's *The Irish Mimick*, for the first time, on 26 September 1804.

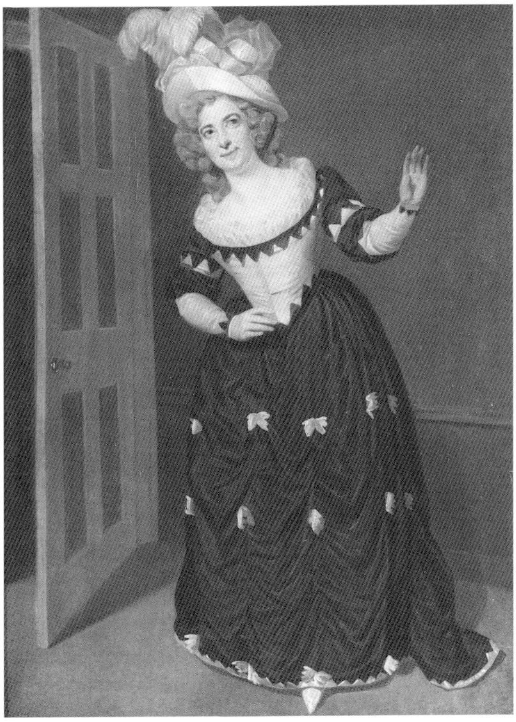

724
MRS ROCK
as Viletta in *She Wou'd and She Wou'd Not*
by Colley Cibber

Samuel De Wilde

Oil on canvas 37.1 x 28.5
INV: Mathews 382; RW/CKA 225
PROV: John Bell; Charles Mathews
EXH: 1833 London (382); 1962 Chichester (18)
ENGR: J. Thornthwaite for Bell's British Library 27 October 1791, line 11.5 x 8, pub. Bell's *British Theatre* (1797), vol 5

In Act III, scene 1, Viletta, the avaricious maid to Rosaria, fends off Trappanti, who has just tried to kiss her. Trappanti tosses her a purse, and she changes her mind, 'Well, if I must, come then – to see how a woman may be deceived at first sight of a man'. The engraving carries the line: 'Indeed my friend, you are too ugly for me; tho' I am not handsome myself, I love to play with those that are.'

Viletta is rather grandly dressed for a lady's maid in the costume of the 1780s. She wears a large straw hat with white satin ribbons and ostrich feathers. Her dress has a white silk bodice and sleeves with purple-black puffs at the elbows and zigzag bands of decoration round the low-cut neck and at the waist. The full skirt is also of purple-black, gathered into two rows of white bows, and has a white zigzag decoration round the hem. She stands in a listening attitude beside a half-open door.

Cibber's comedy was originally performed at Drury Lane on 26 November 1702, with the author as Don Manuel and Mrs Knight as Viletta. Mrs Rock never played Viletta in London; she appeared in the play once, at Covent Garden on 16 July 1790, when she acted Rosa and Mrs Lee Lewes played Viletta.

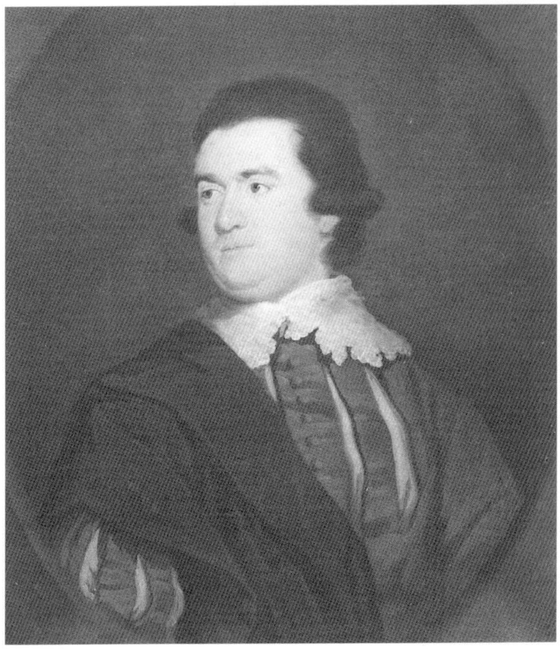

725
DAVID ROSS
as Kiteley in *Every Man in his Humour*
by Ben Jonson

Tilly Kettle

Oil on canvas 76.2 x 62.2
INV: Mathews 359 (artist unknown);
RW/CKA 471 (artist unknown)
PROV: Charles Mathews
EXH: 1833 London (359)

Kiteley is probably shown in Act V, scene 2, 'The Street before Cobb's house', when he enters 'muffled in a cloak' to accuse his wife and Knowell of criminal conduct. Kiteley's hair is brushed back with curls over his ears. He wears a red doublet slashed with white and with red buttons, and a vandyke collar. He has a blue drapery over his right shoulder.

The first Covent Garden performance of Jonson's comedy was on 25 October 1762, with William Smith as Kiteley. He retained the part for the entire period of Ross's career at the theatre, and Ross appears never to have played it. No. 725 was presumably painted during Kettle's residence in England between 1776 and 1783.

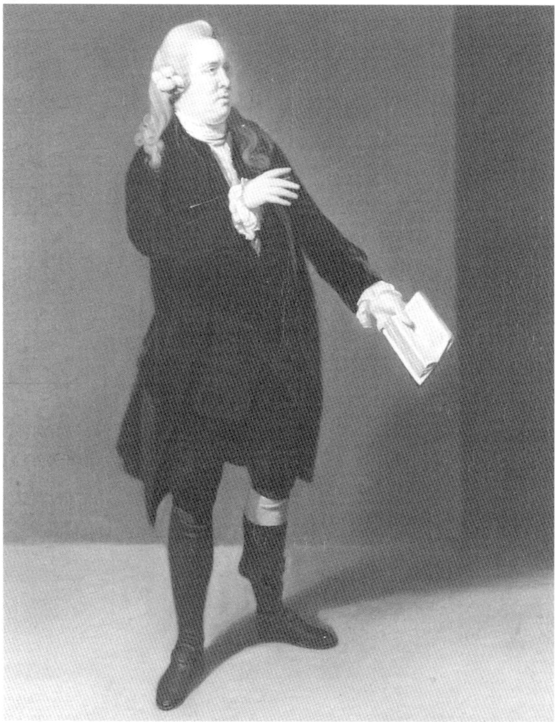

726
DAVID ROSS
as Hamlet in *Hamlet*
by William Shakespeare

Johan Zoffany

Oil on canvas 77 x 64
INV: Mathews 62; RW/CKA 120
PROV: Charles Mathews
EXH: 1833 London (62); 1951 London (42)
LIT: Lady Victoria Manners & Dr G.C. Williamson, *John Zoffany* (1920), pp. 144–46 & 199; Fitzgerald, p. 167; Griffiths, p. 324
REL: [Another version by Zoffany, with the same measurements, was sold at Sotheby's on 24 February 1960, bt. by Constantine for £200]

Ross is dressed in Hamlet black, with the traditional left stocking undone to show his madness and reveal his undergarments. He wears an elaborate wig, with curls over his right ear and a long queue over both shoulders. He gestures with his right hand and holds his book of words in his left.

Ross acted Hamlet for the first time in London at Covent Garden on 8 October 1757, just after he had moved from Drury Lane, where Garrick usually played the role. Ross gave his last Hamlet at Covent Garden on 26 January 1767.

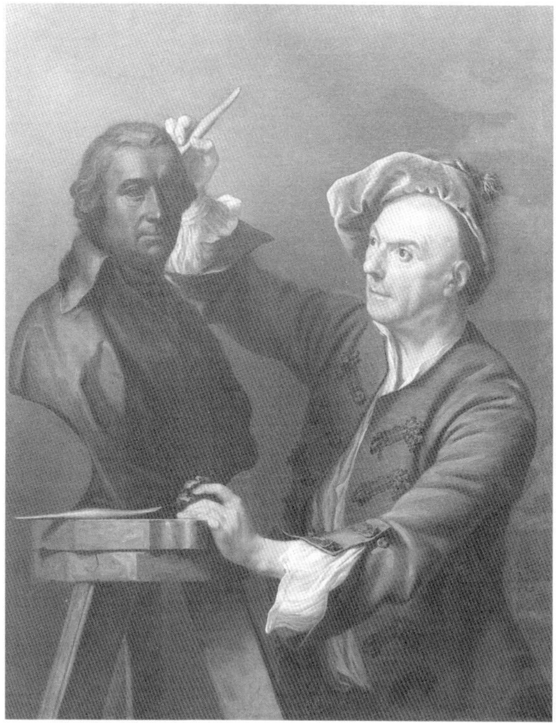

727*
LOUIS FRANÇOIS ROUBILIAC
at work on a bust of David Garrick

Andrea Soldi

Oil on canvas 112.4 x 91.5
INSCR: 'Andrea Soldi / Pinxt ft / 1757 / 8' (grey paint b.r.)
INV: CKA 601; Gift 337
PROV: Presented by Alderson Burrell Horne, 1909
LIT: Walpole Society

Roubiliac's brown hair is just visible under his purple velvet cap. He raises a modelling tool in his right hand to jab at the wet green clay bust of Garrick, and with his left holds a rag or piece of sponge, stained with clay, to the base of the bust. He wears a purple coat and a loose, open-necked shirt.

For Roubiliac's work for Garrick and the versions of the bust of Garrick, see S15. Adrien Carpentiers painted a portrait of Roubiliac, signed and dated 1762 (oil on canvas 125.7 x 100.3, National Portrait Gallery 303), showing him in similar studio garb, at work on the model for his statue of Shakespeare for Garrick's Shakespeare Temple at Hampton.

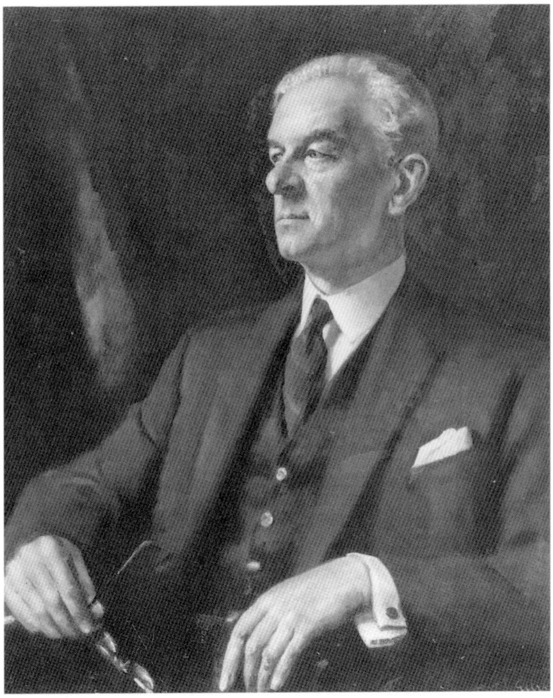

728
LORD CHARLES RUSSELL

John Gilroy

Oil on canvas 76.3 x 63.5
INSCR: 'Gilroy' (red paint b.r.)
INV: Not listed
PROV: Presented by the artist?

Russell holds a pair of spectacles in his right hand and wears a grey coat, a green cardigan with pearl buttons, a white shirt with gold cuff-links, and a purple striped tie. There is a white handkerchief in his jacket pocket and a red-purple curtain hangs behind the figure.

Lord Justice Russell was a member of the Garrick from 1939 until his death.

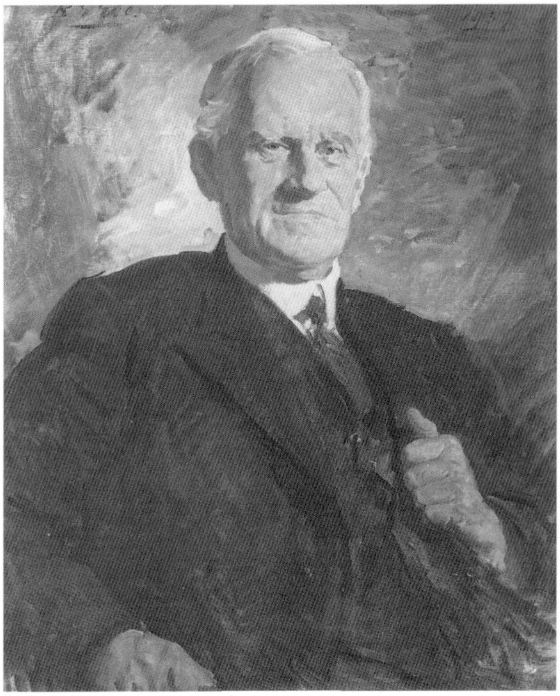

729
LORD FRANCIS XAVIER RUSSELL

Reginald Grenville Eves

Oil on canvas 76.2 x 63.5
INSCR: 'R. G. Eves' (dark brown paint t.l.);
'1937' (dark brown paint t.r.)
INV: CKA 652
PROV: Presented by a number of members, 1947
EXH: 1938 R.A. (141)
REL: Lincoln's Inn, oil on canvas 60 x 49.5
s. and d: 'R G Eves' (t.l.), '1937' (t.r.)
LIT: Adrian Bury, *The Art of Reginald Grenville Eves* (1940), pl. 21

With his left hand Russell holds the lapel of his jacket, which is of the same brown-grey material as his waistcoat. He has a white shirt with stiff collar and a blue tie.

The Lincoln's Inn version of No. 729 is probably the picture that was exhibited at the R.A.

Lord Russell of Killowen was a member of the Garrick Club from 1893 until his death; he was also a Trustee of the Club. In the Club's 'Roll of Members' he is listed as 'Frank' Russell.

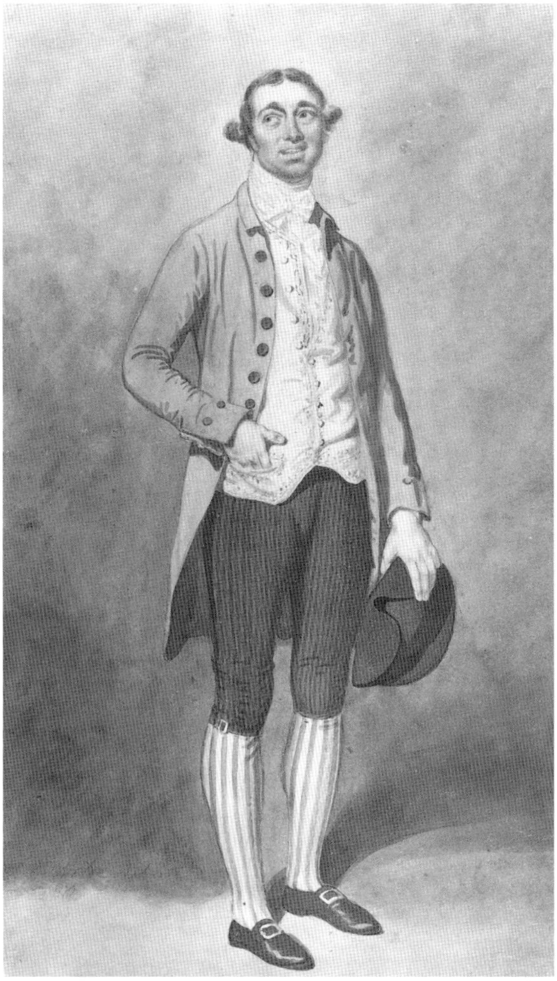

730
SAMUEL THOMAS RUSSELL
as Jerry Sneak in *The Mayor of Garratt*
by Samuel Foote

Samuel De Wilde

Pencil and watercolour
on wove paper 37 x 23.5
INSCR: 'S De Wilde delin / ...' (pencil b.l.)
INV: Mathews 218; RW/CKA 61A (framed as 61B)
PROV: Charles Mathews
EXH: 1833 London (218)
ENGR: Anon. pub. Bell and De Camp 1808,
stipple and line 12.4 x 7.5
REL: Christie's November 1974 oil on canvas n.s.
[Yale Center for British Art, oil on canvas
62.3 x 39.3, prov: Christie's 22 November 1974,
bt. by Baskett & Day for 3200 guineas]

Sneak's silliness is emphasised by his hair, parted in the middle with curls over the ears. He wears black shoes with gold buckles, blue and white striped stockings, green and black striped breeches with buckles at the knees, a pale purple coat with silver buttons, a white waistcoat embroidered around the edges in pink and green, and a high white stock with rosette and frill.

Foote's comedy was first performed at the Haymarket on 20 June 1763, with Thomas Weston as Jerry Sneak. It was revived at Drury Lane on 2 February 1808 – for the first time in five years, according to the playbill – with Russell as Jerry Sneak, Dowton as Major Sturgeon, and Mrs Harlowe as Mrs Sneak. There were 12 performances before the end of the season, the last on 16 June 1808.

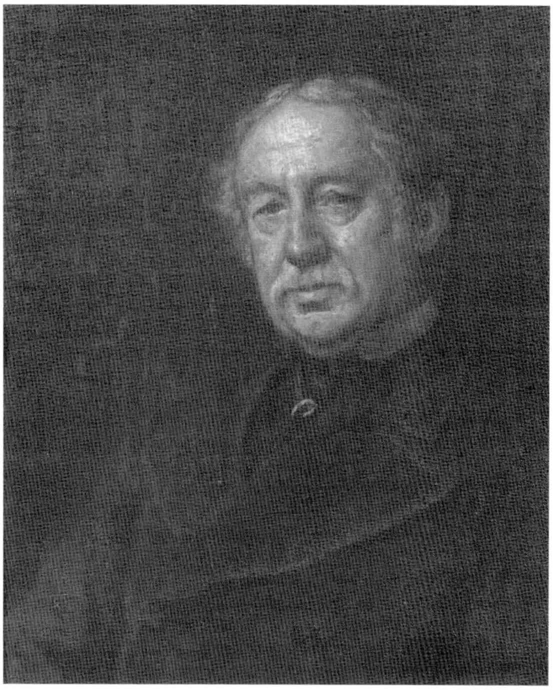

731
SIR WILLIAM HOWARD RUSSELL

Carlo Pellegrini ('Ape')

Oil on canvas 59.7 x 49.5
INSCR: 'C. Pellegrini' (green paint t.l.)
INV: RW/CKA 322; Gift 269
PROV: Lord Ronald Sutherland Gower, by whom
presented to the Garrick Club, 1899

Head and shoulders, seated. The sitter wears a brown frock-coat. He has a horseshoe pin in his cravat.

Sir William Howard Russell was a member of the Garrick Club from 1853 until his death.

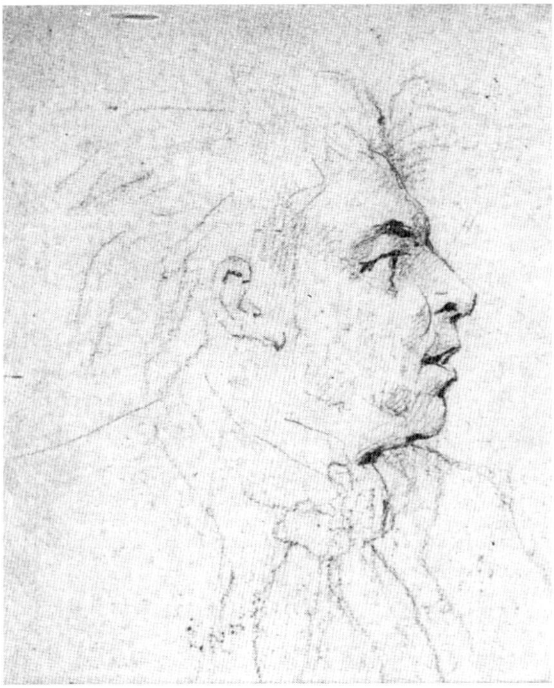

732
THOMAS RYDER

James Roberts

Pencil on laid paper 8.2 x 7.5
INSCR: 'Ryder' (pen and brown ink on mount b.c., in Mathews's hand)
INV: RW/CKA 493A
PROV: Charles Mathews (not in catalogue)

Head and shoulders in profile to right.

The Irish actor and sometime manager Thomas Ryder made his first appearance in London at Covent Garden on 25 October 1786, as Sir John Brute in *The Provok'd Wife*. He was engaged in London until 1790 then returned to Ireland, where he died a year later. He was accounted an excellent and versatile actor in such roles as Falstaff, Romeo, and Peachum in *The Beggar's Opera*.

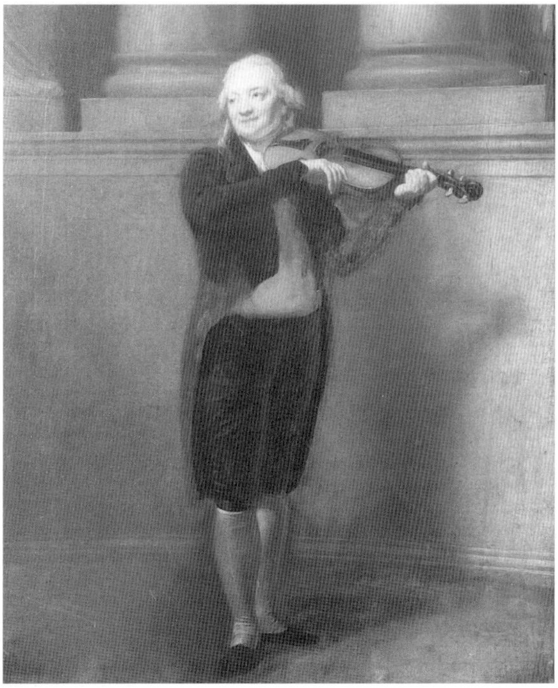

733 *Johann Peter Salomon*

733
JOHANN PETER SALOMON

Circle of G.H. Harlow

Oil on canvas 44 x 35.5
INV: RW/CKA 374; Gift 125
PROV: David Roberts, by whom presented to the Garrick Club, 1854 (as by Lawrence)

LIT: Fitzgerald, p. 245:
'There is in the drawing room, close to the window, a very interesting ... picture, highly finished, and representing a benevolent-looking old violinist in the act of drawing music from his instrument. It is the likeness of John Salomons [*sic*], a professional of reputation, and claims to have been painted by Sir Thomas Laurence ... But it could hardly have been painted by Laurence, as the style shows, which is quite German, and the delicate and minute touchings of the face is not in Laurence's way...'

Salomon, the great impresario and concertmaster, plays a viola or violin. He wears black slippers, silver stockings, blue breeches, a blue jacket with a high black collar, and an orange-yellow waistcoat. The left arm, lower parts of the jacket and areas around the feet are unfinished.

Salomon came to England in 1781 and played in concerts and performed as a conductor until 1789. As an impresario he brought Haydn to England in 1790 and 1794, and he resumed his own concert career in 1796. The picture depicts an elderly man, and it is tempting to suppose that it celebrates the first concert of the Philharmonic Society in the Argyll Rooms on 8 March 1813, when Salomon led the orchestra.

The picture has been optimistically attributed to Lawrence but is probably by a younger artist from his circle, of the generation of George Henry Harlow.

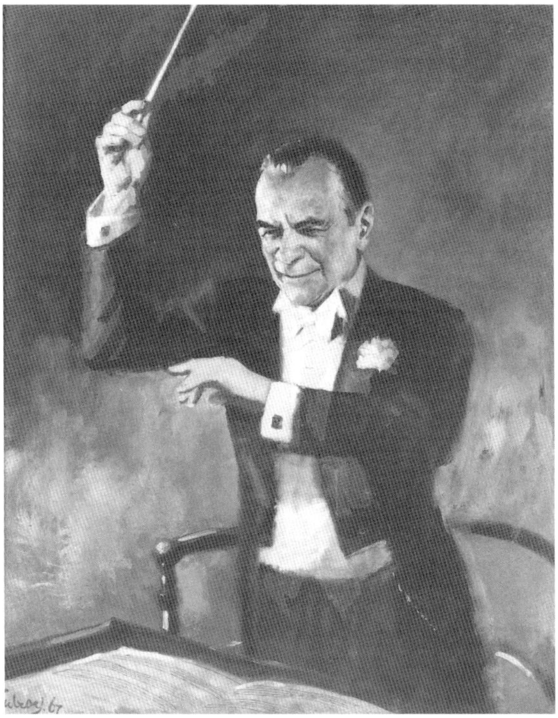

734

SIR MALCOLM SARGENT

John Gilroy

Oil on panel 75 x 63
INSCR: 'Gilroy. 67' (green paint b.l.)
INV: GCL 693
PROV: Presented by the artist?
REL: Royal Albert Hall, oil on canvas

Sir Malcolm conducts with his eyes half-closed, his famously shiny black hair flashing in the light. He wears evening dress with a watch chain and has a pink carnation in his buttonhole. Given the fact that the final or original version of this picture is in the Albert Hall, Sir Malcolm is undoubtedly shown conducting the BBC Symphony Orchestra at the Last Night of the Proms – presumably on the last occasion on which he did so. The picture, painted in 1967, was no doubt intended as a memorial to the sitter, who died that year.

Sir Malcolm was a member of the Garrick Club from 1927 until his death.

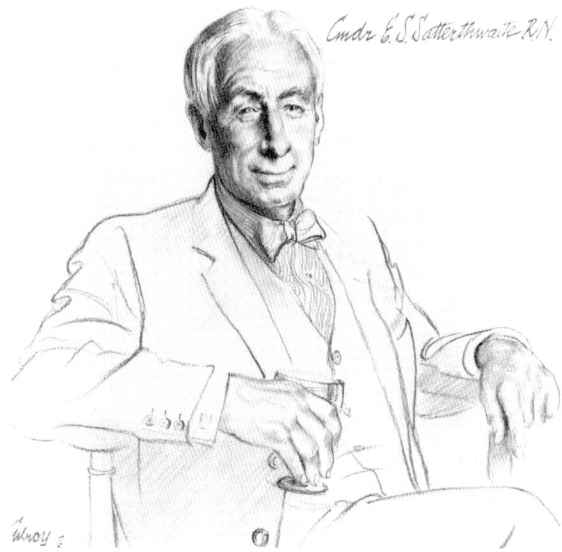

735

E. S. SATTERTHWAITE

John Gilroy

Black chalk and some brown wash
on wove paper 30.2 x 30.5 (sight)
INSCR: 'Gilroy 70' (pencil b.l.);
'Cmdr E. S. Satterthwaite R.N.' (pencil t.r.)
INV: Not listed
PROV: Presented by the artist

Commander Satterthwaite wears a suit and waistcoat, a striped shirt, and a bow tie. He is relaxing with a glass of Beaumes de Venise.

On his retirement as Club Secretary in 1972, Commander Satterthwaite became a Life Member of the Garrick Club.

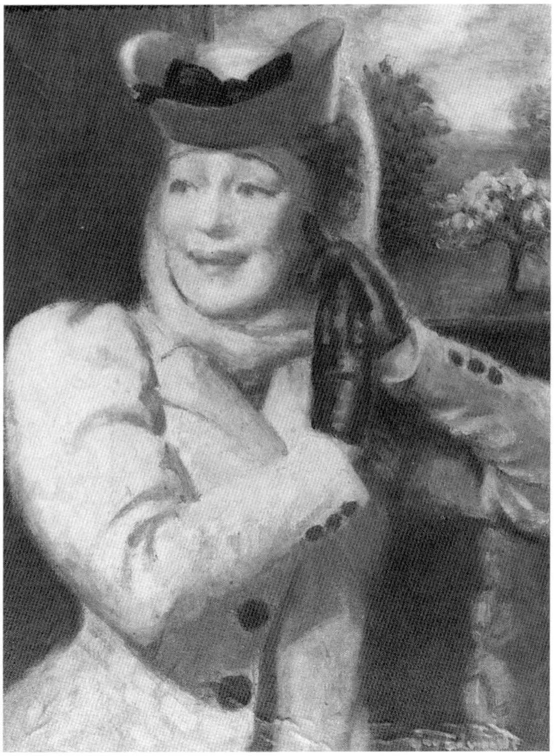

736
ATHENE SEYLER
as Lyubov Andreyevna
in *The Cherry Orchard* by Anton Chekhov

Mrs Grey-Edwards

Oil on canvas 35.5 x 28
INSCR: 'Grey Edwards' (white paint b.r.)
INV: GCL 695
PROV: Unknown

Lyubov Andreyevna has a yellow straw hat with a black bow. She wears black gloves, a yellow-brown jacket with padded shoulders and trimmed with black buttons, and a yellow scarf. To the left is a red curtain and to the right a view of the cherry orchard.

Athene Seyler played Lyubov Andreyevna in a production of *The Cherry Orchard* that entered the repertory of the Old Vic on 9 October 1933. The producer was Tyrone Guthrie. The cast included Charles Laughton as Lopakin, Marius Goring as Epihodov, Ursula Jeans as Anya, Flora Robson as Varya, Leon Quartermaine as Leonid Andreyevitch, Elsa Lanchester as Charlotta Ivanovna, Roger Livesey as Semyonov-Pischchik, James Mason as Yasha, and Dennis Arundel as Trofimov. Athene Seyler played Mme Ranevska in a subsequent revival at the New Theatre on 28 August 1941, with her husband Nicholas Hannen in the role of Gaev.

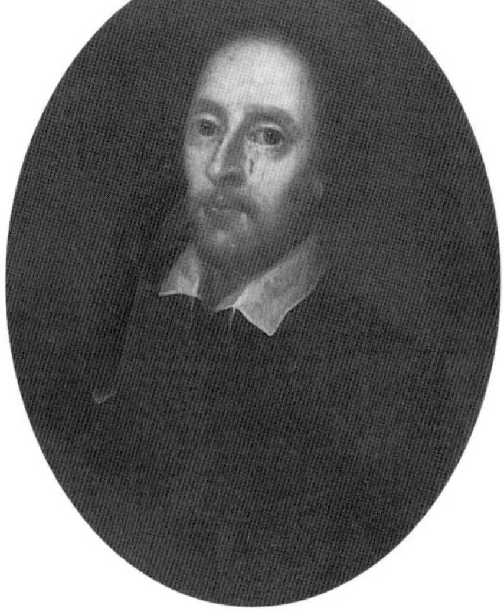

737
WILLIAM SHAKESPEARE

Unknown Artist

Oil on canvas 21.6 x 16.5
INV: RW/CKA 477; Gift O or 64
PROV: H. Broadwood, presented to the Garrick Club, 1831 or 1841
REL: Original: NPG 1 oil on canvas 55.2 x 43.8

In this bust portrait, in oval, Shakespeare has a gold earring in his left ear. He wears a dark doublet and has a loose collared shirt with tassels.

NPG 1, the 'Chandos Portrait', is the source, several times removed, for the Garrick Club picture.

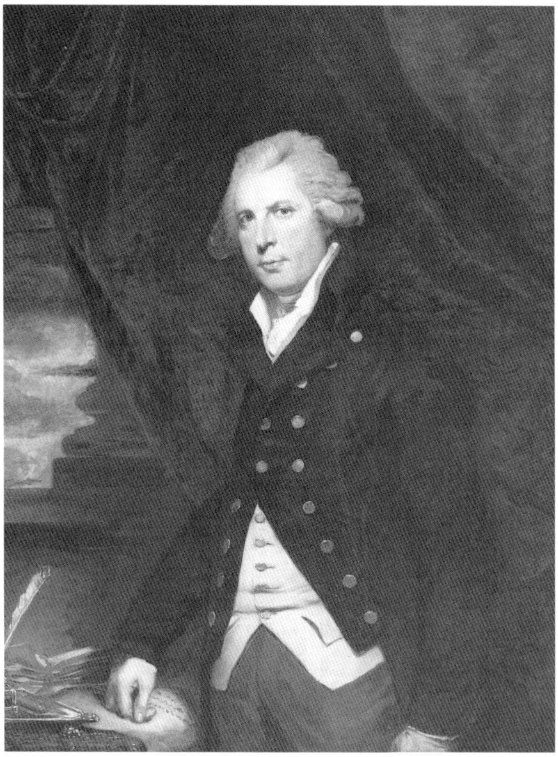

738*

RICHARD BRINSLEY SHERIDAN

Sir Joshua Reynolds (studio)

Oil on canvas 123.2 x 100.3
INV: RW 39 (after Sir Joshua Reynolds); CKA 39; Gift 168
PROV: Edward Tredcroft, by whom presented to the Garrick Club, 1862
REL: Original: ex. Sheridan Coll., Frampton Court, Dorchester (Sotheby's 23 March 1960 [80]?), exh: R.A. 1789 (259), engr: John Hall pub. J. Hall 1791, line 45.7 x 35.5
[For details of the Frampton Court original, sold at Sotheby's on 23 March 1960 and bought by Frost & Reed for £1600 for an anonymous owner, and for other versions and engravings, see BD 13: 321–22]

Sheridan has a yellow glove on his left hand, and wears brown breeches, a black coat, and a yellow waistcoat. The setting is grand, with a red tasselled curtain hanging in front of a balustrade and the base of a large column. On the table, which is covered by a red cloth decorated with blue and yellow, is a quill pen and inkwell. This is a good studio version of a popular portrait.

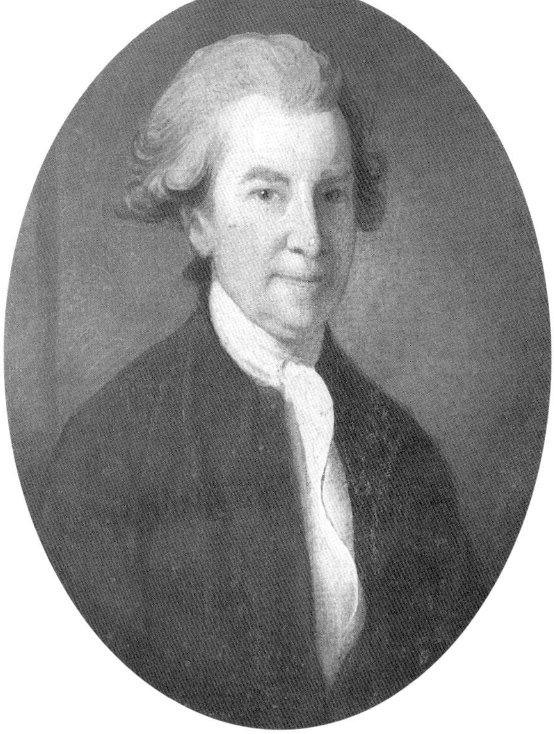

739

THOMAS SHERIDAN

Gilbert Stuart (copy after)

Oil on canvas 25.4 x 21.6
INV: Mathews 148 (artist unknown); RW 366 (artist unknown); CKA 366
PROV: Charles Mathews
EXH: 1833 London (148)
ENGR: Scott pub. C. Dilly 1789, as a plate to Sheridan's *Dictionary*, stipple 16.2 x 12.7; P. Maguire, stipple 13.8 x 10.4

Thomas Sheridan wears a powdered wig, a collarless mulberry velvet jacket, and a white stock.

When manager in Dublin, Sheridan, father of the playwright R.B. Sheridan, was often at odds with his audience. He was, however, a fine tragic actor, both in Dublin and London, who excelled in such roles as Hamlet, Brutus and Cato. A man of substantial intellect, he also wrote important treatises on language and oratory, among them *A General Dictionary of the English Language* (1780), *Lectures on the Art of Reading* (1785), and *A View of the State of School Education in Ireland* (1787).

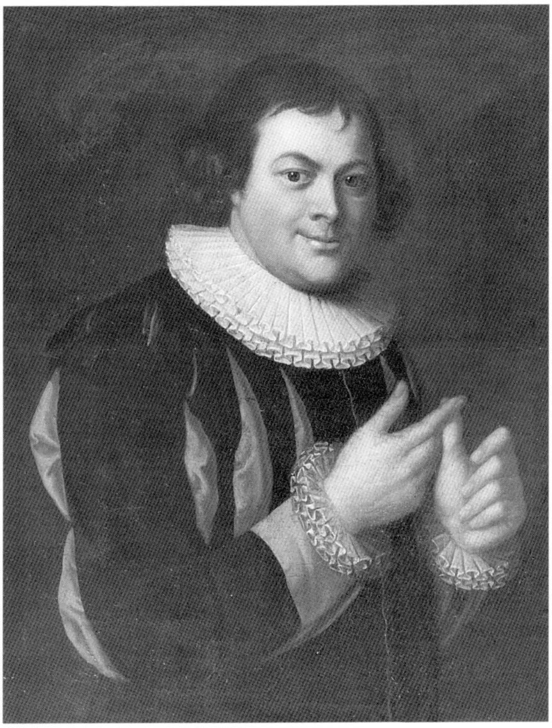

740
EDWARD SHUTER
as Scapin in *The Cheats of Scapin*
by Thomas Otway

Bernard Downes (?)

Oil on canvas 74.9 x 62.2
INV: Mathews 364 (artist unknown);
RW 418 (artist unknown);
CKA 418 (as Scapin in 'The Rival Queens')
PROV: Charles Mathews
EXH: 1762 S.A. (28); 1833 London (364)

Scapin is shown half-length, smiling and making a gesture expressive of his cunning and impudence; his hands are raised to the right, with the forefinger of the right hand touching the thumb of the left. He wears a black doublet slashed to reveal red around the chest and down the sleeves, red cuffs with lace at the wrists, and a double lace ruff.

Otway's comedy was originally performed in 1676. Edward Shuter played Scapin for the first time at Covent Garden on 8 January 1755, and the performance nearest to the date of this picture – assuming that it is Downes's 1762 exhibit – was given as part of Shuter's benefit at Covent Garden on 26 March 1761.

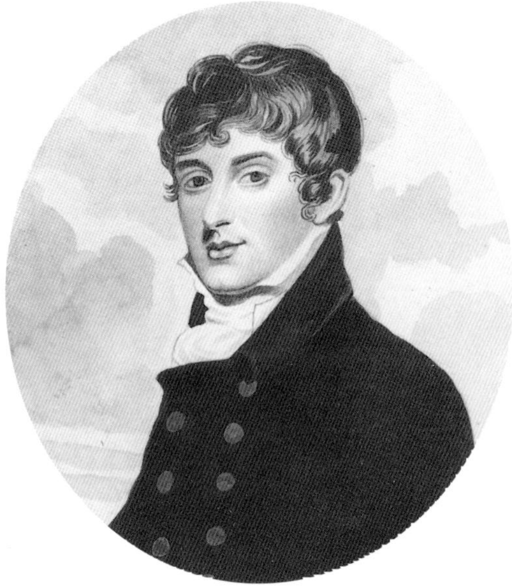

741
HENRY SIDDONS

Sylvester Harding (after Henry Edridge)

Watercolour on wove paper 9.5 x 7.8 (oval)
INSCR: 'H. Siddons' (pen and brown ink on mount below CM)
INV: Not listed
PROV: Charles Mathews (Print collection Vol IV f. 114)
ENGR: William Ridley for the *Monthly Mirror* pub.
Vernor & Hood 1 January 1802, stipple 8.9 x 7.2

Head and shoulders, half-left, wearing a blue coat.

The eldest child of the great Sarah Siddons, the sitter acted children's roles on the London stage in the 1780s and later enjoyed some success as an adult actor in the provinces, playing such parts as Othello, Richmond in *Richard III*, and Zanga in *The Revenge*. In 1801 he returned to London to act at Covent Garden, where he performed Othello to 'great applause' on 28 October. After the 1804–5 season he went over to Drury Lane, remaining there until he obtained the patent of the Edinburgh Theatre, which he managed until his death in 1814, at the age of 40. See also No. 749.

742*
SARAH SIDDONS
as Lady Macbeth
in *Macbeth* by William Shakespeare

George Henry Harlow

Oil on canvas 61 x 38
INV: Mathews 147; RW/CKA 31
PROV: Charles Mathews
EXH: 1833 London (147); 1964 London [2] (35);
1975 London (100)

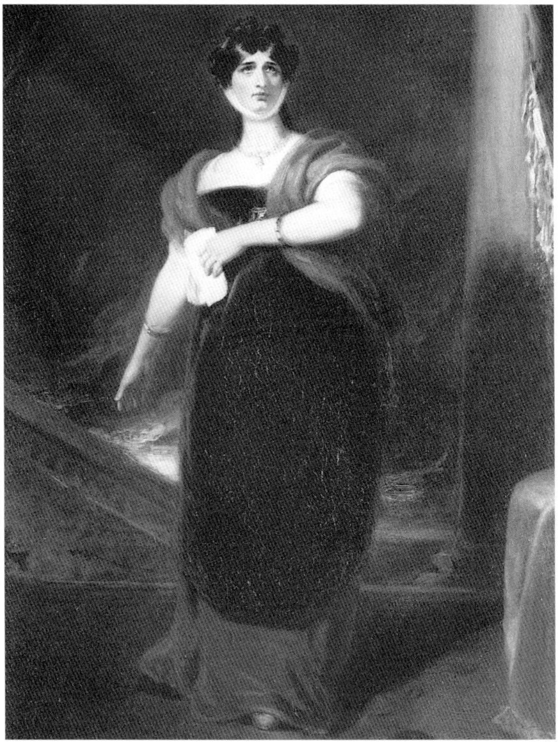

742 *Sarah Siddons as Lady Macbeth*

ENGR: C. Rolls for the *Literary Souvenir*
pub. Longman November 1829, line 11.5 x 7
REL: Original: Bob Jones University, S. Carolina,
oil on canvas 231.1 x 144.8, exh: B.I. 1814 (93)
LIT: Griffiths, p.327

The moment illustrated is Act I, scene V. Lady Macbeth holds Macbeth's letter in her left hand across her chest. She wears a short-sleeved overdress of dark red velvet with a brown underskirt and has a red drapery round her shoulders. Under her chin is a white Siddonian wimple. A stormy night sky suits the drama of the moment. See also No. 748.

Lady Macbeth was the role associated most closely with Sarah Siddons, from her first appearance in London in the part on 2 February 1785 until her last official appearance on the stage, at Covent Garden on 22 June 1812, when the audience would not allow the play to continue after the sleepwalking scene. In the famous words of William Hazlitt in *The Examiner* on 16 June 1816, as an actress: 'She raised the tragedy to the skies ... It was something above nature. We can conceive of nothing grander ... She was Tragedy, personified.'

Harlow charged 20 guineas for this sort of small full-length. It is likely that Nos. 742 and 743 were commissioned directly from the artist by Mathews, a close friend and patron (see No. 471). For details on the provenance of the original at Bob Jones University, see BD 14: 60–61.

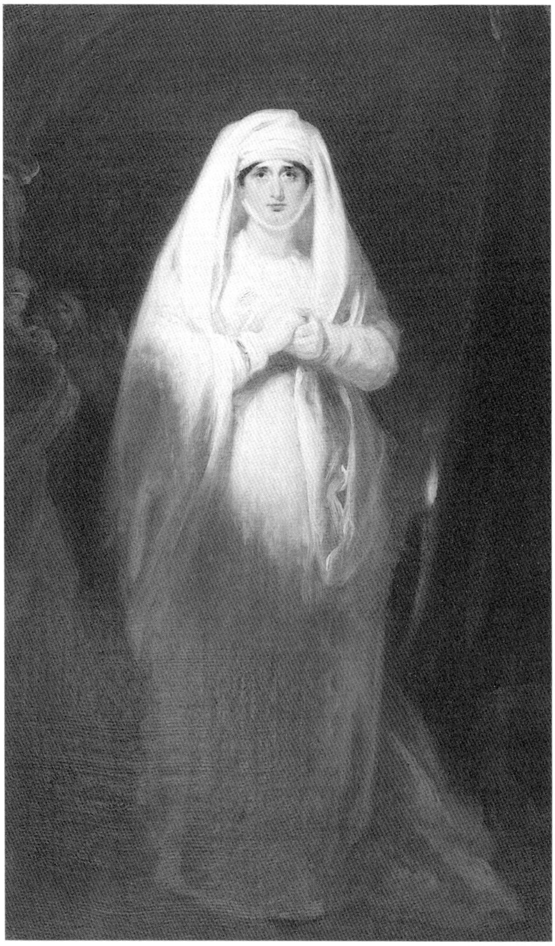

743*
SARAH SIDDONS
as Lady Macbeth
in *Macbeth* by William Shakespeare

George Henry Harlow

Oil on canvas 64 x 39.4
INV: Mathews 137; RW/CKA 43
PROV: Charles Mathews
EXH: 1833 London (137); 1964 London [2] (33);
1975 London (101)
ENGR: Robert Cooper for Terry's *Theatrical Gallery*
pub. H. Berthoud 28 September 1822,
stipple and line 20 x 14.6 ('From an Original Painting
in the possession of Charles Mathews, Esquire');
J. Rogers for Oxberry's *Dramatic Biography*
pub. G. Virtue 19 February 1825, stipple and line
REL: Private coll., London, black chalk and wash on
wove paper 21.6 x 18.4, inscr: 'G.H.H. / December 1813'
(half-length); Marquess of Lansdowne, Bowood,
black chalk and wash on wove paper (half-length);
Huntington Library, black and red chalk and wash
on wove paper 22.8 x 18.4 (half-length)
LIT: Griffiths, p.327

For the sleepwalking scene, Mrs Siddons is seen in stylised nightwear: a long-sleeved white gown with a white wimple, and a large white shawl over her head and shoulders. To the left are the shadowy figures of the Doctor and Woman, standing under an arch. The red drapery on the right partly conceals a lighted candle.

See No. 742. For details about other versions, see BD 14: 60–61.

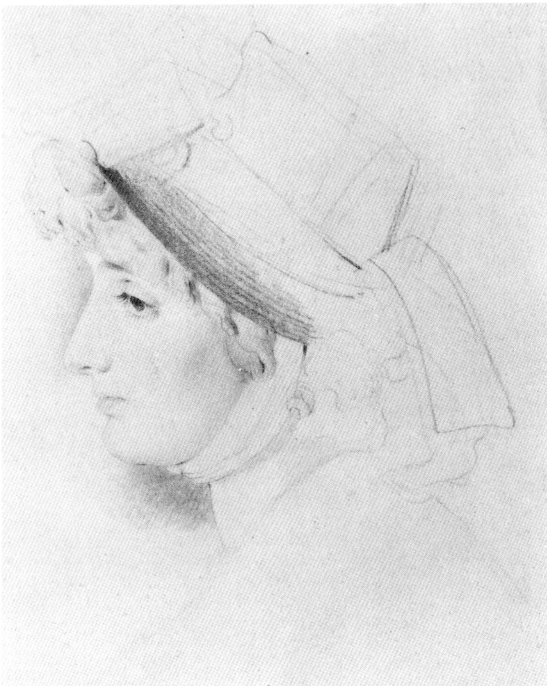

744*

SARAH SIDDONS

Sir Thomas Lawrence

Black chalk on wove paper 22.2 x 17.8
INV: RW/CKA 137
PROV: R.R. Willett, by whom presented to the Garrick Club, 1835?
EXH: 1975 London (103)
ENGR: W. Nicholls pub. J. Hassell 1 December 1810, stipple 28 x 24.1
LIT: Fitzgerald, p. 245

Mrs Siddons is shown head and shoulders, in profile to the left. Her straw bonnet, tied under her chin, has a pale band around the crown, with the ends hanging down over her shoulders, and plumes at the front.

For details of Lawrence's many portraits of Sarah Siddons, see BD 14: 44–47.

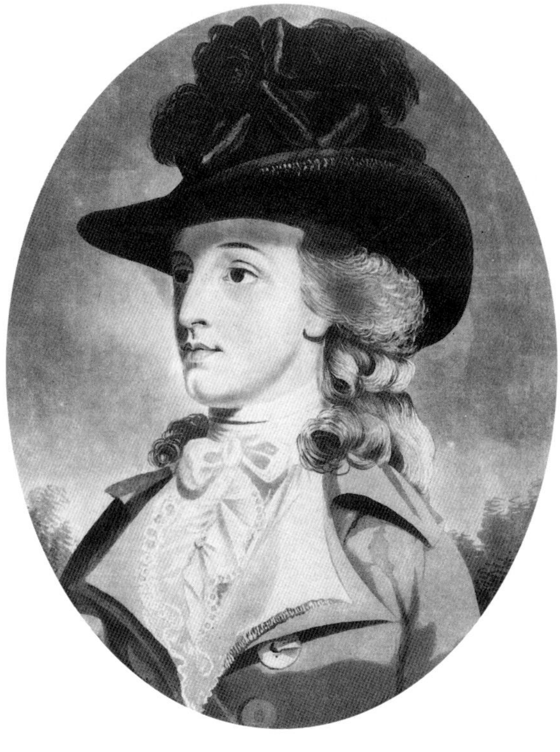

745

SARAH SIDDONS

Sir Thomas Lawrence (after)

Watercolour on wove paper 15 x 10.7 (oval)
INSCR: 'MRS SIDDONS / BY HORACE HONE A.R.A. / FROM A PAINTING BY LAWRENCE OF BATH 1782' (pen and ink with watercolour on mount b.)
INV: GCL 736C; Gift 883
PROV: Sophie Andrae, by whom presented to the Garrick Club, 1978
REL: Pastel portrait by Lawrence, location unknown, engr: Anon. for the *Westminster Magazine* pub. John Walker 31 January 1783, line 14.5 x 9.5 ('From a crayon painting in her own possession'); Francis Jukes pub. F. Jukes 15 May 1783, aquatint 30.5 x 24.5

Mrs Siddons is shown head and shoulders looking to left. She wears a large black hat trimmed with black ribbons and feathers, and a pale blue-grey riding habit with a white stock.

The work does not appear to be of sufficiently high quality to be by Hone, and is likely to have been copied from the aquatint by Jukes. It was mounted in the late 19th century with a letter from Mrs Siddons to Lord Avon and a coloured woodcut showing her birthplace, the Shoulder of Mutton Inn at Brecon (see No. 936).

746

NO CATALOGUE ENTRY

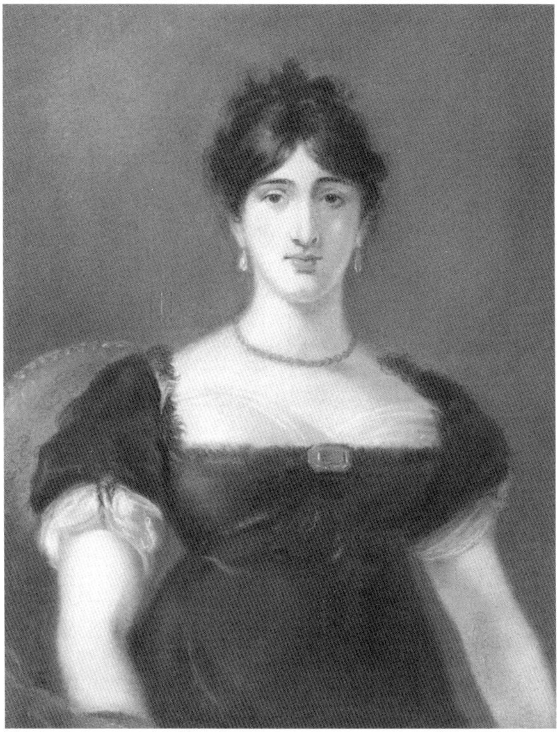

747*
SARAH SIDDONS

John Raphael Smith (?)
(after Lawrence)

Pastel on paper 30.5 x 25.5
INSCR: Label on verso: 'B/1755 Mrs Siddons D/1831 / In the dress she wore when reading / Shakespeare before Royalty &c / Pastel by John Raphael Smith from the fine picture by Sir / Thomas Lawrence (now in the / National Portrait Gallery) / painted in 1804' (pen and black ink)
INV: GCL 735; Gift 889
PROV: Bequeathed by the Hon. Sir Ralph Cusack, 1978
REL: Original: Tate 188, oil on canvas 254 x 148.6, exh: R.A. 1804 (193) (full-length)

Mrs Siddons is shown half-length, seated in a red upholstered chair. She has pearl drop earrings, a single rope of coral beads, and a jewel in a gold setting at her breast. She wears a high-waisted black dress with short sleeves over a white underdress.

Lawrence's original shows Mrs Siddons standing, with her hand on a book. It is not certain that this copy is by J.R. Smith.

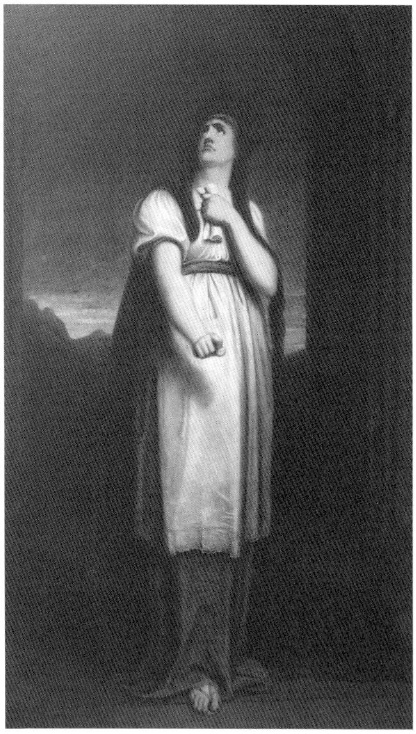

748
Called
SARAH SIDDONS
as Lady Macbeth in *Macbeth* by William Shakespeare

Richard Westall

Oil on canvas 229.9 x 138.5
INV: RW/CKA 434; Gift 262
PROV: Commissioned by John Boydell; Shakespeare Lottery 1804; William Tassie; Christie's 20 May 1805; Sir Squire Bancroft, by whom presented to the Garrick Club, 1899
EXH: 1800–5 London 'Shakspeare Gallery'
ENGR: James Parker for Boydell's *Shakespeare Gallery* pub. John & Josiah Boydell 4 June 1800, line
REL: Priv. Coll., Boston, 1968, watercolour study
LIT: Winifred H. Friedman, *Boydell's Shakespeare Gallery* (New York 1976); Fitzgerald, pp. 193–94

Lady Macbeth is shown in a room in Macbeth's castle at Inverness, having just read her letter from Macbeth (compare No. 742). She strikes a heroic attitude of determination, with clenched right fist, the letter clutched in her left hand. She wears blue sandals, a brown sleeveless dress under a white overskirt with a fringe below the knee, a gold belt, and a long dark brown cloak.

Westall probably never intended this painting to be a portrait of Sarah Siddons, but the inevitable comparison was made the moment the picture was exhibited. It is, however, quite clear that Siddons's performance of Lady Macbeth inspired the picture.

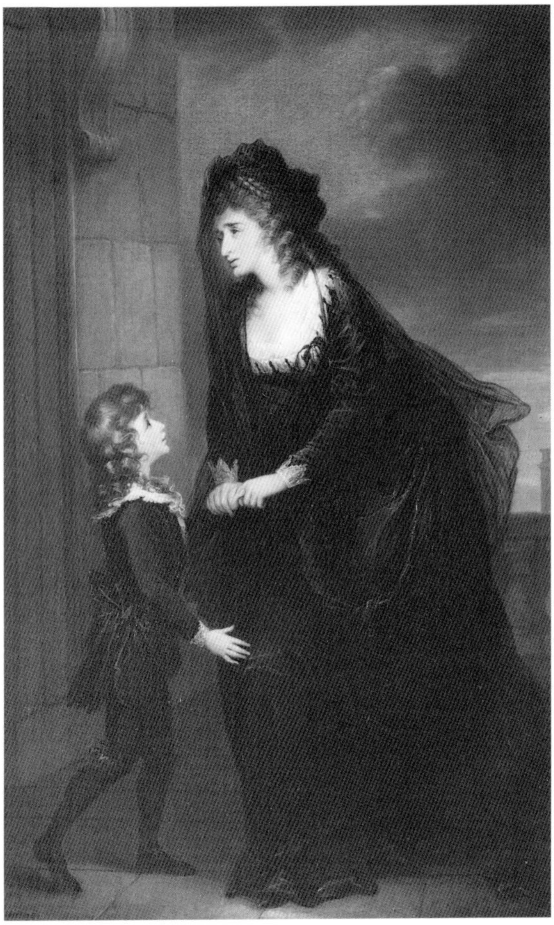

749*
SARAH SIDDONS as Isabella
and *HENRY SIDDONS* as the Child
in *Isabella or The Fatal Marriage*
by David Garrick,
altered from Thomas Southerne

William Hamilton

Oil on canvas 82.5 x 57.1
INSCR: 'W. Hamilton 1784' (black paint b.l.)
INV: CKA 638; Gift 589
PROV: The Rt. Hon. Lord Aberdare; Christie's 3 June 1932 (95); bt. Strauss for £6; F. J. Nettlefold, by whom presented 1940
ENGR: James Caldwell pub. W. Hamilton & J. Caldwell 1 June 1785, line 61.6 x 45.1; H.R. Cook for Oxberry's *New English Drama* pub. Simpkin & Marshall 1 September 1831, stipple 10.8 x 7.9 [half-length only, no child]
REL: Original missing, presumed destroyed, exh: R.A. 1785 (98); Private collection, London, oil on canvas 76 x 63 (bust only) dated 1783, ex. coll. Earl of Harcourt 1820; SNPG 1487, oil on canvas 68.3 x 52.9 (bust of boy) ex. coll. Dame Sarah Siddons Mair
LIT: Mrs C. Parsons, *The Incomparable Siddons* (1909), p. 60–61; William Whitley, *Artists and their Friends in England 1700–1799* (1928), 2: 62; C. Reginald Grundy, *A Catalogue of the Pictures and Drawings in the Collection of Frederick John Nettlefold* (1933–38), 2: 142; *The Connoisseur*, October 1938, p. 193 (illustrated in colour)

Isabella, dressed in mourning for her supposedly dead husband, wears a full-skirted black dress, and a black hat with ribbons and a veil. Her young son also wears black, with a lace collar and cuffs.

Garrick's adaptation of Southerne's 1694 tragedy was first performed at Drury Lane on 2 December 1757, with Mrs Cibber in the role of Isabella. Sarah Siddons returned to the London stage as Isabella at Drury Lane on 10 October 1782, an event that marked the beginning of her career as the greatest of all tragic actresses. Henry Siddons played his mother's son. Mrs Siddons acted Isabella frequently the following season.

For additional information on various versions of this picture, see BD 14: 57–58.

750
SARAH SIDDONS,
JOHN ANDREWS, WILLIAM BLANCHARD,
JOHANN BAPTISTE CRAMER,
WILLIAM AUGUSTUS CONWAY,
GEORGE HENRY HARLOW,
HENRY HARRIS, CHARLES KEMBLE,
JOHN PHILIP KEMBLE,
STEPHEN KEMBLE, CHARLES KNYVETT,
WILLIAM KNYVETT, JOHN PARKE,
FREDERICK REYNOLDS,
MR SHUTER, CATHERINE STEPHENS,
GEORGE YOUNG and *MISS TORR*
in the Court Scene for the Trial of Queen Katherine
in Act II, scene 4 of *Henry VIII*
by William Shakespeare

George Henry Harlow (after)

Oil on canvas 86.35 x 113
INV: CKA 180; Gift 427
PROV: Sir Squire Bancroft, by whom presented to the Garrick Club, 1924
REL: Original: Walter Morrison Collection, Sudeley Castle, Winchcombe, oil on panel 160 x 218.5, exh. 1817 R.A. (17), engr: George Clint pub. William Cribb 1 January 1819, mezzotint, and again on separate plate 2 March 1829, mezzotint; John Sartain for *Campbell's Foreign Semi-Monthly Magazine* 1 January 1844, two states;

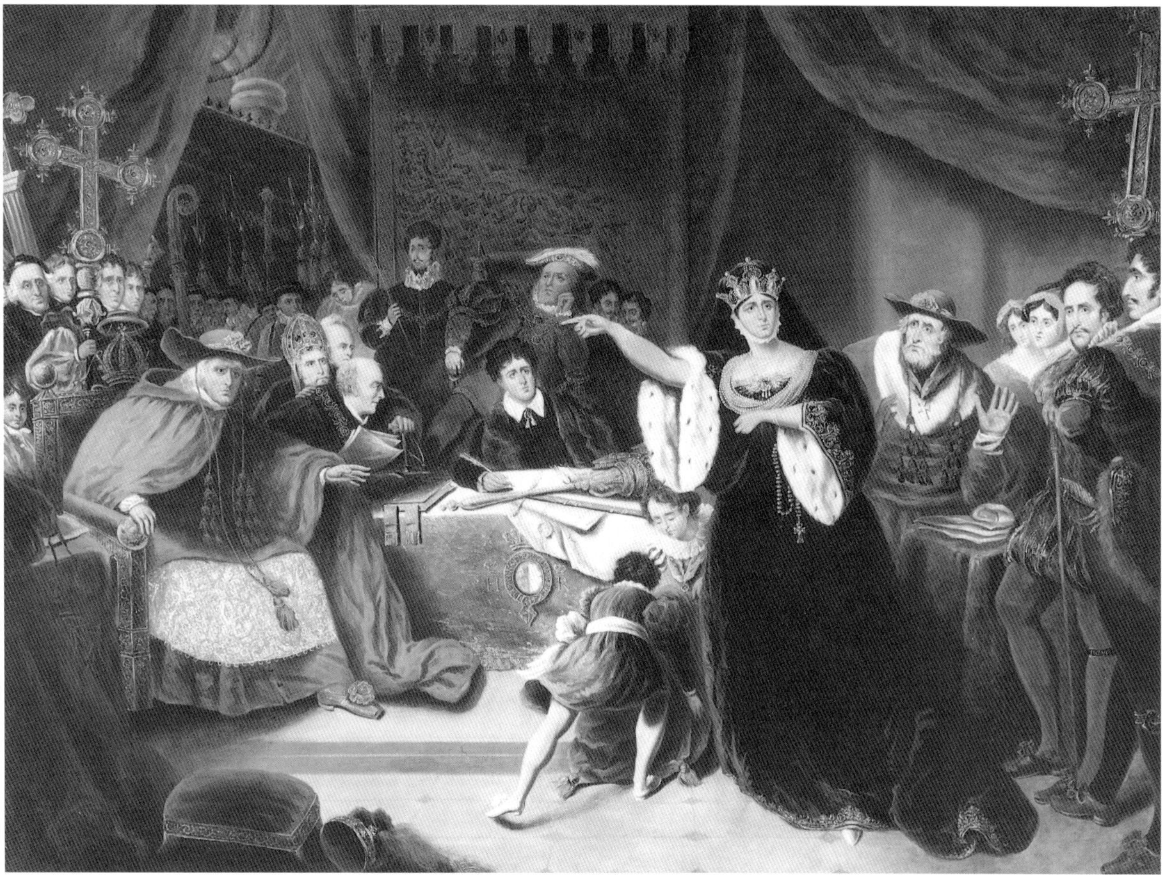

750 *Sarah Siddons and others in the Court Scene for the Trial of Queen Katherine in* Henry VIII

Private collection, oil on panel; Picture Gallery, Royal Shakespeare Theatre, Stratford-upon-Avon [The single figure of Mrs Siddons in this pose was painted by an anonymous artist (American school?), after Harlow, and is now in the Folger Library (see Pressly, *Folger*, 130)]

Queen Katherine is making her famous 'Siddonian' gesture across the canvas to the left. She wears a very full and rich black velvet dress, white slippers, copious pearls, and a jewelled spiked crown. Cardinal Wolsey (J.P. Kemble), responding to her gesture, wears a splendid cardinal's costume with a rich lace apron and gold slippers. King Henry (Stephen Kemble), seated on his throne in the centre, has a red and gold doublet and a hat with white plumes. Cromwell (Charles Kemble), sitting in front of him recording the proceedings of the trial, is dressed in black with a loose white collar. Cardinal Campeius (Charles Knyvett) on the right, behind the Queen, is dressed in cardinal red, with a large white fur collar.

There are numerous other figures, the most prominent being the two full-length male figures in green and gold doublet and hose on the right, both men wearing shoes with blue rosettes. The boy introduced in the centre foreground is dressed in blue, with white stockings and sash. He is bolstering a large red velvet cushion with gold tassels, helped by another boy in a red doublet slashed in white, with a gold chain and white ruff.

The splendid setting deploys the regal authority of the throne in the centre, under a large red canopy, and the authority of the church on either side, with a large cross suspended above each of the two cardinals. The table, on which lies the mace, a variety of papers, and a book with two blue bookmarks fringed with gold, is covered by a cloth of gold, embroidered with the royal insignia. There is a red-padded gilt stool bottom left and an overturned golden crown.

That Harlow's picture was one of the most enduring theatrical images of the 19th century is demonstrated by the fact that most subsequent productions of *Henry VIII* during that century used it as the basis for their arrangement of the trial scene. Even 70 years later, Ellen Terry based her interpretation of Queen Katherine on that of Sarah Siddons and her trial scene on Harlow's picture. Whenever photographed as Queen Katherine, she invariably adopted Sarah Siddons's pose as recorded by Harlow.

Harlow first saw Sarah Siddons act Queen Katherine in Kemble's revival at Covent Garden in 1806. It was one of her most admired interpretations in later life, and she played the role twice during her 1812 retirement season, and twice in 1816, for the benefit of her brother Charles Kemble and for the Theatrical Fund. Harlow had a particular attachment to the play, and one of his first finished exhibition drawings was of Sarah Siddons in the vision scene.

When Thomas Welsh, a music teacher, commissioned a small full-length of Sarah Siddons as Queen Katherine for 20 guineas, Harlow already had a stock of ideas for the subject, and probably planned a painting based on the earlier drawings of Sarah Siddons in the vision scene. However, it seems that when Welsh managed to get Sarah Siddons and her brothers Charles and Stephen Kemble to sit for Harlow, the artist's ideas grew. According to John Timbs's *Anecdote Biography* (of Thomas Lawrence), 1860, p. 248, John Philip Kemble did not sit. Welsh, alarmed at the development of his commission, felt obliged to pay Harlow 100 guineas, although the artist expected no more than the 20 agreed. Harlow hoped that the picture would establish his reputation when shown at the R.A. in 1817, and indeed, the *Trial Scene* was widely admired at that exhibition. The mezzotint by Clint was also a success, and supposedly made Clint's reputation.

The picture excited a peculiar furore concerning the category into which it should be put – Historical or Theatrical. Harlow saw his work as a development of the historical paintings of the Boydell Shakespeare Gallery, but as one using real portraits to make the historical event more immediate. However, despite the array of portraits of Harlow's friends and acquaintances, most contemporaries thought of it as an accurate representation of a stage performance, and therefore a theatrical picture.

No. 750 is a copy of Harlow's original painting; the artist was aware of the correct colours and presumably did not work from the engraving. The sale of Charles Kemble's wardrobe, Robins, 15 June 1837, included, as lot 17, 'Cromwell's dress, a beautiful black cloth suit' and as lot 94 'Cardinal Wolsey's dress, with hat and robe and pair of gold tissue shoes with rosettes'.

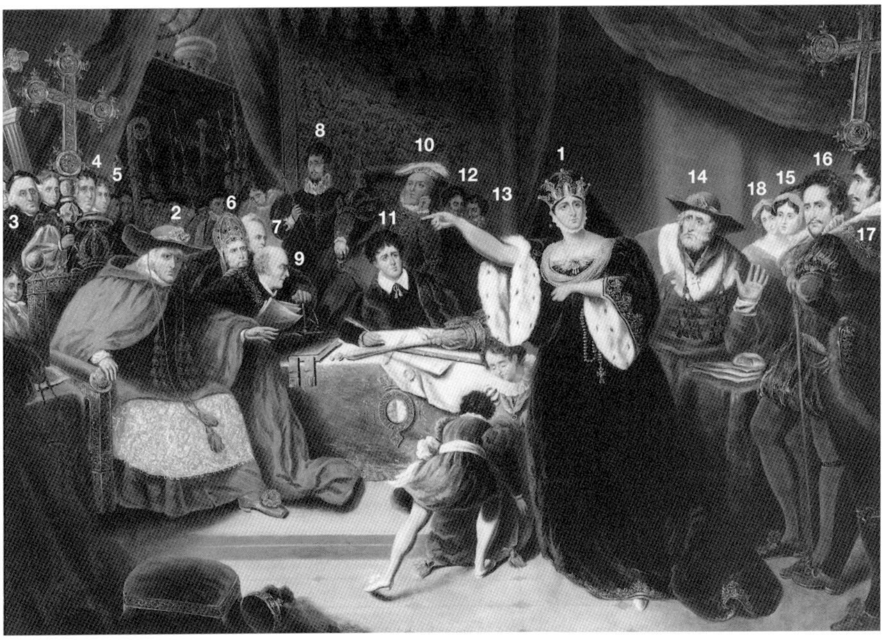

1. Mrs Siddons (1755–1831)
2. John Philip Kemble (1757–1823)
3. George Henry Harlow (1787–1819)
4. William Knyvett (1779–1856)
5. Johann Baptist Cramer (1771–1858)
6. William Blanchard (1769–1835)
7. John Parke (1745–1829)
8. John Andrews
9. —— Shuter
10. Stephen Kemble (1758–1822)
11. Charles Kemble (1775–1854)
12. T. Reynolds (Frederick Reynolds? 1764–1841)
13. Henry Harris
14. Charles Knyvett (1752–1822)
15. Catherine Stephens (1794–1882)
16. George Young (Charles Mayne Young? 1777–1856)
17. William Augustus Conway (1789–1828)
18. Miss Torr

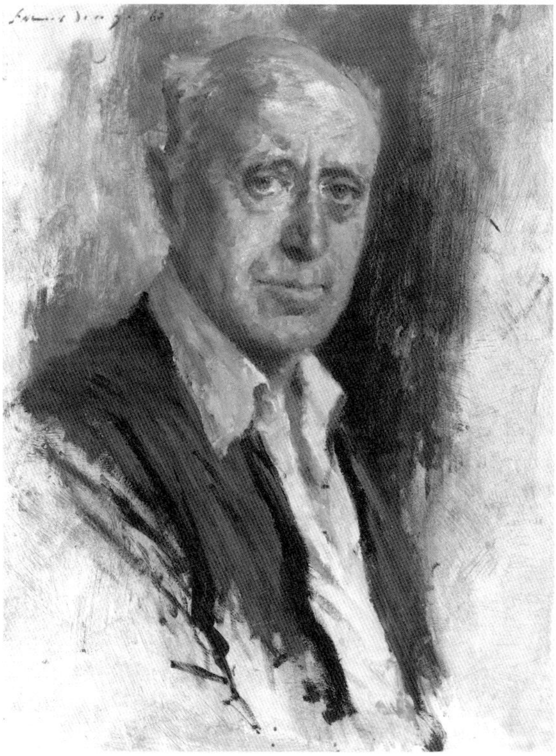

751

ALISTAIR SIM

Edward Seago

Oil on canvas 66 x 48.2

INSCR: 'Edward Seago' (brown paint t.l.)

INV: GCL 692; Gift 775

PROV: Presented by the artist, 1960

EXH: 1974 London

LIT: Jean Goodman, *Edward Seago – the other side of the canvas* (1978), p. 231

Sim, who was a member of the Garrick Club from 1943 until his death in 1976, wears a red pullover edged in brown, and an open-necked shirt.

752

SAMUEL SIMMONS

as Beau Mordecai in *Love à la Mode* by Charles Macklin

Samuel De Wilde

Oil on canvas 36.5 x 28

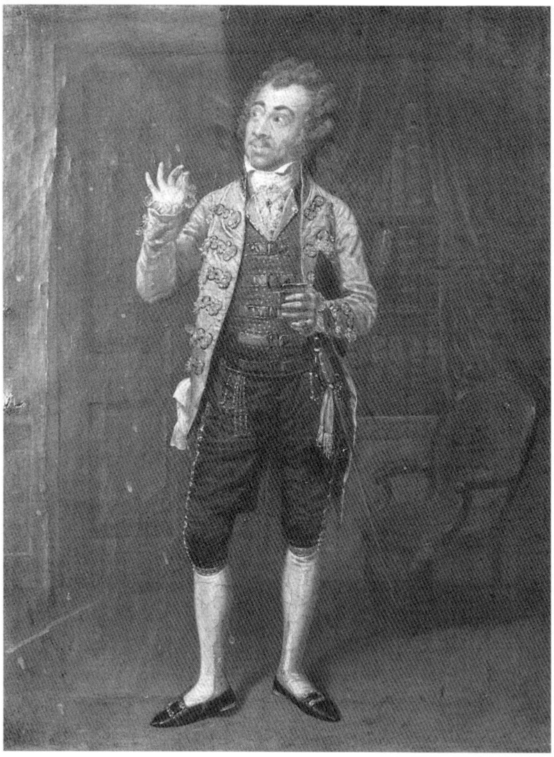

752 *Samuel Siddons as Beau Mordecai*

INV: RW/CKA 467; Gift 119

PROV: William A. Commerell, by whom presented to the Garrick Club, 1854

EXH: 1951 London (14)

ENGR: [An engraving by E. Scriven, after De Wilde, published as a plate to the *Theatrical Inquisitor*, is different from this portrait and No. 753]

REL: See No. 753

Beau Mordecai is a Jewish dandy with a sharp tongue. On his entrance in Act I he is praised by Miss Charlotte, who 'never saw anything better fancied than that suit of yours, Mr Mordecai'. The Beau is taking a pinch of snuff from his gold snuffbox, and has gold rings on both little fingers and a curly powdered wig with a black bow. He wears black shoes with paste buckles and pink heels, white stockings with scarlet clocks, green breeches with a silver stripe, and several fobs. His coat is of pink silk with silver braid fastenings and is worn over a silver-spotted lilac short waistcoat ornamented with five pale blue bands, each fastened with a square silver buckle; the waistcoat has green and yellow revers.

Macklin's farce was first performed at Drury Lane on 12 December 1759, with John Quick as Beau Mordecai. Simmons played the role for the first time at Covent Garden on 14 November 1800.

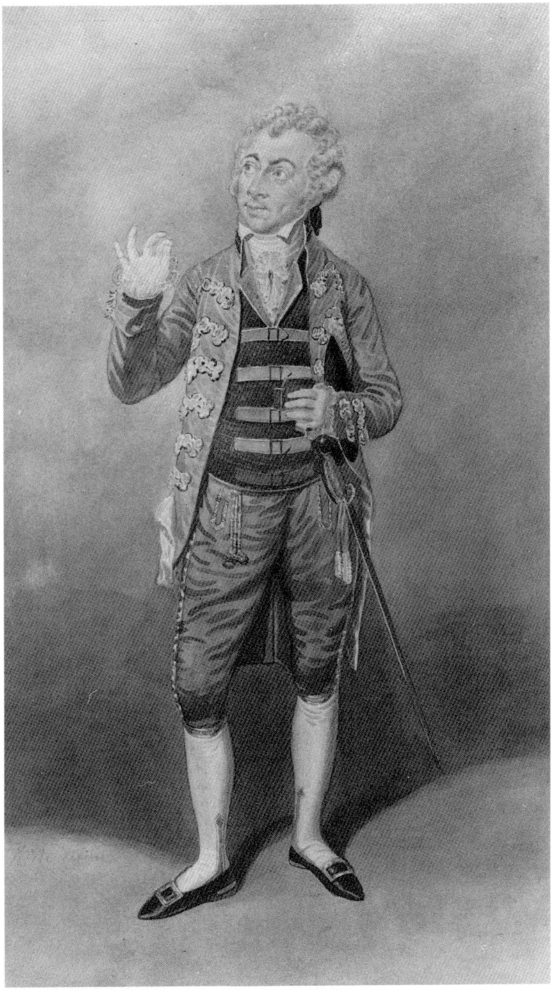

753
SAMUEL SIMMONS
as Beau Mordecai
in *Love à la Mode* by Charles Macklin

Samuel De Wilde

Pencil and watercolour on wove paper 35.5 x 22.8
INSCR: 'S. De Wilde delin' (pencil b.l.)
INV: RW 67? (unknown sitter and artist); CKA 67
PROV: Unknown
REL: See No. 752

Beau Mordecai's pose and costume are similar to No. 752, with a few minor differences: the purple waistcoat has yellow spots, and the belts are grey rather than blue. No. 753 is probably a repetition of No. 752, although it might easily have preceded the oil painting.

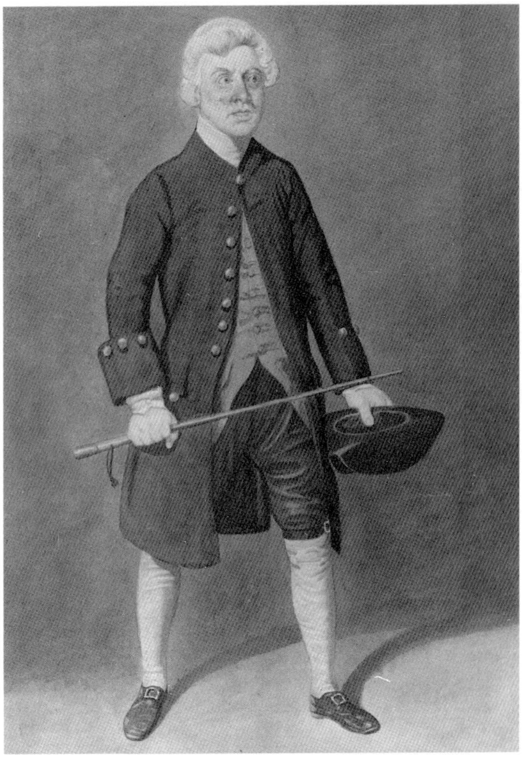

754
SAMUEL SIMMONS
as Jonathan Oldskirt in *Who Wants a Guinea?*
by George Colman the Younger

Samuel De Wilde

Pencil and watercolour on wove paper 36.2 x 24.8
INSCR: 'Mr Simmonds of Covent Garden, as Jonathan old Skirt, In Who Wants a Guinea.' (pen and brown ink on mount b.c.)
INV: (not in RW); CKA 47; Gift 84
PROV: Major-General Wood, by whom presented to the Garrick Club, 1842

Jonathan Oldskirt is shown on his first entrance, in Act II, scene I, 'A cross Road', where he has just emerged dishevelled from the London coach to 'Yorkshire, near the Coast'. He is a remnant-seller from the back of St Clements. There are several references in the play to the wig worn by Simmons, and to his small stature, which was, it seems, 'but five foot three'. His powdered wig is slightly askew; he holds a stick and a black tricorn hat and wears black breeches, a mulberry coat with large buttons, and a pink waistcoat.

The younger Colman's comedy was first performed at Covent Garden on 18 April 1805, with Simmons as the original Jonathan Oldskirt. There were 10 performances during the season; the seventh, on 30 April 1805, and the last, on 7 May 1805, were both by Royal Command.

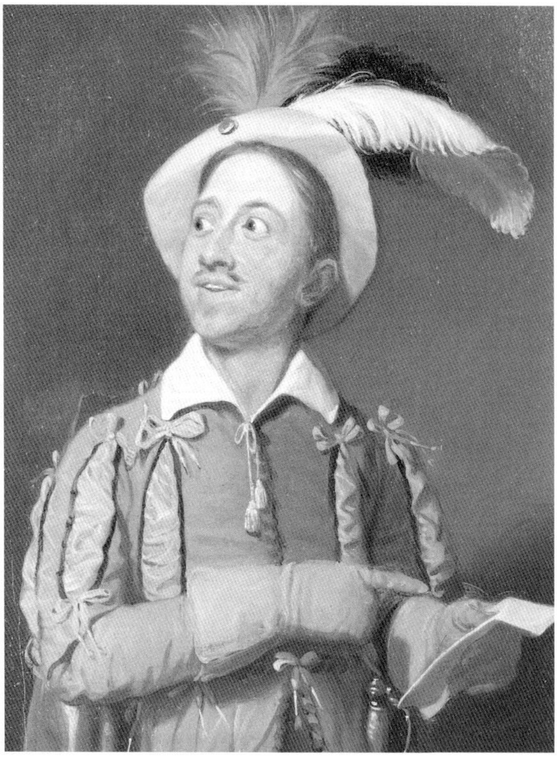

755
SAMUEL SIMMONS
as Master Matthew
in *Every Man in His Humour* by Ben Jonson

Samuel De Wilde

Oil on panel 23.5 x 19.5
INV: Mathews 31; RW/CKA 232
PROV: Charles Mathews
EXH: 1833 London (31)
REL: Earl of Leicester Holkham 108, black chalk and watercolour on panel 25.4 x 19.7, inscr: 'De Wilde / Delin 1802' (black chalk c.r.), exh: R.A. 1802 (670)

Half-length. Master Matthew is shown as he visits Captain Bobadil in Act I, scene 4. He gestures with his right forefinger to the poem held in his left hand that he will presently read to Bobadil. He wears a hat with a yellow brim, buff gauntlets, a lilac doublet slashed to reveal a yellow lining, and a cloak with a silver lining. The same costume is shown in De Wilde's watercolour, No. 756.

Simmons played Master Matthew in London for the first time at Covent Garden on 4 November 1798.

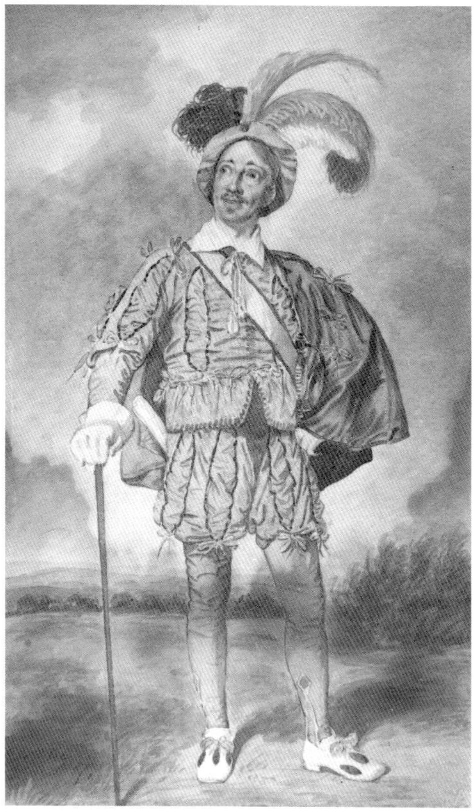

756
SAMUEL SIMMONS
as Master Matthew
in *Every Man in His Humour* by Ben Jonson

Samuel De Wilde

Pencil and watercolour on wove paper 37 x 23.5
INSCR: 'S De Wilde. / delin 1807.' (black chalk b.l., possibly over the original signature)
INV: Mathews 199; RW/CKA 69B
PROV: Charles Mathews
EXH: 1833 London (199)

According to Mathews, Master Matthew is shown on his first entrance in Act I, scene 3, greeting Cob the water-bearer in front of his house. The landscape setting does not match the stage scene, 'The Street before Cob's House', but the rolled-up paper in Matthew's right pocket is called for in the next scene, when he 'pulls out a paper' and reads a poem to Captain Bobadil (see No. 755). Master Matthew has a small fair moustache and a tiny goatee. His yellow hat is adorned with flamboyant multi-coloured plumes. His doublet and hose are pale lilac, slashed to reveal a yellow lining and with yellow laces. He has a short pale brown cloak, blue stockings with white clocks, and white shoes, slashed in blue and with yellow laces.

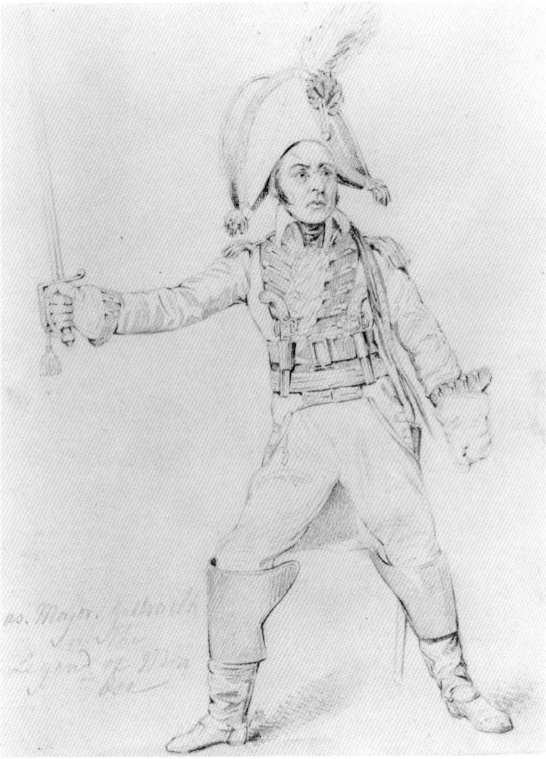

757
SAMUEL SIMMONS
as Baron Munchausen
in *Harlequin Munchausen*
or The Fountain of Love
by Charles Farley

Samuel De Wilde (after?)

Pencil on wove paper 18.5 x 14.5
INSCR: 'as Major Galbraith / in the / Legend of Mon / trose' (pencil b.c. CM?)
INV: Not listed
PROV: Charles Mathews (Print collection Vol. v f. 37)
ENGR: R. Cooper for Daniel Terry's *British Theatrical Gallery* pub. H. Berthoud Jnr, 16 September 1822, line 19.5 x 14.5

The Baron has an amusing pantomime costume, with a half-moon hat with a band around the edge, tassels at the points, and a cockade with a plume over the left eye. There is a tassel on the hilt of the sword he holds to the left. He wears high boots with spurs, tight breeches, and a cutaway military jacket with darker panels down the front and at the wrists. Two pistols are pushed into one of his belts.

No. 757 is either a sketch for, or more probably a tracing after, De Wilde's portrait of Simmons as Baron Munchausen which was engraved by R. Cooper for Terry's *Theatrical Gallery*. Farley's pantomime was first performed at Covent Garden on 26 December 1818 and played a total of 42 times until 1 March 1819. Simmons was the original Baron Munchausen.

The irrelevant inscription by Mathews refers to Thomas John Dibdin's play *Montrose*, based on the Scott novel *The Legend of Montrose* given at the Surrey Theatre on 5 June 1819. Captain Dugald Dalgetty is probably the character Mathews had in mind; Major Galbraith is a character in *Rob Roy MacGregor* (see No. 774).

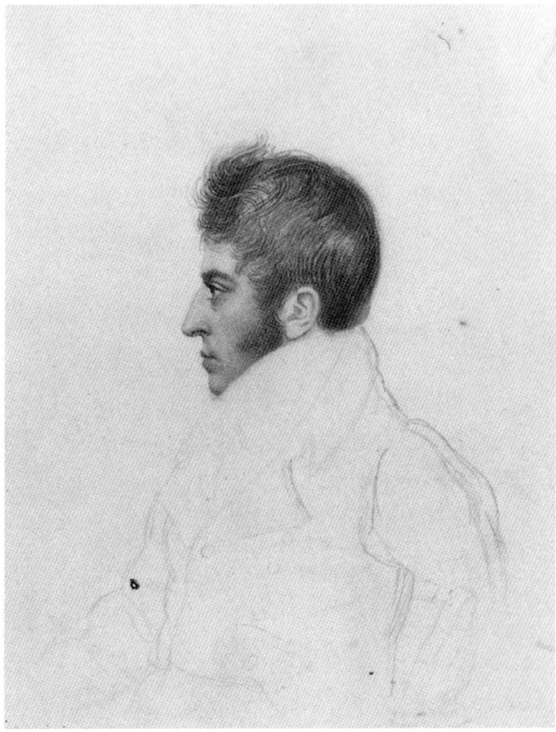

758
SAMUEL SIMMONS

John Turmeau

Pencil and watercolour on wove paper 14.6 x 11.7
INSCR: 'Turmeau Fecit' (pen and brown ink on mount b.l. CM); 'Mr Simmons.' (pen and brown ink on mount b.c. CM)
INV: RW 561B (artist unknown); CKA 561B
PROV: Charles Mathews (not in catalogue)

Simmons is shown in profile to the left, half-length, in a coat with a high stock. Only the head is coloured. See No. 759.

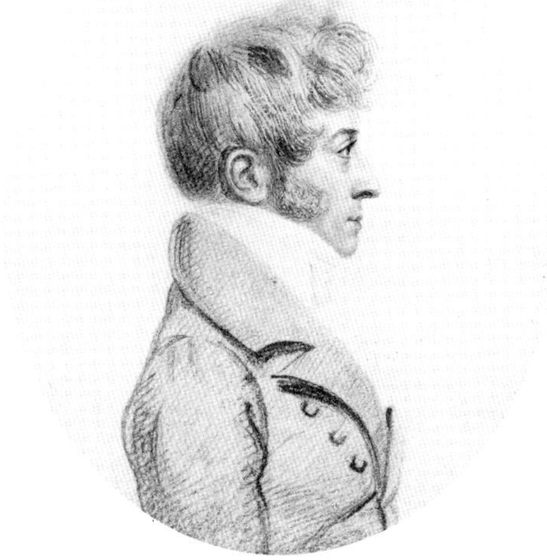

759
SAMUEL SIMMONS

John Turmeau

Pencil and watercolour on wove paper 15.2 x 12 (oval)
INSCR: 'Turmeau Fecit' (pen and brown ink on mount b.l. CM); 'Mr Simmons.' (pen and brown ink on mount b.c. CM)
INV: Mathews 346; RW 545 (artist unknown); CKA 545
PROV: Charles Mathews
EXH: 1833 London (346)

Simmons's other profile view, to the right, with his hair similarly brushed forward. He wears a pale blue coat, and a high white stock. See No. 758.

From the time of his début on 4 November 1783, at the age of 10, when he played the Boy in *The Poor Soldier*, until his death in 1819, Simmons passed almost his entire career at Covent Garden, acting dozens of supporting characters. He specialised in simpletons and coxcombs. Hazlitt called him 'one of the most correct, pointed, *naive*, and whimsical comic actors, we have for a long time had...'.

760
JOHN SINCLAIR
as Apollo in *Midas* by Kane O'Hara

Samuel De Wilde

Pencil and watercolour on wove paper 37 x 23.5
INSCR: 'S De Wilde delin. / 1812.' (pencil b.l.)
INV: Mathews 237; RW/CKA 46F
PROV: Charles Mathews
EXH: 1833 London (237)
ENGR: Similar to: Middlemist for the *Theatrical Inquisitor* pub. C. Chapple 1814, stipple 16.2 x 11.1 (r.h. to waist, hat in l.h. extended to r.)

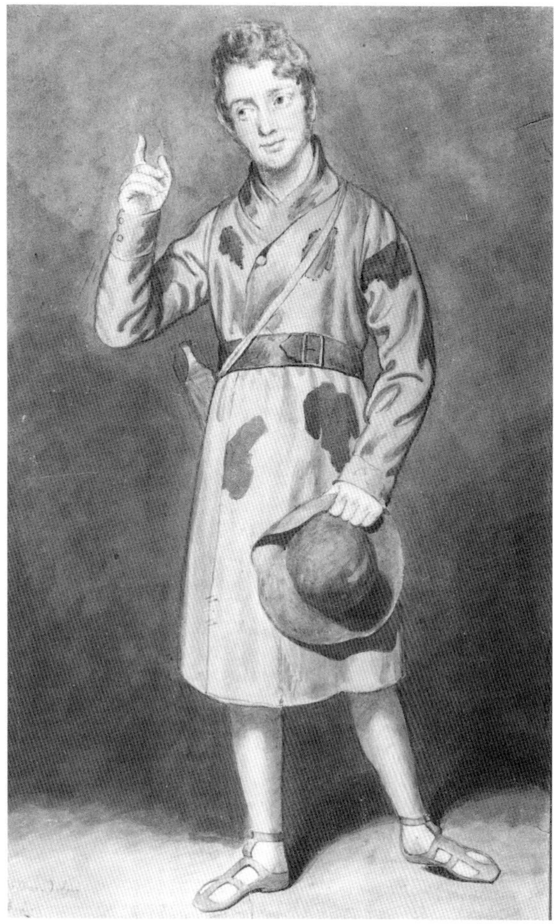

760 *John Sinclair*

Apollo points up to Olympus, whence he has just been thrown. His shepherd's disguise consists of a ginger wig brushed up on top of his head, brown sandals, and a long white tunic with dark brown patches, perhaps to indicate that the garment is made of animal skins. His lyre, mostly hidden, is suspended from a blue band. He has a brown belt with a gold buckle, and in his left hand he holds a reddish soft hat.

Kane O'Hara's two-act burletta was first perfomed at the Crow Street Theatre, Dublin, on 22 January 1762. The first London performance was at Covent Garden on 22 February 1764, with George Mattocks as Apollo. There was a revival of the piece at Covent Garden on 17 September 1812, with a cast that included Tinney as Jupiter, Emery as Pan, Master Wilson as Cupid, Liston as Midas, Fawcett as Sileno and Mrs Stirling as Daphne, as well as Sinclair as Apollo. There were 54 performances that season, including Sinclair's benefit on 30 June 1813. In Act 1, Sinclair sang a 'favourite air of "Pray Goody"' in the character of Apollo; it is this moment that Mathews considered to be represented here.

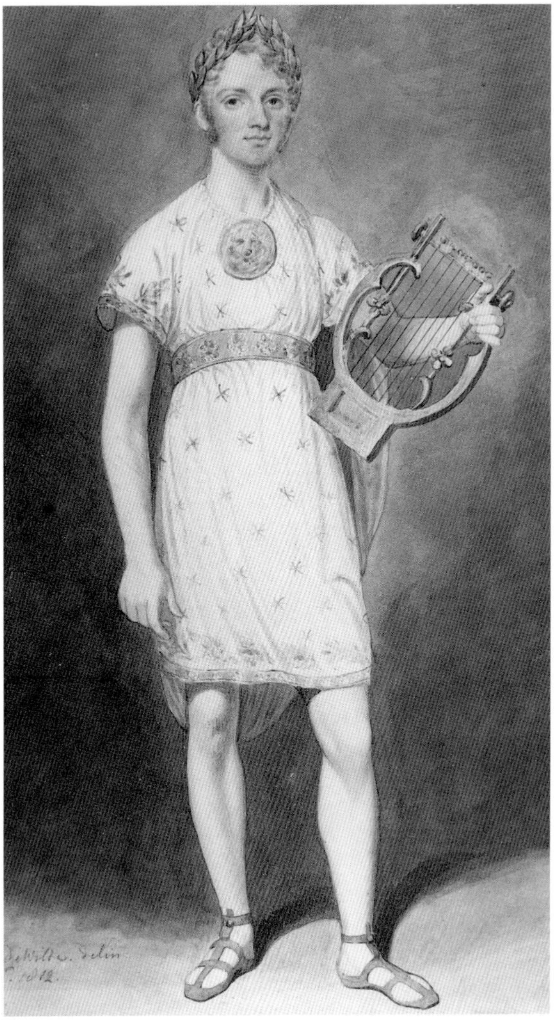

761
JOHN SINCLAIR
as Apollo
in *Midas* by Kane O'Hara

Samuel De Wilde

Pencil and watercolour on wove paper 37 x 23.5
INSCR: 'S De Wilde delin / Octr. 1812.' (pencil b.l.)
INV: Mathews 236; RW/CKA 63C
PROV: Charles Mathews
EXH: 1833 London (236); 1975 London (145)

Here Apollo appears in his second-act glory in god-like apparel – a short white tunic decorated with gold stars, with a blue and gold hem. He has an encrusted gold belt and a large, gold sun medallion round his neck. See No. 760.

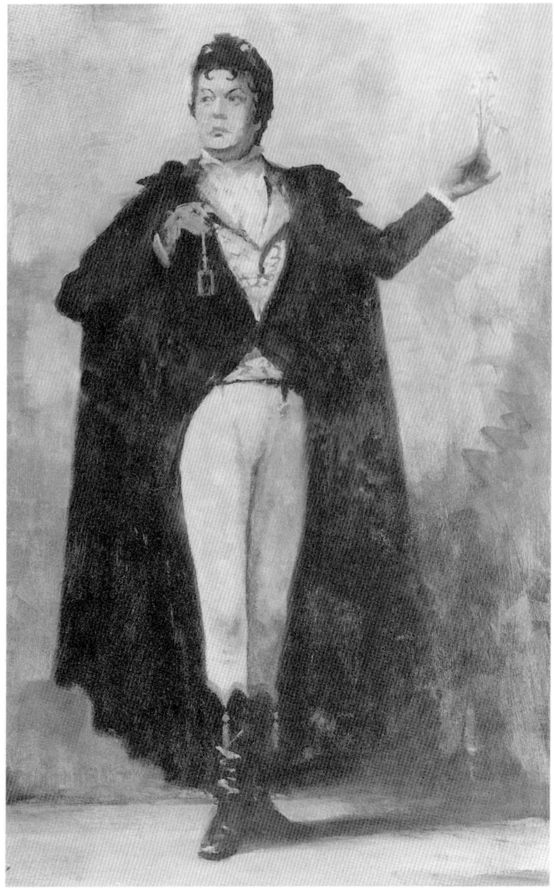

762
DONALD SINDEN
as Sir Harcourt Courtley
in *London Assurance* by Dion Boucicault

Edward Seago

Oil on canvas 76.5 x 63.5
INSCR: 'Edward Seago' (brown paint b.l.)
INV: GCL 723; Gift 853
PROV: Presented by the artist, 1973
EXH: 1974 London (28)

Sir Harcourt Courtley is shown at his entry in Act II: 'Cool, am I the thing?' He wears a 'Prinny' dandified wig, with brown hair curled on the forehead and at the sides. A rectangular spy-glass dangles from his right hand and he holds up a small bunch of white daisies in his upraised left hand. His pose is somewhat balletic. His fashionable dress consists of black boots with curved tops and tassels, white trousers, a purple coat edged in black, a creamy waistcoat decorated in brown with yellow lapels, a high white stock, and a long dark cloak.

Boucicault's comedy was first performed at Covent Garden on 4 March 1841, with William Farren as Sir

Harcourt Courtley. The Royal Shakespeare Company revival, directed by Ronald Eyre, opened at the Aldwych on 23 June 1970, with Donald Sinden as Sir Harcourt Courtley, Judi Dench as Grace Harkaway, Michael Williams as Charles Courtley, Barrie Ingham as Dazzle and Elizabeth Spriggs as Lady Gay Spanker. The settings were by Alan Tagg, the costumes by David Walker and the music by Guy Woolfenden. The production transferred to the New Theatre (Albery) on 5 April 1972 and ran for 390 performances.

Donald Sinden, CBE, became a member of the Garrick Club in 1960. See also No. 965.

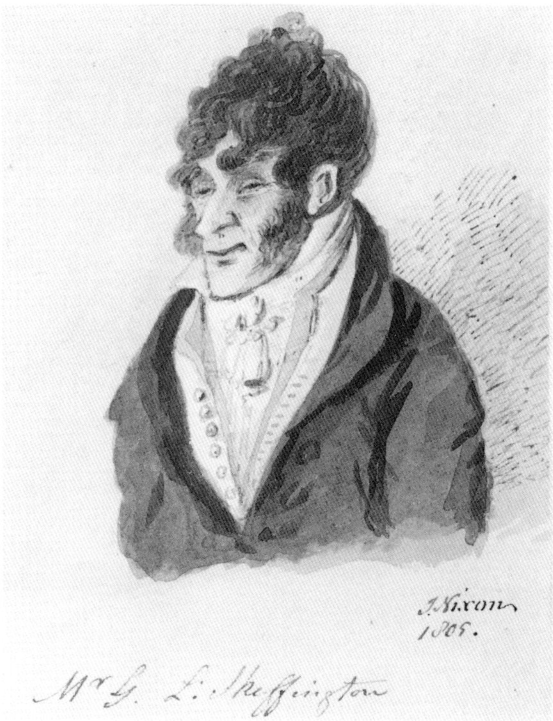

763

SIR LUMLEY ST GEORGE SKEFFINGTON

John Nixon

Pencil, pen and black ink and watercolour
on wove paper 11.8 x 9.6
INSCR: 'J. Nixon / 1805' (pen and black ink b.r.);
'Mr G.L. Skeffington' (pen and brown ink b.c.)
INV: Not listed
PROV: John Nixon, *Dramatic Annals*, 2: 490

Half-length, half to left. Skeffington wears a brown jacket and two waistcoats, a white one over a pink one. Skeffington was the amateur author of a 'New Legendary Melo-Drame', *The Sleeping Beauty in the Wood*, which was given at Drury Lane on 6 December 1805.

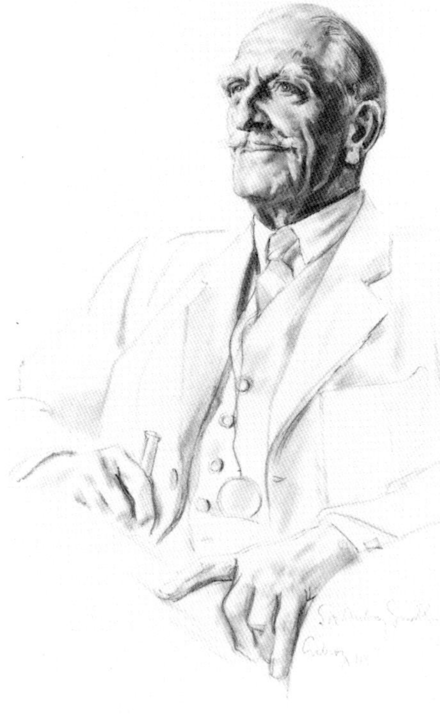

764

SIR C. AUBREY SMITH

John Gilroy

Pencil, grey wash and watercolour
on wove paper 35.5 x 28
INSCR: 'Sir Aubrey Smith / Gilroy 48'' (pencil b.r.)
INV: GCL 712; Gift 811
PROV: Presented by the artist, 1966

Sir Aubrey has a monocle, and holds a pipe in his right hand. He wears a badly-cut coat, a waistcoat with large buttons, a white shirt, and, possibly, a Garrick Club tie. He became a member in 1906.

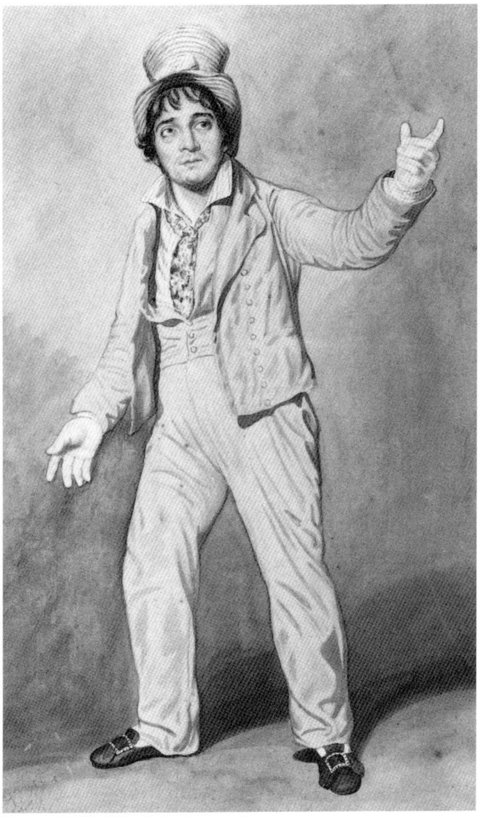

765
GEORGE SMITH
as Peter in *Up All Night*
by Samuel James Arnold

Samuel De Wilde

Pencil and watercolour on wove paper 37 x 23.5
INSCR: 'S De Wilde delin / J 1810.' (pencil b.l.)
INV: Mathews 291 (no character); RW/CKA 65F
PROV: Charles Mathews
EXH: 1833 London (291); 1975 London (154)
ENGR: Similar to: H.R. Cook for the *Theatrical Inquisitor* pub. W. Oxberry 1 October 1812, stipple 14.9 x 9.8 (to front, legs apart, r.h. to waist, money in open r.h. to r., looking to r.); W. Symms for *The Drama* pub. T. & I. Elvey 1 June 1823, stipple and line (bust only)
REL: 1811 R.A. (55), oil on canvas

Peter, a blunt sailor, has one song in *Up All Night*. In Act II he sings of a British naval victory over the French: 'On board the Termagent we sail'd / Mann'd by a gallant crew.' His raised forefinger may signify the lines 'The sailor from aloft, with glee / Shouts out – a sail! – a sail!'. The engraving in the *Theatrical Inquisitor* does not relate to the song.

Peter is unshaven, his dark hair unkempt beneath a striped yellow straw hat with a bow above its curled brim. He wears loose-fitting trousers and waistcoat of faded pink, a jacket with a limp collar, a white shirt with green stripes, and a green and white neckerchief.

Arnold's comic opera, with music by M.P. King, was first performed at the Lyceum on 26 June 1809, with George Smith as Peter. The *Monthly Mirror* of July 1809 reported that 'his voice is little, but pretty, and capable of improvement; his acting is incapable of deterioration'.

The R.A. exhibit is likely to have been a version of the Garrick Club picture, but in oil on canvas. De Wilde produced another drawing of Smith as a jolly tar, in the role of Robin in *No Song, No Supper*, which was engraved by R. Cooper for Terry's *Theatrical Gallery*, published by H. Berthoud Jnr on 24 June 1822.

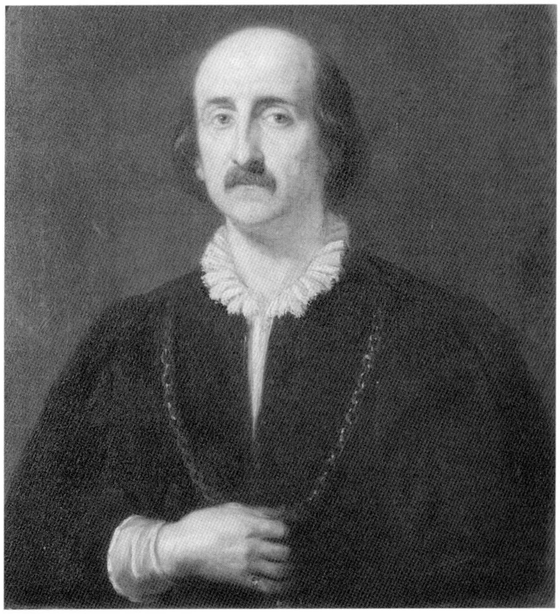

766
RICHARD SMITH
as Don Quixote
in *Don Quixote* by George Almar

Edward Matthew Ward

Oil on canvas 35 x 29.5
INV: RW/CKA 85; Gift 260
PROV: T.F. Dillon Croker, by whom presented to the Garrick Club, 1898
EXH: 1834 R.A. (15) 'Portrait of Mr O. Smith, comedian, in the character of Don Quixote'

Half-length. Smith has been given a Shakespearean aspect, with his bald pate, ruff and black doublet.

This picture may be Ward's earliest exhibited work.

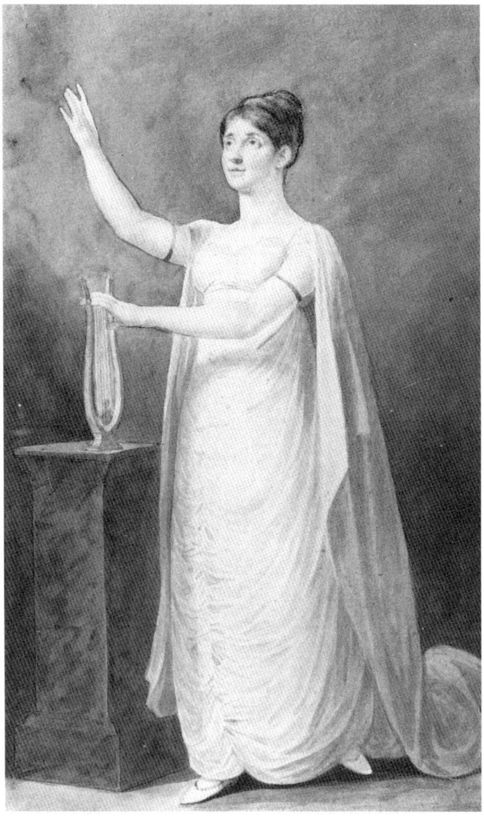

767
SARAH SMITH
reciting Collins's 'Ode to the Passions'

Samuel De Wilde

Pencil and watercolour on wove paper 37 x 23.5
INV: Mathews 196; RW/CKA 60E
PROV: Charles Mathews
EXH: 1833 London (196)

Mrs Smith wears a classically-inspired costume consisting of gold-edged pink slippers and a short-sleeved dress with several layers of white gauze. She has gold bracelets round her upper arms.

Mrs Smith's benefit at Covent Garden on 9 May 1806 included her recital of William Collins's 'Ode to the Passions', with instrumental accompaniment.

768
MARIA SMITH
as Sylvia in *Cymon* by David Garrick

Thomas Parkinson

Oil on canvas 33 x 28
INV: Mathews 294 (artist unknown);
RW 459 (by De Wilde); CKA 459 (artist unknown)

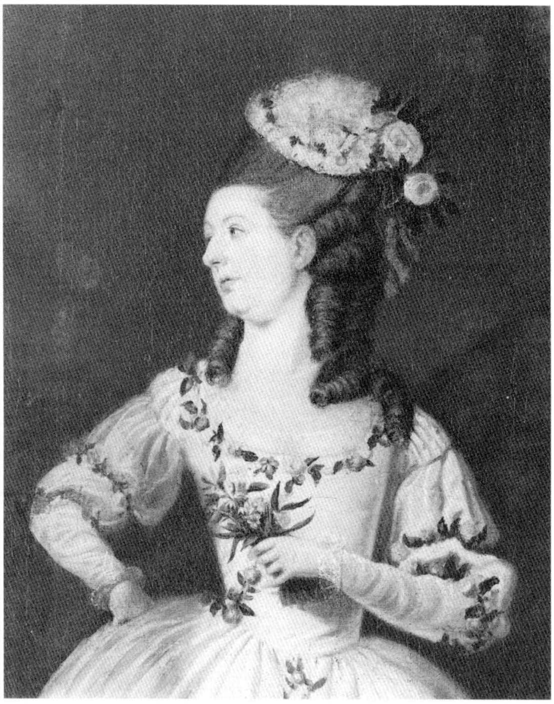

768 *Maria Smith as Sylvia*

PROV: Charles Mathews
EXH: 1775 R.A. (217) 'A scene in Cymon, Act III, scene 1; small whole lengths'; 1833 London (294); 1983 Buxton (21)

Sylvia leaves Dorcas's cottage with Linco to see Dorus, the magistrate. She has been wrongly accused by a jealous shepherdess of philandering with Damon. Her right hand is in the left arm of the truncated figure of Linco (see below). In her left hand she holds a bunch of blue, orange and yellow flowers. Her long-sleeved dress is panniered, flounced from elbow to shoulder, and embroidered with flowers around the neckline and sleeves and up the bodice.

Garrick's dramatic opera, with music by Michael Arne, was first performed at Drury Lane on 2 January 1767, with Mrs Arne playing Sylvia. Mrs Smith made her first appearance on the stage as Sylvia at Drury Lane on 20 October 1772. The performance closest to the date of Parkinson's picture was at Drury Lane on 24 May 1773, and the one before that, on 20 April 1773, was given as part of Mrs Smith's benefit.

When the painting was cleaned in 1987, part of a male figure appeared to the left of Mrs Smith, making it clear that the picture had been cut down and was originally a scene. The figure is that of Linco, who wears a grey doublet with flounced sleeves and a large pink bow at his waist. The role of Linco was performed by Joseph Vernon on both 20 April and 24 May 1773.

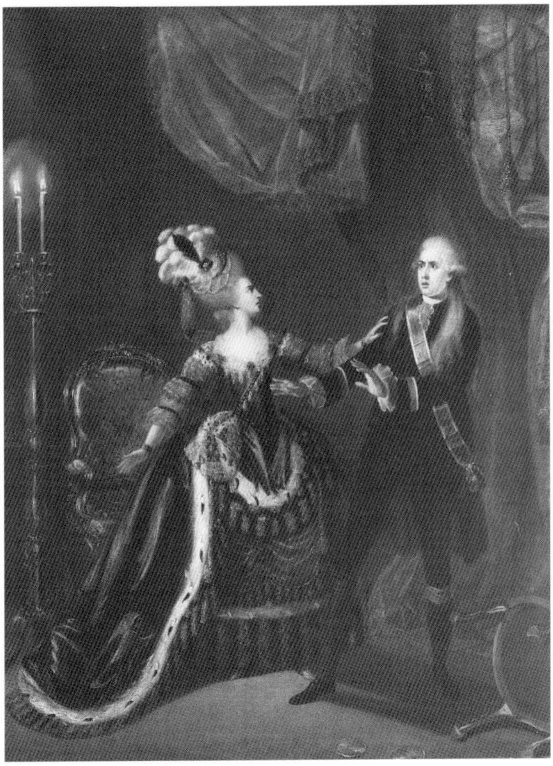

769

WILLIAM SMITH as Hamlet and
ELIZABETH HOPKINS as Gertrude
in *Hamlet*
by William Shakespeare

James Roberts

Oil on canvas 127 x 101
INV: Mathews 126 (Barry as Hamlet,
Mrs Barry as the Queen. Artist unknown);
RW 439 (Barry as Hamlet, Mrs Elmy as the Queen);
CKA 439 (Spranger Barry as Hamlet
and his wife as the Queen)
PROV: Thomas Harris; Harris sale, Robins 12 July 1819 (56)
('A scene in Hamlet, with Hamlet, the Queen and
the Ghost, painted in the costume of the day');
Charles Mathews
EXH: 1833 London (126); 1947 London (31);
1951 London (34)
LIT: Fitzgerald, p.165 (as by Zoffany)

Gertrude stands on the left. On her pile of powdered hair is a gold cap with loops of pearls and a white drapery with horizontal gold bands, innumerable white plumes and a single black plume – perhaps a reminder of Hamlet's father, her dead first husband. She wears gold slippers and a very elaborate full-panniered dress with a blue skirt with horizontal bands of gold fringe. The blue velvet overskirt is edged in ermine with a blue and gold fringe. The narrow bodice has a blue and gold band round the waist, and a blue and gold band from the left shoulder supports a gauze bag. The white sleeves are heavily embroidered in gold and have blue bands and lace cuffs. Hamlet, gesturing dramatically to the invisible ghost, is dressed in his mourning black, with his left stocking undone at the knee.

One of the two carved and gilt chairs, upholstered in red with a floral design, is overturned, showing that Betterton's stage business was still being followed in the late 1770s. (The overturned chair is shown in the illustration to the closet scene in the Rowe edition of Shakespeare of 1709, in which Betterton is depicted as Hamlet.) The miniatures of Hamlet's father and Claudius, called for earlier in the text, are on the floor. To the right hang red curtains with a red and gold fringe.

William Smith played Hamlet in London for the first time at Covent Garden on 2 January 1769, with Mrs Ward as Gertrude. When Smith moved to Drury Lane in 1774–75, he acted Hamlet on 4 October 1774, with Mrs Hopkins as Gertrude. At Drury Lane Hamlet was usually Garrick's role until his last performance of the play on 30 May 1776, but Smith again played the part with Mrs Hopkins as Gertrude on 3 October 1775. After Garrick's retirement, Smith acted Hamlet on 23 October and 30 December 1776 and on 1 January 1777, each time with Mrs Hopkins as Gertrude. On 3 February 1777 he was replaced by John Henderson as the Drury Lane Hamlet.

The picture has been called Spranger Barry and Mrs Barry (or Mrs Elmy) in *Hamlet*, but Barry did not play Hamlet in the late 1770s, nor did his wife play Gertrude. Stylistically Roberts's picture is similar in date to his portrait of Jane Pope as Mrs Page (No. 685), which was shown at the Royal Academy in 1778.

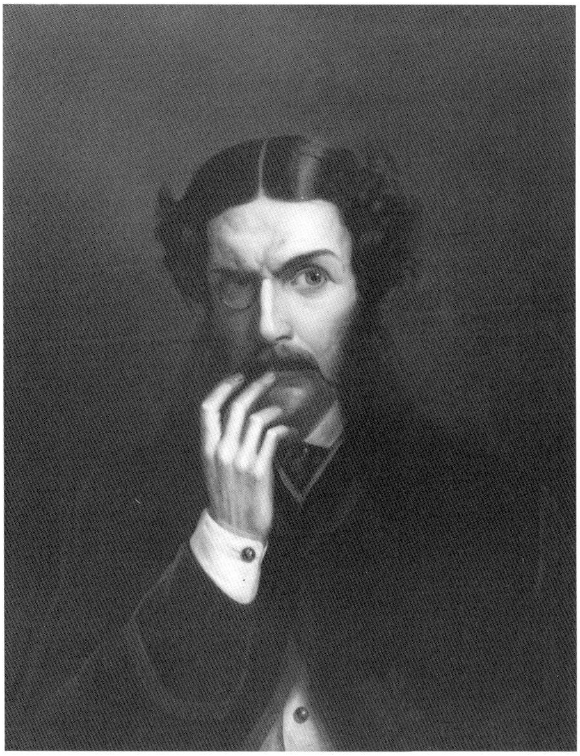

770
EDWARD SOTHERN
as Lord Dundreary
in *Our American Cousin*
by Tom Taylor

G.E. Tuson

Oil on canvas 65.5 x 54.5
INSCR: 'G.E. Tuson, 1862'
INV: RW/CKA 77; Gift 214
PROV: Sir Squire Bancroft, by whom presented to the Garrick Club, 1888

Lord Dundreary holds his right hand to his mouth and wears a dark jacket, light waistcoat, white shirt and dark tie.

Taylor's comic drama was first performed in London at the Haymarket on 11 November 1861, with Sothern as Lord Dundreary. It had been given previously in New York at Laura Keene's Theatre, on 18 October 1858.

Sothern, who became a member of the Garrick Club in 1864, was best known in his time in this role. Though he possessed a somewhat eccentric talent, he enjoyed success in America, especially in New York and Boston. In London he set a style with his characteristic long side-whiskers, which became popularly known as 'dundrearies'.

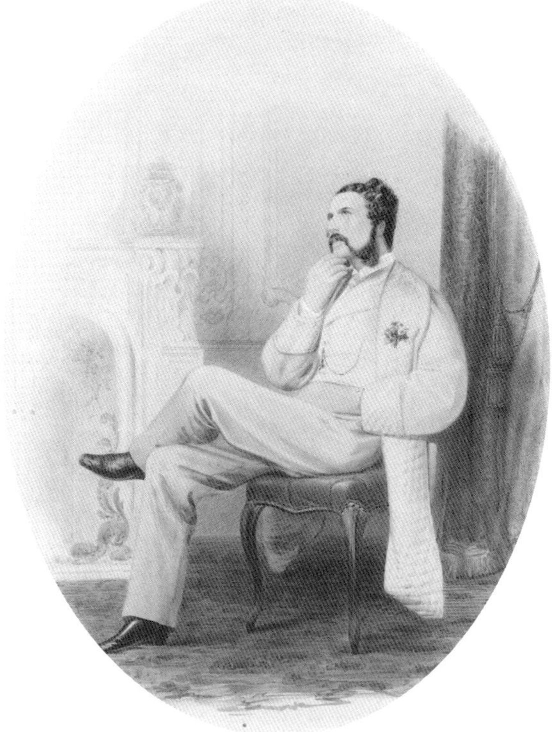

771
EDWARD SOTHERN
as Lord Dundreary
in *Our American Cousin*
by Tom Taylor

Unknown Artist

Pen and brown ink with watercolour on wove paper 45.7 x 30.5 (oval)
INSCR: 'Ward and Co' (pen and brown ink b.l.)
INV: RW 141; omitted by CKA who listed it as a photograph in his appendix
PROV: Unknown

Lord Dundreary sports his whiskers and a monocle and wears grey trousers, a cream smoking jacket with long quilted revers, cuffs and lining, a white waistcoat, and a pink tie. The chair is upholstered in blue. The Victorian interior includes a carved mantel with a Chinese pot on it, blue drapery with tassels and gold decoration, and a green-blue carpet with a yellow and red pattern.

The picture is taken from a photograph. See also No. 770.

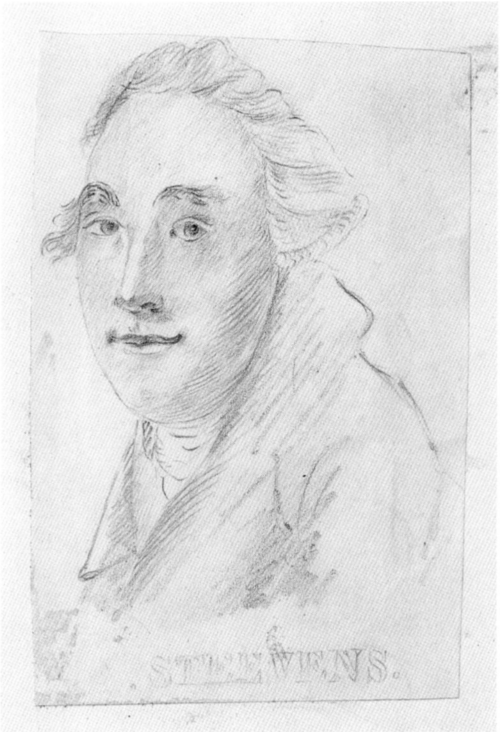

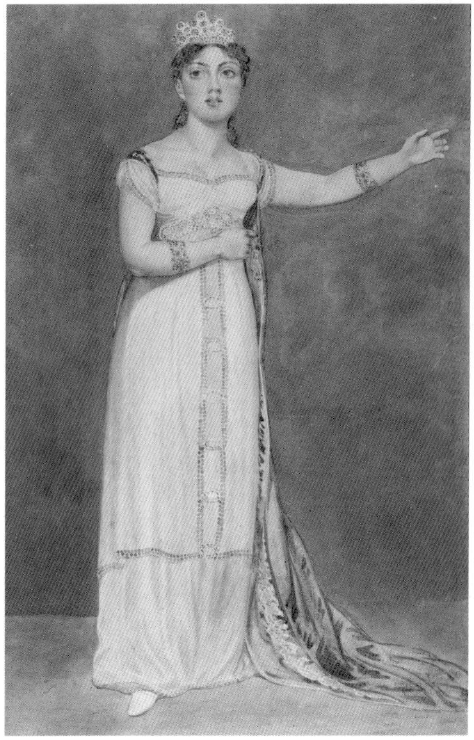

773 *Catherine Stephens as Mandane*

772
GEORGE STEEVENS

Johan Zoffany (after, by Harding?)

Pencil on roughly cut wove paper 11.6 x 8.3
INSCR: 'STEEVENS' (open-letter caps, pencil b.c.)
INV: Not listed
PROV: Charles Mathews (Print Collection Vol. II f. 63)
ENGR: W. Evans pub. S. Harding 1800, stipple 14.9 x 11.4

The sitter, in a brushed-back wig, wears a jacket with a broad collar.

This copy may have been made by Sylvester Harding in 1800. Zoffany's original portrait was produced about 1780; its present location is unknown.

773
CATHERINE STEPHENS
as Mandane in *Artaxerxes*
by Dr Thomas Augustine Arne

Samuel De Wilde

Pencil and watercolour on wove paper 37 x 23.5
INSCR: 'S De Wilde delin / Nov 14 1813' (pencil b.r.)
INV: Mathews 238; RW/CKA 65D
PROV: Charles Mathews
EXH: 1833 London (238); 1975 London (152)
ENGR: Freeman for the *Theatrical Inquisitor*
pub. C. Chapple 1 December 1813, stipple 15.9 x 10.5

Mandane enters in Act II, scene 4, to announce that her lover, Arbaces, has defeated an uprising led by Rimenes and saved the life and throne of her brother Artaxerxes, the King of Persia. She sings of Arbaces's valour with the air 'The soldier tired of war's alarms'. The Duncombe edition of the play (*c.*1835) gives a cast list that includes Miss Stephens as Mandane and Mme Vestris as Artaxerxes. Mandane's costume is described as 'a superb long train satin robe, embroidered; body of silver cloth; loose trousers; silver cloth slippers; elegant turban, with superb feathers – the whole dress elegantly and richly ornamented with jewels and &c.'. The costume in De Wilde's drawing is no less grandiose, and is crowned by a tiara with yellow and green stones in a silver setting. Mandane has filigree bracelets in silver and green around her arms and wears white slippers, a short-sleeved dress edged in sequins around the hem, an overskirt to below the knee, profusely decorated with sequins, and a long red velvet cloak with the edges embroidered in silver.

The first performance of Arne's version of Metastasio's *Artaxerxes* was at Drury Lane on 2 February 1762, with Miss Brent in the role of Mandane, John Beard as Artabanes, Tenducci as Arbanes, Mattocks as Rimenes and Niccolo Peretti as Artaxerxes. Catherine Stephens made her first appearance on the stage as Mandane, at Covent Garden on 23 September 1813.

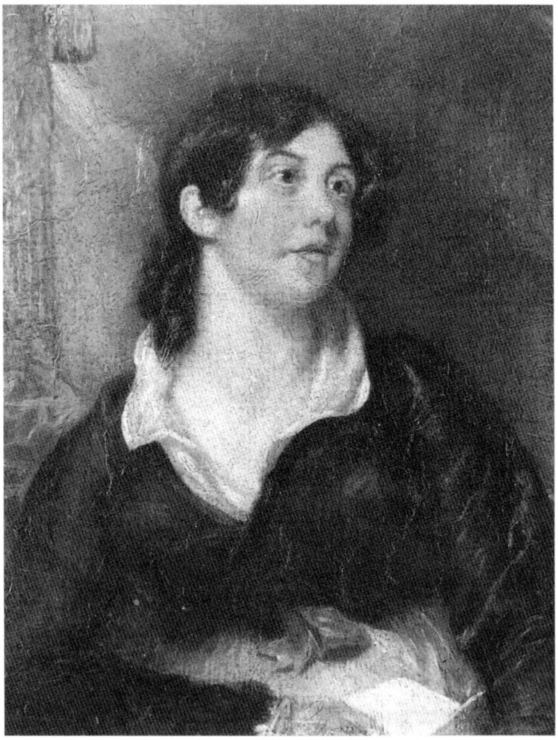

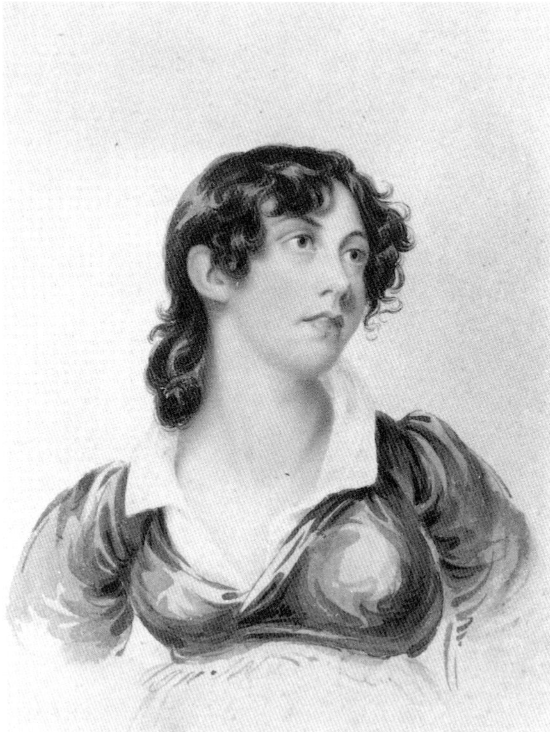

775 *Catherine Stephens as Diana Vernon*

774

CATHERINE STEPHENS

as Diana Vernon in *Rob Roy MacGregor*
by Isaac Pocock, adapted from Sir Walter Scott

George Henry Harlow

Oil on canvas 29.8 x 25.4
INV: RW 286 (as Mandane by De Wilde); CKA 286
PROV: Thomas Welsh; presented by an unknown donor at an unknown date
ENGR: Cooke for Oxberry's *New English Drama* pub. Simpkin & Marshall 1820, stipple 11.7 x 8 (inscr: 'From an original painting in the possession of T. Welsh')
REL: See No. 775

Pocock's *Rob Roy MacGregor*, set in Scotland in the early part of the 18th century, concerns the imminent demise of the financial house of Osbaldistone and Co. The Lacy edition of the play, which includes the 1818 cast list with Catherine Stephens, describes Diana Vernon's first-act costume as 'Plaid silk open dress, high-heeled shoes and broad bows, short full sleeves, lace ruffles' and dates the period 'from 1700 to 1715'. In Harlow's portrait, Diana Vernon wears green silk trimmed with gold, rather than plaid silk, and a loose, open-necked chemise. She is shown in her father's library, which is clearly rather grand, with a gold column to the left, wrapped about with a red and gold band with tassels. There is blue drapery bottom left and a vague arch to the right. Harlow painted No. 774 shortly before he left for Italy on 22 June 1818.

Pocock's operatic drama in three acts, with an overture by J. Davy and 'music composed and selected, chiefly from Old Scottish Airs by Mr Bishop and Mr Davy', was first performed at Covent Garden on 12 March 1818. Catherine Stephens was the original Diana Vernon. That season there were 34 performances of this adaptation of Scott's novel (published in 1817).

775

CATHERINE STEPHENS

as Diana Vernon in *Rob Roy MacGregor*
by Isaac Pocock, adapted from Sir Walter Scott

George Henry Harlow (copy after)

Pencil and watercolour on wove paper 10.5 x 8.2
INSCR: 'Miss Stephens.' (pen and brown ink on mount b.c. CM)
INV: Mathews 339 (artist unknown); RW 560A (artist unknown); CKA 560A
PROV: Charles Mathews
EXH: 1833 London (339)
REL: See No. 774

No. 775 is a reduced copy of No. 774.

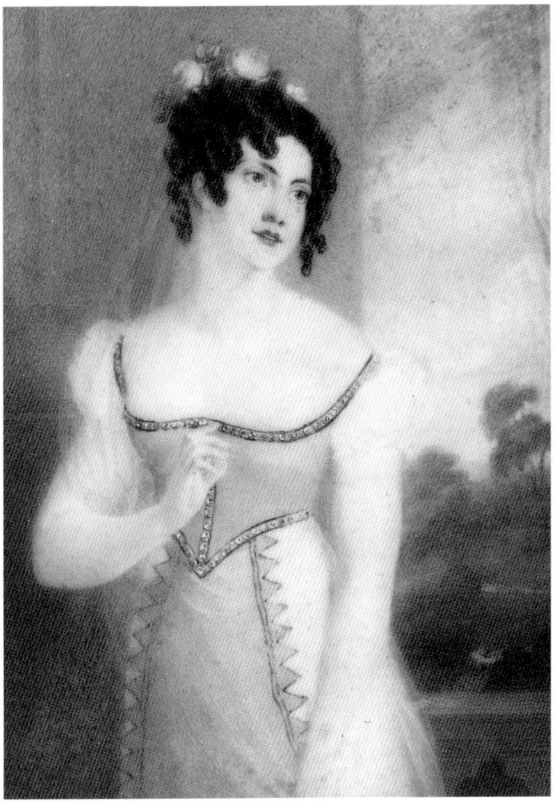

776
CATHERINE STEPHENS
as Mrs Ford
in *The Merry Wives of Windsor*
by William Shakespeare

Louisa Sharpe

Watercolour on ivory 14.8 x 11.5
INV: RW 427E (unknown by Richard Cosway); CKA 427E
PROV: Unknown, but acquired before 1909
EXH: 1824 R.A. (736)
(Portrait of Miss Stephens, in the character of Mrs Ford, in the Merry Wives of Windsor)

Mrs Ford wears a headpiece with roses and a veil. Her pink dress is decorated with gold bands edged in black. The dog-toothing down the skirt is a romantic indication that the costume is meant to reflect 16th-century fashion. A view of Windsor Great Park is seen to the right.

The Merry Wives was revived at Drury Lane on 20 February 1824, with Catherine Stephens as Mrs Ford. It was performed frequently until 8 April 1824, and was then seen occasionally until 24 May 1824, but with Mme Vestris in the part of Mrs Page.

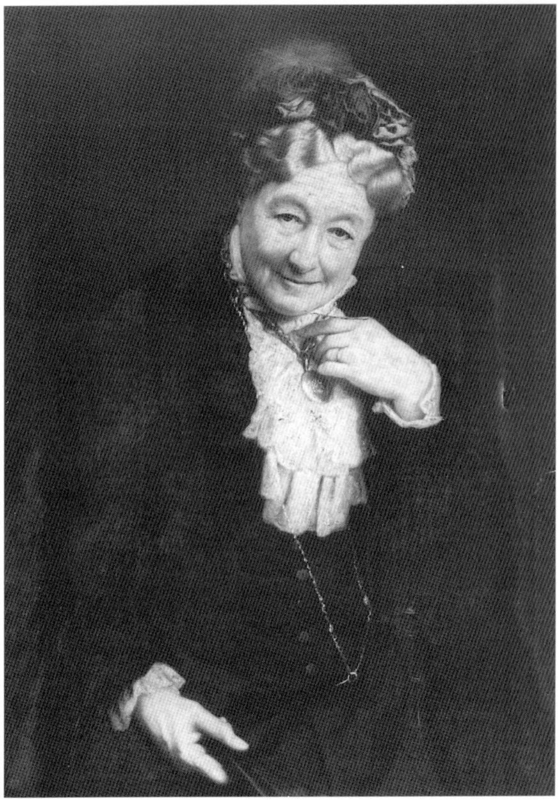

777
FANNY STIRLING

Walter Goodman

Oil on canvas 101.2 x 72
INV: RW/CKA 357; Gift 205
PROV: Spencer Brunton, by whom presented to the Garrick Club, 1886
LIT: Walter Goodman, *The Keeleys* (1895), p. 308 (bust reproduced in photogravure)

The elderly Fanny Stirling wears a bright yellow wig with a centre parting under a hat made of red, orange and blue silk, with a blue feather. She holds a black and white fan in her right hand, and wears a wedding ring. Her black dress has a separate bodice with long sleeves and black buttons, and lace collar and cuffs. She has a black shawl, and round her neck are a thin gold chain possibly supporting an eyeglass, and a heavy gold chain from which hangs a gold medallion studded with red stones. The padded chair is upholstered in red.

Mrs Stirling performed in the middle years of the 19th century at the Adelphi under the management of her husband, Edward Stirling, who was also a very prolific playwright. 'In later years ... she had no equal as Mrs Malaprop, Mrs Candour, and Juliet's Nurse.' (OC) See No. 804.

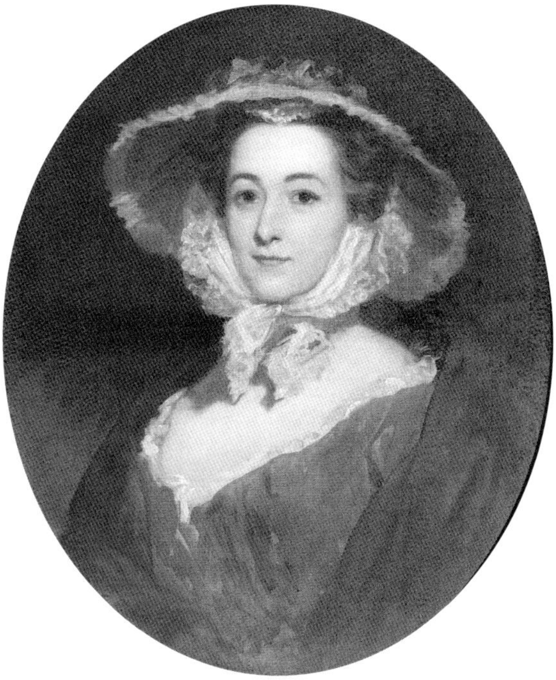

778
FANNY STIRLING
as Peg Woffington in *Masks and Faces*
by Tom Taylor and Charles Reade

Henry Wyndham Phillips

Oil on canvas 74.9 x 62.2, in oval
INV: RW/CKA 96; Gift 148
PROV: Presented by the artist, 1857
REL: Royal Shakespeare Theatre Picture Gallery 85 (1961 catalogue), oil on canvas 73.7 x 57.2 oval, unfinished; presented by the sitter, 1894

Fanny Stirling, as Peg Woffington, wears a broad-brimmed red hat trimmed with lace and a red dress with a green shawl.

Reade and Taylor's comedy was first performed at the Haymarket on 20 November 1852, with Fanny Stirling as Peg. The following year Reade published his novel *Peg Woffington*, based on the play.

In the Club's 1909 catalogue, Roberts Walters stated that the original of this portrait was painted for Tom Taylor and was later in Mrs Stirling's possession. That is the version now at Stratford. The sittings, according to Walters, were given after the performances, late at night, in Phillips's studio. The picture used during representation at the Haymarket Theatre was also a sketch by the artist, with a cut-out available for inserting a face. Henry O'Neil includes No. 778 among the paintings hanging in the Morning Room in his group portrait, No. 793.

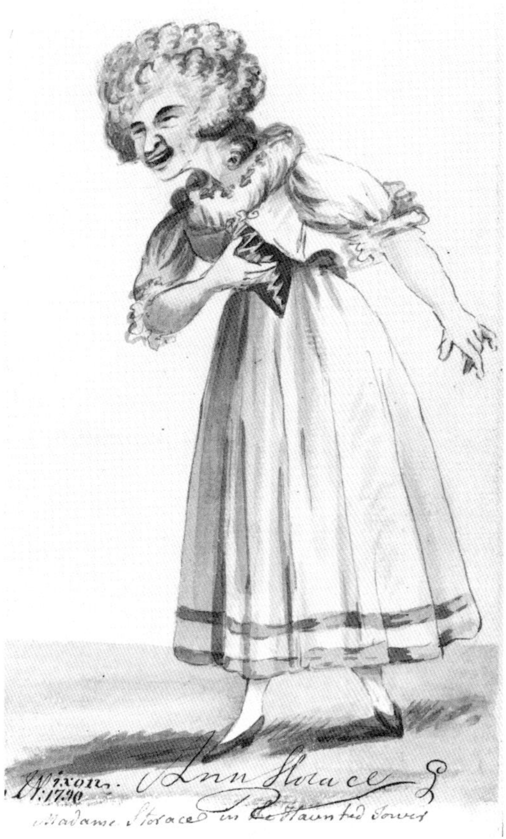

779
ANNA STORACE
as Adelina in *The Haunted Tower*
by James Cobb

John Nixon

Pencil, grey wash and watercolour on laid paper 19.8 x 11.5
INSCR: 'J NIXON /: 1790' (pen and black ink b.l.); 'Anne Storace' (pen and black ink b.c., possibly the sitter's signature); 'Madame Storace in the Haunted Tower' (pen and brown ink b.c.)
INV: Not listed
PROV: John Nixon, *Dramatic Annals*, 2:180

In this caricature, Anna Storace wears a white ankle-length dress with a laced bodice and two blue stripes round the hem.

Cobb's musical drama, with music by Anna's brother, Stephen Storace, and selections from other composers, was first performed at Covent Garden on 24 November 1789. Anna Storace, as Adelina, was making her début in a speaking part, although she had appeared in concerts since 1774 and at the King's Theatre from 24 April 1787.

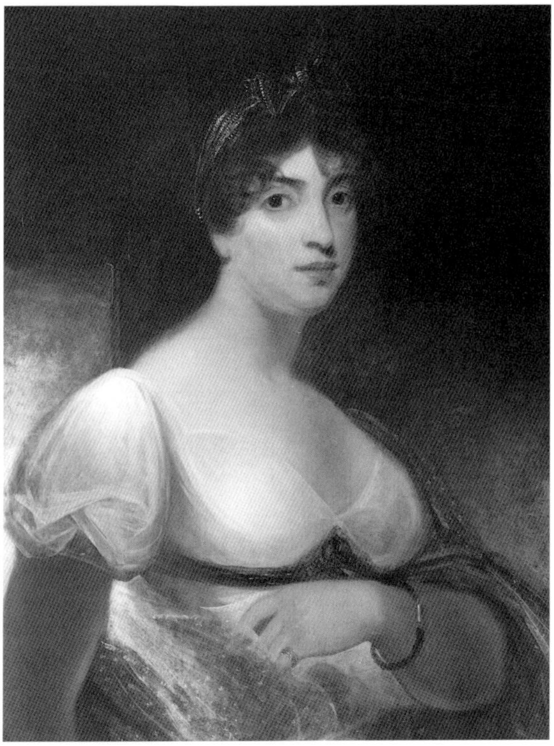

780*

ANNA STORACE

Michael William Sharp

Oil on canvas 76 x 63

INV: Mathews 158; RW/CKA 416

PROV: Thomas Harris; Harris sale, 12 July 1819 (26); Charles Mathews

EXH: 1833 London (158)

Anne Storace's hair is gathered up with a green and silver ribbon tied in a large bow on top of her head. She wears a short-sleeved white muslin dress and has a shawl over her left shoulder.

M.W. Sharp exhibited at the Royal Academy in 1804 (302) a portrait of Anne Storace as Katherine in *The English Fleet in 1342*, by Thomas Frognall Dibdin; but it seems unlikely that the costume seen in No. 780 can relate to that part, or, indeed, to a play set in 1342. Signora Storace would appear to be dressed for a concert performance.

She was a fine actress and an admirable singer, who enjoyed great success on the Continent as well as in England. In Vienna she was the original Rosina in Paisiello's *Barbiere di Seviglia* and the original Susanna in Mozart's sequel, *Le Nozze di Figaro*.

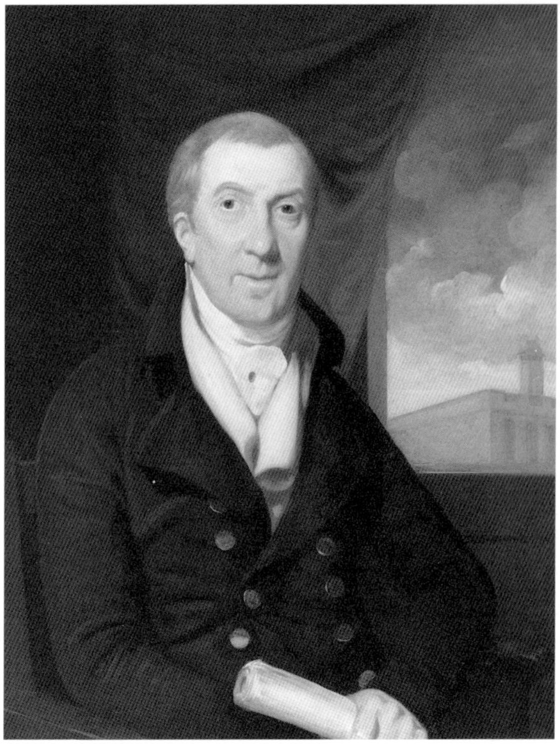

781

RICHARD SUETT

Samuel De Wilde

Oil on canvas 74.3 x 61.6

INV: Mathews 188; RW/CKA 196

PROV: Charles Mathews

EXH: 1833 London (188)

ENGR: William Ridley for the *Monthly Mirror* pub. Vernor & Hood 26 August 1803, stipple 8.7 x 7.2 (bust, no background); Anon. pub. S. De Wilde & J. Cawthorn 1811, mezzotint 24 x 19.9

Suett holds a roll of paper in his left hand and wears a dark brown jacket with double row of brass buttons, a white waistcoat with rolled collar, and a high white stock with rosette and a ruby pin. The view of the building through the rectangular opening to the right appears to be Henry Holland's Drury Lane Theatre, which was built in 1794 and burned down on 24 February 1809.

Suett spent 24 seasons at Drury Lane, from 1780 to 1805, acting mostly a line of low comedy characters such as the Clown in *The Winter's Tale* and *Twelfth Night*, Touchstone in *As You Like It*, and a Gravedigger in *Hamlet*. Charles Lamb (*Essays of Elia*) called him 'the Robin Goodfellow of the stage'. Suett was also a good musician and wrote a number of published songs.

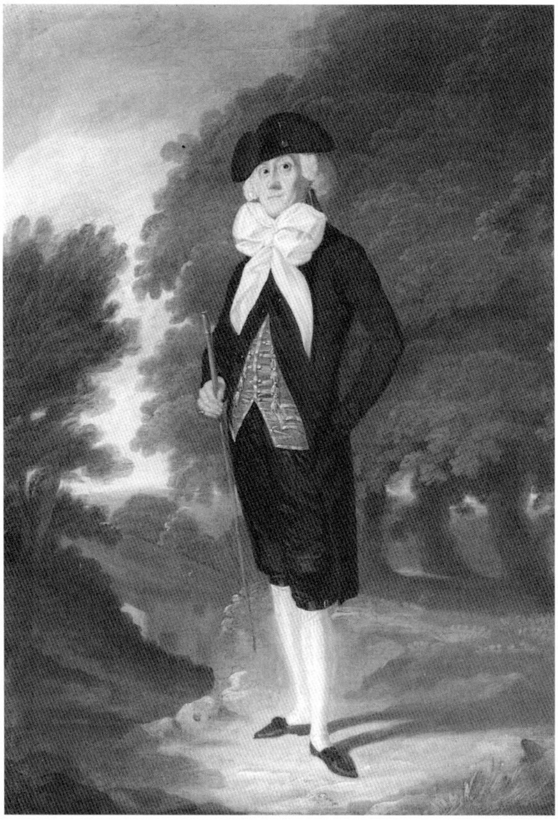

782
RICHARD SUETT
as Endless in *No Song, No Supper*
by Prince Hoare

Samuel De Wilde

Oil on canvas 43.8 x 34.3
INV: Mathews 370; RW/CKA 479
PROV: Charles Mathews
EXH: 1833 London (370)
REL: See No. 783

Endless is a nefarious lawyer who hopes, by a law-suit, to turn Farmer Crop out of his house. He plans to forward his cause by insinuating himself into the affections of Dorothea, Crop's ill-tempered and disaffected wife. In Act I, scene 3, he arrives outside Crop's house and congratulates himself on his appearance, saying: 'This dress, I think, cannot fail of captivating Dorothea's heart' (the line provided by Mathews) 'but the best of the joke is, she fancies I am in love with her.'

Endless stands in front of Crop's cottage, which is in the middle of a wood. Suett's powdered wig with curls was apparently particularly memorable and ridiculous. The costume in which he hopes to charm Dorothea consists of black shoes with rosettes, white hose, black breeches, a black coat, a green waistcoat decorated in gold, and an outrageous white bow at his neck. His black tricorn hat is placed jauntily askew, and he holds a cane in his right hand.

Hoare's entertainment, with music written chiefly by Stephen Storace, was first performed at Drury Lane on 16 April 1790, with Suett as the original Endless. He played the role at the Haymarket for the first time on 6 August 1793 and remained popular in it until the end of the century.

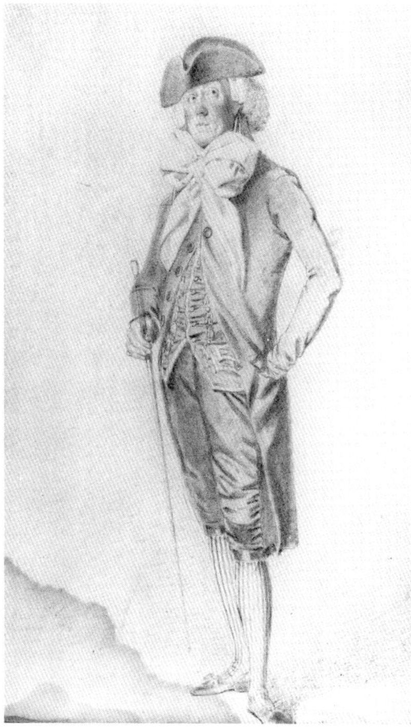

783
RICHARD SUETT
as Endless in *No Song, No Supper*
by Prince Hoare

Samuel De Wilde

Pencil and watercolour on wove paper 38.1 x 23.5
INSCR: 'De Wilde ft / June 17 1794' (pencil b.l.)
INV: RW 552 (artist unknown); CKA 552
PROV: Acquired from unknown source before 1888
REL: See No. 782

Apart from the flesh tints, the drawing consists of blue and grey washes, which presumably do not reflect the correct colours of the costume. Suett wears rosettes on his white pumps, stockings with blue and white vertical stripes, grey breeches and jacket, and a blue waistcoat with white trimming. At his neck is an immense white bow. This is apparently the study on which No. 782 is based.

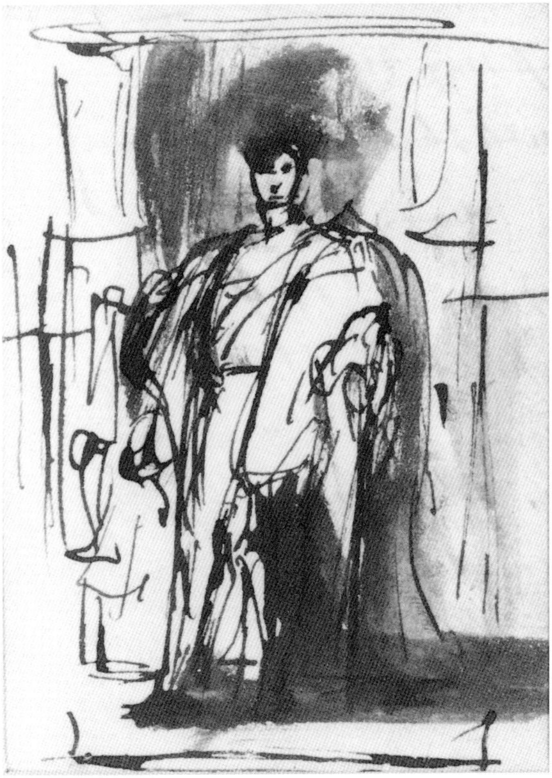

784
AUGUSTUS FREDERICK,
DUKE OF SUSSEX

Sir David Wilkie

Pen and brown ink with brown wash
on wove paper 8.9 x 6.3
INSCR: 'This is an authentic sketch of the Duke of Sussex
by Sir David Wilkie, S.B.C.' (pencil on verso)
INV: CKA 641; Gift 610
PROV: Captain C. Riddell Williams, by whom
presented to the Garrick Club, 1942
REL: Royal Collection Millar 1186, oil on canvas
252.7 x 162.6, inscr: 'DAVID WILKIE f. 1833',
exh: R.A. 1833 (207); Coll: Mrs George Dawnay,
oil on canvas n.s. (sketch); Royal Library 17777–9,
pen and brown ink on wove paper n.s. (sketches for
figure and studies of dead eagle in final picture)
LIT: A. Cunningham, *The Life of Sir David Wilkie* (1843), 3: 70,
514, 529; Sir Oliver Millar, *The Late Georgian Pictures in the
Collection of Her Majesty the Queen* (1969), 1: 143 (No. 1186)

A study for the monumental full-length figure painted for the sitter, which he gave to Queen Victoria on 24 February 1838. In her journal entry for that day, the Queen wrote that she had met the Duke in the Throne Room at Buckingham Palace, 'where he presented me with his full length (size of life) portrait in the Highland dress, painted by Sir David Wilkie'.

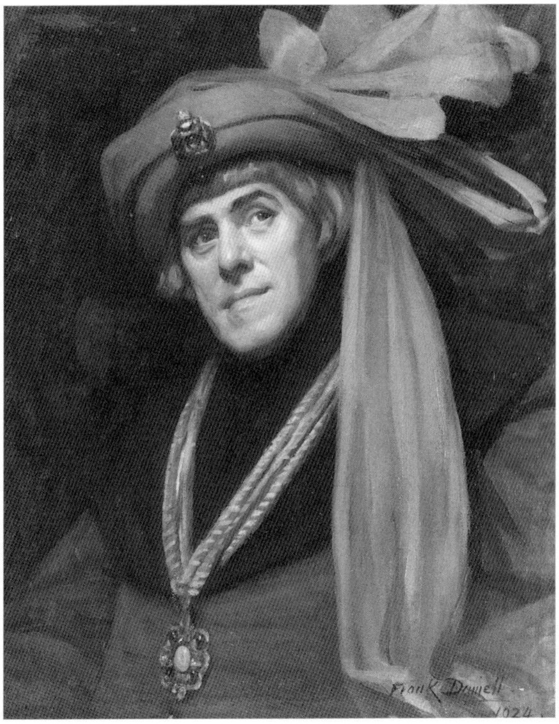

785
E. LYALL SWETE
as Richard de Beauchamp, Earl of Warwick
in *Saint Joan*
by George Bernard Shaw

Frank Dowell

Oil on canvas 74.9 x 62.8
INSCR: 'Frank Dowell / 1924.' (black paint b.r.)
INV: CKA 572; Gift 468
PROV: Bequeathed by the sitter, 1930

Warwick has grey hair and a huge 15th-century hat with liripipe and a jewel above his forehead. He wears a red doublet with a fur collar and has a jewelled pendant round his neck.

Shaw's *Saint Joan* was performed for the first time by the New York Theatre Guild at the Garrick Theatre, New York, on 28 December 1923. The production ran for 214 performances, with Winifred Leniham as Joan. The play then opened in London at the New Theatre on 26 March 1924, in a production mounted by Mary Moore and Sybil Thorndike, and ran for 244 performances. It was directed by the author and Lewis Casson and designed by Charles Ricketts. Sybil Thorndike played Joan, with a supporting cast that included Lewis Casson as Chaplain de Stogumber and E. Lyall Swete as Warwick. Swete became a member of the Garrick Club in 1904.

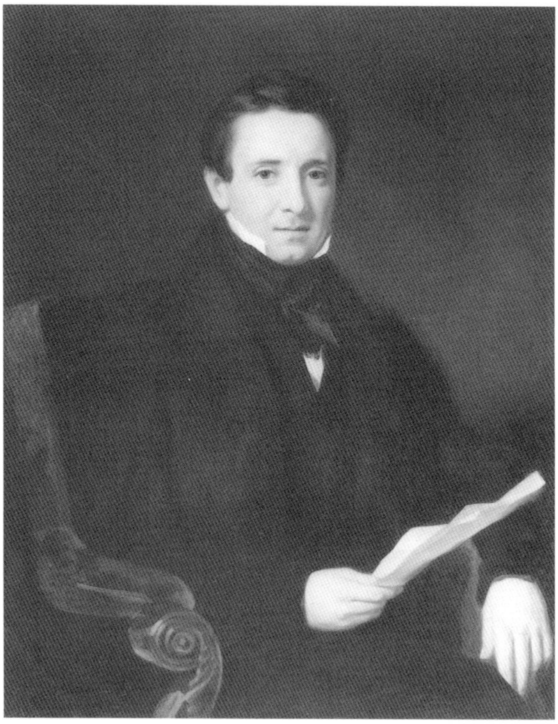

786

SIR THOMAS NOON TALFOURD

John Lucas

Oil on canvas 90.2 x 69.8
INV: RW/CKA 326; Gift 281
PROV: Sir Henry Bodkin Poland, K.C., by whom presented to the Garrick Club, 1902

Talfourd wears a dark suit, white shirt and dark cravat, and sits in a carved and gilt chair upholstered in red.

Another portrait of Talfourd by Lucas was engraved by S. Freeman for the *New Monthly Magazine*, published by Henry Colburn, October 1837.

The Hon. Mr Justice Talfourd was an original member of the Garrick Club in 1831.

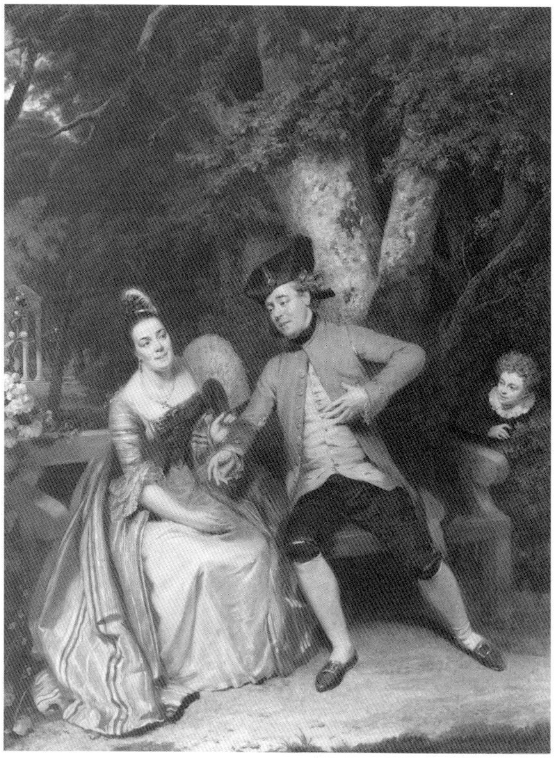

787

JOHN TAYLEURE as Tag,
CLARA FISHER as Little Pickle and
SARAH HARLOWE as Miss Pickle
in *The Spoiled Child*
by Isaac Bickerstaffe

George Clint

Oil on Canvas 97.5 x 77
INV: CKA 184; Gift 429
PROV: F.J. Nettlefold, by whom presented to the Garrick Club, 1924
EXH: 1823 R.A. (13) 'A scene from the Spoiled Child – Mrs Harlowe, Mr. Tayleure, and Miss Clara Fisher, as Miss Pickle, Tag, and Little Pickle' (with quotation of first line of Tag's song: 'O thou wert born to please me')

Act II, scene 2 is 'A Garden – A Seat in a Bower, much shaded with Trees', where Tag and Miss Pickle make love; Tag sings, although the line in the R.A. catalogue does not appear in the printed text. The lines added for Tag's burlesque song in the 1822 Oxberry edition were rather more jaunty: 'A pickle 'tis of virgin fame, / And Bridget Pickle is its name. / Then Billy Cupid, be not fickle, / Inspire the heart of sweet Miss Pickle / To reap love's harvest with thy sickle, – / Oh! Pickle! Pickle! Pickle! Pickle!!' Whilst he is singing, Little Pickle 'steals round the Stage and gets behind the Bower, and sews their cloaths together, and then goes out unperceived by them'. Presumably the moment before the stitching is depicted here. No. 653 shows the result of this prank.

Tag wears black shoes with paste buckles, white stockings, dark blue breeches, a red jacket with brass buttons, white waistcoat, black stock and black tricorn hat. Miss Pickle wears a pink dress with blue and white stripes, and a white underskirt. Both costumes are of the 1760s. Little Pickle, however, is in late 18th-century boy's dress, with a dark green jacket and frilled white collar.

Bickerstaffe's two-act farce was first performed at Drury Lane on 22 March 1790, with Robert Palmer as Tag, Mrs Jordan as Little Pickle, and Mrs Hopkins as Miss Pickle. It was given five times at Drury Lane during the 1822–23 season, on 3 and 30 December 1822, and on 4 January, 22 February and 15 March 1823. The first of these was Clara Fisher's first appearance as Little Pickle; she played at all the performances with Sarah Harlowe as Miss Pickle. John Pritt Harley is given as Tag in the playbills for all the performances, but John Tayleure is named in the R.A. catalogue, so perhaps he stood in for Harley at one or more of the performances. He did play the role at the Haymarket, and would have been an obvious substitute. The actor depicted here is clearly not Harley (see Clint's portrait, No. 286).

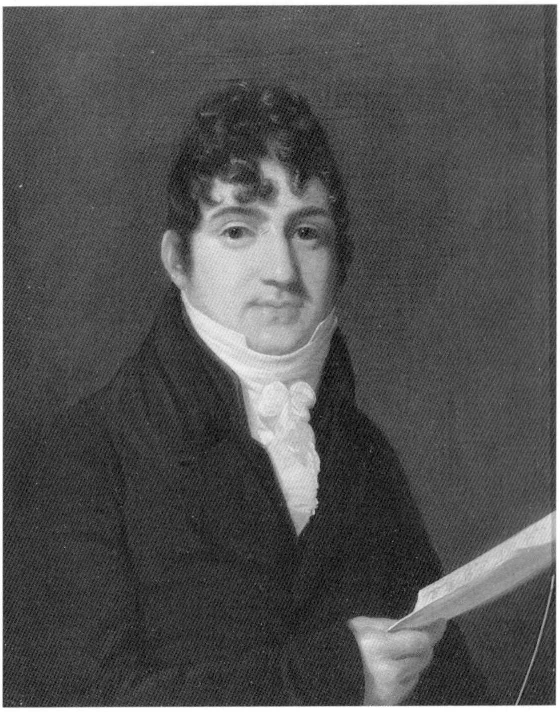

788

CHARLES TAYLOR

Samuel De Wilde

Oil on panel 23.2 x 19.1
INSCR: 'S De Wilde 1805' (black paint b.r.)
INV: Mathews 358; RW/CKA 224
PROV: Charles Mathews
EXH: 1833 London (224)
ENGR: William Ridley for the *Monthly Mirror* pub. Vernor & Hood 31 July 1805, stipple 8.7 x 7.3 (bust in oval)

Half-length, holding a sheet of music and wearing a black coat. Taylor was an original member of the Garrick Club in 1831 and resigned in 1845, two years before he died. He is shown here at about the age of 24.

789

CHARLES TAYLOR

as Lubin in *The Quaker*

by Charles Dibdin

Samuel De Wilde

Pencil and watercolour on wove paper 37 x 23.5
INV: Mathews 335; RW/CKA 66D
PROV: Charles Mathews
EXH: 1833 London (335)
ENGR: Richard Cooper for Cawthorn's *Minor British Theatre* pub. John Cawthorn 7 December 1805, stipple 12 x 7.8 (background with cottage at l., gate at r.)

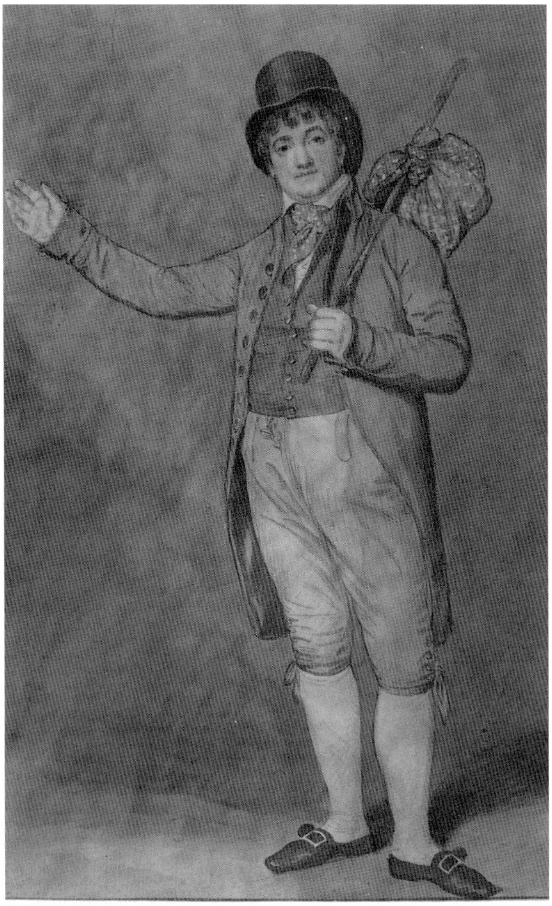

789 *Charles Taylor as Lubin*

Lubin Blackthorn opens the play with an air which begins 'Midst thrushes, blackbirds, nightingales &c', the line quoted on the engraving. The scene is 'An irregular Hill carried quite to the back of the Stage, so situated that Lubin, who comes from it during the Symphony of the Duet, is sometimes seen and sometimes concealed by the Trees. A Cottage right hand near the front' (Oxberry edition 1822). 'Lubin comes over the Stile with a Stick and Bundle on his shoulder.' Lubin's bundle is wrapped in a blue cloth with white spots. He has a black top hat and wears black shoes, white stockings, fawn breeches, a blue coat with silver buttons, a red waistcoat with silver buttons, a white shirt, and a blue neckerchief with white spots.

Charles Dibdin's comic opera was first performed at Drury Lane on 7 October 1777, with Joseph Vernon as Lubin. There is a drawing of Taylor as Lubin, ascribed to De Wilde, in the Westminster Public Library, pencil and watercolour on wove paper 37.5 x 22.8, s. and d: 1821?, full-length, standing to front, stick in sitter's right hand.

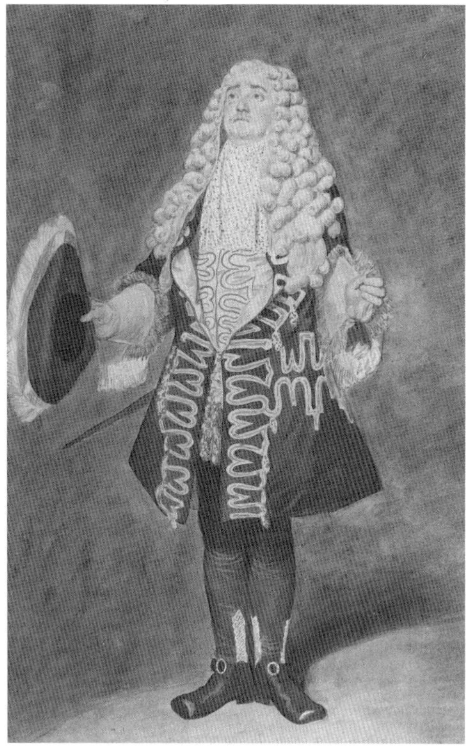

790

CHARLES TAYLOR

as Noodle in *Tom Thumb the Great*

by Kane O'Hara, altered from Henry Fielding

Samuel De Wilde

Pencil and watercolour on wove paper 37 x 23.5

INSCR: '2' (pencil on uncoloured fringe of gauntlet on r. h.)

INV: Mathews 234; RW/CKA 60D

PROV: Charles Mathews

EXH: 1833 London (234)

REL: Similar to NT 50, pencil and watercolour on wove paper 38 x 23.8, inscr: 'S De Wilde delin / March 1815' (costume less striking and wig shorter)

At the beginning of Act III, Noodle comes on and sings a brief air describing the state of King Arthur's court. Noodle's right hand is raised, holding a grey tricorn hat. His courtier's costume consists of large white gauntlets, square-toed black boots with silver buckles, silver clocks on his stockings, grey breeches, a grey coat with silver braid, a silvery waistcoat, and a neckerchief with green flecks tied high round the neck and falling onto his chest.

O'Hara's burletta, based on Henry Fielding's *Tom Thumb the Great* of 1730, was first performed at Covent Garden on 2 October 1780, with Thomas Robson as Noodle. Taylor was playing Noodle as early as 1806, when there were 18 performance of the piece over the summer season at the Haymarket. See No. 434.

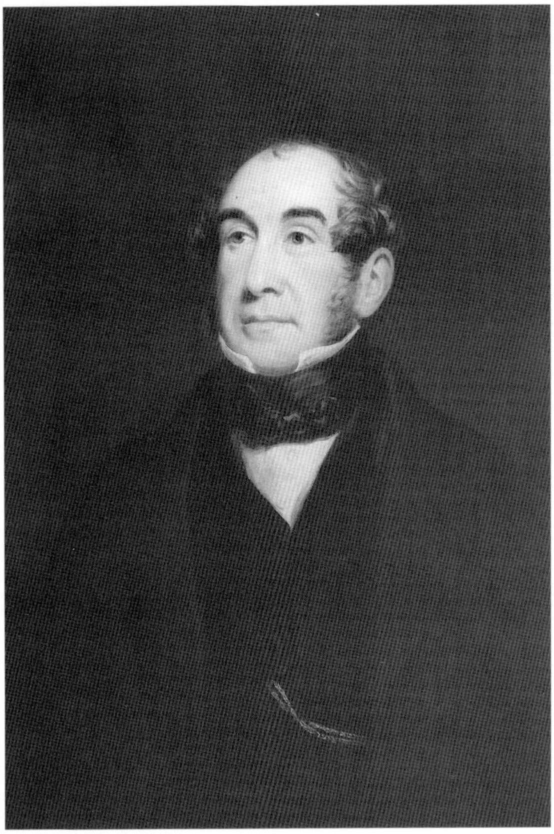

791
CHARLES TAYLOR

Thomas Ellerby

Oil on canvas 73.7 x 61
INV: RW/CKA 358; Gift III
PROV: Andrew Arcedeckne, by whom presented to the Garrick Club, 1850

A more mature Taylor wears a dark jacket and waistcoat, with a white shirt and black stock with bow.

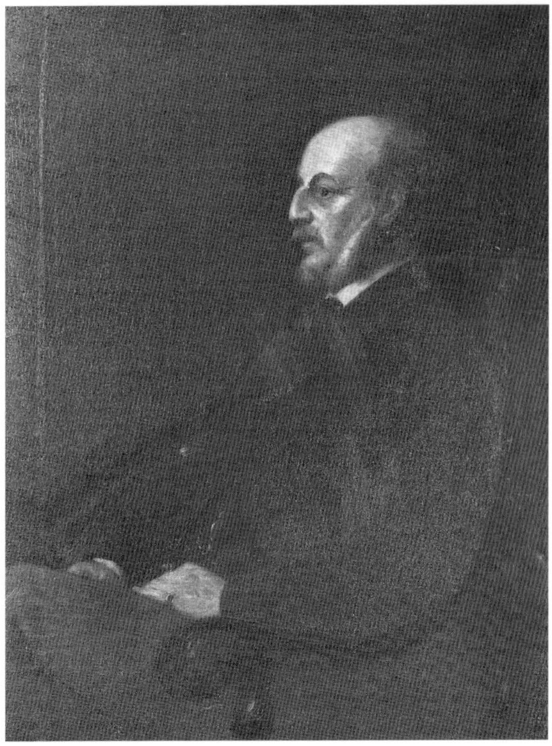

792
SIR CHARLES TAYLOR

Henry O'Neil

Oil on canvas 58.4 x 48.2
INSCR: 'H. O'Neil' (red paint b.r.)
INV: RW/CKA 331
PROV: Presented by the artist before 1880

Sir Charles wears dark brown trousers, a brown jacket, a white collar and a cravat. The padded chair is upholstered in red.

This canvas, without frame and badly damaged, was in storage in 1994.

The sitter became a member of the Garrick Club in 1847.

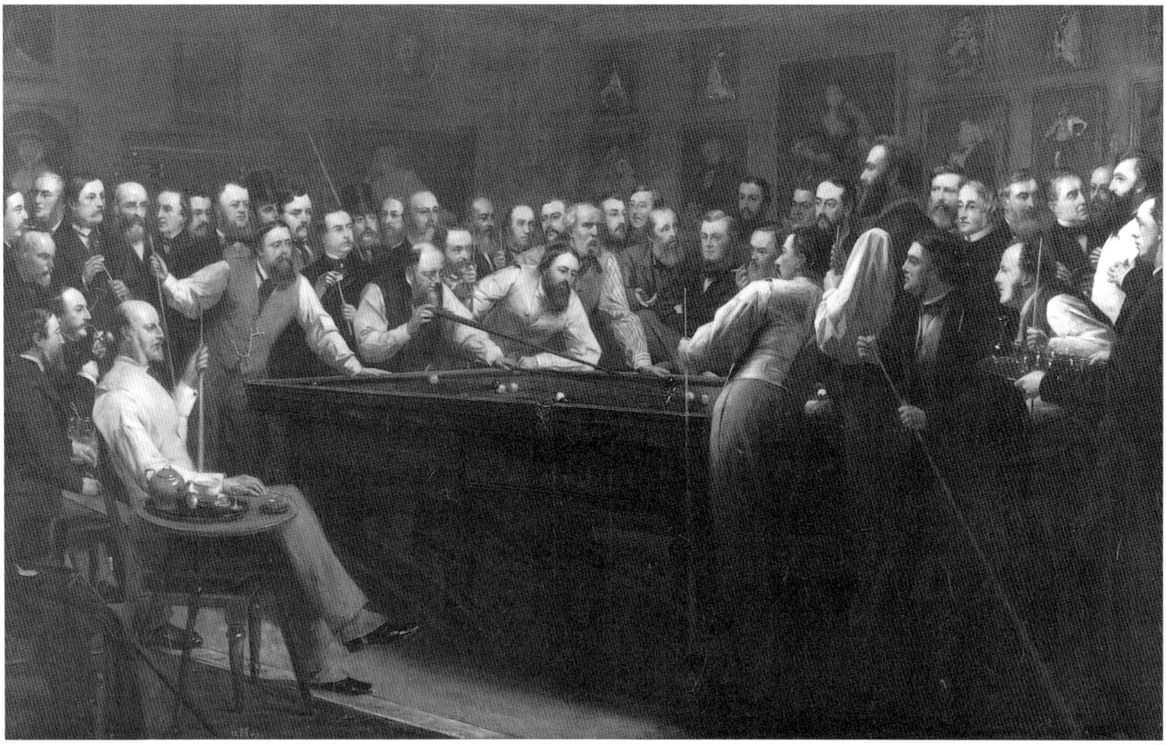

793*
SIR CHARLES TAYLOR and others
(Forty-three members in the
Billiard Room of the Garrick Club)

Henry O'Neil

Oil on canvas 95.2 x 155
INV: RW/CKA 333; Gift 240
PROV: Presented by the artist, *c.*1890
LIT: Fitzgerald, p.232; Griffiths, p.294;
Derek Hudson 'Billiards at the Garrick in 1869',
Connoisseur (December 1969), p.274;
Alan Hankinson *William Howard Russell* (1982),
reproduced

Members of the Garrick Club in 1869 play a game of pool at the billiard table. Sir Charles Taylor, seated at his coffee table, seems to be in control of events as he watches Edward Tredcroft take an awkward long shot. Twelve other members are taking part in the game; the other gentlemen look on. The billiard table is shown in the first floor Morning Room of the new club house, finished only five years before the picture was painted. It is possible that the table was placed in this room, but it seems more likely that O'Neil set the scene in the large downstairs room in order to squeeze in all the portraits. There is no evidence that the billiard table was ever to be found anywhere but in the billiard room on the second floor – where it is today and where it certainly was when Robert Walters produced his catalogue of the Garrick Club pictures in 1904.

The members shown in the picture are identified in the list below, along with the date on which each joined the Garrick Club. There is a remarkable preponderance of artist members, including John Gilbert, William Powell Frith, Frederick Leighton, Alfred Elmore, Val Prinsep, Thomas Creswick, John Millais and O'Neil himself. The principal literary members shown are Trollope and Charles Reade, and O'Neil includes Gilbert's posthumous portrait of Thackeray (No. 805) as a tribute to another recently deceased literary member.

O'Neil's choice of pictures is interesting, and probably does not relate to the arrangement of the pictures in the Morning Room in 1869. Fifteen pictures or parts of pictures are shown, some of them indecipherable. On the wall to the left there are four, including, on either side of the scoreboard, Henry Wyndham Phillips's portrait of Fanny Stirling as Peg Woffington (No. 778) and Mercier's fancy picture, then regarded as a portrait of Peg Woffington herself (No. 847). Above the Mercier is the Zoffany head of David Garrick (No. 249). The large picture in the centre of the long wall on the right is the portrait of a lady in masquerade costume called Mrs Bracegirdle (No. 88). To the right of it is the

Thackeray portrait, and to the right of that De Wilde's portrait of Charles Mathews as Somno (No. 469). Above Thackeray is De Wilde's portrait of Charles Lee Lewes as Bobadil (No. 421), and to the right of that an unidentified male figure in a red cloak. On the top row to the right are two more De Wildes: Moody as Commodore Flip (No. 610) and a female full-length. Below Bobadil is an unidentified male half-length in a red jacket, and below the female portrait is what appears to be an enlarged version of Thomas Carrick's miniature of William Farren the Younger (No. 212). The Farren portrait, like that of Thackeray, may have been intended as a sort of memorial to this famous actor, who was the grand old man of the British theatre by the time he died in 1861, shortly after O'Neil became a member of the Garrick. This curious enlargement illustrates the fact that O'Neil altered the proportions of the pictures to fit the wall space.

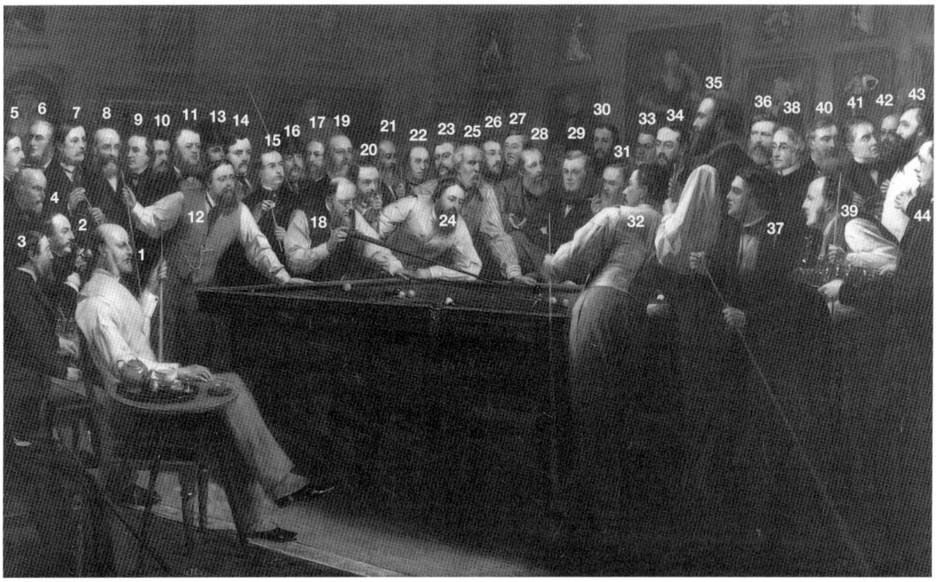

Key (the dates in brackets indicate the year in which each sitter became a member of the Garrick Club):

1. Sir Charles Taylor, BT [1847]
2. Captain Synge, C.E. [1855]
3. James Christie [1851]
4. Henry Nelson O'Neil, A.R.A. [1860]
5. Captain the Hon. Charles William White, M.P. [1864]
6. (Sir) Maurice James O'Connell (or Morgan John O'Connell) [1864]
7. Lieutenant-Colonel Richard Bateson, C.V.O. [1862]
8. Anthony Trollope [1862]
9. James Clay, M.P. [1866]
10. Lieutenant-Colonel Arthur Lambton, C.B. [1854]
11. T.H. Powell [1862]
12. Edward Tredcroft [1849]
13. Charles T. Hebbert [1847]
14. (Sir) James Cornelius O'Dowd, C.B. [1854]
15. (Sir) William Howard Russell, LL.D., C.V.O. [1853]
16. Major-General George Thomas Conolly Napier, C.B. [1868]
17. Henry William George Paget, 3rd Marquess of Anglesey [1845]
18. Henry King [1847]
19. E.A. Breedon [1868]
20. Edward Crabb [1853]
21. Sir John Gilbert (R.A.) [1852]
22. William Powell Frith, R.A. [1864]
23. Shirley Brooks [1850]
24. Arthur Warre [1856]
25. James Robertson Anderson [1843]
26. Frederic (Lord) Leighton, (P.)R.A. [1864]
27. Henry Allworth Merewether, Q.C. [1864]
28. Joseph Arden, F.S.A. (1834]
29. Charles George Merewether, Q.C. [1851]
30. W.M. Praed [1862]
31. Alfred Elmore, R.A. [1863]
32. Frederick Clay [1862]
33. John Connellan Deane [1854]
34. F. Boileau Elliott [1866]
35. Valentine Cameron Prinsep (R.A.) [1864]
36. Thomas Creswick, R.A. [1864]
37. Henry (Lord) James, Q.C., M.P. (1862]
38. I. Brasseur [1871]
39. (Sir) John Everett Millais (BT.), P.R.A. (1855]
40. Joseph Munt Langford [1850]
41. Francis Fladgate [1832]
42. Charles Reade [1839]
43. Eneas Sweetland Dallas [1862]
44. John, a Club servant

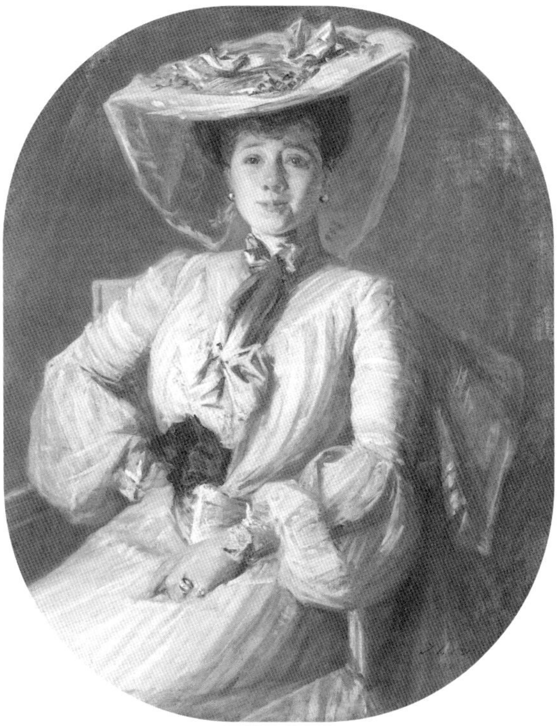

794
DAME MARIE TEMPEST

Jacques-Emile Blanche

Oil on canvas 101.5 x 81.5
INSCR: 'J.E. Blanche / 1903' (brown paint b.r.)
INV: CKA 640; Gift 613
PROV: Presented by Alderson Burrell Horne,
Sir Alfred Webb-Johnson & Lt. Col. Philip Walker, 1943
EXH: 1949 Birmingham (5); 1949 Port Sunlight (9);
1951 London (2); 1974 Folkestone; 1975 Bradford
LIT: J.E. Blanche, *Portraits of a Lifetime* (1937), p.96

Marie Tempest sits wearing a long-sleeved dress of blue and white vertical stripes, with a broad blue belt and blue bows at the wrists, and a broad blue ribbon round the neck, tied in a bow at the front with ends hanging down. She wears a broad-brimmed straw hat with blue ribbons on top.

Marie Tempest met her second husband, Cosmo Gordon-Lennox, in 1898. They married soon afterwards and subsequently spent much of their time in France, where they became important social figures in the British colony at Dieppe. Their neighbours included Max Beerbohm, Percy Grainger and Walter Sickert, as well as the anglophile Jacques-Emile Blanche. Blanche was a particular friend of Gordon-Lennox, who, with Harry Melville, wrote a skit entitled *A Painting Class as Boarding House*, based on incidents taking place in Blanche's studio in Dieppe. As Blanche frequently commuted to London, his portrait of Marie Tempest could have been painted either there or in Dieppe – or even in Paris, where Gordon-Lennox and his wife spent several days every month.

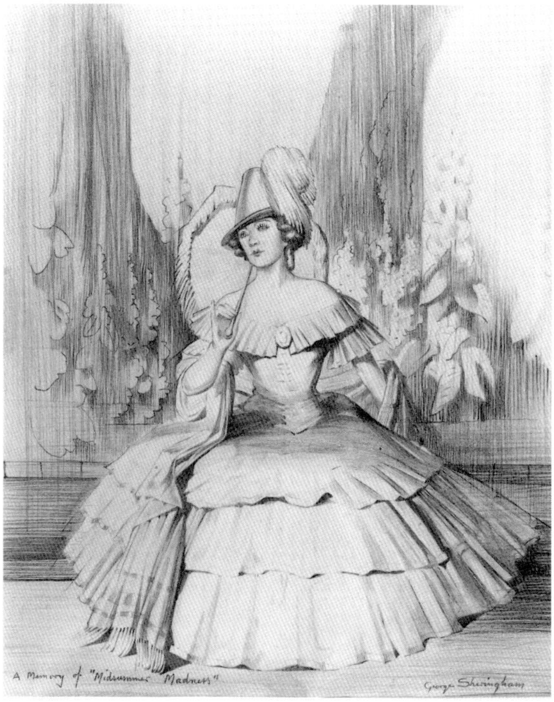

795
DAME MARIE TEMPEST
as Mrs Nolan in *Midsummer Madness*
by Clifford Bax and Armstrong Gibbs

George Sheringham

Pencil on wove paper 22.4 x 18
INSCR: 'A Memory of "Summer Madness"' (b.l.)
INV: GCL 659; Gift 688
PROV: Bequeathed by the artist, 1949
EXH: 1980 Nottingham

Mrs Nolan wears an elaborately decorated dress.

Midsummer Madness, a 'comedy with music', with book by Clifford Bax and music by Armstrong Gibbs, opened at the Lyric, Hammersmith on 3 July 1924. It ran for 115 performances until 11 October 1924. The production was designed by George Sheringham, and the music was directed by Alfred Reynolds. The play was a 'four-hander', with Marie Tempest as Mrs Nolan and Frederick Ranalow as Pat Nolan.

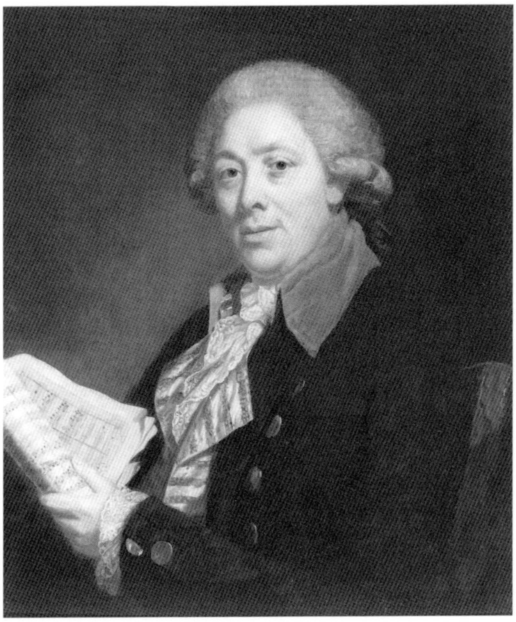

796
GIUSTO FERDINANDO TENDUCCI

Thomas Beach

Oil on canvas 74.9 x 61
INV: Mathews 362 (artist unknown);
RW/CKA 411 (by Gainsborough Dupont)
PROV: Thomas Harris?; Harris sale, Robins 12 July 1819 (2)
(by Gainsborough); Charles Mathews
EXH: 1833 London (362); 1982–83 London (123)
ENGR: Anon. pub. Longman & Broderip, line
(in reverse, oval), inscr: 'Instruction of /
MR TENDUCCI / to his Scholars' (below)
REL: Coll: Lord Hylton, oil on canvas 76.2 x 63.6?
inscr: 'Thomas Beach', exh: 1783 (18, 23 or 29)
[*The Connoisseur* of July 1913 reported it then to be in the
collection of Lord Hylton, Radstock, Somerset], engr:
W. Dickinson pub. W. Dickinson 1782, mezzotint
33 x 27.6 LIT: E. S. Beach, *Thomas Beach* (1934),
p. 72 (No. 281); Hayes, 1968

Tenducci wears a dark blue jacket with gold buttons and a red turned-down collar, a green and white silk waistcoat, and a stock with lace at the collar and cuffs. He holds sheets of music.

The version in the collection of Lord Hylton shows the sitter wearing a hat and with a slightly different style of wig. It has been assumed that this picture was one of Dupont's series painted for Thomas Harris and that the attribution to Gainsborough in the Harris sale catalogue was an optimistic attribution to the artist's uncle. However, there can be no doubt that it is a second version of the Beach in Lord Hylton's collection, possibly a little later than 1782 but certainly dating from the early 1780s.

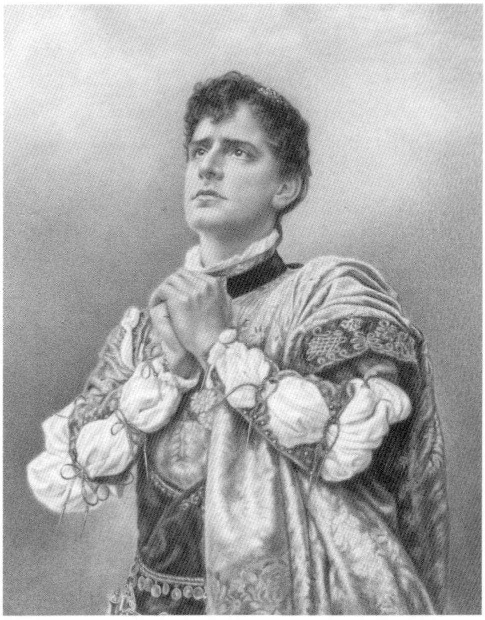

797
WILLIAM TERRISS
as Romeo in *Romeo and Juliet*
by William Shakespeare

Fanny Gibson

Watercolour on wove paper 40.6 x 30.5
INV: Not listed
PROV: Presented by Major Rowland R. Gibson

Romeo, shown half-length, clasps his hands passionately together and looks up (at Juliet?). The picture is taken from a photograph available from Barraud, 263 Oxford Street. The costume is immediately recognisable from other photographs taken of the 1879 Haymarket production. It consists of a bluish doublet, the upper part in a paler blue with a white floral design, with sleeves of the same material, open at the sides to reveal a white shirt and tied together with small gold strings. Gold coins and a gold dagger are suspended from Romeo's gold belt.

Terriss played Romeo on three occasions: at Drury Lane in 1874 with Ellen Wallis as Juliet, at the Haymarket in 1879 with Adelaide Neilson as Juliet, and at the Lyceum in 1884 with Mary Anderson.

William Terriss (real name William Charles James Lewin) acted at the Adelphi and Lyceum theatres during the last three decades of the 19th century. One of the most popular players of his day, Terriss's 'charm and gusto' delighted audiences (OC). His best work was done at the Adelphi, earning him the sobriquet 'No. 1, Adelphi Terriss'. He was killed by a madman in front of that theatre in 1897.

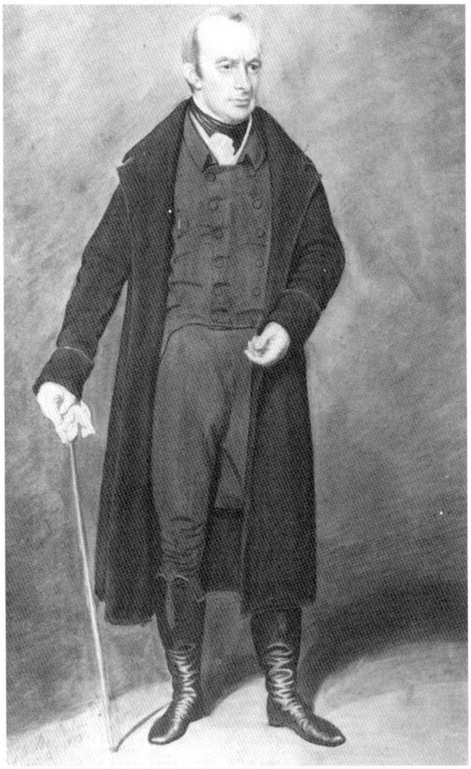

798
DANIEL TERRY
as Barford in *Who Wants a Guinea?*
by George Colman the Younger

Samuel De Wilde

Pencil and watercolour on wove paper 37 x 23.5
INSCR: 'S De Wilde delin / October 19 1812' (pencil b.l.)
INV: Mathews 251; RW/CKA 65A
PROV: Charles Mathews
EXH: 1833 London (251); 1975 London (149)

Barford, or Captain Delamere, is a misanthropic bluff soldier who long ago lost his wife and, he thinks, his daughter. In Act I, scene 2, 'A Room in the Village Inn', Barford enters with a small bundle, all that was salvaged from his burned-down house, saying: 'Rest there, my whole property...' He encounters Torrent, a wealthy do-gooder, who asks how all his property can be tied up 'in such a cursed small pocket-handkerchief'. Barford's reply is gruff: 'By what right, Sir, do you inquire?' – the line cited by Mathews. He eventually finds his daughter Fanny, who has answered Torrent's advertisement for a housekeeper.

The younger Colman's comedy was first performed at Covent Garden on 18 April 1805, with a cast that included Kemble as Barford and Simmons as Jonathan Oldskirt (see No. 754)

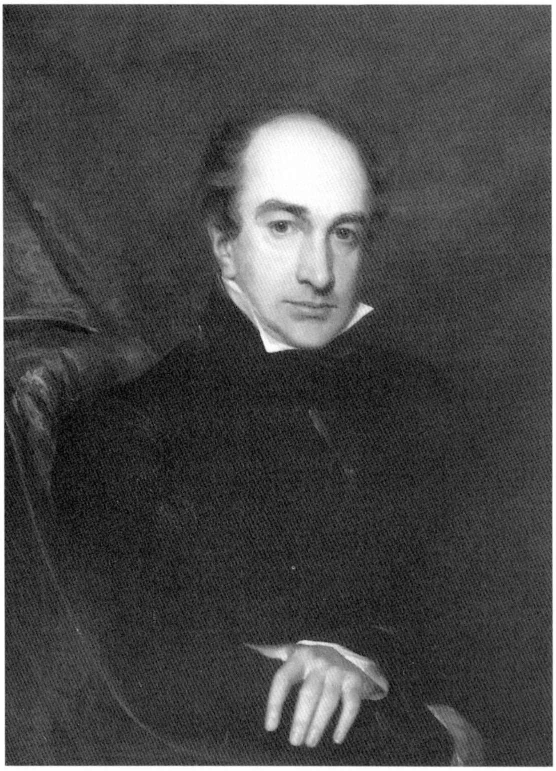

799
DANIEL TERRY

John Prescott Knight

Oil on canvas 76.5 x 63.5
INV: Mathews 112; RW/CKA 70
PROV: Charles Mathews
EXH: 1825 R.A. (552); 1833 London (112)
LIT: Herman Dyson, *John Prescott Knight, R.A., a catalogue* (1971), No. 5

Terry sits with his arms folded in a wooden tub chair with a red cushion, in front of red drapery. He wears a dark jacket with a high collar fastened down the front.

Daniel Terry, who was not related to the more illustrious theatrical dynasty of that name, made his first appearance in London in 1812 at the Haymarket, as Lord Ogleby in *The Clandestine Marriage*. He acted at Covent Garden from 1813 to 1822, and later appeared at Drury Lane and in Edinburgh. For Covent Garden he dramatised some of Sir Walter Scott's novels.

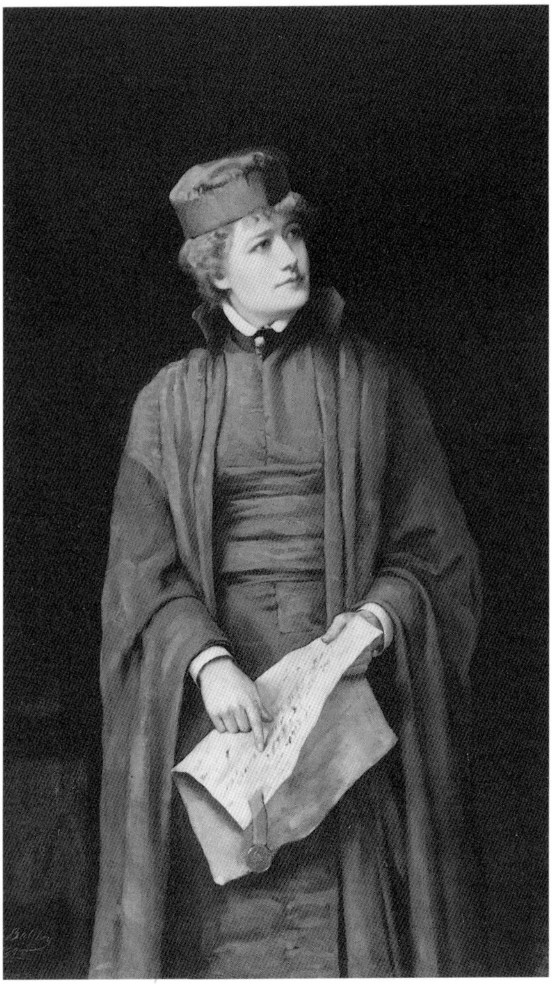

800*

DAME ELLEN TERRY

as Portia in *The Merchant of Venice*

by William Shakespeare

G.W. Baldry

Oil on canvas 92 x 61.5

INSCR: 'G.W. Baldry / 1883' (red paint b.l.)

INV: GCL 707

PROV: Bequeathed by the Baroness de Satje, 1964

EXH: 1981 Tokyo (YM15)

Portia's legal costume for the Trial Scene (Act IV, scene I), is red with a cylindrical soft-topped cap, a long gown with wide sleeves and high collar, and a long robe with a broad sash.

Millais borrowed the same costume from Ellen Terry for his portrait of Portia – which was sat for by a glamorous substitute – signed and dated 1884 (Metropolitan Museum, New York, 06.1328); his fair-haired model does not wear the cap.

Ellen Terry played Portia for the first time at the Prince of Wales Theatre on 17 April 1875, in a famous Bancroft production designed by Godwin. Her first peerformance in the role at the Lyceum took place in 1879; that production, with Henry Irving as Shylock, ran for 250 nights.

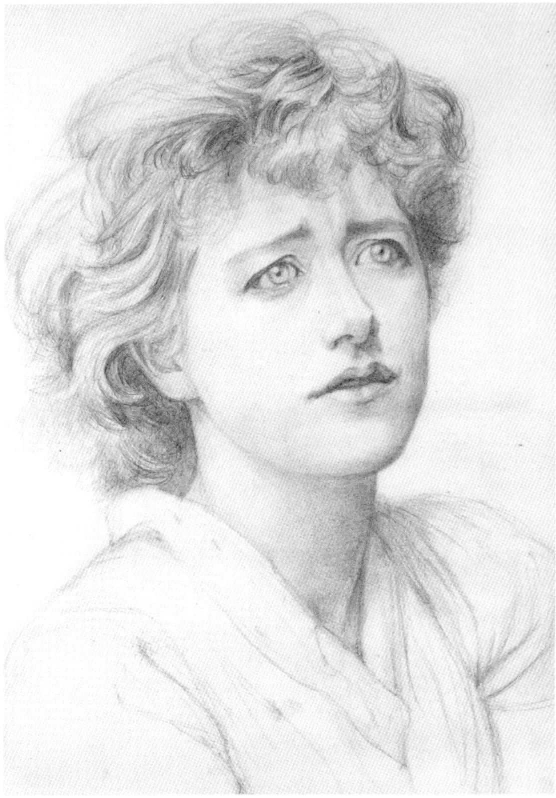

801

DAME ELLEN TERRY

as Ophelia (?) in *Hamlet*

by William Shakespeare

Violet Lindsay, Duchess of Rutland

Pencil on wove paper 35.1 x 25 (sight)

INV: CKA 614 (artist unknown, no character); Gift 461

PROV: R.H. Benson, by whom presented to the Garrick Club, 1928

REL: Watts Gallery pencil on wove paper 24 x 16.5 s. and d: '1879'

The sitter, shown head and shoulders, wears a V-necked dress or jacket.

802

PICTURE DISPOSED OF

DAME ELLEN TERRY

as Lady Macbeth

in *Macbeth*

by William Shakespeare

John Singer Sargent (copy after)

Oil on canvas 127 x 100.3 (disposed of)

INV: CKA 610; Gift 814?

PROV: Miss Clarke Gervaise, by whom presented to the Garrick Club, 1966 (?)

EXH: (1889 New Gallery [110])

REL: Tate 2053, oil on canvas 221 x 114.5, inscr: 'John S. Sargent'

LIT: See Ashton, 1980

The sitter wears the beetle-wing dress which is now in the Ellen Terry museum at Smallhythe. Lady Macbeth is shown about to place Duncan's crown on her own head, an incident that does not occur in the play.

Ellen Terry first played Lady Macbeth in Irving's new production at the Lyceum on 29 December 1888. Sargent saw this performance, was greatly excited by it, and asked Ellen Terry to sit for him in the part. His initial idea had been to show her sweeping out of the castle to greet Duncan between the rows of bobbing court ladies. The final composition is simpler and strikingly dramatic.

This picture, a copy of the famous portrait in the Tate Gallery, has been disposed of because it was so badly damaged.

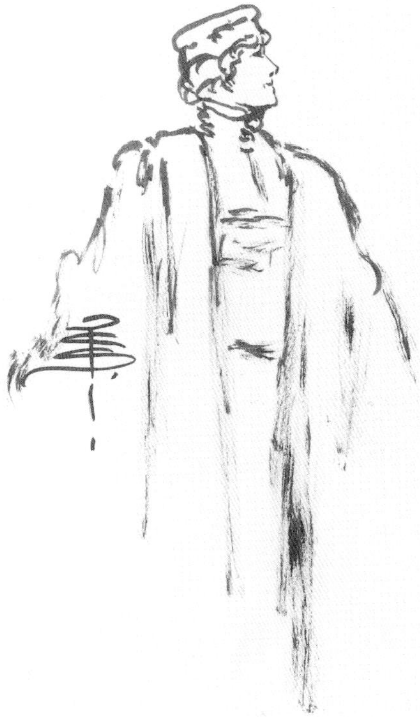

803

DAME ELLEN TERRY

as Portia

in *The Merchant of Venice*

by William Shakespeare

Unknown Artist

Brush and black ink with wash on wove paper 30.5 x 22.8

INSCR: illegible (see below)

INV: GCL 721; Gift 849

PROV: Brigadier Cudden, by whom presented to the Garrick Club, 1973

This economical sketch records the actress in the lawyers' robes she wore for Act IV, scene I of *The Merchant of Venice* (see No. 800).

The monogram may be that of Percy John Delf Smith (1882–1948).

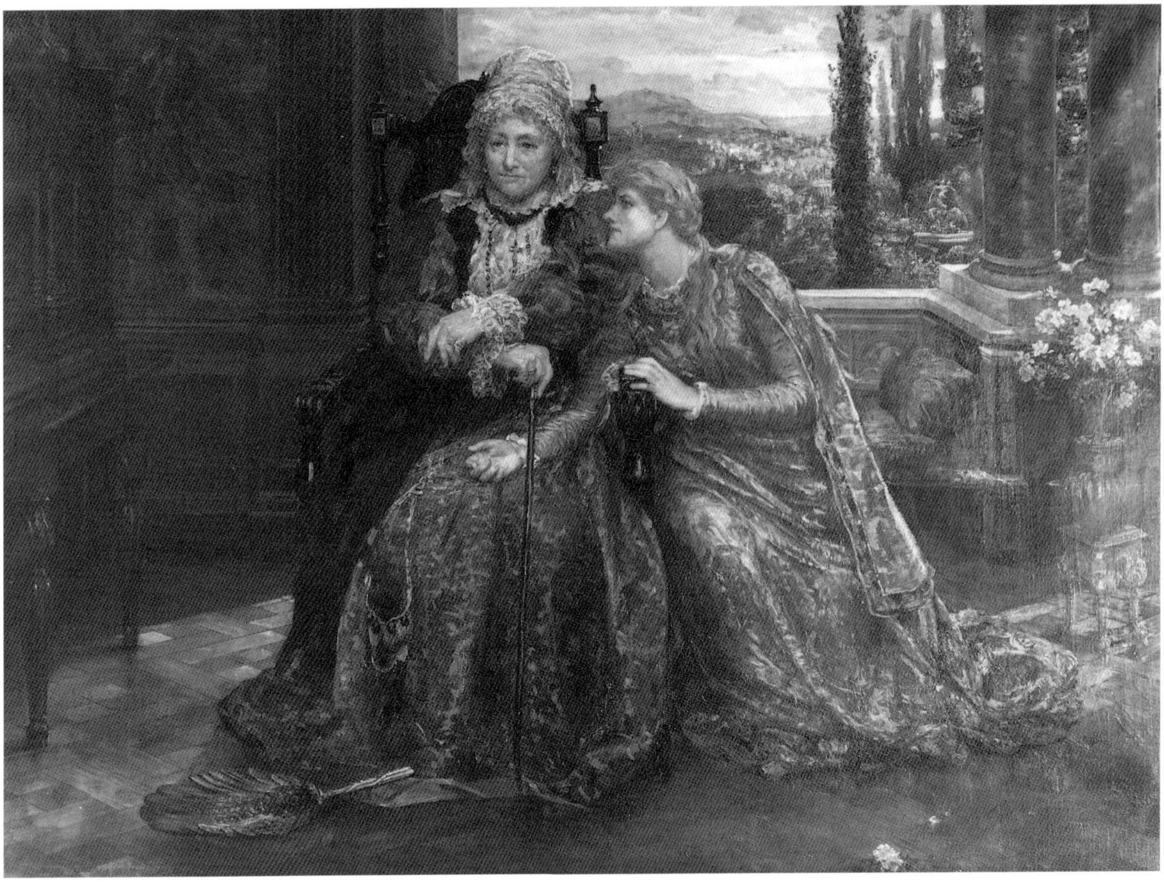

804

DAME ELLEN TERRY as Juliet and

FANNY STIRLING as the Nurse

in *Romeo and Juliet*

by William Shakespeare

Anna Lea Merritt

Oil on canvas 88.9 x 125.7

INSCR: 'Anna Lea Merritt / 1883' (b.r.)

INV: CKA 577; Gift 462

PROV: Mrs Warren de la Rue; Maurice Oswald Smith, by whom presented to the Garrick Club, 1928

EXH: 1980 Buxton (25)

REL: Royal Shakespeare Theatre Picture Gallery 72, oil on canvas 92 x 54.6, inscr: 'Anna Lea Merritt 1884' (figure of nurse only)

LIT: Anna Lea Merritt, *My Journey Through Life from 1924* (1928, 1986)

The Nurse wears a dark green dress with sleeves slashed to reveal a dull red. Her underskirt is of green and gold brocade. Juliet sits on a low stool beside her. Her blue and gold brocade dress and cloak are edged with a band of red and gold embroidery. An Italian landscape is visible beyond the balcony behind them.

Anna Lea Merritt described sittings for this picture in her memoirs:

> Mrs de la Rue ... ordered a picture to represent Ellen Terry and Mrs Stirling as the Nurse and Juliet they had recently acted. This was a great pleasure, for both the famous actresses gladly gave sittings in the costumes they had worn and the many choice pieces of Italian furniture, which my husband had left, fitted the scene to perfection. It was a pleasure too that the more I saw of Miss Terry the more sincerely I liked her, always generous and sympathetic and gifted. Mrs Stirling had given my [younger sister] Marion lessons in elocution when she lived with me in her childhood; lessons to cure a Yankee inflection, which she did not forget.

The production on which the picture is based opened at the Lyceum on 8 March 1882, and ran for 24 weeks. Irving spent £7,500 on an enormously elaborate staging and restored Shakespeare's text – the first time it had been heard since before Garrick's 'improvements'. When she tried to reform the traditional interpretation of Juliet, Ellen Terry faced opposition from Mrs Stirling, who had came out of retirement to play the nurse.

See also Nos. 953 and 954.

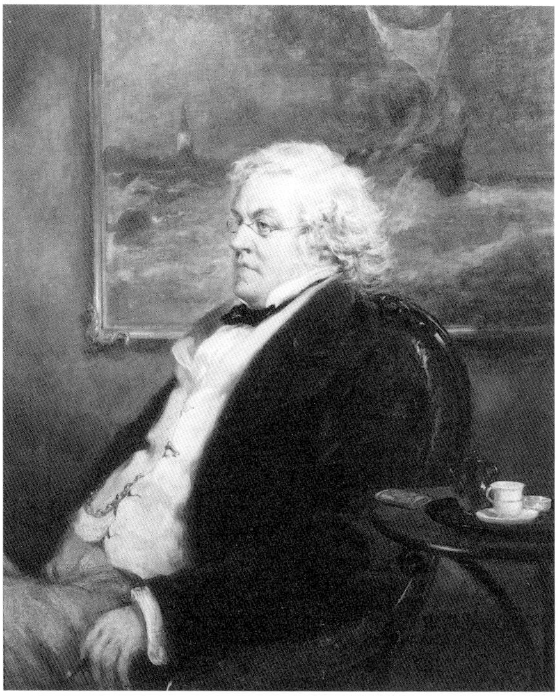

805
WILLIAM MAKEPEACE THACKERAY

Sir John Gilbert

Oil on canvas 59.7 x 49.5
INSCR: 'W.M. Thackeray / presented to / the Garrick Club / by John Gilbert / 1864' (black paint b.r.)
INV: RW/CKA 334; Gift 177
PROV: Presented by the artist, 1864
EXH: 1951 London (19); 1979 Bonn & Sunderland (272)
ENGR: L. Rousseau for the *Magazine of Art* (1891), p. 294
LIT: F.G. Kitton, 'The Portraits of Thackeray', *Magazine of Art* (July 1891), reproduced p. 194; Fitzgerald, p. 247

Thackeray, who became a member of the Garrick Club in 1833, has long grey hair and steel-rimmed spectacles. He wears greyish trousers, a black coat with a large collar, a yellow waistcoat with a thick gold watch-chain, a white shirt, and a black bow tie. On the table are a red cigarette box, a Garrick Club coffee pot, a white cup and saucer with green lines, and a glass ashtray. He sits in front of the Garrick Club Clarkson Stanfield (see No. 935).

Gilbert told F.G. Kitton that 'the picture was posthumous and was based on a drawing by him, aided by his recollection and photographs' (CKA). No. 805 is depicted in O'Neil's Billiard Room group (No. 793).

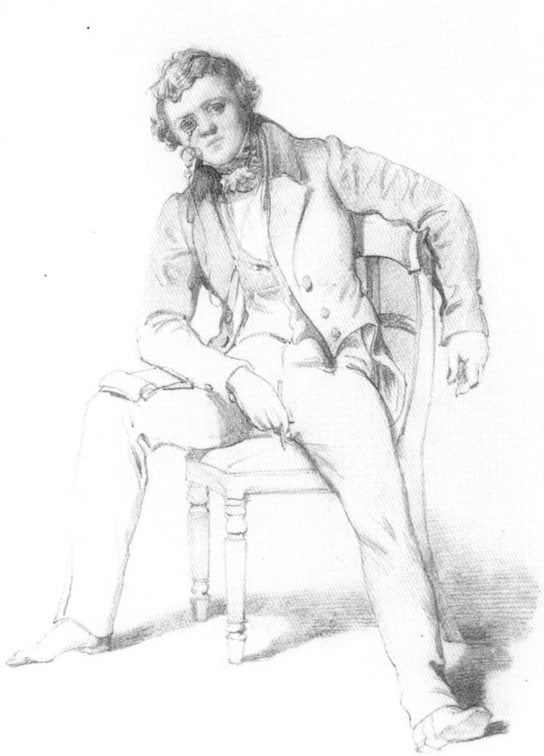

806
WILLIAM MAKEPEACE THACKERAY

Daniel Maclise

Pencil on wove paper 25.4 x 17.8
INSCR: 'W. M. T / 1832' (pencil b.l.); 'D M' (pencil b.r.)
INV: RW/CKA 503; Gift 173
PROV: Presented by the artist, 1864
EXH: 1972 London and Dublin (37)
REL: See No. 807
LIT: F.G. Kitton, 'The Portraits of Thackeray', *Magazine of Art* (July 1891), pp. 289–90; R.L. Ormond, *Catalogue of Early Victorian Portraits in the National Portrait Gallery* (1973), p. 464; G.N. Ray, *The Letters and Private Papers of W.M. Thackeray* (1945–46), I: 238

The young Thackeray sits casually, with a writing pad on his right knee and a pen in his right hand. He wears a cutaway coat and his spectacles dangle, with one lens in his right eye. See No. 807.

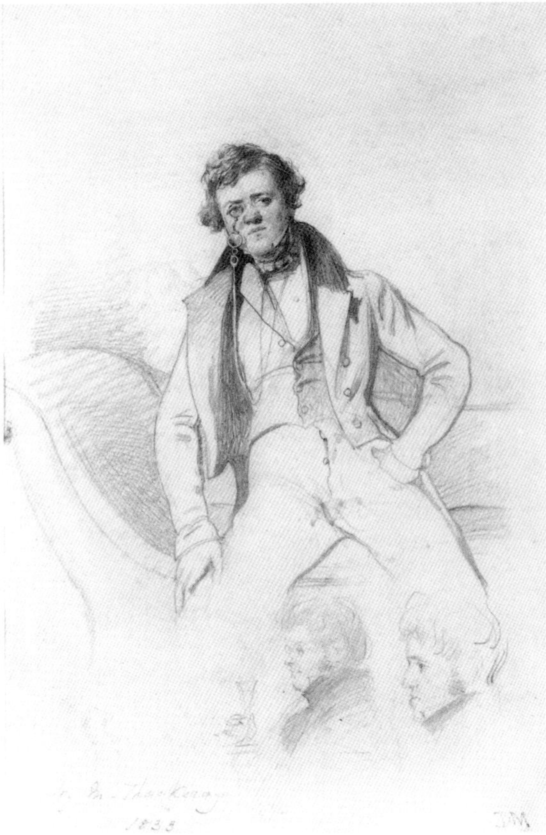

807

WILLIAM MAKEPEACE THACKERAY

Daniel Maclise

Pencil on wove paper 22.8 x 15.9
INSCR: 'W. M. Thackeray / 1833' (pencil b.l.);
'D M' (pencil b.r.)
INV: RW/CKA 507; Gift 173
PROV: Presented by the artist, 1864
REL: See No. 806

Thackeray sits on a chaise-longue, his left hand to his hip and his right resting on his thigh. He wears a cutaway coat and waistcoat, eyeglasses worn as a monocle (as in No. 806), a jacket and waistcoat with high collar, and a decorated neckerchief. Below the main figure are two male heads in profile to the left: one of these men holds a glass of champagne.

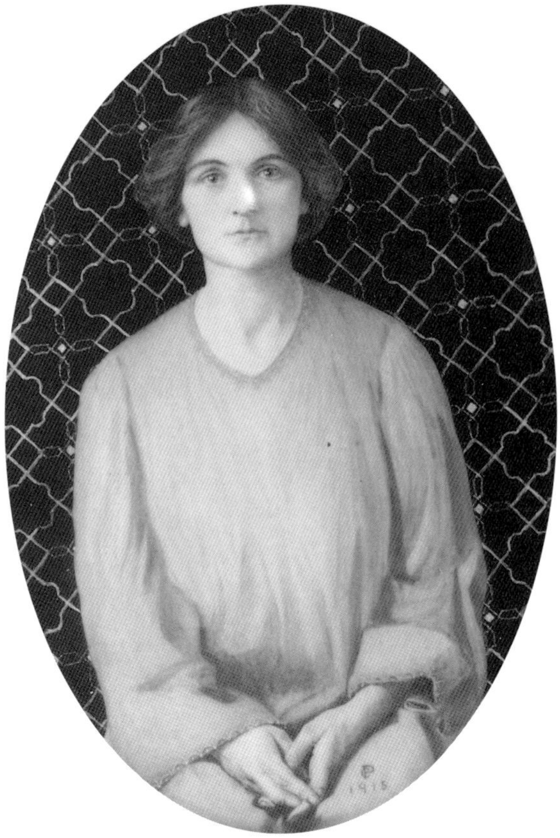

808

DAME SYBIL THORNDIKE

Cushla Parker

Watercolour on card 10.7 x 8.2 (oval)
INSCR: 'CP [in monogram] / 1915' (b.r.);
'Miss Cushla Parker / 9 Ann St / Edin / Miss Sybil Thorndike / Sold' (pen and ink on back-board)
INV: GCL 678; Gift 740
PROV: Bequeathed by Alderson Burrell Horne, 1954

Sybil Thorndike wears a plain, loose red dress. The background is black with a strapwork pattern in gold.

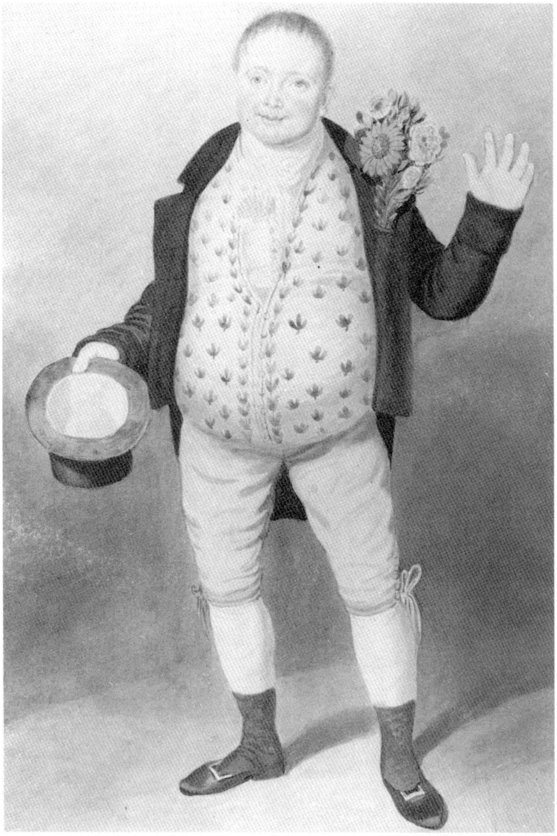

809

JAMES TOKELY

as Peter Pastoral in *Teasing Made Easy*

by Robert Francis Jameson

Samuel De Wilde

Pencil and watercolour on wove paper 37 x 23.5

INSCR: 'De Wilde / Sep 1817' (pencil b.l.)

INV: Mathews 224; RW/CKA 59B

PROV: Charles Mathews

EXH: 1833 London (224)

Peter Pastoral holds a black tall hat with white lining and green under-brim. He wears silver-buckled black shoes, black socks, white stockings, light brown breeches, a black coat wide open at the front, a white waistcoat decorated with green clover leaves, a high white stock, and a veritable bouquet of flowers in his buttonhole.

Jameson's operatic farce, with music by Henry Bishop, was first performed at the Haymarket on 30 July 1817, with Tokely as the original Peter Pastoral. There were 35 performances over the summer season, the last on 15 September 1817. The *Theatrical Inquisitor* described the action of the piece and then stuck its quill into Peter Pastoral: 'If Mr Tokely be excepted, the author has written much below the standard of his actors' abilities.'

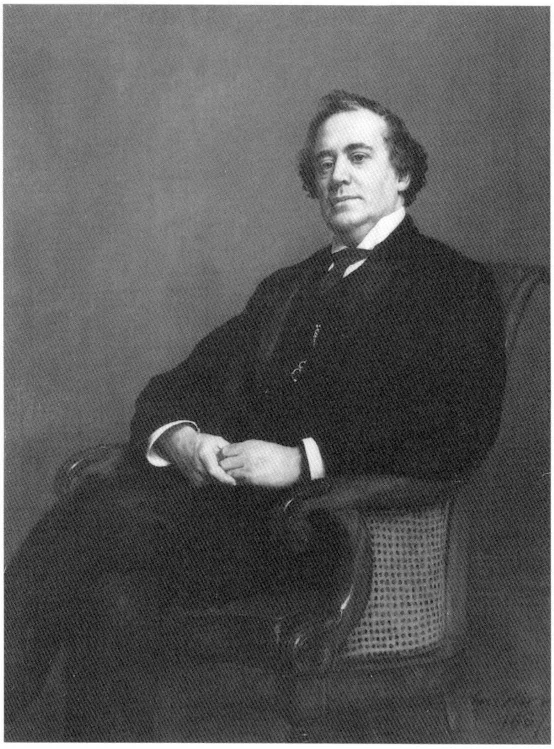

810

JOHN LAWRENCE TOOLE

The Hon. John Collier

Oil on canvas 125.7 x 100.3

INSCR: 'John Collier / 1887' (black paint b.r.)

INV: RW/CKA 340; Gift 248

PROV: Sir Henry Irving, by whom presented to the Garrick Club, 1895

LIT: Fitzgerald, p. 239

Toole wears a dark grey suit with satin lapels, white wing collar, stiff cuffs and a red tie. A gold chain hangs at his breast. He sits in a mahogany chair, upholstered in green leather.

Toole, actor and manager, became a member of the Garrick Club in 1864. His close friend Irving owned this picture. He was also a friend of Dickens, in whose *A Christmas Carol* he appeared as Bob Cratchit in 1859.

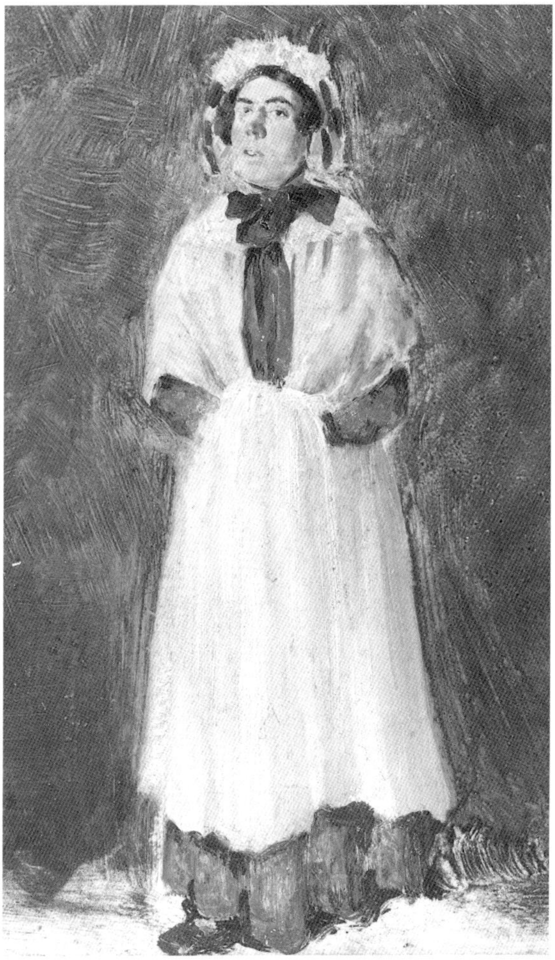

811

JOHN LAWRENCE TOOLE

dressed as a woman

John Keeley

Oil on panel 31 x 26

INSCR: '299 / J. L. Toole / as .../ by Keeley'

(pencil on verso)

INV: Not listed

PROV: Unknown

Toole *en travestie* presents an unprepossessing aspect, with prominent teeth, a big red nose, and black hair parted in the middle under a white bonnet decorated with blue ribbons and tied under the chin with a large blue bow. He wears a dark dress in brown and grey, a long white apron hiding his hands, and a large white shawl over his shoulders, tucked into the apron.

The identification of the sitter is thought by Toole scholars to be secure, though the role in which he is shown cannot be specified.

Toole excelled in Cockney humour and *opéra bouffe*.

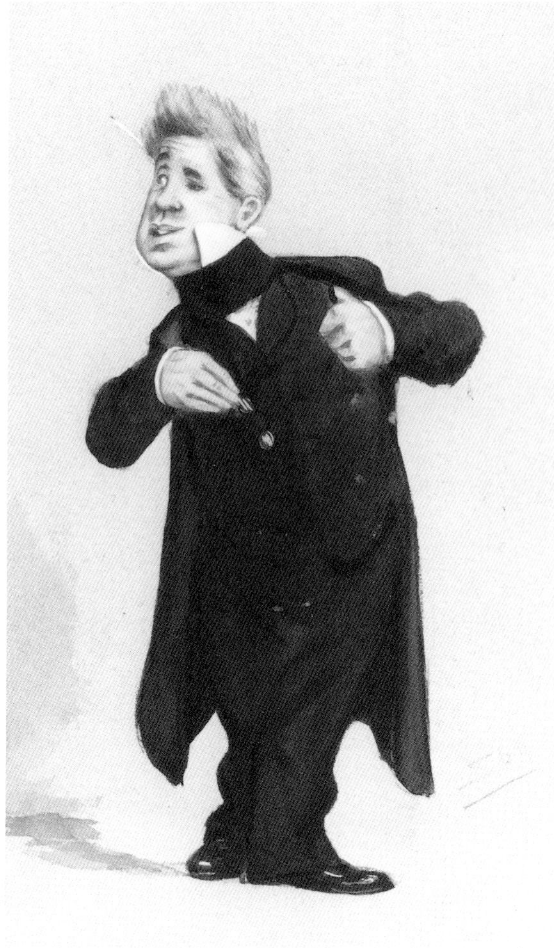

812

JOHN LAWRENCE TOOLE

as Professor Muddle in *A Spelling Bee*

by Robert Reece

Sir Leslie Ward ('Spy')

Caricature, pencil and watercolour

on blue-grey wove paper 30.8 x 18.1

INSCR: 'Spy' (pencil b.r.)

INV: CKA 617; Gift 359

PROV: Presented by R. Woodhouse, 1912

LIT: *Vanity Fair*, 29 June 1876, inscr: 'A Spelling Bee'

Professor Muddle wears black shoes, black crumpled trousers, a long black coat and waistcoat, and a high white collar with a broad black band.

Reece's farce was first performed at the Gaiety on 16 February 1876.

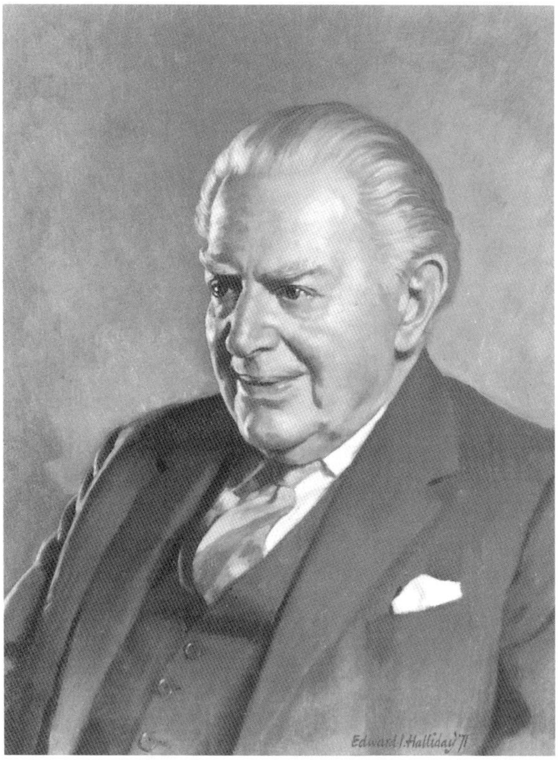

813
BEN TRAVERS

Edward Halliday

Oil on canvas 50.5 x 41
INSCR: 'Edward I. Halliday '71' (grey paint b.r.)
INV: GCL 709; Gift 839
PROV: Presented by the artist, 1971
EXH: 1972 R.S.P.P. (5)

Ben Travers wears a grey coat and waistcoat, a Garrick Club tie, and a white shirt. The background is a striking pale green.

Travers became a member of the Club in 1929.

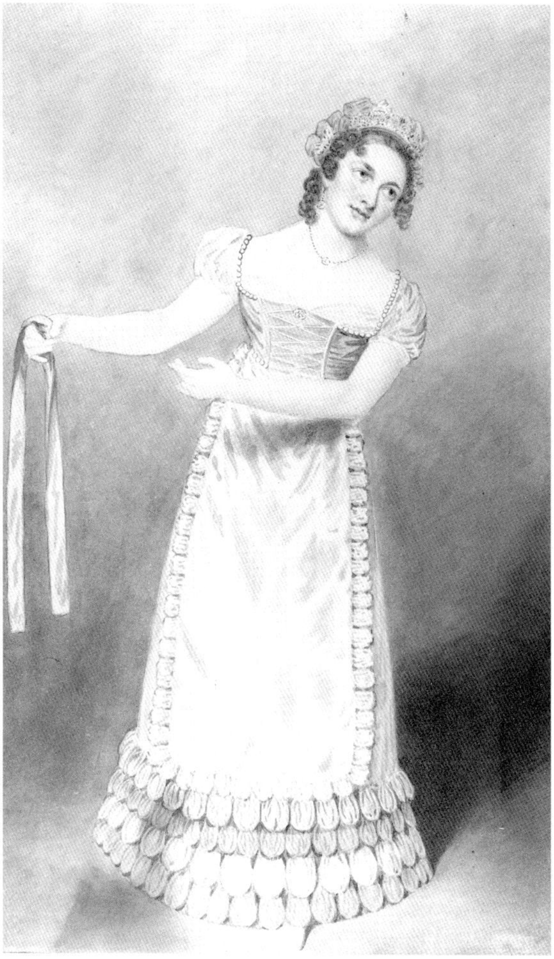

814
ANNA MARIA TREE
as Susanna in *The Marriage of Figaro*
by Wolfgang Amadeus Mozart
and Lorenzo Da Ponte,
after P. Beaumarchais

Samuel De Wilde

Pencil and watercolour on wove paper 37 x 23.5
INSCR: 'S De Wilde / 18...'
(pencil lower l., much rubbed)
INV: Mathews 240; RW/CKA 68B
PROV: Charles Mathews
EXH: 1833 London (240)

As Susanna, Anna Maria Tree holds a green ribbon in her right hand and gestures to it with her left. She wears white slippers and a silvery dress which has short flounced sleeves and four layers of lotus flower decoration around the hem.

No. 814 possibly commemorates a benefit performance for Anna Maria Tree given at Covent Garden on 21 May 1822, when she acted Viola to her sister Ellen's Olivia in *Twelfth Night* and Susanna in a truncated adaptation of *The Marriage of Figaro*. Anna Maria included the song 'Rose d'Amour' and performed a castanet dance; according to a manuscript note on the playbill in the Garrick Club, she also danced a pas seul, by permission of R.W. Elliston. That night marked the first appearance on stage of her sister, Ellen Tree, who subsequently became a formidable actress as Mrs Charles Kean.

Mozart's opera buffa, with a libretto by Lorenzo da Ponte after Beaumarchais, was first staged at the Burgtheater, Vienna, on 1 May 1786, with a cast that included Anna Storace as Susanna (see Nos. 779 and 780). The piece was first performed in England (in Italian) at the King's Theatre in 1812, and the first performance in English was given at Covent Garden in 1819, with Jones, Liston, Isaacs, Mrs Dickens, Miss Beaumont and Catherine Stephens.

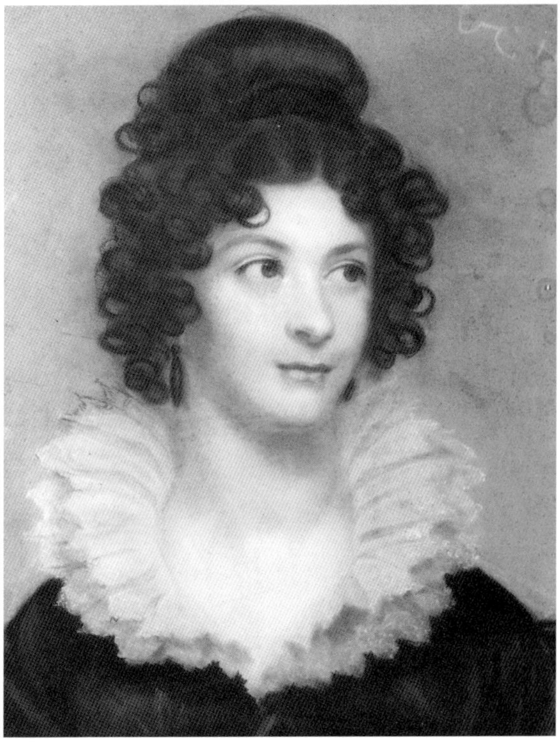

815

ANNA MARIA TREE

Alexander Pope

Pastel on paper 48.9 x 40.6
INV: RW 301 (Mrs Pope [Elizabeth Younge]);
CKA 301; Gift 50
PROV: Bequeathed by the artist's widow, 1838
ENGR: Anon. for *La Belle Assemblée* (1 June 1820), stipple (vignette, with more of the arm visible and the dress to below waist)

The actress is presented as a fashionable young woman of 1820 with ringlets and a 'betsey' collar. She wears pendant jet earrings.

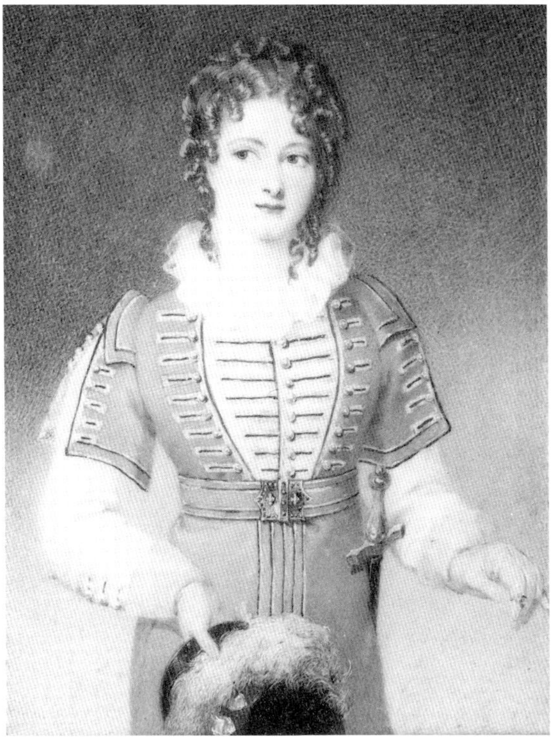

816

ANNA MARIA TREE

as Viola in *Twelfth Night*

by William Shakespeare

Louisa Sharpe

Watercolour on ivory 13.4 x 10.5
INV: RW 427A? (unknown sitter by Richard Cosway); CKA 427A
PROV: Unknown, acquired before 1909
EXH: 1821 R.A. (868)
ENGR: William Holl for *Dramatical and Musical Magazine* (April 1823) pub. Beale & T. Holt, stipple (vignette, cut at elbows and either side of shoulders)

Viola looks after the departing Malvolio, who has given her the ring that Olivia pretends Viola left behind (Act II, scene 2). She holds the ring gingerly in her yellow-gloved left hand and has a black hat with a feather round the brim in her right. Her male costume consists of a vaguely military brown-orange tunic with black and white piping, an orange-brown belt with a gold buckle, and a dagger with a gold hilt. The costume is similar to, and a foretaste of, principal boy costumes of the later 19th century.

Twelfth Night was revived at Covent Garden on 8 November 1820, with Anna Maria Tree as Viola, and played for 17 nights during the season.

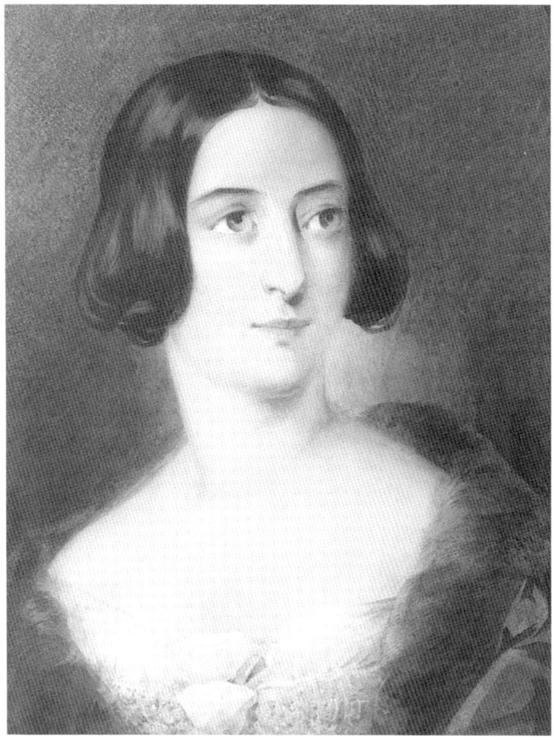

817

ELLEN TREE

Unknown Artist

Watercolour and body colour on paper 51.5 x 43.1
INV: RW/CKA 86; Gift 280
PROV: Sir Squire Bancroft, by whom presented to the Garrick Club, 1902

Ellen Tree's low-cut white dress has an orange bow at the front and she has a fur-trimmed cloak over her shoulders.

Ellen Tree was the wife of the great actor–manager Charles Kean and appeared in his lavish historical productions at the Princess's Theatre, 1851–59.

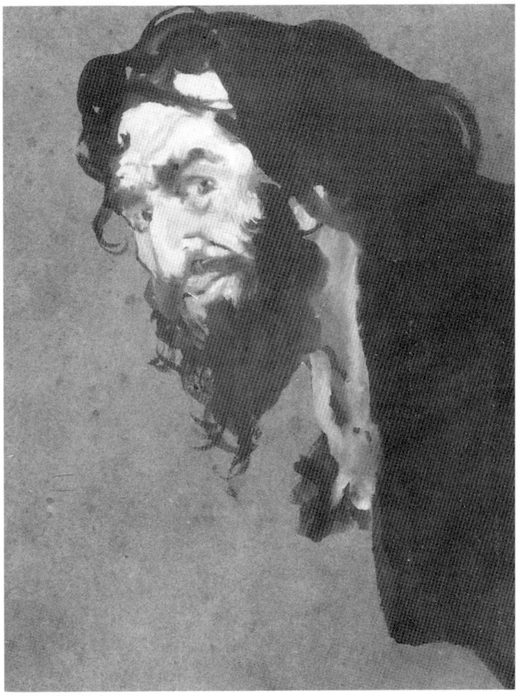

818

SIR HERBERT BEERBOHM TREE

as Svengali in *Trilby* by Paul M. Potter, after George Du Maurier

Albert Morrow

Watercolour on dark grey wove paper 39.1 x 21.6
INSCR: 'A / MORROW' (red paint b.l.)
INV: CKA 582; Gift 383
PROV: R.R.M. See, by whom presented to the Garrick Club, 1919

Svengali is shown almost in caricature, with a demonic stare and long, dark grey hair.

Potter's adaptation of Du Maurier's novel was first performed at the Theatre Royal, Manchester, on 7 September 1895. It moved into the Haymarket on 30 October 1895 and ran for 254 performances, in which Tree played Svengali and Dorothea Baird played Trilby. An anonymous American version had previously opened at the Novelty Theatre on 20 July 1895, with Trant Fisher as Svengali and V. St. Lawrence as Trilby, but had an unimpressive run of only six performances. This version was probably the one Tree had seen in Philadelphia, which inspired him to commission Potter to adapt the novel. Svengali became his best-known role. There was a brief revival of seven performances at Her Majesty's on 7 June 1897, with Tree and Dorothea Baird. The money made out of the first run of the play provided the initial funds for the building of Her Majesty's.

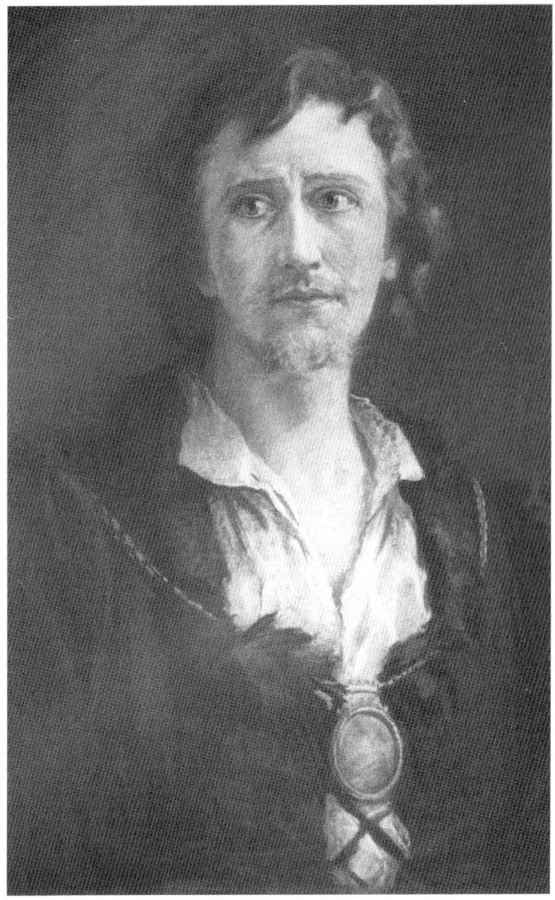

819

SIR HERBERT BEERBOHM TREE

as Hamlet in *Hamlet* by William Shakespeare

Ethel Webling

Pastel on paper 76.2 x 61
INSCR: 'Ethel Webling 1892' (pale blue chalk b.r.)
INV: GCL 665; Gift 705
PROV: Mrs L.B. McRaye, by whom presented to the Garrick Club, 1951
EXH: 1892 R.A. (1327)

Hamlet has Tree's pale blue eyes, ginger hair and florid complexion. He wears a fur-edged black doublet laced at the front, over a white shirt with open collar. A large oval miniature hangs from a gold chain round his neck.

Beerbohm Tree gave his first Hamlet in Manchester on 9 September 1891. His first London Hamlet was performed at the Haymarket on 21 January 1892 and was a great success.

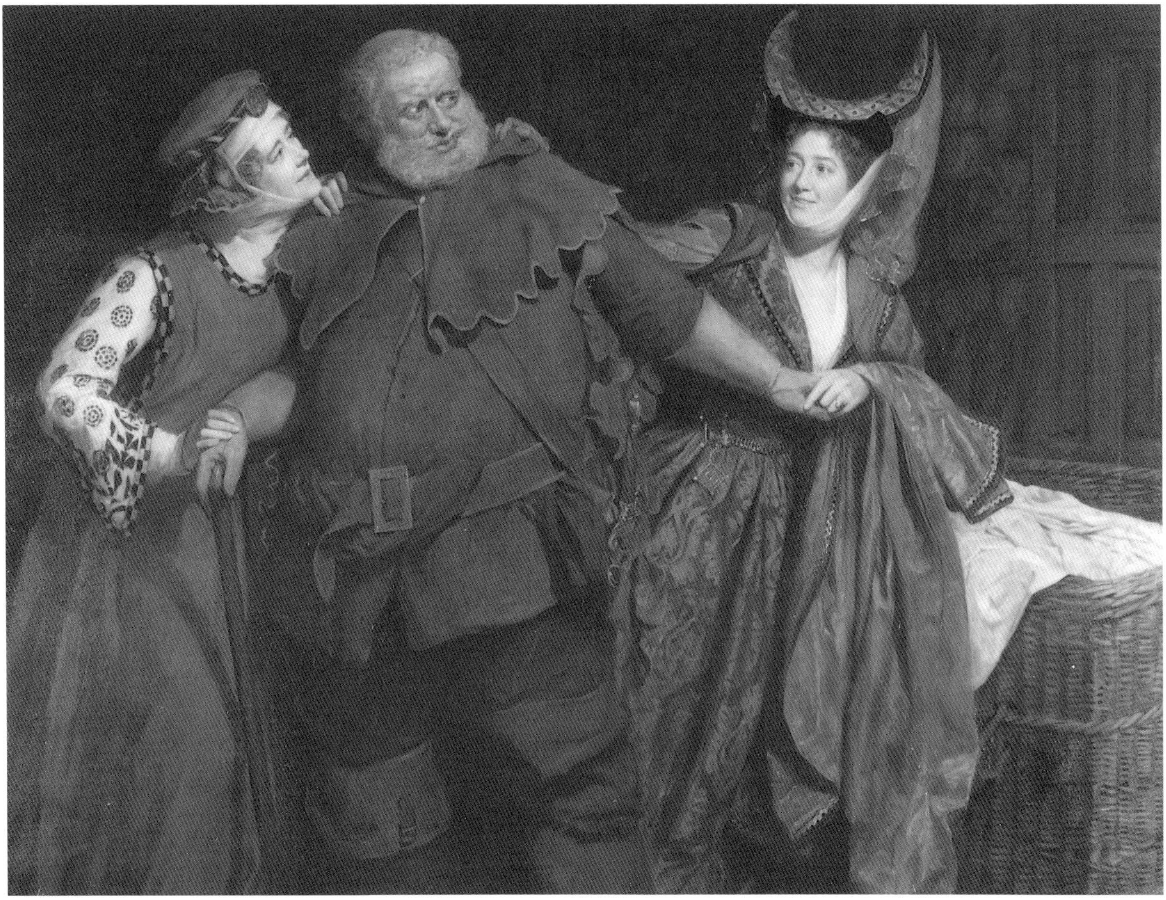

820*

SIR HERBERT BEERBOHM TREE as Falstaff, *DAME ELLEN TERRY* as Mrs Page and *DAME MADGE KENDAL* as Mrs Ford in *The Merry Wives of Windsor* by William Shakespeare

The Hon. John Collier

Oil on canvas 156.2 x 221
INSCR: 'John Collier / 1904' (dark brown paint b.l.)
INV: CKA 599; Gift 382
PROV: Presented by 100 members, 1919
EXH: 1904 R.A. (470)

Collier shows a comic climax of the play, in Act III, scene 3, when the Merry Wives wreak their revenge on the libidinous Falstaff for wooing them both at the same time. Mistress Ford is entertaining Falstaff when Mistress Page enters to warn her that her husband is on his way home. Falstaff is bundled into the buck basket (seen bottom right) and carried out by the servants, to be dumped in the muddy ditch at Datchet Mead on the Thames. Mistress Page (Ellen Terry) stands on the left, her chin and left hand resting on Falstaff's shoulder. She wears a flat red cap, a long red sleeveless overgown, and a long-sleeved white underdress embroidered in black. Falstaff (Tree) wears brown boots with paler brown tops, fawn gauntlets, brown breeches, a brown tunic, and a broad brown belt with a brass buckle. Mistress Ford (Madge Kendal) has red hair. She wears a horned headdress with a white wimple, a long-sleeved green-blue dress with a floral design, and a long red cloak with a gold pattern, edged in gold.

Tree presented *The Merry Wives of Windsor* at His Majesty's in 1902 as his contribution to the glittering Coronation season. It was a typically lavish Tree production, with scenery by W. Telbin, Walter Johnstone and Hawes Craven, and costumes designed by Percy Anderson. The incidental music was by Sir Arthur Sullivan, Raymond Roze and Norman Bath. Tree achieved the diplomatic coup of having Ellen Terry and Madge Kendal together on the same stage after Oscar Ashe suggested the idea as a joke. This highly successful production opened on 2 June 1902.

Sir Herbert, who was half-brother to Max Beerbohm, became a member of the Garrick Club in 1884.

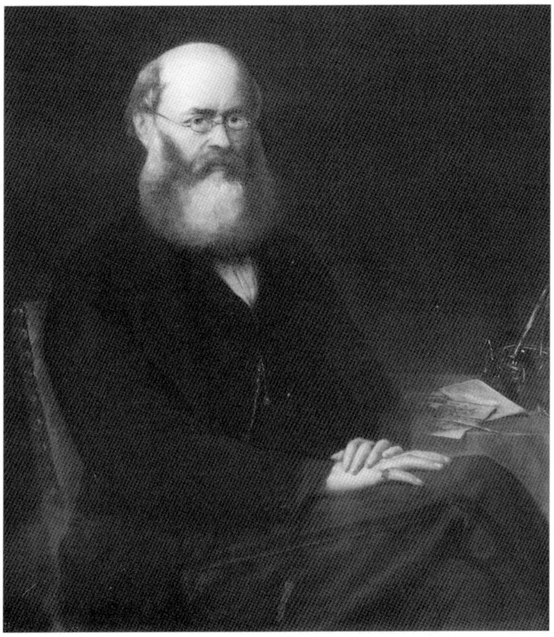

821*

ANTHONY TROLLOPE

Henry O'Neil

Oil on canvas 59 x 49.5
INSCR: '18 [monogram] 73' (b.l.)
INV: RW/CKA 337
PROV: Presented by the artist between 1873 and 1880
LIT: Michael Sadleir, *Trollope: A Commentary* (1927), p. 215, reproduced facing p. 214; C.P. Snow, *Trollope* (1975), p. 145, reproduced

Trollope, with full beard and a moustache, sits in a padded leather chair. He wears wire-rimmed spectacles and is in evening dress. Trollope became a member of the Club in 1862.

822

CAVE UNDERHILL
as Obadiah in *The Committee*
by Sir Robert Howard

Robert Bing

Oil on canvas 33.2 x 24.5 (damaged)
INV: Mathews 83; RW/CKA 273
PROV: Charles Mathews
EXH: 1833 London (83)
ENGR: John Faber Jnr 1712, mezzotint 11.7 x 8.9, inscr: 'Mr Cave Underhill ye Famous Comedian / in ye Habit of Obadiah ye Fanatick Elder / R. Bing pinx. J. Faber Junior fecit 1712'; John Faber Jnr, etching 12 x 8.6; W. Parsons, etching 11.5 x 8.2 (reversed); Anon. pub. J. Caulfield 1825, line 12 x 8.9; Anon., line 12 x 8.9
LIT: Fitzgerald, p. 212; Griffiths, p. 294

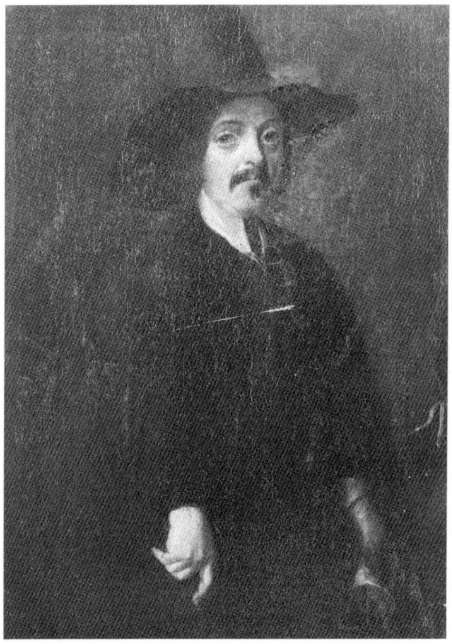

822 *Cave Underhill as Obadiah*

Obadiah is the clerk to the Honourable Committee of Sequestration (see No. 613). He looks the perfect Presbyterian with his high-crowned hat and a black cloak over a black doublet. He has grey gloves, a goatee and a drooping moustache.

Despite its poor condition, this picture appears to be an original work rather than a copy of the mezzotint of 1712 – or, indeed, of any of the later engravings.

Howard's comedy was originally performed at the Theatre Royal, Vere Street, on 27 November 1662.

823

LOCATION UNKNOWN

KATE VAUGHAN
in Egyptian character

Unknown Artist

Pencil on fine wove paper 27.3 x 18.2
INSCR: 'Kate Vaughan' (pencil b.c.)
INV: Not listed
PROV: Unknown

Kate Vaughan's Egyptian character dress includes a headdress and a short-sleeved skirt with hieroglyphs down the front and round the hem. In her left hand she holds an Egyptian lotus-leaf fan. She strikes an exotic dancing attitude. There is a pyramid bottom right.

A music hall dancer and comic actress from 1876 to 1883, the sitter was one of the famous Gaiety quartet, with Nellie Farren, Edway Terry and Royce. After giving up dancing she played such comedy roles as Lydia Languish, Miss Hardcastle and Lady Teazle (OC).

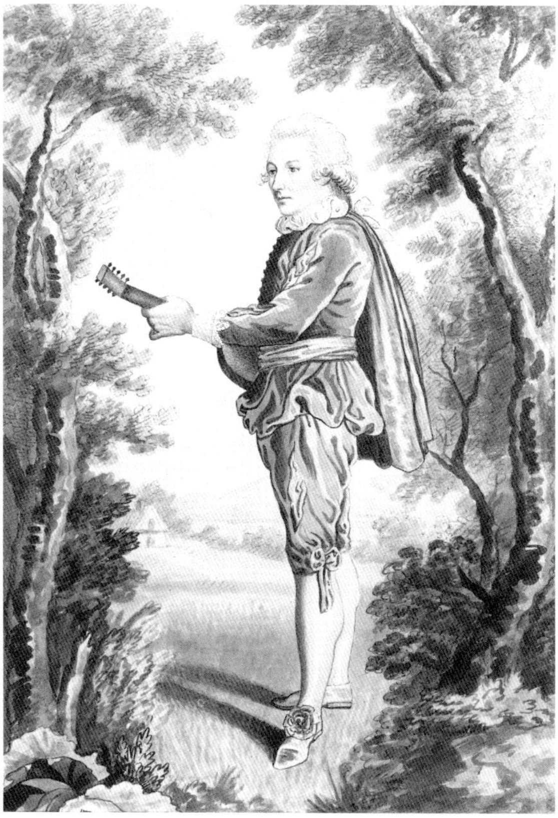

824
JOSEPH VERNON
as Cymon in *Cymon*
by David Garrick

Unknown Artist

Pencil and watercolour
on wove paper 23.8 x 16.8
INSCR: 'Mr Vernon' (pen and brown ink
on mount below CM)
INV: Not listed
PROV: Charles Mathews
(Print collection Vol. III f. 30)

Cymon has a powdered wig and wears blue shoes with red rosettes, blue stockings, blue breeches with pink bows at the knee, a blue doublet slashed with pink, a pink sash, lace cuffs and collar, and a short pink cloak. He is in a woodland setting with trees to either side, and a cottage can be seen in the distance.

This full-length miniature portrait is in the style of Cosway, and is possibly copied from an original by him.

Garrick's dramatic romance was first performed at Drury Lane on 2 January 1767, with Vernon as Cymon. He played the role in the revival at Drury Lane on 17 January 1778, and his last appearance in the part was at Drury Lane on 16 April 1781.

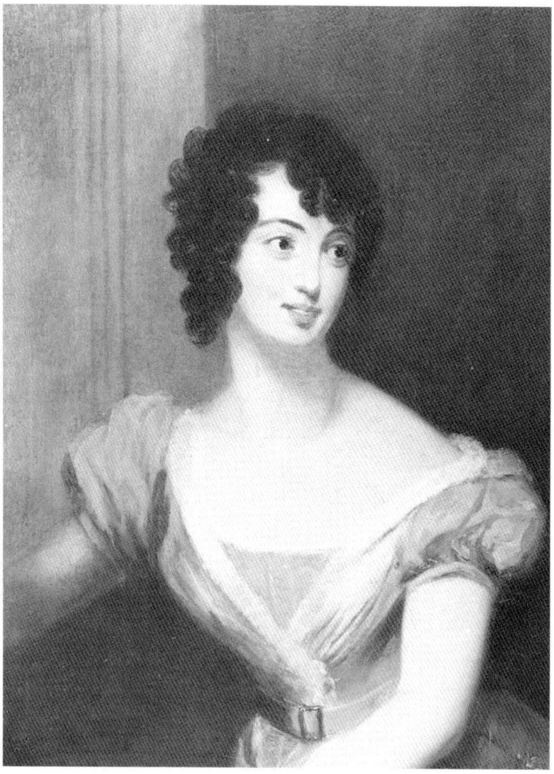

825
LUCIA ELIZABETH VESTRIS
as Phoebe in *Paul Pry*
by John Poole

Robert William Buss
(copy after George Clint)

Oil on panel 32 x 24.5
INV: Mathews 122; RW/CKA 275
PROV: Charles Mathews
EXH: 1833 London (122); 1958 London
REL: Original: Theatre Museum TM 27, oil on canvas
127.4 x 101.7, exh: R.A. 1827 (222), engr: Thomas Lupton
pub. Moon, Boys & Graves 1 July 1828, mezzotint

Phoebe wears a pink, fur-trimmed dress which has short flounced sleeves, a transparent white gauze over the bodice and a pink belt.

This painting is a copy of a detail from Clint's scene from *Paul Pry*, with Liston in the title role. The comedy was performed for the first time at the Haymarket on 13 September 1825, with Liston, and with Mme Vestris as Phoebe, singing 'Cherry Ripe' and 'The Lover's Mistake'.

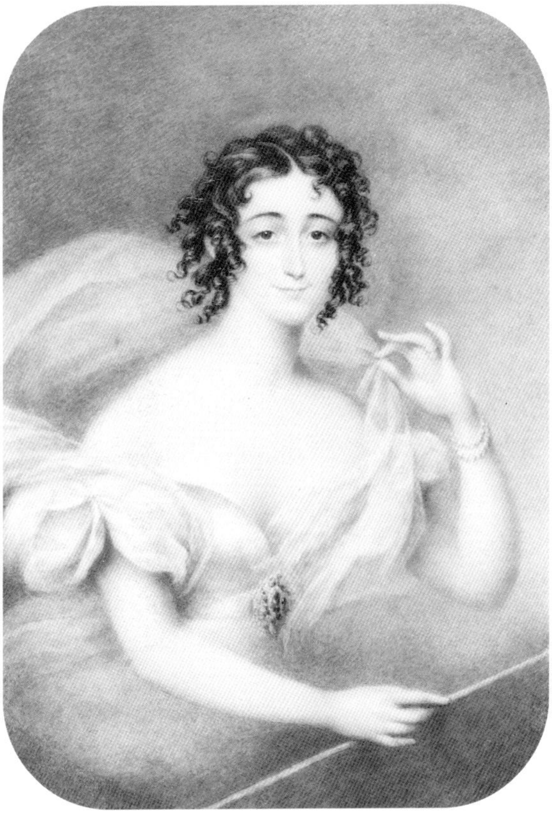

826

LUCIA ELIZABETH VESTRIS

in allegorical character

James Warren Childe

Watercolour on ivory 17.1 x 12
INSCR: 'Childe' (b.l.)
INV: CKA 542; Gift 345
PROV: Duke of Cambridge;
Rear-Admiral Sir Adolphus Fitz George,
by whom presented to the Garrick Club, 1910
EXH: 1958 London

Mme Vestris floats in the clouds, a wand in her right hand, her left elegantly pinching the gauze that floats over her shoulder. She wears a low-cut dress with puff sleeves and a large jewel at the waist. On her left wrist is a double-stranded pearl bracelet.

Her distinguished career on the English stage included singing and acting in burlesque and light comedies, excelling in the roles of fashionable ladies, and managing the Olympic Theatre from 1830 and later the Lyceum with strong discipline. Mme Vestris is credited with many improvements in scenery and accurate costume, and with introducing the box-set, with realistic ceiling, in 1832. In 1838 she married one of her actors, Charles James Mathews (see Nos. 479–594).

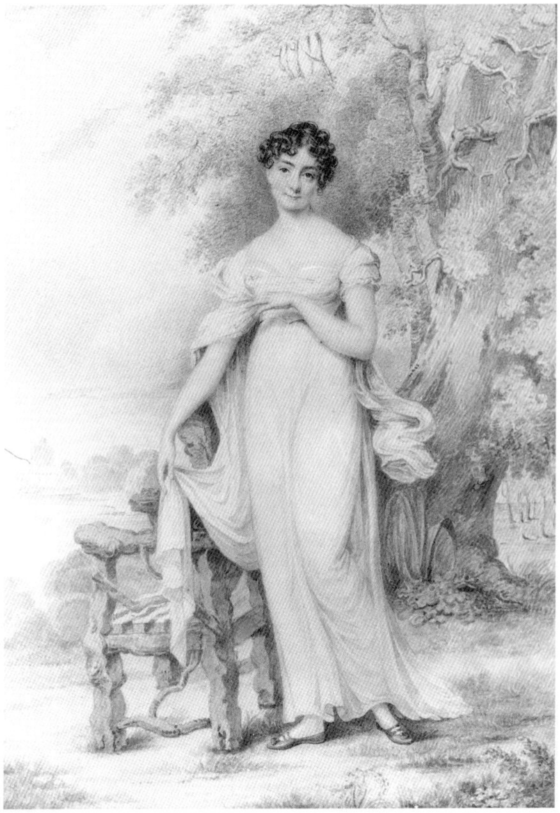

827

LUCIA ELIZABETH VESTRIS

Louisa Sharpe (?)

Pencil and grey wash with watercolour
and a little white body colour
on wove paper 33 x 24.1
INV: RW 320? (unknown sitter and artist);
CKA 320
PROV: Unknown
EXH: 1958 London
ENGR: Similar to: John Cook after Louisa Sharpe
1828 pub. Richard Bentley 1847, stipple and line
10.8 x 8.9 (half-length only; same hair and angle
of head and frock, r. elbow resting
on bank, hands down in front)

Mme Vestris, standing by a rustic garden seat in front of a large, gnarled tree, strikes a pose of elegant whimsy. She wears a simple short-sleeved Empire dress, with a flowing scarf. A church tower is seen across a stretch of water to the left.

No. 827 is similar (hair, angle of head and dress) to a drawing by Louisa Sharpe dated 1828 and published by Richard Bentley in 1847.

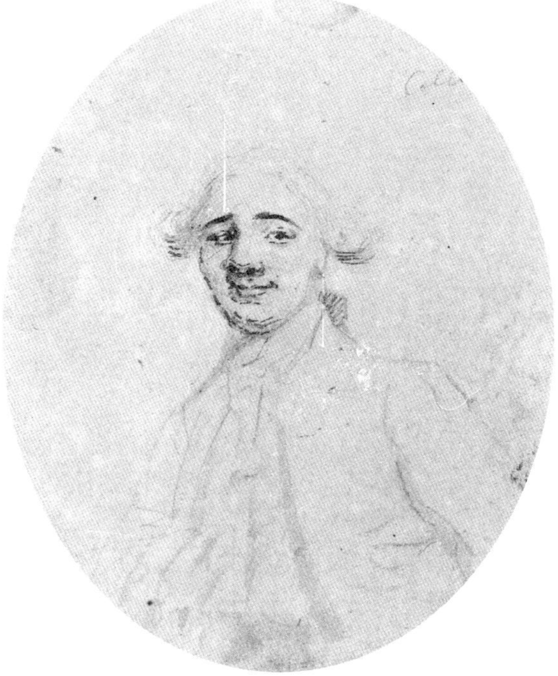

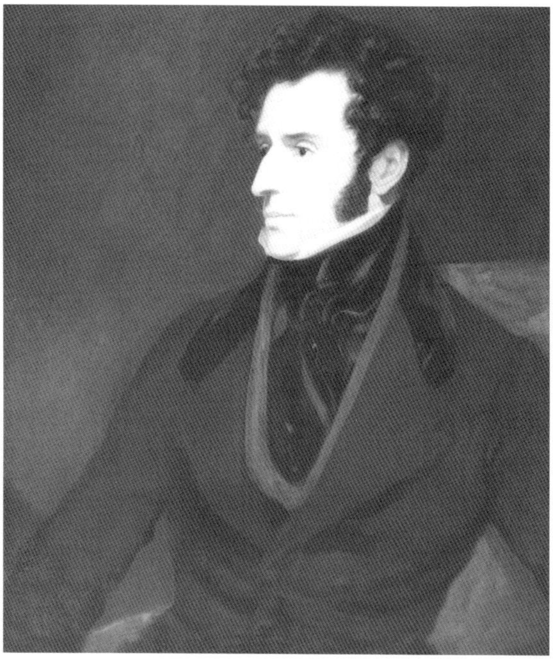

829 *James William Wallack*

828

MR WAKER

James Dowling Herbert

Pencil with some brown and grey wash
on discoloured wove paper 10.2 x 8.9 (oval)
INSCR: 'Collar …'? (pencil t.r.); 'Herbert fecit.'
(pen and brown ink on mount b.l. CM);
'Waker Comedian / Dublin.'
(pen and brown ink on mount b.c. CM)
INV: RW/CKA 491A (Walker)
PROV: Charles Mathews (not in catalogue)

The Dublin painter Francis Robert West portrayed Waker as Roger in *The Ghost*, engraved by Jonathan Fisher. Mathews's inscription certainly refers to this Irish actor and not to the imaginary 'Walker' invented by RW.

829

JAMES WILLIAM WALLACK

George Clint

Oil on canvas 74.3 x 61.6
INV: RW/CKA 71
PROV: Purchased, 1858

Wallack wears a brown jacket with broad lapels, a pale brown waistcoat, a high white collar, and a complicated black cravat. He sits in a red upholstered armchair.

Son of the English actors William and Elizabeth Wallack, the sitter acted for several years at Drury Lane and in 1818 went to New York, where he became an important actor and manager for many years. Dividing his time between London and New York, Wallack was said to have crossed the Atlantic some 35 times (OC). His son, the American actor Lester Wallack (1820–1888), married Emily Millais, sister of the artist Sir John Everett Millais (see No. 604).

James William Wallack was one of the original members of the Garrick Club in 1831.

830

LOCATION UNKNOWN

DAME GENEVIÈVE WARD

Sir Arthur Stockdale Cope

Charcoal on wove paper, bust
INV: GCL 676; Gift 730 (not located 1988)
PROV: Mrs M.C. Percival, by whom
presented to the Garrick Club, 1953

The accomplished actress Geneviève Ward appeared in London in 1874 in a number of capital roles, including Antigone, Belvidera, Portia, and Emilia in *Othello*. She made her American début in New York in 1878. Her performance in *Forget-Me-Not*, brought on in London under her own management, was seen in many countries. In 1921 she was made a DBE.

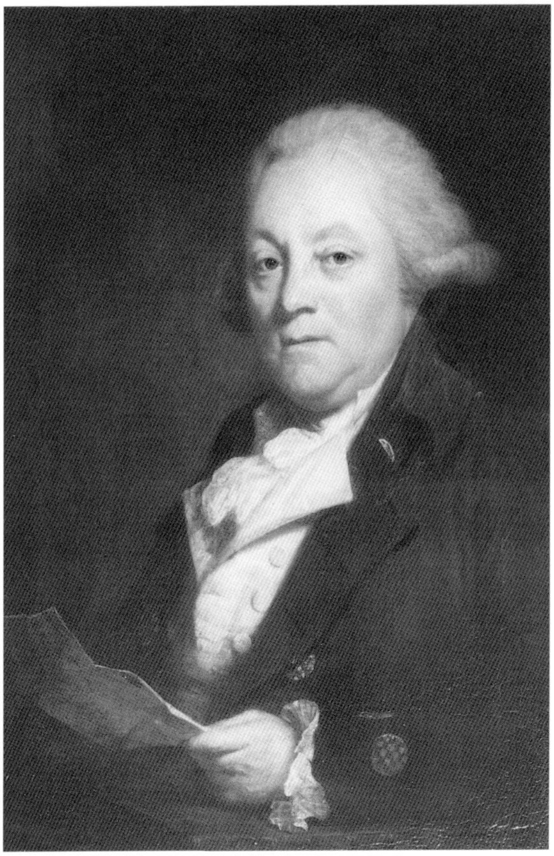

831
JOHN WARD

Thomas Beach (attr.)

Oil on canvas 74.3 x 61
INV: Mathews 255 (artist unknown);
RW/CKA 417 (artist unknown)
PROV: Charles Mathews
EXH: 1833 London (255)

Ward has a powdered wig and a florid complexion, and wears a dark green or blue jacket, a white waistcoat and a white stock. He holds a paper in his left hand.

The sitter and his wife Sarah (née Butcher), mainly provincial actors, were the parents of Sarah Ward, who married Roger Kemble, the couple becoming progenitors of the Kemble clan.

832
JOHN WARD (?)

Unknown Artist

Oil on canvas 35.5 x 28, bust in false oval
INV: RW/CKA 268
PROV: Unknown

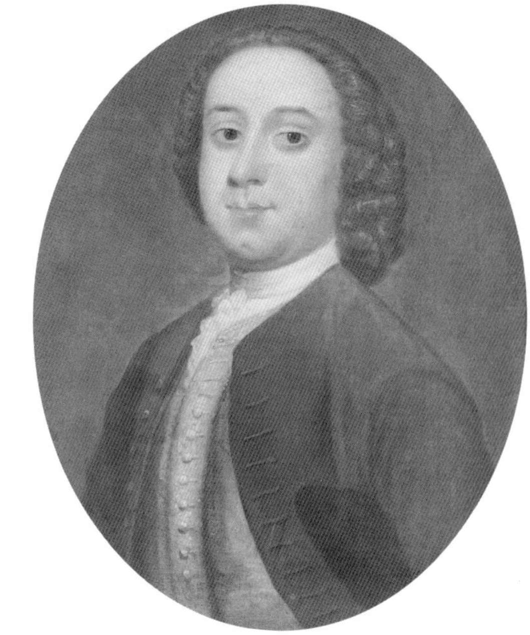

832 *John Ward*

Ward has a curly, pale brown wig. He wears a brown collarless coat, a green waistcoat edged in gold with gold buttons, and a white stock with frill. The tip of a tricorn hat is visible under his left arm. The identity of the sitter is doubtful.

833
SARAH WARD
as Octavia in *All for Love*
by John Dryden

Samuel De Wilde

Oil on canvas 37 x 28.4
INV: Mathews 380; RW/CKA 269
PROV: John Bell; Thomas Harris; Harris sale, 12 July 1819 (66); Charles Mathews
EXH: 1833 London (380)
ENGR: Philippe Audinet for Bell's British Library 24 March 1792, line 11.2 x 8, pub. Bell's *British Theatre* (1797), vol 16

In Act III of Dryden's answer to Shakespeare's *Antony and Cleopatra* there is a marvellous confrontation scene between Octavia (Antony's second wife and Caesar Augustus's sister) and Cleopatra. It follows the arrival of Octavia in Egypt, accompanied by her two little daughters, to plead for Antony's return to the Roman camp. Octavia recognises Cleopatra by her 'haughty carriage'. Cleopatra retorts that her haughty carriage 'shows I am a queen. Nor need I ask who you are'. Octavia replies with the line quoted on the engraving:

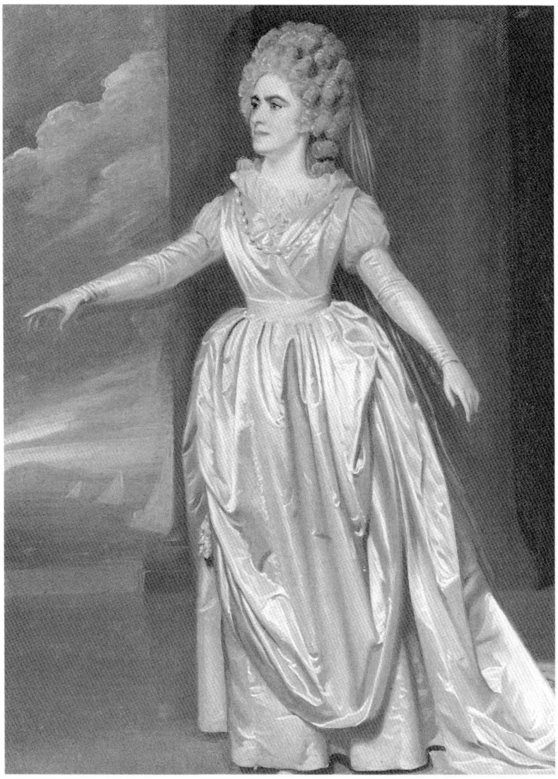

833 *Sarah Ward as Octavia*

'A Roman: A name that makes and can unmake a Queen.' In the Bell edition it is noted that the whole scene was 'omitted in the Representation'. Whether or not the actress ever said the lines, the pose is noble and declamatory. Octavia wears a long-sleeved silver dress and underskirt, with a silver belt and stiffened lace collar, and a single strand of large white beads. A veil falls from the back of her head.

Dryden's tragedy was originally staged at Drury Lane on 12 December 1677. Mrs Ward first performed the role of Octavia in London on 13 November 1780, at Drury Lane. For Mrs Siddons's benefit on 5 May 1788 she played Octavia to Mrs Siddons's Cleopatra and J.P. Kemble's Antony. That performance was the last before De Wilde painted his picture.

This Sarah Ward (née Hoare) – not to be confused with the actress who married Roger Kemble – became the wife of the Manchester actor–manager Thomas Achurch Ward (1747–1835). She played many leading roles at Drury Lane, including Juliet, Zara in *The Mourning Bride*, Millwood in *The London Merchant*, the Queen in *Hamlet* and *Cymbeline*, Jane Shore, and Mrs Oakly in *The Jealous Wife*. After 1793 she joined her husband in Manchester, where she remained a mainstay of the company until 1812.

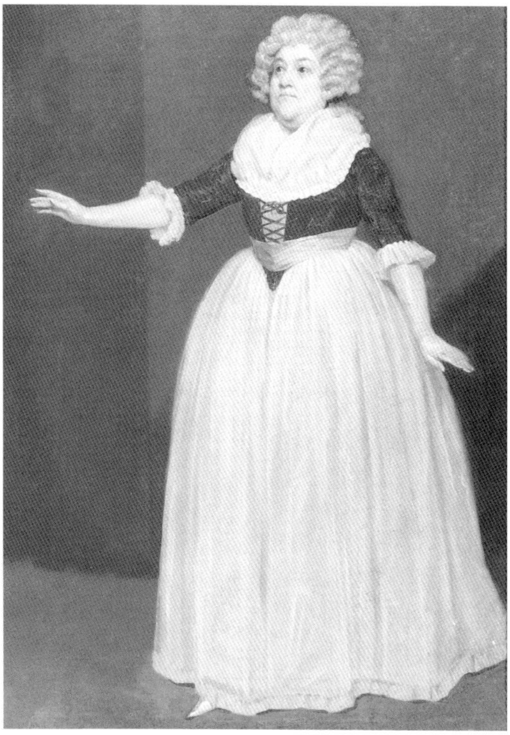

834
MRS WEBB
as Lady Dove in *The Brothers* by Richard Cumberland

Samuel De Wilde

Oil on canvas 37.2 x 28.5
INV: Mathews 373; RW/CKA 237
PROV: John Bell; Charles Mathews
EXH: 1833 London (373)
ENGR: Philippe Audinet for Bell's British Library 22 September 1792, line 11.1 x 8, pub. Bell's *British Theatre* (1797), vol 12, with the quotation: 'I insist upon your turning that old porpoise out of the house' (Act II, scene 2); J. Chapman (after H. Moses) printed C. Cooke 1808 and plate to *British Drama* (1817), stipple and line

It has been suggested that the sitter is Ludia Webb (*fl.* 1788–1812) but it is more likely that she is Mrs Richard Webb, Ludia's mother (see BD 15: 318). Ludia Webb did not perform at Covent Garden (and acted very infrequently in London) in the 1780s.

Lady Dove wears long white gloves and a full pink skirt under a gauze, with a purple bodice and pink stomacher and sash.

Cumberland's comedy was first performed at Covent Garden on 2 December 1769, with Mrs Green as the original Lady Dove. Mrs Webb took the role of Lady Dove for the first time at Covent Garden on 25 April 1787.

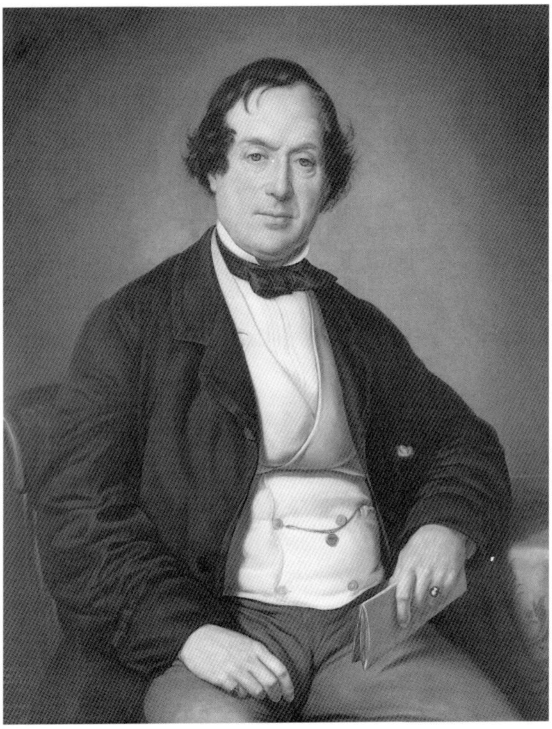

835
BENJAMIN WEBSTER
Philip Hoyoll
Oil on canvas 88.9 x 71.1
INSCR: 'Contributed / to the / Dramatic College / Fancy-Fair / by / Philip Hoyoll / the Artist / London...)' (red paint b.l.)
INV: RW/CKA 343; Gift 217
PROV: Royal Dramatic College; RDC sale at Fairbrother, Lye and Palmer, 24 February 1881 (lot 53), bt. Mowbray, by whom presented to the Junior Garrick Club; JGC sale 1889, bt. by T.H. Bolton, by whom presented to the Garrick Club, 1889

Webster holds a folded paper in his left hand, on the third finger of which is a cameo ring with a bust of Shakespeare. He has a signet ring on the little finger of his right hand. He wears grey trousers, a black jacket, and a white waistcoat, white shirt and black bow tie; there is a pink handkerchief in his breast pocket. He sits in a mahogany chair with a curved back. The table to the right is covered with a red cloth, with a darker red floral design.

The Junior Garrick Club was established in 1868 at No. 1A Adelphi Terrace, not far from a house in which Garrick had lived. According to the rules, 'All members of the dramatic profession or any branch of the dramatic art ... shall always be eligible for admission as members of the club'. (See Charles Dickens [Jr], *Dickens's Dictionary of London, 1879* and *The Era* [1872], 9: 15). The first Secretary was A. Mowbray, and a subsequent Secretary was Charles Harcourt, who was also Secretary of the Drury Lane Theatrical Fund. The Junior Garrick closed in 1889.

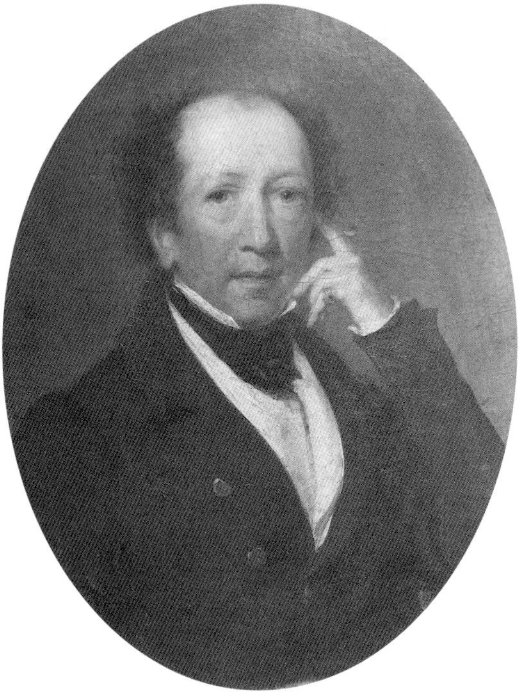

836
BENJAMIN WEBSTER
Unknown Artist
Oil on canvas 33.7 x 25.4 (oval)
INV: RW/CKA 429
PROV: The 1st Lord Burnham, by whom presented to the Garrick Club, 1905

Webster wears a dark brown jacket, a white waistcoat, a high white collar, and a dark green cravat.

Webster, who became a member of the Garrick Club in 1838, acted with Mme Vestris at the Olympic and managed the Haymarket for 16 years, from 1837. He opened the New Adelphi in 1859. His grandson Benjamin Webster (1864–1947) was a prominent actor in London and New York, who married the actress Dame May Whitty (1865–1948); their daughter, Margaret Webster, an outstanding director of Shakespeare's plays, was instrumental in reintroducing the Bard to American audiences.

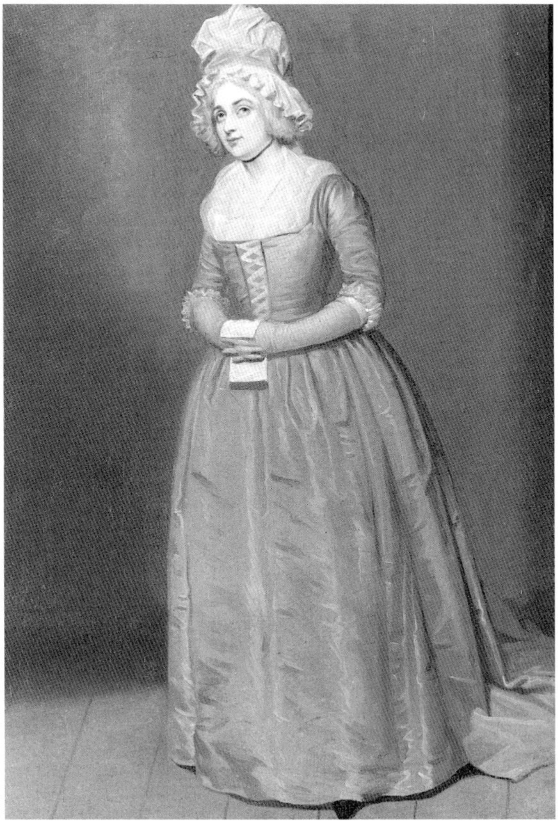

837
MARY WELLS
as Anne Lovely in *A Bold Stroke for a Wife*
by Susannah Centlivre

Samuel De Wilde

Oil on canvas 35.5 x 26.7
INV: Mathews 371; RW/CKA 265
PROV: John Bell; Charles Mathews
EXH: 1833 London (371); 1971 Northampton (7)
ENGR: William S. Leney for Bell's British Library
19 November 1791, line 10.3 x 7.3, pub. Bell's *British Theatre*
(1797), vol 12, with the quotation 'I greatly fear the flesh, and
the weakness thereof hum' (Act v); William S. Leney
printed C. Cooke 1807 as plate to *British Drama* 1817, line

Anne Lovely, who has 'a fortune of thirty thousand pounds', is shown as a Quaker in Obadiah Prim's house in Bath. Prim, a hypocritical Quaker, is one of Anne's four guardians. Anne's Quaker costume consists of long yellow mittens, a pale purple silk dress with touches of silver, a white fichu, a black ribband collier, and a white cap with a blue ribbon.

Mrs Centlivre's comedy was first performed at Lincoln's Inn Fields on 3 February 1718. Mrs Wells played Anne Lovely for the first time at Covent Garden on 31 May 1787.

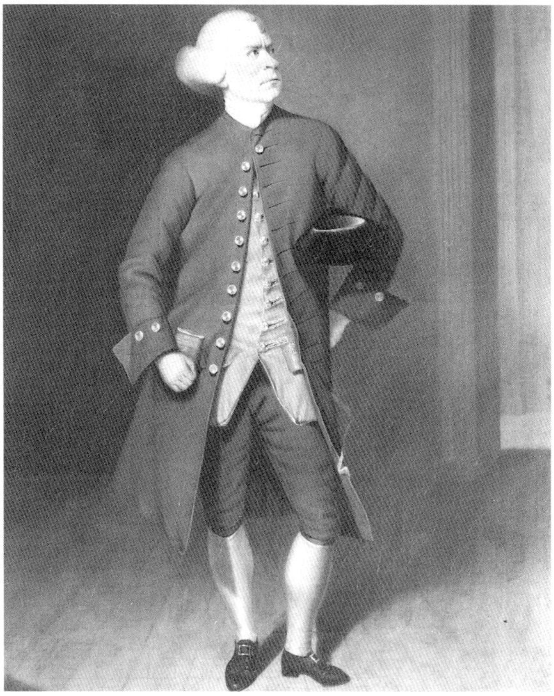

838
THOMAS WESTON
as Billy Button in *The Maid of Bath*
by Samuel Foote

Thomas Parkinson

Oil on canvas 74.9 x 61.6
INSCR: 'T. Parkinson Pinxt 1772' (dark red paint b.l.)
INV: Mathews 69; RW 101 (by J. Zoffany); CKA 101
PROV: Charles Mathews
EXH: 1772 S.A. (253); 1833 London (69); 1951 London (52)
ENGR: Anon. for the *London Magazine* February 1776,
line 9.9 x 8.2 (bust in oval in reverse,
a multitude of warts on the face)
LIT: Lady Victoria Manners & Dr G.C. Williamson,
John Zoffany (1920), p. 148

Billy Button, a tailor, enters the Bear Inn in Act I to apologise to Sir Christopher for the late delivery of some patterns, presumably for new garments. In the picture the patterns are in Button's coat pocket. He has a black tricorn hat under his left arm and wears black shoes with gold buckles, white hose, brown breeches, a brown collarless coat trimmed with silver buttons, a red waistcoat edged in silver, and a high white stock.

Foote's play caused some controversy. It was based on the notorious mismatch between the young singer Elizabeth Linley and the elderly Walter Long, a wealthy bachelor. Long objected to his portrayal as a rich old rake, under the guise of the character of the miser Flint, and Foote was obliged to pay him £3,000 in damages.

The character of Miss Linnet was based on Elizabeth Linley, whose betrothal to Long became a *cause célèbre* in Bath. Released from that engagement, she later married R.B. Sheridan. Foote's three-act comedy was first performed at the Haymarket on 26 June 1771, with Weston as the original Billy Button and Foote as Flint.

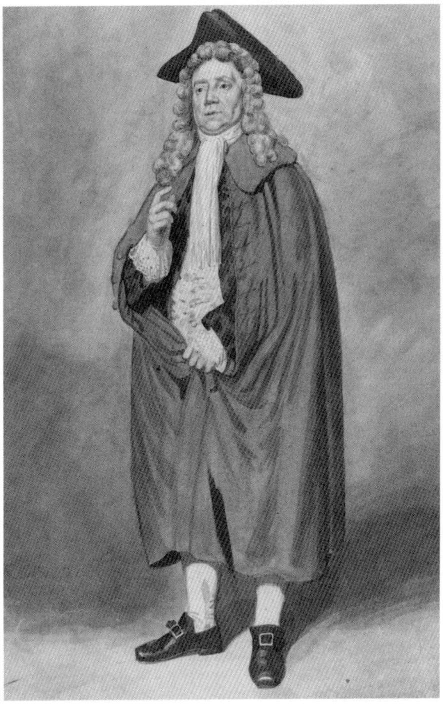

839

RALPH WEWITZER

as Dr Caius in *The Merry Wives of Windsor*

by William Shakespeare

Samuel De Wilde

Pencil and watercolour on wove paper 37 x 23.5

INSCR: 'S De Wilde delin / November (?) 1808' (pencil b.l.)

INV: Mathews 210; RW/CKA 59F

PROV: Charles Mathews

EXH: 1833 London (210)

Dr Caius has a full-bottomed wig and a black tricorn hat. His right hand is raised in a gesture of admonition, as if he addresses Shallow, Slender, Master Page, and the Host of the Garter Inn. His white stockings have yellow clocks, and he wears a long red cloak over a coat of blotched grey and black fabric, and a pale waistcoat.

A drawing by T.C. Wageman, engraved by the artist for Oxberry's *New English Drama* (1819), shows the sitter looking very much as he does in the De Wilde watercolour, even though he is there turned to the front and hides his hands in a muff.

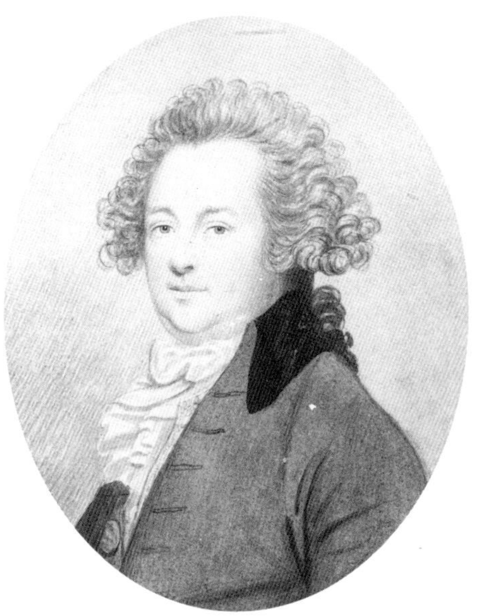

840

JOHN WHITFIELD

Sylvester Harding

Pencil and watercolour 12 x 9.5 (oval)

INSCR: 'Harding fecit.' (pen and brown ink on mount b.l. CM); 'Whitfield Comedian of / Drury Lane Theatre.' (pen and brown ink on mount b.c. CM)

INV: Mathews 311 (artist unknown); RW/CKA 183

PROV: Charles Mathews

EXH: 1833 London (311)

ENGR: Similar to: William Ridley 'from an original miniature' for Parsons's *Minor Theatre* February 1794, stipple 7.6 x 6 (but balding with copious hair at sides)

Head and shoulders, facing spectator, in a green coat.

841

ELIZABETH WHITLOCK

as Margaret in *The Earl of Warwick*

by Thomas Francklin

Samuel De Wilde

Oil on canvas 36.5 x 28.3

INV: Mathews 173; RW/CKA 450

PROV: John Bell; Thomas Harris; Harris sale, 12 July 1819 (62); Charles Mathews

EXH: 1833 London (173)

ENGR: Philippe Audinet for Bell's British Library 6 October 1792, line 11.1 x 8, pub. Bell's *British Theatre* (1797), vol 17

In Act V, scene 5, Margaret of Anjou has just informed King Edward and Lady Elizabeth Grey, the Earl of Warwick's wife, that she has fatally stabbed Warwick in revenge for the death of her child: ' – From my breast

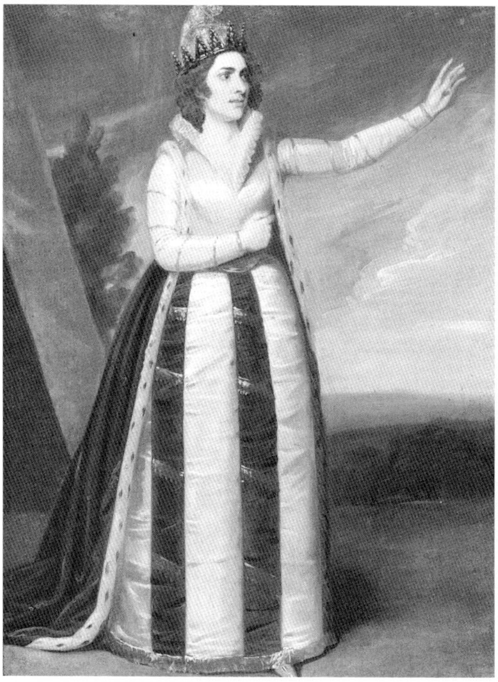

841 *Elizabeth Whitlock as Margaret*

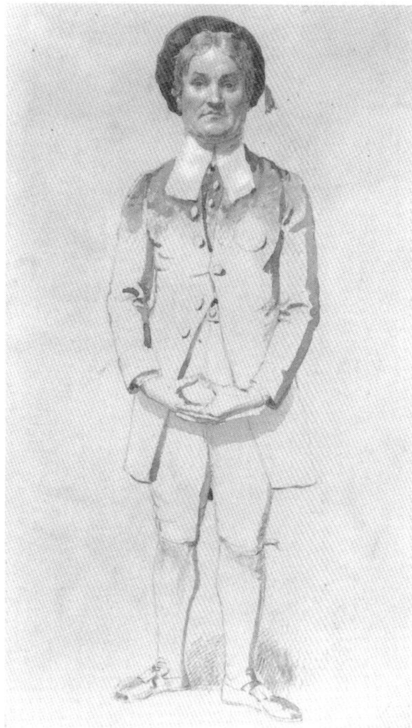

842 *James Pimbury Wilkinson as Geoffrey Muffincap*

I drew / A poignard forth and plunged it in his heart' (quoted on the engraving). She strikes a dramatic attitude, her right hand to her heart and her left arm extended. She has a spiked steel crown with yellow cap of liberty and wears a long silver dress with vertical purple panels, each with four diagonal gold fringes, a long sleeveless cloak of purple velvet edged in ermine, and a V-shaped ruff.

Francklin's tragedy was first performed at Drury Lane on 13 December 1766, with Mrs Yates as the original Margaret of Anjou. Elizabeth Whitlock never acted the role in London, but she did appear in the play as Lady Elizabeth Grey at Drury Lane on 3 November 1784, when Mrs Siddons (her sister) played Margaret.

See also No. 374.

842

JAMES PIMBURY WILKINSON

as Geoffrey Muffincap in *Amateurs and Actors*
by Richard Brinsley Peake

Richard Brinsley Peake

Pencil with some watercolour and body colour
on buff wove paper 34.3 x 20.7
INV: Mathews 314; (not in RW); CKA 525
PROV: Charles Mathews
EXH: 1833 London (314)
ENGR: Richard Brinsley Peake pub. Colnaghi & Co.
and by Fearman 1 December 1818, stipple and line
(vignette); Charles Picart for the *Theatrical Inquisitor*
pub. C. Chapple 1 January 1820, stipple (vignette);
Robert Cooper for *The Drama* pub. T. & I. Elvey
1 January 1822, stipple and line (vignette, half-length only);
Rogers for *The Stage; or, Theatrical Inquisitor* pub. G. Creed
November 1828, stipple (vignette)

Geoffrey Muffincap is 'an elderly Charity Boy, let out as a servant at Bustle's lodging'. Mr O.P. Bustle is 'a Provincial Manager, but engaged to superintend some Private Theatricals'. Mathews identified the moment as being in Act I, scene 2, when Geoffrey, having just arrived from the charity school, introduces himself to Mr Bustle. The quotation on the engraving – 'Gemini Cracks if he isn't going to give me as much trouble as any of the others' – is from a later moment, in Act II, scene 1, when Muffincap comes across Elderberry, a retired manufacturer, who is searching amongst the theatricals of Mr Bustle's company for his ward, Miss Mary Hardacre. The stage directions in the Cumberland edition describe Geoffrey Muffincap's costume as 'A charity boy's dress, cap, leather breeches short at knees, worsted stockings, and shoes'. He wears a blue coat (only partially coloured) with a large round badge and white bands. On the back of his head he has a round black cap with a red tassel.

Peake's musical farce in two acts was first performed at the English Opera House on 29 August 1818, with Wilkinson as the original Geoffrey Muffincap.

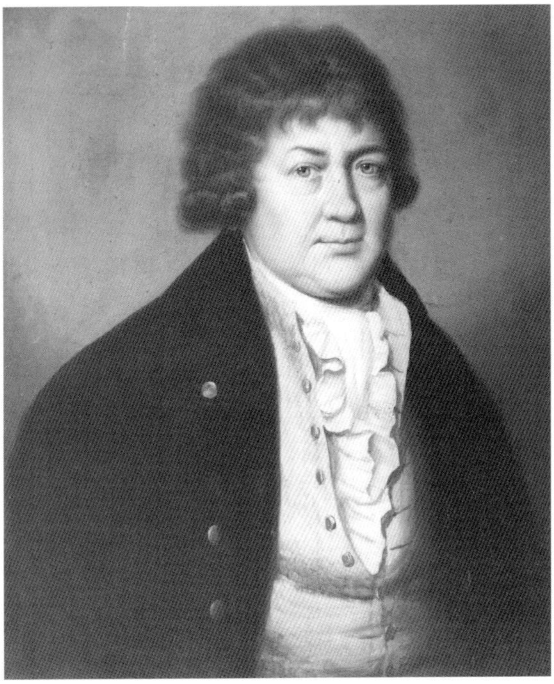

843

TATE WILKINSON

Stephen Hewson

Oil on canvas 66.7 x 56.5
INSCR: 'S. Henson [*sic*]/ 1791'
INV: Mathews 74 (by Atkinson); RW 346 (by Frederick Atkinson); CKA 346 (by S. Henson)
PROV: Charles Mathews
EXH: 1833 London (74)
REL: York 475, oil on canvas 127 x 101.6 (three-quarter-length, seated to r. in red chair, r. arm on chair, l. arm on table with inkstand, quill and paper, blue coat and yellow waistcoat, white stock), engr: M.U. Sears pub. Moon, Boys & Greaves and Rees Davies, Hull, 1 July 1829, mezzotint 21.6 x 18.1

Wilkinson wears a blue coat and yellow waistcoat, both with gold buttons, and a frilled white stock.

This portrait is clearly a smaller version of the York picture, which is, however, unsigned and is catalogued as 'attributed to Stephen Hewson'. [The Garrick Club version is similar to an engraved portrait of Wilkinson by W. Ridley, after F. Atkinson, that was published in the *Monthly Mirror*, 1791.

Though he had several engagements at Drury Lane and the Haymarket in the late 1750s and 1760s, Wilkinson is best remembered as the very successful manager of the York Theatre and Yorkshire circuit from 1766 to 1803. His *Memoirs* (1790) and four-volume *Wandering Patentee* (1795) constitute an invaluable chronicle of provincial theatre in the north of England and Scotland.]

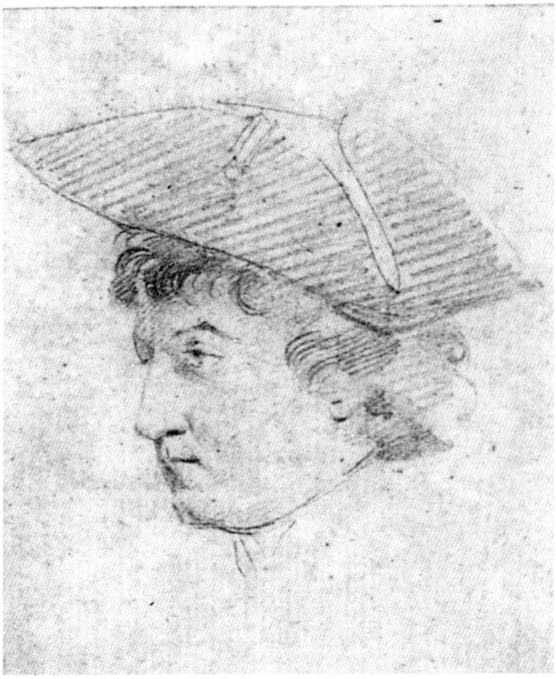

844

RICHARD WILSON

James Roberts

Pencil on slightly discoloured laid paper 8 x 7.3
INSCR: 'Wilson' (pen and brown ink on mount b.c. CM); 'Roberts fecit' (pen and brown ink on mount b.r. CM – this refers to all five drawings mounted in the same frame)
INV: RW/CKA 493D
PROV: Charles Mathews (not in catalogue)

Head only, looking down, almost in profile to the left, with a tricorn hat.

[Wilson was a favourite low comedian at Edinburgh before he made his first London appearance, at the Haymarket on 30 May 1774, as Mungo in *The Padlock*. He continued performing at that theatre during the summer and at Covent Garden in winter until November 1792. Wilson excelled at playing ludicrous old men and was pronounced by Joseph De Castro 'for years the best actor in hearty old men the stage has ever had to boast of'. He died in 1796 in the King's Bench prison, heavily in debt.]

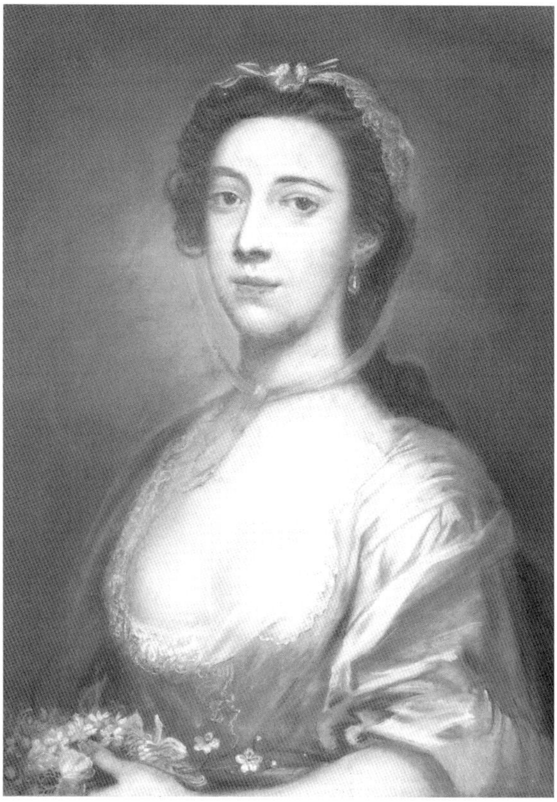

845

MARGARET ('PEG') WOFFINGTON

Arthur Pond

Pastel on laid paper 61 x 48.9
INV: RW/CKA 308; Gift 21
PROV: Francis Andrews, Provost's House, Dublin: John Dawkins, by whom presented to the Garrick Club, 1835
EXH: 1949 Birmingham (122); 1949 Port Sunlight (167); 1974 Twickenham (8)
ENGR: James McArdell, mezzotint 27.3 x 22.2; S. Freeman for *The Cabinet* pub. Matthews & Leigh 1 May 1807, stipple 14.2 x 9.5 (bust only); W. Read for *Dramatic Table Talk*, 1825, stipple (vignette, bust only); S.A. Edwards pub. Wm. Clausen & Co., New York, mezzotint 12.4 x 9.8 (bust in oval); C.K., woodcut 9.5 x 6.3; E.M., lithograph (vignette, bust only); Anon., etching 9.5 x 7.6 (bust only)

Peg Woffington has a lace cap with blue ribbons tied under the chin, and a pearl drop earring in her left ear. She wears a white silk décolleté dress edged with lace and with sleeves to the elbow. There is a blue cloak over her right shoulder, and she carries a bouquet of silvery flowers in her left hand.

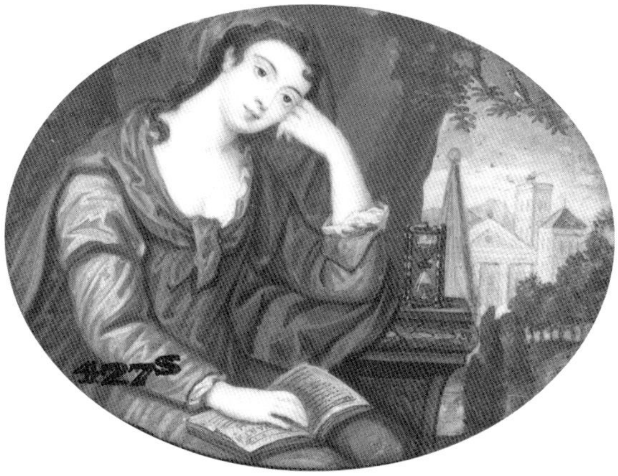

846

MARGARET WOFFINGTON

(called)

Bernard Lens III

Watercolour on ivory 6 x 8.1
INSCR: '137 / PART III / ...H' (on book in lap)
INV: RW 427S (Peg Woffington studying Ophelia by R. Cosway); CKA 427S; Gift 96
PROV: Presented by the 15th Lord Saye and Sele, before 1844
LIT: Fitzgerald, p. 183

The romantic sitter contemplates her reading matter and conjures up the vision seen on the right, an architectural fantasy that includes a pedimented building, two towers and an obelisk. A half-full hour-glass rests on a wooden bracket and a robin sings from the branch of the tree top right. The sitter wears a grey long-sleeved dress and has a blue drapery over her head and under her left elbow, with another round her shoulders.

[J.F. Kerslake writes in *Early Georgian Portraits in the National Portrait Gallery*: 'A number of portraits of unknown ladies, whose features somewhat resemble her, and an even larger number whose features bear almost no resemblance, have been called Woffington, and the subject should be approached with caution.']

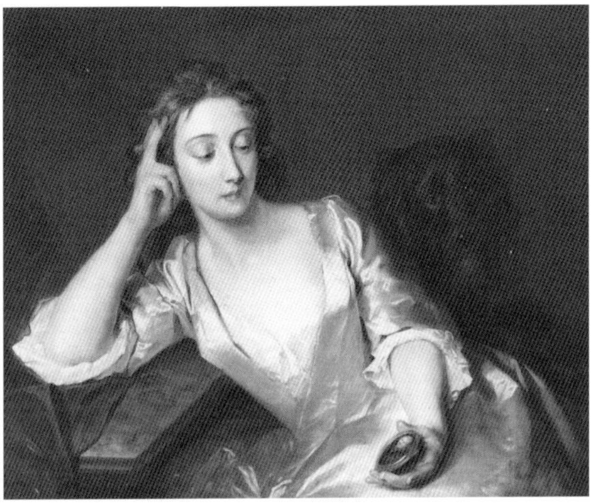

847*
MARGARET WOFFINGTON
(called)

Philip Mercier

Oil on canvas 70 x 91.5
INSCR: 'Reicrem' (brown paint b.l.)
INV: Mathews 11; RW/CKA 402 (repr.)
PROV: Charles Mathews
EXH: 1833 London (11); 1950–51 London (180); 1951 London (28); 1958 Liverpool (33); 1969 York and Kenwood (35)
LIT: Fitzgerald, p. 181 (said to have been commissioned by David Garrick); Griffiths, p. 315; John Ingamells & Robert Raines, *A Catalogue of the Paintings, Drawings and Etchings of Philip Mercier* (Walpole Society 1976–78), 46: 49, No. 203

The sitter contemplates the miniature of a man (said to be Garrick) in a red jacket. She wears a low-necked silver silk dress trimmed with pink ribbon. A large brown dog peers over from the right.

Ingamells and Raines date this picture about 1735–36 and call it 'Woman in Love', noting that the identification with Peg Woffington is unconvincing and the subject evidently fanciful.

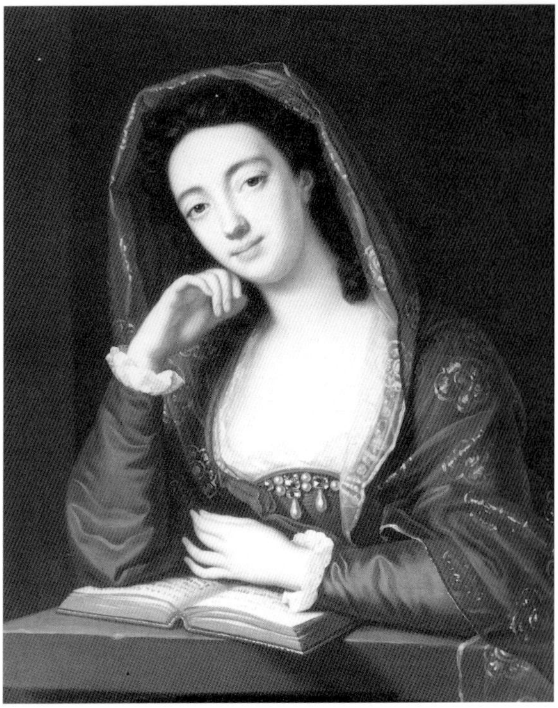

848
MARGARET WOFFINGTON
as Elvira in *The Spanish Fryar*
by John Dryden (?)

Benjamin Wilson (?)

Oil on canvas 73 x 61
INV: Mathews 10; RW/CKA 425
PROV: Charles Mathews
EXH: 1833 London (10)
REL: NG Dublin 776, oil on canvas 77 x 64

The sitter wears a dark dress with long sleeves, with frills at the cuffs and around the neckline. She sits at a table with her left arm resting on an open book.

The pose and costume are taken from John Giles Eccardt's portrait of Lady Mary Walpole (who married Colonel Charles Churchill), painted for Horace Walpole, her brother. There are a number of versions, but the original appears to be that in the W.S. Lewis Walpole Collection at Farmington.

[In *Richard Wilson* (1953), W.G. Constable makes the comment that the picture 'in style has nothing to do with [Richard] Wilson'. In the *Connoisseur* of December 1940, Maj.-Gen. Sir John Hanbury-Williams referred to the Dublin portrait as being similar to one he had recently acquired, which he believed to be a Highmore. Janet Lucey in *Lovely Peggy* is of the opinion that it is a copy by an unknown artist, after Benjamin Wilson. See BD 16: 224 (No. 68).]

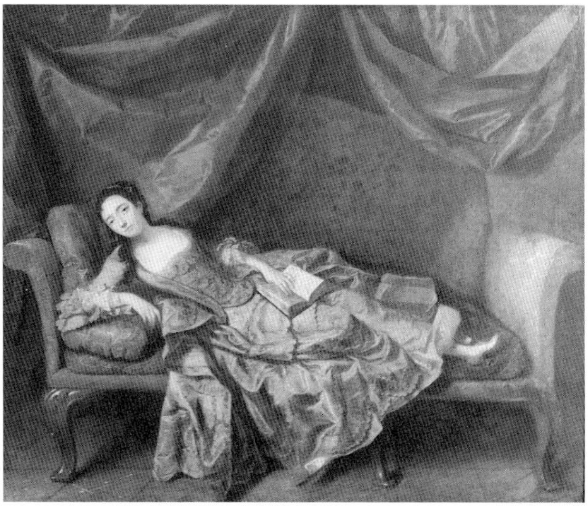

849
MARGARET WOFFINGTON

Unknown Artist

Oil on canvas 73.7 x 61.6
INV: Mathews 85 (by Hogarth);
RW 398 (by W. Hogarth);
CKA 398 (probably by a French artist)
PROV: Henry Angelo; Charles Mathews
EXH: 1833 London (85)
LIT: Henry Angelo, *Reminiscences* (1830), 2: 177–78;
Fitzgerald, p.181; Griffiths, p.124

A charming, but somewhat naïve work, this picture is probably by an English hand, despite CKA's conjecture. The sitter reclines upon a red damask sofa beneath a lifted green curtain. She wears a flounced gold dress embroidered in red and black.

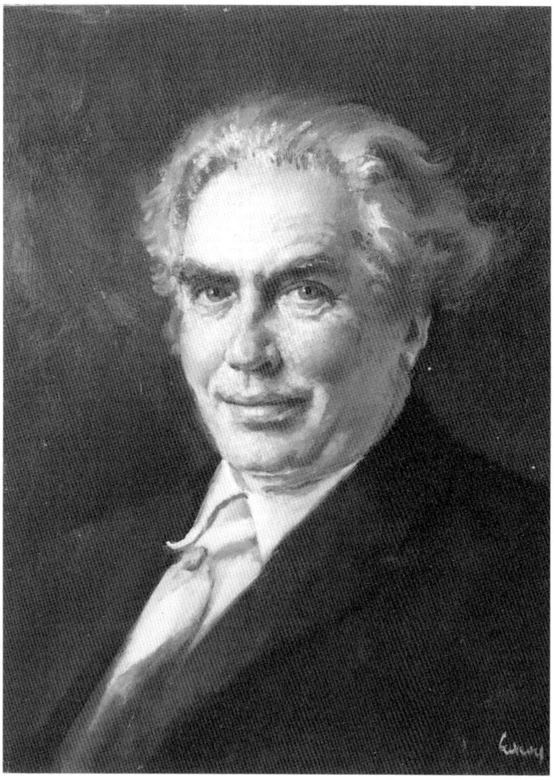

850
SIR DONALD WOLFIT

John Gilroy

Oil on canvas 53.3 x 43.2
INSCR: 'Gilroy' (white paint b.r.)
INV: GCL 705; Gift 805
PROV: Presented by the artist, 1964

Sir Donald is shown with grey hair brushed back and wears a dark jacket, a Garrick Club tie, and a white shirt. He became a member of the Garrick Club in 1942.

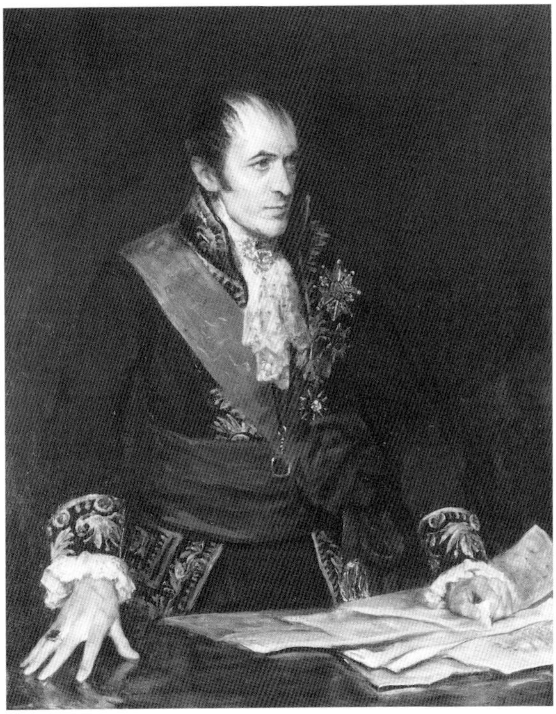

851*
ARTHUR WONTNER
as Joseph Fouché
in *Napoleon: The Hundred Days*
by Benito Mussolini and Giovacchino Forzano,
adapted by John Drinkwater

Sir Arthur Stockdale Cope

Oil on canvas 127 x 106.7
INSCR: 'A. Cope / 1933' (brown paint b.r.)
INV: GCL 697
PROV: Loaned by the late Sir Hugh Wontner (still on loan)
EXH: 1933 R.A. (141); 1934 Salon

Napoleon's thinning black hair is brushed forward. He holds a document in his left hand, which rests on a pile of papers spread on a table. He wears dark trousers, a black coat richly trimmed with gold braid, a broad purple sash, and on his chest various orders including a star hanging from a blue ribbon. [Cope ingeniously suggests the portraits of Goya in his treatment of costume and lighting.]

Robert Atkins's production of *Napoleon* opened at the New Theatre on 18 April 1932. Atkins played Napoleon with a huge cast that included Wontner as Fouché and Frederick Lloyd as General Count Carnot.

Wontner became a member of the Garrick Club in 1916.

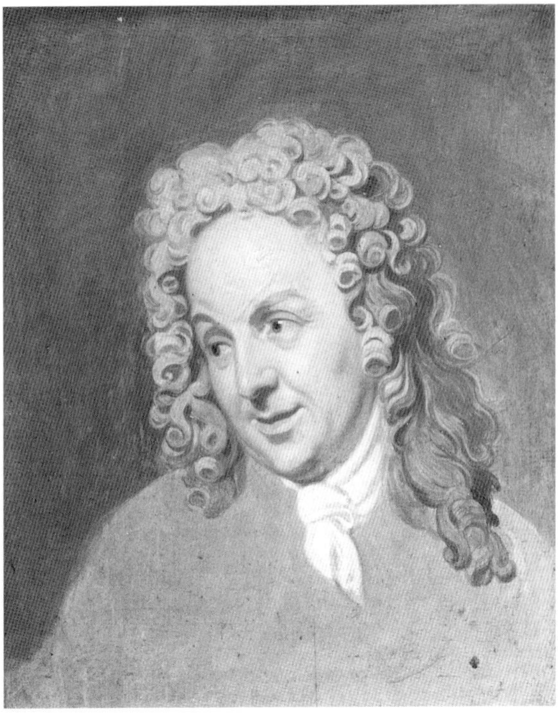

852
HENRY WOODWARD
as Razor in *The Upholsterer*
by Arthur Murphy

Samuel De Wilde (after Johan Zoffany)

Oil on panel 23 x 18.5
INV: Mathews 354 (A sketch from Zoffany, by Dewilde);
RW/CKA 238
PROV: Charles Mathews
EXH: 1833 London (354); 1971 Northampton (17)
ENGR: Anon. pub. J. Smith & R. Sayer 20 March 1771,
line (vignette, full-length holding a barber's basin)

Razor, a barber, is shown head and shoulders, with a full brown curly wig and white stock. Only the head is finished.

Murphy's farce was first performed at Drury Lane on 30 March 1758, with Woodward as the original Razor. De Wilde noted in his diary for 13 December and 30 January 1811 that he was working on a portrait of Woodward, and on 16 February 1811 he wrote that Mathews had taken the picture.

[Woodward held the stage for 48 years of the 18th century. He possessed enormous talent and versatility. As a comedian he was 'Proteus', according to a critic writing for the *Theatrical Review* (1757). Among his best roles were Mercutio, Petruchio, Sir Andrew Aguecheek, Bobadil in *Every Man in his Humour* and the Fine Gentleman in *Lethe*.]

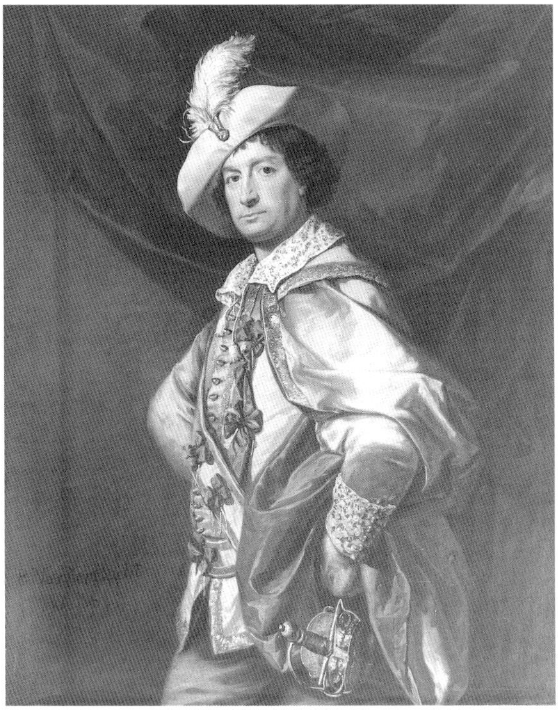

853*

HENRY WOODWARD

as Petruchio in *Catherine and Petruchio*

by David Garrick, adapted from Shakespeare

Benjamin Vandergucht

Oil on canvas 125 x 100.5 (127 x 103 lining canvas)
INSCR: 'B. VanderGucht / pxt. 1775' (dark brown paint b.l.)
INV: Mathews 106; RW/CKA 27
PROV: Thomas Harris; Harris sale, Robins 12 July 1819 (47); Charles Mathews
EXH: 1833 London (106); 1975 London (35)
REL: [Original: Yale Center for British Art, oil on canvas 124.5 x 99, exh: R.A. 1774 (305), prov: given by the artist to London Lock Hospital, where it hung until the beginning of the 20th century; Phillips 22 January 1973 (51); Agnew 1973; then acquired by Paul Mellon, engr: John Raphael Smith pub. J.R. Smith 1774, mezzotint 34.6 x 26.7; Anon. for Bell's *Shakespeare* 3 January 1776, line 15 x 9.2 (f.l.); S. Freeman for *The Cabinet* pub. Matthews & Leigh 1 August 1807, stipple and line 9 x 7 (bust only)]
LIT: Fitzgerald, p.175; Griffiths, p.321

Petruchio, standing three-quarter length with his left hand on his hip, wears a yellow hat and breeches, a pink doublet with long sleeves, lace cuffs with pearl buttons, a lace collar, and a pink and yellow cloak.

Garrick's farce, a three-act adaptation of *The Taming of the Shrew*, was originally performed at Drury Lane on 21 January 1756, with Woodward as Petruchio and Kitty Clive as Catherine. At the first performance Mrs Clive tumbled over, and accused Woodward of pushing her. Woodward's last performances as Petruchio before the original version of Vandergucht's picture was exhibited were at Covent Garden on 16 and 27 November 1773.

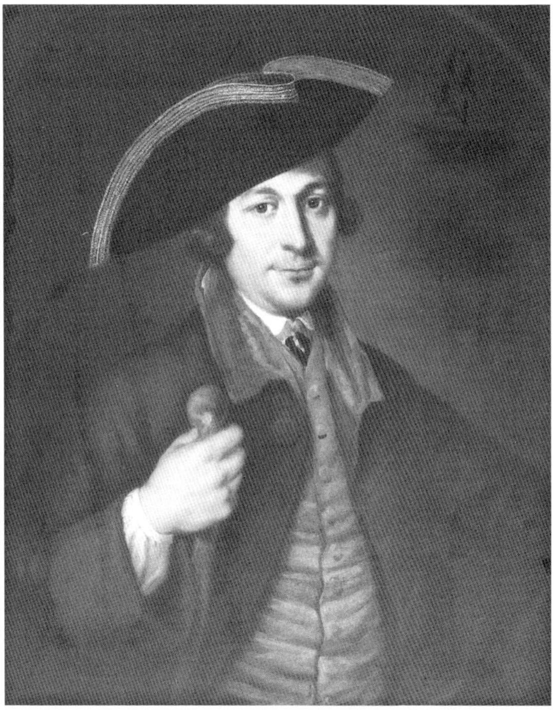

854

HENRY WOODWARD

as Brass in *The Confederacy*

by Sir John Vanbrugh

Thomas Worlidge

Oil on canvas 74.9 x 61.6
INV: Mathews 56; RW/CKA 409
PROV: Charles Mathews
EXH: 1833 London (56)

Brass has a black tricorn hat and holds a knobby stick is in his right hand. He wears a dark brown coat with furled collar and turned-up cuffs, a red waistcoat with red buttons, and a white stock.

Vanbrugh's comedy was originally performed at the King's Theatre on 30 October 1705. Woodward played Brass for the first time at Drury Lane on 15 September 1748, succeeding Charles Macklin in the role. He also acted the role in a revival at Covent Garden on 26 September 1767, and gave six performances before his last on 20 May 1769.

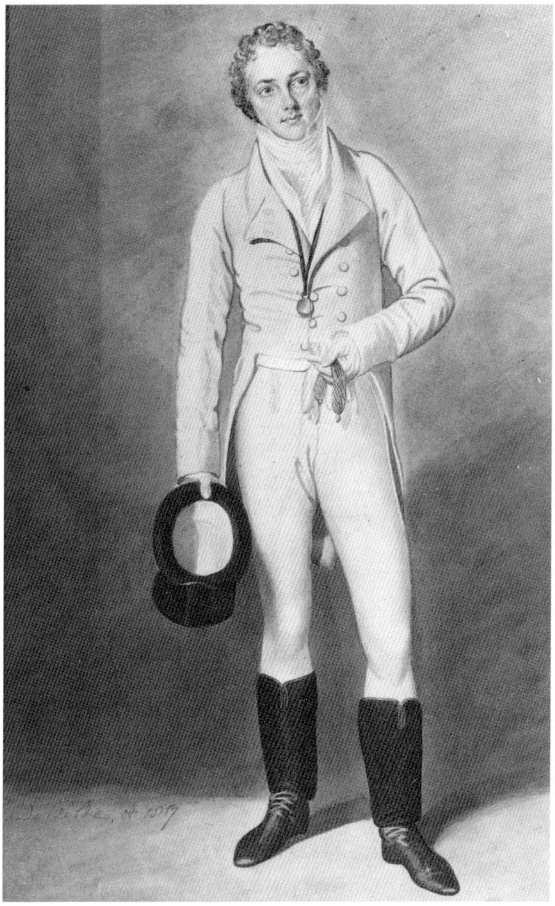

855
BENJAMIN WRENCH
as Sir John Freeman in *Free and Easy*
by Samuel James Arnold

Samuel De Wilde

Pencil and watercolour on wove paper 37 x 23.5
INSCR: 'S De Wilde, A. 1817' (pencil b.l.)
INV: Mathews 217; RW/CKA 45A
PROV: Charles Mathews
EXH: 1833 London (217); 1975 London (137)

The scene for Act I, scene I is Charles Courtley's garden. Wrench holds a black hat in his right hand and has yellow gloves. He wears black boots with decorated tops, creamy yellow tights, a pink cutaway coat with a double row of buttons at the front and a turned-back collar with wide lapels, a white waistcoat with a high collar, and a high white stock and collar.

Arnold's comic opera, with music by Addison, was first performed at the English Opera House on 16 September 1816, with Wrench as Sir John Freeman. The *Theatrical Inquisitor* of September 1816 called the piece 'a farce with songs'.

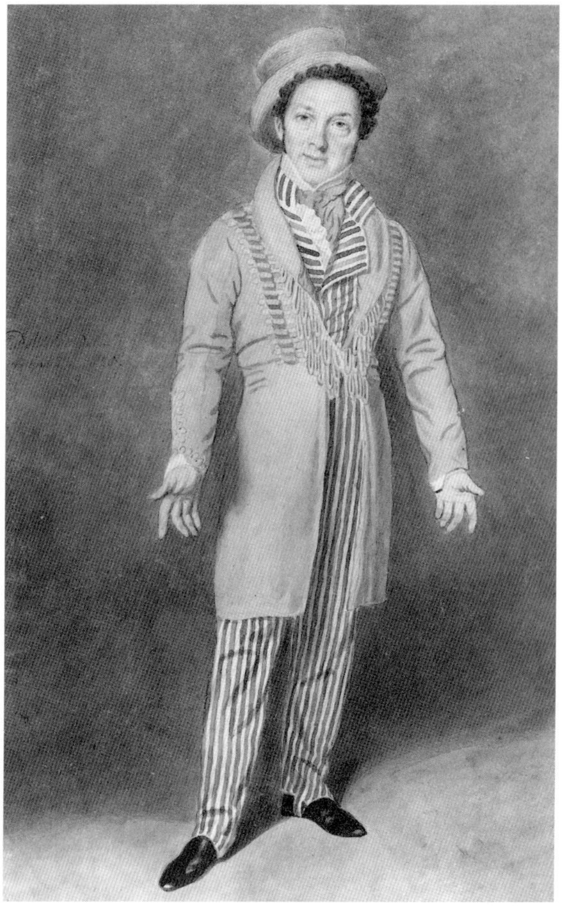

856
BENJAMIN WRENCH
in character

Samuel De Wilde

Pencil and watercolour on wove paper 37 x 23.5
INSCR: 'S De Wilde delin / August 6 1825' (pencil c.l.)
INV: Not listed; Gift 892
PROV: Bequest of Sir St Vincent Troubridge, 1981

Wrench wears a straw hat on the back of his head and a pale fawn coat with elaborate frogging over a striking blue and white striped waistcoat and matching trousers.

Wrench left the Drury Lane company in 1815 and divided his time between the Lyceum and the provinces. His greatest success was as Corinthian Tom in Moncrieff's *Tom and Jerry; or, Life in London*, which opened at the Adelphi on 26 November 1821. He joined the Covent Garden company on 4 October 1826.

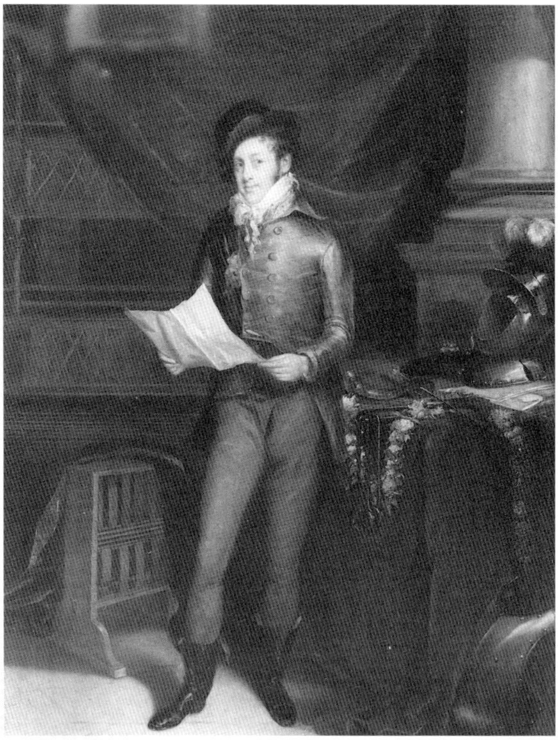

857

BENJAMIN WRENCH

as Wing in *Amateurs and Actors*
by Richard Brinsley Peake

Michael William Sharp

Oil on canvas 61.2 x 46.7
INV: Mathews 84; RW/CKA 102
PROV: Charles Mathews
EXH: 1833 London (84)

Wing is 'a poor Country Actor' who is to be auditioned for leading parts by the provincial manager O.P. Bustle; in Act I he is given a song to study. In Sharp's painting Wing holds the song and seems to be performing for Bustle in the stage box of a rather grand provincial theatre. About the place are various stage properties mentioned in the text, including a contraption on the left (covered in drapery) called a 'crash', which was used to produce sound effects, when, according to Bustle, 'we knock down towns and towers, break bridges, and upset tilburies'.

Wing wears a battered black top hat jauntily cocked over his right ear, black boots, grey-blue trousers, a brownish silk cutaway jacket with silver buttons, and a white stock.

Peake's operatic farce was first performed at the English Opera House on 29 August 1818, with Wrench as the original Wing.

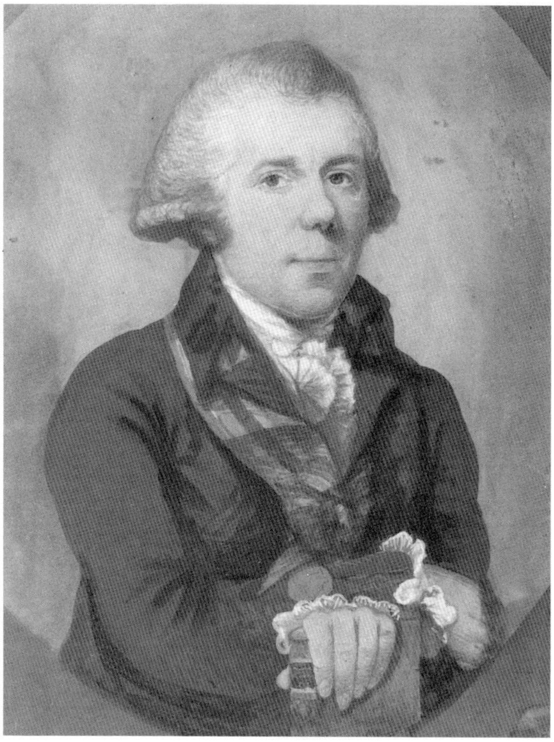

858

JAMES WRIGHTEN

Henry Spicer

Pencil and watercolour on laid paper 26.5 x 21
INV: Mathews 264; RW/CKA 50F
PROV: Charles Mathews
EXH: 1833 London (264)

Wrighten has a powdered wig and wears a grey-blue jacket with the collar turned down over a rainbow ribbon, and a white stock. He rests his right hand on a closed book, suggesting his position as prompter at Drury Lane. He also appeared occasionally on the boards. See No. 6.

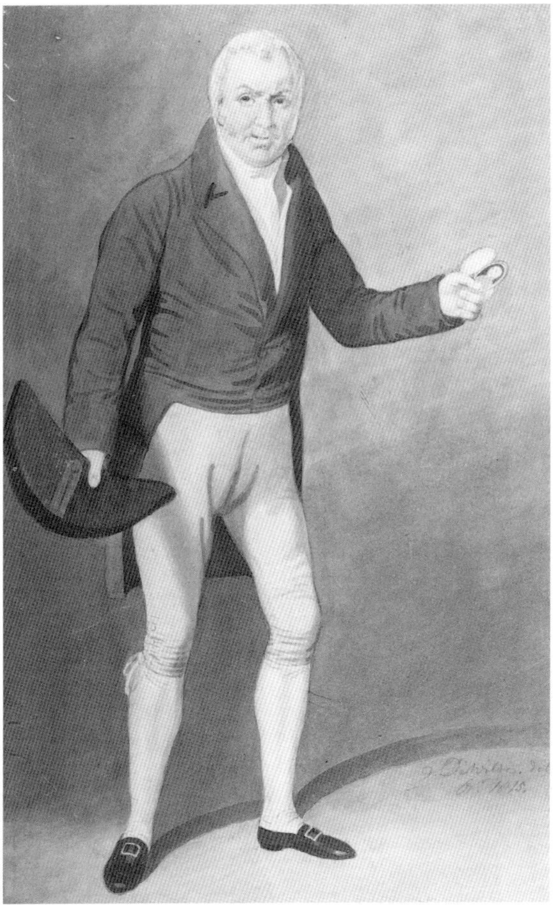

859
RICHARD WROUGHTON
as Sir John Restless in *All in the Wrong*
by Arthur Murphy

Samuel De Wilde

Pencil and watercolour on wove paper 37 x 23.5
INSCR: 'S De Wilde delin / Ocr 1815.' (pencil b.r.)
INV: Mathews 203; RW/CKA 63A
PROV: Charles Mathews
EXH: 1833 London (203); 1975 London (143)

The miniature that Sir John holds in his left hand identifies a moment in Act II, scene 2. Thinking it is a picture of his wife's lover, he shows it to his servant Robert, asking him if he knows the man. Sir John wears shoes with gold buckles, white stockings, yellowish breeches with bows at the knee, a brown cutaway jacket with a high collar, a light waistcoat, and a high white cravat. He holds a hat in his right hand.

Murphy's comedy was first performed at Drury Lane on 15 June 1761, with Richard Yates as Sir John Restless. Wroughton played the role for the first time in London at Drury Lane on 18 May 1790.

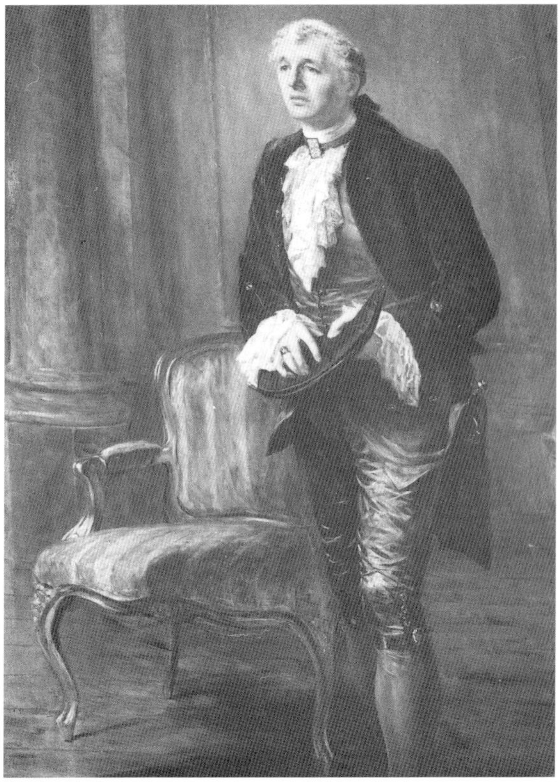

860
SIR CHARLES WYNDHAM
as Garrick in *David Garrick*
by Thomas William Robertson

John Pettie

Oil on canvas 167.6 x 113
INSCR: 'J. Pettie' (dark brown paint b.r.)
INV: CKA 566; Gift 389/401
PROV: Thomas McLean; bequeathed by the sitter, 1919
EXH: 1888 R.A. (1065)
LIT: T. Edgar Pemberton, *Sir Charles Wyndham: A Biography* (1904), repr. opposite p. 204

Wyndham as Garrick wears reddish stockings and silvery-green breeches and waistcoat with a red coat. The carved and gilt chair, with padded back, arms and seat, is upholstered in green and pink stripes.

Robertson's comedy was first performed at the Prince of Wales Theatre, Birmingham, during April 1864. The first London performance followed at the Haymarket on 30 April, when E.A. Sothern enjoyed one of his greatest successes in the title role. Wyndham saw the piece as a potential vehicle for his comic talents, and engaged James Albery and Alfred C. Calmour to polish up the dialogue. The reworked play opened at the Criterion on 13 November 1886, with Wyndham as David Garrick. The production was an immense success, and Garrick remained the role most closely associated with Wyndham throughout his life. On 7 January 1887 the play was performed at Sandringham for the Prince and Princess of Wales, and in the autumn of the same year Wyndham took it to Silesia and Berlin, where he spoke the part in German. He also performed in German in Moscow and St Petersburg. On Wyndham's return to the Criterion in February 1888, the auditorium was filled with the laurel wreaths that had been presented to him on the tour. On 10 August 1888 *David Garrick* received its 376th performance.

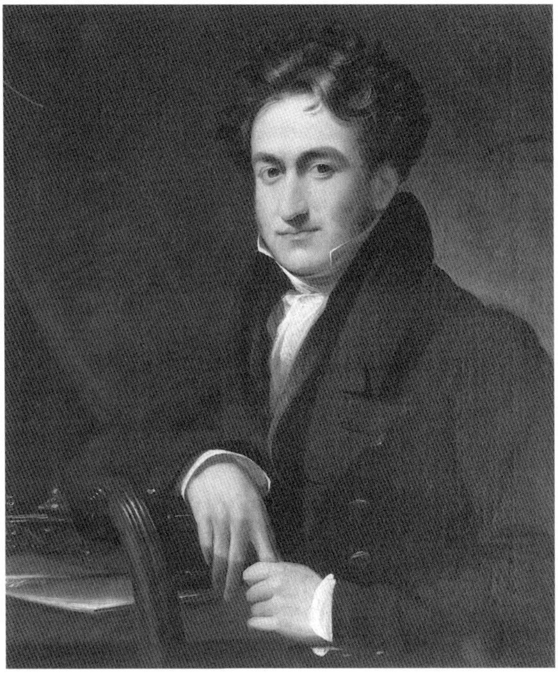

861
FREDERICK YATES

James Lonsdale

Oil on canvas 74.9 x 62.2
INV: Mathews 191; RW/CKA 73
PROV: Charles Mathews
EXH: 1833 London (191)
ENGR: William Say pub. W. Sams 1826, mezzotint 31.1 x 24.7; Joseph Brown for Edmund Yates's *Recollections and Experiences* (1884), stipple and line 11.6 x 10

Yates, sitting sideways on a chair with his right arm on the back, wears a dark grey coat with high collar, a grey waistcoat, and a high white collar and stock.

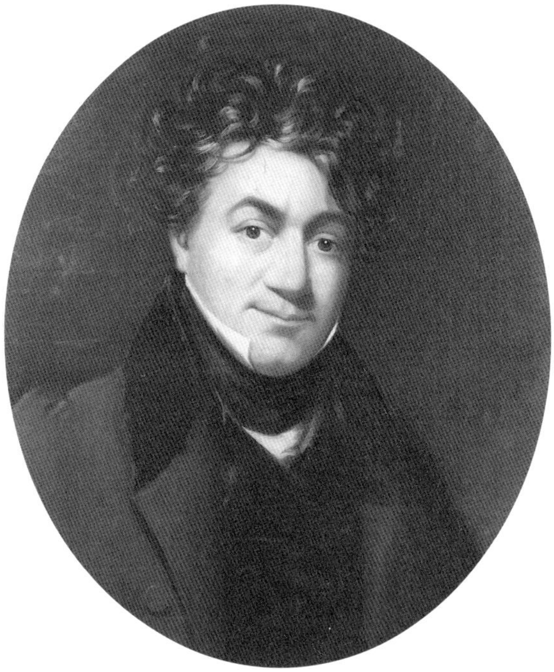

862
FREDERICK YATES

Unknown Artist

Oil on canvas 59.7 x 45.7 (framed in oval)
INV: RW/CKA 325; Gift 301
PROV: J.C. Parkinson, by whom presented to the Garrick Club, 1905

Head and shoulders, looking out at spectator. Yates wears a brown coat with a black velvet collar and a black stock.

A good comic actor, he and Daniel Terry assumed the management of the Adelphi in 1825; after Terry's death in 1829, Yates was joined by his friend Charles Mathews.

Yates was an original member of the Garrick Club in 1831 but resigned in 1840, two years before he died.

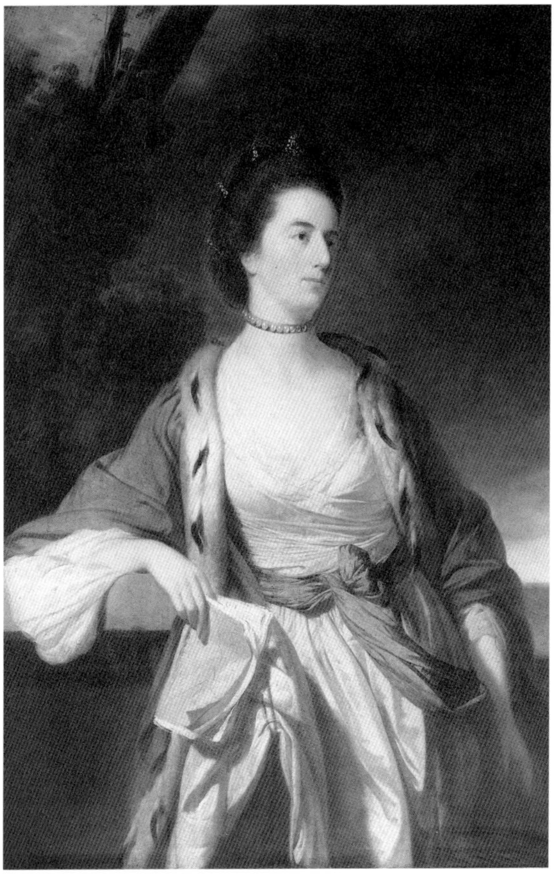

863

MARY ANN YATES

Francis Cotes

Oil on canvas 127.5 x 102
INSCR: '21' (black paint on page of booklet c.l.)
INV: Mathews 142; RW/CKA 21
PROV: Thomas Harris; Harris sale, Robins 12 July 1819 (44); Charles Mathews
EXH: 1833 London (142); 1951 London (4)
LIT: Fitzgerald, p. 223; Griffiths, p. 319; Edward Mead Johnson, *Francis Cotes* (1976), p. 79 No. 184

Mrs Yates, with her brown hair brushed back and folded into a band round her head, decorated with a rope of pearls, wears a dark choker also decorated with large pearls, a yellow dress with a blue sash round the waist, and a brown drapery edged in ermine over her shoulder. In her right hand she holds a soft-bound book, the bottom of the open page inscribed '21'.

Johnson dates this picture about 1765 because of its similarity to Cotes's portrait of the Hon. Mrs Campbell (Johnson No. 172), which is signed and dated 1765.

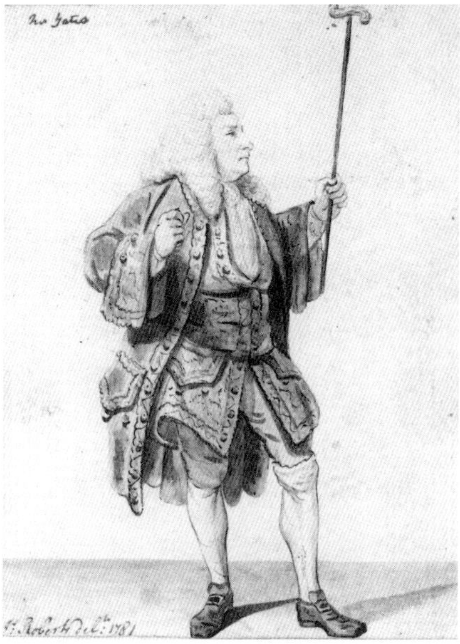

864

RICHARD YATES

as Malvolio in *Twelfth Night*
by William Shakespeare

James Roberts

Brush and grey wash and watercolour on laid paper 11.1 x 8.2
INSCR: 'Mr Yates' (pen and brown ink t.l.); 'J. Roberts delt. 1781' (pen and brown ink b.l.)
INV: RW 560C (artist and character unknown); CKA 560C (character unknown)
PROV: Unknown, but acquired before 1888
REL: [British Museum (Burney X, No. 151), coloured drawing on vellum 10.5 x 7.9, prov: John Bell sale at Christie's 27 March 1793 (lot 40), bt. by Gretton (the catalogue for the Bell sale states that the drawing was by Edwards, but Roberts's signature is clearly on both the Garrick Club and British Museum versions, which seem identical), engr: Anon. for Bell's *Shakespeare* 24 February 1776, with quotation: 'Sweet Lady, ha, ha.' The engraving does not show the name of the artist or the engraver.]

Yates, holding up a walking stick in his left hand, wears a powdered full wig and a pink suit with rich, gold-embroidered cuffs and waistcoat.

[Ashton had identified this picture as Yates in the role of Sir Oliver Surface in Sheridan's *The School for Scandal.* However, when the engraving of the BM version (original or copy?) was published with *Twelfth Night* in Bell's *Shakespeare*, it was clearly called 'Mr Yates as Malvolio'. The BM version is reproduced BD 16: 314.]

Yates first played Malvolio in London on 7 January 1751 at Drury Lane; previously his regular role in that comedy had been the Clown.

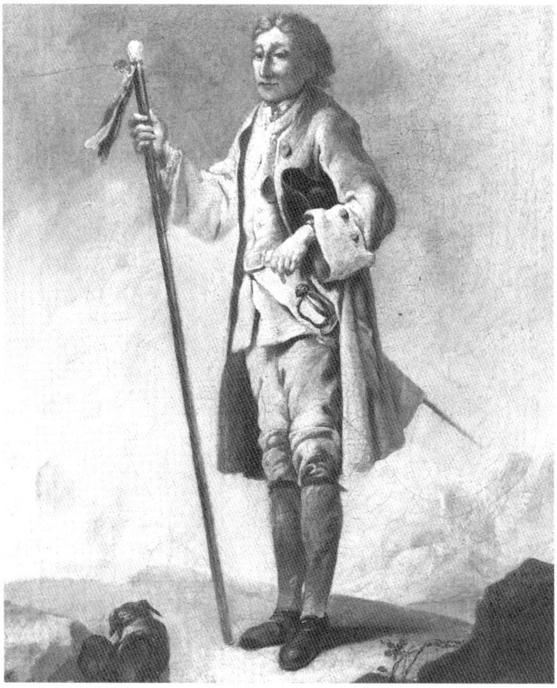

865
RICHARD YATES (?)
as Launce in *The Two Gentlemen of Verona*
by William Shakespeare

Philippe Jacques de Loutherbourg

Oil on canvas 41.5 x 31.5
INSCR: 'De Loutherbourg. / Number 15'
(pen and black ink on verso)
INV: Not listed
PROV: Possibly purchased from Walter H.Ferry, Cowley Grove Private Hotel, Uxbridge, for 12 gns. 1950; it was bought as a portrait of David Garrick attributed to Loutherbourg, oil on canvas 17″ x 12½″

Yates, standing outdoors and holding a long brown stick with a silver top above blue and silver ribbons, has a brown tricorn hat under his left arm. He wears brown shoes with silver buckles, blue stockings pulled over red breeches, garters below the knee, a red collarless frock-coat and waistcoat, a grey belt with a gold buckle, and a gold medallion hanging from a blue ribbon. The identity of the sitter is uncertain. The picture appears to have been purchased as a portrait of David Garrick.

[Yates, a popular low-comedy actor described by Francis Gentleman in *The Theatres* (1772) as 'the king of smiles', acted the role of Launce for the first time on 22 December 1762 at Drury Lane. He was depicted as Launce, standing with his dog Crab, in an engraving by H. Roberts, after T. Bonnor.]

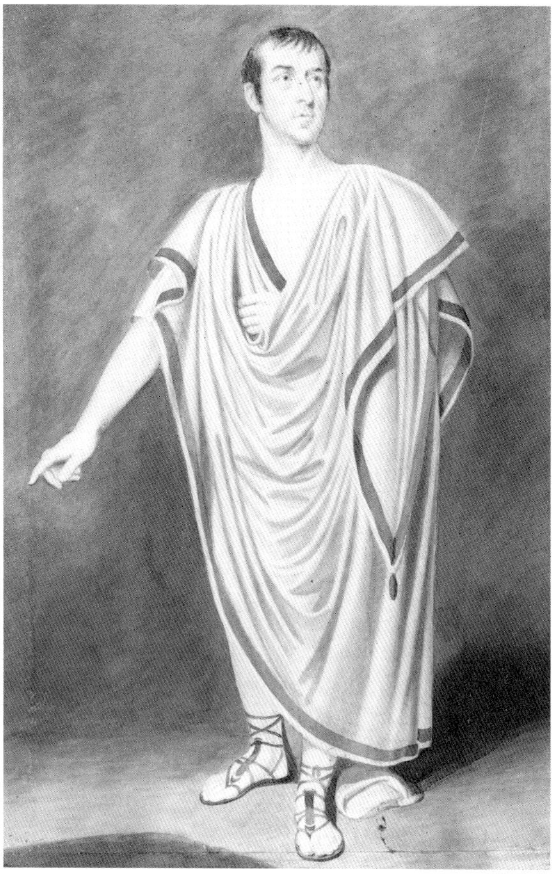

866
CHARLES MAYNE YOUNG
as Cassius in *Julius Caesar*
by William Shakespeare

Samuel De Wilde

Pencil and watercolour on wove paper 35.5 x 22.2
(band 3 high along bottom edge, includes toes of l.f.)
INSCR: 'S De Wilde / ...1817' (pencil l. l.)
INV: RW/CKA 52
PROV: Charles Mathews
EXH: 1964 London [2] (38)

Cassius, in an authoritative pose, wears grey sandals and a white toga with a red band along the border.

Julius Caesar was revived at Covent Garden on 29 February 1812, with Young as Cassius. The cast also included John Philip Kemble as Brutus, Charles Kemble as Mark Antony, and Egerton as Caesar. There were 19 performances during the season, the last taking place on 12 June 1812.

CKA suggests that this drawing might be the portrait that appears in Mathews's catalogue as No. 333 and is identified by Mathews as being of James Warde and attributed to Thurston.

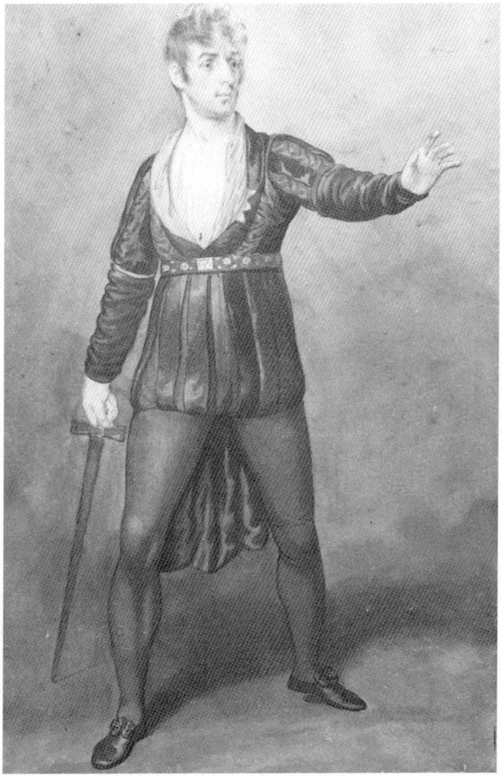

867

CHARLES MAYNE YOUNG

as Hamlet in *Hamlet*

by William Shakespeare

Samuel De Wilde

Pencil and watercolour on wove paper 37 x 23.5
INV: Mathews 248; RW/CKA 69A
PROV: Charles Mathews
EXH: 1833 London (248)
ENGR: Edward Scriven pub. Bell & De Camp
1 October 1808, stipple 12.5 x 7.7, with quotation
'Whither wilt thou lead me? Speak, I'll go no further';
same plate used for *Dramatic Memoirs* pub.
Bell & De Camp 1808, and for the *Theatrical Inquisitor*
pub. C. Chapple 1 May 1813

Young, wearing black doublet and hose with blue at the collar, holds his sword drawn, apparently challenging his father's ghost (Act I, scene 5).

Young's London début was in the role of Hamlet at the Haymarket on 22 June 1807, with a cast that included Mathews as Polonius, De Camp as Osrick, and Mrs Litchfield as Gertrude. His first Hamlet with the Covent Garden company was also given at the Haymarket, on 12 December 1808. Fourteen years later he made his début at Drury Lane, again as Hamlet, on 17 October 1822.

868

NOT ILLUSTRATED

CHARLES MAYNE YOUNG

as the Stranger in *The Stranger*

by Benjamin Thompson,

after August von Kotzebue

Samuel De Wilde

Pencil and watercolour on wove paper
36.8 x 22.8
INSCR: 'S De Wilde delin / June 181–' (pencil b.r.);
'Mr Young / by De Wilde, signed L2.2.0'
(pencil on verso t.c.); 'Griffith' (pen and brown ink
on verso t.c.; '12' (pencil on verso t.r.);
'C. Young' (pen and brown ink on verso c.);
'J.W. Anson / Secy / Royal Dramatic / College /
1872' (pen and brown ink on verso b.r.);
(watermark with date 1815?);
[see provenance]
INV: CKA 486; Gift 457
PROV: [Two portraits of Young, signed and dated by
De Wilde, were in the Royal Dramatic College sale
at Fairbrother, Lye and Palmer on 24 February 1881
(lots 100H and I)]; Sir Arthur Wing Pinero, by whom
presented to the Garrick Club, 1929

The Stranger is Charles, Count Waldburg, whose wife Adelaide has left him and their children. In dismay, he takes to the forest and rivals in charity the acts of the equally mysterious Mrs Haller. She turns out to be the Countess of Waldburg, and at the end the couple are reconciled. In De Wilde's drawing the Stranger is shown seated and melancholic, wearing black boots with high tops, black trousers, and a black military jacket.

Thompson's translation (and adaptation) of Kotzebue's *Menschenhaß und die Reue* was first performed at Drury Lane on 24 March 1798, with Kemble as the Stranger and Mrs Siddons as Mrs Haller. Young played the Stranger for the first time in London at the Haymarket on 3 July 1807, with Mrs Litchfield as Mrs Haller. There were six performances in the summer season during which De Wilde produced this drawing. No. 632 shows Tobias in the same production.

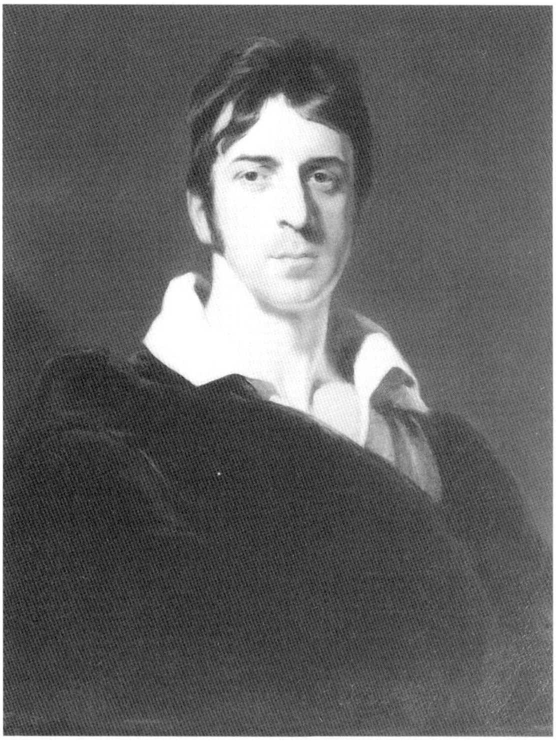

869
CHARLES MAYNE YOUNG

George Henry Harlow
Oil on canvas 77 x 63
INV: Mathews 160; RW/CKA 5
PROV: Charles Mathews
EXH: 1833 London (160)
ENGR: Charles Turner pub. J.P. Thompson 1809, mezzotint 27 x 21.9
LIT: *British Galleries of Art* (1825), p. 27

Young is shown as a romantic hero, unshaven, with sideburns, wrapped in a dark red cloak and wearing an open-necked white shirt.

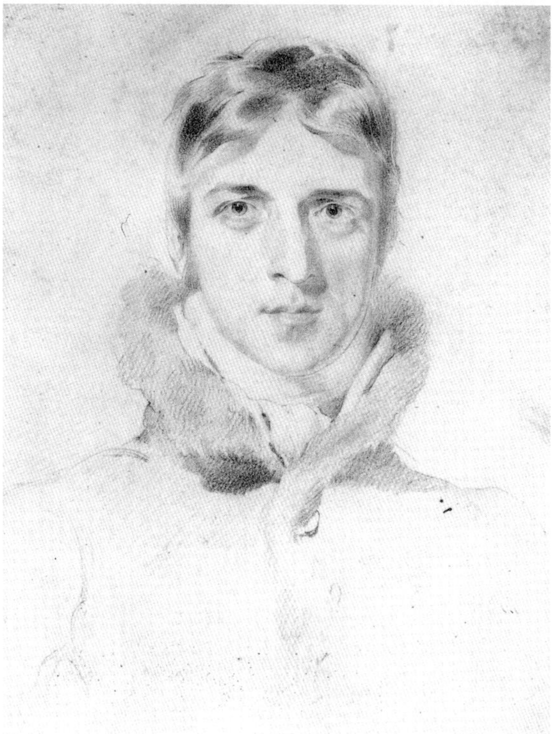

870
CHARLES MAYNE YOUNG

George Henry Harlow
Black and red chalk on wove paper 22 x 17.5
INV: Mathews 298; (not in RW); CKA 594
PROV: Charles Mathews
EXH: 1833 London (298)
ENGR: T. Blood for the *European Magazine* pub. J. Asperne 1 April 1812, stipple 9.3 x 7.5; C.H. Jeens as frontispiece to Julian Charles Young's *A Memoir of Charles Mayne Young/ Tragedian with extracts from his son's Journal* (1871), stipple (vignette, inscr: 'at 40')

Head and shoulders, looking out at spectator. Young wears a jacket with a high collar edged with fur.

Young was an original member of the Garrick Club in 1831; he resigned in 1840.

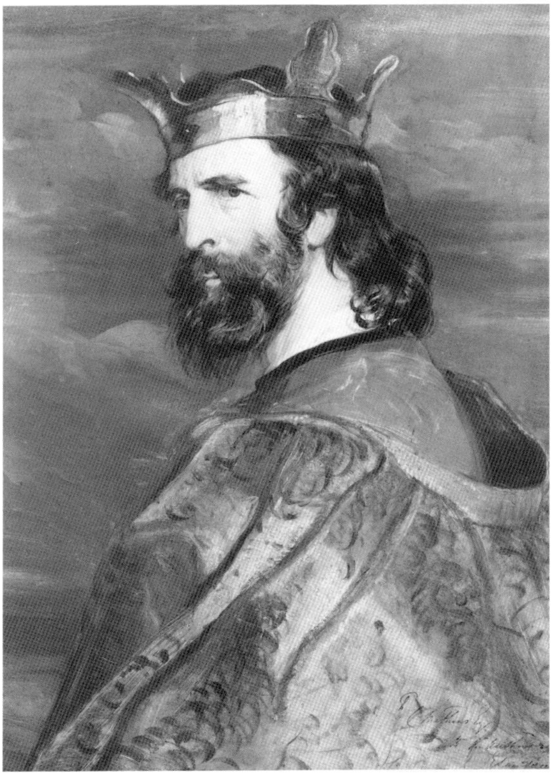

871

CHARLES MAYNE YOUNG

as John in *King John*

by William Shakespeare

Sir Edwin Landseer

Oil on panel 52.7 x 40.6

INSCR: 'To / C. Mathews Esq / with the author's regards / Edwin Landseer' (brown paint b.r.)

INV: Mathews 136; RW/CKA 92

PROV: Charles Mathews

EXH: 1833 London (136)

ENGR: C.H. Jeens for Julian Charles Young's *A Memoir of Charles Mayne Young / Tragedian with extracts from his son's Journal* (1871), stipple (head only on title page of Vol. I)

LIT: Fitzgerald, p. 232; Griffiths, p. 331

King John wears a simple gold crown with jewels, a gold brocade cloak over his shoulders, a red tunic with a narrow black collar, and a white shirt.

Young's first performance as King John appears to have been at Covent Garden on 17 December 1817.

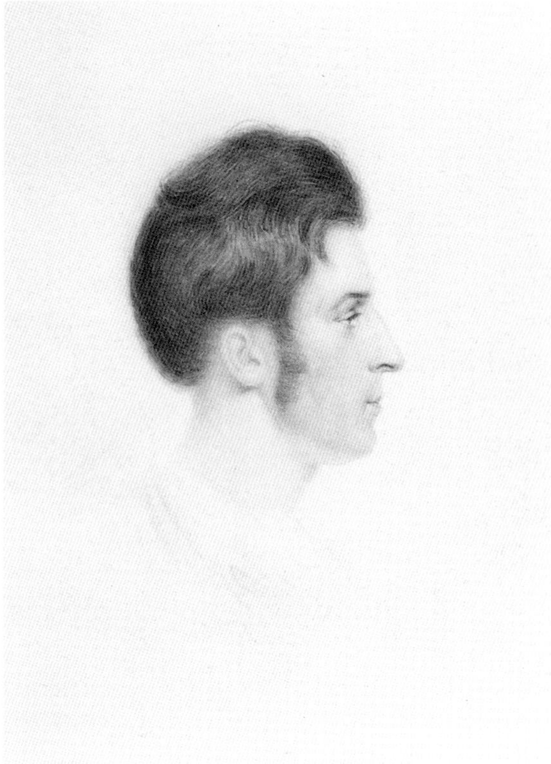

872

CHARLES MAYNE YOUNG

John Turmeau

Pencil and watercolour on wove paper 16.5 x 14.6

INSCR: 'Turmeau Fecit.' (pen and brown ink on mount b.l. CM); 'Mr Charles Young.' (pen and brown ink on mount b.c. CM)

INV: RW 561A (artist unknown); CKA 561A

PROV: Charles Mathews (not in catalogue)

Young is shown in profile to the right. He has blue eyes and brown hair with long sideburns.

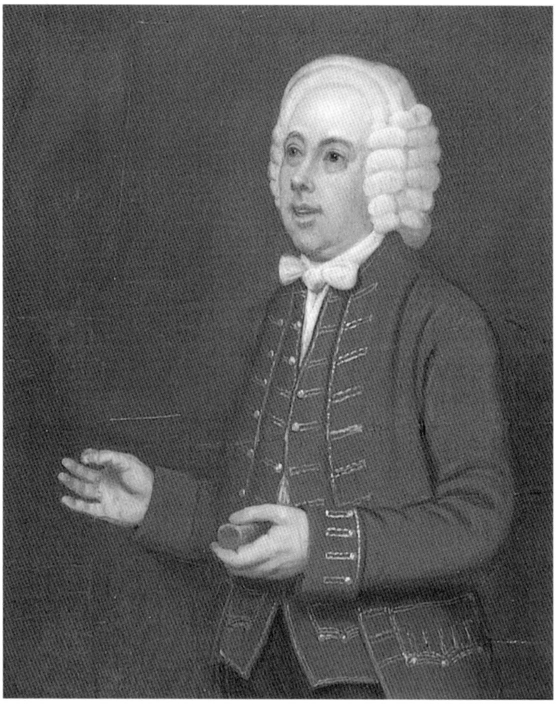

873
UNKNOWN ACTOR
in character

Samuel De Wilde

Oil on panel 22.8 x 19
INV: CKA 567B (William Farren I); Gift 390
PROV: Sir Henry Irving; Irving sale, Christie's 16 December 1905 (149) (Mr D. Meadows); presented by Mrs Weedon Grossmith, 1919
EXH: 1971 Northampton (18)

The sitter is depicted in the costume of about 1770–80. He wears a white powdered wig, black breeches, a reddish-brown coat and waistcoat decorated with gold braid, and a white stock.

874
LOCATION UNKNOWN
UNKNOWN MAN

Henry Kirchoffer

Watercolour on ivory 6 x 5
INSCR: 'Cork, H. Kirchoffer'
INV: CKA 540; Gift 330 (Earl of Cork) [not located 1988]
PROV: S.G. Kirchoffer, by whom presented to the Garrick Club, 1908

The sitter has dishevelled brown hair and wears a dark blue jacket with frills at the neck and a black stock.

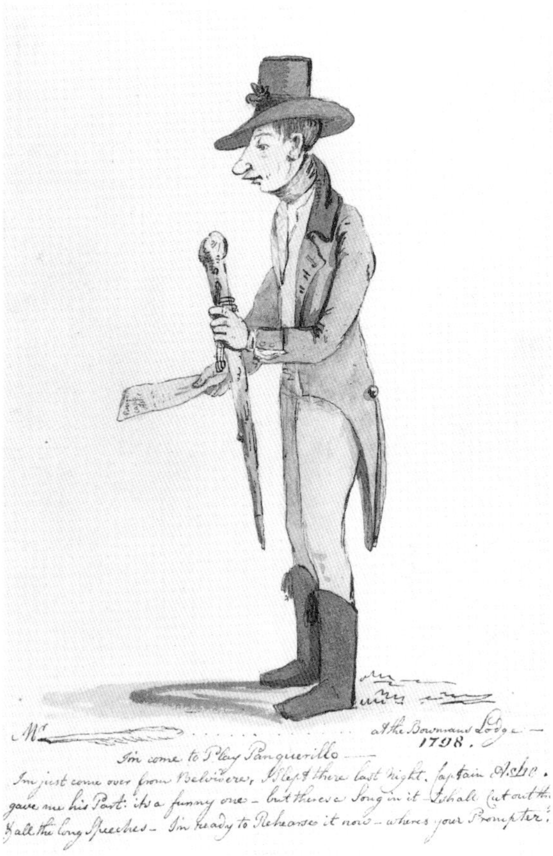

875
UNKNOWN MAN

John Nixon

Pencil, pen and black ink with watercolour on wove paper 16.5 x 11.5
INSCR: 'Mr [drawing of quill] ...at the Bowmans Lodge / 1798. / I'm come to Play Panquerillo – / Im just come over from Belvidere, I Slept there last night. Captain Ashe. / gave me his Part: it's a funny one – but theres a Song in it – I shall cut out that / & all the long Speeches – I'm ready to Rehearse it now – wheres your Prompter? –' (pen and black ink below)
INV: Not listed
PROV: John Nixon *Dramatic Annals* 3: 229
LIT: Sybil Rosenfeld, 'Private Theatricals at Bowman's Lodge, Dartford', *Theatre Notebook* (1961–62), 16: 125–26

Caricature, standing, in profile to left, wearing a brown cutaway coat and high-crowned hat, and holding a rough-knobbed stick. Possibly a self-portrait.

Nixon played the part of the Old Citizen in the younger Colman's *The Surrender of Calais* when the Royal Kentish Bowman's Lodge performed the play in 1798.

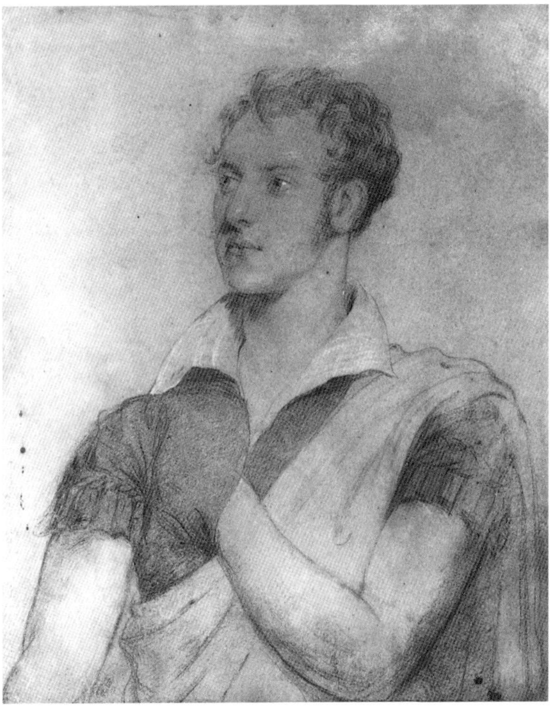

876
UNKNOWN MAN

Unknown Artist

Pencil 25.4 x 21
INV: RW/CKA 548A
PROV: Unknown, but acquired before 1909

The sitter is evidently shown in character, with a loose open collar and drapery over his left shoulder.

877
LOCATION UNKNOWN
UNKNOWN MAN

Unknown Artist

Pencil 25.1 x 18.7
INV: CKA 497 (not located 1988)
PROV: Unknown, but apparently acquired since 1909

Half-length, head slightly to right. The sitter wears a dark coat, a waistcoat unbuttoned at the top, and a black stock.

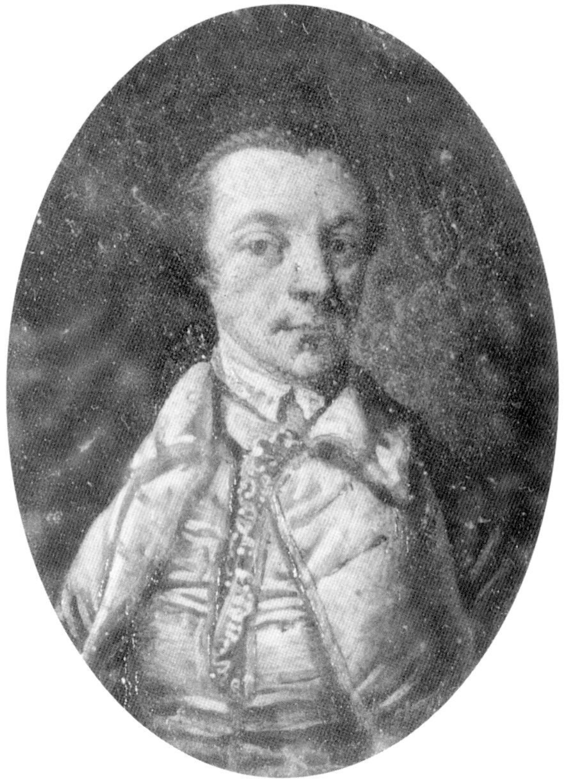

878
UNKNOWN MAN

Unknown Artist

Oil on copper 5.3 x 3.8 (oval)
INV: RW 427G (by Richard Cosway); CKA 427G
PROV: Unknown, but acquired before 1909

The sitter (Spranger Barry?) wears a white jacket with turned-down collar and pink edging, and a white waistcoat with silver buttons and pink edging.

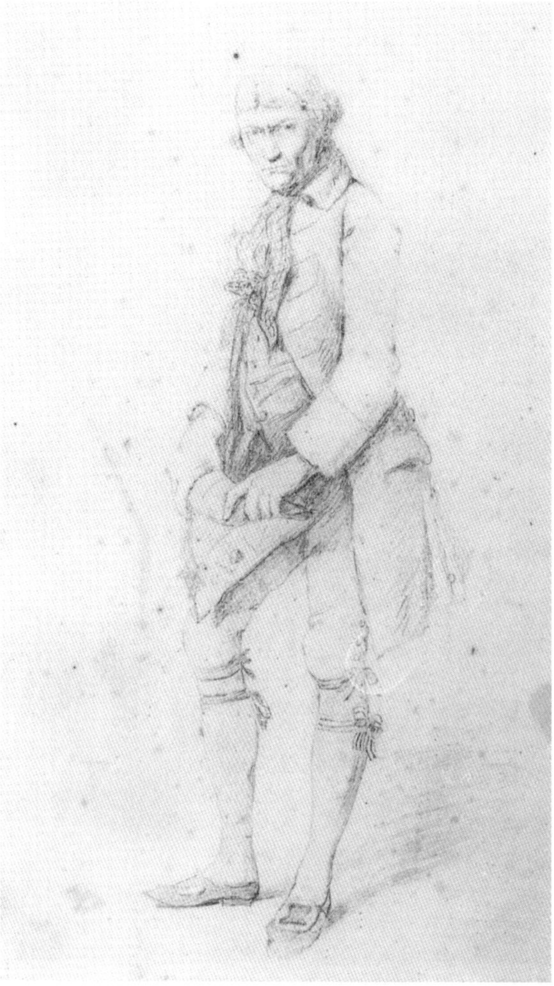

879

UNKNOWN MAN

Unknown Artist

Pencil on laid paper 26 x 15.2
INV: RW/CKA 553A
PROV: Charles Mathews (not in catalogue but framed with (?) Noad's portrait of William Parsons in *The Mountaineers*, which is inscribed by Mathews)

This is an accomplished and expressive drawing, which may well show an actor in character. He has a sullen and frowning expression, and his unpretentious late 18th-century costume is distinguished by the double striped ribbons that he wears at his knees.

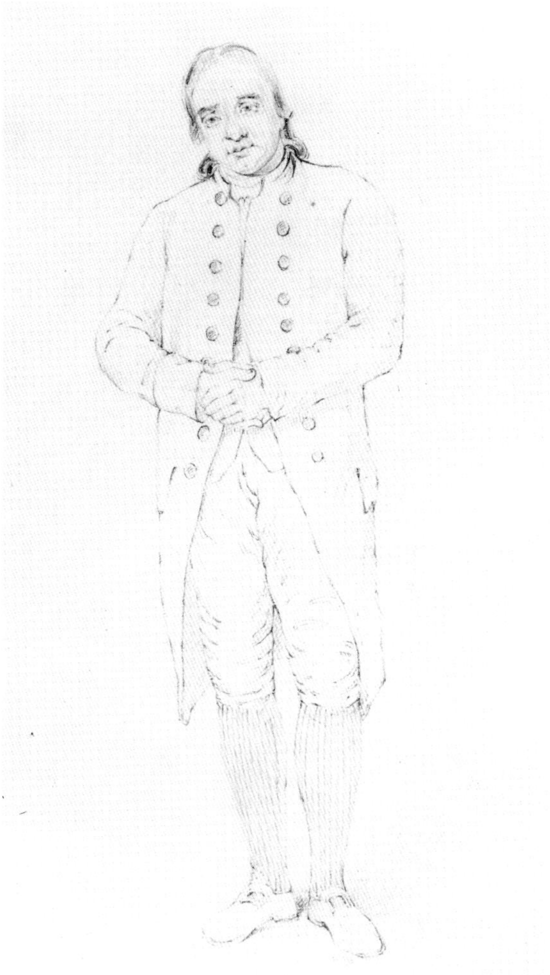

880

UNKNOWN MAN

as Old Strickland in *Love's Secret* by J.R. Brown (?)

Unknown Artist (C. Wageman?)

Oil on canvas 34.3 x 29.8
INSCR: 'Old Strickland / in Love's Secret' (pen and black ink on verso)
INV: CKA 591; Gift 454
PROV: F.J. Anderson, by whom presented to the Garrick Club, 1928

No. 880 is in poor condition. The sitter stands full-length. He has dark eyes and a large nose and wears black shoes with white bows, red stockings, dark breeches, and a black and red striped coat.

Brown's comedietta was first given at Ladbroke Hall on 2 January 1888. The drawing shown, however, seems to have been made much earlier (*c.*1800).

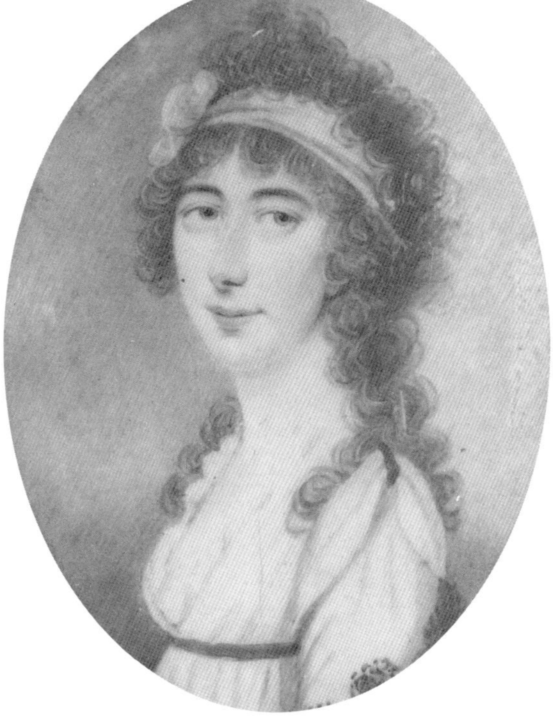

881

UNKNOWN WOMAN

Horace Hone (attr.)

Watercolour on ivory 5.6 x 4.5 (oval)
INV: RW 427T (by Horace Hone); CKA 427T
PROV: Unknown, but acquired before 1909

Head and shoulders, bust to left, head turned to face spectator. The sitter has dark hair falling over her shoulders and wears a white dress. Isabella Mattocks has the same cast of features, but this miniature was probably painted too late to show her. CKA suggests a date of *c.*1795 and unconvincingly attributes the miniature to Hone.

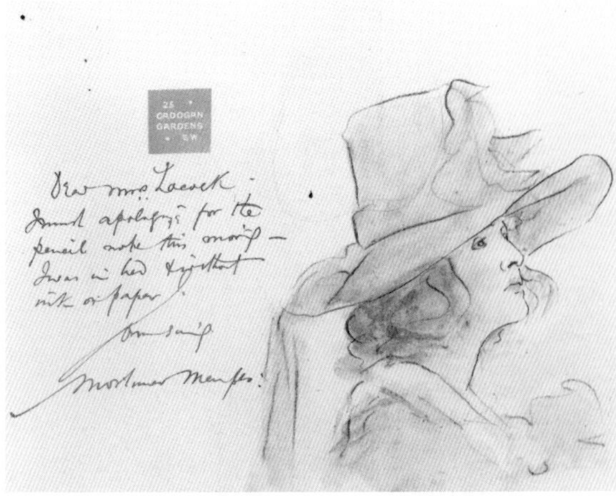

882

UNKNOWN WOMAN

Mortimer Menpes

Pencil and watercolour on wove paper
12 x 20 (whole sheet)
INSCR: (see below)
INV: Not listed; Gift 752
PROV: Guy Knowles, by whom presented to the Garrick Club, 1956

The sitter, with head and shoulders in profile, wears a large, broad-brimmed pink hat and a blue dress. The letter on the writing paper is headed '25, Cadogan Gardens SW' and written in pen and brown ink: 'Dear Mrs Lacock, / I must apologize for the / pencil note this morning – / I was in bed & without / ink or paper. / Yours truly (?) / Mortimer Menpes.' See also No. 322.

Stylistically, the sketch resembles the many drawings of women in large hats signed 'J. Reynolds' which were in circulation early in the century as genuine works of Reynolds.

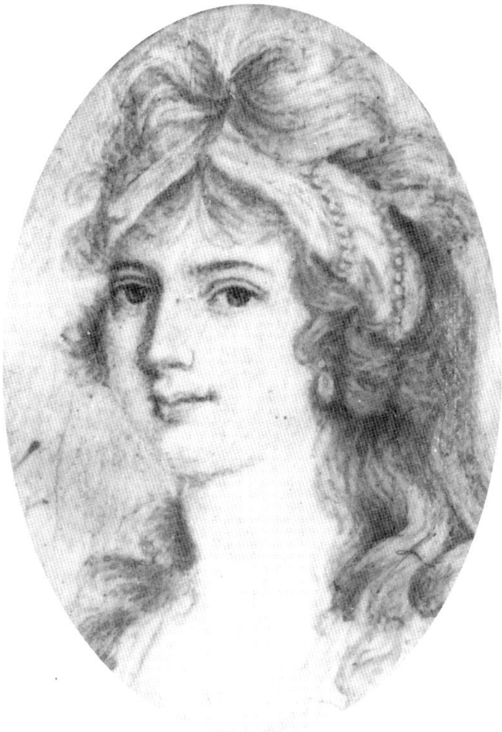

883
UNKNOWN WOMAN

Unknown Artist

Watercolour on ivory 4.5 x 3.1 (oval)
INV: RW 427H (Margaret Woffington); CKA 427H
PROV: The 15th Lord Saye and Sele, by whom presented to the Garrick Club, 1846

The sitter has long, greyish hair tumbling over her shoulders and wears a pearl earring on her left ear, and a turban with bands of pearls and a pink bow.

This miniature was presented as a portrait of Peg Woffington. It probably dates from about 1800.

884
LOCATION UNKNOWN
UNKNOWN WOMAN
as Viola (?) in *Twelfth Night*
by William Shakespeare

Unknown Artist

Oil on canvas 34.3 x 27.9
INV: RW 278 (Jane Pope, character unknown); CKA 278
PROV: Unknown

The sitter wears a blue jacket with gold edging, and a blue waistcoat.

This portrait was called 'Jane Pope' in the 1909 catalogue, following the identification given on the frame. CKA dates it about 1820, but it seems to be much earlier.

PAINTINGS & DRAWINGS OTHER THAN PORTRAITS

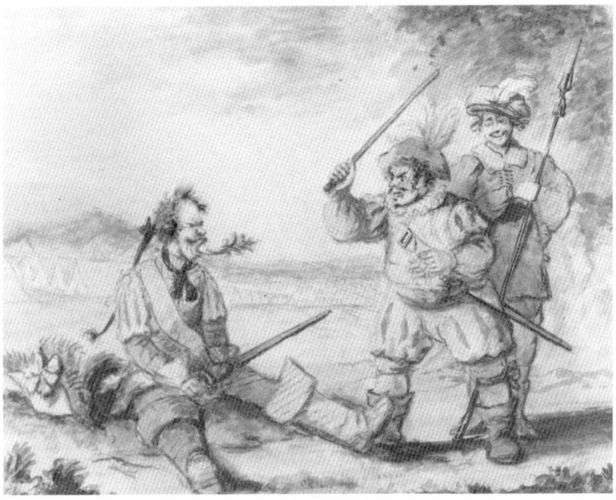

885
FLUELLEN making *PISTOL* eat the leek
in *Henry V* (Act v, scene 1)

Henry William Bunbury

Pencil and watercolour with some body colour
on wove paper 35 x 44.5
INV: RW/CKA 62
PROV: T.H. Powell, by whom presented
to the Garrick Club in or before 1888
ENGR: Meddows pub. Thomas Macklin
1 August 1795, stipple

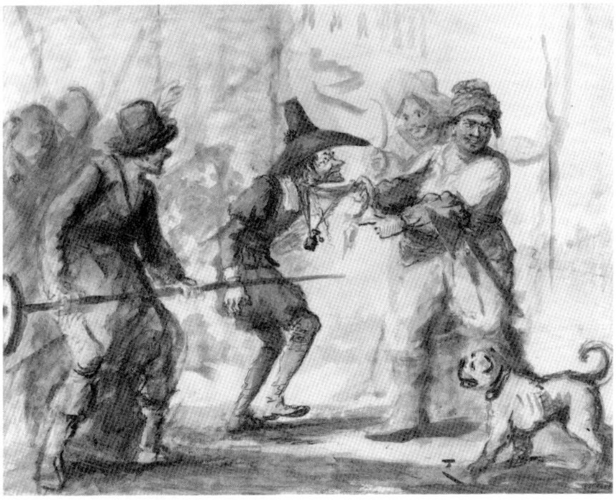

886
DICK THE BUTCHER and *SMITH THE WEAVER* seizing the *CLERK OF CHATHAM*
in *2 Henry VI* (Act IV, scene 2)

Henry William Bunbury

Pencil and watercolour on laid paper 35 x 44.5
INV: RW/CKA 57
PROV: T.H. Powell, by whom presented
to the Garrick Club in or before 1888
ENGR: Coles pub. Thomas Macklin 20 August 1795, stipple

Nos. 885 and 886 were engraved and included in a collection of 22 Shakespeare subjects published by Thomas Macklin at his Poets' Gallery in the Strand. The earliest plate in the series is dated 1 June 1792 and the latest 21 March 1796. Seventeen of the plates, but not those engraved after Nos. 885 and 886, bear an inscription stating that the original drawings were then in the possession of the Duchess of York, the wife of Bunbury's patron. However, the use of a royal owner's name may have had more to do with encouraging sales of the prints than regard for a correct provenance. Some plates, but not those taken from Nos. 885 and 886, describe the artist as the 'late' H.W. Bunbury – another commercial ploy, perhaps, as Bunbury still had 15 years to live.

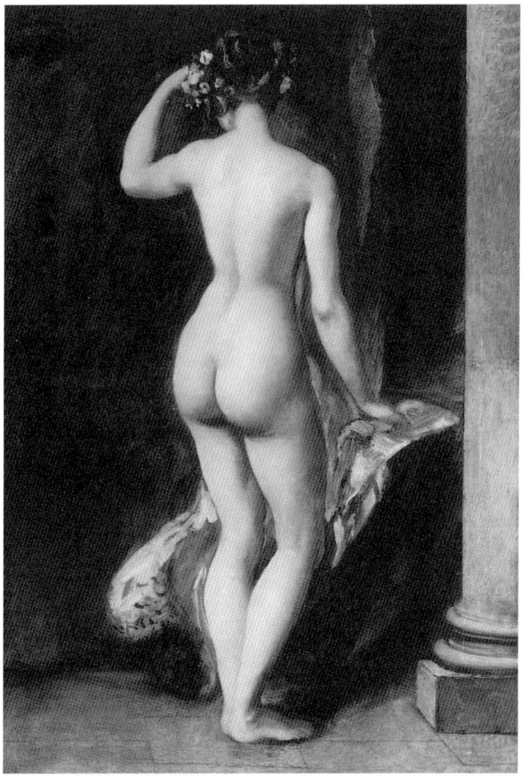

887
The Bath

William Etty

Oil on canvas 70.5 x 49.5
INV: CKA 613; Gift 358
PROV: Bequeathed by A.M. Spalding, 1912

The nude figure, with her back to the viewer, has brown hair piled on top of her head; into it are entwined blue and pink flowers. Decorations include a red drapery which tumbles onto a chair behind the sitter, and a blue cloth on another chair.

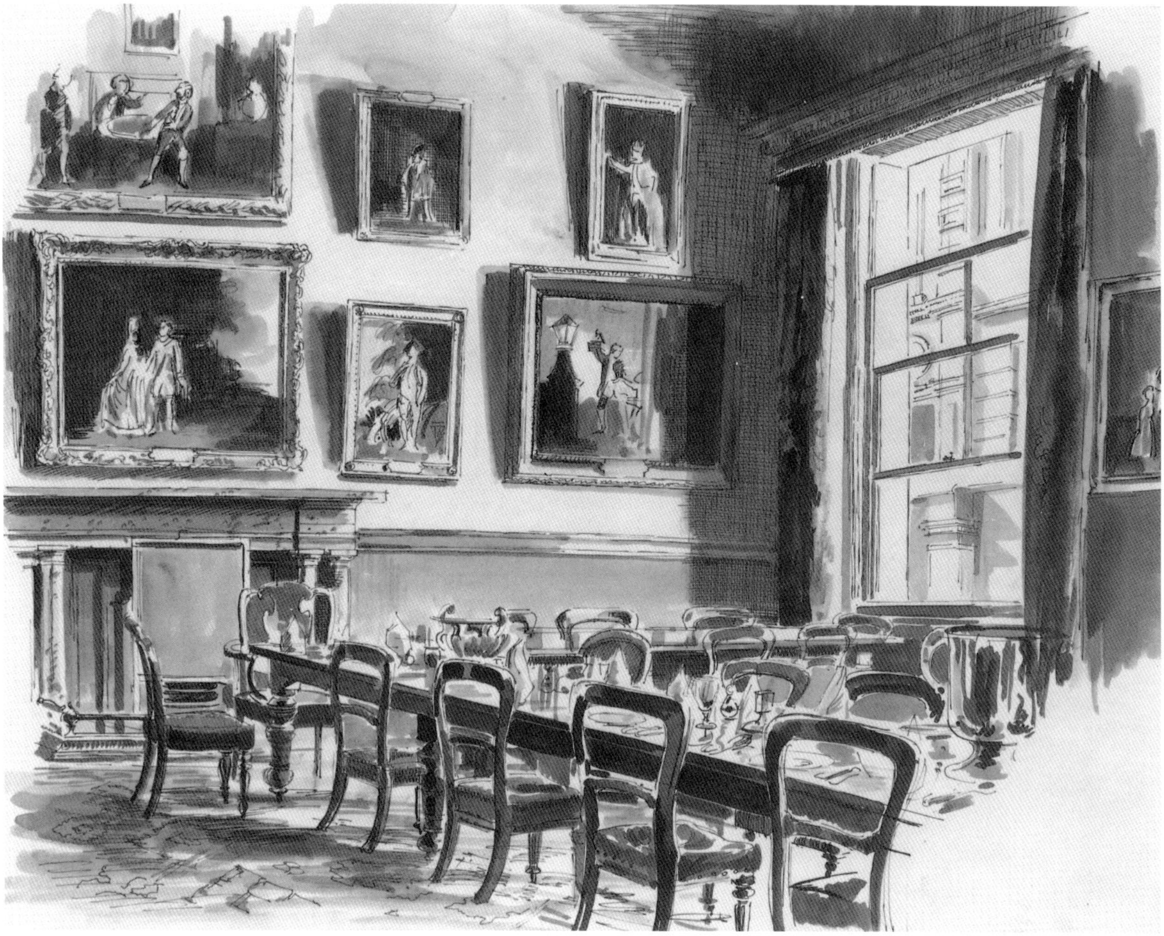

888
The Coffee Room at the Garrick Club

Geoffrey Fletcher

Pen and black ink on wove paper 45.7 x 58.4
INV: GCL 732A; Gift 878
PROV: Presented to Gerald C. Rivington, chairman of the General Committee from 1948 to 1962, by members who served on the Committee with him; bequeathed by Gerald Rivington, 1978

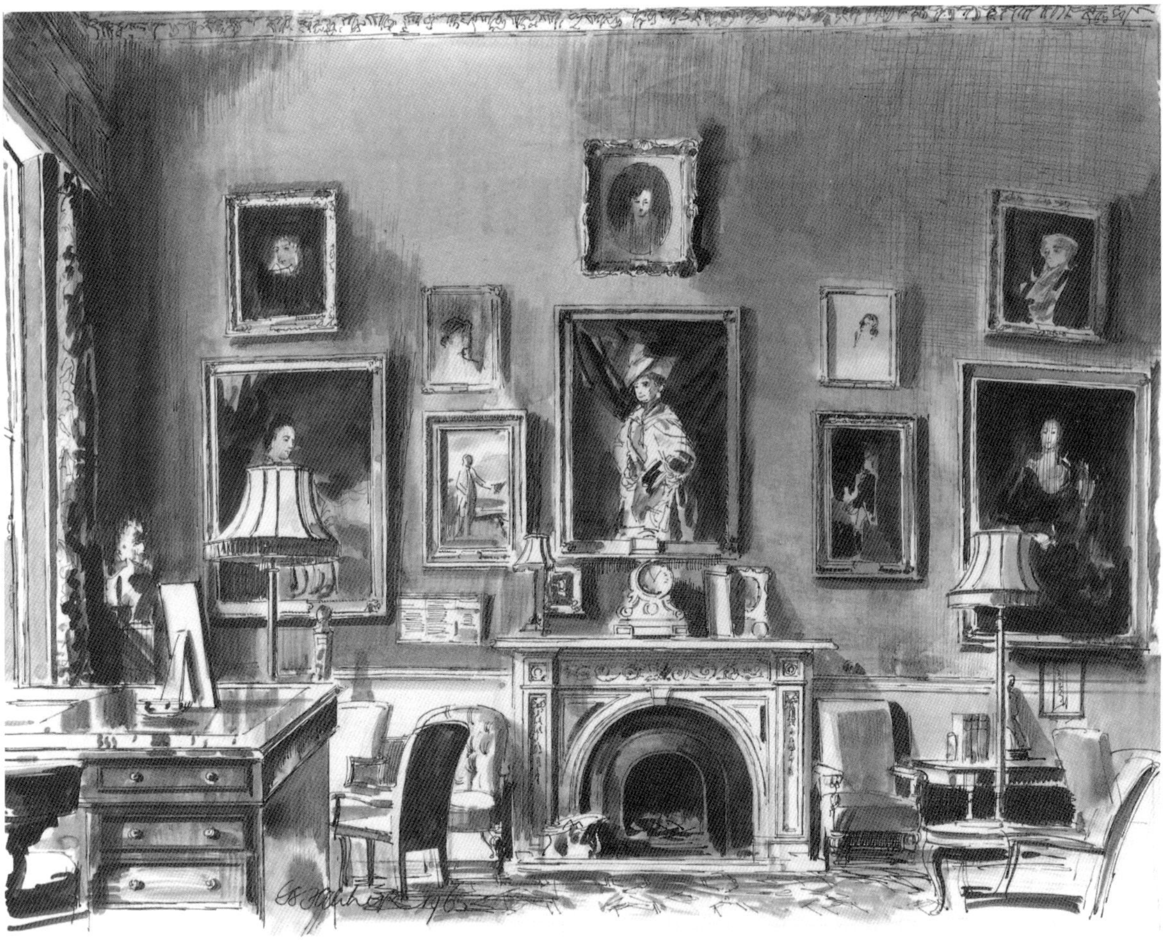

889
The Morning Room at the Garrick Club

Geoffrey Fletcher

Pen and black ink on wove paper 45.7 x 58.4
INV: GCL 732B; Gift 878
PROV: Presented to Gerald C. Rivington, chairman of the General Committee from 1948 to 1962, by members who served on the Committee with him; bequeathed by Gerald Rivington, 1978

890
LOCATION UNKNOWN
First Floor Landing of the Garrick Club

Hanslip Fletcher

Pen and ink on wove paper 33.7 x 52.7
INSCR: 'Hanslip Fletcher, 1945' (b.r.)
INV: CKA 648; Gift 636
PROV: Viscount Kemsley, by whom presented to the Garrick Club, 1946
LIT: Drawn for the *Sunday Times*

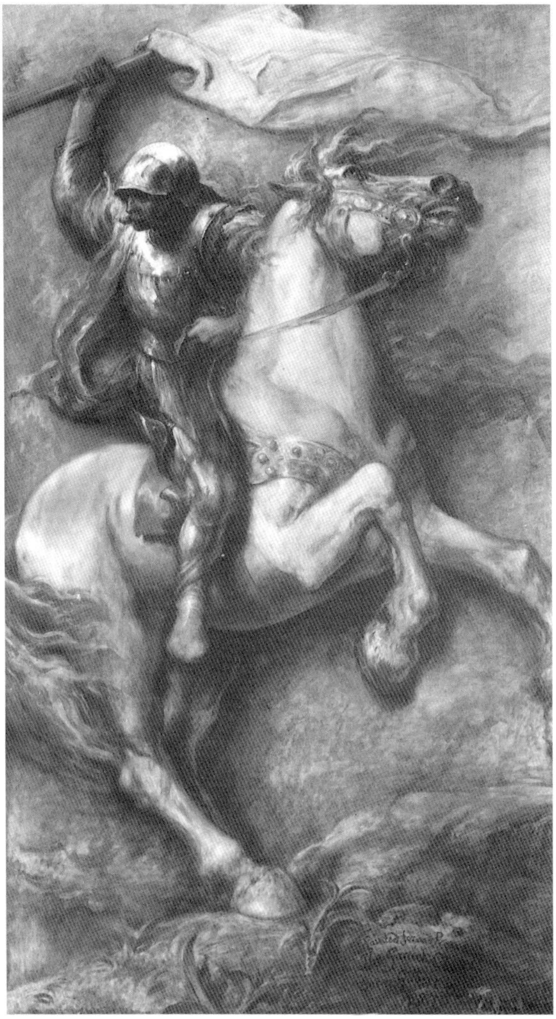

891
The Standard Bearer

Sir John Gilbert

Oil on canvas 210.8 x 123.2
INSCR: 'Painted for and Presented to / The Garrick Club by / John Gilbert PRWS R.A. / 1887' (brown paint b.r.)
INV: RW/CKA 130; Gift 209
PROV: Presented by the artist, 1887

The artist, a prolific painter and illustrator specialising in historical subjects, became a member of the Garrick Club in 1852.

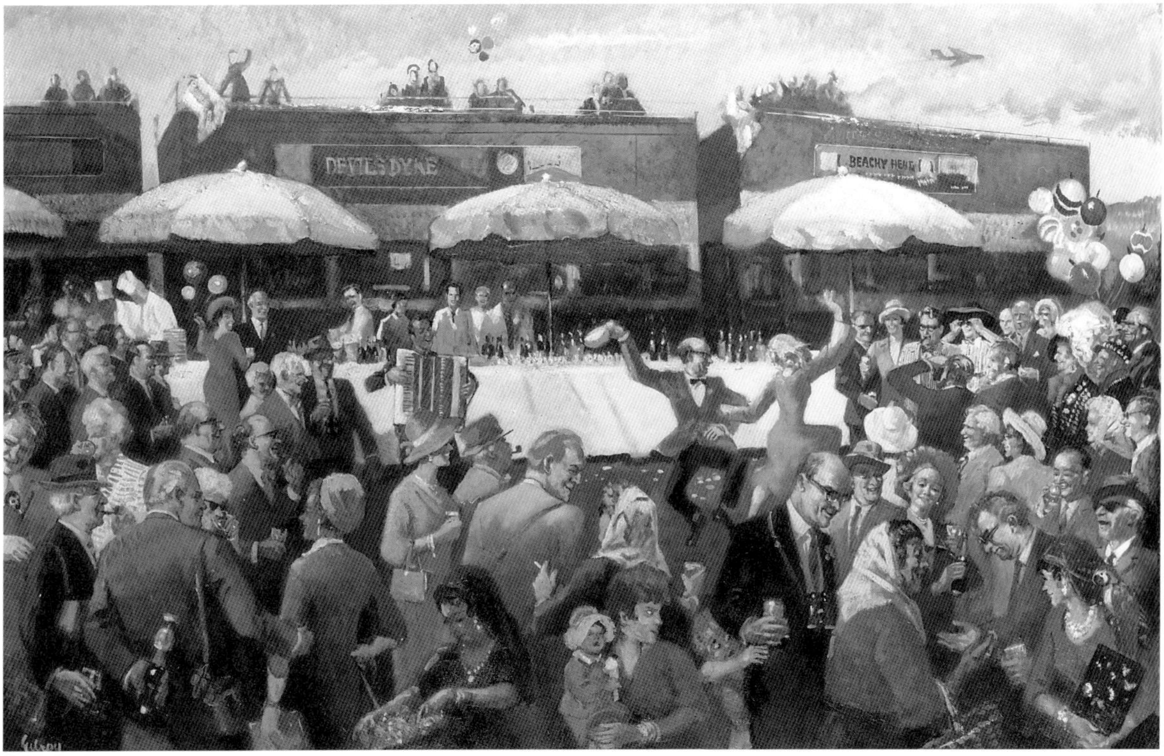

892

The 1967 Garrick Club Outing to The Derby

John Gilroy

Oil on panel 83.5 x 129
(painted in frame)
INV: GCL 662
PROV: Presented by the artist, 1967
EXH: 1979 London (13.29)

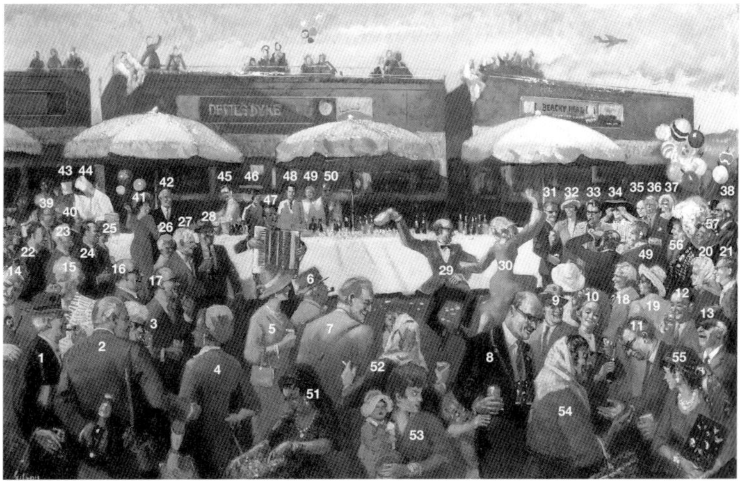

1. Trevor Fenwick
2. John Dykes
3. Mrs Trevor Fenwick
4. Mrs John Dykes
5. Guest
6. Alban Jeynes
7. Sebastian Earl
8. Jimmy Doggart
9. Nigel Patrick
10. Miss Evelyn Laye
11. Kenneth More
12. Frank Lawton
13. George Malcolm Thomson
14. Ian Parsons
15. Guest
16. G.O. Nickalls
17. Jack Gilroy
18. Hubert Gregg
19. Pat Kirkwood
20. Mrs Jack Evans
21. Jack Evans
22. Ian Samuel
23. Unknown
24. Grahame Martin-Turner
25. Trevor Fenwick, jnr
26. Mrs Satterthwaite
27. Cmdr Satterthwaite
28. Dr Cuthbert Cane
29. Freddie Barker
30. Mrs Rutherston
31. Michael Havers
32. Mrs Donald Sinden
33. Sir Robin Day
34. Mrs Robin Day
35. Guest
36. Eric Hawkesley
37. Gate-crasher
38. Kenneth Benda
39. Horace Parshall
40. Mrs Horace Parshall
41. Guest
42. Clive Burt
43. Chef's friend
44. Chef
45. Michael Hart
46. Mrs Help
47. Busker
48. Peter Ellick
49. 'Sir Basil Bartlett' deleted, 'Staff' added
50. Nobby Clarke

51, 53, 54 & 55: Gypsies

52. Mrs Sebastian Earl
56. Pearly Queen
57. Pearly King

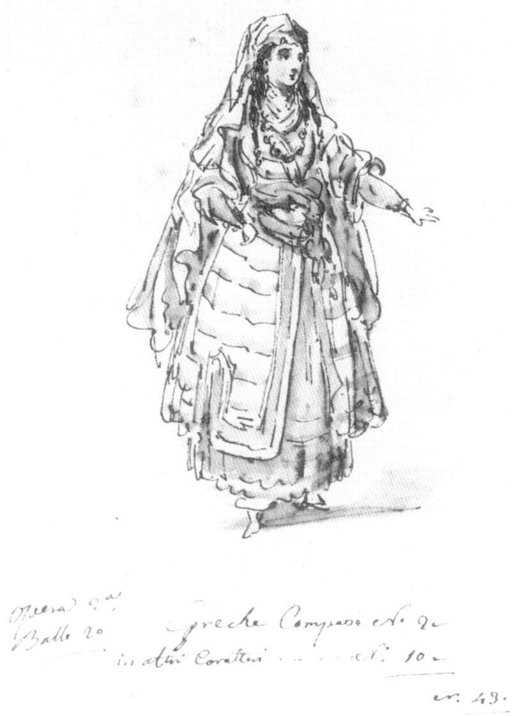

893

Costume sketch for an Opera or Masquerade

18th-Century Italian School

Pen and brown ink with watercolour
on laid paper 26.3 x 18.7
INSCR: 'Opera 2a. / Ballo 20'
(pen and brown ink b.l.);
'Greche Compasi No. 2– / in altri Caratteri ... :
No 10–' (pen and brown ink b.c.);
'N. 43' (pen and brown b.r.)
INV: CKA 514
PROV: Unknown, but apparently acquired since 1909

See No. 894 for a male costume design for the same work.

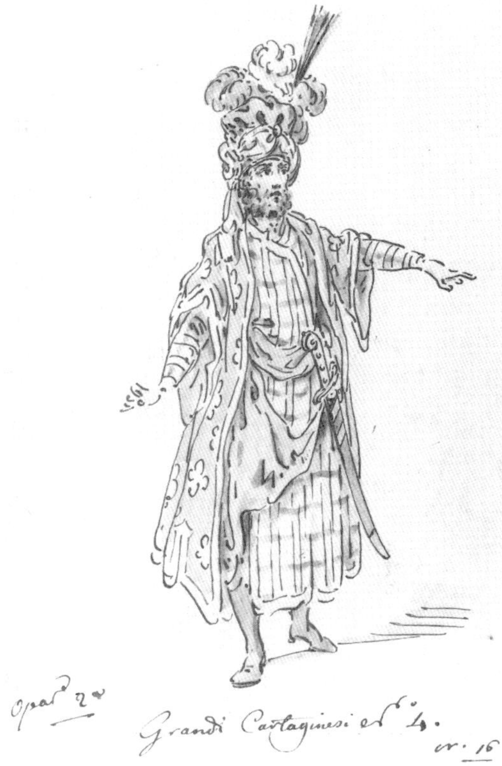

894

Costume sketch for an Opera or Masquerade

18th-Century Italian School

Pen and brown ink with watercolour
on laid paper 26 x 18.4
INSCR: 'Opera 2a' (pen and brown ink b.l.);
'Grandi Cartaginesi No 4.' (pen and brown ink b.c.);
'N. 16' (pen and brown ink b.r.)
INV: CKA 513
PROV: Unknown, but apparently acquired since 1909

The Turkish costume consists of a high green and white turban with a jewel at the front and feathers, purplish stockings, a hanging garment with brown vertical and red horizontal lines, and a long robe decorated in green with a floral design.

See No. 893. There are three similar drawings by the same artist in the Harvard Theatre Collection.

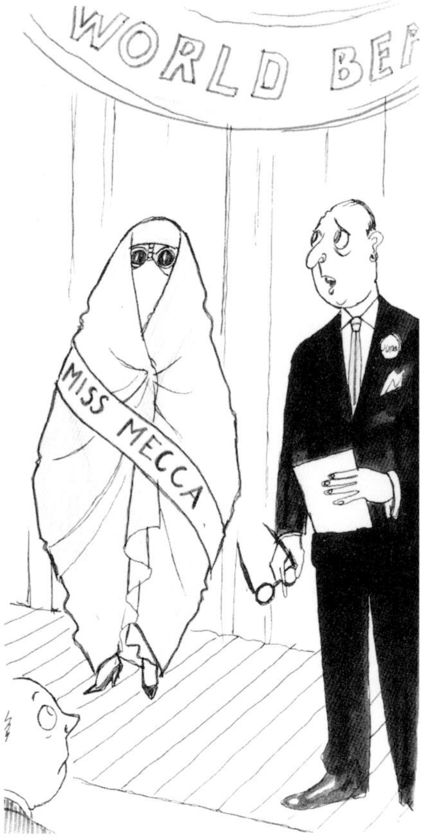

895
'Is there a eunuch in the house?'

Sir Osbert Lancaster

Pen and ink 25.5 x 14 on paper 46 x 36
INSCR: '13.11.65' (pen and ink, l.r.)
INV: Not listed; Gift 922
PROV: Presented by the artist's widow, 1987

The artist (1908–1986), who was also a writer and educator, painted scenery for many productions in the West End and at Glyndebourne. He became a member of the Garrick Club in 1962.

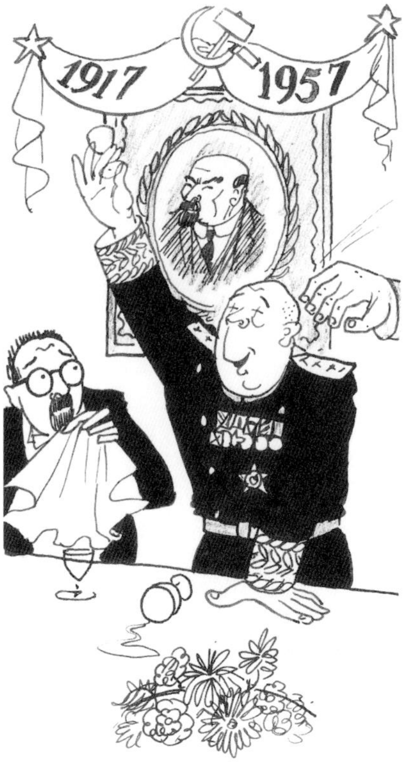

896
'Comrades! I give you the toast to "Absent Friends", coupled with names of…'

Sir Osbert Lancaster

Pen and ink 23.5 x 14 on paper 46 x 36
INSCR: '8.11.57' (pen and ink, l.r.)
INV: Not listed; Gift 922
PROV: Presented by the artist's widow, 1987

See No. 895.

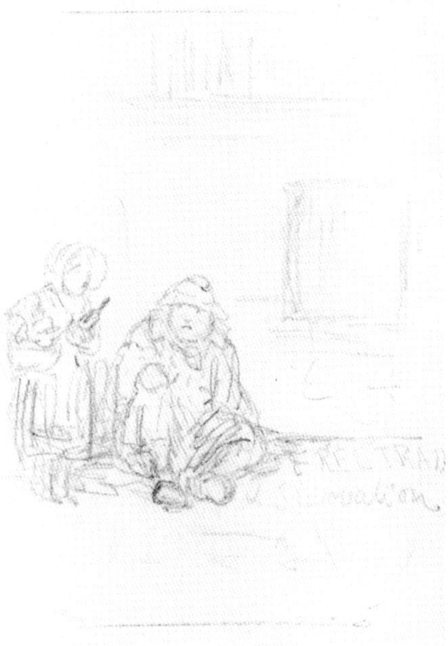

897
Two Figures

John Leech

Pencil on wove paper 10.4 x 11.5
INV: RW 502; CKA 502A; Gift 172 (some or all of 897–922)
PROV: Presented by the artist

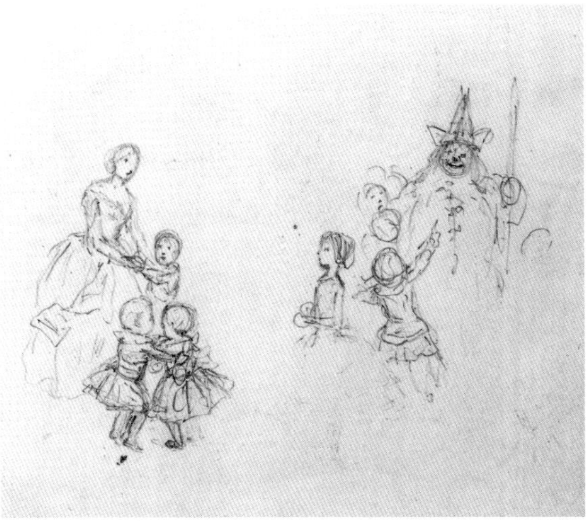

898
Children at a Dance

John Leech

Pencil with pen and black ink on wove paper 13.3 x 18.3
INV: RW 515; CKA 515B
PROV: Probably presented by the artist

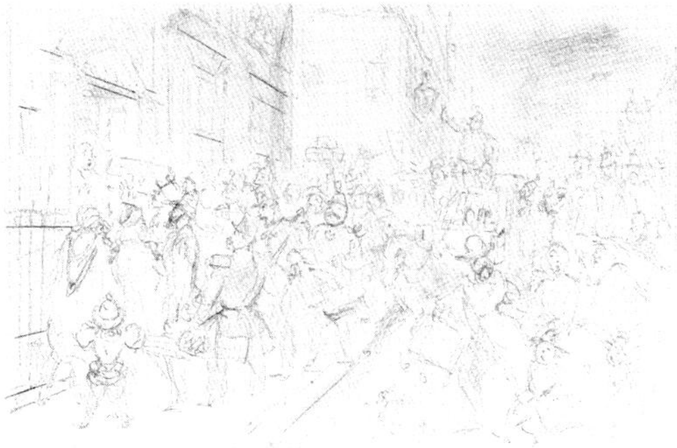

899
A Crowd outside a House

John Leech

Pencil on wove paper 11.5 x 18
INV: RW 511; CKA 511D
PROV: Probably presented by the artist

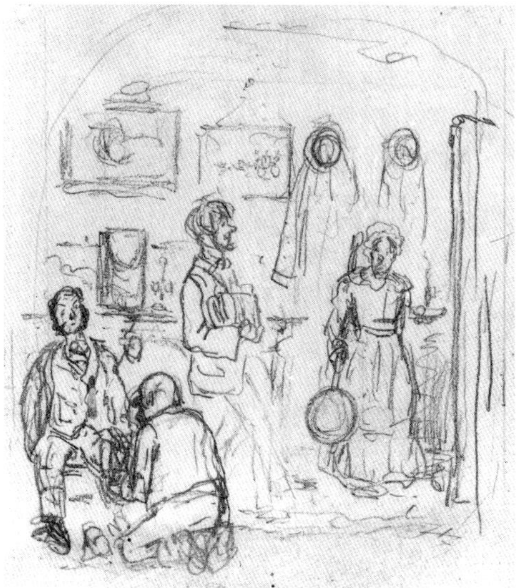

900
Four Men and a Woman in an Interior

John Leech

Pencil with pen and black ink on wove paper 11.8 x 10.6
INV: RW 515; CKA 515C
PROV: Probably presented by the artist

901
NOT ILLUSTRATED
'Free Trade and Starvation'

John Leech

Pencil on wove paper 13 x 9.3
INSCR: 'FREE TRADE and Starvation' (pencil).
INV: RW 502; CKA 502B
PROV: Presented by the artist

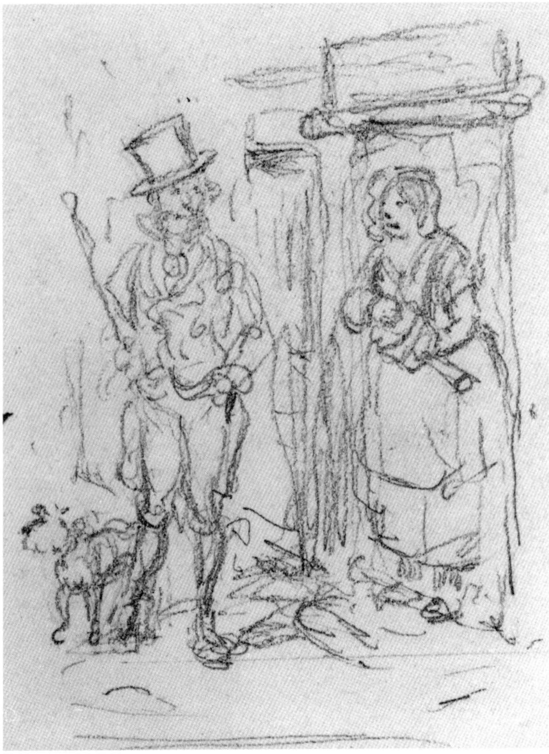

902
A Man and Woman at a Front Door

John Leech

Pencil on wove paper 12 x 9.6
INV: RW 511; CKA 511B
PROV: Probably presented by the artist

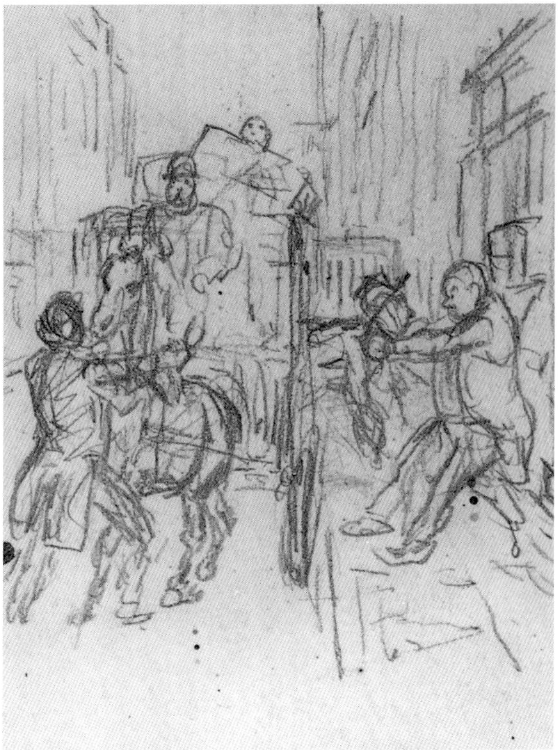

903
A Man being pulled out of a Four-Wheeler

John Leech

Pencil on wove paper 10.7 x 8.3
INV: RW 515; CKA 515D
PROV: Probably presented by the artist

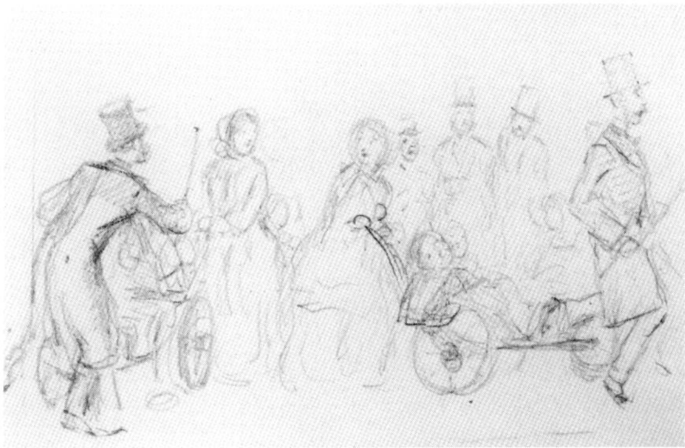

904
Men and Women with Children in Pushchairs

John Leech

Pencil on wove paper 12.1 x 19.1
INV: RW 517; CKA 517D
PROV: Probably presented by the artist

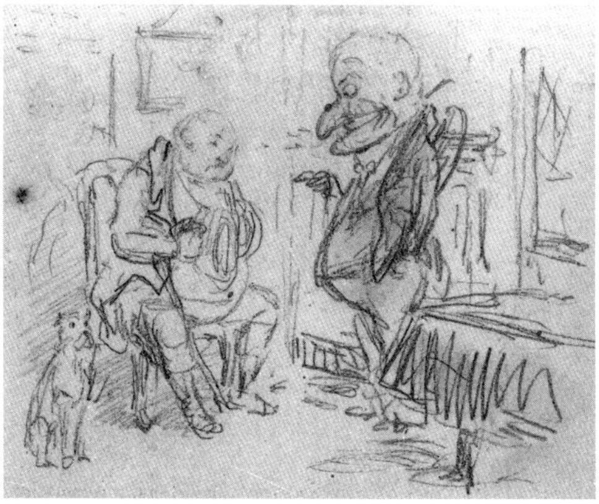

905
Punch and John Bull before a Fire

John Leech

Black chalk on wove paper 9.5 x 12.1
INV: RW 515; CKA 515A
PROV: Probably presented by the artist

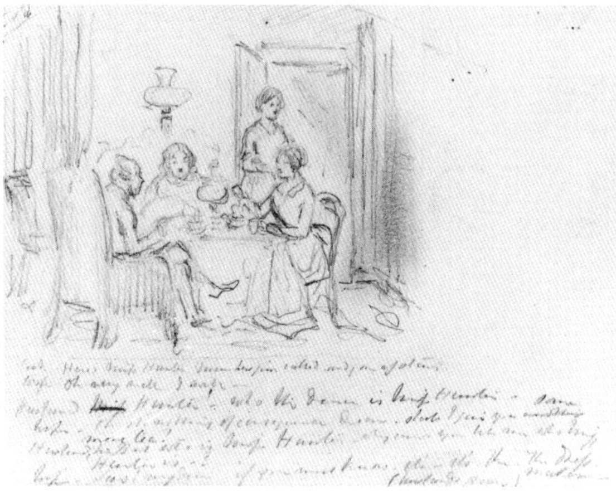

906
Tea-time with Cook at the Door

John Leech

Pencil on wove paper 12.8 x 17.2
INV: RW 502; CKA 502E
PROV: Presented by the artist

Underneath the drawing is a long caption:

Cook: Here's Miss Hunter Mum, her Jim (?) called, and … stairs.
Wife: Oh very well I will –
Husband: Hunter! Who the devil is Miss Hunter?
Wife: Oh it's nothing of consequence dear – shall I give you some more tea?
Husband: But who is Miss Hunter? – why can't you tell me who Miss Hunter is?
Wife: Law! my dear – if you must know – it's – it's – the – Dressmaker.

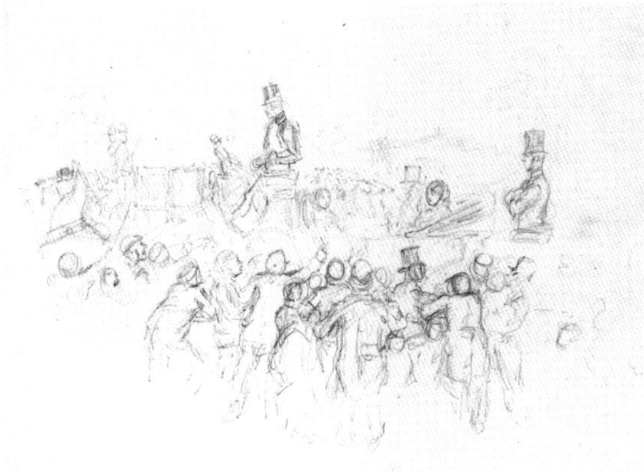

907
The Drive in Rotten Row, Hyde Park

John Leech

Pencil on wove paper 25.5 x 35.4
INV: RW/CKA 500
PROV: Probably presented by the artist

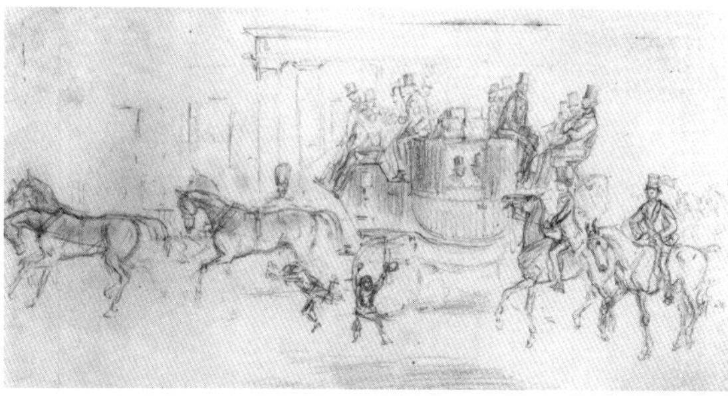

908
The Four-in-Hand Club

John Leech

Pencil on wove paper 22 x 38.6
INV: RW/CKA 506
PROV: Probably presented by the artist

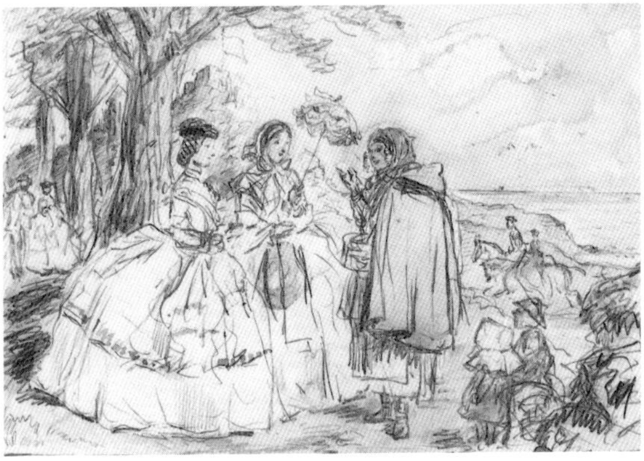

909

'The Gypsey's Prophecy'

John Leech

Pencil and watercolour on wove paper 10.8 x 15.9
INSCR: 'The Gypsey's Prophecy' (pencil b.c.);
'Please let me have a *Laid* paper proof in
colour as pattern [?] JL' (pencil t.r.);
'Bite up all this vigorously' (pencil r.);
'Plain or Ringlets / B & Evans' (pencil b.l.);
'Please send title to B & E / with the Plate' (pencil b.r.)
INV: RW/CKA 504
PROV: Probably presented by the artist

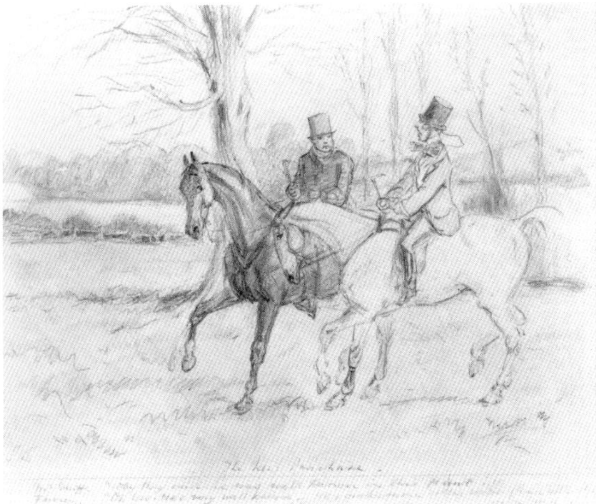

910

'The New Purchase'

John Leech

Pencil and watercolour on wove paper 20.5 x 26.5 (sight)
INSCR: 'The New Purchase / Mr Muff. "Why, they said
he was well known in this Hunt!" / Farmer. "Oh yes!
He's very well known – He's broke more collar bones
than all the osses / in England!" ' (pencil b.)
INV: RW/CKA 520
PROV: Presented by Maitland Dashwood,
member 1856 to 1883

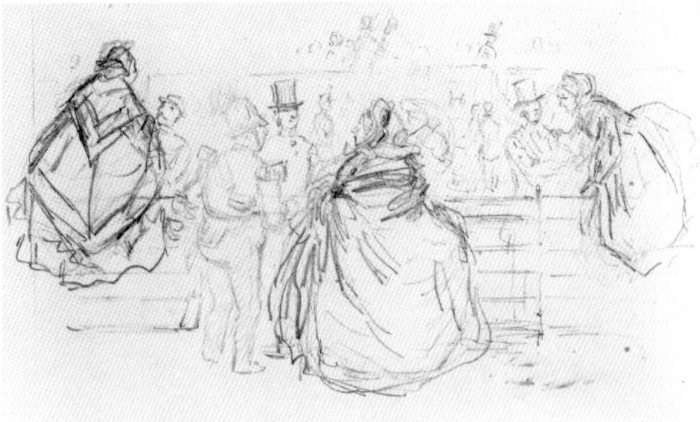

911

Three Fat Ladies over the Railings

John Leech

Black chalk and pencil on wove paper 12 x 18.7
INV: RW 517; CKA 517C
PROV: Probably presented by the artist

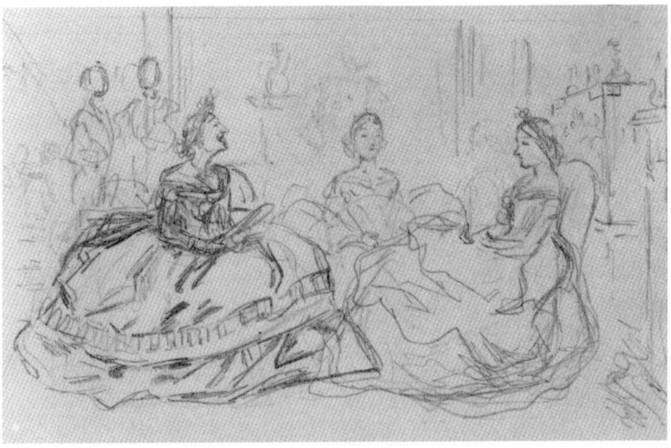

912

'A Serious Drawback'

John Leech

Black chalk and pencil on wove paper 12.8 x 18.7
INV: RW 517; CKA 517A
PROV: Probably presented by the artist
ENGR: *Punch*, illustration inscr: 'Hideous Old Lady of
Fashion (with Plain Daughter). "Charming Ball at Sir
Charles's last night. Everybody there – good rooms, not
over-crowded – capital supper! Dearest Barbara enjoyed
herself prodigiously! I don't see, however, how I can avoid
asking HIS sister and niece to MY ball, next week, he is so
fond of them; And yet you know that they are people
who do not go out nearly as much as we do, and
are not at all in our position in society!" '
LIT: *Punch* (n.d.); *John Leech*, 3: 9

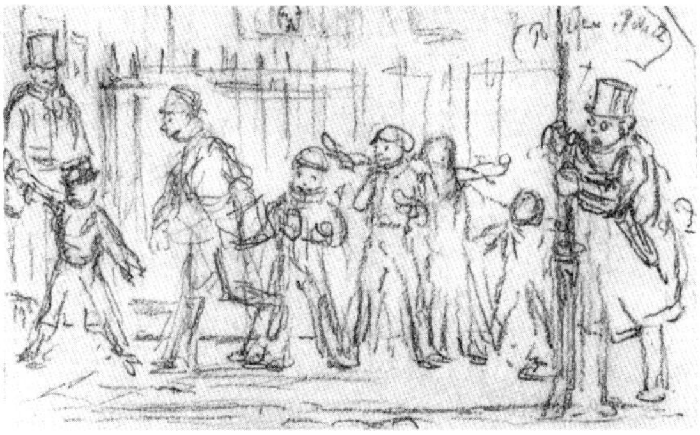

913
Three Men and Children beside Railings

John Leech

Pencil on wove paper 9.3 x 14.8
INV: RW 502; CKA 502C
PROV: Presented by the artist

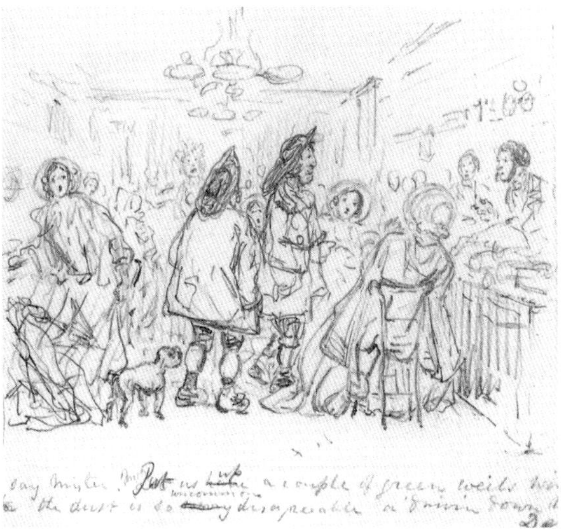

914
Two Men buying Veils

John Leech

Pencil with pen and black ink on wove paper 11.7 x 16.2
INSCR: 'I say Mister. Put us up a couple of green veils will you. / the dust is so uncommon disagreeable a drivin' down to the / Derby' (pencil b.)
INV: RW 502; CKA 502F
PROV: Presented by the artist

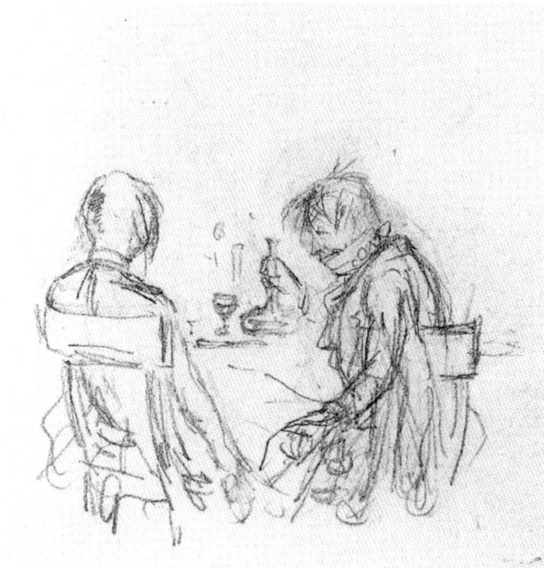

915
Study of Two Small Figures

John Leech

Pencil on wove paper 8.7 x 8.2
INV: RW 511; CKA 511A
PROV: Probably presented by the artist

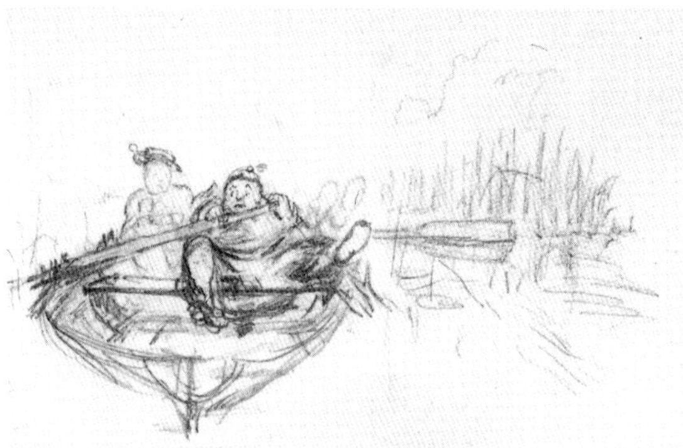

916
'Aquatics'

John Leech

Black chalk and pencil on paper 9.6 x 15.2
INV: RW 502; CKA 502D
PROV: Presented by the artist
ENGR: The *Punch* illustration is inscr: 'Who is this? Why, this is Mr John Chubb pulling one of his long steady strokes. He is taking more pains than usual, because those pretty girls in the round hats are sitting on the lawn drawing from nature.'
LIT: *Punch* (n.d.); *John Leech*, 2: 169

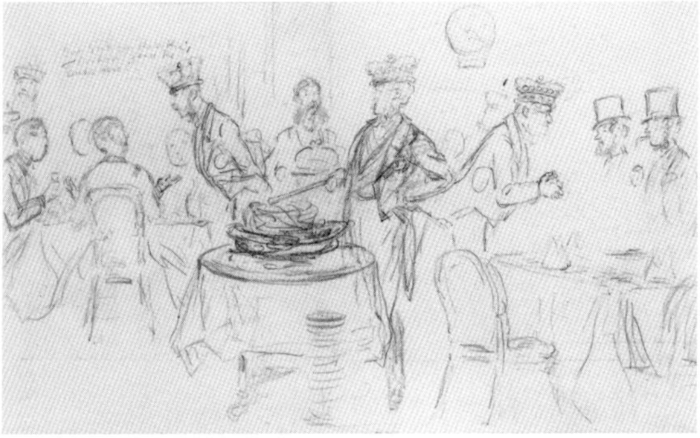

917
'The Aristocratic Hotel Company (Limited)'

John Leech

Pencil on wove paper 21.6 x 36.8
INSCR: 'But I tell you the Wine's / Corked! Send the / Duke here!' (pencil t.l.)
INV: RW/CKA 498
PROV: Probably presented by the artist
ENGR: The *Punch* illustration is inscr: 'But I tell you the wine / is Corked! Send the Duke / here Immediately' (balloon from figure on left); 'ATTENDANCE / IS / CHARGED / IN THE / BILL' (sign on wall l. of c.); 'Dinners for two! Yes Sir – let me take / your hat Gents – Nice Haunch of Venison / from my own place just up!' (balloon from peer at r.); 'THE ARISTOCRATIC HOTEL COMPANY (LIMITED) / A probable scene, if our Noble Lords go on dabbling in business' (under)
LIT: *Punch* (n.d.); *John Leech* 3: 42–43

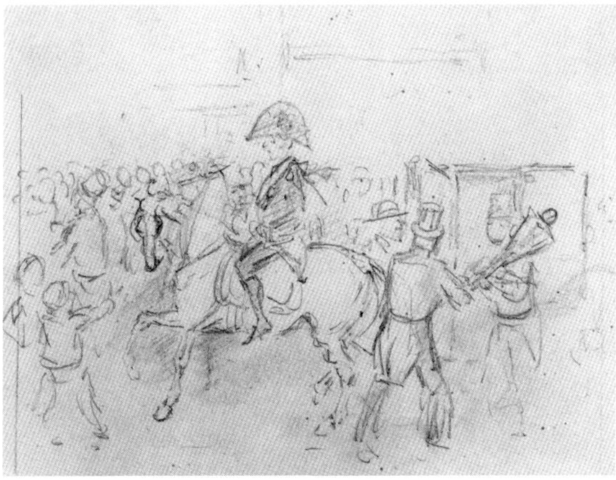

918
THE DUKE OF WELLINGTON
Followed by the Mace

John Leech

Pencil on wove paper 13.5 x 17.8
INV: RW/CKA 517F
PROV: Probably presented by the artist

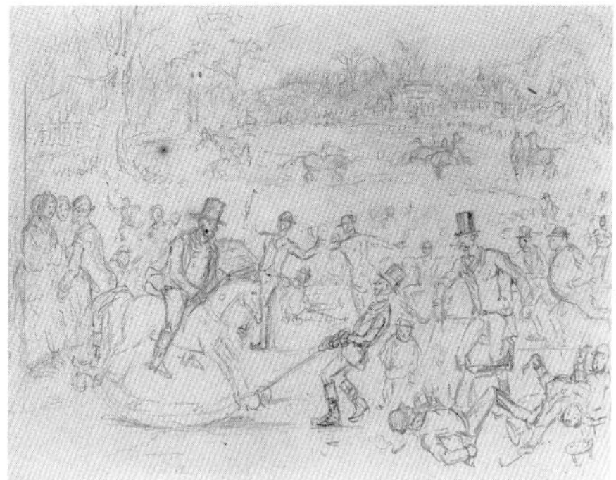

919
'Frozen-out Foxhunters'

John Leech

Pencil on wove paper 17.1 x 22.2
INV: RW/CKA 511C
PROV: Probably presented by the artist
ENGR: The *Punch* illustration is inscr: 'Frozen-out Foxhunters'
LIT: *Punch* (n.d.); *John Leech*, 1: 31

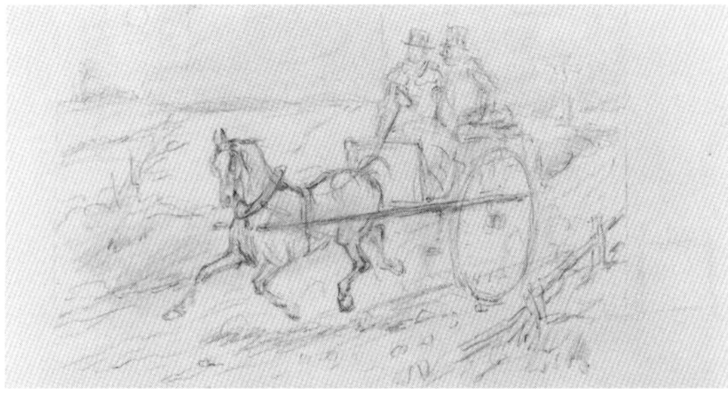

920
'Pleasant'

John Leech

Pencil on wove paper 14.7 x 22.5
INSCR: 'Pleasant'; 'Nervous Gentleman from Town. "Don't you think Robert – going so fast down hill is very likely to / make the horse fall?" – / Robert. "Lor bless yer / no / Sir! I never throwed a oss down in my life 'xcept once – and that / was this werry oss in this werry place, a bringing a gent as might be you / from the Station" ' (pencil b.)
INV: RW/CKA 517B
PROV: Probably presented by the artist
ENGR: The *Punch* illustration is entitled 'PLEASANT' and is inscr. 'Nervous Gentleman. "Don't you think Robert, going so fast down hill is very likely to make the horse fall?" / Robert. "Lor Bless Yer – no, sir! I never throwed a oss down in my life, 'xept once and that was one frosty moonlight night (just such a night as this it was), as I was a-drivin' a gent (as might be you) from the station, when I throwed down this wery oss in this wery identical place" '
LIT: *Punch* (n.d.); *John Leech*, 2: 92

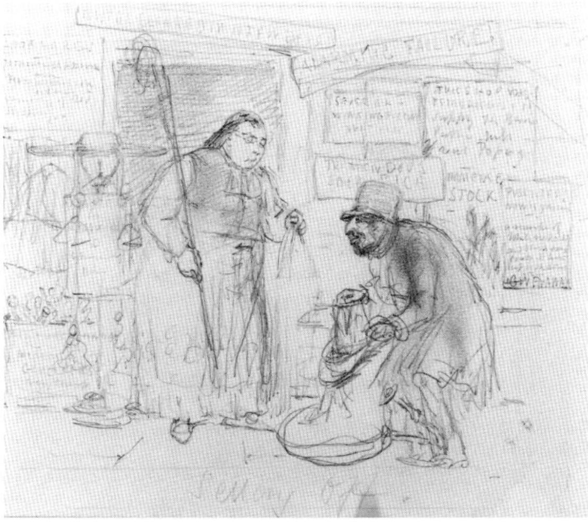

921
'Selling Off!!'

John Leech

Pencil on wove paper 19.1 x 21.7
INSCR: 'Selling Off' (pencil b.c.) (numerous notices indicating reduced prices and the like)
INV: RW/CKA 508
PROV: Probably presented by the artist
ENGR: The *Punch* illustration is entitled 'SELLING OFF'
LIT: *Punch* (n.d.); 'E.P.' Vol. I

In 1851 Lord Russell brought in a bill to counteract the aggressive policy of the Church of Rome, and carried it by 395 to 53.

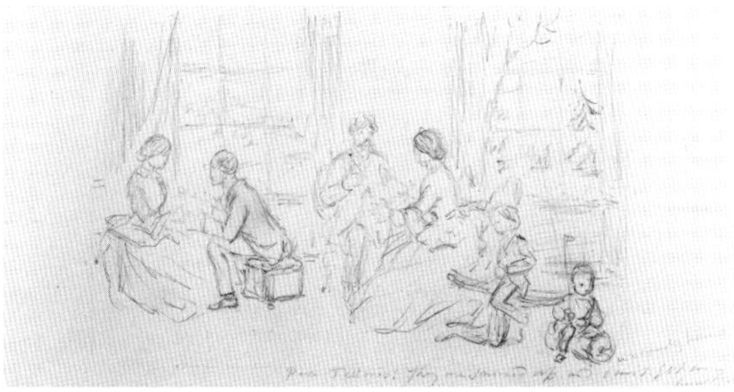

922
'Snowed Up'

John Leech

Pencil on wove paper 18.3 x 24.3
INSCR: 'Poor Fellows! They are snowed up / in a country house / and can't get any hunting' (pencil b.)
INV: RW/CKA 517E
PROV: Probably presented by the artist
ENGR: The *Punch* illustration is entitled 'SNOWED UP' and is inscribed 'Poor Fellow! They can't get any hunting, and are obliged to play at scratch cradle with their cousins.'
LIT: *Punch* (n.d.); *John Leech*, I: 151

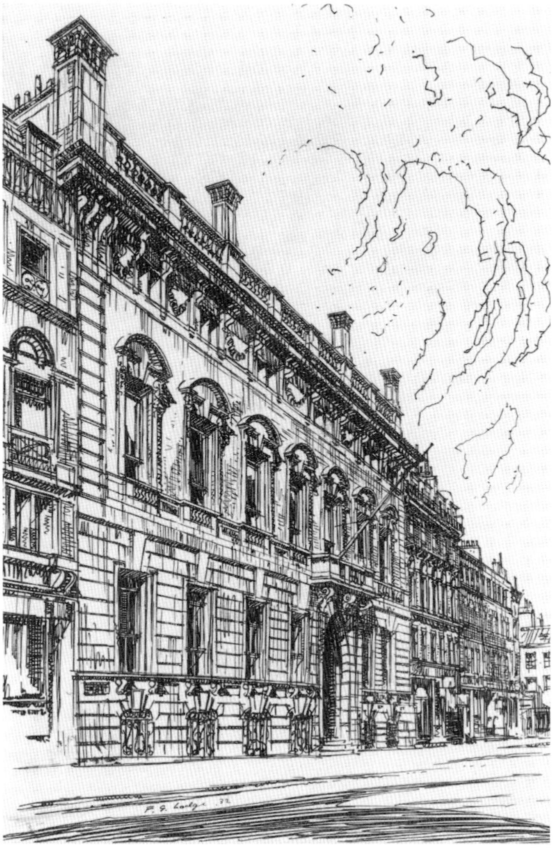

923
The Garrick Club

F.G. Lodge

Pen and ink on fine wove yellow paper 32.4 x 22.2
INSCR: 'F.G. Lodge 32' (pen and black ink)
INV: CKA 629
PROV: Purchased 1935
LIT: *The Observer*, 12 February 1933 (reproduced)

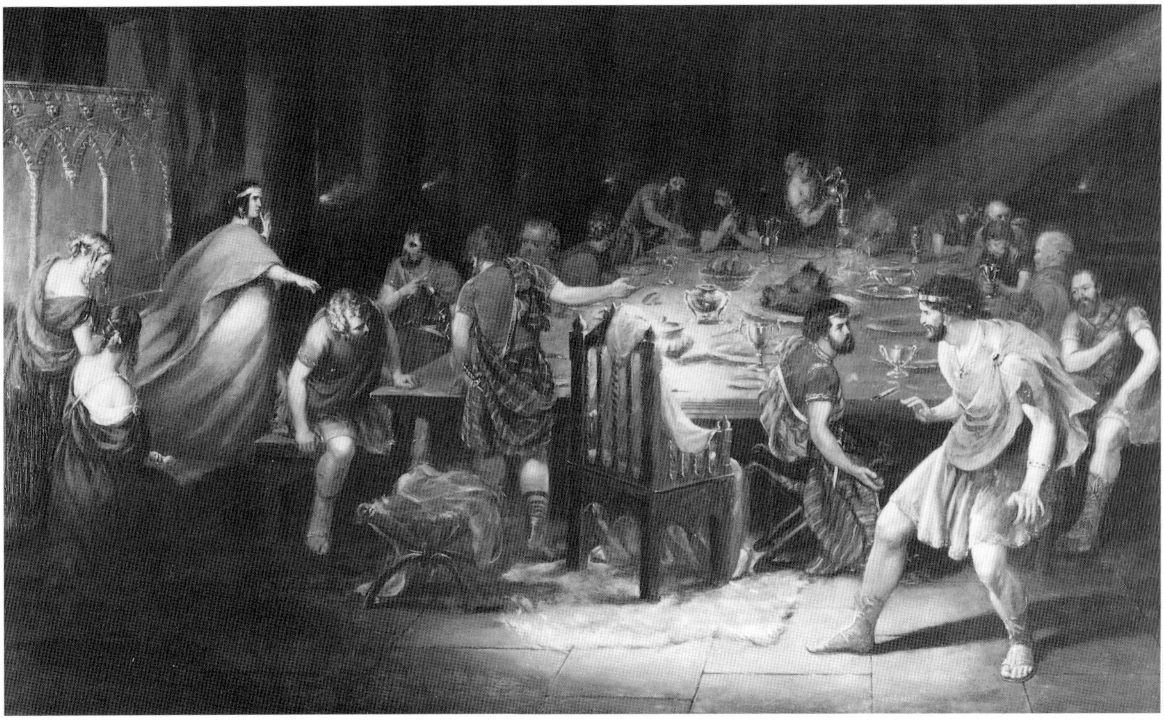

924*
The Banqueting Scene from *Macbeth*
by William Shakespeare

Unknown Artist

Oil on canvas 111.7 x 188
INV: RW 369 (by D. Maclise – replica); CKA 368
PROV: Sir Squire Bancroft, by whom presented
to the Garrick Club, 1906

This picture was acquired with an attribution to David Maclise, whose famous picture of this scene (Guildhall Art Gallery) is, however, quite different.

The picture shows a large number of men in Scottish garb, with Macbeth at the right startled by the appearance of Banquo at left. None of the figures can be identified as actors.

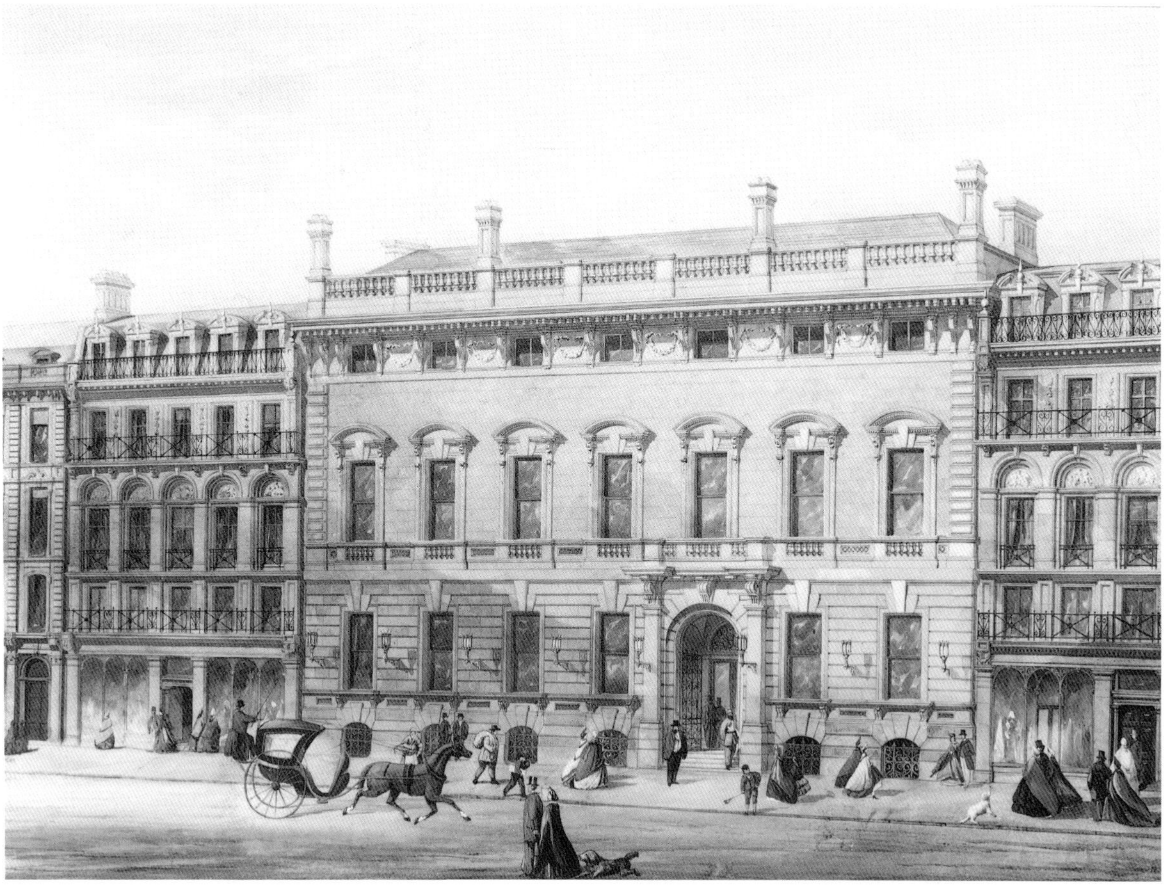

925
The Exterior of the Garrick Club

Frank Marrable

Pencil, pen and brown ink and watercolour on wove paper 64.8 x 88.2
INSCR: 'GARRICK CLUB AND ADJOINING BUILDINGS / IN THE NEW STREET LEADING TO COVENT GARDEN' (pen and ink and watercolour on mount b.c.)
INV: (not in RW); CKA 539; Gift 200
PROV: Mr Grisbrook, by whom presented to the Garrick Club, 1886
EXH: 1863 R.A. (909) 'The Garrick Club and adjoining buildings now erecting in the new street leading to Covent Garden, from the designs and under the superintendance of – F. MARRABLE'
LIT: Anthony Trollope, *Autobiography* (1950), reproduced opposite p. 140

Marrable also exhibited a drawing of the proposed Garrick Club staircase at the Royal Academy in 1863 (931), entitled: 'Staircase of the Garrick Club, now erecting from the designs and under the superintendence of – F. MARRABLE.'

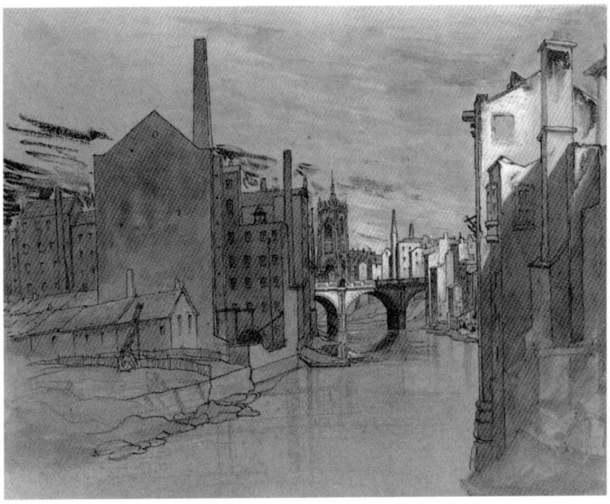

926
Manchester

Charles James Mathews

Pencil, pen and brown ink, brown wash, watercolour
and body colour on grey wove paper 27.3 x 35.5
INSCR: 'Manchester' (pen and brown ink on mount b.c.);
'C J Mathews' (pen and brown ink on mount b.r.)
INV: CKA 606; Gift 447
PROV: Lady Mathews, by whom presented
to the Garrick Club, 1927

This drawing gives a view up the Irwell to Manchester Cathedral, with a bridge in the middle distance, warehouses and mills on the left and ruins on the right, under a dark, stormy sky. The technique of this competent drawing seems to indicate the influence of John Ruskin.

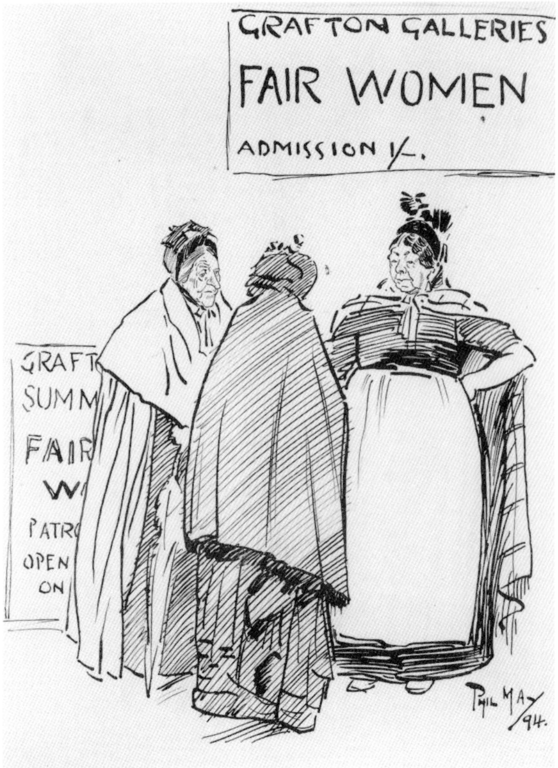

927
'Fair Women'

Phil May

Pen and black ink on wove paper 24.5 x 20.5 (sight)
INSCR: 'PHIL MAY /94' (pen and black ink b.r.)
INV: Not listed; Gift 619
PROV: Mrs Goetze, by whom presented
to the Garrick Club, 1943

928
LOCATION UNKNOWN
Sketch for the Back of a Menu Card

Sir Alfred Munnings

Pencil on wove paper 23.5 x 35.5
INSCR: 'for centre of back of menu';
'about in this proportion'; 'A.J.M.'
INV: CKA 630 (Not located 1988)
PROV: Presented by the artist

Probably the companion design to No. 671.

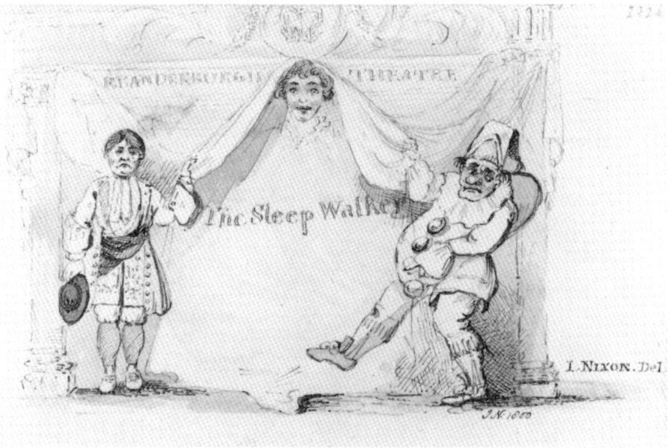

929
Ticket for the Brandenburg Theatre

John Nixon

Pencil, pen and grey ink
with green and brown wash
on wove paper 10.1 x 14.6
INSCR: 'J.N: 1800' (pen and black ink b.r.);
'I. NIXON DEL.' (pen and black ink b.r.);
'BRANDENBURG THEATRE'
(brown wash over proscenium t.c.);
'The Sleep Walker'
(brown wash on drop cloth c.)
INV: Not listed
PROV: John Nixon, *Dramatic Annals*

There are two figures, one on either side of the proscenium arch: a Fool on the left and a Punch on the right. This is a design for a ticket to the private theatre at Brandenburg House, on the banks of the Thames at Hammersmith.

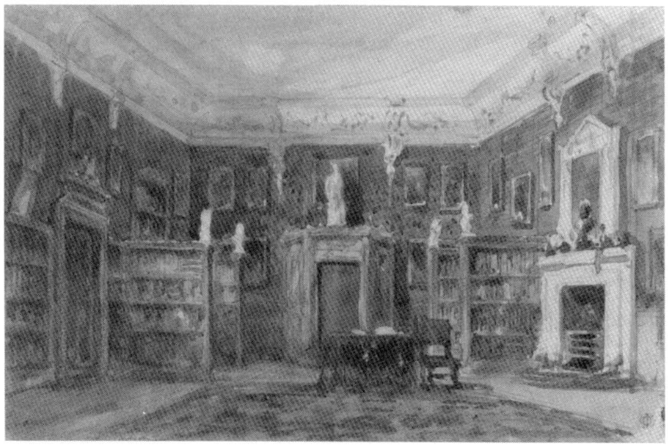

930
Scene Design for *David Garrick*
by Thomas William Robertson

John O'Connor

Pencil and watercolour on wove paper 15.5 x 24.3
INSCR: 'JOC' (in monogram, pen and ink b.r.);
'Sketch of Scene for "David Garrick" / by J. O'Connor.
Haymarket Theatre' (pencil below drawing b.l.);
'To Lennox Browne Esq / with Kind regards from /
Tom Robertson' (pencil below drawing b.r.)
INV: CKA 618; Gift 363
PROV: Tom Robertson; Lennox Browne;
Richard Kershaw, by whom presented
to the Garrick Club, 1913

The first production of this play was given at the Haymarket on 30 April 1864. For the play *David Garrick*, see No. 860.

931
LOCATION UNKNOWN
'A Composition from Fancy'

William Parsons

Pencil and watercolour on laid paper
11.5 x 14.6 (sheet 14.4 x 18)
INSCR: 'Mr Kirkman will honour T. Bellamy
by accepting this drawing by his late dear friend
W. Parsons Esq' (pen and brown ink t.);
'I received from Bill Parsons this Sketch
as a result as a treasure /
Which to none, but Nat Kirkman,
I'd give up with pleasure. /
Thomas Bellamy / 20th August 1798'
(pen and brown ink on verso)
INV: Not listed
PROV: Thomas Bellamy; Nathaniel Kirkman
ENGR: Angus pub. Bellamy & Roberts
1 December 1790, line 9.8 x 15.8

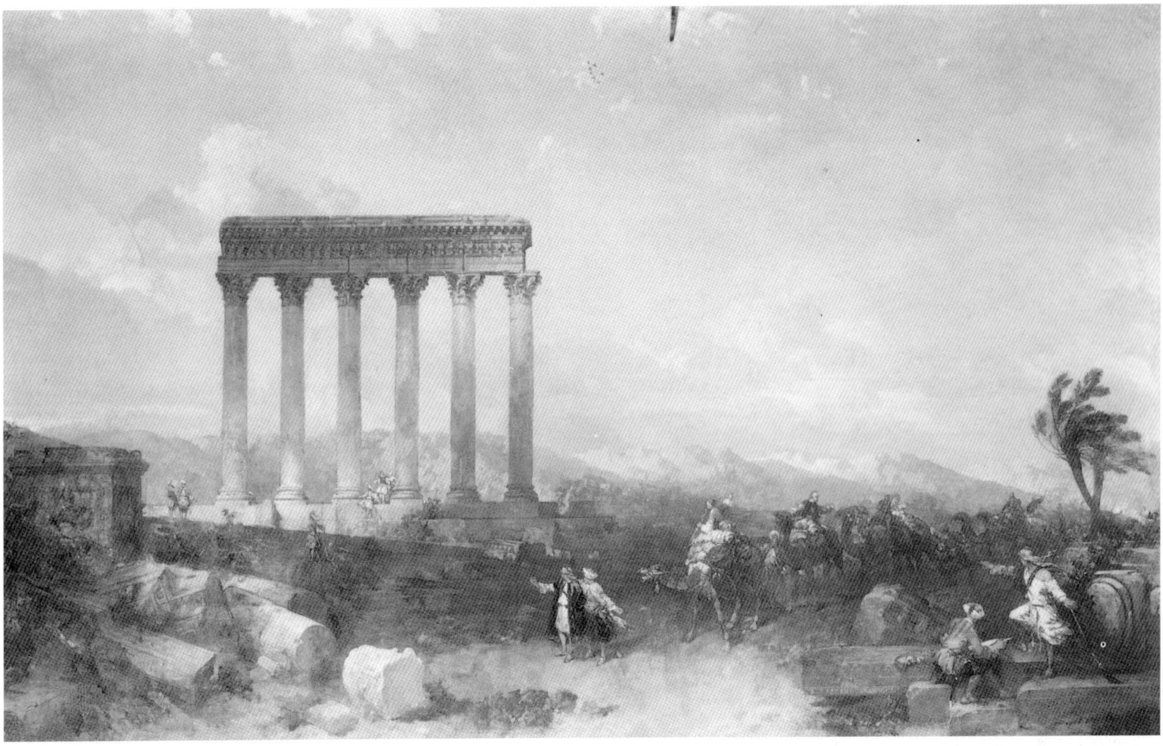

932*
View of the Temple of the Sun
at Baalbec

David Roberts

Oil on canvas 205.7 x 358.1
INSCR: 'Remains of the Temple of the Sun / at BAALBEC'
(brown paint on stone b.l.);
'Presented to the Garrick Club 1847 / by
David Roberts R.A.' (brown paint on stone b.r.)
INV: RW/CKA 132; Gift 227
PROV: Presented by the artist, 1847
EXH: R.A. 1846 (209) as 'Ruins of the Temple
of the Sun, Baalbec'
LIT: Helen Guiterman & Briony Llewellyn,
David Roberts (1986), pp. 76 (repr.) & 84

The artist became a member of the Garrick Club in 1835.

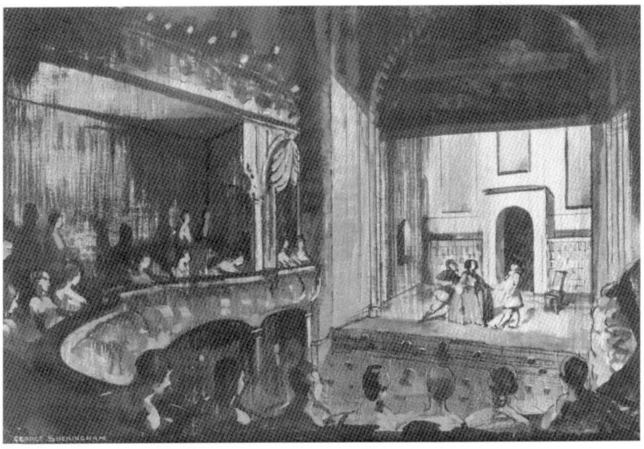

933
Interior of the Lyric Theatre, Hammersmith,
during a performance of *The Duenna*

George Sheringham

Pencil, watercolour and body colour
on wove paper 35.5 x 54 (sight)
INSCR: 'Nigel Playfair / memoria XIV annorum apud
Theatrum Lyricum' &c.
INV: CKA 633; Gift 526
PROV: Given, in 1932, by the artist to Sir Nigel Playfair,
who bequeathed it to the Garrick Club, 1935
EXH: 1935 London; 1945–46 London and tour (35);
1980 Nottingham

Sheridan's *The Duenna* was revived at the Lyric Theatre, Hammersmith, in October 1924.

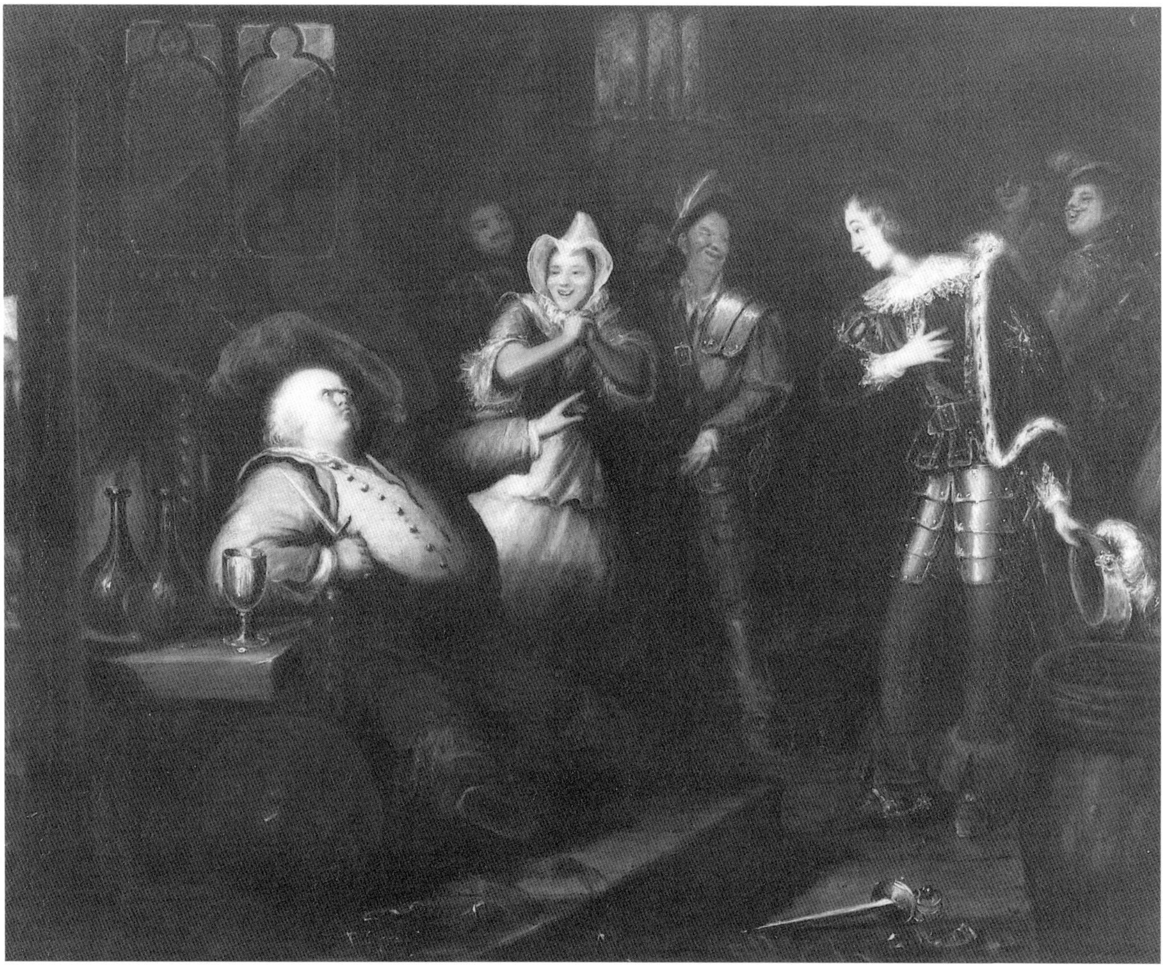

934
Scene from *2 Henry IV*
by William Shakespeare

Robert Smirke (?)

Oil on canvas 71.1 x 91.5
INV: GCL 701; Gift 787
PROV: Mr R. Armstrong-Jones, by whom presented
to the Garrick Club, 1961
REL: Similar to: Coll: Julian Clint pencil on paper
19 x 16.5 (by Clint)

This painting does not appear to be by Smirke. It may perhaps be by Cawse.

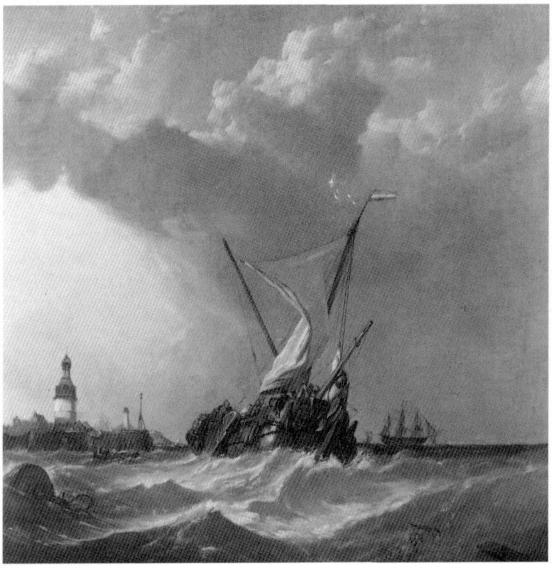

935*
A Dutch Blazer
Coming Out of Monnickendam,
Zuyder Zee

Clarkson Stanfield

Oil on canvas 208.3 x 208.3
INSCR: 'Painted For and Presented to the Garrick Club / Decr. 1856 by Clarkson Stanfield, R.A.'
(brown paint on floating board b.r.)
INV: RW/CKA 126; Gift 146
PROV: Presented by the artist, 1857
EXH: 1979 Bonn & Sunderland (313)
REL: Private owner, oil 56.7 x 31.5, s. & d. 'CS 1856', prov: Sotheby's 11 May 1994 (89); No. 935 is seen in Lake Price's photograph (1857) of Stanfield 'at work', reproduced in Malcolm Rogers's NPG exhibition catalogue *Camera Portraits 1839–1989* (1990–91)
LIT: Peter van der Merwe, *Clarkson Stanfield* (1979), No. 313

Stanfield, a marine artist and scene painter, was an original member of the Garrick Club in 1831.

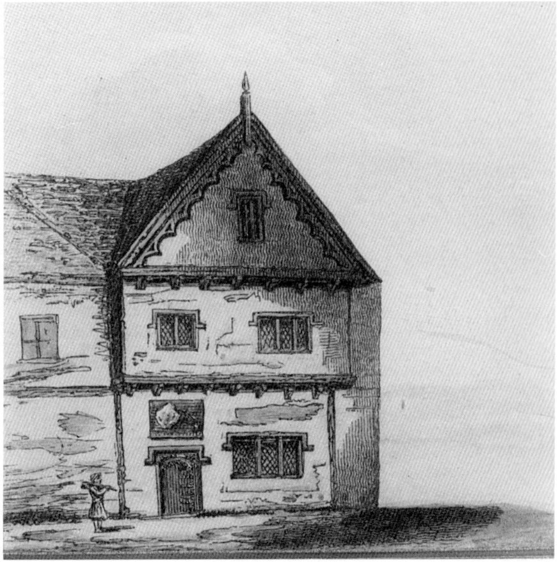

936
The House in which Mrs Siddons was born

Unknown Artist

Watercolour on wove paper 17.5 x 17.5
INV: GCL 736A; Gift 883
PROV: Miss Sophie Andreae, by whom presented to the Garrick Club, 1978

Sarah Siddons was born at the Shoulder of Mutton Inn in Brecon, South Wales. The house still stands, with her name prominently displayed; it was once known as the Siddons Wine Vaults.

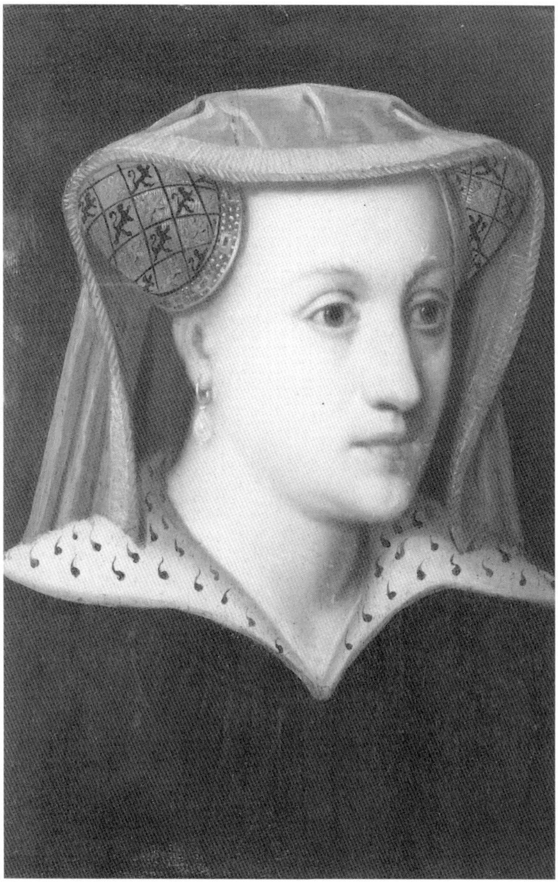

937
MARY, QUEEN OF SCOTS (?)

Unknown Artist

Oil on canvas 40.6 x 29.2
INV: RW 296 (by François Clouet);
CKA 298; Gift 152
PROV: Colonel G.A.K. D'Arcy, by whom
presented to the Garrick Club, 1859

This appears to be a late 18th-century fancy portrait of a historical figure, wearing a costume that seems to be intended to suggest the late 14th or early 15th century – a date inconsistent with its identification with Mary, Queen of Scots.

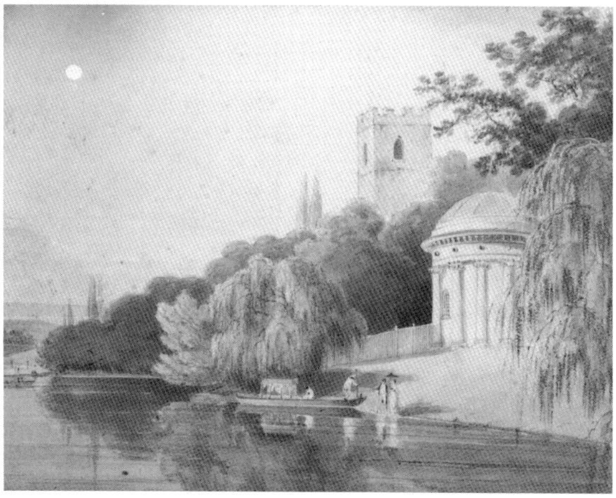

938
Garrick's Temple, Hampton

Unknown Artist

Pencil, pen and brown ink with watercolour
on wove paper 19.3 x 26
INV: (not in RW); CKA 578
('Garrick's Temple to Shakespeare')
PROV: Albert Smith, by whom presented
to the Garrick Club, 1856

A classical temple with Ionic columns stands on an incline which descends to the water. A white fence joins the building and a clump of trees at the water's edge. In front of the trees is a boat with a canopied bower in the middle; a man sits in the boat while another pushes it away from the shore. On the shore are two figures: a man in black hat, blue jacket and white breeches, and a woman with a parasol.

The circular building appears to be the Shakespeare's Temple in the garden of David Garrick's villa at Hampton, well known from Zoffany's views painted in the early 1760s.

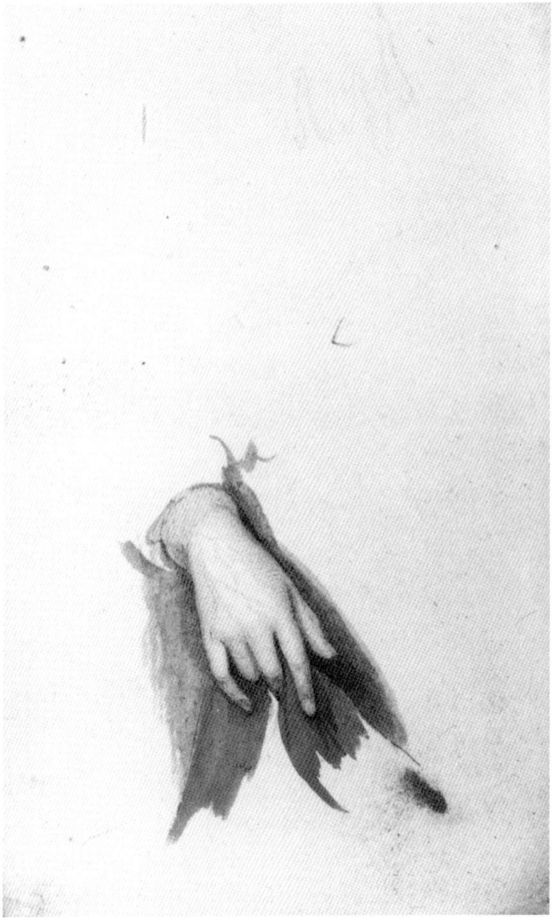

939
The Right Hand of
CHARLES THE FIRST

Edwin Long (?)

Pencil and watercolour on wove paper 10.8 x 7
INSCR: 'Miniature of hand of King Charles I / painted for Henry Irving and / hung in his study at Grafton / St. for many years / given me by Walter Collinson / TH' (pen and ink on label on verso)
INV: Not listed
PROV: Sir Henry Irving; Tom Haslewood, by whom presented to the Garrick Club

See Nos. 940 and 942.

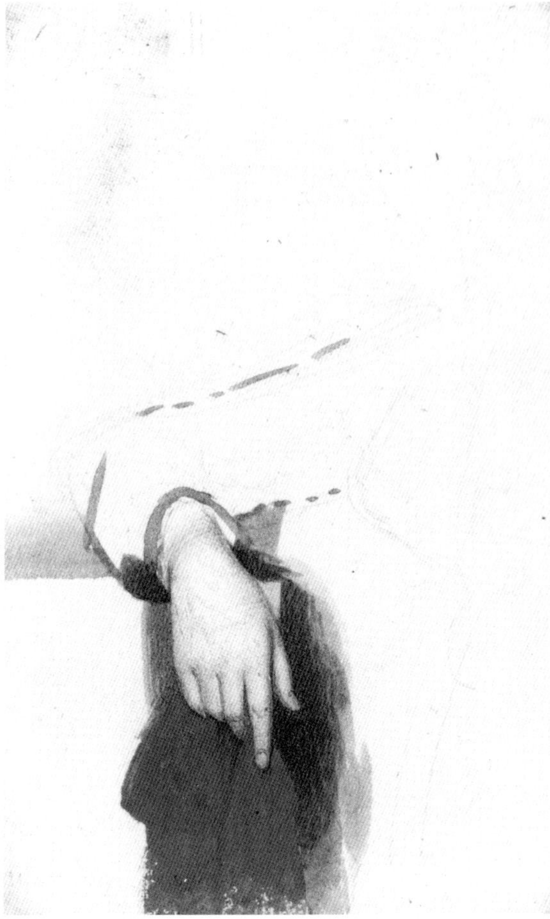

940
The Right Hand of
CHARLES THE FIRST

Edwin Long (?)

Pen and watercolour on wove paper 11 x 7.2
INSCR: 'Tom Haslewood' (pencil on verso)
INV: Not listed
PROV: Sir Henry Irving; Tom Haslewood, by whom presented to the Garrick Club

See Nos. 939 and 942.

ACQUISITIONS SINCE 1988
& RECENT ADDITIONS

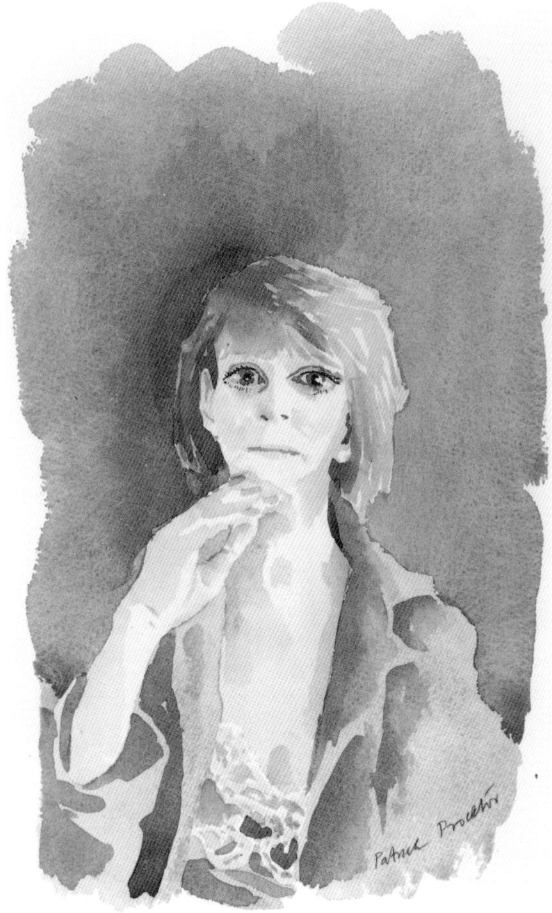

941
JILL BENNETT
in *Infidelities*
by Sean Mathias

Patrick Procktor

Watercolour on paper 36.8 x 24.8, with violet wash background (within mount 41.9 x 54.6)
PROV: The artist, Patrick Procktor, by whom presented to the Garrick Club, 1994

The sitter, facing front with her right hand under her chin, wears a loose blue jacket over a décolleté frilly blouse.

The artist was a close friend of the actress Jill Bennett,of whom he writes fondly in his *Self-Portrait* (1991).

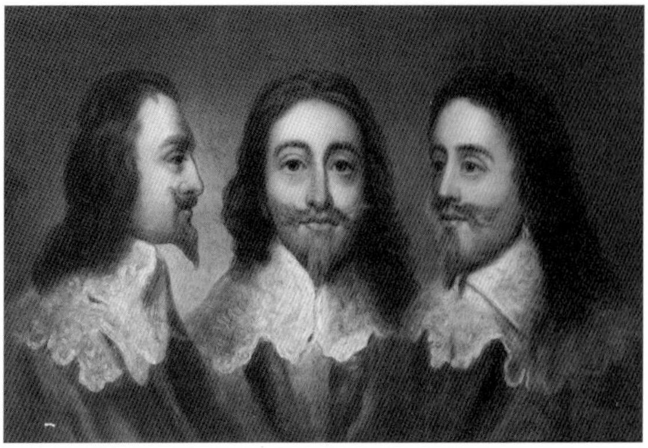

942
Three Heads of
CHARLES THE FIRST

Edwin Long

Oil on millboard 19 x 29.2
INSCR: 'Study of three heads of Charles the First used by Sir Henry Irving in his dressing room to make up from. Painted by Edwin Long R.A. given him by Walter Collinson, Irving's dresser.' (on back of board)
PROV: Walter Collinson; Henry Irving; T. Haslewood 1934; Mrs Pamela Hilton, by whom presented to the Garrick Club, 1994
REL: Triple portrait of Charles I by Sir Anthony Van Dyck 1635, Royal Collection, oil on canvas 84.5 x 99.7, as a guide to Bernini's carving (lost)

The left head looks right, the middle head front and the right head left. In all three, the King has a beard and wears a vandyke collar and a brown coat with a blue ribbon at the front.

See Nos. 939 and 940.

943
LOCATION UNKNOWN
JULIANA GLOVER

Samuel Drummond

Pastel drawing on paper 57.8 x 41.9
(missing in 1988)
INV: CKA 313
PROV: Unknown

Head and shoulders, front. In this missing portrait Mrs Glover has black hair and wears a simple white low-cut dress of about 1805.

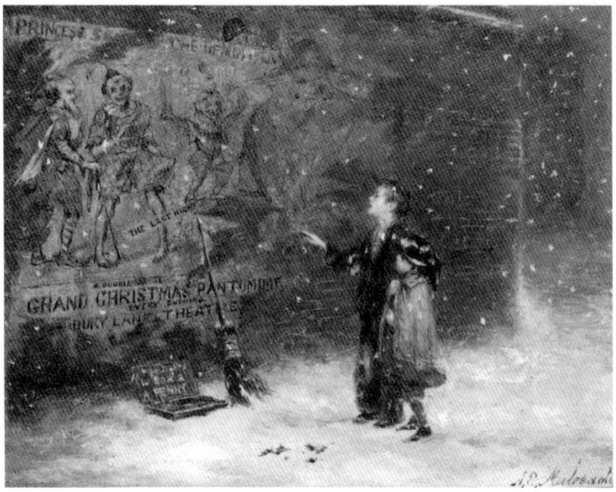

944
JOSEPH GRIMALDI
'The Match Seller'

A.E. Mulready

Oil on board 11.4 x 16.5
PROV: Hugh Clifford, Vancouver, 1978; his sister
Mrs K.A. Lamboit, by whom bequeathed
to the Garrick Club, 1994

Two children stand in a snowy street looking up at a large billboard advertising the 'Grand Christmas Pantomime' at Drury Lane, which shows Grimaldi as Clown in the centre. A broom leans against the poster.

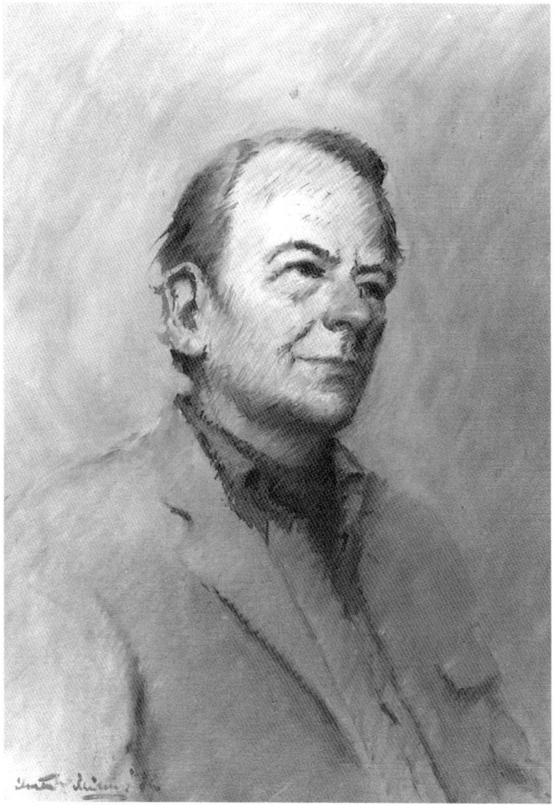

945
ROBERT HARRIS

Chester Williams

1973
Oil on canvas 50.8 x 38.1
PROV: Robert Harris, by whom presented
to the Garrick Club, 1989

Half-length; the sitter wears a tan jacket with an open-necked blue shirt and a blue cravat.

Harris became a member of the Garrick Club in 1952.

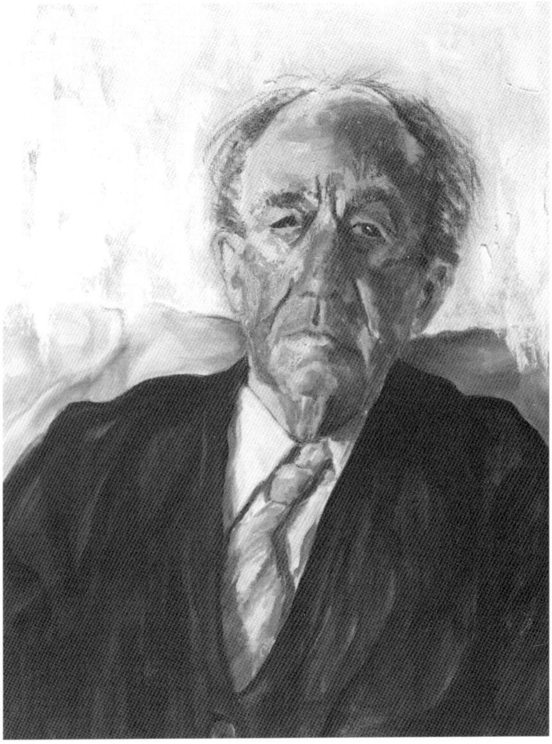

946
SIR MICHAEL HORDERN

Sheila Staefel

Oil on canvas 50.8 x 38.1
PROV: Sir Michael Hordern, by whom presented to the Garrick Club, 1991

Half-length. Sir Michael wears a black jacket and a white shirt with a Garrick Club tie.

He became a member of the Garrick Club in 1953.

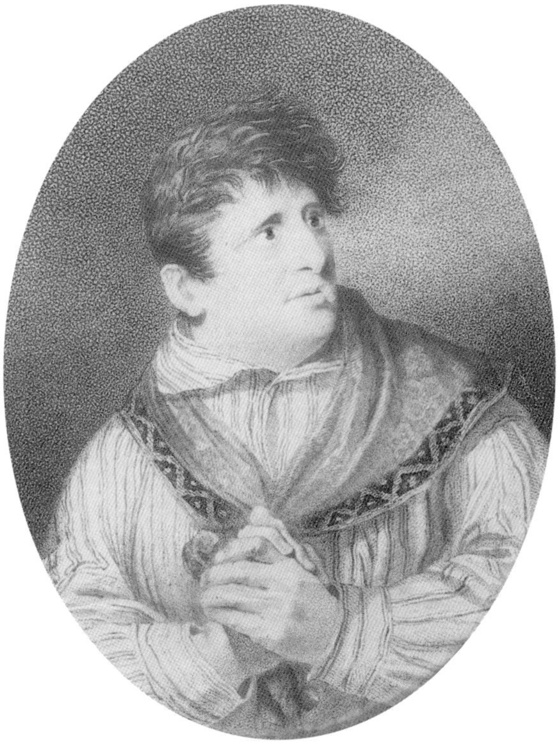

947
BENJAMIN CHARLES INCLEDON
singing 'The Storm'

Richard Cosway (?)
(after John Thomas Barber-Beaumont)

Watercolour 11.4 x 11.4 in oval frame
INSCR: 'To be given to the Garrick Club / (Charles Keen) the original miniature is in the Club / Impression by Richard Cosway / Bequeathed by Malcolm Graham.' (label on back of frame);
another inscripton on back is crossed out
ENGR: See No. 315
PROV: Malcolm Graham, date received by the Club unknown, but after 1988?
REL: Original exh: 1804 R.A. (737); Garrick Club No. 315

In this half-length portrait, Incledon is shown in his own brown hair, with his hands clasped at his chest. He wears a loose white shirt with blue stripes and round his shoulders is a red neckerchief edged in blue and patterned in gold. This picture is a version of a miniature in the Club, No. 315. See also No. 957.

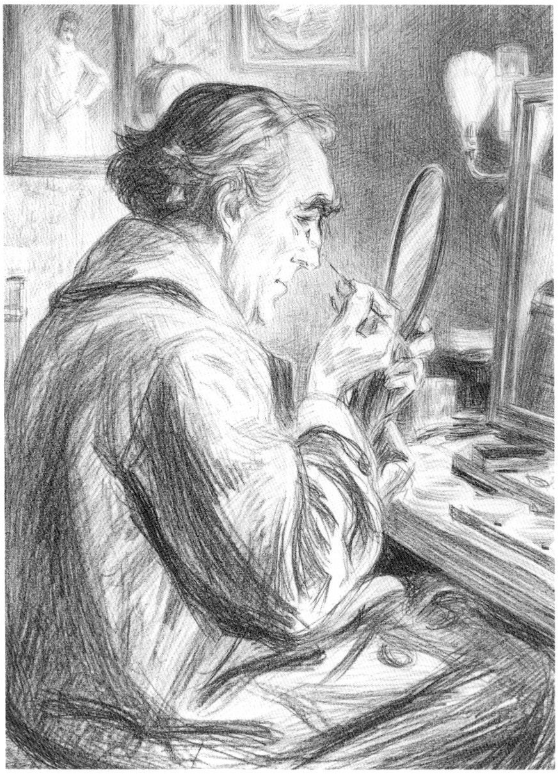

948
SIR HENRY IRVING

Paul Renouard

Pencil drawing 35.5 x 26.7
PROV: Unknown; reproduced in Gordon Craig's *Henry Irving*, opp. p. 21

Irving is shown seated at his dressing-table, making up for a performance.

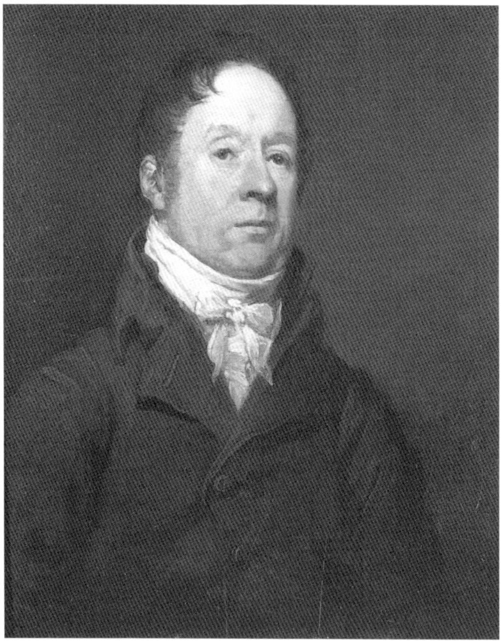

949
JOHN LISTON

James Ward

Oil on board panel 21.5 x 16.2, signed
PROV: D.C. Bell; H.N. Pym; Christopher Fry, by whom presented to the Garrick Club, 1989
EXH: Burlington House 1885; Victorian Exh. New Gallery 1892

Shown half-length, Liston wears a dark coat buttoned at the front, with a white shirt and stock. He has black hair.

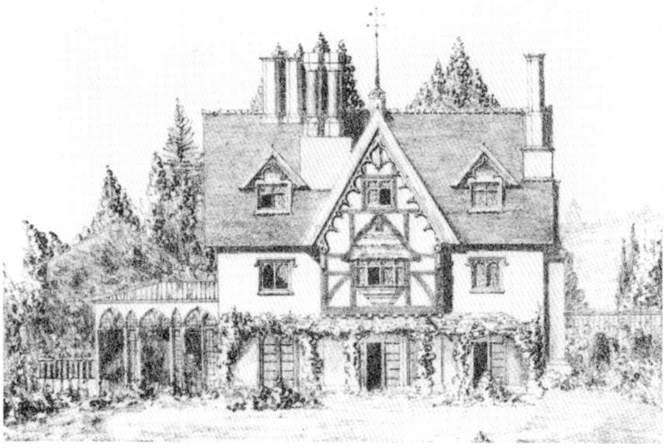

950
'Mr Mathews's Cottage Highgate Hill'

Charles James Mathews

Pencil drawing on paper 14 x 19.7
PROV: Ben Weinreb, by whom presented to the Garrick Club, 1994

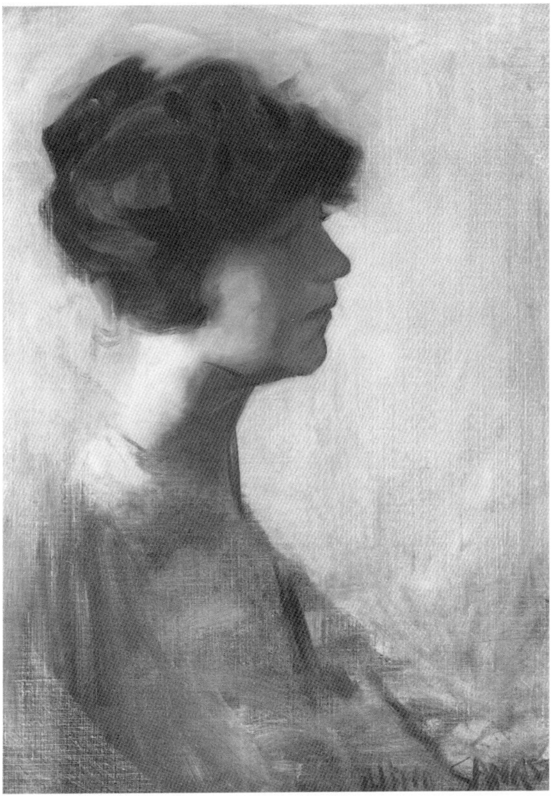

951
ATHENE SEYLER

A. Sangster

Oil on canvas 76.2 x 63.5
PROV: Mrs J.A. Jones (Athene Seyler's daughter), by whom presented to the Garrick Club, 1990

The sitter, shown in profile to the right, is believed to have been about 35 when this portrait was painted.

Athene Seyler lived to the age of 101; she died on 12 September 1990. The artist was one of her friends.

952
LOCATION UNKNOWN
HARRIET DEBORAH TAYLOR

Samuel Drummond

Pastel drawing 47 x 40.6 (missing 1988)
INV: CKA 302
PROV: Unknown

This missing drawing shows the sitter head and shoulders only, wearing a 'brown flat hat with yellow tassel, black hair, yellow dress with white ruff and laced with blue' (CKA).

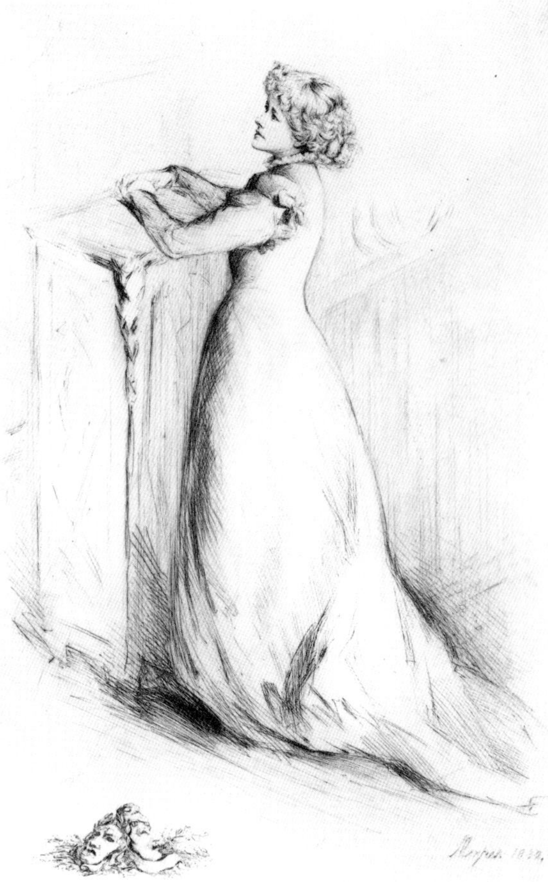

953
DAME ELLEN TERRY

Mortimer Menpes

Pencil on paper 47 x 29.8
INSCR: 'Menpes 1882' (l.r.); 'M.L. Menpes Ellen Terry' (lower border); 'Presented by Charles P. Johnson. "No 12 in 26 Remarque Proofs. M.L.M."' (on back of frame)
PROV: Charles P. Johnson, by whom presented to the Garrick Club

Ellen Terry, in a long dress, stands at a podium.

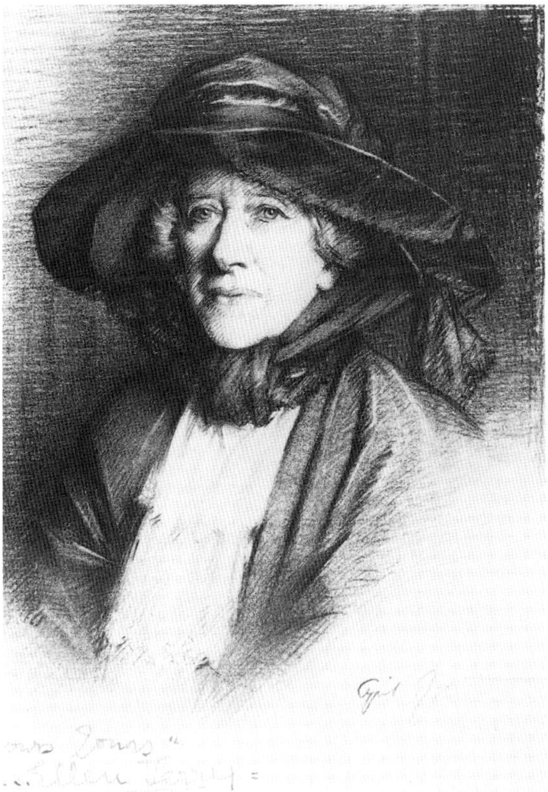

954
DAME ELLEN TERRY

April Roberts

1923
Pencil drawing 28.6 x 21.6
INSCR: 'Presented to the Garrick Club / by / Marjorie Clarke Jervaise / (a friend of both artist and sitter)' (label on back); 'Yours Truly / 1923 *Ellen Terry*' lower left; 'April Roberts / 1923' (lower right)
PROV: Marjorie Clarke Jervaise, by whom presented to the Garrick Club

The sitter wears a dark jacket with a white blouse and has a large, dark hat tied under her chin.

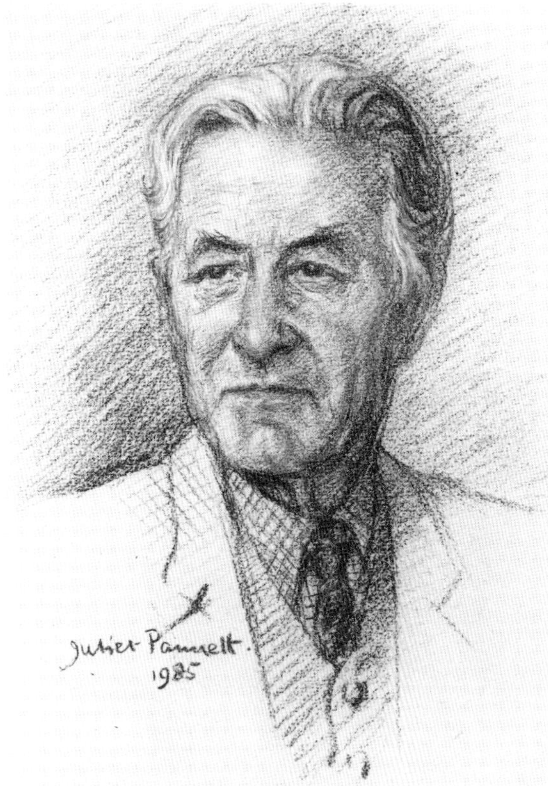

955
SIR JOHN RAMSAY WILLIS

Juliet Pannett

Drawing in chalks and crayons 71.1 x 54.6
INSCR: 'Juliet Pannett 1985' (b.r.); 'From Julie Harris / Presented to the Garrick Club / as a reminder of the / many many happy evenings / spent therein by Jack Willis' (back of frame)
PROV: Julie Harris, by whom presented to the Garrick Club, 1990

Willis, a barrister, became a member of the Garrick Club in 1955.

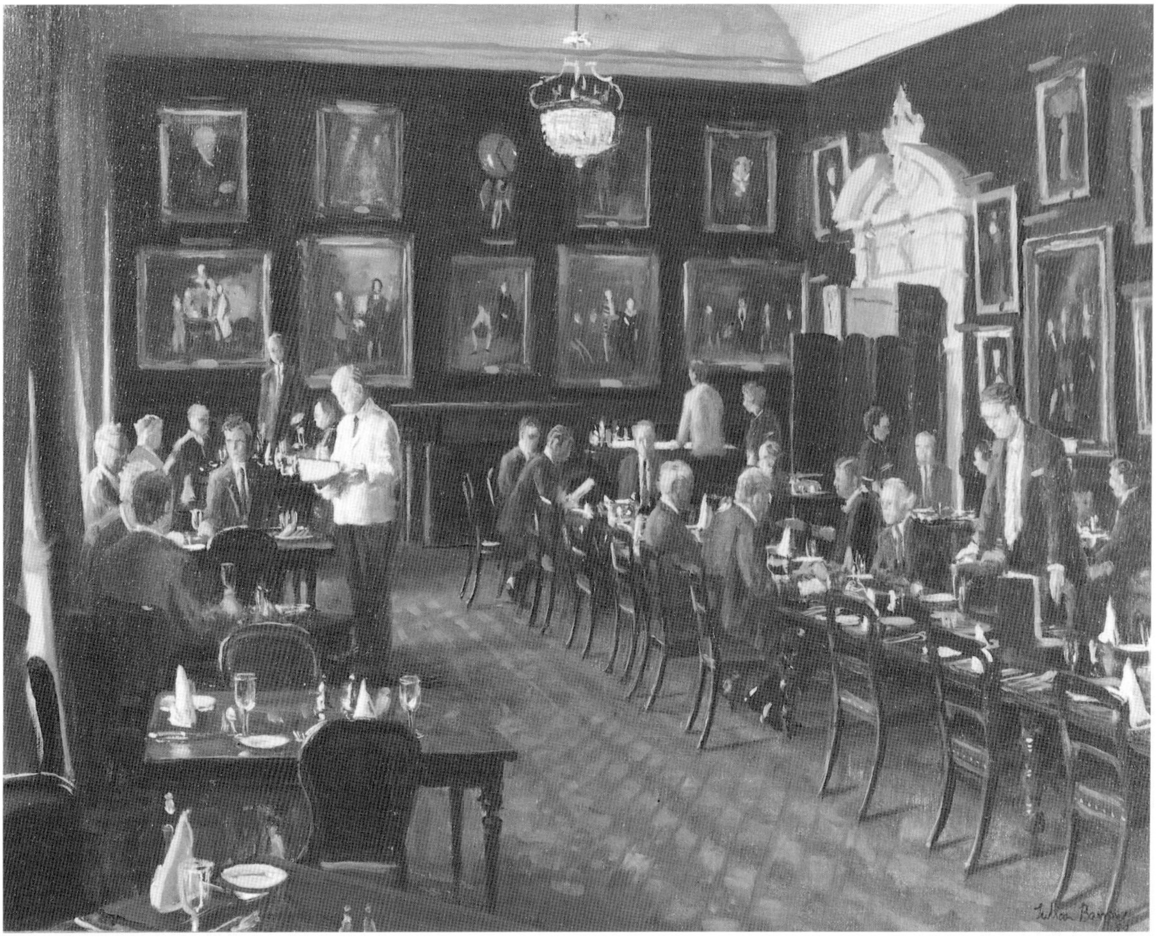

956
'Members Dining in the Coffee Room'

Julian Barrow

Oil on canvas 34.3 x 44.5
PROV: Arthur Grimwade, by whom presented to the Garrick Club, 1990

Barrow depicts the familiar scene of a number of members dining, with waiters in attendance. The figures are fictitious.

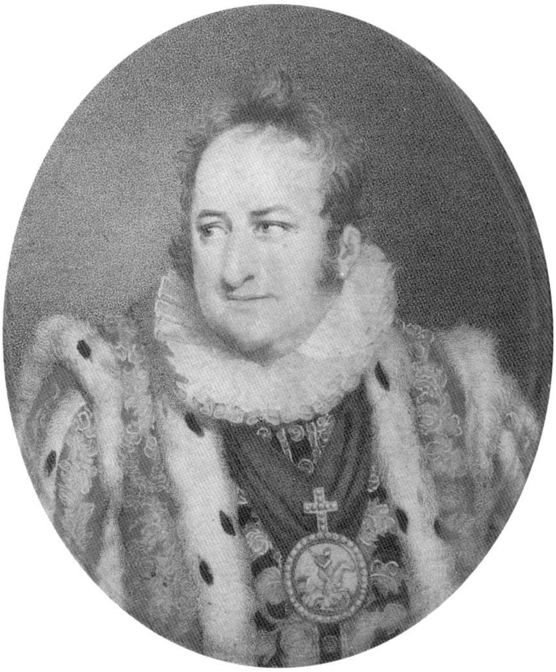

957
GEORGE FREDERICK COOKE
as Richard in *Richard III*
by William Shakespeare

J.T. Barber-Beaumont (after)

Watercolour 11.4 x 8.9 in oval frame
INSCR: 'To be given to the Garrick / Club. London; / (Edmund Keen) / Bequeathed by Malcolm Graham/ Presumed to be in the / Character of Richard III / painted I expect by R. Cosway.' (label on back of frame)
PROV: Malcolm Graham
REL: Coll: the late Robert Eddison, original miniature by J.T. Barber-Beaumont, exh: 'Shakespeare and the Theatre', Guildhall Art Gallery in collaboration with the Society for Theatre Research, 1964, engr: A. Cardon pub. J.P. Thompson 1805; see BD 3: 32

Half-length, the partially bald sitter wears an ermine robe with pink embroidery, a white ruff, and a cross and order at his chest.

[The editors are grateful to Henry McGee for the identification of the sitter. The drawing is a copy after A. Cardon's engraving of J.T. Barber-Beaumont's miniature of 1805. It seems to be a pair with No. 947.]

See Nos. 128, 130 and 132 for other portraits of the same actor in the same role.

958
LOCATION UNKNOWN
UNKNOWN MAN

S. Ransome (?)

Miniature 10.16 diam. on oval top of box
INSCR: 'S. [Ransome?] Pinxt / Patronized by H.R.H. The Duke of Sussex and Prince Leopold' (back)
PROV: Unknown

The sitter, with black hair, wears a black coat and cape, a white shirt and a blue stock.

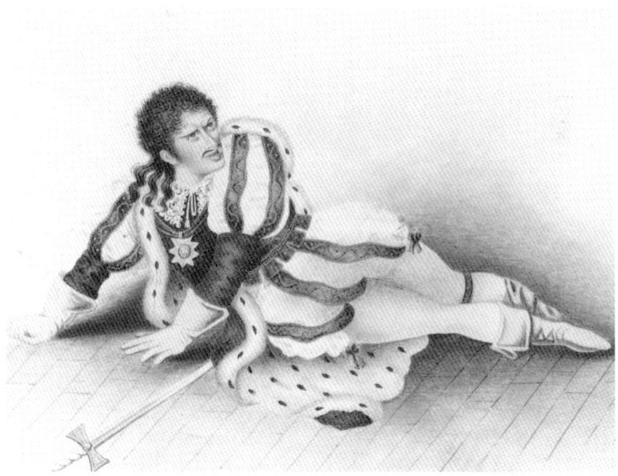

959
EDMUND KEAN
as Richard in *Richard III*
by William Shakespeare

Unknown Artist

Coloured drawing 15.9 x 21.6
PROV: From the Collection of Lord Olivier, presented to the Garrick Club, 1992

[An identification of this actor as Edmund Kean has recently been confirmed by Henry McGee, who points out that the figure may have been the basis of a popular 'penny-plain, twopence-coloured' print.]

See Nos. 345, 346, 348, 352 and 353 for other portraits of the same actor in the same role.

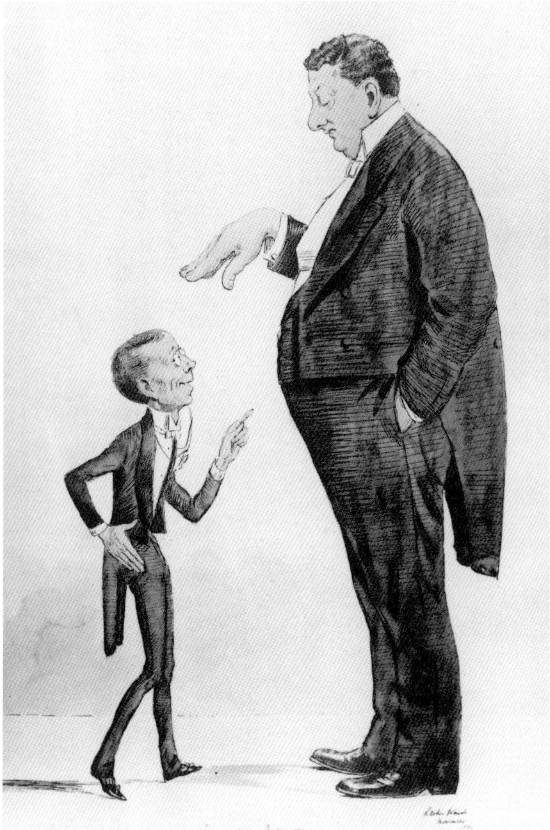

960
A Study from Memory

Sir Leslie Ward ('Spy')

Pencil and black ink on paper 36.8 x 25.4
INSCR: 'A Study from Memory' (bottom c.);
'Leslie Ward / November 1888' (bottom r.)

Two figures. A large portly man on the right, wearing evening dress, with his left hand in his trouser pocket, holds his right hand over the head of a small, thin man who is also in evening dress.

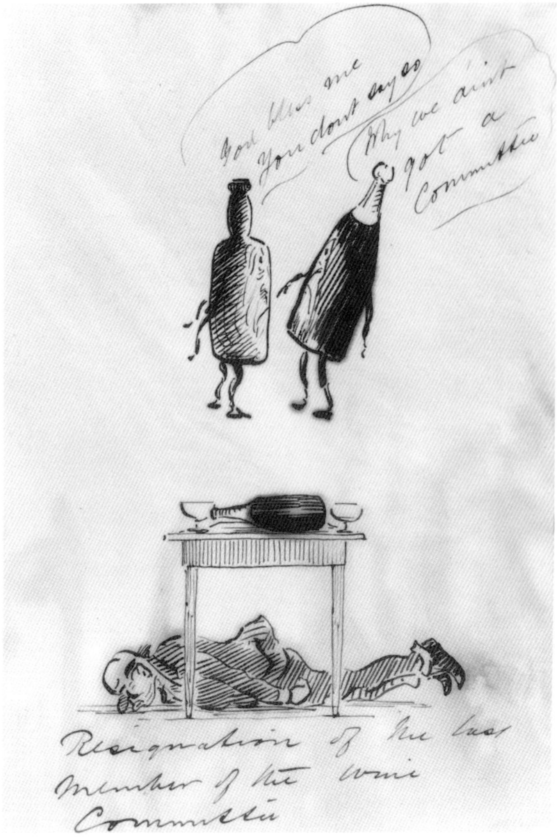

961
'Resignation of the Last Member
of the Wine Committee'

Unknown Artist

Pen and black ink on paper 26.7 x 19
INSCR: 'Resignation of the Last Member of the Wine Committee' (top); two cartoon balloons, one over figure on left 'God bless me / You don't say so' and over right figure 'Why we ain't / got a / Committee'

Two bottle figures walk away from a table, under which lies a drunken man.

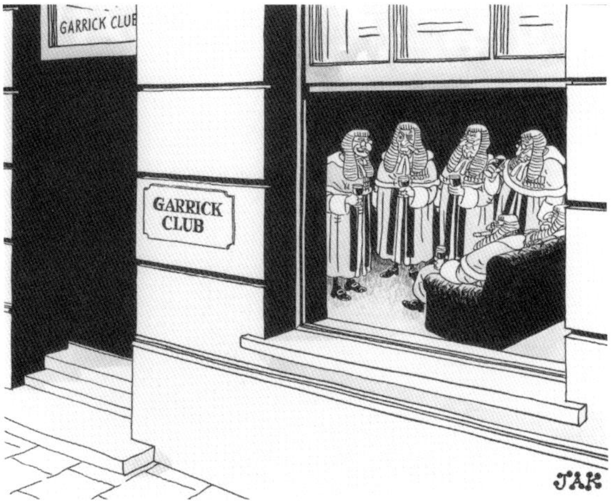

962
Judges at the Garrick Club

Raymond Jackson (JAK)

Pen and black ink 50 x 59.5
INSCR: 'JAK' (lower right corner); 'Well, I think we should join Rod Todd's union, just think what he'd save in legal fees', with line below indicating insert after 'what' – 'we could save him' (below in pencil); 'Garrick Club' (on outer wall of building and over entry); 'x 4 cols Mon 17th April 1989 30% tint' (lower left); '24 JPW' (top picture); '24' (on masking tape label on back); '16' (white sticker on back)

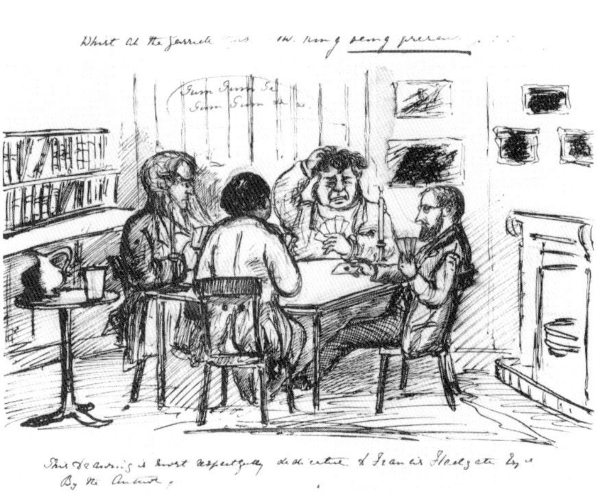

963
'Whist at the Garrick Club – Mr King being present'

Unknown Artist

Pen and ink on paper 20.5 x 33
on paper mount on board 25.5 x 45
INSCR: 'Whist at the Garrick Club. Mr King *being present!!!*' (top of mount); 'This drawing is most respectfully dedicated to Francis Fladgate Esqre By the Author' (bottom of mount)

Four members of the Garrick Club sit at a table in the card room. The fireplace is right, a bookcase left, and there is a small table with a jug and glass left. A balloon emanates from the figure on the right (who is dealing a card) that seems to read 'Gum Gum &c Gum Gum &c'. Possibly one of the figures represents Francis Fladgate (see No. 227).

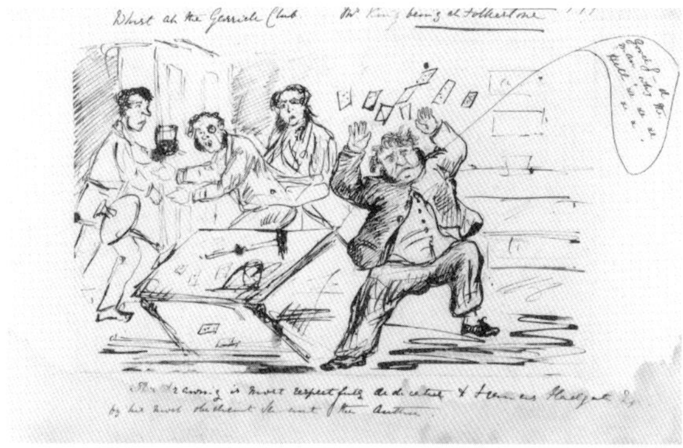

964
'Whist at the Garrick Club – Mr King being at Folkestone'

Unknown Artist

Pen and ink on paper 20.5 x 34
on paper mount on board 27.5 x 45
INSCR: 'Whist at the Garrick Club. Mr King *being at Folkestone!!!*' (top of mount); 'This drawing is most respectfully dedicated to Francis Fladgate Esq. by his most obedient Servant the Author' (bottom of mount)

In the card room there is an overturned card table, with a figure at right throwing cards in the air. Two figures behind seem to be fleeing. A figure standing at left holds a wine glass. A balloon emanates from the mouth of the figure at right which contains the words: 'Good G–d man why the Hell &c &c &c.' Possibly one of the figures represents Francis Fladgate (see No. 227).

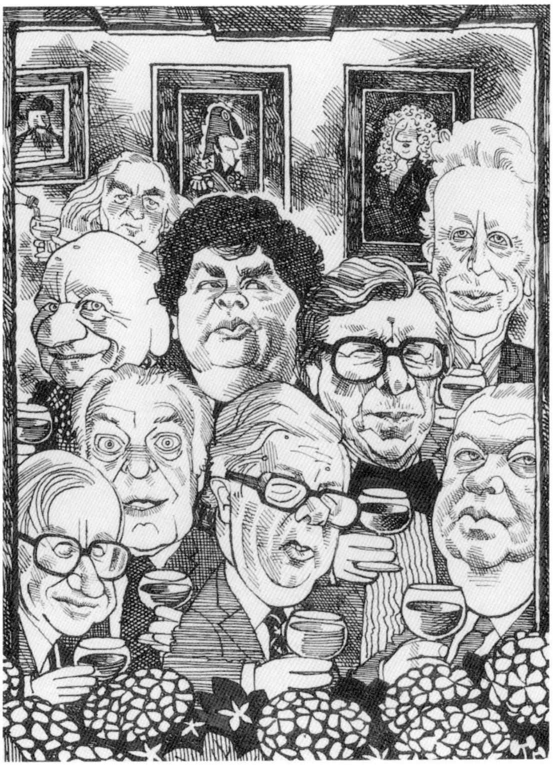

965
Members of the Garrick Club

Wally Fawkes ('Trog')

Cartoon in black ink on paper 25 x 19
PROV: Presented to the Garrick Club by Donald Trelford, editor of *The Observer*, July 1992, accepted October 1992 (information on label on back)
LIT: *The Observer*, 5 July 1992

According to the label on the back of the picture, shown are nine members at the A.G.M. on 6 July 1992, when the vote was taken not to extend membership to women. The members, holding wine glasses, are identified as: (*top*) Keith Waterhouse; (*middle row, left to right*) Sir John Gielgud, Nigel Lawson, Sir Robin Day, Sir Peregrine Worsthorne; (*bottom row, left to right*) Lord Rees-Mogg, Donald Sinden, Sir Geoffrey Howe, Kingsley Amis.

The cartoons of Wally Fawkes, an accomplished satirist, have appeared in *Punch*, *The Spectator*, *London Illustrated News* and elsewhere. Fawkes has been a political cartoonist on *The Observer* since 1965. He has also published a number of books.

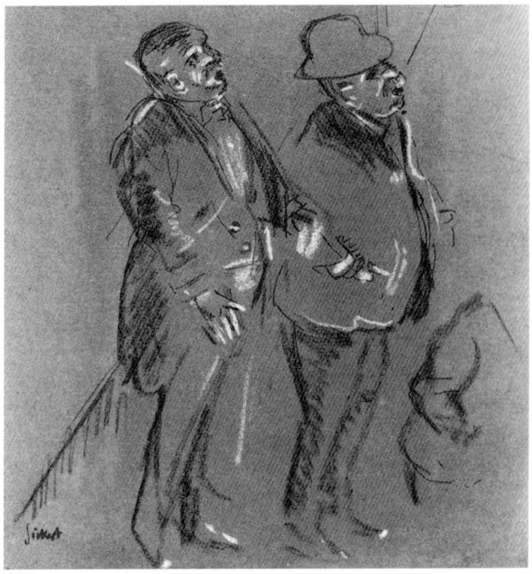

966
Memorial to
HARRY ANDERSON

Walter Richard Sickert

Black and white chalk on brown paper on gold backing 23.1 x 21.6, signed
PROV: Kenneth Snowman, by whom presented to the Garrick Club 1995, in memory of his wife
EXH: *Sickert and the Theatre*, November–December 1992 (27)
ENGR: Etching 12.7 x 10.8, inscr. 'Harry Anderson eheu! / Beer beer glorious / Silence is the gold / My new pal / Is my ole gal' (t.l.) and 'Sickert 1918' (b.l.), pub. Robert Emmons, *The Life and Opinions of Walter Richard Sickert* (London, 1941), p. 25
REL: Aberdeen Art Gallery pencil on buff paper 25.5 x 15.6, inscr: 'Study of Harry Anderson "In Memoriam"', reproduced in Lillian Browse, *Sickert*, p. 11

Two men standing full-length, facing right. The figure on the left wears a patched dress suit, the one on the right wears a short jacket and has his hand in his right pocket. Both figures may be Anderson in two different roles.

Harry Anderson, who died in 1918, was a performer principally in South London music halls in the late 19th and early 20th centuries. In his *The Melodies Linger on: The Story of the Music Hall* (1950), p. 378, W. McQueen Pope writes: 'The songs of Harry Anderson are part of the heritage of the Music Hall, especially "Beer, Beer, Glorious Beer" and "All Sorts of Boys". He sang those songs of his, always full of bonhomie and beer … in a simple blue serge suit and bowler hat.' *Beer* is a song from the 1890s, 'Silence is the Gold' is part of a line from the song *A Woman Without a Tongue* (1907), and 'My New Pal' is from *She's a Jolly Good Fellow* (1906).

Another portrait of Anderson by Sickert, a pencil sketch, is in the Aberdeen Art Gallery.

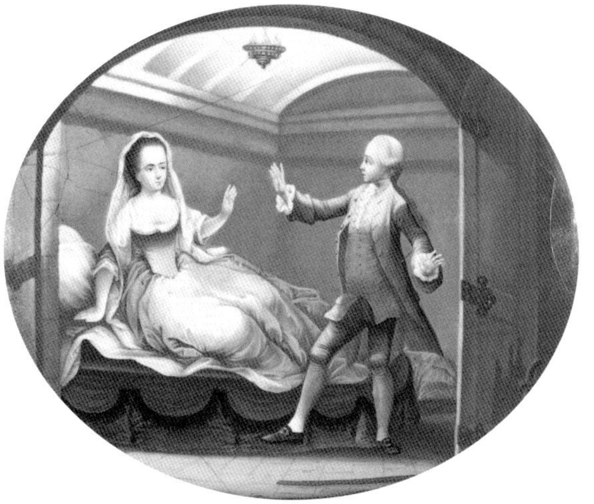

967*
DAVID GARRICK as Romeo and
GEORGE ANN BELLAMY as Juliet
in *Romeo and Juliet*
by William Shakespeare

Christian Frederick Zincke (?)
(after Benjamin Wilson *c.*1765)

Enamel plaque, oval 12.06, in a gilt copper frame
PROV: R. Walker, the Hon. Mrs Nellie Ionides, by descent to Toby Jessel, MP; presented to the Garrick Club by Mr Jessel and his wife, 1995
REL: Theatre Museum (8), original, oil on canvas 63.5 x 76.2, 1751 or 1752, prov: Iain Mackintosh & Geoffrey Ashton, engr: S. Ravenet, after Wilson, 43.2 x 54, pub. 5 April 1783, republished 1765 by Boydell; also an inferior engraving by R. Laurie pub. R. Stayner, and by Stayner pub. C. Shepherd; Yale Center for British Art, oil on canvas 137.2 x 190.5, prov: American Shakespeare Festival Theatre, Paul Mellon; Stourhead, Wilts., oil on canvas, prov: Henry Hoare 1775
LIT: Iain Mackintosh, 'David Garrick and Benjamin Wilson', *Apollo* (May 1985), 314–320; Ashton, TM, No. 8

This painting on enamel is a version of Benjamin Wilson's picture (see also No. 246). Although somewhat crude, it may be by the enameller Christian Frederick Zincke, who was called by Wilson 'the celebrated Mr Zink' and at whose lodgings Wilson resided when he painted this scene. Zincke died at Lambeth on 24 March 1767.

The scene shown is Garrick's alteration, in which Juliet awakens before Romeo has died and 65 lines of Garrick's interpolated dialogue follow. The phial from which Romeo has taken his poison is on the floor of the tomb in the painting and the engraving, but not in the Yale version or the enamel. Garrick's production in 1750, in which he acted Romeo to Mrs Bellamy's Juliet, began a three-year rivalry with the production of the play at Covent Garden, where Spranger Barry and Mrs Cibber were featured as the young lovers. See K.A. Burnim, *David Garrick: Director* (Pittsburgh, 1961), pp. 129–133, and Iain Mackintosh (above).

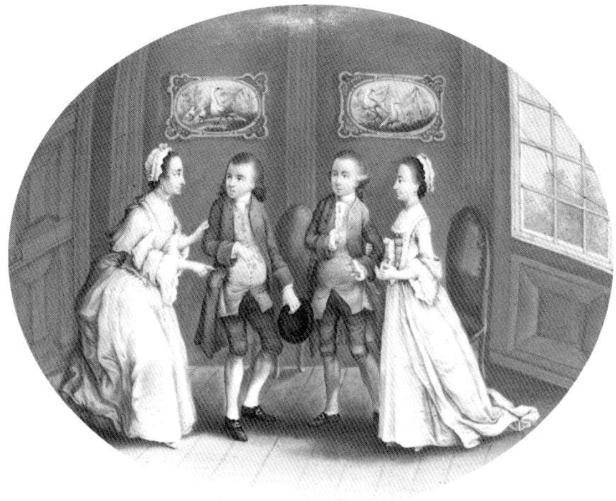

968
A Scene from *Oroonoko*
by Thomas Southerne

Christian Frederick Zincke (?)

*c.*1765 (?)
Enamel plaque, 12.06 oval in a gilt copper frame
PROV: R. Walker, the Hon. Mrs Nellie Ionides, then by descent to Toby Jessel, MP, by whom presented to the Garrick Club, 1995

Four characters standing in a room, women left and right and two men centre. This enamel, a pair with No. 967, is also probably by Zincke. It may represent a scene in the play as acted at either of the patent houses, and if it does, perhaps it shows Act 1, when Lucy Wellborn, Charlotte Wellborn (in breeches), Widow Lackit and Stanmore appear together. But costume traditions were so erratic at this time that the characters could be any of those in this exotic drama about slavery, set in the West Indies.

In the mid-1760s at Covent Garden, Stanmore was usually played by Davis, Charlotte by Miss Macklin, Lucy by Miss Stephens, and Widow Lackit by Mrs Pitt. The cast at Drury Lane varied considerably during those years, and these roles were usually not listed in the bills.

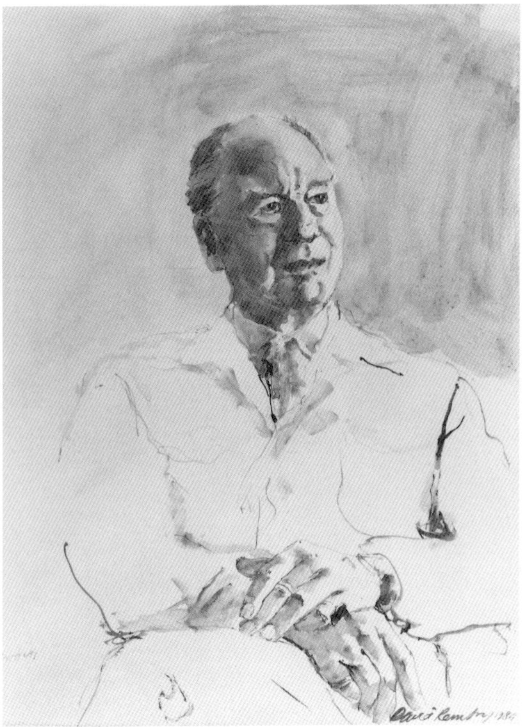

969
SIR JOHN GIELGUD

David Remfry

1984
Pen and watercolour with body colour 51.4 x 40.6
INSCR: (?) 'corsets' (b.l.); s. & d. (l.r.)
PROV: Sir John Gielgud, by whom
presented to the Garrick Club, 1996
EXH: NPG 'Drawing of Sir John Gielgud';
Ankrum Gallery, Los Angeles; O.W.C.S.
'Study for a Portrait' (labels on back of frame)
REL: NPG 5780, oil 101.2 x 80.7, s. & d. 1984

This watercolour study of Sir John for the painting in the NPG shows him half-length, seated and looking three-quarters right.

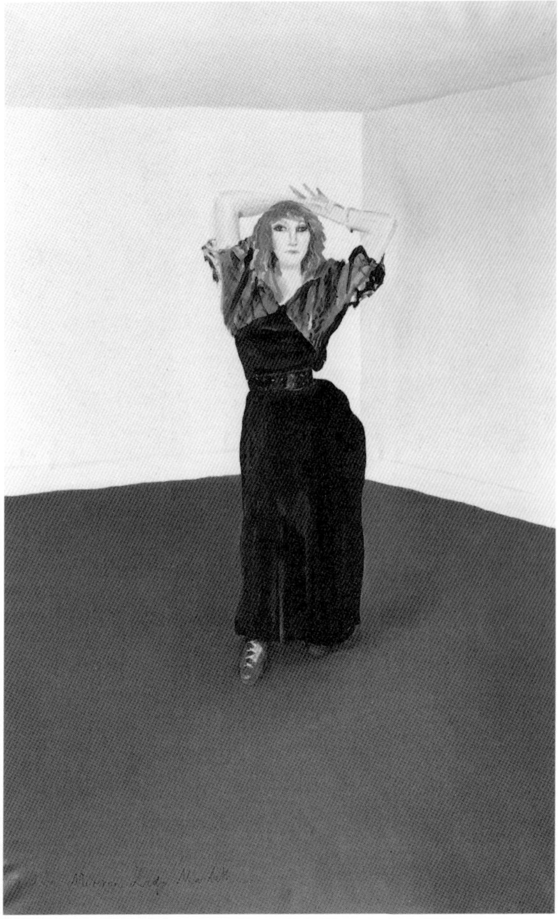

970
HELEN MIRREN
as Lady Macbeth

Patrick Procktor

Oil on canvas 137 x 91
INSCR: 'Helen Mirren Lady Macbeth' (pencil b.l.);
'Patrick Procktor' (b.r.)
PROV: The artist, by whom presented
to the Garrick Club, 1996

Standing full-length in a bare white interior, the sitter has her arms raised behind her head and wears a black dress with a belt, and laced red shoes. Helen Mirren played Lady Macbeth with the Royal Shakespeare Company in 1974 .

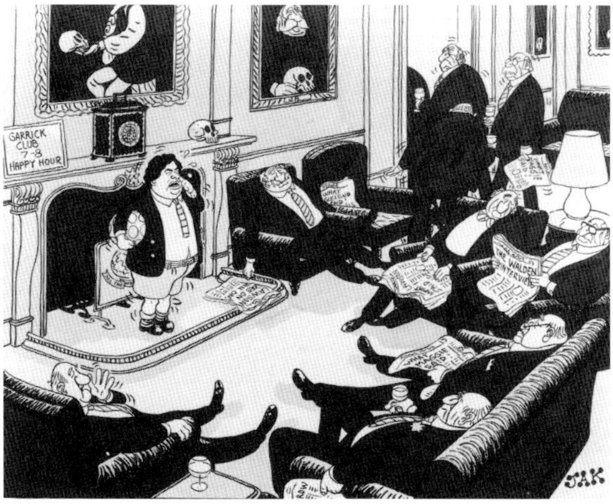

971
Members of the Garrick Club

Raymond Jackson (JAK)

Black ink and blue wash 52 x 60
INSCR: 'JAK' (b.r.); ' "IT'S NOT FAIR! EVERYONE KNEW I WAS MUCH CLEVERER THAN ALAN WALTERS!" / x 4 cols TUES 7th NOV 1989 15% TINT' (in pencil below)
PROV: Timothy Stanley-Clarke, by whom presented to the Garrick Club, May 1996

Ten members are seated in various states of relaxation on chairs and a sofa in a room which is probably intended to be the Newspaper Room off the Bar; some hold wine glasses. A sign over the fireplace reads: 'GARRICK / CLUB / 7–8 / HAPPY HOUR'; newspapers held by some members show various headlines: 'What Lawson said!'; 'What Maggie said!'; 'What Gielgud said!'; 'Lawson Goes On an' On!'; 'The Walden Interview'.

JAK's cartoons appear in the London *Evening Standard*. See Nos. 11, 962 and 972.

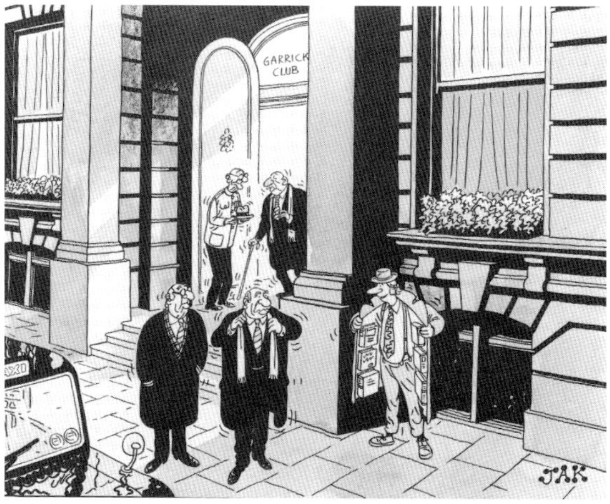

972
Members Leaving the Garrick Club

Raymond Jackson (JAK)

Black ink and blue wash 52 x 60
INSCR: 'JAK' (b.r.); ' "SHORTLISTED BOOKER PRIZE NOVELS, JUST OFF A LORRY?" / x 4 cols MON 15th OCT 1990 25% TINT MAN, TIES, SCARF, HAT. / CURTAINS – GLASS + MIRROR / ON TAXI' (in pencil below)
PROV: Timothy Stanley-Clarke, by whom presented to the Garrick Club, May 1996

The front of the Garrick Club is shown. Three members are leaving the Club and a porter hands one of them his hat. A huckster stands on the pavement with his overcoat open to reveal books attached to the lining. A taxi waits. For the London *Evening Standard*. See Nos. 11, 962 and 971.

SCULPTURE

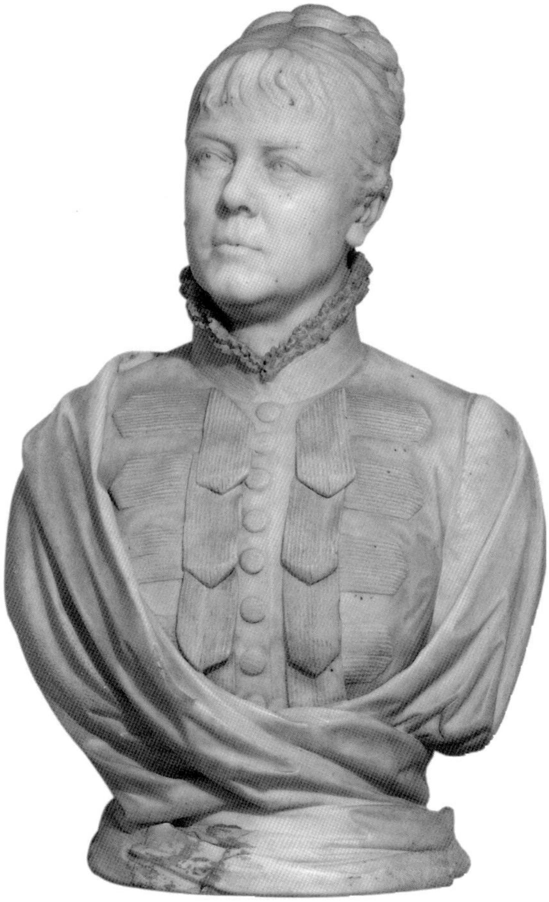

S1

MARIE BANCROFT

H.S.H. Count Gleichen

1879

White marble 70 x 47 x 26 (on red composition column with black base 107 high, *c.* 25 diam., base 27.5 sq.)

INSCR: *G / 1879* (verso); *MARIE BANCROFT / H.S.H. COUNT GLEICHEN / PRESENTED TO THE GARRICK CLUB / BY S.B. BANCROFT* (incised in column and touched in with gold)

INV: Gift 238

PROV: Sir Squire Bancroft, by whom presented *c.* 1893

EXH: 1880 R.A. (1583)

There is some damage to the base of this bust.

Lady Bancroft was the wife of Sir Squire Bancroft. See S2.

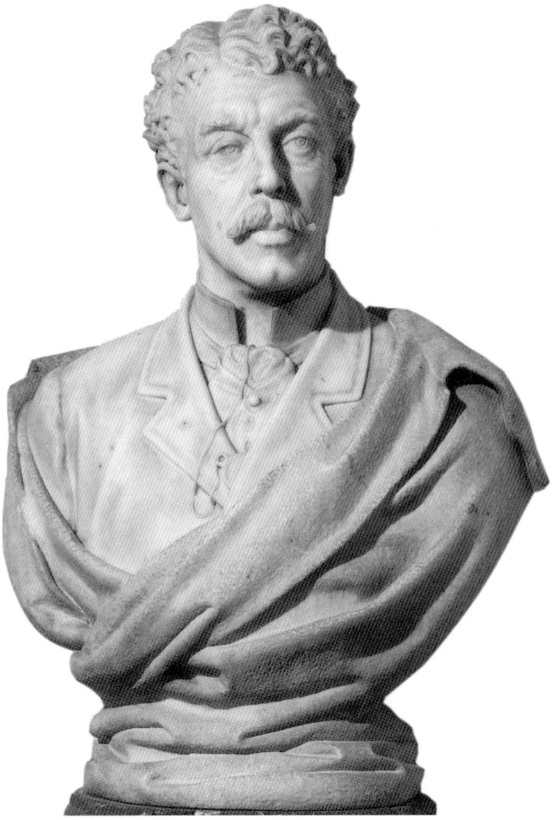

S2

SIR SQUIRE BANCROFT

H.S.H. Count Gleichen

1880

White marble 75.5 x 56 x 27 (on damaged red composition column with black base 107 high, *c.* 25 diam., base 27.5 sq.)

INSCR: *G / 1880* (on verso, touched in with black paint); *S.B. BANCROFT / H.S.H. COUNT GLEICHEN / PRESENTED TO THE GARRICK CLUB / BY S.B. BANCROFT* (incised in column and touched in with gold)

INV: Gift No. 237

PROV: Sir Squire Bancroft, by whom presented *c.* 1893

EXH: 1881 R.A. (1458)

The Bancrofts took over the Haymarket in 1879 and their management opened there on 31 January 1880. It seems likely that the busts were commissioned to celebrate the event, and, possibly, to decorate one of the foyers.

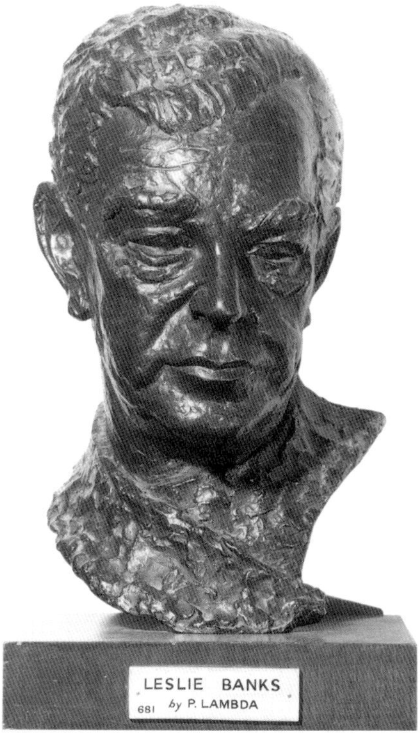

S3

LESLIE JAMES BANKS

Peter Lambda

1953
Bronze 38 x 22 x 26 (wooden support 17 x 28.4 x 28)
INSCR: *LESLIE BANKS / by P. LAMBDA / 681*
(plaque on base)
PROV: Purchased by the Garrick Club for £140, 1953

The head was cast by Mr Forini of the Forini Art Bronze Foundry in Fulham. The purchase of the bust was suggested by Roger Furse in a letter to the Club Secretary, dated 8 August 1953:

> I am enclosing a photograph of what I personally think a realy [*sic*] excellent portrait bust of Leslie Banks. It was done by a sculptor called Peter Lambda. I met him the other day and he told me that as he planned to go away for some time he was trying to clear his studio of as much as possible and was willing to reduce his prices considerably. He asked my advice and I told him that I would send this photograph to you in case the club might be interested – He has other portraits of well known Theatre people including a head of Sir Laurence Olivier.

Peter Lambda wrote on 17 August 1953 suggesting a price of '100 guineas plus the expenses of casting it, which would be about 40 guineas in bronze (or about 8 to 10 in plaster – but I advise strongly against that)'.

The Secretary replied on 10 November 1953:

> I have pleasure in informing you that my Committee would be very pleased to have your bust of Leslie Banks cast in bronze at about 140 guineas. They would like your assurance that the bust will not be cast for any other person or society without reference to them.

Lambda also modelled in clay a small full-length figure of Leslie Banks in *Love for Love* and produced a similar figure of John Gielgud as Hamlet. He exhibited at the Royal Academy in 1952 and 1955.

Banks became a member of the Club in 1928.

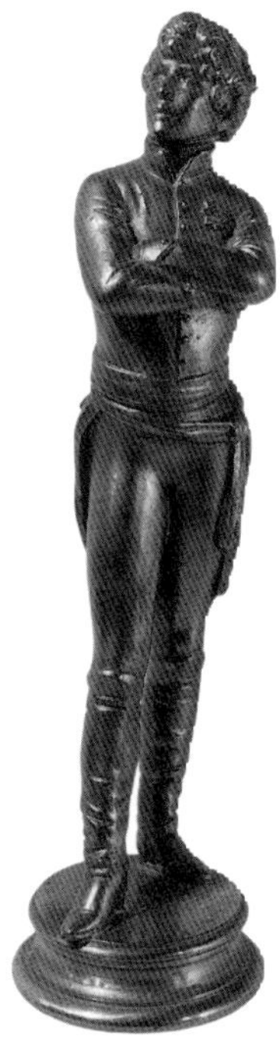

S4

SARAH BERNHARDT

as L'Aiglon in *L'Aiglon* by Edmond Rostand

France Raphael

c. 1900
Bronze 18.5 x 4.5 x 4.5, bronze base 2 x 6 diam.; white marble plinth striped with orange and green 9 x 5.5 diam.; decorative bronze base 4 x 7.5 x 7.5
INSCR: *SARAH BERNHARDT / dans L'AIGLON / par F. Raphael* (bronze plaque on marble plinth)
INV: Gift 915
PROV: Peter Machi Brown (City Tavern Club), by whom presented to the Garrick Club, 1985

The figure has been broken off at the ankles and repaired. There is a (casting?) hole in the top of the head.

Rostand's popular play about Napoleon's son, the King of Rome, was first performed in Paris at the Théâtre Sarah Bernhardt on 15 March 1900. Bernhardt had opened the theatre with her Hamlet on 16 December 1899, but *L'Aiglon* was the theatre's first great success and ran for 237 performances until 30 October 1900. The cast also included Lucien Guitry as Flambeau and André Calmettes as Metternich. Bernhardt took the play on tour to the United States, where it opened at the Garden Theater in New York on 26 November 1900. At the end of the tour the play was given a two-week run at the Metropolitan Opera House, from 8 April 1901. The statuette seems to have been inspired by production photographs showing Bernhardt in costume upon the plain of Wagram.

The sculptor is apparently France Raphael, who was born in Amsterdam in 1877 and exhibited at the Salon d'Automne and the Salon des Tuileries.

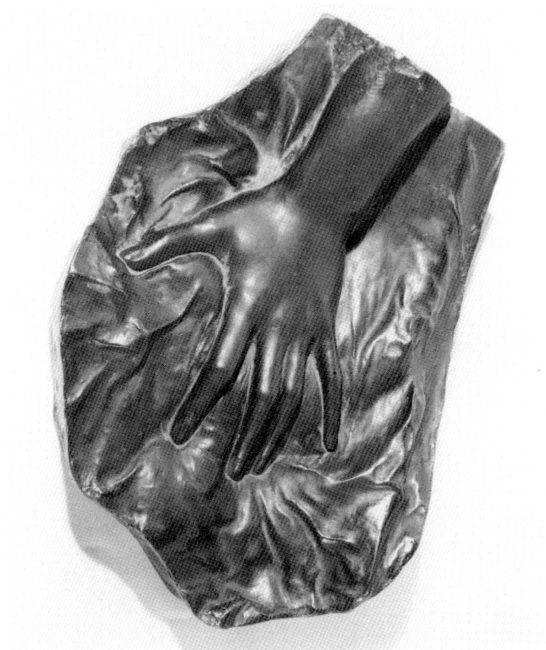

S5

Cast of the Left Hand of

MRS PATRICK CAMPBELL

Madeleine Wyndham

1898

Bronze 10 x 34.5 x 26

INSCR: *Beatrice Stella Campbell's hand / Moulded by / Madeleine Wyndham / Clouds 1898* (on edge above wrist)

INV: Gift 859

PROV: Charles Collingwood, by whom presented to the Garrick Club, 1974

LIT: Mrs Patrick Campbell, *My Life and Some Letters* (1922)

Mrs Patrick Campbell mentions the casting of her hand in her memoirs: 'I look my best when I am very ill, which means the bones of my face are good and my features are placed well. My hands were Italian in shape. "Aunt Madeleine" took a plaster cast of one for me and Lord Wemyss had it done into bronze, and the hand looks lovely.'

The Hon. Mrs Percy Scawen Wyndham, formerly Miss Madeleine Caroline Frances Eden Campbell, exhibited at the Royal Academy as an enamel painter in 1898. Her contribution (1872) was an enamel of *St Francis receiving the stigmata*.

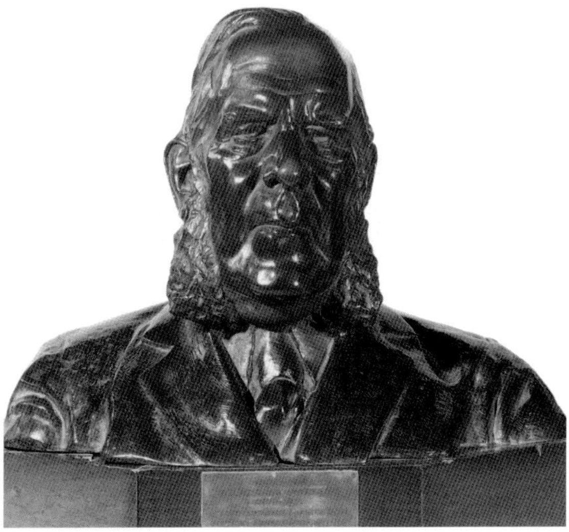

S6

SIR EDWARD CLARKE

Joan Dummett

1929

Bronze 36 x 48 x 24 (set in wooden base shaped around the base of the bust 11.2 x 51.5 x 29)

INSCR: *JD* (in monogram on side of left shoulder); *THE RT. HON. / SIR EDWARD CLARKE K.C. / 1841–1931 / PRESENTED TO THE GARRICK CLUB / OF WHICH HE WAS A MEMBER 1884–1931 / BY / SIR PERCIVAL CLARKE / Joan Dummett Sculpt.* (brass plaque on wooden base)

INV: Gift 485

PROV: Sir Percival Clarke, by whom presented to the Garrick Club, 1931

EXH: 1929 R.A. (1563)

Sir Edward Clarke was the Member of Parliament for Plymouth for 20 years, from 1880. He held the post of Solicitor-General from 1885 to 1892.

Joan Dummett exhibited another bronze at the 1929 Royal Academy (1468): a bronze head of *R.E. Dummett, Esq., Metropolitan Police Court Magistrate.*

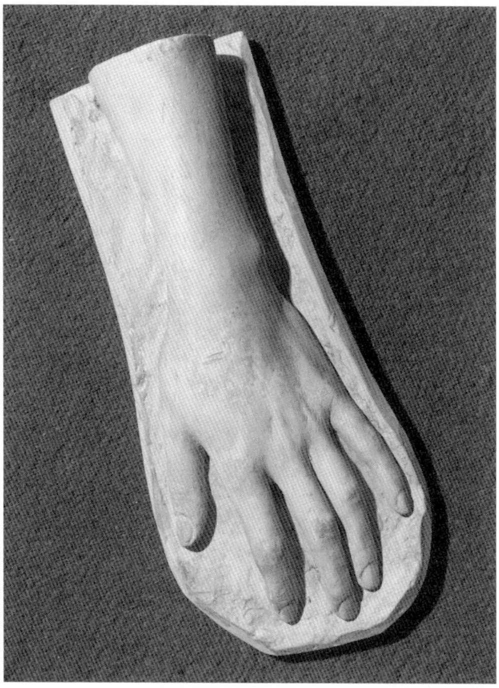

S7
Cast of the Left Hand of
ELEANORA DUSE

Anonymous

Plaster 8 x 31 x 14
INV: Gift 652
PROV: Charles Burlingham of the United States,
by whom presented, 1946

The hand was possibly produced in a commercial edition, although no number is evident. Such things are very fragile, however, and the Garrick Club copy may be a rare survivor.

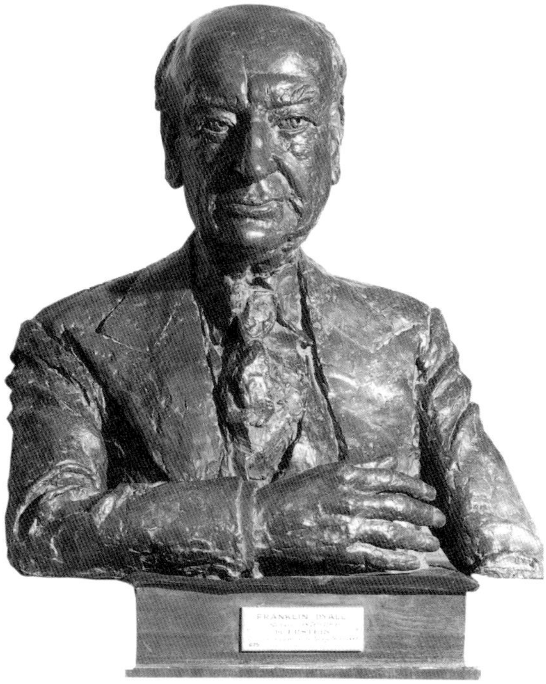

S8
FRANKLIN DYALL

Sir Jacob Epstein

1948
Bronze 53 x 55 x 34
(on wooden plinth 119.5 x 35.5 x 35.5)
INSCR: *FRANKLIN DYALL / Actor 1870–1950 / by EPSTEIN / Presented by his wife, Mary Merrall / 675*
(gold-painted wooden plaque on base)
INV: Gift 728
PROV: Mrs Franklin Dyall (Miss Mary Merrall),
by whom presented to the Garrick Club, 1953
LIT: Richard Buckle, *Jacob Epstein, Sculptor* (1963),
illustrated p. 317, No. 487, p. 428; Evelyn Silber,
The Sculpture of Epstein (1986), p. 202, No. 396

In December 1953 a man giving his name as M. Brandon and his address as the Carco Theatre, Montreal, offered £750 for the bust. After trans-Atlantic enquiries, both M. Brandon and his theatre were found not to exist. Buckle lists nine 1948 portrait busts in his catalogue of Epstein's work, including those of Jill Balcon and Joan Greenwood.

Dyall became a member of the Garrick Club in 1934.

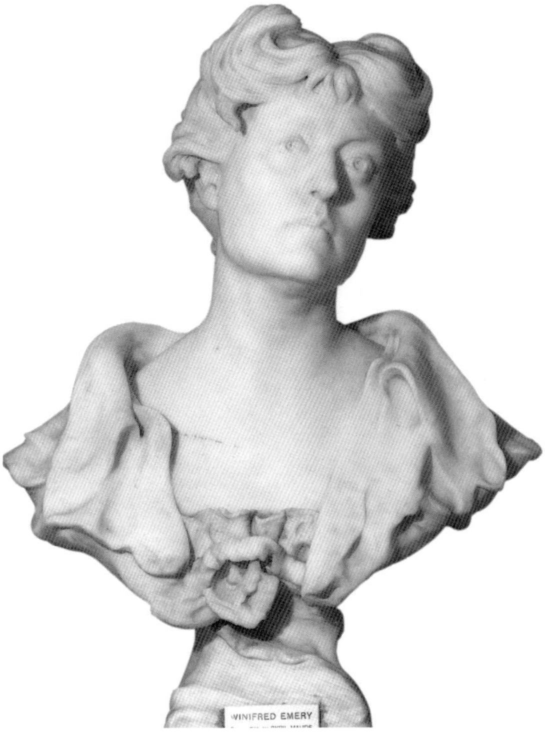

S9
WINIFRED EMERY

Albert Toft

*c.*1915
White marble 66.4 x 50 x 31.5, base 19.2 x 20.7
INSCR: *WINIFRED EMERY / PRESENTED BY CYRIL MAUDE / 10th JULY 1915*
(on ivory plaque attached to base)
INV: Gift 373
PROV: Cyril Maude, by whom presented to the Garrick Club, 1915
LIT: Cyril Maude, *Behind the Scenes with Cyril Maude* (1927), reproduced opposite p. 132

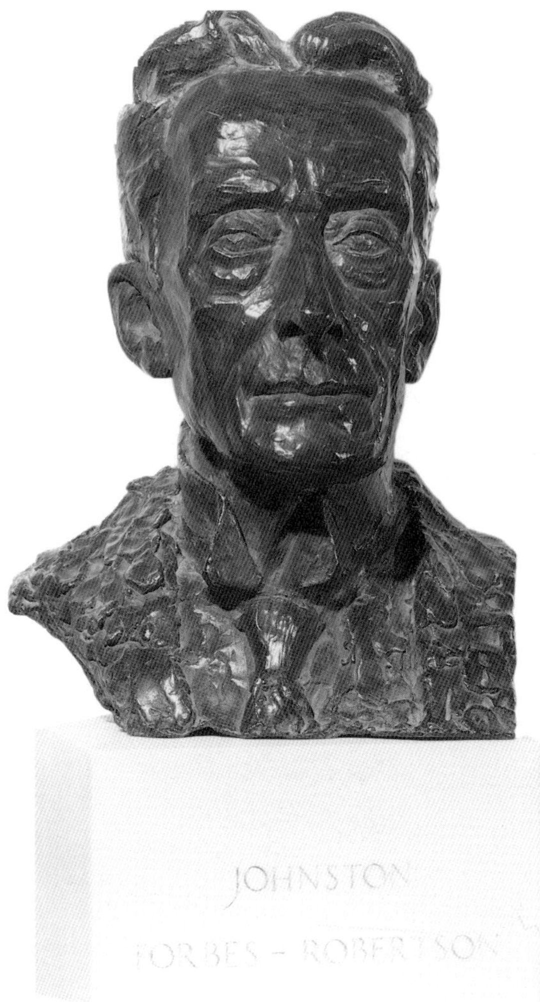

S10
SIR JOHNSTON FORBES-ROBERTSON

Sarah Bobsaris

c. 1930?
Bronze 37 x 29 x 22.5, no base but attached to grey and white marble plinth 127 x 25 x 23.5; the plinth is in three sections: a white marble rectangular base, a tapering grey marble centre section and a rectangular white block above
INSCR: *JOHNSTON / FORBES-ROBERTSON / 1853–1937 / GIFT OF HIS WIFE,* inscribed on upper part of plinth
INV: Gift 578
PROV: Lady Forbes-Robertson, by whom presented to the Garrick Club, 1939

The head has been cast from a very vigorously modelled terracotta.

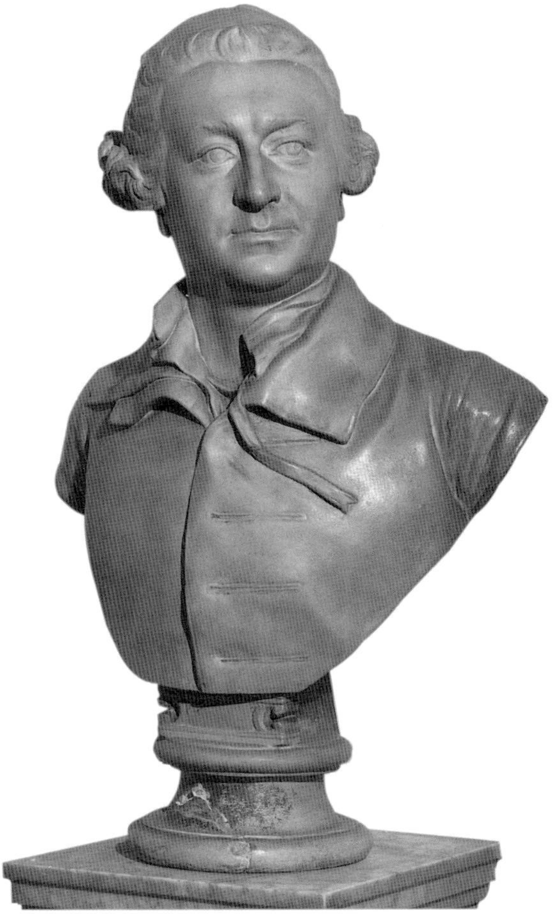

S11

DAVID GARRICK

After John Van Nost the Younger

1765?
Plaster 54 x 50 20, socle 14.5 x 20 diam.
INV: Gift 22 or 67
PROV: Theodore Hook, by whom presented
to the Garrick Club, 1835 or 1841
EXH: 1958, loaned to the BBC for use as a property
in a production of *The Royal Family of Broadway*

The younger Van Nost took a life mask of Garrick which was later owned by Charles Mathews (see S13). From the mask Van Nost made a bust which became one of the most popular images of Garrick. There were so many copies that according to Macklin there was one 'in every Barber's shop-window, as a block for wigs' (reported in J.T. Smith's *Nollekens and His Times*, 2: 207).

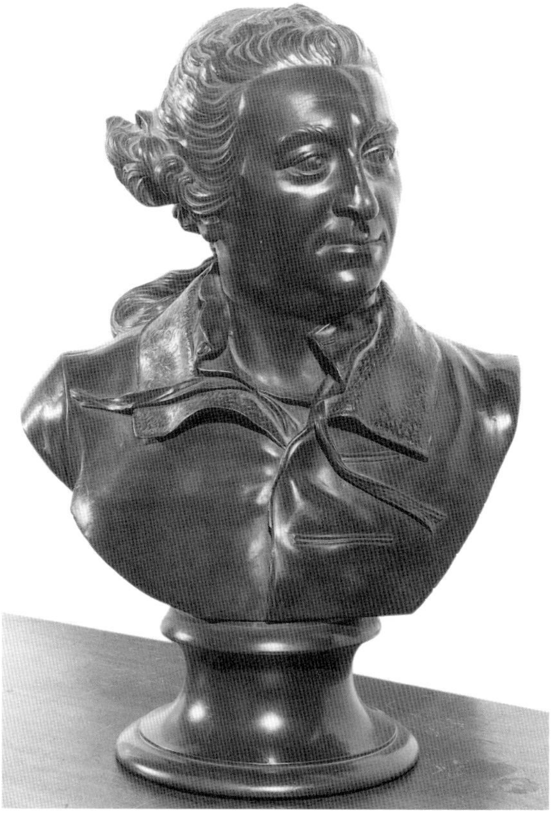

S12

DAVID GARRICK

James Hoskins & Benjamin Grant (after John Van Nost the Younger)

1779
Wedgwood black basalt 43.5 x 30.5 x 18
(including attached socle)
INSCR: *WEDGWOOD* (back of neck)
INV: Gift 684
PROV: Presented by H. Austen Hall & James Gunn, 1949

According to the Wedgwood archives, James Hoskins and Benjamin Grant supplied Wedgwood with busts of Garrick and Sterne in 1779. Other busts supplied over the previous four years had included Swift, Milton, Spenser, Chaucer, Addison, Pope, Locke, Dryden, Dr Johnson, Ben Jonson, Sir William Reigley, Prior, Congreve, Fletcher, Beaumont, Bacon, Boyle, Harvey and Newton. The bust is based on an example of the Van Nost bust; the ribbons and folds around the neck are reproduced exactly. However, there is much more flair in the modelling of the hair, and the face is modelled with greater distinction.

A smaller version of the bust, 9.5 high, is in the Folger Library, Washington. Another example of the large size is at Wimpole Hall.

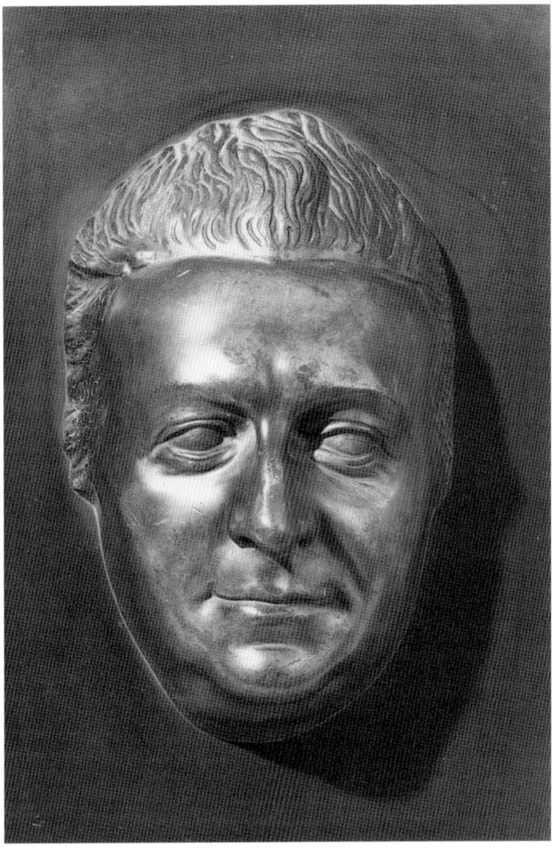

S13
Life Mask of
DAVID GARRICK

Possibly John Van Nost the Younger

1765?
Plaster painted to resemble bronze, mounted on slate
25.5 x 16.5 x 10.5 (head only); 36 x 28.3 (slate);
51.5 x 44.5 x 4.5 (oak frame)
INSCR: *DAVID GARRICK / PRESENTED BY W.O. DANCKWERTS, ESQRE K.C. / 1913.* cream paint (on frame below head); *304 GARRICK. Plaster cast of the head of David Garrick, life size, / relief, on a slab of black polished slate, enclosed in broad flat oak frame, with gilt fillet. / From the Theatrical Collection of the late Mrs. C. Wylie, of Chelsea* printed label (verso)
INV: Gift 363
PROV: Mrs Wylie; her sale; W.O. Danckwerts K.C., by whom presented to the Garrick Club, 1912

Possibly a version of the mask that Van Nost took of Garrick's face prior to modelling his bust (see S11). Another example of this mask, also in plaster and mounted on slate, is in the Folger Library, Washington.

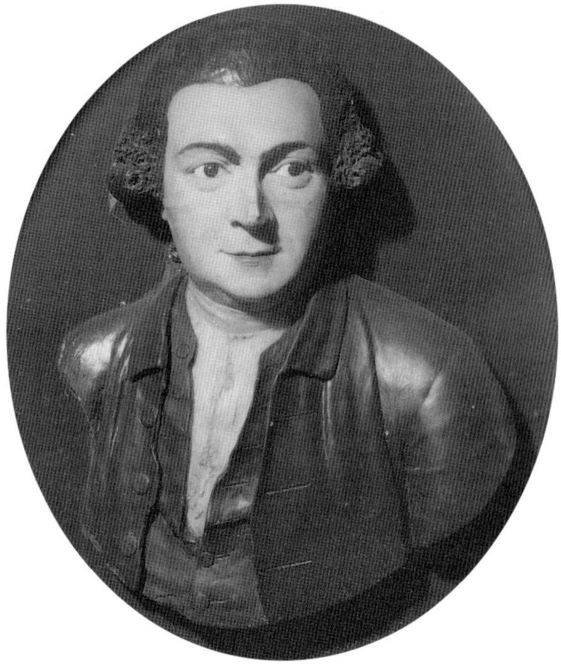

S14
DAVID GARRICK (?)

Unknown Wax Modeller (after Sir Joshua Reynolds?)

c. 1776
Coloured and painted wax
mounted on oval glass disc 18 x 14 x 7 (bust only);
25.5 x 19 (glass disc); 34 x 29 x 9.5 (frame)
INSCR: *This Wax Portrait of / David Garrick / came from the sale of / his house at Hampton at the death of / his wife. It was bought in 1890 / from the purchaser's widow. / who lived in the NEXT house to ME / F.W. Lockwood WED.*, in pen and ink (on label stuck on verso); *F.W. Lockwood F.S.A. / Appledore / Kent,* in pen and ink on a copy of W. Watt's view of Garrick's house at Hampton, published 1 November 1784; a copy of Garrick's book-plate is attached to verso
INV: Gift 464?
PROV: David Garrick; Mrs David Garrick; her sale, Christie's 23 June 1823; unknown buyer; his widow, from whom purchased by F.W. Lockwood, 1890; F.H. Cripps-Day, by whom presented to the Garrick Club, 1930?

The waistcoat, jacket and hair are made of brown wax, the face is painted flesh colour, and the stock and shirt are of white wax. There has been a horizontal repair across the face.

Identification with Garrick is not altogether convincing, but if Garrick is meant to be represented, the inspiration is almost certainly Reynolds's Thrale portrait of 1776, the best surviving version of which is at Knole (see No. 241).

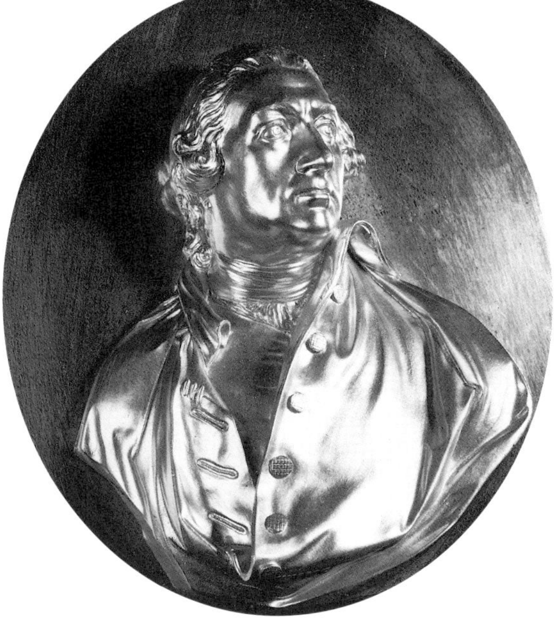

S15*

DAVID GARRICK

Louis François Roubiliac

1758

Gilt bronze 25 x 21 x 6 (oval); bust only 18.5 x 15.5 x 6

INSCR: *DAVID GARRICK. Arm, / L. F.Roubiliac Sct. ad Vivum / 1758* (verso); *DAVID GARRICK. Armr, L.F. Roubiliac Sct. ad Vivum. 1758 / Presented to the Garrick Club, by Peter Norton. Esqr.*, in cream paint on wooden label loosely attached to bottom of frame

INV: Gift 4

PROV: Presented by Peter Norton, 1833

EXH: 1985 Museum of London *The Quiet Conquest: The Huguenots (1685–1985)*, (201)

LIT: Katherine A. Esdaile, *The Life and Works of Louis François Roubiliac* (1928), p. 110; J.V.G. Mallet, 'Some Portrait Medallions by Roubiliac', *Burlington Magazine* (1962), 104: 153–58, figs. 27 & 31

The oval plaque is made of highly polished bronze. The bust itself is attached to the plaque and is in gilded bronze; the gilding, which is matt, may not be original.

Roubiliac was closely involved with Garrick in 1758, in which year he completed the statue of Shakespeare for the Shakespeare temple in Garrick's riverside garden at Hampton (see No. 938). He also produced a terracotta bust of Garrick, seen in Soldi's portrait of Roubiliac in the Garrick Club (No. 727). The Soldi is signed and dated 1757/58, and although the terracotta bust is lost, there is a plaster cast of it in the National Portrait Gallery (707A). It is similar in many ways to S15, though the bronze has a much brighter feel to it, with the head lifted, the stoop alleviated, and details such as the buttons added. The bronze clearly dates slightly later than the terracotta. Roubiliac's posthumous sale, 12–15 May 1762, included a set of plaster medallions depicting Garrick, Pope, Conyers Middleton, Handel, Inigo Jones, Oliver Cromwell and Isaac Newton. In addition, the sale included four plaster medallions of Garrick and three medallions in wax as well as two terracotta busts, a plaster bust, and a mould for the bust. Roubiliac's marble bust of Garrick was sold at Mrs Garrick's sale, Christie's 23 June 1823. Mallet discusses five other bronze busts by Roubiliac, similar to S15, which depict Alexander Pope, Conyers Middleton and George Frederick Handel (three versions).

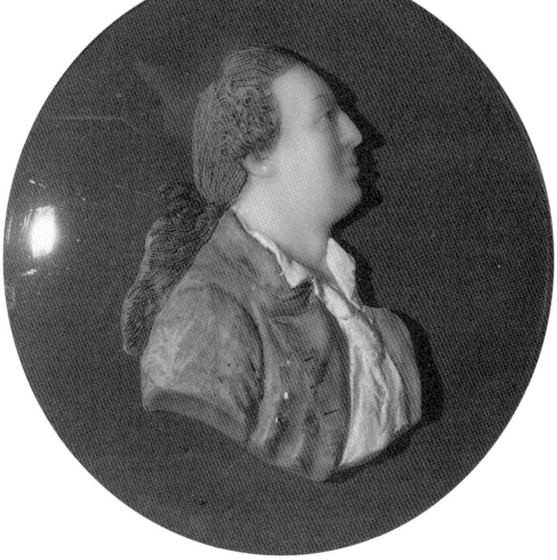

S16

DAVID GARRICK

Gardener (after John Keyse Sherwin)

*c.*1774

Uncoloured wax mounted on oval glass disc 10 x 9 (bust only); 14.5 x 11.5 (glass disc); 24.5 x 21.5 (frame)

PROV: Unknown

LIT: E.J. Pyke, *A Biographical Dictionary of Wax Modellers* (1973), p. 52, pl. 103 (e.g. in Royal Collection)

The wax, of which two examples are recorded (in the Royal Collection and Christie's 11 December 1978, lot 134), is based on a small portrait bust drawn and engraved by J.K. Sherwin. It is a tentative work and is likely to have been produced shortly after Sherwin completed his apprenticeship with Bartolozzi in 1774.

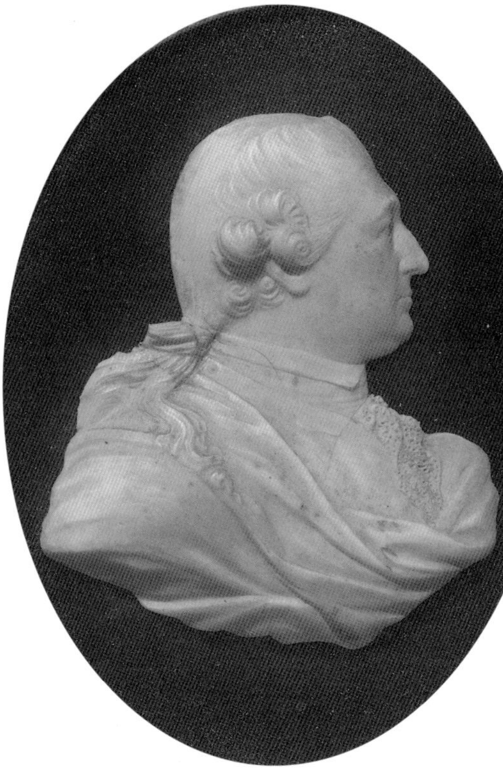

S17
Called
DAVID GARRICK

Unknown artist

c. 1770?
Tinted wax mounted on black paper
8 x 5.6 (bust only); 15.2 diam. (frame)
PROV: Ludo Foster, by whom presented, 1944

The sitter has a brown wig tied with black bow and a purple jacket with three gold buttons.

The profile does not resemble Garrick – despite the sagging chin. Both sitter and workmanship may be Continental, perhaps French.

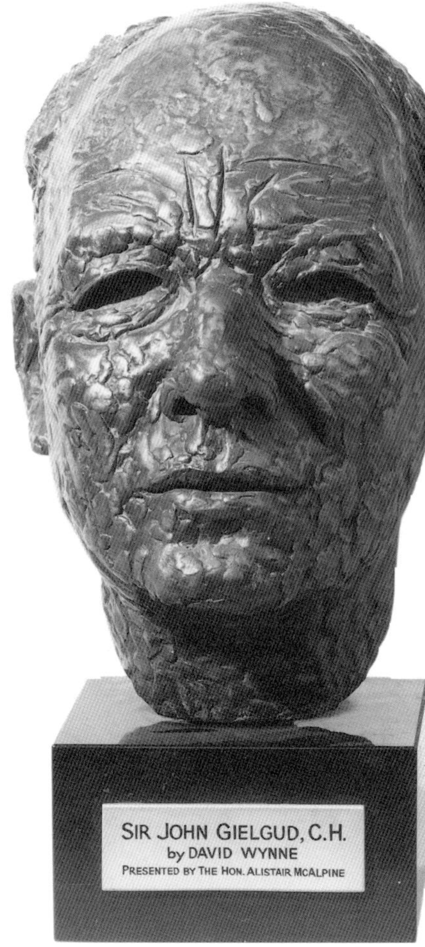

S18
SIR JOHN GIELGUD

David Wynne

1962
Bronze 30.5 x 22 x 29.5, black marble base
INSCR: *DAVID WYNNE / 3 /* (back of neck, left side);
SIR JOHN GIELGUD, C.H. */ by DAVID WYNNE / PRESENTED BY THE HON. ALISTAIR MCALPINE*
(on gold-painted wooden plaque on marble base)
INV: Gift 896
PROV: Presented by the Hon. Alistair McAlpine, 1981
EXH: 1964 *Exhibition of New Sculpture by David Wynne*, Arthur Tooth & Sons Ltd (7)

Number 3 of an edition of 6. In the catalogue of the Tooth exhibition, David Wynne commented: 'The head of the great Shakespearean actor was conceived as a mask whereon moods and passions follow one another at will.' The cast in the collection of the Royal Shakespeare Memorial Theatre was loaned to the David Wynne exhibition at the Fitzwilliam Museum, Cambridge, in 1972 (12).

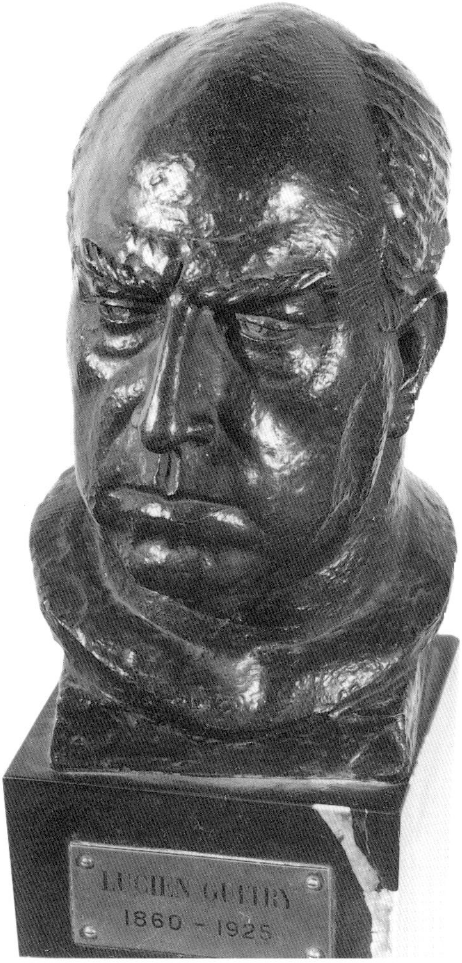

S19

LUCIEN-GERMAIN GUITRY

Paul Rothlisberger

1922

Bronze 20.5 x 12 x 12.5, mottled black and yellow marble plinth 32 x 11 (9 at base) x 11; black marble base 10 x 19.5 x 19.5

INSCR: *Rothlisberger / 1922* (left side below overhang of neck); *ANDRO, Fondeur, Paris* (right side, below neck); *LUCIEN GUITRY / 1860–1925 / OFFERT / AU / GARRICK CLUB / DE LONDRES / PAR / SACHA GUITRY* (bronze plaque on plinth)

INV: Gift 435

PROV: Sacha Guitry, by whom presented to the Garrick Club, 1925

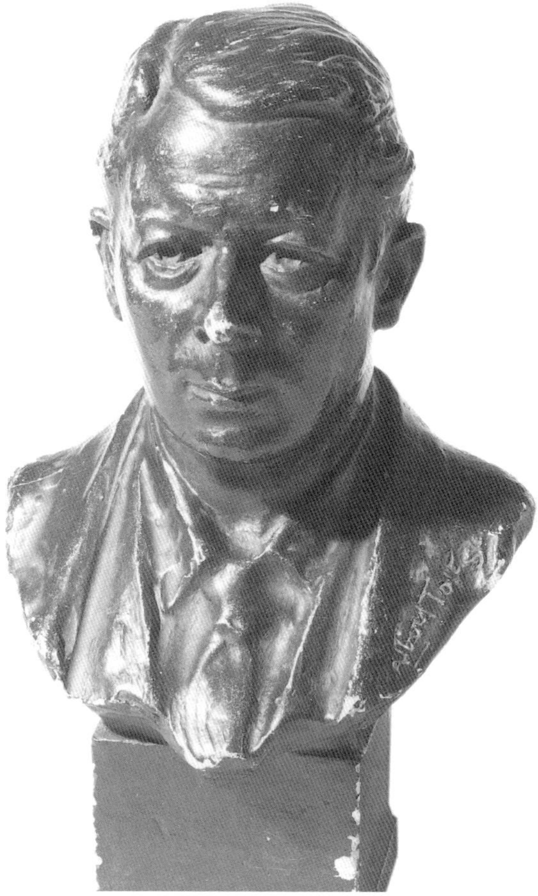

S20

SIR SEYMOUR HICKS

Albert Toft

1924

Plaster 24 x 14 x 10.5 (including attached rectangular base)

INSCR: *Albert Toft sc.* (on left shoulder)

INV: Gift 708

PROV: W. Colbourne Baber, by whom presented to the Garrick Club, 1951

EXH: 1924 R.A. (1555)?

Toft exhibited a bronze bust of Seymour Hicks at the Royal Academy in 1905 (1687). That bust is reproduced in *Pall Mall Magazine Pictures of 1905* (p. 96), and shows a much younger man than does S20. It is probable that S20 relates to the 1924 bust, although it may be a third likeness of the sitter.

See also No. 299.

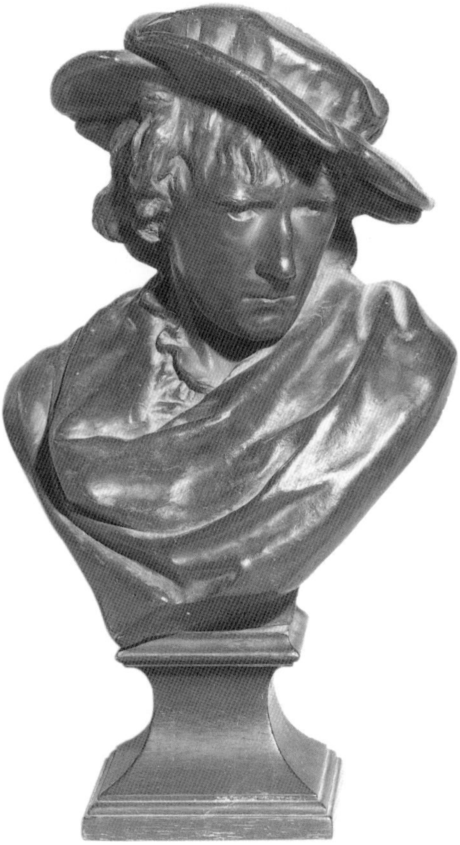

S21
SIR HENRY IRVING
as Hamlet in *Hamlet*
by William Shakespeare

Edward Onslow Ford

1885?
Bronze 23.5 x 18.5 x 13.5 (wooden base 8 x 9.5 x 9.5)
INSCR: *E Onslow* (behind left shoulder)
INV: Gift 903
PROV: Ifan Kyrle Fletcher catalogue No. 90 (1959), item 85; bought by Lincoln Kirstein, by whom presented to the American Shakespeare Theater, Stratford, Connecticut; returned to Lincoln Kirstein 1975; presented by Lincoln Kirstein to the Garrick Club, 1983
EXH: 1885 R.A. (2131)?

Onslow Ford made something of a speciality of portraying Irving as Hamlet. His life-sized seated figure in white marble, now in the Guildhall Art Gallery, was shown at the Royal Academy in 1883 (1628). S21 may be the Hamlet shown at the R.A. in 1885; and another Hamlet was shown posthumously at the R.S.P.P. in 1909 (181). The *Magazine of Art* (1902), p. 181, illustrated another full-length figure of Irving as Hamlet by the same artist.

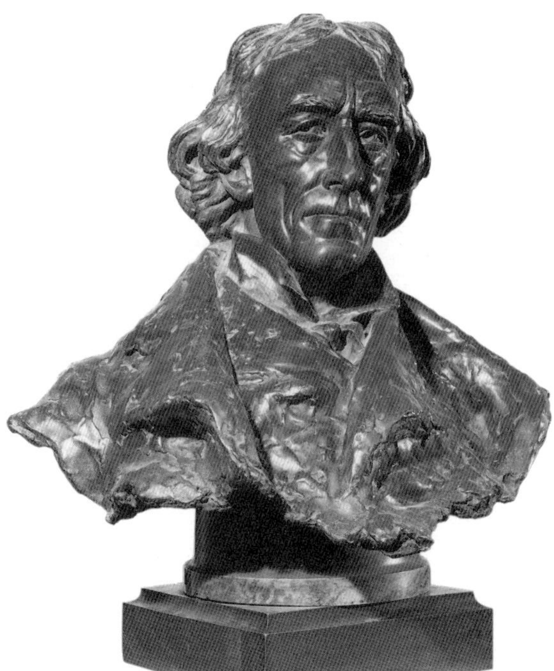

S22*
SIR HENRY IRVING

Courtney Edward Maxwell Pollock

c. 1905
Bronze 53 x 53 x 39
(green marble socle 24 diam. largely hidden; on wooden base 8 x 27.5 x 27.5; on green marble plinth 122 x 36 x 35.7; base of plinth 26 x 53 x 53)
INSCR: *Courtney Pollock* (behind left shoulder); *HENRY IRVING / BORN FEBRUARY 6TH 1838 / DIED OCTOBER 13TH 1905 / BY COURTNEY POLLOCK R.B.A. / PRESENTED TO THE GARRICK CLUB BY SEYMOUR HICKS* (on front of plinth)
INV: Gift 325
PROV: Seymour Hicks, by whom presented to the Garrick Club, 1907

Since it was presented to the Garrick Club in 1907, S22 has to be a fairly early work by Courtney Pollock (1877–1943). He did not exhibit at the Royal Academy until 1912; he continued to exhibit until 1920 but none of his sitters was theatrical. There is another cast of this bust in the Russell Coates Art Gallery, Bournemouth.

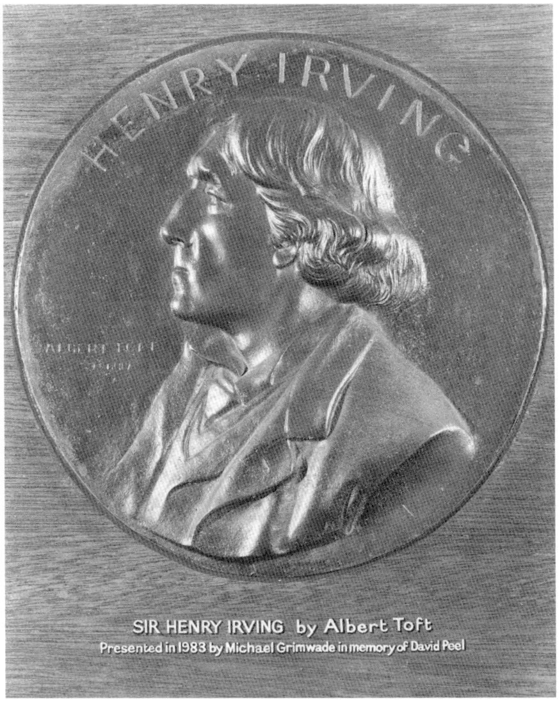

S23
SIR HENRY IRVING

Albert Toft

1887
Bronze medallion 24.5 diam. (wooden frame 39 x 35.5)
INSCR: *HENRY IRVING* (over Irving's head);
ALBERT TOFT / S. 1887 (to left of neck);
SIR HENRY IRVING by Albert Toft / Presented in 1983 by Michael Grimwade in memory of David Peel
(gold and black letters on frame)
INV: Gift 901
PROV: Michael Grimwade, by whom presented in memory of David Peel, 1983

A variant of this medallion was sold at Sotheby's, Belgravia, on 19 March 1975 (lot 34A). It has no lettering above the head, but is signed and dated *Albert Toft '87* below the left shoulder. Another variant in the Mander and Mitchenson Theatre Collection has no lettering at all.

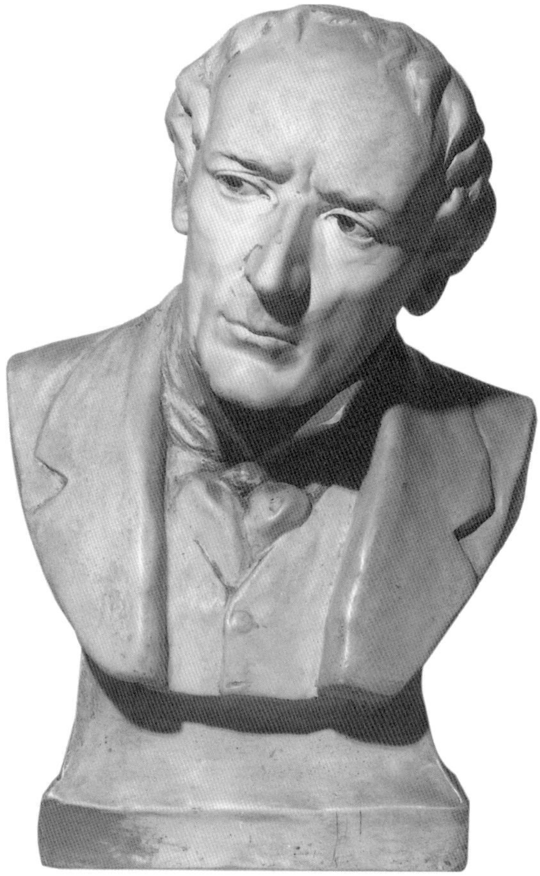

S24
HENRY BRODRIBB IRVING

Doris L.M. Lindner

1917
Plaster 39 x 25 x 16 (including attached base)
INSCR: *D Lindner / 1917* (on back of base)
INV: Gift 383A
PROV: Gerald Du Maurier & A. Sutro, by whom presented to the Garrick Club, 1919

This is an early work by Doris Lindner (*b.*1896). She exhibited portraits and figurative sculpture at the Royal Academy from 1927 to 1957. Her sitters included Her Majesty The Queen when she was Princess Elizabeth in 1949 (1372).

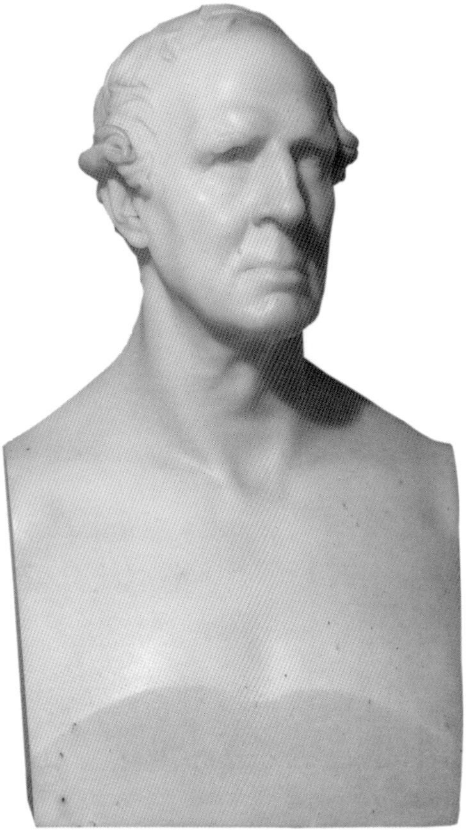

S25

CHARLES KEMBLE

Timothy Butler (?)

1844?
White marble 63 x 37 x 24, plinth of mottled red marble on black marble base, with strip of white marble between, 124.5 x 38 x 38
INSCR: *CHARLES KEMBLE / PRESENTED BY / EDWARD SARTORIS ESQ RE / 1886*
(front of plinth, incised letters touched with gold)
INV: Gift 201; (pedestal Gift 221)
PROV: Edward Sartoris, by whom presented to the Garrick Club, 1886 (pedestal presented by Henry Kemble, 1889)
EXH: 1844 R.A. (1322)?
ENGR: *Illustrated London News*, 18 November 1854 (woodcut), when the bust was in the possession of the family

In this spare neo-classical likeness, Kemble is shown in distinguished old age.

Butler also exhibited a *Bust of Charles Kemble* at the 1846 R.A. (1426). The sculptor exhibited about 100 busts at the Royal Academy between 1828 and 1879. His best-known works are the lamp standards along the Thames Embankment at Westminster.

Edward Sartoris, who gave the bust to the Club, was Charles Kemble's son-in-law.

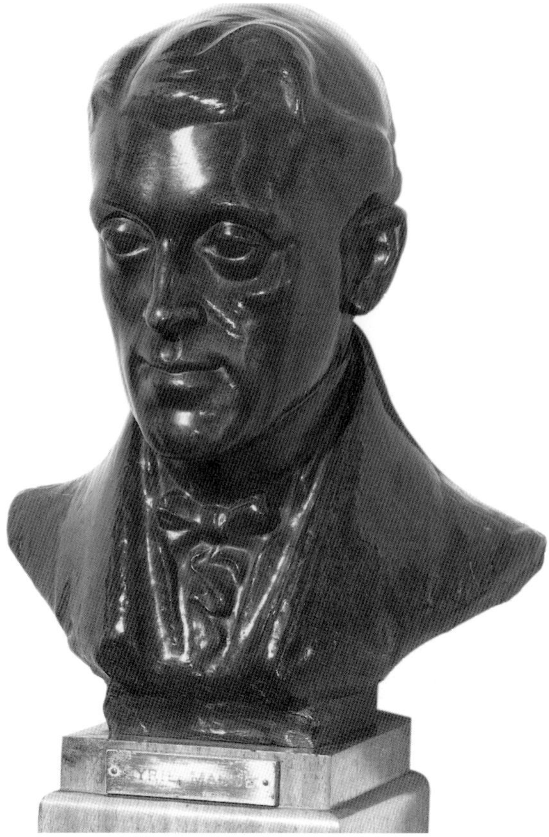

S26

CYRIL MAUDE

Basil Gotto

Bronze 40 x 30.5 x 23.5
INSCR: *Gotto* (under left shoulder)
INV: Gift 622
PROV: Presented by the sitter, 1943

Maude became a member of the Garrick Club in 1894.

Gotto (1866–1954), who studied in Paris under Bouguereau and in London at the Royal Academy Schools, exhibited at the Royal Academy from 1892 to 1935, and also at the Paris Salon.

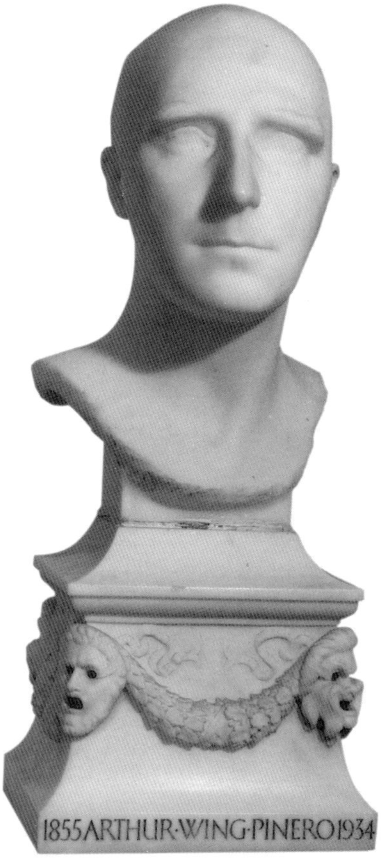

S27*
SIR ARTHUR WING PINERO

Emil Fuchs

*c.*1900?
White marble 46 x 25 x 25
(white marble decorated socle 25.5 x 27.5 x 22.5);
carved wooden plinth 112 x 35.5 x 35.5
INSCR: *1855 ARTHUR·WING·PINERO 1934*
(base of socle, picked out in gold)
INV: Gift 527
PROV: Bequeathed by the sitter, 1934

An austerely simple head on a socle ornamented with masks of comedy and tragedy at the corners, joined by swags of laurel and ribbons.

The surmised date is based on the similarity to photographs of Pinero of around 1900.

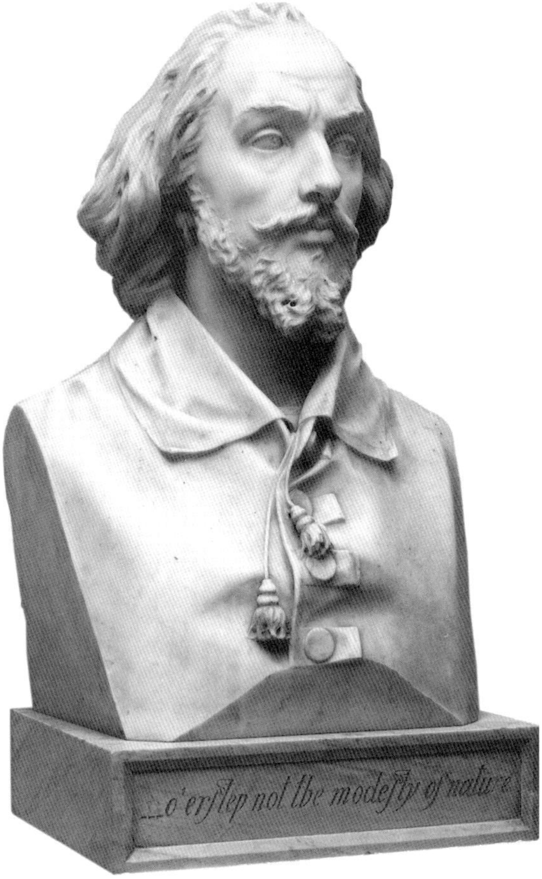

S28
WILLIAM SHAKESPEARE

Augusto Passaglia

*c.*1884
White marble 69 x 39 x 30,
rectangular grey marble base 11 x 44.5 x 34.5
INSCR: *Augto Passaglia Fece / Firenze* (on left shoulder);
– o'erstep not the modesty of nature
(on front of grey marble base)
INV: Gift 232
PROV: Tommaso Salvini, by whom presented
to the Garrick Club, 1884?

The donor, Salvini, paid his first visit to England in 1875, opening with his Othello at Drury Lane on 1 April. He returned the following year and in 1882, and made his farewell appearances at Covent Garden in 1884.

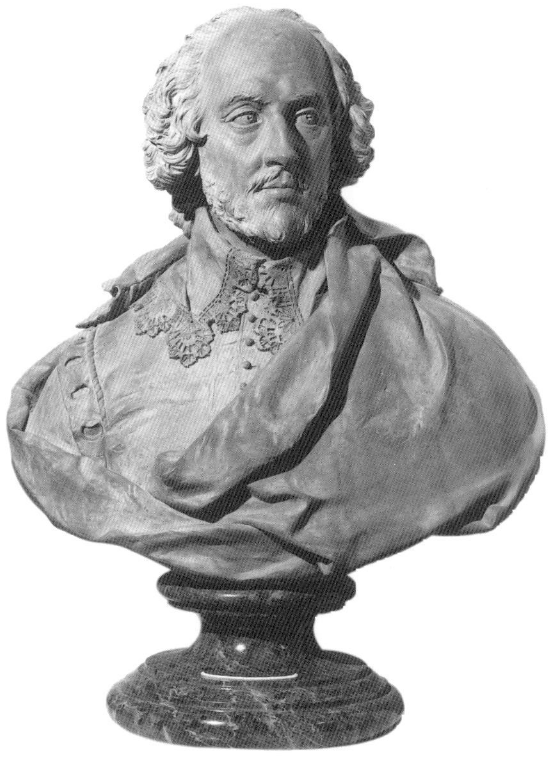

S29*

WILLIAM SHAKESPEARE

Louis François Roubiliac

*c.*1758

Terracotta 62 x 59 x 29, pink marble socle 17 x 35 diam.
(painted terracotta veined with green to complement
the colour of the cleaned bust)
INSCR: *WILLIAM SHAKESPEARE / BY / LOUIS FRANÇOIS ROUBILIAC* in black lettering
on gilded wooden plaque on socle
INV: Gift 139
PROV: Lincoln's Inn Fields Theatre?; Mr Cliff; Professor Owen; the Duke of Devonshire, by whom presented, 1855
EXH: 1896 Shakespeare Memorial Exhibition p. 89
LIT: H. & C. Wood, *Shakespeare's Town and Times* (1896) (frontispiece); Katharine A. Esdaile, *The Life and Works of Louis François Roubiliac* (1928), p. 127, illustrated XLI

The minutes of the Club for 15 December 1855 contain the following letter from the Duke of Devonshire, headed Brighton, 8 December 1855:

> Sir, I have for some time wished to pay a visit to the Garrick Club, and ask you to show me that most interesting collection which belongs to it; but having again left London for some time another delay is caused, and I must write to you to say that there is in my possession a very interesting Bust of Shakespeare, which I wish to present to the Club, as a token of goodwill and also of regrets that the state of my health has hitherto obliged me to appear so remiss as a President. The Bust, which is in terra cotta, was in the possession of Professor Owen of the College of Surgeons, from whom I purchased it. It was discovered in pulling down the old Duke's Theatre in Lincoln's Inn Fields, where it was placed over one of the Stage doors, the Bust of Ben Jonson (accidentally destroyed by the workmen) occupying a corresponding place over the other door – Shakespeare having been rescued by the timely interposition of Mr Cliff (Professor Owen's father-in-law) the Bust became his property and was given by him to Professor Owen. It is my wish to know at what time it will be convenient for the Bust to be received, and Sir Joseph Paxton, in whose possession the Bust now is in Sydenham, will forward it any time if you will inform him or me at what time it should be sent.
>
> Yours &c. *Devonshire*

The provenance is extremely suspect. Lincoln's Inn Fields was built in 1714 and vacated in 1732 when the manager, John Rich, moved to his new theatre in Covent Garden. There were occasional performances for 12 years, the last taking place on 11 December 1744. During the 1745 rebellion, Rich handed over the theatre to the Government to be used as a garrison. It is inconceivable that Roubiliac produced his bust before 1732, and extremely unlikely that it was made before 1744. It appears to relate to the life-size marble figure he produced for Garrick's Shakespeare Temple at Hampton (now in the King's Library in the British Museum). This figure dates from 1758, and although the features of the bust are less lively, the costume is exactly the same.

The bust was cleaned in 1986–87 by J.H. Larson, who produced an important conservation report:

> *Condition before treatment*
>
> The sculpture was not only very dirty but covered with a thick dark brown varnish, which made the terracotta look like bronze.
>
> That this was not likely to be an original treatment was indicated by the number of restorations that were visible through it. Also, at the back of the bust, an iron bar (nearly two feet long) had become detached from the cavity beneath the shoulders and the fact that this had been covered with painted plaster suggested that there had been more than one phase of repair.
>
> The bust was mounted on a large pink marble socle. When it was lifted from the socle the bust, although large, was found to be very light. During transport to my studio some of the terracotta at the back of the bust became detached.
>
> *Treatment*
>
> A range of cleaning tests with various reagents and solvents was carried out on the surface of the sculpture. Of these Nitromors Varnish Remover

proved to be the most effective. This was removed with acetone. However, tests with a Derotor steam cleaner showed that the varnish could be even more effectively removed and with less likelihood of chemical contamination to the terracotta. This system was finally adopted for the full cleaning of the sculpture.

As the surface was gradually revealed by cleaning, several repairs came to light. On Shakespeare's face several long cracks were uncovered. Their position on the face and their precision suggested that they might be the result of a moulding process. It also became clear that the head had been very carefully jointed around the neck and that the head and body had originally been made as two separate pieces.

At the back of the sculpture (along the rim of the shoulders) a great deal of plaster filling was uncovered. Embedded in this was a square-sectioned iron bar (1 [cm] diameter) about 50 [cm] long and this had corroded; it had caused severe cracking of both the plaster and terracotta in this area. With the iron bar removed I could see that the back of the sculpture was in fact hollow. As I chipped away some of the pink plaster infill a gap between the plaster and the back of the terracotta was uncovered. With the removal of a lot more plaster the back of the terracotta was clearly revealed and I could see that it had been carefully roughened with tools very much as one would expect in an 18th century terracotta bust. The back was also very dirty, indicating that this plaster filling had been added some time after the bust had been made.

When I cleared the back of plaster I found that there were two clay ribs running up the centre of the sculpture below the neck. I now concentrated on the joint around the neck. A thin metal band protruded from the neck. I chipped around this and removed it. The band appeared to be made of tin and could well have been the handle from a jug or drinking vessel. With this support removed, the plaster around the neck began to crack. With a little more careful chipping I was able to remove the head from the neck and as I did so two bones were uncovered acting as dowels to secure the head to the neck. It was quite clear that the head and bust had originally been made as separate pieces for both were carefully smoothed along the line of the neck to form a close-fitting joint.

Once the old repairs had been removed and the bust fully dismantled, all of the pieces were carefully cleaned with steam. After drying the pieces were carefully assembled using a polyester adhesive (Sintolit) to bond them together. The joints were then filled with Polyfilla mixed with Artists' dry powder pigment. Then the whole bust was treated with a sealing coat of polyvinyl alcohol and the repairs were retouched with Rowney's Cryla Colour.

A light protective coating of French chalk and dry pigment was dusted over the surface to protect the bust from grease staining produced by handling.

Technique of the Bust

Several discoveries were made during the treatment of the bust, throwing light on the manner in which it was originally made. The sculpture was originally made in a mould and was probably one of a small edition of terracottas of Shakespeare produced by Roubiliac (there is an almost identical bust in the British Museum). Proof that this bust was made in a mould can be deduced from its extreme thinness (little more than 1 [cm] in places) and the fact that the clear joint lines usually the result of piece-moulding were found on the face. The precise jointing of head and neck also suggests that separate elements were made in moulds and joined together with coloured plaster after firing.

The use of bones for dowels (i.e. to secure head to neck) is a technique typically associated with 18th century English sculptures. Also I found in some places a wax-resin adhesive that was in common use at that time. The reason for all this original 18th century restoration can be explained be the fact that damage during firing of the clay into terracotta was a regular occurrence. Rysbrack, Roubiliac, Nollekens and Scheemakers all at one time or another had to restore their own terracottas after firing. They all used very similar techniques and all tended to paint their sculptures after restoration. The Roubiliac Shakespeare was originally painted a dark reddish brown very like that found on his model for the Duke of Argyll monument in the Victoria & Albert Museum.

It is quite clear that this bust had undergone two major restorations, one in the 18th century under the supervision of Roubiliac and a second during the 19th century when the back was filled with plaster and the terracotta was painted to look like bronze.

Two other casts of Roubiliac's bust of Shakespeare are known: that in the British Museum mentioned by Larson and another in the Royal Shakespeare Theatre Memorial Gallery, Stratford-upon-Avon (207). There are differences in the modelling of the head in the British Museum example, although the lower parts are identical. The Shakespeare items in Roubiliac's posthumous sale included eight plaster figures and the mould for the figure, as well as three terracotta and three plaster busts. There was also a mould for the bust and a marble bust.

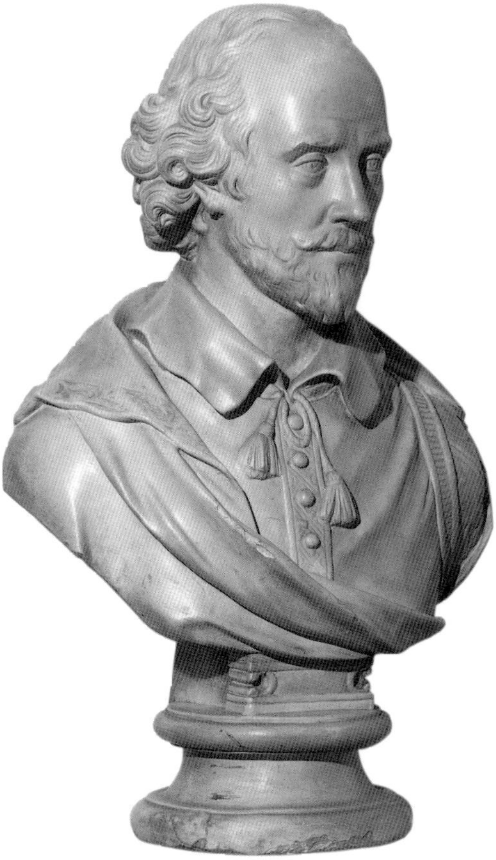

S30
WILLIAM SHAKESPEARE

Benjamin & Robert Shout

*c.*1806
Plaster 55 x 45 x 22, socle 11.5 x 23 diam.
INSCR: *SHOUT* (verso, base of support)
INV: Gift 7, 18 or 33
PROV: Presented by Thomas F. Savany, 1834,
or George Raymond, 1835, or John Poole, 1836

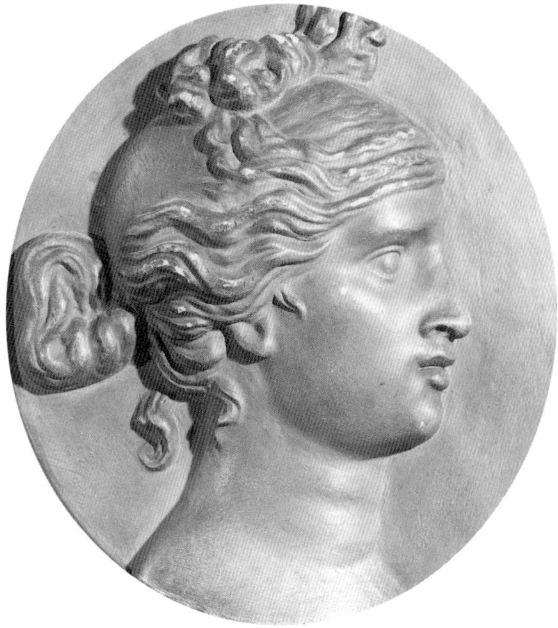

S31
Called
SARAH SIDDONS

Sarah Siddons (attr.)

*c.*1820?
Plaster medallion painted to resemble terracotta
24.5 x 22 (oval)
(ebonised wooden frame 33.5 x 31.5)
INSCR: *Mrs Sarah Siddons / Who lived at 27 Upper ......* (pen & ink on paper covering verso);
Terra Cotta Placque / supposed to have / been modelled / by Sarah Siddons / personally (pen & ink on Miss Dethridge's visiting card);
to the Garrick Club / July 1932 (verso of visiting card)
INV: Gift 491
PROV: Miss Dethridge, by whom presented
to the Garrick Club, 1932

S30 is a copy of a marble bust at Windsor Castle which relates closely to the documented busts of Shakespeare by Scheemakers. Frederick, Prince of Wales, gave busts of Milton, Spenser, Shakespeare and Dryden, all by Scheemakers, to Alexander Pope. There are busts of Shakespeare, Locke, Homer, Cicero and Milton by Scheemakers in Trinity College, Dublin. However, the stamp on the verso of S30 indicates that the bust was produced by the Shout firm, which was active from 1778 to 1827 and was well known for producing plaster casts. In 1806 they made a series of plaster busts for Lord Bridport's library; Shakespeare would have been included. Another series of busts was provided for Salters's Hall in 1827; they were destroyed in 1940.

Although this profile bears some general resemblance to Siddons, it is perhaps simply an ideal head of a type popular in the neo-classical period. It has the soft modelling seen in the self-portrait bust in the Theatre Museum.

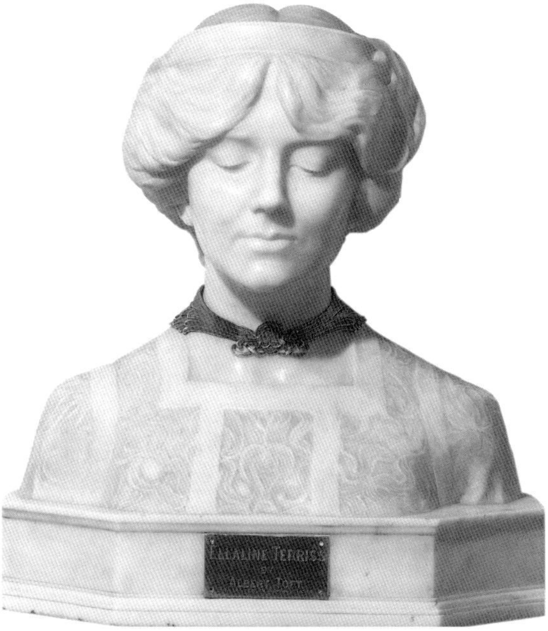

S32

ELLALINE TERRISS

Albert Toft

1901
White marble and enamelled metal 48.5 x 46 x 24
INSCR: *ELLA* (monogram at front of metal necklet);
ELLALINE TERRISS / BY / ALBERT TOFT / PRESENTED BY SEYMOUR HICKS / 1923
(on brass plaque on base)
INV: Gift 411
PROV: Presented by the sitter and her husband, Seymour Hicks, 1923

A small bronze version (on a marble base) of S32 was sold at Sotheby's, Belgravia, on 28 May 1975 (lot 39). It was signed and dated *10.9.1*.

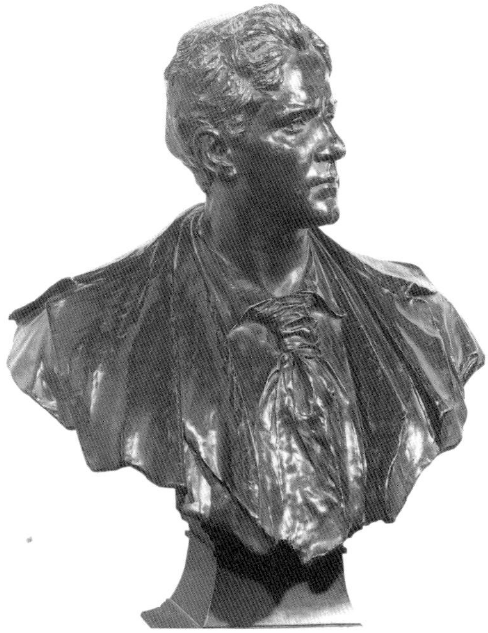

S33

WILLIAM TERRISS

Albert Toft

1908
Bronze 64 x 65 x 42 (red marble base 21 x 28 x 26)
INSCR: *Albert Toft / 1908* (on left shoulder);
WILLIAM TERRISS / 1847–1897 / PRESENTED / BY / SEYMOUR HICKS ESQ. / 1927
(on brass plaque on wooden base)
INV: Gift 445
PROV: Sir Seymour Hicks, by whom presented to the Garrick Club, 1927
EXH: 1909 R.A. (1806) 'The late William Terriss';
1909 S.P.P. (172) 'The late William Terriss'

See also No. 797.

S34

NOT ILLUSTRATED

WILLIAM MAKEPEACE THACKERAY

Sir Joseph Edgar Boehm

1864
Plaster 53.3 high
INV: Gift 174
PROV: Presented by the artist, 1864
EXH: 1864 R.A. (959) (one of an unknown number of casts)

Thackeray is shown full-length, standing, hands in pockets. Further examples of this edition are in the National Portrait Gallery (1282) and the Athenæum Club.

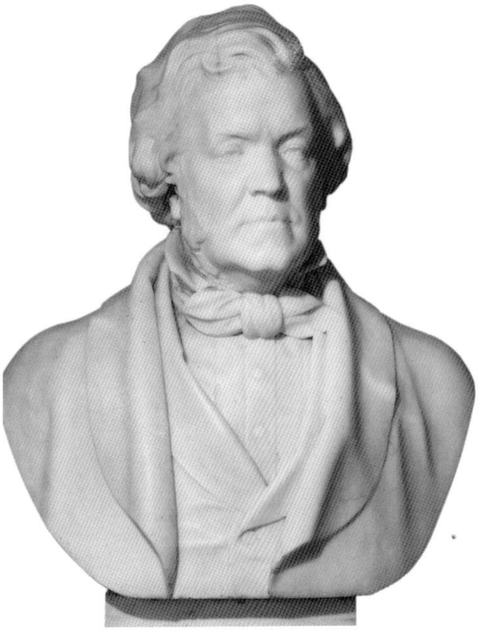

S35*
WILLIAM MAKEPEACE THACKERAY

Joseph Durham

*c.*1863
White marble 67 x 63 x 28 (white marble socle with bowed front 8 x 31 x 17.5; red & green marble plinth 99 x 35.5 x 35; white marble base 24 x 55 x 55)
INSCR: *W.M. THACKERAY / BY / JOSEPH DURHAM, A.R.A. / PRESENTED TO THE GARRICK CLUB / BY THE SCULPTOR* (on front of marble plinth, touched in gold)
INV: Gift 178
PROV: Presented by the artist, 1864

See also Nos. 805–807.

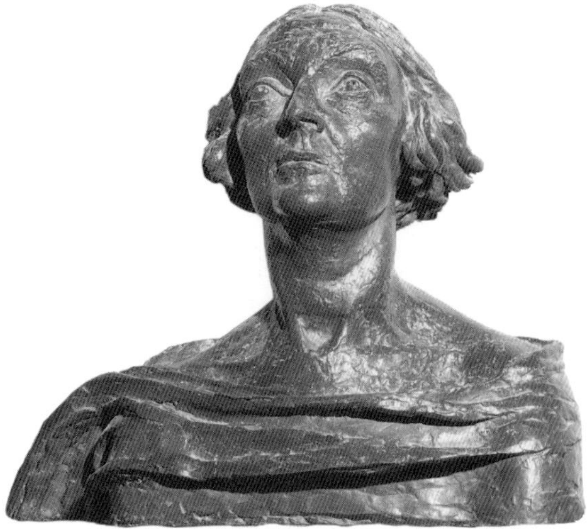

S36
DAME SYBIL THORNDIKE

Sir Jacob Epstein

1925
Bronze 49.5 x 62 x 26.5 (wooden plinth 119.5 x 35.5 x 35.5)
INSCR: *SYBIL THORNDIKE / by EPSTEIN / PRESENTED BY SIR BRONSON ALBERY / 693* (gold painted plaque on plinth)
INV: Gift 777
PROV: Sir Bronson Albery, by whom presented to the Garrick Club, 1960
LIT: *The Sculptor Speaks: Jacob Epstein to Arnold L. Haskell* (1931) illustrated opposite p. 34, listed in catalogue as 1925, p. 184; Richard Buckle, *Jacob Epstein, Sculptor* (1963), p. 140, No. 216, p. 426; Evelyn Silber, *The Sculpture of Epstein* (1986), p. 158, No. 161

There is a version of this bust in the collection of John Casson dated 1924, although Buckle lists it as one of Epstein's eight 1925 portrait busts. Buckle suggests that the upward gaze and bobbed hair are reminders of the sitter's great success as St Joan (1924–25).

Sybil Thorndike was one of the signatories to Muirhead Bone's letter to *The Times* of 23 November 1925 objecting to a proposal to remove Epstein's controversial sculpture *Rima* from Hyde Park.

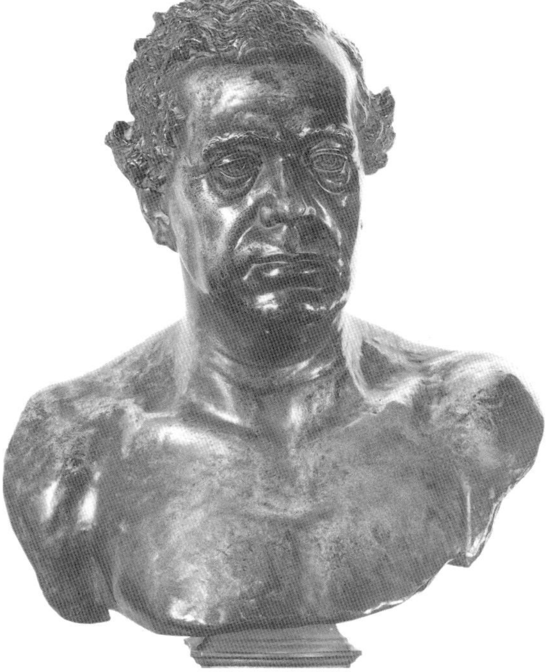

S37
JOHN LAWRENCE TOOLE

Richard C. Belt

1885
Bronze 60.3 x 41.5 x 27.5 (base 19 x 16.5)
INSCR: *R. Belt* (verso)
INV: Gift 321
PROV: Bequeathed by the sitter, 1906
EXH: 1885 R.A. (2004)

See also Nos. 810–812.

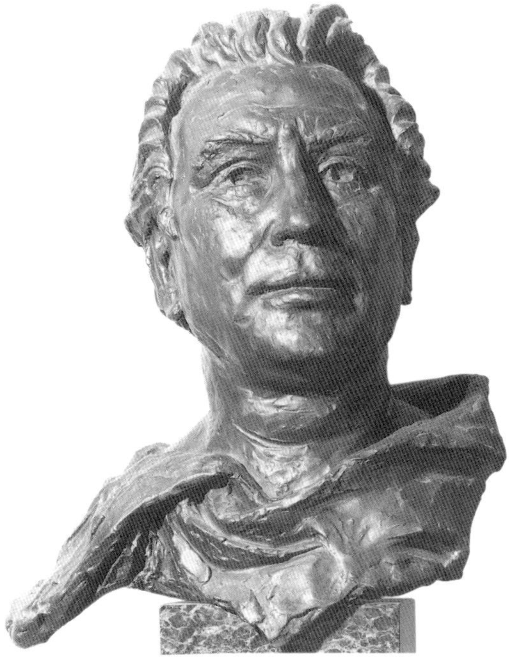

S38
SIR DONALD WOLFIT

Sir Charles Wheeler

1962
Bronze 46 x 37 x 25 (green marble base 12.7 x 17 x 16, on wooden base 18.5 x 32.5 x 25)
INSCR: *CW/1962* (in drapery on left shoulder); *SIR DONALD WOLFIT / by Sir Charles Wheeler, P.R.A.* (plaque in base)
INV: Gift 875
PROV: Presented by the Robin Hood Theatre, Averham, 1977
EXH: 1962 R.A. (1121)

See also Nos. 43 and 850.

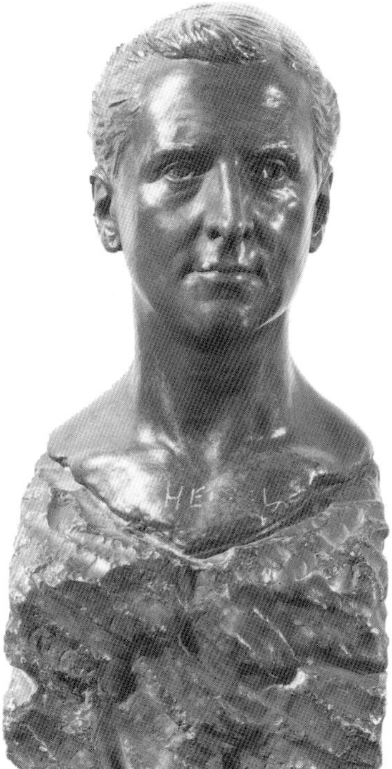

S39
SIR CHARLES YOUNG (?)

A.C. Lauder (?)

1889?
Bronze on brown mottled marble base 14.5 x 11 x 7
(head only); 22 x 11 x 8.5 (with base)
INSCR: *A.C. Lauder 89* (on verso, almost illegible)
INV: Gift 222?
PROV: Lady Alcock, by whom presented
to the Garrick Club, 1890?

If this bust is No. 222 in the list of gifts, then it is of Sir Charles Young.

S40
NOT ILLUSTRATED
UNKNOWN SITTER

Anonymous British School

c. 1850?
Plaster 29 x 19 x 11.5 (including attached socle);
some damage to nose
INV: Not listed
PROV: Unknown

Bust, head turned slightly to left; stiff dog-collar, cravat with pin, and jacket.

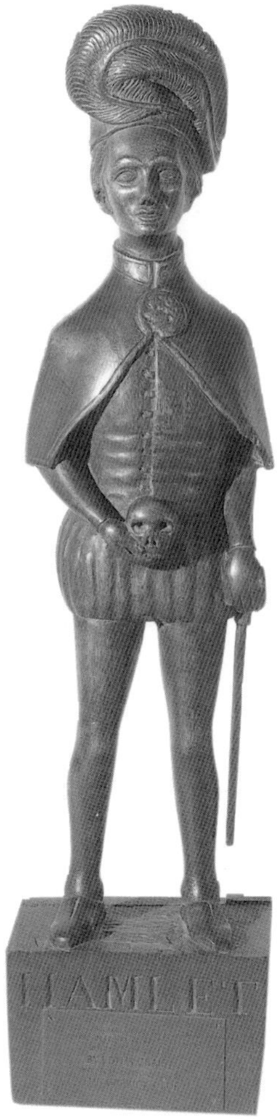

S41
Figure of Hamlet

Anonymous Amateur

19th century
Oak 58 x 16.5 x 11 (figure only); 67.5 x 16.5 x 11
(including 2 pieces fixed to back of base as support)
INSCR: *HAMLET* on front of base; *FIGURE OF HAMLET / FOUND IN HENRY IRVING'S DRESSING / ROOM AT THE LYCEUM / BY EDITH CRAIG / AND BEQUEATHED BY HER TO / THE GARRICK CLUB*
on brass plaque attached to base
INV: Gift 769
PROV: Henry Irving; Edith Craig, by whom
bequeathed to the Garrick Club, 1959

A crude work, ultimately based on Lawrence's portrait of John Philip Kemble as Hamlet (see No. 386). From the painting derive the plumed hat and the casually placed skull. The carver did not understand the point of the Order of the Elephant, which has been turned into a clasp. If the provenance is correct, it is likely that Irving was given this carving by an admirer.

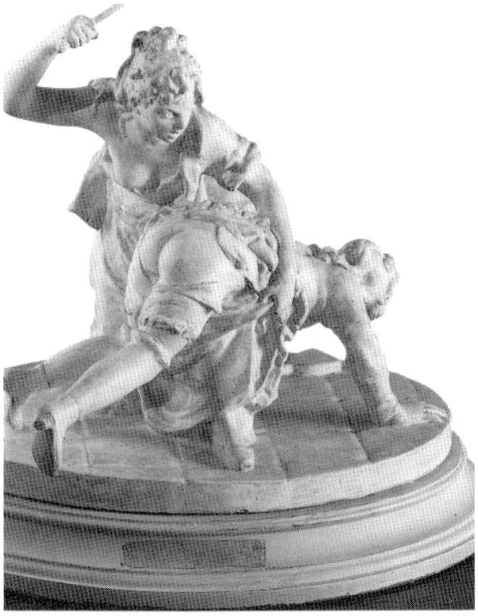

S42
'The Clumsy Dairy Maid'

French School?

*c.*1890?
Plaster 24 x 29 x 19.5 (wooden base 4.5 x 34.5 x 22.5)
INSCR: (Old label on base has been peeled off)
INV: Not in inventory
PROV: Unknown

The subject matter is characteristic of certain works of decorative sculpture produced in France in the late 19th century.

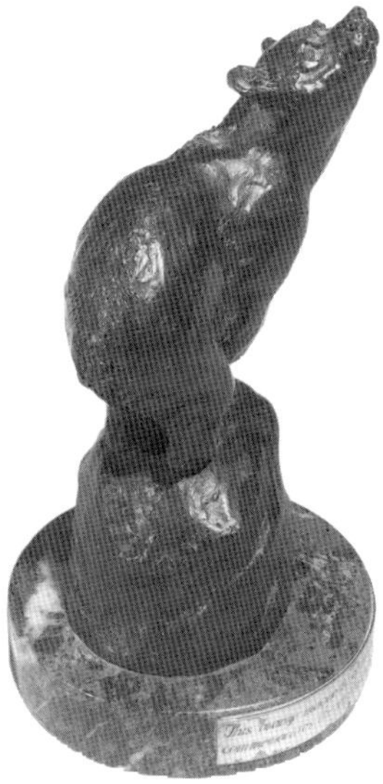

S43
A Bear on a Rock

Laura McKean

Bronze 16 x 9 x 6.5 (green marble base 2 x 10 diam.)
INSCR: *Laura / McKean II* (verso on base of rock);
This bronze maquette of the memorial to A.A. Milne at the London Zoo / commemorates the refurbishment and naming of the A.A. Milne room. Sept. 1964
(brass plaque on base)
PROV: Unknown

RECENT ACQUISITIONS & ADDITIONS

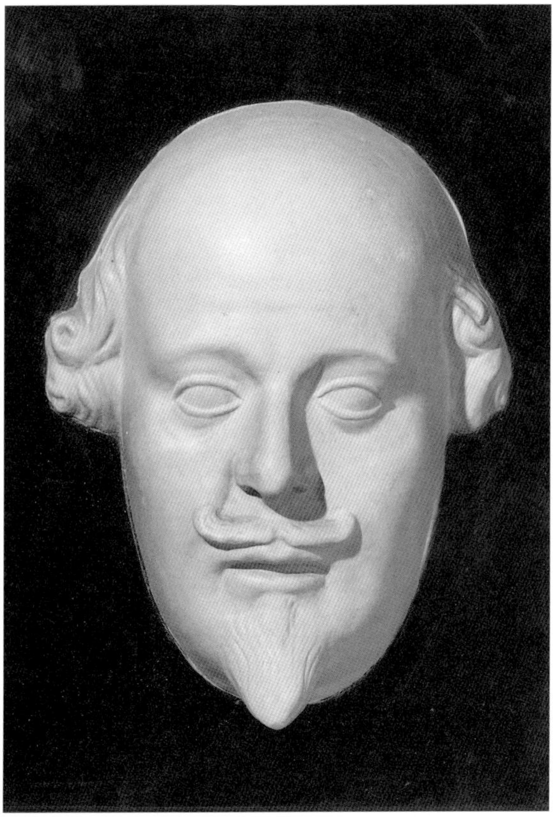

S44
Face Mask of
WILLIAM SHAKESPEARE
1564–1616

Cast by Warner

White mask on black frame, approx. 26 high,
cast from the Stratford monument
PROV: Harold Rubenstein; Michael Rubenstein, who inherited from his father Harold Rubenstein; presented to the Garrick Club by Hilary & Harold Rubenstein, 1992
REL: National Portrait Gallery

Appended to the back of the frame was a label stating:

> Shakespeare's Death Mask. Taken from the monument in Holy Trinity Church, Stratford-upon-Avon. One of a small number of casts made by one Warner, in 1840, without authority. He was ordered to destroy the matrix and casts, which was duly done before witnesses, but a few survived; one of these was bequeathed by Mr. Kite, Parish Clerk at the time of the incident, to Mr. R. Savage, then librarian of the birthplace, and another is in the National Portrait Gallery. Extremely rare.

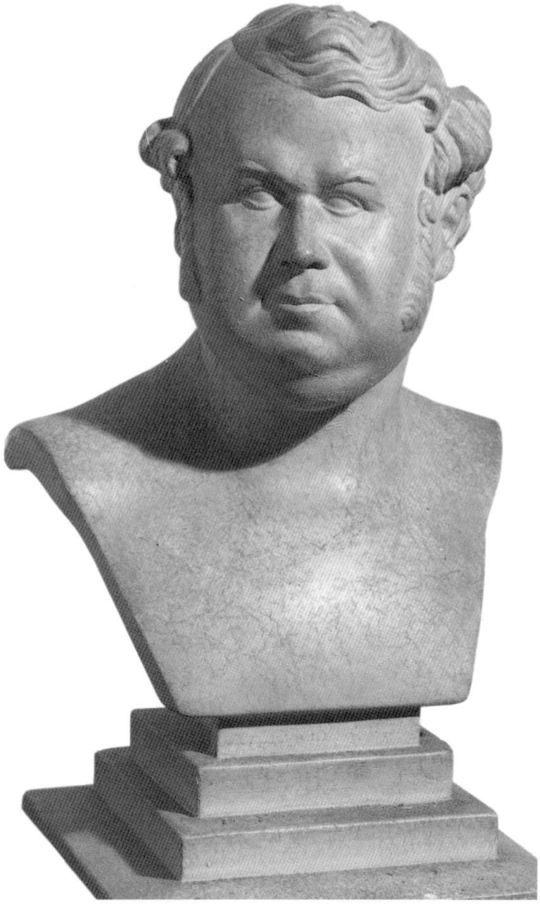

S45
WILLIAM ROBERT HICKS
1808–1868

Unknown artist

Plaster bust, head 22 high on plaster base
INSCR: *With native intellect and polish'd mind*
Keen to perceive and in perception kind;
With store of humour and with matchless power
To make e'en dulness pass a joyous hour
With social magic to make pride unbend,
The foe of selfishness, – the firmest friend.
(ink on paper on base)
PROV: Unknown

If you add to that a mordant wit, princely reserve, a touching vulnerability and sensitivity, and an overwhelming charm, you knew that this was a performance in which all choices had been considered and made, and all avenues explored.'

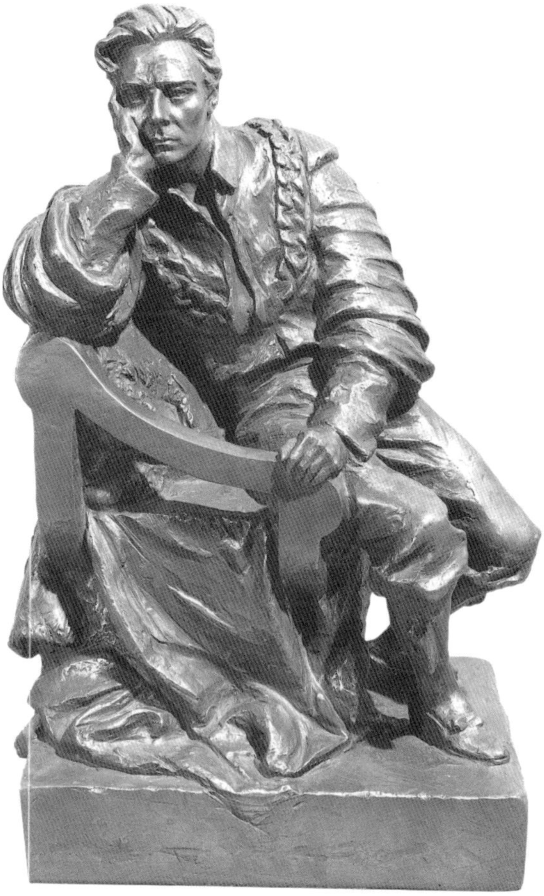

S46
SIR JOHN GIELGUD
as Hamlet in *Hamlet*
by William Shakespeare

Irena Sedlecka

1993
Resin bronze cast 32.5 high, including base
(No. 22 of an edition of 250)
PROV: C. Anthony Hart R.I.B.A.; Richard Bebb, by whom presented to the Garrick Club, 1996
(see also S47, S50, S51, S52 and S53)

Gielgud first acted Hamlet at the Old Vic in 1928 'with electrifying success' and the production was later transferred to the West End. He played the role again at the New Theatre in 1934, in a production directed by himself and with costumes by Motley; the figure has been modelled in the costume designed for this production.

Richard Bebb, in his catalogue *Great Actors and Singers*, writes about seeing Gielgud in a revival of the play at the Haymarket in 1944: 'He is the only actor I have ever seen who has the swiftness of thought and mercuriality of temperament to embrace Hamlet's "racing mind".

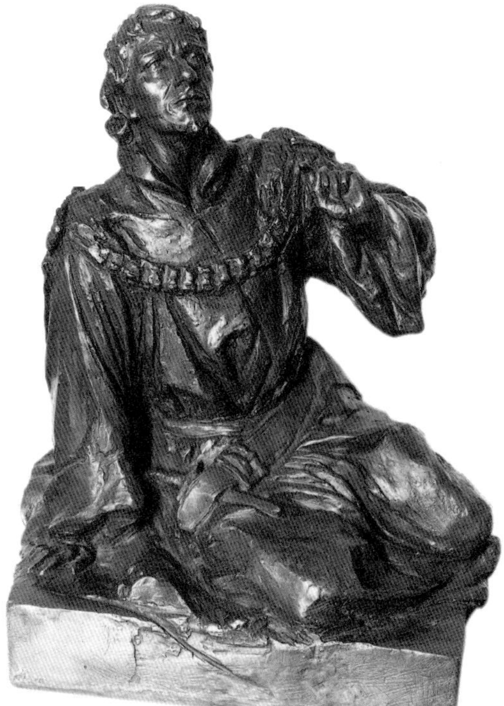

S47
SIR JOHN GIELGUD
as Richard in *Richard II*
by William Shakespeare

Irena Sedlecka

1993
Resin bronze cast 29.2 high, including base
(No. 19 of an edition of 250)
INSCR: '© I. Sedlecka '93' with '19' below (back of base)
PROV: Commissioned by Richard Bebb (see also S46, S50, S51, S52 and S53); C. Anthony Hart R.I.B.A., by whom presented to the Garrick Club, 1996

Richard is seated on the ground, evoking his speech in Act III, scene 2: 'For God's sake, let us sit upon the ground, / And tell sad stories of the death of kings.' Gielgud was a great success when he first acted Richard II, a role 'he was born to play', in the 1929–30 season at the Old Vic.

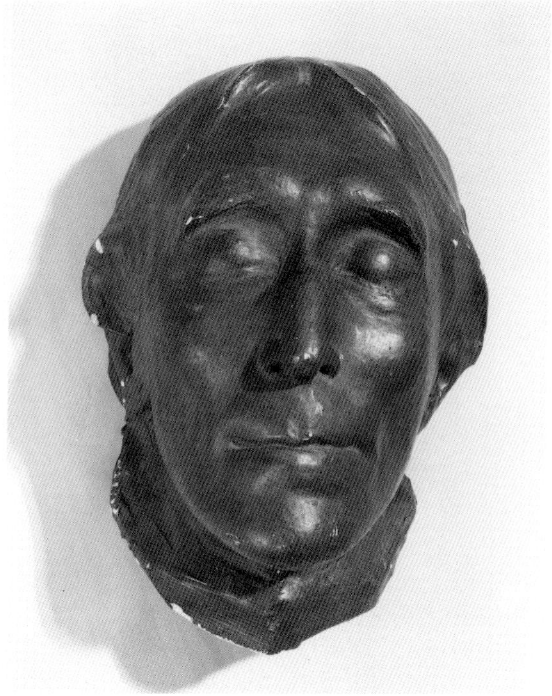

S48
SIR HENRY IRVING
Death Mask

Unknown Sculptor

Plaster approx. 31 x 22

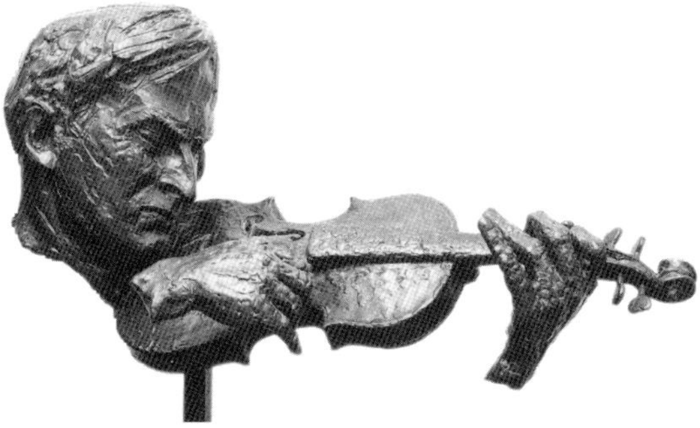

S49
SIR YEHUDI MENUHIN
*b.*1916

David Wynne

Bronze 77 high, including base (one of 12)
PROV: David Wynne, by whom presented to the Club, 1996

The bronze includes only the head, slightly over life-size, and the hands holding a violin. It is the artist's cast of an edition of 12, 1962. Menuhin became a member of the Garrick Club in 1956.

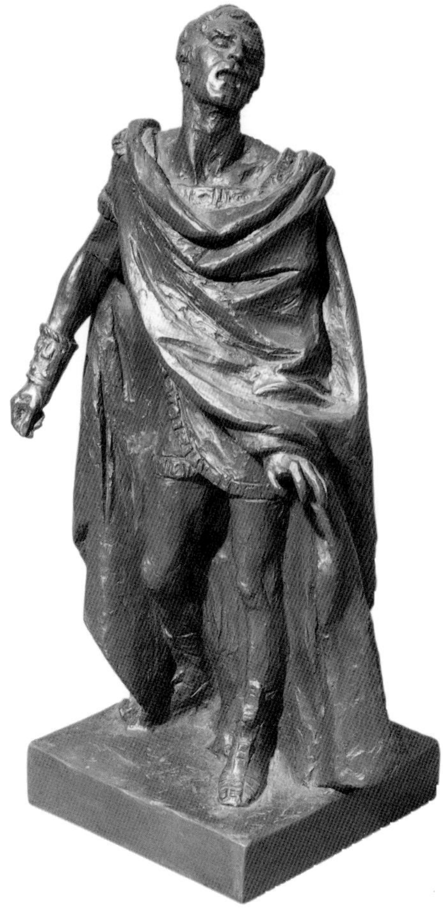

S50
SIR LAURENCE OLIVIER
as Œdipus in *Œdipus* by Sophocles

Irena Sedlecka

1990
Resin bronze cast 43.2 high, including base
(No. 21 of an edition of 250)
PROV: Commissioned by Richard Bebb
(see also S46, S47, S51, S52 and S53)
by whom presented to the Garrick Club, 1996

Olivier's agonised expression marks the moment of the great scream, when Œdipus realises that he has killed his father and slept with his mother. It is described by Richard Bebb in his catalogue *Great Actors and Singers*: 'There was a long pause while the whole house held its breath. He stood perfectly still, threw his head back, and emitted from a distended throat two of the most blood-curdling screams that can ever be heard in any theatre.' Olivier's performance as *Œdipus* was presented by the Old Vic Company at the New Theatre in 1945 as part of an astonishing double bill that also included *The Critic* (see S51).

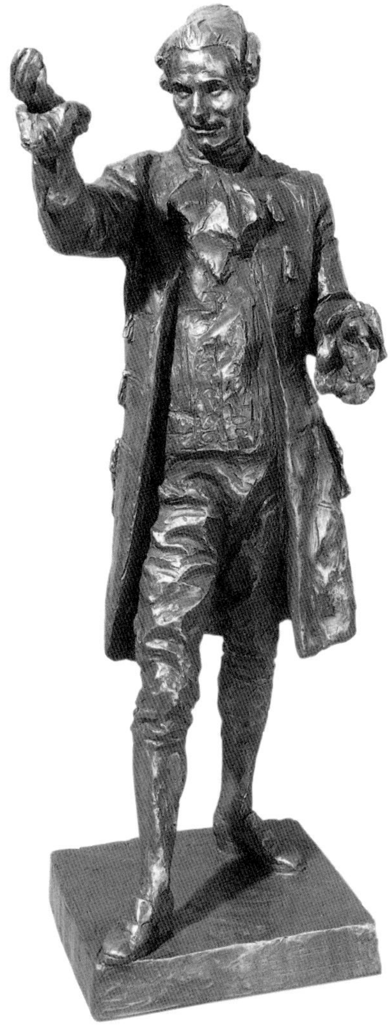

S51
SIR LAURENCE OLIVIER
as Mr Puff in *The Critic*
by Richard Brinsley Sheridan

Irena Sedlecka

1991
Resin bronze cast 43.2 high, including base
(No. 22 of an edition of 250)
PROV: Commissioned by Richard Bebb
(see also S46, S47, S50, S52 and S53), by whom
presented to the Garrick Club, 1996

The Critic formed part of a double bill with *Œdipus* (see S50) at the New Theatre in 1945.

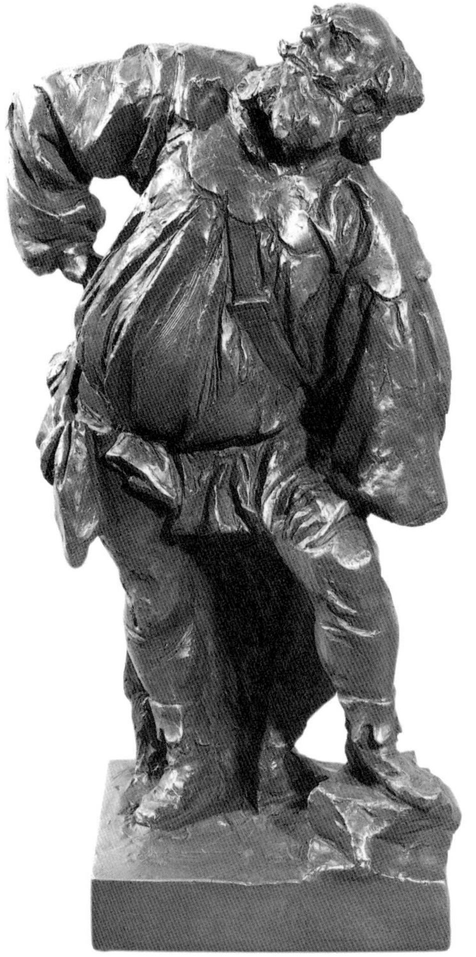

S52
SIR RALPH RICHARDSON
as Falstaff in *1 Henry IV*
by William Shakespeare

Irena Sedlecka

1994
Resin bronze cast 42.3 high, including base
(No. 16 of an edition of 250)
PROV: Commissioned by Richard Bebb
(see also S46, S47, S50, S51 and S53), by whom
presented to the Garrick Club, 1996

The figure captures the moment when Falstaff, thinking himself abandoned at Gadshill, cries out 'Poins! Hal! A plague upon you both!' (Act II, scene 2).

Richardson played Falstaff in a revival of *1 Henry IV* during the 1945–46 Old Vic season at the New Theatre, when his portrayal was described as 'overwhelmingly loveable' whilst shrewd, garrulous and unprincipled. Richard Bebb declared: 'Every Falstaff I have seen since has seemed no more than an impostor.'

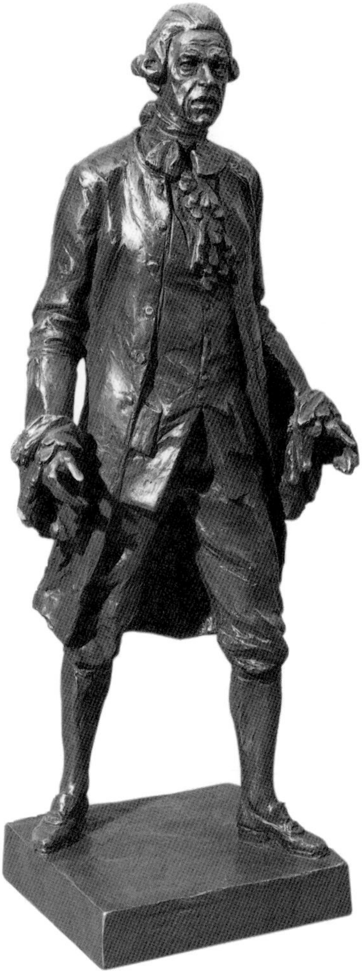

S53
PAUL SCOFIELD
as Salieri in *Amadeus*
by Peter Shaffer

Irena Sedlecka

1992
Resin bronze cast 43.8 high, including base
(No. 12 of an edition of 250)
PROV: Commissioned by Richard Bebb
(see also S46, S47, S50, S51 and S52), by whom
presented to the Garrick Club, 1996

Amadeus opened at the National Theatre on 2 November 1979 with Scofield as Salieri. The performance was one of his greatest triumphs, described by Richard Bebb in his catalogue, *Great Actors and Singers*: '... his grace, intelligence and hypnotic charm mesmerised the audience into a complete understanding of the struggle raging within him which eventually would destroy his very soul ... It is impossible to believe that his wonderful performance will ever be equalled, let alone surpassed.'

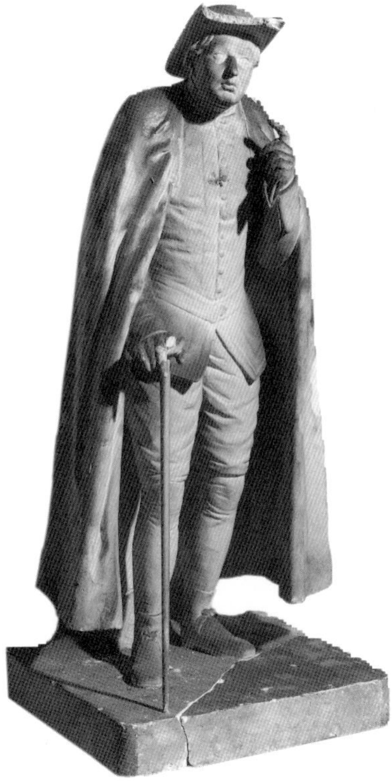

S54
UNKNOWN MAN

Unknown Sculptor

Plaster approx. 67 high

The subject, evidently in character, stands on a plaster base, which is cracked.

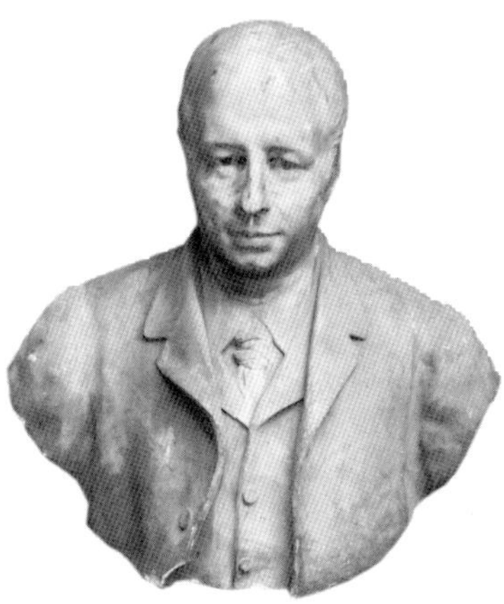

S55
UNKNOWN MAN

Conrad Dressler

Marble bust approx. 62 high
INSCR: 'Conrad Dressler 1888' (back left shoulder)

INDEX OF SITTERS

with bibliographical references (see page LXI for abbreviations)

INDEX OF ARTISTS

INDEX OF PLAYS

The plays are arranged alphabetically, with the author's name followed by catalogue number(s), in bold type, and the name(s) of performer(s) and part(s) played. Full names of performers are to be found in the Index of Sitters.

INDEX OF FORMER OWNERS

The numbers in bold type following owners' names refer to the relevant catalogue entries.

EXHIBITIONS

Exhibitions are arranged chronologically, followed by catalogue numbers in bold type. Exhibition numbers may be found in the relevant catalogue entries.

1864 LONDON: *Royal Academy*: **S34**

1880 LONDON: *Royal Academy*: **S1**

1881 LONDON: *Royal Academy*: **S2**; Grosvenor Gallery, *Summer Exhibition*: **102**

1883 LONDON: *Royal Academy*: **395**

1884 LONDON: *Royal Academy*: **323**; *Royal Institute*: **356**

1885 LONDON: *Royal Academy*: **949**; **S21** (?); **S37**

1886 LONDON: Grosvenor Gallery, *Summer Exhibition*: **323**; *Royal Academy*: **414**

1888 LONDON: *Royal Academy*: **356**; **860**

1889 LONDON: *New Gallery*: **802**

1892 LONDON: New Gallery, *Victorian Exhibition*: **949**

1893 LONDON: *Royal Academy*: **282**

1896 STRATFORD-UPON-AVON: *Shakespeare Memorial Exhibition*: **S29**

1897 LONDON: *Victorian Exhibition*: **270**

1902 LONDON: *Royal Academy*: **7**; **91**

1903 LONDON: *Royal Society of Portrait Painters*: **200**

1904 LONDON: *Royal Academy*: **820**

1908 LONDON: *Royal Academy*: **283**

1909 LONDON: *Royal Academy*: **S33**; *Royal Society of Portrait Painters*: **7**; **S33**

1913 LONDON: *Royal Academy*: **230**

1915 LONDON: *Royal Academy*: **138**

1917 LONDON: *Royal Society of Portrait Painters*: **638**

1919 LONDON: *Royal Society of Portrait Painters*: **230** (?)

1920 LONDON: *Royal Society of Portrait Painters*: **329**

1923 LONDON: *Royal Society of Portrait Painters*: **173**

1924 LONDON: *Royal Academy*: **86**; **S20** (?)

1925 LONDON: *Royal Academy*: **457**

1928 LONDON: *Royal Academy*: **60**

1929 LONDON: *Royal Academy*: **S6**

1931 LONDON: *Royal Academy*: **299**

1933 LONDON: Dudley House, *Theatre Exhibition*: **390**; *Royal Academy*: **851**

1934 LONDON: Royal Academy, *British Art*: **1**; **23**; **42**; **147**; **260**; **267**; **336**; **458**; **680**
PARIS: Salon: **851**

1935 LONDON: Victoria & Albert Museum, *George Sheringham Memorial Exhibition*: **933**; *Royal Academy*: **18**

1938 LONDON: *Royal Academy*: **729**; *Royal Society of Portrait Painters*: **444**

1940 LONDON: *Royal Academy*: **53**

1945/46 LONDON (Kensington Art Gallery), NOTTINGHAM, BURTON-ON-TRENT, SUNDERLAND, LIVERPOOL, ROTHERHAM &C.: *George Sheringham 1884–1937 Memorial Exhibition*: **933**

1947 LONDON: Arts Council, National Book League, *A History of Shakespeare Production*: **49**; **651**; **769**

1948 PARIS: Bibliothèque nationale (British Council exhibition), *La Vie Britannique à Paris*: **249**

1949 BIRMINGHAM: City Museum and Art Gallery, *Painters and the Theatre*: **23**; **116**; **669**; **794**; **845**;
PORT SUNLIGHT: Lady Lever Art Gallery, *Theatre Exhibition*: **23**; **116**; **261**; **276**; **323**; **671**; **794**; **845**

1950 LONDON: *George Harcourt Memorial Exhibition*: **230**

1950–51 LONDON: Royal Academy, *British Painting* (?): **39**; **124**; **151**; **171**; **411**; **463**; **468**; **469**; **477**; **613**; **630**; **847**

1951 EXETER: Royal Albert Memorial Museum, *Exeter Artists* (?): **696**

1951 LONDON: Tate Gallery, *Pictures from the Garrick Club*: **1**; **12**; **23**; **33**; **39**; **40**; **42**; **49**; **71**; **98**; **116**; **117**; **124**; **147**; **151**; **184**; **210**; **229**; **240**; **249**; **250**; **252**; **253**; **256**; **317**; **323**; **352**; **385**; **399**; **401**; **415**; **429**; **468**; **469**; **477**; **622**; **639**; **662**; **672**; **675**; **676**; **680**; **704**; **715**; **726**; **752**; **769**; **794**; **805**; **838**; **847**; **863**

1951–52 LONDON: Royal Academy, *The First 100 Years of the Royal Academy 1769–1868*: **39**; **124**; **151**; **171**; **196**; **411**; **463**; **468**; **469**; **477**; **613**; **630**; **653**

1954–55 LONDON: Royal Academy, *European Masters of the Eighteenth Century*: **23**

1955–56 LONDON: Royal Academy, *English Taste in the Eighteenth Century*: **471**; **715**

1956–57 LONDON: Royal Academy, *British Portraits*: **40**

1957 LONDON: Guildhall Art Gallery, *William Hogarth*: **98**; **672**; **706**; **717**

1958 LIVERPOOL: Walker Art Gallery, *Painting and Sculpture in England 1700–1750*: **116**; **847**;
LONDON: Arts Council, St. James's Square, *Royal Opera House, Covent Garden 100th Anniversary*: **154**; **717**; **825**; **826**; **827**

1959 LICHFIELD: Lichfield Public Library and Museum, *Johnson Anniversary Exhibition*: **252**;
LONDON: Art Exhibitions Arena (?), *Maurice Codner Memorial Exhibition*: **299**

1960 LONDON: Kenwood House, *Francis Hayman*: **49**; Arts Council, *Johann Zoffany*: **429**; *Royal Society of Portrait Painters*: **53**

1962 LONDON: *Royal Academy*: **S38**;
CHICHESTER: Chichester Antiques Ltd., *The Painter and the Stage*: **121**; **202**; **209**; **268**; **285**; **303**; **366**; **371**; **378**; **451**; **471**; **602**; **657**; **715**; **724**

1964 LONDON: Arts Council, *Shakespeare in Art*: **49**; **253**; Guildhall Art Gallery, *Shakespeare and the Theatre*: **94**; **123**; **246**; **297**; **386**; **391**; **394**; **401**; **620**; **651**; **742**; **743**; **866**; Arthur Tooth & Sons, *Exhibition of New Sculpture by David Wynne*: **S18**;
NOTTINGHAM: Nottingham University Art Gallery, *Shakespeare in Art*: **253** (in catalogue but not loaned)

1965 LONDON: Kenwood House, *The Conversation Piece in Georgian London*: **39**; **471**; **695**; **717**

1968 EASTBOURNE / LONDON: Towner Art Gallery / Kenwood House, *John Hamilton Mortimer A.R.A. 1740–1779*: **59**

1968–69 LONDON: Royal Academy, *Royal Academy Bicentenary Exhibition 1768–1968*: **23**

1969 YORK / LONDON: York City Art Gallery / Kenwood House, *Philip Mercier*: **847**

1971 NORTHAMPTON: Northampton Central Art Gallery, *The De Wildes*: **12**; **71**; **80**; **303**; **394**; **434**; **438**; **607**; **644**; **656**; **658**; **698**; **837**; **852**; **873**

1972 LONDON / DUBLIN: National Portrait Gallery / National Gallery of Ireland, *Daniel Maclise 1806–1870*: **806**;
LONDON: *Royal Society of Portrait Painters*: **813**; TUNBRIDGE WELLS: Tunbridge Wells Civic Society, *Les eaux de Scandal*: **242**

1973 YORK: York City Art Gallery, *'A Candidate for Praise', William Mason (1725–97), Precentor of York*: **123**; **239**

1974 FOLKESTONE: Arts Centre, New Metropole, The Leas, *Edwardian Exhibition*: **794**;
LONDON: Marlborough Fine Art, *Edward Seago Memorial Loan Exhibition*: **139**; **751**; **762**;
TWICKENHAM: Orleans House Gallery, *Garrick to Kean*: **121**; **125**; **201**; **244**; **343**; **349**; **845**

1975 BRADFORD: Cartwright Hall, *Edwardian Reflections*: **794**;
BRIGHTON: Brighton Art Gallery and Museum, *Gothick*: **55**; **237**; **351**;
LONDON: Hayward Gallery, *The Georgian Playhouse*: **3**; **35**; **72**; **116**; **130**; **146**; **220**; **235**; **239**; **249**; **258**; **272**; **334**; **384**; **390**; **469**; **471**; **619**; **632**; **646**; **653**; **742**; **743**; **744**; **761**; **765**; **773**; **798**; **853**; **855**; **859**;
MILAN: Palazzo Reale (British Council exhibition), *British Painting*: **39**; **401**; **651**; **715**

1977 LONDON: National Portrait Gallery, *Johan Zoffany 1733–1810*: **23**; **411**; **429**; South London Art Gallery, *Val Prinsep – a Jubilee Painter*: **395**

1979 BONN / SUNDERLAND: Rheinisches Landesmuseum / Tyne & Wear County Council Museum, *The Spectacular Career of Clarkson Stanfield 1793–1867*: **156**; **270**; **805**; **935**;
LONDON: Royal Academy, *Derby Day 200*: **892**; Old Vic Theatre Outer Foyer & Circle Bar Gallery, *We shall not look upon his like again*: **248**

1980 BUXTON: Buxton Museum and Art Gallery, *Shakespeare Heroines in the Nineteenth Century*: **266**; **804**;
NOTTINGHAM: Castle Museum, *George Sheringham*: **795**; **933**;
TWICKENHAM: Orleans House Gallery, *Horace Walpole and Strawberry Hill*: **290**

1981 BUXTON: Buxton Museum and Art Gallery, *Thirty Different Likenesses: David Garrick in Portrait and in Performance*: **235**; **237**; **239**; **245**;
TOKYO: Mitsukoshi Museum of Art, *Age of Shakespeare*: **244**; **386**; **800**

1982–83 LONDON: Royal Academy, *Royal Opera House Retrospective 1732–1982*: **59**; **87**; **120**; **132**; **210**; **306**; **352**; **460**; **477**; **597**; **603**; **633**; **677**; **683**; **701**; **716**; **717**; **796**

1983 BUXTON: Buxton Museum and Art Gallery, *Tale Retold. Boccaccio's Decameron 17th Century to 19th Century*: **89**; **364**; **395**; **768**

1984 LONDON: Museum of London, *Paintings, Politics and Porter. Samuel Whitbread II (1764–1815) and British Art*: **352**

1986 MONTGOMERY, ALABAMA: Montgomery Museum of Fine Arts, *A Brush with Shakespeare*: **123**

1987 TWICKENHAM: Orleans House Gallery, *Music Hath Charms*: **716**

1987 YALE / LONDON: British Art Center / Kenwood House, *Francis Hayman*: **49**

1987–88 LONDON: Theatre Museum, *Sir John Gielgud Exhibition*: **262**

1988 LONDON: Sotheby's, *Childhood Exhibition*: **608**

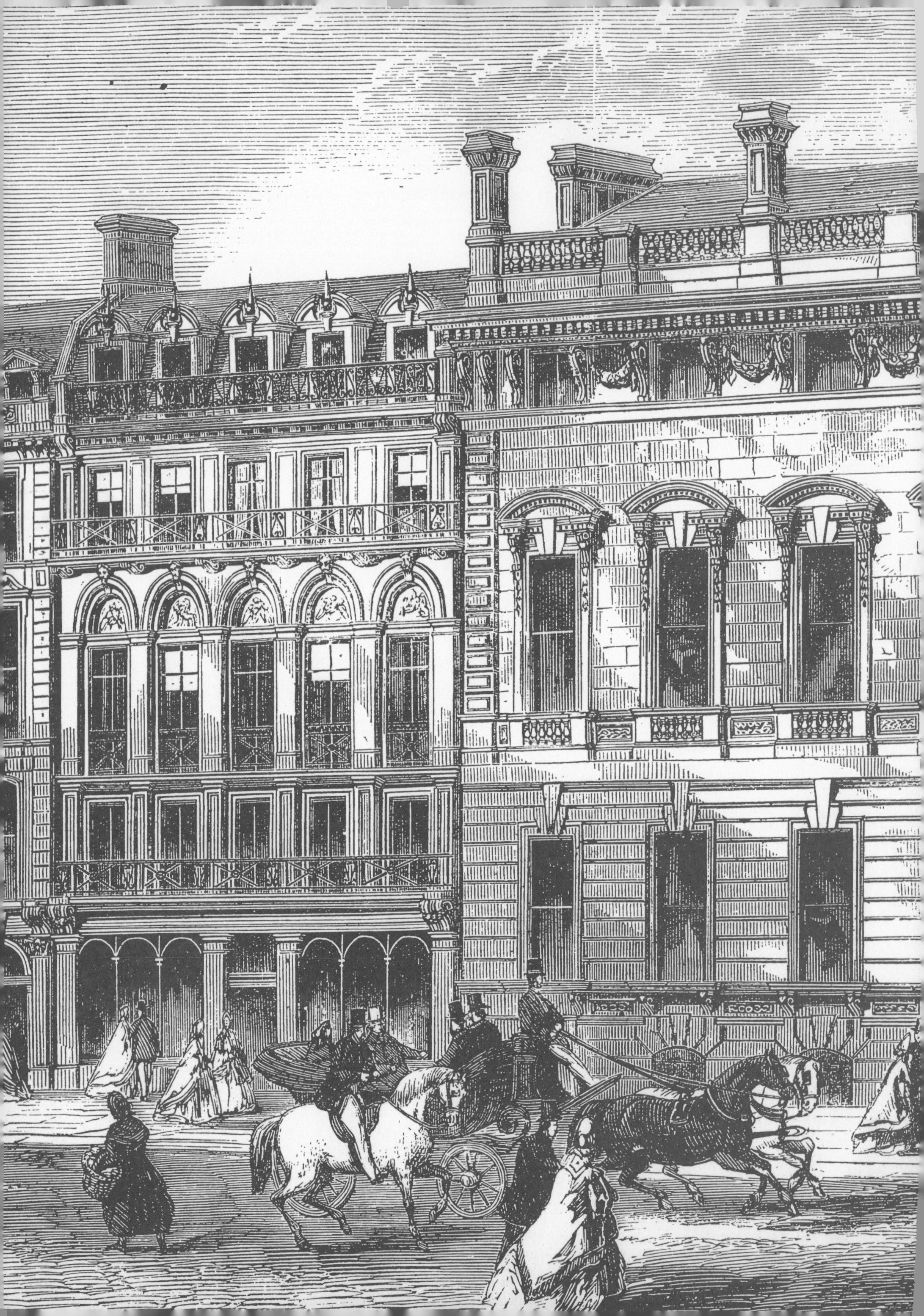